Tours

There's a business school for everyone—meet yours!

The world's top business schools are coming to a free GMAC Tours event in a city near you. Connect in-person with admissions decision-makers or through virtual 1:1 meetings. Meeting representatives is crucial to your application; don't miss out!

Find an event near you

 mba.com/gmactours

Learn the skills you need to succeed in your program

GMAC Business Fundamentals is designed to give you the confidence and fundamental quantitative knowledge you need to start business school.

Learn at Your Own Pace

Access a variety of resources including videos, quizzes, and practical exercises.

Showcase Your Learning

Earn digital badges that highlight your skills and achievements.

Master Core Concepts

Gain a solid foundation in Statistics, Accounting, and Finance, ensuring you're ready to excel from day one.

"I am very grateful that I took the Business Fundamentals courses. My classmates who didn't are struggling in classes where **I feel confident.**"

— MBA Candidate, Portland State University

"The courses provided exactly what I was looking for. The instructors were great, the content was well delivered, and I now **feel back-to-school ready.**"

— MBA Candidate, Emory University

Start business school off right

mba.com/businessfundamentals

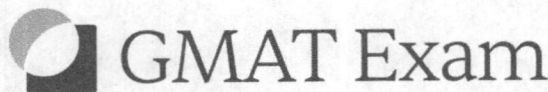

Power up your prep with Official Practice Exams!

Research shows that first-time GMAT test takers can **increase their scores by up to 75 points** after taking all Official Practice Exams!

GMAC GMAT Exam
Practice Exams 3 & 4

GMAC GMAT Exam
Practice Exam 5

GMAC GMAT Exam
Practice Exam 6

Full-length, adaptive GMAT practice exams that simulate the real test-taking experience

Scaled section scores and a total score that aligns to the actual test

Detailed score performance report, including time management

Get started with GMAT Official Practice Exams

 mba.com/gmatprep

 GradSelect

Want to get noticed by top business schools?

GradSelect is your connection to more than 500 global business and management programs that are looking for the best candidate — YOU. Plus, receive exclusive information on school programs, financial aid, and scholarships.

Why connect with schools through GradSelect?

 GradSelect is part of the Graduate Management Admission Council (GMAC), a global mission-driven organization of top business schools.

 Through GradSelect, you can receive exclusive information on school programs, financial aid, and scholarships.

 You can quickly connect with the world's leading schools and discover new opportunities you may not have been familiar with.

 It's free to use!

Join GradSelect

 mba.com/gradselect

GMAT Exam
Official Guide
2026-2027

From the makers of the GMAT Exam

The only test preparation guide with real GMAT Exam questions

More than **975 practice questions** with detailed answer explanations

Includes **digital flashcards, practice games, and a customizable question bank**

Get **exclusive strategies and insights** straight from the exam creators

INCLUDES
newly released
GMAT Exam
questions

GMAT™ OFFICIAL GUIDE 2026–2027

The manufacturer's authorized representative according to the EU General Product Safety Regulation is Wiley-VCH GmbH, Boschstr. 12, 69469 Weinheim, Germany, e-mail: Product_Safety@wiley.com.

For general information on our other products and services or for technical support, please contact our Customer Care Department within the United States at (800) 762-2974, outside the United States at (317) 572-3993 or fax (317) 572-4002.

Wiley also publishes its books in a variety of electronic formats. Some content that appears in print may not be available in electronic formats. For more information about Wiley products, visit our web site at www.wiley.com.

Library of Congress Cataloging-in-Publication Data:
978-1-394-41280-8 (pbk); ISBN 978-1-394-41281-5 (ePub)

Cover Design: GMAC
Cover Icons: Phosphor Icons
Printed and bound by CPI Group (UK) Ltd, Croydon, CR0 4YY

C9781394412808_080426

Table of Contents

Dear GMAT™ Test Taker,

Thank you for taking this important step toward your graduate management education. The GMAT exam remains one of the most trusted indicators of readiness for rigorous business study, relied on by more than 7,700 MBA, business master's, and other graduate-level degree programs worldwide to help identify candidates who are prepared to excel.

By choosing the GMAT™ Official Guide, you are preparing with the only study resource developed by the makers of the exam. Together with the tools available at **mba.com**, this guide is designed to build the skills and confidence you need for your best performance on test day.

The GMAT exam, which has been available to business aspirants like you for more than seven decades, provides schools with meaningful insight into your potential, complementing your academic record and offering a reliable way to demonstrate readiness. It helps signal that you can successfully engage with analytical coursework and thrive in a demanding academic environment.

But the value of the GMAT extends well beyond the classroom. Today's employers continue to prioritize problem-solving, strategic thinking, and data literacy. GMAC's own industry-leading **survey** of the world's top corporate recruiters—the majority of them with Fortune Global 500 companies—has perennially shown these abilities remain among the most sought-after skills for hiring and long-term career growth. Preparing for the GMAT strengthens precisely these capabilities. The exam's emphasis on higher-order reasoning—particularly in the Data Insights section—develops analytical fluency and evidence-based decision-making, competencies that leaders use daily in modern organizations.

In this way, the GMAT serves not only as a trusted admissions tool but also as an early investment in your professional future. By preparing for and taking the exam, you are building the mindset and skill set that drive success in business school, enhance employability upon graduation, and support lasting career advancement.

We applaud your commitment and wish you every success on your exam and in the opportunities that lie ahead.

Warm regards,

Joy J. Jones
CEO, GMAC

GMAT™ Official Guide 2026–2027

1.0   What Is the GMAT™ Exam?

1.1 What Is the GMAT™ Exam?

The Graduate Management Admission Test™ (GMAT™) is used in admissions decisions by more than 7,700 graduate management programs at over 2,400 business schools worldwide. Unlike undergraduate grades and courses, whose meanings vary across regions and institutions, your GMAT scores are a standardized, statistically valid, and reliable measure for both you and these schools to predict your future performance and success in core courses of graduate-level management programs.

Hundreds of studies across hundreds of schools have demonstrated the validity of GMAT scores as being an accurate indicator of business school success. Together, these studies have shown that performance on the GMAT predicts success in business school even better than undergraduate grades.

The exam tests you on skills expected by management faculty and admissions professionals for incoming graduate students. These skills include problem-solving, data analysis, and critical thinking, which all require complex judgments and are tested in the three sections of the GMAT exam: Quantitative Reasoning, Data Insights, and Verbal Reasoning. These three sections feature content relevant to today's business challenges and opportunities, ensuring you are prepared for graduate business school and beyond.

Your GMAT Official Score is meant to be an objective, numeric measure of your ability and potential for success. Business schools will use it as part of their holistic admissions processes, which may also consider recommendation letters, essays, interviews, work experiences, and other signs of social and emotional intelligence, as well as leadership. Even if your program does not require a GMAT score, you can stand out from the crowd by doing well on the exam to show you are serious about business school and have the skills to succeed.

The exam is always delivered in English on a computer, either online (such as at home) or at a test center. The exam tests your ability to apply foundational knowledge in the following areas: algebra and arithmetic, analyzing and interpreting data, reading and comprehending written material, and reasoning and evaluating arguments.

Myth -vs- **FACT**

M – My GMAT score does not predict my success in business school.

F – The GMAT exam measures your critical thinking skills, which you will need in business school and your career.

1.2 Why Take the GMAT™ Exam?

Taking the exam helps you stand out as an applicant and shows you're ready for and committed to a graduate management education. Schools use GMAT scores in choosing the most qualified applicants. They know an applicant who has taken the exam is serious about earning a graduate business degree, and they know the exam scores reliably predict how well applicants can do in graduate business programs.

No matter how you do on the exam, you should contact schools that interest you to learn more about them, and to ask how they use GMAT scores and other criteria in admissions decisions. School admissions offices, websites, and publications are key sources of information when you are researching business schools. Note that schools' published GMAT scores are *averages* of the scores of their admitted students, not minimum scores needed for admission.

While you might aim to get a high or perfect score, such a score is not required to get into top business school programs around the world. You should try your best to achieve a competitive score that aligns with the ranges provided by the schools of your choice. Admissions officers will use GMAT scores as one factor in admissions decisions along with undergraduate records, application essays, interviews, letters of recommendation, and other information.

To learn more about the exam, test preparation materials, registration, and how to use your GMAT Official Score in applying to business schools, please visit **www.mba.com/gmat**.

Myth -vs- **FACT**

M – If I don't get a high GMAT score, I won't get into my top-choice schools.

F – Schools use your GMAT score as a part of their holistic evaluation process.

1.3 GMAT™ Exam Format

The GMAT exam has three separately timed sections (see the table on the following page). The Quantitative Reasoning section and the Verbal Reasoning section consist of only multiple-choice questions. The Data Insights section includes multiple-choice questions along with other kinds of graphical and data analysis questions. Before you start the exam, you can choose any order in which you will take the three sections. For example, you can choose to start with Verbal Reasoning, then do Quantitative Reasoning, and end with Data Insights. Or you can choose to do Data Insights first, followed by Verbal Reasoning, and then Quantitative Reasoning. You can take one optional ten-minute break after either the first or second section.

All three GMAT sections are computer adaptive. This means the test chooses from a large bank of questions to adjust itself to your ability level, so you will not get many questions that are too hard or too easy for you. The first question will be of medium difficulty. As you answer each question, the computer uses your answer, along with your responses to earlier questions, to choose the next question with the right level of difficulty. Because the computer uses your answers to choose your next question, you cannot skip questions.

Computer adaptive tests get harder as you answer more questions correctly. But getting a question that seems easier than the last one doesn't always mean your last answer was wrong. At the end of each section, you can review any question(s) and edit up to three answers within the allotted section time.

Though each test taker gets different questions, the mix of question types is always consistent. Your score depends on the difficulty and statistical traits of the questions you answer, as well as on which of your answers are correct. If you don't know how to answer a question, try to rule out as many wrong answer choices as possible. Then pick the answer choice you think is best. By adapting to each test taker, the exam can accurately and efficiently gauge a full range of skill levels, from very high to very low. Many factors may make the questions easier or harder, so don't waste time worrying if some questions seem easy.

To make sure every test taker gets equivalent content, the test gives specific numbers of questions of each type. While the test covers the same kinds of questions for everyone, some questions may seem harder or easier for you because you may be stronger in some questions than in others.

At the end of the exam, you will see your unofficial score displayed on the screen. A few days after your exam, you will receive your Official Score Report, which includes detailed performance insights. Once you receive your report, you can select to send your Official Score to schools of your choice.

Format of the GMAT™ Exam

	Questions	Timing
Quantitative Reasoning Problem-Solving	21	45 min.
Data Insights Data Sufficiency Multi-Source Reasoning Table Analysis Graphics Interpretation Two-Part Analysis	20	45 min.
Verbal Reasoning Reading Comprehension Critical Reasoning	23	45 min.
	Total Time	135 min.

A ten-minute optional break can be taken after the first or the second section.

Each section of the GMAT exam contains the following features:

- **Bookmarking:** Mark any questions you are unsure about so you can easily get back to them after you complete the section. Bookmarking can make the Question Review & Edit process more efficient.

- **Question Review & Edit:** Review as many questions as you would like (whether or not they're bookmarked) and change or edit up to three answers per section, within the section's allotted time.

1.4 What Is the Testing Experience Like?

You can take the exam either online (such as at home) or at a test center—whichever you prefer. You may feel more comfortable at home with the online delivery format. Or you may prefer the uninterrupted, structured environment of a test center. It is your choice. Both options have the same content, structure, features, optional ten-minute break, scores, and score scales.

At the Test Center: Over 700 test centers worldwide administer the GMAT exam under standardized conditions. Each test center has proctored testing rooms with individual computer workstations that allow you to take the exam in a peaceful, quiet setting, with some privacy. To learn more about exam day, visit **www.mba.com/gmat.**

Online: In available regions, the GMAT exam is delivered online and is proctored remotely, so you can take it in the comfort of your home or office. You will need a quiet workspace with a desktop or laptop computer that meets minimum system requirements, a webcam, microphone, and a reliable internet connection. For more information about taking the exam online, visit **www.mba.com/gmat.**

Whether you're taking the GMAT exam online or at a test center, there are several accommodations available. To learn more about available accommodations for the exam, visit **www.mba.com/accommodations.**

1.5 What Is the Exam Content Like?

The GMAT exam measures several types of analytical reasoning skills. The Quantitative Reasoning section gives you basic arithmetic and algebra problems. The questions present you with a mix of word or pure math problems. The Data Insights section asks you to use diverse reasoning skills to solve real-world problems involving data. It also asks you to interpret and combine data from different sources and in different formats to reach conclusions. The Verbal Reasoning section tests your ability to read and comprehend written material and to reason through and evaluate arguments.

The test questions are contextualized in various subject areas, but each question provides you everything you need to know to answer it correctly. In other words, you do not need detailed outside knowledge of the subject areas.

1.6 Quantitative Reasoning Section

The GMAT Quantitative Reasoning section measures how well you solve math problems and interpret graphs. All questions in this section require solving problems using basic arithmetic, algebra, or both. Some are practical word problems, while others are pure math. Answering these questions correctly relies on logic, analytical skills, and basic knowledge of algebra and arithmetic skills. You **cannot** use a calculator while working on this section.

Chapter 3 of this book, "Math Review," reviews the basic math you need to know to answer questions in the Quantitative Reasoning section. Chapter 4, "Quantitative Reasoning," includes test-taking tips, as well as practice questions and answer explanations both in this book and in the Online Question Bank.

1.7 Data Insights Section

The GMAT Data Insights section tests the skills that today's business managers need to analyze intricate data sources and solve complex real-world problems. It tests how well you can assess multiple sources and types of information—graphic, numeric, and verbal—as they relate to one another. It also tests how well you can analyze a practical math and non-math problem to determine if enough data is given to solve it.

The Data Insights section has five types of questions:

- **Data Sufficiency:** Measures your ability to analyze a quantitative or logical problem, recognize which data is relevant, and determine at what point there is enough data to solve the problem. Questions can be presented in mathematical or non-mathematical real-world contexts.

- **Multi-Source Reasoning:** Measures your ability to examine data from several sources including text passages, tables, or graphics, and analyze each source of data carefully to answer multiple questions. Some questions will require you to recognize discrepancies among different sources of data, while others will ask you to draw inferences, or require you to determine whether data is relevant.

- **Table Analysis:** Measures your ability to sort and analyze a table of data, similar to a spreadsheet, in order to determine what information is relevant or meets certain conditions.

- **Graphics Interpretation:** Measures your ability to interpret the information presented in a graph or other graphical image (scatter plot, *x/y* graph, bar chart, pie chart, or statistical curve distribution) to discern relationships and make inferences.

- **Two-Part Analysis:** Measures your ability to solve complex problems. They could be quantitative, verbal, or a combination of both. The format is intentionally versatile to cover a wide range of content. These questions measure your ability to evaluate trade-offs, solve simultaneous equations, and discern relationships between two entities.

Data Insights questions may require math, data analysis, verbal reasoning, or all three. You will have to interpret graphs and sort data tables to answer some questions, but you won't need advanced statistics or spreadsheet skills. For both online and test center exam delivery, you will have access to an on-screen calculator with basic functions. It should be noted that this calculator is provided for the Data Insights section **only**, and **not** for the Quantitative Reasoning section.

Chapter 5 of this book, "Data Insights Review," reviews the basic data analysis skills you need to answer questions in the Data Insights section. Chapter 6, "Data Insights," explains the Data Insights question types, provides practice questions and answer explanations both in this book and in the Online Question Bank, and offers test-taking tips.

Because the Data Insights questions need to be rendered online, certain question types, such as Multi-Source Reasoning, Table Analysis, and Graphics Interpretation, are only available in the **Online Question Bank** that is included as a part of this guide.

You can access the **Online Question Bank** by going to **www.mba.com/my-account** and using your unique Access Code on the inside front cover of this book.

1.8 Verbal Reasoning Section

The GMAT Verbal Reasoning section measures how well you reason, understand what you read, and evaluate arguments. The Verbal Reasoning section includes passages about many topics. Verbal Reasoning questions do not assume you have any background knowledge on the topic. Therefore, all of the information you need to answer the questions correctly is contained in the passages.

The Verbal Reasoning section has two types of questions:

- **Reading Comprehension:** These questions measure your ability to read and understand written statements, understand logical relationships between significant points, and draw inferences and conclusions. More specifically, you'll be asked to identify main and supporting ideas, draw inferences from information presented in the passage, apply knowledge learned from the passage to unrelated contexts, and recognize the logical structures and style of the passage.

- **Critical Reasoning:** These questions measure your ability to make valid arguments, evaluate different lines of reasoning, and formulate or assess a plan of action. Critical Reasoning questions are based on a short reading passage, usually fewer than 100 words. Typically, the short text is followed by a question that asks you which of the five answer options strengthens or weakens the argument, tells why the argument is flawed, or strongly supports or damages the argument. You will not need specialized knowledge of the subject matter to answer the questions.

Chapter 7 of this book, "Verbal Review," reviews the basic verbal analysis and reasoning skills you need for the Verbal Reasoning section. Chapter 8, "Verbal Reasoning," explains the Verbal Reasoning question subtypes. It also provides test-taking tips for each subtype, as well as practice questions and answer explanations both in this book and in the Online Question Bank.

1.9 How Are Scores Calculated?

The Quantitative Reasoning, Data Insights, and Verbal Reasoning sections are each scored on a scale from 60 to 90, in 1-point increments. You will get four scores: a Section Score each for Quantitative Reasoning, Data Insights, and Verbal Reasoning, along with a Total Score based on your three section scores. The Total Score ranges from 205 to 805. Your scores depend on:

- Which questions you answered correctly.

- How many questions you answered.

- Each question's difficulty and other statistical characteristics.

There is a penalty for not completing each section of the exam. If you do not finish in the allotted time, your score will be penalized, reflecting the number of unanswered questions. Your GMAT exam score will be the best reflection of your performance when all questions are answered within the time limit.

Immediately after completing the exam, your unofficial scores and percentile for the Quantitative Reasoning, Data Insights, and Verbal Reasoning, as well as your Total Score, are displayed on-screen. You are **not** allowed to record, save, screenshot, or print your unofficial score. You will receive an email notification when your Official Score Report is available in your **www.mba.com** account.

The following table summarizes the different types of scores and their scale properties.

Score Type	Scale	Increment
Quantitative Reasoning	60–90	1
Data Insights	60–90	1
Verbal Reasoning	60–90	1
Total	205–805	10

Your GMAT Official Scores are valid for five years from your exam date. Your Total GMAT Score includes a percentile ranking, which shows the percentage of tests taken with scores lower than your score.

In addition to reviewing your Total and Section Scores, it's important to pay attention to your percentile ranking. Percentile rankings indicate what percentage of test takers you performed better than. For example, a percentile ranking of 75% means that you performed better than 75% of other test takers, and 25% of test takers performed better than you. Percentile ranks are calculated using scores from the most recent five years. Visit **www.mba.com/scores** to view the most recent predicted percentile rankings tables.

To better understand the exam experience and view score reports before exam day, we recommend taking at least one GMAT official practice exam to simulate the test-taking experience and gauge your potential score. The more practice exams you take, the better prepared you will be on your actual testing day. Visit **www.mba.com/examprep** to learn more about the practice exams offered by GMAC.

To register for the GMAT™ exam, go to www.mba.com/register

2.0   How to Prepare

2.1 How Should I Prepare for the GMAT™ Exam?

The GMAT™ exam has several unique question formats. We recommend that you familiarize yourself with the test format and the different question types before you take the test. The key to prepping for any exam is setting a pace that works for you and your lifestyle. That might be easier said than done, but the *GMAT™ Official 6-Week Study Planner* does the planning for you! Our step-by-step planner will help you stick to a schedule, inform your activities, and track your progress. Go to **www.mba.com/examprep** to download the planner.

Here are our recommended steps to starting your prep journey with your best foot forward.

1. **Study the structure.** Use the study plan in our **free GMAT™ Official Starter Kit** to become familiar with the exam format and structure. The study plan will guide you through each question type and give you sample questions. This will boost your confidence come test day when you know what to expect.

2. **Understand the question types.** Beyond knowing how to answer questions correctly, learn what each type of question is asking of you. GMAT questions rely on logic and analytical skills, not underlying subject matter mastery, as detailed in the *GMAT™ Official Guide 2026–2027* **and Online Question Bank.**

3. **Establish your baseline.** Take the **GMAT™ Official Practice Exam 1 (FREE)** to establish your baseline. It uses the same format and scoring algorithm as the real test, so you can use the Official Score Report to accurately assess your strengths and growth areas.

4. **Study the answer explanations.** Take advantage of each question you get wrong by studying the correct answers, so you know how to get it right the next time. **GMAT™ Official Practice Questions** provide detailed answer explanations for hundreds of real GMAT questions. This will help you understand why you got a question right or wrong.

5. **Simulate the test-taking experience.** Take the **GMAT™ Official Practice Exams.** All GMAT™ Official Practice Exams use the same algorithm, scoring, and timing as the real exam, so take them with test-day-like conditions (e.g., quiet space, use the tools allowed on test day) for the truest prep experience.

Remember, the exam is timed, so learning to pace yourself and understanding the question formats and the skills you need can be a stepping stone to achieving your desired score. The timed practice in the **Online Question Bank** can help you prepare for this. The time management performance chart provided in practice exam score reports can also help you practice your pacing.

Because the exam assesses reasoning rather than knowledge, memorizing facts probably won't help you. You don't need to study advanced math, but you should know basic arithmetic and algebra. Likewise, you don't need to study advanced vocabulary words, but you should know English well enough to understand writing at an undergraduate level.

> "The GMAT is not a math test. 'Textbook' math will work—but you'll take longer than you need to. Approach the GMAT from a business mindset: What's the least-effort path to a legitimate answer? Estimate, logic it out, test real numbers—whatever works for each problem."
>
> — A test instructor from Manhattan Prep Powered by Kaplan

2.2 Getting Ready for Exam Day

Whether you take the exam online or in a test center, knowing what to expect will help you feel confident and succeed. To understand which exam delivery is right for you, visit **www.mba.com/ plan-for-exam-day**.

Our Top Exam Day Strategies:

1. Get a good night's sleep the night before.

2. Pacing is key. Consult your on-screen timer periodically to avoid having to rush through sections.

3. Read each question carefully to fully understand what is being asked.

4. Don't waste time trying to solve a problem you recognize as too difficult or time-consuming. Instead, eliminate answers you know are wrong and select the best from the remaining choices.

5. Leverage the bookmarking tool to make your question review and edit process more efficient.

> "Don't take a 'brute force' approach to GMAT questions—think strategically instead."
>
> — A test instructor from GMAT Genius

> "Compile summarized notes that can be reviewed on the morning of the test. Awareness of the key points and types of mistakes will boost your scores."
>
> — A test instructor from LeadersMBA

Myth -vs- FACT

M – You need advanced math skills to get a high GMAT score.

F – The exam measures your reasoning ability rather than your advanced math skills.

2.3 How to Use the *GMAT™ Official Guide 2026–2027*

The GMAT™ Official Guide series is the largest official source of actual GMAT questions. You can use this series of books and the included Online Question Bank to practice answering the different types of questions. Each section of this Official Guide has a large set of practice questions split into categories of easy, medium, and hard. Your rate of accuracy in each category might differ from what you expect. You might be able to answer the "hard" questions easily, while the "easy" ones are challenging. This is common and is not an indicator of exam performance. The questions in this book are not adaptive based on your performance but are meant to serve as exposure to the range of question types and formats you might encounter on the exam. Also, the proportions of questions about different content areas in this book don't reflect the proportions in the actual exam. To find questions of a specific type and difficulty level (for example, easy arithmetic questions), use the index of questions in Chapter 9.

We recommend the steps below for how to best use this book:

1. Start with the review chapters to gain an overview of the required concepts.

    > "Building a strong foundation is crucial to achieve a high score. If you struggle with fundamental questions, your progress on more advanced questions will be hindered."
    >
    > — A test instructor from XY Education

2. Go through the practice questions in this book. Once you've familiarized yourself with the concepts and question types, use the **Online Question Bank** to further customize your practice by choosing your preferred level of difficulty, category of concepts, or question types.

    > "The Official Guide offers in-depth answer explanations. After completing a question, reviewing it alongside the explanation helps you gain a deeper understanding of the question's key concepts and solution strategies. On the result interface of the online question bank, it serves a dual purpose: on one hand, it encourages us to review incorrect answers; on the other hand, it provides detailed insights into the time spent on each question, aiding in optimizing our pace during exercises."
    >
    > — A test instructor from Jiangjiang GMAT

3. Use the **Online Question Bank** to continue practicing based on your progress. To better customize and enhance your practice, use the Online Question Bank to:

    a. Review and retry practice questions to improve performance by using the untimed or timed features along with a study mode or an exam mode.

    b. Analyze key performance metrics to help assess focus area and track improvement.

    c. Use flashcards to master key concepts.

    > "The biggest mistake students make is completing too many new problems. Completing problems doesn't move your score! Learning from problems does. Keep a list of questions you want to go back to and redo. Redo at least three of these questions every time you study. This book is one of the most important resources you can use to create the future you want. Make sure you understand every question you complete extremely well. You should be able to explain every problem you complete to someone who is new to the exam. Don't focus on simply 'getting through' the book. That mindset will work against you and your dreams."
    >
    > — A test instructor from The GMAT Strategy

 TIP

Since the exam is given on a computer, we suggest you practice the questions in this book using the **Online Question Bank** accessed via **www.mba.com/my-account**. It includes all the questions in this book, and it lets you create practice sets—both timed and untimed—and track your progress more easily. The Online Question Bank is also available on your mobile device through the GMAT™ Official Practice mobile app. To access the Online Question Bank on your mobile device, first create an account at **www.mba.com**, and then sign into your account on the mobile app.

TIP

Remember: Some of the Data Insights section questions are only available in the **Online Question Bank**.

2.4 How to Use Other GMAT™ Official Prep Products

We recommend using our other GMAT™ Official Prep products along with this guidebook.

- **For a realistic simulation of the exam:** GMAT™ Official Practice Exams 1–6 are the only practice exams that use real exam questions along with the scoring algorithm and user interface from the actual exam. The first two practice exams are free to all test takers at **www.mba.com/gmatprep**.

- **For more practice questions:** *GMAT™ Official Guide Data Insights Review 2026–2027*, *GMAT™ Official Guide Verbal Review 2026–2027*, and *GMAT™ Official Guide Quantitative Review 2026–2027* offer over 350 additional practice questions not included in this book.

- **For focused practice:** GMAT™ Official Practice Questions for Quantitative, Data Insights, and Verbal products offer 100+ questions that are not included in the Official Guide series.

" **Build teaching-level depth; don't just finish content mindlessly. Even if you solve thousands of questions on a shaky foundation, you will remain stuck on a really low accuracy.** "

— **A test instructor from Top One Percent**

2.5 Tips for Taking the Exam

Tips for answering questions of the different types are given later in this book. Here are some general tips to help you do your best on the test.

1. **Before the actual exam, decide in what order to take the sections.**
The exam lets you choose in which order you'll take the sections. Use the GMAT™ Official Practice Exams to practice and find your preferred order. No order is "wrong." Some test takers prefer to complete the section that challenges them the most first, while others prefer to ease into the exam by starting with a section that they're stronger in. Practice each order and see which one works best for you.

2. **Try the practice questions and practice exams.**
Timing yourself as you answer the practice questions and taking the practice exams can give you a sense of how long you will have for each question on the actual test, and whether you are answering them fast enough to finish in time.

TIP

After you've learned about all the question types, use the practice questions in this book and practice them online at **www.mba.com/my-account** to prepare for the actual test. Reminder: Most types of Data Insights practice questions are only available online.

3. **Review all test directions ahead of time.**

   The directions explain exactly what you need to do to answer questions of each type. You can review the directions in the GMAT™ Official Practice Exams ahead of time so that you don't miss anything you need to know to answer properly. To review directions during the test, you can click on the Help icon. But note that your time spent reviewing directions counts against your available time for that section of the test.

4. **Study each question carefully.**

   Before you answer a question, understand exactly what it is asking, then pick the best answer choice. Never skim a question. Skimming may make you miss important details or nuances.

5. **Use your time wisely.**

   Although the exam stresses accuracy over speed, you should use your time wisely. On average, you have just about 2 minutes and 9 seconds per Quantitative Reasoning question; 2 minutes and 15 seconds per Data Insights question; and under 2 minutes per Verbal Reasoning question. Once you start the test, an on-screen clock shows how much time you have left. You can hide this display if you want, but by checking the clock periodically, you can make sure to finish in time.

6. **Do not spend too much time on any one question.**

   If finding the right answer is taking too long, try to rule out answer choices you know are wrong. Then pick the best of the remaining choices and move on to the next question.

   Not finishing sections or randomly guessing answers can lower your score significantly. As long as you've worked on each section, you will get a score even if you didn't finish one or more sections in time. You don't earn points for questions you never get to see.

   Pacing is important. If a question stumps you, pick the answer choice that seems best and move on. If you guess wrong, the computer will likely give you an easier question, which you're more likely to answer correctly. Soon the computer will return to giving you questions matched to your ability. You can bookmark questions you get stuck on, then return to change up to three of your answers if you still have time left at the end of the section. But if you don't finish the section, your score will be reduced.

7. **Confirm your answers ONLY when you are ready to move on.**

   In the GMAT Quantitative Reasoning, Data Insights, and Verbal Reasoning sections, once you choose your answer to a question, you are asked to confirm it. As soon as you confirm your response, the next question appears. You can't skip questions. In the Data Insights and Verbal Reasoning sections, several questions based on the same prompt may appear at once. When more than one question is on a single screen, you can change your answers to any questions on that screen before moving on to the next screen. But until you've reached the end of the section, you can't navigate back to a previous screen to change any answers.

Myth -vs- **FACT**

M – Avoiding wrong answers is more important than finishing the test.

F – Not finishing can lower your score a lot.

2.6 Section Strategies

Utilize the strategies below to better prepare for each section of the exam. Creating a solid study plan and selecting the right prep materials are two key elements of getting accepted into your top business schools. But knowing how to strategically approach the exam is another crucial factor that can increase your confidence going into test day and help you perform your best.

> " Don't just read explanations. Review your notes and learn from your mistakes.**"**
>
> — **A test instructor from Admit Master**

Quantitative Reasoning

Problem-Solving Questions

- Familiarize yourself with the rules and concepts of arithmetic and algebra.

- For questions that require approximations, skim answer choices first. If you are unable to get some idea of how close the approximation should be, you may waste time on long computations when a short mental process would serve you better.

- Take advantage of your whiteboard or note board. Solving problems in writing may help you avoid errors. Make sure you understand how the whiteboard will work on test day. If you are taking the exam online, you also have the option to use an online whiteboard tool—make sure you understand how the online whiteboard works and practice using it before test day.

Data Insights

Data Sufficiency Questions

- Decide whether the problem allows only one value or a range of values. Remember: You are only determining whether you have enough data to solve the problem.

- Avoid making unwarranted assumptions based on figures. Figures are not necessarily drawn to scale.

Multi-Source Reasoning Questions

- Don't expect to be completely familiar with the material. All of the information you need to answer the questions is provided.

- Analyze each source of data carefully, as the questions require detailed understanding of the data presented. Text passages often build ideas in sequences, so be mindful of how each statement adds to the main idea of the passage. Graphic elements come in various forms, such as tables, graphs, diagrams, or charts.

- Make sure you understand what is being asked for each question. Some questions will require recognizing discrepancies among different sources of data. Others will ask you to draw inferences. Still others may require you to determine which one of the data sources is relevant.

- Select the answer choices that have the most support based on the data provided. Don't let your knowledge of the subject matter influence your answer choice. Answer the questions using only the data provided to you.

Table Analysis Questions

- Examine the table and accompanying text to determine the type of information provided.

- Read the question carefully to determine the data analysis required and know the choices you have to make by reviewing the answers.

- Judge each answer statement carefully based on the condition specified (i.e., yes or no, true or false). Focus your attention on whether the given condition has been met.

Graphics Interpretation Questions

- Familiarize yourself with the data presented in the graphic. Make note of the scales on the axis, marked values, and labels. Pay attention to any discrepancies between the units in the graph and the units discussed in the text.

- Read any accompanying text carefully. The text might present data that isn't contained in the graphic but that you need to answer the question.

- Make sure you understand what the problem is asking you to do. You will interpret and integrate data, discern relationships, and make inferences from a set of data.

- Read all the choices in the drop-down menu. By checking the menu options, you will get additional information about your assigned task.

- Choose the option that best completes the statement. More than one option in the drop-down menu may seem plausible. You will need to choose the one that makes the statement most accurate or logical.

Two-Part Analysis Questions

- Read the information carefully. It may cover a wide range of content, including quantitative, verbal, or some combination of both. All the material presented is designed to be challenging. Don't let any familiarity with the subject matter influence your response. Only use the data presented in the question.

- Determine exactly what the question is asking. Pay close attention to how the question describes the tasks. Sometimes the response column headings lack the details that could help you better understand what you are supposed to do.

- When making your answer choices, determine whether your tasks are dependent or independent. Some questions will pose two tasks that can be carried out individually. Others pose one task with two dependent parts.

- Keep in mind that the same answer choice might be the correct response for both columns. It is possible that one answer option satisfies the conditions of both response columns.

Important Note for Data Insights Practice

Multi-Source Reasoning, Table Analysis, and Graphics Interpretation questions are only available in the Online Question Bank. To access the Online Question Bank, go to **www.mba.com/my-account** and use your unique Access Code, which can be found on the inside front cover of this book.

Verbal Reasoning

Reading Comprehension Questions

- Do not expect to be completely familiar with the material presented in passages. Your understanding of the subject matter is not required to answer the question.

- Read and analyze the passage carefully before reading the questions.

- Focus on key words and phrases to maintain an overall sense about the context of the passage.

- Select the answer that fits based on the information given in the passage.

- Don't rush through the passages. This section is about comprehension, not speed.

Critical Reasoning Questions

- Determine exactly what the question is asking. For this section, read the question first and then the material on which it is based.

- Keep the following in mind as you read through the passage:

  - What is put forward as factual information?

  - What is not said but necessarily follows from what is said?

  - What is claimed to follow from facts that have been put forward?

  - How well are those claims substantiated?

- When reading arguments, determine how sound the reasoning is. It is not necessary to pass judgment on the actual truth of anything put forward as fact.

- If a question is based on an argument, identify what part of the argument is its conclusion.

3.0   Math Review

3.0 Math Review

This chapter reviews the math you need to answer GMAT™ Quantitative Reasoning questions and Data Insights questions. This is only a brief overview. If you find unfamiliar terms, consult other resources to learn more.

Unlike some math problems you may have solved in school, GMAT math questions ask you to **apply** your math knowledge. For example, rather than asking you to list a number's prime factors to show you understand prime factorization, a GMAT question may ask you to **use** prime factorization and exponents to simplify an algebraic expression with a radical.

To prepare for the GMAT Quantitative Reasoning section and the Data Insights section, first review basic math to make sure you know enough to answer the questions. Then practice with GMAT questions from past exams.

Section 3.1, "Value, Order, and Factors," includes:

1. Numbers and the Number Line
2. Factors, Multiples, and Remainders
3. Exponents
4. Decimals and Place Value
5. Arithmetic Shortcuts and Properties of Operations

Section 3.2, "Algebra, Equalities, and Inequalities," includes:

1. Algebraic Expressions and Equations
2. Linear Equations
3. Factoring and Quadratic Equations
4. Inequalities
5. Functions
6. Graphing
7. Formulas and Measurement Conversion

Section 3.3, "Rates, Ratios, and Percents," includes:

1. Ratio and Proportion
2. Fractions
3. Percents
4. Converting Decimals, Fractions, and Percents
5. Working with Decimals, Fractions, and Percents
6. Rate, Work, and Mixture Problems

Section 3.4, "Statistics, Sets, Counting, Probability, Estimation, and Series," includes:

1. Statistics
2. Sets
3. Counting Methods
4. Probability
5. Estimation
6. Sequences and Series

Section 3.5, "Reference Sheets"

3.1 Value, Order, and Factors

1. Numbers and the Number Line

A. All *real numbers* match points on *the number line*, and all points on the number line represent real numbers.

The figure below shows the number line with labeled points standing for the real numbers $-\frac{3}{2}$, 0.2, and $\sqrt{2}$.

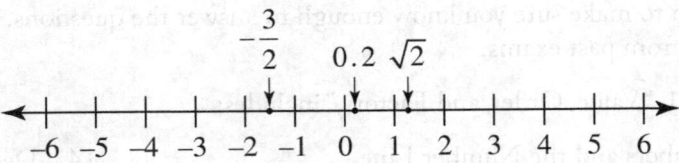

The Number Line

B. On the number line, points to the left of zero stand for *negative* numbers, and points to the right of zero stand for *positive* numbers. Every real number except zero is either positive or negative.

C. On the number line, each number is less than any number to its right. So, as the figure above shows, $-4 < -3 < -\frac{3}{2} < -1$, and $1 < \sqrt{2} < 2$.

D. If a number n is between 1 and 4 on the number line, then $n > 1$ and $n < 4$; that is, $1 < n < 4$. If n is "between 1 and 4, inclusive," then $1 \le n \le 4$.

E. The *absolute value* of a real number x, written as $|x|$, is x if $x \ge 0$ and $-x$ if $x < 0$. A number's absolute value is the distance between that number and zero on the number line. Thus, -3 and 3 have the same absolute value since each is three units from zero on the number line. The absolute value of any nonzero number is positive.

Examples:

$|-5| = |5| = 5$, $|0| = 0$, and

$\left|-\frac{7}{2}\right| = \frac{7}{2}.$

For any real numbers x and y, $|x + y| \le |x| + |y|$, and $|xy| = |x||y|$.

Examples:

If $x = 10$ and $y = 2$, then $|x + y| = |12| = 12 = |x| + |y|$.

And $|xy| = |20| = 20 = |x||y|$.

If $x = 10$ and $y = -2$, then $|x + y| = |8| = 8 < 12 = |x| + |y|$.

And $|xy| = |-20| = 20 = |x||y|$.

2. Factors, Multiples, and Remainders

A. An *integer* is any number in the set $\{\ldots -3, -2, -1, 0, 1, 2, 3, \ldots\}$. For any integer n, the numbers in the set $\{n, n + 1, n + 2, n + 3, \ldots\}$ are *consecutive integers*.

B. For integers x and y, if $x \neq 0$, x is a *divisor* or *factor* of y if $y = xn$ for some integer n. Then y is *divisible* by x and is a *multiple* of x.

> *Example:*
>
> Since $28 = (7)(4)$, both 4 and 7 are divisors or factors of 28.
>
> But 8 isn't a divisor or factor of 28 since n isn't an integer if $28 = 8n$.

C. Dividing a positive integer y by a positive integer x and then rounding down to the nearest nonnegative integer gives the *quotient* of the division.

To find the *remainder* of the division, multiply x by the quotient, then subtract the result from y. The quotient and the remainder are the unique positive integers q and r, respectively, such that $y = xq + r$ and $0 \leq r < x$.

> *Example:*
>
> When 28 is divided by 8, the quotient is 3 and the remainder is 4 because $28 = (8)(3) + 4$.

The remainder r is 0 if and only if y is *divisible* by x. Then x is a divisor or factor of y, and y is a multiple of x.

> *Example:*
>
> Since 32 divided by 8 has a remainder of 0, 32 is divisible by 8. So, 8 is a divisor of 32, and 32 is a multiple of 8.

When a smaller integer is divided by a larger integer, the quotient is 0 and the remainder is the smaller integer.

> *Example:*
>
> When 5 is divided by 7, the quotient is 0 and the remainder is 5 since $5 = (7)(0) + 5$.

D. For any positive integers x, y, and z, suppose that r is the remainder when x is divided by z, and that s is the remainder when y is divided by z. Then the remainder when $x + y$ is divided by z equals the remainder when $r + s$ is divided by z. Similarly, the remainder when xy is divided by z equals the remainder when rs is divided by z.

Examples:

When 142 is divided by 13, the remainder is 12 because $132 = (13 \times 10) + 12$. And when 29 is divided by 13, the remainder is 3 because $29 = (13 \times 2) + 3$.

So, the remainder when $142 + 29$ is divided by 13 equals the remainder when $12 + 3 = 15$ is divided by 13; that is, it's 2.

And the remainder when 142×29 is divided by 13 equals the remainder when $12 \times 3 = 36$ is divided by 13; that is, it's 10.

E. Any integer divisible by 2 is *even*. The set of even integers is $\{\dots -4, -2, 0, 2, 4, 6, 8, \dots\}$. Integers not divisible by 2 are *odd*, so $\{\dots -3, -1, 1, 3, 5, \dots\}$ is the set of odd integers. For any integer n, the numbers in the set $\{2n, 2n + 2, 2n + 4, \dots\}$ are **consecutive even integers**, and the numbers in $\{2n + 1, 2n + 3, 2n + 5, \dots\}$ are **consecutive odd integers**.

If a product of integers has at least one even factor, the product is even; otherwise, it's odd. If two integers are both even or both odd, their sum and their difference are even. Otherwise, their sum and their difference are odd.

F. A *prime* number is a positive integer with exactly two positive divisors: 1 and itself. That is, a prime number is divisible by no integer but itself and 1.

Examples:

The first six prime numbers are 2, 3, 5, 7, 11, and 13.

But 15 is not a prime number because it has four positive divisors: 1, 3, 5, and 15.

Nor is 1 a prime number because it has only one positive divisor: itself.

3. Exponents

A. An expression of the form k^n means the nth **power** of k, or k raised to the nth power, where n is the **exponent** and k is the **base**.

B. A positive integer exponent shows how many instances of the base are multiplied together. That is, when n is a positive integer, k^n is the product of n instances of k.

Examples:

x^5 is $(x)(x)(x)(x)(x)$; that is, the product in which x is a factor 5 times with no other factors. We can also say x^5 is the 5th power of x, or x raised to the 5th power.

The second power of 2, also called 2 **squared**, is $2^2 = 2 \times 2 = 4$. The third power of 2, also called 2 **cubed**, is $2^3 = 2 \times 2 \times 2 = 8$.

Squaring a number greater than 1, or raising it to any power greater than 1, gives a larger number.

Squaring a number between 0 and 1 gives a smaller number.

Examples:

$3^2 = 9$, and $9 > 3$.

$(0.1)^2 = 0.01$, and $0.01 < 0.1$.

C. A *composite number* is an integer greater than 1 that's not prime. Any composite number is a product of a unique set of prime factors, each raised to some positive integer power. The *prime factorization* of a composite number shows it as such a product.

Examples:

Some prime factorizations of composite numbers are $14 = (2)(7)$, $81 = 3^4$, and $484 = (2^2)(11^2)$.

D. For any two positive integers x and y, y is divisible by x if and only if the prime factorization of y includes each prime number in the prime factorization of x, raised to at least as great a power as it is in the prime factorization of x.

Examples:

$1080 = (2^3)(3^3)(5)$ is divisible by $24 = (2^3)(3)$, because the prime factorization of 1080 includes both 2 and 3, which are the only prime factors in the prime factorization of 24, and each is raised to at least as great a power as it is in the prime factorization of 24.

But 1080 is not divisible by $16 = 2^4$, because the prime factor 2 in the prime factorization of 16 is raised to a higher power than it is in the prime factorization of 1080.

Nor is 1080 divisible by $21 = (3)(7)$, because its prime factor 7 isn't in the prime factorization of 1080.

E. A *square root* of a number n is a number x such that $x^2 = n$. Every positive number has two real square roots, one positive and the other negative. The positive square root of n is written as $\sqrt{n}$ or $n^{\frac{1}{2}}$.

Example:

The two square roots of 9 are $\sqrt{9} = 3$ and $-\sqrt{9} = -3$.

For any x, the nonnegative square root of x^2 equals the absolute value of x; that is, $\sqrt{x^2} = |x|$.

The square root of a negative number is not a real number. Only real numbers appear on the GMAT.

F. Every real number r has exactly one real *cube root*, the number s such that $s^3 = r$. The real cube root of r is written as $\sqrt[3]{r}$ or $r^{\frac{1}{3}}$.

Examples:

Since $2^3 = 8$, $\sqrt[3]{8} = 2$.

Likewise, $\sqrt[3]{-8} = -2$ because $(-2)^3 = -8$.

4. Decimals and Place Value

A. A *decimal* is a real number written as a series of digits, often with a period called a *decimal point*. The decimal point's position sets the *place values* of the digits.

Example:

The digits in the decimal 7,654.321 have these place values:

Thousands		Hundreds	Tens	Ones or units		Tenths	Hundredths	Thousandths
7	,	6	5	4	.	3	2	1

B. Some decimal numbers extend rightward by infinitely many digits. In a *repeating decimal*, a finite sequence of digits that are not all 0s repeats forever. A repeating decimal may be written showing the finite sequence of digits to the right of the decimal point only once, with a bar over them. There are never digits to the right of the repeating sequence.

Example:

The repeating decimal $12.34\overline{56}$ has the digits 12.3456565656..., with the digit sequence 56 repeating forever.

C. In *scientific notation*, a decimal is written with only one nonzero digit to the decimal point's left, multiplied by an integer power of 10. To convert a number from scientific notation to regular decimal notation, move the decimal point by the number of places equal to the absolute value of the exponent on the 10. Move the decimal point to the right if the exponent is positive or to the left if the exponent is negative.

Examples:

In scientific notation, 231 is written as 2.31×10^2, and 0.0231 is written as 2.31×10^{-2}.

To convert 2.013×10^4 to regular decimal notation, move the decimal point 4 places to the right, giving 20,130.

Likewise, to convert 1.91×10^{-4} to regular decimal notation, move the decimal point 4 places to the left, giving 0.000191.

D. To add or subtract decimals with many finite digits, line up their decimal points. If one decimal has fewer digits to the right of its decimal point than another, insert zeros to the right of its last digit.

Examples:

To add 17.6512 and 653.27, insert zeros to the right of the last digit in 653.27 to line up the decimal points when the numbers are in a column:

$$17.6512$$
$$+\ 653.2700$$
$$\overline{670.9212}$$

Likewise for 653.27 minus 17.6512:

$$653.2700$$
$$-\ 17.6512$$
$$\overline{635.6188}$$

E. Multiply decimals with many finite digits as if they were integers. Then insert the decimal point in the product so that the number of digits to the right of the decimal point is the sum of the numbers of digits to the right of the decimal points in the numbers being multiplied.

Example:

To multiply 2.09 by 1.3, first multiply the integers 209 and 13 to get 2,717. Since 2 + 1 = 3 digits are to the right of the decimal points in 2.09 and 1.3, put 3 digits in 2,717 to the right of the decimal point to find the product:

$$2.09 \quad \text{(2 digits to the right)}$$
$$\times\ 1.3 \quad \text{(1 digit to the right)}$$
$$\overline{627}$$
$$\underline{2090}$$
$$2.717 \quad \text{(2 + 1 = 3 digits to the right)}$$

F. To divide a number (the *dividend*) by a decimal (the *divisor*), when both have many finite digits, move the decimal points of the dividend and divisor the same number of digits to the right until the divisor is an integer. Then divide as you would integers. The decimal point in the quotient goes directly above the decimal point in the new dividend.

Example:

To divide 698.12 by 12.4, first move the decimal points in both the divisor 12.4 and the dividend 698.12 one place to the right to make the divisor an integer. That is, replace 698.12/12.4 with 6981.2/124. Then do the long division normally:

```
              56.3
        124)6981.2
             620
             781
             744
             372
             372
               0
```

5. Arithmetic Shortcuts and Properties of Operations

A. For any two nonnegative integers x and y, the final digit of $x + y$ is the final digit of the sum of x's final digit and y's final digit. And for any two integers x and y, the final digit of xy is the final digit of the product of x's final digit and y's final digit.

Examples:

The final digit of 345 + 789 is the final digit of 5 + 9 = 14, which is 4.

The final digit of 345 × 789 is the final digit of 5 × 9 = 45, which is 5.

B. Here are some shortcuts to help tell whether one integer is divisible by another:

An integer is divisible by 2 if and only if its final digit is even.

An integer is divisible by 3 if and only if the sum of its digits is divisible by 3.

An integer with 3 or more digits is divisible by 4 if and only if its final 2 digits make a number divisible by 4.

An integer is divisible by 5 if and only if its final digit is 5 or 0.

An integer is divisible by 9 if and only if the sum of its digits is divisible by 9.

An integer is divisible by 10 if and only if its final digit is 0.

Examples:

The integer 180 is divisible by 2, 5, and 10, because its final digit is 0. It's also divisible by 3 and 9, because its digits sum to $1 + 8 + 0 = 9$, which is divisible by both 3 and 9. And it's divisible by 4, because its final 2 digits, 80, make a number divisible by 4.

But the integer 121 is not divisible by 2, because its final digit is odd. Nor is it divisible by 3 or 9, because its digits sum to $1 + 2 + 1 = 4$, which is divisible by neither 3 nor 9. And it's not divisible by 4, because its final two digits, 21, make a number not divisible by 4. Finally, because its final digit is neither 5 nor 0, it's not divisible by 5 or 10.

C. Here are some basic properties of arithmetical operations for any real numbers x, y, and z:

- Addition and Subtraction

$x + 0 = x = x - 0$

$x - x = 0$

$x + y = y + x$

$x - y = -(y - x) = x + (-y)$

$(x + y) + z = x + (y + z)$

If x and y are both positive, then $x + y$ is positive.

If x and y are both negative, then $x + y$ is negative.

- Multiplication and Division

$x \times 1 = x = \dfrac{x}{1}$

$x \times 0 = 0$

If $x \neq 0$, then $\dfrac{x}{x} = 1$.

$\dfrac{x}{0}$ is undefined.

$xy = yx$

If $x \neq 0$ and $y \neq 0$, then $\dfrac{x}{y} = \dfrac{1}{\left(\frac{y}{x}\right)}$.

$(xy)z = x(yz)$

$xy + xz = x(y + z)$

If $y \neq 0$, then $\left(\dfrac{x}{y}\right) + \left(\dfrac{z}{y}\right) = \dfrac{(x + z)}{y}$.

If x and y are both positive, then xy is positive.

If x and y are both negative, then xy is positive.

If x is positive and y is negative, then xy is negative.

If $xy = 0$, then $x = 0$ or $y = 0$, or both.

- Exponentiation

$x^1 = x$

If $x \neq 0$, then $x^0 = 1$.

If $x \neq 0$, then $x^{-1} = \frac{1}{x}$.

$(x^y)^z = x^{yz} = (x^z)^y$

$x^{y+z} = x^y x^z$

If $x \neq 0$, then $x^{y-z} = \frac{x^y}{x^z}$.

$(xz)^y = x^y z^y$

If $z \neq 0$, then $\left(\frac{x}{z}\right)^y = \frac{x^y}{z^y}$.

If $z \neq 0$, then $x^{\frac{y}{z}} = (x^y)^{\frac{1}{z}} = \left(x^{\frac{1}{z}}\right)^y$.

3.2 Algebra, Equalities, and Inequalities

1. Algebraic Expressions and Equations

A. Algebra is based on arithmetic and on the concept of an ***unknown quantity***. Letters like *x* or *n* are ***variables*** that stand for unknown quantities. Other numerical expressions called ***constants*** stand for known quantities. A combination of variables, constants, and arithmetical operations is an ***algebraic expression***.

Solving word problems often requires translating words into algebraic expressions. The table below shows how some words and phrases can be translated as math operations in algebraic expressions:

3.2 Translating Words into Math Operations				
$x + y$	$x - y$	xy	$\frac{x}{y}$	x^y
x added to *y* *x* increased by *y* *x* more than *y* *x* plus *y* the sum of *x* and *y* the total of *x* and *y*	*x* decreased by *y* difference of *x* and *y* *y* fewer than *x* *y* less than *x* *x* minus *y* *x* reduced by *y* *y* subtracted from *x*	*x* multiplied by *y* the product of *x* and *y* *x* times *y*	*x* divided by *y* *x* over *y* the quotient of *x* and *y* the ratio of *x* to *y*	*x* to the power of *y* *x* to the yth power
		If *y* = 2: double *x* twice *x*	If *y* = 2: half of *x* *x* halved	If *y* = 2: *x* squared
		If *y* = 3: triple *x*		If *y* = 3: *x* cubed

B. In an algebraic expression, a *term* is a constant, a variable, or a product of terms that are each a constant or a variable. A variable in a term may be raised to an exponent. A term with no variables is a *constant term*. A constant in a term with one or more variables is a *coefficient*.

> *Example:*
>
> Suppose Pam has 5 more pencils than Fred. If F is the number of pencils Fred has, then Pam has $F + 5$ pencils. The algebraic expression $F + 5$ has two terms: the variable F and the constant 5.

C. A *polynomial* is an algebraic expression that's a sum of terms and has exactly one variable. Each term in a polynomial is a variable raised to some power and multiplied by some coefficient. If the highest power a variable is raised to is 1, the expression is a *first degree* (or *linear*) *polynomial* in that variable. If the highest power a variable is raised to is 2, the expression is a *second degree* (or *quadratic*) *polynomial* in that variable.

> *Examples:*
>
> $F + 5$ is a linear polynomial in F, since the highest power of F is 1.
>
> $19x^2 - 6x + 3$ is a quadratic polynomial in x, since the highest power of x is 2.
>
> $\dfrac{3x^2}{(2x - 5)}$ is not a polynomial because it's not a sum of powers of x multiplied by coefficients.

D. You can simplify many algebraic expressions by factoring or combining *like* terms.

> *Examples:*
>
> In the expression $6x + 5x$, x is a factor common to both terms. So, $6x + 5x$ is equivalent to $(6 + 5)x$, or $11x$.
>
> In the expression $9x - 3y$, 3 is a factor common to both terms: $9x - 3y = 3(3x - y)$.
>
> The expression $5x^2 + 6y$ has no like terms and no common factors.

E. In a fraction $\dfrac{n}{d}$, n is the *numerator* and d is the *denominator*. In a numerator and denominator, you can divide out any common factors not equal to zero.

> *Example:*
>
> If $x \neq 3$, then $\dfrac{(x - 3)}{(x - 3)} = 1$.
>
> So, $\dfrac{(3xy - 9y)}{(x - 3)} = \dfrac{3y(x - 3)}{(x - 3)} = 3y(1) = 3y$.

F. To multiply two algebraic expressions, multiply each term of one expression by each term of the other.

Example:

$$(3x - 4)(9y + x) = 3x(9y + x) - 4(9y + x)$$
$$= 3x(9y) + 3x(x) - 4(9y) - 4(x)$$
$$= 27xy + 3x^2 - 36y - 4x$$

G. To *evaluate* an algebraic expression, replace its variables with constants.

Example:

If $x = 3$ and $y = -2$, we can evaluate $3xy - x^2 + y$ as

$$3(3)(-2) - (3)^2 + (-2) = -18 - 9 - 2 = -29.$$

H. An *algebraic equation* is an equation with only algebraic expressions. An algebraic equation's *solutions* are the sets of assignments of constant values to its variables that make it true, or "satisfy the equation." An equation may have no solution, one solution, or more than one solution. For equations solved together, the solutions must satisfy all the equations at once. An equation's solutions are also called its *roots*. To confirm the roots are correct, you can substitute them into the equation.

I. Two equations with the same solution or solutions are *equivalent*.

Examples:

The equations $2 + x = 3$ and $4 + 2x = 6$ are equivalent, because each has the unique solution $x = 1$. Notice the second equation is the first equation multiplied by 2.

Likewise, the equations $3x - y = 6$ and $6x - 2y = 12$ are equivalent, although each has infinitely many solutions. For any value of x, giving the value $3x - 6$ to y satisfies both these equations. For example, $x = 2$ with $y = 0$ is a solution to both equations, and so is $x = 5$ with $y = 9$.

2. Linear Equations

A. A *linear equation* has a linear polynomial on one side of the equals sign and either a linear polynomial or a constant on the other side—or can be converted to that form. A linear equation with only one variable is a *linear equation with one unknown*. A linear equation with two variables is *a linear equation with two unknowns*.

Examples:

$5x - 2 = 9 - x$ is a linear equation with one unknown.

$3x + 1 = y - 2$ is a linear equation with two unknowns.

B. To solve a linear equation with one unknown (that is, to find what value of the unknown satisfies the equation), isolate the unknown on one side of the equation by doing the same operations on both sides. Adding or subtracting the same number on both sides of the equation doesn't change the equality. Likewise, multiplying or dividing both sides by the same nonzero number doesn't change the equality.

Example:

To solve the equation $\frac{5x - 6}{3} = 4$, isolate the variable x like this:

$$5x - 6 = 12 \quad \text{multiply both sides by 3}$$
$$5x = 18 \quad \text{add 6 to both sides}$$
$$x = \frac{18}{5} \quad \text{divide both sides by 5}$$

To check the answer $\frac{18}{5}$, substitute it for x in the original equation to confirm it satisfies that equation:

$$\frac{\left(5\left(\frac{18}{5}\right) - 6\right)}{3} = \frac{(18 - 6)}{3} = \frac{12}{3} = 4$$

So, $x = \frac{18}{5}$ is the solution.

C. Two equivalent linear equations with the same two unknowns have infinitely many solutions, as in the example of the equivalent equations $3x - y = 6$ and $6x - 2y = 12$ in Section 3.2.1.I above. But if two linear equations with the same two unknowns aren't equivalent, they have at most one solution.

When solving two linear equations with two unknowns, if you reach a trivial equation like $0 = 0$, the equations are equivalent and have infinitely many solutions. But if you reach a contradiction, the equations have no solution.

Example:

Consider the two equations $3x + 4y = 17$ and $6x + 8y = 35$. Note that $3x + 4y = 17$ implies $6x + 8y = 34$, contradicting the second equation. So, no values of x and y can satisfy both equations at once. The two equations have no solution.

If neither a trivial equation nor a contradiction is reached, a unique solution can be found.

D. To solve two linear equations with two unknowns, you can use one of the equations to express one unknown in terms of the other unknown. Then substitute this result into the second equation to make a new equation with only one unknown. Next, solve this new equation. Substitute the value of its unknown into either original equation to solve for the remaining unknown.

Example:

Let's solve these two equations for x and y:

$$(1) \quad 3x + 2y = 11$$
$$(2) \quad x - y = 2$$

In equation (2), $x = 2 + y$. So, in equation (1), substitute $2 + y$ for x:

$$3(2 + y) + 2y = 11$$
$$6 + 3y + 2y = 11$$
$$6 + 5y = 11$$
$$5y = 5$$
$$y = 1$$

Since $y = 1$, we find $x - 1 = 2$, so $x = 2 + 1 = 3$.

E. Another way to remove one unknown and solve for x and y is to make the coefficients of one unknown the same in both equations (ignoring the sign). Then either add the equations or subtract one from the other.

Example:

Let's solve the equations:

$$(1) \quad 6x + 5y = 29 \text{ and}$$
$$(2) \quad 4x - 3y = -6$$

Multiply equation (1) by 3 and equation (2) by 5 to get

$$18x + 15y = 87 \text{ and}$$
$$20x - 15y = -30$$

Add the two equations to remove y. This gives us $38x = 57$, or $x = \frac{3}{2}$.

Substituting $\frac{3}{2}$ for x in either original equation gives $y = 4$. To check these answers, substitute both values into both the original equations.

3. Factoring and Quadratic Equations

A. Some equations can be solved by *factoring*. To do this, first add or subtract to bring all the expressions to one side of the equation, with 0 on the other side. Then try to express the nonzero side as a product of factors that are algebraic expressions. When that's possible, setting any of these factors equal to 0 makes a simpler equation. The solutions of the simpler equations made this way are also solutions of the factored equation.

Example:

Factor to find the solutions of the equation $x^3 - 2x^2 + x = -5(x-1)^2$:

$$x^3 - 2x^2 + x + 5(x-1)^2 = 0$$
$$x(x^2 - 2x + 1) + 5(x-1)^2 = 0$$
$$x(x-1)^2 + 5(x-1)^2 = 0$$
$$(x+5)(x-1)^2 = 0$$
$$x+5 = 0 \text{ or } x-1 = 0$$
$$x = -5 \text{ or } x = 1$$

So, $x = -5$ or $x = 1$.

B. When factoring to solve equations with algebraic fractions, note that a fraction equals 0 if and only if its numerator equals 0 and its denominator doesn't.

Example:

Find the solutions of the equation $\dfrac{x(x-3)(x^2+5)}{x-4} = 0$.

The denominator must not equal 0, so $x - 4 \neq 0$. Thus, $x \neq 4$.

But the numerator must equal 0: $x(x-3)(x^2+5) = 0$.

Thus, $x = 0$, or $x - 3 = 0$, or $x^2 + 5 = 0$. So, $x = 0$, or $x = 3$, or $x^2 + 5 = 0$.

But $x^2 + 5 = 0$ has no real solution because $x^2 + 5 \geq 0$ for every real number x. So, the original equation's solutions are 0 and 3.

C. Here are some common algebraic equations used for factoring. They hold for any real numbers x, y, and z:

Examples:

$(x + \frac{1}{x})^2 = x^2 + \dfrac{1}{x^2} + 2$

$(x+y)^2 = x^2 + 2xy + y^2$

$(x-y)^2 = x^2 - 2xy + y^2$

$(x+y)(x-y) = x^2 - y^2$

$x^2 + y^2 = (x+y)^2 - 2xy = (x-y)^2 + 2xy$

$(x+y+z)^2 = x^2 + y^2 + z^2 + 2xy + 2xz + 2yz$

$(x+y)^3 = x^3 + 3x^2y + 3xy^2 + y^3$

$(x-y)^3 = x^3 - 3x^2y + 3xy^2 - y^3$

D. A **_quadratic equation_** has the standard form $ax^2 + bx + c = 0$, where a, b, and c are real numbers and $a \neq 0$.

Examples:

$$x^2 + 6x + 5 = 0,$$
$$3x^2 - 2x = 0, \text{ and}$$
$$x^2 + 4 = 0.$$

E. Some quadratic equations are easily solved by factoring.

Example (1):

$$x^2 + 6x + 5 = 0$$
$$(x + 5)(x + 1) = 0$$
$$x + 5 = 0 \text{ or } x + 1 = 0$$
$$x = -5 \text{ or } x = -1$$

Example (2):

$$3x^2 - 3 = 8x$$
$$3x^2 - 8x - 3 = 0$$
$$(3x + 1)(x - 3) = 0$$
$$3x + 1 = 0 \text{ or } x - 3 = 0$$
$$x = -\frac{1}{3} \text{ or } x = 3$$

F. A quadratic equation has at most two real roots but may have just one or even no real root.

Examples:

The equation $x^2 - 6x + 9 = 0$ can be written as $(x - 3)^2 = 0$ or $(x - 3)(x - 3) = 0$. So, its only root is 3.

The equation $x^2 + 4 = 0$ has no real root. Since any real number squared is greater than or equal to zero, $x^2 + 4$ must be greater than or equal to 4 if x is a real number.

G. An expression of the form $a^2 - b^2$ can be factored as $(a - b)(a + b)$.

Example:

We can solve the quadratic equation $9x^2 - 25 = 0$ like this:

$$(3x - 5)(3x + 5) = 0$$
$$3x - 5 = 0 \text{ or } x + 5 = 0$$
$$x = \frac{5}{3} \text{ or } x = -\frac{5}{3}$$

H. If a quadratic expression isn't easily factored, we can still find its roots with the *quadratic formula*: If $ax^2 + bx + c = 0$ and $a \neq 0$, the roots are

$$x = \frac{-b + \sqrt{b^2 - 4ac}}{2a} \text{ and } x = \frac{-b - \sqrt{b^2 - 4ac}}{2a}$$

These roots are two distinct real numbers unless $b^2 - 4ac \leq 0$.

If $b^2 - 4ac = 0$, the two root expressions both equal $-\frac{b}{2a}$, so the equation has only one root.

If $b^2 - 4ac < 0$, then $\sqrt{b^2 - 4ac}$ is not a real number, so the equation has no real root.

4. Inequalities

A. An *inequality* is a statement with one of these symbols:

$\neq$ is not equal to

$>$ is greater than

$\geq$ is greater than or equal to

$<$ is less than

$\leq$ is less than or equal to

Examples:

$5x - 3 < 9$ and $6x \geq y$

B. Solve a linear inequality with one unknown the same way you solve a linear equation: isolate the unknown on one side. As in an equation, the same number can be added to or subtracted from both sides of the inequality. And you can multiply or divide both sides by a positive number without changing the order of the inequality. However, multiplying or dividing an inequality by a negative number reverses the order of the inequality. Thus, $6 > 2$, but $(-1)(6) < (-1)(2)$.

Example (1):

To solve the inequality $3x - 2 > 5$ for x, isolate x:

$3x - 2 > 5$

$3x > 7$ (add 2 to both sides)

$x > \frac{7}{3}$ (divide both sides by 3)

Example (2):

To solve the inequality $\frac{5x - 1}{-2} < 3$ for x, isolate x:

$\frac{5x - 1}{-2} < 3$

$5x - 1 > -6$ (multiply both sides by -2)

$5x > -5$ (add 1 to both sides)

$x > -1$ (divide both sides by 5)

5. Functions

A. An algebraic expression in one variable can define a *function* of that variable. A function is written as a letter like f or g along with the variable in the expression. Function notation is a short way to express that a value is being substituted for a variable.

Examples:

(i) The expression $x^3 - 5x^2 + 2$ can define a function f written as $f(x) = x^3 - 5x^2 + 2$.

(ii) The expression $\dfrac{2z + 7}{\sqrt{z + 1}}$ can define a function g written as $g(z) = \dfrac{2z + 7}{\sqrt{z + 1}}$.

In these examples, the symbols "$f(x)$" and "$g(z)$" don't stand for products. Each is just a symbol for a function. Pronounce "$f(x)$" as "f of x" and "$g(z)$" as "g of z."

The substitution of 1 for x in the first expression can be written as $f(1) = -2$. Then $f(1)$ is called the "value of f at $x = 1$."

Likewise, in the second expression the value of g at $z = 0$ is $g(0) = 7$.

B. Once a function $f(x)$ is defined, think of x as an input and $f(x)$ as the output. In any function, any one input gives at most one output. But different inputs can give the same output.

Example:

If $h(x) = |x + 3|$, then $h(-4) = 1 = h(-2)$.

C. The set of all allowed inputs for a function is the function's ***domain***. In the examples in Section 3.2.5.A above, the domain of f is the set of all real numbers, and the domain of g is the set of all numbers greater than -1.

Any function's definition can restrict the function's domain. For example, the definition "$a(x) = 9x - 5$ for $0 \le x \le 10$" restricts the domain of a to real numbers greater than or equal to 0 but less than or equal to 10. If the definition has no restrictions, the domain is the set of all values of x that each give a real output when input into the function.

D. The set of a function's outputs is the function's ***range***.

Examples:

(i) For the function $h(x) = |x + 3|$ in the example in Section 3.2.5.B above, the range is the set of all numbers greater than or equal to 0.

(ii) For the function $a(x) = 9x - 5$ for $0 \le x \le 10$ defined in Section 3.2.5.C above, the range is the set of all real numbers y such that $-5 \le y \le 85$.

E. A ***quadratic function*** has the form $f(x) = ax^2 + bx + c$ where a, b, and c are constants and $a \ne 0$. If $a > 0$, then $f(x)$ has a unique minimum value but no maximum value. Otherwise, it has a unique maximum value but no minimum value. In either case, the unique minimum or maximum value of $f(x)$ is $c - \dfrac{b^2}{4a}$. This value occurs only when $x = -\dfrac{b}{2a}$.

Examples:

(i) The quadratic function $f(x) = 2x^2 - 3x + 4$ has a unique minimum value of $4 - \dfrac{(-3)^2}{4 \times 2} =$ $4 - \dfrac{9}{8} = \dfrac{25}{8}$. This minimum value occurs only when $x = -\left(\dfrac{-3}{2 \times 2}\right) = \dfrac{3}{4}$.

(ii) The quadratic function $g(x) = -3x^2 + 2x + 1$ has a unique maximum value of $1 - \dfrac{2^2}{4 \times -3} =$ $1 - \dfrac{-1}{3} = \dfrac{4}{3}$. This maximum value occurs only when $x = -\left(\dfrac{2}{2 \times -3}\right) = \dfrac{1}{3}$.

6. Graphing

A. The figure below shows the rectangular *coordinate plane.* The horizontal line is the *x-axis* and the vertical line is the *y-axis*. These two axes intersect at the *origin*, called O. The axes divide the plane into four quadrants: I, II, III, and IV, as shown.

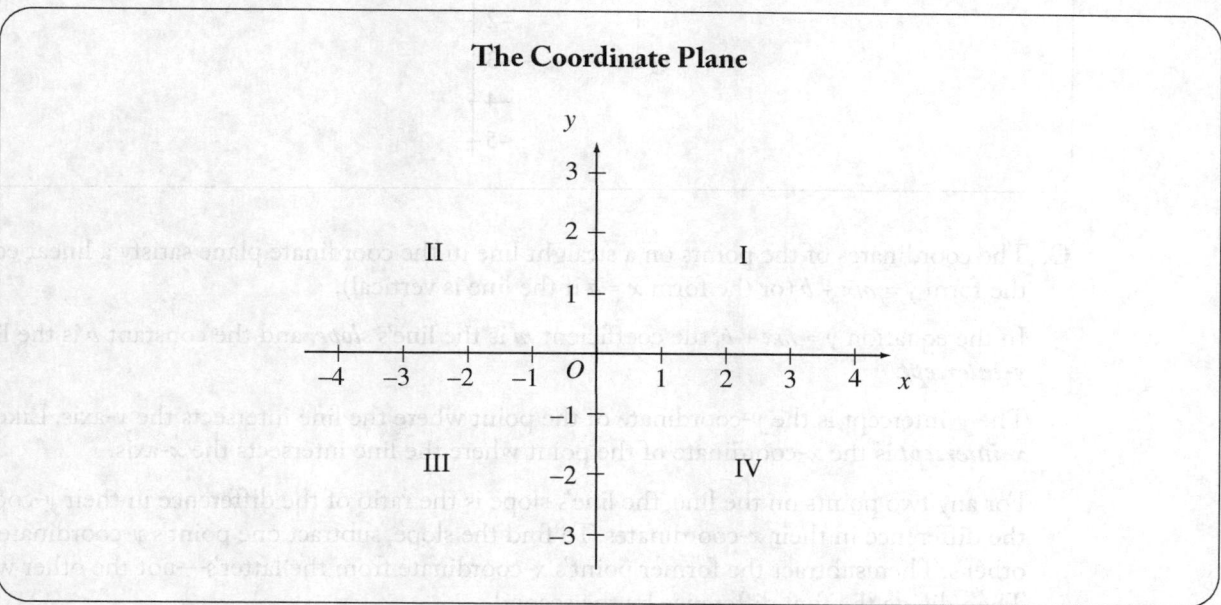

The Coordinate Plane

B. Any ordered pair (x, y) of real numbers defines a point in the coordinate plane. The point's *x-coordinate* is the first number in this pair. It shows how far the point is to the right or left of the *y*-axis. If the *x*-coordinate is positive, the point is to the right of the *y*-axis. If it's negative, the point is to the left of the *y*-axis. If it's 0, the point is on the *y*-axis. The point's *y-coordinate* is the second number in the ordered pair. It shows how far the point is above or below the *x*-axis. If the *y*-coordinate is positive, the point is above the *x*-axis. If it's negative, the point is below the *x*-axis. If it's 0, the point is on the *x*-axis.

Example:

In the graph below, the (x, y) coordinates of point P are $(2, 3)$. P is 2 units to the right of the y-axis, so $x = 2$. Since P is 3 units above the x-axis, $y = 3$.

Likewise, the (x, y) coordinates of point Q are $(-4, -3)$. The origin O has coordinates $(0, 0)$.

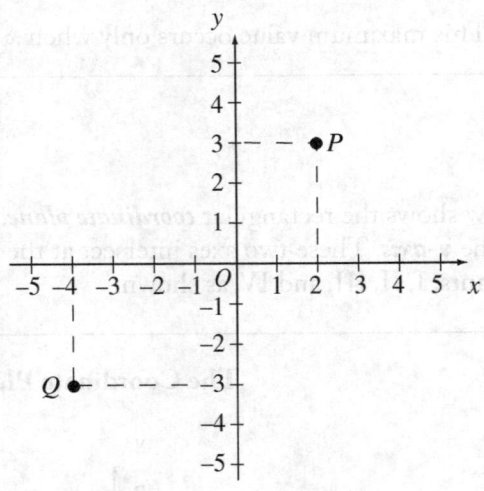

C. The coordinates of the points on a straight line in the coordinate plane satisfy a linear equation of the form $y = mx + b$ (or the form $x = a$ if the line is vertical).

In the equation $y = mx + b$, the coefficient m is the line's **slope**, and the constant b is the line's **y-intercept**.

The y-intercept is the y-coordinate of the point where the line intersects the y-axis. Likewise, the **x-intercept** is the x-coordinate of the point where the line intersects the x-axis.

For any two points on the line, the line's slope is the ratio of the difference in their y-coordinates to the difference in their x-coordinates. To find the slope, subtract one point's y-coordinate from the other's. Then subtract the former point's x-coordinate from the latter's—not the other way around! Then divide the first difference by the second.

If a line's slope is negative, the line slants down from left to right.

If the slope is positive, the line slants up.

If the slope is 0, the line is horizontal. A horizontal line's equation has the form $y = b$, since $m = 0$.

A vertical line's slope is undefined.

Example:

In the graph below, each point on the line satisfies the equation $y = -\frac{1}{2}x + 1$. To check this for the points $(-2, 2)$, $(2, 0)$, and $(0, 1)$, substitute each point's coordinates for x and y in the equation.

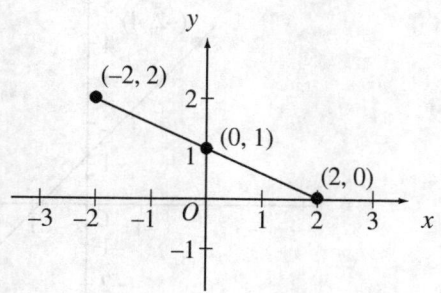

You can use the points $(-2, 2)$ and $(2, 0)$ to find the line's slope:

$$\frac{\text{the difference in the } y\text{-coordinates}}{\text{the difference in the } x\text{-coordinates}} = \frac{0 - 2}{2 - (-2)} = \frac{-2}{4} = -\frac{1}{2}.$$

The y-intercept is 1. That's y's value when x is 0 in $y = -\frac{1}{2}x + 1$.

To find the x-intercept, set y to 0 in the same equation:

$$-\frac{1}{2}x + 1 = 0$$
$$-\frac{1}{2}x = -1$$
$$x = 2$$

Thus, the x-intercept is 2.

D. You can use the definition of slope to find an equation of the line through two points (x_1, y_1) and (x_2, y_2) with $x_1 \neq x_2$. The slope is $m = \frac{y_2 - y_1}{x_2 - x_1}$. Given the known point (x_1, y_1) and the slope m, any other point (x, y) on the line satisfies the equation $m = \frac{(y - y_1)}{(x - x_1)}$, or equivalently $(y - y_1) = m(x - x_1)$. Using (x_2, y_2) instead of (x_1, y_1) as the known point gives an equivalent equation.

Example:

The graph below shows points (–2, 4) and (3, –3).

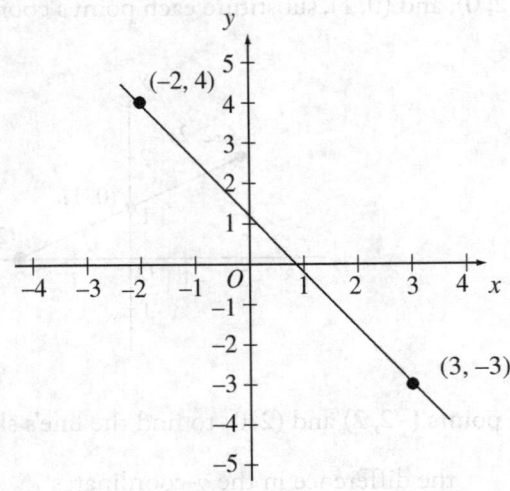

The line's slope is $\dfrac{(-3-4)}{(3-(-2))} = -\dfrac{7}{5}$. To find an equation of this line, let's use the point (3, –3):

$$y - (-3) = \left(-\frac{7}{5}\right)(x - 3)$$

$$y + 3 = \left(-\frac{7}{5}\right)x + \frac{21}{5}$$

$$y = \left(-\frac{7}{5}\right)x + \frac{6}{5}$$

So, the *y*-intercept is $\dfrac{6}{5}$.

Find the *x*-intercept like this:

$$0 = -\frac{7}{5}x + \frac{6}{5}$$

$$\frac{7}{5}x = \frac{6}{5}$$

$$x = \frac{6}{7}$$

The graph shows both these intercepts.

E. If two linear equations with unknowns *x* and *y* have a unique shared solution, their graphs are two lines intersecting at the shared point that is the solution.

If two linear equations are equivalent, they both stand for the same line and have infinitely many shared solutions.

Two linear equations with no shared solution stand for two parallel lines.

F. Graph any function $f(x)$ in the coordinate plane by equating *y* with the function's value: $y = f(x)$. For any *x* in the function's domain, the point $(x, f(x))$ is on the function's graph. For every point on the graph, the *y*-coordinate is the function's value at the *x*-coordinate.

Example:

Consider the function $f(x) = -\frac{7}{5}x + \frac{6}{5}$.

If $f(x)$ is equated with the variable y, the function's graph is the graph of $y = -\frac{7}{5}x + \frac{6}{5}$ in the example above.

G. For any function f, the x-intercepts are the solutions of the equation $f(x) = 0$. The y-intercept is the value $f(0)$.

Example:

To see how the quadratic function $f(x) = x^2 - 1$ relates to its graph, let's plot some points $(x, f(x))$ in the coordinate plane:

x	$f(x)$
-2	3
-1	0
0	-1
1	0
2	3

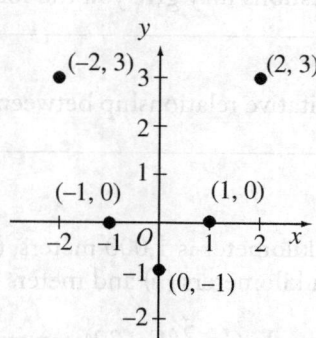

The graph below shows all the points for $-2 \le x \le 2$:

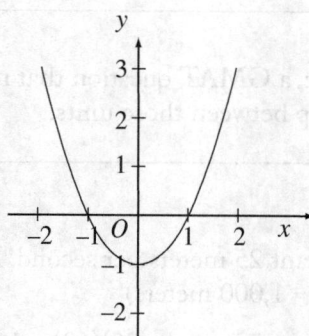

The roots of this equation $f(x) = x^2 - 1 = 0$ are $x = 1$ and $x = -1$. They match the x-intercepts since x-intercepts are found by setting $y = 0$ and solving for x.

The y-intercept is $f(0) = -1$ because that's the value of y for $x = 0$.

7. Formulas and Measurement Conversion

A. A *formula* is an algebraic equation with variables that have specific meanings. To use a formula, assign quantities to its variables to match these meanings.

> *Example:*
>
> In the physics formula $F = ma$, the variable F stands for force, the variable m stands for mass, and the variable a stands for acceleration. The standard metric unit of force, the newton, is just enough force to accelerate a mass of 1 kilogram by 1 meter/second^2.
>
> If we know a rock with a mass of 2 kilograms is accelerating at 5 meters/second^2, we can use the formula $F = ma$ by setting the variable m to 2 kilograms, and the variable a to 5 meters/second^2. Then we find that 10 newtons of force F are pushing the rock.
>
> Note: You don't need to learn physics formulas or terms like this for the GMAT, but some specific GMAT questions may give you the formulas and terms you need to solve them.

B. Any quantitative relationship between units of measure can be written as a formula.

> *Examples:*
>
> (i) Since 1 kilometer is 1,000 meters, the formula $m = 1000k$ can stand for the relationship between kilometers (k) and meters (m).
>
> (ii) The formula $C = \frac{5}{9}(F - 32)$ can stand for the relationship between temperature measurements in degrees Celsius (C) and degrees Fahrenheit (F).

C. Except for units of time, a GMAT question that requires converting one unit of measure to another will give the relationship between those units.

> *Example:*
>
> A train travels at a constant 25 meters per second. How many kilometers does it travel in 5 minutes? (1 kilometer = 1,000 meters)
>
> *Solution:* In 1 minute the train travels $(25)(60) = 1,500$ meters, so in 5 minutes it travels 7,500 meters. Since 1 kilometer = 1,000 meters, we find 7,500 meters = 7.5 kilometers.

3.3 Rates, Ratios, and Percents

1. Ratio and Proportion

A. The *ratio* of a number x to a nonzero number y may be written as $x{:}y$, or $\frac{x}{y}$, or x to y. In each of these expressions, x is the numerator and y is the denominator. The order of a ratio's terms is important. Unless the absolute values of x and y are equal, $\frac{x}{y} \neq \frac{y}{x}$.

Examples:

The ratio of 2 to 3 may be written as 2:3, or $\frac{2}{3}$, or 2 to 3.

The ratio of the number of months with exactly 30 days to the number of months with exactly 31 days is 4:7, not 7:4.

B. A ***proportion*** is an equation between two ratios. Remember, the denominator on either side of the proportion must not equal zero.

Example:

2:3 = 8:12 is a proportion.

C. One way to solve for an unknown in a proportion is to cross multiply, then solve the resulting equation.

Example:

To solve for n in the proportion $\frac{2}{3} = \frac{n}{12}$, cross multiply to get $3n = 24$, then divide both sides by 3 to find $n = 8$.

D. Some word problems can be solved using ratios.

Example:

If 5 shirts cost a total of $44, then what is the total cost of 8 shirts at the same cost per shirt?

Solution: If c is the cost of the 8 shirts, then $\frac{5}{44} = \frac{8}{c}$. Cross multiplying gives $5c = 8 \times 44 = 352$, so $c = \frac{352}{5} = 70.4$. Thus, the 8 shirts cost a total of $70.40.

2. Fractions

A. In a fraction $\frac{n}{d}$, n is the ***numerator*** and d is the ***denominator***. A fraction's denominator can never be 0 because division by 0 is undefined.

B. ***Equivalent*** fractions stand for the same number. To check whether two fractions with numerators and denominators that are integers are equivalent, divide each fraction's numerator and denominator by the largest factor common to that numerator and that denominator, their ***greatest common divisor*** (GCD). This is called ***reducing each fraction to its lowest terms***. Two fractions are equivalent if and only if reducing each to its lowest terms makes them identical.

Example:

To check whether $\frac{8}{36}$ and $\frac{14}{63}$ are equivalent, first reduce each to its lowest terms. In the first fraction, 4 is the GCD of the numerator 8 and the denominator 36. Dividing both the numerator and the denominator of $\frac{8}{36}$ by 4 gives $\frac{2}{9}$. In the second fraction, 7 is the GCD of the numerator 14 and the denominator 63. Dividing both the numerator and the denominator of $\frac{14}{63}$ by 7 also gives $\frac{2}{9}$. Since reducing $\frac{8}{36}$ and $\frac{14}{63}$ to their lowest terms makes them identical, they're equivalent.

C. To add or subtract two fractions with the same denominator, just add or subtract the numerators, leaving the denominators the same.

Examples:

$\frac{3}{5} + \frac{4}{5} = \frac{3+4}{5} = \frac{7}{5}$ and

$\frac{5}{7} - \frac{2}{7} = \frac{5-2}{7} = \frac{3}{7}$

D. To add or subtract two fractions with different denominators, first express them as fractions with the same denominator.

Example:

To add $\frac{3}{5}$ and $\frac{4}{7}$, multiply the numerator and denominator of $\frac{3}{5}$ by 7 to get $\frac{21}{35}$. Then multiply the numerator and denominator of $\frac{4}{7}$ by 5 to get $\frac{20}{35}$. Since both fractions now have the same denominator 35, you can easily add them: $\frac{3}{5} + \frac{4}{7} = \frac{21}{35} + \frac{20}{35} = \frac{41}{35}$

E. To multiply two fractions, multiply their numerators, and also multiply their denominators.

Example:

$\frac{2}{3} \times \frac{4}{7} = \frac{2 \times 4}{3 \times 7} = \frac{8}{21}$

F. The *reciprocal* of a fraction $\frac{n}{d}$ is $\frac{d}{n}$ if neither n nor d is 0.

Example:

The reciprocal of $\frac{4}{7}$ is $\frac{7}{4}$.

G. To divide by a fraction, multiply by its reciprocal.

> *Example:*
>
> $$\frac{2}{3} \div \frac{4}{7} = \frac{2}{3} \times \frac{7}{4} = \frac{14}{12} = \frac{7}{6}$$

H. A *mixed number* is written as an integer next to a fraction. It equals the integer plus the fraction.

> *Example:*
>
> The mixed number $7\frac{2}{3} = 7 + \frac{2}{3}$

I. To write a mixed number as a fraction, multiply the integer part of the mixed number by the denominator of the fractional part. Add this product to the numerator. Then put this sum over the denominator.

> *Example:*
>
> $$7\frac{2}{3} = \frac{(7 \times 3) + 2}{3} = \frac{23}{3}$$

3. Percents

A. The word *percent* means *per hundred* or *number out of 100*.

> *Example:*
>
> Saying that 37 percent, or 37%, of the houses in a city are painted blue means that 37 houses per 100 in the city are painted blue.

B. A percent may be greater than 100.

> *Example:*
>
> Saying that the number of blue houses in a city is 150% of the number of red houses means the city has 150 blue houses for every 100 red houses. Since 150:100 = 3:2, this means the city has 3 blue houses for every 2 red houses.

C. A percent need not be an integer.

> *Example:*
>
> Saying that the number of pink houses in a city is 0.5% of the number of blue houses means the city has 0.5 of a pink house for every 100 blue houses. Since 0.5:100 = 1:200, this means the city has 1 pink house for every 200 blue houses.
>
> Likewise, saying that the number of orange houses is 12.5% of the number of blue houses means the ratio of orange houses to blue houses is 12.5:100 = 1:8. Therefore, there is 1 orange house for every 8 blue houses.

4. Converting Decimals, Fractions, and Percents

A. Decimals with many finite digits can be rewritten as fractions or sums of fractions.

> *Examples:*
>
> $$0.321 = \frac{3}{10} + \frac{2}{100} + \frac{1}{1,000} = \frac{321}{1,000}$$
>
> $$0.0321 = \frac{0}{10} + \frac{3}{100} + \frac{2}{1,000} + \frac{1}{10,000} = \frac{321}{10,000}$$
>
> $$1.56 = 1 + \frac{5}{10} + \frac{6}{100} = \frac{156}{100}$$

B. Repeating decimals can also be rewritten as fractions. To do this, set a variable x equal to the repeating decimal. Next multiply both sides by a power of 10 just large enough to make the repeating digits start right after the decimal if they don't already. Call this Equation A. Then make another equation by multiplying both sides of Equation A by a power of 10 just large enough to move one copy of the repeating digits from the right to the left of the decimal point. From this, subtract Equation A, and solve for x.

> *Examples:*
>
> (i) To rewrite the repeating decimal $3.\overline{6}$ as a fraction, first let $x = 3.\overline{6}$. This equation already has the repeating digit 6 starting right after the decimal, so it's our Equation A. Next we multiply both sides by 10 to move one repeating 6 from the right to the left of the decimal point: $10x = 36.\overline{6}$. From this, subtract Equation A to get $9x = 36.\overline{6} - 3.\overline{6} = 33$. Finally divide both sides by 9 to solve for x: $x = \frac{33}{9} = 3\frac{2}{3}$.
>
> (ii) To rewrite the repeating decimal $1.2\overline{79}$ as a fraction, first let $x = 1.2\overline{79}$. Next multiply both sides by 10 to make the repeating digits start right after the decimal: $10x = 12.\overline{79}$. This is our Equation A. Then multiply both sides by 100 to move one copy of the repeating digits 79 from the right to the left of the decimal point: $1000x = 1279.\overline{79}$. From this, subtract Equation A to get $990x = 1279.\overline{79} - 12.\overline{79} = 1267$. Finally divide both sides by 990 to solve for x: $x = \frac{1267}{990} = 1\frac{277}{990}$.

C. To rewrite a percent as a fraction, write the percent number as the numerator over a denominator of 100. To rewrite a percent as a decimal, move the decimal point in the percent two places to the left and drop the percent sign. To rewrite a decimal as a percent, move the decimal point two places to the right, then add a percent sign.

Examples:

$37\% = \dfrac{37}{100} = 0.37$

$300\% = \dfrac{300}{100} = 3$

$0.5\% = \dfrac{0.5}{100} = 0.005$

D. To find a percent of a number, multiply the number by the percent written as a fraction or decimal.

Examples:

20% of $90 = 90\left(\dfrac{20}{100}\right) = 90\left(\dfrac{1}{5}\right) = \dfrac{90}{5} = 18$

20% of $90 = 90(0.2) = 18$

250% of $80 = 80\left(\dfrac{250}{100}\right) = 80(2.5) = 200$

0.5% of $12 = 12\left(\dfrac{0.5}{100}\right) = 12(0.005) = 0.06$

5. Working with Decimals, Fractions, and Percents

A. To find the percent increase or decrease from one positive quantity to another, first find the amount of increase or decrease. Then divide this amount by the original quantity. Write this quotient as a percent.

Examples:

Suppose a price increases from $24 to $30. To find the percent increase, first find the amount of increase: $30 − $24 = $6. Divide this $6 by the original price of $24 to find the percent increase: $\dfrac{6}{24} = 0.25 = 25\%$.

Now suppose a price falls from $30 to $24. The amount of decrease is $30 − $24 = $6. So, the percent decrease is $\dfrac{6}{30} = 0.20 = 20\%$.

Notice the percent **increase** from 24 to 30 (25%) doesn't equal the percent **decrease** from 30 to 24 (20%).

A percent increase may be greater than 100%, but a percent decrease cannot be.

Example:

Suppose a house's price in 2018 was 300% of its price in 2003, which was above 0. By what percent did the price increase?

Solution: If n is the price in 2003, the percent increase is $\left|\frac{(3n-n)}{n}\right| = \left|\frac{2n}{n}\right| = 2, \frac{(3n-n)}{n} = \frac{2n}{2} = 2$, or 200%.

B. A price discounted by n percent is $(100 - n)$ percent of the original price.

Example:

A customer paid $24 for a dress. If the customer got a 25% discount off the original price of the dress, what was the original price before the discount?

Solution: The discounted price is 100% − 25% = 75% of the original price. So, if p is the original price, $0.75p = \$24$ is the discounted price. Thus, $p = (\$24/0.75) = \$32$, the original price before the discount.

Two discounts can be combined to make a larger discount.

Example:

A price is discounted 20%. Then this reduced price is discounted another 30%. These two discounts together make an overall discount of what percent?

Solution: If p is the original price, then $0.8p$ is the price after the first discount. The price after the second discount is $(0.7)(0.8)\,p = 0.56p$. The overall discount is 100% − 56% = 44%.

C. *Profit* equals revenues minus expenses, or selling price minus total costs.

Example:

A certain appliance costs a merchant a total of $30 to acquire and sell. At what price should the merchant sell the appliance to make a profit of 50% of the appliance's total cost to the merchant?

Solution: The merchant should sell the appliance for a price $\$s$ such that $s - 30 = (0.5)(30)$. So, $\$s = \$30 + \$15 = \$45$.

D. *Simple annual interest* on a loan or investment is based only on the original loan or investment amount (the *principal*). It equals (principal) × (interest rate) × (time).

Example:

If $8,000 is invested at 6% simple annual interest, how much interest is earned in 3 months?

Solution: Since the annual interest rate is 6%, the interest for 1 year is $(0.06)(\$8,000) = \$480$. A year has 12 months, so the interest earned in 3 months is $\left(\frac{3}{12}\right)(\$480) = \$120$.

E. ***Compound interest*** is based on the principal plus any interest already earned.

Compound interest over n periods = (principal) $\times$ (1 + interest per period)^n – principal.

Example:

If \$10,000 is invested at 10% annual interest, compounded every 6 months, what is the investment's value after 1 year?

Solution: Since the interest is compounded every 6 months, or twice a year, the interest rate for each 6-month period is 5%, half the 10% annual rate. So, the investment's value after the first 6 months is 10,000 + (10,000)(0.05) = \$10,500.

For the second 6 months, the interest is based on the \$10,500 balance after the first 6 months. So, the investment's value after 1 year is 10,500 + (10,500)(0.05) = \$11,025.

The investment's value after 1 year can also be written as $10,000 \times \left(1 + \dfrac{0.10}{2}\right)^2$ dollars.

F. To solve some word problems with percents and fractions, you can organize the information in a table.

Example:

In a production lot, 40% of the toys are red, and the rest are green. Half of the toys are small, and half are large. If 10% of the toys are red and small, and 40 toys are green and large, how many of the toys are red and large?

Solution: First make a table to organize the information:

	Red	Green	Total
Small	10%		50%
Large			50%
Total	40%	60%	100%

Then fill in the missing percents so that the "Red" and "Green" percents in each row add up to that row's total, and the "Small" and "Large" percents in each column add up to that column's total:

	Red	Green	Total
Small	10%	40%	50%
Large	30%	20%	50%
Total	40%	60%	100%

The number of large green toys, 40, is 20% of the total number of toys (n), so $0.20n = 40$. Thus, the total number of toys $n = 200$. So, 30% of the 200 toys are red and large. Since $(0.3)(200) = 60$, we find that 60 of the toys are red and large.

---

6. Rate, Work, and Mixture Problems

A. The distance an object travels is its average speed multiplied by the time it takes to travel that distance. That is, ***distance = rate × time.***

Example:

How many kilometers did a car travel in 4 hours at an average speed of 70 kilometers per hour?

Solution: Since distance = rate × time, multiply 70 kilometers/hour × 4 hours to find that the car went 280 kilometers.

B. To find an object's average travel speed, divide the total travel distance by the total travel time.

Example:

On a 600-kilometer trip, a car went half the distance at an average speed of 60 kilometers per hour (kph), and the other half at an average speed of 100 kph. The car didn't stop between the two halves of the trip. What was the car's average speed over the whole trip?

Solution: First find the total travel time. For the first 300 kilometers, the car went at 60 kph, taking $\frac{300 \text{ kilometers}}{60 \text{ kph}}$ = 5 hours. For the second 300 kilometers, the car went at 100 kph, taking $\frac{300 \text{ kilometers}}{100 \text{ kph}}$ = 3 hours. So, the total travel time was 5 + 3 = 8 hours. The car's average speed was $\frac{600 \text{ kilometers}}{8 \text{ hours}}$ = 75 kph. Notice the average speed was not $\frac{(60 + 100) \text{ kilometers}}{2 \text{ hours}}$ = 80 kph.

C. A ***work problem*** usually says how fast certain individuals work alone, then asks you to find how fast they work together, or vice versa.

The basic formula for work problems is $\frac{1}{r} + \frac{1}{s} = \frac{1}{h}$, where r is how long an amount of work takes a certain individual, s is how long that much work takes a different individual, and h is how long that much work takes both individuals working at the same time.

Example:

Suppose one machine takes 4 hours to make 1,000 bolts, and a second machine takes 5 hours to make 1,000 bolts. How many hours do both machines working at the same time take to make 1,000 bolts?

Solution:

$$\frac{1}{4} + \frac{1}{5} = \frac{1}{h}$$

$$\frac{5}{20} + \frac{4}{20} = \frac{1}{h}$$

$$\frac{9}{20} = \frac{1}{h}$$

$$9h = 20$$

$$h = \frac{20}{9} = 2\frac{2}{9}$$

Working together, the two machines can make 1,000 bolts in $2\frac{2}{9}$ hours.

If a work problem says how long it takes two individuals to do an amount of work together, and how long it takes one of them to do that much work alone, you can use the same formula to find how long it takes the other individual to do that much work alone.

Example:

Suppose Art and Rita both working at the same time take 4 hours to do an amount of work, and Art alone takes 6 hours to do that much work. Then how many hours does Rita alone take to do that much work?

Solution:

$$\frac{1}{6} + \frac{1}{R} = \frac{1}{4}$$

$$\frac{1}{R} = \frac{1}{4} - \frac{1}{6} = \frac{1}{12}$$

$$R = 12$$

Rita alone takes 12 hours to do that much work.

D. In *mixture problems*, substances with different properties are mixed, and you must find the mixture's properties.

Example:

If 6 kilograms of nuts that cost $1.20 per kilogram are mixed with 2 kilograms of nuts that cost $1.60 per kilogram, how much does the mixture cost per kilogram?

Solution: The 8 kilograms of nuts cost a total of 6($1.20) + 2($1.60) = $10.40. So, the cost per kilogram of the mixture is $\frac{\$10.40}{8}$ = $1.30.

Some mixture problems use percents.

Example:

How many liters of a solution that is 15% salt must be added to 5 liters of a solution that is 8% salt to make a solution that is 10% salt?

Solution: Let n be the needed number of liters of the 15% solution. The amount of salt in n liters of 15% solution is $0.15n$. The amount of salt in the 5 liters of 8% solution is $(0.08)(5)$. These amounts add up to the amount of salt in the 10% mixture, which is $0.10(n + 5)$. So,

$$0.15n + 0.08(5) = 0.10(n + 5)$$

$$15n + 40 = 10n + 50$$

$$5n = 10$$

$$n = 2 \text{ liters}$$

So, 2 liters of the 15% salt solution must be added to the 8% solution to make the 10% solution.

3.4 Statistics, Sets, Counting, Probability, Estimation, and Series

1. Statistics

A. A common statistical measure is the *average* or *(arithmetic) mean*, a type of center for the numerical values in a data set. The average or mean of n values is the sum of the n values divided by n. If a number appears more than once in the data set, each instance of that number is a separate value and is added separately to find the sum. To learn more about values in data sets, see Chapter 5, "Data Insights Review."

> *Example:*
>
> The average of the 5 values 6, 4, 7, 10, and 4 is $\frac{(6 + 4 + 7 + 10 + 4)}{5} = \frac{31}{5} = 6.2$. Notice that 4 appears twice in the list of 5 values, so it is added twice when finding the sum.

B. The *median* is another type of center for ordered values in a data set. As above, if a number appears more than once in the data set, each instance of that number is a separate value. To find the median, list the values from least to greatest. If the number of entries in the list is odd, the median is the middle entry in the list. But if the number of entries in the list is even, the median is the average of the two middle entries. The median may be less than, equal to, or greater than the mean.

> *Example:*
>
> To find the median of the 5 values 6, 4, 7, 10, and 4, arrange them from least to greatest: 4, 4, 6, 7, 10. The median is 6, the middle entry in this list.
>
> The median of the 6 values 4, 6, 6, 8, 9, and 12 is $\frac{(6 + 8)}{2} = 7$. But the mean of these 6 values is $\frac{(4 + 6 + 6 + 8 + 9 + 12)}{6} = \frac{45}{6} = 7.5$.

Often about half the values in a data set are less than the median, and about half are greater than the median. But not always.

> *Example:*
>
> For the 15 values 3, 5, 7, 7, 7, 7, 7, 7, 8, 9, 9, 9, 9, 10, and 10, the median is 7. Only $\frac{2}{15}$ of the values are less than the median.

C. The *mode* of a data set is the value appearing most often in the list.

> *Example:*
>
> The mode of the list of values 1, 3, 6, 4, 3, and 5 is 3, since 3 is the only value appearing more than once in the list.

A list may have more than one mode.

> *Example:*
>
> The list 1, 2, 3, 3, 3, 5, 7, 10, 10, 10, and 20 has two modes, 3 and 10.

D. The ***dispersion*** of numerical data is how spread out the data is. The simplest measure of dispersion is the ***range***, which is the greatest value in the data minus the least value.

> *Example:*
>
> The range of the values 11, 10, 5, 13, and 21 is $21 - 5 = 16$. Notice the range depends on only 2 of the values.

E. Another common measure of dispersion is the ***standard deviation***. Generally, the farther the values are from the mean, the greater the standard deviation. To find the standard deviation of n values:

(1) Find their mean

(2) Find the differences between the mean and each of the n values

(3) Square each difference

(4) Find the average of the squared differences, and

(5) Take the nonnegative square root of this average

> *Examples:*
>
> Let's use the table below to find the standard deviation of the 5 values 0, 7, 8, 10, and 10, which have the mean 7.
>
> | x | $x - 7$ | $(x - 7)^2$ |
> |-----|---------|-------------|
> | 0 | −7 | 49 |
> | 7 | 0 | 0 |
> | 8 | 1 | 1 |
> | 10 | 3 | 9 |
> | 10 | 3 | 9 |
> | | Total | 68 |
>
> The standard deviation is $\sqrt{\dfrac{68}{5}} \approx 3.7$

The standard deviation depends on every value in the data set, but more on those farther from the mean. This is why the standard deviation is smaller for a data set grouped closer around its mean.

As a second example, consider the values 6, 6, 6.5, 7.5, and 9, which also have the mean 7. These values are grouped closer around the mean 7 than are those in the first example. That makes the standard deviation in this second example only about 1.1, far below the standard deviation of 3.7 in the first example.

F. How many times a value occurs in a data set is its *frequency* in the set. When different values have different frequencies, a *frequency distribution* can help show how the values are distributed.

Example:

Consider this data set of 20 numbers:

$$-4 \quad 0 \quad 0 \quad -3 \quad -2 \quad -1 \quad -1 \quad 0 \quad -1 \quad -4$$
$$-1 \quad -5 \quad 0 \quad -2 \quad 0 \quad -5 \quad -2 \quad 0 \quad 0 \quad -1$$

We can show its frequency distribution in a table showing each value x and x's frequency f:

Value x	Frequency f
−5	2
−4	2
−3	1
−2	3
−1	5
0	7
Total	20

This frequency distribution table makes finding statistical measures easier:

Mean: $= \dfrac{(-5)(2) + (-4)(2) + (-3)(1) + (-2)(3) + (-1)(5) + (0)(7)}{20} = -1.6$

Median: −1 (the average of the 10th and 11th numbers)

Mode: 0 (the number that occurs most often)

Range: $0 - (-5) = 5$

Standard deviation: $\sqrt{\dfrac{(-5 + 1.6)^2(2) + (-4 + 1.6)^2(2) + \ldots + (0 + 1.6)^2(7)}{20}} \approx 1.7$

2. Sets

A. In math, a *set* is a collection of numbers or other things. The things in the set are its *elements*. A list of a set's elements between braces stands for the set. The list's order doesn't matter.

Example:

$\{-5, 0, 1\}$ is the same set as $\{0, 1, -5\}$. That is, $\{-5, 0, 1\} = \{0, 1, -5\}$.

B. The number of elements in a finite set S is written as $|S|$.

> *Example:*
>
> $S = \{-5, 0, 1\}$ is a set with $|S| = 3$.

C. If all the elements in a set S are also in a set T, then S is a ***subset*** of T. This is written as $S \subseteq T$ or $T \supseteq S$.

> *Example:*
>
> $\{-5, 0, 1\}$ is a subset of $\{-5, 0, 1, 4, 10\}$. That is, $\{-5, 0, 1\} \subseteq \{-5, 0, 1, 4, 10\}$.

D. The ***union*** of two sets A and B is the set of all elements that are each in A or in B or both. The union is written as $A \cup B$.

> *Example:*
>
> $\{3, 4\} \cup \{4, 5, 6\} = \{3, 4, 5, 6\}$

E. The ***intersection*** of two sets A and B is the set of all elements that are each in **both** A and B. The intersection is written as $A \cap B$.

> *Example:*
>
> $\{3, 4\} \cap \{4, 5, 6\} = \{4\}$

F. Two sets sharing no elements are ***disjoint*** or ***mutually exclusive***.

> *Example:*
>
> $\{-5, 0, 1\}$ and $\{4, 10\}$ are disjoint.

G. The *empty set* is the set with no elements. It's written as $\varnothing$ or $\{\}$.

H. A ***Venn diagram*** shows the unions and intersections of two or more sets. Suppose sets S and T aren't disjoint, and neither is a subset of the other. The Venn diagram below shows their intersection $S \cap T$ as a shaded area.

A Venn Diagram of Two Intersecting Sets

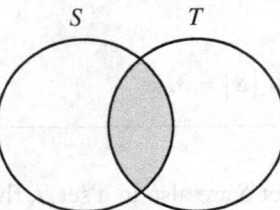

A Venn diagram of sets S and T, with their intersection $S \cap T$ shaded.

I. The number of elements in the union of two finite sets S and T is the number of elements in S, plus the number of elements in T, minus the number of elements in the intersection of S and T. That is, $|S \cup T| = |S| + |T| - |S \cap T|$. This is the ***general addition rule for two sets***.

Example:

$$|\{3, 4\} \cup \{4, 5, 6\}| = |\{3, 4\}| + |\{4, 5, 6\}| - |\{3, 4\} \cap \{4, 5, 6\}| =$$

$$|\{3, 4\}| + |\{4, 5, 6\}| - 1\{4\} = 2 + 3 - 1 = 4.$$

If S and T are disjoint, then $|S \cup T| = |S| + |T|$, since $|S \cap T| = 0$.

J. You can often solve word problems involving sets by using Venn diagrams and the general addition rule.

Example:

Each of 25 students is taking history, mathematics, or both. If 20 of them are taking history and 18 of them are taking mathematics, how many of them are taking both history and mathematics?

Solution: Separate the 25 students into three disjoint sets: the students taking history only, those taking mathematics only, and those taking both history and mathematics. This gives us the Venn diagram below, where n is the number of students taking both courses, $20 - n$ is the number taking history only, and $18 - n$ is the number taking mathematics only.

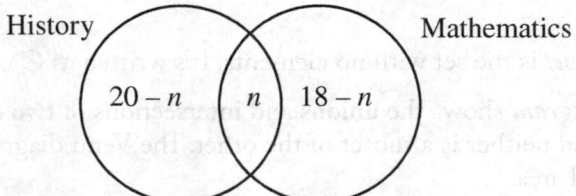

Since there are 25 students total, $(20 - n) + n + (18 - n) = 25$, so $n = 13$. So, 13 students are taking both history and mathematics. Notice that $20 + 18 - 13 = 25$ uses the general addition rule for two sets.

3. Counting Methods

A. To count elements in sets without listing them, you can sometimes use this *multiplication principle*:

If an object will be chosen from a set of m different objects, and another object will be chosen from a disjoint set of n different objects, then mn different choices are possible.

> *Example:*
>
> Suppose a meal at a restaurant must include exactly 1 entree and 1 dessert. The entree can be any 1 of 5 options, and the dessert can be any 1 of 3 options. Then $5 \times 3 = 15$ different meals are available.

B. Here's a more general version of the multiplication principle: The number of possible choices of 1 object apiece out of any number of sets is the product of the numbers of objects in those sets. For example, when choosing 1 object apiece out of 3 sets with x, y, and z elements, respectively, xyz different choices are possible. The general multiplication principle also means that when choosing 1 object apiece out of n sets of exactly m objects apiece, m^n different choices are possible.

> *Example:*
>
> Each time a coin is flipped, the 2 possible results are heads and tails. In a sequence of 8 consecutive coin flips, think of each flip as a set of those 2 possible results. The 8 flips give us a sequence of 8 of these 2-element sets. So, the sequence of 8 flips has 2^8 possible results.

C. A concept often used with the multiplication principle is the *factorial*. For any integer $n > 1$, n factorial is written as $n!$ and is the product of all the integers from 1 through n. Also, by definition, $0! = 1! = 1$.

> *Examples:*
>
> $2! = 2 \times 1 = 2$
>
> $3! = 3 \times 2 \times 1 = 6$
>
> $4! = 4 \times 3 \times 2 \times 1 = 24$, etc.

A useful equation with factorials is $n! = (n-1)!(n)$.

D. Any sequential ordering of a set's elements is a *permutation* of the set. A permutation is a way to choose elements one by one in a certain order.

The factorial is useful for finding how many permutations a set has. If a set of n objects is being ordered from 1st to n^{th}, there are n choices for the 1st object, $n-1$ choices left for the 2nd object, $n-2$ choices left for the 3rd object, and so on, until only 1 choice is left for the nth object. So, by the multiplication principle, a set of n objects has $n(n-1)(n-2) \ldots (3)(2)(1) = n!$ permutations.

> *Example:*
>
> The set of letters A, B, and C has $3! = 6$ permutations: ABC, ACB, BAC, BCA, CAB, and CBA.

E. When $0 \le k \le n$, each possible choice of k objects out of n objects is a ***combination*** of n objects taken k at a time. The number of these combinations is written as $\binom{n}{k}$. This is also the number of k-element subsets of a set with n elements, since the combinations simply are these subsets. It can be calculated as $\binom{n}{k} = \frac{n!}{k!(n-k)!}$. Note that $\binom{n}{k} = \binom{n}{n-k}$.

Example:

The 2-element subsets of $S = \{A, B, C, D, E\}$ are the combinations of the 5 letters in S taken 2 at a time. There are $\binom{5}{2} = \frac{5!}{2!3!} = \frac{120}{(2)(6)} = 10$ of these subsets: $\{A, B\}, \{A, C\}, \{A, D\}, \{A, E\}, \{B, C\},$ $\{B, D\}, \{B, E\}, \{C, D\}, \{C, E\},$ and $\{D, E\}$.

For each of its 2-element subsets, a 5-element set also has exactly one 3-element subset containing the elements not in that 2-element subset. For example, in S the 3-element subset $\{C, D, E\}$ contains the elements not in the 2-element subset $\{A, B\}$, the 3-element subset $\{B, D, E\}$ contains the elements not in the 2-element subset $\{A, C\}$, and so on. This shows that a 5-element set like S has exactly as many 2-element subsets as 3-element subsets, so $\binom{5}{2} = 10 = \binom{5}{3}$.

---

4. Probability

A. Sets and counting methods are also important to ***discrete probability***. Discrete probability involves ***experiments*** with finitely many possible ***outcomes***. An ***event*** is a set of an experiment's possible outcomes.

Example:

Rolling a 6-sided die with faces numbered 1 to 6 is an experiment with 6 possible outcomes. Let's call these outcomes 1, 2, 3, 4, 5, and 6, each number being the one facing up after the roll. Notice that no two outcomes can occur together.

One event in this experiment is that the outcome is 4. This event is written as $\{4\}$. Another event in the experiment is that the outcome is an odd number. This event has the three outcomes 1, 3, and 5. It is written as $\{1, 3, 5\}$.

B. The probability of an event E is written as $P(E)$ and is a number between 0 and 1, inclusive. If E is the empty set of no possible outcomes, then E is ***impossible***, and $P(E) = 0$. If E is the set of all possible outcomes of the experiment, then E is ***certain***, and $P(E) = 1$. Otherwise, E is possible but not certain, and $0 < P(E) < 1$. If F is a subset of E, then $P(F) \le P(E)$.

C. If the probabilities of two or more outcomes are equal, those outcomes are ***equally likely***. For an experiment with outcomes that are all equally likely, the probability of an event E is

$$P(E) = \frac{\text{the number of outcomes in } E}{\text{the total number of possible outcomes}}.$$

Example:

In the earlier example of a 6-sided die rolled once, suppose all 6 outcomes are equally likely. Then each outcome's probability is $\frac{1}{6}$. The probability that the outcome is an odd number is

$$P(\{1, 3, 5\}) = \frac{|\{1, 3, 5\}|}{6} = \frac{3}{6} = \frac{1}{2}.$$

D. Given two events E and F, these further events are defined:

(i) "not E" is the set of outcomes not in E;

(ii) "E or F" is the set of outcomes in E or F or both, that is, $E \cup F$;

(iii) "E and F" is the set of outcomes in both E and F, that is, $E \cap F$.

The probability that E doesn't occur is $P(\text{not } E) = 1 - P(E)$.

The probability that "E or F" occurs is $P(E \text{ or } F) = P(E) + P(F) - P(E \text{ and } F)$. This is based on the general addition rule for two sets, given above in Section 3.4.2.I.

Example:

In the example above of a 6-sided die rolled once, let E be the event $\{1, 3, 5\}$ that the outcome is an odd number. Let F be the event $\{2, 3, 5\}$ that the outcome is a prime number. Then

$P(E \text{ and } F) = P(E \cap F) = P(\{3, 5\}) = \dfrac{|\{3, 5\}|}{6} = \dfrac{2}{6} = \dfrac{1}{3}$. So, $P(E \text{ or } F) = P(E) + P(F) -$

$P(E \text{ and } F) = \dfrac{3}{6} + \dfrac{3}{6} - \dfrac{2}{6} = \dfrac{4}{6} = \dfrac{2}{3}$.

We get the same result by noticing that the event "E or F" is $E \cup F = \{1, 2, 3, 5\}$, so $P(E \text{ or } F)$

$= \dfrac{|\{1, 2, 3, 5\}|}{6} = \dfrac{4}{6} = \dfrac{2}{3}$.

Events E and F are ***mutually exclusive*** if no outcomes are in $E \cap F$. Then the event "E and F" is impossible: $P(E \text{ and } F) = 0$. The special addition rule for the probability of two mutually exclusive events is $P(E \text{ or } F) = P(E) + P(F)$.

E. Two events A and B are ***independent*** if neither changes the other's probability. The multiplication rule for independent events E and F is $P(E \text{ and } F) = P(E)P(F)$.

Example:

In the example above of the 6-sided die rolled once, let A be the event $\{2, 4, 6\}$ and B be the

event $\{5, 6\}$. Then A's probability is $P(A) = \dfrac{|A|}{6} = \dfrac{3}{6} = \dfrac{1}{2}$. The probability of A occurring **if B**

occurs is $\dfrac{|A \cap B|}{|B|} = \dfrac{|\{6\}|}{|\{5, 6\}|} = \dfrac{1}{2}$, the same as $P(A)$.

Likewise, B's probability is $P(B) = \dfrac{|B|}{6} = \dfrac{2}{6} = \dfrac{1}{3}$. The probability of B occurring **if A occurs**

is $\dfrac{|B \cap A|}{|A|} = \dfrac{\{6\}}{|\{2, 4, 6\}|} = \dfrac{1}{3}$, the same as $P(B)$.

So, neither event changes the other's probability. Thus, A and B are independent. Therefore, by the

multiplication rule for independent events, $P(A \text{ and } B) = P(A)P(B) = \left(\dfrac{1}{2}\right)\left(\dfrac{1}{3}\right) = \dfrac{1}{6}$.

Notice the event "A and B" is $A \cap B = \{6\}$, so $P(A \text{ and } B) = P(\{6\}) = \dfrac{1}{6}$.

The general addition rule and the multiplication rule discussed above imply that if E and F are independent, $P(E \text{ or } F) = P(E) + P(F) - P(E)P(F)$.

F. An event A is *dependent* on a nonempty event B if B changes the probability of A.

The probability of A occurring if B occurs is written as $P(A|B)$. So, the statement that A is dependent on B can be written as $P(A|B) \neq P(A)$.

A general multiplication rule for any dependent or independent events A and B is $P(A \text{ and } B) = P(A|B)P(B)$.

Example:

In the example of the 6-sided die rolled once, let A be the event $\{4, 6\}$ and B be the event $\{4, 5, 6\}$.

Then the probability of A is $P(A) = \dfrac{|A|}{6} = \dfrac{2}{6} = \dfrac{1}{3}$. But the probability that A occurs **if B occurs** is

$P(A|B) = \dfrac{|A \cap B|}{|B|} = \dfrac{|\{4, 6\}|}{|\{4, 5, 6\}|} = \dfrac{2}{3}$. Thus, $P(A|B) \neq P(A)$, so A is dependent on B.

Likewise, the probability that B occurs is $P(B) = \dfrac{|B|}{6} = \dfrac{3}{6} = \dfrac{1}{2}$. But the probability that B occurs **if**

A occurs is $P(B|A) = \dfrac{|B \cap A|}{|A|} = \dfrac{|\{4, 6\}|}{|\{4, 6\}|} = 1$. Thus, $P(B|A) \neq P(B)$, so B is dependent on A.

In this example, by the general multiplication rule for events,

$P(A \text{ and } B) = P(A|B)P(B) = \left(\dfrac{2}{3}\right)\left(\dfrac{1}{2}\right) = \dfrac{1}{3}$. Likewise, $P(A \text{ and } B) = P(B|A)P(A) = (1)\left(\dfrac{1}{3}\right) = \dfrac{1}{3}$.

Notice the event "A and B" is $A \cap B = \{4, 6\} = A$, so $P(A \text{ and } B) = P(\{4, 6\}) = \dfrac{1}{3} = P(A)$.

G. The rules above can be combined for more complex probability calculations.

Example:

In an experiment with events A, B, and C, suppose $P(A) = 0.23$, $P(B) = 0.40$, and $P(C) = 0.85$. Also suppose events A and B are mutually exclusive, and events B and C are independent. Since A and B are mutually exclusive, $P(A \text{ or } B) = P(A) + P(B) = 0.23 + 0.40 = 0.63$.

Since B and C are independent, $P(B \text{ or } C) = P(B) + P(C) - P(B)P(C) = 0.40 + 0.85 - (0.40)(0.85) = 0.91$.

$P(A \text{ or } C)$ and $P(A \text{ and } C)$ can't be found from the information given. But we can find that $P(A) + P(C) = 1.08 > 1$. So, $P(A) + P(C)$ can't equal $P(A \text{ or } C)$, which like any probability cannot be greater than 1. This means that A and C can't be mutually exclusive, and that $P(A \text{ and } C) \geq 0.08$.

Since $A \cap B$ is a subset of A, we can also find that $P(A \text{ and } C) \leq P(A) = 0.23$.

And C is a subset of $A \cup C$, so $P(A \text{ or } C) \geq P(C) = 0.85$.

Thus, we've found that $0.85 \leq P(A \text{ or } C) \leq 1$ and that $0.08 \leq P(A \text{ and } C) < 0.23$.

---

5. Estimation

A. Calculating exact answers to complex math questions is often too hard or slow. Estimating the answers by simplifying the questions may be easier and faster.

One way to estimate is to **round** the numbers in the original question: replace each number with a nearby number that has fewer digits.

For any integer n and real number m, you can **round m down** to a multiple of 10^n by deleting all of m's digits to the right of the digit that stands for multiples of 10^n.

To **round m up** to a multiple of 10^n, first add 10^n to m, then round the result down.

To **round m to the nearest** 10^n, first find the digit in m that stands for a multiple of 10^{n-1}. If this digit is 5 or higher, round m up to a multiple of 10^n. Otherwise, round m down to a multiple of 10^n.

Examples:

(i) To round 7651.4 to the nearest hundred (multiple of 10^2), first notice the digit standing for tens (multiples of 10^1) is 5.

Since this digit is 5 or higher, round up:

First add 100 to the original number: 7651.4 + 100 = 7751.4.

Then drop all the digits to the right of the one standing for multiples of 100 to get 7700.

Notice that 7700 is closer to 7651.4 than 7600 is, so 7700 is the nearest 100.

(ii) To round 0.43248 to the nearest thousandth (multiple of 10^{-3}), first notice the digit standing for ten-thousandths (multiples of 10^{-4}) is 4. Since 4 < 5, round down: just drop all the digits to the right of the digit standing for thousandths to get 0.432.

B. Rounding can simplify complex calculations and give rough answers. If you keep more digits of the original numbers, the answers are usually more exact, but the calculations take longer.

Example:

You can estimate the value of $\dfrac{(298.534+58.296)}{1.4822+0.937+0.014679}$ by rounding the numbers in the dividend to the nearest 10 and the numbers in the divisor to the nearest 0.1:

$$\frac{(298.534+58.296)}{1.4822+0.937+0.014679} \approx \frac{300+60}{1.5+0.9+0} = \frac{360}{2.4} = 150$$

C. Sometimes it's easier to estimate by rounding to a multiple of a number other than 10, like the nearest square or cube of an integer.

Examples:

(i) You can estimate the value of $\frac{2447.13}{11.9}$ by noting first that both the dividend and the divisor are near multiples of 12: 2448 and 12. So, $\frac{2447.13}{11.9} \approx \frac{2448}{12} = 204$.

(ii) You can estimate the value of $\sqrt{\frac{8.96}{24.82 \times 4.057}}$ by noting first that each decimal number in the expression is near the square of an integer: $8.96 \approx 9 = 3^2$, $24.82 \approx 25 = 5^2$, and $4.057 \approx 4 = 2^2$. So, $\sqrt{\frac{8.96}{24.82 \times 4.057}} \approx \sqrt{\frac{3^2}{5^2 \times 2^2}} = \sqrt{\frac{3^2}{10^2}} = \frac{3}{10}$.

D. Sometimes finding a *range* of possible values for an expression is more useful than finding a single estimated value. The range's **upper bound** is the smallest number found to be greater than (or no less than) the expression's value. The range's **lower bound** is the largest number found to be less than (or no greater than) the expression's value.

Example:

In the equation $x = \frac{2.32^2 - 2.536}{2.68^2 + 2.79}$, each decimal is greater than 2 and less than 3. So, $\frac{2^2 - 3}{3^2 + 3} < x < \frac{3^2 - 2}{2^2 + 2}$. Simplifying these fractions, we find that x is in the range $\frac{1}{12} < x < \frac{7}{6}$. The range's lower bound is $\frac{1}{12}$, and the upper bound is $\frac{7}{6}$.

6. Sequences and Series

A. A *sequence* is an ordered list of elements, starting with a first element. Any sequence may be defined as the range of a function $a(n)$ with a domain that is the positive integers. Its value a_i for a specific positive integer i is its ***i*th term**.

An ***arithmetic sequence*** has the form $a_n = b + cn$, where b and c are constants. The first term of an arithmetic sequence is $a_1 = b + c$. For each term a_i, the next term $a_{i+1} = a_i + c$.

A ***geometric sequence*** has the form $a_n = bc^n$, where b and c are constants. The first term of an arithmetic sequence is $a_1 = bc$. For each term a_i, the next term $a_{i+1} = a_i c$.

Sometimes a sequence is defined only by giving the value of the first term or terms, then giving an equation for finding each subsequent term's value based on the value of one or more earlier terms.

Examples:

(i) The function $a(n) = n^2 + \left(\frac{n}{5}\right)$ with a domain that is the positive integers is an infinite

sequence $a_1, a_2, a_3, \ldots$. Its third term is its value at $n = 3$, which is $a_3 = 3^2 + \frac{3}{5} = 9.6$.

(ii) $a(n) = n^2 + \left(\frac{n}{5}\right) b_n = (-1)^n (n!)$ The function $a(n) = 2 + 3n$ with a domain that is the positive integers is an arithmetic sequence. Its first term $a_1 = 5$. For any positive integer i, $a_{i+1} = ai + 3$. Thus, $a_2 = a_1 + 3 = 8$.

(iii) The function $b(n) = 2(3^n)$ with a domain that is the positive integers is a geometric sequence. Its first term $b_1 = 6$. For any positive integer i, $b_{i+1} = 3b_i$. Thus, $b_2 = 3 \times 6 = 18$.

(iv) We can define a sequence $c(n)$ just by stating that its first term $c_1 = 1$, its second term $c_2 = 1$, and each subsequent term $c_{n+2} = c_n + c_{n+1}$. Thus, $c_3 = c_1 + c_2 = 1 + 1 = 2$.

B. A *series* is the sum of a sequence's terms.

For an infinite sequence $a(n)$, the ***infinite series*** $\sum_{n=1}^{\infty} a(n)$ adds up the sequence's infinitely many

terms, $a_1 + a_2 + a_3 + \ldots$. Some infinite series add up to finite sums, but others don't.

Example:

The infinite series based on the function $a(n) = n^2 + \left(\frac{n}{5}\right)$ is $\sum_{i=1}^{\infty} n^2 + \left(\frac{n}{5}\right)$. It adds up the

infinitely many terms $\left(1^2 + \frac{1}{5}\right) + \left(2^2 + \frac{2}{5}\right) + \left(3^2 + \frac{3}{5}\right) + \ldots$. This series has no finite sum.

But the sum of its first three terms $a(n) = n^2 + \left(\frac{n}{5}\right)$ is

$$\sum_{i=1}^{3} a_i = \left(1^2 + \frac{1}{5}\right) + \left(2^2 + \frac{2}{5}\right) + \left(3^2 + \frac{3}{5}\right) = 1.2 + 4.4 + 9.6 = 15.2.$$

3.5   Reference Sheets

Arithmetic and Decimals

ABSOLUTE VALUE:

$|x|$ is x if $x \geq 0$ and $-x$ if $x < 0$.

For any x and $y, |x + y| < |x| + |y|$, and $|xy| = |x||y|$.
$\sqrt{x^2} = |x|$.

EVEN AND ODD NUMBERS:

Even × Even = Even	Even × Odd = Even
Odd × Odd = Odd	Even + Even = Even
Even + Odd = Odd	Odd + Odd = Even

ADDITION AND SUBTRACTION:

$x + 0 = x = x - 0$

$x - x = 0$

$x + y = y + x$

$x - y = -(y - x) = -y + x$

$(x + y) + z = x + (y + z)$

If x and y are both positive, then $x + y$ is positive.

If x and y are both negative, then $x + y$ is negative.

DECIMALS WITH MANY FINITE DIGITS:

Add or subtract decimals by lining up their decimal points:

17.6512	653.2700
+ 653.2700	−17.6512
670.9212	635.6188

To multiply decimal A by decimal B:

First, ignore the decimal points and multiply A and B as if they were integers.

Next, if decimal A has n digits to the right of its decimal point and decimal B has m digits to the right of its decimal point, place the decimal point in $A \times B$ so it has $m + n$ digits to its right.

To divide decimal A by decimal B, first move the decimal points of A and B equally many digits to the right until B is an integer. Then divide as you would integers.

QUOTIENTS AND REMAINDERS:

The quotient q and the remainder r of dividing positive integer x by positive integer y are unique positive integers such that

$y = xq + r$ and $0 < r < x$.

The remainder r is 0 if and only if y is divisible by x. Then x is a factor of y.

MULTIPLICATION AND DIVISION:

$x \times 1 = x = \frac{x}{1}$

$x \times 0 = 0$

If $x \neq 0$, then $\frac{x}{x} = 1$.

$\frac{x}{0}$ is undefined.

$xy = yx$

If $x \neq 0$ and $y \neq 0$, then $\frac{x}{y} = \frac{1}{\left(\frac{y}{x}\right)}$.

$(xy)z = x(yz)$

$xy + xz = x(y + z)$

If $y \neq 0$, then $\left(\frac{x}{y}\right) + \left(\frac{z}{y}\right) = \frac{(x + z)}{y}$.

If x and y are both positive, then xy is positive.

If x and y are both negative, then xy is positive.

If x is positive and y is negative, then xy is negative.

If $xy = 0$, then $x = 0$ or $y = 0$, or both.

SCIENTIFIC NOTATION:

To convert a number in scientific notation $A \times 10^n$ into regular decimal notation, move A's decimal point n places to the right if n is positive, or $|n|$ places to the left if n is negative.

To convert a decimal to scientific notation, move the decimal point n spaces so that exactly one nonzero digit is to its left. Multiply the result by 10^n if you moved the decimal point to the left or by 10^{-n} if you moved it to the right.

ARITHMETIC SHORTCUTS:

For any two nonnegative integers x and y, the final digit of $x + y$ is the final digit of the sum of x's final digit and y's final digit. And for any two integers x and y, the final digit of xy is the final digit of the product of x's final digit and y's final digit.

An integer is divisible by	if and only if
2	its final digit is 0, 2, 4, 6, or 8.
3	the sum of its digits is divisible by 3.
4	its final two digits make a number divisible by 4.
5	its final digit is 5 or 0.
9	the sum of its digits is divisible by 9.
10	its final digit is 0.

Exponents

SQUARES, CUBES, AND SQUARE ROOTS:

Every positive number has two real square roots, one positive and the other negative. The table below shows the positive square roots rounded to the nearest hundredth.

n	n^2	n^3	$\sqrt{n}$
1	1	1	1
2	4	8	1.41
3	9	27	1.73
4	16	64	2
5	25	125	2.24
6	36	216	2.45
7	49	343	2.65
8	64	512	2.83
9	81	729	3
10	100	1,000	3.16

EXPONENTIATION:

Formula	Example
$x^1 = x$	$2^1 = 2$
If $x \neq 0$, then $x^0 = 1$.	$2^0 = 1$
If $x \neq 0$, then $x^{-1} = \frac{1}{x}$.	$2^{-1} = \frac{1}{2}$
If $x > 1$ and $y > 1$, then $x^y > x$.	$2^3 = 8 > 2$
If $0 < x < 1$ and $y > 1$, then $x^y < x$.	$0.2^3 = 0.008 < 0.2$
$(x^y)^z = x^{yz} = (x^z)^y$	$(2^3)^4 = 2^{12} = (2^4)^3$
$x^{y+z} = x^y x^z$	$2^7 = 2^3 2^4$
If $x \neq 0$, then $x^{y-z} = \dfrac{x^y}{x^z}$.	$2^{5-3} = \dfrac{2^5}{2^3}$
$(xz)^y = x^y z^y$	$6^4 = 2^4 3^4$
If $z \neq 0$, then $\left(\dfrac{x}{z}\right)^y = \dfrac{x^y}{z^y}$.	$\left(\dfrac{3}{4}\right)^2 = \dfrac{3^2}{4^2} = \dfrac{9}{16}$
If $z \neq 0$, then $x^{\frac{y}{z}} = (x^y)^{\frac{1}{z}} = (x^{\frac{1}{z}})^y$.	$4^{\frac{2}{3}} = (4^2)^{\frac{1}{3}} = (4^{\frac{1}{3}})^2$

Algebraic Expressions and Linear Equations

TRANSLATING WORDS INTO MATH OPERATIONS:

$x + y$	$x - y$	xy	$\dfrac{x}{y}$	x^y
x added to y x increased by y x more than y x plus y the sum of x and y the total of x and y	x decreased by y difference of x and y y fewer than x y less than x x minus y x reduced by y y subtracted from x	x multiplied by y the product of x and y x times y	x divided by y x over y the quotient of x and y the ratio of x to y	x to the power of y x to the yth power
		If $y = 2$: double x twice x	If $y = 2$: half of x x halved	If $y = 2$: x squared
		If $y = 3$: triple x		If $y = 3$: x cubed

MANIPULATING ALGEBRAIC EXPRESSIONS:

Technique	Example
Factor to combine like terms	$3xy - 9y = 3y(x - 3)$
Divide out common factors	$\dfrac{(3xy - 9y)}{(x - 3)} = \dfrac{3y(x - 3)}{(x - 3)} = 3y\,(1) = 3y$
Multiply two expressions by multiplying each term of one expression by each term of the other	$(3x - 4)(9y + x) = 3x(9y + x) - 4(9y + x)$ $\qquad = 3x(9y) + 3x(x) - 4(9y) - 4(x)$ $\qquad = 27xy + 3x^2 - 36y - 4x$
Substitute constants for variables	If $x = 3$ and $y = -2$, then $3xy - x^2 + y =$ $3(3)(-2) - (3)^2 + (-2) = -18 - 9 - 2 = -29$.

SOLVING LINEAR EQUATIONS:

Technique	Example
Isolate a variable on one side of an equation by doing the same operations on both sides of the equation.	Solve the equation $\frac{(5x-6)}{3} = 4$ like this: (1) Multiply both sides by 3 to get $5x - 6 = 12$. (2) Add 6 to both sides to get $5x = 18$. (3) Divide both sides by 5 to get $x = \frac{18}{5}$.
To solve two equations with two variables x and y: (1) Express x in terms of y using one of the equations. (2) Substitute that expression for x to make the second equation have only the variable y. (3) Solve the second equation for y. (4) Substitute the solution for y into the first equation to solve for x.	Solve the equations A: $x - y = 2$ and B: $3x + 2y = 11$: (1) From A, $x = 2 + y$. (2) In B, substitute $2 + y$ for x to get $3(2 + y) + 2y = 11$. (3) Solve B for y: $6 + 3y + 2y = 11$ $\qquad 6 + 5y = 11$ $\qquad\quad 5y = 5$ $\qquad\quad\ y = 1$ (4) Since $y = 1$, from A we find $x = 2 + 1 = 3$.
Alternative technique: (1) Multiply both sides of one equation or both equations so that the coefficients on y have the same absolute value in both equations. (2) Add or subtract the two equations to remove y and solve for x. (3) Substitute the solution for x into the first equation to find the value of y.	Solve the equations A: $x - y = 2$ and B: $3x + 2y = 11$: (1) Multiply both sides of A by 2 to get $2x - 2y = 4$. (2) Add the equation in (1) to equation B: $\quad 2x - 2y + 3x + 2y = 4 + 11$ $\qquad\qquad\qquad 5x = 15$ $\qquad\qquad\qquad\ x = 3$ (3) Since $x = 3$, from A we find $3 - y = 2$, so $y = 1$.

Factoring, Quadratic Equations, and Inequalities

SOLVING EQUATIONS BY FACTORING:

Techniques	Example
(1) Start with a polynomial equation. (2) Add or subtract from both sides until 0 is on one side of the equation. (3) Write the nonzero side as a product of factors. (4) Set each factor to 0 to find simple equations giving the solutions to the original equation.	$x^3 - 2x^2 + x = -5(x-1)^2$ $x^3 - 2x^2 + x + 5(x-1)^2 = 0$ (i) $\quad x(x^2 - 2x + 1) + 5(x-1)^2 = 0$ (ii) $\quad x(x-1)^2 + 5(x-1)^2 = 0$ (iii) $\quad (x+5)(x-1)^2 = 0$ $x + 5 = 0$ or $x - 1 = 0$. So, $x = -5$ or $x = 1$.

FORMULAS FOR FACTORING:

$\left(a + \dfrac{1}{a}\right)^2 = a^2 + \dfrac{1}{a^2} + 2$

$a^2 - b^2 = (a - b)(a + b)$

$a^2 + 2ab + b^2 = (a + b)^2$

$a^2 - 2ab + b^2 = (a - b)^2$

$a^2 + b^2 = (a + b)^2 - 2ab = (a - b)^2 + 2ab$

$(a + b + c)^2 = a^2 + b^2 + c^2 + 2ab + 2ac + 2bc$

$(a + b)^3 = a^3 + 3a^2b + 3ab^2 + b^3$

THE QUADRATIC FORMULA:

For any quadratic equation $ax^2 + bx + c = 0$ with $a \neq 0$, the roots are

$$x = \frac{-b + \sqrt{b^2 - 4ac}}{2a} \text{ and } x = \frac{-b - \sqrt{b^2 - 4ac}}{2a}$$

These roots are two distinct real numbers if $b^2 - 4ac \geq 0$.

If $b^2 - 4ac = 0$, the equation has only one root: $-\dfrac{b}{2a}$.

If $b^2 - 4ac < 0$, the equation has no real roots.

SOLVING INEQUALITIES:

Explanation	Example
As in solving an equation, the same number can be added to or subtracted from both sides of the inequality, or both sides can be multiplied or divided by a positive number, without changing the order of the inequality. But multiplying or dividing an inequality by a negative number reverses the order of the inequality. Thus, $6 > 2$, but $(-1)(6) < (-1)(2)$.	To solve the inequality $\dfrac{(5x-1)}{-2} < 3$ for x, isolate x: (1) $5x - 1 > -6$ (multiplying both sides by -2, reversing the order of the inequality) (2) $5x > -5$ (add 1 to both sides) (3) $x > -1$ (divide both sides by 5)

LINES IN THE COORDINATE PLANE:

An equation $y = mx + b$ defines a line with slope m, which has a y-intercept that is b.

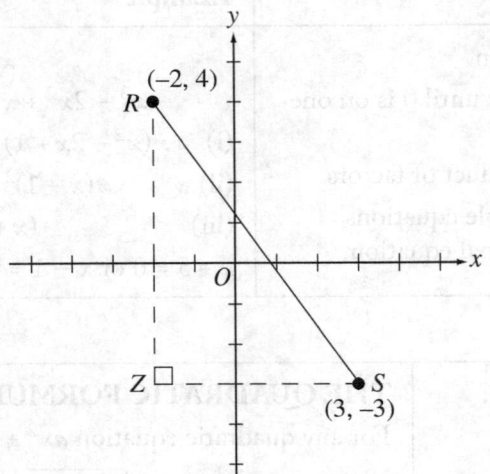

For a line through two points (x_1, y_1) and (x_2, y_2) with $x_1 \neq x_2$, the slope is $m = \dfrac{(y_2 - y_1)}{(x_2 - x_1)}$. Given the known point (x_1, y_1) and the slope m, any other point (x, y) on the line satisfies the equation $m = \dfrac{(y - y_1)}{(x - x_1)}$.

Above, the line's slope is $\dfrac{(-3 - 4)}{(3 - (-2))} = -\dfrac{7}{5}$. To find an equation of the line, we can use the point $(3, -3)$:

$$y - (-3) = \left(-\frac{7}{5}\right)(x - 3)$$

$$y + 3 = \left(-\frac{7}{5}\right)x + \frac{21}{5}$$

$$y = \left(-\frac{7}{5}\right)x + \frac{6}{5}$$

So, the y-intercept is $\dfrac{6}{5}$.

Find the x-intercept like this:

$$0 = \left(-\frac{7}{5}\right)x + \frac{6}{5}$$

$$\left(\frac{7}{5}\right)x = \frac{6}{5}$$

$$x = \frac{6}{7}$$

The graph shows both these intercepts.

Rates, Ratios, and Percents

FRACTIONS:

Equivalent or Equal Fractions:
Two fractions stand for the same number if dividing each fraction's numerator and denominator by their greatest common divisor makes the fractions identical.

Adding, Subtracting, Multiplying, and Dividing Fractions:

$\frac{a}{b} + \frac{c}{d} = \frac{ad}{bd} + \frac{bc}{bd}; \frac{a}{b} - \frac{c}{d} = \frac{ad}{bd} - \frac{bc}{bd}$

$\frac{a}{b} \times \frac{c}{d} = \frac{ac}{bd}; \frac{a}{b} \div \frac{c}{d} = \frac{ad}{bc}$

MIXED NUMBERS:

A mixed number of the form $a\frac{b}{c}$ equals the fraction $\frac{ac+b}{c}$.

RATE:

distance = rate × time

PROFIT:

Profit = Revenues − Expenses, or

Profit = Selling price − Cost.

INTEREST:

Simple annual interest =

(principal) × (interest rate) × (time)

Compound interest over n periods =

(principal) × (1 + interest per period)^n − principal

PERCENTS:

$x\% = \frac{x}{100}$.

$x\%$ of y equals $\frac{xy}{100}$.

To convert a percent to a decimal, drop the percent sign, then move the decimal point two digits left.

To convert a decimal to a percent, add a percent sign, then move the decimal point two digits right.

PERCENT INCREASE OR DECREASE:

The percent increase from x to y is $100\left(\frac{y-x}{x}\right)\%$.

The percent decrease from x to y is $100\left(\frac{x-y}{x}\right)\%$.

DISCOUNTS:

A price discounted by n percent becomes $(100 - n)$ percent of the original price.

A price discounted by n percent and then by m percent becomes $(100 - n)(100 - m)$ percent of the original price.

WORK:

$\frac{1}{r} + \frac{1}{s} = \frac{1}{h}$, where r is how long one individual takes to do an amount of work, s is how long a second individual takes to do that much work, and h is how long they take to do that much work when both are working at the same time.

MIXTURES:

	Number of units of a substance or mixture	Amount of an ingredient per unit of the substance or mixture	Total amount of that ingredient in the substance or mixture
Substance A	X	M	X × M
Substance B	Y	N	Y × N
Mixture of A and B	X + Y	$\frac{(X \times M) + (Y \times N)}{X + Y}$	(X × M) + (Y × N)

Statistics, Sets, and Counting Methods

STATISTICS:

Concept	Definition for a data set of n values ordered from least to greatest	Example with data set $\{4, 4, 5, 7, 10\}$
Mean	The sum of the n values, divided by n	$\dfrac{(4 + 4 + 5 + 7 + 10)}{5} = \dfrac{30}{5} = 6$
Median	The middle value if n is odd; The mean of the two middle values if n is even.	5 is the middle value in $\{4, 4, 5, 7, 10\}$.
Mode	The value that appears most often in the data set.	4 is the only value that appears more than once in $\{4, 4, 5, 7, 10\}$.
Range	The largest value in the data set minus the smallest	$10 - 4 = 6$
Standard Deviation	Calculate like this: (1) Find the arithmetic mean (2) Find the differences between each of the n values and the mean (3) Square each of the differences (4) Find the average of the squared differences, and (5) Take the nonnegative square root of this average	(1) The mean is 6. (2) $-2, -2, -1, 1, 4$ (3) $4, 4, 1, 1, 16$ (4) $\dfrac{26}{5} = 5.2$ (5) $\sqrt{5.2}$

SETS:

Concept	Notation for finite sets S and T	Example
Number of elements	$\lvert S \rvert$	$S = \{-5, 0, 1\}$ is a set with $\lvert S \rvert = 3$.
Subset	$S \subseteq T$ (S is a subset of T); $S \supseteq T$ (T is a subset of S)	$\{-5, 0, 1\}$ is a subset of $\{-5, 0, 1, 4, 10\}$.
Union	$S \cup T$	$\{3, 4\} \cup \{4, 5, 6\} = \{3, 4, 5, 6\}$
Intersection	$S \cap T$	$\{3, 4\} \cap \{4, 5, 6\} = \{4\}$
The general addition rule for two sets	$\lvert S \cup T \rvert = \lvert S \rvert + \lvert T \rvert - \lvert S \cap T \rvert$	$\lvert \{3, 4\} \cup \{4, 5, 6\} \rvert =$ $\lvert \{3, 4\} \rvert + \lvert \{4, 5, 6\} \rvert - \lvert \{3, 4\} \cap \{4, 5, 6\} \rvert =$ $\lvert \{3, 4\} \rvert + \lvert \{4, 5, 6\} \rvert - \lvert \{4\} \rvert = 2 + 3 - 1 = 4.$

COUNTING METHODS:

Concept and Equations	Examples
Multiplication Principle: The number of possible choices of 1 element apiece from the data sets $A_1, A_2, \ldots, A_n$ is $\lvert A_1 \rvert \times \lvert A_2 \rvert \times \ldots \times \lvert A_n \rvert$.	The number of possible choices of 1 element apiece from the data sets $S = \{-5, 0, 1\}$, $T = \{3, 4\}$, and $U = \{3, 4, 5, 6\}$ is $\lvert S \rvert \times \lvert T \rvert \times \lvert U \rvert = 3 \times 2 \times 4 = 24$.
Factorial: $n! = n \times (n-1) \times \ldots \times 1$ $0! = 1! = 1$ $n! = (n-1)!(n)$	$4! = 4 \times 3 \times 2 \times 1 = 24$ $4! = 3! \times 4$
Permutations: A data set of n objects has $n!$ permutations	The data set of letters A, B, and C has $3! = 6$ permutations: ABC, ACB, BAC, BCA, CAB, and CBA.
Combinations: The number of possible choices of k objects from a data set of n objects is $\binom{n}{k} = \dfrac{n!}{k!(n-k)!}$.	The number of 2-element subsets of data set $\{A, B, C, D, E\}$ is $$\binom{5}{2} = \frac{5!}{2!3!} = \frac{120}{(2)(6)} = 10.$$ The 10 subsets are: $\{A, B\}, \{A, C\}, \{A, D\}, \{A, E\}, \{B, C\}, \{B, D\}, \{B, E\}, \{C, D\}, \{C, E\}$, and $\{D, E\}$.

Probability and Sequences

PROBABILITY:

Concept	Definition, Notation, and Equations	Example: Rolling a die with 6 numbered sides once
Event	A set of outcomes of an experiment	The event of the outcome being an odd number is the set $\{1, 3, 5\}$.
Probability	The probability $P(E)$ of an event E is a number between 0 and 1, inclusive. If each outcome is equally likely, $P(E) =$ $\dfrac{\text{(the number of possible outcomes in E)}}{\text{(the total number of possible outcomes)}}$.	If the 6 outcomes are equally likely, the probability of each outcome is $\dfrac{1}{6}$. The probability that the outcome is an odd number is $P(\{1, 3, 5\}) =$ $\dfrac{|\{1, 3, 5\}|}{6} = \dfrac{3}{6} = \dfrac{1}{2}$.
Conditional Probability	The probability that E occurs if F occurs is $P(E\|F) = \dfrac{|E \cap F|}{|F|}$.	$P(\{1, 3, 5\}\|\{1, 2\}) = \dfrac{|\{1\}|}{|\{1, 2\}|} = \dfrac{1}{2}$
Not E	The set of outcomes not in event E: $P(\text{not } E) = 1 - P(E)$.	$P(\text{not}\{3\}) = \dfrac{6 - 1}{6} = \dfrac{5}{6}$
E and F	The set of outcomes in both E and F, that is, $E \cap F$; $P(E \text{ and } F) = P(E \cap F) = P(E\|F)\,P(F)$.	For $E = \{1, 3, 5\}$ and $F = \{2, 3, 5\}$: $P(E \text{ and } F) = P(E \cap F) = P(\{3, 5\}) =$ $\dfrac{|\{3, 5\}|}{6} = \dfrac{2}{6} = \dfrac{1}{3}$
E or F	The set of outcomes in E or F or both, that is, $E \cup F$; $P(E \text{ or } F) = P(E) + P(F) - P(E \text{ and } F)$.	For $E = \{1, 3, 5\}$ and $F = \{2, 3, 5\}$: $P(E \text{ or } F) = P(E) + P(F) - P(E \text{ and } F)$ $= \dfrac{3}{6} + \dfrac{3}{6} - \dfrac{2}{6} = \dfrac{4}{6} = \dfrac{2}{3}$.
Dependent and Independent Events	E is dependent on F if $P(E\|F) \neq P(E)$. E and F are independent if neither is dependent on the other. If E and F are independent, $P(E \text{ and } F) = P(E)P(F)$.	For $E = \{2, 4, 6\}$ and $F = \{5, 6\}$: $P(E\|F) = P(E) = \dfrac{1}{2}$, and $P(F\|E) = P(F) = \dfrac{1}{3}$, so E and F are independent. Thus $P(E \text{ and } F) = P(E)P(F) = \left(\dfrac{1}{2}\right)\left(\dfrac{1}{3}\right) = \dfrac{1}{6}$.

SEQUENCE:

An ordered list of elements, starting with a first element.

Example: The function $a(n) = n^2 + \left(\dfrac{n}{5}\right)$ with the domain of all positive integers $n = 1, 2, 3, \ldots$ is an infinite sequence a_n.

4.0 Quantitative Reasoning

4.0 Quantitative Reasoning

The GMAT™ exam's Quantitative Reasoning section tests your math skills in the areas reviewed in Chapter 3, "Math Review": Value, Order, Factors, Algebra, Equalities, Inequalities, Rates, Ratios, Percents, Statistics, Sets, Counting, Probability, Estimation, and Series. Quantitative Reasoning questions also test how well you reason mathematically, solve math problems, and interpret graphic data. All the math needed to answer the questions is generally taught in secondary school (or high school) math classes.

To answer a Quantitative Reasoning question, you pick one of five answer choices. First study the question to see what information it gives and what it's asking you to do with that information. Then scan the answer choices. If the problem seems simple, try to find the answer quickly. Then check your answer against the choices. If your answer isn't among the choices, or if the problem is complicated, think again about what the problem is asking you to do. Try to rule out some of the choices. If you still can't narrow down the answer to one choice, reread the question. It gives all the information you need to find the right answer. If you already know about the topic, don't use that knowledge to answer. Use only the information given.

You have 45 minutes to answer the 21 questions in the section. That's an average of about two minutes and nine seconds per question. You may run out of time if you spend too long on any one question. If you find yourself stuck on a question, just pick the answer that seems best, even if you're not sure. Guessing is not usually the best way to score high on the GMAT, but making an educated guess is better than not answering.

Below are question-solving tips, directions for the section, and sample questions with an answer key and answer explanations. These explanations also show strategies that may help you solve other Quantitative Reasoning questions.

4.1 Tips for Answering Quantitative Reasoning Questions

1. **Pace yourself.**

   Check the on-screen timer to see how much time you have left. Work carefully, but don't take too long double-checking an answer or struggling with a problem.

2. **Use the erasable notepad provided.**

   Solving a problem step by step on the notepad may help you avoid mistakes. If the problem doesn't show a diagram, drawing your own may help.

3. **Study each question to understand what it's asking.**

   Approach word problems one step at a time. Read each sentence. When useful, translate the problem into math expressions.

4. **Scan all the answer choices before working on the problem.**

   By scanning the answer choices, you can avoid finding the answer in the wrong form. For example, if the choices are all fractions like $\frac{1}{4}$, work out the answer as a fraction, not as a decimal like 0.25.

   Similarly, if the choices are all estimates, you can often take shortcuts. For example, you may be able to estimate by rounding 48% to 50% if every answer choice is an estimate.

5. **Don't waste time on a problem that's too hard for you.**

   Make your best guess. Then move on to the next question.

4.2 Practice Questions

Solve the problem and pick the best answer choice given.

<u>Numbers:</u> **All numbers used are real numbers.**

<u>Figures:</u> **A figure in a Quantitative Reasoning question gives information useful in solving the problem. Figures are drawn as accurately as possible, except as noted. Lines shown as straight are straight. Lines that look jagged may also be straight. Points, angles, regions, etc., are positioned as shown. All figures are flat unless otherwise noted.**

Questions 1 to 103 — Difficulty: Easy

1. In the graduating class of a certain college, 48 percent of the students identify exclusively as male and 52 percent identify exclusively as female. In this class, 40 percent of the students who identify as male and 20 percent of the students who identify as female are 25 years old or older. If one student in the graduating class is randomly selected, approximately what is the probability that the student will be <u>less</u> than 25 years old?

    (A) 0.90
    (B) 0.70
    (C) 0.45
    (D) 0.30
    (E) 0.25

2. In a certain board game, a stack of 48 cards, 8 of which represent a single share of stock, are shuffled and then placed face down. If the first 2 cards selected do <u>not</u> represent shares of stock, what is the probability that the third card selected will represent a share of stock?

    (A) $\dfrac{1}{8}$

    (B) $\dfrac{1}{6}$

    (C) $\dfrac{1}{5}$

    (D) $\dfrac{3}{23}$

    (E) $\dfrac{4}{23}$

3. During a trip that they took together, Carmen, Juan, Maria, and Rafael drove an average (arithmetic mean) of 80 miles each. Carmen drove 72 miles, Juan drove 78 miles, and Maria drove 83 miles. How many miles did Rafael drive?

    (A) 80
    (B) 82
    (C) 85
    (D) 87
    (E) 89

4. Each week, a clothing salesperson receives a commission equal to 15 percent of the first $500 in sales and 20 percent of all additional sales that week. What commission would the salesperson receive on total sales for the week of $1,300?

    (A) $195
    (B) $227
    (C) $235
    (D) $260
    (E) $335

5. Five batches of 100 nails each are taken from a production line. The numbers of defective nails in the first four batches are 2, 4, 3, and 5, respectively. If the fifth batch has either 1, 2, or 6 defective nails, for which of these values does the average (arithmetic mean) number of defective nails per batch for the five batches equal the median number of defective nails for the five batches?

    I.   1
    II.   2
    III. 6

    (A) I only
    (B) II only
    (C) III only
    (D) I and III only
    (E) I, II, and III

6. List *S* consists of 10 consecutive odd integers, and list *T* consists of 5 consecutive even integers. If the least integer in *S* is 7 more than the least integer in *T*, how much greater is the average (arithmetic mean) of the integers in *S* than the average of the integers in *T*?

   (A)   2
   (B)   7
   (C)   8
   (D)   12
   (E)   22

Lane number	Number in line
1	5
2	4
3	3
4	4
5	2

7. A certain grocery store has 5 checkout lanes. The table above shows the amount of carts the last person waiting in each checkout lane had at closing time yesterday. What was the median number of carts?

   (A) $2\frac{4}{5}$
   (B)   3
   (C) $3\frac{1}{2}$
   (D) $3\frac{3}{5}$
   (E)   4

8. $\left(\frac{1}{2}-\frac{1}{3}\right)+\left(\frac{1}{3}-\frac{1}{4}\right)+\left(\frac{1}{4}-\frac{1}{5}\right)+\left(\frac{1}{5}-\frac{1}{6}\right)=$

   (A) $-\frac{1}{6}$
   (B)   0
   (C) $\frac{1}{3}$
   (D) $\frac{1}{2}$
   (E) $\frac{2}{3}$

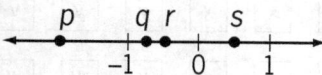

9. If *p*, *q*, *r*, and *s* are as shown on the number line above, which of the following products is greatest?

   (A)   *pq*
   (B)   *pr*
   (C)   *qr*
   (D)   *qs*
   (E)   *rs*

10. Last year $48,000 of a certain store's profit was shared by its 2 owners and their 10 employees. Each of the 2 owners received 3 times as much as each of their 10 employees. How much did each owner receive from the $48,000?

    (A) $12,000
    (B) $9,000
    (C) $6,000
    (D) $4,000
    (E) $3,000

11. On a vacation, Rose exchanged $500.00 for euros at an exchange rate of 0.80 euro per dollar and spent $\frac{3}{4}$ of the euros she received. If she exchanged the remaining euros for dollars at an exchange rate of $1.20 per euro, what was the dollar amount she received?

    (A) $60.00
    (B) $80.00
    (C) $100.00
    (D) $120.00
    (E) $140.00

x	x	x	y	y	v
v	x	x	y	w	w

12. Each of the 12 squares shown is labeled x, y, v, or w. What is the ratio of the number of these squares labeled x or y to the number of these squares labeled v or w?

    (A) 1:2
    (B) 2:3
    (C) 4:3
    (D) 3:2
    (E) 2:1

Number of Solid-Colored Marbles in Three Jars

Jar	Number of red marbles	Number of green marbles	Total number of red and green marbles
P	x	y	80
Q	y	z	120
R	x	z	160

13. In the table above, what is the number of green marbles in Jar R?

    (A) 70
    (B) 80
    (C) 90
    (D) 100
    (E) 110

14. Bouquets are to be made using white tulips and red tulips, and the ratio of the number of white tulips to the number of red tulips is to be the same in each bouquet. If there are 15 white tulips and 85 red tulips available for the bouquets, what is the greatest number of bouquets that can be made using all the tulips available?

    (A) 3
    (B) 5
    (C) 8
    (D) 10
    (E) 13

County	Amount Recycled	Amount Disposed of
A	16,700	142,800
B	8,800	48,000
C	13,000	51,400
D	3,900	20,300
E	3,300	16,200

15. The table above shows the amount of waste material, in tons, recycled by each of five counties in a single year and the amount of waste material, also in tons, that was disposed of in landfills by the five counties in that year. Which county had the lowest ratio of waste material disposed of to waste material recycled in the year reported in the table?

    (A) A
    (B) B
    (C) C
    (D) D
    (E) E

16. 125% of 5 =

    (A) 5.125
    (B) 5.25
    (C) 6
    (D) 6.125
    (E) 6.25

17. Each day Linda spends 6 hours at her dog-walking job, for which she is paid $15.00 per hour. In addition, Linda spends a total of 1.5 hours each day, (for which she is not paid), traveling to and from the job. What is Linda's hourly rate of pay for the total amount of time that she spends each day at her dog-walking job and traveling to and from that job?

    (A) $7.50
    (B) $9.00
    (C) $10.00
    (D) $10.75
    (E) $12.00

18. When traveling at a constant speed of 32 miles per hour, a certain motorboat consumes 24 gallons of fuel per hour. What is the fuel consumption of this boat at this speed measured in miles traveled per gallon of fuel?

    (A) $\frac{2}{3}$

    (B) $\frac{3}{4}$

    (C) $\frac{4}{5}$

    (D) $\frac{4}{3}$

    (E) $\frac{3}{2}$

19. If snow accumulation increased at a constant rate of 30 millimeters per hour during a certain snowstorm, how many <u>seconds</u> did it take for snow accumulation to increase by 1 millimeter?

    (A) $\frac{1}{120}$

    (B) $\frac{1}{60}$

    (C) $\frac{1}{20}$

    (D) 20

    (E) 120

20. From 2000 to 2003, the number of employees at a certain company increased by a factor of $\frac{1}{4}$. From 2003 to 2006, the number of employees at this company decreased by a factor of $\frac{1}{3}$. If there were 100 employees at the company in 2006, how many employees were there at the company in 2000?

    (A) 200

    (B) 120

    (C) 100

    (D) 75

    (E) 60

21. Working alone at its own constant rate, machine R fills 10,000 boxes with pins in 9 hours, and working alone at its own constant rate, machine S fills 5,000 boxes with pins in 3 hours. If machine R and machine S, each working at its own constant rate and for the same period of time, together filled a certain number of boxes with pins, what percent of the boxes were filled by machine R?

    (A) 25%

    (B) 33%

    (C) 40%

    (D) 66%

    (E) 75%

22. A collection of 16 coins, each with a face value of either 10 cents or 25 cents, has a total face value of $2.35. How many of the coins have a face value of 25 cents?

    (A) 3

    (B) 5

    (C) 7

    (D) 9

    (E) 11

23. A retailer purchased eggs at $2.80 per dozen and sold the eggs at 3 eggs for $0.90. What was the retailer's gross profit from purchasing and selling 5 dozen eggs? (1 dozen eggs = 12 eggs)

    (A) $0.90

    (B) $2.40

    (C) $4.00

    (D) $11.30

    (E) $12.00

24. In a set of 24 cards, each card is numbered with a different positive integer from 1 to 24. One card will be drawn at random from the set. What is the probability that the card drawn will have either a number that is divisible by both 2 and 3 or a number that is divisible by 7?

(A) $\dfrac{3}{24}$

(B) $\dfrac{4}{24}$

(C) $\dfrac{7}{24}$

(D) $\dfrac{8}{24}$

(E) $\dfrac{17}{24}$

25. As a salesperson, Phyllis can choose one of two methods of annual payment: either an annual salary of $35,000 with no commission or an annual salary of $10,000 plus a 20% commission on her total annual sales. What must her total annual sales be to give her the same annual pay with either method?

(A) $100,000
(B) $120,000
(C) $125,000
(D) $130,000
(E) $132,000

26. If $1 < x < y < z$, which of the following has the greatest value?

(A) $z(x + 1)$
(B) $z(y + 1)$
(C) $x(y + z)$
(D) $y(x + z)$
(E) $z(x + y)$

27. Set X consists of eight consecutive integers. Set Y consists of all the integers that result from adding 4 to each of the integers in Set X and all the integers that result from subtracting 4 from each of the integers in Set X. How many more integers are there in Set Y than in Set X?

(A) 0
(B) 4
(C) 8
(D) 12
(E) 16

28. Of the following, which is the closest to $\dfrac{60.2}{1.03 \times 4.86}$?

(A) 10
(B) 12
(C) 13
(D) 14
(E) 15

29. Thabo owns exactly 140 books, and each book is either paperback fiction, paperback nonfiction, or hardcover nonfiction. If he owns 20 more paperback nonfiction books than hardcover nonfiction books, and twice as many paperback fiction books as paperback nonfiction books, how many hardcover nonfiction books does Thabo own?

(A) 10
(B) 20
(C) 30
(D) 40
(E) 50

30. What is 35 percent of the sum of 1.4 and $\dfrac{1}{5}$?

(A) 0.42
(B) 0.56
(C) 0.85
(D) 1.55
(E) 1.95

31. If $x > 0$, $\dfrac{x}{50} + \dfrac{x}{25}$ is what percent of x?

    (A)   6%
    (B)   25%
    (C)   37%
    (D)   60%
    (E)   75%

32. During a certain time period, Car X traveled north along a straight road at a constant rate of 1 mile per minute and used fuel at a constant rate of 5 gallons every 2 hours. During this time period, if Car X used exactly 3.75 gallons of fuel, how many miles did Car X travel?

    (A)   36
    (B)   37.5
    (C)   40
    (D)   80
    (E)   90

33. Which of the following is closest to the value of $\dfrac{999}{100 + \dfrac{1}{999}}$?

    (A)   10
    (B)   1
    (C)   0.1
    (D)   0.01
    (E)   0.001

34. The population of City X is 50 percent of the population of City Y. The population of City X is what percent of the total population of City X and City Y?

    (A)   25%
    (B) $33\dfrac{1}{3}$%
    (C)   40%
    (D)   50%
    (E) $66\dfrac{2}{3}$%

35. A bicycle store purchased two bicycles, one for $250 and the other for $375, and sold both bicycles at a total gross profit of $250. If the store sold one of the bicycles for $450, which of the following could be the store's gross profit from the sale of the other bicycle?

    (A) $75
    (B) $100
    (C) $125
    (D) $150
    (E) $175

36. If $k^2 = m^2$, which of the following must be true?

    (A) $k = m$
    (B) $k = -m$
    (C) $k = |m|$
    (D) $k = -|m|$
    (E) $|k| = |m|$

37. Makoto, Nishi, and Ozuro were paid a total of $780 for waxing the floors at their school. Each was paid in proportion to the number of hours he or she worked. If Makoto worked 15 hours, Nishi worked 20 hours, and Ozuro worked 30 hours, how much was Makoto paid?

    (A) $52
    (B) $117
    (C) $130
    (D) $180
    (E) $234

38. If x is a positive integer and $4^x - 3 = y$, which of the following CANNOT be a value of y?

    (A)   1
    (B)   7
    (C)   13
    (D)   61
    (E)   253

39. The regular price per can of a certain brand of soda is $0.40. If the regular price per can is discounted 15 percent when the soda is purchased in 24-can cases, what is the price of 72 cans of this brand of soda purchased in 24-can cases?

    (A) $16.32
    (B) $18.00
    (C) $21.60
    (D) $24.48
    (E) $28.80

40. The quotient when a certain number is divided by $\frac{2}{3}$ is $\frac{9}{2}$. What is the number?

    (A) $\frac{4}{27}$
    (B) $\frac{1}{3}$
    (C) 3
    (D) 6
    (E) $\frac{27}{4}$

41. The price of gasoline at a service station increased from $1.65 per gallon last week to $1.82 per gallon this week. Sally paid $26.40 for gasoline last week at the station. How much more will Sally pay this week at the station for the same amount of gasoline?

    (A) $1.70
    (B) $2.55
    (C) $2.64
    (D) $2.72
    (E) $2.90

42. Harry spent 25% of his $2,200 May take-home pay on rent and 30% of the remainder on food. How much of his May take-home pay did Harry spend on food?

    (A) $165
    (B) $495
    (C) $550
    (D) $660
    (E) $1,045

43. If $2x + y = 7$ and $x + 2y = 5$, then $\frac{x+y}{3} =$

    (A) 1
    (B) $\frac{4}{3}$
    (C) $\frac{17}{5}$
    (D) $\frac{18}{5}$
    (E) 4

44. City X has a population 4 times as great as the population of City Y, which has a population twice as great as the population of City Z. What is the ratio of the population of City X to the population of City Z?

    (A) 1:8
    (B) 1:4
    (C) 2:1
    (D) 4:1
    (E) 8:1

Total Membership of Organization *X*, 1988

Emeritus	78
Fellows	9,209
Partners	35,509
Associates	27,909
Affiliates	2,372

45. According to the table above, the number of fellows was approximately what percent of the total membership of Organization *X*? **Note: All categories of membership are mutually exclusive.**

(A)   9%

(B)   12%

(C)   18%

(D)   25%

(E)   35%

46. If $S = 1 + \frac{1}{2^2} + \frac{1}{3^2} + \frac{1}{4^2} + \frac{1}{5^2} + \frac{1}{6^2} + \frac{1}{7^2} + \frac{1}{8^2} + \frac{1}{9^2} + \frac{1}{10^2}$, which of the following is true?

(A) $S > 3$

(B) $S = 3$

(C) $2 < S < 3$

(D) $S = 2$

(E) $S < 2$

47. A manufacturer of a certain product can expect that between 0.3 percent and 0.5 percent of the units manufactured will be defective. If the retail price is $2,500 per unit and the manufacturer offers a full refund for defective units, how much money can the manufacturer expect to need to cover the refunds on 20,000 units?

(A)   Between $15,000 and $25,000

(B)   Between $30,000 and $50,000

(C)   Between $60,000 and $100,000

(D)   Between $150,000 and $250,000

(E)   Between $300,000 and $500,000

48. Which of the following is closest to $\sqrt{\frac{4.2(1,590)}{15.7}}$?

(A)   20

(B)   40

(C)   60

(D)   80

(E)   100

49. What is the value of $\sqrt{17} + \sqrt{47}$, to the nearest whole number?

(A)   8

(B)   11

(C)   12

(D)   15

(E)   32

50. Last week Chris earned *x* dollars per hour for the first 40 hours worked plus 22 dollars per hour for each hour worked beyond 40 hours. If last week Chris earned a total of 816 dollars by working 48 hours, what is the value of *x*?

(A)   13

(B)   14

(C)   15

(D)   16

(E)   17

51. The value of $\dfrac{\frac{7}{8} + \frac{1}{9}}{\frac{1}{2}}$ is closest to which of the following?

(A)   2

(B) $\frac{3}{2}$

(C)   1

(D) $\frac{1}{2}$

(E)   0

52. The positive two-digit integers x and y have the same digits, but in reverse order. Which of the following must be a factor of $x + y$?

(A)   6
(B)   9
(C)   10
(D)   11
(E)   14

53. In a certain sequence of 8 numbers, each number after the first is 1 more than the previous number. If the first number is −5, how many of the numbers in the sequence are positive?

(A)   None
(B)   One
(C)   Two
(D)   Three
(E)   Four

54. A total of s oranges are to be packaged in boxes that will hold r oranges each, with no oranges left over. When n of these boxes have been completely filled, what is the number of boxes that remain to be filled?

(A) $s - nr$

(B) $s - \dfrac{n}{r}$

(C) $rs - n$

(D) $\dfrac{s}{n} - r$

(E) $\dfrac{s}{r} - n$

55. If $0 < a < b < c$, which of the following statements must be true?

I. $2a > b + c$

II. $c - a > b - a$

III. $\dfrac{c}{a} < \dfrac{b}{a}$

(A)   I only
(B)   II only
(C)   III only
(D)   I and II
(E)   II and III

	Monday	Tuesday	Wednesday	Thursday
Company A	45	55	50	50
Company B	10	30	30	10
Company C	34	28	28	30
Company D	39	42	41	38
Company E	50	60	60	70

56. The table shows the numbers of packages shipped daily by each of five companies during a 4-day period. The standard deviation of the numbers of packages shipped daily during the period was greatest for which of the five companies?

(A)   A
(B)   B
(C)   C
(D)   D
(E)   E

57. Company Q plans to make a new product next year and sell each unit of this new product at a selling price of $2. The variable costs per unit in each production run are estimated to be 40% of the selling price, and the fixed costs for each production run are estimated to be $5,040. Based on these estimated costs, how many units of the new product will Company Q need to make and sell in order for their revenue to equal their total costs for each production run?

(A)   4,200
(B)   3,150
(C)   2,520
(D)   2,100
(E)   1,800

58. A small business invests $9,900 in equipment to produce a product. Each unit of the product costs $0.65 to produce and is sold for $1.20. How many units of the product must be sold before the revenue received equals the total expense of production, including the initial investment in equipment?

    (A) 12,000
    (B) 14,500
    (C) 15,230
    (D) 18,000
    (E) 20,000

Estimated Number of Home-Schooled Students by State, January 2001

State	Number (in thousands)
A	181
B	125
C	103
D	79
E	72

59. According to the table shown, the estimated number of home-schooled students in State A is approximately what percent greater than the number in State D?

    (A) 25%
    (B) 55%
    (C) 100%
    (D) 125%
    (E) 155%

60. When n liters of fuel were added to a tank that was already $\frac{1}{3}$ full, the tank was filled to $\frac{7}{9}$ of its capacity. In terms of n, what is the capacity of the tank, in liters?

    (A) $\frac{10}{9}n$

    (B) $\frac{4}{3}n$

    (C) $\frac{3}{2}n$

    (D) $\frac{9}{4}n$

    (E) $\frac{7}{3}n$

61. A bicycle race on a mountain trail began at an elevation 850 meters above Town X. The race course consisted of 5 phases, with the following elevation changes: a descent of 280 meters, an ascent of 350 meters, a descent of 620 meters, an ascent of 100 meters, and a descent of 400 meters. At what elevation, in meters above or below Town X, did the race end?

    (A) 850 below Town X
    (B) Same elevation as Town X
    (C) 850 above Town X
    (D) 1,700 above Town X
    (E) 2,600 above Town X

62. The harvest yield from a certain apple orchard was 350 bushels of apples. If x of the trees in the orchard each yielded 10 bushels of apples, what fraction of the harvest yield was from these x trees?

    (A) $\frac{x}{35}$

    (B) $1 - \frac{x}{35}$

    (C) $10x$

    (D) $35 - x$

    (E) $350 - 10x$

63. In a certain fraction, the denominator is 16 greater than the numerator. If the fraction is equivalent to 80 percent, what is the denominator of the fraction?

    (A) 32
    (B) 64
    (C) 72
    (D) 80
    (E) 120

64. Jonathan, Kyle, and Michael agreed to pay equal shares of the monthly rent on an apartment. Because Jonathan has a cat, he paid a one-time pet deposit of $250. The pet deposit and Jonathan's share of the monthly rent for the first month totaled $525. How much is the monthly rent on the apartment?

    (A) $1,575
    (B) $1,075
    (C) $1,025
    (D) $825
    (E) $775

65. The ratio of the amount of Alex's fuel oil bill for the month of February to the amount of his fuel oil bill for the month of January was $\frac{3}{2}$. If the fuel oil bill for February had been \$40 more, the corresponding ratio would have been $\frac{5}{3}$. How much was Alex's fuel oil bill for January?

    (A) \$240
    (B) \$300
    (C) \$360
    (D) \$450
    (E) \$540

66. Al and Ben are drivers for SD Trucking Company. One snowy day, Ben left SD at 8:00 a.m. heading east and Al left SD at 11:00 a.m. heading west. At a particular time later that day, the dispatcher retrieved data from SD's vehicle tracking system. The data showed that, up to that time, Al had averaged 40 miles per hour and Ben had averaged 20 miles per hour. It also showed that Al and Ben had driven a combined total of 240 miles. At what time did the dispatcher retrieve data from the vehicle tracking system?

    (A) 1:00 p.m.
    (B) 2:00 p.m.
    (C) 3:00 p.m.
    (D) 5:00 p.m.
    (E) 6:00 p.m.

67. If $f = 3r \left(\frac{s}{1,000} \right)^2$ and if $s = 2,000$, what is r in terms of f?

    (A) $\frac{f}{6}$

    (B) $\frac{f}{12}$

    (C) $\frac{f}{36}$

    (D) $\frac{f^2}{36}$

    (E) $\frac{3f}{4}$

68. At the start of an experiment, a certain population consisted of 3 animals. At the end of each month after the start of the experiment, the population size was double its size at the beginning of that month. Which of the following represents the population size at the end of 10 months?

    (A) 2^3
    (B) 3^2
    (C) $2(3^{10})$
    (D) $3(2^{10})$
    (E) $3(10^2)$

69. The formula $F = \frac{9C}{5} + 32$ gives the relationship between the temperature in degrees Fahrenheit, F, and the temperature given in degrees Celsius, C. If the temperature is 85 degrees Fahrenheit, what is the temperature, to the nearest degree, in degrees Celsius?

    (A) 18°C
    (B) 23°C
    (C) 29°C
    (D) 47°C
    (E) 51°C

70. If x and y are positive integers such that y is a multiple of 5 and $3x + 4y = 200$, then x must be a multiple of which of the following?

    (A) 3
    (B) 6
    (C) 7
    (D) 8
    (E) 10

71. Which of the following expressions can be written as an integer?

    I. $\left(\sqrt{82} + \sqrt{82}\right)^2$

    II. $(82)\left(\sqrt{82}\right)$

    III. $\dfrac{\left(\sqrt{82}\right)\left(\sqrt{82}\right)}{82}$

    (A) None
    (B) I only
    (C) III only
    (D) I and II
    (E) I and III

72. Which of the following is equal to the average (arithmetic mean) of $(x + 2)^2$ and $(x - 2)^2$?

    (A) x^2
    (B) $x^2 + 2$
    (C) $x^2 + 4$
    (D) $x^2 + 2x$
    (E) $x^2 + 4x$

73. If $x^2 - 2 < 0$, which of the following specifies all the possible values of x?

    (A) $0 < x < 2$
    (B) $0 < x < \sqrt{2}$
    (C) $-\sqrt{2} < x < \sqrt{2}$
    (D) $-2 < x < 0$
    (E) $-2 < x < 2$

Book Number	Pages in Book	Total Pages Read
1	253	253
2	110	363
3	117	480
4	170	650
5	155	805
6	50	855
7	205	1,060
8	70	1,130
9	165	1,295
10	105	1,400
11	143	1,543
12	207	1,750

74. Shawana made a schedule for reading books during 4 weeks (28 days) of her summer vacation. She has checked out 12 books from the library. The number of pages in each book and the order in which she plans to read the books are shown in the table above. She will read exactly 50 pages each day. The only exception will be that she will never begin the next book on the same day that she finishes the previous one, and therefore on some days she may read fewer than 50 pages. At the end of the 28th day, how many books will Shawana have finished?

    (A) 7
    (B) 8
    (C) 9
    (D) 10
    (E) 11

75. In Western Europe, x bicycles were sold in each of the years 1990 and 1993. The bicycle producers of Western Europe had a 42 percent share of this market in 1990 and a 33 percent share in 1993. Which of the following represents the decrease in the annual number of bicycles produced and sold in Western Europe from 1990 to 1993?

   (A) 9% of $\dfrac{x}{100}$

   (B) 14% of $\dfrac{x}{100}$

   (C) 75% of $\dfrac{x}{100}$

   (D) 9% of x

   (E) 14% of x

76. If k is a positive integer, what is the remainder when $(k + 2)(k^3 - k)$ is divided by 6?

   (A) 0
   (B) 1
   (C) 2
   (D) 3
   (E) 4

77. Which of the following fractions is closest to $\dfrac{1}{2}$?

   (A) $\dfrac{4}{7}$

   (B) $\dfrac{5}{9}$

   (C) $\dfrac{6}{11}$

   (D) $\dfrac{7}{13}$

   (E) $\dfrac{9}{16}$

78. If $p \neq 0$ and $p - \dfrac{1 - p^2}{p} = \dfrac{r}{p}$, then $r =$

   (A) $p + 1$
   (B) $2p - 1$
   (C) $p^2 + 1$
   (D) $2p^2 - 1$
   (E) $p^2 + p - 1$

79. If $\dfrac{|z|}{w} = 1$, which of the following must be true?

   (A) $z = -w$
   (B) $z = w$
   (C) $z^2 = w^2$
   (D) $z^2 = w^3$
   (E) $z^3 = w^3$

80. What number is 108 more than two-thirds of itself?

   (A) 72
   (B) 144
   (C) 162
   (D) 216
   (E) 324

81. A service provider charges c dollars for the first 50 hours of service used per month and 40 cents for each 30 minutes in excess of 50 hours used during the month. If x is an integer greater than 50, which of the following expressions gives this service provider's charge, in dollars, for a month in which x hours of service were used?

   (A) $c + 0.40x$
   (B) $c + 0.80x$
   (C) $c + 0.40(x - 50)$
   (D) $c + 0.80(x - 50)$
   (E) $c + 0.40(2x - 50)$

82. A salesperson who had been driving at a speed of 100 kilometers per hour slowed down to a speed of 47 kilometers per hour. Approximately how many miles per hour was the speed reduced? (1 kilometer $\approx$ 0.625 mile)

   (A) 29
   (B) 33
   (C) 53
   (D) 63
   (E) 75

83. If $5x - 8 = 12$ and $x = y + 3$, then $y =$

    (A) $\dfrac{4}{5}$

    (B) 1

    (C) $\dfrac{17}{5}$

    (D) 4

    (E) 7

	Recording Time	Viewing Time
Tuesday	4 hours	None
Wednesday	None	1 to 2 hours
Thursday	2 hours	None
Friday	None	2 to 3 hours

84. The table above shows the numbers of hours of television programs that Jane recorded last week and the numbers of hours she spent viewing these recorded programs. No recorded program was viewed more than once. If h is the number of hours of recorded programs she had not yet viewed by the end of Friday, which of the following intervals represents all of the possible values of h?

    (A) $0 \leq h \leq 1$

    (B) $1 \leq h \leq 2$

    (C) $2 \leq h \leq 3$

    (D) $0 \leq h \leq 2$

    (E) $1 \leq h \leq 3$

85. A dance troupe has a total of 50 dancers split into 2 groups. The costumes worn by Group A cost $80 each, and those worn by Group B cost $90 each. If the total cost of all the costumes is $4,270, what is the total cost of the costumes worn by Group B?

    (A) $1,840

    (B) $2,070

    (C) $2,135

    (D) $2,160

    (E) $2,430

86. A doctor prescribed 18 cubic centimeters of a certain drug to a patient whose body weight was 120 pounds. If the typical dosage is 2 cubic centimeters per 15 pounds of body weight, by what percent was the prescribed dosage greater than the typical dosage?

    (A) 8%

    (B) 9%

    (C) 11%

    (D) 12.5%

    (E) 14.8%

87. The function f is defined by $f(x) = \sqrt{x} - 10$ for all positive numbers x. If $u = f(t)$ for some positive numbers t and u, what is t in terms of u?

    (A) $\sqrt{\sqrt{u} + 10}$

    (B) $\left(\sqrt{u} + 10\right)^2$

    (C) $\sqrt{u^2 + 10}$

    (D) $(u + 10)^2$

    (E) $(u^2 + 10)^2$

88. If 35% of a number is decreased by 15, then the result is 25% of the original number. What is the original number?

    (A) 1.5

    (B) 9

    (C) 25

    (D) 150

    (E) 900

89. A flower arrangement consists of 30 roses, each of which is either white or red. If a rose is to be selected at random from the flower arrangement, the probability that the rose selected will be white is twice the probability that it will be red. How many white roses are in the flower arrangement?

    (A) 5

    (B) 10

    (C) 15

    (D) 20

    (E) 25

90. Sixty percent of the people who responded to a company's advertisement for a job opening were interviewed over the phone. Twenty percent of those interviewed over the phone, that is, 3 people, were asked to come to the company for a personal interview. How many people responded to the advertisement?

    (A) 16
    (B) 20
    (C) 25
    (D) 40
    (E) 64

91. $(-3)^{-2} =$

    (A) -9
    (B) -6
    (C) $-\dfrac{1}{9}$
    (D) $\dfrac{1}{9}$
    (E) 9

92. Mark bought a set of 6 flowerpots of different sizes at a total cost of $8.25. Each pot cost $0.25 more than the next one below it in size. What was the cost, in dollars, of the largest pot?

    (A) $1.75
    (B) $1.85
    (C) $2.00
    (D) $2.15
    (E) $2.30

93. If r and s are positive integers and $r - s = 6$, which of the following has the greatest value?

    (A) $2r$
    (B) $2s$
    (C) $r + s$
    (D) $2r - s$
    (E) $2s - r$

94. An auction house charges a commission of 15 percent on the first $50,000 of the sale price of an item, plus 10 percent on the amount of the sale price in excess of $50,000. What was the sale price of a painting for which the auction house charged a total commission of $24,000?

    (A) $115,000
    (B) $160,000
    (C) $215,000
    (D) $240,000
    (E) $365,000

95. At a certain college there are twice as many English majors as history majors and three times as many English majors as mathematics majors. What is the ratio of the number of history majors to the number of mathematics majors?

    (A) 6 to 1
    (B) 3 to 2
    (C) 2 to 3
    (D) 1 to 5
    (E) 1 to 6

96. A certain method for calculating pediatric drug dosages states that if d is the adult dosage, in milligrams, and y is the child's age, in years, then the child's dosage, in milligrams, is $d\left(\dfrac{y+1}{24}\right)$. If the adult dosage for a particular drug is 800 milligrams, what is an 8-year-old child's dosage, in milligrams, according to this method?

    (A) 200
    (B) 225
    (C) 250
    (D) 275
    (E) 300

97. 1, 2, 3, 4, 5, 6, 7, 8, 9, 10
    How many different ordered pairs of numbers (s, t) can be formed such that $t = 3s$, where s and t are numbers from the list above?

    (A) Two
    (B) Three
    (C) Five
    (D) Six
    (E) Ten

98. If $|x - 2| > 3$, then x could be equal to any of the following EXCEPT

    (A)   −3

    (B)   −2

    (C)   4

    (D)   6

    (E)   8

99. If the average (arithmetic mean) of 7, 16, and h is greater than or equal to 7, what is the least possible value of h?

    (A)   −16

    (B)   −2

    (C)   7

    (D)   21

    (E)   23

100. Norman is scheduled to write computer programs during a 15-week period beginning this week. Norman will write 5 computer programs this week, 6 computer programs next week, and each week thereafter, he will write 1 computer program more than he did in the previous week. What is the total number of computer programs that Norman will write during the 15-week period?

    (A)   180

    (B)   190

    (C)   200

    (D)   210

    (E)   225

101. Which of the following fractions has the greatest value?

    (A) $\dfrac{5}{13}$

    (B) $\dfrac{3}{11}$

    (C) $\left(\dfrac{5}{13}\right)^2$

    (D) $\left(\dfrac{3}{11}\right)^3$

    (E) $\left(\dfrac{5}{13}\right)^3$

Fee	Plan A	Plan B
Line 1, Activation Fee	$0	$50
Line 2, Activation Fee	$0	$30
Line 1, Monthly Fee	$40	$35
Line 2, Monthly Fee	$15	$10

102. The table above shows all applicable charges for 2 phone lines, Line 1 and Line 2, under 2 plans, Plan A and Plan B. Both plans require a monthly fee per phone line, and Plan B requires an additional one-time Line Activation Fee. If n is the number of months for which the total charges for 2 lines under Plan A are equal to the total charges for 2 lines under Plan B, what is n?

    (A)   4

    (B)   5

    (C)   8

    (D)   10

    (E)   16

103. The prices for 5 textbooks on a certain shelf are $40, $50, $40, $45, and $50, respectively. In which of the following intervals does the standard deviation of the prices of the 5 textbooks lie?

    (A)   Between $0 and $10

    (B)   Between $10 and $20

    (C)   Between $20 and $30

    (D)   Between $40 and $45

    (E)   Between $45 and $50

Questions 104 to 191 — Difficulty: **Medium**

104. The sides of each of two plastic cubes are numbered 1 through 6, and each number is equally likely to appear face up after either cube is rolled. What is the probability that after the two cubes are rolled, the sum of the two numbers appearing face up will be greater than 9?

(A) $\dfrac{1}{6}$

(B) $\dfrac{1}{5}$

(C) $\dfrac{1}{4}$

(D) $\dfrac{5}{18}$

(E) $\dfrac{1}{3}$

105. On Saturday morning, Malachi will begin a camping vacation, and he will return home at the end of the first day on which it rains. If on the first three days of the vacation the probability of rain on each day is 0.2, what is the probability that Malachi will return home at the end of the day on the following Monday?

(A) 0.008

(B) 0.128

(C) 0.488

(D) 0.512

(E) 0.640

106. According to a survey of 200 people, 60 enjoy skiing and 80 enjoy skating. If the number of people who enjoy neither skiing nor skating is 2 times the number of people who enjoy both skiing and skating, how many people surveyed enjoy neither skiing nor skating?

(A) 20

(B) 40

(C) 50

(D) 80

(E) 120

$$m \oplus p = n$$
$$n \oplus r = m$$
$$n \oplus q = q$$
$$p \oplus q = p$$
$$q \oplus p = r$$

107. If the relations shown hold for the operation $\oplus$ and the numbers m, n, p, q, and r, then $[(m \oplus p) \oplus q] \oplus p =$

(A) m

(B) n

(C) p

(D) q

(E) r

108. To rent a tractor, it costs a total of x dollars for the first 24 hours, plus y dollars per hour for each hour in excess of 24 hours. Which of the following represents the cost, in dollars, to rent a tractor for 36 hours?

(A) $x + 12y$

(B) $x + 36y$

(C) $12x + y$

(D) $24x + 12y$

(E) $24x + 36y$

109. If the mass of 1 cubic centimeter of a certain substance is 7.3 grams, what is the mass, in kilograms, of 1 cubic meter of this substance? (1 cubic meter = 1,000,000 cubic centimeters; 1 kilogram = 1,000 grams)

(A) 0.0073

(B) 0.73

(C) 7.3

(D) 7,300

(E) 7,300,000

110. If $z \neq 0$ and $z + \dfrac{1 - 2z^2}{z} = \dfrac{w}{z}$, then $w =$

(A) $z + 1$

(B) $z^2 + 1$

(C) $-z^2 + 1$

(D) $-z^2 + z + 1$

(E) $-2z^2 + 1$

111. For all real numbers a, b, c, d, e, and f, the operation $\ominus$ is defined by the equation $(a, b, c) \ominus (d, e, f) = ad + be + cf$. What is the value of $(1, -2, 3) \ominus \left(1, -\frac{1}{2}, \frac{1}{3}\right)$?

   (A) -1

   (B) $\dfrac{5}{6}$

   (C) 1

   (D) $\dfrac{5}{2}$

   (E) 3

Absences from a Certain Math Class During the Spring Semester

Number of Absences	Number of Students
0	4
1	3
2	10
3	3
4	5
5 or more	3

112. The table above shows the distribution of the number of absences from a certain Math class during the spring semester. For those students who had at least 1 absence, what was the median number of absences?

   (A) 1.5

   (B) 2

   (C) 2.5

   (D) 3

   (E) 3.5

113. If $\dfrac{x}{y} = \dfrac{c}{d}$ and $\dfrac{d}{c} = \dfrac{b}{a}$, which of the following must be true?

   I. $\dfrac{y}{x} = \dfrac{b}{a}$

   II. $\dfrac{x}{a} = \dfrac{y}{b}$

   III. $\dfrac{y}{a} = \dfrac{x}{b}$

   (A) I only

   (B) II only

   (C) I and II only

   (D) I and III only

   (E) I, II, and III

114. If $[x]$ denotes the least integer greater than or equal to x and $\left[\dfrac{x}{2}\right] = 0$, which of the following could be the value of x?

   (A) -2

   (B) $-\dfrac{3}{2}$

   (C) $\dfrac{1}{2}$

   (D) 1

   (E) 2

115. If $a(a + 2) = 24$ and $b(b + 2) = 24$, where $a \neq b$, then $a + b =$

   (A) -48

   (B) -2

   (C) 2

   (D) 46

   (E) 48

116. In a recent election, Ms. Robbins received 8,000 votes cast by independent voters, that is, voters not registered with a specific political party. She also received 10 percent of the votes cast by those voters registered with a political party. If N is the total number of votes cast in the election and 40 percent of the votes cast were cast by independent voters, which of the following represents the number of votes that Ms. Robbins received?

    (A) $0.06N + 3,200$
    (B) $0.1N + 7,200$
    (C) $0.4N + 7,200$
    (D) $0.1N + 8,000$
    (E) $0.06N + 8,000$

117. The profit P, in dollars, for any given month at a certain company is defined by $P = I - C$, where I represents total income, in dollars, and C represents total costs, in dollars, for the month. For each of the first 4 months of the year, $C = I + 32,000$; and for each of the next 3 months, $I = C + 36,000$. If $I = C + 10,000$ for each of the 5 remaining months of the year, what was the company's total profit for the 12-month year?

    (A) $10,000
    (B) $30,000
    (C) $40,000
    (D) $50,000
    (E) $70,000

118. A manufacturer makes and sells 2 products, P and Q. The revenue from the sale of each unit of P is $20.00 and the revenue from the sale of each unit of Q is $17.00. Last year the manufacturer sold twice as many units of Q as P. What was the manufacturer's average (arithmetic mean) revenue per unit sold of these 2 products last year?

    (A) $28.50
    (B) $27.00
    (C) $19.00
    (D) $18.50
    (E) $18.00

119. A worker carries jugs of liquid soap from a production line to a packing area, carrying 4 jugs per trip. If the jugs are packed into cartons that hold 7 jugs each, how many jugs are needed to fill the last partially filled carton after the worker has made 17 trips?

    (A)   1
    (B)   2
    (C)   4
    (D)   5
    (E)   6

120. Last year a state senate consisting of only Republican and Democrat members had 20 more Republican members than Democrat members. This year the senate has the same number of members as last year, but it has 2 fewer Republican members than last year.

    If this year the number of Republican members is $\frac{2}{3}$ the number of senate members, how many members does the senate have this year?

    (A)   33
    (B)   36
    (C)   42
    (D)   45
    (E)   48

121. Sam has $800 in his account. He will deposit $1 in his account one week from now, $2 two weeks from now, and each week thereafter he will deposit an amount that is $1 greater than the amount that he deposited one week before. If there are no other transactions, how much money will Sam have in his account 50 weeks from now?

    (A) $850
    (B) $1,200
    (C) $1,675
    (D) $2,075
    (E) $3,350

122. A certain state's milk production was 980 million pounds in 2007 and 2.7 billion pounds in 2014. Approximately how many more million <u>gallons</u> of milk did the state produce in 2014 than in 2007? (1 billion = 10^9 and 1 gallon = 8.6 pounds.)

    (A)   100
    (B)   200
    (C)   1,700
    (D)   8,200
    (E)   14,800

123. Working simultaneously and independently at an identical constant rate, four machines of a certain type can produce a total of x units of Product P in 6 days. How many of these machines, working simultaneously and independently at this constant rate, can produce a total of $3x$ units of Product P in 4 days?

    (A)   24
    (B)   18
    (C)   16
    (D)   12
    (E)   8

124. The symbol Δ denotes one of the four arithmetic operations: addition, subtraction, multiplication, or division. If $6 \Delta 3 \leq 3$, which of the following must be true?

    I. $2 \Delta 2 = 0$
    II. $2 \Delta 2 = 1$
    III. $4 \Delta 2 = 2$

    (A)   I only
    (B)   II only
    (C)   III only
    (D)   I and II only
    (E)   I, II, and III

125. If $mn \neq 0$ and 25 percent of n equals $37\frac{1}{2}$ percent of m, what is the value of $\frac{12n}{m}$?

    (A)   18
    (B) $\frac{32}{3}$
    (C)   8
    (D)   3
    (E) $\frac{9}{8}$

126. N and M are each 3-digit integers. Each of the numbers 1, 2, 3, 6, 7, and 8 is a digit of either N or M. What is the smallest possible positive difference between N and M?

    (A)   29
    (B)   49
    (C)   58
    (D)   113
    (E)   131

Technique	Percent of Consumers
Television ads	35%
Coupons	22%
Store displays	18%
Samples	15%

127. The table shows <u>partial</u> results of a survey in which consumers were asked to indicate which one of six promotional techniques most influenced their decision to buy a new food product. Of those consumers who indicated one of the four techniques listed, what fraction indicated either coupons or store displays?

    (A) $\frac{2}{7}$

    (B) $\frac{1}{3}$

    (C) $\frac{2}{5}$

    (D) $\frac{4}{9}$

    (E) $\frac{1}{2}$

128. If 65 percent of a certain firm's employees are full-time and if there are 5,100 more full-time employees than part-time employees, how many employees does the firm have?

(A)   8,250
(B)   10,200
(C)   11,050
(D)   16,500
(E)   17,000

129. The cost C, in dollars, to remove p percent of a certain pollutant from a pond is estimated by using the formula $C = \dfrac{100{,}000p}{100 - p}$. According to this estimate, how much more would it cost to remove 90 percent of the pollutant from the pond than it would cost to remove 80 percent of the pollutant?

(A) $500,000
(B) $100,000
(C) $50,000
(D) $10,000
(E) $5,000

130. If $xy \neq 0$ and $x^2y^2 - xy = 6$, which of the following could be y in terms of x?

I. $\dfrac{1}{2x}$

II. $-\dfrac{2}{x}$

III. $\dfrac{3}{x}$

(A)   I only
(B)   II only
(C)   I and II
(D)   I and III
(E)   II and III

131. If the positive number d is the standard deviation of n, k, and p, then the standard deviation of $n + 1$, $k + 1$, and $p + 1$ is

(A) $d + 3$
(B) $d + 1$
(C) $6d$
(D) $3d$
(E) d

132. In a certain high school, 80 percent of the seniors are taking calculus, and 60 percent of the seniors who are taking calculus are also taking physics. If 10 percent of the seniors are taking neither calculus nor physics, what percent of the seniors are taking physics?

(A)   40%
(B)   42%
(C)   48%
(D)   58%
(E)   80%

133. If the units digit of $\dfrac{5{,}610.37}{10^k}$ is 6, what is the value of k?

(A)   3
(B)   2
(C)   1
(D)   −1
(E)   −2

134. Three printing presses, R, S, and T, working together at their respective constant rates, can do a certain printing job in 4 hours. S and T, working together at their respective constant rates, can do the same job in 5 hours. How many hours would it take R, working alone at its constant rate, to do the same job?

(A)   8
(B)   10
(C)   12
(D)   15
(E)   20

Results of a Poll

Company	Number Who Own Stock in the Company
AT&T	30
IBM	48
GM	54
FORD	75
US Air	83

135. In a poll, 200 subscribers to *Financial Magazine X* indicated which of five specific companies they own stock in. The results are shown in the table above. If 15 of the 200 own stock in both IBM and AT&T, how many of those polled own stock in neither company?

    (A) 63
    (B) 93
    (C) 107
    (D) 122
    (E) 137

136. The sum of all the integers k such that $-26 < k < 24$ is

    (A)   0
    (B) −2
    (C) −25
    (D) −49
    (E) −51

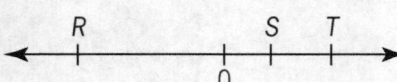

137. The number line shown contains three points R, S, and T, whose coordinates have absolute values r, s, and t, respectively. Which of the following equals the average (arithmetic mean) of the coordinates of the points R, S, and T?

    (A) s
    (B) $s + t - r$
    (C) $\dfrac{r - s - t}{3}$
    (D) $\dfrac{r + s + t}{3}$
    (E) $\dfrac{s + t - r}{3}$

138. Mark and Ann together were allocated n boxes of cookies to sell for a club project. Mark sold 10 boxes less than n and Ann sold 2 boxes less than n. If Mark and Ann have each sold at least one box of cookies, but together they have sold less than n boxes, what is the value of n?

    (A) 11
    (B) 12
    (C) 13
    (D) 14
    (E) 15

$$\begin{array}{r} 3P5 \\ + \, 4QR \\ \hline 8S4 \end{array}$$

139. In the correctly worked addition problem shown, P, Q, R, and S are digits. If $Q = 2P$, which of the following could be the value of S?

    (A) 3
    (B) 4
    (C) 5
    (D) 7
    (E) 9

140. A certain high school has 5,000 students. Of these students, x are taking music, y are taking art, and z are taking both music and art. How many students are taking neither music nor art?

    (A) $5{,}000 - z$
    (B) $5{,}000 - x - y$
    (C) $5{,}000 - x + z$
    (D) $5{,}000 - x - y - z$
    (E) $5{,}000 - x - y + z$

141. Each person who attended a company meeting was either a stockholder in the company, an employee of the company, or both. If 62 percent of those who attended the meeting were stockholders and 47 percent were employees, what percent were stockholders who were NOT employees?

    (A) 34%
    (B) 38%
    (C) 45%
    (D) 53%
    (E) 62%

142. If *M* is the least common multiple of 90, 196, and 300, which of the following is <u>not</u> a factor of *M*?

    (A)   600

    (B)   700

    (C)   900

    (D)   2,100

    (E)   4,900

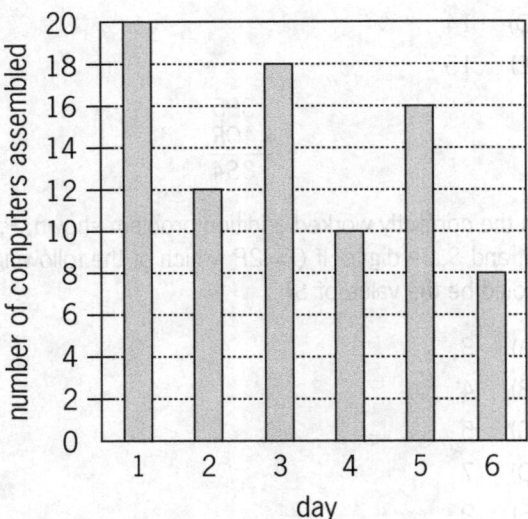

143. The graph shows the number of computers assembled during each of 6 consecutive days. From what day to the next day was the percent change in the number of computers assembled the greatest in magnitude?

    (A)   From Day 1 to Day 2

    (B)   From Day 2 to Day 3

    (C)   From Day 3 to Day 4

    (D)   From Day 4 to Day 5

    (E)   From Day 5 to Day 6

144. If *n* = 20! + 17, then *n* is divisible by which of the following?

    I.   15

    II.   17

    III.   19

    (A)   None

    (B)   I only

    (C)   II only

    (D)   I and II

    (E)   II and III

145. Exchange Rates in a Particular Year

$$\$1 = 5.3 \text{ francs}$$
$$\$1 = 1.6 \text{ marks}$$

An American dealer bought a table in Germany for 480 marks and sold the same table in France for 2,385 francs. What was the dealer's gross profit on the two transactions in dollars?

    (A) $0

    (B) $50

    (C) $100

    (D) $150

    (E) $200

146. The product of two negative numbers is 160. If the lesser of the two numbers is 4 less than twice the greater, what is the greater number?

    (A)   −20

    (B)   −16

    (C)   −10

    (D)   −8

    (E)   −4

147. According to a certain estimate, the depth *N*(*t*), in centimeters, of the water in a certain tank at *t* hours past 2:00 in the morning is given by $N(t) = -20(t - 5)^2 + 500$ for $0 \leq t \leq 10$. According to this estimate, at what time in the morning does the depth of the water in the tank reach its maximum?

    (A)   5:30

    (B)   7:00

    (C)   7:30

    (D)   8:00

    (E)   9:00

148. After driving to a riverfront parking lot, Bob plans to run south along the river, turn around, and return to the parking lot, running north along the same path. After running 3.25 miles south, he decides to run for only 50 minutes more. If Bob runs at a constant rate of 8 minutes per mile, how many miles farther south can he run and still be able to return to the parking lot in 50 minutes?

    (A) 1.5
    (B) 2.25
    (C) 3.0
    (D) 3.25
    (E) 4.75

149. Alex deposited x dollars into a new account that earned 8 percent annual interest, compounded annually. One year later Alex deposited an additional x dollars into the account. If there were no other transactions and if the account contained w dollars at the end of two years, which of the following expresses x in terms of w?

    (A) $\dfrac{w}{1+1.08}$

    (B) $\dfrac{w}{1.08+1.16}$

    (C) $\dfrac{w}{1.16+1.24}$

    (D) $\dfrac{w}{1.08+(1.08)^2}$

    (E) $\dfrac{w}{(1.08)^2+(1.08)^3}$

150. M is the sum of the reciprocals of the consecutive integers from 201 to 300, inclusive. Which of the following is true?

    (A) $\dfrac{1}{3}<M<\dfrac{1}{2}$

    (B) $\dfrac{1}{5}<M<\dfrac{1}{3}$

    (C) $\dfrac{1}{7}<M<\dfrac{1}{5}$

    (D) $\dfrac{1}{9}<M<\dfrac{1}{7}$

    (E) $\dfrac{1}{12}<M<\dfrac{1}{9}$

151. Working simultaneously at their respective constant rates, Machines A and B produce 800 nails in x hours. Working alone at its constant rate, Machine A produces 800 nails in y hours. In terms of x and y, how many hours does it take Machine B, working alone at its constant rate, to produce 800 nails?

    (A) $\dfrac{x}{x+y}$

    (B) $\dfrac{y}{x+y}$

    (C) $\dfrac{xy}{x+y}$

    (D) $\dfrac{xy}{x-y}$

    (E) $\dfrac{xy}{y-x}$

152. Carol purchased one basket of fruit consisting of 4 apples and 2 oranges and another basket of fruit consisting of 3 apples and 5 oranges. Carol is to select one piece of fruit at random from each of the two baskets. What is the probability that one of the two pieces of fruit selected will be an apple and the other will be an orange?

    (A) $\dfrac{1}{4}$

    (B) $\dfrac{1}{2}$

    (C) $\dfrac{1}{24}$

    (D) $\dfrac{5}{24}$

    (E) $\dfrac{13}{24}$

153. Last year Brand X shoes were sold by dealers in 403 different regions worldwide, with an average (arithmetic mean) of 98 dealers per region. If last year these dealers sold an average of 2,488 pairs of Brand X shoes per dealer, which of the following is closest to the total number of pairs of Brand X shoes sold last year by the dealers worldwide?

    (A) 10^4
    (B) 10^5
    (C) 10^6
    (D) 10^7
    (E) 10^8

154. A positive integer is divisible by 3 if and only if the sum of its digits is divisible by 3. If the six-digit integer n is divisible by 3 and n is of the form $1k2,k24$, where k represents a digit that occurs twice, how many values could n have?

    (A) Two
    (B) Three
    (C) Four
    (D) Five
    (E) Ten

	Number of Marbles in Each of Three Bags	Percent of Marbles in Each Bag That Are Blue (to the nearest tenth)
Bag P	37	10.8%
Bag Q	x	66.7%
Bag R	32	50.0%

155. If $\frac{1}{3}$ of the total number of marbles in the three bags listed in the table above are blue, how many marbles are there in Bag Q?

    (A) 5
    (B) 9
    (C) 12
    (D) 23
    (E) 46

Age Category (in years)	Number of Employees
Less than 20	29
20–29	58
30–39	36
40–49	21
50–59	10
60–69	5
70 and over	2

156. The table above gives the age categories of the 161 employees at Company X and the number of employees in each category. According to the table, if m is the median age, in years, of the employees at Company X, then m must satisfy which of the following?

    (A) $20 \leq m \leq 29$
    (B) $25 \leq m \leq 34$
    (C) $30 \leq m \leq 39$
    (D) $35 \leq m \leq 44$
    (E) $40 \leq m \leq 49$

157. If k and n are positive integers such that $n > k$, then $k! + (n - k) \cdot (k - 1)!$ is equivalent to which of the following?

    (A) $k \cdot n!$
    (B) $k! \cdot n$
    (C) $(n - k)!$
    (D) $n \cdot (k + 1)!$
    (E) $n \cdot (k - 1)!$

158. Ron is 4 inches taller than Amy, and Barbara is 1 inch taller than Ron. If Barbara's height is 65 inches, what is the median height, in inches, of these three people?

    (A) 60
    (B) 61
    (C) 62
    (D) 63
    (E) 64

159. If x and y are positive numbers such that $x + y = 1$, which of the following could be the value of $100x + 200y$?

   I.   80
   II. 140
   III. 199

   (A)   II only
   (B)   III only
   (C)   I and II
   (D)   I and III
   (E)   II and III

160. If X is the hundredths digit in the decimal $0.1X$ and if Y is the thousandths digit in the decimal $0.02Y$, where X and Y are nonzero digits, which of the following is closest to the greatest possible value of $\dfrac{0.1X}{0.02Y}$?

   (A)   4
   (B)   5
   (C)   6
   (D)   9
   (E)   10

161. If each of the 12 teams participating in a certain tournament plays exactly one game with each of the other teams, how many games will be played?

   (A)   144
   (B)   132
   (C)   66
   (D)   33
   (E)   23

162. For which of the following values of x is $\sqrt{1 - \sqrt{2 - \sqrt{x}}}$ not defined as a real number?

   (A)   1
   (B)   2
   (C)   3
   (D)   4
   (E)   5

163. What is the remainder when 3^{19} is divided by 10?

   (A)   1
   (B)   3
   (C)   5
   (D)   7
   (E)   9

164. Of 200 people surveyed, 80 percent own a cellular phone and 45 percent own a pager. If all 200 people surveyed own a cellular phone, or a pager, or both, what percent of those surveyed either do not own a cellular phone or do not own a pager?

   (A)   35%
   (B)   45%
   (C)   55%
   (D)   65%
   (E)   75%

165. At the end of the first quarter, the share price of a certain mutual fund was 20 percent higher than it was at the beginning of the year. At the end of the second quarter, the share price was 50 percent higher than it was at the beginning of the year. What was the percent increase in the share price from the end of the first quarter to the end of the second quarter?

   (A)   20%
   (B)   25%
   (C)   30%
   (D)   33%
   (E)   40%

$$\frac{1}{2}, \frac{1}{4}, \frac{1}{8}, \frac{1}{16}, \frac{1}{32}, \ldots$$

166. In the sequence above, each term after the first is one-half the previous term. If x is the tenth term of the sequence, then x satisfies which of the following inequalities?

   (A) $0.1 < x < 1$
   (B) $0.01 < x < 0.1$
   (C) $0.001 < x < 0.01$
   (D) $0.0001 < x < 0.001$
   (E) $0.00001 < x < 0.0001$

167. If $xy + z = x(y + z)$, which of the following must be true?

(A) $x = 0$ and $z = 0$

(B) $x = 1$ and $y = 1$

(C) $y = 1$ and $z = 0$

(D) $x = 1$ or $y = 0$

(E) $x = 1$ or $z = 0$

168. Two water pumps, working simultaneously at their respective constant rates, took exactly 4 hours to fill a certain swimming pool. If the constant rate of one pump was 1.5 times the constant rate of the other, how many hours would it have taken the faster pump to fill the pool if it had worked alone at its constant rate?

(A) 5

(B) $\dfrac{16}{3}$

(C) $\dfrac{11}{2}$

(D) 6

(E) $\dfrac{20}{3}$

169. If $0 < x < 1$, what is the median of the values x, x^{-1}, x^2, $\sqrt{x}$, and x^3?

(A) x

(B) x^{-1}

(C) x^2

(D) $\sqrt{x}$

(E) x^3

170. The number of stamps that Kaye and Alberto had were in the ratio 5:3, respectively. After Kaye gave Alberto 10 of her stamps, the ratio of the number Kaye had to the number Alberto had was 7:5. As a result of this gift, Kaye had how many more stamps than Alberto?

(A) 20

(B) 30

(C) 40

(D) 60

(E) 90

7.51	8.22	7.86	8.36
8.09	7.83	8.30	8.01
7.73	8.25	7.96	8.53

171. A vending machine is designed to dispense 8 ounces of coffee into a cup. After a test that recorded the number of ounces of coffee in each of 1,000 cups dispensed by the vending machine, the 12 listed amounts, in ounces, were selected from the data. If the 1,000 recorded amounts have a mean of 8.1 ounces and a standard deviation of 0.3 ounce, how many of the 12 listed amounts are within 1.5 standard deviations of the mean?

(A) Four

(B) Six

(C) Nine

(D) Ten

(E) Eleven

172. In a certain quiz that consists of 10 questions, each question after the first is worth 4 points more than the preceding question. If the 10 questions on the quiz are worth a total of 360 points, how many points is the third question worth?

(A) 18

(B) 24

(C) 26

(D) 32

(E) 44

173. A car traveling at a certain constant speed takes 2 seconds longer to travel 1 kilometer than it would take to travel 1 kilometer at 75 kilometers per hour. At what speed, in kilometers per hour, is the car traveling?

(A) 71.5

(B) 72

(C) 72.5

(D) 73

(E) 73.5

174. If the speed of x meters per second is equivalent to the speed of y kilometers per hour, what is y in terms of x? (1 kilometer = 1,000 meters)

   (A) $\dfrac{5x}{18}$

   (B) $\dfrac{6x}{5}$

   (C) $\dfrac{18x}{5}$

   (D) $60x$

   (E) $3,600,000x$

175. The function f is defined by $f(x) = -\dfrac{1}{x}$ for all nonzero numbers x. If $f(a) = -\dfrac{1}{2}$ and $f(ab) = \dfrac{1}{6}$, then $b =$

   (A) 3

   (B) $\dfrac{1}{3}$

   (C) $-\dfrac{1}{3}$

   (D) -3

   (E) -12

176. If $5^x - 5^{x-3} = (124)(5^y)$, what is y in terms of x?

   (A) x

   (B) $x - 6$

   (C) $x - 3$

   (D) $2x + 3$

   (E) $2x + 6$

177. The total of Company C's assets in 1994 was 300 percent greater than the total in 1993, which in turn was 400 percent greater than the total in 1992. If the total of Company C's assets in 1992 was N dollars, which of the following represents the total of Company C's assets, in dollars, in 1994?

   (A) $7N$

   (B) $8N$

   (C) $9N$

   (D) $12N$

   (E) $20N$

178. If $\dfrac{x}{|y|} = -1$, which of the following must be true?

   (A) $x = -y$

   (B) $x = y$

   (C) $x = y^2$

   (D) $x^2 = y^2$

   (E) $x^3 = y^3$

A	1	$2\sqrt{3}$
B	$\sqrt{6}$	C
$\sqrt{3}$	6	D

179. The table above is a 3 by 3 grid of 9 numbers, 5 of which are given. The 4 numbers that are not given are denoted by A, B, C, and D. The product of the numbers in each row and in each column is the same for all rows and columns. What is the value of the product $ABCD$?

   (A) 36

   (B) 72

   (C) $36\sqrt{2}$

   (D) $36\sqrt{3}$

   (E) $72\sqrt{6}$

180. In May, Mrs. Lee's earnings were 60 percent of the Lee family's total income. In June, Mrs. Lee earned 20 percent more than in May. If the rest of the family's income was the same both months, then in June, Mrs. Lee's earnings were approximately what percent of the Lee family's total income?

   (A) 64%

   (B) 68%

   (C) 72%

   (D) 76%

   (E) 80%

181. John would have reduced the time it took him to drive from his home to a certain store by $\frac{1}{3}$ if he had increased his average speed by 15 miles per hour. What was John's actual average speed, in miles per hour, when he drove from his home to the store?

   (A)   25
   (B)   30
   (C)   40
   (D)   45
   (E)   50

182. Which of the following inequalities has a solution set that, when graphed on a number line, is a single line segment of finite length?

   (A) $x^4 \geq 1$
   (B) $x^3 \leq 27$
   (C) $x^2 \geq 16$
   (D) $2 \leq |x| \leq 5$
   (E) $2 \leq 3x + 4 \leq 6$

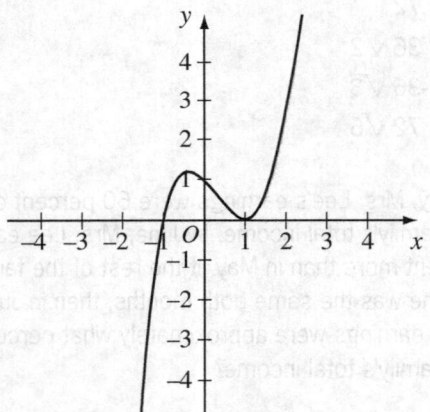

183. The figure shows the graph of $y = (x + 1)(x - 1)^2$ in the xy-plane. At how many points does the graph of $y = (x + 1)(x - 1)^2 + 2$ intercept the x-axis?

   (A)   None
   (B)   One
   (C)   Two
   (D)   Three
   (E)   Four

184. If the average (arithmetic mean) of positive integers 2, 5, 1, x, and y is 4, what is the greatest possible value of y?

   (A)   10
   (B)   11
   (C)   12
   (D)   13
   (E)   14

185. A jeweler bought a necklace at a wholesale price of $135 and then sold it at a 10 percent discount off the suggested retail price. If the jeweler made a 40 percent profit on the wholesale price, what was the suggested retail price of the necklace?

   (A) $139
   (B) $189
   (C) $199
   (D) $210
   (E) $220

186. The weights of 6 packages are 12, 10, 11, 10, 12, and 10 pounds, respectively. In which of the following intervals does the standard deviation of the weights of the packages lie?

   (A)   Between 0 and 3
   (B)   Between 6 and 7
   (C)   Between 8 and 10
   (D)   Between 10 and 11
   (E)   Between 11 and 12

187. In one week a certain taxicab company's cabs used a total of 600 gallons of gasoline, and each gallon of gasoline cost $1.20. If the cabs traveled a total of 9,000 miles that week, what was the company's average gasoline cost per mile traveled by the cabs?

   (A) $0.08
   (B) $0.12
   (C) $0.15
   (D) $0.18
   (E) $0.20

188. For a fundraiser, each of 20 people walked a total of either 2 miles or 5 miles. If they walked a total of 76 miles, how many <u>more</u> people walked 5 miles than walked 2 miles?

    (A)   2
    (B)   4
    (C)   6
    (D)   8
    (E)   10

189. Last Monday the price per share of Company X stock at the end of the first hour of trading was 30 percent lower than the opening price per share. If the price per share at the end of the second hour was 10 percent greater than the price per share at the end of the first hour, then the price per share at the end of the second hour was what percent less than the opening price per share?

    (A)   20%
    (B)   23%
    (C)   24%
    (D)   27%
    (E)   33%

190. The average (arithmetic mean) selling price of 5 houses in a certain neighborhood was $250,000. If the average selling price of 3 of the houses was $280,000, what was the average selling price of the other 2 houses?

    (A) $205,000
    (B) $215,000
    (C) $220,000
    (D) $240,000
    (E) $250,000

191. Which of the following fractions has the greatest value?

    (A) $\dfrac{11}{13}$

    (B) $\dfrac{13}{15}$

    (C) $\left(\dfrac{11}{13}\right)^2$

    (D) $\left(\dfrac{11}{13}\right)^4$

    (E) $\left(\dfrac{13}{15}\right)^4$

Questions 192 to 293 — Difficulty: **Hard**

192. The cost to rent a small bus for a trip is x dollars, which is to be shared equally among the people taking the trip. If 10 people take the trip rather than 16, how many more dollars, in terms of x, will it cost per person?

    (A) $\dfrac{x}{6}$

    (B) $\dfrac{x}{10}$

    (C) $\dfrac{x}{16}$

    (D) $\dfrac{3x}{40}$

    (E) $\dfrac{3x}{80}$

193. Clarissa will create her summer reading list by randomly choosing 4 books from the 10 books approved for summer reading. She will list the books in the order in which they are chosen. How many different lists are possible?

    (A)   6
    (B)   40
    (C)   210
    (D)   5,040
    (E)   151,200

194. If n is a positive integer and the product of all the integers from 1 to n, inclusive, is divisible by 990, what is the least possible value of n?

    (A)   8
    (B)   9
    (C)   10
    (D)   11
    (E)   12

195. The probability that event M will NOT occur is 0.8 and the probability that event R will NOT occur is 0.6. If events M and R CANNOT both occur, which of the following is the probability that either event M or event R will occur?

(A) $\frac{1}{5}$

(B) $\frac{2}{5}$

(C) $\frac{3}{5}$

(D) $\frac{4}{5}$

(E) $\frac{12}{25}$

196. The total cost for Company X to produce a batch of tools is $10,000 plus $3 per tool. Each tool sells for $8. The gross profit earned from producing and selling these tools is the total income from sales minus the total production cost. If a batch of 20,000 tools is produced and sold, then Company X's gross profit per tool is

(A) $3.00
(B) $3.75
(C) $4.50
(D) $5.00
(E) $5.50

197. If Q is an odd number and the median of Q consecutive integers is 120, what is the largest of these integers?

(A) $\frac{Q-1}{2}+120$

(B) $\frac{Q}{2}+119$

(C) $\frac{Q}{2}+120$

(D) $\frac{Q+119}{2}$

(E) $\frac{Q+120}{2}$

198. If there are fewer than 8 zeros between the decimal point and the first nonzero digit in the decimal expansion of $\left(\frac{t}{1,000}\right)^4$, which of the following numbers could be the value of t?

I.   3
II. 5
III. 9

(A) None
(B) I only
(C) II only
(D) III only
(E) II and III

199. A three-digit code for certain locks uses the digits 0, 1, 2, 3, 4, 5, 6, 7, 8, 9 according to the following constraints. The first digit cannot be 0 or 1, the second digit must be 0 or 1, and the second and third digits cannot both be 0 in the same code. How many different codes are possible?

(A) 144
(B) 152
(C) 160
(D) 168
(E) 176

200. Jackie has two solutions that are 2 percent sulfuric acid and 12 percent sulfuric acid by volume, respectively. If these solutions are mixed in appropriate quantities to produce 60 liters of a solution that is 5 percent sulfuric acid, approximately how many liters of the 2 percent solution will be required?

(A) 18
(B) 20
(C) 24
(D) 36
(E) 42

201. If Jake loses 8 pounds, he will weigh twice as much as his sister. Together they now weigh 278 pounds. What is Jake's present weight, in pounds?

    (A) 131
    (B) 135
    (C) 139
    (D) 147
    (E) 188

202. For each student in a certain class, a teacher adjusted the student's test score using the formula $y = 0.8x + 20$, where x is the student's original test score and y is the student's adjusted test score. If the standard deviation of the original test scores of the students in the class was 20, what was the standard deviation of the adjusted test scores of the students in the class?

    (A) 12
    (B) 16
    (C) 28
    (D) 36
    (E) 40

203. Last year 26 members of a certain club traveled to England, 26 members traveled to France, and 32 members traveled to Italy. Last year no members of the club traveled to both England and France, 6 members traveled to both England and Italy, and 11 members traveled to both France and Italy. How many members of the club traveled to at least one of these three countries last year?

    (A) 52
    (B) 67
    (C) 71
    (D) 73
    (E) 79

204. A store reported total sales of $385 million for February of this year. If the total sales for the same month last year were $320 million, approximately what was the percent increase in sales?

    (A) 2%
    (B) 17%
    (C) 20%
    (D) 65%
    (E) 83%

205. When positive integer x is divided by positive integer y, the remainder is 9. If $\dfrac{x}{y} = 96.12$, what is the value of y?

    (A) 96
    (B) 75
    (C) 48
    (D) 25
    (E) 12

206. If $x(2x + 1) = 0$ and $\left(x + \frac{1}{2}\right)(2x - 3) = 0$, then $x =$

    (A) -3
    (B) $-\dfrac{1}{2}$
    (C) 0
    (D) $\dfrac{1}{2}$
    (E) $\dfrac{3}{2}$

207. A certain experimental mathematics program was tried out in 2 classes in each of 32 elementary schools and involved 37 teachers. Each of the classes had 1 teacher and each of the teachers taught at least 1, but not more than 3, of the classes. If the number of teachers who taught 3 classes is n, then the least and greatest possible values of n, respectively, are

    (A) 0 and 13
    (B) 0 and 14
    (C) 1 and 10
    (D) 1 and 9
    (E) 2 and 8

208. For the positive numbers, n, $n + 1$, $n + 2$, $n + 4$, and $n + 8$, the mean is how much greater than the median?

    (A) 0
    (B) 1
    (C) $n + 1$
    (D) $n + 2$
    (E) $n + 3$

209. The present ratio of students to teachers at a certain school is 30 to 1. If the student enrollment were to increase by 50 students and the number of teachers were to increase by 5, the ratio of students to teachers would then be 25 to 1. What is the present number of teachers?

    (A)   5
    (B)   8
    (C)   10
    (D)   12
    (E)   15

210. What is the smallest integer n for which $25^n > 5^{12}$?

    (A)   6
    (B)   7
    (C)   8
    (D)   9
    (E)   10

211. Sixty percent of the members of a study group are women, and 45 percent of those women are lawyers. If one member of the study group is to be selected at random, what is the probability that the member selected is a woman lawyer?

    (A)   0.10
    (B)   0.15
    (C)   0.27
    (D)   0.33
    (E)   0.45

212. Each year for 4 years, a farmer increased the number of trees in a certain orchard by $\frac{1}{4}$ of the number of trees in the orchard the preceding year. If all of the trees thrived and there were 6,250 trees in the orchard at the end of the 4-year period, how many trees were in the orchard at the beginning of the 4-year period?

    (A)   1,250
    (B)   1,563
    (C)   2,250
    (D)   2,560
    (E)   2,752

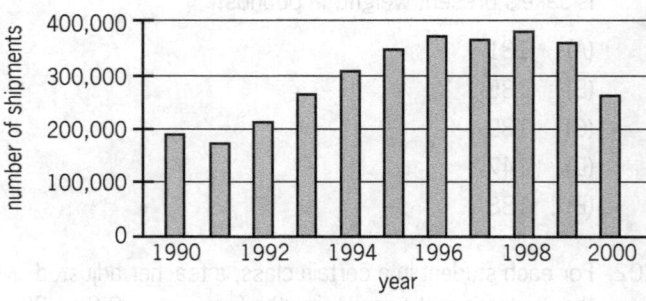

Number of Shipments of Manufactured Homes in the United States, 1990–2000

213. According to the chart shown, which of the following is closest to the median annual number of shipments of manufactured homes in the United States for the years from 1990 to 2000, inclusive?

    (A)   250,000
    (B)   280,000
    (C)   310,000
    (D)   325,000
    (E)   340,000

214. For the positive integers a, b, and k, $a^k \| b$ means that a^k is a divisor of b, but a^{k+1} is not a divisor of b. If k is a positive integer and $2^k \| 72$, then k is equal to

    (A)   2
    (B)   3
    (C)   4
    (D)   8
    (E)   18

215. A certain characteristic in a large population has a distribution that is symmetric about the mean m. If 68 percent of the distribution lies within one standard deviation d of the mean, what percent of the distribution is less than $m + d$?

    (A)   16%
    (B)   32%
    (C)   48%
    (D)   84%
    (E)   92%

216. Four extra-large sandwiches of exactly the same size were ordered for m students, where $m > 4$. Three of the sandwiches were evenly divided among the students. Since 4 students did not want any of the fourth sandwich, it was evenly divided among the remaining students. If Carol ate one piece from each of the four sandwiches, the amount of sandwich that she ate would be what fraction of a whole extra-large sandwich?

(A) $\dfrac{m+4}{m(m-4)}$

(B) $\dfrac{2m-4}{m(m-4)}$

(C) $\dfrac{4m-4}{m(m-4)}$

(D) $\dfrac{4m-8}{m(m-4)}$

(E) $\dfrac{4m-12}{m(m-4)}$

217. Which of the following equations has $1 + \sqrt{2}$ as one of its roots?

(A) $x^2 + 2x - 1 = 0$
(B) $x^2 - 2x + 1 = 0$
(C) $x^2 + 2x + 1 = 0$
(D) $x^2 - 2x - 1 = 0$
(E) $x^2 - x - 1 = 0$

218. In Country C, the unemployment rate among construction workers dropped from 16 percent on September 1, 1992, to 9 percent on September 1, 1996. If the number of construction workers was 20 percent greater on September 1, 1996, than on September 1, 1992, what was the approximate percent change in the number of unemployed construction workers over this period?

(A) 50% decrease
(B) 30% decrease
(C) 15% decrease
(D) 30% increase
(E) 55% increase

219. In a box of 12 pens, a total of 3 are defective. If a customer buys 2 pens selected at random from the box, what is the probability that neither pen will be defective?

(A) $\dfrac{1}{6}$

(B) $\dfrac{2}{9}$

(C) $\dfrac{6}{11}$

(D) $\dfrac{9}{16}$

(E) $\dfrac{3}{4}$

220. At a certain fruit stand, the price of each apple is 40 cents and the price of each orange is 60 cents. Mary selects a total of 10 apples and oranges from the fruit stand, and the average (arithmetic mean) price of the 10 pieces of fruit is 56 cents. How many oranges must Mary put back so that the average price of the pieces of fruit that she keeps is 52 cents?

(A) 1
(B) 2
(C) 3
(D) 4
(E) 5

221. A pharmaceutical company received $3 million in royalties on the first $20 million in sales of the generic equivalent of one of its products and then $9 million in royalties on the next $108 million in sales. By approximately what percent did the ratio of royalties to sales decrease from the first $20 million in sales to the next $108 million in sales?

(A) 8%
(B) 15%
(C) 45%
(D) 52%
(E) 56%

Times at Which the Door
Opened from 8:00 to 10:00

8:00	8:06	8:30	9:05
8:03	8:10	8:31	9:11
8:04	8:18	8:54	9:29
8:04	8:19	8:57	9:31

222. The light in a restroom operates with a 15-minute timer that is reset every time the door opens as a person goes in or out of the room. Thus, after someone enters or exits the room, the light remains on for only 15 minutes unless the door opens again and resets the timer for another 15 minutes. If the times listed above are the times at which the door opened from 8:00 to 10:00, approximately how many minutes during this two-hour period was the light off?

(A)   10
(B)   25
(C)   35
(D)   40
(E)   70

223. If p is the product of the integers from 1 to 30, inclusive, what is the greatest integer k for which 3^k is a factor of p?

(A)   10
(B)   12
(C)   14
(D)   16
(E)   18

224. If $n = 3^8 - 2^8$, which of the following is NOT a factor of n?

(A)   97
(B)   65
(C)   35
(D)   13
(E)   5

225. Club X has more than 10 but fewer than 40 members. Sometimes the members sit at tables with 3 members at one table and 4 members at each of the other tables, and sometimes they sit at tables with 3 members at one table and 5 members at each of the other tables. If they sit at tables with 6 members at each table except one and fewer than 6 members at that one table, how many members will be at the table that has fewer than 6 members?

(A)   1
(B)   2
(C)   3
(D)   4
(E)   5

226. In order to complete a reading assignment on time, Terry planned to read 90 pages per day. However, she read only 75 pages per day at first, leaving 690 pages to be read during the last 6 days before the assignment was to be completed. How many days in all did Terry have to complete the assignment on time?

(A)   15
(B)   16
(C)   25
(D)   40
(E)   46

227. If $s > 0$ and $\sqrt{\dfrac{r}{s}} = s$, what is r in terms of s?

(A) $\dfrac{1}{s}$
(B) $\sqrt{s}$
(C) $s\sqrt{s}$
(D) s^3
(E) $s^2 - s$

228. If $3 < x < 100$, for how many values of x is $\dfrac{x}{3}$ the square of a prime number?

(A)   Two
(B)   Three
(C)   Four
(D)   Five
(E)   Nine

229. A researcher plans to identify each participant in a certain medical experiment with a code consisting of either a single letter or a pair of distinct letters written in alphabetical order. What is the least number of letters that can be used if there are 12 participants, and each participant is to receive a different code?

    (A) 4
    (B) 5
    (C) 6
    (D) 7
    (E) 8

230. An object thrown directly upward is at a height of h feet after t seconds, where $h = -16(t-3)^2 + 150$. At what height, in feet, is the object 2 seconds after it reaches its maximum height?

    (A)   6
    (B)   86
    (C) 134
    (D) 150
    (E) 166

231. Which of the following is equivalent to the pair of inequalities $x + 6 > 10$ and $x - 3 \leq 5$?

    (A) $2 \leq x < 16$
    (B) $2 \leq x < 4$
    (C) $2 < x \leq 8$
    (D) $4 < x \leq 8$
    (E) $4 \leq x < 16$

232. David has d books, which is 3 times as many as Jeff and $\frac{1}{2}$ as many as Paula. How many books do the three of them have altogether, in terms of d?

    (A) $\frac{5}{6}d$

    (B) $\frac{7}{3}d$

    (C) $\frac{10}{3}d$

    (D) $\frac{7}{2}d$

    (E) $\frac{9}{2}d$

233. There are 8 teams in a certain league and each team plays each of the other teams exactly once. If each game is played by 2 teams, what is the total number of games played?

    (A) 15
    (B) 16
    (C) 28
    (D) 56
    (E) 64

234. At his regular hourly rate, Don had estimated the labor cost of a repair job as $336 and he was paid that amount. However, the job took 4 hours longer than he had estimated and, consequently, he earned $2 per hour less than his regular hourly rate. What was the time Don had estimated for the job, in hours?

    (A) 28
    (B) 24
    (C) 16
    (D) 14
    (E) 12

235. If $\frac{p}{q} < 1$, and p and q are positive integers, which of the following must be greater than 1?

    (A) $\sqrt{\dfrac{p}{q}}$

    (B) $\dfrac{p}{q^2}$

    (C) $\dfrac{p}{2q}$

    (D) $\dfrac{q}{p^2}$

    (E) $\dfrac{q}{p}$

236. To mail a package, the rate is x cents for the first pound and y cents for each additional pound, where x > y. Two packages weighing 3 pounds and 5 pounds, respectively, can be mailed separately or combined as one package. Which method is cheaper, and how much money is saved?

    (A) Combined, with a savings of x – y cents
    (B) Combined, with a savings of y – x cents
    (C) Combined, with a savings of x cents
    (D) Separately, with a savings of x – y cents
    (E) Separately, with a savings of y cents

237. If money is invested at r percent interest, compounded annually, the amount of the investment will double in approximately $\frac{70}{r}$ years. If Pat's parents invested $5,000 in a long-term bond that pays 8 percent interest, compounded annually, what will be the approximate total amount of the investment 18 years later, when Pat is ready for college?

    (A) $20,000
    (B) $15,000
    (C) $12,000
    (D) $10,000
    (E) $9,000

238. On a recent trip, Cindy drove her car 290 miles, rounded to the nearest 10 miles, and used 12 gallons of gasoline, rounded to the nearest gallon. The actual number of miles per gallon that Cindy's car got on this trip must have been between

    (A) $\frac{290}{12.5}$ and $\frac{290}{11.5}$
    (B) $\frac{295}{12}$ and $\frac{285}{11.5}$
    (C) $\frac{285}{12}$ and $\frac{295}{12}$
    (D) $\frac{285}{12.5}$ and $\frac{295}{11.5}$
    (E) $\frac{295}{12.5}$ and $\frac{285}{11.5}$

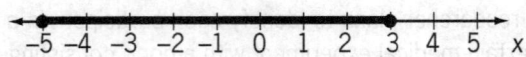

239. Which of the following inequalities is an algebraic expression for the shaded part of the number line above?

    (A) $|x| \leq 3$
    (B) $|x| \leq 5$
    (C) $|x - 2| \leq 3$
    (D) $|x - 1| \leq 4$
    (E) $|x + 1| \leq 4$

240. In a small snack shop, the average (arithmetic mean) revenue was $400 per day over a 10-day period. During this period, if the average daily revenue was $360 for the first 6 days, what was the average daily revenue for the last 4 days?

    (A) $420
    (B) $440
    (C) $450
    (D) $460
    (E) $480

241. If y is the smallest positive integer such that 3,150 multiplied by y is the square of an integer, then y must be

    (A)   2
    (B)   5
    (C)   6
    (D)   7
    (E) 14

242. If [x] is the greatest integer less than or equal to x, what is the value of [–1.6] + [3.4] + [2.7]?

    (A) 3
    (B) 4
    (C) 5
    (D) 6
    (E) 7

243. In the first week of the year, Nancy saved $1. In each of the next 51 weeks, she saved $1 more than she had saved in the previous week. What was the total amount that Nancy saved during the 52 weeks?

    (A) $1,326
    (B) $1,352
    (C) $1,378
    (D) $2,652
    (E) $2,756

244. In a certain sequence, the term x_n is given by the formula $x_n = 2x_{n-1} - \frac{1}{2}(x_{n-2})$ for all $n \geq 2$. If $x_0 = 3$ and $x_1 = 2$, what is the value of x_3?

    (A)   2.5
    (B)   3.125
    (C)   4
    (D)   5
    (E)   6.75

245. During a trip, Francine traveled x percent of the total distance at an average speed of 40 miles per hour and the rest of the distance at an average speed of 60 miles per hour. In terms of x, what was Francine's average speed for the entire trip?

    (A) $\dfrac{180 - x}{2}$

    (B) $\dfrac{x + 60}{4}$

    (C) $\dfrac{300 - x}{5}$

    (D) $\dfrac{600}{115 - x}$

    (E) $\dfrac{12,000}{x + 200}$

246. If $n = (33)^{43} + (43)^{33}$, what is the units digit of n?

    (A)   0
    (B)   2
    (C)   4
    (D)   6
    (E)   8

247. Team A and Team B are competing against each other in a game of tug-of-war. Team A, consisting of 3 males and 3 females, decides to line up male, female, male, female, male, female. The lineup that Team A chooses will be one of how many different possible lineups?

    (A)   9
    (B)   12
    (C)   15
    (D)   36
    (E)   720

248. If $d = \dfrac{1}{2^3 \times 5^7}$ is expressed as a terminating decimal, how many nonzero digits will d have?

    (A)   One
    (B)   Two
    (C)   Three
    (D)   Seven
    (E)   Ten

249. For any positive integer n, the sum of the first n positive integers equals $\dfrac{n(n + 1)}{2}$. What is the sum of all the even integers between 99 and 301?

    (A)   10,100
    (B)   20,200
    (C)   22,650
    (D)   40,200
    (E)   45,150

250. November 16, 2001, was a Friday. If each of the years 2004, 2008, and 2012 had 366 days, and the remaining years from 2001 through 2014 had 365 days, what day of the week was November 16, 2014?

(A) Sunday
(B) Monday
(C) Tuesday
(D) Wednesday
(E) Thursday

251. How many prime numbers between 1 and 100 are factors of 7,150?

(A) One
(B) Two
(C) Three
(D) Four
(E) Five

252. A sequence of numbers a_1, a_2, a_3, ... is defined as follows: $a_1 = 3$, $a_2 = 5$, and every term in the sequence after a_2 is the product of all terms in the sequence preceding it, e.g., $a_3 = (a_1)(a_2)$ and $a_4 = (a_1)(a_2)(a_3)$. If $a_n = t$ and $n > 2$, what is the value of a_{n+2} in terms of t?

(A) $4t$
(B) t^2
(C) t^3
(D) t^4
(E) t^8

253. Last year the price per share of Stock X increased by k percent and the earnings per share of Stock X increased by m percent, where k is greater than m. By what percent did the ratio of price per share to earnings per share increase, in terms of k and m?

(A) $\dfrac{k}{m}\%$

(B) $(k-m)\%$

(C) $\dfrac{100(k-m)}{100+k}\%$

(D) $\dfrac{100(k-m)}{100+m}\%$

(E) $\dfrac{100(k-m)}{100+k+m}\%$

254. Of the 300 subjects who participated in an experiment using virtual-reality therapy to reduce their fear of heights, 40 percent experienced sweaty palms, 30 percent experienced vomiting, and 75 percent experienced dizziness. If all of the subjects experienced at least one of these effects and 35 percent of the subjects experienced exactly two of these effects, how many of the subjects experienced only one of these effects?

(A) 105
(B) 125
(C) 130
(D) 180
(E) 195

255. If $m^{-1} = -\dfrac{1}{3}$, then m^{-2} is equal to

(A) -9
(B) -3
(C) $-\dfrac{1}{9}$
(D) $\dfrac{1}{9}$
(E) 9

256. A photography dealer ordered 60 Model X cameras to be sold for $250 each, which represents a 20 percent markup over the dealer's initial cost for each camera. Of the cameras ordered, 6 were never sold and were returned to the manufacturer for a refund of 50 percent of the dealer's initial cost. What was the dealer's approximate profit or loss as a percent of the dealer's initial cost for the 60 cameras?

    (A)   7% loss
    (B)   13% loss
    (C)   7% profit
    (D)   13% profit
    (E)   15% profit

257. Seven pieces of rope have an average (arithmetic mean) length of 68 centimeters and a median length of 84 centimeters. If the length of the longest piece of rope is 14 centimeters more than 4 times the length of the shortest piece of rope, what is the maximum possible length, in centimeters, of the longest piece of rope?

    (A)   82
    (B)   118
    (C)   120
    (D)   134
    (E)   152

258. What is the difference between the sixth and the fifth terms of the sequence 2, 4, 7, … whose nth term is $n + 2^{n-1}$?

    (A)   2
    (B)   3
    (C)   6
    (D)   16
    (E)   17

259. From the consecutive integers −10 to 10, inclusive, 20 integers are randomly chosen with repetitions allowed. What is the least possible value of the product of the 20 integers?

    (A) $(-10)^{20}$
    (B) $(-10)^{10}$
    (C)   0
    (D) $-(10)^{19}$
    (E) $-(10)^{20}$

260. The letters D, G, I, I, and T can be used to form 5-letter strings such as DIGIT or DGIIT. Using these letters, how many 5-letter strings can be formed in which the two occurrences of the letter I are separated by at least one other letter?

    (A)   12
    (B)   18
    (C)   24
    (D)   36
    (E)   48

261. $\dfrac{0.99999999}{1.0001} - \dfrac{0.99999991}{1.0003} =$

    (A) 10^{-8}
    (B) $3(10^{-8})$
    (C) $3(10^{-4})$
    (D) $2(10^{-4})$
    (E) 10^{-4}

262. Last Sunday a certain store sold copies of Newspaper A for $1.00 each and copies of Newspaper B for $1.25 each, and the store sold no other newspapers that day. If r percent of the store's revenue from newspaper sales was from Newspaper A and if p percent of the newspapers that the store sold were copies of Newspaper A, which of the following expresses r in terms of p?

(A) $\dfrac{100p}{125 - p}$

(B) $\dfrac{150p}{250 - p}$

(C) $\dfrac{300p}{375 - p}$

(D) $\dfrac{400p}{500 - p}$

(E) $\dfrac{500p}{625 - p}$

263. For the past n days, the average (arithmetic mean) daily production at a company was 50 units. If today's production of 90 units raises the average to 55 units per day, what is the value of n?

(A) 30
(B) 18
(C) 10
(D) 9
(E) 7

264. If a two-digit positive integer has its digits reversed, the resulting integer differs from the original by 27. By how much do the two digits differ?

(A) 3
(B) 4
(C) 5
(D) 6
(E) 7

265. In an electric circuit, two resistors with resistances x and y are connected in parallel. In this case, if r is the combined resistance of these two resistors, then the reciprocal of r is equal to the sum of the reciprocals of x and y. What is r in terms of x and y?

(A) xy

(B) $x + y$

(C) $\dfrac{1}{x + y}$

(D) $\dfrac{xy}{x + y}$

(E) $\dfrac{x + y}{xy}$

266. Xavier, Yvonne, and Zelda each try independently to solve a problem. If their individual probabilities for success are $\dfrac{1}{4}$, $\dfrac{1}{2}$, and $\dfrac{5}{8}$, respectively, what is the probability that Xavier and Yvonne, but not Zelda, will solve the problem?

(A) $\dfrac{11}{8}$

(B) $\dfrac{7}{8}$

(C) $\dfrac{9}{64}$

(D) $\dfrac{5}{64}$

(E) $\dfrac{3}{64}$

267. If $\dfrac{1}{x} - \dfrac{1}{x+1} = \dfrac{1}{x+4}$, then x could be

(A) 0
(B) −1
(C) −2
(D) −3
(E) −4

268. $\left(\frac{1}{2}\right)^{-3}\left(\frac{1}{4}\right)^{-2}\left(\frac{1}{16}\right)^{-1}=$

(A) $\left(\frac{1}{2}\right)^{-48}$

(B) $\left(\frac{1}{2}\right)^{-11}$

(C) $\left(\frac{1}{2}\right)^{-6}$

(D) $\left(\frac{1}{8}\right)^{-11}$

(E) $\left(\frac{1}{2}\right)^{-6}$

269. List T consists of 30 positive decimals, none of which is an integer, and the sum of the 30 decimals is S. The estimated sum of the 30 decimals, E, is defined as follows. Each decimal in T whose tenths digit is even is rounded up to the nearest integer, and each decimal in T whose tenths digit is odd is rounded down to the nearest integer; E is the sum of the resulting integers.

If $\frac{1}{3}$ of the decimals in T have a tenths digit that is even, which of the following is a possible value of $E - S$?

  I.   −16
  II.   6
  III.   10

(A) I only

(B) I and II only

(C) I and III only

(D) II and III only

(E) I, II, and III

270. If $5 - \frac{6}{x} = x$, then x has how many possible values?

(A) None

(B) One

(C) Two

(D) A finite number greater than two

(E) An infinite number

271. Seed mixture X is 40 percent ryegrass and 60 percent bluegrass by weight; seed mixture Y is 25 percent ryegrass and 75 percent fescue. If a mixture of X and Y contains 30 percent ryegrass, what percent of the weight of the mixture is X?

(A) 10%

(B) $33\frac{1}{3}\%$

(C) 40%

(D) 50%

(E) $66\frac{2}{3}\%$

272. How many of the integers that satisfy the inequality $\frac{(x+2)(x+3)}{x-2} \geq 0$ are less than 5?

(A) 1

(B) 2

(C) 3

(D) 4

(E) 5

273. Of the 150 houses in a certain development, 60 percent have air-conditioning, 50 percent have a sunporch, and 30 percent have a swimming pool. If 5 of the houses have all three of these amenities and 5 have none of them, how many of the houses have exactly two of these amenities?

(A) 10

(B) 45

(C) 50

(D) 55

(E) 65

274. The value of $\dfrac{2^{-14} + 2^{-15} + 2^{-16} + 2^{-17}}{5}$ is how many times the value of 2^{-17}?

(A) $\dfrac{3}{2}$

(B) $\dfrac{5}{2}$

(C) 3

(D) 4

(E) 5

275. Which of the following fractions has a decimal equivalent that is a terminating decimal?

(A) $\dfrac{10}{189}$

(B) $\dfrac{15}{196}$

(C) $\dfrac{16}{225}$

(D) $\dfrac{25}{144}$

(E) $\dfrac{39}{128}$

276. If $\left(\dfrac{1}{5}\right)^m \left(\dfrac{1}{4}\right)^{18} = \dfrac{1}{2(10)^{35}}$, then $m =$

(A) 17

(B) 18

(C) 34

(D) 35

(E) 36

277. From a group of 8 volunteers, including Andrew and Karen, 4 people are to be selected at random to organize a charity event. What is the probability that Andrew will be among the 4 volunteers selected and Karen will not?

(A) $\dfrac{3}{7}$

(B) $\dfrac{5}{12}$

(C) $\dfrac{27}{70}$

(D) $\dfrac{2}{7}$

(E) $\dfrac{9}{35}$

278. An investor purchased 100 shares of Stock X at $6\dfrac{1}{18}$ dollars per share and sold them all a year later at 24 dollars per share. If the investor paid a 2 percent brokerage fee on both the total purchase price and the total selling price, which of the following is closest to the investor's percent gain on this investment?

(A) 92%

(B) 240%

(C) 280%

(D) 300%

(E) 380%

279. If x is the product of the integers from 1 to 150, inclusive, and 5^y is a factor of x, what is the greatest possible value of y?

(A) 30

(B) 34

(C) 36

(D) 37

(E) 39

280. The number of defects in the first five cars to come through a new production line are 9, 7, 10, 4, and 6, respectively. If the sixth car through the production line has either 3, 7, or 12 defects, for which of these values does the mean number of defects per car for the first six cars equal the median?

I.   3

II. 7

III. 12

(A) I only

(B) II only

(C) III only

(D) I and III only

(E) I, II, and III

281. A furniture dealer purchased a desk for $150 and then set the selling price equal to the purchase price plus a markup that was 40 percent of the selling price. If the dealer sold the desk at the selling price, what was the amount of the dealer's gross profit from the purchase and the sale of the desk?

    (A) $40
    (B) $60
    (C) $80
    (D) $90
    (E) $100

282. How many odd numbers between 10 and 1,000 are the squares of integers?

    (A)   12
    (B)   13
    (C)   14
    (D)   15
    (E)   16

283. Three grades of milk are 1 percent, 2 percent, and 3 percent fat by volume. If x gallons of the 1 percent grade, y gallons of the 2 percent grade, and z gallons of the 3 percent grade are mixed to give $x + y + z$ gallons of a 1.5 percent grade, what is x in terms of y and z?

    (A) $y + 3z$
    (B) $\dfrac{y + z}{4}$
    (C) $2y + 3z$
    (D) $3y + z$
    (E) $3y + 4.5z$

284. There are 8 books on a shelf, of which 2 are paperbacks and 6 are hardbacks. How many possible selections of 4 books from this shelf include at least one paperback?

    (A)   40
    (B)   45
    (C)   50
    (D)   55
    (E)   60

285. If $M = \sqrt{4} + \sqrt[3]{4} + \sqrt[4]{4}$, then the value of M is

    (A)   less than 3
    (B)   equal to 3
    (C)   between 3 and 4
    (D)   equal to 4
    (E)   greater than 4

286. When a certain tree was first planted, it was 4 feet tall, and the height of the tree increased by a constant amount each year for the next 6 years. At the end of the 6th year, the tree was $\dfrac{1}{5}$ taller than it was at the end of the 4th year. By how many feet did the height of the tree increase each year?

    (A) $\dfrac{3}{10}$
    (B) $\dfrac{2}{5}$
    (C) $\dfrac{1}{2}$
    (D) $\dfrac{2}{3}$
    (E) $\dfrac{6}{5}$

287. A certain musical scale has 13 notes, each having a different frequency, measured in cycles per second. In the scale, the notes are ordered by increasing frequency, and the highest frequency is twice the lowest. For each of the 12 lower frequencies, the ratio of a frequency to the next higher frequency is a fixed constant. If the lowest frequency is 440 cycles per second, then the frequency of the seventh note in the scale is how many cycles per second?

    (A) $440\sqrt{2}$
    (B) $440\sqrt{2^7}$
    (C) $440\sqrt{2^{12}}$
    (D) $440\sqrt[12]{2^7}$
    (E) $440\sqrt[7]{2^{12}}$

288. Five machines at a certain factory operate at the same constant rate. If all five machines, operating simultaneously, take 27 hours to fill a certain production order, how many <u>more</u> hours does it take three of these machines, operating simultaneously, to fill the same production order?

    (A) 45
    (B) 36
    (C) 24
    (D) 18
    (E) 9

289. If w is an integer and $(21.6)(36)(0.0006)(60)(10^w)$ is an integer, what is the least possible value of w?

    (A) 4
    (B) 3
    (C) 0
    (D) −3
    (E) −4

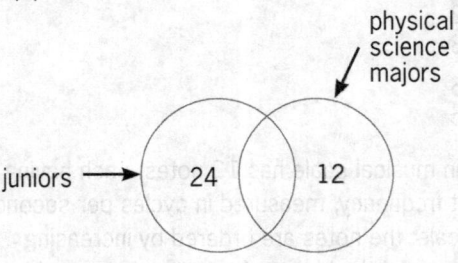

290. According to the diagram, if there are 18 physical science majors altogether, what percent of the juniors are physical science majors?

    (A) 6%
    (B) 20%
    (C) 25%
    (D) $33\frac{1}{3}$%
    (E) 50%

291. At a certain photo processing shop, the first standard-size print of a negative costs $4, and each additional print of the same negative costs $1. What is the total cost, in dollars, of y standard-size prints of each of x different negatives?

    (A) $4xy + (x − 1)y$
    (B) $4xy + (y − 1)x$
    (C) $4x + xy$
    (D) $4x + xy − 1$
    (E) $4x + x(y − 1)$

292. For 6 days of work, a carpenter had daily earnings of $110, $120, $110, $100, $100, and $120, respectively. In which of the following intervals does the standard deviation of the daily earnings lie?

    (A) Between $110 and $120
    (B) Between $100 and $110
    (C) Between $50 and $60
    (D) Between $10 and $20
    (E) Between $0 and $10

293. When the positive integer n is divided by 5, the remainder is 2. When n is divided by 8, the remainder is 3. The least possible value of n lies between

    (A) 5 and 10
    (B) 10 and 15
    (C) 15 and 20
    (D) 20 and 25
    (E) 25 and 30

4.3 Answer Key

1.	B	42.	B	83.	B	124.	C
2.	E	43.	B	84.	E	125.	A
3.	D	44.	E	85.	E	126.	A
4.	C	45.	B	86.	D	127.	D
5.	D	46.	E	87.	D	128.	E
6.	D	47.	D	88.	D	129.	A
7.	E	48.	A	89.	D	130.	E
8.	C	49.	B	90.	C	131.	E
9.	A	50.	D	91.	D	132.	D
10.	B	51.	A	92.	C	133.	B
11.	D	52.	D	93.	A	134.	E
12.	E	53.	C	94.	C	135.	E
13.	D	54.	E	95.	B	136.	D
14.	B	55.	B	96.	E	137.	E
15.	C	56.	B	97.	B	138.	A
16.	E	57.	A	98.	C	139.	A
17.	E	58.	D	99.	B	140.	E
18.	D	59.	D	100.	A	141.	D
19.	E	60.	D	101.	A	142.	A
20.	B	61.	B	102.	C	143.	D
21.	C	62.	A	103.	A	144.	C
22.	B	63.	D	104.	A	145.	D
23.	C	64.	D	105.	B	146.	D
24.	C	65.	A	106.	E	147.	B
25.	C	66.	B	107.	E	148.	A
26.	E	67.	B	108.	A	149.	D
27.	C	68.	D	109.	D	150.	A
28.	B	69.	C	110.	C	151.	E
29.	B	70.	E	111.	E	152.	E
30.	B	71.	E	112.	B	153.	E
31.	A	72.	C	113.	C	154.	C
32.	E	73.	C	114.	B	155.	B
33.	A	74.	B	115.	B	156.	A
34.	B	75.	D	116.	E	157.	E
35.	E	76.	A	117.	B	158.	E
36.	E	77.	D	118.	E	159.	E
37.	D	78.	D	119.	B	160.	D
38.	B	79.	C	120.	E	161.	C
39.	D	80.	E	121.	D	162.	E
40.	C	81.	D	122.	B	163.	D
41.	D	82.	B	123.	B	164.	E

165.	B	186.	A
166.	D	187.	A
167.	E	188.	B
168.	E	189.	B
169.	A	190.	A
170.	C	191.	B
171.	E	192.	E
172.	C	193.	D
173.	B	194.	D
174.	C	195.	C
175.	D	196.	C
176.	C	197.	A
177.	E	198.	A
178.	D	199.	B
179.	A	200.	E
180.	A	201.	E
181.	B	202.	B
182.	E	203.	B
183.	B	204.	C
184.	B	205.	B
185.	D		

206.	B	224.	C	242.	A	260.	D	278.	C
207.	A	225.	E	243.	C	261.	D	279.	D
208.	B	226.	B	244.	C	262.	D	280.	D
209.	E	227.	D	245.	E	263.	E	281.	E
210.	B	228.	B	246.	A	264.	A	282.	C
211.	C	229.	B	247.	D	265.	D	283.	A
212.	D	230.	B	248.	B	266.	E	284.	D
213.	C	231.	D	249.	B	267.	C	285.	E
214.	B	232.	C	250.	A	268.	B	286.	D
215.	D	233.	C	251.	D	269.	B	287.	A
216.	E	234.	B	252.	D	270.	C	288.	D
217.	D	235.	E	253.	D	271.	B	289.	A
218.	B	236.	A	254.	D	272.	D	290.	B
219.	C	237.	A	255.	D	273.	D	291.	E
220.	E	238.	D	256.	D	274.	C	292.	E
221.	C	239.	E	257.	D	275.	E	293.	E
222.	B	240.	D	258.	E	276.	D		
223.	C	241.	E	259.	E	277.	D		

4.4 Answer Explanations

The following discussion is intended to familiarize you with the most efficient and effective approaches to the kinds of problems common to Quantitative Reasoning questions. The particular questions in this chapter are generally representative of the kinds of Quantitative Reasoning questions you will encounter on the GMAT exam. Remember that it is the problem-solving strategy that is important, not the specific details of a particular question.

Questions 1 to 103 — Difficulty: **Easy**

1. In the graduating class of a certain college, 48 percent of the students identify exclusively as male and 52 percent identify exclusively as female. In this class, 40 percent of the students who identify as male and 20 percent of the students who identify as female are 25 years old or older. If one student in the graduating class is randomly selected, approximately what is the probability that the student will be <u>less</u> than 25 years old?

    (A) 0.90
    (B) 0.70
    (C) 0.45
    (D) 0.30
    (E) 0.25

Arithmetic Statistics

In the class, the percentage of students who identify exclusively as male and are less than 25 years old is $48\% \times (100 - 40)\% = 28.8\%$. The percentage who identify exclusively as female and are less than 25 years old is $52\% \times (100 - 20)\% = 41.6\%$. So, the percentage of students who are less than 25 years old is $28.8\% + 41.6\% = 70.4\% \approx 70\%$. Thus, the probability of a randomly selected student in the class being less than 25 years old is about 70%.

The correct answer is B.

2. In a certain board game, a stack of 48 cards, 8 of which represent a single share of stock, are shuffled and then placed face down. If the first 2 cards selected do <u>not</u> represent shares of stock, what is the probability that the third card selected will represent a share of stock?

    (A) $\dfrac{1}{8}$

    (B) $\dfrac{1}{6}$

    (C) $\dfrac{1}{5}$

    (D) $\dfrac{3}{23}$

    (E) $\dfrac{4}{23}$

Arithmetic Statistics

After the first 2 cards have been drawn, 46 cards remain, including all 8 of those representing one share of stock apiece. So, assuming that any of those 46 cards is equally likely to be the third card drawn, the probability that the third card drawn represents a share of stock is $\dfrac{8}{46} = \dfrac{4}{23}$.

The correct answer is E.

3. During a trip that they took together, Carmen, Juan, Maria, and Rafael drove an average (arithmetic mean) of 80 miles each. Carmen drove 72 miles, Juan drove 78 miles, and Maria drove 83 miles. How many miles did Rafael drive?

   (A) 80
   (B) 82
   (C) 85
   (D) 87
   (E) 89

Arithmetic Statistics

Let C, J, M, and R be the numbers of miles, respectively, that Carmen, Juan, Maria, and Rafael drove. Since the average of the numbers of miles they drove is 80, it follows that

$\dfrac{C+J+M+R}{4} = 80$, or $C+J+M+R = 4(80) =$

320. It is given that $C = 72$, $J = 78$, and $M = 83$. Therefore, $72 + 78 + 83 + R = 320$, or $R = 87$.

The correct answer is D.

4. Each week, a clothing salesperson receives a commission equal to 15 percent of the first $500 in sales and 20 percent of all additional sales that week. What commission would the salesperson receive on total sales for the week of $1,300?

   (A) $195
   (B) $227
   (C) $235
   (D) $260
   (E) $335

Arithmetic Applied Problems

The commission on the total sales can be calculated as follows:

$$\begin{aligned} &\text{commission on} \atop \text{first \$500}} + {\text{commission on} \atop \text{amount over \$500}} \\ &= (0.15)(\$500) + (0.20)(\$1,300 - \$500) \\ &= \$75 + \$160 \end{aligned}$$

Therefore, the commission on the total sales is $75 + $160 = $235.

The correct answer is C.

5. Five batches of 100 nails each are taken from a production line. The numbers of defective nails in the first four batches are 2, 4, 3, and 5, respectively. If the fifth batch has either 1, 2, or 6 defective nails, for which of these values does the average (arithmetic mean) number of defective nails per batch for the five batches equal the median number of defective nails for the five batches?

   I.   1
   II. 2
   III. 6

   (A) I only
   (B) II only
   (C) III only
   (D) I and III only
   (E) I, II, and III

Arithmetic Statistics

If the fifth batch has just 1 defective nail, the numbers of defective nails in the five batches are 2, 4, 3, 5, and 1. Then the mean number of defective nails per batch is $\dfrac{(1 + 2 + 3 + 4 + 5)}{5} = \dfrac{15}{5} = 3$. The median is also 3, since exactly 2 batches have fewer than 3 defective nails apiece and exactly 2 have more than 3 defective nails apiece. So, in this first case, the median and mean are equal. Now consider the second case, in which the fifth batch has 2 defective nails. In this case, the mean number of defective nails per batch is $\dfrac{16}{5} = 3.2$, whereas the median is still 3. In this second case, the median and the mean are not equal. And in the third case, the fifth batch has 6 defective nails, so the mean number of defective nails per batch is $\dfrac{20}{5} = 4$. The median is also 4, since 2 batches have fewer than 4 defective nails apiece and 2 have more than 4 apiece. Thus, in the third case, the median and mean are equal.

The correct answer is D.

6. List S consists of 10 consecutive odd integers, and list T consists of 5 consecutive even integers. If the least integer in S is 7 more than the least integer in T, how much greater is the average (arithmetic mean) of the integers in S than the average of the integers in T?

   (A) 2
   (B) 7
   (C) 8
   (D) 12
   (E) 22

Arithmetic Statistics

Let the integers in S be $s, s + 2, s + 4, \ldots, s + 18$, where s is odd. Let the integers in T be $t, t + 2, t + 4, t + 6, t + 8$, where t is even. Given that $s = t + 7$, it follows that $s - t = 7$. The average of the integers in S is $\dfrac{10s + 90}{10} = s + 9$, and, similarly, the average of the integers in T is $\dfrac{5t + 20}{5} = t + 4$. The difference in these averages is $(s + 9) - (t + 4) = (s - t) + (9 - 4) = 7 + 5 = 12$. Thus, the average of the integers in S is 12 greater than the average of the integers in T.

The correct answer is D.

Lane number	Number in line
1	5
2	4
3	3
4	4
5	2

7. A certain grocery store has 5 checkout lanes. The table above shows the number of people who were waiting in line at each checkout lane at closing time yesterday. What was the median number of people waiting in line?

   (A) $2\dfrac{4}{5}$

   (B) 3

   (C) $3\dfrac{1}{2}$

   (D) $3\dfrac{3}{5}$

   (E) 4

Arithmetic Statistics

To find the median number of people in line in the 5 checkout lanes, we take the 5 numbers of people in line, shown in the table's "Number in line" column, and list them from least to greatest: 2, 3, 4, 4, 5. The middle number in this list is a 4, so 4 is the median.

The correct answer is E.

8. $\left(\dfrac{1}{2} - \dfrac{1}{3}\right) + \left(\dfrac{1}{3} - \dfrac{1}{4}\right) + \left(\dfrac{1}{4} - \dfrac{1}{5}\right) + \left(\dfrac{1}{5} - \dfrac{1}{6}\right) =$

   (A) $-\dfrac{1}{6}$

   (B) 0

   (C) $\dfrac{1}{3}$

   (D) $\dfrac{1}{2}$

   (E) $\dfrac{2}{3}$

Arithmetic Operations with Rational Numbers

The parentheses can be removed without any change of signs, and after doing this, most of the terms can be additively cancelled as shown below.

$$\frac{1}{2} - \frac{\cancel{1}}{\cancel{3}} + \frac{\cancel{1}}{\cancel{3}} - \frac{\cancel{1}}{\cancel{4}} + \frac{\cancel{1}}{\cancel{4}} - \frac{\cancel{1}}{\cancel{5}} + \frac{\cancel{1}}{\cancel{5}} - \frac{1}{6} = \frac{1}{2} - \frac{1}{6}$$
$$= \frac{1}{3}$$

The correct answer is C.

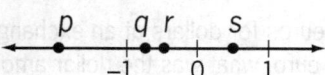

9. If p, q, r, and s are as shown on the number line above, which of the following products is greatest?

   (A) pq

   (B) pr

   (C) qr

   (D) qs

   (E) rs

Arithmetic Number Line

The number line shows that p, q, and r are all negative, while s is positive. The product of any two negative numbers is positive. That means pq, pr, and qr are each positive, so each is greater than qs and rs, which are both negative. And since $p < q < r < 0$, then $pq > pr > qr$. Thus, pq is the greatest of the 5 products.

The correct answer is A.

10. Last year $48,000 of a certain store's profit was shared by its 2 owners and their 10 employees. Each of the 2 owners received 3 times as much as each of their 10 employees. How much did each owner receive from the $48,000?

(A) $12,000
(B) $9,000
(C) $6,000
(D) $4,000
(E) $3,000

Algebra First-Degree Equations

Let A be the amount received by each owner and let B be the amount received by each employee. From the given information, it follows that $A = 3B$ and $2A + 10B = 48,000$. Thus, $2(3B) + 10B = 48,000$, or $16B = 48,000$, or $B = 3,000$. Therefore, the amount received by each owner was $A = 3B = 3($3,000$) = $9,000$.

The correct answer is B.

11. On a vacation, Rose exchanged $500.00 for euros at an exchange rate of 0.80 euro per dollar and spent $\frac{3}{4}$ of the euros she received. If she exchanged the remaining euros for dollars at an exchange rate of $1.20 per euro, what was the dollar amount she received?

(A) $60.00
(B) $80.00
(C) $100.00
(D) $120.00
(E) $140.00

Arithmetic Operations with Rational Numbers

At the exchange rate of 0.80 euro per dollar, Rose exchanged $500.00 for $(0.80)(500) = 400$ euros. She spent $\frac{3}{4}(400) = 300$ euros, had $400 - 300 = 100$ euros left, and exchanged them for dollars at the exchange rate of $1.20 per euro. Therefore, the dollar amount she received was $(1.20)(100) = 120.00.

The correct answer is D.

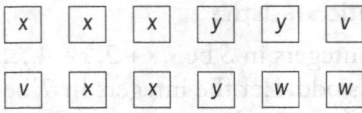

12. Each of the 12 squares shown is labeled x, y, v, or w. What is the ratio of the number of these squares labeled x or y to the number of these squares labeled v or w?

(A) 1:2
(B) 2:3
(C) 4:3
(D) 3:2
(E) 2:1

Arithmetic Ratio and Proportion

By a direct count, there are 8 squares labeled x or y (5 labeled x, 3 labeled y) and there are 4 squares labeled v or w (2 labeled v, 2 labeled w). Therefore, the ratio of the number of squares labeled x or y to the number of squares labeled v or w is 8:4, which reduces to 2:1.

The correct answer is E.

Number of Solid-Colored Marbles in Three Jars			
Jar	Number of red marbles	Number of green marbles	Total number of red and green marbles
P	x	y	80
Q	y	z	120
R	x	z	160

13. In the table above, what is the number of green marbles in Jar R?

(A) 70
(B) 80
(C) 90
(D) 100
(E) 110

Arithmetic Algebra Interpretation of Tables; Applied Problems

First, set up an equation to find the total number of marbles in the three jars as follows:

$$x + y + y + z + x + z = 80 + 120 + 160$$
$$2x + 2y + 2z = 360 \quad \text{combine the like terms}$$
$$x + y + z = 180 \quad \text{divide both sides by 2}$$

Then, since it can be seen from the table that the number of green marbles in Jar R is z, solve for z to answer the problem. To do this most efficiently, use the information from the table for Jar P, which is that $x + y = 80$.

$x + y + z = 180$

$80 + z = 180$ substitute 80 for $x + y$

$z = 100$

The correct answer is D.

14. Bouquets are to be made using white tulips and red tulips, and the ratio of the number of white tulips to the number of red tulips is to be the same in each bouquet. If there are 15 white tulips and 85 red tulips available for the bouquets, what is the greatest number of bouquets that can be made using all the tulips available?

    (A) 3
    (B) 5
    (C) 8
    (D) 10
    (E) 13

Arithmetic Applied Problems; Properties of Numbers

Because all the tulips are to be used and the same number of white tulips will be in each bouquet, the number of white tulips in each bouquet times the number of bouquets must equal the total number of white tulips, or 15. Thus, the number of bouquets must be a factor of 15, and so the number must be 1, 3, 5, or 15. Also, the number of red tulips in each bouquet times the number of bouquets must equal the total number of red tulips, or 85. Thus, the number of bouquets must be a factor of 85, and so the number must be 1, 5, 17, or 85. Since the number of bouquets must be 1, 3, 5, or 15, and the number of bouquets must be 1, 5, 17, or 85, it follows that the number of bouquets must be 1 or 5, and thus the greatest number of bouquets that can be made is 5. Note that each of the 5 bouquets will have 3 white tulips, because $(5)(3) = 15$, and each of the 5 bouquets will have 17 red tulips, because $(5)(17) = 85$.

The correct answer is B.

County	Amount Recycled	Amount Disposed of
A	16,700	142,800
B	8,800	48,000
C	13,000	51,400
D	3,900	20,300
E	3,300	16,200

15. The table above shows the amount of waste material, in tons, recycled by each of five counties in a single year and the amount of waste material, also in tons, that was disposed of in landfills by the five counties in that year. Which county had the lowest ratio of waste material disposed of to waste material recycled in the year reported in the table?

    (A) A
    (B) B
    (C) C
    (D) D
    (E) E

Arithmetic Ratio and Proportion

To quickly estimate each county's ratio of waste material disposed of to waste material recycled, find the row representing that county in the table. Then in that row, roughly estimate the ratio of the number in the "Amount Disposed of" column to that in the "Amount Recycled" column. You can just divide by 1,000 and round to get nice simple ratios. County A's ratio (142,800:16,700) is more than 140:20, which is 7:1. County B's is more than 45:9, which is 5:1. County C's is less than 52:13, which is 4:1. County D's is more than 20:4, which is 5:1. County E's is more than 16:4, which is 4:1. Thus, County C has the lowest ratio of material disposed of to material recycled.

The correct answer is C.

16. 125% of 5 =

    (A) 5.125
    (B) 5.25
    (C) 6
    (D) 6.125
    (E) 6.25

Arithmetic Percents

125% of 5 represents $\dfrac{125}{100} \times 5$, or $1.25 \times 5 = 6.25$.

The correct answer is E.

17. Each day Linda spends 6 hours at her dog-walking job, for which she is paid $15.00 per hour. In addition, Linda spends a total of 1.5 hours each day, (for which she is not paid), traveling to and from the job. What is Linda's hourly rate of pay for the total amount of time that she spends each day at her dog-walking job and traveling to and from that job?

    (A) $7.50
    (B) $9.00
    (C) $10.00
    (D) $10.75
    (E) $12.00

Arithmetic Applied Problems

Linda is paid $15/hour for 6 hours of dog-walking job each day, totaling $90. She's not paid for her 1.5 hours of commuting each day. So, her total daily pay for the dog-walking job and commuting combined is $90 for 7.5 hours. Thus, her hourly rate of pay for the dog-walking job and commuting combined is $90/7.5 hours = $12/hour.

The correct answer is E.

18. When traveling at a constant speed of 32 miles per hour, a certain motorboat consumes 24 gallons of fuel per hour. What is the fuel consumption of this boat at this speed measured in miles traveled per gallon of fuel?

    (A) $\dfrac{2}{3}$
    (B) $\dfrac{3}{4}$
    (C) $\dfrac{4}{5}$
    (D) $\dfrac{4}{3}$
    (E) $\dfrac{3}{2}$

Arithmetic Operations with Rational Numbers

If the motorboat consumes 24 gallons of fuel in 1 hour, then it consumes 1 gallon of fuel in $\dfrac{1}{24}$ hour. If the motorboat travels 32 miles in 1 hour, then it travels $\dfrac{32}{24} = \dfrac{4}{3}$ miles in $\dfrac{1}{24}$ hour, which is the length of time it takes to consume 1 gallon of fuel. Thus, the motorboat travels $\dfrac{4}{3}$ miles per gallon of fuel.

The correct answer is D.

19. If snow accumulation increased at a constant rate of 30 millimeters per hour during a certain snowstorm, how many <u>seconds</u> did it take for snow accumulation to increase by 1 millimeter?

    (A) $\dfrac{1}{120}$
    (B) $\dfrac{1}{60}$
    (C) $\dfrac{1}{20}$
    (D) 20
    (E) 120

Arithmetic Applied Problems

Since the snow accumulation increased at a constant 30 mm/hour, a 1-mm increase in snow accumulation took 1/30 of an hour, which is 2 minutes or 120 seconds.

The correct answer is E.

20. From 2000 to 2003, the number of employees at a certain company increased by a factor of $\frac{1}{4}$. From 2003 to 2006, the number of employees at this company decreased by a factor of $\frac{1}{3}$. If there were 100 employees at the company in 2006, how many employees were there at the company in 2000?

    (A) 200
    (B) 120
    (C) 100
    (D) 75
    (E) 60

Algebra First-Degree Equations

Let N be the number of employees in 2000. In 2003 there were $\frac{1}{4}(\text{number in 2000}) = \frac{1}{4}N$ more employees than in 2000, for a total of $N + \frac{1}{4}N = \frac{5}{4}N$ employees. In 2006 there were $\frac{1}{3}(\text{number in 2003}) = \frac{1}{3}\left(\frac{5}{4}\right)N$ fewer employees than in 2003, for a total of $\frac{5}{4}N - \frac{1}{3}\left(\frac{5}{4}N\right) = \frac{5}{6}N$ employees. It is given that there were 100 employees in 2006, so $\frac{5}{6}N = 100$, or $N = \frac{6}{5}(100) = 120$.

The correct answer is B.

21. Working alone at its own constant rate, machine R fills 10,000 boxes with pins in 9 hours, and working alone at its own constant rate, machine S fills 5,000 boxes with pins in 3 hours. If machine R and machine S, each working at its own constant rate and for the same period of time, together filled a certain number of boxes with pins, what percent of the boxes were filled by machine R?

    (A) 25%
    (B) 33%
    (C) 40%
    (D) 66%
    (E) 75%

Arithmetic Applied Problems

In the 9 hours machine R takes to fill 10,000 boxes of pins, machine S fills (5,000 boxes/ 3 hours) × 3 hours = 15,000 boxes of pins. So, each working at its own constant rate for 9 hours, the two machines together fill 10,000 + 15,000 = 25,000 boxes of pins. Therefore, machine R fills 10,000/25,000 = 0.4 = 40% of that total.

The correct answer is C.

22. A collection of 16 coins, each with a face value of either 10 cents or 25 cents, has a total face value of $2.35. How many of the coins have a face value of 25 cents?

    (A) 3
    (B) 5
    (C) 7
    (D) 9
    (E) 11

Algebra First-Degree Equations

Let x represent the number of coins each with a face value of 25 cents. Then, since there are 16 coins in all, $16 - x$ represents the number of coins each with a face value of 10 cents. The total face value of the coins is $2.35 or 235 cents so,

$$
\begin{aligned}
25x + 10(16 - x) &= 235 && \text{given} \\
25x + 160 - 10x &= 235 && \text{distributive property} \\
15x + 160 &= 235 && \text{combine like terms} \\
15x &= 75 && \text{subtract 160 from both sides} \\
x &= 5 && \text{divide both sides by 15}
\end{aligned}
$$

Therefore, 5 of the coins have a face value of 25 cents.

The correct answer is B.

23. A retailer purchased eggs at $2.80 per dozen and sold the eggs at 3 eggs for $0.90. What was the retailer's gross profit from purchasing and selling 5 dozen eggs? (1 dozen eggs = 12 eggs)

    (A) $0.90
    (B) $2.40
    (C) $4.00
    (D) $11.30
    (E) $12.00

Arithmetic Applied Problems

The retailer's cost was $2.80 per dozen eggs and the retailer's revenue was $0.90 per 3 eggs, or 4($0.90) = $3.60 per dozen eggs. Therefore, the retailer's profit for 5 dozen eggs—revenue minus cost for 5 dozen eggs—was 5($3.60 − $2.80) = 5($0.80) = $4.00.

The correct answer is C.

24. In a set of 24 cards, each card is numbered with a different positive integer from 1 to 24. One card will be drawn at random from the set. What is the probability that the card drawn will have either a number that is divisible by both 2 and 3 or a number that is divisible by 7?

    (A) $\dfrac{3}{24}$
    (B) $\dfrac{4}{24}$
    (C) $\dfrac{7}{24}$
    (D) $\dfrac{8}{24}$
    (E) $\dfrac{17}{24}$

Arithmetic Probability

The desired probability is N divided by 24, where N is the number of positive integers from 1 through 24 that are either divisible by both 2 and 3, or divisible by 7. Since an integer is divisible by both 2 and 3 if and only if the integer is divisible by 6, it follows that N is the number of positive integers from 1 through 24 that are either divisible by 6 or divisible by 7. There are 4 numbers from 1 through 24 that are divisible by 6, namely 6, 12,

18, and 24. There are 3 numbers from 1 through 24 that are divisible by 7, namely 7, 14, and 21. Since these numbers are all different from each other, it follows that $N = 4 + 3 = 7$ and the desired probability is $\dfrac{N}{24} = \dfrac{7}{24}$.

The correct answer is C.

25. As a salesperson, Phyllis can choose one of two methods of annual payment: either an annual salary of $35,000 with no commission or an annual salary of $10,000 plus a 20% commission on her total annual sales. What must her total annual sales be to give her the same annual pay with either method?

    (A) $100,000
    (B) $120,000
    (C) $125,000
    (D) $130,000
    (E) $132,000

Algebra Applied Problems

Letting s be Phyllis's total annual sales needed to generate the same annual pay with either method, the given information can be expressed as $35,000 = $10,000 + 0.2s$. Solve this equation for s.

$$\$35{,}000 = \$10{,}000 + 0.2s$$
$$\$25{,}000 = 0.2s$$
$$\$125{,}000 = s$$

The correct answer is C.

26. If $1 < x < y < z$, which of the following has the greatest value?

    (A) $z(x + 1)$
    (B) $z(y + 1)$
    (C) $x(y + z)$
    (D) $y(x + z)$
    (E) $z(x + y)$

Algebra Inequalities

This problem can be solved by calculating each of the options for a fixed and appropriate choice of values of the variables. For example, if $x = 2$, $y = 3$, and $z = 4$, then $1 < x < y < z$ and the values of the options are as follows:

(A) $z(x + 1) = 4(2 + 1) = 12$

(B) $z(y + 1) = 4(3 + 1) = 16$

(C) $x(y + z) = 2(3 + 4) = 14$

(D) $y(x + z) = 3(2 + 4) = 18$

(E) $z(x + y) = 4(2 + 3) = 20$

Alternatively, this problem can also be solved algebraically.

Answer choice E is greater than each of answer choice A and B:

$z(x + 1) = zx + z$ $\quad<\quad$ $zx + zy = z(x + y)$
Answer choice A   use $1 < y$ Answer choice E

$z(y + 1) = zy + z$ $\quad<\quad$ $zy + zx = z(y + 1)$
Answer choice B   use $1 < x$ Answer choice E

Answer choice E is greater than each of answer choice C and D:

$x(y + z) = xy + xz$ $\quad<\quad$ $zy + xz = z(y + x)$
Answer choice C   use $x < z$ Answer choice E

$y(x + z) = yx + yz$ $\quad<\quad$ $zx + yz = z(x + y)$
Answer choice D   use $y < z$ Answer choice E

The correct answer is E.

27. Set X consists of eight consecutive integers. Set Y consists of all the integers that result from adding 4 to each of the integers in Set X and all the integers that result from subtracting 4 from each of the integers in Set X. How many more integers are there in Set Y than in Set X?

(A) 0

(B) 4

(C) 8

(D) 12

(E) 16

Arithmetic Operations with Integers

Since the 8 consecutive integers in Set X are not specified, let Set $X = \{3, 4, 5, 6, 7, 8, 9, 10\}$. The following table shows Set X and Set Y whose elements were obtained by adding 4 to each

element of Set X and subtracting 4 from each element of Set X. The elements of Set Y that are also in Set X are marked with an asterisk, *. There are 8 unmarked elements in Set Y, so Set Y has 8 more elements than Set X.

Set X	Set Y	
	Add 4	Subtract 4
3	7*	−1
4	8*	0
5	9*	1
6	10*	2
7	11	3*
8	12	4*
9	13	5*
10	14	6*

The correct answer is C.

28. Of the following, which is the closest to $\dfrac{60.2}{1.03 \times 4.86}$?

(A) 10

(B) 12

(C) 13

(D) 14

(E) 15

Arithmetic Estimation

Replace the three numbers appearing in the expression with three nearby integers that allow the arithmetic operations to be carried out easily to get an approximation.

$$\frac{60.2}{1.03 \times 4.86} \approx \frac{\overset{12}{\cancel{60}}}{1 \times \underset{1}{\cancel{5}}} = \frac{12}{1 \times 1} = 12$$

The correct answer is B.

29. Thabo owns exactly 140 books, and each book is either paperback fiction, paperback nonfiction, or hardcover nonfiction. If he owns 20 more paperback nonfiction books than hardcover nonfiction books, and twice as many paperback fiction books as paperback nonfiction books, how many hardcover nonfiction books does Thabo own?

   (A)   10
   (B)   20
   (C)   30
   (D)   40
   (E)   50

Algebra Simultaneous First-Degree Equations

Let F represent the number of paperback fiction books that Thabo owns; N_p, the number of paperback nonfiction books; and N_h, the number of hardcover nonfiction books. It is given that $F + N_p + N_h = 140$, $N_p = N_h + 20$, and $F = 2N_p = 2(N_h + 20)$. It follows that

$$F + N_p + N_h = 140 \text{ given}$$
$$2(N_h + 20) + (N_h + 20) + N_h = 140 \text{ by substitution}$$
$$4N_h + 60 = 140 \text{ combine like terms}$$
$$4N_h = 80 \text{ subtract 60 from both sides}$$
$$N_h = 20 \text{ divide both sides by 4}$$

The correct answer is B.

30. What is 35 percent of the sum of 1.4 and $\frac{1}{5}$?

   (A)   0.42
   (B)   0.56
   (C)   0.85
   (D)   1.55
   (E)   1.95

Arithmetic Applied Problems

Thirty-five percent of the sum of 1.4 and $\frac{1}{5}$ is $0.35(1.4 + 0.2) = 0.35(1.6) = 0.56$.

The correct answer is B.

31. If $x > 0$, $\frac{x}{50} + \frac{x}{25}$ is what percent of x?

   (A)   6%
   (B)   25%
   (C)   37%
   (D)   60%
   (E)   75%

Algebra; Arithmetic Simplifying Algebraic Expressions; Percents

Because we want a percent, use a common denominator of 100 to combine the two terms. $\frac{x}{50} + \frac{x}{25} = \frac{2x}{100} + \frac{4x}{100} = \frac{6x}{100} = \left(\frac{6}{100}\right)x$, which is 6% of x.

The correct answer is A.

32. During a certain time period, Car X traveled north along a straight road at a constant rate of 1 mile per minute and used fuel at a constant rate of 5 gallons every 2 hours. During this time period, if Car X used exactly 3.75 gallons of fuel, how many miles did Car X travel?

   (A)   36
   (B)   37.5
   (C)   40
   (D)   80
   (E)   90

Arithmetic Applied Problems

The car used fuel at the rate of 5 gallons every 2 hours, and thus after using 3.75 gallons of fuel, the car had traveled for $(3.75)\left(\frac{2}{5}\right)$ hours.

One way to obtain this value is indicated by the calculations in the following table.

5 gal	corresponds to	2 hr	Given
1 gal	corresponds to	$\frac{2}{5}$ hr	Divide by 5
3.75 gal	corresponds to	$(3.75)\left(\frac{2}{5}\right)$ hr	Multiply by 3.75

Since $(3.75)\left(\dfrac{2}{5}\right) = \left(\dfrac{15}{4}\right)\left(\dfrac{2}{5}\right) = \dfrac{3}{2}$ hours = 90 minutes, the car drove for 90 minutes at a rate of 1 mile per minute. Therefore, the total distance the car drove was

distance = rate × time = $\left(1\,\dfrac{\text{mi}}{\text{min}}\right)(90\ \text{min}) =$ 90 miles.

The correct answer is E.

33. Which of the following is closest to the value of $\dfrac{999}{100 + \dfrac{1}{999}}$?

(A) 10
(B) 1
(C) 0.1
(D) 0.01
(E) 0.001

Arithmetic Estimation

$\dfrac{999}{100 + \dfrac{1}{999}}$ is close to $\dfrac{1000}{100} = 10$.

The correct answer is A.

34. The population of City X is 50 percent of the population of City Y. The population of City X is what percent of the total population of City X and City Y?

(A) 25%
(B) $33\dfrac{1}{3}$%
(C) 40%
(D) 50%
(E) $66\dfrac{2}{3}$%

Arithmetic Percents

Let x be the population of City X and y be the population of City Y. Since $x = 0.5y$, then $y = 2x$. So, the total population of City X and City Y is $x + y = x + 2x = 3x$. Thus, x is $\dfrac{1}{3}$, or $33\dfrac{1}{3}$%, of $x + y$.

The correct answer is B.

35. A bicycle store purchased two bicycles, one for $250 and the other for $375, and sold both bicycles at a total gross profit of $250. If the store sold one of the bicycles for $450, which of the following could be the store's gross profit from the sale of the other bicycle?

(A) $75
(B) $100
(C) $125
(D) $150
(E) $175

Arithmetic Profit and Loss

Let $450 and $R be the individual revenues from selling the two bicycles. Then the unknown profit from selling one of the bicycles is either $R − $250 or $R − $375.

$$\text{total profit} = (\text{total revenue}) - (\text{total cost})$$
$$\$250 = (\$450 + \$R) - (\$250 + \$375)$$
$$\$250 = \$R - \$175$$
$$\$425 = \$R$$

From this it follows that the unknown profit is either $425 − $250 = $175 or $425 − $375 = $50.

The correct answer is E.

36. If $k^2 = m^2$, which of the following must be true?

(A) $k = m$
(B) $k = -m$
(C) $k = |m|$
(D) $k = -|m|$
(E) $|k| = |m|$

Algebra Simplifying Algebraic Expressions

One method of solving this problem is to take the nonnegative square root of both sides of the equation $k^2 = m^2$ and then since $\sqrt{u^2} = |u|$ for all real numbers u, it follows that $|k| = \sqrt{k^2} = \sqrt{m^2} = |m|$.

The table below shows that each of the other answer choices can be true but can also be false. For each pair of values for k and m, it is true that $k^2 = m^2$.

	True for		False for	
	k	m	k	m
A $k = m$	3	3	3	−3
B $k = -m$	−3	3	3	3
C $k = \|m\|$	3	−3	−3	−3
D $k = -\|m\|$	−3	−3	3	−3

The correct answer is E.

37. Makoto, Nishi, and Ozuro were paid a total of $780 for waxing the floors at their school. Each was paid in proportion to the number of hours he or she worked. If Makoto worked 15 hours, Nishi worked 20 hours, and Ozuro worked 30 hours, how much was Makoto paid?

(A) $52
(B) $117
(C) $130
(D) $180
(E) $234

Arithmetic Ratio and Proportion

Makoto, Nishi, and Ozuro worked a total of 15 + 20 + 30 = 65 hours and were paid a total of $780. Since Makoto worked 15 of the 65 hours and he was paid in proportion to the number of hours he worked, his pay was $\frac{15}{65}$ ($780). To determine which of the answer choices equals this amount of money, note that $\frac{15}{65}$ can be reduced to $\frac{3}{13}$ by dividing the numerator and denominator by 5. Also note that 780 can be factored as $(10)(78) = (10)(2)(39) = (10)(2)(3)(13)$. Then calculate $\frac{3}{13}(10)(2)(3)(13) = (3)(10)(2)(3) = 180$.

Tip: In problems requiring calculations with fractions, it can be helpful to reduce fractions and utilize cancellation as much as possible.

The correct answer is D.

38. If x is a positive integer and $4^x - 3 = y$, which of the following CANNOT be a value of y?

(A) 1
(B) 7
(C) 13
(D) 61
(E) 253

Arithmetic Exponents

This can be solved by calculating the value of $4^x - 3$ for the first few positive integer values of x.

x	4^x	$4^x - 3$	answer choice
1	4	1	A
2	16	13	C
3	64	61	D
4	256	253	E

Alternatively, this can be solved by observing that 4^x always has units digit 4 or 6—the product of two integers with units digit 4 has units digit 6, the product of two integers with units digit 6 has units digit 4, etc.—and therefore any integer that does not have units digit 4 − 3 = 1 or 6 − 3 = 3 cannot be the value of $4^x - 3$ for some positive integer value of x.

The correct answer is B.

39. The regular price per can of a certain brand of soda is $0.40. If the regular price per can is discounted 15 percent when the soda is purchased in 24-can cases, what is the price of 72 cans of this brand of soda purchased in 24-can cases?

(A) $16.32
(B) $18.00
(C) $21.60
(D) $24.48
(E) $28.80

Arithmetic Percents

The price per can with the 15% discount is 100% − 15% = 85% of the regular price of 40 cents per can; that is, the discounted price is 0.85(40) = 34 cents per can. So, 72 cans at 34 cents apiece cost 72 × 34 cents = 2,448 cents, or $24.48.

The correct answer is D.

40. The quotient when a certain number is divided by $\frac{2}{3}$ is $\frac{9}{2}$. What is the number?

    (A) $\frac{4}{27}$

    (B) $\frac{1}{3}$

    (C) 3

    (D) 6

    (E) $\frac{27}{4}$

Arithmetic Operations with Rational Numbers

Let N be the unknown number. The quotient when N is divided by $\frac{2}{3}$ is $N \div \frac{2}{3}$, which equals $N \times \frac{3}{2} = \frac{3}{2}N$ (invert and multiply). Since this quotient equals $\frac{9}{2}$, it follows that $\frac{3}{2}N = \frac{9}{2}$.

Therefore, $N = \left(\frac{9}{2}\right)\left(\frac{2}{3}\right) = 3$.

Tip: Sometimes a correct method of calculation will be intuitively evident if difficult-to-conceptualize numbers are replaced with easy-to-conceptualize numbers. For example, if the first sentence had instead been "The quotient when a certain number is divided by 2 is 3" (i.e., after dividing a certain number by 2, the result is 3), then it may be intuitively evident that the number can be obtained by multiplying 2 and 3. Thus, for this problem, the number can be obtained by multiplying $\frac{2}{3}$ and $\frac{9}{2}$.

The correct answer is C.

41. The price of gasoline at a service station increased from $1.65 per gallon last week to $1.82 per gallon this week. Sally paid $26.40 for gasoline last week at the station. How much more will Sally pay this week at the station for the same amount of gasoline?

    (A) $1.70

    (B) $2.55

    (C) $2.64

    (D) $2.72

    (E) $2.90

Arithmetic Applied Problems

Since $1.82 − $1.65 = $0.17, Sally paid $0.17 per gallon more this week than last week. Therefore, the total additional amount that Sally paid this week over last week is the number of gallons Sally purchased times $0.17.

Number of gallons purchased last week:

$$\frac{\text{total paid last week}}{\text{price per gallon last week}} = \frac{26.40}{1.65}$$

Number of gallons purchased this week: $\frac{26.40}{1.65}$

Total additional amount paid this week:

$$(\$0.17)\frac{26.40}{1.65} = (\$0.17)(16) = \$2.72.$$

One way to lessen the arithmetic computations is to work with integers and factor.

$0.17\left(\dfrac{26.4}{1.65}\right) = \dfrac{(17)(264)}{1,650}$	multiply numerator and denominator by 1,000 for ease of calculation
$= \dfrac{(17)(3 \times 8 \times 11)}{3 \times 5 \times 11 \times 10}$	factor
$= \dfrac{(17)(\cancel{3} \times 8 \times \cancel{11})}{\cancel{3} \times 5 \times \cancel{11} \times 10}$	identify common factors
$= \dfrac{17 \times 8}{5 \times 10}$	cancel common factors
$= \dfrac{136}{50}$	multiply
$= \dfrac{13.6}{5}$	divide numerator and denominator by 10
$= 2.72$	divide

The correct answer is D.

Monthly Charge for Low-Use Telephone
Contract Offered by Company X

Monthly rate (up to 75 message units)	20% less than standard rate of $10.00
Per unit in excess of 75 message units	$0.065

42. Harry spent 25% of his $2,200 May take-home pay on rent and 30% of the remainder on food. How much of his May take-home pay did Harry spend on food?

(A) $165
(B) $495
(C) $550
(D) $660
(E) $1,045

Arithmetic Percents

Since Harry spent 25% of the $2,200 May take-home pay on rent, the remainder was 75% × $2,200 = $1,650. So, of his May take-home pay, Harry spent 30% × $1,650 = $495 on food.

The correct answer is B.

43. If $2x + y = 7$ and $x + 2y = 5$, then $\dfrac{x+y}{3} =$

(A) 1
(B) $\dfrac{4}{3}$
(C) $\dfrac{17}{5}$
(D) $\dfrac{18}{5}$
(E) 4

Algebra Simultaneous Equations

Adding the equations $2x + y = 7$ and $x + 2y = 5$ gives $3x + 3y = 12$, or $x + y = 4$. Dividing both sides of the last equation by 3 gives $\dfrac{x+y}{3} = \dfrac{4}{3}$.

The correct answer is B.

44. City X has a population 4 times as great as the population of City Y, which has a population twice as great as the population of City Z. What is the ratio of the population of City X to the population of City Z?

(A) 1:8
(B) 1:4
(C) 2:1
(D) 4:1
(E) 8:1

Arithmetic Ratio and Proportion

Let X, Y, and Z be the populations of Cities X, Y, and Z, respectively. It is given that $X = 4Y$, and $Y = 2Z$ or $Z = \dfrac{Y}{2}$. Then, $\dfrac{X}{Z} = \dfrac{4Y}{\dfrac{Y}{2}} =$

$(4Y)\left(\dfrac{2}{Y}\right) = \dfrac{8}{1}$.

The correct answer is E.

Total Membership of Organization X, 1988

Emeritus	78
Fellows	9,209
Partners	35,509
Associates	27,909
Affiliates	2,372

45. According to the table above, the number of fellows was approximately what percent of the total membership of Organization X? **Note: All categories of membership are mutually exclusive.**

(A) 9%
(B) 12%
(C) 18%
(D) 25%
(E) 35%

Arithmetic Percents

Since no one is in more than one of the categories listed in the table, the total membership is the sum of the numbers in the table. We're just asked to find an approximate percentage, so let's round each number to the nearest thousand and then divide each by a thousand. Thus, we find that the approximate percentage of the total membership who are fellows was $100\% \times \dfrac{9}{(9+36+28+2)} = 100\% \times \dfrac{9}{75} = 12\%$.

The correct answer is B.

46. If $S = 1 + \dfrac{1}{2^2} + \dfrac{1}{3^2} + \dfrac{1}{4^2} + \dfrac{1}{5^2} + \dfrac{1}{6^2} + \dfrac{1}{7^2} + \dfrac{1}{8^2} + \dfrac{1}{9^2} + \dfrac{1}{10^2}$, which of the following is true?

(A) $S > 3$
(B) $S = 3$
(C) $2 < S < 3$
(D) $S = 2$
(E) $S < 2$

Arithmetic Estimation

Because $\dfrac{1}{3^2}$ is less than $\dfrac{1}{2^2}$ and each of $\dfrac{1}{5^2}$, $\dfrac{1}{6^2}, \dfrac{1}{7^2}, \dfrac{1}{8^2}, \dfrac{1}{9^2}$, and $\dfrac{1}{10^2}$ is less than $\dfrac{1}{4^2}$,

$$\underbrace{1 + \dfrac{1}{2^2} + \dfrac{1}{3^2}}_{< 1 + 2\left(\dfrac{1}{2^2}\right) = 1\dfrac{1}{2}} + \underbrace{\dfrac{1}{4^2} + \dfrac{1}{5^2} + \dfrac{1}{6^2} + \dfrac{1}{7^2} + \dfrac{1}{8^2} + \dfrac{1}{9^2} + \dfrac{1}{10^2}}_{+ 7\left(\dfrac{1}{4^2}\right) = \dfrac{7}{16}}$$

Therefore, $S < 1\dfrac{1}{2} + \dfrac{7}{16} < 2$.

The correct answer is E.

47. A manufacturer of a certain product can expect that between 0.3 percent and 0.5 percent of the units manufactured will be defective. If the retail price is $2,500 per unit and the manufacturer offers a full refund for defective units, how much money can the manufacturer expect to need to cover the refunds on 20,000 units?

(A) Between $15,000 and $25,000
(B) Between $30,000 and $50,000
(C) Between $60,000 and $100,000
(D) Between $150,000 and $250,000
(E) Between $300,000 and $500,000

Arithmetic Applied Problems

The expected number of defective units is between 0.3% and 0.5% of 20,000, or between $(0.003)(20,000) = 60$ and $(0.005)(20,000) = 100$. Since each unit has a retail price of $2,500, the amount of money needed to cover the refunds for the expected number of defective units is between $60(\$2,500)$ and $100(\$2,500)$, or between $150,000 and $250,000.

The correct answer is D.

48. Which of the following is closest to $\sqrt{\dfrac{4.2(1,590)}{15.7}}$?

(A) 20
(B) 40
(C) 60
(D) 80
(E) 100

Arithmetic Estimation

Replace the numbers that appear with nearly equal values that are perfect squares and then evaluate the resulting expression:

$$\sqrt{\dfrac{4(1,600)}{16}} = \sqrt{\dfrac{4 \times 16 \times 100}{16}} = \sqrt{4 \times 100}$$

$$= \sqrt{4} \times \sqrt{100} = 2 \times 10 = 20$$

The correct answer is A.

49. What is the value of $\sqrt{17} + \sqrt{47}$, to the nearest whole number?

    (A) 8
    (B) 11
    (C) 12
    (D) 15
    (E) 32

Arithmetic Equations

$\sqrt{17}$ is slightly greater than $\sqrt{16} = 4$, while $\sqrt{47}$ is slightly less than $\sqrt{49} = 7$. Thus, $\sqrt{17} + \sqrt{47} \approx 4 + 7 = 11$.

The correct answer is B.

50. Last week Chris earned x dollars per hour for the first 40 hours worked plus 22 dollars per hour for each hour worked beyond 40 hours. If last week Chris earned a total of 816 dollars by working 48 hours, what is the value of x?

    (A) 13
    (B) 14
    (C) 15
    (D) 16
    (E) 17

Algebra Applied Problems

Chris worked 40 hours at a rate of \$x per hour, $48 - 40 = 8$ hours at a rate of \$22 per hour, and earned a total of \$816.

$$40x + 8(22) = 816 \quad \text{given information}$$
$$40x + 176 = 816 \quad \text{multiply 8 and 22}$$
$$40x = 640 \quad \text{subtract 176 from both sides}$$
$$x = 16 \quad \text{divide both sides by 40}$$

The correct answer is D.

51. The value of $\dfrac{\frac{7}{8}+\frac{1}{9}}{\frac{1}{2}}$ is closest to which of the following?

    (A) 2
    (B) $\frac{3}{2}$
    (C) 1
    (D) $\frac{1}{2}$
    (E) 0

Arithmetic Estimation

First, note that division by $\frac{1}{2}$ is the same as multiplication by $\frac{2}{1}$ (invert and multiply), so,

$\left(\frac{7}{8}+\frac{1}{9}\right) \div \frac{1}{2} = \left(\frac{7}{8}+\frac{1}{9}\right) \times \frac{2}{1} = \left(\frac{7}{8}+\frac{1}{9}\right) \times 2$. Then, because the question asks for the value "closest to" and not the exact value, estimate $\left(\frac{7}{8}+\frac{1}{9}\right) \times 2 \approx$ $\left(\frac{7}{8}+\frac{1}{8}\right) \times 2$ and calculate $\left(\frac{7+1}{8}\right) \times 2 = \frac{8}{8} \times 2 = 2$.

Alternatively, calculate $\frac{7}{8}+\frac{1}{9}$ using the common denominator of 72, $\frac{7}{8}+\frac{1}{9} = \frac{63}{72} + \frac{8}{72} = \frac{71}{72}$, then estimate $\frac{71}{72} \approx \frac{72}{72} = 1$, then calculate $1(2) = 2$.

The correct answer is A.

52. The positive two-digit integers x and y have the same digits, but in reverse order. Which of the following must be a factor of x + y?

    (A) 6
    (B) 9
    (C) 10
    (D) 11
    (E) 14

Arithmetic Properties of Numbers

Let m and n be digits. If $x = 10m + n$, then $y = 10n + m$. Adding x and y gives $x + y = (10m + n) + (10n + m) = 11m + 11n = 11(m + n)$, and therefore 11 is a factor of $x + y$.

The correct answer is D.

53. In a certain sequence of 8 numbers, each number after the first is 1 more than the previous number. If the first number is –5, how many of the numbers in the sequence are positive?

    (A) None
    (B) One
    (C) Two
    (D) Three
    (E) Four

Arithmetic Sequences

The sequence consists of eight consecutive integers beginning with –5:

$$-5, \ -4, \ -3, \ -2, \ -1, \ 0, \ 1, \ 2$$

In this sequence exactly two of the numbers are positive.

The correct answer is C.

54. A total of s oranges are to be packaged in boxes that will hold r oranges each, with no oranges left over. When n of these boxes have been completely filled, what is the number of boxes that remain to be filled?

    (A) $s - nr$
    (B) $s - \dfrac{n}{r}$
    (C) $rs - n$
    (D) $\dfrac{s}{n} - r$
    (E) $\dfrac{s}{r} - n$

Algebra Algebraic Expressions

If s oranges are packed r oranges to a box with no oranges left over, then the number of boxes that will be filled is $\dfrac{s}{r}$. If n of these boxes are already filled, then $\dfrac{s}{r} - n$ boxes remain to be filled.

The correct answer is E.

55. If $0 < a < b < c$, which of the following statements must be true?

    I. $2a > b + c$
    II. $c - a > b - a$
    III. $\dfrac{c}{a} < \dfrac{b}{a}$

    (A) I only
    (B) II only
    (C) III only
    (D) I and II
    (E) II and III

Algebra Inequalities

Given $0 < a < b < c$, Statement I is not necessarily true. If, for example, $a = 1$, $b = 2$, and $c = 3$, then $0 < a < b < c$, but $2a = 2(1) < 2 + 3 = b + c$.

Given $0 < a < b < c$, then $c > b$, and subtracting a from both sides gives $c - a > b - a$. Therefore, Statement II is true.

Given $0 < a < b < c$, Statement III is not necessarily true. If, for example, $a = 1$, $b = 2$, and $c = 3$, then $0 < a < b < c$, but $\dfrac{c}{a} = \dfrac{3}{1} > \dfrac{2}{1} = \dfrac{b}{a}$.

The correct answer is B.

	Monday	Tuesday	Wednesday	Thursday
Company A	45	55	50	50
Company B	10	30	30	10
Company C	34	28	28	30
Company D	39	42	41	38
Company E	50	60	60	70

56. The table shows the numbers of packages shipped daily by each of five companies during a 4-day period. The standard deviation of the numbers of packages shipped daily during the period was greatest for which of the five companies?

    (A) A
    (B) B
    (C) C
    (D) D
    (E) E

Arithmetic Statistics

Since the standard deviation of a data set is a measure of how widely the data are scattered about their mean, find the mean number of packages shipped by each company and then calculate the deviations of the company's data from its mean.

For Company A, the mean number of packages shipped is $\dfrac{45 + 55 + 2(50)}{4} = 50$ and the deviations from this mean are $-5, 5, 0,$ and 0. Note that the numbers of packages allow for quick calculations of the means. For example, for Company A the total number of packages is the sum of $45 + 55 = 100$ and $50 + 50 = 100$, and for Company D the total number of packages is the sum of $39 + 41 = 80$ and $42 + 38 = 80$.

The following table shows the means and deviations for the 5 companies.

	mean	deviations from mean
Company A	50	$-5, 5, 0, 0$
Company B	**20**	**$-10, 10, 10, -10$**
Company C	30	$4, -2, -2, 0$
Company D	40	$-1, 2, 1, -2$
Company E	60	$-10, 0, 0, 10$

This table shows that the magnitude of each of the 4 deviations for Company B is greater than or equal to the magnitude of any of the other deviations, which strongly suggests that the standard deviation is greatest for Company B.

For those interested, the standard deviations can be calculated as $\sqrt{\dfrac{\text{sum of (deviations)}^2}{4}}$. However, since we only wish to determine which company has the greatest standard deviation, it suffices to calculate the values of "sum of (deviations)^2," because dividing these values by 4 followed by taking a square root will not change their order (that is, the greatest will still be the greatest).

	(deviations)^2	sum of (deviations)^2
Company A	25, 25, 0, 0	50
Company B	**100, 100, 100, 100**	**400**
Company C	16, 4, 4, 0	24
Company D	1, 4, 1, 4	10
Company E	100, 0, 0, 100	200

The correct answer is B.

57. Company Q plans to make a new product next year and sell each unit of this new product at a selling price of \$2. The variable costs per unit in each production run are estimated to be 40% of the selling price, and the fixed costs for each production run are estimated to be \$5,040. Based on these estimated costs, how many units of the new product will Company Q need to make and sell in order for their revenue to equal their total costs for each production run?

(A) 4,200
(B) 3,150
(C) 2,520
(D) 2,100
(E) 1,800

Algebra Applied Problems

Let x be the desired number of units to be sold at a price of \$2 each. Then the revenue for selling these units is \$2x, and the total cost for selling these units is $(40\%)(\$2.00)x = \$0.80x$ plus a fixed cost of \$5,040.

revenue = total cost	given requirement
$2x = 0.8x + 5{,}040$	given information
$1.2x = 5{,}040$	subtract $0.8x$ from both sides
$x = 4{,}200$	divide both sides by 1.2

The correct answer is A.

58. A small business invests $9,900 in equipment to produce a product. Each unit of the product costs $0.65 to produce and is sold for $1.20. How many units of the product must be sold before the revenue received equals the total expense of production, including the initial investment in equipment?

    (A) 12,000
    (B) 14,500
    (C) 15,230
    (D) 18,000
    (E) 20,000

Arithmetic Rate

Let n be the number of units desired. Then, in dollars, the revenue received is $1.2n$ and the total expense is $9,900 + 0.65n$. These two amounts are equal when $1.2n = 9,900 + 0.65n$, or $0.55n = 9,900$. Therefore,

$$n = \frac{9,900}{0.55} = \frac{990,000}{55} = \frac{90,000}{5} = 18,000.$$

The correct answer is D.

Estimated Number of Home-Schooled
Students by State, January 2001

State	Number (in thousands)
A	181
B	125
C	103
D	79
E	72

59. According to the table shown, the estimated number of home-schooled students in State A is approximately what percent greater than the number in State D?

    (A) 25%
    (B) 55%
    (C) 100%
    (D) 125%
    (E) 155%

Arithmetic Percents

The percent increase from the number in State D to the number in State A is

$$= \left(\frac{181,000 - 79,000}{79,000} \times 100 \right)\% \quad \text{expression for percent increase}$$

$$= \left(\frac{181 - 79}{79} \times 100 \right)\% \quad \text{reduce fraction}$$

$$= \left(\frac{102}{79} \times 100 \right)\% \quad \text{subtract}$$

$$\approx \left(\frac{100}{80} \times 100 \right)\% \quad \text{approximate}$$

$$= (1.25 \times 100)\% \quad \text{divide}$$

$$= 125\% \quad \text{multiply}$$

The correct answer is D.

60. When n liters of fuel were added to a tank that was already $\frac{1}{3}$ full, the tank was filled to $\frac{7}{9}$ of its capacity. In terms of n, what is the capacity of the tank, in liters?

    (A) $\frac{10}{9}n$

    (B) $\frac{4}{3}n$

    (C) $\frac{3}{2}n$

    (D) $\frac{9}{4}n$

    (E) $\frac{7}{3}n$

Algebra Applied Problems

Let C represent the capacity of the tank, in liters. It follows that

$$\frac{1}{3}C + n = \frac{7}{9}C \quad \text{given}$$

$$n = \frac{7}{9}C - \frac{1}{3}C \quad \text{subtract } \frac{1}{3}C \text{ from both sides}$$

$$n = \frac{4}{9}C \quad \text{combine like terms}$$

$$\frac{9}{4}n = C \quad \text{divide both sides by } \frac{4}{9}$$

The correct answer is D.

61. A bicycle race on a mountain trail began at an elevation 850 meters above Town X. The race course consisted of 5 phases, with the following elevation changes: a descent of 280 meters, an ascent of 350 meters, a descent of 620 meters, an ascent of 100 meters, and a descent of 400 meters. At what elevation, in meters above or below Town X, did the race end?

    (A)   850 below Town X
    (B)   Same elevation as Town X
    (C)   850 above Town X
    (D)   1,700 above Town X
    (E)   2,600 above Town X

Arithmetic Applied Problems

Starting at 850 meters above Town X and adjusting for the 5 elevation changes, we find that the race ended at an elevation of 850 – 280 + 350 – 620 + 100 – 400 = 0 meters above Town X; that is, at the same elevation as Town X.

The correct answer is B.

62. The harvest yield from a certain apple orchard was 350 bushels of apples. If x of the trees in the orchard each yielded 10 bushels of apples, what fraction of the harvest yield was from these x trees?

    (A) $\dfrac{x}{35}$

    (B) $1 - \dfrac{x}{35}$

    (C) $10x$

    (D) $35 - x$

    (E) $350 - 10x$

Algebra Algebraic Expressions

Since each of the x trees yielded 10 bushels, the total number of bushels yielded by these trees was $10x$. Since the yield of the entire orchard was 350 bushels, $\dfrac{10x}{350} = \dfrac{x}{35}$ was the fraction of the total yield from these x trees.

The correct answer is A.

63. In a certain fraction, the denominator is 16 greater than the numerator. If the fraction is equivalent to 80 percent, what is the denominator of the fraction?

    (A)   32
    (B)   64
    (C)   72
    (D)   80
    (E)   120

Algebra First-Degree Equations

Let n be the numerator of the fraction. Then $n + 16$ is the denominator of the fraction. From the given information it follows that $\dfrac{n}{n+16} = 80\%$, which is solved below.

$$\dfrac{n}{n+16} = \dfrac{4}{5} \qquad \text{convert 80\% to a fraction}$$

$$5n = 4(n+16) \qquad \text{clear fractions}$$

$$5n = 4n + 64 \qquad \text{simplify}$$

$$n = 64 \qquad \text{subtract } 4n \text{ from both sides}$$

Therefore, the denominator of the fraction is $n + 16 = 64 + 16 = 80$.

The correct answer is D.

64. Jonathan, Kyle, and Michael agreed to pay equal shares of the monthly rent on an apartment. Because Jonathan has a cat, he paid a one-time pet deposit of $250. The pet deposit and Jonathan's share of the monthly rent for the first month totaled $525. How much is the monthly rent on the apartment?

    (A) $1,575
    (B) $1,075
    (C) $1,025
    (D) $825
    (E) $775

Arithmetic Applied Problems

Jonathan's share of the monthly rent was $525 minus the $250 pet deposit, which comes to $275. Since his two roommates also agreed to pay equal $275 thirds of the monthly rent, the total monthly rent was $3 \times \$275 = \$825$.

The correct answer is D.

65. The ratio of the amount of Alex's fuel oil bill for the month of February to the amount of his fuel oil bill for the month of January was $\frac{3}{2}$. If the fuel oil bill for February had been $40 more, the corresponding ratio would have been $\frac{5}{3}$. How much was Alex's fuel oil bill for January?

    (A) $240
    (B) $300
    (C) $360
    (D) $450
    (E) $540

Algebra Ratio and Proportion

Let x be the amount of Alex's fuel bill for January. Then the amount of his fuel bill for February is $\frac{3x}{2}$. We're also told that $\frac{3x}{2} + \$40 = \frac{5x}{3}$, so $\$40 = \frac{5x}{3} - \frac{3x}{2} = \frac{10x - 9x}{6} = \frac{x}{6}$. Thus, $x = 6(\$40) = \$240$.

The correct answer is A.

66. Al and Ben are drivers for SD Trucking Company. One snowy day, Ben left SD at 8:00 a.m. heading east and Al left SD at 11:00 a.m. heading west. At a particular time later that day, the dispatcher retrieved data from SD's vehicle tracking system. The data showed that, up to that time, Al had averaged 40 miles per hour and Ben had averaged 20 miles per hour. It also showed that Al and Ben had driven a combined total of 240 miles. At what time did the dispatcher retrieve data from the vehicle tracking system?

    (A) 1:00 p.m.
    (B) 2:00 p.m.
    (C) 3:00 p.m.
    (D) 5:00 p.m.
    (E) 6:00 p.m.

Algebra Applied Problems

Let t be the number of hours after 8:00 a.m. that Ben drove. Then Al, who began 3 hours after Ben began and thus drove 3 hours less than Ben, drove $(t - 3)$ hours. First, find the total distance each drove in terms of t.

	rate	time	distance = rate × time
Al	40	$t - 3$	$40(t - 3)$
Ben	20	t	$20t$

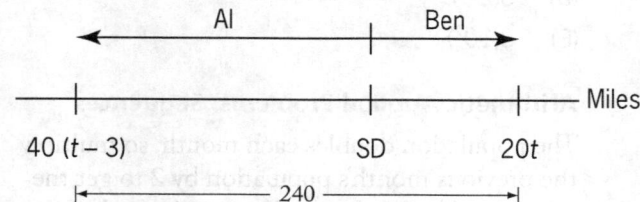

Since the combined total distance that Al and Ben drove was 240 miles, it follows that $40(t - 3) + 20t = 240$. Solve for t.

$40(t - 3) + 20t = 240$	given
$60t - 120 = 240$	expand and combine like terms
$60t = 360$	add 120 to both sides
$t = 6$	divide both sides by 60

Therefore, the data was retrieved 6 hours after 8:00 a.m., which was 2:00 p.m.

The correct answer is B.

67. If $f = 3r\left(\frac{s}{1,000}\right)^2$ and if $s = 2,000$, what is r in terms of f?

    (A) $\frac{f}{6}$

    (B) $\frac{f}{12}$

    (C) $\frac{f}{36}$

    (D) $\frac{f^2}{36}$

    (E) $\frac{3f}{4}$

Algebra Formulas

Since $f = 3r\left(\frac{2,000}{1,000}\right)^2 = 3r(2)^2 = 12r$, then $r = \frac{f}{12}$.

The correct answer is B.

68. At the start of an experiment, a certain population consisted of 3 animals. At the end of each month after the start of the experiment, the population size was double its size at the beginning of that month. Which of the following represents the population size at the end of 10 months?

(A) 2^3
(B) 3^2
(C) $2(3^{10})$
(D) $3(2^{10})$
(E) $3(10^2)$

Arithmetic Applied Problems; Sequences

The population doubles each month, so multiply the previous month's population by 2 to get the next month's population. Thus, at the end of the 1st month the population will be (3)(2), at the end of the 2nd month the population will be (3)(2)(2), at the end of the 3rd month the population will be (3)(2)(2)(2), and so on. Therefore, at the end of the 10th month the population will be the product of 3 and ten factors of 2, which equals $3(2^{10})$.

The correct answer is D.

69. The formula $F = \frac{9C}{5} + 32$ gives the relationship between the temperature in degrees Fahrenheit, F, and the temperature given in degrees Celsius, C. If the temperature is 85 degrees Fahrenheit, what is the temperature, to the nearest degree, in degrees Celsius?

(A) 18°C
(B) 23°C
(C) 29°C
(D) 47°C
(E) 51°C

Algebra Formulas

Using the given formula to convert 85 degrees Fahrenheit to Celsius, we get $85 = \frac{9}{5}C + 32$, so $53 = \frac{9}{5}C$, which means $C = 53\left(\frac{5}{9}\right) = \frac{265}{9} = 29\frac{4}{9}$. So, rounding to the nearest degree Celsius, we find that 85 degrees Fahrenheit is 29 degrees Celsius.

The correct answer is C.

70. If x and y are positive integers such that y is a multiple of 5 and $3x + 4y = 200$, then x must be a multiple of which of the following?

(A) 3
(B) 6
(C) 7
(D) 8
(E) 10

Arithmetic Properties of Numbers

Since y is a multiple of 5, consider the following table:

y	$4y$	$3x = 200 - 4y$	$x = \frac{200 - 4y}{3}$	Is x a positive integer?
5	20	180	60	**yes**
10	40	160	$\frac{160}{3}$	no
15	60	140	$\frac{140}{3}$	no
20	80	120	40	**yes**
25	100	100	$\frac{100}{3}$	no
30	120	80	$\frac{80}{3}$	no
35	140	60	20	**yes**
40	160	40	$\frac{40}{3}$	no
45	180	20	$\frac{20}{3}$	no
50	200	0	0	no

The only positive integers x that satisfy the $3x + 4y = 200$, where y is a multiple of 5, are 60, 40, and 20; each is a multiple of 10.

Note: It is not necessary to perform all of the calculations shown here, nor is it necessary to fill out the table completely. Using "number sense" to see the patterns (e.g., numbers in the second column increase by 20 while numbers in the third column decrease by 20) will shorten the work considerably.

The correct answer is E.

71. Which of the following expressions can be written as an integer?

    I. $\left(\sqrt{82} + \sqrt{82}\right)^2$

    II. $(82)\left(\sqrt{82}\right)$

    III. $\dfrac{\left(\sqrt{82}\right)\left(\sqrt{82}\right)}{82}$

    (A) None
    (B) I only
    (C) III only
    (D) I and II
    (E) I and III

Arithmetic Operations with Radical Expressions

Expression I represents an integer because $\left(\sqrt{82} + \sqrt{82}\right)^2 = \left(2\sqrt{82}\right)^2 = (4)(82)$.
Expression II does not represent an integer because $(82)\sqrt{82} = \sqrt{82^3}$ and $82^3 = 2^3 \times 41^3$ is not a perfect square. Regarding this last assertion, note that the square of any integer has the property that each of its distinct prime factors is repeated an even number of times. For example, $24^2 = (2^3 \times 3)^2 = 2^6 \times 3^2$ has the prime factor 2 repeated 6 times and the prime factor 3 repeated twice. Expression III represents an integer, because $\dfrac{\left(\sqrt{82}\right)\left(\sqrt{82}\right)}{82} = \dfrac{82}{82} = 1$.

The correct answer is E.

72. Which of the following is equal to the average (arithmetic mean) of $(x + 2)^2$ and $(x - 2)^2$?

    (A) x^2
    (B) $x^2 + 2$
    (C) $x^2 + 4$
    (D) $x^2 + 2x$
    (E) $x^2 + 4x$

Algebra Statistics

The average of $(x + 2)^2$ and $(x - 2)^2$ is
$$\dfrac{(x + 2)^2 + (x - 2)^2}{2} = \dfrac{x^2 + 4x + 4 + x^2 - 4x + 4}{2} =$$
$$\dfrac{2x^2 + 8}{2} = x^2 + 4.$$

The correct answer is C.

73. If $x^2 - 2 < 0$, which of the following specifies all the possible values of x?

    (A) $0 < x < 2$
    (B) $0 < x < \sqrt{2}$
    (C) $-\sqrt{2} < x < \sqrt{2}$
    (D) $-2 < x < 0$
    (E) $-2 < x < 2$

Algebra Inequalities

The corresponding equality $x^2 - 2 = 0$ has two solutions, $x = \sqrt{2}$ and $x = -\sqrt{2}$, and thus there are three intervals to test for inclusion in the solution of the inequality: $x < -\sqrt{2}$, $-\sqrt{2} < x < \sqrt{2}$, and $x > \sqrt{2}$, labeled I_1, I_2, and I_3, respectively, in the figure below.

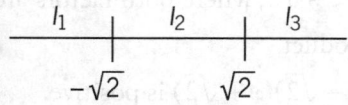

Next, choose a value from each of these intervals to test whether the inequality holds:

From I_1, for example, choose $x = -2$; the inequality becomes $(-2)^2 - 2 < 0$ (False).

From I_2, for example, choose $x = 0$; the inequality becomes $(0)^2 - 2 < 0$ (True).

From I_3, for example, choose $x = 2$; the inequality becomes $(2)^2 - 2 < 0$ (False).

Therefore, the solution consists of only values in I_2.

Alternatively, the expression $x^2 - 2$ can be factored as $(x - \sqrt{2})(x + \sqrt{2})$. The value of the factor $(x - \sqrt{2})$ is 0 at $x = \sqrt{2}$, negative for values of x less than $\sqrt{2}$, and positive for values of x greater than $\sqrt{2}$. Similarly, the value of the factor $(x + \sqrt{2})$ is 0 at $x = -\sqrt{2}$, negative for values of x less than $-\sqrt{2}$, and positive for values of x greater than $-\sqrt{2}$. Using the number line, this information can be summarized as shown below:

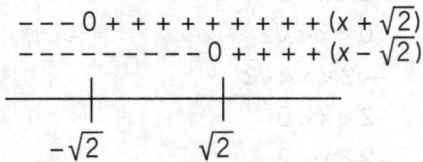

Then, as shown below, vertical lines through the zeros partition the number line into three intervals I_1, I_2, and I_3.

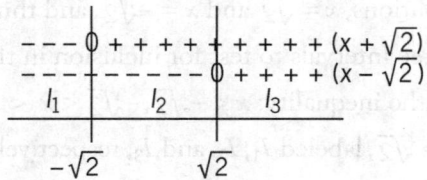

I_1: $x < -\sqrt{2}$, where both factors are negative, so the product

$(x - \sqrt{2})(x + \sqrt{2})$ is positive.

I_2: $-\sqrt{2} < x < \sqrt{2}$, where one factor is positive and the other is negative, so the product

$(x - \sqrt{2})(x + \sqrt{2})$ is negative.

I_3: $x > \sqrt{2}$, where both factors are positive, so the product

$(x - \sqrt{2})(x + \sqrt{2})$ is positive.

Therefore, the solution consists of only values in I_2.

The correct answer is C.

Book Number	Pages in Book	Total Pages Read
1	253	253
2	110	363
3	117	480
4	170	650
5	155	805
6	50	855
7	205	1,060
8	70	1,130
9	165	1,295
10	105	1,400
11	143	1,543
12	207	1,750

74. Shawana made a schedule for reading books during 4 weeks (28 days) of her summer vacation. She has checked out 12 books from the library. The number of pages in each book and the order in which she plans to read the books are shown in the table above. She will read exactly 50 pages each day. The only exception will be that she will never begin the next book on the same day that she finishes the previous one, and therefore on some days she may read fewer than 50 pages. At the end of the 28th day, how many books will Shawana have finished?

(A)   7

(B)   8

(C)   9

(D)   10

(E)   11

Arithmetic Operations with Integers

Book 1: 6 days—50 pages on each of Days 1–5, 3 pages on Day 6 [5(50) + 3 = 253]

Book 2: 3 days—50 pages on each of Days 7 and 8, 10 pages on Day 9 [2(50) + 10 = 110]

Book 3: 3 days—50 pages on each of Days 10 and 11, 17 pages on Day 12 [2(50) + 17 = 117]

Book 4: 4 days—50 pages on each of Days 13–15, 20 pages on Day 16 [3(50) + 20 = 170]

Book 5: 4 days—50 pages on each of Days 17–19, 5 pages on Day 20 [3(50) + 5 = 155]

Book 6: 1 day—50 pages on Day 21 [1(50) = 50]

Book 7: 5 days—50 pages on each of Days 22–25, 5 pages on Day 26 [4(50) + 5 = 205]

Book 8: 2 days—50 pages on Day 27, 20 pages on Day 28 [50 + 20 = 70]

At this point, Shawana has read on a total of 28 days and has finished 8 books.

The correct answer is B.

75. In Western Europe, x bicycles were sold in each of the years 1990 and 1993. The bicycle producers of Western Europe had a 42 percent share of this market in 1990 and a 33 percent share in 1993. Which of the following represents the decrease in the annual number of bicycles produced and sold in Western Europe from 1990 to 1993?

(A) 9% of $\frac{x}{100}$

(B) 14% of $\frac{x}{100}$

(C) 75% of $\frac{x}{100}$

(D) 9% of x

(E) 14% of x

Arithmetic Percents

Of the x bicycles sold in Western Europe in 1990, 42% of them were produced in Western Europe. It follows that the number of bicycles produced and sold in Western Europe in 1990 was 0.42x. Similarly, of the x bicycles sold in Western Europe in 1993, 33% were produced in Western Europe. It follows that the number of bicycles produced and sold in Western Europe in 1993 was 0.33x. Therefore, the decrease in the annual number of bicycles produced and sold in Western Europe from 1990 to 1993 was 0.42x − 0.33x = 0.09x, which is 9% of x.

The correct answer is D.

76. If k is a positive integer, what is the remainder when $(k + 2)(k^3 - k)$ is divided by 6?

(A) 0
(B) 1
(C) 2
(D) 3
(E) 4

Algebra Properties of Numbers

Since k can be any positive integer, the remainder must be the same regardless of the value of k. If k = 2, for example, then $(k + 2)(k^3 - k) = (2 + 2)(2^3 - 2) = (4)(6)$, which is a multiple of 6, and therefore, the remainder when divided by 6 is 0.

Alternatively, factor the given expression:

$$(k + 2)(k^3 - k) = (k + 2)(k)(k^2 - 1)$$
$$= (k + 2)(k)(k + 1)(k - 1)$$

Now, rearrange the factors in ascending order $(k - 1)(k)(k + 1)(k + 2)$, and observe that for any positive integer k, the factors are four consecutive integers, two of which are even and one of which is divisible by 3. Therefore, $(k + 2)(k^3 - k)$ is divisible by both 2 and 3. Thus, $(k + 2)(k^3 - k)$ is divisible by 6 with 0 remainder.

The correct answer is A.

77. Which of the following fractions is closest to $\frac{1}{2}$?

(A) $\frac{4}{7}$

(B) $\frac{5}{9}$

(C) $\frac{6}{11}$

(D) $\frac{7}{13}$

(E) $\frac{9}{16}$

Arithmetic Fractions

A fraction equals $\frac{1}{2}$ if its numerator is half its denominator. Thus, to compare the answer choices with $\frac{1}{2}$, rewrite $\frac{1}{2}$ to have the same denominators as the answer choices. This will allow for an easy determination of the distance to $\frac{1}{2}$.

answer choice	value	rewrite of $\frac{1}{2}$	distance to $\frac{1}{2}$
A	$\frac{4}{7}$	$\frac{3.5}{7}$	$\frac{0.5}{7}$
B	$\frac{5}{9}$	$\frac{4.5}{9}$	$\frac{0.5}{9}$
C	$\frac{6}{11}$	$\frac{5.5}{11}$	$\frac{0.5}{11}$
D	$\frac{7}{13}$	$\frac{6.5}{13}$	$\frac{0.5}{13}$
E	$\frac{9}{16}$	$\frac{8}{16}$	$\frac{1}{16}$

Clearly, $\frac{0.5}{13}$ is smaller than each of $\frac{0.5}{7}$, $\frac{0.5}{9}$, and $\frac{0.5}{11}$ because the numerators are equal, and thus larger denominators correspond to smaller values. Also, $\frac{0.5}{13} = \frac{1}{26}$ is smaller than $\frac{1}{16}$. Therefore, $\frac{7}{13}$ is closest to $\frac{1}{2}$.

The correct answer is D.

78. If $p \neq 0$ and $p - \frac{1-p^2}{p} = \frac{r}{p}$, then $r =$

(A) $p + 1$
(B) $2p - 1$
(C) $p^2 + 1$
(D) $2p^2 - 1$
(E) $p^2 + p - 1$

Algebra Simplifying Algebraic Expressions

$p - \frac{1-p^2}{p} = \frac{r}{p}$ given

$p^2 - (1 - p^2) = r$ multiply both sides by p

$2p^2 - 1 = r$ combine like terms

The correct answer is D.

79. If $\frac{|z|}{w} = 1$, which of the following must be true?

(A) $z = -w$
(B) $z = w$
(C) $z^2 = w^2$
(D) $z^2 = w^3$
(E) $z^3 = w^3$

Algebra Absolute Value

If $\frac{|z|}{w} = 1$, then $|z| = w$. That is, either $z = w$ or $-z = w$. In either case, $z^2 = w^2$, so option C is correct. Option A is wrong because if z and w are both positive, then $z \neq -w$. Option B is wrong because if z is negative and w is positive, then $z \neq w$. To see that options D and E are wrong, suppose $z = -2$, so that $w = 2$. In that case $z^2 = 4 \neq w^3 = 8$, contrary to option D, and $z^3 = -8 \neq w^3 = 8$, contrary to option E.

The correct answer is C.

80. What number is 108 more than two-thirds of itself?

(A) 72
(B) 144
(C) 162
(D) 216
(E) 324

Algebra First-Degree Equations

Let x be the number that is 108 more than two-thirds of itself. Then, $108 + \frac{2}{3}x = x$. Solve for x as follows:

$108 + \frac{2}{3}x = x$

$108 = \frac{1}{3}x$

$324 = x$

The correct answer is E.

81. A service provider charges c dollars for the first 50 hours of service used per month and 40 cents for each 30 minutes in excess of 50 hours used during the month. If x is an integer greater than 50, which of the following expressions gives this service provider's charge, in dollars, for a month in which x hours of service were used?

    (A) $c + 0.40x$
    (B) $c + 0.80x$
    (C) $c + 0.40(x - 50)$
    (D) $c + 0.80(x - 50)$
    (E) $c + 0.40(2x - 50)$

Algebra Algebraic Expressions

For x hours of service used in the month, the charge is c dollars for the first 50 hours used, leaving $(x - 50)$ hours to be charged at 40 cents per half hour, which is equivalent to 80 cents per hour. Therefore, the total charge, in dollars, for a month in which x hours of service were used is $c + 0.80(x - 50)$.

The correct answer is D.

82. A salesperson who had been driving at a speed of 100 kilometers per hour slowed down to a speed of 47 kilometers per hour. Approximately how many miles per hour was the speed reduced? (1 kilometer ≈ 0.625 mile)

    (A) 29
    (B) 33
    (C) 53
    (D) 63
    (E) 75

Arithmetic Measurement Conversion

$$(100 - 47)\ \frac{\text{km}}{\text{hr}} \quad \text{amount of reduction}$$

$$53\ \frac{\text{km}}{\text{hr}} \quad \text{subtract}$$

$$\left(53\ \frac{\text{km}}{\text{hr}}\right)\left(0.625\ \frac{\text{mi}}{\text{km}}\right) \quad 1\ \text{km} = 0.625\ \text{mi}$$

$$(50)(0.6)\ \frac{\text{mi}}{\text{hr}} \quad \text{estimate}$$

$$30\ \frac{\text{mi}}{\text{hr}} \quad \text{multiply}$$

From the calculations it follows that speed was reduced, in miles per hour, by a little more than 30; among the answer choices, only 33 is a reasonable choice. The exact value is 33.125, and this can be found by multiplying 53 and 0.625 or, since $(53)\left(\dfrac{625}{1,000}\right) = (53)\left(\dfrac{5}{8}\right) = \dfrac{265}{8}$, dividing 265 by 8.

The correct answer is B.

83. If $5x - 8 = 12$ and $x = y + 3$, then $y =$

    (A) $\dfrac{4}{5}$
    (B) 1
    (C) $\dfrac{17}{5}$
    (D) 4
    (E) 7

Algebra Simultaneous Equations

If $5x - 8 = 12$, then $5x = 20$, so $x = 4$. Thus, if $x = y + 3$, then $y = 4 - 3 = 1$.

The correct answer is B.

	Recording Time	Viewing Time
Tuesday	4 hours	None
Wednesday	None	1 to 2 hours
Thursday	2 hours	None
Friday	None	2 to 3 hours

84. The table above shows the numbers of hours of television programs that Jane recorded last week and the numbers of hours she spent viewing these recorded programs. No recorded program was viewed more than once. If h is the number of hours of recorded programs she had not yet viewed by the end of Friday, which of the following intervals represents all of the possible values of h?

    (A) $0 \le h \le 1$
    (B) $1 \le h \le 2$
    (C) $2 \le h \le 3$
    (D) $0 \le h \le 2$
    (E) $1 \le h \le 3$

Arithmetic Inequalities

By the end of Friday, Jane had recorded a total of $4 + 2 = 6$ hours of programs, and she had viewed between $1 + 2 = 3$ hours and $2 + 3 = 5$ hours of these programs. Therefore, the number of hours of recorded programs that Jane had not yet viewed by the end of Friday was between $6 - 5 = 1$ and $6 - 3 = 3$.

The correct answer is E.

85. A dance troupe has a total of 50 dancers split into 2 groups. The costumes worn by Group A cost $80 each, and those worn by Group B cost $90 each. If the total cost of all the costumes is $4,270, what is the total cost of the costumes worn by Group B?

    (A) $1,840
    (B) $2,070
    (C) $2,135
    (D) $2,160
    (E) $2,430

Algebra Applied Problems; First-Degree Equations

Let n be the number of dancers in Group B. Then the number of dancers in Group A is $50 - n$, and we are given that $(50 - n)(\$80) + (n)(\$90) = \$4,270$.

$(50 - n)(80) + 90n = 4{,}270$	given
$(50 - n)(8) + 9n = 427$	divide both sides by 10
$400 - 8n + 9n = 427$	distributive law
$n = 27$	combine like terms and subtract 400 from each side

Therefore, the total cost of the costumes worn by Group B is $27(\$90) = \$2,430$.

The correct answer is E.

86. A doctor prescribed 18 cubic centimeters of a certain drug to a patient whose body weight was 120 pounds. If the typical dosage is 2 cubic centimeters per 15 pounds of body weight, by what percent was the prescribed dosage greater than the typical dosage?

    (A) 8%
    (B) 9%
    (C) 11%
    (D) 12.5%
    (E) 14.8%

Arithmetic Percents

If the typical dosage is 2 cubic centimeters per 15 pounds of body weight, then the typical dosage for a person who weighs 120 pounds is $2\left(\dfrac{120}{15}\right) = 2(8) = 16$ cubic centimeters. The prescribed dosage of 18 cubic centimeters is, therefore, $\left(\left(\dfrac{18 - 16}{16}\right) \times 100\right)\%$ or 12.5% greater than the typical dosage.

The correct answer is D.

87. The function f is defined by $f(x) = \sqrt{x} - 10$ for all positive numbers x. If $u = f(t)$ for some positive numbers t and u, what is t in terms of u?

    (A) $\sqrt{\sqrt{u} + 10}$
    (B) $\left(\sqrt{u} + 10\right)^2$
    (C) $\sqrt{u^2 + 10}$
    (D) $(u + 10)^2$
    (E) $(u^2 + 10)^2$

Algebra Functions

Because $f(x) = \sqrt{x} - 10$, it follows that $f(t) = \sqrt{t} - 10$. The problem states that $u = f(t)$, so by substitution, $u = \sqrt{t} - 10$. To express t in terms of u, isolate t on one side of the equation:

u	$=$	$\sqrt{t} - 10$	given
$u + 10$	$=$	$\sqrt{t}$	add 10 to both sides
$(u + 10)^2$	$=$	t	square both sides

Therefore, t in terms of u is $(u + 10)^2$.

The correct answer is D.

88. If 35% of a number is decreased by 15, then the result is 25% of the original number. What is the original number?

    (A) 1.5
    (B) 9
    (C) 25
    (D) 150
    (E) 900

Arithmetic Percents

We need to find x such that $0.35x - 15 = 0.25x$. Adding $15 - 0.25x$ to both sides of the equation gives us $0.1x = 15$, so $x = 150$.

The correct answer is D.

89. A flower arrangement consists of 30 roses, each of which is either white or red. If a rose is to be selected at random from the flower arrangement, the probability that the rose selected will be white is twice the probability that it will be red. How many white roses are in the flower arrangement?

(A) 5
(B) 10
(C) 15
(D) 20
(E) 25

Algebra Applied Problems

Let W be the number of white roses and R be the number of red roses. From the given information, $W + R = 30$ and $\frac{W}{30} = 2 \times \frac{R}{30}$, where $\frac{W}{30}$ is the probability that the rose selected will be white and $\frac{R}{30}$ is the probability that the rose selected will be red. Multiplying both sides of $\frac{W}{30} = 2 \times \frac{R}{30}$ by 30 gives $W = 2R$. Substituting $W = 2R$ into $W + R = 30$ gives $2R + R = 30$, or $R = 10$. Therefore, $W = 2R = 2(10) = 20$.

The correct answer is D.

90. Sixty percent of the people who responded to a company's advertisement for a job opening were interviewed over the phone. Twenty percent of those interviewed over the phone, that is, 3 people, were asked to come to the company for a personal interview. How many people responded to the advertisement?

(A) 16
(B) 20
(C) 25
(D) 40
(E) 64

Arithmetic Percents

Since 20% of the 60% who responded were the 3 people who were asked to come for an interview, it follows that 12% of those who responded were the 3 people who were asked to come for an interview. Therefore, the number of those who responded is $3 \div 0.12 = 25$.

The correct answer is C.

91. $(-3)^{-2} =$

(A) -9
(B) -6
(C) $-\frac{1}{9}$
(D) $\frac{1}{9}$
(E) 9

Arithmetic Negative Exponents

$$(-3)^{-2} = \frac{1}{(-3)^2} = \frac{1}{9}$$

The correct answer is D.

92. Mark bought a set of 6 flowerpots of different sizes at a total cost of $8.25. Each pot cost $0.25 more than the next one below it in size. What was the cost, in dollars, of the largest pot?

(A) $1.75
(B) $1.85
(C) $2.00
(D) $2.15
(E) $2.30

Algebra Applied Problems; First-Degree Equations

Let C be the cost of the largest pot in dollars. Then, in dollars, the total cost 8.25 is equal to $C + (C - 0.25) + (C - 0.50) + (C - 0.75) + (C - 1.00) + (C - 1.25)$, or $6C - 3.75$. Therefore, $6C - 3.75 = 8.25$, which when solved gives $C = 2$.

The correct answer is C.

93. If r and s are positive integers and $r - s = 6$, which of the following has the greatest value?

(A) $2r$

(B) $2s$

(C) $r + s$

(D) $2r - s$

(E) $2s - r$

Arithmetic Order

Since we can assume that only one of the answer choices has the greatest value, any two positive integers r and s such that $r - s = 6$ can be used to identify that answer choice. The table below shows the values of the answer choices for $r = 7$ and $s = 1$.

answer choice	value when $r = 7$ and $s = 1$
$2r$	14
$2s$	2
$r + s$	8
$2r - s$	13
$2s - r$	-5

From the table it follows that the first answer choice has the greatest value.

Alternatively, an algebraic approach can be used to identify the greatest value without making the assumption that only one of the answer choices always has the greatest value. First, using $s = r - 6$, express each of the answer choices in terms of r. For example, in terms of r the answer choice $2s - r$ is equal to $2(r - 6) - r = r - 12$. The table below shows the answer choices in terms of r.

answer choice	answer choice in terms of r
$2r$	$2r$
$2s$	$2r - 12$
$r + s$	$2r - 6$
$2r - s$	$r + 6$
$2s - r$	$r - 12$

From the second column of the table, it follows that, for each possible value of r, the first answer choice $2r$ is the greatest of the first three answer choices and the fourth answer choice $2r - s = r + 6$ is the greater of the remaining two answer

choices. Therefore, the greater of the first and fourth answer choices, $2r$ and $r + 6$, will be the greatest of the answer choices. To determine which of $2r$ and $r + 6$ is greater, note that since s is a positive integer, we have $s + 6 > 6$. Now use $r = s + 6$ to get $r > 6$, from which it follows that $r + r > r + 6$, or $2r > r + 6$.

The correct answer is A.

94. An auction house charges a commission of 15 percent on the first $50,000 of the sale price of an item, plus 10 percent on the amount of the sale price in excess of $50,000. What was the sale price of a painting for which the auction house charged a total commission of $24,000?

(A) $115,000

(B) $160,000

(C) $215,000

(D) $240,000

(E) $365,000

Arithmetic Applied Problems; Percents

Since the commission on $50,000 is $(0.15)(\$50,000) = \$7,500$ and the total commission of $24,000 is $16,500 greater than $7,500, it follows that $16,500 of the total commission arises from the sale price in excess of $50,000. Therefore, 10% of the sale price in excess of $50,000 is equal to $16,500, and hence the sale price in excess of $50,000 is $165,000 (because 10% of $165,000 is $16,500). Thus, the sale price is $50,000 + $165,000 = $215,000.

Alternatively, let P be the sale price in dollars. Then the given information can be expressed as a first-degree equation which can be solved for the value of P.

$$24,000 = 0.15(50,000) + 0.10(P - 50,000)$$

$$24,000 = 7,500 + 0.10P - 5,000$$

$$21,500 = 0.10P$$

$$P = 215,000$$

The correct answer is C.

95. At a certain college there are twice as many English majors as history majors and three times as many English majors as mathematics majors. What is the ratio of the number of history majors to the number of mathematics majors?

    (A)   6 to 1
    (B)   3 to 2
    (C)   2 to 3
    (D)   1 to 5
    (E)   1 to 6

Algebra Ratios

Let E, H, and M denote, respectively, the number of English, history, and mathematics majors. From the given information, it follows that $E = 2H$ and $E = 3M$, or equivalently, $H = \frac{1}{2}E$ and $M = \frac{1}{3}E$. Therefore, $\dfrac{H}{M} = \dfrac{\frac{1}{2}\cancel{E}}{\frac{1}{3}\cancel{E}} = \dfrac{3}{2}$, and hence the ratio of the number of history majors to the number of mathematics majors is 3 to 2.

The correct answer is B.

96. A certain method for calculating pediatric drug dosages states that if d is the adult dosage, in milligrams, and y is the child's age, in years, then the child's dosage, in milligrams, is $d\left(\dfrac{y+1}{24}\right)$. If the adult dosage for a particular drug is 800 milligrams, what is an 8-year-old child's dosage, in milligrams, according to this method?

    (A)   200
    (B)   225
    (C)   250
    (D)   275
    (E)   300

Algebra Formulas

From the given information, we know that $d = 800$ and $y = 8$. Therefore, the dosage, in milligrams, for the 8-year-old child is

$$d\left(\frac{y+1}{24}\right) = 800\left(\frac{8+1}{24}\right) = 800 \times \frac{3}{8} = 300.$$

The correct answer is E.

97. 1, 2, 3, 4, 5, 6, 7, 8, 9, 10

    How many different ordered pairs of numbers (s, t) can be formed such that $t = 3s$, where s and t are numbers from the list above?

    (A)   Two
    (B)   Three
    (C)   Five
    (D)   Six
    (E)   Ten

Algebra Statistics

Since $t = 3s$ and s is an integer, it follows that t is a multiple of 3, and hence t can only be one of the numbers 3, 6, and 9 in the given list. Moreover, for each of these choices of t, there is exactly one choice of s (one-third the value of t), so exactly three different ordered pairs satisfy the given requirements:

(1,3), (2,6), and (3,9).

The correct answer is B.

98. If $|x - 2| > 3$, then x could be equal to any of the following EXCEPT

    (A) -3
    (B) -2
    (C) 4
    (D) 6
    (E) 8

Algebra Statistics

The inequality $|x - 2| > 3$ is equivalent to $x - 2 < -3$ or $x - 2 > 3$, which in turn is equivalent to $x < -1$ or $x > 5$. Of the five numbers to consider, both -3 and -2 are less than -1, and thus are possible values of x; both 6 and 8 are greater than 5, and thus are also possible values of x; but 4 is neither less than -1 nor greater than 5, and thus is not a possible value of x.

The correct answer is C.

99. If the average (arithmetic mean) of 7, 16, and h is greater than or equal to 7, what is the least possible value of h?

    (A) −16
    (B) −2
    (C) 7
    (D) 21
    (E) 23

Algebra Inequalities

$\dfrac{7 + 16 + h}{3} \geq 7$ from given information

$7 + 16 + h \geq 21$ multiply both sides by 3

$h \geq -2$ subtract 23 from both sides

The last row above implies that the possible values of h are the numbers greater than or equal to −2. Therefore, the least possible value of h is −2.

The correct answer is B.

100. Norman is scheduled to write computer programs during a 15-week period beginning this week. Norman will write 5 computer programs this week, 6 computer programs next week, and each week thereafter, he will write 1 computer program more than he did in the previous week. What is the total number of computer programs that Norman will write during the 15-week period?

    (A) 180
    (B) 190
    (C) 200
    (D) 210
    (E) 225

Arithmetic Series and Sequences

Since 5 programs will be written during the 1st week, $(5 + 1)$ programs will be written during the 2nd week, $(5 + 2)$ programs will be written during the 3rd week, etc., it follows that $(5 + 14) = 19$ programs will be written during the 15th week. Therefore, the total number of programs written during the 15-week period will be the following sum:

$$S = 5 + 6 + 7 + \dots + 19$$

The sum above is an arithmetic series whose value (denoted here by S) can be quickly found in several ways. One way is to add the series in a term-by-term manner to a reverse-ordered version of the series to obtain a series all of whose terms are the same number.

$$\begin{aligned} S &= 5 + 6 + \dots + 18 + 19 \\ S &= 19 + 18 + \dots + 6 + 5 \\ S + S &= 24 + 24 + \dots + 24 + 24 \end{aligned}$$

From the last equation above, it follows that $S + S$ is equal to 24 added to itself 15 times, so $2S = 15 \times 24$, and therefore $S = 15 \times 12 = 180$.

Another way is to apply the following formula, where a_1 is the 1st term, a_n is the last term, and n is the number of terms.

$$S = \frac{n}{2}(a_1 + a_n) = \frac{15}{2}(5 + 19) = \frac{15}{2} \times 24 = 180$$

The correct answer is A.

101. Which of the following fractions has the greatest value?

    (A) $\dfrac{5}{13}$

    (B) $\dfrac{3}{11}$

    (C) $\left(\dfrac{5}{13}\right)^2$

    (D) $\left(\dfrac{3}{11}\right)^3$

    (E) $\left(\dfrac{5}{13}\right)^3$

Arithmetic Fractions

The statements below show that the greatest is either $\frac{5}{13}$ or $\frac{3}{11}$.

$\left(\frac{5}{13}\right)^2 = \frac{5}{13} \times \frac{5}{13}$ is less than $1 \times \frac{5}{13}$

$\left(\frac{3}{11}\right)^3 = \left(\frac{3}{11} \times \frac{3}{11}\right) \times \frac{3}{11}$ is less than $1 \times \frac{3}{11}$

$\left(\frac{5}{13}\right)^3 = \left(\frac{5}{13} \times \frac{5}{13}\right) \times \frac{5}{13}$ is less than $1 \times \frac{5}{13}$

One way to determine which of $\frac{5}{13}$ or $\frac{3}{11}$ is greater is to use a common denominator. Since $\frac{5}{13} = \frac{5}{13} \times \frac{11}{11} = \frac{55}{143}$ and $\frac{3}{11} = \frac{3}{11} \times \frac{13}{13} = \frac{39}{143}$, it follows that $\frac{5}{13}$ is greater.

The correct answer is A.

Fee	Plan A	Plan B
Line 1, Activation Fee	$0	$50
Line 2, Activation Fee	$0	$30
Line 1, Monthly Fee	$40	$35
Line 2, Monthly Fee	$15	$10

102. The table above shows all applicable charges for 2 phone lines, Line 1 and Line 2, under 2 plans, Plan A and Plan B. Both plans require a monthly fee per phone line, and Plan B requires an additional one-time Line Activation Fee. If n is the number of months for which the total charges for 2 lines under Plan A are equal to the total charges for 2 lines under Plan B, what is n?

(A)   4
(B)   5
(C)   8
(D)   10
(E)   16

Algebra Applied Problems; First-Degree Equations

For each of the plans, the total charges for n months under that plan is the sum of the two activation fees for that plan added to n times the sum of the two monthly fees for that plan.

Each plan's total charges: (sum of activation fees) + n(sum of monthly fees)

Plan A total charges: $(0 + 0) + n(40 + 15) = 55n$

Plan B total charges: $(50 + 30) + n(35 + 10) = 80 + 45n$

The two plans will have the same total charges when $55n = 80 + 45n$.

$55n = 80 + 45n$ equation to solve
$10n = 80$ subtract $45n$ from both sides
$n = 8$ divide both sides by 10

Therefore, for 8 months the total charges for 2 lines under Plan A is equal to the total charges for 2 lines under Plan B.

The correct answer is C.

103. The prices for 5 textbooks on a certain shelf are $40, $50, $40, $45, and $50, respectively. In which of the following intervals does the standard deviation of the prices of the 5 textbooks lie?

(A)   Between $0 and $10
(B)   Between $10 and $20
(C)   Between $20 and $30
(D)   Between $40 and $45
(E)   Between $45 and $50

The standard deviation of a data set is the square root of the average of the squared differences from the mean. To find the standard deviation, first find the mean of the data set:

$$\frac{40 + 50 + 40 + 45 + 50}{5} = 45$$

Next, find the differences and the squared differences from the mean:

x	$x - 45$	$(x - 45)^2$
40	−5	25
50	5	25
40	−5	25
45	0	0
50	5	25

Now use the right-most column of the table to find the average of the squared differences:

$$\frac{25 + 25 + 25 + 0 + 25}{5} = \frac{100}{5} = 20$$

Thus, the square root of the average of the squared differences from the mean (i.e., the standard deviation) is $\sqrt{20}$, which is between 0 and 10 (since 20 is between $0^2 = 0$ and $10^2 = 100$).

The correct answer is A.

Questions 104 to 191 — Difficulty: **Medium**

104. The sides of each of two plastic cubes are numbered 1 through 6, and each number is equally likely to appear face up after either cube is rolled. What is the probability that after the two cubes are rolled, the sum of the two numbers appearing face up will be greater than 9?

(A) $\frac{1}{6}$

(B) $\frac{1}{5}$

(C) $\frac{1}{4}$

(D) $\frac{5}{18}$

(E) $\frac{1}{3}$

Arithmetic Statistics

For either cube, any 1 of the 6 numbers is equally likely to appear face up after rolling the cube. Thus, $6 \times 6 = 36$ equally likely outcomes of rolling both cubes are possible. Of these 36, only 6 outcomes have sums greater than 9. These are $\{4, 6\}, \{5, 5\}, \{5, 6\}, \{6, 4\}, \{6, 5\}$, and $\{6, 6\}$, where the first number in each set is face up on the first cube and the second is face up on the second cube. Since each outcome is equally probable, the probability of the sum of the numbers facing up being greater than 9 is $\frac{6}{36} = \frac{1}{6}$.

The correct answer is A.

105. On Saturday morning, Malachi will begin a camping vacation, and he will return home at the end of the first day on which it rains. If on the first three days of the vacation the probability of rain on each day is 0.2, what is the probability that Malachi will return home at the end of the day on the following Monday?

(A) 0.008

(B) 0.128

(C) 0.488

(D) 0.512

(E) 0.640

Algebra Statistics

The first three days of Malachi's vacation are Saturday, Sunday, and Monday. On each of these days, if Malachi is still camping, the probability that it will rain and thus he'll return home that day is 0.2, which means the probability that he won't return home that day is $1 - 0.2 = 0.8$. So, the probability that he'll still be camping Sunday is 0.8, and the probability that he'll still be camping Monday is $0.8 \times 0.8 = 0.64$. Therefore, the probability that he'll return home Monday is $0.64 \times 0.2 = 0.128$.

The correct answer is B.

106. According to a survey of 200 people, 60 enjoy skiing and 80 enjoy skating. If the number of people who enjoy neither skiing nor skating is 2 times the number of people who enjoy both skiing and skating, how many people surveyed enjoy neither skiing nor skating?

(A) 20

(B) 40

(C) 50

(D) 80

(E) 120

Algebra Sets

Determine the number of people who enjoy neither skiing nor skating.

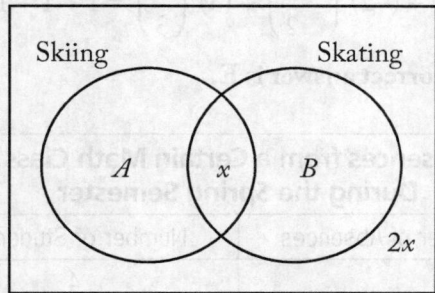

Consider the Venn diagram on the previous page, where A represents the number of people who enjoy skiing only, B represents the number of people who enjoy skating only, and x is the number of people who enjoy both skiing and skating. As stated, the number of people who enjoy neither is twice the number who enjoy both, so $2x$ represents the number of people who enjoy neither skiing nor skating. From the given information, it follows that $60 = A + x$, $80 = B + x$, and $200 = A + x + B + 2x = (A + x) + (B + x) + x$. By substitution, $200 = 60 + 80 + x$, so $x = 60$ and $2x = 120$.

The correct answer is E.

$$m \oplus p = n$$
$$n \oplus r = m$$
$$n \oplus q = q$$
$$p \oplus q = p$$
$$q \oplus p = r$$

107. If the relations shown hold for the operation $\oplus$ and the numbers m, n, p, q, and r, then $[(m \oplus p) \oplus q] \oplus p =$

(A) m
(B) n
(C) p
(D) q
(E) r

Algebra Formulas

$$[(m \oplus p) \oplus q] \oplus p \quad \text{given}$$
$$[n \oplus q] \oplus p \quad m \oplus p = n$$
$$q \oplus p \quad n \oplus q = q$$
$$r \quad q \oplus p = r$$

The correct answer is E.

108. To rent a tractor, it costs a total of x dollars for the first 24 hours, plus y dollars per hour for each hour in excess of 24 hours. Which of the following represents the cost, in dollars, to rent a tractor for 36 hours?

(A) $x + 12y$
(B) $x + 36y$
(C) $12x + y$
(D) $24x + 12y$
(E) $24x + 36y$

Algebra Algebraic Expressions

Determine the cost to rent a tractor for 36 hours if the cost is x dollars for the first 24 hours and y dollars for each hour in excess of 24 hours.

The cost will be x dollars for the first 24 hours plus y dollars for each of $36 - 24 = 12$ hours. Thus, the total cost of renting the tractor for 36 hours is $(x + 12y)$ dollars.

The correct answer is A.

109. If the mass of 1 cubic centimeter of a certain substance is 7.3 grams, what is the mass, in kilograms, of 1 cubic meter of this substance? (1 cubic meter = 1,000,000 cubic centimeters; 1 kilogram = 1,000 grams)

(A) 0.0073
(B) 0.73
(C) 7.3
(D) 7,300
(E) 7,300,000

Arithmetic Measurement Conversion

Determine the mass, in kilograms, of 1 cubic meter of a substance if the mass of 1 cubic centimeter of this substance is 7.3 grams.

1 cubic meter is 1,000,000 cubic centimeters and each cubic centimeter has a mass of 7.3 grams, so 1 cubic meter has a mass of $7.3(1,000,000) = 7,300,000$ grams. Then, since 1 kilogram = 1,000 grams,

$$7,300,000 \text{ grams} = \frac{7,300,000}{1,000}$$

$$= 7,300 \text{ kilograms.}$$

The correct answer is D.

110. If $z \neq 0$ and $z + \dfrac{1 - 2z^2}{z} = \dfrac{w}{z}$, then $w =$

(A) $z + 1$

(B) $z^2 + 1$

(C) $-z^2 + 1$

(D) $-z^2 + z + 1$

(E) $-2z^2 + 1$

Algebra Simplifying Algebraic Expressions

Multiplying both sides of $\dfrac{w}{z} = z + \dfrac{1 - 2z^2}{z}$ by z

gives $w = z\left(z + \dfrac{1 - 2z^2}{z}\right) = z^2 + (1 - 2z^2) = 1 - z^2$.

The correct answer is C.

111. For all real numbers a, b, c, d, e, and f, the operation Θ is defined by the equation $(a, b, c) \Theta (d, e, f) = ad + be + cf$. What is the value of $(1, -2, 3) \Theta \left(1, -\dfrac{1}{2}, \dfrac{1}{3}\right)$?

(A) -1

(B) $\dfrac{5}{6}$

(C) 1

(D) $\dfrac{5}{2}$

(E) 3

Algebra Formulas

By definition, $(1, -2, 3) \Theta \left(1, -\dfrac{1}{2}, \dfrac{1}{3}\right) =$

$(1)(1) + (-2)\left(-\dfrac{1}{2}\right) + (3)\left(\dfrac{1}{3}\right) = 1 + 1 + 1 = 3.$

The correct answer is E.

Absences from a Certain Math Class During the Spring Semester	
Number of Absences	Number of Students
0	4
1	3
2	10
3	3
4	5
5 or more	3

112. The table above shows the distribution of the number of absences from a certain Math class during the spring semester. For those students who had at least 1 absence, what was the median number of absences?

(A) 1.5

(B) 2

(C) 2.5

(D) 3

(E) 3.5

Arithmetic Statistics

The table shows that the total number of students who each had at least 1 absence was $3 + 10 + 3 + 5 + 3 = 24$. To find the median number of absences for these 24 students, we list the students' numbers of absences from least to greatest, giving us a list of 24 numbers (one per student): three 1s, ten 2s, three 3s, five 4s, and three numbers that are each at least 5. Since 24 is even, the median is the mean of the two middle numbers in the list—the twelfth number and the thirteenth number. These numbers are both 2s. So, 2 is the median.

The correct answer is B.

113. If $\dfrac{x}{y} = \dfrac{c}{d}$ and $\dfrac{d}{c} = \dfrac{b}{a}$, which of the following must be true?

   I. $\dfrac{y}{x} = \dfrac{b}{a}$

   II. $\dfrac{x}{a} = \dfrac{y}{b}$

   III. $\dfrac{y}{a} = \dfrac{x}{b}$

   (A) I only
   (B) II only
   (C) I and II only
   (D) I and III only
   (E) I, II, and III

Algebra Ratio and Proportion

Equation I is true:

$$\dfrac{x}{y} = \dfrac{c}{d} \qquad \text{given}$$

$$\dfrac{y}{x} = \dfrac{d}{c} \qquad \text{take reciprocals}$$

$$\dfrac{d}{c} = \dfrac{b}{a} \qquad \text{given}$$

$$\dfrac{y}{x} = \dfrac{b}{a} \qquad \text{use last two equations}$$

Equation II is true:

$$\dfrac{y}{x} = \dfrac{b}{a} \qquad \text{Equation I (shown true)}$$

$$y = \dfrac{bx}{a} \qquad \text{multiply both sides by } x$$

$$\dfrac{y}{b} = \dfrac{x}{a} \qquad \text{divide both sides by } b$$

Equation III is false, since otherwise it would follow that:

$$y = \dfrac{bx}{a} \qquad \text{from earlier}$$

$$\dfrac{y}{a} = \dfrac{bx}{a^2} \qquad \text{divide both sides by } a$$

$$\dfrac{x}{b} = \dfrac{bx}{a^2} \qquad \text{use Equation III (assumed true)}$$

$$x = \dfrac{b^2 x}{a^2} \qquad \text{multiply both sides by } b$$

From this it follows that Equation III will hold only if $\dfrac{b^2}{a^2} = 1$, which can be false. For example, if $x = a = c = 1$ and $y = b = d = 2$ (a choice of values for which $\dfrac{x}{y} = \dfrac{c}{d}$ and $\dfrac{d}{c} = \dfrac{b}{a}$ are true), then $\dfrac{b^2}{a^2} \neq 1$ and Equation III is $\dfrac{2}{1} = \dfrac{1}{2}$, which is false.

The correct answer is C.

114. If [x] denotes the least integer greater than or equal to x and $\left[\dfrac{x}{2}\right] = 0$, which of the following could be the value of x?

   (A) -2
   (B) $-\dfrac{3}{2}$
   (C) $\dfrac{1}{2}$
   (D) 1
   (E) 2

Arithmetic Formulas

Since the least integer greater than or equal to $\dfrac{x}{2}$ is 0, then $-1 < \dfrac{x}{2} \leq 0$. Thus, $-2 < x \leq 0$. Among the 5 options, $-\dfrac{3}{2}$ is the only number greater than -2 and less than or equal to 0, and therefore the only one that could be the value of x.

The correct answer is B.

115. If $a(a + 2) = 24$ and $b(b + 2) = 24$, where $a \neq b$, then
$a + b =$

   (A) −48
   (B) −2
   (C)   2
   (D) 46
   (E) 48

Algebra Second-Degree Equations

$a(a + 2) = 24$ given
$a^2 + 2a = 24$ use distributive property
$a^2 + 2a - 24 = 0$ subtract 24 from both sides
$(a + 6)(a - 4) = 0$ factor

So, $a + 6 = 0$, which means that $a = -6$, or
$a - 4 = 0$, which means $a = 4$. The equation with
the variable b has the same solutions, and so
$b = -6$ or $b = 4$.

Since $a \neq b$, then $a = -6$ and $b = 4$, which means
$a + b = -6 + 4 = -2$, or $a = 4$ and $b = -6$, which
means that $a + b = 4 + (-6) = -2$

The correct answer is B.

116. In a recent election, Ms. Robbins received 8,000 votes cast by independent voters, that is, voters not registered with a specific political party. She also received 10 percent of the votes cast by those voters registered with a political party. If N is the total number of votes cast in the election and 40 percent of the votes cast were cast by independent voters, which of the following represents the number of votes that Ms. Robbins received?

   (A) $0.06N + 3,200$
   (B) $0.1N + 7,200$
   (C) $0.4N + 7,200$
   (D) $0.1N + 8,000$
   (E) $0.06N + 8,000$

Algebra Percents

If N represents the total number of votes cast and 40% of the votes cast were cast by independent voters, then 60% of the votes cast, or $0.6N$ votes, were cast by voters registered with a political party. Ms. Robbins received 10% of these, and so Ms. Robbins received $(0.10)(0.6N) = 0.06N$ votes

cast by voters registered with a political party. Thus, Ms. Robbins received $0.06N$ votes cast by voters registered with a political party and 8,000 votes cast by independent voters, so she received $0.06N + 8,000$ votes in all.

The correct answer is E.

117. The profit P, in dollars, for any given month at a certain company is defined by $P = I - C$, where I represents total income, in dollars, and C represents total costs, in dollars, for the month. For each of the first 4 months of the year, $C = I + 32,000$; and for each of the next 3 months, $I = C + 36,000$. If $I = C + 10,000$ for each of the 5 remaining months of the year, what was the company's total profit for the 12-month year?

   (A) $10,000
   (B) $30,000
   (C) $40,000
   (D) $50,000
   (E) $70,000

Arithmetic Applied Problems

For each of the first 4 months, total costs exceeded total income by $32,000, and hence for each of 4 months total profit was −$32,000. Also, for each of the next 3 months, total income exceeded total costs by $36,000, and hence for each of 3 months total profit was $36,000. Finally, for each of the remaining 5 months, total income exceeded total costs by $10,000, and hence for each of 5 months total profit was $10,000. Therefore, the total profit for the 12-month year was $4(-\$32,000) + 3(\$36,000) + 5(\$10,000) = \$30,000$.

Alternatively, the given equations can be easily manipulated to obtain the values of $I - C$ for each month, as shown below.

Given Equation	Value of $I - C$	Number of Months	Net Profit
$C = I + 32,000$	$I - C = -32,000$	4	−$128,000
$I = C + 36,000$	$I - C = 36,000$	3	$108,000
$I = C + 10,000$	$I - C = 10,000$	5	$50,000

Adding the values in the right-most column gives the total profit for the 12-month year: –$128,000 + $108,000 + $50,000 = $30,000.

The correct answer is B.

118. A manufacturer makes and sells 2 products, P and Q. The revenue from the sale of each unit of P is $20.00 and the revenue from the sale of each unit of Q is $17.00. Last year the manufacturer sold twice as many units of Q as P. What was the manufacturer's average (arithmetic mean) revenue per unit sold of these 2 products last year?

    (A) $28.50
    (B) $27.00
    (C) $19.00
    (D) $18.50
    (E) $18.00

Arithmetic Statistics

Let x represent the number of units of Product P the manufacturer sold last year. Then $2x$ represents the number of units of Product Q the manufacturer sold, and $x + 2x = 3x$ represents the total number of units of Products P and Q the manufacturer sold. The total revenue from the sale of Products P and Q was $\$(20x) + \$(17(2x)) = \$(54x)$, so the average revenue per unit sold was $\dfrac{\$(54x)}{3x} = \$18$.

The correct answer is E.

119. A worker carries jugs of liquid soap from a production line to a packing area, carrying 4 jugs per trip. If the jugs are packed into cartons that hold 7 jugs each, how many jugs are needed to fill the last partially filled carton after the worker has made 17 trips?

    (A) 1
    (B) 2
    (C) 4
    (D) 5
    (E) 6

Arithmetic Remainders

Carrying 4 jugs per trip, the worker carries a total of 4(17) = 68 jugs in 17 trips. At 7 jugs per carton, these jugs will completely fill 9 cartons

with 5 jugs left over since (9)(7) + 5 = 68. To fill the 10th carton, 7 – 5 = 2 jugs are needed.

The correct answer is B.

120. Last year a state senate consisting of only Republican and Democrat members had 20 more Republican members than Democrat members. This year the senate has the same number of members as last year, but it has 2 fewer Republican members than last year. If this year the number of Republican members is $\dfrac{2}{3}$ the number of senate members, how many members does the senate have this year?

    (A) 33
    (B) 36
    (C) 42
    (D) 45
    (E) 48

Algebra First-Degree Equations

Let D be the number of Democrat members last year. Then $D + 20$ is the number of Republican members last year and $(D + 20) – 2 = D + 18$ is the number of Republican members this year. Since the total number of members this year is the same as last year, it follows that there are 2 more Democrat members this year than last year, and so the number of Democrat members this year is $D + 2$ and the total number of members this year is $2D + 20$. Using the fact that this year the number of Republican members is $\dfrac{2}{3}$ the total number of members, the value of D can be found.

$$D + 18 = \frac{2}{3}(2D + 20) \quad \text{given}$$
$$3(D + 18) = 2(2D + 20) \quad \text{multiply both sides by 3}$$
$$3D + 54 = 4D + 40 \quad \text{distributive law}$$
$$D = 14 \quad \begin{array}{l}\text{subtract both } 3D \text{ and} \\ 40 \text{ from both sides}\end{array}$$

Therefore, the total number of members this year is $2D + 20 = 2(14) + 20 = 48$.

The correct answer is E.

121. Sam has $800 in his account. He will deposit $1 in his account one week from now, $2 two weeks from now, and each week thereafter he will deposit an amount that is $1 greater than the amount that he deposited one week before. If there are no other transactions, how much money will Sam have in his account 50 weeks from now?

(A) $850
(B) $1,200
(C) $1,675
(D) $2,075
(E) $3,350

Arithmetic Series and Sequences

Determine the amount Sam will have in his account after 50 weeks if the account starts with $800 and Sam deposits $1 more each week than he deposited the week before.

Sam's deposits over the 50-week period will be $1 + 2 + 3 + \ldots + 48 + 49 + 50 = (1 + 50) + (2 + 49) + (3 + 48) + \ldots + (25 + 26) = (25)(51) = \$1,275$. Thus, after 50 weeks Sam will have $800 + $1,275 = $2,075.

The correct answer is D.

122. A certain state's milk production was 980 million pounds in 2007 and 2.7 billion pounds in 2014. Approximately how many more million <u>gallons</u> of milk did the state produce in 2014 than in 2007? (1 billion = 10^9 and 1 gallon = 8.6 pounds.)

(A)   100
(B)   200
(C)   1,700
(D)   8,200
(E)   14,800

Arithmetic Measurement Conversion

Using 2.7 billion = 2,700 million, the amount of increase in millions of gallons can be calculated as follows.

The amount of increase is:
(2,700 − 980) million pounds = 1,720 million pounds

To convert pounds into gallons:

$$(1{,}720 \text{ million } \cancel{\text{pounds}})\left(\frac{1 \text{ gallon}}{8.6 \ \cancel{\text{pounds}}}\right)$$
$$= 200 \text{ million gallons}$$

The correct answer is B.

123. Working simultaneously and independently at an identical constant rate, 4 machines of a certain type can produce a total of x units of Product P in 6 days. How many of these machines, working simultaneously and independently at this constant rate, can produce a total of 3x units of Product P in 4 days?

(A)   24
(B)   18
(C)   16
(D)   12
(E)   8

Algebra Applied Problems

Define a *machine day* as 1 machine working for 1 day. Then 4 machines each working 6 days is equivalent to (4)(6) = 24 machine days. Thus, x units of Product P were produced in 24 machine days, and 3x units of Product P will require (3)(24) = 72 machine days, which is equivalent to $\frac{72}{4} = 18$ machines working independently and simultaneously for 4 days.

The correct answer is B.

124. The symbol Δ denotes one of the four arithmetic operations: addition, subtraction, multiplication, or division. If 6 Δ 3 ≤ 3, which of the following must be true?

I.   2 Δ 2 = 0
II.   2 Δ 2 = 1
III.   4 Δ 2 = 2

(A)   I only
(B)   II only
(C)   III only
(D)   I and II only
(E)   I, II, and III

Arithmetic Operations with Integers

If Δ represents addition, subtraction, multiplication, or division, then $6 \Delta 3$ is equal to either $6 + 3 = 9$, or $6 - 3 = 3$, or $6 \times 3 = 18$, or $6 \div 3 = 2$. Since it is given that $6 \Delta 3 \leq 3$, Δ represents either subtraction or division.

Statement I is true for subtraction since $2 - 2 = 0$ but not true for division since $2 \div 2 = 1$.

Statement II is not true for subtraction since $2 - 2 = 0$ but is true for division since $2 \div 2 = 1$.

Statement III is true for subtraction since $4 - 2 = 2$ and is true for division since $4 \div 2 = 2$. Therefore, only Statement III must be true.

The correct answer is C.

125. If $mn \neq 0$ and 25 percent of n equals $37\frac{1}{2}$ percent of m, what is the value of $\dfrac{12n}{m}$?

(A)   18

(B) $\dfrac{32}{3}$

(C)   8

(D)   3

(E) $\dfrac{9}{8}$

Algebra Percents; First-Degree Equations

It is given that $(25\%)n = (37.5\%)m$, or $0.25n = 0.375m$. The value of $\dfrac{12n}{m}$ can be found by first finding the value of $\dfrac{n}{m}$ and then multiplying the result by 12. Doing this gives $\dfrac{12n}{m} = \left(\dfrac{0.375}{0.25}\right)(12) = 18$. Alternatively, the numbers involved allow for a series of simple equation transformations to be carried out, such as the following:

$0.25n = 0.375m$	given
$25n = 37.5m$	multiply both sides by 100
$50n = 75m$	multiply both sides by 2
$2n = 3m$	divide both sides by 25
$12n = 18m$	multiply both sides by 6
$\dfrac{12n}{m} = 18$	divide both sides by m

The correct answer is A.

126. N and M are each 3-digit integers. Each of the numbers 1, 2, 3, 6, 7, and 8 is a digit of either N or M. What is the smallest possible positive difference between N and M?

(A)   29

(B)   49

(C)   58

(D)   113

(E)   131

Arithmetic Applied Problems

Suppose $N > M$. Let's represent N with its digits abc and M with its digits def, where each of a, b, c, d, e, and f is a different one of the numbers 1, 2, 3, 6, 7, or 8. We want to assign these numbers to the letters to minimize the difference between abc and def. To do this, first we minimize the difference between a and d. That is, $a - d$ must equal 1. Thus, $\{a, d\}$ must be either $\{2, 1\}$, $\{3, 2\}$, $\{7, 6\}$, or $\{8, 7\}$. Next, to make the larger number abc as close as possible to the smaller number def, we assign the smallest available digit to b and the largest to e. That is, we set $b = 1$ and $e = 8$. Since each digit can occur only once, this means $\{a, d\}$ cannot contain 8 or 1. That means $\{a, d\}$ cannot be $\{2, 1\}$ or $\{8, 7\}$, so it must be either $\{3, 2\}$ or $\{7, 6\}$. Finally, the last two digits f and c must be whichever two digits have not yet been assigned as values of a, b, d, or e. We again minimize the difference between the larger number abc and the smaller number def by assigning the smaller of these two remaining digits to c and the larger to f, so $f > c$. Given these constraints, we find that either $N = 316$ and $M = 287$ or else $N = 712$ and $M = 683$. In either case, $N - M = 29$. Therefore, 29 is the smallest possible positive difference between N and M.

The correct answer is A.

Technique	Percent of Consumers
Television ads	35%
Coupons	22%
Store displays	18%
Samples	15%

127. The table shows partial results of a survey in which consumers were asked to indicate which one of six promotional techniques most influenced their decision to buy a new food product. Of those consumers who indicated one of the four techniques listed, what fraction indicated either coupons or store displays?

(A) $\dfrac{2}{7}$

(B) $\dfrac{1}{3}$

(C) $\dfrac{2}{5}$

(D) $\dfrac{4}{9}$

(E) $\dfrac{1}{2}$

Arithmetic Percents; Ratio and Proportion

Let T be the total number of consumers who were asked. Then the table shows $35\% + 22\% + 18\% + 15\% = 90\%$ of this total, or $0.9T$ consumers. Also, the number of consumers who indicated either coupons or store displays was $0.22T + 0.18T = 0.4T$. Therefore, the number of consumers who indicated either coupons or store displays divided by the number of consumers shown in the table is $\dfrac{0.4T}{0.9T} = \dfrac{4}{9}$.

The correct answer is D.

128. If 65 percent of a certain firm's employees are full-time and if there are 5,100 more full-time employees than part-time employees, how many employees does the firm have?

(A) 8,250
(B) 10,200
(C) 11,050
(D) 16,500
(E) 17,000

Algebra Simultaneous Equations

Let T represent the total number of employees the firm has; F, the number of full-time employees; and P, the number of part-time employees. Since 65 percent of the firm's employees are full-time, it follows that 35 percent are part-time. Thus, $F = 0.65T$ and $P = 0.35T$. However, $F = P + 5,100$, so $0.65T = 0.35T + 5,100$, so $0.30T = 5,100$, and $T = \dfrac{5,100}{0.30} = 17,000$.

The correct answer is E.

129. The cost C, in dollars, to remove p percent of a certain pollutant from a pond is estimated by using the formula $C = \dfrac{100,000p}{100 - p}$. According to this estimate, how much more would it cost to remove 90 percent of the pollutant from the pond than it would cost to remove 80 percent of the pollutant?

(A) $500,000
(B) $100,000
(C) $50,000
(D) $10,000
(E) $5,000

Algebra; Arithmetic Simplifying Algebraic Expressions; Operations on Rational Numbers

Removing 90% of the pollutant from the pond would cost $\dfrac{(100,000)(90)}{100 - 90} = \dfrac{9,000,000}{10} = 900,000$ dollars, and removing 80% of the pollutant would cost $\dfrac{(100,000)(80)}{100 - 80} = \dfrac{8,000,000}{20} = 400,000$ dollars. The difference is, then, $900,000 - 400,000 = 500,000$.

The correct answer is A.

130. If $xy \neq 0$ and $x^2y^2 - xy = 6$, which of the following could be y in terms of x?

    I. $\dfrac{1}{2x}$

    II. $-\dfrac{2}{x}$

    III. $\dfrac{3}{x}$

    (A) I only
    (B) II only
    (C) I and II
    (D) I and III
    (E) II and III

Algebra Second-Degree Equations

$$x^2y^2 - xy = 6 \quad \text{given}$$
$$x^2y^2 - xy - 6 = 0 \quad \text{subtract 6 from both sides}$$
$$(xy + 2)(xy - 3) = 0 \quad \text{factor}$$

So, $xy + 2 = 0$, which means $xy = -2$ and $y = -\dfrac{2}{x}$, or $xy - 3 = 0$, which means that $xy = 3$ and $y = \dfrac{3}{x}$. Thus, y in terms of x could be given by the expressions in II or III.

The correct answer is E.

131. If the positive number d is the standard deviation of n, k, and p, then the standard deviation of $n + 1$, $k + 1$, and $p + 1$ is

    (A) $d + 3$
    (B) $d + 1$
    (C) $6d$
    (D) $3d$
    (E) d

Arithmetic Statistics

To find the standard deviation of the numbers in a set, we find their arithmetic mean, then find the differences between the mean and each number in the set, then square each difference, then average the squared differences, and finally find the nonnegative square root of this average. Let x be the mean of n, k, and p. Then $x + 1$ is the mean of $n + 1$, $k + 1$, and $p + 1$. The differences between x and each of n, k, and p exactly equal the differences between $x + 1$ and each of $n + 1$, $k + 1$, and $p + 1$,

respectively. Thus, the squares of the differences, the average of the squared differences, and the nonnegative square root of that average are exactly the same for $\{n, k, p\}$ as for $\{n + 1, k + 1, p + 1\}$. Therefore, the standard deviation d of n, k, and p is also the standard deviation of $n + 1$, $k + 1$, and $p + 1$.

The correct answer is E.

132. In a certain high school, 80 percent of the seniors are taking calculus, and 60 percent of the seniors who are taking calculus are also taking physics. If 10 percent of the seniors are taking neither calculus nor physics, what percent of the seniors are taking physics?

    (A) 40%
    (B) 42%
    (C) 48%
    (D) 58%
    (E) 80%

Arithmetic Sets

Determine what percent of the seniors at a certain high school are taking physics.

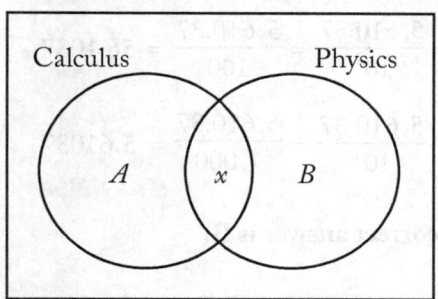

Consider the Venn diagram on the previous page, where A represents the percent of the seniors who are taking calculus only, B represents the percent of the seniors who are taking physics only, and x is the percent of the seniors who are taking both calculus and physics. As stated, 80 percent of the seniors are taking calculus, so $A + x = 0.8$, and 60 percent of the seniors taking calculus are taking physics, so $x = (0.8)(0.6) = 0.48$. Also, $A + x + B = 0.9$ since 10 percent of the seniors are taking neither calculus nor physics. It follows that $B = 0.9 - (A + x) = 0.9 - 0.8 = 0.1$. Therefore, the percent of the seniors who are taking physics is given by $B + x = 0.1 + 0.48 = 0.58$ or 58 percent.

The correct answer is D.

133. If the units digit of $\dfrac{5,610.37}{10^k}$ is 6, what is the value of k?

  (A) 3
  (B) 2
  (C) 1
  (D) −1
  (E) −2

Arithmetic Exponents

As shown in the table below, the units digit of $\dfrac{5,610.37}{10^k}$ is 6 when $k = 2$.

$$\frac{5,610.37}{10^{-2}} = \frac{5,610.37}{0.01} = 561,037$$

$$\frac{5,610.37}{10^{-1}} = \frac{5,610.37}{0.1} = 56,103.7$$

$$\frac{5,610.37}{10^{0}} = \frac{5,610.37}{1} = 5,610.37$$

$$\frac{5,610.37}{10^{1}} = \frac{5,610.37}{10} = 561.037$$

$$\frac{5,610.37}{10^{2}} = \frac{5,610.37}{100} = 56.1037$$

$$\frac{5,610.37}{10^{3}} = \frac{5,610.37}{1,000} = 5.61037$$

The correct answer is B.

134. Three printing presses, R, S, and T, working together at their respective constant rates, can do a certain printing job in 4 hours. S and T, working together at their respective constant rates, can do the same job in 5 hours. How many hours would it take R, working alone at its constant rate, to do the same job?

  (A) 8
  (B) 10
  (C) 12
  (D) 15
  (E) 20

Algebra Applied Problems

Let r be the portion of the job that printing press R, working alone, completes in 1 hour, and let s and t be the corresponding portions, respectively, for printing press S and printing press T. From the given information, it follows that $r + s + t = \dfrac{1}{4}$ and $s + t = \dfrac{1}{5}$. Subtracting these two equations gives $r = \dfrac{1}{4} - \dfrac{1}{5} = \dfrac{1}{20}$. It follows that printing press R, working alone, will complete $\dfrac{1}{20}$ of the job in 1 hour, and therefore printing press R, working alone, will complete the job in 20 hours.

The correct answer is E.

Results of a Poll

Company	Number Who Own Stock in the Company
AT&T	30
IBM	48
GM	54
FORD	75
US Air	83

135. In a poll, 200 subscribers to *Financial Magazine X* indicated which of five specific companies they own stock in. The results are shown in the table above. If 15 of the 200 own stock in both IBM and AT&T, how many of those polled own stock in neither company?

  (A) 63
  (B) 93
  (C) 107
  (D) 122
  (E) 137

Arithmetic Sets; Interpretation of Tables

Since 48 of the 200 subscribers polled own stock in IBM and 15 of these 48 subscribers also own stock in AT&T, it follows that $48 - 15 = 33$ subscribers own stock in IBM but not in AT&T, as shown in the Venn diagram below. Similarly, $30 - 15 = 15$ of the 200 subscribers own stock in AT&T but not in IBM. Therefore, if n is the number of those polled who do not own stock in either IBM or AT&T, then $33 + 15 + 15 + n = 200$, or $n = 137$.

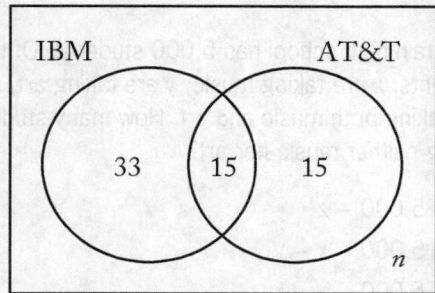

The correct answer is E.

136. The sum of all the integers k such that $-26 < k < 24$ is

(A)   0
(B)   −2
(C)   −25
(D)   −49
(E)   −51

Arithmetic Operations on Integers

In the sum of all integers k such that $-26 < k < 24$, the positive integers from 1 through 23 can be paired with the negative integers from −1 through −23. The sum of these pairs is 0 because $a + (-a) = 0$ for all integers a. Therefore, the sum of all integers k such that $-26 < k < 24$ is $-25 + (-24) + (23)(0) = -49$.

The correct answer is D.

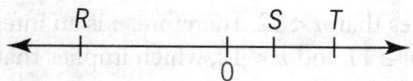

137. The number line shown contains three points R, S, and T, whose coordinates have absolute values r, s, and t, respectively. Which of the following equals the average (arithmetic mean) of the coordinates of the points R, S, and T?

(A) s

(B) $s + t - r$

(C) $\dfrac{r - s - t}{3}$

(D) $\dfrac{r + s + t}{3}$

(E) $\dfrac{s + t - r}{3}$

Arithmetic Absolute Value; Number Line

Because point R is to the left of 0 on the number line, the coordinate of R is negative. It is given that r is the absolute value of the coordinate of R, and so the coordinate of R is $-r$. Because points S and T are to the right of 0 on the number line, their coordinates are positive. It is given that s and t are the absolute values of the coordinates of S and T, and so the coordinates of S and T are s and t. The arithmetic mean of the coordinates of R, S, and T is $\dfrac{s + t - r}{3}$.

The correct answer is E.

138. Mark and Ann together were allocated n boxes of cookies to sell for a club project. Mark sold 10 boxes less than n and Ann sold 2 boxes less than n. If Mark and Ann have each sold at least one box of cookies, but together they have sold less than n boxes, what is the value of n?

(A)   11
(B)   12
(C)   13
(D)   14
(E)   15

Algebra Inequalities

Mark sold $n - 10$ boxes and Ann sold $n - 2$ boxes. Because each person sold at least one box, it follows that $n - 10 \geq 1$ and $n - 2 \geq 1$, which implies that $n \geq 11$. On the other hand, together they sold less than n boxes, so $(n - 10) + (n - 2) < n$, which implies that $n < 12$. Therefore, n is an integer such that $n \geq 11$ and $n < 12$, which implies that $n = 11$.

The correct answer is A.

$$\begin{array}{r} 3P5 \\ + 4QR \\ \hline 8S4 \end{array}$$

139. In the correctly worked addition problem shown, P, Q, R, and S are digits. If $Q = 2P$, which of the following could be the value of S?

(A)   3
(B)   4
(C)   5
(D)   7
(E)   9

Arithmetic Place Value

Step 1: Analysis of the units column.

By considering the sum of the unit digits, $5 + R = 4$ or $5 + R = 14$. Since $R \geq 0$, we have $5 + R \geq 5$, and thus $5 + R = 4$ is not possible. Therefore, $5 + R = 14$. It follows that $R = 9$ and 1 is carried to the tens column.

Step 2: Analysis of the tens and hundreds columns.

Since $3 + 4 = 7$ and the hundreds digit of $8S4$ is 8, it follows that 1 must have been carried from the tens column to the hundreds column. Therefore, the sum of the tens digits must be $S + 10$, and hence $1 + P + Q = S + 10$, where the 1 was carried from the units column.

Step 3: Apply the assumption $Q = 2P$ to rule out answer choices B, C, and D.

Substituting $2P$ for Q in the equation $1 + P + Q = S + 10$ gives $1 + P + 2P = S + 10$, which can be rewritten as $S = 3P - 9 = 3(P - 3)$. This shows that S is divisible by 3, and therefore, answer choices B, C, and D CANNOT be correct.

Step 4: Show that $S = 9$ is not possible.

If $S = 9$, then we have $9 = 3(P - 3)$. Solving this equation gives $P = 6$. However, from $Q = 2P$, it follows that $Q = 12$, which is not a digit.

Therefore, $S = 9$ is not possible and answer choice E is NOT correct.

The only possibility remaining is $S = 3$. Although it is not necessary to verify that $S = 3$ is consistent, one can show that $S = 3$ leads to the following for the sum:

$$\begin{array}{r} 345 \\ + 489 \\ \hline 834 \end{array}$$

The correct answer is A.

140. A certain high school has 5,000 students. Of these students, x are taking music, y are taking art, and z are taking both music and art. How many students are taking neither music nor art?

(A) $5{,}000 - z$
(B) $5{,}000 - x - y$
(C) $5{,}000 - x + z$
(D) $5{,}000 - x - y - z$
(E) $5{,}000 - x - y + z$

Algebra Sets

Since x students are taking music, y students are taking art, and z students are taking both music and art, the number of students taking only music is $x - z$, and the number of students taking only art is $y - z$, as illustrated by the Venn diagram below.

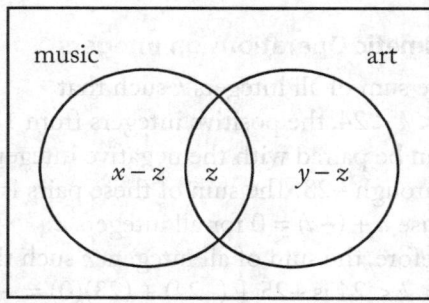

Therefore, the number of students taking neither music nor art is $5{,}000 - [(x - z) + z + (y - z)] = 5{,}000 - x - y + z$.

The correct answer is E.

141. Each person who attended a company meeting was either a stockholder in the company, an employee of the company, or both. If 62 percent of those who attended the meeting were stockholders and 47 percent were employees, what percent were stockholders who were NOT employees?

    (A) 34%
    (B) 38%
    (C) 45%
    (D) 53%
    (E) 62%

Arithmetic Sets

Let M represent the number of meeting attendees. Then, since 62% of M or $0.62M$ were stockholders and 47% of M or $0.47M$ were employees, it follows that $0.62M + 0.47M = 1.09M$ were either stockholders, employees, or both. Since $1.09M$ exceeds M, the excess $1.09M - M = 0.09M$ must be the number of attendees who were both stockholders and employees, leaving the rest $0.62M - 0.09M = 0.53M$, or 53%, of the meeting attendees to be stockholders but not employees.

The correct answer is D.

142. If M is the least common multiple of 90, 196, and 300, which of the following is not a factor of M?

    (A) 600
    (B) 700
    (C) 900
    (D) 2,100
    (E) 4,900

Arithmetic Applied Problems

Let x be the least common multiple of 90, 196, and 300. To find x, first use prime factorization to express 90, 196, and 300 as products of prime factors: $90 = 2 \times 3 \times 3 \times 5$, while $196 = 2 \times 2 \times 7 \times 7$, and $300 = 2 \times 2 \times 3 \times 5 \times 5$. Then x is the smallest number with a prime factorization including at least as many 2s, 3s, 5s, and 7s as are in the prime factorization of any one of 90, 196, and 300: that is, $x = 2 \times 2 \times 3 \times 3 \times 5 \times 5 \times 7 \times 7$. Since this prime factorization includes two 2s, two 3s, two 5s, and two 7s, any factor of x will

have a prime factorization that includes only at most two 2s, at most two 3s, at most two 5s, and at most two 7s. Thus, $600 = 2 \times 2 \times 2 \times 3 \times 5 \times 5$ can't be a factor of x, because 600 has three 2s among its prime factors whereas x only has two 2s. But x's factors do include 700 ($2 \times 2 \times 5 \times 5 \times 7$), 900 ($2 \times 2 \times 3 \times 3 \times 5 \times 5$), 2,100 ($2 \times 2 \times 3 \times 5 \times 5 \times 7$), and 4,900 ($2 \times 2 \times 5 \times 5 \times 7 \times 7$), because x includes at least as many 2s, 3s, 5s, and 7s in its prime factorization as any one of these numbers does.

The correct answer is A.

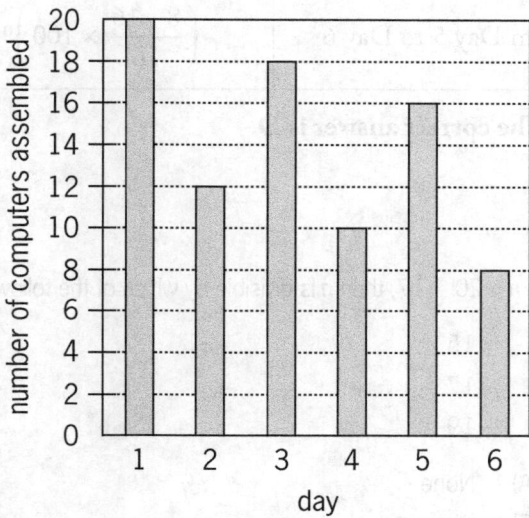

143. The graph shows the number of computers assembled during each of 6 consecutive days. From what day to the next day was the percent change in the number of computers assembled the greatest in magnitude?

    (A) From Day 1 to Day 2
    (B) From Day 2 to Day 3
    (C) From Day 3 to Day 4
    (D) From Day 4 to Day 5
    (E) From Day 5 to Day 6

Arithmetic Percents

The following table shows the percent change from each day to the next and the magnitude of the percent change.

Time Period	Percent Change	Magnitude of Percent Change
From Day 1 to Day 2	$\left(\dfrac{12-20}{20}\times 100\right)\% = \left(-\dfrac{8}{20}\times 100\right)\% = -40\%$	40
From Day 2 to Day 3	$\left(\dfrac{18-12}{12}\times 100\right)\% = \left(\dfrac{6}{12}\times 100\right)\% = 50\%$	50
From Day 3 to Day 4	$\left(\dfrac{10-18}{18}\times 100\right)\% = \left(-\dfrac{8}{18}\times 100\right)\% \approx -44\%$	44
From Day 4 to Day 5	$\left(\dfrac{16-10}{10}\times 100\right)\% = \left(\dfrac{6}{10}\times 100\right)\% = 60\%$	60
From Day 5 to Day 6	$\left(\dfrac{8-16}{16}\times 100\right)\% = \left(-\dfrac{8}{16}\times 100\right)\% = -50\%$	50

The correct answer is D.

144. If $n = 20! + 17$, then n is divisible by which of the following?

   I.   15
   II.   17
   III. 19

   (A) None
   (B) I only
   (C) II only
   (D) I and II
   (E) II and III

Arithmetic Properties of Numbers

Because 20! is the product of all integers from
1 through 20, it follows that 20! is divisible
by each integer from 1 through 20. In particular,
20! is divisible by each of the integers 15, 17, and
19. Since 20! and 17 are both divisible by 17,
their sum is divisible by 17, and hence the correct
answer will include Statement II. If n were
divisible by 15, then $n - 20!$ would be divisible by
15. But $n - 20! = 17$, and 17 is not divisible by 15.

Therefore, the correct answer does not include
Statement I. If n were divisible by 19, then
$n - 20!$ would be divisible by 19. But $n - 20! =$
17, and 17 is not divisible by 19. Therefore, the
correct answer does not include Statement III.

The correct answer is C.

145. Exchange Rates in a Particular Year

   $1 = 5.3 francs
   $1 = 1.6 marks

An American dealer bought a table in Germany for
480 marks and sold the same table in France for
2,385 francs. What was the dealer's gross profit on
the two transactions in dollars?

   (A) $0
   (B) $50
   (C) $100
   (D) $150
   (E) $200

Arithmetic Measurement Conversion

Given that $1 = 1.6 marks, it follows that
$\dfrac{\$1}{1.6} = 1$ mark and 480 marks $= 480\left(\dfrac{\$1}{1.6}\right) =$
$300. Similarly, given that $1 = 5.3 francs,
it follows that $\dfrac{\$1}{5.3} = 1$ franc and
2,385 francs $= 2,385\left(\dfrac{\$1}{5.3}\right) = \$450$. The gross profit
on the two transactions is $450 - $300 = $150.

The correct answer is D.

146. The product of two negative numbers is 160. If the lesser of the two numbers is 4 less than twice the greater, what is the greater number?

    (A) −20
    (B) −16
    (C) −10
    (D) −8
    (E) −4

Algebra Second-Degree Equations

Let x and y be the two numbers, where x is the lesser of the two numbers and y is the number desired. From the given information, it follows that $xy = 160$ and $x = 2y - 4$, from which it follows that $(2y - 4)y = 160$. Dividing both sides of the last equation by 2 gives $(y - 2)y = 80$. Thus, 80 is to be written as a product of two negative numbers, one that is 2 less than the other. Trying simple factorizations of 80 quickly leads to the value of y: $(−40)(−2) = 80$, $(−20)(−4) = 80$, $(−10)(−8) = 80$. Therefore, $y = −8$. Note that because −8 is one of the answer choices, it is not necessary to ensure there are no other negative solutions to the equation $(y - 2)y = 80$.

Alternatively, $(y - 2)y = 80$ can be written as $y^2 - 2y - 80 = 0$. Factoring the left side gives $(y + 8)(y - 10) = 0$, and $y = −8$ is the only negative solution.

The correct answer is D.

147. According to a certain estimate, the depth $N(t)$, in centimeters, of the water in a certain tank at t hours past 2:00 in the morning is given by $N(t) = −20(t − 5)^2 + 500$ for $0 \leq t \leq 10$. According to this estimate, at what time in the morning does the depth of the water in the tank reach its maximum?

    (A) 5:30
    (B) 7:00
    (C) 7:30
    (D) 8:00
    (E) 9:00

Algebra Functions

When $t = 5$, the value of $−20(t − 5)^2 + 500$ is 500. For all values of t between 0 and 10, inclusive, except $t = 5$, the value of $−20(t − 5)^2$ is negative

and $−20(t − 5)^2 + 500 < 500$. Therefore, the tank reaches its maximum depth 5 hours after 2:00 in the morning, which is 7:00 in the morning.

The correct answer is B.

148. After driving to a riverfront parking lot, Bob plans to run south along the river, turn around, and return to the parking lot, running north along the same path. After running 3.25 miles south, he decides to run for only 50 minutes more. If Bob runs at a constant rate of 8 minutes per mile, how many miles farther south can he run and still be able to return to the parking lot in 50 minutes?

    (A) 1.5
    (B) 2.25
    (C) 3.0
    (D) 3.25
    (E) 4.75

Algebra Applied Problems

After running 3.25 miles south, Bob has been running for $(3.25 \text{ miles})\left(8 \dfrac{\text{minutes}}{\text{mile}}\right) = 26$ minutes. Thus, if t is the number of additional minutes that Bob can run south before turning around, then the number of minutes that Bob will run north, after turning around, will be $t + 26$. Since Bob will be running a total of 50 minutes after the initial 26 minutes of running, it follows that $t + (t + 26) = 50$, or $t = 12$. Therefore, Bob can run south an additional

$$\dfrac{12 \text{ minutes}}{8 \dfrac{\text{minutes}}{\text{mile}}} = 1.5 \text{ miles before turning around.}$$

The correct answer is A.

149. Alex deposited x dollars into a new account that earned 8 percent annual interest, compounded annually. One year later Alex deposited an additional x dollars into the account. If there were no other transactions and if the account contained w dollars at the end of two years, which of the following expresses x in terms of w?

    (A) $\dfrac{w}{1 + 1.08}$

    (B) $\dfrac{w}{1.08 + 1.16}$

(C) $\dfrac{w}{1.16+1.24}$

(D) $\dfrac{w}{1.08+(1.08)^2}$

(E) $\dfrac{w}{(1.08)^2+(1.08)^3}$

Algebra Applied Problems

At the end of the first year, the value of Alex's initial investment was $x(1.08)$ dollars, and after he deposited an additional x dollars into the account, its value was $[x(1.08)+x]$ dollars. At the end of the second year, the value was w dollars, where $w=[x(1.08)+x](1.08)=x(1.08)^2+x(1.08)=x[(1.08)^2+1.08]$. Thus, $x=\dfrac{w}{1.08+(1.08)^2}$.

The correct answer is D.

150. M is the sum of the reciprocals of the consecutive integers from 201 to 300, inclusive. Which of the following is true?

(A) $\dfrac{1}{3}<M<\dfrac{1}{2}$

(B) $\dfrac{1}{5}<M<\dfrac{1}{3}$

(C) $\dfrac{1}{7}<M<\dfrac{1}{5}$

(D) $\dfrac{1}{9}<M<\dfrac{1}{7}$

(E) $\dfrac{1}{12}<M<\dfrac{1}{9}$

Arithmetic Estimation

$M=$	$\dfrac{1}{201}+$	$\dfrac{1}{202}+$	$\dfrac{1}{203}+$	$\cdots+$	$\dfrac{1}{298}+$	$\dfrac{1}{299}+\dfrac{1}{300}$	Given
$>$	$\dfrac{1}{300}+$	$\dfrac{1}{300}+$	$\dfrac{1}{300}+$	$\cdots+$	$\dfrac{1}{300}+$	$\dfrac{1}{300}+\dfrac{1}{300}$	See Note 1 below

Note 1: 300 is greater than each of 201, 202, 203, ... , 298, and 299, so the reciprocal of 300 is less than the reciprocal of each of 201, 202, 203, ... , 298, and 299 and the sum in line 2 of the table above, $(100)\left(\dfrac{1}{300}\right)=\dfrac{1}{3}$, is less than the sum of line 1. Thus, $\dfrac{1}{3}<M$.

$M=$	$\dfrac{1}{201}+$	$\dfrac{1}{202}+$	$\dfrac{1}{203}+$	$\cdots+$	$\dfrac{1}{298}+$	$\dfrac{1}{299}+\dfrac{1}{300}$	Given
$<$	$\dfrac{1}{200}+$	$\dfrac{1}{200}+$	$\dfrac{1}{200}+$	$\cdots+$	$\dfrac{1}{200}+$	$\dfrac{1}{200}+\dfrac{1}{200}$	See Note 2 below

Note 2: 200 is less than each of 201, 202, 203, ..., 298, and 299, so the reciprocal of 200 is greater than the reciprocal of each of 201, 202, 203, ... , 298, and 299 and the sum in line 2 of the table above, $(100)\left(\dfrac{1}{200}\right)=\dfrac{1}{2}$, is greater than the sum of line 1. Thus, $\dfrac{1}{2}>M$ or $M<\dfrac{1}{2}$. Combining the results $\dfrac{1}{3}<M$ and $M<\dfrac{1}{2}$ gives $\dfrac{1}{3}<M<\dfrac{1}{2}$.

The correct answer is A.

151. Working simultaneously at their respective constant rates, Machines A and B produce 800 nails in x hours. Working alone at its constant rate, Machine A produces 800 nails in y hours. In terms of x and y, how many hours does it take Machine B, working alone at its constant rate, to produce 800 nails?

(A) $\dfrac{x}{x+y}$

(B) $\dfrac{y}{x+y}$

(C) $\dfrac{xy}{x+y}$

(D) $\dfrac{xy}{x-y}$

(E) $\dfrac{xy}{y-x}$

Algebra Applied Problems

Let R_A and R_B be the constant rates, in nails per hour, at which Machines A and B work, respectively. Then it follows from the given information that $R_A+R_B=\dfrac{800}{x}$ and $R_A=\dfrac{800}{y}$.

Hence, $\dfrac{800}{y}+R_B=\dfrac{800}{x}$, or

$$R_B=\dfrac{800}{x}-\dfrac{800}{y}=800\left(\dfrac{1}{x}-\dfrac{1}{y}\right)=800\left(\dfrac{y-x}{xy}\right).$$

Therefore, the time, in hours, it would take Machine B to produce 800 nails is given by

$$\dfrac{800}{800\left(\dfrac{y-x}{xy}\right)}=\dfrac{xy}{y-x}.$$

The correct answer is E.

152. Carol purchased one basket of fruit consisting of 4 apples and 2 oranges and another basket of fruit consisting of 3 apples and 5 oranges. Carol is to select one piece of fruit at random from each of the two baskets. What is the probability that one of the two pieces of fruit selected will be an apple and the other will be an orange?

(A) $\dfrac{1}{4}$

(B) $\dfrac{1}{2}$

(C) $\dfrac{1}{24}$

(D) $\dfrac{5}{24}$

(E) $\dfrac{13}{24}$

Arithmetic Probability

There are 6 pieces of fruit in the first basket and 8 pieces of fruit in the second basket. By the multiplication principle, the number of selections of a piece of fruit from the first basket and a piece of fruit from the second basket is $(6)(8) = 48$. Of these selections, $(4)(5) = 20$ are such that an apple is selected from the first basket and an orange is selected from the second basket, and $(2)(3) = 6$ are such that an orange is selected from the first basket and an apple is selected from the second basket. Therefore, there is a total of $20 + 6 = 26$ selections in which one apple is chosen and one orange is chosen, and hence the probability of such a selection is $\dfrac{26}{48} = \dfrac{13}{24}$.

Alternatively, the desired probability is the sum of the probabilities of two disjoint events. In the first event, an apple is selected from the first basket and an orange is selected from the second basket; the probability of this event is $\left(\dfrac{4}{6}\right)\left(\dfrac{5}{8}\right) = \dfrac{20}{48}$.

In the second event, an orange is selected from the first basket and an apple is selected from the second basket; the probability of this event is $\left(\dfrac{2}{6}\right)\left(\dfrac{3}{8}\right) = \dfrac{6}{48}$. Therefore, the desired probability is $\dfrac{20}{48} + \dfrac{6}{48} = \dfrac{26}{48} = \dfrac{13}{24}$.

The correct answer is E.

153. Last year Brand X shoes were sold by dealers in 403 different regions worldwide, with an average (arithmetic mean) of 98 dealers per region. If last year these dealers sold an average of 2,488 pairs of Brand X shoes per dealer, which of the following is closest to the total number of pairs of Brand X shoes sold last year by the dealers worldwide?

(A) 10^4

(B) 10^5

(C) 10^6

(D) 10^7

(E) 10^8

Arithmetic Estimation; Exponents

Since the average number of dealers per region is 98, it follows that $\dfrac{\text{number of dealers}}{403} = 98$, and thus the number of dealers is $(98)(403)$. Also, since the average number of pairs sold per dealer is 2,488, it follows that $\dfrac{\text{number of pairs sold}}{(98)(403)} = 2{,}488$, and thus the number of pairs sold is $(98)(403)(2{,}488)$, which is approximately $(100)(400)(2500) = (10^2)(4 \times 10^2)(25 \times 10^2)$. Therefore, the total number of pairs sold is approximately $(4)(25) \times 10^{2+2+2} = 100 \times 10^6 = 10^8$.

The correct answer is E.

154. A positive integer is divisible by 3 if and only if the sum of its digits is divisible by 3. If the six-digit integer n is divisible by 3 and n is of the form $1k2,k24$, where k represents a digit that occurs twice, how many values could n have?

(A) Two

(B) Three

(C) Four

(D) Five

(E) Ten

Arithmetic Equations

Since n is divisible by 3, the six digits of n sum to a number divisible by 3. So, $1 + k + 2 + k + 2 + 4 = 9 + 2k$ must be divisible by 3. The first term of $9 + 2k$ is 9, which is divisible by 3, so the other term $2k$ must be either 0 or else itself divisible by 3.

That means k is either 0 or divisible by 3. Thus, since k is a single digit, it must be either 0, 3, 6, or 9. Each of these four values of k generates a different value for n: 102,024, 132,324, 162,624, or 192,924. Since no other value of k generates a six-digit number of the form $1k2,k24$ divisible by 3, but n must be a number of this form divisible by 3, these are the only four possible values of n.

The correct answer is C.

	Number of Marbles in Each of Three Bags	Percent of Marbles in Each Bag That Are Blue (to the nearest tenth)
Bag P	37	10.8%
Bag Q	x	66.7%
Bag R	32	50.0%

155. If $\frac{1}{3}$ of the total number of marbles in the three bags listed in the table above are blue, how many marbles are there in Bag Q?

(A) 5
(B) 9
(C) 12
(D) 23
(E) 46

Algebra Percents

What is the value of x, the number of marbles in Bag Q? From the given information and rounded to the nearest integer, Bag P has $(37)(0.108) = 4$ blue marbles, Bag Q has $(x)(0.667) = \frac{2}{3}x$ blue marbles, and Bag R has $(32)(0.5) = 16$ blue marbles. Therefore, the total number of blue marbles is equal to $4 + \frac{2}{3}x + 16 = 20 + \frac{2}{3}x$. It is given that $\frac{1}{3}$ of the total number of marbles are blue, so the total number of blue marbles is also equal to $\frac{1}{3}(37 + x + 32) = \frac{1}{3}x + 23$. It follows that $20 + \frac{2}{3}x = \frac{1}{3}x + 23$, or $\frac{1}{3}x = 3$, or $x = 9$.

The correct answer is B.

Age Category (in years)	Number of Employees
Less than 20	29
20–29	58
30–39	36
40–49	21
50–59	10
60–69	5
70 and over	2

156. The table above gives the age categories of the 161 employees at Company X and the number of employees in each category. According to the table, if m is the median age, in years, of the employees at Company X, then m must satisfy which of the following?

(A) $20 \le m \le 29$
(B) $25 \le m \le 34$
(C) $30 \le m \le 39$
(D) $35 \le m \le 44$
(E) $40 \le m \le 49$

Arithmetic Statistics

The median of 161 ages is the 81st age when the ages are listed in order. Since 29 of the ages are less than 20, the median age must be greater than or equal to 20. Since 58 of the ages are between 20 and 29, a total of $29 + 58 = 87$ of the ages are less than or equal to 29, and thus the median age is less than or equal to 29. Therefore, the median age is greater than or equal to 20 and less than or equal to 29.

The correct answer is A.

157. If k and n are positive integers such that $n > k$, then $k! + (n - k) \cdot (k - 1)!$ is equivalent to which of the following?

(A) $k \cdot n!$
(B) $k! \cdot n$
(C) $(n - k)!$
(D) $n \cdot (k + 1)!$
(E) $n \cdot (k - 1)!$

Algebra Simplifying Algebraic Expressions

$k! + (n - k) \cdot (k - 1)!$ given

$k \cdot (k - 1)! + (n - k) \cdot (k - 1)!$ $k! = k \cdot (k - 1)!$

$[k + (n - k)] \cdot (k - 1)!$ factor out $(k - 1)!$

$n \cdot (k - 1)!$ combine like terms

The correct answer is E.

158. Ron is 4 inches taller than Amy, and Barbara is 1 inch taller than Ron. If Barbara's height is 65 inches, what is the median height, in inches, of these three people?

    (A) 60
    (B) 61
    (C) 62
    (D) 63
    (E) 64

Arithmetic Operations with Integers

Let $R, A,$ and B be the heights, respectively and in inches, of Ron, Amy, and Barbara. It is given that $R = 4 + A, B = 1 + R,$ and $B = 65.$ Therefore, $R = B - 1 = 65 - 1 = 64$ and $A = R - 4 = 64 - 4 = 60.$ From this it follows that the three heights, in inches, are 60, 64, and 65. The median of these three heights is 64.

The correct answer is E.

159. If x and y are positive numbers such that x + y = 1, which of the following could be the value of 100x + 200y?

    I. 80
    II. 140
    III. 199

    (A) II only
    (B) III only
    (C) I and II
    (D) I and III
    (E) II and III

Algebra Simultaneous Equations; Inequalities

Since $x + y = 1,$ then $y = 1 - x$ and $100x + 200y$ can be expressed as $100x + 200(1 - x) = 200 - 100x.$ Test each value.

    I. If $200 - 100x = 80,$ then $x = \dfrac{200 - 80}{100} = 1.2$ and $y = 1 - 1.2 = -0.2.$

Since y must be positive, 80 cannot be a value of $100x + 200y.$

    II. If $200 - 100x = 140,$ then $x = \dfrac{200 - 140}{100} = 0.6$ and $y = 1 - 0.6 = 0.4,$ so 140 can be a value of $100x + 200y.$

    III. If $200 - 100x = 199,$ then $x = \dfrac{200 - 199}{100} = 0.01$ and $y = 1 - 0.01 = 0.99,$ so 199 can be a value of $100x + 200y.$

The correct answer is E.

160. If X is the hundredths digit in the decimal 0.1X and if Y is the thousandths digit in the decimal 0.02Y, where X and Y are nonzero digits, which of the following is closest to the greatest possible value of $\dfrac{0.1X}{0.02Y}$?

    (A) 4
    (B) 5
    (C) 6
    (D) 9
    (E) 10

Arithmetic Operations with Decimals; Place Value

The greatest possible value of $\dfrac{0.1X}{0.02Y}$ will occur when $0.1X$ has the greatest possible value and $0.02Y$ has the least possible value. Since X and Y are nonzero digits, this means that X must be 9 and Y must be 1. The greatest possible value of $\dfrac{0.1X}{0.02Y}$ is then $\dfrac{0.19}{0.021} \approx 9.05,$ which is closest to 9.

The correct answer is D.

161. If each of the 12 teams participating in a certain tournament plays exactly one game with each of the other teams, how many games will be played?

    (A) 144
    (B) 132
    (C) 66
    (D) 33
    (E) 23

Arithmetic Elementary Combinatorics

Since each of the 12 teams will play exactly one game with each of the other teams, the number of games that will be played is equal to the number of selections of 2 teams, without regard to order, from 12 teams. This is the number of combinations of 12 teams taken 2 at a time, which is equal to

$$\binom{12}{2} = \frac{12!}{2!(12-2)!} = \frac{(10!)\,(11)(12)}{(2)\,(10!)} = 66.$$

Alternatively, each of the 12 teams will play each of the 11 other teams. The product $(12)(11)$ counts each of the games twice since, for example, this product separately counts "Team A plays Team B" and "Team B plays Team A." Therefore, the number of games that will be played is $\frac{(12)(11)}{2} = 66$.

The correct answer is C.

162. For which of the following values of x is $\sqrt{1 - \sqrt{2 - \sqrt{x}}}$ **not** defined as a real number?

(A) 1
(B) 2
(C) 3
(D) 4
(E) 5

Algebra Equations

For the difference between two numbers to be a real number, those two numbers must both be real themselves. So, for $\sqrt{1 - \sqrt{2 - \sqrt{x}}}$ to be a real number, $\sqrt{2 - \sqrt{x}}$ must be a real number. Thus, since only a nonnegative real number has a real square root, $2 - \sqrt{x}$ must be a nonnegative real number. It follows that $\sqrt{x}$ must be a real number no greater than 2, so x must be a real number no greater than 4. Therefore, for $x = 5$, $\sqrt{1 - \sqrt{2 - \sqrt{x}}}$ is not defined as a real number.

The correct answer is E.

163. What is the remainder when 3^{19} is divided by 10?

(A) 1
(B) 3
(C) 5
(D) 7
(E) 9

Arithmetic Properties of Integers; Series and Sequences

When a positive integer is divided by 10, the remainder is the units digit of that positive integer. For example, when 584 is divided by 10, the quotient is 58 and the remainder is 4. Thus, the remainder when 3^{19} is divided by 10 is the units digit when 3^{19} is written as a decimal numeral. The table shows the units digits for the first few powers of 3.

number	decimal numeral	units digit
3^1	3	3
3^2	9	9
3^3	27	7
3^4	81	1
3^5	243	3
3^6	729	9
3^7	2,187	7
3^8	6,561	1
⋮	⋮	⋮

The table, along with thinking about the standard method for multiplying decimal numerals by hand, shows that the units digits of the powers of 3 form a sequence in which the digits 3, 9, 7, and 1 repeat indefinitely in that order. By following this pattern, the units digit of 3^{19} is seen to be 7.

The correct answer is D.

164. Of 200 people surveyed, 80 percent own a cellular phone and 45 percent own a pager. If all 200 people surveyed own a cellular phone, or a pager, or both, what percent of those surveyed either do <u>not</u> own a cellular phone or do <u>not</u> own a pager?

    (A)   35%
    (B)   45%
    (C)   55%
    (D)   65%
    (E)   75%

Algebra Sets (Venn Diagrams)

From the given information, $(0.8)(200) = 160$ of the people surveyed own a cellular phone and $(0.45)(200) = 90$ of the people surveyed own a pager. The Venn diagram shows this information, where N denotes the number of people who own both.

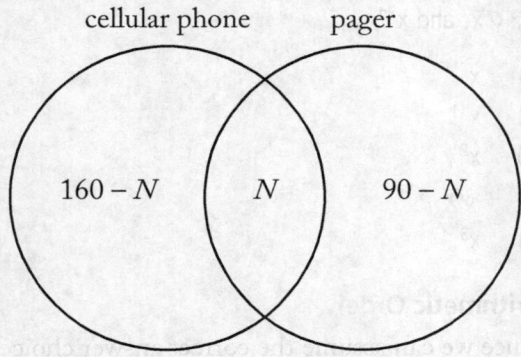

cellular phone   pager

$160 - N$ N $90 - N$

Since a total of 200 people were surveyed, it follows that $(160 - N) + N + (90 - N) = 200$, or $N = 50$. Therefore, the number of people surveyed who do not own a cellular phone is $90 - 50 = 40$ and the number of people surveyed who do not own a pager is $160 - 50 = 110$, which together account for $40 + 110 = 150$ of the 200 people surveyed, or $\frac{150}{200} \times 100\% = 75\%$ of the people surveyed.

The correct answer is E.

165. At the end of the first quarter, the share price of a certain mutual fund was 20 percent higher than it was at the beginning of the year. At the end of the second quarter, the share price was 50 percent higher than it was at the beginning of the year. What was the percent increase in the share price from the end of the first quarter to the end of the second quarter?

    (A)   20%
    (B)   25%
    (C)   30%
    (D)   33%
    (E)   40%

Arithmetic Applied Problems; Percents

Let P be the sale price of the mutual fund at the beginning of the year. Then at the end of the first quarter the sale price was $1.2P$, and at the end of the second quarter the sale price was $1.5P$. Therefore, the percent increase in the sale price from the end of the first quarter to the end of the second quarter is $\frac{1.5P - 1.2P}{1.2P} \times 100\% = \frac{15 - 12}{12} \times 100\% = 25\%$.

The correct answer is B.

$$\frac{1}{2}, \frac{1}{4}, \frac{1}{8}, \frac{1}{16}, \frac{1}{32}, \dots$$

166. In the sequence above, each term after the first is one-half the previous term. If x is the tenth term of the sequence, then x satisfies which of the following inequalities?
    (A) $0.1 < x < 1$
    (B) $0.01 < x < 0.1$
    (C) $0.001 < x < 0.01$
    (D) $0.0001 < x < 0.001$
    (E) $0.00001 < x < 0.0001$

Arithmetic Series and Sequences; Decimals

The first, second, third, fourth, etc. terms are, respectively, the reciprocals of $2^1, 2^2, 2^3, 2^4$, etc. Therefore, the tenth term x is the reciprocal of $2^{10} = 1,024$, or $\frac{1}{1,024}$. Since $1,000 < 1,024 < 10,000$, it follows that $\frac{1}{10,000} < \frac{1}{1,024} < \frac{1}{1,000}$, so $0.0001 < \frac{1}{1,024} < 0.001$, or $0.0001 < x < 0.001$.

The correct answer is D.

167. If $xy + z = x(y + z)$, which of the following must be true?

    (A) $x = 0$ and $z = 0$
    (B) $x = 1$ and $y = 1$
    (C) $y = 1$ and $z = 0$
    (D) $x = 1$ or $y = 0$
    (E) $x = 1$ or $z = 0$

Algebra Equations

$$\begin{aligned}
xy + z &= x(y + z) & &\text{given} \\
xy + z &= xy + xz & &\text{distributive property} \\
z &= xz & &\text{subtract } xy \text{ from both sides} \\
0 &= xz - z & &\text{subtract } z \text{ from both sides} \\
0 &= (x - 1)z & &\text{factor} \\
x - 1 &= 0 \text{ or } z = 0 & &\text{property of } 0 \\
x &= 1 \text{ or } z = 0 & &\text{solve for } x
\end{aligned}$$

The correct answer is E.

168. Two water pumps, working simultaneously at their respective constant rates, took exactly 4 hours to fill a certain swimming pool. If the constant rate of one pump was 1.5 times the constant rate of the other, how many hours would it have taken the faster pump to fill the pool if it had worked alone at its constant rate?

   (A) $\quad$ 5

   (B) $\quad \dfrac{16}{3}$

   (C) $\quad \dfrac{11}{2}$

   (D) $\quad$ 6

   (E) $\quad \dfrac{20}{3}$

Arithmetic Work Problem

Let t be the number of hours it would take the slower pump to fill the pool working alone. Since the faster pump works $1.5 = \dfrac{3}{2}$ times faster than the slower pump, the faster pump will take $\dfrac{1}{1.5}t = \dfrac{2}{3}t$ hours to fill the pool working alone. It follows that $\dfrac{1}{t} + \dfrac{1}{\frac{2}{3}t} = \dfrac{1}{4}$, or $\left(1 + \dfrac{3}{2}\right)\left(\dfrac{1}{t}\right) = \dfrac{1}{4}$.

Solving, we get $\dfrac{1}{t} = \dfrac{1}{4} \div \dfrac{5}{2} = \dfrac{1}{10}$, and hence $t = 10$.

Therefore, the faster pump would have taken $\dfrac{2}{3}t = \dfrac{2}{3} \times 10 = \dfrac{20}{3}$ hours to fill the pool if it had worked alone.

Alternatively, let r and $1.5r = \dfrac{3}{2}r$ be the rates, respectively, at which the slower and faster pumps work. Working together, the pumps work at a combined rate of $r + \dfrac{3}{2}r = \dfrac{5}{2}r$ and can fill 1 pool in 4 hours. Therefore, when working alone, the faster pump, which works at a rate that is $\dfrac{3}{5}$ times as fast as their combined rate (because $\dfrac{3}{2}r = \dfrac{3}{5} \times \dfrac{5}{2}r$), will take $\dfrac{1}{\frac{3}{5}} = \dfrac{5}{3}$ times as long as than when they are working together, or $\dfrac{5}{3} \times 4 = \dfrac{20}{3}$ hours to fill the pool.

The correct answer is E.

169. If $0 < x < 1$, what is the median of the values x, x^{-1}, x^2, $\sqrt{x}$, and x^3?

   (A) $\quad x$

   (B) $\quad x^{-1}$

   (C) $\quad x^2$

   (D) $\quad \sqrt{x}$

   (E) $\quad x^3$

Arithmetic Order

Since we can assume the correct answer choice does not depend on the value of x between 0 and 1 that is used, choose a value of x between 0 and 1 for which all of these expressions can be easily evaluated, such as $x = \dfrac{1}{4}$.

x	x^{-1}	x^2	$\sqrt{x}$	x^3
$\dfrac{1}{4}$	4	$\dfrac{1}{16}$	$\dfrac{1}{2}$	$\dfrac{1}{64}$

When these values are arranged in ascending order,

$\dfrac{1}{64}$	$\dfrac{1}{16}$	$\dfrac{1}{4}$	$\dfrac{1}{2}$	4

the median of the values will be the middle value, which is $x = \dfrac{1}{4}$.

The correct answer is A.

...

170. The number of stamps that Kaye and Alberto had were in the ratio 5:3, respectively. After Kaye gave Alberto 10 of her stamps, the ratio of the number Kaye had to the number Alberto had was 7:5. As a result of this gift, Kaye had how many more stamps than Alberto?

    (A) 20
    (B) 30
    (C) 40
    (D) 60
    (E) 90

Algebra Ratio and Proportion

Let x be the number of stamps Alberto had at first. Then Kaye had $\frac{5x}{3}$ stamps at first. So, after Kaye gave Alberto 10 of her stamps, she had $\frac{5x}{3} - 10$ stamps and Alberto had $x + 10$ stamps. Since Kaye then had 7 stamps for every 5 Alberto had,

$$7(x + 10) = 5\left(\frac{5x}{3} - 10\right) = 7x + 70 = \frac{25x}{3} - 50.$$

Thus, $120 = \frac{(25 - 21)x}{3} = \frac{4x}{3}$, so $360 = 4x$, and $x = 90$. Therefore, after Kaye gave Alberto 10 of her stamps, she had $\frac{5(90)}{3} - 10 = 5(30) - 10 = 140$ stamps, while Alberto had $90 + 10 = 100$ stamps. So, as a result of the gift, Kaye had $140 - 100 = 40$ more stamps than Alberto.

The correct answer is C.

7.51	8.22	7.86	8.36
8.09	7.83	8.30	8.01
7.73	8.25	7.96	8.53

171. A vending machine is designed to dispense 8 ounces of coffee into a cup. After a test that recorded the number of ounces of coffee in each of 1,000 cups dispensed by the vending machine, the 12 listed amounts, in ounces, were selected from the data. If the 1,000 recorded amounts have a mean of 8.1 ounces and a standard deviation of 0.3 ounce, how many of the 12 listed amounts are within 1.5 standard deviations of the mean?

    (A) Four
    (B) Six
    (C) Nine
    (D) Ten
    (E) Eleven

Arithmetic Statistics

Since 1.5 standard deviations is equal to $(1.5)(0.3) = 0.45$, it follows that a recorded number of ounces of coffee is within 1.5 standard deviations of the mean if that number of ounces is within 0.45 of 8.1, or between $8.1 - 0.45 = 7.65$ and $8.1 + 0.45 = 8.55$. Since 7.51 is the only one of the 12 listed amounts that is not between 7.65 and 8.55, there are $12 - 1 = 11$ listed amounts that are between 7.65 and 8.55.

The correct answer is E.

172. In a certain quiz that consists of 10 questions, each question after the first is worth 4 points more than the preceding question. If the 10 questions on the quiz are worth a total of 360 points, how many points is the third question worth?

    (A) 18
    (B) 24
    (C) 26
    (D) 32
    (E) 44

Algebra Series and Sequences

Suppose the first question on the quiz is worth x points. Then the 10 questions together are worth $10x + 4(1 + 2 + 3 + 4 + 5 + 6 + 7 + 8 + 9) = 10x + 4(45) = 10x + 180 = 360$ points. So, $10x = 180$, and $x = 18$. Since the third question is worth 8 points more than the first, it must be worth $18 + 8 = 26$ points.

The correct answer is C.

173. A car traveling at a certain constant speed takes 2 seconds longer to travel 1 kilometer than it would take to travel 1 kilometer at 75 kilometers per hour. At what speed, in kilometers per hour, is the car traveling?

    (A) 71.5
    (B) 72
    (C) 72.5
    (D) 73
    (E) 73.5

Algebra Applied Problems

An hour is 3,600 seconds. At 75 kilometers per hour, the car would take 3,600 seconds to travel 75 kilometers, so it would take $\frac{3600}{75} = 48$ seconds to travel 1 kilometer. But we're told that the car actually takes 2 seconds longer than that, or 50 seconds, to travel 1 kilometer. Therefore, in 1 hour, or 3,600 seconds, it travels $\frac{3600}{50} \times$ 1 kilometer/hour = 72 kilometers/hour.

The correct answer is B.

174. If the speed of *x* meters per second is equivalent to the speed of *y* kilometers per hour, what is *y* in terms of *x*? (1 kilometer = 1,000 meters)

(A) $\frac{5x}{18}$

(B) $\frac{6x}{5}$

(C) $\frac{18x}{5}$

(D) $60x$

(E) $3,600,000x$

Algebra Measurement Conversion

We are given that *y* kilometers per hour is the same speed as *x* meters per second. By converting from meters to kilometers using 1 km = 1,000 m and seconds to hours using 1 hr = 3,600 sec, we can obtain *y* in terms of *x*.

$$y \frac{\text{km}}{\text{hr}} = x \frac{\text{m}}{\text{sec}}$$

$$y \frac{\text{km}}{\text{hr}} = x \frac{\text{m}}{\text{sec}} \times \frac{1 \text{ km}}{1,000 \text{ m}} \times \frac{3,600 \text{ sec}}{1 \text{ hr}}$$

$$y \frac{\text{km}}{\text{hr}} = \left(\frac{3,600}{1,000}\right) x \frac{\text{km}}{\text{hr}}$$

$$y \frac{\text{km}}{\text{hr}} = \frac{18x}{5} \frac{\text{km}}{\text{hr}}$$

From the last equality above it follows that $y = \frac{18x}{5}$.

The correct answer is C.

175. The function *f* is defined by $f(x) = -\frac{1}{x}$ for all nonzero numbers *x*. If $f(a) = -\frac{1}{2}$ and $f(ab) = \frac{1}{6}$, then *b* =

(A) 3

(B) $\frac{1}{3}$

(C) $-\frac{1}{x}$

(D) -3

(E) -12

Algebra Functions

From $f(x) = -\frac{1}{x}$ and $f(a) = -\frac{1}{2}$ we have $-\frac{1}{a} = -\frac{1}{2}$, or $a = 2$. From $f(x) = -\frac{1}{x}$ and $f(ab) = \frac{1}{6}$ we have $-\frac{1}{ab} = \frac{1}{6}$, or $ab = -6$. Since $a = 2$, it follows from $ab = -6$ that $2b = -6$, or $b = -3$.

The correct answer is D.

176. If $5^x - 5^{x-3} = (124)(5^y)$, what is *y* in terms of *x*?

(A) x

(B) $x - 6$

(C) $x - 3$

(D) $2x + 3$

(E) $2x + 6$

Algebra Equations; Factoring

A strategy that is useful in rewriting sums and/or differences of exponential terms having the same base is to use the term with the least exponent as a common factor. For example, in $5^x - 5^{x-3}$, factor out 5^{x-3} since $x - 3$ is less than x. This gives $5^x - 5^{x-3} = 5^{x-3}(5^3 - 1)$. Therefore, the given equation is equivalent to $5^{x-3}(5^3 - 1) = (124)(5^y)$, or $5^{x-3}(124) = (124)(5^y)$. Dividing both sides of the last equation by 124 gives $5^{x-3} = 5^y$, and hence $y = x - 3$.

The correct answer is C.

177. The total of Company C's assets in 1994 was 300 percent greater than the total in 1993, which in turn was 400 percent greater than the total in 1992. If the total of Company C's assets in 1992 was N dollars, which of the following represents the total of Company C's assets, in dollars, in 1994?

(A) $7N$
(B) $8N$
(C) $9N$
(D) $12N$
(E) $20N$

Algebra Percents

The total in 1993 was 400% greater than N; that is, it was $5N$. The total in 1994 was 300% greater than the total in 1993; that is, it was 4 times the total in 1993. Thus, the total in 1994 was $4(5N) = 20N$.

The correct answer is E.

178. If $\frac{x}{|y|} = -1$, which of the following must be true?

(A) $x = -y$
(B) $x = y$
(C) $x = y^2$
(D) $x^2 = y^2$
(E) $x^3 = y^3$

Algebra Equations

When $y \neq 0$, the given equation is equivalent to $x = (-1)|y|$. Since $|y|$ is equal to y or $-y$, depending on whether $y > 0$ or $y < 0$, and $y^2 = (-y)^2$, it follows that $|y|^2 = y^2$. Therefore, squaring both sides of $x = (-1)|y|$ gives $x^2 = (-1)^2|y|^2 = y^2$.

Alternatively, if $x = -1$, then for both $y = 1$ and $y = -1$ we have $\frac{x}{|y|} = -1$. The table shows that among the answer choices, only $x^2 = y^2$ is true for both of these choices of x and y.

	$x = -y$	$x = y$	$x = y^2$	$x^2 = y^2$	$x^3 = y^3$
$x = -1$ and $y = 1$	true	false	false	**true**	false
$x = -1$ and $y = -1$	false	true	false	**true**	true

The correct answer is D.

179. The table above is a 3 by 3 grid of 9 numbers, 5 of which are given. The 4 numbers that are not given are denoted by A, B, C, and D. The product of the numbers in each row and in each column is the same for all rows and columns. What is the value of the product $ABCD$?

(A) 36
(B) 72
(C) $36\sqrt{2}$
(D) $36\sqrt{3}$
(E) $72\sqrt{6}$

Algebra Simultaneous Equations; Computation with Radical Expressions

For each of the 3 rows and 3 columns, let x be the common product of the numbers in that row or column. The table below shows the products associated with the 3 rows and 3 columns. For example, the product of the numbers in the rightmost column is $(2\sqrt{3})(C)(D)$, and so we have $2\sqrt{3}\,CD = x$.

row products	column products
$2\sqrt{3}A = x$	$\sqrt{3}AB = x$
$\sqrt{6}BC = x$	$6\sqrt{6} = x$
$6\sqrt{3}D = x$	$2\sqrt{3}CD = x$

Multiplying together the 3 left-hand sides and the 3 right-hand sides of the 3 column product equations gives $(\sqrt{3}AB)(6\sqrt{6})(2\sqrt{3}\,CD) = x^3$, or $36\sqrt{6}\,ABCD = x^3$. Since $x = 6\sqrt{6}$ (the middle column product), it follows that $36\sqrt{6}\,ABCD = (6\sqrt{6})^3$. Therefore,

$$ABCD = \frac{(6\sqrt{6})(6\sqrt{6})(6\sqrt{6})}{(36\sqrt{6})} = 36.$$

Alternatively, begin with $(\sqrt{3}AB)(x)(2\sqrt{3}\,CD) = x^3$ instead of $(\sqrt{3}AB)(6\sqrt{6})(2\sqrt{3}\,CD) = x^3$.

Now divide both sides by x and use $(\sqrt{3})(2\sqrt{3}) = 6$ to get $6ABCD = (6\sqrt{6})^2$, or $ABCD = 36$.

The correct answer is A.

180. In May, Mrs. Lee's earnings were 60 percent of the Lee family's total income. In June, Mrs. Lee earned 20 percent more than in May. If the rest of the family's income was the same both months, then in June, Mrs. Lee's earnings were approximately what percent of the Lee family's total income?

(A) 64%
(B) 68%
(C) 72%
(D) 76%
(E) 80%

Algebra Percents

Let x be the Lee family's total income in May. In May, Mrs. Lee earned $0.6x$, so the rest of the family's income was $(1 - 0.6x) = 0.4x$. In June, the rest of the family still just earned $0.4x$, but Mrs. Lee earned 20 percent more than in May; that is, she earned $1.2(0.6x) = 0.72x$. So in June, Mrs. Lee earned $\frac{0.72}{1.12} = \frac{72}{112} = \frac{9}{14} \approx 64\%$ of the family's income.

The correct answer is A.

181. John would have reduced the time it took him to drive from his home to a certain store by $\frac{1}{3}$ if he had increased his average speed by 15 miles per hour. What was John's actual average speed, in miles per hour, when he drove from his home to the store?

(A) 25
(B) 30
(C) 40
(D) 45
(E) 50

Algebra Applied Problems

Let R be John's actual average speed (in miles per hour) and let T be John's actual travel time (in hours). Then it follows from ***distance = rate × time*** that the distance (in miles) from John's home to the store is RT. Since the same distance can be traveled when R is replaced by $R + 15$ and T is replaced by $\frac{2}{3}T$, we have $RT = (R + 15)\left(\frac{2}{3}T\right)$. Now solve this eequation for R.

$$RT = (R + 15)\left(\frac{2}{3}T\right) \quad \text{from above}$$

$$R = (R + 15)\left(\frac{2}{3}\right) \quad \text{divide both sides by } T$$

$$R = \frac{2}{3}R + 10 \quad \text{expand right side}$$

$$\frac{1}{3}R = 10 \quad \text{subtract } \frac{2}{3}R \text{ from both sides}$$

$$R = 30 \quad \text{multiply both sides by 3}$$

Therefore, John's actual average speed was 30 miles per hour.

The correct answer is B.

182. Which of the following inequalities has a solution set that, when graphed on the number line, is a single line segment of finite length?

(A) $x^4 \geq 1$
(B) $x^3 \leq 27$
(C) $x^2 \geq 16$
(D) $2 \leq |x| \leq 5$
(E) $2 \leq 3x + 4 \leq 6$

Algebra Number Line

For option A, $x^4 \geq 1$, the solution set includes every $x \geq 1$ and also every $x \leq -1$. On the number line this is graphed as two line segments, one extending infinitely leftward from -1 and the other infinitely rightward from 1.

For option B, $x^3 \leq 27$, the solution set includes every $x \leq 3$. This is graphed as a line segment extending infinitely leftward from 3.

For option C, $x^2 \geq 16$, the solution set includes every $x \geq 4$ and also every $x \leq -4$. As with option A, this is graphed as two line segments extending infinitely in opposite directions.

For option D, $2 \leq |x| \leq 5$, the solution set includes every x from 2 through 5 and also every x from -2 through -5. This is graphed as two separate finite line segments.

For option E, $2 \leq 3x + 4 \leq 6$, the solution set includes only every x from $-\frac{2}{3}$ through $\frac{2}{3}$. This is graphed as a single line segment of finite length.

The correct answer is E.

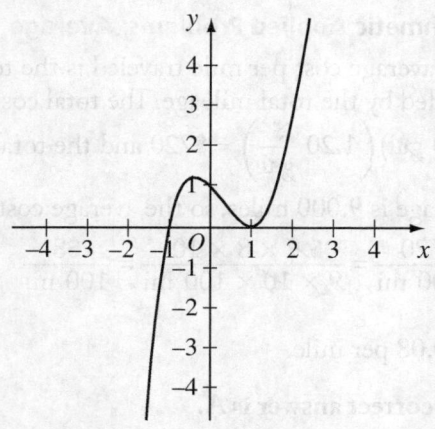

183. The figure shows the graph of $y = (x + 1)(x - 1)^2$ in the xy-plane. At how many points does the graph of $y = (x + 1)(x - 1)^2 + 2$ intercept the x-axis?

    (A) None
    (B) One
    (C) Two
    (D) Three
    (E) Four

Algebra Applied Problems

The graph of $y = (x + 1)(x - 1)^2 + 2$ is the graph of $y = (x + 1)(x - 1)^2$ shifted upward by 2. So, looking at the given graph of $y = (x + 1)(x - 1)^2$, we can see the graph of $y = (x + 1)(x - 1)^2 + 2$ intercepts the x-axis at only one point, left of the y-axis.

The correct answer is B.

184. If the average (arithmetic mean) of positive integers 2, 5, 1, x, and y is 4, what is the greatest possible value of y?

    (A) 10
    (B) 11
    (C) 12
    (D) 13
    (E) 14

Arithmetic Elementary Combinatorics

First, find an expression for y from the given information as follows:

$$\frac{2 + 5 + 1 + x + y}{5} = 4 \qquad \text{from given information}$$

$$2 + 5 + 1 + x + y = 20 \qquad \text{multiply both sides by 5}$$

$$x + y = 12 \qquad \text{subtract 8 from both sides}$$

$$y = 12 - x \qquad \text{subtract } x \text{ from both sides}$$

From the last row above, it follows that the greatest possible value of y is the greatest possible value of $12 - x$, which is its value at the least possible value of x. Since x is a positive integer, its least possible value is 1. Therefore, the greatest possible value of y is $12 - 1 = 11$.

The correct answer is B.

185. A jeweler bought a necklace at a wholesale price of $135 and then sold it at a 10 percent discount off the suggested retail price. If the jeweler made a 40 percent profit on the wholesale price, what was the suggested retail price of the necklace?

    (A) $139
    (B) $189
    (C) $199
    (D) $210
    (E) $220

Algebra Simultaneous Equations

Let R be the suggested retail price. Then the jeweler sold the necklace for $0.9R$, and thus the jeweler made a profit of $(0.9R - 135)$ on the wholesale price. Since the jeweler's profit is 40% of $135, it follows that $0.9R - 135 = (0.4)(135)$, or $0.9R - 135 = 54$. Now solve this last equation for R:

$$0.9R - 135 = 54 \qquad \text{given equation}$$

$$0.9R = 189 \qquad \text{add 135 to both sides}$$

$$R = 210 \qquad \text{divide both sides by 0.9}$$

The correct answer is D.

186. The weights of 6 packages are 12, 10, 11, 10, 12, and 10 pounds, respectively. In which of the following intervals does the standard deviation of the weights of the packages lie?

    (A) Between 0 and 3
    (B) Between 6 and 7
    (C) Between 8 and 10
    (D) Between 10 and 11
    (E) Between 11 and 12

Algebra Systems of Equations

The standard deviation of a data set is the square root of the average of the squared differences from the mean. To estimate the standard deviation, first find an approximate mean of the data set:

$$\frac{12 + 10 + 11 + 10 + 12 + 10}{6} = \frac{65}{6} \approx 11$$

Next, find the approximate differences and the approximate squared differences from the mean:

x	$x - 11$	$(x - 11)^2$
12	1	1
10	–1	1
11	0	0
10	–1	1
12	1	1
10	–1	1

Now use the right-most column of the table to find the approximate average of the squared differences:

$$\frac{1 + 1 + 0 + 1 + 1 + 1}{6} = \frac{5}{6}$$

Finally, the square root of the average of the squared differences from the mean (i.e., the standard deviation) is approximately $\sqrt{\frac{5}{6}}$, which is greater than 0 but less than $\sqrt{1} = 1$, and hence is between 0 and 3.

The correct answer is A.

187. In one week a certain taxicab company's cabs used a total of 600 gallons of gasoline, and each gallon of gasoline cost $1.20. If the cabs traveled a total of 9,000 miles that week, what was the company's average gasoline cost per mile traveled by the cabs?

(A) $0.08
(B) $0.12
(C) $0.15
(D) $0.18
(E) $0.20

Arithmetic Applied Problems; Average

The average cost per mile traveled is the total cost divided by the total mileage. The total cost is

$$(600 \text{ gal})\left(1.20 \frac{\$}{\text{gal}}\right) = \$720 \text{ and the total}$$

mileage is 9,000 miles, so the average cost is

$$\frac{\$720}{9{,}000 \text{ mi}} = \frac{\$9 \times 8 \times 10}{9 \times 10 \times 100 \text{ mi}} = \frac{\$8}{100 \text{ mi}}$$

$$= \$0.08 \text{ per mile.}$$

The correct answer is A.

188. For a fundraiser, each of 20 people walked a total of either 2 miles or 5 miles. If they walked a total of 76 miles, how many more people walked 5 miles than walked 2 miles?

(A) 2
(B) 4
(C) 6
(D) 8
(E) 10

Algebra Applied Problems

Let x be the number of people who walked 2 miles. These people walked a total of $2x$ miles. Since there were 20 people altogether, the number of people who walked 5 miles is $20 - x$, and these people walked a total of $5(20 - x)$ miles. Because the total number of miles all 20 people walked is 76, it follows that $2x + 5(20 - x) = 76$.

$$2x + 5(20 - x) = \ 76 \quad \text{initial equation}$$

$$2x + 100 - 5x = \ 76 \quad \text{distributive law}$$

$$-3x + 100 = \ 76 \quad \text{combine like terms}$$

$$-3x = -24 \quad \text{subtract 100 from both sides}$$

$$x = \ 8 \quad \text{divide both sides by } -3$$

Therefore, 8 people walked 2 miles and $20 - 8 = 12$ people walked 5 miles, and hence $12 - 8 = 4$ more people walked 5 miles than walked 2 miles.

The correct answer is B.

189. Last Monday the price per share of Company X stock at the end of the first hour of trading was 30 percent lower than the opening price per share. If the price per share at the end of the second hour was 10 percent greater than the price per share at the end of the first hour, then the price per share at the end of the second hour was what percent less than the opening price per share?

    (A)   20%
    (B)   23%
    (C)   24%
    (D)   27%
    (E)   33%

Arithmetic Percents

Assume the opening price per share was $100. Then the price per share at the end of the first hour decreased by 30% to (70%)($100) = (0.7)($100) = $70, and the price per share at the end of the second hour increased by 10% to (110%)($70) = (1.1)($70) = $77, which is $23 less than $100, and hence 23% less than $100.

Alternatively, without making the assumption above, let p denote the opening price per share. After a 30% decrease, the price per share will be $0.7p$, and when this is followed by a 10% increase, the price per share will be $(1.1)(0.7p) = 0.77p$, which is 23% less than p.

The correct answer is B.

190. The average (arithmetic mean) selling price of 5 houses in a certain neighborhood was $250,000. If the average selling price of 3 of the houses was $280,000, what was the average selling price of the other 2 houses?

    (A) $205,000
    (B) $215,000
    (C) $220,000
    (D) $240,000
    (E) $250,000

Arithmetic Statistics

Since the average selling price of the 5 houses is $250,000, the sum of the selling prices of the 5 houses is (5)($250,000). Similarly, the sum of the selling prices of 3 of the houses is (3)($280,000). Therefore, the sum of the selling prices of the other 2 houses is (5)($250,000) − (3)($280,000) = $410,000, and hence the average selling price of the other 2 houses is $\frac{\$410,000}{2} = \$205,000$.

The correct answer is A.

191. Which of the following fractions has the greatest value?

    (A) $\frac{11}{13}$
    (B) $\frac{13}{15}$
    (C) $\left(\frac{11}{13}\right)^2$
    (D) $\left(\frac{11}{13}\right)^4$
    (E) $\left(\frac{13}{15}\right)^4$

Arithmetic Fractions

The statements below show that the greatest is either $\frac{11}{13}$ or $\frac{13}{15}$.

$\left(\frac{11}{13}\right)^2 = \frac{11}{13} \times \frac{11}{13}$ is less than $1 \times \frac{11}{13}$

$\left(\frac{11}{13}\right)^4 = \left(\frac{11}{13} \times \frac{11}{13} \times \frac{11}{13}\right) \times \frac{11}{13}$ is less than $1 \times \frac{11}{13}$

$\left(\frac{13}{15}\right)^4 = \left(\frac{13}{15} \times \frac{13}{15} \times \frac{13}{15}\right) \times \frac{13}{15}$ is less than $1 \times \frac{13}{15}$

One way to determine which of $\frac{11}{13}$ or $\frac{13}{15}$ is greater is to use a common denominator. Since $\frac{11}{13} = \frac{11}{13} \times \frac{15}{15} = \frac{165}{195}$ and $\frac{13}{15} = \frac{13}{15} \times \frac{13}{13} = \frac{169}{195}$, it follows that $\frac{13}{15}$ is greater.

The correct answer is B.

Questions 192 to 293 — Difficulty: Hard

192. The cost to rent a small bus for a trip is x dollars, which is to be shared equally among the people taking the trip. If 10 people take the trip rather than 16, how many more dollars, in terms of x, will it cost per person?

    (A) $\dfrac{x}{6}$

    (B) $\dfrac{x}{10}$

    (C) $\dfrac{x}{16}$

    (D) $\dfrac{3x}{40}$

    (E) $\dfrac{3x}{80}$

Algebra Applied Problems

If 16 people take the trip, the cost per person would be $\dfrac{x}{16}$ dollars. If 10 people take the trip, the cost would be $\dfrac{x}{10}$ dollars. (Note that the lowest common multiple of 10 and 16 is 80.) Thus, if 10 people take the trip, the increase in dollars per person would be

$$\frac{x}{10} - \frac{x}{16} = \frac{8x}{80} - \frac{5x}{80} = \frac{3x}{80}.$$

The correct answer is E.

193. Clarissa will create her summer reading list by randomly choosing 4 books from the 10 books approved for summer reading. She will list the books in the order in which they are chosen. How many different lists are possible?

    (A) 6
    (B) 40
    (C) 210
    (D) 5,040
    (E) 151,200

Arithmetic Elementary Combinatorics

Any of the 10 books can be listed first. Any of the 9 books remaining after the first book is listed can be listed second. Any of the 8 books remaining after the first and second books are listed can be

listed third. Any of the 7 books remaining after the first, second, and third books are listed can be listed fourth. By the multiplication principle, there are $(10)(9)(8)(7) = 5,040$ different lists possible.

The correct answer is D.

194. If n is a positive integer and the product of all the integers from 1 to n, inclusive, is divisible by 990, what is the least possible value of n?

    (A) 8
    (B) 9
    (C) 10
    (D) 11
    (E) 12

Arithmetic Properties of Numbers

For convenience, let N represent the product of all integers from 1 through n. Then, since N is divisible by 990, every prime factor of 990 must also be a factor of N. The prime factorization of 990 is $2 \times 3^2 \times 5 \times 11$, and therefore, 11 must be a factor of N. Then the least possible value of N with factors of $2, 5, 3^2$, and 11 is $1 \times 2 \times 3 \times \cdots \times 11$, and the least possible value of n is 11.

The correct answer is D.

195. The probability that event M will NOT occur is 0.8 and the probability that event R will NOT occur is 0.6. If events M and R CANNOT both occur, which of the following is the probability that either event M or event R will occur?

    (A) $\dfrac{1}{5}$

    (B) $\dfrac{2}{5}$

    (C) $\dfrac{3}{5}$

    (D) $\dfrac{4}{5}$

    (E) $\dfrac{12}{25}$

Arithmetic Probability

Let $P(M)$ be the probability that event M will occur, let $P(R)$ be the probability that event R will occur, and let $P(M \text{ and } R)$ be the probability that events M and R both occur. Then the probability that either event M or event R will occur is $P(M) + P(R) - P(M \text{ and } R)$. From the given information, it follows that $P(M) = 1.0 - 0.8 = 0.2$, $P(R) = 1.0 - 0.6 = 0.4$, and $P(M \text{ and } R) = 0$. Therefore, the probability that either event M or event R will occur is

$$0.2 + 0.4 - 0 = 0.6 = \frac{3}{5}.$$

The correct answer is C.

196. The total cost for Company X to produce a batch of tools is $10,000 plus $3 per tool. Each tool sells for $8. The gross profit earned from producing and selling these tools is the total income from sales minus the total production cost. If a batch of 20,000 tools is produced and sold, then Company X's gross profit per tool is

    (A) $3.00
    (B) $3.75
    (C) $4.50
    (D) $5.00
    (E) $5.50

Arithmetic Applied Problems

The total cost to produce 20,000 tools is $10,000 + $3(20,000) = $70,000. The revenue resulting from the sale of 20,000 tools is $8(20,000) = $160,000. The gross profit is $160,000 − $70,000 = $90,000, and the gross profit per tool is $\frac{\$90,000}{20,000} = \$4.50$.

The correct answer is C.

197. If Q is an odd number and the median of Q consecutive integers is 120, what is the largest of these integers?

    (A) $\frac{Q-1}{2} + 120$
    (B) $\frac{Q}{2} + 119$
    (C) $\frac{Q}{2} + 120$
    (D) $\frac{Q+119}{2}$
    (E) $\frac{Q+120}{2}$

Arithmetic Statistics

For an odd number of data values, the median is the middle number. Thus, 120 is the middle number, and so half of the $Q - 1$ remaining values are at most 120 and the other half of the $Q - 1$ remaining values are at least 120. In particular, $\frac{Q-1}{2}$ data values lie to the right of 120 when the data values are listed in increasing order from left to right, and so the largest data value is $120 + \frac{Q-1}{2}$. Alternatively, it is evident that answer choice B, answer choice C, or answer choice E cannot be correct since these expressions do not have an integer value when Q is odd. For the list consisting of the single number 120 (i.e., if $Q = 1$), answer choice D fails because $\frac{Q+119}{2} = \frac{1+119}{2} = 60 \neq 120$ and answer choice A does not fail because $\frac{Q-1}{2} + 120 = \frac{1-1}{2} + 120 = 120$.

The correct answer is A.

198. If there are fewer than 8 zeros between the decimal point and the first nonzero digit in the decimal expansion of $\left(\dfrac{t}{1{,}000}\right)^4$, which of the following numbers could be the value of t?

I.   3
II.   5
III. 9

(A) None
(B) I only
(C) II only
(D) III only
(E) II and III

Arithmetic Properties of Numbers; Decimals

Since $\left(\dfrac{t}{1{,}000}\right)^4 = \left(t \times \dfrac{1}{1{,}000}\right)^4 = t^4 \times \left(\dfrac{1}{1{,}000}\right)^4 = t^4 \times \dfrac{1}{1{,}000^4}$ and $(1{,}000)^4 = (10^3)^4 = 10^{12}$, it follows that $\left(\dfrac{t}{1{,}000}\right)^4 = t^4 \times \dfrac{1}{10^{12}} = t^4 \times 10^{-12}$.

The following table illustrates the effect that multiplication by 10^{-1}, 10^{-2}, 10^{-3}, and 10^{-4} has on the placement of the decimal point of 52.7, a number chosen only for illustrative purposes.

multiplication by	resulting number	placement of decimal point
10^{-1}	5.27	1 place left of original
10^{-2}	0.527	2 places left of original
10^{-3}	0.0527	3 places left of original
10^{-4}	0.00527	4 places left of original

Therefore, the decimal point of $t^4 \times 10^{-12}$ is 12 positions to the left of the decimal point of t^4. Now consider the value of $t^4 \times 10^{-12}$ for the three given values of t.

t	t^4	$t^4 \times 10^{-12}$	# zeros after decimal point
3	81	0.000000000081	10
5	625	0.000000000625	9
9	6,561	0.000000006561	8

From the prior table it follows that NONE of these values of t is such that $t^4 \times 10^{-12}$ has fewer than 8 zeros between the decimal point and the first nonzero digit.

The correct answer is A.

199. A three-digit code for certain locks uses the digits 0, 1, 2, 3, 4, 5, 6, 7, 8, 9 according to the following constraints. The first digit cannot be 0 or 1, the second digit must be 0 or 1, and the second and third digits cannot both be 0 in the same code. How many different codes are possible?

(A) 144
(B) 152
(C) 160
(D) 168
(E) 176

Arithmetic Elementary Combinatorics

Since the first digit cannot be 0 or 1, there are 8 digits possible for the first digit. Since the second digit must be 0 or 1, there are 2 digits possible for the second digit. If there were no other restrictions, all 10 digits would be possible for the third digit, making the total number of possible codes $8 \times 2 \times 10 = 160$. But the additional restriction that the second and third digits cannot both be 0 in the same code eliminates the 8 codes 2-0-0, 3-0-0, 4-0-0, 5-0-0, 6-0-0, 7-0-0, 8-0-0, and 9-0-0. Therefore, there are $160 - 8 = 152$ possible codes.

The correct answer is B.

200. Jackie has two solutions that are 2 percent sulfuric acid and 12 percent sulfuric acid by volume, respectively. If these solutions are mixed in appropriate quantities to produce 60 liters of a solution that is 5 percent sulfuric acid, approximately how many liters of the 2 percent solution will be required?

    (A) 18
    (B) 20
    (C) 24
    (D) 36
    (E) 42

Algebra Simultaneous Equations

Let x represent the quantity of the 2% sulfuric acid solution in the mixture, from which it follows that the 2% sulfuric acid solution contributes $0.02x$ liters of sulfuric acid to the mixture. Let y represent the quantity of the 12% sulfuric acid solution in the mixture, from which it follows that the 12% sulfuric acid solution contributes $0.12y$ liters of sulfuric acid to the mixture. Since there are 60 liters of the mixture, $x + y = 60$. The quantity of sulfuric acid in the mixture, which is 5% sulfuric acid, is then $(0.05)(60) = 3$ liters. Therefore, $0.02x + 0.12y = 3$. Substituting $60 - x$ for y gives $0.02x + 0.12(60 - x) = 3$. Then,

$0.02x + 0.12(60 - x) = 3$	given
$0.02x + 7.2 - 0.12x = 3$	use distributive property
$7.2 - 0.1x = 3$	combine like terms
$-0.1x = -4.2$	subtract 7.2 from both sides
$x = 42$	divide both sides by -0.1

The correct answer is E.

201. If Jake loses 8 pounds, he will weigh twice as much as his sister. Together they now weigh 278 pounds. What is Jake's present weight, in pounds?

    (A) 131
    (B) 135
    (C) 139
    (D) 147
    (E) 188

Algebra Systems of Equations

Let J represent Jake's weight and S represent his sister's weight. Then $J - 8 = 2S$ and $J + S = 278$. Solve the second equation for S and get $S = 278 - J$. Substituting the expression for S into the first equation gives

$$J - 8 = 2(278 - J)$$
$$J - 8 = 556 - 2J$$
$$J + 2J = 556 + 8$$
$$3J = 564$$
$$J = 188$$

The correct answer is E.

202. For each student in a certain class, a teacher adjusted the student's test score using the formula $y = 0.8x + 20$, where x is the student's original test score and y is the student's adjusted test score. If the standard deviation of the original test scores of the students in the class was 20, what was the standard deviation of the adjusted test scores of the students in the class?

    (A) 12
    (B) 16
    (C) 28
    (D) 36
    (E) 40

Arithmetic Statistics

The solution to this problem relies on the statistical properties summarized in the following table:

Data Set Values	Mean	Standard Deviation
x	μ	σ
$ax + b$	$a\mu + b$	$a\sigma$

The standard deviation of the original test scores was 20. Therefore, when the teacher multiplied each student's score by 0.8 and then added 20, the standard deviation of the set of adjusted scores is $0.8(20) = 16$.

The correct answer is B.

203. Last year 26 members of a certain club traveled to England, 26 members traveled to France, and 32 members traveled to Italy. Last year no members of the club traveled to both England and France, 6 members traveled to both England and Italy, and 11 members traveled to both France and Italy. How many members of the club traveled to at least one of these three countries last year?

(A) 52
(B) 67
(C) 71
(D) 73
(E) 79

Arithmetic Applied Problems

The numbers in the Venn diagram below represent the numbers of members of the club who traveled to the indicated countries, and these numbers can be determined as follows. Since no members traveled to both England and France, both regions that form the overlap of England and France are labeled with 0. It follows that none of the 6 members who traveled to both England and Italy traveled to France, and so the region corresponding to England and Italy only is labeled with 6. It also follows that none of the 11 members who traveled to both France and Italy traveled to England, and so the region corresponding to France and Italy only is labeled with 11. At this point it can be determined that 26 − 6 = 20 members traveled to England only, 26 − 11 = 15 members traveled to France only, and 32 − (6 + 11) = 15 members traveled to Italy only.

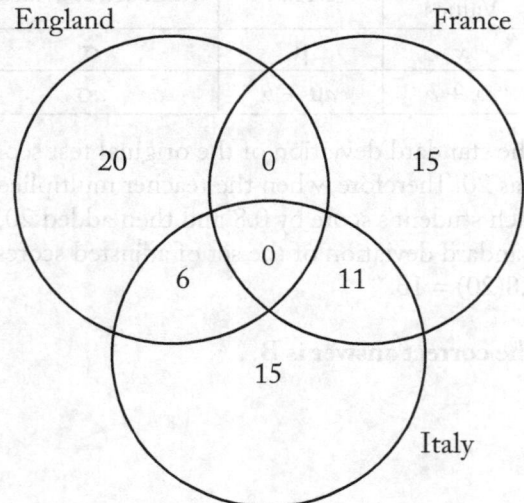

England   France

Italy

From the diagram it follows that 20 + 15 + 6 + 11 + 15 = 67 members traveled to at least one of these three countries.

The correct answer is B.

204. A store reported total sales of $385 million for February of this year. If the total sales for the same month last year were $320 million, approximately what was the percent increase in sales?

(A) 2%
(B) 17%
(C) 20%
(D) 65%
(E) 83%

Arithmetic Percents

The percent increase in sales from last year to this year is 100 times the quotient of the difference in sales for the two years divided by the sales last year. Thus, the percent increase is

$$\frac{385-320}{320}\times100 = \frac{65}{320}\times100$$

$$= \frac{13}{64}\times100$$

$$\approx \frac{13}{65}\times100$$

$$= \frac{1}{5}\times100$$

$$= 20\%$$

The correct answer is C.

205. When positive integer x is divided by positive integer y, the remainder is 9. If $\frac{x}{y} = 96.12$, what is the value of y?

(A) 96
(B) 75
(C) 48
(D) 25
(E) 12

Arithmetic Properties of Numbers

The remainder is 9 when x is divided by y, so $x = yq + 9$ for some positive integer q. Dividing both sides by y gives $\frac{x}{y} = q + \frac{9}{y}$. But $\frac{x}{y} = 96.12 = 96 + 0.12$.

Equating the two expressions for $\frac{x}{y}$ gives

$q + \frac{9}{y} = 96 + 0.12$. Thus, $q = 96$ and $\frac{9}{y} = 0.12$.

$$9 = 0.12y$$

$$y = \frac{9}{0.12}$$

$$y = 75$$

The correct answer is B.

206. If $x(2x + 1) = 0$ and $\left(x + \frac{1}{2}\right)(2x - 3) = 0$, then $x =$

(A) -3

(B) $-\frac{1}{2}$

(C) 0

(D) $\frac{1}{2}$

(E) $\frac{3}{2}$

Algebra Second-Degree Equations; **Simultaneous Equations**

Setting each factor equal to 0, it can be seen that the solution set to the first equation is $\left\{0, -\frac{1}{2}\right\}$ and the solution set to the second equation is

$\left\{-\frac{1}{2}, \frac{3}{2}\right\}$. Therefore, $-\frac{1}{2}$ is the solution to both equations.

The correct answer is B.

207. A certain experimental mathematics program was tried out in 2 classes in each of 32 elementary schools and involved 37 teachers. Each of the classes had 1 teacher and each of the teachers taught at least 1, but not more than 3, of the classes. If the number of teachers who taught 3 classes is n, then the least and greatest possible values of n, respectively, are

(A)   0 and 13

(B)   0 and 14

(C)   1 and 10

(D)   1 and 9

(E)   2 and 8

Algebra Simultaneous Equations; Inequalities

It is given that $2(32) = 64$ classes are taught by 37 teachers. Let k, m, and n be the number of teachers who taught, respectively, 1, 2, and 3 of the classes. Then $k + m + n = 37$ and $k + 2m + 3n = 64$. Subtracting these two equations gives $m + 2n = 64 - 37 = 27$, or $2n = 27 - m$, and therefore $2n \leq 27$. Because n is an integer, it follows that $n \leq 13$ and answer choice B cannot be the answer. Since $n = 0$ is possible, which can be seen by using $m = 27$ and $k = 10$ (obtained by solving $2n = 27 - m$ with $n = 0$, then by solving $k + m + n = 37$ with $n = 0$ and $m = 27$), the answer must be answer choice A.

It is not necessary to ensure that $n = 13$ is possible to answer the question. However, it is not difficult to see that $k = 23$, $m = 1$, and $n = 13$ satisfy the given conditions.

The correct answer is A.

208. For the positive numbers n, $n + 1$, $n + 2$, $n + 4$, and $n + 8$, the mean is how much greater than the median?

(A) 0

(B) 1

(C) $n + 1$

(D) $n + 2$

(E) $n + 3$

Algebra Statistics

Since the five positive numbers n, $n + 1$, $n + 2$, $n + 4$, and $n + 8$ are in ascending order, the median is the third number, which is $n + 2$. The mean of the five numbers is

$$\frac{n + (n+1) + (n+2) + (n+4) + (n+8)}{5}$$

$$= \frac{5n + 15}{5}$$

$$= n + 3$$

Since $(n + 3) - (n + 2) = 1$, the mean is 1 greater than the median.

The correct answer is B.

209. The present ratio of students to teachers at a certain school is 30 to 1. If the student enrollment were to increase by 50 students and the number of teachers were to increase by 5, the ratio of students to teachers would then be 25 to 1. What is the present number of teachers?

(A) 5
(B) 8
(C) 10
(D) 12
(E) 15

Algebra Applied Problems

After noting that $\dfrac{\text{number of students}}{\text{number of teachers}} = \dfrac{30}{1}$ implies that the number of students is 30 times the number of teachers, this problem can be solved with arithmetic, as shown in the table below, by guessing the present number of teachers, increasing the numbers of students and teachers as specified, then checking to see if the resulting ratio is equal to $\dfrac{25}{1}$.

Present Number of Teachers	Present Number of Students	Teachers Increased by 5	Students Increased by 50	Resulting Ratio	Equal to $\dfrac{25}{1}$?
5	150	10	200	$\dfrac{200}{10} = \dfrac{20}{1}$	no
8	240	13	290	$\dfrac{290}{13} = \dfrac{22\frac{4}{13}}{1}$	no
10	300	15	350	$\dfrac{350}{15} = \dfrac{23\frac{1}{3}}{1}$	no
12	360	17	410	$\dfrac{410}{17} = \dfrac{24\frac{2}{17}}{1}$	no
15	450	20	500	$\dfrac{500}{20} = \dfrac{25}{1}$	yes

Therefore, the present number of teachers is 15.

Alternatively, the problem can be solved using algebra.

The following table summarizes the given information, where s represents the present number of students and t represents the present number of teachers:

	Number of Students	Number of Teachers	$\dfrac{\text{Students}}{\text{Teachers}}$	Equation After Cross Multiplying
Present	s	t	$\dfrac{s}{t} = \dfrac{30}{1}$	$s = 30t$
After Increases	$s + 50$	$t + 5$	$\dfrac{s+50}{t+5} = \dfrac{25}{1}$	$s + 50 = 25(t + 5)$

Determine the value of t using $s = 30t$ (Equation 1) and $s + 50 = 25(t + 5) = 25t + 125$ (Equation 2).

$s + 50 = 25t + 125$	Equation 2
$30t + 50 = 25t + 125$	substitution from Equation 1
$5t + 50 = 125$	subtract $25t$ from both sides
$5t = 75$	subtract 50 from both sides
$t = 15$	divide both sides by 5

Therefore, the present number of teachers is 15.

The correct answer is E.

210. What is the smallest integer n for which $25^n > 5^{12}$?

    (A) 6
    (B) 7
    (C) 8
    (D) 9
    (E) 10

Arithmetic Operations with Rational Numbers

Because $5^2 = 25$, a common base is 5. Rewrite the left side with 5 as a base: $25^n = (5^2)^n = 5^{2n}$. It follows that the desired integer is the least integer n for which $5^{2n} > 5^{12}$. This will be the least integer n for which $2n > 12$, or the least integer n for which $n > 6$, which is 7.

The correct answer is B.

211. Sixty percent of the members of a study group are women, and 45 percent of those women are lawyers. If one member of the study group is to be selected at random, what is the probability that the member selected is a woman lawyer?

    (A) 0.10
    (B) 0.15
    (C) 0.27
    (D) 0.33
    (E) 0.45

Arithmetic Probability

For simplicity, suppose there are 100 members in the study group. Since 60 percent of the members are women, there are 60 women in the group. Also, 45 percent of the women are lawyers so there are $0.45(60) = 27$ women lawyers in the study group. Therefore, the probability of selecting a woman lawyer is $\dfrac{27}{100} = 0.27$.

The correct answer is C.

212. Each year for 4 years, a farmer increased the number of trees in a certain orchard by $\dfrac{1}{4}$ of the number of trees in the orchard the preceding year. If all of the trees thrived and there were 6,250 trees in the orchard at the end of the 4-year period, how many trees were in the orchard at the beginning of the 4-year period?

    (A) 1,250
    (B) 1,563
    (C) 2,250
    (D) 2,560
    (E) 2,752

Arithmetic Operations on Rational Numbers

Let N be the number of trees in the orchard at the beginning of the 4-year period. Since the number of trees increases by a factor of $\dfrac{1}{4}$ each year, the number of trees after the first year is $N + \dfrac{1}{4}N = \dfrac{5}{4}N$. Note that this shows algebraically that an increase by a factor of $\dfrac{1}{4}$ corresponds to multiplication by $\dfrac{5}{4}$. Therefore, the number of trees after the second year is $\dfrac{5}{4}$ times $\dfrac{5}{4}N$, which equals $\left(\dfrac{5}{4}\right)^2 N$. Similarly, the number of trees after the third year is $\left(\dfrac{5}{4}\right)^3 N$ and the number of trees after the fourth year is $\left(\dfrac{5}{4}\right)^4 N$. Since the number of trees after the fourth year is 6,250, it follows that $\left(\dfrac{5}{4}\right)^4 N = 6,250$. Next, solve for N:

$\left(\dfrac{5}{4}\right)^4 N = 6{,}250$	given
$\left(\dfrac{5^4}{4^4}\right) N = 6{,}250$	property of exponents
$N = 6{,}250 \div \dfrac{5^4}{4^4}$	divide both sides by $\dfrac{5^4}{4^4}$
$N = 6{,}250 \times \dfrac{4^4}{5^4}$	invert and multiply
$N = 2 \times 5^5 \times \dfrac{4^4}{5^4}$	factor 6,250
$N = 2 \times 5 \times 4^4$	cancel common factors
$N = 2{,}560$	multiply

The correct answer is D.

Number of Shipments of Manufactured Homes
in the United States, 1990–2000

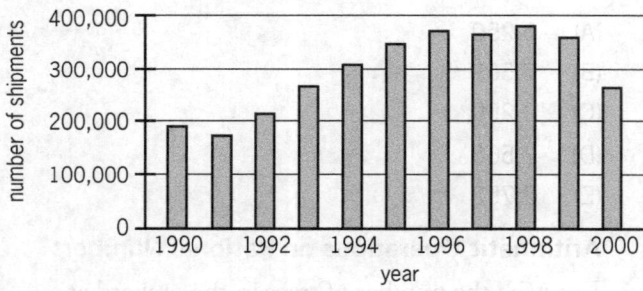

213. According to the chart shown, which of the following is closest to the median annual number of shipments of manufactured homes in the United States for the years from 1990 to 2000, inclusive?

(A) 250,000
(B) 280,000
(C) 310,000
(D) 325,000
(E) 340,000

Arithmetic Interpretation of Graphs and Tables; Statistics

From the chart, the approximate numbers of shipments are as follows:

Year	Number of Shipments
1990	190,000
1991	180,000
1992	210,000
1993	270,000
1994	310,000
1995	350,000
1996	380,000
1997	370,000
1998	390,000
1999	360,000
2000	270,000

Since there are 11 entries in the table and 11 is an odd number, the median of the numbers of shipments is the 6th entry when the numbers of shipments are arranged in order from least to greatest. In order, from least to greatest, the first 6 entries are:

Number of Shipments
180,000
190,000
210,000
270,000
270,000
310,000

The 6th entry is 310,000.

The correct answer is C.

214. For the positive integers a, b, and k, $a^k \| b$ means that a^k is a divisor of b, but a^{k+1} is not a divisor of b. If k is a positive integer and $2^k \| 72$, then k is equal to

(A) 2
(B) 3
(C) 4
(D) 8
(E) 18

Arithmetic Property of Numbers

Since $72 = (2^3)(3^2)$, it follows that 2^3 is a divisor of 72 and 2^4 is not a divisor of 72. Therefore, $2^3 \| 72$, and hence $k = 3$.

The correct answer is B.

215. A certain characteristic in a large population has a distribution that is symmetric about the mean m. If 68 percent of the distribution lies within one standard deviation d of the mean, what percent of the distribution is less than $m + d$?

    (A) 16%
    (B) 32%
    (C) 48%
    (D) 84%
    (E) 92%

Arithmetic Statistics

Since 68% lies between $m - d$ and $m + d$, a total of $(100 - 68)\% = 32\%$ lies to the left of $m - d$ and to the right of $m + d$. Because the distribution is symmetric about m, half of the 32% lies to the right of $m + d$. Therefore, 16% lies to the right of $m + d$, and hence $(100 - 16)\% = 84\%$ lies to the left of $m + d$.

The correct answer is D.

216. Four extra-large sandwiches of exactly the same size were ordered for m students, where $m > 4$. Three of the sandwiches were evenly divided among the students. Since 4 students did not want any of the fourth sandwich, it was evenly divided among the remaining students. If Carol ate one piece from each of the four sandwiches, the amount of sandwich that she ate would be what fraction of a whole extra-large sandwich?

    (A) $\dfrac{m+4}{m(m-4)}$
    (B) $\dfrac{2m-4}{m(m-4)}$
    (C) $\dfrac{4m-4}{m(m-4)}$
    (D) $\dfrac{4m-8}{m(m-4)}$
    (E) $\dfrac{4m-12}{m(m-4)}$

Algebra Applied Problems

Since each of 3 of the sandwiches was evenly divided among m students, each piece was $\frac{1}{m}$ of a sandwich. Since the fourth sandwich was evenly divided among $m - 4$ students, each piece was

$\dfrac{1}{m-4}$ of the fourth sandwich. Carol ate 1 piece from each of the four sandwiches, so she ate a total of

$$(3)\frac{1}{m} + \frac{1}{m-4} = \frac{3(m-4)+m}{m(m-4)} = \frac{4m-12}{m(m-4)}$$

The correct answer is E.

217. Which of the following equations has $1 + \sqrt{2}$ as one of its roots?

    (A) $x^2 + 2x - 1 = 0$
    (B) $x^2 - 2x + 1 = 0$
    (C) $x^2 + 2x + 1 = 0$
    (D) $x^2 - 2x - 1 = 0$
    (E) $x^2 - x - 1 = 0$

Algebra Second-Degree Equations

This problem can be solved by working backward to construct a quadratic equation with $1 + \sqrt{2}$ as a root that does not involve radicals.

$x = 1 + \sqrt{2}$	set x to the desired value
$x - 1 = \sqrt{2}$	subtract 1 from both sides
$(x-1)^2 = 2$	square both sides
$x^2 - 2x + 1 = 2$	expand the left side
$x^2 - 2x - 1 = 0$	subtract 2 from both sides

The correct answer is D.

218. In Country C, the unemployment rate among construction workers dropped from 16 percent on September 1, 1992, to 9 percent on September 1, 1996. If the number of construction workers was 20 percent greater on September 1, 1996, than on September 1, 1992, what was the approximate percent change in the number of unemployed construction workers over this period?

    (A) 50% decrease
    (B) 30% decrease
    (C) 15% decrease
    (D) 30% increase
    (E) 55% increase

Arithmetic Percents

Letting N represent the number of construction workers on September 1, 1992, the information given in the problem is as follows:

(1) On September 1, 1992, the unemployment rate among construction workers was 16 percent, so the **number** of unemployed construction workers on September 1, 1992, was **$0.16N$**.

(2) On September 1, 1996, the **number** of construction workers was 20 percent greater than on September 1, 1992, so the **number** of construction workers on September 1, 1996, was **$1.2N$**.

(3) On September 1, 1996, the unemployment rate among construction workers was 9 percent, so the **number** of unemployed construction workers on September 1, 1996, was **$0.09(1.2N)$**.

As a fraction, the percent change in the **number** of unemployed construction workers from September 1, 1992, to September 1, 1996, is given by:

$$\frac{\text{number in 1996} - \text{number in 1992}}{\text{number in 1992}}$$

$= \dfrac{0.09(1.2N) - 0.16N}{0.16N}$	substitution of expressions from (1) and (3)
$= \dfrac{(0.09)(1.2) - 0.16}{0.16}$	divide numerator and denominator by N
$= \dfrac{9(12) - 160}{160}$	multiply numerator and denominator by 1,000 for ease of calculation
$= \dfrac{108 - 160}{160}$	multiply
$= -\dfrac{52}{160}$	subtract
$= -\dfrac{13}{40}$	divide numerator and denominator by 4
$\approx -\dfrac{13}{39}$	$39 \approx 40$
$\approx -\dfrac{1}{3}$	divide numerator and denominator by 13

Then, as a percent, $-\dfrac{1}{3}$ represents a decrease of about 30%.

The correct answer is B.

219. In a box of 12 pens, a total of 3 are defective. If a customer buys 2 pens selected at random from the box, what is the probability that neither pen will be defective?

(A) $\dfrac{1}{6}$

(B) $\dfrac{2}{9}$

(C) $\dfrac{6}{11}$

(D) $\dfrac{9}{16}$

(E) $\dfrac{3}{4}$

Arithmetic Probability

The probability that the first pen selected is not defective is $\dfrac{9}{12} = \dfrac{3}{4}$ (9 pens are not defective out of a total of 12 pens). Assuming the first pen selected is not defective, the probability that the second pen is not defective is $\dfrac{8}{11}$ (this time 8 pens are not defective out of a total of 11 pens). Therefore, using the multiplication rule for dependent events, the probability that both pens are not defective is $\left(\dfrac{3}{4}\right)\left(\dfrac{8}{11}\right) = \dfrac{6}{11}$.

Alternatively, by a direct count using the number of combinations of n objects taken k at a time (see Section 3.4.3, "Counting Methods," in the Math Review chapter), there are $\binom{9}{2} = \dfrac{(9)(8)}{2} = 36$ ways to select 2 non-defective pens from the 9 non-defective pens, and there are $\binom{12}{2} = \dfrac{(12)(11)}{2} = 66$ ways to select 2 pens from the 12 pens. Therefore, the probability that the 2 pens selected are not defective is

$$\frac{\text{number of ways to select 2 non-defective pens}}{\text{number of ways to select 2 pens}} =$$

$$\frac{36}{66} = \frac{6}{11}.$$

The correct answer is C.

220. At a certain fruit stand, the price of each apple is 40 cents and the price of each orange is 60 cents. Mary selects a total of 10 apples and oranges from the fruit stand, and the average (arithmetic mean) price of the 10 pieces of fruit is 56 cents. How many oranges must Mary put back so that the average price of the pieces of fruit that she keeps is 52 cents?

(A) 1
(B) 2
(C) 3
(D) 4
(E) 5

Algebra Statistics

This problem can be solved using arithmetic or algebra.

<u>With algebra</u>

Let x be the number of oranges Mary selected originally. It follows that the number of apples Mary selected is $10 - x$ since the number of pieces of fruit she selected originally was 10. The average price of the 10 pieces of fruit is 56 cents so,

$\dfrac{40(10-x)+60x}{10} = 56$	given
$40(10-x)+60x = 560$	multiply both sides by 10
$400 - 40x + 60x = 560$	distributive property
$400 + 20x = 560$	combine like terms
$20x = 160$	subtract 400 from each term
$x = 8$	divide both sides by 20

Thus, Mary originally selected 8 oranges and 2 apples.

If y represents the number of oranges that Mary must put back, then $8 - y$ is the number of oranges she keeps. So, with the 2 apples, the total number of pieces of fruit she keeps is $2 + (8 - y)$. The average price of these $2 + (8 - y)$ pieces of fruit is 52 cents so,

$\dfrac{40(2)+60(8-y)}{2+(8-y)} = 52$	given
$40(2)+60(8-y) = 52[2+(8-y)]$	multiply both sides by $2 + (8 - y)$
$40(2)+60(8-y) = 52(10-y)$	combine like terms
$80 + 480 - 60y = 520 - 52y$	distributive property
$560 - 60y = 520 - 52y$	combine like terms
$560 = 520 + 8y$	add $60y$ to both sides
$40 = 8y$	subtract 520 from both sides
$5 = y$	divide both sides by 8

Therefore, Mary must put back 5 oranges so that the average price of the 2 apples and 3 oranges she keeps is $\dfrac{40(2)+60(3)}{5} = \dfrac{260}{5} = 52$ cents.

<u>With arithmetic</u>

In order to know how many oranges Mary should put back to decrease the average price of the pieces of fruit she is buying to 52 cents, the number of oranges she originally selected needs to be determined. Consider the following table:

Number of apples	Number of oranges	Average price (cents)	Average = 56 cents?
1	9	$\dfrac{1(40)+9(60)}{10} = \dfrac{580}{10} = 58$	no
2	8	$\dfrac{2(40)+8(60)}{10} = \dfrac{560}{10} = 56$	**yes**

Thus, Mary originally selected 2 apples and 8 oranges.

203

Next, determine how many oranges Mary must put back so that the average price of the pieces of fruit she keeps is 52 cents, consider the following table:

Number of apples	Number of oranges put back	Number of oranges kept	Average price (cents)	Average = 52 cents?
2	1	7	$\frac{2(40)+7(60)}{9} = \frac{500}{9} = 55\frac{5}{9}$	no
2	2	6	$\frac{2(40)+6(60)}{8} = \frac{440}{8} = 55$	no
2	3	5	$\frac{2(40)+5(60)}{7} = \frac{380}{7} = 54\frac{2}{7}$	no
2	4	4	$\frac{2(40)+4(60)}{6} = \frac{320}{6} = 53\frac{1}{3}$	no
2	5	3	$\frac{2(40)+3(60)}{5} = \frac{260}{5} = 52$	**yes**

Therefore, Mary must put back 5 oranges.

Note: It is not necessary to perform all of the calculations shown here. It should be obvious, for example, that $\frac{500}{9}, \frac{380}{7}$, and $\frac{320}{6}$ are not whole numbers and therefore cannot equal 52. Nor is it necessary to increment the number of oranges she must put back by 1. For this problem, a good guess might be 4, thinking she might need to put back half the oranges she selected originally. Since putting back 4 oranges doesn't bring the average price down enough, the only other choice is 5, which is the correct answer.

Note that the steps are explained in great detail here. Having good algebraic manipulation skills would make most of the steps fairly automatic.

The correct answer is E.

221. A pharmaceutical company received $3 million in royalties on the first $20 million in sales of the generic equivalent of one of its products and then $9 million in royalties on the next $108 million in sales. By approximately what percent did the ratio of royalties to sales decrease from the first $20 million in sales to the next $108 million in sales?

(A)   8%
(B)   15%
(C)   45%
(D)   52%
(E)   56%

Arithmetic Percents

The ratio of royalties to sales for the first $20 million in sales is $\frac{3}{20}$, and the ratio of royalties to sales for the next $108 million in sales is $\frac{9}{108} = \frac{1}{12}$.

Now calculate the percent decrease from $\frac{3}{20}$ to $\frac{1}{12}$.

$$\frac{\frac{1}{12} - \frac{3}{20}}{\frac{3}{20}} \times 100 = \left(\frac{1}{12} - \frac{3}{20}\right) \times \frac{20}{3} \times 100$$

$$= \left(\frac{1 \times 20}{12 \times 3} - \frac{3 \times 20}{20 \times 3}\right) \times 100$$

$$= \left(\frac{5}{9} - 1\right) \times 100$$

$$= -\frac{4}{9} \times 100$$

$$\approx -0.44 \times 100$$

$$\approx 45\% \text{ decrease}$$

An alternative way to calculate the percent decrease from $\frac{3}{20}$ to $\frac{1}{12}$ is to scale the values up until they are integers, which allows for a simpler calculation. Multiplying each of these values by 60 gives $60 \times \frac{3}{20} = 9$ and $60 \times \frac{1}{12} = 5$, respectively, so the problem reduces to calculating the percent decrease from 9 to 5. Therefore,

$$\frac{5-9}{9} \times 100 = -\frac{4}{9} \times 100 \approx -0.44 \times 100 \approx 45\%$$

decrease.

The correct answer is C.

Times at Which the Door
Opened from 8:00 to 10:00

8:00	8:06	8:30	9:05
8:03	8:10	8:31	9:11
8:04	8:18	8:54	9:29
8:04	8:19	8:57	9:31

222. The light in a restroom operates with a 15-minute timer that is reset every time the door opens as a person goes in or out of the room. Thus, after someone enters or exits the room, the light remains on for only 15 minutes unless the door opens again and resets the timer for another 15 minutes. If the times listed above are the times at which the door opened from 8:00 to 10:00, approximately how many minutes during this two-hour period was the light off?

(A) 10
(B) 25
(C) 35
(D) 40
(E) 70

Arithmetic Operations with Integers

In the table given above, read down the columns looking for pairs of consecutive times that are more than 15 minutes apart. The following table shows all such pairs:

Consecutive times more than 15 minutes apart	Minutes between times door opens	Minutes that light is on	Minutes that light is off
8:31 and 8:54	54 − 31 = 23	15	23 − 15 = 8
9:11 and 9:29	29 − 11 = 18	15	18 − 15 = 3
9:31 and 10:00	60 − 31 = 29	15	29 − 15 = 14
Total time light is off			25

The correct answer is B.

223. If p is the product of the integers from 1 to 30, inclusive, what is the greatest integer k for which 3^k is a factor of p?

(A) 10
(B) 12
(C) 14
(D) 16
(E) 18

Arithmetic Properties of Numbers

The table below shows the numbers from 1 to 30, inclusive, that have at least one factor of 3 and how many factors of 3 each has.

Multiples of 3 Between 1 and 30	Number of Factors of 3
3	1
$6 = 2 \times 3$	1
$9 = 3 \times 3$	2
$12 = 2 \times 2 \times 3$	1
$15 = 3 \times 5$	1
$18 = 2 \times 3 \times 3$	2
$21 = 3 \times 7$	1
$24 = 2 \times 2 \times 2 \times 3$	1
$27 = 3 \times 3 \times 3$	3
$30 = 2 \times 3 \times 5$	1

The sum of the numbers in the right column is 14. Therefore, 3^{14} is the greatest power of 3 that is a factor of the product of the first 30 positive integers.

The correct answer is C.

224. If $n = 3^8 - 2^8$, which of the following is NOT a factor of n?

(A) 97

(B) 65

(C) 35

(D) 13

(E)   5

Arithmetic Properties of Numbers

Since $3^8 - 2^8$ is the difference of the perfect squares $(3^4)^2$ and $(2^4)^2$, then $3^8 - 2^8 = (3^4 + 2^4)(3^4 - 2^4)$. But $3^4 - 2^4$ is also the difference of the perfect squares $(3^2)^2$ and $(2^2)^2$ so $3^4 - 2^4 = (3^2 + 2^2)(3^2 - 2^2)$ and therefore $3^8 - 2^8 = (3^4 + 2^4)(3^2 + 2^2)(3^2 - 2^2)$. It follows that $3^8 - 2^8$ can be factored as $(81 + 16)(9 + 4)(9 - 4) = (97)(13)(5)$. Therefore, 7 is not a factor of $3^8 - 2^8$, and hence $35 = 5 \times 7$ is not a factor of $3^8 - 2^8$. It is easy to see that each of 97, 13, and 5 is a factor of $3^8 - 2^8$, and so is 65, since $65 = 5 \times 13$, although this additional analysis is not needed to arrive at the correct answer.

The correct answer is C.

225. Club X has more than 10 but fewer than 40 members. Sometimes the members sit at tables with 3 members at one table and 4 members at each of the other tables, and sometimes they sit at tables with 3 members at one table and 5 members at each of the other tables. If they sit at tables with 6 members at each table except one and fewer than 6 members at that one table, how many members will be at the table that has fewer than 6 members?

(A) 1

(B) 2

(C) 3

(D) 4

(E) 5

Arithmetic Properties of Numbers

Let n be the number of members that Club X has. Since the members can be equally divided into groups of 4 each with 3 left over, and the members can be equally divided into groups of 5 each with 3 left over, it follows that $n - 3$ is divisible by both 4 and 5. Therefore, $n - 3$ must be

a multiple of $(4)(5) = 20$. Also, because the only multiple of 20 that is greater than 10 and less than 40 is 20, it follows that $n - 3 = 20$, or $n = 23$. Finally, when these 23 members are divided into the greatest number of groups of 6 each, there will be 5 members left over, since $23 = (3)(6) + 5$.

The correct answer is E.

226. In order to complete a reading assignment on time, Terry planned to read 90 pages per day. However, she read only 75 pages per day at first, leaving 690 pages to be read during the last 6 days before the assignment was to be completed. How many days in all did Terry have to complete the assignment on time?

(A) 15

(B) 16

(C) 25

(D) 40

(E) 46

Algebra Applied Problems

Let n be the number of days that Terry read at the slower rate of 75 pages per day. Then $75n$ is the number of pages Terry read at this slower rate, and $75n + 690$ is the total number of pages Terry needs to read. Also, $n + 6$ is the total number of days that Terry will spend on the reading assignment. The requirement that Terry average 90 pages per day is equivalent to $\dfrac{75n + 690}{n + 6} = 90$. Then

$$\frac{75n + 690}{n + 6} = 90$$
$$75n + 690 = 90n + 540$$
$$150 = 15n$$
$$10 = n$$

Therefore, the total number of days that Terry has to complete the assignment on time is $n + 6 = 10 + 6 = 16$.

The correct answer is B.

227. If $s > 0$ and $\sqrt{\dfrac{r}{s}} = s$, what is r in terms of s?

    (A) $\dfrac{1}{s}$

    (B) $\sqrt{s}$

    (C) $s\sqrt{s}$

    (D) s^3

    (E) $s^3 - s$

Algebra Equations

Solve the equation for r as follows:

$$\sqrt{\dfrac{r}{s}} = s$$

$\quad \dfrac{r}{s} = s^2 \quad$ square both sides of the equation

$\quad r = s^3 \quad$ multiply both sides by s

The correct answer is D.

228. If $3 < x < 100$, for how many values of x is $\dfrac{x}{3}$ the square of a prime number?

    (A) Two

    (B) Three

    (C) Four

    (D) Five

    (E) Nine

Arithmetic Properties of Numbers

If $\dfrac{x}{3}$ is the square of a prime number, then possible values of $\dfrac{x}{3}$ are $2^2, 3^2, 5^2, 7^2, \ldots$.
Therefore, possible values of x are $3 \times 2^2 = 12$, $3 \times 3^2 = 27$, $3 \times 5^2 = 75$, $3 \times 7^2 = 147$, $\ldots$. Since only three of these values, namely $12, 27$, and 75, are between 3 and 100, there are three values of x such that $\dfrac{x}{3}$ is the square of a prime number.

The correct answer is B.

229. A researcher plans to identify each participant in a certain medical experiment with a code consisting of either a single letter or a pair of distinct letters written in alphabetical order. What is the least number of letters that can be used if there are 12 participants, and each participant is to receive a different code?

    (A) 4

    (B) 5

    (C) 6

    (D) 7

    (E) 8

Arithmetic Elementary Combinatorics

None of the essential aspects of the problem is affected if the letters are restricted to be the first n letters of the alphabet, for various positive integers n. With the 3 letters a, b, and c, there are 6 codes: a, b, c, ab, ac, and bc. With the 4 letters a, b, c, and d, there are 10 codes: a, b, c, d, ab, ac, ad, bc, bd, and cd. Clearly, more than 12 codes are possible with 5 or more letters, so the least number of letters that can be used is 5.

The correct answer is B.

230. An object thrown directly upward is at a height of h feet after t seconds, where $h = -16(t-3)^2 + 150$. At what height, in feet, is the object 2 seconds after it reaches its maximum height?

    (A) 6

    (B) 86

    (C) 134

    (D) 150

    (E) 166

Algebra Applied Problems

Since $(t-3)^2$ is positive when $t \neq 3$ and zero when $t = 3$, it follows that the *minimum* value of $(t-3)^2$ occurs when $t = 3$. Therefore, the *maximum* value of $-16(t-3)^2$, and also the maximum value of $-16(t-3)^2 + 150$, occurs when $t = 3$. Hence, the height 2 seconds after the maximum height is the value of h when $t = 5$, or $-16(5-3)^2 + 150 = 86$.

The correct answer is B.

231. Which of the following is equivalent to the pair of inequalities $x + 6 > 10$ and $x - 3 \le 5$?

    (A) $2 \le x < 16$
    (B) $2 \le x < 4$
    (C) $2 < x \le 8$
    (D) $4 < x \le 8$
    (E) $4 \le x < 16$

Algebra Inequalities

Solve the inequalities separately and combine the results.

$$x + 6 > 10$$
$$x > 4$$
$$x - 3 \le 5$$
$$x \le 8$$

Since $x > 4$, then $4 < x$. Combining $4 < x$ and $x \le 8$ gives $4 < x \le 8$.

The correct answer is D.

232. David has d books, which is 3 times as many as Jeff and $\frac{1}{2}$ as many as Paula. How many books do the three of them have altogether, in terms of d?

    (A) $\frac{5}{6}d$
    (B) $\frac{7}{3}d$
    (C) $\frac{10}{3}d$
    (D) $\frac{7}{2}d$
    (E) $\frac{9}{2}d$

Algebra Applied Problems; Simultaneous Equations

Let J be the number of books that Jeff has, and let P be the number of books Paula has. Then the given information about David's books can be expressed as $d = 3J$ and $d = \frac{1}{2}P$. Solving these

two equations for J and P gives $\frac{d}{3} = J$ and $2d = P$.

Thus, $d + J + P = d + \frac{d}{3} + 2d = 3\frac{1}{3}d = \frac{10}{3}d$.

The correct answer is C.

233. There are 8 teams in a certain league and each team plays each of the other teams exactly once. If each game is played by 2 teams, what is the total number of games played?

    (A) 15
    (B) 16
    (C) 28
    (D) 56
    (E) 64

Arithmetic Operations on Rational Numbers

Since no team needs to play itself, each team needs to play 7 other teams. In addition, each game needs to be counted only once, rather than once for each team that plays that game. Since two teams play each game, $\frac{8 \times 7}{2} = 28$ games are needed.

The correct answer is C.

234. At his regular hourly rate, Don had estimated the labor cost of a repair job as \$336 and he was paid that amount. However, the job took 4 hours longer than he had estimated and, consequently, he earned \$2 per hour less than his regular hourly rate. What was the time Don had estimated for the job, in hours?

    (A) 28
    (B) 24
    (C) 16
    (D) 14
    (E) 12

Algebra Second-Degree Equations

For ease of calculation later, note that $336 = 6 \times 7 \times 8$.

To avoid fairly extensive algebraic manipulation, consider starting with the answer choices by checking to see which one satisfies the conditions of the problem.

Estimated		Actual	
Number of hours	Per hour pay†	Number of hours	Per hour pay
A 28	$\dfrac{\$336}{28} = \$12^*$	32	$\dfrac{\$336}{32} \neq \$10^{**}$
B 24	$\dfrac{\$336}{24} = \$14$	28	$\dfrac{\$336}{28} = \$12$
C 16	$\dfrac{\$336}{16} = \$21$	20	$\dfrac{\$336}{20} \neq \$19$
D 14	$\dfrac{\$336}{14} = \$24$	18	$\dfrac{\$336}{18} \neq \$22$
E 12	$\dfrac{\$336}{12} = \$28$	16	$\dfrac{\$336}{16} \neq \$26$

† Note that Don used his regular hourly rate to estimate the labor cost of the repair job, so if he estimated $336 for his labor for a t-hour job, then his regular hourly rate was $\dfrac{\$336}{t}$.

*Cancel wherever possible

$$\frac{336}{28} = \frac{6 \times \cancel{7} \times 8^{\,2}}{\cancel{7} \times \cancel{4}} = 6 \times 2 = 12$$

**This would need to be $12 − $2 = $10 in order for (A) 28 to be correct.

The correct answer is B.

235. If $\dfrac{p}{q} < 1$, and p and q are positive integers, which of the following must be greater than 1?

(A) $\sqrt{\dfrac{p}{q}}$

(B) $\dfrac{p}{q^2}$

(C) $\dfrac{p}{2q}$

(D) $\dfrac{q}{p^2}$

(E) $\dfrac{q}{p}$

Arithmetic Properties of Numbers

Since p and q are positive integers, $0 < \dfrac{p}{q} < 1$.

A   Since $\dfrac{p}{q} < 1$, then $q > p$. Taking the square root of both sides of the inequality gives $\sqrt{q} > \sqrt{p}$. Then, $\sqrt{\dfrac{p}{q}} = \dfrac{\sqrt{p}}{\sqrt{q}}$, so here the denominator will still be larger than the numerator. CANNOT be greater than 1.

B   Squaring the denominator increases the denominator, which decreases the value of the fraction. CANNOT be greater than 1.

C   Multiplying the denominator by 2 increases the denominator, which decreases the value of the fraction. CANNOT be greater than 1.

D   Since $\dfrac{p}{q} < 1$, then $q > p$. When $p^2 < q$, this expression will be greater than 1, but p^2 need not be less than q. For example, if $p = 2$ and $q = 100$, $\dfrac{p}{q} = \dfrac{2}{100}$ and $\dfrac{q}{p^2} = \dfrac{100}{2^2} = \dfrac{100}{4} = 25 > 1$. However, if $p = 3$ and $q = 4$, then $\dfrac{p}{q} = \dfrac{3}{4}$ and $\dfrac{q}{p^2} = \dfrac{4}{3^2} = \dfrac{4}{9} < 1$. NEED NOT be greater than 1.

E   Again, since $\dfrac{p}{q} < 1$, then $q > p$. Thus, the reciprocal, $\dfrac{q}{p}$, always has a value greater than 1 because the numerator will always be a larger positive integer than the denominator. MUST be greater than 1.

The correct answer is E.

236. To mail a package, the rate is x cents for the first pound and y cents for each additional pound, where $x > y$. Two packages weighing 3 pounds and 5 pounds, respectively, can be mailed separately or combined as one package. Which method is cheaper, and how much money is saved?

(A) Combined, with a savings of $x - y$ cents
(B) Combined, with a savings of $y - x$ cents
(C) Combined, with a savings of x cents
(D) Separately, with a savings of $x - y$ cents
(E) Separately, with a savings of y cents

Algebra Applied Problems

Shipping the two packages separately would cost $1x + 2y$ for the 3-pound package and $1x + 4y$ for the 5-pound package. Shipping them together (as a single 8-pound package) would cost $1x + 7y$. By calculating the sum of the costs for shipping the two packages separately minus the cost for shipping the one combined package, it is possible to determine the difference in cost, as shown.

$$\big((1x + 2y) + (1x + 4y)\big) - (1x + 7y)$$ (cost for 3 lbs + cost for 5 lbs) − cost for 8 lbs

$$= (2x + 6y) - (1x + 7y)$$ combine like terms

$$= 2x + 6y - 1x - 7y$$ distribute the negative

$$= x - y$$ combine like terms

Since $x > y$, this value is positive, which means it costs more to ship two packages separately. Thus, it is cheaper to mail one combined package at a cost savings of $x - y$ cents.

The correct answer is A.

237. If money is invested at r percent interest, compounded annually, the amount of the investment will double in approximately $\frac{70}{r}$ years. If Pat's parents invested $5,000 in a long-term bond that pays 8 percent interest, compounded annually, what will be the approximate total amount of the investment 18 years later, when Pat is ready for college?

(A) $20,000
(B) $15,000
(C) $12,000
(D) $10,000
(E) $9,000

Algebra Applied Problems

Since the investment will double in $\frac{70}{r} = \frac{70}{8} = 8.75 \approx 9$ years, the value of the investment over 18 years can be approximated by doubling its initial value twice. Therefore, the approximate value will be $(\$5,000)(2)(2) = \$20,000$.

The correct answer is A.

238. On a recent trip, Cindy drove her car 290 miles, rounded to the nearest 10 miles, and used 12 gallons of gasoline, rounded to the nearest gallon. The actual number of miles per gallon that Cindy's car got on this trip must have been between

(A) $\frac{290}{12.5}$ and $\frac{290}{11.5}$

(B) $\frac{295}{12}$ and $\frac{285}{11.5}$

(C) $\frac{285}{12}$ and $\frac{295}{12}$

(D) $\frac{285}{12.5}$ and $\frac{295}{11.5}$

(E) $\frac{295}{12.5}$ and $\frac{285}{11.5}$

Arithmetic Estimation

The lowest number of miles per gallon can be calculated using the lowest possible miles and the highest amount of gasoline. Also, the highest number of miles per gallon can be calculated using the highest possible miles and the lowest amount of gasoline.

Since the miles are rounded to the nearest 10 miles, the number of miles is between 285 and 295. Since the gallons are rounded to the nearest gallon, the number of gallons is between 11.5 and 12.5. Therefore, the lowest number of miles per gallon is $\frac{\text{lowest miles}}{\text{highest gallons}} = \frac{285}{12.5}$

and the highest number of miles per gallon is

$$\frac{\text{highest miles}}{\text{lowest gallons}} = \frac{295}{11.5}$$

The correct answer is D.

239. Which of the following inequalities is an algebraic expression for the shaded part of the number line above?

(A) $|x| \leq 3$

(B) $|x| \leq 5$

(C) $|x - 2| \leq 3$

(D) $|x - 1| \leq 4$

(E) $|x + 1| \leq 4$

Algebra Inequalities

The number line above shows $-5 \leq x \leq 3$. To turn this into absolute value notation, as all the choices are written, the numbers need to be opposite signs of the same value.

Since the distance between -5 and 3 is 8 $(3 - (-5) = 8)$, that distance needs to be split in half with -4 to one side and 4 to the other. Each of these two values is 1 more than the values in the inequality above, so adding 1 to all terms in the inequality gives $-4 \leq x + 1 \leq 4$, which is the same as $|x + 1| \leq 4$.

The correct answer is E.

240. In a small snack shop, the average (arithmetic mean) revenue was $400 per day over a 10-day period. During this period, if the average daily revenue was $360 for the first 6 days, what was the average daily revenue for the last 4 days?

(A) $420

(B) $440

(C) $450

(D) $460

(E) $480

Arithmetic; Algebra Statistics; Applied Problems

Let x be the average daily revenue for the last 4 days. Using the formula

$$\text{average} = \frac{\text{sum of values}}{\text{number of values}},$$ the information

regarding the average revenues for the 10-day and 6-day periods can be expressed as follows and solved for x:

$$\$400 = \frac{6(\$360) + 4x}{10}$$

$\$4{,}000 = \$2{,}160 + 4x$ multiply both sides by 10

$\$1{,}840 = 4x$ subtract $2,160 from both sides

$\$460 = x$ divide both sides by 4

The correct answer is D.

241. If y is the smallest positive integer such that 3,150 multiplied by y is the square of an integer, then y must be

(A) 2

(B) 5

(C) 6

(D) 7

(E) 14

Arithmetic Properties of Numbers

To find the smallest positive integer y such that $3{,}150y$ is the square of an integer, first find the prime factorization of 3,150 by a method similar to the following:

$$3{,}150 = 10 \times 315$$
$$= (2 \times 5) \times (3 \times 105)$$
$$= 2 \times 5 \times 3 \times (5 \times 21)$$
$$= 2 \times 5 \times 3 \times 5 \times (3 \times 7)$$
$$= 2 \times 3^2 \times 5^2 \times 7$$

To be a perfect square, $3{,}150y$ must have an even number of each of its prime factors. At a minimum, y must have one factor of 2 and one factor of 7 so that $3{,}150y$ has two factors of each of the primes 2, 3, 5, and 7. The smallest positive integer value of y is then $(2)(7) = 14$.

The correct answer is E.

242. If $[x]$ is the greatest integer less than or equal to x, what is the value of $[-1.6]+[3.4]+[2.7]$?

(A) 3
(B) 4
(C) 5
(D) 6
(E) 7

Arithmetic Profit and Loss

The greatest integer that is less than or equal to -1.6 is -2. It cannot be -1 because -1 is greater than -1.6. The greatest integer that is less than or equal to 3.4 is 3. It cannot be 4 because 4 is greater than 3.4. The greatest integer that is less than or equal to 2.7 is 2. It cannot be 3 because 3 is greater than 2.7. Therefore, $[-1.6]+[3.4]+[2.7] = -2 + 3 + 2 = 3$.

The correct answer is A.

243. In the first week of the year, Nancy saved $1. In each of the next 51 weeks, she saved $1 more than she had saved in the previous week. What was the total amount that Nancy saved during the 52 weeks?

(A) $1,326
(B) $1,352
(C) $1,378
(D) $2,652
(E) $2,756

Arithmetic Operations on Rational Numbers

In dollars, the total amount saved is the sum of $1, (1 + 1), (1 + 1 + 1)$, and so on, up to and including the amount saved in the 52nd week, which was $52. Therefore, the total amount saved in dollars was $1 + 2 + 3 + \ldots + 50 + 51 + 52$. This sum can be easily evaluated by grouping the terms as $(1 + 52) + (2 + 51) + (3 + 50) + \ldots + (26 + 27)$, which results in the number 53 added to itself 26 times. Therefore, the sum is $(26)(53) = 1,378$.

Alternatively, the formula for the sum of the first n positive integers is $\dfrac{n(n+1)}{2}$. Therefore, the sum of the first 52 positive integers is $\dfrac{52(53)}{2} = 26(53) = 1,378$.

The correct answer is C.

244. In a certain sequence, the term x_n is given by the formula $x_n = 2x_{n-1} - \dfrac{1}{2}(x_{n-2})$ for all $n \geq 2$. If $x_0 = 3$ and $x_1 = 2$, what is the value of x_3?

(A) 2.5
(B) 3.125
(C) 4
(D) 5
(E) 6.75

Algebra Simplifying Algebraic Expressions

Given the formula $x_n = 2x_{n-1} - \dfrac{1}{2}(x_{n-2})$ with $x_0 = 3$ and $x_1 = 2$, then

$$x_2 = 2x_1 - \frac{1}{2}x_0$$
$$= 2(2) - \frac{1}{2}(3)$$
$$= \frac{5}{2}$$
$$x_3 = 2x_2 - \frac{1}{2}x_1$$
$$= 2\left(\frac{5}{2}\right) - \frac{1}{2}(2)$$
$$= 5 - 1$$
$$= 4$$

The correct answer is C.

245. During a trip, Francine traveled x percent of the total distance at an average speed of 40 miles per hour and the rest of the distance at an average speed of 60 miles per hour. In terms of x, what was Francine's average speed for the entire trip?

(A) $\dfrac{180 - x}{2}$

(B) $\dfrac{x + 60}{4}$

(C) $\dfrac{300 - x}{5}$

(D) $\dfrac{600}{115 - x}$

(E) $\dfrac{12,000}{x + 200}$

Algebra Applied Problems

Assume for simplicity that the total distance of Francine's trip is 100 miles. Then the following table gives all of the pertinent information.

Distance	Rate	Time = $\dfrac{\text{Distance}}{\text{Rate}}$
x	40	$\dfrac{x}{40}$
$100 - x$	60	$\dfrac{100 - x}{60}$

The total time for Francine's trip is

$$\frac{x}{40} + \frac{100 - x}{60} = \frac{3x}{120} + \frac{2(100 - x)}{120}$$

$$= \frac{3x + 2(100 - x)}{120}$$

$$= \frac{3x + 200 - 2x}{120}$$

$$= \frac{x + 200}{120}$$

Francine's average speed over the entire trip is

$$\frac{\text{total distance}}{\text{total time}} = \frac{100}{\dfrac{x + 200}{120}} = \frac{12,000}{x + 200}.$$

The correct answer is E.

246. If $n = (33)^{43} + (43)^{33}$, what is the units digit of n?

(A)   0
(B)   2
(C)   4
(D)   6
(E)   8

Arithmetic Properties of Numbers

When a polynomial is raised to a power, the last term in the expression is the last term of the polynomial raised to that power. For example, $(a + b)^2 = a^2 + 2ab + b^2$. We can think of 33 as the binomial $10 \cdot 3 + 3$ whose last term is the units digit 3. Thus, the units digit of 33^2 is $3^2 = 9$. Similarly, for 33^3 we have $3^3 = 27$, so the units digit of 33^3 is 7. The patterns for powers of 33 and 43 are shown in the following table.

power of 33	units digit	power of 43	units digit
33^1	3	43^1	3
33^2	9	43^2	9
33^3	7	43^3	7
33^4	1	43^4	1
33^5	3	43^5	3
33^6	9	43^6	9
33^7	7	43^7	7
33^8	1	43^8	1
⋮	⋮	⋮	⋮
33^{32}	1	43^{32}	1
33^{33}	3	43^{33}	3
⋮	⋮		
33^{40}	1		
33^{41}	3		
33^{42}	9		
33^{43}	7		

From the table above, the units digit of 3^{43} is 7 and the units digit of 43^{33} is 3. Since $7 + 3 = 10$, the units digit of $33^{43} + 43^{33}$ is 0.

The correct answer is A.

247. Team A and Team B are competing against each other in a game of tug-of-war. Team A, consisting of 3 males and 3 females, decides to line up male, female, male, female, male, female. The lineup that Team A chooses will be one of how many different possible lineups?

(A)   9
(B)   12
(C)   15
(D)   36
(E)   720

Arithmetic Elementary Combinatorics

Any of the 3 males can be first in the line, and any of the 3 females can be second. Either of the 2 remaining males can be next, followed by either of the 2 remaining females. The last 2 places in the line are filled with the only male left followed by the only female left. By the multiplication principle, there are $3 \times 3 \times 2 \times 2 \times 1 \times 1 = 36$ different lineups possible.

The correct answer is D.

248. If $d = \dfrac{1}{2^3 \times 5^7}$ is expressed as a terminating decimal, how many nonzero digits will d have?

   (A) One
   (B) Two
   (C) Three
   (D) Seven
   (E) Ten

Arithmetic Operations on Rational Numbers

It will be helpful to use the fact that a factor that is an integer power of 10 has no effect on the number of nonzero digits a terminating decimal has.

$$\frac{1}{2^3 \times 5^7} = \frac{1}{2^3 \times 5^3} \times \frac{1}{5^4}$$

$$= \left(\frac{1}{2 \times 5}\right)^3 \times \left(\frac{1}{5}\right)^4$$

$$= \left(\frac{1}{10}\right)^3 \times \left(\frac{1}{5}\right)^4$$

$$= 10^{-3} \times (0.2)^4$$

$$= 10^{-3} \times (0.0016)$$

$$= 0.0000016$$

The correct answer is B.

249. For any positive integer n, the sum of the first n positive integers equals $\dfrac{n(n+1)}{2}$. What is the sum of all the even integers between 99 and 301?

   (A) 10,100
   (B) 20,200
   (C) 22,650
   (D) 40,200
   (E) 45,150

Algebra Simplifying Expressions; Arithmetic Computation with Integers

Note: The following approach does not rely on the given formula.

To determine how many integers are to be summed, consider the following:

5 even integers have 10 as their first two digits, namely 100, 102, 104, 106, 108; 5 even integers have 11 as their first two digits, namely 110, 112, 114, 116, 118;

$\vdots$

5 even integers have 28 as their first two digits, namely 280, 282, 284, 286, 288;

5 even integers have 29 as their first two digits, namely 290, 292, 294, 296, 298.

The first two digits range from 10 through 29, so there are $29 - 10 + 1 = 20$ such pairs of two digits. Thus, there are $20(5) = 100$ even integers between 100 and 298. Including 300, there are 101 even integers between 99 and 301.

These even integers are listed below.

1st	2nd	3rd	4th	...	50th	51st	52nd	...	98th	99th	100th	101st
100	102	104	106	...	198	200	202	...	294	296	298	300

To sum, pair the integers

$$
\left.
\begin{array}{ll}
\text{1}^{st} \text{ and } 101^{st} & 100 + 300 = 400 \\
\text{2}^{nd} \text{ and } 100^{th} & 102 + 298 = 400 \\
\text{3}^{rd} \text{ and } 99^{th} & 104 + 296 = 400 \\
\text{4}^{th} \text{ and } 98^{th} & 106 + 294 = 400 \\
\quad\quad\vdots & \\
50^{th} \text{ and } 52^{nd} & 198 + 202 = 400
\end{array}
\right\} \; 50(400) = 20{,}000
$$

$$51^{st} \qquad\qquad\qquad\qquad = 200 \qquad\qquad + \quad 200$$

$$\overline{\qquad\qquad\qquad\qquad\qquad\qquad\qquad\qquad 20{,}200}$$

Alternatively, let S represent the sum. Then,

$$S = 100 + 102 + 104 + \ldots + 296 + 298 + 300$$

next, rewrite the sum

$$S = 300 + 298 + 296 + \ldots + 104 + 102 + 100$$

then add the two equations

$$2S = 400 + 400 + 400 + \ldots + 400 + 400 + 400$$

now divide by 2

$$S = 200 + 200 + 200 + \ldots + 200 + 200 + 200$$

there are 101 terms in S, so

$$S = 101(200) = 20{,}200.$$

The correct answer is B.

250. November 16, 2001, was a Friday. If each of the years 2004, 2008, and 2012 had 366 days, and the remaining years from 2001 through 2014 had 365 days, what day of the week was November 16, 2014?

(A) Sunday
(B) Monday
(C) Tuesday
(D) Wednesday
(E) Thursday

Arithmetic Operations with Integers

The number of days between November 16, 2001, and November 16, 2014, is $10(365) + 3(366) = 4,748$ and, because $4,748 = 7(678) + 2$, it follows that 4,748 days is 678 weeks plus 2 days. Then, 678 weeks from Friday, November 16, 2001, is Friday, November 14, 2014, and 2 days from Friday, November 14, 2014, is Sunday, November 16, 2014.

The correct answer is A.

251. How many prime numbers between 1 and 100 are factors of 7,150?

(A) One
(B) Two
(C) Three
(D) Four
(E) Five

Arithmetic Rate

To find the number of prime numbers between 1 and 100 that are factors of 7,150, find the prime factorization of 7,150 using a method similar to the following:

$7,150 = 10 \times 715$

$= (2 \times 5) \times (5 \times 143)$

$= 2 \times 5 \times 5 \times (11 \times 13)$

Thus, 7,150 has four prime factors: 2, 5, 11, and 13.

The correct answer is D.

252. A sequence of numbers a_1, a_2, a_3, ... is defined as follows: $a_1 = 3$, $a_2 = 5$, and every term in the sequence after a_2 is the product of all terms in the sequence preceding it, e.g., $a_3 = (a_1)(a_2)$ and $a_4 = (a_1)(a_2)(a_3)$. If $a_n = t$ and $n > 2$, what is the value of a_{n+2} in terms of t?

(A) $4t$
(B) t^2
(C) t^3
(D) t^4
(E) t^8

Algebra Sequences

It is given that $a_n = (a_1)(a_2) \ldots (a_{n-1})$ and $a_n = t$. Therefore, $a_{n+1} = (a_1)(a_2) \ldots (a_{n-1})(a_n) = (a_n)(a_n) = t^2$ and $a_{n+2} = (a_1)(a_2) \ldots (a_n)(a_{n+1}) = (a_{n+1})(a_{n+1}) = (t^2)(t^2) = t^4$.

The correct answer is D.

253. Last year the price per share of Stock X increased by k percent and the earnings per share of Stock X increased by m percent, where k is greater than m. By what percent did the ratio of price per share to earnings per share increase, in terms of k and m?

(A) $\dfrac{k}{m}\%$
(B) $(k-m)\%$
(C) $\dfrac{100(k-m)}{100+k}\%$
(D) $\dfrac{100(k-m)}{100+m}\%$
(E) $\dfrac{100(k-m)}{100+k+m}\%$

Algebra Percents

Although this problem can be solved algebraically, the answer can also be identified by choosing numerical values for the variables, calculating the percent increase in the ratio, and comparing the result with the corresponding numerical values of the answer choices. To this end, let the original price per share be $1,000 and earnings per share be $200, where $k = 10$ and $m = 5$. Note that $k > m$ for these values.

	Before increase	After increase
price	$1,000	1.1($1,000) = $1,100
earnings	$200	1.05($200) = $210
$\dfrac{\text{price}}{\text{earnings}}$	$\dfrac{1,000}{200} = 5$	$\dfrac{1,100}{210} = \dfrac{110}{21}$

Therefore, the percent increase in the ratio of price per share to earnings per share is

$$\left(\frac{\frac{110}{21} - 5}{5} \times 100\right)\% = \left(\frac{110 - 105}{(5)(21)} \times 100\right)\% = \frac{500}{105}\%$$

Now substitute $k = 10$ and $m = 5$ into the answer choices to determine which answer choice gives $\dfrac{500}{105}\%$.

A $\dfrac{10}{5}\%$ NO

B $(10 - 5)\%$ NO

C $\dfrac{100(5)}{100 + 10}\% = \dfrac{500}{110}\%$ NO

D $\dfrac{100(5)}{100 + 5}\% = \dfrac{500}{105}\%$ **YES**

E $\dfrac{100(5)}{100 + 10 + 5}\% = \dfrac{500}{115}\%$ NO

The correct answer is D.

254. Of the 300 subjects who participated in an experiment using virtual-reality therapy to reduce their fear of heights, 40 percent experienced sweaty palms, 30 percent experienced vomiting, and 75 percent experienced dizziness. If all of the subjects experienced at least one of these effects and 35 percent of the subjects experienced exactly two of these effects, how many of the subjects experienced only one of these effects?

(A) 105
(B) 125
(C) 130
(D) 180
(E) 195

Arithmetic Applied Problems

Let a be the number who experienced only one of the effects, b be the number who experienced exactly two of the effects, and c be the number who experienced all three of the effects. Then $a + b + c = 300$, since each of the 300 participants experienced at least one of the effects. From the given information, $b = 105$ (35% of 300), which gives $a + 105 + c = 300$, or $a + c = 195$ (Equation 1). Also, if the number who experienced sweaty palms (40% of 300, or 120) is added to the number who experienced vomiting (30% of 300, or 90), and this sum is added to the number who experienced dizziness (75% of 300, or 225), then each participant who experienced only one of the effects is counted exactly once, each participant who experienced exactly two of the effects is counted exactly twice, and each participant who experienced all three of the effects is counted exactly 3 times. Therefore, $a + 2b + 3c = 120 + 90 + 225 = 435$. Using $b = 105$, it follows that $a + 2(105) + 3c = 435$, or $a + 3c = 225$ (Equation 2). Then, solving the system defined by Equation 1 and Equation 2,

$$\begin{cases} a + c = 195 \\ a + 3c = 225 \end{cases} \quad \text{multiply 1}^{\text{st}} \text{ equation by } -3$$

$$\begin{cases} -3a - 3c = -585 \\ a + 3c = 225 \end{cases} \quad \text{add equations}$$

$-2a = -360$, or $a = 180$

The correct answer is D.

255. If $m^{-1} = -\dfrac{1}{3}$, then m^{-2} is equal to

(A) -9
(B) -3
(C) $-\dfrac{1}{9}$
(D) $\dfrac{1}{9}$
(E) 9

Arithmetic Negative Exponents

Using rules of exponents, $m^{-2} = m^{-1 \times 2} = \left(m^{-1}\right)^2$, and since $m^{-1} = -\dfrac{1}{3}$, $m^{-2} = \left(-\dfrac{1}{3}\right)^2 = \dfrac{1}{9}$.

The correct answer is D.

256. A photography dealer ordered 60 Model X cameras to be sold for $250 each, which represents a 20 percent markup over the dealer's initial cost for each camera. Of the cameras ordered, 6 were never sold and were returned to the manufacturer for a refund of 50 percent of the dealer's initial cost. What was the dealer's approximate profit or loss as a percent of the dealer's initial cost for the 60 cameras?

    (A) 7% loss
    (B) 13% loss
    (C) 7% profit
    (D) 13% profit
    (E) 15% profit

Arithmetic Percents

Given that $250 is 20% greater than a camera's initial cost, it follows that the initial cost for each camera was $\left(\$\dfrac{250}{1.2}\right)$. Therefore, the initial cost for the 60 cameras was $60\left(\$\dfrac{250}{1.2}\right)$. The total revenue is the sum of the amount obtained from selling $60 - 6 = 54$ cameras for $250 each and the $\left(\dfrac{1}{2}\right)\left(\$\dfrac{250}{1.2}\right)$ refund for each of 6 cameras, or $(54)(\$250)+(6)\left(\dfrac{1}{2}\right)\left(\$\dfrac{250}{1.2}\right)$. The total profit, as a percent of the total initial cost, is

$$\left(\frac{(\text{total revenue})-(\text{total initial cost})}{(\text{total initial cost})}\times 100\right)\%=$$

$$\left(\left(\frac{(\text{total revenue})}{(\text{total initial cost})}-1\right)\times 100\right)\%.\ \text{Using}$$

the numerical expressions obtained above,

$$\frac{(\text{total revenue})}{(\text{total initial cost})}-1$$

$$=\frac{(54)(250)+6\left(\dfrac{1}{2}\right)\left(\dfrac{250}{1.2}\right)}{(60)\left(\dfrac{250}{1.2}\right)}-1 \quad \text{by substitution}$$

$$=\frac{54+3\left(\dfrac{1}{1.2}\right)}{(60)\left(\dfrac{1}{1.2}\right)}-1 \quad \text{by canceling 250s}$$

$$=\frac{54(1.2)+3}{60}-1 \quad \begin{array}{l}\text{by multiplying}\\ \text{top and bottom by 1.2}\\ \text{and then canceling 1.2}\end{array}$$

$$=\frac{67.8}{60}-1$$

$$=1.13-1$$

$$=0.13$$

Finally, $(0.13 \times 100)\% = 13\%$, which represents a profit since it is positive.

The correct answer is D.

257. Seven pieces of rope have an average (arithmetic mean) length of 68 centimeters and a median length of 84 centimeters. If the length of the longest piece of rope is 14 centimeters more than 4 times the length of the shortest piece of rope, what is the maximum possible length, in centimeters, of the longest piece of rope?

    (A)   82
    (B)   118
    (C)   120
    (D)   134
    (E)   152

Algebra Statistics

Let a, b, c, d, e, f, and g be the lengths, in centimeters, of the pieces of rope, listed from least to greatest. From the given information, it follows that $d = 84$ and $g = 4a + 14$. Therefore, listed from least to greatest, the lengths are $a, b, c, 84, e, f$, and $4a + 14$. The maximum value of $4a + 14$ will occur when the maximum value of a is used, and this will be the case only if the shortest 3 pieces all have the same length. Therefore, listed from least to greatest, the lengths are a, a, a, 84, e, f, and $4a + 14$. The maximum value for $4a + 14$ will occur when e and f are as small as possible. Since e and f are to the right of the median, they must be at least 84 and so 84 is the least possible value for each of e and f. Therefore, listed from least to greatest, the lengths are a, a, a, 84, 84, 84, and $4a + 14$. Since the average length is 68, it follows that $\frac{a+a+a+84+84+84+(4a+14)}{7} = 68$, or $a = 30$.

Hence, the maximum length of the longest piece is $(4a + 14) = [4(30) + 14] = 134$ centimeters.

The correct answer is D.

258. What is the difference between the sixth and the fifth terms of the sequence 2, 4, 7, … whose n^{th} term is $n + 2^{n-1}$?

(A)   2
(B)   3
(C)   6
(D)   16
(E)   17

Algebra Simplifying Algebraic Expressions

According to the given formula, the sixth term of the sequence is $6 + 2^{6-1} = 6 + 2^5$ and the fifth term is $5 + 2^{5-1} = 5 + 2^4$. Then,

$$\left(6 + 2^5\right) - \left(5 + 2^4\right) = (6 - 5) + \left(2^5 - 2^4\right)$$
$$= 1 + 2^4(2 - 1)$$
$$= 1 + 2^4$$
$$= 1 + 16$$
$$= 17$$

The correct answer is E.

259. From the consecutive integers –10 to 10, inclusive, 20 integers are randomly chosen with repetitions allowed. What is the least possible value of the product of the 20 integers?

(A) $(-10)^{20}$
(B) $(-10)^{10}$
(C)   0
(D) $-(10)^{19}$
(E) $-(10)^{20}$

Arithmetic Properties of Numbers

If –10 is chosen an odd number of times and 10 is chosen the remaining number of times (for example, choose –10 once and choose 10 nineteen times, or choose –10 three times and choose 10 seventeen times), then the product of the 20 chosen numbers will be $-(10)^{20}$. Note that $-(10)^{20}$ is less than $-(10)^{19}$, the only other negative value among the answer choices.

The correct answer is E.

260. The letters D, G, I, I, and T can be used to form 5-letter strings such as DIGIT or DGIIT. Using these letters, how many 5-letter strings can be formed in which the two occurrences of the letter I are separated by at least one other letter?

(A)   12
(B)   18
(C)   24
(D)   36
(E)   48

Arithmetic Elementary Combinatorics

There are 6 ways to select the locations of the two occurrences of the letter I, and this number can be determined by listing all such ways as shown below, where the symbol * is used in place of the letters D, G, and T:

I*I**, I**I*, I***I, *I*I*, *I**I, **I*I

Alternatively, the number of ways to select the locations of the 2 occurrences of the letter I can be determined by using $\binom{5}{2} - 4 =$ $\frac{5!}{(2!)(3!)} - 4 = 10 - 4 = 6$, which is the number of ways to select 2 of the 5 locations minus the 4 ways in which the 2 selected locations are adjacent.

For each of these 6 ways to select the locations of the 2 occurrences of the letter I, there are 6 ways to select the locations of the letters D, G, and T, which can be determined by using 3! = 6 or by listing all such ways:

$$DGT, DTG, GDT, GTD, TDG, TGD$$

It follows that the number of ways to select the locations of the 5 letters to form 5-letter strings is $(6)(6) = 36$.

The correct answer is D.

261. $\dfrac{0.99999999}{1.0001} - \dfrac{0.99999991}{1.0003} =$

(A) 10^{-8}

(B) $3(10^{-8})$

(C) $3(10^{-4})$

(D) $2(10^{-4})$

(E) 10^{-4}

Arithmetic Operations on Rational Numbers

Calculations with lengthy decimals can be avoided by writing 0.99999999 as $1 - 10^{-8}$, 0.99999991 as $1 - 9(10^{-8})$, 1.0001 as $1 + 10^{-4}$, and 1.0003 as $1 + 3(10^{-4})$. Doing this gives

$$\frac{1-10^{-8}}{1+10^{-4}} - \frac{1-9(10^{-8})}{1+3(10^{-4})}$$

$$= \frac{\left[1+10^{-4}\right]\left[1-10^{-4}\right]}{1+10^{-4}} - \frac{1-9(10^{-8})}{1+3(10^{-4})}$$

$$= \frac{1-10^{-4}}{1} - \frac{1-9(10^{-8})}{1+3(10^{-4})}$$

$$= \frac{\left[1-10^{-4}\right]\left[1+3(10^{-4})\right] - \left[1-9(10^{-8})\right]}{1+3(10^{-4})}$$

$$= \frac{1+3(10^{-4})-10^{-4}-3(10^{-8})-1+9(10^{-8})}{1+3(10^{-4})}$$

$$= \frac{2(10^{-4})+6(10^{-8})}{1+3(10^{-4})}$$

$$= \frac{\left[2(10^{-4})\right]\left[1+3(10^{-4})\right]}{1+3(10^{-4})}$$

$$= 2(10^{-4})$$

The correct answer is D.

262. Last Sunday a certain store sold copies of Newspaper A for $1.00 each and copies of Newspaper B for $1.25 each, and the store sold no other newspapers that day. If r percent of the store's revenue from newspaper sales was from Newspaper A and if p percent of the newspapers that the store sold were copies of Newspaper A, which of the following expresses r in terms of p?

(A) $\dfrac{100p}{125-p}$

(B) $\dfrac{150p}{250-p}$

(C) $\dfrac{300p}{375-p}$

(D) $\dfrac{400p}{500-p}$

(E) $\dfrac{500p}{625-p}$

Algebra Percents

Because the number of newspapers sold at the store last Sunday is not given, assume for simplicity that number is 1,000. Also, the value of p is not given, so choose a convenient value to work with, say $p = 60$. In the table that follows, the chosen numbers are in **boldface**.

	Newspaper A	Newspaper B	Total
Percent of papers sold	$p = \mathbf{60}$	40	100
Number sold	600	400	**1,000**
Revenue	600($1) = $600	400($1.25) = $500	$1,100
Percent of revenue (r)	$\dfrac{600}{1,100} \times 100 = \dfrac{600}{11}$		

Now, check the answer choices using $p = 60$ to see which one yields $\dfrac{600}{11}$.

(A) $\dfrac{100p}{125-p} = \dfrac{100(60)}{125-60} = \dfrac{6,000}{65}$

No (65 doesn't have 11 as a factor)

(B) $\dfrac{150p}{250-p} = \dfrac{150(60)}{250-60} = \dfrac{9,000}{190}$

No (190 doesn't have 11 as a factor)

(C) $\dfrac{300p}{375-p} = \dfrac{300(60)}{375-60} = \dfrac{18,000}{315}$

No (315 doesn't have 11 as a factor)

(D) $\dfrac{400p}{500-p} = \dfrac{400(60)}{500-60} = \dfrac{24,000}{440}$

Yes (440 has 11 as a factor) $\dfrac{24,000}{440} = \dfrac{600}{11}$

(E) $\dfrac{500p}{625-p} = \dfrac{500(60)}{625-60} = \dfrac{30,000}{565}$

No (565 doesn't have 11 as a factor)

The correct answer is D.

263. For the past n days, the average (arithmetic mean) daily production at a company was 50 units. If today's production of 90 units raises the average to 55 units per day, what is the value of n?

(A) 30
(B) 18
(C) 10
(D) 9
(E) 7

Arithmetic; Algebra Statistics; Applied Problems; Simultaneous Equations

Let x be the total production of the past n days.

Using the formula $\text{average} = \dfrac{\text{sum of values}}{\text{number of values}}$, the information in the problem can be expressed in the following two equations

$50 = \dfrac{x}{n}$ — daily average of 50 units over the past n days

$55 = \dfrac{x+90}{n+1}$ — increased daily average when including today's 90 units

Solving the first equation for x gives $x = 50n$. Then substituting $50n$ for x in the second equation gives the following that can be solved for n:

$55 = \dfrac{50n+90}{n+1}$

$55(n+1) = 50n + 90$ — multiply both sides by $(n+1)$

$55n + 55 = 50n + 90$ — distribute the 55

$5n = 35$ — subtract $50n$ and 55 from both sides

$n = 7$ — divide both sides by 5

The correct answer is E.

264. If a two-digit positive integer has its digits reversed, the resulting integer differs from the original by 27. By how much do the two digits differ?

(A) 3
(B) 4
(C) 5
(D) 6
(E) 7

Algebra Applied Problems

Let the one two-digit integer be represented by $10t + s$, where s and t are digits, and let the other integer with the reversed digits be represented by $10s + t$. The information that the difference between the integers is 27 can be expressed in the following equation, which can be solved for the answer.

$(10s + t) - (10t + s) = 27$

$10s + t - 10t - s = 27$ — distribute the negative

$9s - 9t = 27$ — combine like terms

$s - t = 3$ — divide both sides by 9

Thus, it is seen that the two digits s and t differ by 3.

The correct answer is A.

265. In an electric circuit, two resistors with resistances x and y are connected in parallel. In this case, if r is the combined resistance of these two resistors, then the reciprocal of r is equal to the sum of the reciprocals of x and y. What is r in terms of x and y?

(A) xy

(B) $x + y$

(C) $\dfrac{1}{x + y}$

(D) $\dfrac{xy}{x + y}$

(E) $\dfrac{x + y}{xy}$

Algebra Applied Problems

Note that two numbers are reciprocals of each other if and only if their product is 1. Thus, the reciprocals of r, x, and y are $\dfrac{1}{r}, \dfrac{1}{x}$, and $\dfrac{1}{y}$, respectively. So, according to the problem, $\dfrac{1}{r} = \dfrac{1}{x} + \dfrac{1}{y}$. To solve this equation for r, begin by creating a common denominator on the right side by multiplying the first fraction by $\dfrac{y}{y}$ and the second fraction by $\dfrac{x}{x}$:

$\dfrac{1}{r} = \dfrac{1}{x} + \dfrac{1}{y}$

$\dfrac{1}{r} = \dfrac{y}{xy} + \dfrac{x}{xy}$

$\dfrac{1}{r} = \dfrac{x + y}{xy}$ combine the fractions on the right side

$r = \dfrac{xy}{x + y}$ invert the fractions on both sides

The correct answer is D.

266. Xavier, Yvonne, and Zelda each try independently to solve a problem. If their individual probabilities for success are $\dfrac{1}{4}$, $\dfrac{1}{2}$, and $\dfrac{5}{8}$, respectively, what is the probability that Xavier and Yvonne, but not Zelda, will solve the problem?

(A) $\dfrac{11}{8}$

(B) $\dfrac{7}{8}$

(C) $\dfrac{9}{64}$

(D) $\dfrac{5}{64}$

(E) $\dfrac{3}{64}$

Arithmetic Probability

Since the individuals' probabilities are independent, they can be multiplied to figure out the combined probability. The probability of Xavier's success is given as $\dfrac{1}{4}$, and the probability of Yvonne's success is given as $\dfrac{1}{2}$. Since the probability of Zelda's success is given as $\dfrac{5}{8}$, then the probability of her NOT solving the problem is

$1 - \dfrac{5}{8} = \dfrac{3}{8}$.

Thus, the combined probability is

$\left(\dfrac{1}{4}\right)\left(\dfrac{1}{2}\right)\left(\dfrac{3}{8}\right) = \dfrac{3}{64}$.

The correct answer is E.

267. If $\dfrac{1}{x} - \dfrac{1}{x + 1} = \dfrac{1}{x + 4}$, then x could be

(A) 0

(B) −1

(C) −2

(D) −3

(E) −4

Algebra Second-Degree Equations

Solve the equation for x. Begin by multiplying all the terms by $x(x+1)(x+4)$ to eliminate the denominators.

$$\frac{1}{x} - \frac{1}{x+1} = \frac{1}{x+4}$$

$$(x+1)(x+4) - x(x+4) = x(x+1)$$

$(x+4)(x+1-x) = x(x+1)$ factor the $(x+4)$ out front on the left side

$(x+4)(1) = x(x+1)$ simplify

$(x+4) = x^2 + x$ distribute the x on the right side

$4 = x^2$ subtract x from both sides

$\pm 2 = x$ take the square root of both sides

Both -2 and 2 are square roots of 4 since $\left(-2^2\right) = 4$ and $\left(2^2\right) = 4$. Thus, x could be -2.

This problem can also be solved as follows. Rewrite the left side as, $\dfrac{(x+1)-x}{x(x+1)} = \dfrac{1}{x(x+1)}$, then set equal to the right side to get $\dfrac{1}{x(x+1)} = \dfrac{1}{x+4}$. Next, cross multiply: $(1)(x+4) = x(x+1)(1)$. Therefore, $x+4 = x^2 + x$, or $x^2 = 4$, so $x = \pm 2$.

The correct answer is C.

268. $\left(\dfrac{1}{2}\right)^{-3} \left(\dfrac{1}{4}\right)^{-2} \left(\dfrac{1}{16}\right)^{-1} =$

(A) $\left(\dfrac{1}{2}\right)^{-48}$

(B) $\left(\dfrac{1}{2}\right)^{-11}$

(C) $\left(\dfrac{1}{2}\right)^{-6}$

(D) $\left(\dfrac{1}{8}\right)^{-11}$

(E) $\left(\dfrac{1}{8}\right)^{-6}$

Arithmetic Operations on Rational Numbers

It is clear from the answer choices that all three factors need to be written with a common denominator, and they thus become

$$\left(\frac{1}{2}\right)^{-3} = \left(\frac{1}{2}\right)^{-3}$$

$$\left(\frac{1}{4}\right)^{-2} = \left(\left(\frac{1}{2}\right)^2\right)^{-2} = \left(\frac{1}{2}\right)^{-4}$$

$$\left(\frac{1}{16}\right)^{-1} = \left(\left(\frac{1}{2}\right)^4\right)^{-1} = \left(\frac{1}{2}\right)^{-4}$$

So, $\left(\dfrac{1}{2}\right)^{-3} \left(\dfrac{1}{4}\right)^{-2} \left(\dfrac{1}{16}\right)^{-1} =$

$$\left(\frac{1}{2}\right)^{-3}\left(\frac{1}{2}\right)^{-4}\left(\frac{1}{2}\right)^{-4} = \left(\frac{1}{2}\right)^{-3-4-4} = \left(\frac{1}{2}\right)^{-11}.$$

The correct answer is B.

269. List T consists of 30 positive decimals, none of which is an integer, and the sum of the 30 decimals is S. The estimated sum of the 30 decimals, E, is defined as follows. Each decimal in T whose tenths digit is even is rounded up to the nearest integer, and each decimal in T whose tenths digit is odd is rounded down to the nearest integer; E is the sum of the resulting integers. If $\dfrac{1}{3}$ of the decimals in T have a tenths digit that is even, which of the following is a possible value of $E - S$?

I. -16

II.   6

III.   10

(A) I only

(B) I and II only

(C) I and III only

(D) II and III only

(E) I, II, and III

Arithmetic Operations on Rational Numbers

First, consider $E - S$ as the total of the "contributions" made by the decimals in T with even tenths digits and the "contributions" made by the decimals in T with odd tenths digits, as shown in the following tables.

	Decimals with even tenth digit	Example
Number that occurs in T	$\frac{1}{3}(30)=10$	
Max possible tenth digit	8	14.89999
Contribution each makes to $E-S$	Greater than 0.1	$15-14.89999$ $=0.10001$
Total contribution to $E-S$	Greater than $10(0.1)$ $=1$	
Min possible tenth digit	0	14.00001
Contribution each makes to $E-S$	Less than 1	$15-14.00001$ $=0.99999$
Total contribution to $E-S$	Less than $10(1)=10$	
Summary	$1<$ (evens' contribution to $E-S$) <10	

	Decimals with odd tenth digit	Example
Number that occurs in T	$\frac{2}{3}(30)=20$	
Max possible tenth digit	9	14.9999
Contribution each makes to $E-S$	Greater than -1	$14-14.9999$ $=-0.9999$
Total contribution to $E-S$	Greater than $20(-1)$ $=-20$	
Min possible tenth digit	1	14.1
Contribution each makes to $E-S$	Less than or equal to -0.1	$14-14.1$ $=-0.1$
Total contribution to $E-S$	Less than or equal to $20(-0.1)=-2$	
Summary	$-20<$ (odds' contribution to $E-S$) ≤-2	

Adding the summary inequalities from the tables gives

$1+(-20)<$ (evens' contribution to $E-S$) + (odds' contribution to $E-S$) $<10+(-2)$ or $-19<E-S<8$. Thus, the possible values of $E-S$ include -16 and 6, but not 10.

Note that if T contains 10 repetitions of 1.8 and 20 repetitions of 1.9, then $S=10(1.8)+20(1.9)=18+38=56$, $E=10(2)+20(1)=20+20=40$, and $E-S=40-56=-16$.

However, if T contains 10 repetitions of 1.2 and 20 repetitions of 1.1, then $S=10(1.2)+20(1.1)=12+22=34$, $E=10(2)+20(1)=20+20=40$, and $E-S=40-34=6$.

The correct answer is B.

270. If $5-\dfrac{6}{x}=x$, then x has how many possible values?

(A) None
(B) One
(C) Two
(D) A finite number greater than two
(E) An infinite number

Algebra Second-Degree Equations

Solve the equation to determine how many values are possible for x.

$$5-\frac{6}{x}=x$$
$$5x-6=x^2$$
$$0=x^2-5x+6$$
$$0=(x-3)(x-2)$$
$$x=3 \text{ or } 2$$

The correct answer is C.

271. Seed mixture X is 40 percent ryegrass and 60 percent bluegrass by weight; seed mixture Y is 25 percent ryegrass and 75 percent fescue. If a mixture of X and Y contains 30 percent ryegrass, what percent of the weight of the mixture is X?

(A)   10%

(B) $33\frac{1}{3}$%

(C)   40%

(D)   50%

(E) $66\frac{2}{3}$%

Algebra Applied Problems

Let X be the amount of seed mixture X in the final mixture, and let Y be the amount of seed mixture Y in the final mixture. The final mixture of X and Y needs to contain 30 percent ryegrass seed, so any other kinds of grass seed are irrelevant to the solution to this problem. The information about the ryegrass percentages for X, Y, and the final mixture can be expressed in the following equation and solved for X.

$$0.40X + 0.25Y = 0.30(X + Y)$$

$0.40X + 0.25Y = 0.30X + 0.30Y$	distribute the 0.30 on the right side
$0.10X = 0.05Y$	subtract $0.30X$ and $0.25Y$ from both sides
$X = 0.5Y$	divide both sides by 0.10

Using this, the percent of the weight of the combined mixture $(X + Y)$ that is X is

$$\frac{X}{X+Y} = \frac{0.5Y}{0.5Y+Y} = \frac{0.5Y}{1.5Y} = \frac{0.5}{1.5} = 0.33\overline{3} = 33\frac{1}{3}\%$$

The correct answer is B.

272. How many of the integers that satisfy the inequality $\frac{(x+2)(x+3)}{x-2} \geq 0$ are less than 5?

(A)   1

(B)   2

(C)   3

(D)   4

(E)   5

Algebra Inequalities

Note: This explanation is very detailed. However, many of the steps should become more automatic with additional practice in solving nonlinear inequalities.

The expression $\frac{(x+2)(x+3)}{x-2}$ contains three binomials, namely $x + 2$, $x + 3$, and $x - 2$, that determine for what values of x each binomial is zero, negative, and positive. The table below summarizes these values.

Binomial	Zero for	Negative for	Positive for
$x + 3$	$x = -3$	$x < -3$	$x > -3$
$x + 2$	$x = -2$	$x < -2$	$x > -2$
$x - 2$	$x = 2$	$x < 2$	$x > 2$

Note that, although $x - 2 = 0$ when $x = 2$, $\frac{(x+2)(x+3)}{x-2}$ is undefined for $x = 2$. However, $\frac{(x+2)(x+3)}{x-2} = 0$ when $x = -3$ and when $x = -2$. Both of these values are integers less than 5. (i)

The following number line shows the information in the table above. The vertical segments at $x = -3$, $x = -2$, and $x = 2$ partition the number line into 4 intervals:

I_1, where $x < -3$

I_2, where $-3 < x < -2$

I_3, where $-2 < x < 2$

I_4, where $x > 2$.

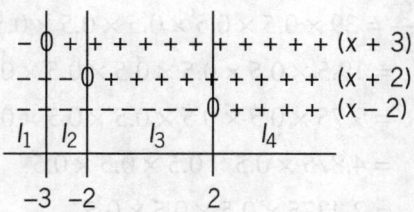

I_1: All three binomials are negative, so the inequality $\dfrac{(x+2)(x+3)}{x-2} \geq 0$ is NOT satisfied.

I_2: Contains no integers, so need not be considered further.

I_3: Two binomials are positive, one is negative, so the inequality $\dfrac{(x+2)(x+3)}{x-2} \geq 0$ is NOT satisfied.

I_4: All three binomials are positive, so the inequality $\dfrac{(x+2)(x+3)}{x-2} \geq 0$ is satisfied. The integers in this interval that are less than 5 are 3 and 4. (ii)

From (i) and (ii), there are 4 integers, namely -3, -2, 3, and 4, for which $\dfrac{(x+2)(x+3)}{x-2} \geq 0$.

The correct answer is D.

273. Of the 150 houses in a certain development, 60 percent have air-conditioning, 50 percent have a sunporch, and 30 percent have a swimming pool. If 5 of the houses have all three of these amenities and 5 have none of them, how many of the houses have exactly two of these amenities?

   (A)   10
   (B)   45
   (C)   50
   (D)   55
   (E)   65

Arithmetic Sets

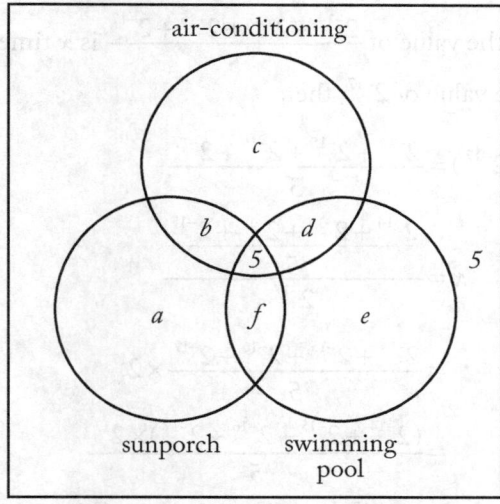

Since 60% of the 150 houses have air-conditioning, $b + c + d + 5 = 0.6(150) = 90$, so $b + c + d = 85$ (i). Similarly, since 50% have a sunporch, $a + b + f + 5 = 0.5(150) = 75$, so $a + b + f = 70$ (ii). Likewise, since 30% have a swimming pool, $d + e + f + 5 = 0.3(150) = 45$, so $d + e + f = 40$ (iii). Adding equations (i), (ii), and (iii) gives $(b + c + d) + (a + b + f) + (d + e + f) = 195$, or $a + 2b + c + 2d + e + 2f = 195$ (iv). But $a + b + c + d + e + f + 5 + 5 = 150$, or $a + b + c + d + e + f = 140$ (v). Subtracting equation (v) from equation (iv) gives $b + d + f = 55$, so 55 houses have exactly two of the amenities.

The correct answer is D.

274. The value of $\dfrac{2^{-14} + 2^{-15} + 2^{-16} + 2^{-17}}{5}$ is how many times the value of 2^{-17}?

   (A) $\dfrac{3}{2}$
   (B) $\dfrac{5}{2}$
   (C)   3
   (D)   4
   (E)   5

Arithmetic Negative Exponents

If the value of $\dfrac{2^{-14}+2^{-15}+2^{-16}+2^{-17}}{5}$ is x times the value of 2^{-17}, then

$$x(2^{-17})=\frac{2^{-14}+2^{-15}+2^{-16}+2^{-17}}{5}$$

$$x=\frac{\dfrac{2^{-14}+2^{-15}+2^{-16}+2^{-17}}{5}}{2^{-17}}$$

$$=\frac{2^{-14}+2^{-15}+2^{-16}+2^{-17}}{5}\times 2^{17}$$

$$=\frac{(2^{-14}+2^{-15}+2^{-16}+2^{-17})\times 2^{17}}{5}$$

$$=\frac{2^{-14+17}+2^{-15+17}+2^{-16+17}+2^{-17+17}}{5}$$

$$=\frac{2^{3}+2^{2}+2^{1}+2^{0}}{5}$$

$$=\frac{8+4+2+1}{5}$$

$$=3$$

The correct answer is C.

275. Which of the following fractions has a decimal equivalent that is a terminating decimal?

(A) $\dfrac{10}{189}$

(B) $\dfrac{15}{169}$

(C) $\dfrac{16}{225}$

(D) $\dfrac{25}{144}$

(E) $\dfrac{39}{128}$

Arithmetic Fractions; Decimals

Since the denominator of $\dfrac{39}{128}$, which is 128, has only factors of 2, and $\dfrac{1}{2}=0.5$, the following shows that $\dfrac{39}{128}=39\times\dfrac{1}{2}\times\dfrac{1}{2}\times\dfrac{1}{2}\times\dfrac{1}{2}\times\dfrac{1}{2}\times\dfrac{1}{2}\times\dfrac{1}{2}$ has a terminating decimal.

$$\frac{39}{128}=39\times 0.5\times 0.5\times 0.5\times 0.5\times 0.5\times 0.5\times 0.5$$

$$=19.5\times 0.5\times 0.5\times 0.5\times 0.5\times 0.5\times 0.5$$

$$=9.75\times 0.5\times 0.5\times 0.5\times 0.5\times 0.5$$

$$=4.875\times 0.5\times 0.5\times 0.5\times 0.5$$

$$=2.4375\times 0.5\times 0.5\times 0.5$$

$$=1.21875\times 0.5\times 0.5$$

$$=0.609375\times 0.5$$

$$=0.3046875$$

Moreover, the fact that each of the other answer choices, when expanded in this way, involves at least one factor of $\dfrac{1}{3}=0.\overline{3}=0.333...$ and/or $\dfrac{1}{7}=0.\overline{142857}$, neither of which has a terminating decimal expansion, suggests that none of the other answer choices has a terminating decimal.

denominator	prime factors
189	3 and 7
196	2 and 7
225	3 and 5
144	2 and 3
128	only 2

In fact, it can be proved that a fraction (numerator and denominator both integers, denominator an integer greater than 1) has a terminating decimal if and only if its denominator has only prime factors of 2 and/or 5, although this result is not needed to solve the present problem.

The correct answer is E.

276. If $\left(\dfrac{1}{5}\right)^{m}\left(\dfrac{1}{4}\right)^{18}=\dfrac{1}{2(10)^{35}}$, then $m=$

(A) 17

(B) 18

(C) 34

(D) 35

(E) 36

Arithmetic Exponents

$$\left(\frac{1}{5}\right)^m \left(\frac{1}{4}\right)^{18} = \frac{1}{2(10)^{35}} \qquad \text{given}$$

$$\left(\frac{1^m}{5^m}\right)\left(\frac{1^{18}}{4^{18}}\right) = \frac{1}{2(10)^{35}} \qquad \text{use } \left(\frac{a}{b}\right)^x = \frac{a^x}{b^x}$$

$$\frac{1^m \times 1^{18}}{5^m \times 4^{18}} = \frac{1}{2 \times 10^{35}} \qquad \text{use } \left(\frac{a}{b}\right)\left(\frac{c}{d}\right) = \frac{ac}{bd}$$

$$\frac{1}{5^m \times 4^{18}} = \frac{1}{2 \times 10^{35}} \qquad \text{property of 1}$$

$$5^m \times 4^{18} = 2 \times 10^{35} \qquad \text{take reciprocal of both sides}$$

$$5^m \times (2^2)^{18} = 2 \times 10^{35} \qquad 4 = 2^2$$

$$5^m \times 2^{36} = 2 \times 10^{35} \qquad \text{use } (a^x)^y = a^{xy}$$

$$5^m \times 2^{36} = 2 \times (2 \times 5)^{35} \qquad 10 = 2 \times 5$$

$$5^m \times 2^{36} = 2 \times 2^{35} \times 5^{35} \qquad \text{use } (ab)^x = a^x b^x$$

$$5^m \times 2^{36} = 2^{36} \times 5^{35} \qquad \text{use } a^x a^y = a^{x+y}$$

$$5^m = 5^{35} \qquad \text{divide both sides by } 2^{36}$$

$$m = 35 \qquad \text{exponents must be equal}$$

The correct answer is D.

277. From a group of 8 volunteers, including Andrew and Karen, 4 people are to be selected at random to organize a charity event. What is the probability that Andrew will be among the 4 volunteers selected and Karen will not?

    (A) $\frac{3}{7}$

    (B) $\frac{5}{12}$

    (C) $\frac{27}{70}$

    (D) $\frac{2}{7}$

    (E) $\frac{9}{35}$

Arithmetic Probability; Elementary Combinatorics

The probability that Andrew will be among the 4 volunteers selected and Karen will not is equal to $\frac{A}{T}$, where A is the number of possible selections of the 4 volunteers that include Andrew and do not include Karen, and T is the total number of

possible selections of the 4 volunteers. Since T is the number of combinations of 8 objects taken 4 at a time, it follows that $T = \binom{8}{4} = \frac{8!}{4!(8-4)!} = \frac{(5)(6)(7)(8)}{(1)(2)(3)(4)} = 70$. Since A is the number of combinations of 6 objects taken 3 at a time (select 3 volunteers from the 6 volunteers other than Andrew and Karen; including Andrew as a 4th selected volunteer will not change the number), it follows that $A = \binom{6}{3} = \frac{6!}{3!(6-3)!} = \frac{(4)(5)(6)}{(1)(2)(3)} = 20$.

Therefore, the desired probability is $\frac{A}{T} = \frac{20}{70} = \frac{2}{7}$.

The correct answer is D.

278. An investor purchased 100 shares of Stock X at $6\frac{1}{18}$ dollars per share and sold them all a year later at 24 dollars per share. If the investor paid a 2 percent brokerage fee on both the total purchase price and the total selling price, which of the following is closest to the investor's percent gain on this investment?

    (A) 92%

    (B) 240%

    (C) 280%

    (D) 300%

    (E) 380%

Arithmetic Applied Problems; Estimation

In dollars, the investor's total cost was

$$100\left(6 + \frac{1}{18}\right) + (2\%)100\left(6 + \frac{1}{18}\right), \text{which}$$

is equal to $102\left(6 + \frac{1}{18}\right) = 612 + 5\frac{2}{3} \approx 618$,

and the investor's total revenue was $100(24) -$ $(2\%)100(24)$, which is equal to $2{,}400 - 48 =$ $2{,}352$. Therefore, the percent gain on the investment is very nearly $\left(\frac{2{,}352 - 618}{618}\right) \times$

$100\% = \left(\frac{867}{309}\right) \times 100\%$, or $\left(2 + \frac{249}{309}\right) \times 100\%$.

Since $\frac{249}{309} \approx \frac{250}{300} = \frac{5}{6} \approx 0.8$, it follows that the percent gain on the investment is closest to $(2 + 0.8) \times 100\% = 280\%$.

The correct answer is C.

279. If x is the product of the integers from 1 to 150, inclusive, and 5^y is a factor of x, what is the greatest possible value of y?

(A)   30
(B)   34
(C)   36
(D)   37
(E)   39

Arithmetic Properties of Integers

The greatest possible value of y such that 5^y is a factor of x is equal to the number of factors of 5 in the prime factorization of x. Because 5 is a prime number, only multiples of 5 will contribute factors of 5. Each multiple of 5 that is not a multiple of 25 contributes exactly one factor of 5, each multiple of $25 = 5 \times 5$ that is not a multiple of 125 contributes one additional factor of 5 beyond that already counted for multiples of 5, and $125 = 5 \times 5 \times 5$ contributes one additional factor of 5 beyond that already counted for multiples of 25. From 1 to 150, inclusive, there are 30 multiples of 5, 6 multiples of 25, and the number 125. Therefore, the number of factors of 5 in the prime factorization of x is $30 + 6 + 1 = 37$, and hence the value of y is 37.

The correct answer is D.

280. The number of defects in the first five cars to come through a new production line are 9, 7, 10, 4, and 6, respectively. If the sixth car through the production line has either 3, 7, or 12 defects, for which of these values does the mean number of defects per car for the first six cars equal the median?

I.   3
II.   7
III. 12

(A)   I only
(B)   II only
(C)   III only
(D)   I and III only
(E)   I, II, and III

Arithmetic Statistics

The table shows, for each of the possible number of defects in the sixth car (shown in bold), the list of the number of defects in the first six cars in ascending order, the mean of this list, and the median of this list. For example, if the sixth car has 7 defects, then the list of the number of defects in ascending order is 4, 6, **7**, 7, 9, 10; the mean of this list is the sum of these numbers divided by 6, or $\frac{43}{6}$, which is approximately 7.2; and the median of this list when in ascending order is the average of the 3rd and 4th numbers in this list, which is 7. For this example, the mean is NOT equal to the median.

list of the number of defects	mean	median
3, 4, 6, 7, 9, 10	$\frac{39}{6} = 6.5$	6.5
4, 6, **7**, 7, 9, 10	$\frac{43}{6} \approx 7.2$	7
4, 6, 7, 9, 10, **12**	$\frac{48}{6} = 8$	8

From the table it follows that the mean equals the median ONLY when the number of defects in the sixth car is 3 or 12.

The correct answer is D.

281. A furniture dealer purchased a desk for $150 and then set the selling price equal to the purchase price plus a markup that was 40 percent of the selling price. If the dealer sold the desk at the selling price, what was the amount of the dealer's gross profit from the purchase and the sale of the desk?

(A) $40
(B) $60
(C) $80
(D) $90
(E) $100

Algebra Applied Problems; First-Degree Equations

Let S be the selling price in dollars. From the first sentence of the problem, we have $S = 150 + 0.4S$. Thus, $0.6S = 150$ and $S = \frac{150}{0.6} = 250$. Therefore, the selling price was $250, and hence the gross profit was $250 – $150 = $100.

The correct answer is E.

282. How many odd numbers between 10 and 1,000 are the squares of integers?

(A) 12
(B) 13
(C) 14
(D) 15
(E) 16

Arithmetic Properties of Integers

A quick way to determine which squares of integers are less than 1,000 is to observe that $30^2 = 900$ (easily done mentally) is relatively close to 1,000 and then, since odd numbers that are the squares of integers correspond exactly to the squares of odd numbers, consider the squares of odd numbers beginning with 3. This leads to the following list:

$$3^2 = 9, 5^2 = 25, \ldots, 31^2 = 961, 33^2 = 1,089$$

It follows that the odd numbers between 10 and 1,000 that are the squares of integers are $5^2, 7^2, 9^2, \ldots, 31^2$. By a direct count one finds that there are 14 squares of integers in this list. A direct count can be avoided by using the computation $\dfrac{31 - 5}{2} + 1$.

The correct answer is C.

283. Three grades of milk are 1 percent, 2 percent, and 3 percent fat by volume. If x gallons of the 1 percent grade, y gallons of the 2 percent grade, and z gallons of the 3 percent grade are mixed to give $x + y + z$ gallons of a 1.5 percent grade, what is x in terms of y and z?

(A) $y + 3z$
(B) $\dfrac{y + z}{4}$
(C) $2y + 3z$
(D) $3y + z$
(E) $3y + 4.5z$

Algebra Applied Problems

Since the milk, when mixed, is 1.5 percent fat, the number of gallons of fat in the mixed milk is

$0.015(x + y + z)$. This is also equal to the sum of the numbers of gallons of fat in the three grades of milk before they are mixed, which is $0.01x + 0.02y + 0.03z$, so

$$0.015(x + y + z) = 0.01x + 0.02y + 0.03z.$$

Multiplying both sides by 1,000 (to remove the decimal fractions) and expanding the left side gives

$$15x + 15y + 15z = 10x + 20y + 30z.$$

To solve for x, isolate the terms involving x on one side, combine like terms, and divide by the coefficient of x.

$$15x - 10x = 20y - 15y + 30z - 15z$$
$$5x = 5y + 15z$$
$$x = y + 3z$$

The correct answer is A.

284. There are 8 books on a shelf, of which 2 are paperbacks and 6 are hardbacks. How many possible selections of 4 books from this shelf include at least one paperback?

(A) 40
(B) 45
(C) 50
(D) 55
(E) 60

Arithmetic Elementary Combinatorics

The number of possible selections of 4 books that have at least 1 paperback is the number of possible selections of 4 books having 1 paperback and 3 hardbacks added to the number of possible selections of 4 books having 2 paperbacks and 2 hardbacks. In the case of 1 paperback and 3 hardbacks, this will be the number of combinations of 2 objects taken 1 at a time (i.e., the number of ways to choose the paperback) multiplied by the number of combinations of 6 objects taken 3 at a time (i.e., the number of ways to choose the hardbacks), which is equal to

$$\binom{2}{1} \times \binom{6}{3} = \frac{2!}{1!(2-1)!} \times \frac{6!}{3!(6-3)!}$$

$$= 2 \times \frac{(4)(5)(6)}{(1)(2)(3)} = 40.$$

Similarly, the analogous calculation for the number of possible selections of having 2 paperbacks and 2 hardbacks is

$$\binom{2}{2} \times \binom{6}{2} = \frac{2!}{2!(2-2)!} \times \frac{6!}{2!(6-2)!}$$

$$= 1 \times \frac{(5)(6)}{(1)(2)} = 15.$$

Thus, the number of possible selections of 4 books that have at least 1 paperback is $40 + 15 = 55$.

Alternatively, determine the number of possible selections of 4 books that do NOT include at least 1 paperback and then subtract this number from the number of possible selections of 4 books without regard to how many are paperback. The number of possible selections of 4 books that do NOT include at least 1 paperback (i.e., the number of ways to choose 4 hardback books from the 6 hardback books) is the number of combinations of 6 objects taken 4 at a time, which is equal to $\binom{6}{4} = \frac{6!}{4!(6-4)!} = \frac{(5)(6)}{(1)(2)} = 15$.

The number of possible selections of 4 books without regard to how many are paperback is the number of combinations of 8 objects taken 4 at a time, which is equal to $\binom{8}{4} = \frac{8!}{4!(8-4)!} = \frac{(5)(6)(7)(8)}{(1)(2)(3)(4)} = 70$. Therefore, the number of possible selections of 4 books that include at least 1 paperback is $70 - 15 = 55$.

The correct answer is D.

285. If $M = \sqrt{4} + \sqrt[3]{4} + \sqrt[4]{4}$, then the value of M is

(A) less than 3

(B) equal to 3

(C) between 3 and 4

(D) equal to 4

(E) greater than 4

Arithmetic Estimation; Operations on Radical Expressions

Note that $\sqrt{4} = 2$. Also, $\sqrt[3]{4} > 1$ because if $\sqrt[3]{4} \leq 1$ then $\left(\sqrt[3]{4}\right)^3 \leq 1^3$, or $4 \leq 1$, which is not true.

Similarly, $\sqrt[4]{4} > 1$. Therefore, $\sqrt{4} + \sqrt[3]{4} + \sqrt[4]{4} > 2 + 1 + 1 = 4$.

The correct answer is E.

286. When a certain tree was first planted, it was 4 feet tall, and the height of the tree increased by a constant amount each year for the next 6 years. At the end of the 6th year, the tree was $\frac{1}{5}$ taller than it was at the end of the 4th year. By how many feet did the height of the tree increase each year?

(A) $\frac{3}{10}$

(B) $\frac{2}{5}$

(C) $\frac{1}{2}$

(D) $\frac{2}{3}$

(E) $\frac{6}{5}$

Algebra Series and Sequences; First-Degree Equations

Let H be the constant amount, in feet, that the height of the tree increased each of the 6 years after the tree was planted. Since the height of the tree when planted was 4 feet, its height at the end of the 4th year was $(4 + 4H)$ feet and its height at the end of the 6th year was $(4 + 6H)$ feet. We are given that its height at the end of the 6th year was $\frac{1}{5}$ greater than its height at the end of the 4th year.

$4 + 6H = (4 + 4H) + \frac{1}{5}(4 + 4H)$	given
$4 + 6H = \frac{24}{5} + \frac{24}{5}H$	distributive property, collect like terms
$6H = \frac{4}{5} + \frac{24}{5}H$	subtract $4 = \frac{20}{5}$ from both sides
$\frac{6}{5}H = \frac{4}{5}$	subtract $\frac{24}{5}H$ from both sides
$H = \frac{2}{3}$	divide both sides by $\frac{6}{5}$

Alternatively, fractions can be mostly avoided by recognizing that $\frac{1}{5}$ greater is equivalent to 20% greater.

$4 + 6H = 1.2(4 + 4H)$	given
$4 + 6H = 4.8 + 4.8H$	distributive property
$6H = 0.8 + 4.8H$	subtract 4 from both sides
$1.2H = 0.8$	subtract $4.8H$ from both sides
$H = \dfrac{0.8}{1.2} = \dfrac{2}{3}$	divide both sides by 1.2

Therefore, the height of the tree increased by $\frac{2}{3}$ feet each year.

The correct answer is D.

287. A certain musical scale has 13 notes, each having a different frequency, measured in cycles per second. In the scale, the notes are ordered by increasing frequency, and the highest frequency is twice the lowest. For each of the 12 lower frequencies, the ratio of a frequency to the next higher frequency is a fixed constant. If the lowest frequency is 440 cycles per second, then the frequency of the seventh note in the scale is how many cycles per second?

(A) $440\sqrt{2}$

(B) $440\sqrt{2^7}$

(C) $440\sqrt{2^{12}}$

(D) $440\sqrt[12]{2^7}$

(E) $440\sqrt[7]{2^{12}}$

Algebra Series and Sequences

Let x be the constant ratio of the frequency of each of the 12 notes above the lowest to that of the note right below it, so that each frequency is x times the next lower one. Then the frequency n musical notes above the lowest note is x^n times the lowest frequency. The highest frequency is 12 musical notes above the lowest, and is also twice the lowest. Since the lowest frequency is 440 cycles per second, the highest is $440x^{12} = 440(2)$ cycles per second. Thus, $x^{12} = 2$. Therefore, since the seventh note in the scale is 6 musical notes above the lowest, the frequency of the seventh note must be $440x^6 = 440\sqrt{x^{12}} = 440\sqrt{2}$ cycles per second.

The correct answer is A.

288. Five machines at a certain factory operate at the same constant rate. If all five machines, operating simultaneously, take 27 hours to fill a certain production order, how many <u>more</u> hours does it take three of these machines, operating simultaneously, to fill the same production order?

(A) 45

(B) 36

(C) 24

(D) 18

(E) 9

Arithmetic Ratio and Proportion

Since five machines operating simultaneously take 27 hours to fill the production order, a single machine takes five times as long, $(27)(5 \text{ hours}) = 135$ hours, to fill the production order. Three machines operating simultaneously perform the task three times as fast as a single machine, and thus take one-third as long as a single machine. Therefore, three machines operating simultaneously take $135/3 = 45$ hours to fill the production order, which is $45 - 27 = 18$ more hours than five machines operating simultaneously take.

The correct answer is D.

289. If w is an integer and $(21.6)(36)(0.0006)(60)(10^w)$ is an integer, what is the least possible value of w?

(A) 4

(B) 3

(C) 0

(D) −3

(E) −4

Arithmetic Applied Problems

To find the least possible value of w, first express the given product as the product of a power of 10 and an integer not divisible by 10, as follows:

$(21.6)(36)(0.0006)(60)(10^w)$

$= (216 \times 10^{-1})(36)(6 \times 10^{-4})(6 \times 10^1)(10^w)$

$= (216)(36)(6)(6) \times (10^{-1})(10^{-4})(10^1)(10^w)$

$= (216)(36)(36) \times 10^{-1-4+1+w}$

$= (216)(36)(36) \times 10^{w-4}$

The units digit of $(216)(36)(36)$ is 6 because the product of the units digits of 216, 36, and 36 is $6 \times 6 \times 6 = 216$, which has units digit 6. Thus, $(216)(36)(36)$ is not divisible by 10. So for $(216)(36)(36) \times 10^{w-4}$ to be an integer, we must have $w - 4 \geq 0$, or $w \geq 4$. Therefore, the least possible value of w is 4.

The correct answer is A.

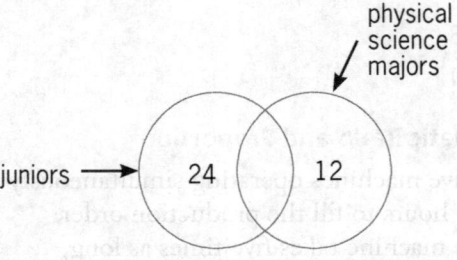

290. According to the diagram, if there are 18 physical science majors altogether, what percent of the juniors are physical science majors?

    (A)   6%
    (B)   20%
    (C)   25%
    (D) $33\frac{1}{3}$%
    (E)   50%

Arithmetic Sets (Venn Diagrams)

The diagram above divides the physical science majors into two groups, an unknown number who are juniors and 12 who are not juniors. Since there are 18 physical science majors altogether, there are $18 - 12 = 6$ physical science majors who are juniors.

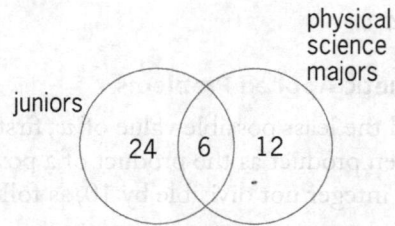

Hence, there are $24 + 6 = 30$ juniors altogether, of whom 6 are physical science majors. Therefore, $\frac{6}{30} \times 100\% = \frac{1}{5} \times 100\% = 20\%$ of the juniors are physical science majors.

The correct answer is B.

291. At a certain photo processing shop, the first standard-size print of a negative costs $4, and each additional print of the same negative costs $1. What is the total cost, in dollars, of y standard-size prints of each of x different negatives?

    (A) $4xy + (x - 1)y$
    (B) $4xy + (y - 1)x$
    (C) $4x + xy$
    (D) $4x + xy - 1$
    (E) $4x + x(y - 1)$

Algebra Applied Problems; Formulas

For each negative, the cost of y standard-size prints of that negative is the sum of the cost of the first negative ($4) and the cost of the $(y - 1)$ remaining negatives ($1 each):

$$\$4 + (y - 1)(\$1) = [4 + (y - 1)] \text{ dollars}$$

Therefore, for x different negatives, the total cost is x times this amount:

$$x[4 + (y - 1)] \text{ dollars} = 4x + x(y - 1) \text{ dollars}$$

The correct answer is E.

292. For 6 days of work, a carpenter had daily earnings of $110, $120, $110, $100, $100, and $120, respectively. In which of the following intervals does the standard deviation of the daily earnings lie?

    (A)   Between $110 and $120
    (B)   Between $100 and $110
    (C)   Between $50 and $60
    (D)   Between $10 and $20
    (E)   Between $0 and $10

Arithmetic Statistics

The standard deviation of a data set is the square root of the average of the squared differences from the mean. To unpack this, first find the mean of the data set:

$$\frac{110 + 120 + 110 + 100 + 100 + 120}{6} = 110$$

Next, find the differences and the squared differences from the mean:

x	$x - 110$	$(x - 110)^2$
110	0	0
120	10	100
110	0	0
100	−10	100
100	−10	100
120	10	100

Now use the right-most column of the table to find the average of the squared differences:

$$\frac{0 + 100 + 0 + 100 + 100 + 100}{6} = \frac{400}{6}$$

Finally, the square root of the average of the squared differences from the mean (i.e., the standard deviation) is $\sqrt{\frac{400}{6}} = \frac{\sqrt{400}}{\sqrt{6}} = \frac{20}{\sqrt{6}}$, which is between $\frac{20}{\sqrt{4}} = \frac{20}{2} = 10$ and $\frac{20}{\sqrt{9}} = \frac{20}{3} \approx 6.7$.

The correct answer is E.

293. When the positive integer n is divided by 5, the remainder is 2. When n is divided by 8, the remainder is 3. The least possible value of n lies between

(A) 5 and 10
(B) 10 and 15
(C) 15 and 20
(D) 20 and 25
(E) 25 and 30

Arithmetic Properties of Integers

The set of positive integers having remainder 2 when divided by 5 is the same as the set of positive integers that are 2 more than a multiple of 5:

$$2, 7, 12, 17, 22, \textbf{27}, 32, \ldots$$

The set of positive integers having remainder 3 when divided by 8 is the same as the set of positive integers that are 3 more than a multiple of 8:

$$3, 11, 19, \textbf{27}, 35, \ldots$$

The smallest integer that appears in both lists is 27. Therefore, the least possible value of n lies between 25 and 30.

The correct answer is E.

5.0   Data Insights Review

5.0 Data Insights Review

For the GMAT™ Data Insights section, and for graduate business programs, you need basic skills in analyzing data. This chapter is about the kinds of data in tables and charts. It's only a brief overview. If you find unfamiliar terms, consult outside resources to learn more. Before reading this chapter, read this book's Section 3.4.1, "Statistics," and Section 7.2.2, "Generalizations and Predictions," to review basic statistics and inductive generalization.

Section 5.1, "Data Sets and Types," includes:

1. Data Sets
2. Qualitative Data
3. Quantitative Data

Section 5.2, "Data Displays," includes:

1. Tables
2. Qualitative Charts
3. Quantitative Charts

Section 5.3, "Data Patterns" includes:

1. Distributions
2. Trends and Correlations

5.1 Data Sets and Types

1. Data Sets

A. A *data set* is an organized collection of data about a specific topic. A data set can be shown with one or more tables, charts, or both.

> *Example:*
>
> A data set might have data about all the employees in a company's human resources department, such as their first names, last names, home addresses, phone numbers, positions, salaries, hiring dates, and full-time or part-time statuses.

B. A *case* is an individual or thing that a data set holds data about. Often a data set has the same types of data about many cases together. Then a table or chart can show those types of data for all the cases.

> *Example:*
>
> In the example above, each employee in the human resources department is a case.

C. A *variable* is any specific type of data a data set holds about its cases. For each case, the variable has a *value*.

> *Example:*
>
> In the example above, each type of data held about the employees is a variable: *first name* is one variable, *home address* is another variable, *phone number* is a third variable, and so on. If Zara is an employee in the human resources department, one value of the variable *first name* is "Zara."

In a simple table, the top row often names the variables. Each column shows one variable's values for all the cases. In a chart, labels usually say which variables are shown.

D. The value of a *dependent variable* depends on the values of one or more other variables in the data set. An *independent variable* is not dependent.

> *Example:*
>
> In a data set of revenues, expenses, and profits, *revenue* and *expense* are independent variables. But *profit* is a dependent variable because profit is calculated as revenue minus expense. For each case, the value of the variable *profit* depends on the values of the variables *revenue* and *expense*.

E. A *data point* gives the value of one variable in one case. A cell in a table usually stands for a data point.

> *Example:*
>
> In the example above, one data point might be that Zara's position is assistant manager. That is, the data point gives the value "assistant manager" for the variable *position* in Zara's case.

F. A *record* is a set of the data points for one case. A row in a table usually shows one record. In a chart, a record might be shown as a point, a line, a bar, or a small shape with a specific position or length.

> *Example:*
>
> In the example above, one record might list Zara's first name, last name, home address, phone number, position, salary, hiring date, and full-time or part-time status.

2. Qualitative Data

A. *Qualitative data* is any type of data that doesn't use numbers to stand for a quantity. Statements, words, names, letters, symbols, algebraic expressions, colors, images, sounds, computer files, and web links can all be qualitative data. Even data that looks numeric is qualitative if the numbers don't stand for quantities.

> *Example:*
>
> Phone numbers are qualitative data. That's because they don't stand for quantities and aren't used in math—for example, they're generally not summed, multiplied, or averaged.

B. *Nominal data* is any type of qualitative data that's not ordered in any relevant way. The statistical measures of mean, median, and range don't apply to nominal data, because those measures need an ordering that nominal data lacks. But even in a set of nominal data, some values may appear more often than others. So, the statistical measure of mode does apply to nominal data, because the mode is simply the value that appears most often. To review these statistical terms, refer to Section 3.4.1, "Statistics."

> *Example:*
>
> In the example above, the first names of the human resources department's employees are nominal data if their alphabetical order doesn't matter in the data set. Suppose three of the employees share the first name "Amy," but no more than two of the employees share any other first name. Then "Amy" is the mode of the first names of the department's employees, because it's the first name that appears most often in the data set.

C. **Ordinal data** is qualitative data ordered in a way that matters in the data set. Because ordinal data is qualitative, its values can't be added, subtracted, multiplied, or divided. So, the statistical measures of mean and range don't apply to ordinal data, because they require those arithmetic operations. However, the statistical measure of median does apply to ordinal data, because finding a median only requires putting the values in an order. The statistical measure of mode also applies, just as it does for nominal data.

> *Example:*
>
> In a data set for a weekly schedule of appointments, the weekdays Monday, Tuesday, Wednesday, Thursday, and Friday are ordinal data. These days are in an order that matters to the schedule, but they're not numbers and don't measure quantities. Suppose the data set lists seven appointments: two on Monday, two on Tuesday, and three on Thursday. The fourth appointment is the median in the schedule, because three appointments are before it and three are after it. The fourth appointment is on Tuesday, so "Tuesday" is the median value of the variable *weekday* for these appointments. "Thursday" is the mode, because more of the appointments are on Thursday than on any other day.

D. **Binary data** takes only two values, like "true" and "false." Binary data is ordinal if the order of the two values matters, but nominal otherwise. Tables may show binary values with two words like "yes" and "no," or with two letters like "T" and "F," or with a check mark or "X" standing for one of the two values and a blank space standing for the other.

> *Example:*
>
> In the example above of the data set of employees in a human resources department, their employment status is a binary variable with two values: "full time" and "part time." A table might show the employment status data in a column simply titled "Full Time," with a check mark for each full-time employee and a blank for each part-time employee.

E. **Partly ordered data** has an order among some cases but not others. The statistical measure of median does not apply to a set of partly ordered values, though it might apply to a subset whose values are fully ordered.

> *Example:*
>
> Suppose a family tree shows how people over several generations are related as parents, children, and siblings, but doesn't show when each person was born. This tree lets us partly order the family members by the variable *age*. For example, suppose the family tree shows that Haruto's children are Honoka and Akari, and that Honoka's child is Minato. Since we know that all parents are older than their children, we can tell that Haruto is older than Honoka and Akari, and that Honoka is older than Minato. That also means Haruto is older than Minato. But we can't tell whether Akari is older or younger than her sister Honoka. We can't even tell whether Akari is older or younger than her nephew Minato. So, the family tree only partly orders the family members by age.

3. Quantitative Data

A. ***Quantitative data*** is data about quantities measured in numbers. Quantitative values can be added, multiplied, averaged, and so on. The statistical measures of mean, median, mode, range, and standard deviation all apply to quantitative data.

> *Example:*
>
> In the example above of the data set of the employees in the human resources department, the salaries are quantitative data. They're amounts of money shown as numbers.

B. Quantitative data is ***continuous*** if it measures something that can be infinitely divided.

> *Examples:*
>
> Temperatures are continuous data. That's because for any two temperatures, some third temperature is between them—warmer than one and cooler than the other. Likewise, altitudes are continuous data. For any two altitudes, some third altitude is higher than one and lower than the other.

A set of continuous quantitative values rarely has a mode. Because infinitely many of these values are possible, usually no two of them in a data set are exactly alike.

C. Quantitative data that isn't continuous is ***discrete***.

> *Examples:*
>
> The numbers of students taking different university courses are discrete data, because they're whole numbers. A course normally can't have a fractional number of students.
>
> As another example, prices in a currency are discrete data, because they can't be divided beyond the currency's smallest denomination. Suppose one price in euros is €3.00, and another is €3.01. No price in euros is larger than the first and smaller than the second, because the currency has no denomination below one euro cent (1/100 of a euro). That means you can't have a price of €3.005, for example. The prices in euros aren't continuous, so they're discrete.
>
> Counted numbers of people, objects, or events are generally discrete data.

D. *Interval data* uses a measurement scale whose number zero doesn't stand for a complete absence of the factor measured. So, for interval data, a measurement above zero doesn't show how much greater than nothing the measured quantity is. Because of this, the ratio of two measurements in interval data isn't the ratio of the two measured quantities.

Examples:

Dates given in years are interval data. In different societies' calendars, the year 0 stands for different years. The year 0 in the Gregorian calendar was roughly the year 3760 in the Hebrew calendar, −641 in the Islamic calendar, and −78 in the Indian National calendar. In none of these calendars does 0 stand for the very first year ever. This means, for example, that the ratio of the numbers in the two years 500 CE and 1500 CE in the Gregorian calendar isn't the ratio of two amounts: the year 500 CE isn't 1/3 the amount of the year 1500 CE.

As another example, temperatures in Celsius or Fahrenheit are also interval data. The temperature 0 degrees Celsius is 32 degrees Fahrenheit. Neither temperature scale uses 0 degrees to mean absolute zero, the complete absence of heat. This means, for example, that the ratio of the numbers in the temperatures 30°F and 60°F isn't the ratio of two amounts of heat. Thus, 60°F isn't twice as hot as 30°F.

In a measurement scale for interval data, each unit stands for the same amount. That is, any two measurements that differ by the same number of units stand for two quantities that differ by the same amount.

Examples:

In the example above of dates given in years, the year 1500 CE was 1000 years after 500 CE, because $1500 - 500 = 1000$. Likewise, the year 1600 CE was 1000 years after 600 CE, because $1600 - 600 = 1000$. Although you can't divide one year by another to find a real ratio, you can subtract one year from another to find a real length of time—in this case, 1000 years.

Likewise, 60°F is the same amount warmer than 40°F as it is cooler than 80°F. A 20°F difference in two temperatures always stands for the same real difference in heat between those temperatures.

E. *Ratio data* uses a measurement scale whose number zero stands for the absence of the measured factor. In ratio data, as in interval data, the difference between two measurements stands for the actual difference between the measured amounts. However, in ratio data, unlike interval data, the ratio of two measurements also stands for the actual ratio of the measured amounts.

Examples:

Measured weights are ratio data, whether they're in kilograms or pounds. That's because 0 kilograms stands for a complete absence of weight, as does 0 pounds. So, the ratio of 10 kilograms to 5 kilograms is a ratio of two real weights. Because the ratio of 10 to 5 is 2 to 1, 10 kilograms is twice as heavy as 5 kilograms, and 10 pounds is twice as heavy as 5 pounds.

As another example, temperatures in Kelvin are ratio data. That's because 0 K stands for absolute zero, the complete absence of heat. Thus, 200 K is really twice as hot as 100 K. As explained above, this isn't true for temperatures in Celsius or Fahrenheit, which are interval data.

F. *Logarithmic data* use a measurement scale whose higher units stand for amounts exponentially farther apart. For logarithmic data, as for ratio data, the number zero stands for a complete absence. But in logarithmic data, when two measurements a certain number of units apart are higher, the real difference between the measured amounts is greater.

Example:

Noise measured in decibels is logarithmic data. Although 0 decibels means complete silence, 30 decibels is 10 times as loud as 20 decibels, not just 1.5 times as loud. And the real difference in loudness between 40 decibels and 30 decibels is 10 times the real difference in loudness between 30 decibels and 20 decibels, even though the two differences are each 10 decibels.

Because higher units on a logarithmic scale stand for greater amounts of difference, you can't just sum and divide logarithmic data to find a statistical mean. Nor can you subtract one logarithmic measurement from another to find a statistical range. Finding the mean and range requires more complex calculations, which you won't have to do on the GMAT.

5.2 Data Displays

1. Tables

A. A *table* shows data in rows and columns. In a simple table, the top row shows the names of the variables and is called the *header*. Below the header, usually each row shows one record, each column shows one variable, and each cell shows one data point. Sometimes another row above the header has the table's title or description. Sometimes a column or a few rows within the table are used only to group the records by category. Likewise, a row or a few columns within the table are sometimes used only to group the variables by category. Sometimes a row or column shows totals, averages, or other operations on the values in other rows or columns.

Example:

The table below shows revenues, expenses, and profits for two branches of Village Shoppe for one year. The top row is the header listing the independent variables *revenue* and *expense* and the dependent variable *profit*. In each row, the profit is just the revenue minus the expense.

The table has only four rows of records. These are the third row showing the Mapleton branch's January–June finances, the fourth row showing the Mapleton branch's July–December finances, the sixth row showing the Elmville branch's January–June finances, and the seventh row showing the Elmville branch's July–December finances. The second row "Mapleton branch" serves to group the third and fourth rows together. Likewise, the fifth row "Elmville branch" serves to group the sixth and seventh rows together. The bottom row "Annual grand totals" doesn't show a record but rather sums the values in the four records for each of the three variables.

Village Shoppe	Revenue	Expense	Profit
Mapleton branch			
January–June	125000	40000	85000
July–December	90000	35000	55000
Elmville branch			
January–June	85000	30000	55000
July–December	115000	25000	90000
Annual grand totals	**415000**	**130000**	**285000**

B. Sometimes a table's title or description explains the data shown. To understand the data, always study any title or description.

Example:

In the table below, the title says the populations are in **thousands**. So, to find the total population aged 44 and under, add 63,376 thousand and 86,738 thousand. This gives 150,114 thousand, which is 150,114,000. If you only read the numbers without noticing the title, you'll get the wrong result for the total population aged 44 and under.

Population by Age Group (in thousands)	
Age	Population
17 years and under	63,376
18–44 years	86,738
45–64 years	43,845
65 years and over	24,051

2. Qualitative Charts

A. Many different types of charts show qualitative data. This book's Section 3.4.2, "Sets," discusses one type of qualitative chart, the ***Venn diagram***. Here we describe a few other common types. But the GMAT may also challenge you with unfamiliar types of charts this book doesn't discuss. To understand any type of chart, study its labels. The labels will tell you how to read the chart's various points, lines, shapes, symbols, and colors. Several labels may be together, sometimes inside a rectangle on the chart, to make a ***legend***.

B. A *network diagram* has lines connecting small circles or other shapes. Each small shape is a *node* standing for an individual, and each line stands for a relationship between two individuals. In some network diagrams, the lines are one-way or two-way arrows standing for one-way or two-way relationships.

Example:

In the network diagram below, the lettered nodes stand for six pen pals: Alice, Ben, Cathy, Dave, Ellen, and Frank. The arrows show who got a letter from whom in the past month. Each arrow points from the pen pal who sent the letter to the one who got it. A two-way arrow means both the pen pals got letters from each other. This diagram tells us many facts about the pen pals and their relationships over the past month. For example, it shows who got the most letters (Cathy received three) and who got the fewest (Frank received none).

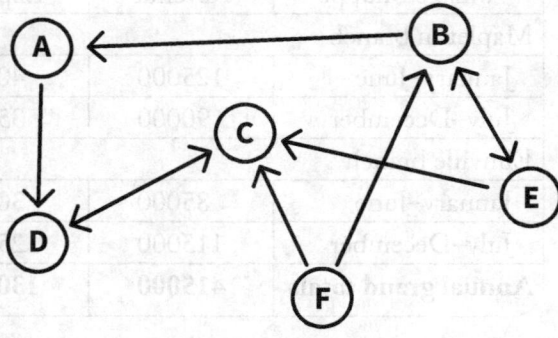

C. A *tree diagram* is a type of network diagram that shows partly ordered data like organizational structures, ancestral relationships, or conditional probabilities. In a tree diagram, each relationship is one way.

Example:

Expanding on the example in Section 5.1.2.E above, the tree diagram below shows how Haruto and his descendants are related. Each line connects a parent above to his or her child below. The diagram shows that Haruto has two children, four grandchildren, and one great-grandchild. From the diagram we can tell that Akari is older than her grandchild Mei, and that Himari and Minato are cousins. But we can't tell whether Akari, Mei, or Himari is older than Minato.

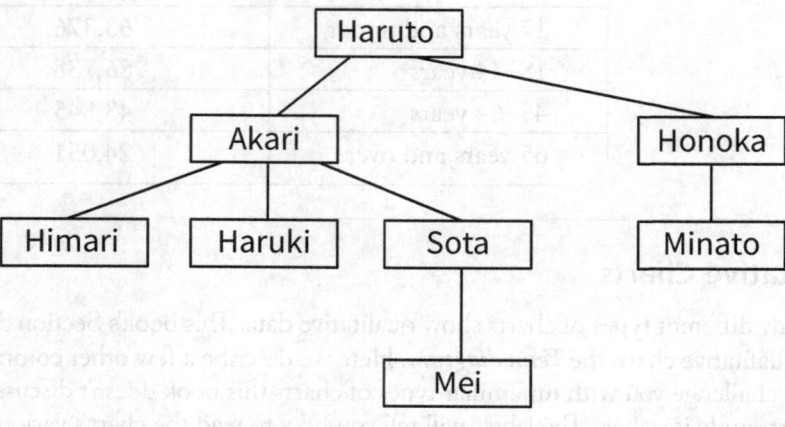

D. In a *flowchart*, each node stands for a step in a process. Arrows direct you from each step to the next. An arrow pointing back to an earlier step tells you to repeat that step. A flowchart usually has at least three types of nodes. *Process nodes* stand for actions to take and are usually rectangles. *Decision nodes* show questions to answer and are usually diamond shaped. At least two labeled arrows lead from each decision node to show how choosing the next step depends on how you answer the question. *Terminal nodes* show the start or end of the process and are usually oval.

Example:

The flowchart below shows a simple process for getting cereal from a store. The top oval shows the first step, going to the store. The arrow below it then takes us to a process node saying to look for a cereal we like. For the third step, we reach a decision node asking whether we've found the cereal we want. If we have, we follow the decision node's "Yes" arrow to another process node telling us to buy the cereal we found, and then we move on to the bottom terminal node telling us to go home. On the other hand, if we haven't found the cereal we want, we follow the decision node's "No" arrow to a second decision node asking whether the store offers other good cereal choices. If it doesn't, we follow another "No" arrow telling us to give up and go home. But if the store does offer other good cereal choices, we follow a "Yes" arrow back to the "Look for a cereal you like" step to peruse the choices again. We repeat the loop until we either find a cereal we want to buy or else decide the store has no more good cereal choices. Since the store won't have infinitely many cereals, we eventually end at the bottom terminal node and go home.

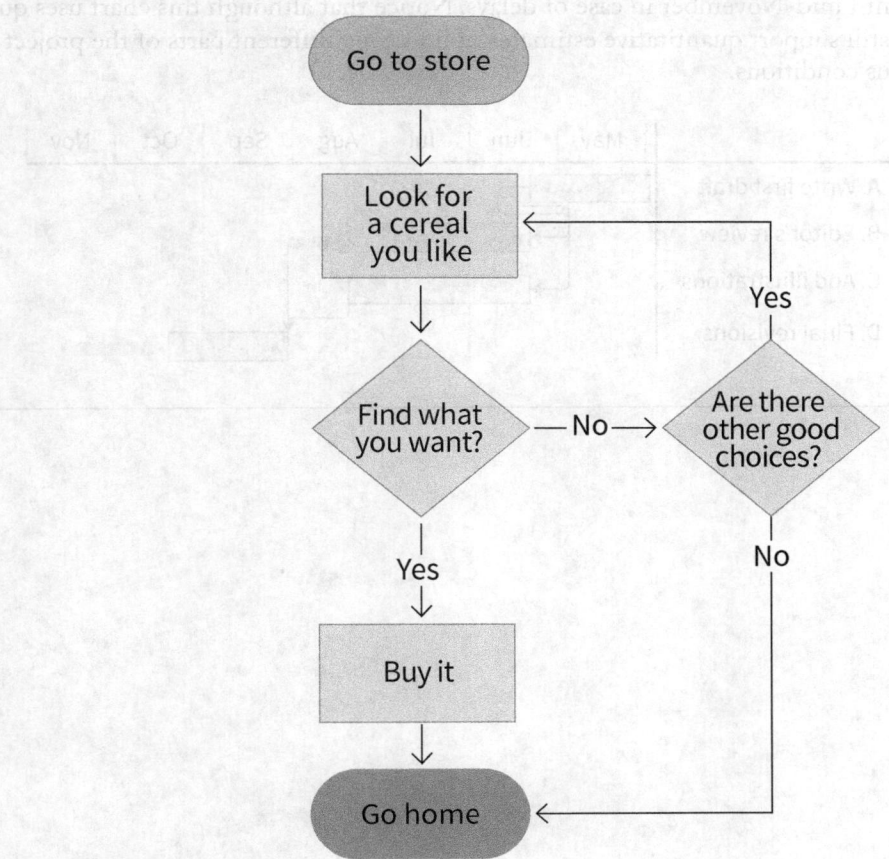

E. A *Gantt chart* is used to plan and schedule projects. The horizontal axis has a time scale showing the period planned for a project. The time units usually are qualitative ordinal units, such as months or calendar dates. The vertical axis is divided into labeled rows, each typically standing for one task in the project. In each row, a bar stretches from the planned start time to the planned end time for that row's task. Sometimes a second bar stretches out past the first to show how a task might take longer than expected. An arrow pointing from the end of one task's bar to the beginning of another's bar means the second task can't begin until the first is finished.

Example:

The Gantt chart below shows a schedule for writing a children's book. The top bar shows that Task A, writing the first draft, should be done over about five weeks in May and early June. Task B, the editor's review, and Task C, adding illustrations, start when Task A ends. The lines pointing from the end of Task A to the beginnings of Tasks B and C mean that Tasks B and C can't start until Task A is finished. So, if Task A isn't finished on time, Tasks B and C will both have to be delayed. Tasks B and C are both scheduled to be finished by mid-August. But the thinner gray bar at the end of Task B's main bar means the plan allows the editor's review to take until the beginning of September if necessary—perhaps in case the editor needs extra time to review the illustrations. The arrows from Tasks B and C to Task D, the final revisions, mean that the final revisions can't start until Tasks B and C are finished. Although Task D is supposed to be done by mid-October, a final thinner gray bar at the end of Task D's main bar shows that the plan allows Task D to take until mid-November in case of delays. Notice that although this chart uses qualitative data, it can still support quantitative estimates of how long different parts of the project may take under various conditions.

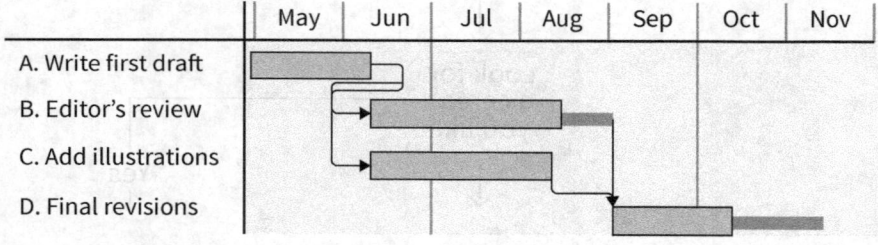

3. Quantitative Charts

A. Here we discuss a few common types of charts that normally show quantitative data. The GMAT may also use rarer types this book doesn't discuss. To understand any type of quantitative chart, study the description and any labels to find out what cases and variables are shown, and how. Also notice any axes. These show the measurement scales. Some quantitative charts have no axes. Others have one, two, or, rarely, three or more. For each axis, notice whether it starts below, at, or above 0. Note the numbers on the axes, as well as the units the numbers stand for. You must read the axes correctly to understand the data.

Example:

In the chart below, labels say that the scale on the left is for temperature data and the scale on the right is for precipitation data. The bottom axis shows four months of the year, spaced three months apart. The chart's title tells us each data point gives the **average** temperature or precipitation in City X during a given month. This implies that the temperatures and precipitations shown are averages over many years. Suppose we're asked to find the average temperature and precipitation in City X in April. To do this, we don't have to calculate averages of any of the values shown. Those values are **already** averages. So, to find the average temperature for April, we simply read the April temperature data point by noting it's slightly lower than the 15 on the temperature scale at the left. Likewise, to find the average precipitation for April, we read the April precipitation data point by noticing it's about as high as the 8 on the precipitation scale on the right. This means the chart says that in April, the average temperature is around 14° Celsius and the average precipitation around 8 centimeters. Since the question is only about April, the data shown for January, July, and October are irrelevant.

AVERAGE TEMPERATURE AND PRECIPITATION IN CITY X

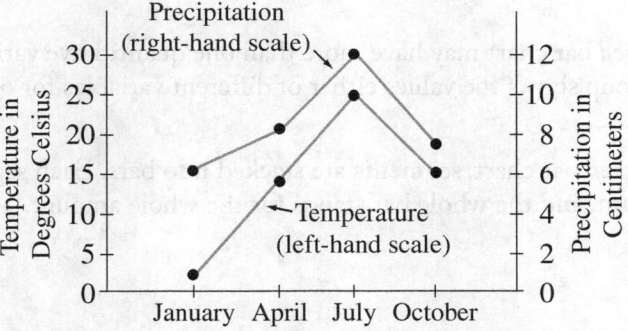

B. A *pie chart* has a circle divided into sections like pie slices. The sections make up the whole circle without overlapping. They stand for parts that together make up some whole amount. Usually, each section is sized in proportion to the part it stands for and labeled with that part's fraction, or percent, of the whole amount. You can use these fractions or percents in calculations. Refer to Section 3.3, "Rates, Ratios, and Percents," to review how.

Example:

In the pie chart below, the sections are sized in proportion to their percent amounts. These percents add up to 100%. Suppose we're told that Al's weekly net salary is $350 and asked how many of the categories shown each individually took at least $80 of that $350. To answer, first we find that $\frac{\$80}{\$350}$ is about 23%. This means each category that took at least $80 of Al's salary took at least 23% of his salary. So, the graph shows exactly two categories that each took at least $80 of Al's salary: *Savings* took 25% of his salary, and *Rent and Utilities* took 30%.

DISTRIBUTION OF AL'S WEEKLY NET SALARY

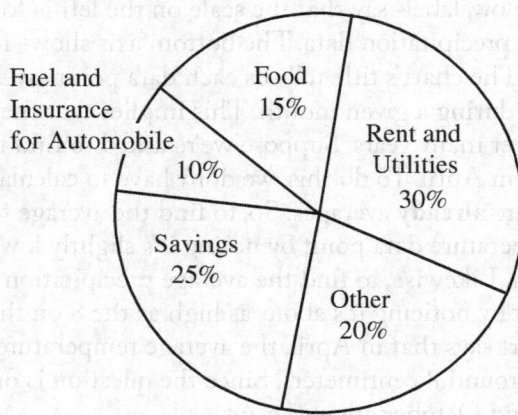

C. A *bar chart* has vertical or horizontal bars standing for cases. A simple bar chart has only one quantitative variable. The bars' different heights or lengths show this variable's values for different cases.

A *grouped* bar chart may have more than one quantitative variable. Its bars are grouped together. Each group shows the values either of different variables for one case or of related cases for one variable.

In a *stacked* bar chart, segments are stacked into bars. Each segment inside a bar stands for part of an amount, and the whole bar stands for the whole amount.

Example:

The bar chart below is both grouped and stacked. Each pair of grouped bars shows population figures for one of three towns. In each pair, the bar on the left shows the town's population in 2010, and the bar on the right shows the town's population in 2020. Inside each bar, the lower segment shows how many people in the town were under age 30, and the upper segment shows how many were age 30 or older. For example, the chart's fifth bar shows that in 2010, Ceburg's population was around 2,000, including about 1,100 people under 30 and 900 people 30 or older. And the chart's sixth bar shows that by 2020, Ceburg's population had grown to around 2,400, including about 1,200 people under 30 and 1,200 people 30 or older. By reading the amounts shown, we can also estimate various other amounts, like the three towns' combined number of residents 30 or older in 2020.

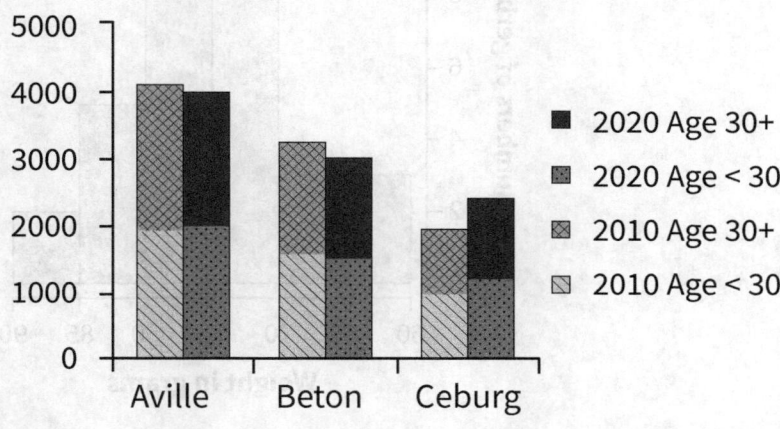

D. A *histogram* looks like a bar chart but works differently. In a histogram, each bar stands for a range of values that the same variable can take. These ranges don't overlap. Together they usually include every value the variable can take, or at least every value it does take in some population. The bars are in order from the one farthest left, which stands for the lowest range of values, to the one farthest right, which stands for the highest range. Each bar's height shows the number or proportion of times the variable's value is in the range the bar stands for. A bar chart shows clearly how the values are distributed.

Example:

The histogram below shows the weights of 31 gerbils. Each bar's height shows how many gerbils were in a specific weight range. For example, the bar farthest left says 3 gerbils each weighed from 60 to 65 grams. The histogram doesn't show any individual gerbil's weight. However, it does give us some statistical information. For example, by adding the numbers of gerbils in the different weight ranges, we can tell that the 16th-heaviest of the 31 gerbils weighed between 75 and 80 grams. This means the gerbils' median weight was in that range. The histogram also shows that the gerbils mainly weighed between 70 and 85 grams apiece, though several weighed less or more.

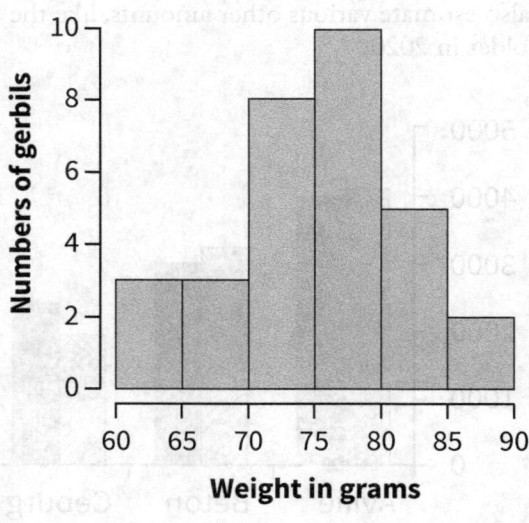

E. A *line chart* often shows how the values of one or more quantitative variables change over time. Typically, the horizontal axis has the time scale, and the vertical axis has one or more scales for the variable or variables. One or more lines connect the data points. Different lines may stand either for different variables or for a single variable applied to different cases. Line charts make it easy to see trends and correlations.

Some line charts show probability distributions instead of changes over time, as we'll see in Section 5.3.1 below.

Examples:

In Section 5.2.3.A above, the chart of average monthly temperatures and precipitations is a line chart whose two variables have two separate scales, one on the left and one on the right.

The line chart below shows how many toasters of three different brands were sold each year from 2017 to 2022. Each sloping line shows how sales changed for one of the brands during those years. The legend on the bottom says which line stands for which brand. All three lines use the scale on the left, whose numbers stand for thousands of units sold annually. The chart shows that over the six years, annual sales of Crispo toasters increased dramatically, annual sales of Brownita toasters declined to almost zero, and annual sales of Toastador toasters fluctuated.

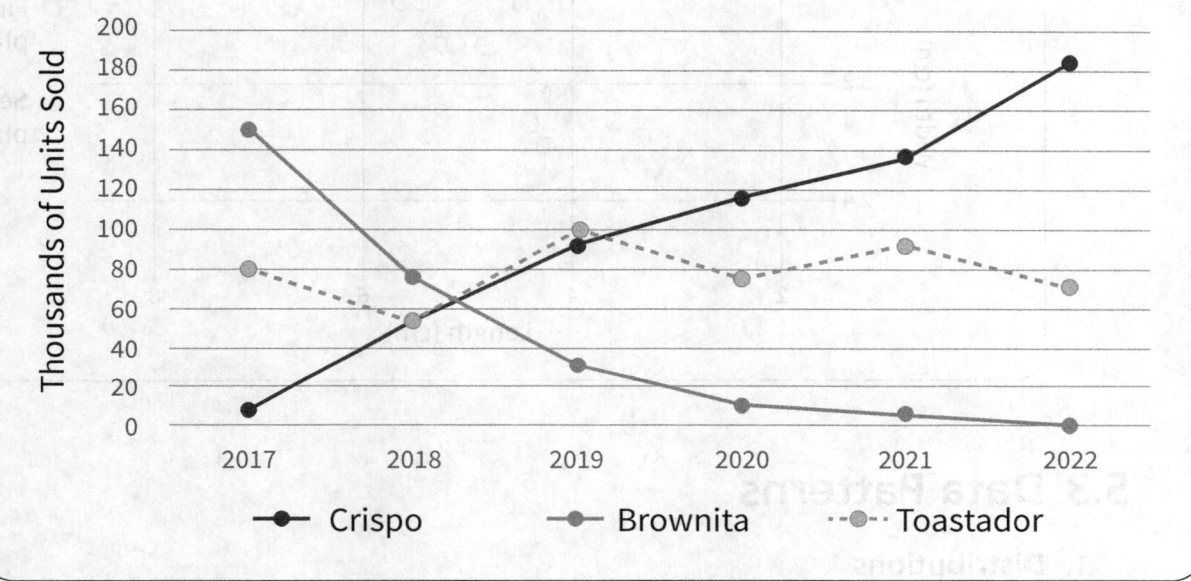

F. A *scatterplot* has at least two quantitative variables, one on each axis. For each case in the data, a dot's position shows the variables' values. No lines connect the scattered dots, but a line through the scatterplot may show an overall trend in the data. Sometimes the dots have a few different shapes or colors to show they stand for cases in different categories. And in scatterplots called *bubble charts*, the dots have different sizes standing for values of a third variable.

Scatterplots are useful for showing correlations. They also show how much individual cases fit an overall correlation or deviate from it.

Example:

The scatterplot below shows measured widths and lengths of leaves on two plants. Each dot stands for one leaf. The dot's position stands for the leaf's width and length in centimeters, as the scatterplot's two axes show. The legend says how one set of dots stands for leaves on the first plant, and another set for leaves on the second. The scatterplot shows that, in general, the longer leaves tend to be wider, and vice versa. It also shows how leaves on the second plant tend to be somewhat longer and wider than those on the first, with some exceptions.

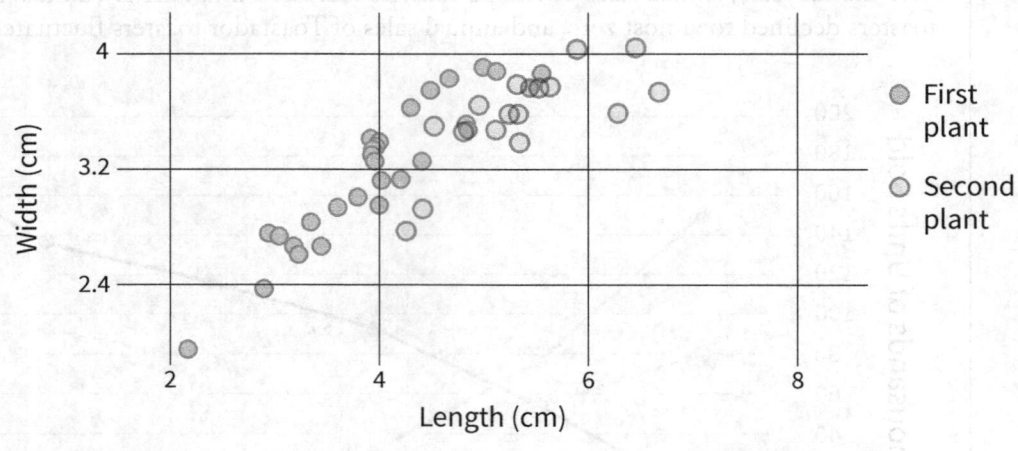

5.3 Data Patterns

1. Distributions

A. A data ***distribution*** is a pattern in how often different values appear in data. How data in a sample is distributed can tell you how likely different values are to appear in the same population outside the sample. In this book, Section 7.2.2, "Generalizations and Predictions," discusses generalizations and predictions based on samples.

B. A distribution is ***uniform*** if the values each occur about equally often. It's less uniform when the values differ more in how often each occurs. The more uniform a distribution is for a sample, the better it supports the conclusion that the distribution for other cases in the population is likewise uniform.

Example:

Suppose the six faces on a die are numbered 1 to 6. And suppose that when rolled sixty times, the die comes up 1 eleven times, 2 nine times, 3 ten times, 4 eleven times, 5 ten times, and 6 nine times. This isn't a **perfectly** uniform distribution, because the six values 1 to 6 didn't occur exactly ten times apiece. But because each value did occur between nine and eleven times, the distribution is **fairly** uniform. This suggests that each of the six values is about equally likely to occur whenever the die is rolled, and that their distribution for future rolls will stay fairly uniform.

C. A variable's values are often distributed unevenly. Sometimes one central value occurs most often, with other values occurring less often the farther they are from the central value. When this type of distribution is *normal*, each value below the central value occurs just as often as the value equally far above the central value. For a perfectly normal distribution, the central value is the mean, the median, and the mode. When plotted on a chart, a normal distribution is bell shaped, with a central hump tapering off equally into tails on both sides. But a distribution with a larger tail on one side of the hump than the other is not normal but *skewed*. For a skewed distribution, the mean is often farther out on the larger tail than the median is.

Example:

The two charts below show distributions of lengths for two beetle species. The chart on the left shows that Species A beetles have roughly a normal distribution of lengths. The central hump is symmetrical, with equal tails on both sides. From the chart on the left, we can tell that the mode, the median, and the mean of the lengths for Species A are all around 5 millimeters. In contrast, the chart on the right shows that Species B beetles have a skewed distribution of lengths. The tail on the right side of the hump is larger than the tail on the left side. This means more beetles of Species B have lengths above the mode than below it. As a result, the median length for Species B is above the mode, and the mean is above the median.

Normal Distribution

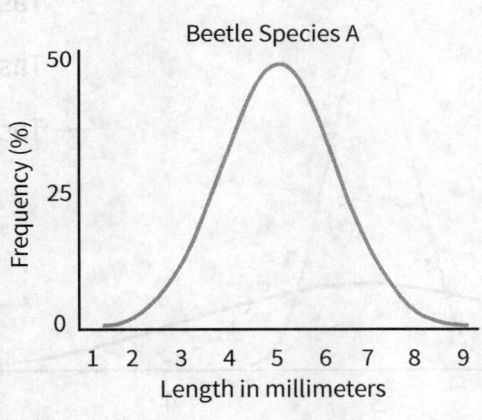

Skewed Distribution

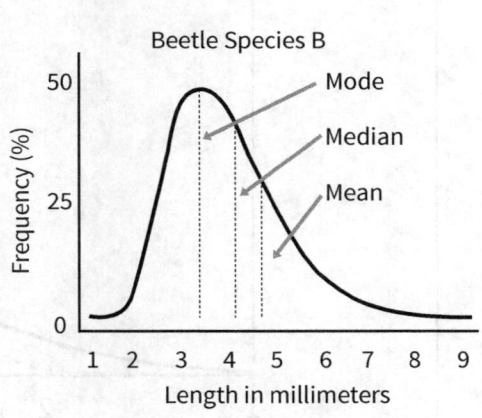

D. The more tightly clustered a distribution is around a central value, the higher and narrower the hump is, and the smaller the tails are. A more tightly clustered distribution also has a smaller standard deviation, as discussed in Section 3.4.1, "Statistics." The more tightly clustered a distribution is for an observed sample, the more likely a new case from the population outside that sample is to have a value near the distribution's central value.

Example:

For each of three tasks, the chart below shows how frequently it takes workers different lengths of time in minutes to complete that task. Even though the bottom axis shows times from 1 to 5 minutes, it doesn't stand for a single period starting at 1 minute and ending at 5 minutes. Instead, it stands for a range of lengths of task completion times.

Notice how the chart uses smooth curves to show the frequencies of different completion times. That suggests it shows trends idealized from the observed data points, which could be shown more precisely as separate dots or bars.

For each task, the distribution of completion times is uniform, with a mode, median, and mean of 3 minutes. But the completion times are most tightly clustered around 3 minutes for Task A, and least tightly clustered for Task C. That means the standard deviation of the completion times is lowest for Task A and highest for Task C. It also means the probability is higher that an individual worker will take close to 3 minutes to complete Task A than to complete Task C. A worker's completion time for Task C is less predictable and likely to be farther from 3 minutes. So, the chart gives **stronger evidence** for the conclusion that finishing Task A will take a worker between 2 and 4 minutes than for the conclusion that finishing Task C will take that worker between 2 and 4 minutes.

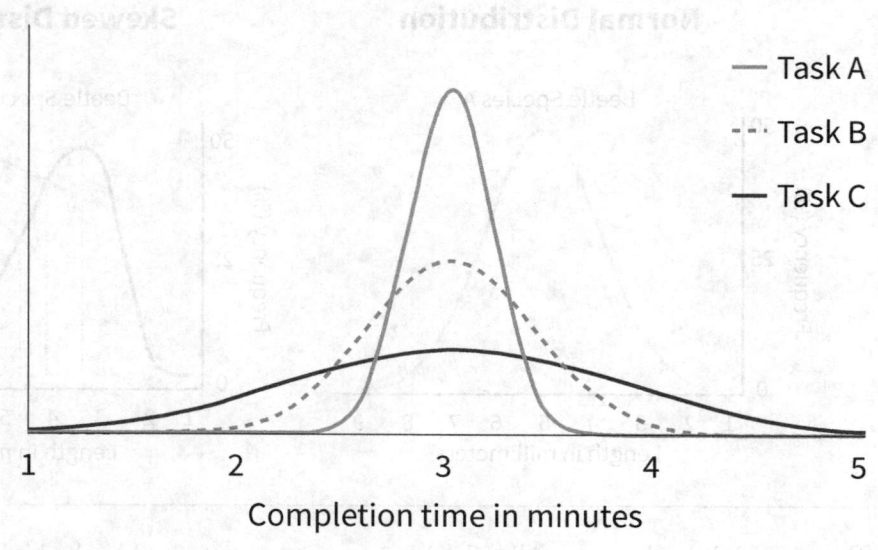

Completion time in minutes

E. Data distributions take many other shapes too. Some have two or more humps, and others have random variations in frequency among adjacent values. In general, the less the values in a sample cluster around one central hump, the larger the standard deviation is, and the less predictable the values are for cases in the population outside the observed sample.

2. Trends and Correlations

A. Charts often show trends over time. They may show that a variable's values increase, decrease, fluctuate, or change in cycles. They may also show values of different plotted variables changing in the same ways or opposite ways.

Usually, an observed trend over a period is evidence that the same trend extends at least slightly before and after that period. This evidence is stronger the longer the observed trend has lasted and the more varied the conditions it's lasted through. Generalizing from a longer observed period with more varied conditions is like generalizing from a larger sample, as discussed in Section 7.2.2, "Generalizations and Predictions." But the odds increase of other factors disrupting the observed trend at times farther from the observed period, and in conditions that differ more from those observed.

Example:

The line chart in Section 5.2.3.E above shows that annual sales of Crispo toasters rose from fewer than 10,000 in 2017 to over 180,000 in 2022. If this trend continued another year, even more than 180,000 Crispo toasters would have been sold in 2023. But many factors might disrupt Crispo's surging popularity. For example, another company might start making better or less expensive toasters, drawing consumers away from Crispo toasters. Or broader social, economic, or technological changes might reduce demand for toasters altogether. The more years that pass outside the observed period of 2017 through 2022, the more likely such disruptions become. So, the observed trend gives stronger evidence that annual Crispo toaster sales would have been over 180,000 in 2023 than it gives that they'll still be over 180,000 in 2050.

B. Two quantitative or ordinal variables are ***positively correlated*** if they both tend to be higher in the same cases. They're ***negatively correlated*** if one tends to be higher in cases where the other is lower.

Examples:

If warmer days tend to be rainier in a certain region, then temperature and precipitation are positively correlated there.

But if warmer days tend to be drier in a different region, then temperature and precipitation are negatively correlated there.

C. On a line chart, the lines standing for positively correlated variables tend to slope up or down together. The more consistently the slopes match, the stronger the positive correlation. But when two variables are negatively correlated, the line standing for one tends to slope up where the other slopes down, and vice versa. The more consistently the lines slope in opposite directions, the stronger the negative correlation.

Examples:

The chart in Section 5.2.3.A shows a positive correlation between average monthly temperature and precipitation in City X. The temperature and precipitation lines both slope up together from January through July, and then slope down together.

The chart in Section 5.2.3.E shows a negative correlation between annual sales of Crispo toasters and annual sales of Brownita toasters. Throughout this chart, the line standing for Crispo toaster sales slopes up and the line standing for Brownita toaster sales slopes down. But the chart shows no clear positive or negative correlation of Crispo or Brownita toaster sales with Toastador toaster sales. The line standing for Toastador toaster sales fluctuates, sometimes sloping up and sometimes down. It shows no consistent trend relative to the other two lines. So, the chart doesn't clearly support a prediction that in future years Toastador sales will increase or decrease as Crispo or Brownita sales do the same or the opposite.

D. When a scatterplot shows a positive correlation, the dots tend to cluster around a line that slopes up. When it shows a negative correlation, they tend to cluster around a line that slopes down. The stronger the correlation, the more tightly the dots cluster around the sloped line. If the dots spread farther away from the sloped line, or cluster around a line with a less consistent slope, the correlation is weaker or nonexistent.

Example:

The scatterplot in Section 5.2.3.F shows leaf width as positively correlated with leaf length for both plants. The dots mostly cluster around a line sloping up, which means wider leaves tend to be longer and vice versa. Thus, the scatterplot supports a prediction that if another leaf on one of the plants is measured, it too will probably be wider if it's longer. But the correlation in the scatterplot isn't perfect. For example, the dot farthest to the right is lower than each of about a dozen dots to its left. That dot farthest to the right stands for a leaf that's both longer and thinner than any of the leaves those other dozen dots stand for. This inconsistency in the correlation somewhat weakens the scatterplot's support for the prediction that another leaf measured on one of the plants will be wider if it's longer.

E. Values of a nominal variable may also be associated with higher or lower values of an ordinal or quantitative variable. Different values of two nominal variables can also be associated with each other.

Examples:

Species is a nominal variable. Individuals of some species tend to weigh more than individuals of other species, so different values of the nominal variable *species* are associated with higher or lower values of the quantitative variable *weight*.

As another example, university students majoring in certain subjects like physics are more likely to take certain courses like statistics than university students majoring in other subjects like theater are, even though a student's *major* and *course enrollment* are both nominal variables.

An association involving a nominal variable like *species* isn't a positive or negative correlation, because nominal variables aren't ordered; one species isn't greater or less than another. Still, these nominal associations can be shown in qualitative charts and tables, and they can support predictions. Knowing an animal's species gives you some evidence about roughly how much it likely weighs. And knowing a student's major gives you some evidence about what courses that student is more likely to take.

6.0   Data Insights

6.0 Data Insights

This chapter describes the Data Insights section of the GMAT™ exam, explains what it measures, discusses the five types of Data Insights questions, and offers strategies for answering them.

Because most Data Insights questions are interactive, you need a computer to access them fully. Among Data Insights questions, only the Data Sufficiency questions and Two-Part Analysis questions can be shown on paper as they are on the test. So, those are the only Data Insights practice questions in this book.

> For practice with other Data Insights practice questions, go to www.mba.com/my-account and access the Online Question Bank using the Access Code inside the front cover of this book.

Overview of the Data Insights Section

The Data Insights section measures your skill at analyzing data shown in formats often used in real business situations. You'll need this skill to make informed decisions as a future business leader. Data Insights questions ask you to assess multiple sources and types of information—graphic, numeric, and verbal—as they relate to one another.

This section asks you to:

- Use math, verbal reasoning, and data analysis,

- Solve connected problems together, and

- Give answers in different formats, not just traditional multiple choice.

Many Data Insights questions ask you to study graphs and sort tables to find information. These questions don't require advanced statistics or spreadsheet expertise. Other Data Insights questions ask you to tell whether given information is enough to answer a question, but don't ask you to actually answer it. You have 45 minutes to respond to the 20 questions in the Data Insights section, an average of 2 minutes and 15 seconds per question. Throughout the section are questions of five types. Some need multiple responses. A question may use math, data analysis, verbal reasoning, or all three. Questions with math require knowing the topics reviewed in Chapter 3, "Math Review": Value, Order, Factors; Algebra, Equalities, Inequalities; Rates, Ratios, Percents; and Statistics, Sets, Counting, Probability, Estimation, and Series. Questions involving data analysis require understanding different types of data in tables or graphs, finding patterns in that data, and using other skills reviewed in Chapter 5, "Data Insights Review." Questions with verbal aspects require reasoning, understanding texts, evaluating arguments, and using other skills reviewed in Chapter 7, "Verbal Review."

To prepare for the Data Insights section, first review basic math, data analysis, and verbal reasoning skills to make sure you know enough to answer the questions. Then practice on GMAT questions from past exams.

Special Features:

- Unlike other sections of the GMAT exam, the Data Insights section sometimes shows two or more questions on one screen. When it does, you can change your answers before clicking "Next" to go on to the next screen. But once you're on a new screen, you can't return to the previous screen.

- The Data Insights section uses some math, but it doesn't ask you to calculate by hand. An onscreen calculator with basic functions is available for this section. For more information, please go to **www.mba.com/exampolicies**.

6.1 What Is Measured

The Data Insights section measures how well you use data to solve problems. Specifically, it tests the skills described below:

Skill Category	Details	Examples
Apply	Understand principles, rules, or other concepts Use them in a new context or say what would follow if new information were added	• Tell if new examples follow or break given rules • Tell how new situations affect a trend • Draw conclusions about new data from given principles
Evaluate	Judge information as evidence	• Tell if information in one source supports or weakens a claim in another source • Tell if information justifies a course of action • Judge how well evidence supports an argument or plan • Find errors or gaps in information
Infer	Draw unstated conclusions from information	• Find an outcome's probability using data • Tell if statements follow logically from given information • Say what a term means in a context • Find a rate of change in data gathered over time
Recognize	Identify information given explicitly, including details or relationships between pieces of information	• Find agreements and disagreements between information sources • Find how strongly two variables are correlated • Give a ranking based on combined factors from a table (for example, saying which product maximizes revenue and minimizes costs) • Tell which data an argument uses as evidence
Strategize	Find ways to work toward a goal given constraints	• Choose a plan that minimizes risks and maximizes value • Identify trade-offs among ways to reach a goal • Tell which math formula gives a desired result • Decide which ways of doing a task meet given needs

6.2 Question Types and Test-Taking Strategies

The Data Insights section has five types of questions: Multi-Source Reasoning, Table Analysis, Graphics Interpretation, Two-Part Analysis, and Data Sufficiency. We describe each below.

1. Multi-Source Reasoning

What you see:

- Two or three tabs on the left side of your screen. Each tab shows a written passage, a table, a graph, or another information source. The different tabs may show information in different forms. Click on the tabs to see what's on them and find what you need to answer the questions.

Example of information sources on multiple tabs:

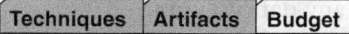

Techniques	Artifacts	Budget

For outside laboratory tests, the museum's first-year budget for the Kaxna collection allows unlimited IRMS testing, and a total of $7,000—equal to the cost of 4 TL tests plus 15 radiocarbon tests, or the cost of 40 ICP-MS tests—for all other tests. For each technique applied by an outside lab, the museum is charged a fixed price per artifact.

- A question with answer choices on the right side of your screen. With each set of tabs, three questions appear one at a time.

The response type:

- Some questions are traditional multiple choice, with five answer choices.

- Others are "conditional statement" questions. Each question gives a condition. Below the condition are three rows with content such as sentences, phrases, words, numbers, or formulas. For each row, mark "yes" or "true" if the row's contents meet the given condition, or mark "no" or "false" if not.

- Mark one answer PER ROW.

- You must mark all three rows correctly to get credit for the question.

Example of a conditional statement question:

For each of the following artifacts in the museum's Kaxna collection, select *Yes* if, based on the museum's assumptions, a range of dates for the object's creation can be obtained using one of the techniques in the manner described. Otherwise, select *No*.

Yes	No	
○	○	Bronze statue of a deer
○	○	Fired-clay pot
○	○	Wooden statue of a warrior

Tips for Answering Multi-Source Reasoning Questions

- **Answer using only the information given.**

  The tabs show all the information you need to answer correctly. If you already know about the topic, don't use that knowledge to answer. Use only the information in the tabs.

- **Analyze each information source.**

  As you read a passage, note each statement's role. Section 7.1, "Analyzing Passages," explains how.

259

Read labels and scales to understand the data in tables and graphs. Chapter 5, "Data Insights Review," explains how.

- **Read the whole question.**

  You need to understand what each question is asking you to do. For example, some questions ask you to spot conflicts between information sources. Others ask you to draw conclusions by combining information from different sources. And some questions ask you to judge which information sources are relevant to an issue.

  While answering the questions, you can always click on the tabs to review any of the information.

2. Table Analysis

What you see:

- A data table. You can sort it by any data column.

Example of data table with sorting drop-down menu:

The table displays data on Brazilian agricultural products in 2009.

Sort By: Production, world share (%) ▼

Commodity	Production, world share (%)	Production, world rank	Exports, world share (%)	Exports, world rank
Pork	4	4	12	4
Cotton	5	5	10	4
Corn	8	4	10	2
Chickens	15	3	38	1
Beef	16	2	22	1
Sugar	21	1	44	1
Soybeans	27	2	40	2
Coffee	40	1	32	1
Orange juice	56	1	82	1

The response type:

- The questions are in "conditional statement" form. Each question gives a condition. Below the condition are three rows with contents such as sentences, phrases, words, numbers, or formulas. For each row, mark "yes" or "true" if the row's contents meet the condition, or mark "no" or "false" if not.

- Mark one answer PER ROW.

- You must mark all three rows correctly to get credit for the question.

Example of a conditional statement question:

For each of the following statements, select *Yes* if the statement can be shown to be true based on the information in the table. Otherwise select *No*.

Yes	No	
○	○	No individual country produces more than one-fourth of the world's sugar.
○	○	If Brazil produces less than 20% of the world's supply of any commodity listed in the table, Brazil is not the world's top exporter of that commodity.
○	○	Of the commodities in the table for which Brazil ranks first in world exports, Brazil produces more than 20% of the world's supply.

Tips for Answering Table Analysis Questions

- **Study the table and any text around it to learn what kind of data it shows.**

  Knowing what kind of data is in the table helps you find the information you need.

- **Study the condition in the question.**

  The question gives a condition like *"is consistent with the information provided"* or *"can be inferred from the information provided."* Understanding that condition helps you understand how to mark each row.

- **Read each answer row to decide how to sort the table.**

  Often an answer row's contents hint at how to sort the table by one or more columns to make the data you need easier to find.

- **Judge whether each answer row's contents meet the given condition.**

  In each row, you can only mark one of the two answer choices, and only one is right. Decide whether the row's contents meet the condition in the question.

3. Graphics Interpretation

What you see:

- A graphic. Section 5.2, "Data Displays," explains some kinds of graphics you might see.

- One or more statements with blanks in missing parts. Each blank part has a drop-down menu you use to fill it in.

Example of graphics:

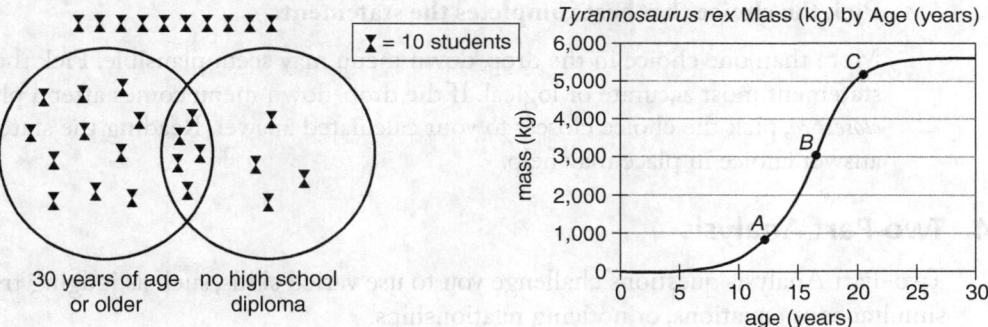

Example of a statement with a drop-down menu to fill in a blank:

Use the drop-down menu to complete the statement according to the information presented in the diagram.

If one student is selected at random from the 300 surveyed, the chance that the student will be under 30 or a high school graduate or both is Select...▾

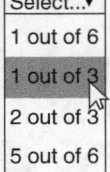

1 out of 6
1 out of 3
2 out of 3
5 out of 6

If one student is selected at random from the 300 surveyed, the chance that the student will be both under 30 and a high school graduate is 1 out of 3▾

The response type:

- Each drop-down menu shows a list of choices such as words, phrases, or numbers. Pick the best choice in the drop-down menu to fill in the blank in the statement.

- If the question has two or more drop-down menus, you must pick the best choices in all of them to get credit for the question.

Tips for Answering Graphics Interpretation Questions

- **Study the graphic.**

  Find the information in the graphic. Notice any marked values on the axes. Also notice any differences between units in the graphic and units the text discusses. Don't assume the graphic is drawn to scale.

- **Read any text around the graphic.**

  Text near the graphic may clarify what the graphic means. The text may also give information that's not in the graphic but is needed to answer the question.

- **Study the statements with drop-down menus.**

  Studying these statements helps you understand what the question is asking you to do. Graphics Interpretation questions may ask you to interpret and connect data, to find how different pieces of data are related, or to draw conclusions from a data set. You may have to do some math, for example to find or compare rates of change.

- **Read all the choices in each drop-down menu.**

  The menu choices may have clues about how to answer the question.

- **Pick the choice that best completes the statement.**

  More than one choice in the drop-down menu may seem plausible. Pick the one that makes the statement most accurate or logical. If the drop-down menu comes after a phrase like *nearest to* or *closest to*, pick the choice closest to your calculated answer. Reading the statement again with your answer choice in place may help.

4. Two-Part Analysis

Two-Part Analysis questions challenge you to use varied skills, such as judging trade-offs, solving simultaneous equations, or noticing relationships.

What you see:

- A passage.

- Instructions saying to use the passage to make two choices that together or separately meet one or more conditions.

- A response table with three columns.

Example of a passage:

A literature department at a small university in an English-speaking country is organizing a two-day festival in which it will highlight the works of ten writers who have been the subjects of recent scholarly work by the faculty. Five writers will be featured each day. To reflect the department's strengths, the majority of writers scheduled for one of the days will be writers whose primary writing language is not English. On the other day of the festival, at least four of the writers will be women. Neither day should have more than two writers from the same country. Departmental members have already agreed on a schedule for eight of the writers. That schedule showing names, along with each writer's primary writing language and country of origin, is shown.

- Day 1:

    Achebe (male, English, Nigeria)

    Weil (female, French, France)

    Gavalda (female, French, France)

    Barrett Browning (female, English, UK)

- Day 2:

    Rowling (female, English, UK)

    Austen (female, English, UK)

    Ocantos (male, Spanish, Argentina)

    Lu Xun (male, Chinese, China)

Example of a response based on passage information:

Select a writer who could be added to the schedule for either day. Then select a writer who could be added to the schedule for neither day. Make only two selections, one in each column.

Either day	Neither day	Writer
○	○	LeGuin (female, English, USA)
○	○	Longfellow (male, English, USA)
○	○	Murasaki (female, Japanese, Japan)
○	○	Colette (female, French, France)
○	○	Vargas Llosa (male, Spanish, Peru)
○	○	Zola (male, French, France)

The response type:

- The response table's top row names the columns. Below that, the first two columns have buttons you click to choose from a list in the third column.

- Pick one answer PER COLUMN, not per row.

- To get credit for the question, you must pick one correct answer in the first column, and one in the second column.

- You can pick the same answer in both columns.

Tips for Answering Two-Part Analysis Questions

- **Answer using only the information given.**

    The question tells you everything you need to know to pick the right answers. If you already know about the topic, don't use that knowledge to answer the question. Rely on the given information to answer the question.

- **Read the instructions below the passage.**

    The table's top row may not fully explain the tasks in the first two columns. Notice how the instructions describe the tasks.

- **Make two choices.**

    Pick one answer in the first column and one answer in the second column.

- **Read all the answer choices before picking any.**

  Before you pick answers in the first two columns, read all the answer choices in the third column.

- **Notice if the instructions say the two answers depend on each other.**

  Some Two-Part Analysis questions ask you to make two independent choices. Others ask you to pick two answers that combine into one correct response. Follow the instructions to make sure your two answer choices combine the right way.

- **Pick the same answer in both columns if it is the best choice for both.**

  Sometimes the same answer is the best choice for both columns.

5. Data Sufficiency

A Data Sufficiency problem asks you to analyze a question. Usually, the question is about an information source such as a written passage, a table, a graph, or an equation. You must then decide whether either or both of two new statements give enough new information to answer the question. But you don't have to give the answer. Instead, you pick one of five response choices to classify how the two statements relate to the question. These five choices are the same for each Data Sufficiency question.

What you see:

- A question, usually with background information.
- Two statements labeled (1) and (2).

Example of a Data Sufficiency Problem and Statements

Kim has a deck of forty colored cards. The deck is comprised of cards of four different colors. Kim shuffles the cards and keeps drawing cards from the deck, one after the other, to count the number of cards of each color. Is there a chance that Kim might draw thirty-one cards without drawing a blue card—and then draw a blue card?

(1) The four colors are red, blue, green, and yellow.

(2) The deck contains the same number of cards of each of the four colors.

The response type:

- Each question is multiple choice, always with these five answer choices:

  (A) Statement (1) ALONE is sufficient, but statement (2) alone is not sufficient.

  (B) Statement (2) ALONE is sufficient, but statement (1) alone is not sufficient.

  (C) BOTH statements TOGETHER are sufficient, but NEITHER statement ALONE is sufficient.

  (D) EACH statement ALONE is sufficient.

  (E) Statements (1) and (2) TOGETHER are NOT sufficient.

Pick exactly one of these answer choices. To answer correctly, you must judge whether statement (1) alone gives enough information to solve the math problem, and whether statement (2) alone does. If neither statement alone gives enough information to solve the problem, you must judge whether both do.

Tips for Answering Data Sufficiency Questions

- **Analyze the question and the two statements step by step.**

  First study the question and any information shown. Then read statement (1). Decide whether it gives enough new information to answer the question. Next go on to statement (2). Ignore statement (1) while you decide whether statement (2) alone gives enough new information to answer the question. If you find that either statement alone gives enough information to answer the question, you now know enough to pick the right answer choice from among answer choice (A), answer choice (B), and answer choice (D).

  If you find that neither statement alone gives enough information to answer the question, decide whether both give enough information together. If so, the right answer choice is answer choice (C). Otherwise, it's answer choice (E).

  Here's a flowchart showing how to find the right answer choice, step by step.

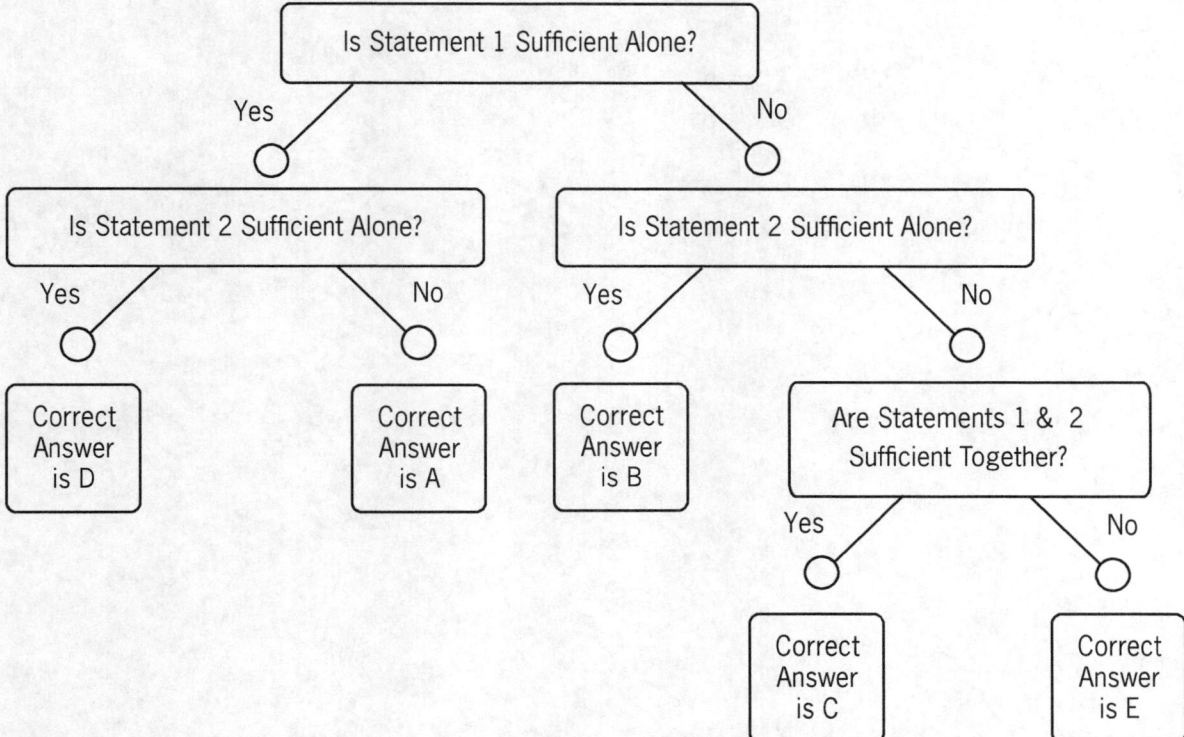

- **Don't waste time finding the answer to the question.**

  You only have to decide whether the two statements give enough information to answer it.

- **Check whether there's enough information to answer the exact question asked.**

  For example, suppose the question is what unique value a variable y must take. Then you have to decide whether either statement alone or both together give enough information to find **one and only one** value for y. Here, the question is not whether the statements give enough information to find an equation like $y = x + 2$. Nor is it whether they give enough information to find a range of values rather than y's unique value. So, ignore those irrelevant questions.

- **Don't assume any images are drawn to scale.**

  They may not be. For example, if a figure described as a rectangle looks like a square, that doesn't mean it is a square.

6.3 Online Question Bank Instructions

Accessing the Data Insights Practice Questions

Below are Data Sufficiency and Two-Part Analysis Data Insights practice questions. Because the Data Insights questions need to be rendered online, certain question types, such as Multi-Source Reasoning, Table Analysis, and Graphics Interpretation, are only available in the **Online Question Bank** that is included as a part of this book.

Use your unique Access Code from the inside front cover of this book to access additional practice questions with answer explanations at **www.mba.com/my-account**. You can buy more Data Insights practice questions on **www.mba.com/gmatprep**.

6.4 Practice Questions: Data Sufficiency

Each Data Sufficiency question has a math problem and two statements, labeled (1) and (2), which present data. Using this data with your knowledge of math and everyday facts (such as the number of days in July or what *counterclockwise* means), decide whether the data in the statements are enough to solve the problem. Then pick one of these answer choices:

A   Statement (1) ALONE is sufficient, but statement (2) alone is not sufficient.
B   Statement (2) ALONE is sufficient, but statement (1) alone is not sufficient.
C   BOTH statements TOGETHER are sufficient, but NEITHER statement ALONE is sufficient.
D   EACH statement ALONE is sufficient.
E   Statements (1) and (2) TOGETHER are NOT sufficient.

<u>Note:</u> In Data Sufficiency questions that ask for a quantity's value, the data given in the statements are sufficient only when they make it possible to find exactly one numerical value for the quantity.

Questions 294 to 344 — Difficulty: Easy

294. What is the number of pages of a certain journal article?

(1)   The size of each page is $5\frac{1}{2}$ inches by 8 inches.

(2)   The average (arithmetic mean) number of words per page is 250.

295. If a certain vase contains only roses and tulips, how many tulips are there in the vase?

(1)   The number of roses in the vase is 4 times the number of tulips in the vase.

(2)   There is a total of 20 flowers in the vase.

296. The cost of 10 pounds of apples and 2 pounds of grapes was $12. What was the cost per pound of apples?

(1)   The cost per pound of grapes was $2.

(2)   The cost of 2 pounds of apples was less than the cost of 1 pound of grapes.

297. What was the median annual salary for the employees at Company X last year?

(1)   Last year, there were 29 employees at Company X.

(2)   Last year, 12 employees at Company X had an annual salary of $24,000.

298. How many basic units of Currency X are equivalent to 250 basic units of Currency Y?

(1)   100 basic units of Currency X are equivalent to 625 basic units of Currency Y.

(2)   2,000 basic units of Currency X are equivalent to 12,500 basic units of Currency Y.

299. A company bought 3 printers and 1 scanner. What was the price of the scanner?

(1)   The total price of the printers and the scanner was $1,300.

(2)   The price of each printer was 4 times the price of the scanner.

300. Each of the 256 solid-colored marbles in a box is either blue, green, or purple. What is the ratio of the number of blue marbles to the number of purple marbles in the box?

(1)   The number of green marbles in the box is 4 times the number of blue marbles in the box.

(2)   There are 192 green marbles in the box.

301. A certain mixture of paint requires blue, yellow, and red paints in ratios of 2:3:1, respectively, and no other ingredients. If there are ample quantities of the blue and red paints available, is there enough of the yellow paint available to make the desired amount of the mixture?

(1)   Exactly 20 quarts of the mixture are needed.

(2)   Exactly 10 quarts of the yellow paint are available.

302. There are 2 groups of students who took a history test. Was the average (arithmetic mean) score of the students in Group A higher than the average score of the students in Group B who took the test?

    (1) Of the students who took the test, 10 were in Group A and 12 were in Group B.

    (2) On the test, the highest score achieved was achieved by a Group B student, and the lowest score achieved was achieved by a Group A student.

303. The research funds of a certain company were divided among three departments, X, Y, and Z. Which one of the three departments received the greatest proportion of the research funds?

    (1) The research funds received by Departments X and Y were in the ratio 3 to 5, respectively.

    (2) The research funds received by Departments X and Z were in the ratio 2 to 1, respectively.

304. In a certain class, some students donated cans of food to a local food bank. What was the average (arithmetic mean) number of cans donated per student in the class?

    (1) The students donated a total of 56 cans of food.

    (2) The total number of cans donated was 40 greater than the total number of students in the class.

305. Each of the n employees at a certain company has a different annual salary. What is the median of the annual salaries of the n employees?

    (1) When the annual salaries of the n employees are listed in increasing order, the median is the 15th salary.

    (2) The sum of the annual salaries of the n employees is $913,500.

306. In a recent town election, what was the ratio of the number of votes in favor of a certain proposal to the number of votes against the proposal?

    (1) There were 60 more votes in favor of the proposal than against the proposal.

    (2) There were 240 votes in favor of the proposal.

307. How many men are in a certain company's vanpool program?

    (1) The ratio of men to women in the program is 3 to 2.

    (2) The men and women in the program fill 6 vans.

308. Last semester, Professor K taught two classes, A and B. Each student in Class A handed in 7 assignments, and each student in Class B handed in 5 assignments. How many students were in Class A?

    (1) The students in both classes combined handed in a total of 85 assignments.

    (2) There were 10 students in Class B.

309. Was the amount of John's heating bill for February greater than it was for January?

    (1) The ratio of the amount of John's heating bill for February to that for January was $\frac{26}{25}$.

    (2) The sum of the amounts of John's heating bills for January and February was $183.60.

310. Machine R and Machine S work at their respective constant rates. How much time does it take Machine R, working alone, to complete a certain job?

    (1) The amount of time that it takes Machine S, working alone, to complete the job is $\frac{3}{4}$ the amount of time that it takes Machine R, working alone, to complete the job.

    (2) Machine R and Machine S, working together, take 12 minutes to complete the job.

311. Beth's bank charges a service fee on a regular checking account for each month in which the balance on the account falls below $100 at any time during the month. Did the bank charge a service fee on Beth's regular checking account last month?

    (1) During last month, a total of $1,000 was withdrawn from Beth's regular checking account.

    (2) At the beginning of last month, Beth's regular checking account balance was $500.

312. Three houses are being sold through a real estate agent. What is the asking price for the house with the second-largest asking price?

    (1) The difference between the greatest and the least asking price is $130,000.
    (2) The difference between the two greater asking prices is $85,000.

313. How many people in a group of 50 own neither a fax machine nor a laser printer?

    (1) The total number of people in the group who own a fax machine or a laser printer or both is less than 50.
    (2) The total number of people in the group who own both a fax machine and a laser printer is 15.

314. A state legislature had a total of 96 members. The members who did not vote on a certain bill consisted of 25 who were absent and 3 who abstained. How many of those voting voted for the bill?

    (1) Exactly $\frac{1}{3}$ of the total membership of the legislature voted against the bill.
    (2) The number of legislators who voted for the bill was 8 more than the total number who were absent or abstained.

315. What is the average (arithmetic mean) of the first 90 measurements in a certain list of 92 measurements?

    (1) The average of the 92 measurements is 7.0 centimeters.
    (2) The average of the last 2 measurements is 7.2 centimeters.

316. How many of the employees of a certain company use both a tablet and an iPhone?

    (1) 60 of the employees use a tablet.
    (2) 45 of the employees use an iPhone.

317. What is the standard deviation of the weights of the 30 samples in a certain experiment?

    (1) The total weight of the 30 samples is 360 grams.
    (2) Each of the 30 samples weighs 12 grams.

318. The people in a line waiting to buy tickets to a show are standing one behind the other. Adam and Beth are among the people in the line, and Beth is standing behind Adam with a number of people between them. If the number of people in front of Adam plus the number of people behind Beth is 18, how many people in the line are behind Beth?

    (1) There are a total of 32 people in the line.
    (2) 23 people in the line are behind Adam.

319. In a certain group of 50 people, how many are doctors who have a law degree?

    (1) In the group, 36 people are doctors.
    (2) In the group, 18 people have a law degree.

320. Of a group of 50 households, how many have at least one cat or at least one dog, but not both?

    (1) The number of households that have at least one cat and at least one dog is 4.
    (2) The number of households that have no cats and no dogs is 14.

321. Robin invested a total of $12,000 in two investments, X and Y, so that the investments earned the same amount of simple annual interest. How many dollars did Robin invest in Investment Y?

    (1) Investment X paid 3 percent simple annual interest, and Investment Y paid 6 percent simple annual interest.
    (2) Robin invested more than $1,000 in Investment X.

322. In a real estate office that employs n salespeople, f of them are females and x of the females are new employees. What is the value of n?

    (1) If an employee were randomly selected from the n employees, the probability of selecting a female would be $\frac{2}{3}$.
    (2) If an employee were randomly selected from the f female employees, the probability of selecting a new employee would be $\frac{1}{2}$.

323. Is the total price of the items in Andrea's shopping cart less than $25.00?

    (1) There are 5 items in Andrea's shopping cart.
    (2) The price of the most expensive item in Andrea's shopping cart is $4.99.

324. A certain plumber charges $92 for each job completed in 4 hours or less and $23 per hour for each job completed in more than 4 hours. If it took the plumber a total of 7 hours to complete two separate jobs, what was the total amount charged by the plumber for the two jobs?

    (1) The plumber charged $92 for one of the two jobs.
    (2) The plumber charged $138 for one of the two jobs.

325. If x and y are positive numbers, is $\frac{x+1}{y+1} > \frac{x}{y}$?

    (1) $x > 1$
    (2) $x < y$

326. If a school district paid a total of $35 per desk for x desks and a total of $30 per table for y tables, what was the total amount that the district paid for these desks and tables?

    (1) The total amount the district paid for the y tables was $900.
    (2) $x = 90$, and the total amount the district paid for the x desks was 3.5 times the total amount the district paid for the y tables.

327. Three children inherited a total of X dollars. If the oldest child inherited $7,000 more than the youngest child, and the youngest child inherited $9,000 less than the middle child, what is the value of X?

    (1) The middle child inherited $27,000.
    (2) The youngest child and the middle child together inherited a total of $45,000.

328. If a building has 6,000 square meters of floor space, how many offices are in the building?

    (1) Exactly $\frac{1}{4}$ of the floor space is not used for offices.
    (2) There are exactly 20 executive offices, and each of these occupies 3 times as much floor space as the average for all of the remaining offices.

329. For which type of investment, J or K, is the annual rate of return greater?

    (1) Type J returns $115 per $1,000 invested for any one-year period, and Type K returns $300 per $2,500 invested for any one-year period.
    (2) The annual rate of return for an investment of Type K is 12%.

330. If Car X followed Car Y across a certain bridge that is $\frac{1}{2}$ mile long, how many seconds did it take Car X to travel across the bridge?

    (1) Car X drove onto the bridge exactly 3 seconds after Car Y drove onto the bridge and drove off the bridge exactly 2 seconds after Car Y drove off the bridge.
    (2) Car Y traveled across the bridge at a constant speed of 30 miles per hour.

331. Will Candidate A win the most votes of any of the competing candidates in the upcoming election?

    (1) An opinion poll, Poll P, indicates that 60% of respondents prefer Candidate A over other candidates competing in the upcoming election.
    (2) An election-forecasting opinion poll is a method to estimate election outcomes based on a sample that is representative of the population of all of those legally entitled to vote.

332. The government of Nation X makes policy decisions intended to advance the public interest, such as policy decisions aiming to promote employment, economic flourishing, and environmental protection. A policy decision can involve a significant trade-off, i.e., it can entail foreseeably giving up part or all of one valued outcome in the pursuit of another valued outcome. Does a policy decision by Nation X to permit extensive clearcutting of forests provide a valued outcome at the expense of another valued outcome?

    (1) Extensive clearcutting of forests is permitted in Nation X because it provides immediate economic gains by enabling businesses such as farming and lumbering to flourish and provide employment.
    (2) Extensive clearcutting of forests is permitted in Nation X even though it reduces forests' absorption of carbon dioxide, and this indirectly contributes to global warming, resulting in adverse climate changes that are certain to be very costly for Nation X to manage.

333. Is Sarah's mathematics test score higher than the class average?

    (1) Sarah scored 90% on her mathematics test, answering 45 out of 50 questions correctly.
    (2) Sarah's high percentage score indicates that she performed exceptionally well, with only a few questions answered incorrectly.

334. On Day X, was the forecast temperature 36°C at noon?

    (1) On Day X, the forecast temperature was 30°C at 9:00 a.m. and 40°C at 2:00 p.m.
    (2) On Day X, every half hour, the forecast temperature increased by 1°C.

335. Benjamin is a salesman working for commission at a shoe store. For the first $1,000 worth of sales in a given month, he earns a commission of 2%. For any sales he makes after the first $1,000 in that month, he earns a commission of 4%. What is the total dollar value of sales made by Benjamin in the month of March?

    (1) Benjamin earned a commission of $120 in March.
    (2) Benjamin doubled the dollar value of his sales in March compared to his sales in February.

336. What is the length of Train A if it crosses Bridge X in 30 seconds from the moment it enters the bridge to the moment its final carriage exits the bridge?

    (1) Train B, which is 200 meters long, traveling at a constant speed of 20 meters per second, crosses Bridge X in 40 seconds.
    (2) The end of Train A, which is traveling at a constant speed, passes a pole in 10 seconds from the moment the train meets the pole.

337. Solomon leases space for his barber shop, and his landlord has recently increased the rent by 40%. Solomon wants to increase his monthly revenue to pay the increased rent without affecting his net income. By what percentage must he increase his revenue?

    (1) 20% of his previous monthly revenue was used to pay the rent before the landlord increased it.
    (2) The new rent is $50 more than the previous rent.

338. What is the ratio of the amount, by weight, of Metal A to Metal B in Alloy K?

    (1) The ratio of Metal A to Metal B in Alloy K becomes 5:6 when 40 pounds of Metal A is added to the alloy.
    (2) The ratio of Metal A to Metal B in Alloy K becomes 7:6 when 60 pounds of Metal A is added to the alloy.

339. Train A started from Station X toward Station Y traveling at a constant speed, and on the same day, on a parallel track, Train B started from Station Y toward Station X at a constant speed. At what time did Train A reach Station Y?

    (1) The two trains met at 3:00 p.m. The distance traveled by Train A was twice the distance traveled by Train B by the time they met.
    (2) The ratio between the speeds of Trains A and B is 3:5. Train B started from Station Y at 6:00 a.m.

340. Pipes A and B are the pipes that fill a tank. Pipes C and D are the pipes that empty the same tank. What is the capacity of the tank?

    (1) Pipe A is twice as efficient as Pipe C, that is, the volume of water per hour that Pipe A moves is twice the volume per hour that Pipe C moves. Pipe A and Pipe B are equally efficient. When Pipes C and D are closed, Pipes A and B together fill the empty tank in 5 hours. Pipe C empties 6,000 liters per hour.
    (2) Pipe B is three times as efficient as Pipe D.

341. The total cost of a car consisted of the price of the car and the sales tax. If the sales tax was $1,000, what was the price of the car?

    (1) The sales tax was 5 percent of the price of the car.
    (2) The sales tax was $\frac{1}{21}$ of the total cost of the car.

342. Yesterday a plane flew from City N to City V within the same time zone and made exactly one stop along the way. What was the total time that elapsed from the time the plane left N until it arrived at V?

    (1) The plane began a 30-minute stop at noon.
    (2) The plane left N at 8:18 a.m. and arrived at V at 4:48 p.m.

343. Raymond's father weighs twice as much as Raymond. How much does Raymond weigh?

    (1) Raymond's father weighs 3 times as much as Raymond weighed 5 years ago.

    (2) If Raymond's father weighed 100 pounds more, he would weigh 3 times as much as Raymond.

344. Of the people who work at Company X, 80% are enrolled in its savings program. How many people work at Company X?

    (1) Exactly 24 people who work at Company X do not belong to its savings program.

    (2) Exactly 96 people who work at Company X belong to its savings program.

Questions 345 to 388 — Difficulty: **Medium**

345. What is the total number of executives at Company P?

    (1) The number of male executives is $\frac{3}{5}$ the number of female executives.

    (2) There are 4 more female executives than male executives.

346. Jack picked 76 apples. Of these, he sold $4y$ apples to Juanita and $3t$ apples to Sylvia. If he kept the remaining apples, how many apples did he keep? (t and y are positive integers.)

    (1) $y \geq 15$ and $t = 2$
    (2) $y = 17$

347. The total price of 5 pounds of regular coffee and 3 pounds of decaffeinated coffee was $21.50. What was the price of the 5 pounds of regular coffee?

    (1) If the price of the 5 pounds of regular coffee had been reduced 10 percent and the price of the 3 pounds of decaffeinated coffee had been reduced 20 percent, the total price would have been $18.45.

    (2) The price of the 5 pounds of regular coffee was $3.50 more than the price of the 3 pounds of decaffeinated coffee.

348. A certain painting job requires a mixture of yellow, green, and white paint. If 12 quarts of paint are needed for the job, how many quarts of green paint are needed?

    (1) The ratio of the amount of green paint to the amount of yellow and white paint combined needs to be 1 to 3.

    (2) The ratio of the amount of yellow paint to the amount of green paint needs to be 3 to 2.

349. A company produces a certain toy in only 2 sizes, small or large, and in only 2 colors, red or green. If, for each size, there are equal numbers of red and green toys in a certain production lot, what fraction of the total number of green toys is large?

    (1) In the production lot, 400 of the small toys are green.

    (2) In the production lot, $\frac{2}{3}$ of the toys produced are small.

350. Jones has worked at Firm X twice as many years as Green, and Green has worked at Firm X four years longer than Smith. How many years has Green worked at Firm X?

    (1) Jones has worked at Firm X 9 years longer than Smith.

    (2) Green has worked at Firm X 5 years less than Jones.

351. On June 1, Mary paid Omar $360 for rent and utilities for the month of June. Mary moved out early, and Omar refunded the money she paid for utilities, but not for rent, for the days in June after she moved out. How many dollars did Omar refund to Mary?

    (1) Mary moved out on June 24.

    (2) The amount Mary paid for utilities was less than $\frac{1}{5}$ the amount Mary paid for rent.

352. A collection of 36 cards consists of 4 sets of 9 cards each. The 9 cards in each set are numbered 1 through 9. If one card has been removed from the collection, what is the number on that card?

    (1) The units digit of the sum of the numbers on the remaining 35 cards is 6.

    (2) The sum of the numbers on the remaining 35 cards is 176.

353. What is the ratio of the number of cups of flour to the number of cups of sugar required in a certain cake recipe?

    (1) The number of cups of flour required in the recipe is 250 percent of the number of cups of sugar required in the recipe.

    (2) $1\frac{1}{2}$ more cups of flour than cups of sugar are required in the recipe.

354. A clothing manufacturer makes jackets that are wool or cotton or a combination of wool and cotton. The manufacturer has 3,000 pounds of wool and 2,000 pounds of cotton on hand. Is this enough wool and cotton to make at least 1,000 jackets?

    (1) Each wool jacket requires 4 pounds of wool, and no cotton.

    (2) Each cotton jacket requires 6 pounds of cotton, and no wool.

355. Are at least 10 percent of the people in Country X who are 65 years old or older employed?

    (1) In Country X, 11.3 percent of the population is 65 years old or older.

    (2) In Country X, of the population 65 years old or older, 20 percent of those with a college degree and 10 percent of those without a college degree are employed.

356. A scientist recorded the number of eggs in each of 10 birds' nests. What was the standard deviation of the numbers of eggs in the 10 nests?

    (1) The average (arithmetic mean) number of eggs for the 10 nests was 4.

    (2) Each of the 10 nests contained the same number of eggs.

357. A paint mixture was formed by mixing exactly 3 colors of paint. By volume, the mixture was $x\%$ blue paint, $y\%$ green paint, and $z\%$ red paint. If exactly 1 gallon of blue paint and 3 gallons of red paint were used, how many gallons of green paint were used?

    (1) $x = y$

    (2) $z = 60$

358. For a basic monthly fee of F yen (¥F), Naoko's first cell phone plan allowed him to use a maximum of 420 minutes on calls during the month. Then, for each of x additional minutes he used on calls, he was charged ¥M, making his total charge for the month ¥T, where $T = F + xM$. What is the value of F?

    (1) Naoko used 450 minutes on calls the first month, and the total charge for the month was ¥13,755.

    (2) Naoko used 400 minutes on calls the second month, and the total charge for the month was ¥13,125.

359. Is the sum of the prices of the 3 books that Shana bought less than $48?

    (1) The price of the most expensive of the 3 books that Shana bought is less than $17.

    (2) The price of the least expensive of the 3 books that Shana bought is exactly $3 less than the price of the second most expensive book.

360. If Elena spent a total of $720 on newspapers, magazines, and books last year, what amount did she spend on newspapers?

    (1) Last year, the amount that Elena spent on magazines was 80 percent of the amount that she spent on books.

    (2) Last year, the amount that Elena spent on newspapers was 60 percent of the total amount that she spent on magazines and books.

361. Of the 800 sweaters at a certain store, 150 are red. How many of the red sweaters at the store are made of pure wool?

    (1) 320 of the sweaters at the store are neither red nor made of pure wool.

    (2) 100 of the red sweaters at the store are not made of pure wool.

362. A certain computer company produces two different monitors, P and Q. In 2010, what was the net profit from the sale of the two monitors?

    (1) Of the company's expenses in 2010, rent and utilities totaled $500,000.

    (2) In 2010, the company sold 50,000 units of Monitor P at $300 per unit and 30,000 units of Monitor Q at $650 per unit.

363. A conveyor belt moves bottles at a constant speed of 120 centimeters per second. If the conveyor belt moves a bottle from a loading dock to an unloading dock, is the distance that the conveyor belt moves the bottle less than 90 meters? (1 meter = 100 centimeters)

    (1) It takes the conveyor belt less than 1.2 minutes to move the bottle from the loading dock to the unloading dock.
    (2) It takes the conveyor belt more than 1.1 minutes to move the bottle from the loading dock to the unloading dock.

364. In a product test of a common cold remedy, x percent of the patients tested experienced side effects from the use of the drug and y percent experienced relief of cold symptoms. What percent of the patients tested experienced both side effects and relief of cold symptoms?

    (1) Of the 1,000 patients tested, 15 percent experienced neither side effects nor relief of cold symptoms.
    (2) Of the patients tested, 30 percent experienced relief of cold symptoms without side effects.

365. Three roommates—Bela, Gyorgy, and Janos—together saved money for a trip. The amount that Bela saved was equal to 8% of his monthly income. The amount that Gyorgy saved was exactly $\frac{1}{3}$ of the total amount saved by all 3 roommates. What was the total amount saved for the trip by all 3 roommates?

    (1) Bela had a monthly income of $2,000.
    (2) Janos saved 1.5 times as much for the trip as Bela.

366. In each game of a certain tournament, a contestant either loses 3 points or gains 2 points. If Pat had 100 points at the beginning of the tournament, how many games did Pat play in the tournament?

    (1) At the end of the tournament, Pat had 104 points.
    (2) Pat played fewer than 10 games.

367. At the beginning of the year, the Finance Committee and the Planning Committee of a certain company each had n members, and no one was a member of both committees. At the end of the year, 5 members left the Finance Committee and 3 members left the Planning Committee. How many members did the Finance Committee have at the beginning of the year?

    (1) The ratio of the total number of members who left at the end of the year to the total number of members at the beginning of the year was 1:6.
    (2) At the end of the year, 21 members remained on the Planning Committee.

368. Some computers at a certain company are Brand X and the rest are Brand Y. If the ratio of the number of Brand Y computers to the number of Brand X computers at the company is 5 to 6, how many of the computers are Brand Y?

    (1) There are 80 more Brand X computers than Brand Y computers at the company.
    (2) There is a total of 880 computers at the company.

369. Was the number of books sold at Bookstore X last week greater than the number of books sold at Bookstore Y last week?

    (1) Last week, more than 1,000 books were sold at Bookstore X on Saturday and fewer than 1,000 books were sold at Bookstore Y on Saturday.
    (2) Last week, less than 20 percent of the books sold at Bookstore X were sold on Saturday and more than 20 percent of the books sold at Bookstore Y were sold on Saturday.

370. From May 1 to May 30 in the same year, the balance in a checking account increased. What was the balance in the checking account on May 30?

    (1) If, during this period of time, the increase in the balance in the checking account had been 12 percent, then the balance in the account on May 30 would have been $504.
    (2) During this period of time, the increase in the balance in the checking account was 8 percent.

371. A merchant discounted the sale price of a coat and the sale price of a sweater. Which of the two articles of clothing was discounted by the greater dollar amount?

    (1) The percent discount on the coat was 2 percentage points greater than the percent discount on the sweater.

    (2) Before the discounts, the sale price of the coat was $10 less than the sale price of the sweater.

372. If the positive integer n is added to each of the integers 69, 94, and 121, what is the value of n?

    (1) $69 + n$ and $94 + n$ are the squares of two consecutive integers.

    (2) $94 + n$ and $121 + n$ are the squares of two consecutive integers.

373. If a merchant purchased a sofa from a manufacturer for $400 and then sold it, what was the selling price of the sofa?

    (1) The selling price of the sofa was greater than 140 percent of the purchase price.

    (2) The merchant's gross profit from the purchase and sale of the sofa was $\frac{1}{3}$ of the selling price.

374. Last year, in a certain housing development, the average (arithmetic mean) price of 20 new houses was $160,000. Did more than 9 of the 20 houses have prices that were less than the average price last year?

    (1) Last year, the greatest price of one of the 20 houses was $219,000.

    (2) Last year, the median of the prices of the 20 houses was $150,000.

375. For a certain city's library, the average cost of purchasing each new book is $28. The library receives $15,000 from the city each year; the library also receives a bonus of $2,000 if the total number of items checked out over the course of the year exceeds 5,000. Did the library receive the bonus last year?

    (1) The library purchased an average of 50 new books each month last year and received enough money from the city to cover this cost.

    (2) The lowest number of items checked out in one month was 459.

7, 9, 6, 4, 5, x

376. If x is a number in the list above, what is the median of the list?

    (1) $x > 7$

    (2) The median of the list equals the arithmetic mean of the list.

377. Three dice, each of which has its 6 sides numbered 1 through 6, are tossed. The sum of the 3 numbers that are facing up is 12. Is at least 1 of these numbers 5?

    (1) None of the 3 numbers that are facing up is divisible by 3.

    (2) Of the numbers that are facing up, 2, but not all 3, are equal.

378. Mohit went cycling on 10 consecutive days. Every day he started from Point X, cycled a certain distance in an easterly direction, and then returned to Point X. What is the total distance he covered in those 10 days?

    (1) From the second day onward, Mohit covered twice the distance he covered the previous day. On the fifth day, he covered 3.2 km from Point X east, and then back to Point X.

    (2) On the first day, Mohit cycled less than 0.3 km.

379. Candidates A, B, and C competed in an election. This election usually comprises two rounds. In the first round, all three candidates compete. A candidate qualifies for the second round only if he/she receives at least 20% of the votes cast in the first round. If two candidates receive less than 20% of the votes cast, the other candidate wins the election by default. If a candidate receives more than 60% of the votes in the first round, he/she wins the election without the second round. Was there a second round of election?

    (1) The votes received by Candidates A and B together is 82% of the total votes cast.

    (2) The votes received by Candidates C and B together is 42% of the total votes cast.

380. There are a certain number of male and female students in a classroom. The weights of the male students range from 80 kg to 85 kg. The weights of the female students range from 70 kg to 75 kg. What is the average (arithmetic mean) weight of all the students in the classroom? All weights are rounded to the nearest 1 kg.

    (1) No two students weigh the same.
    (2) The number of male students is equal to the number of female students.

381. An alloy, Alloy K, is made by mixing certain quantities of iron and lead. The total weight of the alloy is 50 kg. What is the ratio of the weight of iron to the weight of lead in Alloy K?

    (1) If 4 kg of iron were to be replaced with 4 kg of lead, the percentage of lead, by weight, in Alloy K would become 40%.
    (2) The weight of iron per 100 cc is 0.7 times the weight of lead per 100 cc.

382. A box contains exactly 40 bottles, each of which contains only one of three types of soda—orange, lemon, and ginger. What is the probability of randomly selecting a ginger soda, without any replacement in the box, on each of 3 consecutive attempts?

    (1) The number of orange sodas is 5 more than the number of ginger sodas.
    (2) The number of ginger sodas is 10 more than the number of lemon sodas.

383. Workers A, B, and C, working at their individual constant rates, can work together and complete a piece of work in 6 days. How long will it take for B and C alone to complete the work?

    (1) A is twice as efficient as B. B is three times as efficient as C.
    (2) The time taken by A to do 9 units of work is the same as the time taken by B and C together to do 6 units of work.

384. The students in College X must take two, and no more, of these five subjects: computing, electronics, mechanics, architecture, and psychology. Students who take computing cannot take psychology. Students who take electronics cannot take architecture. Students who take mechanics cannot take electronics. Is Student G, a student at College X, taking psychology?

    (1) Student G is taking architecture as one of her two subjects.
    (2) Student G is taking neither electronics nor computing.

385. A candy shop owner must mix three types of sweeteners—A, B, and C—in a certain ratio to get the desired mixture in his candies. What is the ratio of the weights of Sweetener A to Sweetener B to Sweetener C in the final mixture?

    (1) Sweeteners A, B, and C cost $40, $50, and $60 per pound. The average (arithmetic mean) cost of the final mixture is $50 per pound.
    (2) In the final mixture, the average (arithmetic mean) price of Sweeteners A and B together is $45, and the average (arithmetic mean) price of Sweeteners B and C together is $55.

386. A movie theater increased the ticket price for evening shows by 10% and decreased the ticket price for morning shows by 40%. The average number of tickets sold for the morning shows increased by 30%, and the average number of tickets sold for the evening shows decreased by 5%. What was the percentage change in total revenue?

    (1) Prior to the changes in ticket prices, the ticket prices for the morning shows and the evening shows were the same.
    (2) Prior to the changes in ticket prices, the ratio between the number of tickets sold for the morning shows and the evening shows was 5:8.

387. George is an employee at a firm. For each day that he is absent, he forfeits 4% of his monthly salary. For every hour of overtime he does, he receives 1% added to his monthly salary. His salary reduced for the month of June by 5%. How many hours of overtime did George do in that month?

    (1) George was absent for 3 days in the month of June.
    (2) George received 7% of his monthly salary for doing overtime in the month of June.

388. Three teaching assistants—Mike, Rafael, and Joanna—wrote all the questions for the class midterm. If Mike wrote $\frac{1}{3}$ of the questions, what is the number of questions that the three teaching assistants wrote for the midterm?

    (1) Joanna and Rafael wrote a total of 30 questions.
    (2) Joanna wrote $\frac{3}{2}$ the number of questions that Rafael wrote.

Questions 389 to 436 — Difficulty: Hard

389. Did the population of Town C increase by at least 100 percent from the year 2000 to the year 2010?

    (1) The population of Town C in 2000 was $\frac{2}{3}$ of the population in 2005.
    (2) The population of Town C increased by a greater number of people from 2005 to 2010 than it did from 2000 to 2005.

390. In a survey of 200 college graduates, 30% said they had received student loans during their college careers, and 40% said they had received scholarships. What percent of those surveyed said that they had received neither student loans nor scholarships during their college careers?

    (1) 25% of those surveyed said that they had received scholarships but no loans.
    (2) 50% of those surveyed who said that they had received loans also said that they had received scholarships.

391. Stores L and M each sell a certain product at a different regular price. If both stores discount their regular price of the product, is the discount price at Store M less than the discount price at Store L?

    (1) At Store L, the discount price is 10 percent less than the regular price; at Store M, the discount price is 15 percent less than the regular price.
    (2) At Store L, the discount price is $5 less than the regular store price; at Store M, the discount price is $6 less than the regular price.

392. A box contains only red chips, white chips, and blue chips. If a chip is randomly selected from the box, what is the probability that the chip will be either white or blue?

    (1) The probability that the chip will be blue is $\frac{1}{5}$.
    (2) The probability that the chip will be red is $\frac{1}{3}$.

393. Did the sum of the prices of three shirts exceed $60?

    (1) The price of the most expensive of the shirts exceeded $30.
    (2) The price of the least expensive of the shirts exceeded $20.

394. What is the total number of coins that Bert and Claire have?

    (1) Bert has 50 percent more coins than Claire.
    (2) The total number of coins that Bert and Claire have is between 21 and 28.

395. A telephone station has x processors, each of which can process a maximum of y calls at any particular time, where x and y are positive integers. If 500 calls are sent to the station at a particular time, can the station process all of the calls?

    (1) $x = 600$
    (2) $100 < y < 200$

	Price per Flower
Roses	$1.00
Daisies	$0.50

396. Kim and Sue each bought some roses and some daisies at the prices shown above. If Kim bought the same total number of roses and daisies as Sue, was the price of Kim's purchase of roses and daisies higher than the price of Sue's purchase of roses and daisies?

    (1) Kim bought twice as many daisies as roses.
    (2) Kim bought 4 more roses than Sue bought.

397. Jazz and blues recordings accounted for 6 percent of the $840 million revenue from the sales of recordings in Country Y in 2000. What was the revenue from the sales of jazz and blues recordings in Country Y in 1998?

    (1) Jazz and blues recordings accounted for 5 percent of the revenue from the sales of recordings in Country Y in 1998.

    (2) The revenue from the sales of jazz and blues recordings in Country Y increased by 40 percent from 1998 to 2000.

398. On a certain nonstop trip, Marta averaged x miles per hour for 2 hours and y miles per hour for the remaining 3 hours. What was her average speed, in miles per hour, for the entire trip?

    (1) $2x + 3y = 280$
    (2) $y = x + 10$

399. A group consisting of several families visited an amusement park where the regular admission fees were ¥5,500 for each adult and ¥4,800 for each child. Because there were at least 10 people in the group, each paid an admission fee that was 10% less than the regular admission fee. How many children were in the group?

    (1) The total of the admission fees paid for the adults in the group was ¥29,700.

    (2) The total of the admission fees paid for the children in the group was ¥4,860 more than the total of the admission fees paid for the adults in the group.

400. What is the ratio of the average (arithmetic mean) height of students in Class X to the average height of students in Class Y?

    (1) The average height of the students in Class X is 120 centimeters.

    (2) The average height of the students in Class X and Class Y combined is 126 centimeters.

401. Max has $125 consisting of bills each worth either $5 or $20. How many bills worth $5 does Max have?

    (1) Max has fewer than 5 bills worth $5 each.
    (2) Max has more than 5 bills worth $20 each.

402. At a bakery, all donuts are priced equally and all bagels are priced equally. What is the total price of 5 donuts and 3 bagels at the bakery?

    (1) At the bakery, the total price of 10 donuts and 6 bagels is $12.90.

    (2) At the bakery, the price of a donut is $0.15 less than the price of a bagel.

403. Last year, if Arturo spent a total of $12,000 on his mortgage payments, real estate taxes, and home insurance, how much did he spend on his real estate taxes?

    (1) Last year, the total amount that Arturo spent on his real estate taxes and home insurance was $33\frac{1}{3}$ percent of the amount that he spent on his mortgage payments.

    (2) Last year, the amount that Arturo spent on his real estate taxes was 20 percent of the total amount he spent on his mortgage payments and home insurance.

404. Is the number of members of Club X greater than the number of members of Club Y?

    (1) Of the members of Club X, 20 percent are also members of Club Y.

    (2) Of the members of Club Y, 30 percent are also members of Club X.

405. The only articles of clothing in a certain closet are shirts, dresses, and jackets. The ratio of the number of shirts to the number of dresses to the number of jackets in the closet is 9:4:5, respectively. If there are more than 7 dresses in the closet, what is the total number of articles of clothing in the closet?

    (1) The total number of shirts and jackets in the closet is less than 30.

    (2) The total number of shirts and dresses in the closet is 26.

406. Material A costs $3 per kilogram, and Material B costs $5 per kilogram. If 10 kilograms of Material K consists of x kilograms of Material A and y kilograms of Material B, is $x > y$?

    (1) $y > 4$
    (2) The cost of the 10 kilograms of Material K is less than $40.

407. At what speed was a train traveling on a trip when it had completed half of the total distance of the trip?

    (1) The trip was 460 miles long and took 4 hours to complete.

    (2) The train traveled at an average rate of 115 miles per hour on the trip.

408. Tom, Jane, and Sue each purchased a new house. The average (arithmetic mean) price of the three houses was $120,000. What was the median price of the three houses?

    (1) The price of Tom's house was $110,000.

    (2) The price of Jane's house was $120,000.

409. A certain bookcase has 2 shelves of books. On the upper shelf, the book with the greatest number of pages has 400 pages. On the lower shelf, the book with the least number of pages has 475 pages. What is the median number of pages for all of the books on the 2 shelves?

    (1) There are 25 books on the upper shelf.

    (2) There are 24 books on the lower shelf.

410. In planning for a car trip, Joan estimated both the distance of the trip, in miles, and her average speed, in miles per hour. She accurately divided her estimated distance by her estimated average speed to obtain an estimate for the time, in hours, that the trip would take. Was her estimate within 0.5 hours of the actual time that the trip took?

    (1) Joan's estimate for the distance was within 5 miles of the actual distance.

    (2) Joan's estimate for her average speed was within 10 miles per hour of her actual average speed.

Shipment	S1	S2	S3	S4	S5	S6
Fraction of the Total Value of the Six Shipments	$\frac{1}{4}$	$\frac{1}{5}$	$\frac{1}{6}$	$\frac{3}{20}$	$\frac{2}{15}$	$\frac{1}{10}$

411. Six shipments of machine parts were shipped from a factory on two trucks, with each shipment entirely on one of the trucks. Each shipment was labeled either S1, S2, S3, S4, S5, or S6. The table shows the value of each shipment as a fraction of the total value of the six shipments. If the shipments on the first truck had a value greater than $\frac{1}{2}$ of the total value of the six shipments, was S3 shipped on the first truck?

    (1) S2 and S4 were shipped on the first truck.

    (2) S1 and S6 were shipped on the second truck.

	Favorable	Unfavorable	Not Sure
Candidate M	40	20	40
Candidate N	30	35	35

412. The table above shows the results of a survey of 100 voters who each responded "Favorable" or "Unfavorable" or "Not Sure" when asked about their impressions of Candidate M and of Candidate N. What was the number of voters who responded "Favorable" for both candidates?

    (1) The number of voters who did not respond "Favorable" for either candidate was 40.

    (2) The number of voters who responded "Unfavorable" for both candidates was 10.

413. A school administrator will assign each student in a group of n students to one of m classrooms. If $3 < m < 13 < n$, is it possible to assign each of the n students to one of the m classrooms so that each classroom has the same number of students assigned to it?

    (1) It is possible to assign each of $3n$ students to one of m classrooms so that each classroom has the same number of students assigned to it.

    (2) It is possible to assign each of $13n$ students to one of m classrooms so that each classroom has the same number of students assigned to it.

414. At a certain clothing store, customers who buy 2 shirts pay the regular price for the first shirt and a discounted price for the second shirt. The store makes the same profit from the sale of 2 shirts that it makes from the sale of 1 shirt at the regular price. For a customer who buys 2 shirts, what is the discounted price of the second shirt?

    (1) The regular price of each of the 2 shirts the customer buys at the clothing store is $16.
    (2) The cost to the clothing store of each of the 2 shirts the customer buys is $12.

415. What is the median number of employees assigned per project for the projects at Company Z?

    (1) 25 percent of the projects at Company Z have 4 or more employees assigned to each project.
    (2) 35 percent of the projects at Company Z have 2 or fewer employees assigned to each project.

416. Last year, a certain company began manufacturing Product X and sold every unit of Product X that it produced. Last year, the company's total expenses for manufacturing Product X were equal to $100,000 plus 5 percent of the company's total revenue from all units of Product X sold. If the company made a profit on Product X last year, did the company sell more than 21,000 units of Product X last year?

    (1) The company's total revenue from the sale of Product X last year was greater than $110,000.
    (2) For each unit of Product X sold last year, the company's revenue was $5.

417. Beginning in January of last year, Carl made deposits of $120 into his account on the 15th of each month for several consecutive months and then made withdrawals of $50 from the account on the 15th of each of the remaining months of last year. There were no other transactions in the account last year. If the closing balance of Carl's account for May of last year was $2,600, what was the range of the monthly closing balances of Carl's account last year?

    (1) Last year, the closing balance of Carl's account for April was less than $2,625.
    (2) Last year, the closing balance of Carl's account for June was less than $2,675.

418. What amount did Jean earn from the commission on her sales in the first half of 1988?

    (1) In 1988, Jean's commission was 5 percent of the total amount of her sales.
    (2) The amount of Jean's sales in the second half of 1988 averaged $10,000 per month more than in the first half.

419. In a certain business, production index p is directly proportional to efficiency index e, which is in turn directly proportional to investment index i. What is p if i = 70?

    (1) e = 0.5 whenever i = 60.
    (2) p = 2.0 whenever i = 50.

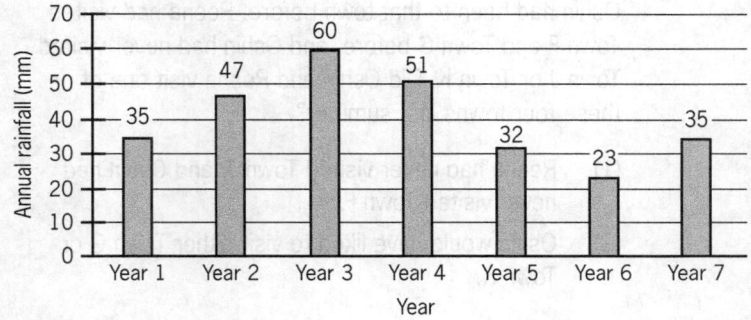

Annual Rainfall in City X Over Seven Years

420. The annual rainfall in a city over the past 50 years is its historical average rainfall (HAR). The graph above shows the annual rainfall in City X over a seven-year period. All figures are rounded to the nearest integer.

    Is it true that the rounded HAR for City X is 47 mm or greater?

    (1) In the seven-year period in City X, the annual rainfall was greater than the HAR in exactly two of the consecutive years.
    (2) In the seven-year period in City X, the annual rainfall was less than the HAR in exactly four of the years.

421. Five coffee-chicory blends—J, K, L, M, and N—are all priced differently. The blends are such that the greater the proportion of coffee, the more expensive the blend, and the greater the proportion of chicory, the stronger the flavor of the blend. If the five blends were ranked in order of cost per kilogram, which would fall in the middle?

    (1) Blend L has a higher proportion of coffee than the other blends except for Blend M.

    (2) Blend K and Blend N both have a stronger flavor than Blend J.

422. Last summer, as with every summer, Oshin and Reena made exactly one long trip together to a town neither of them had visited before. For their long summer trips, Oshin and Reena have always chosen to visit a town that Reena would have liked to visit—unless Oshin had been to that town before. Reena had visited Town F and Town G before, and Oshin had never visited Town J or Town K. Did Oshin and Reena visit one of these four towns last summer?

    (1) Reena had never visited Town J, and Oshin had never visited Town F.

    (2) Oshin would have liked to visit either Town G or Town K.

423. For a new project, an organization is creating a three-member team from among its employees. Selection of members for the team conforms to exactly two rules: no selected member can be working on more than one other project at the time of selection, and at least one of the selected members must have an MBA degree. The organization has selected Paula and Quincy for the team. Neither of these will be replaced before the third member is selected. The organization is about to make the third selection. If the organization adheres to the selection rules for committee membership, is it possible that Rubin will be selected for the team?

    (1) Quincy has an MBA degree, and Rubin is currently working on only one other project.

    (2) Rubin is one of only two employees in the organization who have an MBA degree.

424. All the T-shirts a clothing store stocks are plain, and they are all in one of exactly four colors: blue, green, red, and yellow. On any given day, the store sells about twice as many blue T-shirts as it does green T-shirts. Last week, did the store sell more blue T-shirts than red T-shirts?

    (1) Last week, the store sold fewer blue T-shirts than red T-shirts and green T-shirts combined.

    (2) Last week, the store sold more blue T-shirts than half the total number of red T-shirts and yellow T-shirts combined.

Month	Forecast for Units of Product Z
January	12
February	16
March	16
April	20
May	20
June	24

425. The table above shows the sales forecast from January to June of last year, by the sales team of Company X, for the number of units of Product Z each month.

    Was the actual number of units of Product Z sold in March less than the number sold in April?

    (1) Twelve units of Product Z were sold in March.

    (2) From January through June of last year, there was a constant, linear relationship between the forecast and actual number of units of Product Z sold.

426. Chris was in an electronic appliances store to buy an LED computer monitor. Chris's purchase criteria included screen size, which must be at least 32 inches, and price, which must not exceed $400. A friend made two recommendations: Monitor A and Monitor B. Chris liked both monitors. Did Chris more likely buy Monitor A, Monitor B, or neither?

    (1) Monitor A's screen size was more than 32 inches and it cost less than Monitor B.

    (2) Monitor B cost $390 and its screen size was less than that of Monitor A.

Revenue Share of Most Popular Pizzas

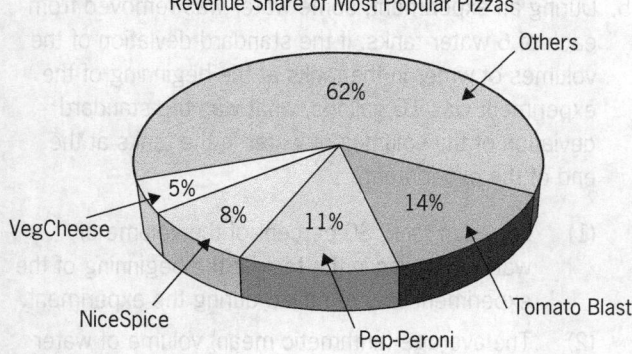

427. A certain pizzeria has more than fifty types of pizza on its menu. The chart above shows the revenue share, in the pizzeria's total revenue in the last month, of its four most popular pizza types. Each pizza type has only a single size and a single price.

    Which was their best-selling pizza last month in terms of number of pizzas sold?

    (1) The number of customers who ordered at least one Pep-Peroni pizza last month was greater than the number of customers who ordered at least one of any other pizza type last month.

    (2) The lowest-priced pizza type on the pizzeria's menu is Tomato Blast, followed by VegCheese.

428. In any twenty-four-hour period, a certain faulty clock gains anywhere from one second to a maximum of three minutes. The clock did not stop or lose time since noon the day before yesterday. At exactly noon today, did the clock show the correct time to an accuracy of five minutes?

    (1) The clock was set to the correct time the day before yesterday at exactly noon.

    (2) At exactly noon yesterday, the clock was set back by one minute.

429. The couple decide one day that they will definitely go to the beach the next evening if it is sunny without rain at the time they plan to go, and that they will definitely not go if such is not the case. The next morning, the hour-by-hour weather forecast says that in the evening, it will be sunny without rain. Will the couple go to the beach that evening?

    (1) It is raining on the morning and in the afternoon of the day of their planned beach outing.

    (2) The couple always believe that the weather forecast is likely to be accurate.

430. A small library has books on twenty different subjects including, most prominently, history. One afternoon, a librarian arbitrarily picks up 100 books for reshelving from among the books returned that day. All the books returned that day were borrowed during the past three weeks. Are fewer than 20 percent of the books the librarian picks up on history?

    (1) Fewer than 20 percent of the books in the library are on history.

    (2) During the past three weeks, exactly 15 books on history were borrowed from the library.

Topic	Alex	Beika	Carlos	Deepa
History	X	X	✓	X
Humor	X	✓	X	✓
Language	X	X	✓	✓
Philosophy	✓	✓	✓	X
Science Fiction	✓	X	✓	✓

431. Four book lovers have recently met and are not sure of the topics that interest the others. The table above indicates the topics that interest each of them with check marks and those that do not with cross marks (Xs).

    One of these persons will gift another of these persons two books, each on a different one of the listed topics. Will at least one of the two books fall under the recipient's broad topic of interest?

    (1) One topic is science fiction and the other is humor.

    (2) The intended recipient is Carlos.

432. In a gas sample, there are, rounded to the nearest order of magnitude (that is, to the nearest power of 10), approximately 10^{21} molecules of H_2 and also 10^{21} molecules of O_2. What is the combined number of H_2 and O_2 molecules in the gas sample, rounded to the nearest order of magnitude?

    (1) The number of H_2 molecules and the number of O_2 molecules are each less than 3×10^{21}.

    (2) The number of H_2 molecules is more than twice the number of O_2 molecules.

433. On Jane's credit card account, the average daily balance for a 30-day billing cycle is the average (arithmetic mean) of the daily balances at the end of each of the 30 days. At the beginning of a certain 30-day billing cycle, Jane's credit card account had a balance of $600. Jane made a payment of $300 on the account during the billing cycle. If no other amounts were added to or subtracted from the account during the billing cycle, what was the average daily balance on Jane's account for the billing cycle?

    (1) Jane's payment was credited on the 21st day of the billing cycle.

    (2) The average daily balance through the 25th day of the billing cycle was $540.

434. The annual rent collected by a corporation from a certain building was x percent more in 1998 than in 1997 and y percent less in 1999 than in 1998. Was the annual rent collected by the corporation from the building more in 1999 than in 1997?

    (1) $x > y$

    (2) $\dfrac{xy}{100} < x - y$

435. During an experiment, some water was removed from each of 6 water tanks. If the standard deviation of the volumes of water in the tanks at the beginning of the experiment was 10 gallons, what was the standard deviation of the volumes of water in the tanks at the end of the experiment?

    (1) For each tank, 30 percent of the volume of water that was in the tank at the beginning of the experiment was removed during the experiment.

    (2) The average (arithmetic mean) volume of water in the tanks at the end of the experiment was 63 gallons.

436. Each member of a team consisting of 6 researchers and 4 assistants received a bonus. If the sum of the researchers' bonuses was $7,200, what was the sum of the assistants' bonuses?

    (1) The average (arithmetic mean) of the researchers' bonuses was $300 greater than the average of the assistants' bonuses.

    (2) The sum of the bonuses of 3 of the researchers and 2 of the assistants was $4,500.

6.5 Answer Key: Data Sufficiency

294.	E	323.	C	352.	D	381.	A	410.	E
295.	C	324.	C	353.	A	382.	C	411.	B
296.	A	325.	B	354.	C	383.	D	412.	A
297.	E	326.	B	355.	B	384.	E	413.	B
298.	D	327.	D	356.	B	385.	C	414.	B
299.	C	328.	E	357.	D	386.	C	415.	C
300.	C	329.	A	358.	B	387.	D	416.	B
301.	C	330.	C	359.	C	388.	A	417.	C
302.	E	331.	B	360.	B	389.	C	418.	E
303.	C	332.	C	361.	B	390.	C	419.	B
304.	C	333.	E	362.	E	391.	C	420.	A
305.	E	334.	A	363.	A	392.	B	421.	C
306.	C	335.	A	364.	E	393.	B	422.	E
307.	E	336.	E	365.	C	394.	C	423.	A
308.	C	337.	C	366.	E	395.	C	424.	E
309.	A	338.	C	367.	D	396.	C	425.	B
310.	C	339.	C	368.	D	397.	B	426.	E
311.	E	340.	A	369.	C	398.	A	427.	B
312.	E	341.	D	370.	C	399.	C	428.	C
313.	E	342.	B	371.	E	400.	E	429.	E
314.	D	343.	B	372.	D	401.	D	430.	B
315.	C	344.	D	373.	B	402.	A	431.	D
316.	E	345.	C	374.	B	403.	B	432.	C
317.	B	346.	C	375.	D	404.	C	433.	D
318.	C	347.	C	376.	A	405.	D	434.	B
319.	E	348.	A	377.	C	406.	B	435.	A
320.	C	349.	B	378.	A	407.	E	436.	A
321.	A	350.	D	379.	B	408.	B		
322.	E	351.	E	380.	E	409.	C		

6.6 Answer Explanations: Data Sufficiency

The following discussion of Data Insights is intended to familiarize you with the most efficient and effective approaches to the kinds of problems common to Data Insights. The particular questions in this chapter are generally representative of the kinds of Data Insights questions you will encounter on the GMAT exam. Remember that it is the problem-solving strategy that is important, not the specific details of a particular question.

Questions 294 to 344 — Difficulty: **Easy**

294. What is the number of pages of a certain journal article?

    (1) The size of each page is $5\frac{1}{2}$ inches by 8 inches.

    (2) The average (arithmetic mean) number of words per page is 250.

Arithmetic Applied Problems

(1) Given that each page is $5\frac{1}{2}$ inches by 8 inches, any positive integer can be the number of pages of the journal article. For example, it is possible that the journal article consists of 10 pages, each $5\frac{1}{2}$ inches by 8 inches. However, it is also possible that the journal article consists of 20 pages, each $5\frac{1}{2}$ inches by 8 inches. Therefore, the number of pages cannot be determined; NOT sufficient.

(2) Given that the average number of words per page is 250, any positive integer can be the number of pages of the journal article. For example, it is possible that the journal article consists of 10 pages and contains a total of $10(250) = 2,500$ words, and in this case the average number of words per page is $\frac{2,500}{10} = 250$. However, it is also possible that the journal article consists of 20 pages and contains a total of $20(250) = 5,000$ words, and in this case the average number of words per page is also $\frac{5,000}{20} = 250$. Therefore, the number of pages cannot be determined; NOT sufficient.

Taking (1) and (2) together, it is still not possible to determine the number of pages because each of the examples used above satisfies both (1) and (2).

The correct answer is E; both statements together are still not sufficient.

295. If a certain vase contains only roses and tulips, how many tulips are there in the vase?

    (1) The number of roses in the vase is 4 times the number of tulips in the vase.

    (2) There is a total of 20 flowers in the vase.

Arithmetic Ratio and Proportion

The task is to determine the number of tulips in the vase.

(1) This says that for every tulip in the vase, there are 4 roses, so the ratio of roses to tulips is 4:1. Because there could be 4 roses and 1 tulip or there could be 20 roses and 5 tulips, the number of tulips cannot be uniquely determined; NOT sufficient.

(2) This says the total number of roses and tulips in the vase is 20. Because there could be 10 roses and 10 tulips or there could be 15 roses and 5 tulips, the number of tulips cannot be uniquely determined; NOT sufficient.

From (1), the ratio of roses to tulips is 4:1 so $\frac{1}{5}$ of the flowers in the vase are tulips. From (2), there are 20 flowers in the vase. So, taking (1) and (2) together, the number of tulips in the vase is $\frac{1}{5}(20) = 4$.

The correct answer is C; both statements together are sufficient.

296. The cost of 10 pounds of apples and 2 pounds of grapes was $12. What was the cost per pound of apples?

    (1) The cost per pound of grapes was $2.
    (2) The cost of 2 pounds of apples was less than the cost of 1 pound of grapes.

Arithmetic Applied Problems

Determine the cost per pound of apples.

    (1) The cost per pound of grapes was $2. The cost of 2 pounds of grapes was 2($2) = $4. The cost of the 10 pounds of apples was $12 − $4 = $8. The cost per pound of the apples was $\frac{\$8}{10}$ = $0.80; SUFFICIENT.

    (2) Intuitively, since (2) involves an inequality, it seems as if it wouldn't give enough information to determine the unique cost per pound of apples. A good strategy might be to guess multiple values for the costs per pound of apples and grapes that satisfy the condition given in the problem (the cost of 10 pounds of apples and 2 pounds of grapes is $12) and look for values that also meet the condition in (2), namely that the cost of 2 pounds of apples is less than the cost of 1 pound of grapes. For example:

Cost per pound of apples	Cost per pound of grapes	Total cost of 10 pounds of apples and 2 pounds of grapes, in dollars	Is total cost $12?	Is the cost of 2 pounds of apples less than the cost of 1 pound of grapes?
$1	$1	10(1) + 2(1)	yes	No, 2(1) $\not<$ 1
$0.50	$3.50	10(0.5) + 2(3.5)	yes	Yes, 2(0.50) < 3.50
$0.60	$3.00	10(0.6) + 2(3)	yes	Yes, 2(0.60) < 3.00

As shown in the table, the cost per pound of apples could be $0.50 or $0.60, so the cost per pound of apples cannot be uniquely determined; NOT sufficient.

The correct answer is A;
statement 1 alone is sufficient.

297. What was the median annual salary for the employees at Company X last year?

    (1) Last year, there were 29 employees at Company X.
    (2) Last year, 12 employees at Company X had an annual salary of $24,000.

Arithmetic Statistics

    (1) Given that there were 29 employees, the median salary is the 15th salary in a list of 29 positive numbers, but we cannot determine the value of any of the numbers; NOT sufficient.

    (2) Given that 12 employees had an annual salary of $24,000, the median salary is the median of a list of 12 or more positive numbers, of which 12 are equal to $24,000. If there were only 12 employees, then the median salary would be $24,000. However, if there were more than 2(12) = 24 employees and all but 12 of the employees had an annual salary of $30,000, then the median salary would be $30,000; NOT sufficient.

Taking (1) and (2) together, if 12 employees had an annual salary of $24,000 and the remaining 17 employees had an annual salary of $20,000, then the median salary would be $20,000. However, if 12 employees had an annual salary of $24,000 and the remaining 17 employees had an annual salary of $30,000, then the median salary would be $30,000.

Tip: If more than half the numbers in a list of numbers have the same value, then the median of the list will be that value, regardless of the values of the remaining numbers.

The correct answer is E;
both statements together are still not sufficient.

298. How many basic units of Currency X are equivalent to 250 basic units of Currency Y?

    (1) 100 basic units of Currency X are equivalent to 625 basic units of Currency Y.
    (2) 2,000 basic units of Currency X are equivalent to 12,500 basic units of Currency Y.

Arithmetic Ratio and Proportion

(1) The equivalency of 100 basic units of Currency X and 625 basic units of Currency Y means that 1 basic unit of Currency Y is equivalent to $\dfrac{100}{625}$ basic units of Currency X. Therefore, 250 basic units of Currency Y are equivalent to $(250)\left(\dfrac{100}{625}\right)$ basic units of Currency X; SUFFICIENT.

(2) The equivalency of 2,000 basic units of Currency X and 12,500 basic units of Currency Y means that 1 basic unit of Currency Y is equivalent to $\dfrac{2,000}{12,500}$ basic units of Currency X. Therefore, 250 basic units of Currency Y are equivalent to $(250)\left(\dfrac{2,000}{12,500}\right)$ basic units of Currency X; SUFFICIENT.

Tip: For Data Insights questions in which the task is to determine a specific value, there is no need to perform calculations to get the value in its simplest form. The goal is to determine whether the value can be uniquely determined, not to find the actual value in its simplest form.

**The correct answer is D;
each statement alone is sufficient.**

299. A company bought 3 printers and 1 scanner. What was the price of the scanner?

(1) The total price of the printers and the scanner was $1,300.

(2) The price of each printer was 4 times the price of the scanner.

Algebra Simultaneous Equations

Let P_1, P_2, and P_3 be the prices, in dollars, of the 3 printers and let S be the price, in dollars, of the scanner. What is the value of S?

(1) Given that $P_1 + P_2 + P_3 + S = 1,300$, it is clear that the value of S cannot be determined; NOT sufficient.

(2) Given that $P_1 = P_2 = P_3 = 4S$, it is possible that $P_1 = P_2 = P_3 = 400$ and $S = 100$. On the other hand, it is also possible that $P_1 = P_2 = P_3 = 800$ and $S = 200$; NOT sufficient.

Taking (1) and (2) together, substituting $P_1 = 4S$, $P_2 = 4S$, and $P_3 = 4S$ into $P_1 + P_2 + P_3 + S = 1,300$ gives $4S + 4S + 4S + S = 1,300$, or $13S = 1,300$, and therefore $S = 100$.

**The correct answer is C;
both statements together are sufficient.**

300. Each of the 256 solid-colored marbles in a box is either blue, green, or purple. What is the ratio of the number of blue marbles to the number of purple marbles in the box?

(1) The number of green marbles in the box is 4 times the number of blue marbles in the box.

(2) There are 192 green marbles in the box.

Arithmetic Ratio and Proportion

Let B, G, and P be the numbers of marbles, respectively, that are blue, green, and purple. From the given information, it follows that $B + G + P = 256$. What is the value of $\dfrac{B}{P}$?

(1) Given that $G = 4B$, it is possible that $\dfrac{B}{P} = \dfrac{1}{251}$ (choose $B = 1$, $G = 4$, and $P = 251$), and it is possible that $\dfrac{B}{P} = \dfrac{1}{123}$ (choose $B = 2$, $G = 8$, and $P = 246$); NOT sufficient.

(2) Given that $G = 192$, it is possible that $\dfrac{B}{P} = \dfrac{1}{63}$ (choose $B = 1$, $G = 192$, and $P = 63$), and it is possible that $\dfrac{B}{P} = \dfrac{1}{31}$ (choose $B = 2$, $G = 192$, and $P = 62$); NOT sufficient.

Taking (1) and (2) together, it follows from $G = 4B$ and $G = 192$ that $192 = 4B$, or $B = 48$. Thus, $B + G + P = 256$ becomes $48 + 192 + P = 256$, and so $P = 256 - 48 - 192 = 16$. Therefore, $\dfrac{B}{P} = \dfrac{48}{16}$.

**The correct answer is C;
both statements together are sufficient.**

301. A certain mixture of paint requires blue, yellow, and red paints in ratios of 2:3:1, respectively, and no other ingredients. If there are ample quantities of the blue and red paints available, is there enough of the yellow

paint available to make the desired amount of the mixture?

(1) Exactly 20 quarts of the mixture are needed.

(2) Exactly 10 quarts of the yellow paint are available.

Arithmetic Ratios

Given that the mixture requires blue paint, yellow paint, and red paint in the ratios 2:3:1, it follows that $\frac{3}{2+3+1} = \frac{1}{2}$ of the mixture will be yellow paint. Determining whether there is enough yellow paint available depends on how much of the mixture is needed and how much yellow paint is available.

(1) This indicates that exactly 20 quarts of the paint mixture are needed, so $\frac{1}{2}(20) =$ 10 quarts of yellow paint are needed. However, there is no information about how much yellow paint is available; NOT sufficient.

(2) This indicates that exactly 10 quarts of yellow paint are available, but there is no information about how much of the mixture or how much yellow paint is needed; NOT sufficient.

Taking (1) and (2) together, 10 quarts of yellow paint are needed, and 10 quarts are available.

The correct answer is C; both statements together are sufficient.

302. There are 2 groups of students who took a history test. Was the average (arithmetic mean) score of the students in Group A higher than the average score of the students in Group B who took the test?

(1) Of the students who took the test, 10 were in Group A and 12 were in Group B.

(2) On the test, the highest score was achieved by a Group B student, and the lowest score was achieved by a Group A student.

Arithmetic Statistics

(1) Given that 10 of the scores were by students in Group A and 12 of the scores were by students in Group B, the following table shows two possibilities.

A scores	B scores	A average	B average	A average > B average?
10 scores of 8	12 scores of 1	8	1	yes
10 scores of 1	12 scores of 8	1	8	no

Therefore, it is not possible to determine whether the average score of the students in Group A is higher than the average score of the students in Group B; NOT sufficient.

(2) Given that the highest score was achieved by a Group B student and the lowest score was achieved by a Group A student, the following table shows two possibilities.

A scores	B scores	A average	B average	A average > B average?
1, 7, 7	2, 2, 8	5	4	yes
1, 1, 1	8, 8, 8	1	8	no

Therefore, it is not possible to determine whether the average score of the students in Group A is higher than the average score of the students in Group B; NOT sufficient.

Taking (1) and (2) together, the table below shows that it is not possible to determine whether the average score of the students in Group A is higher than the average score of the students in Group B.

A scores		B scores		A average	B average	A average > B average?
score	frequency	score	frequency			
2	1	3	11	4.7	4	yes
5	9	15	1			
score	frequency	score	frequency			
2	1	6	12	4.7	6	no
5	9					

The correct answer is E; both statements together are still not sufficient.

303. The research funds of a certain company were divided among three departments, X, Y, and Z. Which one of the three departments received the greatest proportion of the research funds?

    (1) The research funds received by Departments X and Y were in the ratio 3 to 5, respectively.
    (2) The research funds received by Departments X and Z were in the ratio 2 to 1, respectively.

Algebra Order; Ratio

Let x, y, and z be the research funds, respectively, of Departments X, Y, and Z. Which of $\frac{x}{x+y+z}$, $\frac{y}{x+y+z}$, or $\frac{z}{x+y+z}$ is the greatest, or respectively, which of x, y, or z is the greatest?

    (1) Given that $\frac{x}{y} = \frac{3}{5}$ where x and y are positive, it follows that $x < y$. However, nothing is known about z other than z is positive, so it cannot be determined which of x, y, or z is the greatest; NOT sufficient.

    (2) Given that $\frac{x}{z} = \frac{2}{1}$ where x and z are positive, it follows that $z < x$. However, nothing is known about y other than y is positive, so it cannot be determined which of x, y, or z is the greatest; NOT sufficient.

Taking (1) and (2) together, it follows from (1) that $x < y$ and it follows from (2) that $z < x$. Therefore, $z < x < y$, and y is the greatest.

The correct answer is C; both statements together are sufficient.

304. In a certain class, some students donated cans of food to a local food bank. What was the average (arithmetic mean) number of cans donated per student in the class?

    (1) The students donated a total of 56 cans of food.
    (2) The total number of cans donated was 40 greater than the total number of students in the class.

Arithmetic Statistics

Let s be the number of students and let c be the number of cans. What is the value of $\frac{c}{s}$?

    (1) Given that $c = 56$, it is not possible to determine the value of $\frac{c}{s}$ because nothing is known about the value of s other than s is a positive integer; NOT sufficient.

    (2) Given that $c = 40 + s$, it is not possible to determine the value of $\frac{c}{s}$. For example, if $c = 40$ and $s = 40$, then $\frac{c}{s} = 1$. However, if $c = 80$ and $s = 40$, then $\frac{c}{s} = 2$; NOT sufficient.

Taking (1) and (2) together, it follows that $40 + s = c = 56$, or $s = 56 - 40 = 16$. Therefore, $c = 56$, $s = 16$, and $\frac{c}{s} = \frac{56}{16}$.

The correct answer is C; both statements together are sufficient.

305. Each of the n employees at a certain company has a different annual salary. What is the median of the annual salaries of the n employees?

    (1) When the annual salaries of the n employees are listed in increasing order, the median is the 15th salary.
    (2) The sum of the annual salaries of the n employees is $913,500.

Arithmetic Statistics

    (1) Given that the median is the 15th salary and all n salaries are different, it follows that there are 14 salaries less than the 15th salary and 14 salaries greater than the 15th salary, for a total of 29 employee salaries. However, there is no information about what any of the salaries actually are, so the median of the salaries cannot be determined; NOT sufficient.

    (2) Given that the sum of the annual salaries is $913,500, the median salary cannot be uniquely determined. To determine more than one possible value for the median salary, use common divisibility rules to find factors of $913,500.

    For example, 913,500 is divisible by 5 because it ends in 0. Then, because $913,500 = 5(182,700)$, there could be 5 salaries, each $182,700. But the salaries must be all different, so we need 5 different salaries that total $913,500. They could be the salaries shown in the table below. Note that the pattern starts with the 3rd (middle) salary of $182,700, and then the 2nd and 4th salaries are "paired" in that one is decreased and the other is increased by the same amount from $182,700. Likewise, for the 1st and 5th salaries. The median is $182,700.

Salary #	Salary
1	$182,698
2	$182,699
3	**$182,700**
4	$182,701
5	$182,702
Total	$913,500

Also, 913,500 is divisible by 9 because the sum of its digits is divisible by 9, and 913,500 = 9(101,500). Using ideas similar to those used in the first example, there could be 9 different salaries that total $913,500. Using the same technique as in the first example, these salaries could be those shown below. All 9 salaries are listed to reinforce the technique. They need not be written out as part of the solution.

Salary #	Salary
1	$101,496
2	$101,497
3	$101,498
4	$101,499
5	**$101,500**
6	$101,501
7	$101,502
8	$101,503
9	$101,504
Total	$913,500

Therefore, the median salary could be $182,700 or $101,500; NOT sufficient.

Taking (1) and (2) together, there are 29 different salaries and their sum is $913,500, but this information is not sufficient to uniquely determine the median.

Salary number	Salary (Example I)	Salary (Example II)
1	$30,100	$30,100
2	$30,200	$30,200
3	$30,300	$30,300
⋮	⋮	⋮
14	$31,400	$31,380
15	**$31,500**	**$31,540**
16	$31,600	$31,580
⋮	⋮	⋮
27	$32,700	$32,700
28	$32,800	$32,800
29	$32,900	$32,900
Total	$913,500	$913,500

Note that 913,500 = 29(31,500). The table above shows two examples, each consisting of 29 different salaries (not all are shown, however) that were obtained using techniques similar to those used in the previous examples. Note that, in both examples, the 1st salary is $1,400 less than $31,500 and the 29th is $1,400 more than $31,500, the 2nd salary is $1,300 less than $31,500 and the 28th is $1,300 more than $31,500, and so on. The salary columns in both examples are identical except for the 14th, 15th, and 16th salaries, which were used to obtain different medians.

In each example, the median is the 15th salary, so (1) is satisfied, and the sum of the salaries is $913,500, so (2) is satisfied. But the median in one case is $31,500 and the median in the other case is $31,540.

**The correct answer is E;
both statements together are still not sufficient.**

306. In a recent town election, what was the ratio of the number of votes in favor of a certain proposal to the number of votes against the proposal?

   (1)   There were 60 more votes in favor of the proposal than against the proposal.

   (2)   There were 240 votes in favor of the proposal.

Arithmetic Ratio and Proportion

Let F be the number of votes in favor and let A be the number of votes against. What is the value of $\frac{F}{A}$?

(1) Given that $F = 60 + A$, it is possible that $\frac{F}{A} = 2$ (choose $F = 120$ and $A = 60$) and it is possible that $\frac{F}{A} = 3$ (choose $F = 90$ and $A = 30$); NOT sufficient.

(2) Given that $F = 240$, it is possible that $\frac{F}{A} = 1$ (choose $F = 240$ and $A = 240$) and it is possible that $\frac{F}{A} = 2$ (choose $F = 240$ and $A = 120$); NOT sufficient.

Taking (1) and (2) together, substitute $F = 240$ into $F = 60 + A$ to get $240 = 60 + A$, or $A = 180$. Therefore, $\frac{F}{A} = \frac{240}{180}$.

**The correct answer is C;
both statements together are sufficient.**

307. How many men are in a certain company's vanpool program?

(1) The ratio of men to women in the program is 3 to 2.

(2) The men and women in the program fill 6 vans.

Arithmetic Applied Problems

Let m be the number of men in the program and let w be the number of women in the program. What is the value of m?

(1) Given that $\frac{m}{w} = \frac{3}{2}$, it is not possible to determine the value of m. For example, if $m = 3$ and $w = 2$, then $\frac{m}{w} = \frac{3}{2}$ is true; and if $m = 6$ and $w = 4$, then $\frac{m}{w} = \frac{3}{2}$ is true; NOT sufficient.

(2) Given that the men and women fill 6 vans, it is clearly not possible to determine the value of m; NOT sufficient.

Taking (1) and (2) together, it is still not possible to determine the value of m. Even if it is assumed that each van has the same maximum capacity, it is possible that $m = 18$ and $w = 12$ (a total of

30 people, which would fill 6 vans each having a capacity of 5 people), and it is possible that $m = 36$ and $w = 24$ (a total of 60 people, which would fill 6 vans each having a capacity of 10 people).

**The correct answer is E;
both statements together are still not sufficient.**

308. Last semester, Professor K taught two classes, A and B. Each student in Class A handed in 7 assignments, and each student in Class B handed in 5 assignments. How many students were in Class A?

(1) The students in both classes combined handed in a total of 85 assignments.

(2) There were 10 students in Class B.

Algebra Simultaneous Equations

Let a be the number of students in Class A and let b be the number of students in Class B. Then the students in Class A handed in a total of $7a$ assignments, and the students in Class B handed in a total of $5b$ assignments. What is the value of a?

(1) Given that $7a + 5b = 85$, it is not possible to determine the value of a. For example, it is possible that $a = 5$ and $b = 10$, since $7(5) + 5(10) = 85$. On the other hand, it is also possible that $a = 10$ and $b = 3$, since $7(10) + 5(3) = 85$; NOT sufficient.

(2) Given that $b = 10$, it is not possible to determine the value of a. For example, it is possible that $a = b = 10$; and it is also possible that $a = 5$ and $b = 10$; NOT sufficient.

Taking (1) and (2) together, substituting $b = 10$ into $7a + 5b = 85$ gives $7a + 5(10) = 85$, or $7a = 35$, or $a = 5$.

**The correct answer is C;
both statements together are sufficient.**

309. Was the amount of John's heating bill for February greater than it was for January?

(1) The ratio of the amount of John's heating bill for February to that for January was $\frac{26}{25}$.

(2) The sum of the amounts of John's heating bills for January and February was $183.60.

Arithmetic Applied Problems

Let J and F be the amounts, respectively and in dollars, of the heating bills for January and February. Is $F > J$?

(1) Given that $\frac{F}{J} = \frac{26}{25}$, it follows that $\frac{F}{J} > 1$. Multiplying both sides of the inequality $\frac{F}{J} > 1$ by the positive quantity J gives $F > J$; SUFFICIENT.

(2) Given that $J + F = 183.60$, it is not possible to determine whether $F > J$. For example, if $J = 83.60$ and $F = 100.00$, then $J + F = 183.60$ and $F > J$. On the other hand, if $J = 100.00$ and $F = 83.60$, then $J + F = 183.60$ and $F < J$; NOT sufficient.

**The correct answer is A;
statement 1 alone is sufficient.**

310. Machine R and Machine S work at their respective constant rates. How much time does it take Machine R, working alone, to complete a certain job?

(1) The amount of time that it takes Machine S, working alone, to complete the job is $\frac{3}{4}$ the amount of time that it takes Machine R, working alone, to complete the job.

(2) Machine R and Machine S, working together, take 12 minutes to complete the job.

Algebra Applied Problems

(1) Given that Machine S takes $\frac{3}{4}$ as long as Machine R to complete the job, if the rate of each machine were doubled, then Machine S would still take $\frac{3}{4}$ as long as Machine R to complete the job and Machine R, working alone, would then take half as long to complete the job as compared to before the rates were doubled; NOT sufficient.

(2) Given that Machine R and Machine S, working together, take 12 minutes to complete the job, if Machine S is extremely slow and thus contributes very little when the machines are working together, then it would take Machine R, working alone, only a little more than 12 minutes to complete

the job. However, if Machine S, working alone, takes only a few seconds less than 12 minutes to complete the job, and thus Machine R contributes very little when the machines are working together, then it would take Machine R, working alone, a long time to complete the job; NOT sufficient.

Taking (1) and (2) together, let t be the time it takes for Machine R, working alone, to complete the job. Then the time it takes Machine S, working alone, to complete the job is $\frac{3}{4}t$. Thus, the individual constant rates of Machines R and S are, respectively, $\frac{1}{t}$ and $\frac{1}{\frac{3}{4}t} = \left(\frac{4}{3}\right)\frac{1}{t}$, and their combined rate is $\left(1 + \frac{4}{3}\right)\frac{1}{t} = \frac{7}{3t}$. Since it takes 12 minutes to complete the job when the machines are working together, it follows that $\left(\frac{7}{3t}\right)(12) = 1$, which can be solved for t.

**The correct answer is C;
both statements together are sufficient.**

311. Beth's bank charges a service fee on a regular checking account for each month in which the balance on the account falls below $100 at any time during the month. Did the bank charge a service fee on Beth's regular checking account last month?

(1) During last month, a total of $1,000 was withdrawn from Beth's regular checking account.

(2) At the beginning of last month, Beth's regular checking account balance was $500.

Arithmetic Equations

(1) Given that a total of $1,000 was withdrawn from the account last month, it is possible that the bank charged a service fee (for example, if the account had $1,050 at the beginning of the month and no deposits were made), and it is possible that the bank did not charge a service fee (for example, if the account had $1,500 at the beginning of the month); NOT sufficient.

(2) Given that the account had $500 at the beginning of last month, it is possible that the bank charged a service fee (for example, if a withdrawal of $450 was made and no deposits were made), and it is possible that the bank did not charge a service fee (for example, if no withdrawals were made); NOT sufficient.

Taking (1) and (2) together, it is still not possible to determine whether the bank charged a service fee last month. For example, if the account had $500 at the beginning of last month and the only activity was a deposit of $1,000 followed later by a withdrawal of $1,000, then the bank would not have charged a service fee. On the other hand, if the account had $500 at the beginning of last month and the only activity was a deposit of $550 followed by a withdrawal of $1,000, then the bank would have charged a service fee.

The correct answer is E;
both statements together are still not sufficient.

312. Three houses are being sold through a real estate agent. What is the asking price for the house with the second-largest asking price?

(1) The difference between the greatest and the least asking price is $130,000.

(2) The difference between the two greater asking prices is $85,000.

Algebra Simultaneous Equations

Let x, y, and z, where $x \leq y \leq z$, be the asking prices of the three houses. This problem can be solved by determining the value of y.

(1) This indicates that $z - x = \$130,000$, but it does not give the value of y; NOT sufficient.

(2) This indicates that $z - y = \$85,000$, but it does not give the value of y; NOT sufficient.

Taking (1) and (2) together, x, y, and z could be $100,000$, $145,000$, and $230,000$, respectively, in which case the second-largest asking price is $145,000$, or they could be $200,000$, $245,000$, and $330,000$, respectively, in which case the second-largest asking price is $245,000$.

The correct answer is E;
both statements together are still not sufficient.

313. How many people in a group of 50 own neither a fax machine nor a laser printer?

(1) The total number of people in the group who own a fax machine or a laser printer or both is less than 50.

(2) The total number of people in the group who own both a fax machine and a laser printer is 15.

Algebra Sets

(1) This indicates that the total number who own either a fax machine or a laser printer or both is less than 50, but it does not indicate how much less than 50 the total number is. Thus, the number of people in the group who own neither a fax machine nor a laser printer cannot be determined; NOT sufficient.

(2) This indicates that, of the 50 people, 15 own both a fax machine and a laser printer, but it does not indicate how many own one or the other. Thus, the number of people in the group who own neither a fax machine nor a laser printer cannot be determined; NOT sufficient.

Taking (1) and (2) together, it is known that 15 people own both a fax machine and a laser printer and that the total number who own either a fax machine or a laser printer or both is less than 50, but the exact number who own neither still cannot be determined. For example, if 20 people own only a fax machine and 10 people own only a laser printer, then both (1) and (2) are true and the number of people who own neither a fax machine nor a laser printer is $50 - 20 - 10 - 15 = 5$. However, if 10 people own only a fax machine and 10 people own only a laser printer, then both (1) and (2) are true and the number of people who own neither a fax machine nor a laser printer is $50 - 10 - 10 - 15 = 15$.

The correct answer is E;
both statements together are still not sufficient.

314. A state legislature had a total of 96 members. The members who did not vote on a certain bill consisted of 25 who were absent and 3 who abstained. How many of those voting voted for the bill?

(1) Exactly $\frac{1}{3}$ of the total membership of the legislature voted against the bill.

(2) The number of legislators who voted for the bill was 8 more than the total number who were absent or abstained.

Arithmetic Equations

Since there are 96 members and $3 + 25 = 28$ of the members did not vote, it follows that $96 - 28 = 68$ of the members voted. We are to determine the number of members who voted FOR the bill.

(1) We are given that $\frac{1}{3}(96) = 32$ members voted AGAINST the bill. Therefore, $68 - 32 = 36$ members voted FOR the bill; SUFFICIENT.

(2) We are given that $8 + (25 + 3) = 36$ members voted FOR the bill; SUFFICIENT.

The correct answer is D; each statement alone is sufficient.

315. What is the average (arithmetic mean) of the first 90 measurements in a certain list of 92 measurements?

(1) The average of the 92 measurements is 7.0 centimeters.

(2) The average of the last 2 measurements is 7.2 centimeters.

Arithmetic Statistics

(1) Given that the average of all 92 measurements is 7, it follows that the sum of all 92 measurements is $92 \times 7 = 644$. However, the sum of the first 90 measurements could be any number and hence we cannot determine the average of the first 90 measurements. For example, it is possible that the average of the first 90 measurements is 1 (sum of first 90 measurements is 90 and each of the last 2 measurements is 277), and it is possible that the average of the first 90 measurements is 7 (sum of first 90 measurements is 630 and each of the last 2 measurements is 7); NOT sufficient.

(2) Given that the average of the last 2 measurements is 7.2, it follows that the sum of the last 2 measurements is

$2 \times 7.2 = 14.4$. However, the sum of the first 90 measurements, and hence the average of the first 90 measurements, could be any number, and hence we cannot determine the average of the first 90 measurements; NOT sufficient.

Taking (1) and (2) together, the sum of the first 90 measurements is the sum of all 92 measurements minus the sum of the last 2 measurements, or $644 - 14.4 = 629.6$. Therefore, the average of the first 90 measurements is $629.6 \div 90$.

The correct answer is C; both statements together are sufficient.

316. How many of the employees of a certain company use both a tablet and an iPhone?

(1) 60 of the employees use a tablet.

(2) 45 of the employees use an iPhone.

Arithmetic Statistics

(1) Given that 60 of the employees use a tablet, the number of employees who use both a tablet and an iPhone cannot be determined because no information about iPhone use by employees is provided; NOT sufficient.

(2) Given that 45 of the employees use an iPhone, the number of employees who use both a tablet and an iPhone cannot be determined because no information about tablet use by employees is provided; NOT sufficient.

Taking (1) and (2) together, it is still not possible to determine the number of employees who use both a tablet and an iPhone. Indeed, the number of employees who use both could be any integer from 0 to 45, inclusive.

The correct answer is E; both statements together are still not sufficient.

317. What is the standard deviation of the weights of the 30 samples in a certain experiment?

(1) The total weight of the 30 samples is 360 grams.

(2) Each of the 30 samples weighs 12 grams.

Arithmetic Statistics

(1) Given that the total weight of the 30 samples is 360 grams, the standard deviation of the weights cannot be determined. For example, if each of the 30 samples weighed 12 grams (this gives a total weight of 360 grams), then the average weight would be $\frac{360}{30} = 12$ grams, each of the squared distances of the weights from the average weight would be 0, and the average of these squared distances would be 0. Therefore, the standard deviation of the weights—the square root of the average of these squared distances—would be $\sqrt{0} = 0$. On the other hand, if there were 15 samples that each weighed 11 grams and 15 samples that each weighed 13 grams (this gives a total weight of 360 grams), then the average weight would be $\frac{360}{30} = 12$ grams, each of the squared distances of the weights from the average weight would be 1, and the average of these squared distances would be 1. Therefore, the standard deviation of the weights—the square root of the average of these squared distances—would be $\sqrt{1} = 1$; NOT sufficient.

(2) Given that each of the 30 samples weighs 12 grams, the first example above shows the standard deviation of the weights is 0; SUFFICIENT.

The correct answer is B; statement 2 alone is sufficient.

318. The people in a line waiting to buy tickets to a show are standing one behind the other. Adam and Beth are among the people in the line, and Beth is standing behind Adam with a number of people between them. If the number of people in front of Adam plus the number of people behind Beth is 18, how many people in the line are behind Beth?

(1) There are a total of 32 people in the line.
(2) 23 people in the line are behind Adam.

Arithmetic Order

Beth is standing in line behind Adam with a number of people between them. Let x be the number of people ahead of Adam, let y be the number of people between Adam and Beth,

and let z be the number of people behind Beth. It is given that $x + z = 18$. Determine z.

(1) This indicates that there are 32 people in the line. Two of these people are Adam and Beth, so there are 30 other people in line besides Adam and Beth. Therefore, $x + y + z = 30$ and $x + z = 18$. From this, $y = 12$, but z cannot be determined uniquely. For example, if $x = 5$, then $z = 13$, but if $x = 10$, then $z = 8$; NOT sufficient.

(2) This indicates that $y + 1 + z = 23$ because the people behind Adam consist of the people between Adam and Beth, Beth herself, and the people behind Beth. If, for example, $y = 4$, then $z = 18$, but if $y = 9$, then $z = 13$; NOT sufficient.

Taking (1) and (2) together, $y = 12$ from (1) and $y + z = 22$ from (2). Therefore, $z = 10$, and there are 10 people in line behind Beth.

The correct answer is C; both statements together are sufficient.

319. In a certain group of 50 people, how many are doctors who have a law degree?

(1) In the group, 36 people are doctors.
(2) In the group, 18 people have a law degree.

Arithmetic Sets

(1) Given that there are 36 people who are doctors, there is no information about how many of the 36 people have a law degree, and therefore it cannot be determined how many of the 36 people are doctors with a law degree; NOT sufficient.

(2) Given that there are 18 people who have a law degree, there is no information about how many of the 18 people are doctors, and therefore it cannot be determined how many of the 18 people are doctors with a law degree; NOT sufficient.

Taking (1) and (2) together, if n is the number of doctors with a law degree, the contingency table below shows that more than one value of n is possible by assigning appropriate values in the column labeled "not a doctor."

	doctor	not a doctor	total
law degree	n		18
no law degree	$36 - n$		32
total	36	14	50

For example, the first table below gives $n = 10$ and the second table below gives $n = 12$.

	doctor	not a doctor	total
law degree	n	8	18
no law degree	$36 - n$	6	32
total	36	14	50

	doctor	not a doctor	total
law degree	n	6	18
no law degree	$36 - n$	8	32
total	36	14	50

**The correct answer is E;
both statements together are still not sufficient.**

320. Of a group of 50 households, how many have at least one cat or at least one dog, but not both?

(1) The number of households that have at least one cat and at least one dog is 4.

(2) The number of households that have no cats and no dogs is 14.

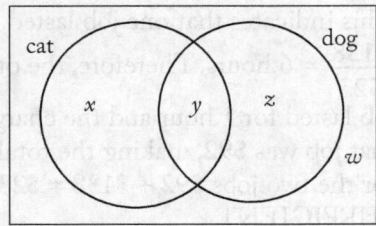

Arithmetic Sets

Using the labels on the Venn diagram above, $w + x + y + z = 50$. Determine the value of $x + z$.

(1) This indicates that $y = 4$, so $w + x + z = 46$, but the value of $x + z$ cannot be uniquely determined; NOT sufficient.

(2) This indicates that $w = 14$, so $x + y + z = 36$, but the value of $x + z$ cannot be uniquely determined; NOT sufficient.

Taking (1) and (2) together, $14 + x + 4 + z = 50$, so $x + z = 50 - 14 - 4 = 32$.

**The correct answer is C;
both statements together are sufficient.**

321. Robin invested a total of $12,000 in two investments, X and Y, so that the investments earned the same amount of simple annual interest. How many dollars did Robin invest in Investment Y?

(1) Investment X paid 3 percent simple annual interest, and Investment Y paid 6 percent simple annual interest.

(2) Robin invested more than $1,000 in Investment X.

Algebra Applied Problems

For Investments X and Y, let r_X and r_Y be the annual percentage interest rates, respectively, and let x and y be the investment amounts, respectively and in dollars. Then $x + y = 12,000$ and $r_X \cdot x = r_Y \cdot y$. What is the value of y?

(1) Given that $r_X = 3$ and $r_Y = 6$, then from $r_X \cdot x = r_Y \cdot y$, it follows that $3x = 6y$, or $x = 2y$. Therefore, $x + y = 12,000$ becomes $2y + y = 12,000$, or $3y = 12,000$, or $y = 4,000$; SUFFICIENT.

(2) Given that $x > 1,000$, it is not possible to determine the value of y. For example, $y = 4,000$ is possible (choose $r_X = 3$, $r_Y = 6$, and $x = 8,000$), and $y = 6,000$ is possible (choose $r_X = 3$, $r_Y = 3$, and $x = 6,000$); NOT sufficient.

**The correct answer is A;
statement 1 alone is sufficient.**

322. In a real estate office that employs n salespeople, f of them are females and x of the females are new employees. What is the value of n?

(1) If an employee were randomly selected from the n employees, the probability of selecting a female would be $\frac{2}{3}$.

(2) If an employee were randomly selected from the f female employees, the probability of selecting a new employee would be $\frac{1}{2}$.

Arithmetic Probability

(1) Given that $\frac{f}{n} = \frac{2}{3}$, it is possible that $n = 3$ (choose $f = 2$ and $x = 1$), and it is possible that $n = 6$ (choose $f = 4$ and $x = 2$); NOT sufficient.

(2) Given that $\frac{x}{f} = \frac{1}{2}$, the value of n cannot be determined because $\frac{x}{f} = \frac{1}{2}$ is true for each of the two choices of values of $n, f,$ and x that were used in (1); NOT sufficient.

Taking (1) and (2) together is still not sufficient because both (1) and (2) hold for each of the two choices of values of $n, f,$ and x that were used in (1).

**The correct answer is E;
both statements together are still not sufficient.**

323. Is the total price of the items in Andrea's shopping cart less than $25.00?

(1) There are 5 items in Andrea's shopping cart.

(2) The price of the most expensive item in Andrea's shopping cart is $4.99.

Arithmetic Estimation

(1) Given that there are 5 items in the cart, the total price of the items in the cart could be less than $25 (for example, if the price of each item was $1), and the total price of the items in the cart could be greater than $25 (for example, if the price of each item was $6); NOT sufficient.

(2) Given that the price of the most expensive item in the cart was $4.99, the total price of the items in the cart could be less than $25 (for example, if the cart contained only 2 items: 1 item with price $4.99 and 1 item with price $4), and the total price of the items in the cart could be greater than $25 (for example, if the cart contained 1 item with price $4.99 and 6 items with price $4); NOT sufficient.

Taking (1) and (2) together, the total price of the 5 items in the cart is at most 5($4.99) = $24.95, which is less than $25.

**The correct answer is C;
both statements together are sufficient.**

324. A certain plumber charges $92 for each job completed in 4 hours or less and $23 per hour for each job completed in more than 4 hours. If it took the plumber a total of 7 hours to complete two separate jobs, what was the total amount charged by the plumber for the two jobs?

(1) The plumber charged $92 for one of the two jobs.

(2) The plumber charged $138 for one of the two jobs.

Arithmetic Applied Problems

Find the total amount charged for two jobs lasting a total of 7 hours if the plumber charges $92 for a job lasting 4 hours or less and $23 per hour for a job lasting more than 4 hours.

(1) This indicates that one of the two jobs lasted 4 hours or less. If that job lasted 2 hours, then the other job lasted 5 hours, and the charge for that job would be ($23)(5) = $115, making the total for the two jobs $92 + $115 = $207. However, if the jobs lasted 1 hour and 6 hours, respectively, then the total charge for the two jobs would be $92 + (6)($23) = $92 + $138 = $230; NOT sufficient.

(2) This indicates that one job lasted $\frac{\$138}{\$23} = 6$ hours. Therefore, the other job lasted for 1 hour and the charge for that job was $92, making the total charge for the two jobs $92 + $138 = $230; SUFFICIENT.

**The correct answer is B;
statement 2 alone is sufficient.**

325. If x and y are positive numbers, is $\frac{x+1}{y+1} > \frac{x}{y}$?

(1) $x > 1$

(2) $x < y$

Algebra Inequalities

Since y is positive, multiplying both sides

of the inequality $\dfrac{x+1}{y+1} > \dfrac{x}{y}$ by $y(y+1)$ gives

$y(x+1) > x(y+1)$ or $xy + y > xy + x$, which is

equivalent to $y > x$. So, determining whether

the inequality $\dfrac{x+1}{y+1} > \dfrac{x}{y}$ is true is equivalent to

determining whether the inequality $y > x$ is true.

(1) This indicates that $x > 1$. If, for example, $x = 3$ and $y = 4$, then $y > x$ is true. However, if $x = 4$ and $y = 3$, then $y > x$ is not true; NOT sufficient.

(2) This indicates that $x < y$, so $y > x$ is true; SUFFICIENT.

The correct answer is B;
statement 2 alone is sufficient.

326. If a school district paid a total of $35 per desk for x desks and a total of $30 per table for y tables, what was the total amount that the district paid for these desks and tables?

(1) The total amount the district paid for the y tables was $900.

(2) $x = 90$, and the total amount the district paid for the x desks was 3.5 times the total amount the district paid for the y tables.

Algebra Simultaneous Equations

Determine the value of $35x + 30y$.

(1) Given that $30y = 900$, it follows that $y = 30$. However, it is not possible to determine the value of $35x + 30y = 35x + 900$ because more than one possible value of x is possible; NOT sufficient.

(2) Given that $x = 90$ and $35x = 3.5(30y)$, it follows that $(35)(90) = (3.5)(30)y$, or $y = \dfrac{35}{3.5} \times \dfrac{90}{30} = 10 \times 3 = 30$, and therefore $35x + 30y = 35(90) + 30(30)$; SUFFICIENT.

The correct answer is B;
statement 2 alone is sufficient.

327. Three children inherited a total of X dollars. If the oldest child inherited $7,000 more than the youngest child, and the youngest child inherited $9,000 less than the middle child, what is the value of X?

(1) The middle child inherited $27,000.

(2) The youngest child and the middle child together inherited a total of $45,000.

Algebra Simultaneous Equations

Let A, B, and C be the amounts inherited, respectively and in dollars, of the oldest, middle, and youngest child. It is given that $A = 7,000 + C$ and $C = B - 9,000$. Then $A = 7,000 + (B - 9,000) = B - 2,000$. Determine the value of $A + B + C$, or equivalently, determine the value of $(B - 2,000) + B + (B - 9,000) = 3B - 11,000$.

(1) Given that $B = 27,000$, it follows that $3B - 11,000 = 70,000$; SUFFICIENT.

(2) Given that $B + C = 45,000$, then, using $C = B - 9,000$, it follows that $B + (B - 9,000) = 45,000$, which can be solved to obtain $B = 27,000$. Therefore, $3B - 11,000 = 70,000$; SUFFICIENT.

The correct answer is D;
each statement alone is sufficient.

328. If a building has 6,000 square meters of floor space, how many offices are in the building?

(1) Exactly $\dfrac{1}{4}$ of the floor space is not used for offices.

(2) There are exactly 20 executive offices, and each of these occupies 3 times as much floor space as the average for all of the remaining offices.

Algebra Simultaneous Equations

(1) This says that exactly $\dfrac{3}{4}(6,000) = 4,500$ square meters of floor space are used for offices, since exactly $\dfrac{1}{4}(6,000) = 1,500$ square meters of the floor space are not used for offices. No information is given about the configuration of the 4,500 square meters used for offices. Therefore, the number of offices in the building cannot be determined; NOT sufficient.

(2)   While this says there are exactly 20 executive offices and each occupies 3 times the average space of the other offices, no information is given about how much of the 6,000 square meters of floor space in the building is used for offices nor how the offices are configured. Therefore, the number of offices in the building cannot be determined; NOT sufficient.

Taking (1) and (2) together, 4,500 square meters of space are used for offices which include 20 executive offices, and each executive office occupies 3 times as much floor space as the average of all of the remaining offices. However, no information is given about the actual size of an executive office or about the actual average size of the remaining offices. Therefore, the number of offices in the building cannot be determined. The examples in the table verify this:

Non-executive		Executive			
Number	Size (m²)	Number	Size (m²)	Total number of offices	Total space used for offices
30	50	20	150	30 + 20 = 50	30(50) + 20(150) = 4,500
15	60	20	180	15 + 20 = 35	15(60) + 20(180) = 4,500

The correct answer is E; both statements together are still not sufficient.

329. For which type of investment, J or K, is the annual rate of return greater?

(1)   Type J returns $115 per $1,000 invested for any one-year period, and Type K returns $300 per $2,500 invested for any one-year period.

(2)   The annual rate of return for an investment of Type K is 12%.

Arithmetic Percents

Compare the annual rates of return for the investment types J and K.

(1)   For Type J, the annual rate of return is $115 per $1,000 for any one-year period, which can be converted to a percent. For Type K, the annual rate of return is $300 per $2,500 for any one-year period, which can also be converted to a percent. These two percents

can be compared to determine which is greater; SUFFICIENT.

(2)   Type K has an annual rate of return of 12%, but no information is given about the annual rate of return for Type J; NOT sufficient.

The correct answer is A; statement 1 alone is sufficient.

330. If Car X followed Car Y across a certain bridge that is $\frac{1}{2}$ mile long, how many seconds did it take Car X to travel across the bridge?

(1)   Car X drove onto the bridge exactly 3 seconds after Car Y drove onto the bridge and drove off the bridge exactly 2 seconds after Car Y drove off the bridge.

(2)   Car Y traveled across the bridge at a constant speed of 30 miles per hour.

Arithmetic Rate Problem

Find the number of seconds that it took Car X to cross the $\frac{1}{2}$-mile bridge.

(1)   If Car X drove onto the bridge 3 seconds after Car Y and drove off the bridge 2 seconds after Car Y, then Car X took 1 second less to cross the bridge than Car Y. Since there is no information on how long Car Y took to cross the bridge, there is no way to determine how long Car X took to cross the bridge; NOT sufficient.

(2)   If the speed of Car Y was 30 miles per hour, it took Car Y $\frac{1}{60}$ hour = 1 minute = 60 seconds to cross the bridge. However, there is no information on how long Car X took to cross the bridge; NOT sufficient.

Taking (1) and (2) together, Car X took 1 second less than Car Y to cross the bridge, and Car Y took 60 seconds to cross the bridge, so Car X took 60 − 1 = 59 seconds to cross the bridge.

The correct answer is C; both statements together are sufficient.

331. Will Candidate A win the most votes of any of the competing candidates in the upcoming election?

    (1) An opinion poll, Poll P, indicates that 60% of respondents prefer Candidate A over other candidates competing in the upcoming election.

    (2) An election-forecasting opinion poll is a method to estimate election outcomes based on a sample that is representative of the population of all of those legally entitled to vote.

Inference

The information provided is capable of providing a prediction of the election outcome based only on probabilistic data, as predictions usually are. So none of the information in the statements, taken either alone or together, can entail a yes or no answer to the question posed.

(1) Of those who responded to Poll P, a subset of a sample of those polled, 60% preferred Candidate A over the other candidates. Was the sample of those eligible to vote truly representative? No answer is provided to this question—important for determining whether the poll is a reliable tool for making a prediction about the election outcome. Therefore, the information in the statement is insufficient by itself to determine a yes or no answer to the question posed; NOT sufficient.

(2) An election-forecasting opinion poll provides data to **estimate** an election outcome. It can do so reliably only if it is based on a random sample representative of the whole population of eligible voters. The information in (2) is insufficient to answer the question posed about Candidate A; for example, it provides no data about the attitudes of voters toward Candidate A. Therefore, it cannot by itself entail an answer to the question posed about Candidate A's performance in the upcoming election; NOT sufficient.

(1) lacks the information to show that the poll mentioned in (1) conforms to the purpose and method of the type of election-forecasting poll that (2) describes. Therefore, (1) and (2), even combined, are insufficient to entail that Candidate A will win the upcoming election or will lose it.

The correct answer is E; both statements together are still not sufficient.

332. The government of Nation X makes policy decisions intended to advance the public interest, such as policy decisions aiming to promote employment, economic flourishing, and environmental protection. A policy decision can involve a significant trade-off, i.e., it can entail foreseeably giving up part or all of one valued outcome in the pursuit of another valued outcome. Does a policy decision by Nation X to permit extensive clearcutting of forests provide a valued outcome at the expense of another valued outcome?

    (1) Extensive clearcutting of forests is permitted in Nation X because it provides immediate economic gains by enabling businesses such as farming and lumbering to flourish and provide employment.

    (2) Extensive clearcutting of forests is permitted in Nation X even though it reduces forests' absorption of carbon dioxide, and this indirectly contributes to global warming, resulting in adverse climate changes that are certain to be very costly for Nation X to manage.

Evaluation

A policy decision involves a significant trade-off whenever the policy sacrifices one valued outcome in pursuit of another outcome that is also valued. Can the policy of permitting extensive clearcutting of forests entail a significant trade-off?

(1) We are told that extensive clearcutting of forests in Nation X produces valued outcomes, but nothing is said or can be concluded about any potential trade-off. So (1) is not sufficient by itself to answer the question asked. This information, by itself, is not sufficient to indicate a trade-off; NOT sufficient.

(2) This information indicates that permitting extensive clearcutting of forest sacrifices a valued outcome, but it does not enable us to conclude that permitting clearcutting of forests produces a valued outcome; NOT sufficient.

Even though (2) by itself is not sufficient to indicate a trade-off, the information in (1) and (2) combined is sufficient to indicate the trade-off involved in permitting extensive clearcutting of forests.

The correct answer is C; both statements together are sufficient.

333. Is Sarah's mathematics test score higher than the class average?

    (1) Sarah scored 90% on her mathematics test, answering 45 out of 50 questions correctly.

    (2) Sarah's high percentage score indicates that she performed exceptionally well, with only a few questions answered incorrectly.

Inference

The question posed is whether Sarah's mathematics test score is higher than the class average. We are given two pieces of information about Sarah's performance, but no information about how other people performed. Without the latter information, we cannot determine what the class average was.

    (1) Some information about Sarah's test score is given, but we are not given any information about the test scores of others in the class. So statement (1) is not sufficient alone; NOT sufficient.

    (2) Knowing that Sarah "performed exceptionally well" on her mathematics test does not allow us to infer that Sarah's performance was above the class average, even if Sarah's performance was exceptional for her. Statement (2) is not sufficient alone; NOT sufficient.

Taking (1) and (2) together does not give us enough information to answer the question asked. (1) does not help to remove the insufficiency described in (2).

The correct answer is E; both statements together are still not sufficient.

334. On Day X, was the forecast temperature 36°C at noon?

    (1) On Day X, the forecast temperature was 30°C at 9:00 a.m. and 40°C at 2:00 p.m.

    (2) On Day X, every half hour, the forecast temperature increased by 1°C.

Inference

    (1) This information provides that the forecast temperature was 30°C at 9:00 a.m., but nothing about the forecast temperatures after 9:00 a.m. except that the forecast temperature was 40°C at 2:00 p.m. By itself, it provides no information about the forecast temperature at noon. Therefore, statement (1) is not sufficient alone to provide a definitive answer to the question posed; NOT sufficient.

    (2) The information that the forecast temperature increased by 1°C on each half hour would enable us to calculate the forecast temperature at each half hour after some earlier given time. But statement (2) gives us no forecast temperature for an earlier time in the 24-hour period. If statement (2) informed us, for example, that the temperature at 9:00 a.m. was 30°C, we could infer that it was 31°C at 9:30 a.m. This means that statement (2) is not sufficient by itself to answer definitively the question posed; NOT sufficient.

If we combine the information in statements (1) and (2), both of which refer to forecast temperatures on Day X, we can infer the forecast temperature at noon on Day X; since it increased by 2°C each hour, it was therefore 36°C at noon.

The correct answer is C; both statements together are sufficient.

335. Benjamin is a salesman working for commission at a shoe store. For the first $1,000 worth of sales in a given month, he earns a commission of 2%. For any sales he makes after the first $1,000 in that month, he earns a commission of 4%. What is the total dollar value of sales made by Benjamin in the month of March?

    (1) Benjamin earned a commission of $120 in March.

    (2) Benjamin doubled the dollar value of his sales in March compared to his sales in February.

Applied Problems

    (1) From the commission amount of $120 for March sales, we can infer the dollar value of those sales. He earned (2%)($1,000) in commission for the first $1,000 in sales. The remaining $100 in commission represented 4% of Benjamin's additional March sales, which therefore were (100 ÷ 0.04) dollars, i.e., $2,500. So total March sales

were $(1,000 + 2,500)$, i.e., $3,500. The information provided is sufficient alone; SUFFICIENT.

(2) The dollar value of Benjamin's March sales was double the value of his February sales. But this information is not sufficient alone to answer the question posed; NOT sufficient.

The correct answer is A; statement 1 alone is sufficient.

336. What is the length of Train A if it crosses Bridge X in 30 seconds from the moment it enters the bridge to the moment its final carriage exits the bridge?

(1) Train B, which is 200 meters long, traveling at a constant speed of 20 meters per second, crosses Bridge X in 40 seconds.

(2) The end of Train A, which is traveling at a constant speed, passes a pole in 10 seconds from the moment the train meets the pole.

Applied Problems

Data is presented about two trains, Train A and Train B, crossing Bridge X. Notice that a train has crossed a bridge when its total length has exited the bridge, so the crossing distance is the length of the bridge plus the length of the train. The question posed is what the length of Train A is.

(1) We are given information about the constant speed of Train B, the length of Train B, its speed crossing the bridge, and how long that takes. That information about Train B is sufficient to establish the length of the bridge, which will be the total crossing distance minus the length of the train. But knowing this is not sufficient to infer the length of Train A, since we are not told the constant speed of Train A. So (1) is not sufficient by itself to enable us to infer a definite answer to the question posed; NOT sufficient.

(2) We are not given the constant speed of Train A nor its length. (2) does not allow us to infer either of those magnitudes. If we knew its speed that enabled it to pass the pole in 10 seconds, then we could infer the train's length. So (2) is not sufficient alone; NOT sufficient.

Even combining the information in (1) and (2) will not be sufficient to allow the length of Train A to be inferred.

The correct answer is E; both statements together are still not sufficient.

337. Solomon leases space for his barber shop, and his landlord has recently increased the rent by 40%. Solomon wants to increase his monthly revenue to pay the increased rent without affecting his net income. By what percentage must he increase his revenue?

(1) 20% of his previous monthly revenue was used to pay the rent before the landlord increased it.

(2) The new rent is $50 more than the previous rent.

Applied Problems

Note that we are asked about a percentage, not a monetary amount.

(1) We have enough information to calculate the percentage increase needed in Solomon's revenue. We have information from the stimulus about the percentage rent increase (40%) and from (1) about what percentage of revenue (20%) went to rent before the increase. To absorb that rent increase, Solomon's revenue will have to increase by 40% of that 20%, which is 0.4 multiplied by 0.2, i.e., 0.08, which is 8%. So the information in the stimulus together with that in (1) has enabled us to provide a definitive answer to the question asked. Therefore, (1) is sufficient alone; SUFFICIENT.

(2) The information provided is that Solomon's rent increase is $50. Combining this information with the information in the stimulus allows us to calculate Solomon's old rent, R1, and his new rent, R2. If $50 = 0.4(R1), then R1 was $50/0.4, i.e., $125, and the new rent R2 is $175, i.e., $50 more than R1. But we lack enough information from the stimulus plus (2) to infer what percentage increase in revenue is needed to absorb the rent increase. We don't have enough information to calculate last year's revenue. So (2) is not sufficient alone; NOT sufficient.

The correct answer is A; statement 1 alone is sufficient.

338. What is the ratio of the amount, by weight, of Metal A to Metal B in Alloy K?

    (1) The ratio of Metal A to Metal B in Alloy K becomes 5:6 when 40 pounds of Metal A is added to the alloy.

    (2) The ratio of Metal A to Metal B in Alloy K becomes 7:6 when 60 pounds of Metal A is added to the alloy.

Applied Problems

We are told how adding two different quantities of Metal A to Alloy K of Metals A and B changes the ratio between the two metals. We are asked to determine what the ratio between Metals A and B was before more of Metal A was added. Let A_1 be the quantity of metal.

    (1) Let A_1 be the original quantity in pounds of Metal A in the alloy before any further additions of Metal A. Let B_1 be the original quantity in pounds of Metal B in the alloy. Then, based on the information in (1), we know that $(A_1 + 40):B_1 = 5:6$. Alternatively, this could be written as an equality of two fractional amounts: $(A_1 + 40)/B_1 = 5/6$. It follows from this that $5(B_1) = 6(A_1 + 40)$. This information is not sufficient alone to determine a unique value for the original ratio of Metal A to Metal B in Alloy K; NOT sufficient.

    (2) A similar approach to the information in (1) is applicable to the information in (2). This allows us to immediately conclude that the information in (2), like the information in (1), is also not sufficient alone to uniquely determine the original ratio of Metal A to Metal B in Alloy K; NOT sufficient.

The information gleaned from (2), as in (1), will give us an equation, derived in the same way as in (1). Then we have two equations, each with two unknowns, A_1 and B_1. Solving for A_1 and B_1 will allow us to provide a definitive answer to the question posed about the ratio of Metal A to Metal B in the original Alloy K before any further additions of Metal A. The answer you should get is the following: $A_1:B_1 = 1:6$.

The correct answer is C; both statements together are sufficient.

339. Train A started from Station X toward Station Y traveling at a constant speed, and on the same day, on a parallel track, Train B started from Station Y toward Station X at a constant speed. At what time did Train A reach Station Y?

    (1) The two trains met at 3:00 p.m. The distance traveled by Train A was twice the distance traveled by Train B by the time they met.

    (2) The ratio between the speeds of Trains A and B is 3:5. Train B started from Station Y at 6:00 a.m.

Applied Problems

We are asked to determine Train A's time of arrival at Station Y.

    (1) This provides us with the ratio between the distance traveled by Train A to the distance traveled by Train B when the trains meet at 3:00 p.m. But we lack enough information about the speeds of the trains, neither the specific speeds nor the ratio between the speeds. Therefore, (1) is not sufficient alone to provide a definitive answer to the question posed; NOT sufficient.

    (2) This provides us with the ratio between the speeds of Trains A and B, and also tells us that Train B left Station Y at 6:00 a.m. But it tells us nothing about the distances that Trains A and B have traveled when they met. Therefore, (2) is not sufficient alone to provide a definitive answer to the question asked; NOT sufficient.

If the information in (1) and (2) is combined, it will be sufficient to determine the time at which Train A will reach Station Y. We have, in total, information concerning speeds, distances, and times. The distance Train A must travel from 3:00 p.m. is the distance Train B has already traveled. Train B covered that distance in 9 hours. The ratio between Train A's speed and Train B's speed is 3:5. So Train A will take 5/3 times 9 hours, i.e. 15 hours after 3:00 p.m., to arrive at Station Y. Therefore, the total information in (1) and (2) is sufficient to provide a definitive answer to the question, but neither (1) nor (2) is sufficient alone.

The correct answer is C; both statements together are sufficient.

340. Pipes A and B are the pipes that fill a tank. Pipes C and D are the pipes that empty the same tank. What is the capacity of the tank?

    (1) Pipe A is twice as efficient as Pipe C, that is, the volume of water per hour that Pipe A moves is twice the volume per hour that Pipe C moves. Pipe A and Pipe B are equally efficient. When Pipes C and D are closed, Pipes A and B together fill the empty tank in 5 hours. Pipe C empties 6,000 liters per hour.

    (2) Pipe B is three times as efficient as Pipe D.

Applied Problems

We are asked to determine the volume of a tank that has two pipes, A and B, that can fill it and two pipes, C and D, that can drain it. Is there sufficient information to find the volume of the tank?

    (1) Since Pipe A is twice as efficient as Pipe C, and Pipe C drains 6,000 liters per hour, Pipe A fills 12,000 liters per hour. Since Pipes A and B are equally efficient, Pipe B also fills 12,000 liters per hour. If Pipes C and D, the drainage pipes, are closed, then Pipes A and B fill the tank in 5 hours. This means that the total volume of the tank is 5 times 24,000 liters, i.e., 120,000 liters. Therefore, (1) is sufficient alone to provide an answer to the question asked; SUFFICIENT.

    (2) The information provided in (2) is irrelevant to determining the volume of the tank. We are not given a rate of filling per hour for Pipes A or B. Therefore, (2) is not sufficient alone to provide an answer to the question asked; NOT sufficient.

**The correct answer is A;
statement 1 alone is sufficient.**

341. The total cost of a car consisted of the price of the car and the sales tax. If the sales tax was $1,000, what was the price of the car?

    (1) The sales tax was 5 percent of the price of the car.

    (2) The sales tax was $\frac{1}{21}$ of the total cost of the car.

Applied Problems

If the sales tax of $1,000 was 5% of the price of the car, then the price of the car must have been $20,000, since $1,000 is 5% of $20,000. So statement (1) alone is sufficient to answer the question.

If the sales tax of $1,000 was $\frac{1}{21}$ of the total cost of the car, then the total cost must have been $21 \times \$1,000 = \$21,000$. Since the price of the car was the total cost minus the sales tax, the price must have been $\$21,000 - \$1,000 = \$20,000$. So statement (2) alone is sufficient to answer the question.

**The correct answer is D;
each statement alone is sufficient.**

342. Yesterday a plane flew from City N to City V within the same time zone and made exactly one stop along the way. What was the total time that elapsed from the time the plane left N until it arrived at V?

    (1) The plane began a 30-minute stop at noon.

    (2) The plane left N at 8:18 a.m. and arrived at V at 4:48 p.m.

Applied Problems

If the stop the plane made along the way from City N to City V lasted 30 minutes, the total time that elapsed from the time the plane left N until it arrived at V must have been more than 30 minutes. But that doesn't tell us how much more than 30 minutes it was. So statement (1) alone is not sufficient to answer the question.

City N and City V are in the same time zone. So if the plane left N at 8:18 a.m. yesterday and arrived at V at 4:48 p.m. yesterday, the total time that elapsed from the time the plane left N until it arrived at V was 8 hours and 30 minutes. Thus, statement (2) alone is sufficient to answer the question.

**The correct answer is B;
statement 2 alone is sufficient.**

343. Raymond's father weighs twice as much as Raymond. How much does Raymond weigh?

   (1) Raymond's father weighs 3 times as much as Raymond weighed 5 years ago.

   (2) If Raymond's father weighed 100 pounds more, he would weigh 3 times as much as Raymond.

Applied Problems

If Raymond's father weighs twice as much as Raymond does now but 3 times as much as Raymond weighed 5 years ago, then Raymond must weigh $\frac{3}{2}$ as much now as he did 5 years ago.

But since we don't know how much Raymond weighed 5 years ago, this doesn't tell us how much he weighs now. So statement (1) alone is not sufficient to answer the question.

Suppose that if Raymond's father weighed 100 pounds more, he would weigh 3 times as much as Raymond. Since he actually weighs twice as much as Raymond, twice Raymond's weight plus 100 pounds must equal 3 times Raymond's weight, so Raymond must weigh 100 pounds. Thus, statement (2) alone is sufficient to answer the question.

**The correct answer is B;
statement 2 alone is sufficient.**

344. Of the people who work at Company X, 80% are enrolled in its savings program. How many people work at Company X?

   (1) Exactly 24 people who work at Company X do not belong to its savings program.

   (2) Exactly 96 people who work at Company X belong to its savings program.

Applied Problems

If 80% of the people who work at the company are enrolled in its savings program, then the other 20% are not. So if, as statement (1) says, exactly 24 people who work at the company do not belong to its savings program, then 24 is $20\% = \frac{1}{5}$ of the total number of people who work at the company. Thus, $5 \times 24 = 120$ people work at the company. Therefore, statement (1) alone is sufficient to answer the question.

If, as statement (2) says, exactly 96 people who work at the company belong to its savings program, then 96 is $80\% = \frac{4}{5}$ of the total number of people who work at the company. Thus, $96 \times \frac{5}{4} = 120$ people work at the company. Therefore, statement (2) alone is also sufficient to answer the question.

**The correct answer is D;
each statement alone is sufficient.**

Questions 345 to 388 — Difficulty: Medium

345. What is the total number of executives at Company P?

   (1) The number of male executives is $\frac{3}{5}$ the number of female executives.

   (2) There are 4 more female executives than male executives.

Algebra Simultaneous Equations

Let M be the number of male executives at Company P and let F be the number of female executives at Company P. Determine the value of $M + F$.

   (1) Given that $M = \frac{3}{5} F$, it is not possible to determine the value of $M + F$. For example, if $M = 3$ and $F = 5$, then $M = \frac{3}{5} F$ and $M + F = 8$. However, if $M = 6$ and $F = 10$, then $M = \frac{3}{5} F$ and $M + F = 16$; NOT sufficient.

   (2) Given that $F = M + 4$, it is not possible to determine the value of $M + F$. For example, if $M = 3$ and $F = 7$, then $F = M + 4$ and $M + F = 10$. However, if $M = 4$ and $F = 8$, then $F = M + 4$ and $M + F = 12$; NOT sufficient.

Taking (1) and (2) together, then $F = M + 4$ and $M = \frac{3}{5} F$, so $F = \frac{3}{5} F + 4$. Now solve for F to get $\frac{2}{5} F = 4$ and $F = 10$. Therefore, using $F = 10$ and $F = M + 4$, it follows that $M = 6$, and hence $M + F = 6 + 10 = 16$.

**The correct answer is C;
both statements together are sufficient.**

346. Jack picked 76 apples. Of these, he sold $4y$ apples to Juanita and $3t$ apples to Sylvia. If he kept the remaining apples, how many apples did he keep? (t and y are positive integers.)

    (1) $y \geq 15$ and $t = 2$
    (2) $y = 17$

Algebra Simultaneous Equations

Determine the value of the nonnegative integer $76 - 4y - 3t$.

(1) Given that $y \geq 15$ and $t = 2$, it follows that $76 - 4y - 3t = 76 - 4y - 6 = 70 - 4y$ could have the value $70 - 4(15) = 10$, $70 - 4(16) = 6$, or $70 - 4(17) = 2$; NOT sufficient.

(2) Given that $y = 17$, it follows that $76 - 4y - 3t = 76 - 68 - 3t = 8 - 3t$ could have the value $8 - 3(1) = 5$ or $8 - 3(2) = 2$; NOT sufficient.

Taking (1) and (2) together, it follows that $76 - 4y - 3t = 76 - 4(17) - 3(2) = 2$.

The correct answer is C; both statements together are sufficient.

347. The total price of 5 pounds of regular coffee and 3 pounds of decaffeinated coffee was $21.50. What was the price of the 5 pounds of regular coffee?

    (1) If the price of the 5 pounds of regular coffee had been reduced 10 percent and the price of the 3 pounds of decaffeinated coffee had been reduced 20 percent, the total price would have been $18.45.
    (2) The price of the 5 pounds of regular coffee was $3.50 more than the price of the 3 pounds of decaffeinated coffee.

Algebra Simultaneous Equations

Let $\$x$ be the price of 5 pounds of regular coffee and let $\$y$ be the price of 3 pounds of decaffeinated coffee. Then $x + y = 21.5$, or $y = 21.5 - x$. Determine the value of x.

(1) Given that $0.9x + 0.8y = 18.45$, the value of x can be determined because substituting $y = 21.5 - x$ into $0.9x + 0.8y = 18.45$ gives a single equation with unknown x, and that equation can be solved for a unique value of x; SUFFICIENT.

Alternatively (see the Tip below), $y = 21.5 - x$ and $0.9x + 0.8y = 18.45$ are equations of nonparallel lines in the coordinate plane and thus have a single point of intersection. One way to ensure that the lines are not parallel is to solve each equation for y in terms of x and note that the coefficients of x are different. In this case, $y = 21.5 - x$ gives a coefficient of x equal to -1 and $0.9x + 0.8y = 18.45$ gives a coefficient of x equal to $-\dfrac{0.9}{0.8}$.

(2) Given that $x = 3.5 + y$, the value of x can be determined because substituting $y = 21.5 - x$ into $x = 3.5 + y$ gives a single equation with unknown x, and that equation can be solved for a unique value of x; SUFFICIENT.

Alternatively (see the Tip below), $y = 21.5 - x$ and $x = 3.5 + y$ are equations of nonparallel lines in the coordinate plane and thus have a single point of intersection. One way to ensure that the lines are not parallel is to solve each equation for y in terms of x and note that the coefficients of x are different. In this case, $y = 21.5 - x$ gives a coefficient of x equal to -1 and $x = 3.5 + y$ gives a coefficient of x equal to 1.

Tip: Data Insights problems involving simultaneous equations usually do not have to be solved. Instead, it is typically enough to determine whether no solution exists, exactly one solution exists, or more than one solution exists, and this can often be accomplished by graphical methods.

The correct answer is D; each statement alone is sufficient.

348. A certain painting job requires a mixture of yellow, green, and white paint. If 12 quarts of paint are needed for the job, how many quarts of green paint are needed?

    (1) The ratio of the amount of green paint to the amount of yellow and white paint combined needs to be 1 to 3.
    (2) The ratio of the amount of yellow paint to the amount of green paint needs to be 3 to 2.

Algebra Ratios; Simultaneous Equations

This problem involves 3 quantities:

The number of quarts of yellow paint, represented by Y; the number of quarts of green paint, represented by G; and the number of quarts of white paint, represented by W.

It is given that $Y + G + W = 12$.

The task is to uniquely determine the value of G, which is possible only if there is enough information to eliminate Y and W from $Y + G + W = 12$, so that only G is left.

(1) Using the variables introduced above, this gives $\frac{G}{Y+W} = \frac{1}{3}$ or $3G = Y + W$. Substituting $3G$ for $Y + W$ in $Y + G + W = 12$ gives $4G = 12$, which yields a unique value of G; SUFFICIENT.

(2) Using the variables introduced above, this gives $\frac{Y}{G} = \frac{3}{2}$ or $Y = \frac{3}{2}G$. Then, by substitution, $\frac{3}{2}G + G + W = 12$. Because the value of W can vary, the value of G cannot be uniquely determined; NOT sufficient.

The correct answer is A; statement 1 alone is sufficient.

349. A company produces a certain toy in only 2 sizes, small or large, and in only 2 colors, red or green. If, for each size, there are equal numbers of red and green toys in a certain production lot, what fraction of the total number of green toys is large?

(1) In the production lot, 400 of the small toys are green.

(2) In the production lot, $\frac{2}{3}$ of the toys produced are small.

Algebra Ratios

Let x be the number of small toys of each color, and let y be the number of large toys of each color. The contingency table below gives a summary of the information given. Determine the value of $\frac{y}{x+y}$.

	small	large	total
red	x	y	$x + y$
green	x	y	$x + y$
total	$2x$	$2y$	$2x + 2y$

(1) Given that $x = 400$, it is clearly not possible to determine the value of $\frac{y}{x+y} = \frac{y}{400+y}$; NOT sufficient.

(2) Given that $\frac{2}{3}$ of the toys are small, then, because there are $(2x + 2y)$ toys altogether and $2x$ small toys, it follows that $\frac{2x}{2x+2y} = \frac{2}{3}$. Therefore, $3(2x) = 2(2x + 2y)$, or $x = 2y$, and hence $\frac{y}{x+y} = \frac{y}{2y+y} = \frac{y}{3y} = \frac{1}{3}$; SUFFICIENT.

The correct answer is B; statement 2 alone is sufficient.

350. Jones has worked at Firm X twice as many years as Green, and Green has worked at Firm X four years longer than Smith. How many years has Green worked at Firm X?

(1) Jones has worked at Firm X 9 years longer than Smith.

(2) Green has worked at Firm X 5 years less than Jones.

Algebra Simultaneous Equations

Let J, G, and S be the number of years Jones, Green, and Smith, respectively, have worked at Firm X. Then $J = 2G$ and $G = 4 + S$. What is the value of G?

(1) Given that $J = 9 + S$, then from $J = 2G$, it follows that $2G = 9 + S$. From $G = 4 + S$, it follows that $S = G - 4$, and therefore $G - 4$ can be substituted for S in the equation $2G = 9 + S$ to obtain $2G = 9 + (G - 4)$, or $G = 5$; SUFFICIENT.

(2) Given that $G = J - 5$, it follows from $J = 2G$ that $G = 2G - 5$, or $G = 5$; SUFFICIENT.

The correct answer is D; each statement alone is sufficient.

351. On June 1, Mary paid Omar $360 for rent and utilities for the month of June. Mary moved out early, and Omar refunded the money she paid for utilities, but not for rent, for the days in June after she moved out. How many dollars did Omar refund to Mary?

(1) Mary moved out on June 24.

(2)   The amount Mary paid for utilities was less than $\frac{1}{5}$ the amount Mary paid for rent.

Algebra Applied Problems; Proportions

This problem could be solved by making a table of possible amounts Mary could have paid for rent and utilities for the month of June, such that they total $360, as shown below.

Rent	Utilities
$300	$60
$310	$50
$320	$40
$330	$30
$340	$20
$350	$10

(1)   Given that Mary moved out on June 24, Omar refunded the amount she paid for 6 days of utilities or $\frac{6}{30} = \frac{1}{5}$ of the amount she paid for the whole month. As seen from the table, this amount varies, so $\frac{1}{5}$ of the total amount varies. Therefore, the amount Omar refunded to Mary cannot be uniquely determined; NOT sufficient.

Note that a third column, as shown below, could be added to the table to confirm that $\frac{1}{5}$ of the amount she paid for utilities for the whole month varies. Adding this column will aid in determining whether (1) and (2) together are sufficient. Amounts shown in **boldface** satisfy (1).

Rent	Utilities	$\frac{1}{5}$ Utilities
$300	$60	**$12**
$310	$50	**$10**
$320	$40	**$8**
$330	$30	**$6**
$340	$20	**$4**
$350	$10	**$2**

(2)   Given that the amount Mary paid for utilities was less than $\frac{1}{5}$ the amount she paid for rent, the amount Omar refunded to Mary cannot be uniquely determined. To verify this, another column can be added to the table to show $\frac{1}{5}$ the amount Mary paid for rent and to show the amounts she paid for utilities that are less than $\frac{1}{5}$ the amount she paid for rent. Amounts shown *underlined* in the table below satisfy (2); NOT sufficient.

Rent	Utilities	$\frac{1}{5}$ Utilities	$\frac{1}{5}$ Rent
$300	$60	**$12**	$60
$310	_$50_	**$10**	$62
$320	_$40_	**$8**	$64
$330	_$30_	**$6**	$66
$340	_$20_	**$4**	$68
$350	_$10_	**$2**	$70

Taking (1) and (2) together, observe that there are several amounts in **boldface** in the third column that satisfy (1) and corresponding amounts underlined in the second column that satisfy (2). Therefore, the amount Omar refunded to Mary cannot be uniquely determined.

The correct answer is E; both statements together are still not sufficient.

352. A collection of 36 cards consists of 4 sets of 9 cards each. The 9 cards in each set are numbered 1 through 9. If one card has been removed from the collection, what is the number on that card?

(1)   The units digit of the sum of the numbers on the remaining 35 cards is 6.

(2)   The sum of the numbers on the remaining 35 cards is 176.

Arithmetic Place Value

The sum of all the numbers on the cards in the collection is $4(1 + 2 + 3 + \ldots + 9) = 4(45) = 180$, and hence the sum of the numbers on the remaining cards is 180 minus the number on the removed card. Therefore, if the number on the removed card is 1, 2, 3, 4, 5, 6, 7, 8, or 9, then the sum of the numbers on the remaining cards is, respectively, 179, 178, 177, 176, 175, 174, 173, 172, or 171.

(1)   Given that the units digit of the sum of the numbers on the remaining cards is 6, the

list above shows the sum of the numbers on the remaining cards must be 176, and hence the number on the removed card must be 4; SUFFICIENT.

(2) Given that the sum of the numbers on the remaining cards is 176, the list above shows the number on the removed card must be 4; SUFFICIENT.

The correct answer is D; each statement alone is sufficient.

353. What is the ratio of the number of cups of flour to the number of cups of sugar required in a certain cake recipe?

(1) The number of cups of flour required in the recipe is 250 percent of the number of cups of sugar required in the recipe.

(2) $1\frac{1}{2}$ more cups of flour than cups of sugar are required in the recipe.

Arithmetic Ratio and Proportion

Let F and S be the number of cups of flour and sugar, respectively, required in the cake recipe. We are to determine the ratio $F:S$.

(1) Given that $F = 2.5S$, it follows that $F:S$ is 2.5:1 (if $S = 1$, then $F = 2.5$), or equivalently, 5:2; SUFFICIENT.

(2) Given that $F = 1.5 + S$, it is not possible to determine the ratio $F:S$. For example, if $F = 2.5$ and $S = 1$, then $F = 1.5 + S$ and $F:S$ is 2.5:1, or equivalently, 5:2. On the other hand, if $F = 10$ and $S = 8.5$, then $F = 1.5 + S$ and $F:S$ is 10:8.5, or equivalently, 20:17; NOT sufficient.

The correct answer is A; statement 1 alone is sufficient.

354. A clothing manufacturer makes jackets that are wool or cotton or a combination of wool and cotton. The manufacturer has 3,000 pounds of wool and 2,000 pounds of cotton on hand. Is this enough wool and cotton to make at least 1,000 jackets?

(1) Each wool jacket requires 4 pounds of wool, and no cotton.

(2) Each cotton jacket requires 6 pounds of cotton, and no wool.

Arithmetic Applied Problems

(1) Given that each wool jacket requires 4 pounds of wool and no cotton, then at most a total of 750 wool jackets can be made (because $\frac{3,000}{4} = 750$), and possibly no other jackets. Therefore, it is possible that there is enough wool and cotton to make at least 1,000 jackets (for example, if there is enough cotton to make 250 cotton jackets), and it is possible that there is not enough wool and cotton to make at least 1,000 jackets (for example, if there is less than the amount of cotton needed to make 250 cotton jackets); NOT sufficient.

(2) Given that each cotton jacket requires 6 pounds of cotton and no wool, then at most a total of 333 cotton jackets can be made (because rounding $\frac{2,000}{6}$ down to the nearest integer gives 333), and possibly no other jackets. Therefore, it is possible that there is enough wool and cotton to make at least 1,000 jackets (for example, if there is enough wool to make 667 wool jackets), and it is possible that there is not enough wool and cotton to make at least 1,000 jackets (for example, if there is less than the amount of wool needed to make 667 wool jackets); NOT sufficient.

Taking (1) and (2) together, there is enough wool and cotton to make 750 wool jackets and 333 cotton jackets for a total of 1,083 jackets.

The correct answer is C; both statements together are sufficient.

355. Are at least 10 percent of the people in Country X who are 65 years old or older employed?

(1) In Country X, 11.3 percent of the population is 65 years old or older.

(2) In Country X, of the population 65 years old or older, 20 percent of those with a college degree and 10 percent of those without a college degree are employed.

Arithmetic Percents

(1) Given that 11.3 percent of the population is 65 years old or older, it is not possible to

determine whether at least 10 percent of those 65 years old or older are employed because no information about employment is provided; NOT sufficient.

(2)　Given that of those 65 years and older, 20 percent of those with a college degree and 10 percent of those without a college degree are employed, it follows that the number of employed is more than the number corresponding to 10 percent of the college degree holders and 10 percent of those without a degree. Therefore, of those 65 or older, more than 10 percent are employed; SUFFICIENT.

The correct answer is B;
statement 2 alone is sufficient.

356.　A scientist recorded the number of eggs in each of 10 birds' nests. What was the standard deviation of the numbers of eggs in the 10 nests?

(1)　The average (arithmetic mean) number of eggs for the 10 nests was 4.

(2)　Each of the 10 nests contained the same number of eggs.

Arithmetic Statistics

(1)　Given that the average number of eggs is 4, the standard deviation of the numbers of eggs cannot be determined. For example, if each of the 10 nests had 4 eggs, then the average number of eggs would be 4, each of the squared distances of these numbers from the average would be 0, and the average of these squared distances would be 0. Therefore, the standard deviation of the numbers of eggs—the square root of the average of these squared distances—would be $\sqrt{0} = 0$. On the other hand, if there were 5 nests each containing 3 eggs and 5 nests each containing 5 eggs, then the average number of eggs would be 4, each of the squared distances of these numbers from the average would be 1, and the average of these squared distances would be 1. Therefore, the standard deviation of the numbers of eggs— the square root of the average of these squared distances—would be $\sqrt{1} = 1$; NOT sufficient.

(2)　Given that each of the 10 nests contains the same number of eggs, the average number of eggs is equal to the number of eggs in each of the 10 nests. Thus, each of the squared distances of these numbers from the average is 0, and hence the average of these squared distances is 0. Therefore, the standard deviation of the numbers of eggs—the square root of the average of these squared distances—is $\sqrt{0} = 0$; SUFFICIENT.

The correct answer is B;
statement 2 alone is sufficient.

357.　A paint mixture was formed by mixing exactly 3 colors of paint. By volume, the mixture was x% blue paint, y% green paint, and z% red paint. If exactly 1 gallon of blue paint and 3 gallons of red paint were used, how many gallons of green paint were used?

(1)　$x = y$

(2)　$z = 60$

Algebra First-Degree Equations

Letting T represent the total number of gallons of the paint in the mixture, and B, G, and R the amounts of blue paint, green paint, and red paint, respectively, in the mixture, then $B = \dfrac{x}{100}T$, $G = \dfrac{y}{100}T$, and $R = \dfrac{z}{100}T$. It is given that $\dfrac{x}{100}T = 1$ and $\dfrac{z}{100}T = 3$, from which it follows that $z = 3x$. Also, since there are exactly three colors of paint, $x + y + z = 100$ and $B + G + R = T$. Determine the value of G, or equivalently, the value $\dfrac{y}{100}T$.

(1)　Given that $x = y$ and $\dfrac{x}{100}T = 1$, it follows that $\dfrac{y}{100}T = 1$; SUFFICIENT.

(2)　Given that $z = 60$ and $\dfrac{z}{100}T = 3$, it follows that $T = 5$. Knowing that the total amount of paint in the mixture is 5 gallons of which 1 gallon is blue paint and 3 gallons are red paint, the amount of green paint can be determined; SUFFICIENT.

The correct answer is D;
each statement alone is sufficient.

358. For a basic monthly fee of F yen (¥F), Naoko's first cell phone plan allowed him to use a maximum of 420 minutes on calls during the month. Then, for each of x additional minutes he used on calls, he was charged ¥M, making his total charge for the month ¥T, where $T = F + xM$. What is the value of F?

 (1) Naoko used 450 minutes on calls the first month, and the total charge for the month was ¥13,755.

 (2) Naoko used 400 minutes on calls the second month, and the total charge for the month was ¥13,125.

Algebra Simultaneous Equations

 (1) Given that Naoko used 450 minutes and was charged ¥13,125, it follows that $F + (450 - 420)$ $M = 13,755$, or $F + 30M = 13,755$. However, the value of F cannot be determined. For example, $F = 13,005$ and $M = 25$ is possible, and $F = 13,035$ and $M = 24$ is possible; NOT sufficient.

 (2) Given that Naoko used 400 minutes and was charged ¥13,125, it follows that $F = 13,125$, since Naoko did not use more than 420 minutes; SUFFICIENT.

**The correct answer is B;
statement 2 alone is sufficient.**

359. Is the sum of the prices of the 3 books that Shana bought less than $48?

 (1) The price of the most expensive of the 3 books that Shana bought is less than $17.

 (2) The price of the least expensive of the 3 books that Shana bought is exactly $3 less than the price of the second most expensive book.

Arithmetic Operations with Integers; Order

Let B_1, B_2, and B_3 be the prices, in dollars and in numerical order, of the 3 books. Thus, $B_1 \le B_2 \le B_3$. Determine whether $B_1 + B_2 + B_3 < 48$.

 (1) Given that $B_3 < 17$, it is possible that $B_1 + B_2 + B_3 < 48$ (choose $B_1 = B_2 = 15$ and $B_3 = 16$), and it is possible that $B_1 + B_2 + B_3 > 48$ (choose $B_1 = B_2 = 16$ and $B_3 = 16.5$); NOT sufficient.

 (2) Given that $B_1 = B_2 - 3$, it is possible that $B_1 + B_2 + B_3 < 48$ (choose $B_1 = 3$, $B_2 = 6$,

and $B_3 = 10$), and it is possible that $B_1 + B_2 + B_3 > 48$ (choose $B_1 = 3$, $B_2 = 6$, and $B_3 = 48$); NOT sufficient.

Taking (1) and (2) together, from (1) and the information given, it follows that $B_3 < 17$ and $B_2 \le B_3 < 17$, or $B_2 < 17$. Also, from $B_2 < 17$ and (2), it follows that $B_1 < 17 - 3$, or $B_1 < 14$. Therefore, $B_1 + B_2 + B_3$ is the sum of 3 numbers—a number less than 14, a number less than 17, and a number less than 17—and thus $B_1 + B_2 + B_3 < 14 + 17 + 17 = 48$.

**The correct answer is C;
both statements together are sufficient.**

360. If Elena spent a total of $720 on newspapers, magazines, and books last year, what amount did she spend on newspapers?

 (1) Last year, the amount that Elena spent on magazines was 80 percent of the amount that she spent on books.

 (2) Last year, the amount that Elena spent on newspapers was 60 percent of the total amount that she spent on magazines and books.

Arithmetic Statistics

Let \$$N$, \$$M$, and \$$B$ be the amount spent, respectively, on newspapers, magazines, and books. We are given that $N + M + B = 720$ and are to determine the value of N.

 (1) Given that $M = 0.8B$, it follows from $N + M + B = 720$ that $N + 1.8B = 720$. By considering different values of B (for example, $B = 10$ and $B = 100$), we can show that more than one value of N is possible, and therefore it is not possible to determine the value of N. For example, if $B = 10$, then $M = 0.8B = 8$ and $N = 720 - 1.8B = 702$. On the other hand, if $B = 100$, then $M = 0.8B = 80$ and $N = 720 - 1.8B = 540$; NOT sufficient.

 (2) Given that $N = 0.6(M + B)$, it follows from $N + M + B = 720$ that $0.6(M + B) + (M + B) = 720$, or $1.6(M + B) = 720$. Therefore, $M + B = 720 \div 1.6 = 450$, and hence $N = 0.6(M + B) = 0.6 \times 450 = 270$; SUFFICIENT.

**The correct answer is B;
statement 2 alone is sufficient.**

361. Of the 800 sweaters at a certain store, 150 are red. How many of the red sweaters at the store are made of pure wool?

    (1) 320 of the sweaters at the store are neither red nor made of pure wool.

    (2) 100 of the red sweaters at the store are not made of pure wool.

    Arithmetic Statistics

    (1) Given that 320 of the sweaters are neither red nor made of pure wool, it follows that the $800 - 320 = 480$ remaining sweaters are red, made of pure wool, or both. Since 150 of the sweaters are red, $480 - 150 = 330$ of the sweaters are not red and are made of pure wool. However, the number of red sweaters made of pure wool cannot be determined. Letting b be this number, the Venn diagram below shows that any integer between 0 and 150, inclusive, can be a possible value of b; NOT sufficient.

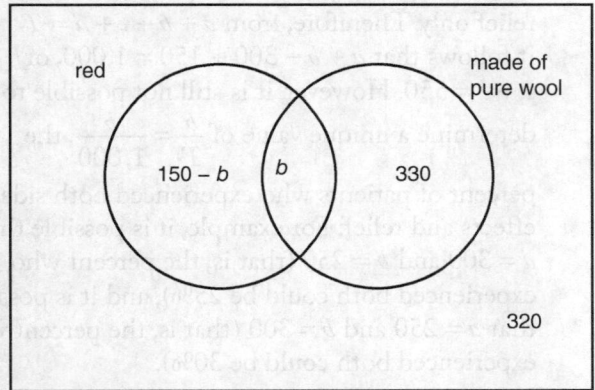

    (2) Given that 100 of the red sweaters are not made of pure wool, it follows that the $150 - 100 = 50$ remaining red sweaters are made of pure wool; SUFFICIENT.

    The correct answer is B; statement 2 alone is sufficient.

362. A certain computer company produces two different monitors, P and Q. In 2010, what was the net profit from the sale of the two monitors?

    (1) Of the company's expenses in 2010, rent and utilities totaled $500,000.

    (2) In 2010, the company sold 50,000 units of Monitor P at $300 per unit and 30,000 units of Monitor Q at $650 per unit.

Arithmetic Applied Problems

The net profit from the sale of the two monitors is the total revenue, R, from the sale of the two monitors minus the total cost, C, of the two monitors, or $R - C$. Determine the value of $R - C$.

(1) Given that the rent and utilities totaled $500,000, it is not possible to determine the value of $R - C$ because we only know that $C \geq 500,000$, and we do not know anything about the value of R; NOT sufficient.

(2) Given that $R = 50,000(\$300) + 30,000(\$650)$, it is not possible to determine the value of $R - C$ because we do not know anything about the value of C; NOT sufficient.

Taking (1) and (2) together, it is not possible to determine the value of $R - C$ because from (2) the value of R is fixed, and from both (1) and (2) we can only conclude that $C \geq 500,000$, and therefore more than one value of $R - C$ is possible.

The correct answer is E; both statements together are still not sufficient.

363. A conveyor belt moves bottles at a constant speed of 120 centimeters per second. If the conveyor belt moves a bottle from a loading dock to an unloading dock, is the distance that the conveyor belt moves the bottle less than 90 meters? (1 meter = 100 centimeters)

    (1) It takes the conveyor belt less than 1.2 minutes to move the bottle from the loading dock to the unloading dock.

    (2) It takes the conveyor belt more than 1.1 minutes to move the bottle from the loading dock to the unloading dock.

Arithmetic Applied Problems

Since the rate at which the conveyor belt moves is given as 120 centimeters per second, which is equivalent to $\frac{120}{100} = 1.2$ meters per second, the conveyor will move less than 90 meters if it moves for less than $\frac{90}{1.2} = 75$ seconds.

(1) This indicates that the length of time the conveyor belt moves is less than 1.2 minutes, which is equivalent to $(1.2)(60) = 72$ seconds and $72 < 75$; SUFFICIENT.

(2) This indicates that the length of time the conveyor belt moves is more than 1.1 minutes, which is equivalent to

$(1.1)(60) = 66$ seconds, but does not indicate how much more than 66 seconds the conveyor moves. If the conveyor moves for 70 seconds $(70 > 66)$, for example, it moves less than 90 meters, since $70 < 75$. However, if the conveyor belt moves for 80 seconds $(80 > 66)$, then it moves more than 90 meters, since $80 > 75$; NOT sufficient.

The correct answer is A;
statement 1 alone is sufficient.

364. In a product test of a common cold remedy, x percent of the patients tested experienced side effects from the use of the drug and y percent experienced relief of cold symptoms. What percent of the patients tested experienced both side effects and relief of cold symptoms?

    (1) Of the 1,000 patients tested, 15 percent experienced neither side effects nor relief of cold symptoms.

    (2) Of the patients tested, 30 percent experienced relief of cold symptoms without side effects.

Algebra Sets

The Venn diagram on the following page represents the numbers of patients who experienced neither, one, or both side effects and relief. In the diagram,

a = number who experienced side effects only,
b = number who experienced both,
c = number who experienced relief only,
d = number who experienced neither,

where $T = a + b + c + d$ is the total number of patients. Note that $a + b = \dfrac{x}{100}T$ and $b + c = \dfrac{y}{100}T$.

Determine the value of $\dfrac{b}{T}$.

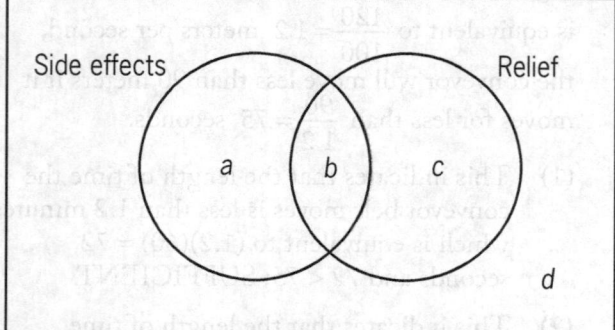

(1) Given that 1,000 patients were tested and $(0.15)(1,000) = 150$ patients experienced neither side effects nor relief, it follows that $a + b + c + d = 1,000$ and $d = 150$. Therefore, $a + b + c + 150 = 1,000$, or $a + b + c = 850$. However, there is no information about how the remaining 850 patients are assigned to the other categories. Thus, the percent of patients who experienced both side effects and relief could be any value between 0% and 85%; NOT sufficient.

(2) Given that 30% of the patients experienced relief without side effects, there is no information about how the remaining 70% of the patients are assigned to the other categories. Thus, the percent of patients who experienced both side effects and relief could be any value between 0% and 70%; NOT sufficient.

Taking (1) and (2) together, it follows that 150 patients experienced neither side effects nor relief and $(0.3)(1,000) = 300$ patients experienced relief only. Therefore, from $a + b + c + d = T$ it follows that $a + b + 300 + 150 = 1,000$, or $a + b = 550$. However, it is still not possible to determine a unique value of $\dfrac{b}{T} = \dfrac{b}{1,000}$, the percent of patients who experienced both side effects and relief. For example, it is possible that $a = 300$ and $b = 250$ (that is, the percent who experienced both could be 25%), and it is possible that $a = 250$ and $b = 300$ (that is, the percent who experienced both could be 30%).

The correct answer is E;
both statements together are still not sufficient.

365. Three roommates—Bela, Gyorgy, and Janos—together saved money for a trip. The amount that Bela saved was equal to 8% of his monthly income. The amount that Gyorgy saved was exactly $\dfrac{1}{3}$ of the total amount saved by all 3 roommates. What was the total amount saved for the trip by all 3 roommates?

    (1) Bela had a monthly income of $2,000.

    (2) Janos saved 1.5 times as much for the trip as Bela.

Algebra First-Degree Equations

Letting B, G, and J represent the amounts saved by Bela, Gyorgy, and Janos, respectively, then $B = 0.08I$, where I represents Bela's monthly income, $G = \frac{1}{3}(B + G + J)$, and $G = \frac{1}{2}(B + J)$. Determine the value of $B + G + J$.

(1) This allows the value of B to be determined but gives no information about the values of G or J; NOT sufficient.

(2) This gives the relationship between the values of J and B but no information to determine the value of either B or J; NOT sufficient.

Taking (1) and (2) together, the values of both B and J can be determined, as can the value of G since $G = \frac{1}{2}(B + J)$. Thus, the value of $B + G + J$ can be determined.

**The correct answer is C;
both statements together are sufficient.**

366. In each game of a certain tournament, a contestant either loses 3 points or gains 2 points. If Pat had 100 points at the beginning of the tournament, how many games did Pat play in the tournament?

(1) At the end of the tournament, Pat had 104 points.

(2) Pat played fewer than 10 games.

Arithmetic Computation with Integers

Pat either lost 3 points or gained 2 points in each game she played. Therefore, since she had 100 points at the beginning of the tournament, her score at the end of the tournament was $100 - 3x + 2y$, where x and y represent, respectively, the number of games in which she lost 3 points and the number of games in which she gained 2 points. Determine the value of $x + y$.

(1) This indicates that $100 - 3x + 2y = 104$, but no information is given about the values of x or y. For example, the values of x and y could be 0 and 2, respectively, so that $x + y = 2$, or the values of x and y could be 2 and 5, respectively, so that $x + y = 7$; NOT sufficient.

(2) This indicates that Pat played fewer than 10 games, but in each of the examples above,

Pat played fewer than 10 games; NOT sufficient.

Since the examples given satisfy both (1) and (2), taking (1) and (2) together does not give enough information to determine the value of $x + y$.

**The correct answer is E;
both statements together are still not sufficient.**

367. At the beginning of the year, the Finance Committee and the Planning Committee of a certain company each had n members, and no one was a member of both committees. At the end of the year, 5 members left the Finance Committee and 3 members left the Planning Committee. How many members did the Finance Committee have at the beginning of the year?

(1) The ratio of the total number of members who left at the end of the year to the total number of members at the beginning of the year was 1:6.

(2) At the end of the year, 21 members remained on the Planning Committee.

Algebra Applied Problems

(1) It is given that $\frac{8}{2n} = \frac{1}{6}$, since a total of $3 + 5 = 8$ members left at the end of the year and there were a total of $n + n = 2n$ members at the beginning of the year. It follows that $(8)(6) = (2n)(1)$, or $n = 24$; SUFFICIENT.

(2) It is given that $n - 3 = 21$, since 3 members from the original n members left the Planning Committee at the end of the year. It follows that $n = 21 + 3 = 24$; SUFFICIENT.

**The correct answer is D;
each statement alone is sufficient.**

368. Some computers at a certain company are Brand X and the rest are Brand Y. If the ratio of the number of Brand Y computers to the number of Brand X computers at the company is 5 to 6, how many of the computers are Brand Y?

(1) There are 80 more Brand X computers than Brand Y computers at the company.

(2) There is a total of 880 computers at the company.

Algebra Simultaneous Equations

Let x be the number of Brand X computers and y be the number of Brand Y computers. We are given that $\frac{y}{x} = \frac{5}{6}$, or $6y = 5x$, and are to determine the value of y.

(1) Given that $x = y + 80$, we have x solved in terms of y. Now replace x with $y + 80$ in the equation $6y = 5x$ to get an equation in which only y appears: $6y = 5(y + 80)$. This linear equation involving only y can be solved for a unique value of y, namely $y = 400$. Alternatively, $x = \left(\frac{6}{5}\right)y = y + \left(\frac{1}{5}y\right)$ and $x = y + 80$, so we have $\left(\frac{1}{5}y\right) = 80$, and hence $y = 400$; SUFFICIENT.

(2) Given that $x + y = 880$, solve for x in terms of y to get $x = 880 - y$. Now replace x with $880 - y$ in the equation $6y = 5x$ to get an equation in which only y appears: $6y = 5(880 - y)$. This linear equation involving only y can be solved for a unique value of y, namely $y = 400$; SUFFICIENT.

Alternatively, in each of (1) and (2), we have two linear equations in two unknowns which, when graphed in the standard xy-coordinate plane, represent two lines having different slopes (hence the lines are not parallel), and therefore the two lines have exactly one point in common. The y-coordinate of that common point is the unique value of y that satisfies both equations.

The correct answer is D;
each statement alone is sufficient.

369. Was the number of books sold at Bookstore X last week greater than the number of books sold at Bookstore Y last week?

(1) Last week, more than 1,000 books were sold at Bookstore X on Saturday and fewer than 1,000 books were sold at Bookstore Y on Saturday.

(2) Last week, less than 20 percent of the books sold at Bookstore X were sold on Saturday and more than 20 percent of the books sold at Bookstore Y were sold on Saturday.

Arithmetic Inequalities

Determine if Bookstore X sold more books last week than Bookstore Y.

(1) This indicates that Bookstore X sold more books on Saturday than Bookstore Y, but it gives no information about the numbers of books sold by the two bookstores on the other days of last week; NOT sufficient.

(2) This gives information about the percents of the books sold last week that were sold on Saturday, but it gives no information about the actual numbers of books sold at the two bookstores last week. Therefore, a comparison of the numbers of books sold last week by Bookstore X and Bookstore Y is not possible; NOT sufficient.

Taking (1) and (2) together, if x represents the number of books that Bookstore X sold on Saturday and T_X represents the total number of books that Bookstore X sold last week, then $x > 1,000$ and $x < 0.2T_X$. It follows that $1,000 < 0.2T_X$, and so $T_X > 5,000$. Similarly, if y represents the number of books that Bookstore Y sold on Saturday and T_Y represents the total number of books that Bookstore Y sold last week, then $y < 1,000$ and $y > 0.2T_Y$. It follows that $0.2T_Y < 1,000$, and so $T_Y < 5,000$. Combining the inequalities gives $T_Y < 5,000 < T_X$, and so $T_Y < T_X$, which means that Bookstore X sold more books last week than Bookstore Y.

The correct answer is C;
both statements together are sufficient.

370. From May 1 to May 30 in the same year, the balance in a checking account increased. What was the balance in the checking account on May 30?

(1) If, during this period of time, the increase in the balance in the checking account had been 12 percent, then the balance in the account on May 30 would have been $504.

(2) During this period of time, the increase in the balance in the checking account was 8 percent.

Arithmetic Applied Problems; Percents

(1) Given that the amount on May 30 would have been \$504 if the increase had been 12%,

it follows that the amount on May 1 was

$\dfrac{504}{1.12}$ = \$450. However, the balance on May 30 cannot be determined because the (actual) percent increase is not given. For example, if the increase had been 10%, then the balance on May 30 would have been (1.1)(\$450) = \$495, which is different from \$504; NOT sufficient.

(2) Given that the increase was 8%, the amount on May 30 could be \$108 (if the amount on May 1 was \$100), and the amount on May 30 could be \$216 (if the amount on May 1 was \$200); NOT sufficient.

Taking (1) and (2) together, it follows that the amount on May 30 was (\$450)(1.08) = \$486.

**The correct answer is C;
both statements together are sufficient.**

371. A merchant discounted the sale price of a coat and the sale price of a sweater. Which of the two articles of clothing was discounted by the greater dollar amount?

(1) The percent discount on the coat was 2 percentage points greater than the percent discount on the sweater.

(2) Before the discounts, the sale price of the coat was \$10 less than the sale price of the sweater.

Arithmetic Applied Problems; Percents

(1) Given that the discount on the coat was 2 percentage points greater than the discount on the sweater, the sweater could have been discounted by the greater dollar amount (\$30 sweater with 10% discount is a discount of \$3; \$20 coat with 12% discount is a discount of \$2.40), and the coat could have been discounted by the greater dollar amount (\$110 sweater with 10% discount is a discount of \$11; \$100 coat with 12% discount is a discount of \$12); NOT sufficient.

(2) Given that the coat's sale price was \$10 less than the sweater's sale price, the same examples used to show that (1) is

not sufficient can be used for (2); NOT sufficient.

Taking (1) and (2) together is of no more help than either (1) or (2) taken separately because the same examples used to show that (1) is not sufficient also show that (2) is not sufficient.

**The correct answer is E;
both statements together are still not sufficient.**

372. If the positive integer n is added to each of the integers 69, 94, and 121, what is the value of n?

(1) $69 + n$ and $94 + n$ are the squares of two consecutive integers.

(2) $94 + n$ and $121 + n$ are the squares of two consecutive integers.

Algebra Computation with Integers

(1) Given that $69 + n$ and $94 + n$ are squares of consecutive integers and differ by 25 (that is, $(94 + n) - (69 + n) = 25$), look for consecutive integers whose squares differ by 25. It would be wise to start with $10^2 = 100$ since $94 + n$ will be greater than 94.

$10^2 = 100$
  } difference is 21
$11^2 = 121$
  } difference is 23
$12^2 = 144$
  } difference is 25
$13^2 = 169$

Then the consecutive integers whose squares differ by 25 are $69 + n = 144$ and $94 + n = 169$. The value of n can be determined from either equation.

To be sure that the value for n is unique, consider algebraically that the difference of the squares of consecutive integers is 25. So, $(x + 1)^2 - x^2 = 25$, from which it follows that $x^2 + 2x + 1 - x^2 = 25$ and $2x + 1 = 25$. This equation has a unique solution; SUFFICIENT.

(2) Given that $94 + n$ and $121 + n$ are squares of consecutive integers and differ by 27 (that is, $(121 + n) - (94 + n) = 27$), look for consecutive integers whose squares differ by 27. It would be wise to start with $12^2 = 144$ since $121 + n$ will be greater than 121.

$12^2 = 144$
} difference is 25
$13^2 = 169$
} difference is 27
$14^2 = 196$

Then the consecutive integers whose squares differ by 27 are $94 + n = 169$ and $121 + n = 196$. The value of n can be determined from either equation; SUFFICIENT.

Tip: Since this and other such problems can be solved quickly using numbers, it might be helpful to have rapid recall of the perfect squares, possibly through 20^2.

The correct answer is D;
each statement alone is sufficient.

373. If a merchant purchased a sofa from a manufacturer for $400 and then sold it, what was the selling price of the sofa?

   (1) The selling price of the sofa was greater than 140 percent of the purchase price.

   (2) The merchant's gross profit from the purchase and sale of the sofa was $\frac{1}{3}$ of the selling price.

Algebra Applied Problems

Letting s represent the selling price of the sofa, in dollars, determine the value of s.

   (1) The condition that the selling price of the sofa was greater than 140 percent of the purchase price is equivalent to $s > 1.4(400)$, from which it is not possible to determine the selling price; NOT sufficient.

   (2) Given that the gross profit from the purchase and sale of the sofa was $\frac{1}{3}$ of the selling price, it follows that $s - 400 = \frac{1}{3}s$, since gross profit is defined to be the selling price minus the purchase price. From this, a unique value of s can be determined; SUFFICIENT.

The correct answer is B;
statement 2 alone is sufficient.

374. Last year, in a certain housing development, the average (arithmetic mean) price of 20 new houses was $160,000. Did more than 9 of the 20 houses have prices that were less than the average price last year?

   (1) Last year, the greatest price of one of the 20 houses was $219,000.

   (2) Last year, the median of the prices of the 20 houses was $150,000.

Arithmetic Statistics

   (1) Given that the greatest of the prices was $219,000, the table below shows two possibilities in which the average price was $160,000.

Example I		Example II	
price	frequency	price	frequency
$101,000	1	$119,000	1
$160,000	18	$159,000	18
$219,000	1	$219,000	1

In Example I, note that $101,000 + 219,000 = 320,000 = 160,000 + 160,000$, so the sum of the prices is $20(\$160,000)$ and the average price is $160,000. Example II is then obtained from Example I by transferring $1,000 from each of the $160,000 prices to the $101,000 price, and thus the sum of the prices in Example II is also $20(\$160,000)$.

Example I shows that only 1 of the prices could have been less than the average price, and Example II shows that 19 of the prices could have been less than the average price; NOT sufficient.

   (2) Given that the median of the 20 prices was $150,000, then when the prices are listed in numerical order from least to greatest, the average of the 10th and 11th prices is $150,000. Therefore, the 10th price must be less than or equal to $150,000, since if the 10th price was greater than $150,000, then both prices would be greater than $150,000 and their average would be greater than $150,000 (the median), contrary to what is given. Moreover, since the first 9 prices are less than or equal to the 10th price, it follows that the first 10 prices are

each less than or equal to $150,000. Therefore, at least 10 of the prices are less than the average price; SUFFICIENT.

**The correct answer is B;
statement 2 alone is sufficient.**

375. For a certain city's library, the average cost of purchasing each new book is $28. The library receives $15,000 from the city each year; the library also receives a bonus of $2,000 if the total number of items checked out over the course of the year exceeds 5,000. Did the library receive the bonus last year?

(1) The library purchased an average of 50 new books each month last year and received enough money from the city to cover this cost.

(2) The lowest number of items checked out in one month was 459.

Arithmetic Applied Problems

(1) Given that the library purchased an average of 50 new books each month, for the entire year the library purchased a total of $(50)(12) = 600$ books for a total cost of $(600)(\$28) = \$16,800$. Excluding any possible bonus, the library received $15,000 from the city. Since this amount received from the city is not enough to cover the cost of the books, and the information provided in (1) says that the total amount received from the city was enough to cover the cost of the books, it follows that the library received a bonus; SUFFICIENT.

(2) Given that the least number of books checked out in one month was 459, it follows that the total number of books checked out for the year was at least $(12)(459) = 5,508$. Since this is greater than 5,000, it follows that the total number of books checked out for the year was greater than 5,000 and the library received a bonus; SUFFICIENT.

**The correct answer is D;
each statement alone is sufficient.**

7, 9, 6, 4, 5, x

376. If x is a number in the list above, what is the median of the list?

(1) $x > 7$

(2) The median of the list equals the arithmetic mean of the list.

Arithmetic Statistics

(1) The given numbers in the list, in order, are 4, 5, 6, 7, 9. From (1), $x > 7$, so the list could be 4, 5, 6, 7, x, 9 or the list could be 4, 5, 6, 7, 9, x. In either case, the two middle numbers are 6 and 7 and the median is $\frac{6+7}{2} = \frac{13}{2}$; SUFFICIENT.

(2) The mean of the list is $\frac{7+9+6+4+5+x}{6} = \frac{31+x}{6}$, which depends on the value of x. Likewise, the median depends on the value of x. If $x = 2$, then the list is 2, 4, 5, 6, 7, 9, which has median $\frac{5+6}{2} = \frac{11}{2}$ and arithmetic mean $\frac{31+2}{6} = \frac{33}{6} = \frac{11}{2}$, thereby satisfying (2). However, if $x = 8$, then the list is 4, 5, 6, 7, 8, 9, which has median $\frac{6+7}{2} = \frac{13}{2}$ and arithmetic mean $\frac{31+8}{6} = \frac{39}{6} = \frac{13}{2}$, thereby satisfying (2); NOT sufficient.

**The correct answer is A;
statement 1 alone is sufficient.**

377. Three dice, each of which has its 6 sides numbered 1 through 6, are tossed. The sum of the 3 numbers that are facing up is 12. Is at least 1 of these numbers 5?

(1) None of the 3 numbers that are facing up is divisible by 3.

(2) Of the numbers that are facing up, 2, but not all 3, are equal.

Arithmetic Properties of Integers

When three dice, each with its 6 faces numbered 1 through 6, are tossed and the sum of the three integers facing up is 12, the possible outcomes are {1, 5, 6}, {2, 4, 6}, {2, 5, 5}, {3, 3, 6}, {3, 4, 5}, and

{4, 4, 4}. Determine if, in the outcome described, at least one of the numbers is 5.

(1) This indicates that none of the numbers is divisible by three. The outcome could be {4, 4, 4}. In this case, none of the three numbers is 5. On the other hand, the outcome could be {2, 5, 5}. In this case, at least one of the numbers is 5; NOT sufficient.

(2) This indicates that two of the numbers, but not all three, are equal. The outcome could be {3, 3, 6}. In this case, none of the three numbers is 5. On the other hand, the outcome could be {2, 5, 5}. In this case, at least one of the numbers is 5; NOT sufficient.

Taking (1) and (2) together, of the possible outcomes, {1, 5, 6}, {2, 4, 6}, {3, 3, 6}, and {3, 4, 5} are eliminated because they do not satisfy (1), and {4, 4, 4} is eliminated because it does not satisfy (2). This leaves only {2, 5, 5}, and at least one number is 5.

**The correct answer is C;
both statements together are sufficient.**

378. Mohit went cycling on 10 consecutive days. Every day he started from Point X, cycled a certain distance in an easterly direction, and then returned to Point X. What is the total distance he covered in those 10 days?

(1) From the second day onward, Mohit covered twice the distance he covered the previous day. On the fifth day, he covered 3.2 km from Point X east, and then back to Point X.

(2) On the first day, Mohit cycled less than 0.3 km.

Applied Problems

A man, Mohit, went cycling for 10 consecutive days. Each day he cycled east, starting from Point X, and back. We are asked to determine his total cycling distance over the 10 days.

(1) On each day successively, Mohit cycled double the previous day's distance. On Day 5, he cycled 3.2 km from Point X east, and then back to Point X, and the total cycling distance on Day 4 was 1.6 km. For the final five days, the distance keeps doubling daily, so, for example, his cycling distance on Day 6 was 6.4 km. The information we have allows

us to calculate the cycling distance on each of the 10 days. Finding the total distance covered in the 10 days is a simple matter of adding the distances for each of the 10 days. (1) is sufficient alone; SUFFICIENT.

(2) This information is not sufficient alone; NOT sufficient.

**The correct answer is A;
statement 1 alone is sufficient.**

379. Candidates A, B, and C competed in an election. This election usually comprises two rounds. In the first round, all three candidates compete. A candidate qualifies for the second round only if he/she receives at least 20% of the votes cast in the first round. If two candidates receive less than 20% of the votes cast, the other candidate wins the election by default. If a candidate receives more than 60% of the votes in the first round, he/she wins the election without the second round. Was there a second round of election?

(1) The votes received by Candidates A and B together is 82% of the total votes cast.

(2) The votes received by Candidates C and B together is 42% of the total votes cast.

Inference

An election had exactly three candidates A, B, and C competing. The election sometimes has two rounds of voting. A candidate who receives less than 20% of the votes cast is eliminated. If all but one candidate is eliminated, there is no second round. A candidate who receives 60% or more of the votes cast in the first round is automatically elected. The question posed is whether there was a second round in the election.

(1) Candidates A and B together got 82% of the votes cast. That means that Candidate C was eliminated from any second round. However, we cannot decide whether another of the candidates was also eliminated; if so, the remaining candidate would have gotten more than 60% of the votes cast and been elected. But if Candidates A and B both got votes exceeding 20% of votes cast, there would be a runoff election. We do not have sufficient information to decide how the 82% of the votes split between Candidates A and B.

So (1) does not provide information sufficient alone to decide whether there was a second round in the election; NOT sufficient.

(2) Candidates C and B together got 42% of the total votes cast. That means that Candidate A got 58% of the votes cast. This means that nobody got 60% of the votes cast, and at least one of Candidate C or Candidate B got 20% or more of the votes cast—in either case, there would be a second round. So (2) is sufficient alone to determine that there was a second round in the election; SUFFICIENT.

**The correct answer is B;
statement 2 alone is sufficient.**

380. There are a certain number of male and female students in a classroom. The weights of the male students range from 80 kg to 85 kg. The weights of the female students range from 70 kg to 75 kg. What is the average (arithmetic mean) weight of all the students in the classroom? All weights are rounded to the nearest 1 kg.

(1) No two students weigh the same.

(2) The number of male students is equal to the number of female students.

Applied Problems

In a classroom of male and female students, weights are recorded to the nearest kilo. Note that we are not told how many students are in the classroom.

(1) No two students have the same recorded weight. This means that the number of males must be 6 or less, and similarly, the number of females must be 6 or less. However, we do not know the total number of students, nor the weights of the students—unless there are exactly 6 males and 6 females. Lacking more specific information, the mean weight of all students in the classroom cannot be calculated. So (1) is not sufficient alone; NOT sufficient.

(2) The number of male students is equal to the number of female students. This does not help us calculate the total number of students in the classroom. And without this information, and without knowing the

distribution of weights, we cannot calculate the mean of the students' weights. So (2) is not sufficient alone; NOT sufficient.

Neither (1) nor (2), whether alone or together, provides enough information about the number of students and distribution of weights.

**The correct answer is E;
both statements together are still not sufficient.**

381. An alloy, Alloy K, is made by mixing certain quantities of iron and lead. The total weight of the alloy is 50 kg. What is the ratio of the weight of iron to the weight of lead in Alloy K?

(1) If 4 kg of iron were to be replaced with 4 kg of lead, the percentage of lead, by weight, in Alloy K would become 40%.

(2) The weight of iron per 100 cc is 0.7 times the weight of lead per 100 cc.

Applied Problems

We are asked to determine the ratio of iron and lead in an alloy weighing 50 kg. We are given a piece of hypothetical information concerning the alloy: what the concentration (i.e., percentage by weight) of lead in the alloy would be if 4 kg of iron were swapped for 4 kg of lead.

(1) If 4 kg of iron in the alloy were to be swapped out for 4 kg of lead, the percentage of lead in the alloy would become 40%. In other words, 0.4 of the alloy would be lead. So there would be 20 kg of lead in the alloy. This means that before the hypothetical swap, there would have been 16 kg of lead and 34 kg of iron. So the ratio of iron to lead in the original alloy was 34:16. This means that (1) is sufficient alone to provide a definitive answer to the question asked; SUFFICIENT.

(2) This information is simply a general fact about iron and lead and does not, by itself, have a bearing on the ratio of iron to lead in Alloy K. So this information is not sufficient alone to answer the question asked; NOT sufficient.

**The correct answer is A;
statement 1 alone is sufficient.**

382. A box contains exactly 40 bottles, each of which contains only one of three types of soda—orange, lemon, and ginger. What is the probability of randomly selecting a ginger soda, without any replacement in the box, on each of 3 consecutive attempts?

    (1) The number of orange sodas is 5 more than the number of ginger sodas.

    (2) The number of ginger sodas is 10 more than the number of lemon sodas.

Evaluation

A box of 40 sodas has 3 flavors, orange, ginger, and lemon, with a different number of sodas in each flavor. How probable is it to randomly select a ginger soda from the box on each of just three consecutive tries? To answer this question, here are pieces of information that will be needed: First, how many ginger sodas are in the box? Second, when a ginger soda is selected from the box, will it be removed and not replaced by a different flavor?

    (1) This information is not sufficient alone to determine the probability, since we don't know how many orange sodas are in the box; NOT sufficient.

    (2) This information is not sufficient alone to determine the number of ginger sodas in the box, since we don't know how many lemon sodas are in the box; NOT sufficient.

Using the information from (1) and (2) combined with the information in the stimulus, we can establish that the number of ginger sodas in the box is 15. When a ginger soda is selected on the first try, the number of ginger sodas left in the box is 14, and there is no addition to the box of a lemon or orange soda. With this information we can calculate the probability of choosing a ginger soda on the first two tries. Given similar information concerning non-replacement—i.e., that 2 ginger sodas chosen on the first two tries would not be replaced by two new sodas, ginger or other—then the probability of choosing 3 ginger sodas on consecutive tries can be calculated. (In that case, the result is $15/40 \times 14/39 \times 13/38$.) So (1) and (2) are sufficient together.

The correct answer is C; both statements together are sufficient.

383. Workers A, B, and C, working at their individual constant rates, can work together and complete a piece of work in 6 days. How long will it take for Workers B and C alone to complete the work?

    (1) Worker A is twice as efficient as Worker B. Worker B is three times as efficient as Worker C.

    (2) The time taken by Worker A to do 9 units of work is the same as the time taken by Workers B and C together to do 6 units of work.

Applied Problems

    (1) This provides the ratio of the three amounts of work completed by each in that 6-day period: A:B:C = 6:3:1. This tells us that in 6 days, Worker A completes 1.5 times the work done by Workers B and C in that time. In other words, Workers B and C working together do 0.4 of all the work done, while Worker A does 0.6 of the work done. For Workers A and B together to do all of the work done by Workers A, B, and C, it will take 2.5 times 6 days, i.e., 15 days. So (1) is sufficient alone to infer an answer to the question asked; SUFFICIENT.

    (2) This provides that Worker A can do 9 units of work in the time that Workers A and B together do 6 units. That is, Worker A does 1.5 times the work that Workers B and C do together in the same time. In other words, we get the ratio in production A:(B + C) = 3:2. So the time it would take Workers B and C together to do all the work is $(5/2 \times 6)$ days, i.e., 15 days. So (2) is sufficient alone to infer an answer to the question asked; SUFFICIENT.

The correct answer is D; each statement alone is sufficient.

384. The students in College X must take two, and no more, of these five subjects: computing, electronics, mechanics, architecture, and psychology. Students who take computing cannot take psychology. Students who take electronics cannot take architecture. Students who take mechanics cannot take electronics. Is Student G, a student at College X, taking psychology?

    (1) Student G is taking architecture as one of her two subjects.

    (2) Student G is taking neither electronics nor computing.

Inference

Every student at College X must take two and no more of the following five subjects: computing, electronics, mechanics, architecture, and psychology. The following constraints apply:

- Students taking computing cannot take psychology.
- Students taking electronics cannot take architecture.
- Students taking mechanics cannot take electronics.

Is Student G at College X taking psychology?

(1) Student G is taking architecture as one of her two required subjects. This implies that she did not take electronics. Given the constraints, she would have taken psychology only if she was not taking computing. But we have no information that she is not taking computing. Therefore, (1) is not sufficient by itself to elicit a definitive answer to the question posed; NOT sufficient.

(2) This provides that Student G is not taking computing. If she were, she would not be free to take psychology. Therefore, (2) is not sufficient alone to elicit a definitive answer to the question posed; NOT sufficient.

The information in (1) and (2) together with the stimulus is not sufficient to provide a definitive answer to the question. (1) tells us neither that Student G is taking psychology nor that she is not. (2) tells us that Student G is free to take psychology, but it tells us neither that she is nor is not taking it.

**The correct answer is E;
both statements together are still not sufficient.**

385. A candy shop owner must mix three types of sweeteners—A, B, and C—in a certain ratio to get the desired mixture in his candies. What is the ratio of the weights of Sweetener A to Sweetener B to Sweetener C in the final mixture?

(1) Sweeteners A, B, and C cost $40, $50, and $60 per pound. The average (arithmetic mean) cost of the final mixture is $50 per pound.

(2) In the final mixture, the average (arithmetic mean) price of Sweeteners A and B together is

$45, and the average (arithmetic mean) price of Sweeteners B and C together is $55.

Applied Problems

Three sweeteners A, B, and C are mixed as ingredients for candy. We are asked to determine the ratio among the weights of each based on information about cost per pound for each of the three ingredients and information about average (arithmetic mean) cost per pound for mixtures of two or three of the ingredients.

(1) This information will not allow us to calculate weights of individual ingredients in the mixture, or even a ratio between individual weights. Therefore, (1) is not sufficient by itself; NOT sufficient.

(2) This information will not allow us to calculate weights of individual ingredients in the mixture or even a ratio between the weights of individual ingredients. Therefore, (2) is not sufficient by itself; NOT sufficient.

If we combine the information provided in (1) and (2), we will be able to calculate the ratio between the weights of each of the three ingredients in the mixture.

Let a be the weight in pounds of Sweetener A, b the weight in pounds of Sweetener B, and c the weight in pounds of Sweetener C. From (1) and (2), we get the following equations:

$$(40a + 50b) = 45(a + b)$$

$$(50b + 60c) = 55(b + c).$$

From the first, we can infer $5b - 5a = 0$, and therefore that $a = b$. Similarly, from the second, we can infer that $b = c$. So $a{:}b{:}c = 1{:}1{:}1$. So (1) and (2) are sufficient together.

**The correct answer is C;
both statements together are sufficient.**

386. A movie theater increased the ticket price for evening shows by 10% and decreased the ticket price for morning shows by 40%. The average number of tickets sold for the morning shows increased by 30% and the average number of tickets sold for the evening shows decreased by 5%. What was the percentage change in total revenue?

(1)   Prior to the changes in ticket prices, the ticket prices for the morning shows and the evening shows were the same.

(2)   Prior to the changes in ticket prices, the ratio between the number of tickets sold for the morning shows and the evening shows was 5:8.

Applied Problems

Two changes are made in a theater's pricing plan for its morning and evening shows. The new plan raises the cost of a ticket for an evening show by 10% and reduces the cost of a ticket for a morning show by 40%. Average attendances at morning shows increased by 30%, and average attendances at evening shows decreased by 5%. These changes affected total revenue. We are asked to determine the net change in revenue that resulted from these changes.

(1)   This provides no information that would tell us, either explicitly or by inference, about the relative sizes of attendances at the morning and evening shows prior to the changes in pricing. To calculate the percentage changes in revenue, we would need such information. Therefore, (1) is not sufficient by itself; NOT sufficient.

(2)   This provides the ratio between total attendances at morning shows and evening shows prior to the changes in pricing, information that is lacking in (1). This information ultimately allows us to calculate a revised ratio for total attendances at morning shows and evening shows after the price changes. However, it lacks another crucial piece of information for calculating the change in total revenue, i.e., the information provided in (1). Therefore (2) is not sufficient by itself; NOT sufficient.

Although neither (1) nor (2) is sufficient alone, the information lacking in (1) is provided in (2), and the information lacking in (2) is provided in (1). Therefore, by combining the information in (1) and (2), the needed calculation can be made.

The correct answer is C; both statements together are sufficient.

387.   George is an employee at a firm. For each day that he is absent, he forfeits 4% of his monthly salary.

For every hour of overtime he does, he receives 1% added to his monthly salary. His salary reduced for the month of June by 5%. How many hours of overtime did George do in that month?

(1)   George was absent for 3 days in the month of June.

(2)   George received 7% of his monthly salary for doing overtime in the month of June.

Applied Problems

For each unpaid absence from work in a given month, an employee, George, loses 4% of his monthly salary. However, for each hour of overtime worked in that month, he can earn an addition of 1% to his salary, which helps to defray some of the salary losses due to absences. In June his monthly salary was reduced by 5%. We need to determine how many overtime hours George worked in June.

(1)   George's absence for 3 days in June would have incurred a salary reduction of 12%. But his total salary reduction was only 5%. The only other way for George to have reduced his net salary loss was by doing overtime. Therefore, George did 7 hours of overtime to defray 7% of the 12% salary loss resulting from unpaid absences. So (1) is sufficient by itself to provide a definitive answer to the question asked; SUFFICIENT.

(2)   Given that each hour of overtime earns an addition of 1% to monthly salary, George must have worked 7 hours of overtime in June. So (2) is sufficient alone; SUFFICIENT.

The correct answer is D; each statement alone is sufficient.

388.   Three teaching assistants—Mike, Rafael, and Joanna—wrote all the questions for the class midterm. If Mike wrote $\frac{1}{3}$ of the questions, what is the number of questions that the three teaching assistants wrote for the midterm?

(1)   Joanna and Rafael wrote a total of 30 questions.

(2)   Joanna wrote $\frac{3}{2}$ the number of questions that Rafael wrote.

Applied Problems

If Mike wrote $\frac{1}{3}$ of the questions, then Joanna and Rafael wrote the other $\frac{2}{3}$. That means together the three teaching assistants wrote $\frac{3}{2}$ the number of questions that Joanna and Rafael wrote. So if Joanna and Rafael wrote a total of 30 questions, then together the three teaching assistants must have written $30 \times \frac{3}{2} = 45$ questions. Thus, statement (1) alone is sufficient to answer the question.

If Mike wrote $\frac{1}{3}$ of the questions, and Joanna wrote $\frac{3}{2}$ the number of questions that Rafael wrote, then we can infer that Joanna wrote $\frac{2}{5}$ of all the questions and Rafael wrote $\frac{4}{15}$ of all the questions. Assuming that none of the teaching assistants wrote just part of a question, we can tell from this that the total number of questions must be a multiple of 15, but we can't tell which multiple of 15 it is. For example, Mike might have written 5 questions, Joanna 6, and Rafael 4. Or Mike might have written 10 questions, Joanna 12, and Rafael 8. So statement (2) alone is not sufficient to answer the question.

The correct answer is A; statement 1 alone is sufficient.

Questions 389 to 436 — Difficulty: Hard

389. Did the population of Town C increase by at least 100 percent from the year 2000 to the year 2010?

   (1) The population of Town C in 2000 was $\frac{2}{3}$ of the population in 2005.

   (2) The population of Town C increased by a greater number of people from 2005 to 2010 than it did from 2000 to 2005.

Algebra Percents

Determine whether the population of Town C increased by at least 100 percent from the year 2000 to the year 2010.

   (1) Given that the population of Town C in 2000 was $\frac{2}{3}$ of the population in 2005, it

is not possible to determine whether the population of Town C increased by at least 100 percent from the year 2000 to the year 2010 because no information is given that helps to determine the population in 2010; NOT sufficient.

   (2) Given that the population of Town C increased by a greater number of people from 2005 to 2010 than it did from 2000 to 2005, it is not possible to determine whether the population of Town C increased by at least 100 percent from the year 2000 to the year 2010 because no information is given that helps determine the increase from 2000 to 2005; NOT sufficient.

Taking (1) and (2) together, from (1) the population in 2000 was $\frac{2}{3}$ of the population in 2005, so if P represents the population in 2005, then the population increase from 2000 to 2005 is $P - \frac{2}{3}P = \frac{1}{3}P$. From (2), the population increase from 2005 to 2010 was greater than $\frac{1}{3}P$, so the population increase from 2000 to 2010 was greater than $\frac{1}{3}P + \frac{1}{3}P = \frac{2}{3}P$. Thus, the percent increase from 2000 to 2010 is given by $\frac{\text{increase in population from 2000 to 2010}}{\text{population in 2000}}$, which is greater than $\frac{\frac{2}{3}P}{\frac{2}{3}P} = 1$ or 100%.

The correct answer is C; both statements together are sufficient.

390. In a survey of 200 college graduates, 30% said they had received student loans during their college careers, and 40% said they had received scholarships. What percent of those surveyed said that they had received neither student loans nor scholarships during their college careers?

   (1) 25% of those surveyed said that they had received scholarships but no loans.

   (2) 50% of those surveyed who said that they had received loans also said that they had received scholarships.

Arithmetic Sets

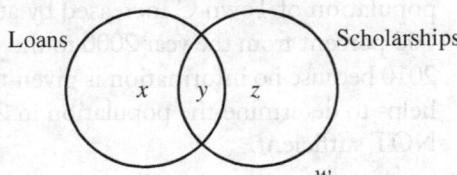

Using the variables shown on the Venn diagram above, determine the value of w. According to the information given, 30% had received student loans, so $x + y = 0.3(200) = 60$ and $x = 60 - y$. Also, 40% had received scholarships, so $y + z = 0.4(200) = 80$ and $z = 80 - y$. Then, since $x + y + z + w = 200$, $w = 200 - x - y - z = 200 - (60 - y) - y - (80 - y) = 60 + y$. Thus, if the value of y can be determined, then the value of w can be determined.

(1) Since 25% received scholarships but no loans, $z = 80 - y = 0.25(200) = 50$ and $y = 30$; SUFFICIENT.

(2) Since 50% of those who had received loans had also received scholarships, $0.5(x + y) = y$ and so $0.5(60) = 30 = y$; SUFFICIENT.

**The correct answer is D;
each statement alone is sufficient.**

391. Stores L and M each sell a certain product at a different regular price. If both stores discount their regular price of the product, is the discount price at Store M less than the discount price at Store L?

(1) At Store L, the discount price is 10 percent less than the regular price; at Store M, the discount price is 15 percent less than the regular price.

(2) At Store L, the discount price is $5 less than the regular store price; at Store M, the discount price is $6 less than the regular price.

Arithmetic Percents

Let L_r and L_d be the regular and discounted prices, respectively, at Store L, and let M_r and M_d be the regular and discounted prices, respectively, at Store M. Determine if $M_d < L_d$.

(1) Knowing that $L_d = (1 - 0.10)L_r = 0.90L_r$ and that $M_d = (1 - 0.15)M_r = 0.85M_r$ gives

no information for comparing M_d and L_d, NOT sufficient.

(2) Knowing that $L_d = L_r - 5$ and that $M_d = M_r - 6$ gives no information for comparing M_d and L_d, NOT sufficient.

Taking (1) and (2) together gives $0.90L_r = L_r - 5$ and $0.85 M_r = M_r - 6$, from which it follows that $0.10L_r = 5$ or $L_r = 50$ and $0.15M_r = 6$ or $M_r = 40$. Then $L_d = 50 - 5 = 45$ and $M_d = 40 - 6 = 34$. Therefore, $M_d < L_d$.

**The correct answer is C;
both statements together are sufficient.**

392. A box contains only red chips, white chips, and blue chips. If a chip is randomly selected from the box, what is the probability that the chip will be either white or blue?

(1) The probability that the chip will be blue is $\frac{1}{5}$.

(2) The probability that the chip will be red is $\frac{1}{3}$.

Arithmetic Probability

(1) Since the probability of drawing a blue chip is known, the probability of drawing a chip that is not blue (in other words, a red or white chip) can also be found. However, the probability of drawing a white or blue chip cannot be determined from this information; NOT sufficient.

(2) The probability that the chip will be either white or blue is the same as the probability that it will NOT be red. Thus, the probability is $1 - \left(\frac{1}{3}\right) = \left(\frac{2}{3}\right)$; SUFFICIENT.

**The correct answer is B;
statement 2 alone is sufficient.**

393. Did the sum of the prices of three shirts exceed $60?

(1) The price of the most expensive of the shirts exceeded $30.

(2) The price of the least expensive of the shirts exceeded $20.

Arithmetic Applied Problems

(1) Given that the price of the most expensive shirt exceeded $30, the sum of the prices of the shirts can be under $60 (if the prices were $10, $10, and $35), and the sum of the prices of the shirts can be over $60 (if the prices were $10, $10, and $50); NOT sufficient.

(2) Given that the price of the least expensive shirt exceeded $20, it follows that the sum of the prices of the shirts exceeds $3($20) = 60; SUFFICIENT.

The correct answer is B; statement 2 alone is sufficient.

394. What is the total number of coins that Bert and Claire have?

(1) Bert has 50 percent more coins than Claire.

(2) The total number of coins that Bert and Claire have is between 21 and 28.

Arithmetic Computation with Integers

Determine the total number of coins Bert and Claire have. If B represents the number of coins that Bert has and C represents the number of coins that Claire has, determine $B + C$.

(1) Bert has 50% more coins than Claire, so $B = 1.5C$, and $B + C = 1.5C + C = 2.5C$, but the value of C can vary; NOT sufficient.

(2) The total number of coins Bert and Claire have is between 21 and 28, so $21 < B + C < 28$ and, therefore, $B + C$ could be 22, 23, 24, 25, 26, or 27; NOT sufficient.

Taking (1) and (2) together, $21 < 2.5C < 28$ and then $\frac{21}{2.5} < C < \frac{28}{2.5}$ or $8.4 < C < 11.2$.

If $C = 9$, then $B = (1.5)(9) = 13.5$; if $C = 10$, then $B = (1.5)(10) = 15$; and if $C = 11$, then $B = (1.5)(11) = 16.5$. Since B represents a number of coins, B is an integer. Therefore, $B = 15$, $C = 10$, and $B + C = 25$.

The correct answer is C; both statements together are sufficient.

395. A telephone station has x processors, each of which can process a maximum of y calls at any particular time, where x and y are positive integers. If 500 calls are sent to the station at a particular time, can the station process all of the calls?

(1) $x = 600$

(2) $100 < y < 200$

Algebra Applied Problems

At a particular time, the telephone station can process a maximum of xy calls, where x and y are positive integers. Determine whether $xy \geq 500$.

(1) Given that $x = 600$, it follows that $xy \geq 600$ since $y \geq 1$ (y is a positive integer); SUFFICIENT.

(2) Given that $100 < y < 200$, $xy < 500$ is possible (if $x = 3$ and $y = 150$), and $xy \geq 500$ is possible (if $x = 10$ and $y = 150$); NOT sufficient.

The correct answer is A; statement 1 alone is sufficient.

	Price per Flower
Roses	$1.00
Daisies	$0.50

396. Kim and Sue each bought some roses and some daisies at the prices shown above. If Kim bought the same total number of roses and daisies as Sue, was the price of Kim's purchase of roses and daisies higher than the price of Sue's purchase of roses and daisies?

(1) Kim bought twice as many daisies as roses.

(2) Kim bought 4 more roses than Sue bought.

Algebra Applied Problems

Let R_K be the number of roses that Kim bought, let R_S be the number of roses that Sue bought, and let T be the total number of roses and daisies each bought. Then Kim bought $(T - R_K)$ daisies and Sue bought $(T - R_S)$ daisies. For the roses and daisies, Kim paid a total of

$\$[R_K + \frac{1}{2}(T - R_K)] = \$\frac{1}{2}(R_K + T)$ and Sue paid a total of $\$[R_S + \frac{1}{2}(T - R_S)] = \$\frac{1}{2}(R_S + T)$. Determine whether $\frac{1}{2}(R_K + T) > \frac{1}{2}(R_S + T)$, or equivalently, determine whether $R_K > R_S$.

(1) Given that $T - R_K = 2R_K$, or $T = 3R_K$, it is not possible to determine whether $R_K > R_S$ because no information is provided about the value of R_S; NOT sufficient.

(2) Given that $R_K = R_S + 4$, it follows that $R_K > R_S$; SUFFICIENT.

**The correct answer is B;
statement 2 alone is sufficient.**

397. Jazz and blues recordings accounted for 6 percent of the $840 million revenue from the sales of recordings in Country Y in 2000. What was the revenue from the sales of jazz and blues recordings in Country Y in 1998?

(1) Jazz and blues recordings accounted for 5 percent of the revenue from the sales of recordings in Country Y in 1998.

(2) The revenue from the sales of jazz and blues recordings in Country Y increased by 40 percent from 1998 to 2000.

Arithmetic Percents

It is given that jazz and blues recordings accounted for 6% of the $840 million revenue of recordings in Country Y in 2000. Determine the revenue from the sales of jazz and blues recordings in 1998.

(1) This indicates that jazz and blues recordings accounted for 5% of the revenue from the sales of recordings in Country Y in 1998. However, no information is given to indicate what the revenue from the sales of recordings was in 1998. Therefore, the revenue from sales of jazz and blues recordings in 1998 cannot be determined; NOT sufficient.

(2) This indicates that the revenue from the sales of jazz and blues recordings in Country Y increased by 40% from 1998 to 2000. Letting R_{1998} and R_{2000} represent the revenue from the sales of jazz and blues recordings in 1998 and 2000,

respectively, then $R_{2000} = 1.4R_{1998}$, and so $(0.06)(\$840 \text{ million}) = 1.4R_{1998}$, from which R_{1998} can be determined; SUFFICIENT.

**The correct answer is B;
statement 2 alone is sufficient.**

398. On a certain nonstop trip, Marta averaged x miles per hour for 2 hours and y miles per hour for the remaining 3 hours. What was her average speed, in miles per hour, for the entire trip?

(1) $2x + 3y = 280$

(2) $y = x + 10$

Algebra Rate Problems

Marta traveled a total of $(2x + 3y)$ miles in $2 + 3 = 5$ hours for an average speed of $\left(\frac{2x + 3y}{5}\right)$ miles per hour. Determine the value of $\frac{2x + 3y}{5}$.

(1) Given that $2x + 3y = 280$, it follows that $\frac{2x + 3y}{5} = \frac{280}{5}$; SUFFICIENT.

(2) Given that $y = x + 10$, it follows that $\frac{2x + 3y}{5} = \frac{2x + 3(x + 10)}{5} = x + 6$. Therefore, the value of $\frac{2x + 3y}{5}$ can be 56 (if $x = 50$ and $y = 60$), and the value of $\frac{2x + 3y}{5}$ can be 61 (if $x = 55$ and $y = 65$); NOT sufficient.

**The correct answer is A;
statement 1 alone is sufficient.**

399. A group consisting of several families visited an amusement park where the regular admission fees were ¥5,500 for each adult and ¥4,800 for each child. Because there were at least 10 people in the group, each paid an admission fee that was 10% less than the regular admission fee. How many children were in the group?

(1) The total of the admission fees paid for the adults in the group was ¥29,700.

(2) The total of the admission fees paid for the children in the group was ¥4,860 more than the total of the admission fees paid for the adults in the group.

Arithmetic Simultaneous Equations

Determine the number of children in a group of at least 10 people who visited an amusement park.

(1) This indicates that $(0.9)(5,500)A = 29,700$, where A represents the number of adults in the group. From this, the number of adults can be determined. However, the number of children in the group cannot be determined without additional information about the exact number of people in the group; NOT sufficient.

(2) If C and A represent the numbers of children and adults, respectively, in the group, this indicates that $(0.9)(4,800)C = (0.9)(5,500)A + 4,860$, or $48C = 55A + 54$, or $48C - 55A = 54$, which is a single equation with two variables from which unique values of C and A cannot be determined, even under the assumptions that C and A are integers such that $C + A \geq 10$. For example, the values of C and A could be 8 and 6, respectively, since $(48)(8) - (55)(6) = 54$, or the values of C and A could be 63 and 54, respectively, since $(48)(63) - (55)(54) = 54$; NOT sufficient.

Taking (1) and (2) together, it follows that

$$A = \frac{29,700}{(0.9)(5,500)} = 6 \text{ and}$$

$$C = \frac{(0.9)(5,500)(6) + 4,860}{(0.9)(4,800)} = 8$$

The correct answer is C; both statements together are sufficient.

400. What is the ratio of the average (arithmetic mean) height of students in Class X to the average height of students in Class Y?

   (1) The average height of the students in Class X is 120 centimeters.

   (2) The average height of the students in Class X and Class Y combined is 126 centimeters.

Arithmetic Statistics

(1) Given that the average height of the students in Class X is 120 cm, but given no information about the average height of the students in Class Y, the desired ratio cannot be determined; NOT sufficient.

(2) Given that the average height of the students in Class X and Class Y combined is 126 cm, the ratio of the averages of the individual classes cannot be determined. For example, if Class X consists of 10 students, each of whom has height 120 cm, and Class Y consists of 10 students, each of whom has height 132 cm, then the average height of the students in Class X and Class Y combined is $\frac{10(120) + 10(132)}{20} = 126$ cm and the ratio of the averages of the individual classes is $\frac{120}{132}$. However, if Class X consists of 10 students, each of whom has height 120 cm, and Class Y consists of 20 students, each of whom has height 129 cm, then the average height of the students in Class X and Class Y combined is $\frac{10(120) + 20(129)}{30} = 126$ cm and the ratio of the averages of the individual classes is $\frac{120}{129}$; NOT sufficient.

Taking (1) and (2) together is of no more help than either (1) or (2) taken separately because the same examples used to show that (2) is not sufficient include the information from (1).

The correct answer is E; both statements together are still not sufficient.

401. Max has $125 consisting of bills each worth either $5 or $20. How many bills worth $5 does Max have?

   (1) Max has fewer than 5 bills worth $5 each.

   (2) Max has more than 5 bills worth $20 each.

Arithmetic Equations

Letting x and y be the numbers, respectively, of $5 bills and $20 bills, it follows from the given information that $5x + 20y = 125$, or equivalently, $x + 4y = 25$. We are to determine the value of x.

(1) Given that $x < 5$ and x is a nonnegative integer, the possible values of x must

be among the integers 0, 1, 2, 3, and 4. Therefore, the possible values of $4y = 25 - x$ must be among the integers 25, 24, 23, 22, and 21. Since y is an integer, $4y$ must also be a multiple of 4, and hence it follows that $4y = 24$. Therefore, $x = 25 - 4y = 25 - 24 = 1$; SUFFICIENT.

(2) Given that $y > 5$, the possible values of y must be among the integers 6, 7, 8, …. Therefore, the possible values of $x = 25 - 4y$ must be among the integers 1, –3, –7, …. Since x is a nonnegative integer and 1 is the only nonnegative integer among the integers 1, –3, –7, …, it follows that $x = 1$; SUFFICIENT.

**The correct answer is D;
each statement alone is sufficient.**

402. At a bakery, all donuts are priced equally and all bagels are priced equally. What is the total price of 5 donuts and 3 bagels at the bakery?

(1) At the bakery, the total price of 10 donuts and 6 bagels is $12.90.

(2) At the bakery, the price of a donut is $0.15 less than the price of a bagel.

Algebra Simultaneous Equations

Let x be the price, in dollars, of each donut and let y be the price, in dollars, of each bagel. Find the value of $5x + 3y$.

(1) Given that $10x + 6y = 12.90$, since

$5x + 3y = \frac{1}{2}(10x + 6y)$, it follows that

$5x + 3y = \frac{1}{2}(12.90)$; SUFFICIENT.

(2) Given that $x = y - 0.15$, then $5x + 3y = 5(y - 0.15) + 3y = 8y - 0.75$, which varies as y varies; NOT sufficient.

**The correct answer is A;
statement 1 alone is sufficient.**

403. Last year, if Arturo spent a total of $12,000 on his mortgage payments, real estate taxes, and home insurance, how much did he spend on his real estate taxes?

(1) Last year, the total amount that Arturo spent on his real estate taxes and home insurance was $33\frac{1}{3}$ percent of the amount that he spent on his mortgage payments.

(2) Last year, the amount that Arturo spent on his real estate taxes was 20 percent of the total amount he spent on his mortgage payments and home insurance.

Arithmetic Applied Problems

Let M, R, and H be the amounts that Arturo spent last year on mortgage payments, real estate taxes, and home insurance, respectively. Given that $M + R + H = 12,000$, determine the value of R.

(1) Given that $R + H = \frac{1}{3}M$ and $M + R + H = 12,000$, then $M + \frac{1}{3}M = 12,000$, or $M = 9,000$. However, the value of R cannot be determined, since it is possible that $R = 2,000$ (use $M = 9,000$ and $H = 1,000$), and it is possible that $R = 1,000$ (use $M = 9,000$ and $H = 2,000$); NOT sufficient.

(2) Given that $R = \frac{1}{5}(M + H)$, or $5R = M + H$ and $M + R + H = 12,000$, which can be rewritten as $(M + H) + R = 12,000$, then $5R + R = 12,000$, or $R = 2,000$; SUFFICIENT.

**The correct answer is B;
statement 2 alone is sufficient.**

404. Is the number of members of Club X greater than the number of members of Club Y?

(1) Of the members of Club X, 20 percent are also members of Club Y.

(2) Of the members of Club Y, 30 percent are also members of Club X.

Arithmetic Sets

(1) Given that 20 percent of the members of Club X are also members of Club Y, these 20 percent could be the only members of Club Y, in which case all the members of Club Y belong to Club X and Club X would have a greater number of members than Club Y. However, these 20 percent could form

only a tiny portion of the members of Club Y and Club Y would have a greater number of members than Club X; NOT sufficient.

(2) Given that 30 percent of the members of Club Y are also members of Club X, these 30 percent could be the only members of Club X, in which case all the members of Club X belong to Club Y and Club Y would have a greater number of members than Club X. However, these 30 percent could form only a tiny portion of the members of Club X and Club X would have a greater number of members than Club Y; NOT sufficient.

Taking (1) and (2) together, the Venn diagram below shows the numbers of members in one or both of Club X and Club Y. For example, b is the number of members of Club X that are also members of Club Y, and b is the number of members of Club Y that are also members of Club X. We are to determine whether $a + b$, the number of members of Club X, is greater than $b + c$, the number of members of Club Y.

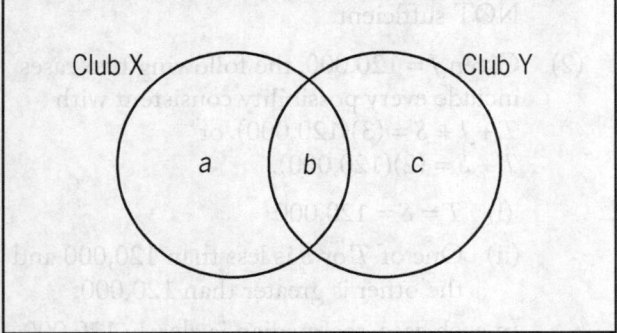

$b = \frac{1}{5}(a + b)$ from (1) and $20\% = \frac{1}{5}$

$5b = a + b$ multiply both sides by 5

$b = \frac{3}{10}(b + c)$ from (2) and $30\% = \frac{3}{10}$

$\frac{10}{3}b = b + c$ multiply both sides by $\frac{10}{3}$

The 2nd equation above says that the number of members of Club X is $5b$ and the 4th equation above says that the number of members of Club Y is $\frac{10}{3}b$. Since 5 is greater than $\frac{10}{3}$, it

follows that the number of members of Club X is greater than the number of members of Club Y.

The correct answer is C; both statements together are sufficient.

405. The only articles of clothing in a certain closet are shirts, dresses, and jackets. The ratio of the number of shirts to the number of dresses to the number of jackets in the closet is 9:4:5, respectively. If there are more than 7 dresses in the closet, what is the total number of articles of clothing in the closet?

(1) The total number of shirts and jackets in the closet is less than 30.

(2) The total number of shirts and dresses in the closet is 26.

Arithmetic Ratio and Proportion

Letting s, d, and j represent, respectively, the numbers of shirts, dresses, and jackets in the closet, then $s = 9x$, $d = 4x$, and $j = 5x$, where x is a positive integer. It is given that $4x > 7$, and so $4x > 8$ or $x \geq 2$ since x is an integer. Determine the value of $9x + 4x + 5x = 18x$.

(1) This indicates that $9x + 5x < 30$, and so $14x \leq 28$ or $x \leq 2$ since x is an integer. It follows from $x \geq 2$ and $x \leq 2$ that $x = 2$ and $18x = 36$; SUFFICIENT.

(2) This indicates that $9x + 4x = 26$ or $13x = 26$, or $x = 2$. It follows that $18x = 36$; SUFFICIENT.

The correct answer is D; each statement alone is sufficient.

406. Material A costs \$3 per kilogram, and Material B costs \$5 per kilogram. If 10 kilograms of Material K consists of x kilograms of Material A and y kilograms of Material B, is $x > y$?

(1) $y > 4$

(2) The cost of the 10 kilograms of Material K is less than \$40.

Algebra Inequalities

Since $x + y = 10$, the relation $x > y$ is equivalent to $x > 10 - x$, or $x > 5$.

(1) The given information is consistent with $x = 5.5$ and $y = 4.5$, and the given information is also consistent with $x = y = 5$. Therefore, it is possible for $x > y$ to be true, and it is possible for $x > y$ to be false; NOT sufficient.

(2) Given that $3x + 5y < 40$, or $3x + 5(10 - x) < 40$, then $3x - 5x < 40 - 50$. It follows that $-2x < -10$, or $x > 5$; SUFFICIENT.

The correct answer is B; statement 2 alone is sufficient.

407. At what speed was a train traveling on a trip when it had completed half of the total distance of the trip?

(1) The trip was 460 miles long and took 4 hours to complete.

(2) The train traveled at an average rate of 115 miles per hour on the trip.

Arithmetic Applied Problems

Determine the speed of the train when it had completed half the total distance of the trip.

(1) Given that the train traveled 460 miles in 4 hours, the train could have traveled at the constant rate of 115 miles per hour for 4 hours, and thus it could have been traveling 115 miles per hour when it had completed half the total distance of the trip. However, the train could have traveled 150 miles per hour for the first 2 hours (a distance of 300 miles) and 80 miles per hour for the last 2 hours (a distance of 160 miles), and thus it could have been traveling 150 miles per hour when it had completed half the total distance of the trip; NOT sufficient.

(2) Given that the train traveled at an average rate of 115 miles per hour, each of the possibilities given in the explanation for (1) could occur, since 460 miles in 4 hours gives an average speed of $\frac{460}{4} = 115$ miles per hour; NOT sufficient.

Assuming (1) and (2), each of the possibilities given in the explanation for (1) could occur. Therefore, (1) and (2) together are not sufficient.

The correct answer is E; both statements together are still not sufficient.

408. Tom, Jane, and Sue each purchased a new house. The average (arithmetic mean) price of the three houses was $120,000. What was the median price of the three houses?

(1) The price of Tom's house was $110,000.

(2) The price of Jane's house was $120,000.

Arithmetic Statistics

Let $T, J,$ and S be the purchase prices for Tom's, Jane's, and Sue's new houses, respectively. Given that the average purchase price is 120,000, or $T + J + S = 3(120,000)$, determine the median purchase price.

(1) Given $T = 110,000$, the median could be 120,000 (if $J = 120,000$ and $S = 130,000$) or 125,000 (if $J = 125,000$ and $S = 125,000$); NOT sufficient.

(2) Given $J = 120,000$, the following two cases include every possibility consistent with $T + J + S = (3)(120,000)$, or $T + S = (2)(120,000)$.

  (i) $T = S = 120,000$

  (ii) One of T or S is less than 120,000 and the other is greater than 120,000.

  In each case, the median is clearly 120,000; SUFFICIENT.

The correct answer is B; statement 2 alone is sufficient.

409. A certain bookcase has 2 shelves of books. On the upper shelf, the book with the greatest number of pages has 400 pages. On the lower shelf, the book with the least number of pages has 475 pages. What is the median number of pages for all of the books on the 2 shelves?

(1) There are 25 books on the upper shelf.

(2) There are 24 books on the lower shelf.

Arithmetic Statistics

(1) The information given says nothing about the number of books on the lower shelf. If there are fewer than 25 books on the lower shelf, then the median number of pages will be the number of pages in one of the books on the upper shelf or the average number of pages in two books on the upper shelf. Hence, the median will be at most 400. If there are more than 25 books on the lower shelf, then the median number of pages will be the number of pages in one of the books on the lower shelf or the average number of pages in two books on the lower shelf. Hence, the median will be at least 475; NOT sufficient.

(2) An analysis very similar to that used in (1) shows the information given is not sufficient to determine the median; NOT sufficient.

Given both (1) and (2), it follows that there is a total of 49 books. Therefore, the median will be the 25th book when the books are ordered by number of pages. Since the 25th book in this ordering is the book on the upper shelf with the greatest number of pages, the median is 400. Therefore, (1) and (2) together are sufficient.

**The correct answer is C;
both statements together are sufficient.**

410. In planning for a trip, Joan estimated both the distance of the trip, in miles, and her average speed, in miles per hour. She accurately divided her estimated distance by her estimated average speed to obtain an estimate for the time, in hours, that the trip would take. Was her estimate within 0.5 hours of the actual time that the trip took?

(1) Joan's estimate for the distance was within 5 miles of the actual distance.

(2) Joan's estimate for her average speed was within 10 miles per hour of her actual average speed.

Arithmetic Applied Problems; Estimating

(1) Given that the estimate for the distance was within 5 miles of the actual distance, it is not possible to determine whether the estimate of the time (that is, the estimated distance divided by the estimated average speed) was within 0.5 hour of the actual time because nothing is known about the estimated average speed; NOT sufficient.

(2) Given that the estimate for the average speed was within 10 miles per hour of the actual average speed, it is not possible to determine whether the estimate of the time (that is, the estimated distance divided by the estimated average speed) was within 0.5 hours of the actual time because nothing is known about the estimated distance; NOT sufficient.

Taking (1) and (2) together, the table below shows two possibilities for the estimated distance, estimated average speed, actual distance, and actual average speed that are consistent with the information given in (1) and (2).

estimated distance	estimated speed	actual distance	actual speed
20 miles	$20 \frac{\text{miles}}{\text{hour}}$	20 miles	$20 \frac{\text{miles}}{\text{hour}}$
20 miles	$20 \frac{\text{miles}}{\text{hour}}$	20 miles	$10 \frac{\text{miles}}{\text{hour}}$

In the first row of the table, the estimate of the time and the actual time are each equal to 1 hour, and so the estimate of the time is within 0.5 hours of the actual time. In the second row of the table, the estimate of the time is 1 hour and the actual time is $\frac{20}{10} = 2$ hours, and so the estimate of the time is not within 0.5 hours of the actual time.

**The correct answer is E;
both statements together are still not sufficient.**

Shipment	S1	S2	S3	S4	S5	S6
Fraction of the Total Value of the Six Shipments	$\frac{1}{4}$	$\frac{1}{5}$	$\frac{1}{6}$	$\frac{3}{20}$	$\frac{2}{15}$	$\frac{1}{10}$

411. Six shipments of machine parts were shipped from a factory on two trucks, with each shipment entirely on one of the trucks. Each shipment was labeled either S1, S2, S3, S4, S5, or S6. The table shows the value of each shipment as a fraction of the total value of the six shipments. If the shipments on the first truck had a value greater than $\frac{1}{2}$ of the total value of the six shipments, was S3 shipped on the first truck?

(1) S2 and S4 were shipped on the first truck.

(2) S1 and S6 were shipped on the second truck.

Arithmetic Operations on Rational Numbers

Given that the shipments on the first truck had a value greater than $\frac{1}{2}$ of the total value of the 6 shipments, determine if S3 was shipped on the first truck.

To avoid dealing with fractions, it will be convenient to create scaled values of the shipments by multiplying each fractional value by 60, which is the least common denominator of the fractions. Thus, the scaled values associated with S1, S2, S3, S4, S5, and S6 are 15, 12, 10, 9, 8, and 6, respectively. The given information is that the scaled value of the shipments on the first truck is greater than $\left(\frac{1}{2}\right)(60) = 30$.

(1) Given that the first truck includes shipments with scaled values 12 and 9, it may or may not be the case that S3 (the shipment with scaled value 10) is on the first truck. For example, the first truck could contain only S2, S3, and S4, for a total scaled value $12 + 10 + 9 = 31 > 30$. Or the first truck could contain only S1, S2, and S4, for a total scaled value $15 + 12 + 9 = 36 > 30$; NOT sufficient.

(2) Given that the second truck includes shipments with scaled values 15 and 6, the second truck cannot contain S3. Otherwise,

the second truck would contain shipments with scaled values 15, 6, and 10, for a total scaled value $15 + 6 + 10 = 31$, leaving at most a total scaled value 29 (which is not greater than 30) for the first truck; SUFFICIENT.

The correct answer is B; statement 2 alone is sufficient.

	Favorable	Unfavorable	Not Sure
Candidate M	40	20	40
Candidate N	30	35	35

412. The table above shows the results of a survey of 100 voters who each responded "Favorable" or "Unfavorable" or "Not Sure" when asked about their impressions of Candidate M and of Candidate N. What was the number of voters who responded "Favorable" for both candidates?

(1) The number of voters who did not respond "Favorable" for either candidate was 40.

(2) The number of voters who responded "Unfavorable" for both candidates was 10.

Arithmetic Sets

Let x, y, and z, respectively, be the numbers of voters who responded "Favorable," "Unfavorable," and "Not Sure" to both candidates. The table below gives a more complete tabulation of the survey results. For example, since 20 voters responded "Unfavorable" for Candidate M and y of those 20 voters also responded "Unfavorable" for Candidate N, it follows that $20 - y$ of those 20 voters responded "Unfavorable" for Candidate M only. Determine the value of x, the number of voters who responded "Favorable" for both candidates.

	Favorable	Unfavorable	Not Sure
M and N	x	y	z
M only	$40 - x$	$20 - y$	$40 - z$
N only	$30 - x$	$35 - y$	$35 - z$

(1) It is given that the number of voters who did not respond "Favorable" for either candidate was 40. Also, from the table above, the number of voters who responded "Favorable" for at least one candidate was $(40 - x) + (30 - x) + x = 70 - x$. Since there were 100 voters, it follows that $(70 - x) + 40 = 100$, which can be solved for a unique value of x; SUFFICIENT.

(2) It is given that the number of voters who responded "Unfavorable" for both candidates was 10, or $y = 10$. However, there is not enough information to determine the value of x. This can be seen by choosing different integer values for x between 0 and 30, inclusive, and using each value to complete the table above (choose $z = 5$ for completeness, for example); NOT sufficient.

The correct answer is A; statement 1 alone is sufficient.

413. A school administrator will assign each student in a group of n students to one of m classrooms. If $3 < m < 13 < n$, is it possible to assign each of the n students to one of the m classrooms so that each classroom has the same number of students assigned to it?

(1) It is possible to assign each of $3n$ students to one of m classrooms so that each classroom has the same number of students assigned to it.

(2) It is possible to assign each of $13n$ students to one of m classrooms so that each classroom has the same number of students assigned to it.

Arithmetic Properties of Numbers

Determine if n is divisible by m.

(1) Given that $3n$ is divisible by m, then n is divisible by m if $m = 9$ and $n = 27$ (note that $3 < m < 13 < n$, $3n = 81$, and $m = 9$, so $3n$ is divisible by m), and n is not divisible by m if $m = 9$ and $n = 30$ (note that $3 < m < 13 < n$, $3n = 90$, and $m = 9$, so $3n$ is divisible by m); NOT sufficient.

(2) Given that $13n$ is divisible by m, then $13n = qm$, or $\dfrac{n}{m} = \dfrac{q}{13}$, for some integer q.

Since 13 is a prime number that divides qm (because $13n = qm$) and 13 does not divide m (because $m < 13$), it follows that 13 divides q.

Therefore, $\dfrac{q}{13}$ is an integer, and since $\dfrac{n}{m} = \dfrac{q}{13}$, then $\dfrac{n}{m}$ is an integer. Thus, n is divisible by m; SUFFICIENT.

The correct answer is B; statement 2 alone is sufficient.

414. At a certain clothing store, customers who buy 2 shirts pay the regular price for the first shirt and a discounted price for the second shirt. The store makes the same profit from the sale of 2 shirts that it makes from the sale of 1 shirt at the regular price. For a customer who buys 2 shirts, what is the discounted price of the second shirt?

(1) The regular price of each of the 2 shirts the customer buys at the clothing store is $16.

(2) The cost to the clothing store of each of the 2 shirts the customer buys is $12.

Arithmetic Applied Problems

Solving this problem relies on the definition of profit: profit = selling price − cost.

(1) Given that the regular price of each of the 2 shirts is $16, the discounted price cannot be uniquely determined because no information is given about the rate of discount, the amount of discount, or the cost; NOT sufficient.

(2) Recall that profit = selling price − cost. Since the store makes the same profit from the sale of 2 shirts as it makes from the sale of 1 shirt at the regular price, the profit from the second shirt is $0. It follows that the selling price (that is, the discounted price) of the second shirt equals its cost.

Given that the cost of each of the shirts is $12, it follows that the discounted price of the second shirt is $12; SUFFICIENT.

The correct answer is B; statement 2 alone is sufficient.

415. What is the median number of employees assigned per project for the projects at Company Z?

    (1) 25 percent of the projects at Company Z have 4 or more employees assigned to each project.

    (2) 35 percent of the projects at Company Z have 2 or fewer employees assigned to each project.

Arithmetic Statistics

(1) Although 25 percent of the projects have 4 or more employees, there is essentially no information about the middle values of the numbers of employees per project. For example, if there were a total of 100 projects, then the median could be 2 (75 projects that have exactly 2 employees each and 25 projects that have exactly 4 employees each) or the median could be 3 (75 projects that have exactly 3 employees each and 25 projects that have exactly 4 employees each); NOT sufficient.

(2) Although 35 percent of the projects have 2 or fewer employees, there is essentially no information about the middle values of the numbers of employees per project. For example, if there were a total of 100 projects, then the median could be 3 (35 projects that have exactly 2 employees each and 65 projects that have exactly 3 employees each) or the median could be 4 (35 projects that have exactly 2 employees each and 65 projects that have exactly 4 employees each); NOT sufficient.

Given both (1) and (2), $100 - (25 + 35)$ percent = 40 percent of the projects have exactly 3 employees. Therefore, when the numbers of employees per project are listed from least to greatest, 35 percent of the numbers are 2 or less and $(35 + 40)$ percent = 75 percent are 3 or less, and hence the median is 3.

The correct answer is C; both statements together are sufficient.

416. Last year, a certain company began manufacturing Product X and sold every unit of Product X that it produced. Last year, the company's total expenses for manufacturing Product X were equal to $100,000 plus 5 percent of the company's total revenue from all units of Product X sold. If the company made a profit on Product X last year, did the company sell more than 21,000 units of Product X last year?

    (1) The company's total revenue from the sale of Product X last year was greater than $110,000.

    (2) For each unit of Product X sold last year, the company's revenue was $5.

Algebra Applied Problems

Recall that Profit = Revenue − Expenses, and for this company, the profit on Product X last year was positive. Then, letting R represent total revenue, in dollars, from all units of Product X sold, profit $= R - (100,000 + 0.05R) = 0.95R - 100,000$. So, $0.95R - 100,000 > 0$.

(1) This says $R > 110,000$ but gives no information on how many units were sold or the price at which they were sold. Therefore, whether the company sold more than 21,000 units cannot be determined; NOT sufficient.

number sold	unit price	R, in dollars	number sold > 21,000?
1,200	$100	120,000	no
22,000	$10	220,000	yes

Note that a calculator is not needed to verify that the profit (which is given in dollars by 95% of $R - 100,000$) is positive for each of these two values of R. For example,

10% of 120,000	=	12,000	move decimal point 1 place to the left
5% of 120,000	=	6,000	5% is $\frac{1}{2}$ of 10%
120,000 − 6,000	=	114,000	$R - 5\%$ of $R =$ 95% of R
114,000 − 100,000	=	14,000	95% of $R - 100,000$

(2)　This says the unit price was $5. If x represents the number of units sold, then $R = 5x$ and, by substitution, the requirement that the profit is positive becomes $0.95(5x) - 100,000 > 0$.

$$
\begin{aligned}
0.95(5x) - 100,000 &> 0 && \text{given} \\
0.95(5x) &> 100,000 && \text{add 100,000 to both sides} \\
0.95x &> 20,000 && \text{divide both sides by 5} \\
x &> \frac{20,000}{0.95} && \text{divide both sides by 0.95} \\
x &> \frac{20,000}{\frac{19}{20}} && 0.95 = \frac{95}{100} = \frac{19}{20} \\
x &> (20,000)\left(\frac{20}{19}\right) && \text{invert divisor and multiply} \\
x &> 20,000 + (20,000)\left(\frac{1}{19}\right) && \frac{20}{19} = 1 + \frac{1}{19} \\
x &> 20,000 + 1,000 && \frac{1}{19} > \frac{1}{20}, (20,000)\left(\frac{1}{20}\right) = 1,000 \\
x &> 21,000 && \text{add}
\end{aligned}
$$

Therefore, the company sold more than 21,000 units; SUFFICIENT.

The correct answer is B; statement 2 alone is sufficient.

417. Beginning in January of last year, Carl made deposits of $120 into his account on the 15th of each month for several consecutive months and then made withdrawals of $50 from the account on the 15th of each of the remaining months of last year. There were no other transactions in the account last year. If the closing balance of Carl's account for May of last year was $2,600, what was the range of the monthly closing balances of Carl's account last year?

(1)　Last year, the closing balance of Carl's account for April was less than $2,625.

(2)　Last year, the closing balance of Carl's account for June was less than $2,675.

Arithmetic Statistics

It is given that the closing balance for May was $2,600 and the closing balance for each month either increases by $120 or decreases by $50 relative to the closing balance for the previous month, depending on when the withdrawals began. Therefore, the closing balance for June was either $2,720 or $2,550, and the closing balance for April was either $2,480 or $2,650. The table below shows these possibilities for 5 of the months that the withdrawals could have begun. The values in the last two rows of the table remain the same for later months that the withdrawals could have begun.

Withdrawals began	Close April	Close May	Close June
Apr 15	$2,650	$2,600	$2,550
May 15	$2,650	$2,600	$2,550
Jun 15	$2,480	$2,600	$2,550
Jul 15	$2,480	$2,600	$2,720
Aug 15	$2,480	$2,600	$2,720

(1) Given that the closing balance for April was less than $2,625, it follows from the table above that the withdrawals could have begun in June or in any later month. For each of these possibilities, the balance at the beginning of January was $2,600 − 5($120) = $2,000, since each of the 5 transactions made before the end of May were $120 deposits. Therefore, the range of the monthly closing balances of the account can vary because the range will depend on how many of the transactions made after May were $120 deposits and how many were $50 withdrawals; NOT sufficient.

(2) Given that the closing balance for June was less than $2,675, it follows from the table above that the withdrawals could have begun in June or in any earlier month. For each of these possibilities, the balance at the end of December was $2,600 − 7($50) = $2,250, since each of the 7 transactions made after the end of May were $50 withdrawals. Therefore, the range of the monthly closing balances of the account can vary because the range will depend on how many of the transactions made before May were $120 deposits and how many were $50 withdrawals; NOT sufficient.

Taking (1) and (2) together, withdrawals started in June or later by (1) and withdrawals started in June

or earlier by (2), so withdrawals started in June. Therefore, each of the monthly closing balances of the account is known, and thus the range of these monthly closing balances can be determined.

The correct answer is C; both statements together are sufficient.

418. What amount did Jean earn from the commission on her sales in the first half of 1988?

(1) In 1988, Jean's commission was 5 percent of the total amount of her sales.

(2) The amount of Jean's sales in the second half of 1988 averaged $10,000 per month more than in the first half.

Arithmetic Applied Problems

Let A be the amount of Jean's sales in the first half of 1988. Determine the value of A.

(1) If the amount of Jean's sales in the first half of 1988 was $10,000, then her commission in the first half of 1988 would have been (5%)($10,000) = $500. On the other hand, if the amount of Jean's sales in the first half of 1988 was $100,000, then her commission in the first half of 1988 would have been (5%)($100,000) = $5,000; NOT sufficient.

(2) No information is given that relates the amount of Jean's sales to the amount of Jean's commission; NOT sufficient.

Given (1) and (2), from (1) the amount of Jean's commission in the first half of 1988 is (5%)A. From (2) the amount of Jean's sales in the second half of 1988 is A + $60,000. Both statements together do not give information to determine the value of A.

The correct answer is E; both statements together are still not sufficient.

419. In a certain business, production index p is directly proportional to efficiency index e, which is in turn directly proportional to investment index i. What is p if i = 70?

(1) e = 0.5 whenever i = 60.

(2) p = 2.0 whenever i = 50.

Arithmetic Proportions

(1) This gives only values for e and i, and, while p is directly proportional to e, the nature of this proportion is unknown. Therefore, p cannot be determined; NOT sufficient.

(2) Since p is directly proportional to e, which is directly proportional to i, then p is directly proportional to i. Therefore, the following proportion can be set up: $\frac{p}{i} = \frac{2.0}{50}$. If $i = 70$, then $\frac{p}{70} = \frac{2.0}{50}$. Through cross multiplying, this equation yields $50p = 140$, or $p = 2.8$; SUFFICIENT.

The preceding approach is one method that can be used. Another approach is as follows: It is given that $p = Ke = K(Li) = (KL)i$, where K and L are the proportionality constants, and the value of $70KL$ is to be determined. Statement (1) allows us to determine the value of L but gives nothing about K, and thus (1) is not sufficient. Statement (2) allows us to determine the value of KL, and thus (2) is sufficient.

The correct answer is B; statement 2 alone is sufficient.

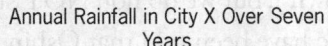

Annual Rainfall in City X Over Seven Years

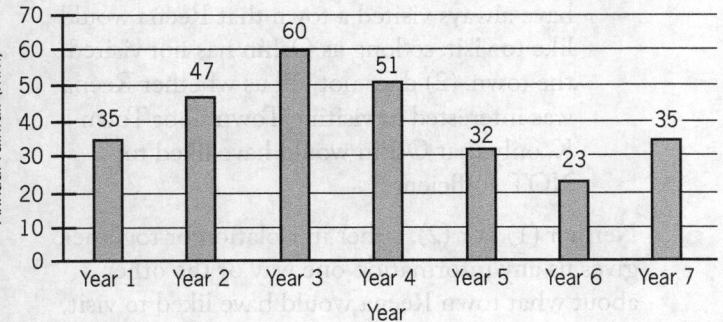

420. The annual rainfall in a city over the past 50 years is its historical average rainfall (HAR). The graph above shows the annual rainfall in City X over a seven-year period. All figures are rounded to the nearest integer.

Is it true that the rounded historical average rainfall (HAR) for City X over the past 50 years is 47 mm or greater?

(1) In the seven-year period in City X, the annual rainfall was greater than the HAR in exactly two of the consecutive years.

(2) In the seven-year period in City X, the annual rainfall was less than the HAR in exactly four of the years.

Inference

(1) According to this statement, in the seven-year period in City X depicted in the graph—a period that falls sometime during the past 50 years—the average annual rainfall was greater than the HAR in only two consecutive years. Those two years must be years 3 and 4, because they are the two years with the greatest annual rainfall. That means that none of the remaining years' average annual rainfalls was greater than the rounded HAR. It can be inferred, then, that the rounded HAR for City X over the past 50 years was at least as great as the average annual rainfall of year 2, that is, 47 mm; SUFFICIENT.

(2) According to this statement, in the seven-year period in City X depicted in the graph—a period that falls sometime during the past 50 years—the average annual rainfall was less than the HAR in exactly four of the years. It can be inferred that those years are years 1, 5, 6, and 7, so the rounded HAR must be at least 36 but no more than 47. Thus, we can infer that the HAR may, but need not be, as great as 47 mm; NOT sufficient.

The correct answer is A; statement 1 alone is sufficient.

421. Five coffee-chicory blends—J, K, L, M, and N—are all priced differently. The blends are such that the greater the proportion of coffee, the more expensive the blend, and the greater the proportion of chicory, the stronger the flavor of the blend. If the five blends were ranked in order of cost per kilogram, which would fall in the middle?

(1) Blend L has a higher proportion of coffee than the other blends except for Blend M.

(2) Blend K and Blend N both have a stronger flavor than Blend J.

Inference

From the stimulus we know that there are five different coffee-chicory blends, J, K, L, M, and

N, and they are differentiated by their relative proportions of coffee to chicory. The greater the proportion of coffee, the greater the price. The greater the proportion of chicory, the stronger the flavor and the less the proportion of coffee. We are told that no two blends have the same prices. We can infer that no two blends are equally strong in flavor. Given those two inferences, we can also infer that the stronger the flavor, the less expensive the blend.

(1) We can infer that Blend M is the most expensive blend and Blend L is the next most expensive. We can infer that Blends J, K, and N are the three least expensive (and thus the three strongest in flavor), but we do not know in what order, so we don't know which would fall in the middle if the five blends were ranked in order of cost per kilogram; NOT sufficient.

(2) We can infer that Blend K and Blend N have stronger flavors than Blend J, and thus are less expensive than Blend J. Therefore, Blend J could be either the most, second-most, or third-most expensive, and thus Blend J might fall in the middle if the five blends were ranked in order of cost per kilogram, but the information in the stimulus and (2) is not sufficient to determine whether it does fall in the middle; it could also be the most or second-most expensive; NOT sufficient.

From the stimulus and (1), we can infer that Blend J is either the third-most, fourth-most, or fifth-most expensive blend. Also, from the stimulus and (2), we can infer that Blend J is either the most, second-most, or third-most expensive blend. Therefore, from the stimulus and (1) and (2) taken together, we can infer that Blend J is the third-most expensive blend, which means that it would fall in the middle if the five blends were ranked in order of cost per kilogram.

The correct answer is C; both statements together are sufficient.

422. Last summer, as with every summer, Oshin and Reena made exactly one long trip together to a town neither of them had visited before. For their long summer trips, Oshin and Reena have always chosen to visit a town that Reena would have liked to visit—unless Oshin had been to that town before. Reena had visited Town F and Town G before, and Oshin had never visited Town J or Town K. Did Oshin and Reena visit one of these four towns last summer?

(1) Reena had never visited Town J, and Oshin had never visited Town F.

(2) Oshin would have liked to visit either Town G or Town K.

Inference

We can infer that they did NOT visit Town F or Town G, because the town they visited had never been visited by either one of them, and Reena had visited Towns F and G. We are told in the stimulus that Oshin has never visited Town J or Town K, but we are not told whether Reena has visited them or has any interest in visiting them.

(1) We already know that Oshin and Reena did not visit Town F (because the prior information had told us that Reena had visited there before). This statement neither rules out nor supports that Oshin and Reena visited Town J. We would need to know whether Reena was interested in visiting Town J, but we do not; NOT sufficient.

(2) We have been told that Oshin and Reena have always visited a town that Reena would like to visit, so long as Oshin has not visited the town. (2) does not tell us whether Reena was interested in visiting Town G or Town K, only that Oshin would have liked to; NOT sufficient.

Neither (1) nor (2), either in isolation or together, gives us any information one way or the other about what town Reena would have liked to visit, but that is information that we would need to answer the question, so statements 1 and 2 taken together are not sufficient.

The correct answer is E; both statements together are still not sufficient.

423. For a new project, an organization is creating a three-member team from among its employees. Selection of members for the team conforms to exactly two rules: no selected member can be working on more than one other project at the time of selection, and at least one

of the selected members must have an MBA degree. The organization has selected Paula and Quincy for the team. Neither of these will be replaced before the third member is selected. The organization is about to make the third selection. If the organization adheres to the selection rules for committee membership, is it possible that Rubin will be selected for the team?

(1) Quincy has an MBA degree, and Rubin is currently working on only one other project.

(2) Rubin is one of only two employees in the organization who have an MBA degree.

Inference

Paula and Quincy were selected to be members, and they remain, on the team. Given the two selection rules, it will be possible for Rubin to be selected so long as he is working on no more than one other project at the time he is selected and either he or at least one of the two already-selected members has an MBA.

(1) This statement informs us that the two requirements are met, namely, that either Rubin or one of the already-selected members has an MBA (we are told Quincy has one) and that Rubin is currently working on only one other project; SUFFICIENT.

(2) This statement informs us that one of the two requirements will be met if Rubin is selected—Rubin has an MBA—but we do not know from this statement alone whether Rubin meets the other requirement for his selection, namely, whether he is working on at most one other project; NOT sufficient.

The correct answer is A; statement 1 alone is sufficient.

424. All the T-shirts a clothing store stocks are plain, and they are all in one of exactly four colors: blue, green, red, and yellow. On any given day, the store sells about twice as many blue T-shirts as it does green T-shirts. Last week, did the store sell more blue T-shirts than red T-shirts?

(1) Last week, the store sold fewer blue T-shirts than red T-shirts and green T-shirts combined.

(2) Last week, the store sold more blue T-shirts than half the total number of red T-shirts and yellow T-shirts combined.

Inference

All the information we are given is that the store sells only blue, green, red, and yellow T-shirts and on any given day it sells about twice as many blue T-shirts as green T-shirts.

(1) From (1) we can infer only that last week the store sold at least slightly more red T-shirts than green T-shirts, but this is compatible with the store having sold anywhere from only slightly more red T-shirts than half the number of blue T-shirts it sold to many more red T-shirts than blue T-shirts; NOT sufficient.

(2) From (2) we can infer only that the store sold at most roughly twice as many red T-shirts as blue T-shirts (in which case the number of yellow T-shirts sold would be close to zero). But (2) is also compatible with the store having sold only as many red T-shirts as a tiny fraction of the number of blue T-shirts it sold, so long as the number of yellow T-shirts was sufficiently great; NOT sufficient.

From (1) and (2) combined, we can infer only that the number of red T-shirts sold last week was somewhere in the range of approximately one-half the number of blue T-shirts sold to approximately twice the number of blue T-shirts sold.

The correct answer is E; both statements together are still not sufficient.

Month	Forecast for Units of Product Z
January	12
February	16
March	16
April	20
May	20
June	24

425. The table above shows the sales forecast from January to June of last year, by the sales team of Company X, for the number of units of Product Z each month.

Was the actual number of units of Product Z sold in March less than the number sold in April?

(1) Twelve units of Product Z were sold in March.

(2) From January through June of last year, there was a constant, linear relationship between the forecast and actual number of units of Product Z sold.

Inference

Note that the graph only tells us what the sales team had forecast for March and April (16 and 20 units sold, respectively), not the actual units sold.

(1) This statement tells us only the actual number of units sold in March but nothing about the actual number of units sold in April. If the actual sales varied from the forecast sales in a random way from month to month, then it is possible that March's sales were less than, more than, or the same as April's sales; NOT sufficient.

(2) Because this statement tells us that there is an unchanging linear relationship between the forecast and the actual number of units of Product Z sold through the months given in the graph, we know that for any month X given in the graph, if another month Y was forecast to have lower sales than X, then the actual sales of Y were lower than the sales of X. Therefore, since the forecast for units sold for March was lower than the forecast for units sold for April, then the actual sales

for March were lower than the actual sales for April; SUFFICIENT.

The correct answer is B; statement 2 alone is sufficient.

426. Chris was in an electronic appliances store to buy an LED computer monitor. Chris's purchase criteria included screen size, which must be at least 32 inches, and price, which must not exceed $400. A friend made two recommendations: Monitor A and Monitor B. Chris liked both monitors. Did Chris more likely buy Monitor A, Monitor B, or neither?

(1) Monitor A's screen size was more than 32 inches, and it cost less than Monitor B.

(2) Monitor B cost $390, and its screen size was less than that of Monitor A.

Inference

Chris is in a store shopping for an LED computer monitor that must meet at least two criteria—the monitor must have a screen size of at least 32 inches and cost no more than $400. Note that we are not told whether these are Chris's only two criteria; there may be others. Chris likes both Monitor A and Monitor B, so presumably they both meet his criteria regarding screen size and price.

(1) From this statement we can be certain that Monitor A's screen size is sufficiently large, but we cannot infer from it whether Monitor A meets Chris's price requirement. We cannot infer anything about Monitor B's screen size, and it may or may not be the case that its screen size is enough larger than Monitor A's that Chris would be willing to pay more for it, assuming neither monitor is more than $400; NOT sufficient.

(2) From this statement we can conclude that Monitor B meets Chris's price criterion, but it does not allow us to infer anything about Monitor A's price—though it does inform us that Monitor B has a smaller screen size than Monitor A. It does not, however, give us information sufficient to infer whether either of the monitors meets his screen size requirement; NOT sufficient.

It might seem that from (1) and (2) taken together, we can infer that Chris would prefer Monitor A to Monitor B and would therefore choose to purchase Monitor A. After all, we can infer from those statements together that Monitor A meets both the screen size requirement and the price requirement (because we can infer that Monitor A costs less than $390) and that Monitor A is both larger and less expensive than Monitor B. But remember that there may be other criteria that Chris may use for assessing which monitor to purchase besides the two criteria mentioned, which might make Monitor B preferable to Monitor A. Furthermore, none of the given information confirms that Monitor A or Monitor B are LED monitors, the kind we are told Chris desires. Furthermore, there may be a third monitor that Chris would choose over either of these two, in which case Chris might be likely to purchase neither. Therefore, (1) and (2) taken together are not sufficient.

The correct answer is E; both statements together are still not sufficient.

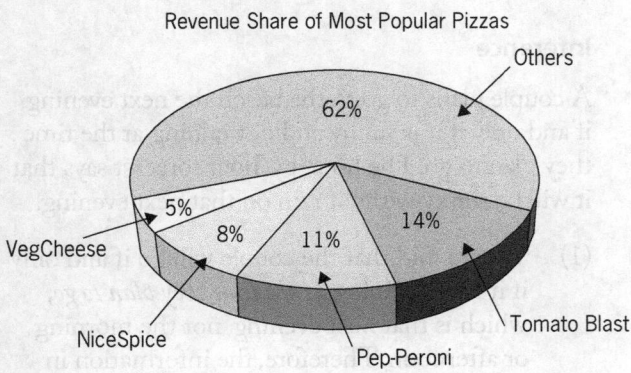

Revenue Share of Most Popular Pizzas

427. A certain pizzeria has more than fifty types of pizza on its menu. The chart above shows the revenue share, in the pizzeria's total revenue in the last month, of its four most popular pizza types. Each pizza type has only a single size and a single price.

Which was their best-selling pizza last month in terms of number of pizzas sold?

(1) The number of customers who ordered at least one Pep-Peroni pizza last month was greater than the number of customers who ordered at least one of any other pizza type last month.

(2) The lowest-priced pizza type on the pizzeria's menu is Tomato Blast, followed by VegCheese.

Inference

The graph shows the revenue share of the pizzeria's total revenue in the last month of its four most popular types. Each type of pizza has only a single size and a single price, but note that nothing in the initially given information indicates how the prices of the various types of pizza relate to one another—for instance, do all the types have the same price or not, and if not, which type is most expensive? Therefore, even though the graph shows that revenue from sales of Tomato Blast made up the greatest share of the total revenue, it is possible that Tomato Blast was not the best-selling pizza last month in terms of number of pizzas sold.

(1) This statement does not allow us to answer the question, because it does not tell us whether the average number of Pep-Peroni pizzas ordered per customer was greater than, less than, or the same as the average number of other types. Therefore, though it is possible that Pep-Peroni was the best-selling pizza last month (in which case Pep-Peroni pizzas must be less expensive than Tomato Blast pizzas), it might not be, if the average number of Pep-Peroni pizzas ordered by customers who bought at least one was less than the average number of pizzas of some other type ordered by customers who bought that type; NOT sufficient.

(2) If Tomato Blast is the lowest-priced pizza type, and yet (as the graph shows) revenue from its sales made up the largest share of total revenue, clearly more Tomato Blast pizzas were sold than any other type of pizza; SUFFICIENT.

The correct answer is B; statement 2 alone is sufficient.

428. In any twenty-four-hour period, a certain faulty clock gains anywhere from one second to a maximum of three minutes. The clock did not stop or lose time since noon the day before yesterday. At exactly noon today, did the clock show the correct time to an accuracy of five minutes?

    (1) The clock was set to the correct time the day before yesterday at exactly noon.
    (2) At exactly noon yesterday, the clock was set back by one minute.

Inference

The clock in question gains anywhere from one second to three minutes in any 24-hour period. Given that we know that the clock never stopped or lost time since noon the day before yesterday, we can answer the question if we could know whether the clock was any more than 5 minutes and one second slow at noon yesterday or any more than two minutes fast at noon yesterday.

    (1) From this statement we only know that the clock could be as much as six minutes fast—in which case the answer to the question is "No." But nothing rules out that the clock gained only, for instance, two seconds, or that at some point in the past 48 hours someone manually changed the time on the clock; NOT sufficient.

    (2) Without the information given in (1), (2) does not help determine an answer to the question, because we do not know what time was on the clock immediately prior to its being reset at noon yesterday. If, for instance, the clock was one minute fast just before noon yesterday, then at most the clock would be three minutes fast at noon today, and the answer would be "Yes." But if the clock at just before noon yesterday was, for instance, four minutes fast, then the clock at noon today could have been as much as six minutes fast, in which case that answer would be "No"; NOT sufficient.

From (1) and (2), we can infer that, as of just before noon yesterday, the clock was at least one second fast and at most three minutes fast. Therefore, when the clock was set back one minute at noon, the clock could have been anywhere from fifty-nine seconds slow to two minutes fast. Therefore, because the clock would have gained a minimum of one second and a maximum of three minutes between noon yesterday and noon today, we can infer that at most the clock was fifty-eight seconds slow and at most five minutes fast at noon today. Given that range, we can infer that at noon today, the clock showed the correct time to an accuracy of five minutes, and thus the answer to the question is "Yes," which makes both statements together sufficient.

**The correct answer is C;
both statements together are sufficient.**

429. The couple decide one day that they will definitely go to the beach the next evening if it is sunny without rain at the time they plan to go, and that they will definitely not go if such is not the case. The next morning, the hour-by-hour weather forecast says that in the evening, it will be sunny without rain. Will the couple go to the beach that evening?

    (1) It is raining on the morning and in the afternoon of the day of their planned beach outing.
    (2) The couple always believe that the weather forecast is likely to be accurate.

Inference

A couple plans to go to the beach the next evening if and only if it is sunny and not raining at the time they plan to go. The hour-by-hour forecast says that it will be sunny without rain on that next evening.

    (1) We are told that the couple will go if and only if it is not raining *at the time they plan to go*, which is that next evening, not the morning or afternoon. Therefore, the information in this statement is irrelevant; NOT sufficient.

    (2) The couple may always believe that the forecast is likely to be accurate, and maybe it is *likely* to be accurate. But that does not mean that it will be accurate this time. Perhaps it will turn out to be one of the rare times when the forecast is inaccurate. The stimulus says that the couple will go if, but only if, it actually is sunny without rain *at the time they plan to go*, not if they have believed on the basis of an earlier forecast that it will not be raining; NOT sufficient.

We cannot infer from (1) and (2) taken together whether or not it is actually sunny and not raining at the time they plan to go to the beach that evening. Therefore, (1) and (2) taken together are not sufficient.

The correct answer is E; both statements together are still not sufficient.

430. A small library has books on twenty different subjects including, most prominently, history. One afternoon, a librarian arbitrarily picks up 100 books for reshelving from among the books returned that day. All the books returned that day were borrowed during the past three weeks. Are fewer than 20 percent of the books the librarian picks up on history?

    (1) Fewer than 20 percent of the books in the library are on history.
    (2) During the past three weeks, exactly 15 books on history were borrowed from the library.

Inference

Are fewer than 20 percent of the 100 books that the librarian has arbitrarily picked up to reshelve—all of which had been returned that day—on history? Note that all the books returned that day had been borrowed during the past three weeks.

(1) Nothing in the stimulus or (1) tells us whether the distribution of subject matter of the books that were returned that day was representative of the distribution of subject matter of the library in general; NOT sufficient.

(2) If during the past three weeks exactly 15 books on history were borrowed from the library, as this statement indicates, and all books returned to the library that day had been borrowed during the past three weeks, it follows that at most 15—and perhaps even none—of the 100 books that the librarian picked up to reshelve were on history. Therefore, no more than 15 percent of those books are on history; SUFFICIENT.

The correct answer is B; statement 2 alone is sufficient.

Topic	Alex	Beika	Carlos	Deepa
History	X	X	✓	X
Humor	X	✓	X	✓
Language	X	X	✓	✓
Philosophy	✓	✓	✓	X
Science Fiction	✓	X	✓	✓

431. Four book lovers have recently met and are not sure of the topics that interest the others. The table above indicates the topics that interest each of them with check marks and those that do not with cross marks (Xs).

One of these persons will gift another of these persons two books, each on a different one of the listed topics. Will at least one of the two books fall under the recipient's broad topic of interest?

    (1) One topic is science fiction and the other is humor.
    (2) The intended recipient is Carlos.

Inference

The chart lists four book lovers and the book topics that interest them. None of these book lovers knows what topics interest the others, but one of the book lovers gifts another one of them two books, each on a different one of the topics.?

(1) One of the two topics is science fiction and the other is humor. Each of the potential recipients is interested in science fiction except for Beika, but Beika is interested in humor. Therefore, no matter which book lover is the recipient, at least one of the two books is on one of the potential recipient's topics of interest; SUFFICIENT.

(2) This tells us that Carlos is the intended recipient, and the chart shows that Carlos is interested in all the topics except for humor. So even if one of the two topics is humor, whatever the other topic is, it will be among the recipient's—i.e., Carlos's—topics of interest; SUFFICIENT.

The correct answer is D; each statement alone is sufficient.

432. In a gas sample, there are, rounded to the nearest order of magnitude (that is, to the nearest power of 10), approximately 10^{21} molecules of H_2 and also 10^{21} molecules of O_2. What is the combined number of H_2 and O_2 molecules in the gas sample, rounded to the nearest order of magnitude?

(1) The number of H_2 molecules and the number of O_2 molecules are each less than 3×10^{21}.

(2) The number of H_2 molecules is more than twice the number of O_2 molecules.

Arithmetic Exponents

We are given that the number of H_2 molecules is greater than 5×10^{20} and the number of O_2 molecules is greater than 5×10^{20}. Therefore, the combined number of molecules is greater than 1×10^{21}, and hence the combined number of molecules is greater than 10^{20} when rounded to the nearest order of magnitude. We are to determine the combined number of molecules when rounded to the nearest order of magnitude.

(1) We are given that each of the numbers of H_2 molecules and O_2 molecules is less than 3×10^{21}. It is possible that the combined number of molecules is 10^{21} when rounded to the nearest order of magnitude. For example, if there are 2×10^{21} molecules of each type, then the combined number of molecules is 4×10^{21}, which when rounded to the nearest order of magnitude is 10^{21}. On the other hand, it is possible that the combined number of molecules is 10^{22} when rounded to the nearest order of magnitude. For example, if there are 2.8×10^{21} molecules of each type, then the combined number of molecules is 5.6×10^{21}, which when rounded to the nearest order of magnitude is 10^{22}; NOT sufficient.

(2) We are given that the number of H_2 molecules is more than twice the number of O_2 molecules. It is possible that the combined number of molecules is 10^{21} when rounded to the nearest order of magnitude. For example, if there are 2×10^{21} molecules of H_2 and 6×10^{20} molecules of O_2 (note that each rounded to the nearest order of magnitude is 10^{21}), then the number of H_2 molecules is more

than twice the number of O_2 molecules, and the combined number of molecules is 2.6×10^{21}, which when rounded to the nearest order of magnitude is 10^{21}. On the other hand, it is possible that the combined number of molecules is 10^{22} when rounded to the nearest order of magnitude. For example, if there are 4.5×10^{21} molecules of H_2 and 2×10^{21} molecules of O_2 (note that each rounded to the nearest order of magnitude is 10^{21}), then the number of H_2 molecules is more than twice the number of O_2 molecules, and the combined number of molecules is 6.5×10^{21}, which when rounded to the nearest order of magnitude is 10^{22}; NOT sufficient.

Taking (1) and (2) together, from (1) we know the number of H_2 molecules is less than 3×10^{21}, and from (2) we know the number of O_2 molecules is less than 1.5×10^{21}. Therefore, the combined number of molecules is less than 4.5×10^{21}, which is less than 10^{22} when rounded to the nearest order of magnitude. We also know from above (before (1) or (2) is considered) that the combined number of molecules is greater than 10^{20} when rounded to the nearest order of magnitude. Since the combined number of molecules, when rounded to the nearest order of magnitude, is less than 10^{22} and greater than 10^{20}, it follows that the combined number of molecules is 10^{21} when rounded to the nearest order of magnitude.

The correct answer is C; both statements together are sufficient.

433. On Jane's credit card account, the average daily balance for a 30-day billing cycle is the average (arithmetic mean) of the daily balances at the end of each of the 30 days. At the beginning of a certain 30-day billing cycle, Jane's credit card account had a balance of $600. Jane made a payment of $300 on the account during the billing cycle. If no other amounts were added to or subtracted from the account during the billing cycle, what was the average daily balance on Jane's account for the billing cycle?

(1) Jane's payment was credited on the 21st day of the billing cycle.

(2) The average daily balance through the 25th day of the billing cycle was $540.

Algebra Statistics

(1) It is given that the $300 payment was credited on the 21st day of the billing cycle. Thus, the 30 daily balances consisted of 20 daily balances of $600 followed by 10 daily balances of $300, and hence the average daily balance for the 30-day billing cycle was $\frac{(20)(\$600) + (10)(\$300)}{30} =$ $(20)(\$20) + (10)(\$10) = \$500$; SUFFICIENT.

(2) It is given that the average daily balance through the 25th day of the billing cycle was $540. If n is the number of days of the billing cycle before the $300 payment was credited, then the 25 daily balances consisted of n daily balances of $600 followed by $(25 - n)$ daily balances of $300. Since the average of these 25 daily balances was $540, it follows that $\frac{(n)(\$600) + (25 - n)(\$300)}{25} =$ 540, which can be solved to obtain $n = 20$. Therefore, the $300 payment was credited on the 21st day of the billing cycle, and the same calculation used to evaluate (1) above shows the average daily balance for the 30-day billing cycle was $500; SUFFICIENT.

**The correct answer is D;
each statement alone is sufficient.**

434. The annual rent collected by a corporation from a certain building was x percent more in 1998 than in 1997 and y percent less in 1999 than in 1998. Was the annual rent collected by the corporation from the building more in 1999 than in 1997?

(1) $x > y$

(2) $\frac{xy}{100} < x - y$

Algebra Percents

We are given that the rent collected increased by $x\%$ from 1997 to 1998 and decreased by $y\%$ from 1998 to 1999. Therefore, if the rent collected in 1997 was R, then the rent collected in 1998 was $(\$R)\left(1 + \frac{x}{100}\right)$ and the rent collected in 1999 was $(\$R)\left(1 + \frac{x}{100}\right)\left(1 - \frac{y}{100}\right)$. Expanding this last expression, the rent collected in 1999 was

$(\$R)\left(1 + \frac{x - y}{100} - \frac{xy}{10,0000}\right)$, which is greater than R—the rent collected in 1997—if and only if $\frac{x - y}{100} - \frac{xy}{10,000} > 0$.

(1) Given that $x > y$, we have $\frac{x - y}{100} > 0$, but it is not possible to determine whether $\frac{x - y}{100} - \frac{xy}{10,000} > 0$. For example, if $x = 20$ and $y = 10$, then $x > y$ and $\frac{x - y}{100} - \frac{xy}{10,000} = \frac{10}{100} - \frac{200}{10,000} > 0$. On the other hand, if $x = 200$ and $y = 100$, then $x > y$ and $\frac{x - y}{100} - \frac{xy}{10,000} = \frac{100}{100} - \frac{20,000}{10,000} < 0$; NOT sufficient.

(2) Given that $\frac{xy}{100} < x - y$, it follows that $\frac{xy}{10,000} < \frac{x - y}{100}$, and hence $\frac{x - y}{100} - \frac{xy}{10,000} > 0$; SUFFICIENT.

**The correct answer is B;
statement 2 alone is sufficient.**

435. During an experiment, some water was removed from each of 6 water tanks. If the standard deviation of the volumes of water in the tanks at the beginning of the experiment was 10 gallons, what was the standard deviation of the volumes of water in the tanks at the end of the experiment?

(1) For each tank, 30 percent of the volume of water that was in the tank at the beginning of the experiment was removed during the experiment.

(2) The average (arithmetic mean) volume of water in the tanks at the end of the experiment was 63 gallons.

Algebra Statistics

Let $T_1, T_2, \ldots, T_6$ be the 6 original volumes of water at the beginning of the experiment and let T_{ave} be the average of the original volumes of water. We are given that the standard deviation of the original volumes of water is 10, namely

$$\sqrt{\frac{(T_1 - T_{ave})^2 + (T_2 - T_{ave})^2 + \ldots + (T_6 - T_{ave})^2}{6}} =$$

10, and are to determine the standard deviation of the 6 new volumes of water at the end of the experiment. Note that one possibility for the 6 original volumes of water is 70, 70, 70, 90, 90, 90, since for these numbers we have $T_{ave} = 80$, and hence $(T_1 - T_{ave})^2 + (T_2 - T_{ave})^2 + \ldots + (T_6 - T_{ave})^2 = 10^2 + 10^2 + \ldots + 10^2 = 600$, so the standard deviation is $\sqrt{\frac{600}{6}} = \sqrt{100} = 10$.

(1) We are given that 30% was removed from each of the 6 tanks, so the 6 new volumes of water are $0.7T_1, 0.7T_2, \ldots, 0.7T_6$. The average of the new volumes of water is 0.7 times the average of the original volumes of water because $\frac{0.7T_1 + 0.7T_2 + \ldots + 0.7T_6}{6} = \frac{0.7(T_1 + T_2 + \ldots + T_6)}{6} = 0.7T_{ave}$.
Therefore, the standard deviation of the 6 new volumes of water is

$\sqrt{\frac{(0.7T_1 - 0.7T_{ave})^2 + (0.7T_2 - 0.7T_{ave})^2 + \ldots + (0.7T_6 - 0.7T_{ave})^2}{6}} =$

$\sqrt{\frac{(0.7)^2(T_1 - T_{ave})^2 + (0.7)^2(T_2 - T_{ave})^2 + \ldots + (0.7)^2(T_6 - T_{ave})^2}{6}} =$

$\sqrt{\frac{(0.7)^2[(T_1 - T_{ave})^2 + (T_2 - T_{ave})^2 + \ldots + (T_6 - T_{ave})^2]}{6}} =$

$0.7\sqrt{\frac{(T_1 - T_{ave})^2 + (T_2 - T_{ave})^2 + \ldots + (T_6 - T_{ave})^2}{6}} = (0.7)(10);$

SUFFICIENT.

(2) Given that the average of the 6 new volumes of water is 63, it is not possible to determine the standard deviation of the 6 new volumes of water. For example, if the original volumes of water were 70, 70, 70, 90, 90, 90 and each of the new volumes of water was 63, then the standard deviation of the original volumes of water would be 10, the average of the new volumes of water would be 63, and the standard deviation of the new volumes of water would be 0. On the other hand, if the original volumes of water were 70, 70,

70, 90, 90, 90 and the new volumes of water were 60, 60, 60, 66, 66, 66, then the standard deviation of the original volumes of water would be 10, the average of the new volumes of water would be 63, and the standard deviation of the new volumes of water would be greater than 0; NOT sufficient.

The correct answer is A; statement 1 alone is sufficient.

436. Each member of a team consisting of 6 researchers and 4 assistants received a bonus. If the sum of the researchers' bonuses was $7,200, what was the sum of the assistants' bonuses?

(1) The average (arithmetic mean) of the researchers' bonuses was $300 greater than the average of the assistants' bonuses.

(2) The sum of the bonuses of 3 of the researchers and 2 of the assistants was $4,500.

Algebra Statistics

If the sum of the 6 researchers' bonuses was $7,200, then the average of their bonuses was $\frac{7,200}{6} = \$1,200$. If, as statement (1) says, this average of the researchers' bonuses was $300 greater than the average of the assistants' bonuses, then the average of the assistants' bonuses was $1,200 − $300 = $900. That tells us that the sum of the 4 assistants' bonuses was $4 \times \$900 = \$3,600$. So statement (1) alone is sufficient to answer the question.

We don't know whether all the researchers got equal bonuses, or whether all the assistants did. So knowing that the sum of the bonuses of 3 of the researchers and 2 of the assistants was $4,500 doesn't even tell us what the sum of those 2 assistants' bonuses was, let alone what the sum of all the assistants' bonuses was. Therefore, statement (2) alone is not sufficient to answer the question.

The correct answer is A; statement 1 alone is sufficient.

6.7 Practice Questions: Two-Part Analysis

Each Two-Part Analysis Question tells you everything you need to know to pick the right answers. Rely on the given information provided to answer the question. Pick one answer in the first column and one answer in the second column.

Questions 437 to 455 — Difficulty: Easy

437. Trains M and N are traveling west on parallel tracks. At exactly noon, the front of Train M, which is traveling at a constant speed of 80 kilometers per hour (km/h), is at the rail crossing at Location X, and the front of Train N, which is traveling at a constant speed of 65 km/h, is 30 km west of the rail crossing at Location X. The trains continue traveling at their respective speeds until the front of Train M and the front of Train N are simultaneously at the rail crossing at Location Y.

In the table, identify the number of kilometers that the front of Train M has traveled between noon and 12:45 p.m. and the number of kilometers that the front of Train N has traveled between noon and 1:00 p.m.

Front of Train M	Front of Train N	
		55
		60
		65
		70
		75

438. An international basketball tournament will be held in either Nation QN or Nation RN. Exactly six nations, including the host, plan to participate, depending on the following conditions:

SN will participate only if TN does. UN will not participate if either VN or WN does. WN will not participate unless the tournament is held in RN.

Based on the information provided, and assuming WN participates, in the first column select the nation that must also participate, and in the second column select the nation that will not participate. Make only two selections, one in each column.

Must participate	Will not participate	
		QN
		RN
		SN
		TN
		UN
		VN

439. A portion of an automobile test track is divided into Segment A, Segment B, and Segment C, in that order. In a performance test on a car, the car traveled Segment A at a constant speed of 140 kilometers per hour (km/h). Immediately after this, the car rapidly slowed on Segment B and then traveled on Segment C at a constant speed of 70 km/h. The length of Segment C is 3 times the length of Segment A, and it took a total of 42 minutes for the car to travel both Segments A and C. In the table, select the length of Segment A, in kilometers, and select the length of Segment C, in kilometers. Make only two selections, one in each column.

Length of Segment A (kilometers)	Length of Segment C (kilometers)	
		8
		14
		24
		42
		72
		126

440. Let *X*, *Y*, and *Z* denote the number of international students, in thousands, that Company U predicted would be studying in the United States (US) during the school years 2014–2015, 2019–2020, and 2024–2025, respectively. The average (arithmetic mean) of *X*, *Y*, and *Z* is 1,128, and *Y* = 1,124. Company U predicted that there would be more international students studying in the US during the 2024–2025 school year than during the 2014–2015 school year.

In the table, identify a value of *X* and a value of *Z* that are jointly consistent with the information provided. Make only two selections, one in each column.

X	Z	
		910
		995
		1,175
		1,350
		1,435

441. Advice from a computer security expert on passwords used for accessing online accounts follows:

Computer users should use a different password for each online account. They should also use *strong passwords*, which are hard for hackers to decipher. However, strong passwords are difficult to remember, and this is especially the case for users who have multiple online accounts.

Fortunately, software is available at no cost that can store and encrypt a user's passwords: the user need only remember one password to access the rest. For users willing to take the time to install the software on a computer and enter all the required data, such software provides one way to comply with my advice. Some versions of the software can even be copied to a portable device, such as a USB drive, whereby a user can access passwords from any compatible computer.

For computer users with multiple accounts who would not otherwise use a different strong password on every account, the expert's advice amounts to suggesting that such users make certain sacrifices in order to make certain gains. Indicate by appropriate selections in the first and second column which of the items in the third column such users would sacrifice and which they would gain. Make only two selections, one in each column.

Sacrifice	Gain	
		Money
		Computing speed
		Security
		Number of online accounts
		Time

442. Some studies of how it was that Prussia resisted the wave of European democratization in the nineteenth century point to Prussia's unequal distribution of land ownership as the principal explanation. And political figures from areas in Prussia with high inequality in land ownership tended to be the staunchest opponents of democratic reforms.

However, **arguments that focus only on those figures' conflicts with landless people ignore the fact that political figures are not only representatives of socioeconomic interests but also political actors embedded in particular contexts that shape whether they support democratic reforms**. Historians must take such contexts into account if they hope to explain what transpired in Prussia during this period.

Select *Passage* for the statement that best describes the purpose of the passage as a whole, and select *Portion in **Boldface*** for the statement that best describes the purpose of the portion in **boldface**. Make only two selections, one in each column.

Passage	Portion in Boldface	
		To offer an alternative to the standard explanation of a particular historical event
		To provide evidence that economic issues were at the root of a particular historical event
		To criticize a certain type of argument about a particular historical event
		To criticize the motives of political figures involved in a particular historical event
		To encourage historians not to approach a particular historical event from too narrow a perspective

443. In September 2010, Armando purchased 5 identically priced shirts and 3 identically priced pairs of trousers from a certain department store. Armando paid a total of €28.85 for the shirts and €38.97 for the trousers. In October 2010, the department store held a sale, taking 25% off the September price of everything in the store. Armando returned to the store during the October 2010 sale and bought 11 of the shirts and 7 pairs of the trousers for some friends.

In the table, select how much Armando paid in October for the 11 shirts and 7 pairs of trousers, rounding for each item to the nearest cent. Make only one selection in each column.

Shirts	Trousers	
		€47.60
		€63.51
		€68.20
		€79.39
		€90.91
		€204.54

444. A city is hosting a table tennis tournament for its residents. Each team has exactly two players, and each player is on exactly one team. In each round, each team plays exactly one other team and either wins or loses. The winning team advances to the next round and the losing team is eliminated. No team or player drops out except by losing a game. The tournament is in progress, and exactly 512 players participated in the first round.

From the available options, select a number of tournament rounds and a number of teams such that after the specified number of rounds there will be the specified number of teams remaining in the tournament. Make only two selections, one in each column.

Rounds Completed	Teams Remaining	
		2
		4
		8
		16
		32

445. Adiliah, Bao, Davi, Laszlo, Saleema, and Yarah work in a firm's legal department. Adiliah supervises Bao and Davi, Davi supervises Laszlo, and Laszlo supervises Saleema and Yarah. These are the only supervisory relationships involving these six employees. Each document that the department processes must be initially reviewed by exactly one department member. Each document reviewed by a department member must then be reviewed by that person's supervisor. No other rules require anyone else to review any document. Anyone not required to review a given document will not review it.

Select *Laszlo among reviewers* for the maximum number of department members who could have reviewed a single document if Laszlo was among the reviewers. Select *Adiliah among reviewers* for the maximum number of department members who could have reviewed a single document if Adiliah was among the reviewers. Make only two selections, one in each column.

Laszlo among reviewers	Adiliah among reviewers	
		1
		2
		3
		4
		5
		6

446. Naturalist: The decline of coral reefs has various causes. One contributing factor is predation on coral by organisms such as the crown-of-thorns sea star, whose preferred food source is coral polyps. Human fishing practices have decreased the sea star's predators, such as the harlequin shrimp. It is also possible that runoff containing nutrients for phytoplankton has resulted in larger phytoplankton blooms: the crown-of-thorns sea star gladly eats phytoplankton.

Indicate which cause-and-effect sequence would most likely, according to the naturalist, result in coral reef decline. Make only two selections, one in each column.

Cause	Effect	
		An increase in phytoplankton
		A decrease in phytoplankton
		An increase in crown-of-thorns sea stars
		A decrease in crown-of-thorns sea stars
		An increase in harlequin shrimp

447. Archaeologist: There were several porcelain-production centers in eighteenth-century Britain, among them Bristol, Plymouth, and New Hall. Each center developed a unique recipe for its porcelain that might include flint glass, soapstone, bone ash, clay, quartz, and so on. We will therefore be able to determine, on the basis of compositional analysis, where the next cup we recover from this archaeological site was made.

Indicate two different statements as follows: one statement identifies an *assumption required* by the archaeologist's argument, and the other identifies a *possible fact* that would, if true, provide significant logical support for the required assumption. Make only two selections, one in each column.

Assumption Required	Possible Fact	
		Other cups have been recovered from the archeological site, all of which were made of porcelain.
		Some of the cups recovered from the archeological site were not made of porcelain.
		The next cup to be recovered from the site will likely be made of porcelain.
		Porcelain makers often traveled between centers, experimenting with one another's recipes.
		There was considerable overlap of materials in the recipes used by the various centers.
		Most porcelain in eighteenth-century Britain was made at one of the several centers.

448. Health advocate: The government's current farm-subsidy system primarily rewards large farms for planting monocultures of corn, soybeans, wheat, and rice. Most of the crops produced in this way go to feed livestock in factory farms, which results in a glut of fatty meats in the marketplace. A large proportion of such crops that are not used to feed livestock are used to make sugary processed foods. These subsidies promote unhealthy diets by making sugary foods and fatty meats artificially cheap. Obviously, it is important for the government to avoid these effects.

On the basis of the information above, select *Recommends* for the option that describes the government action that the health advocate most likely recommends, and select *Intended result* for the option that describes what the health advocate likely hopes will be the result of that action. Make only two selections, one in each column.

Recommends	Intended result	
		Improve the overall quality of livestock feed
		Improve the overall quality of people's diets
		Reduce the overall financial cost of people's diets
		Prevent the manufacture of sugary processed food
		Change the farm-subsidy system

449. An archaeologist studying Artifacts A–D is interested in whether Artifact C is older than Artifact A.

Select an assertion involving Artifact A and an assertion involving Artifact C that together imply the assertion "Artifact C is older than Artifact A." Make only two selections, one in each column.

Assertion involving Artifact A	Assertion involving Artifact C	
		Artifact A is older than Artifact B.
		Artifact A is older than Artifact D.
		Artifact B is older than Artifact A.
		Artifact B is older than Artifact D.
		Artifact C is older than Artifact D.
		Artifact C is older than Artifact B.

450. For a randomly selected day, the probability that a visitor to a certain pond will see at least one swan is 0.35. The probability that a visitor to that pond on a randomly selected day will see at least one heron is

0.2. Furthermore, seeing a swan and seeing a heron are independent of each other.

Based on the information provided, select *Both swan and heron* for the probability that a visitor to the pond will see both at least one swan and at least one heron on any given day, and select *Neither swan nor heron* for the probability that a visitor to the pond will see neither a swan nor a heron on any given day. Make only two selections, one in each column.

Both swan and heron	Neither swan nor heron	
		0.02
		0.07
		0.48
		0.52
		0.70

451. Two primary school teachers are debating the merits of classrooms with highly decorated walls.

Teacher 1: A recent study has shown that highly decorated walls can interfere with learning in the classroom. We should therefore decrease the number of wall decorations in our classrooms.

Teacher 2: The results of that study are correct, but pertain only to the retention of information from single lessons in which the students were in the classroom for only a short period of time. Our students are in the same classroom all day, five days a week. Without some added stimulation, students can become bored and therefore even more distracted than they would be by highly decorated walls. I therefore maintain that highly decorated walls serve to increase learning over the long term.

Select for X and for Y the options such that the following statement, if filled in accordingly, has the most support from the information provided. Make only two selections, one in each column. Teacher 2 suggests that he agrees with Teacher 1 about the effects of wall decorations on ___X___, but disagrees about the effects of wall decorations on ___Y___.

X	Y	
		retention of certain specified types of information
		the effectiveness of teaching methods that eschew rote learning
		the ability of students to maintain skills if practiced in various classrooms
		retention of information from multiple lessons given in the same room over a period of time
		retention of information from lessons given in rooms occupied for only a short time

452. Natalya put 14 blue marbles, 14 red marbles, and no other marbles into 3 empty cups. She put 2 blue marbles and 6 red marbles in Cup A, 6 blue marbles and 4 red marbles in Cup B, and 6 blue marbles and 4 red marbles in Cup C. After this, Dmitry will randomly pick three marbles, one from each cup.

Consistent with the given information, select for *3 blue* the probability that Dmitry will pick 3 blue marbles, and select for *3 red* the probability that Dmitry will pick 3 red marbles. Make only two selections, one in each column.

3 blue	3 red	
		0.090
		0.120
		0.125
		0.150
		0.250
		0.500

453. In recent years, commercial beekeepers have reported *colony collapse:* the disappearance of entire colonies of bees. A biologist, Dr. B, argues that colony collapse is caused by a new parasite to which bees have not acquired immunity. A chemist, Dr. C, argues that colony collapse is caused by genetic damage from pesticides. And an ecologist,

Dr. E, argues that 3 specific commercial beekeeping practices—transportation of hives over long distances, indiscriminate medication, and inbreeding—compromise both the immunity and the genetic diversity of bees, leaving them susceptible to mass die-offs from normally benign microbes.

Complete the table based on the stated views of Dr. B, Dr. C, and Dr. E. In the first column, select the factor common to both Dr. B's and Dr. E's accounts of colony collapse. In the second column, select the factor common to both Dr. C's and Dr. E's accounts of colony collapse. Make two selections, one in each column.

Dr. B and Dr. E	Dr. C and Dr. E	Factor
		Genetics
		Immunity
		Medication
		New parasites
		Normally benign microbes
		Pesticides

454. Martine is scheduling five contractors (Contractors A through E) to do various tasks during Monday through Friday of the upcoming week. For each day, exactly one contractor will be scheduled to work, and each contractor's task will be completed on the day for which that contractor is scheduled. The scheduling must conform to the following constraints:

Contractor A must be scheduled to work on Monday.

Contractor B must be scheduled to work exactly two days after Contractor A.

Contractor E must be scheduled to work exactly three days after Contractor C.

Statement: Given the constraints, Martine must schedule Contractor B to work on ____1____ and Contractor D to work on ____2____.

Select for 1 and for 2 the options that complete the statement so that it is accurate based on the information provided. Make only two selections, one in each column.

1	2	
		Monday
		Tuesday
		Wednesday
		Thursday
		Friday

455. Maria and her companion were given a $20 gift certificate for a restaurant. When they dined at the restaurant, the total amount they originally owed consisted of the total cost of the items they ordered plus a 7 percent sales tax and an 18 percent tip, both calculated on the total cost of the items they ordered. They applied the gift certificate and paid the remainder of the total amount they originally owed.

Let P denote the total cost, in dollars, of the items Maria and her companion ordered. Select *Before gift certificate* for the expression that is equivalent, for all $P > 20$, to the total amount they originally owed, before they applied the gift certificate, and select *After gift certificate* for the expression that is equivalent, for all $P > 20$, to the amount they paid after they applied the gift certificate.

Before gift certificate	After gift certificate	Expressions
		$1.25(P - 20)$
		$1.25P + 20$
		$1.25P - 20$
		$P + 0.25P$
		$0.8P + 0.18P + 0.07P$

Questions 456 to 486 — Difficulty: **Medium**

456. Supervisor's memo: At the present rate of manufacture we will not have the 1,200 circuit boards assembled in time to ship them to the customer. We currently have 10 workers, all working 8 hours a day at the same hourly rate, assembling the boards, and to date they've assembled 400. In order to finish the customer's order in time, I'll need to have each of the workers work an additional 2 hours for each of the 10 workdays between now and the deadline.

One can determine the hourly rate at which each worker assembled circuit boards up to the date of the supervisor's memo by dividing ___1___ circuit boards by the product of ___2___ worker-hours per day and the number of days since the workers began assembling the circuit boards.

Select *Circuit boards* for the option that fills the blank labeled 1 in the given statement, and select *Worker-hours* for the option that fills the blank labeled 2 in the given statement to create the most accurate statement on the basis of the information provided. Make only two selections, one in each column.

Circuit boards	Worker-hours	
		80
		400
		500
		800
		1,000
		1,200

457. In an experiment, one thousand nine-year-old children were allowed to choose whether to participate in a program in which the researchers taught them dance during the daily break from their lessons. Four hundred of the children chose to participate for at least one year. At the end of the year, researchers found that the children who had participated had significantly better balance, on average, than those who had not. The researchers hypothesized that dancing resulted in a sustained improvement in the children's sense of balance.

It would be most helpful in evaluating the researchers' hypothesis to know whether the researchers ___1___ prior to having ___2___.

Select *Researchers* for the phrase that fills the blank labeled 1 in the given statement, and select *Prior to* for the phrase that fills the blank labeled 2 in the given statement to create the most accurate statement on the basis of the information provided. Make only two selections, one in each column.

Researchers	Prior to	
		tested the children's ability to dance
		designed a second experiment
		divided the children into the two experimental groups
		tested the children's sense of balance
		taught dance to the children through the dance program

458. Klaus: Closing our neighborhood's school will mean a major hassle for neighborhood families. Students will have to travel farther to and from school, which means they'll have less time for homework. That will likely affect them academically. Additionally, a vacant school building in our neighborhood is sure to attract crime and drag down home values.

Rena: Our neighborhood's school never had a great reputation anyway. Closing it means students will get to go to a larger school—with a better reputation— just a few kilometers away, where they'll have more opportunities to participate in extracurricular activities. That should make homes here more valuable to potential buyers. And the vacant school building could be converted into a much-needed community center.

Select *Klaus* for the phrase that best describes a factor that is specifically addressed by Klaus but not by Rena, and select *Rena* for the phrase that best describes a factor that is specifically addressed by Rena but not by Klaus. Make only two selections, one in each column.

Klaus	Rena	
		The vacant school building
		The distance students must travel to school
		Extracurricular activities
		Real estate values
		Students' academic performance

459. Alfredo: The United States could make significant progress toward becoming independent of petroleum-derived gasoline as a source of energy by diverting a large proportion of corn grown in the US to the production of ethanol for fuel. Brazil is virtually independent of petroleum as a source of fuel because that country has been very successful in ethanol production.

Mavis: Ethanol derived from corn will never be a viable substitute for petroleum-derived gasoline in the US. While it is true that Brazil has been very successful in replacing gasoline with ethanol, Brazil's ethanol is derived from sugarcane, which is very easy to convert to ethanol and, in Brazil, very easy to cultivate. Corn, on the other hand, is difficult to grow, requiring intensive cultivation. Also, the amount of power that can be garnered from the land is much less per square meter for corn ethanol.

In the table, select the statement about which Alfredo and Mavis would most clearly agree and select the statement about which Alfredo and Mavis would most clearly disagree. Make only two selections, one in each column.

Agree with each other about	Disagree with each other about	
		Corn ethanol produces much less power per square meter of cultivated land than does sugarcane ethanol.
		Ethanol is easier to produce from sugarcane than from corn.
		There are no crops, other than corn, for producing ethanol that could viably be grown in the US.
		Brazil has been very successful at replacing petroleum with ethanol.
		Producing corn ethanol is a viable strategy for a nation intent on reducing dependence on petroleum.

460. Radhika is refinancing a business loan and is considering 2 different loan offers. Under Offer 1, the loan's initial principal would be $190,000, and she would pay down $1,250 in principal with each monthly payment during the first year of the loan. Under Offer 2, $4,000 in refinancing fees would be added to bring the principal to $194,000, but she would pay down $1,775 in principal with each monthly payment during the first year of the loan.

In the first column of the table, select the amount of principal that would remain after 12 monthly payments under Offer 1. In the second column of the table, select the amount of principal that would remain after 12 monthly payments under Offer 2. Make only two selections, one in each column.

Principal remaining after 12 months under Offer 1	Principal remaining after 12 months under Offer 2	
		$168,700
		$171,000
		$172,700
		$175,000
		$176,700
		$179,000

461. Professor A: The field of Artificial Intelligence (AI) was originally aimed exclusively at the construction of *thinking machines,* that is, computer systems with human-like general intelligence. But the difficulty of this goal of general AI has led researchers to shift their focus to producing narrow AI systems: software displaying intelligence regarding specific tasks in relatively narrow domains such as chess. The problem is, narrow AI and general AI are fundamentally and entirely different pursuits. If modeling general intelligence is the objective, AI researchers must redirect themselves toward the original goals of the field and confront the more difficult issues of human-like intelligence.

Professor B: Narrow AI work is producing real results today, such as chess-playing programs that can defeat any human, programs that translate speech to text, and programs that can drive automated vehicles. Achievements in this field will continue to flow, and eventually narrow AI will lead to the creation of systems with general intelligence.

On the basis of the given information, select a claim that *Professor A* would most likely *disagree* with, and select a claim that *Professor B* would most likely *disagree* with. Select only two claims, one in each column.

Professor A disagrees	Professor B disagrees	
		The creation of computer systems that display human-like general intelligence is an important goal.
		The creation of systems that display intelligence regarding specific tasks is an especially important step toward the creation of systems with general intelligence.
		Systems with general intelligence are more difficult to create than are systems with narrow intelligence.
		Research in the narrow AI field is not likely to lead to significant breakthroughs in the general AI field.
		The original aim of AI research was to create systems with general intelligence.
		The research into narrow AI is not producing results that real people can benefit from today.

462. Swamp sparrows live in a variety of wetland habitats. Unlike most swamp sparrows, which live in freshwater habitats, the coastal-plain subspecies lives in tidal wetlands, where freshwater and seawater mix and the mud is gray rather than brown. Coastal-plain swamp sparrows differ from all other populations of swamp sparrows in having plumage that is gray-brown rather than rusty brown. DNA analysis indicates several important genetic differences between swamp sparrows that inhabit tidal marshes and other subspecies of swamp sparrows. Therefore, there must have been genetic-selection pressure on swamp sparrows in tidal marshes to become darker and grayer.

Select *Strengthen* for the statement that would, if true, most strengthen the argument, and select *Weaken* for the statement that would, if true, most weaken the argument. Make only two selections, one in each column.

Strengthen	Weaken	
		None of the genetic differences that have been identified in the genomes of coastal-plain swamp sparrows and freshwater swamp sparrows affect plumage color.
		Mud in tidal marshes tends to be grayish because of the presence of iron sulfide, whereas freshwater mud is browner because of the presence of iron oxide.
		Some species of birds that live in tidal marshes do not have gray plumage.
		The diets of both coastal-plain and freshwater swamp sparrows can change significantly from season to season.
		Baby birds of the coastal-plain subspecies and baby birds of a freshwater swamp subspecies, all raised on an identical diet under controlled conditions, grew plumage similar in color to that of their respective parents.

463. Boppo is a game played by 2 teams for a fixed duration (number of minutes). It is played with 8 members of each team on the floor—actually playing the game—at all times. At any time during the game, exactly one player from each team must be off the floor—not actually playing. Thus, by taking a break, by entering the game after it starts, or by leaving before it finishes, every player on each team must spend exactly 5 minutes resting or otherwise not playing.

In the table, identify a number of players per team and a number of minutes per game that are consistent with the given information about Boppo. Make only two selections, one in each column.

Number of players	Number of minutes	
		9
		11
		18
		30
		45
		50

464. Loan X has a principal of $x and a yearly simple interest rate of 4%. Loan Y has a principal of $y and a yearly simple interest rate of 8%. Loans X and Y will be consolidated to form Loan Z with a principal of $(x + y) and a yearly simple interest rate of r%, where $r = \dfrac{4x + 8y}{x + y}$. Select a value for x and a value for y corresponding to a yearly simple interest rate of 5% for the consolidated loan. Make only two selections, one in each column.

x	y	Value
		21,000
		32,000
		51,000
		64,000
		81,000
		96,000

465. Perry, Maria, and Lorna are painting rooms in a college dormitory. Working alone, Perry can paint a standard room in 3 hours, Maria can paint a standard room in 2 hours, and Lorna can paint a standard room in 2 hours 30 minutes. Perry, Maria, and Lorna have decided that, to speed up the work, 2 of them will paint a standard room together.

Select the value closest to the shortest time in which a 2-person team could paint a standard room, and select the value closest to the longest time in which a 2-person team could paint a standard room, with each person working at his or her respective rate. Make only two selections, one in each column.

Shortest time	Longest time	
		49 minutes
		1 hour 7 minutes
		1 hour 12 minutes
		1 hour 14 minutes
		1 hour 22 minutes
		1 hour 45 minutes

466. A dance show will include exactly five pieces, and each piece will be presented only once: Requiem, Smooth Step, Trampoline, Unleashed, and Waltzy. Requiem will be presented immediately before Smooth Step. Unleashed will be presented earlier than Trampoline, with at least one piece in between. Waltzy will not be the final piece presented.

    In the table, select a piece that cannot be the second piece presented and a piece that cannot be the third piece presented. Make only two selections, one in each column.

Cannot be presented second	Cannot be presented third	
		Requiem
		Smooth Step
		Trampoline
		Unleashed
		Waltzy

467. An American museum of East Asian art reviewed its acquisitions strategy in 2009. As part of that review, a marketing executive recommended purchasing more ceramics, jades, and paintings of people or landscapes because visitor surveys indicated that those types are of greatest interest to museumgoers in the region. The museum's curator recommended purchasing more twenty-first-century East Asian art—particularly abstract (nonrepresentational) paintings and sculptures—because the museum's collection is weakest in that area.

Among the East Asian works of art described below, select a painting and a sculpture, each of which satisfies at least one of the recommendations made by the marketing executive and at least one of the recommendations made by the curator. Make only two selections, one in each column.

Painting	Sculpture	
		Painting of girl's face, in shades of blue and red, acrylic and oil on canvas, 2006
		Chinese brush painting of fish in a tank, ink on paper, 2002
		Fish-shaped vase with dragon head, jade, 1849
		Abstract sequence of interconnected curves, ceramic, 2008
		Fossil-like, jagged sculpture suspended from cables, stainless steel, aluminum, fiberglass, and cable, 2004

468. Professor A: The aid industry should begin to focus its efforts to spending on primary schools in the poorest areas, to providing medicines and other basic supplies for health such as mosquito nets, and to a few key agricultural initiatives.

    Professor B: Much education work has been ineffective. A village or town with poor schooling may be better off getting a road than a teacher. Once local farmers can transport produce to market, they will be willing to pay for schools—and to make sure the schools succeed.

    Suppose that the professors' statements express their genuine opinions. Select statements (1) and (2) as follows: Professor A would likely disagree with (1), and Professor B would take (2) to present logical support for (1). Select only two statements, one per column.

(1)	(2)	
		The aid industry should focus less on the areas of health and agriculture than it now does.
		The aid industry should focus more on primary education than it now does.
		The aid industry should focus its spending less on primary education than it now does.
		Projects in health and agriculture are more likely to be successful if they are not paid for by the aid industry.
		Projects in education are more likely to be successful if they are paid for by the aid industry.
		Projects in education are more likely to be successful if they are paid for by local people.

469. A car is traveling on a straight stretch of roadway, and the speed of the car is increasing at a constant rate with respect to time. At time 0 seconds, the speed of the car is v_0 meters per second; 10 seconds later, the front bumper of the car has traveled 125 meters, and the speed of the car is v_{10} meters per second.

Select values of v_0 and v_{10} that are together consistent with the information provided. Make only two selections, one in each column.

v_0	v_{10}	
		5
		18
		20
		36
		72

470. For each positive integer n, the quantity s_n is defined such that $s_{n+2} = (s_n)^2 - s_{n+1}$. In addition, $s_2 = 1$.

Select values for s_1 and s_4 that are jointly compatible with these conditions. Select only two values, one in each column.

s_1	s_4	
		−12
		−7
		−3
		−1
		0

471. The *finesse* of a gold bar is the weight of the gold present in the bar divided by the total weight of the bar. A jeweler has three gold bars. The three bars have identical weights, and the first two bars have identical finesse. If all three bars were melted and combined into one bar, the finesse of the resulting bar would be 0.96.

Select a finesse of the *First two bars* and a finesse of the *Third bar* that are jointly consistent with the given information. Make only two selections, one in each column.

First two bars	Third bar	
		0.92
		0.93
		0.94
		0.98
		0.99

472. A fair coin has 2 distinct flat sides—one of which bears the image of a face and the other of which does not—and when the coin is tossed, the probability that the coin will land face up is $\frac{1}{2}$. For certain values of M, N, p, and q, when M fair coins are tossed simultaneously, the probability is p that all M coins land face up, and when N fair coins are tossed simultaneously, the probability is q that all N coins land face up. Furthermore, $M < N$ and $\frac{1}{p} + \frac{1}{q} = 72$.

In the table, select a value for M and a value for N that are jointly consistent with the given information. Make only two selections, one in each column.

M	N	
		2
		3
		4
		5
		6
		7

473. Educational policy analyst: To improve the long-term economic benefits that our country's universities provide to their students, the government should provide subsidies enabling the universities to hire more academic staff. Hiring more academic staff would allow smaller class sizes. Statistically, university students in smaller classes tend to receive higher grades than those in larger classes. And on average, a student who earns higher grades in university classes tends to have a higher salary after graduation than a student who earns lower grades. Thus, hiring more academic staff nationwide should improve the economic well-being of graduates nationwide.

Consider the incomplete statement:

According to the analyst's argument, students'
____1____ is bolstered by their ____2____.

Select for *1* and *2* the options that complete the statement in the manner that most accurately reflects the given information. Make only two selections, one in each column.

1	2	
		tendency to earn higher grades in university classes
		economic well-being after graduating from university
		being in larger than average university classes
		receiving better education overall
		learning from a greater number of academic staff

474. The *payload rating* (PR) of a truck is the truck's recommended load weight, which is specified as a number of tonnes (t), where 1 tonne = 1,000 kilograms. A certain truck's PR is a whole number of tonnes. The truck has hauled exactly 7 loads, exactly 3 of which had a greater weight than the truck's PR. The weights of these 7 loads, in tonnes, are as follows:

50, 51, 52, 52, 54, 54, 56.

Select the *Least* and the *Greatest* possible values for the truck's PR, in tonnes. Make only two selections, one in each column.

Least	Greatest	
		49
		50
		51
		52
		53
		54

475. Each of the species of a certain type of insect has at least one of five significant traits: A, B, C, D, and E. Furthermore, one study has determined that any species with Trait A has at least one of the Traits B and C. Another study has determined that any species with Trait C has at least one of the Traits D and E. And a third study has determined that any of the species with Trait B has Trait C. The results of each study are correct.

Select different options for *X* and for *Y* such that the following statement most accurately describes the passage. Make only two selections, one in each column.

In addition to the relationship between Traits B and C that is stated explicitly with respect to the third study, the passage implies that any of the insects that has Trait ____X____ also has Trait ____Y____.

X	Y	
		A
		B
		C
		D
		E

476. Events A, B, and C have the following probabilities of future occurrence:

A: 20%

B: 50%

C: 80%

On the basis of these probabilities, select for *Both A and B* a description that must be true of the probability that both A and B will occur. And select for *B or C or Both* a description that must be true of the probability that B or C or both will occur. Make only two selections, one in each column.

Both A and B	B or C or Both	
		Must be equal to 40%
		Must be equal to 50%
		Must be equal to 70%
		Must be less than or equal to 20%
		Must be greater than or equal to 80%

477. Premiolex Corporation spokesperson: In our survey of Premiolex customers, the majority of respondents rated our services as "Excellent," whereas in our competitor Cretazole's survey, the majority of their respondents rated Cretazole's services as "Very good." That's proof that—on average, at least—our customers have a higher opinion of Premiolex's services than Cretazole's customers have of its services.

Skeptic: I don't think the spokesperson's conclusion necessarily follows from the evidence he cites. What if, for example, the Premiolex survey asked participants to choose from among options that weren't all identical to the ones used in Cretazole's survey?

Select for *Premiolex survey* and *Cretazole survey* the options such that, in combination, the Premiolex survey and Cretazole survey would support the skeptic's position and be consistent with the spokesperson's report of the results but indicate that the spokesperson's conclusion does not necessarily follow. Make only two selections, one in each column.

Premiolex Survey	Cretazole Survey	Condition: 1,000 respondents were asked to choose among these survey options	Results: Number of respondents who chose each survey option
		Excellent	517
		Average	482
		Below average	1
		Poor	0
		Unacceptable	0
		Excellent	463
		Average	501
		Below average	0
		Poor	35
		Unacceptable	1
		Excellent	454
		Average	511
		Below average	34
		Poor	0
		Unacceptable	1
		Excellent	512
		Average	478
		Below average	10
		Poor	0
		Unacceptable	0
		Excellent	23
		Average	516
		Below average	230
		Poor	231
		Unacceptable	0

478. A satellite is currently in a circular orbit with radius 32,714 km about the center of the earth. (Note: The circumference of a circle is given by $C = 2\pi r$, where r is the radius of the circle and, to the nearest 0.01, $\pi \approx 3.14$.)

Select for *0.5 km* the increase, to the nearest whole kilometer, in the distance the satellite travels about the center of the earth during each revolution if the orbital radius of the satellite is increased by 0.5 km. And select for *1.5 km* the increase, to the nearest whole kilometer, in the distance the satellite travels about the center of the earth during each revolution if the orbital radius is increased by 1.5 km. Make only two selections, one in each column.

0.5 km	1.5 km	
		3
		9
		27
		81
		150
		450

479. Some studies of how Prussia resisted the wave of European democratization in the nineteenth century point to Prussia's unequal distribution of land ownership as the principal explanation. Indeed, political figures from areas in Prussia with high inequality in land ownership tended to be the staunchest opponents of democratic reforms. However, arguments that focus so strongly on those figures' conflicts with landless people tend to ignore the fact that political figures are not merely representatives of socioeconomic interests but are also political actors embedded in particular contexts that shape whether they support democratic reforms. Historians must take such contexts into account if they hope to explain what transpired in Prussia during this period.

This argument would be most strengthened if, in the nineteenth century, there were other European countries that ___1___ despite the fact that those countries ___2___.

Select for *1* and *2* the options that complete the statement in the manner that most accurately reflects the given information. Make only two selections, one in each column.

1	2	
		enacted more democratic reforms than did Prussia
		enacted fewer democratic reforms than did Prussia
		had similar inequality in land ownership as did Prussia
		had less inequality in land ownership than did Prussia
		had more complex political contexts than did Prussia

480. Many countries have traditionally used surface-irrigation systems, which use gravity to distribute water over the soil surface. But these systems contribute significantly to groundwater depletion. Many of these countries' governments are not regulating such groundwater extraction properly, resulting in water table depletion in many regions. Therefore governments need to introduce new water-management policies that will curtail such practices, control allocations of water to agriculture and industry, and enable the governments to reduce those allocations when supplies become scarce or demand from other sectors increases.

Select for *Cause* and *Consequence* the options such that the information provided most strongly suggests that if the cause occurs, the consequence is likely to occur. Make only two selections, one in each column.

Cause	Consequence	
		Governments enacting new water-management policies
		Governments failing to enact new water-management policies
		Depletion of groundwater supplies in some regions
		Greater allocation of groundwater for agricultural use than for industrial use
		Agriculture and industry voluntarily curtailing groundwater use

481. A philosophy professor randomly assigned students to either of the two different sides of a debate in an ethics class, regardless of their stance on the issue. The students then researched and prepared arguments for a week. The students had been almost evenly divided on the issue when the assignments were made, according to an anonymous survey, but almost all of the students reported strong agreement with their assigned position in another, postdebate anonymous survey. The professor concluded that the research and preparation for the debate had a polarizing effect, causing many students to change their original positions.

In the columns, select the statement that, if true, would most strengthen the professor's conclusion and the statement that, if true, would most weaken the conclusion. Make only two selections, one in each column.

Strengthens	Weakens	
		Most students learned a great deal about both sides of their debate topic during their week of preparation.
		Most of the students consulted research materials that were outdated and based on incomplete data.
		Prior to the assignment, none of the students had strong feelings about either side of the debate topic.
		By chance, almost all of the students were assigned to the side of the debate that they already agreed with.
		Many students had not reported their original positions to their debate partners at the outset of the project.

482. The results of a large study suggest that television viewers enjoy shows with commercials more than those without them. Test subjects who viewed an episode of a television series with commercials rated it more enjoyable than did subjects who viewed the same episode commercial-free. The study's researchers concluded that a viewer's enjoyment of a program depends a great deal on how well one can maintain attention, reasoning that commercial breaks enable viewers to reset their attention.

In the columns, select the statement that, if true, would most strengthen the argument and the statement that, if true, would most weaken the argument. Make only two selections, one in each column.

Strengthens	Weakens	
		Television programs tend to hold viewers' attention better when they have shorter commercial breaks.
		Television programs with commercial breaks have often been edited to allow time for the insertion of the breaks.
		When the option to pause a commercial-free television program is available, the vast majority of people will do so at least once during a program.
		People shown to have especially long attention spans are no more likely to enjoy commercial-free television programs than are people with short attention spans.
		Commercial-free television programming tends to be of lower production quality than that shown with commercials.

483. The workers in an office are placed into 3 working groups, each containing 20 workers. All workers are in at least one group. Any two groups have exactly 10 members in common.

Identify in the table two numbers that are jointly consistent with the given information: the total number of workers in the office, and the number of workers who are members of all three groups. Make only two selections, one in each column.

Total workers	Workers in all three	Number
		4
		8
		10
		18
		34
		45

484. In a study of human behavior, researchers solicited charitable donations from two different groups of people, those having just donated blood and those having just visited a doctor. Contributions from blood donors were significantly less than contributions from people who had visited a doctor. The researchers concluded that people believe their obligation to behave generously is finite. Therefore those who had donated blood, the researchers explained, believed they had temporarily somewhat satisfied their charitable obligations.

Which of the following would, if true, most weaken the researchers' conclusion, and which would, if true, most strengthen it? Make only two selections, one in each column.

Most weakens	Most strengthens	
		Blood donors are generally allowed to donate whole blood only once every two months.
		People report that they are more likely to make charitable donations when the request is made in person than when it is made over the phone.
		People who placed money in a store's charity collection container before shopping bought fewer groceries, on average, than those who did so after shopping.
		People report that making charitable donations causes them to feel better about themselves.
		People tend to give less to charity during weeks in which they help neighbors by providing a needed good or service.
		A different study found that few blood donors consider donating blood to be comparable to "charitable giving."

485. Organization A currently has 1,050 members. Organization B currently has 1,550 members. The number of members of Organization A and the number of members of Organization B are increasing annually, each at its own constant rate. Analysts project that if each of these organizations maintains its constant annual rate of membership increase, five years from now they will for the first time have the same number of members, and in subsequent years Organization A will have more members than Organization B.

In the following table, identify a rate of increase, in members per year, for Organization A and a rate of increase, in members per year, for Organization B that together are consistent with the analysts' projection. Make only one selection in each column.

Organization A	Organization B	Rate of increase (members per year)
		10
		30
		40
		120
		130
		150

486. A company called the US Copyright Group (USCG) has filed seven lawsuits in Washington, DC, courts, naming over fourteen thousand defendants. The defendants are associated with personal computers implicated in USCG's investigations of unauthorized movie downloads. The USCG contends that the strategy of prosecuting groups makes the most sense because each individual defendant lacks the assets and earning capacity to make individual prosecutions worthwhile financially. The Electronic Frontier Foundation (EFF) claims that USCG's strategy deprives defendants of a fair chance to defend themselves. Because the vast majority of defendants in these cases do not live in Washington, DC—indeed, many live outside the United States—the travel and legal defense costs associated with contesting the charges are likely to be prohibitively high for them.

Select *EFF objects to* for the statement that most accurately describes an aspect of USCG's lawsuits to which the EFF objects; select *On the basis that* for the statement that most accurately describes the EFF's basis for that objection. Make only two selections, one in each column.

EFF objects to	On the basis that	
		The USCG filed multiple cases alleging copyright infringement, rather than naming all individuals in a single case.
		The costs associated with contesting the charges would be high for a large number of the defendants.
		Many defendants named in the cases likely did not infringe on copyrights.
		The USCG investigated IP addresses associated with unauthorized downloading of movies.
		Each of the USCG's suits was filed in a single location and names a large number of defendants in other locations.
		The investigative methods employed by USCG violate the rights of Internet users.

Questions 487 to 504 — Difficulty: Hard

487. Companies A and B are part of the same industry and are located in the same city. For Company A, the average (arithmetic mean) salary of its employees, in United Arab Emirates dirhams (AED), is 10,000 AED higher than that for Company B. However, more than half of the employees at Company A have salaries below the average for Company B.

Statement: If the average salary at Company B is ___1___, then the median salary at Company A is ___2___.

Select for 1 and for 2 the options that complete the statement so that it most accurately reflects the information provided. Make only two selections, one in each column.

1	2	
		(A) greater than 100,000 AED
		(B) less than 100,000 AED
		(C) equal to 110,000 AED
		(D) between 100,000 and 110,000 AED
		(E) greater than 110,000 AED

488. The following statements describe certain characteristics of a certain pool of candidates for a position. Any candidate who did not meet the minimum qualifications for the position was immediately excluded from consideration. The two candidates who met the minimum qualifications for the position and met all of the desired qualifications also had multiple recommendations. All candidates who received a telephone interview also had extensive experience. All candidates who had extensive experience and impressed the hiring committee during the telephone interview were invited to interview on-site. At least one candidate declined an invitation for an on-site interview, and exactly one candidate was interviewed on-site without receiving a telephone interview.

Consider the following incomplete sentence:

If any candidate ___1___, then that candidate ___2___.

Select for 1 and for 2 two different options that best complete the sentence such that it can be logically inferred from the information provided. Make only two selections, one in each column.

1	2	
		did not meet the minimum qualifications
		had multiple recommendations
		had extensive experience
		impressed the hiring committee during the telephone interview
		interviewed on-site

489. In Country C, some but not all eligible voters are required to vote. The particulars of the country's laws governing voting are as follows.

Every citizen who is eligible must vote on Election Day.

A person is eligible if (and only if) that person meets the age requirement and is either a citizen or meets the residency requirement for noncitizens.

The age requirement is that every voter must be at least 19 years old on Election Day.

The residency requirement for noncitizens is that the voter must have been a resident of Country C for at least 5 years on Election Day.

Consider the following individuals:

Abigail: a citizen who is currently 19 years old

Barbara: a 7-year resident noncitizen who is currently 19 years old

Charles: a 7-year resident noncitizen who is currently 18 years old

For an election held today, select the individual or individuals who must vote based on the information provided, and select the individual or individuals who must not vote based on the information provided. Make only two selections, one in each column.

Must vote	Must not vote	
		Abigail only
		Barbara only
		Charles only
		Abigail and Barbara only
		Abigail and Charles only
		Barbara and Charles only

490. Most of the cubicles in the north wing of the Acme Company headquarters are less than 20 meters from the nearest fire escape, whereas half of the cubicles in the east wing are not. In other words, those same east-wing cubicles and ____1____ half the north-wing cubicles are ____2____ 20 meters from the nearest fire escape.

Select for 1 and for 2 two options to create a sentence that most accurately restates the information given in the first sentence. Make only two selections, one in each column.

1	2	
		at least
		at most
		exactly
		greater than
		less than

491. In June 1990, a small academic press published an initial run of 2,500 copies of linguist Chloe Vermeulen's first book, *Speech and Speaking*. Because the first run was selling well, a second, larger run was produced in June 1995. Total sales for the period from June 1995–June 2000 represented an increase of 52 percent over total sales for the preceding five years; by June 2000, Vermeulen's book had sold a total of 3,843 copies. In 2000, *Speech and Speaking* was cited in an influential paper; subsequently, for the period June 2000–June 2005, sales of Vermeulen's book were double the sales for the previous five-year period.

In the table, identify the number of books that most closely approximates the total sales of *Speech and Speaking* for each of the five-year periods June 1990–June 1995 and June 2000–June 2005, based on the information given. Make only two selections, one in each column.

June 1990–June 1995	June 2000–June 2005	Total sales for the period (number of books)
		1,320
		1,530
		2,530
		2,640
		3,800
		4,640

492. Miguel's online banking password is nine characters long and includes at least one character of each of five types: digits, punctuation marks, uppercase (capital) letters, lowercase (noncapital) letters, and certain other characters. The password begins or ends with one of these other characters, of which it contains exactly one. No consecutive characters in the password are of the same one of these types. (For example, no capital letter is preceded or followed by another capital letter.) The password contains more lowercase letters than characters of any one of the other four types. It also contains fewer punctuation marks than digits, lowercase letters, or uppercase letters. The first three characters of the password are M, ?, and G.

In the table, select a type of character that the fifth character in the password must be and a type of character that the seventh character must be. Make only two selections, one in each column.

Fifth character	Seventh character	
		Digit
		Lowercase letter
		Punctuation mark
		Uppercase letter
		Other character

493. Public health professional: The Happydale Department of Environmental Services (DES) has inspected area beaches for pathogenic bacteria for over 20 years. Currently, DES monitors 50 freshwater beaches and 10 coastal beaches on a weekly basis. Program participation by owners of beaches that are open to the public is voluntary. Beach owners who choose not to participate in the program are allowing the public to recreate on entirely unmonitored beaches. The DES now proposes adoption of the Adopt-a-Beach Program, designed to promote health and environmental education as well as public involvement in the protecting of public beaches. The program would require DES to collect biological data from all area beaches. It will also help reduce the number of beach advisories, whereby the public must be warned of dangerous conditions on certain beaches.

On the basis of the public health professional's statement, indicate in the table which of the following is most likely to result if the DES proposal is successfully adopted, and indicate which is most likely to result if the DES proposal is not adopted. Make only two selections, one in each column.

Adopted	Not adopted	
		Incidents of waterborne disease will increase.
		The number of beach advisories will increase.
		DES will shift its principal priorities from monitoring to education.
		There will be fewer, if any, entirely unmonitored beaches.
		Some beaches will remain entirely unmonitored.

494. Marco: Giant kangaroos—one of several extinct species of large mammals (megafauna)—went extinct in Australia around 46,000 years ago. The deposits and wear patterns on the teeth of these animals from around the time of their extinction indicate that they fed mostly on saltbrush shrubs. Saltbrush thrives in arid climates, so it is not likely that the kangaroos' food supply was adversely affected by the increasing aridity of the climate at the time. Thus, something else would have to account for their extinction, and the best candidate for that cause is predation by humans.

Fatima: That argument alone is not likely to satisfy many researchers in this field. Have you found any other evidence to bolster your conclusion?

Select Marco for the statement that, if true, most justifies Marco's assertions, and select Fatima for the statement that, if true, most justifies Fatima's skepticism about Marco's assertions. Make only two selections, one in each column.

Marco	Fatima	
		Giant kangaroos became extinct during a period that was less arid than previous periods they endured.
		Many researchers believe humans first arrived in Australia around 40,000 years ago.
		Approximately 60 different species in Australia died out in the wave of extinctions around 46,000 years ago.
		Fossils of giant kangaroos also show evidence that those animals' diets routinely included plants other than saltbrush.
		Several types of megafauna larger than the giant kangaroo went extinct around 46,000 years ago.

495. A mattress company has two stores, one in City X and the other in City Z. The company has advertised equally in newspapers in both cities but has advertised twice as much on the radio in City Z as in City X. The two cities have similar populations and economies, and the sales at each store have been roughly equal. A consultant claims this shows that the radio advertising has not improved mattress sales. In the table below, select changes that the company could make in City X and City Z, respectively, that together would probably be most helpful in testing the consultant's claim. Make only two selections, one in each column.

City X	City Z	
		Double newspaper advertising
		Eliminate newspaper advertising
		Eliminate radio advertising
		Change the content of radio advertising
		Add television advertising

496. Metro Ballet Company presents high-quality productions of traditional, classical ballet. For the past several years, however, the company's overall profits have been declining, and ticket sales have been flat. Annual audience surveys indicate that a majority of those who attend Metro Ballet productions consistently enjoy the performances and prefer classical ballet to other forms of dance; almost all of them have been attending Metro Ballet for several years. General surveys of area residents indicate, however, that very few are aware of Metro Ballet productions, and most imagine that the performances are boring and the tickets too expensive. In an effort to appeal to a wider audience, over the past decade the company has spent increasing amounts of money on spectacular stage productions, while lowering ticket prices.

In the first column, select the strategy that, in the absence of the other alternatives listed, would lead most directly to decreasing Metro Ballet's expenses for its classical ballet productions. In the second column, select the strategy that, in the absence of the other alternatives listed, would constitute the most direct approach to solving the problem of increasing audience size for Metro Ballet's classical ballet productions. Make only two selections, one in each column.

Decrease expenses	Increase audience size	
		Obtain public funding to double the spending on stage productions without increasing ticket prices
		Return spending on productions to levels of several years ago
		Expand productions to include modern, folk, and tap dance traditions
		Offer special discounts to reward people who have attended the greatest number of performances
		Mount a local advertising campaign emphasizing the affordability and excitement of Metro Ballet's spectacular stage productions

369

497. At XYZ Inc. any employee receives a verbal warning upon accumulating at least 3 unexcused absences within any 365-day period and a written reprimand upon accumulating at least 4 such absences. For any single 8-hour workday, missing between 10 minutes and 2 hours of work counts as one-third of an absence, missing between 2 hours and 4 hours of work counts as half an absence, and missing more than 4 hours counts as a full absence. However, an employee may stay late to make up for up to 1 hour of an unexcused absence on the same day.

The following options are descriptions of the unexcused absences of 5 employees of XYZ Inc. Assume that in each case the employee had no other unexcused absences and made up no other time. Select a description of an employee who qualified for a verbal warning but not a written reprimand, and select a description of an employee who qualified for a written reprimand. Make only two selections, one in each column.

Verbal warning	Written reprimand	
		Absent all day on 5 April 2010, 8 June 2010, 17 April 2011, and 14 June 2011
		Absent 4.5 hours but stayed 1 hour late on 13 May 2010; absent all day on 2 June 2010, 1 May 2011, and 21 July 2011
		Absent 4.5 hours on 19 March 2010; stayed one hour late on 20 March 2010; absent all day on 8 February 2011 and 9 February 2011; arrived 40 minutes late on 17 April 2011
		Absent 3.5 hours on 13 September 2010; absent 1 hour on 15 September 2010; absent 6 hours on 16 September 2010; absent 2.5 hours on 18 September 2010; absent 1 hour on 19 September 2010
		Absent 3 hours on 7 July 2010; absent 2.5 hours on 13 September 2010; absent all day on 31 January 2011 and 4 July 2011; absent 5 hours on 12 March 2011

498. Marketing strategist: Agency A designed an advertising campaign that our company is about to test with a focus group. We are wondering whether a new ad campaign will increase our name recognition among consumers. As a contingency, we have decided that we might ask Agency B to design an alternate campaign. However, if we find that Agency A's campaign elicits positive responses from the focus group, we will not ask Agency B for a campaign.

A statement that must be true if the marketing strategist's statements are true: After the focus testing is complete, if the company ___1___, then it must also be the case that the company ___2___.

Select for 1 if and 2 then the two different options that create a statement that must be true if the marketing strategist's statements are true. Make only two selections, one in each column.

1 if	2 then	
		believes Agency A's campaign will increase the company's name recognition
		believes Agency A's campaign will decrease the company's name recognition
		asks Agency B for a campaign
		asks Agency A for an alternate campaign
		believes the focus group did not respond positively to Agency A's campaign

499. Francois and Pierre each owe Claudine money. Today, Francois will make a payment equal to 50% of the amount he owes Claudine, and Pierre will make a payment equal to 10% of the amount he owes Claudine. Together, the two payments will be equal to 40% of the combined amount that Francois and Pierre owe Claudine.

Select for Francois and Pierre amounts that Francois and Pierre could owe Claudine that are jointly consistent with the given information. Make only two selections, one in each column.

Francois	Pierre	
	€50	
	€250	
	€750	
	€3,750	
	€6,750	

500. Witness testimony: Around 8:00 on the morning of Tuesday, July 6, I saw a man exit from the back entrance of the building. I knew it was McGregor by the man's height and his long, slightly awkward steps, and from the fact that he was wearing a hat—possibly a baseball cap. McGregor always seemed to be wearing some kind of hat. On Tuesdays there are always several groundskeepers scheduled to work on the grounds, and he would very likely have been scheduled that day.

Select *Assumes to be true* for the statement that describes something the testimony implies the witness assumes to be true, and select *Assumes to be false* for the statement that describes something the testimony implies the witness assumes to be false. Make only two selections, one in each column.

Assumes to be true	Assumes to be false	
		McGregor was the only groundskeeper scheduled to work at the building on Tuesday, July 6.
		McGregor exited the rear of the building in question alone at 8:00 on the morning of Tuesday, July 6.
		McGregor was scheduled to work at the building on the morning of Tuesday, July 6.
		McGregor's height, way of walking, and tendency to wear hats distinguish him from the other groundskeepers.
		McGregor often wore a baseball cap prior to the morning of Tuesday, July 6.

501. Ribonucleic acid (RNA) is a molecule built from sequences of smaller molecules called nucleobases. RNA nucleobases are of 4 different types: adenine (A), cytosine (C), guanine (G), and uracil (U). Consider the collection of all possible RNA sequences consisting of 12 nucleobases, 3 of each type. An RNA sequence will be selected at random from this collection, and the first 3 nucleobases of the sequence will be detached from the sequence.

In the table, select the probability that the 3 nucleobases are all of the same type, and select the probability that they are of 3 different types. Make only two selections, one in each column.

All the same type	3 different types	
		$\frac{1}{55}$
		$\frac{9}{220}$
		$\frac{9}{110}$
		$\frac{9}{55}$
		$\frac{27}{55}$

502. Let S be the set of all 7-digit numbers N such that the sum of the digits of N is divisible by 7.

A and B are two 7-digit numbers:

$A = 4,893,P12$

$B = 5,857,0Q5$

Select a value for P so that A is an element of S. Select a value for Q so that B is an element of S. Make two selections, one in each column.

P	Q	
		4
		5
		6
		7
		8

503. Alfredo: The United States could make significant progress toward becoming independent of petroleum-derived gasoline as a source of energy by diverting a large proportion of corn grown in the US to the production of ethanol for fuel. Brazil is virtually independent of petroleum as a source of fuel because that country has been very successful in ethanol production.

Mavis: Ethanol derived from corn will never be a viable substitute for petroleum-derived gasoline in the US. While it is true that Brazil has been very successful in replacing gasoline with ethanol, the US cannot expect the same degree of success with corn-derived ethanol. Brazil's ethanol is derived from sugarcane, which is very easy to convert to ethanol and, in Brazil, very easy to cultivate. Corn, on the other hand, is difficult to grow, requiring intensive cultivation. Also, the amount of fuel energy that can be garnered from the land is much less per square meter for corn ethanol.

Based on the information provided, select for *Alfredo* the statement that best describes the primary purpose of Alfredo's remarks and select for *Mavis* the statement that best describes the primary purpose of Mavis's remarks. Make only two selections, one in each column.

Alfredo	Mavis	
		Critique a line of reasoning
		Compare two strategies aimed at solving a problem
		Provide an alternative to a given proposal
		Illustrate the details of a particular strategy
		Recommend a course of action for reaching a goal

504. Company T projected the number of international students studying in the United States (US) for three consecutive school years from 2014–2015 through 2016–2017. The projected numbers for the 2014–2015 school year and during the 2016–2017 school year would be 880,000 and 1,026,080, respectively. Let X% and Y% denote the company's predicted percentage increase in the number of international students studying in the US from school year 2014–2015 to school year 2015–2016, and from school year 2015–2016 to school year 2016–2017, respectively. Both X and Y are positive integers, and X is less than Y.

In the table, identify the value of X and the value of Y. Make only two selections, one in each column.

X	Y	
		2
		6
		10
		15
		20

6.8 Answer Key: Two-Part Analysis

	Response 1	Response 2
437.	60	65
438.	RN	UN
439.	14	42
440.	910	1,350
441.	Time	Security
442.	To encourage historians not to approach a particular historical event from too narrow a perspective	To criticize a certain type of argument about a particular historical event
443.	€47.60	€68.20
444.	4	16
445.	4	4
446.	An increase in phytoplankton	An increase in crown-of-thorns sea stars
447.	The next cup to be recovered from the site will likely be made of porcelain.	Other cups have been recovered from the archaeological site, all of which were made of porcelain.
448.	Change the farm-subsidy system	Improve the overall quality of people's diets
449.	Artifact B is older than Artifact A.	Artifact C is older than Artifact B.
450.	0.07	0.52
451.	retention of information from lessons given in rooms occupied for only a short time	retention of information from multiple lessons given in the same room over a period of time
452.	0.090	0.120
453.	Immunity	Genetics
454.	Wednesday	Thursday
455.	$P + 0.25\,P$	$1.25\,P - 20$
456.	400	80
457.	tested the children's sense of balance	taught dance to the children through the dance program

	Response 1	Response 2
458.	Students' academic performance	Extracurricular activities
459.	Brazil has been very successful at replacing petroleum with ethanol.	Producing corn ethanol is a viable strategy for a nation intent on reducing dependence on petroleum.
460.	$175,000	$172,700
461.	The creation of systems that display intelligence regarding specific tasks is an especially important step toward the creation of systems with general intelligence.	Research in the narrow AI field is not likely to lead to significant breakthroughs in the general AI field.
462.	Baby birds of the coastal-plain subspecies and baby birds of a freshwater swamp subspecies, all raised on an identical diet under controlled conditions, grew plumage similar in color to that of their respective parents.	None of the genetic differences that have been identified in the genomes of coastal-plain swamp sparrows and freshwater swamp sparrows affect plumage color.
463.	9	45
464.	96,000	32,000
465.	1 hour 7 minutes	1 hour 22 minutes
466.	Trampoline	Waltzy
467.	Painting of girl's face, in shades of blue and red, acrylic and oil on canvas, 2006	Abstract sequence of interconnected curves, ceramic, 2008
468.	The aid industry should focus its spending less on primary education than it now does.	Projects in education are more likely to be successful if they are paid for by local people.
469.	5	20
470.	−3	−7
471.	0.98	0.92
472.	3	6
473.	economic well-being after graduating from university	tendency to earn higher grades in university classes

	Response 1	Response 2
474.	52	53
475.	A	C
476.	Must be less than or equal to 20%	Must be greater than or equal to 80%
477.	1st selection	3rd selection
478.	3	9
479.	enacted more democratic reforms than did Prussia	had similar inequality in land ownership as did Prussia
480.	Governments failing to enact new water-management policies	Depletion of groundwater supplies in some regions
481.	Prior to the assignment, none of the students had strong feelings about either side of the debate topic.	By chance, almost all of the students were assigned to the side of the debate that they already agreed with.
482.	When the option to pause a commercial-free television program is available, the vast majority of people will do so at least once during a program.	People shown to have especially long attention spans are no more likely to enjoy commercial-free television programs than are people with short attention spans.
483.	34	4
484.	A different study found that few blood donors consider donating blood to be comparable to "charitable giving."	People tend to give less to charity during weeks in which they help neighbors by providing a needed good or service.
485.	130	30
486.	Each of the USCG's suits was filed in a single location and names a large number of defendants in other locations.	The costs associated with contesting the charges would be high for a large number of the defendants.
487.	less than 100,000 AED	less than 100,000
488.	impressed the hiring committee during the telephone interview	had extensive experience
489.	Abigail only	Charles only

	Response 1	Response 2
490.	less than	at least
491.	1,530	4,640
492.	Digit	Digit
493.	There will be fewer, if any, entirely unmonitored beaches.	Some beaches will remain entirely unmonitored.
494.	Giant kangaroos became extinct during a period that was less arid than previous periods they endured.	Many researchers believe humans first arrived in Australia around 40,000 years ago.
495.	Eliminate radio advertising.	Eliminate radio advertising.
496.	Return spending on productions to levels of several years ago.	Mount a local advertising campaign emphasizing the affordability and excitement of Metro Ballet's spectacular stage productions.
497.	Absent 4.5 hours on 19 March 2010; stayed one hour late on 20 March 2010; absent all day on 8 February 2011 and 9 February 2011; arrived 40 minutes late on 17 April 2011	Absent 3 hours on 7 July 2010; absent 2.5 hours on 13 September 2010; absent all day on 31 January 2011 and 4 July 2011; absent 5 hours on 12 March 2011
498.	asks Agency B for a campaign	believes the focus group did not respond positively to Agency A's campaign
499.	€750	€250
500.	McGregor's height, way of walking, and tendency to wear hats distinguish him from the other groundskeepers.	McGregor was the only groundskeeper scheduled to work at the building on Tuesday, July 6.
501.	$\frac{1}{55}$	$\frac{27}{55}$
502.	8	5
503.	Recommend a course of action for reaching a goal.	Critique a line of reasoning.
504.	6	10

6.9 Answer Explanations: Two-Part Analysis

The following discussion of Data Insights is intended to familiarize you with the most efficient and effective approaches to the kinds of problems common to Data Insights. The particular questions in this chapter are generally representative of the kinds of Data Insights questions you will encounter on the GMAT exam. Remember that it is the problem-solving strategy that is important, not the specific details of a particular question.

Questions 437 to 455 — Difficulty: Easy

437. Trains M and N are traveling west on parallel tracks. At exactly noon, the front of Train M, which is traveling at a constant speed of 80 kilometers per hour (km/h), is at the rail crossing at Location X, and the front of Train N, which is traveling at a constant speed of 65 km/h, is 30 km west of the rail crossing at Location X. The trains continue traveling at their respective speeds until the front of Train M and the front of Train N are simultaneously at the rail crossing at Location Y.

In the table, identify the number of kilometers that the front of Train M has traveled between noon and 12:45 p.m. and the number of kilometers that the front of Train N has traveled between noon and 1:00 p.m.

Front of Train M	Front of Train N	
		55
		60
		65
		70
		75

Answer Explanation:

Infer

Front of Train M:

The elapsed time between noon and 12:45 p.m. is 45 minutes, which is $\frac{3}{4}$ hour. In traveling at 80 kilometers per hour for $\frac{3}{4}$ hour, the front of Train M traveled $\frac{3}{4}(80) = 60$ kilometers.

The correct answer is *60*.

Front of Train N:

The elapsed time between noon and 1:00 p.m. is 1 hour. In traveling at 65 kilometers per hour for 1 hour, the front of Train N traveled $1(65) = 65$ kilometers.

The correct answer is *65*.

438. An international basketball tournament will be held in either Nation QN or Nation RN. Exactly six nations, including the host, plan to participate, depending on the following conditions:

SN will participate only if TN does. UN will not participate if either VN or WN does. WN will not participate unless the tournament is held in RN.

Based on the information provided, and assuming WN participates, in the first column select the nation that must also participate, and in the second column select the nation that will not participate. Make only two selections, one in each column.

Must participate	Will not participate	
		QN
		RN
		SN
		TN
		UN
		VN

Answer Explanation:

Apply

Must participate:

We are told to assume that WN participates. If so, we know that the tournament will be held in RN, because WN will not participate unless that is where the tournament is held. And if the tournament is held in RN, then it must be that RN will participate, because the host nation will participate in the tournament. Therefore, assuming WN participates, it must be the case that RN will participate as well.

The correct answer is *RN*.

Will not participate:

We are told to assume that WN participates. We are also told that UN will not participate if either VN or WN does. So, assuming that WN participates, it cannot be that UN participates.

The correct answer is *UN*.

439. A portion of an automobile test track is divided into Segment A, Segment B, and Segment C, in that order. In a performance test on a car, the car traveled Segment A at a constant speed of 140 kilometers per hour (km/h). Immediately after this, the car rapidly slowed on Segment B and then traveled on Segment C at a constant speed of 70 km/h. The length of Segment C is 3 times the length of Segment A, and it took a total of 42 minutes for the car to travel both Segments A and C. In the table, select the length of Segment A, in kilometers, and select the length of Segment C, in kilometers. Make only two selections, one in each column.

Length of Segment A (kilometers)	Length of Segment C (kilometers)
	8
	14
	24
	42
	72
	126

Answer Explanation:

Strategize

Length of Segment A (kilometers)

We are asked to determine the lengths of two segments of an automobile test track. The passage states that a car traveled Segment A at a constant rate of 140 km/h and traveled Segment C at a constant rate of 70 km/h, which indicates that it took the car twice as much time to cover a given unit of distance in Segment C as it took to cover the same distance in Segment A. The passage further states that the length of Segment C is 3 times the length of Segment A. Because the car took twice the time to cover a given distance in Segment C as in Segment A, and because Segment C is 3 times as long as Segment A, it can be further determined that the car spent 6 times as much time traveling Segment C as it did traveling Segment A. The passage indicates that it took a total of 42 minutes for the car to travel both Segments A and C, and 42 minutes is equal to 0.7 h (42/60). Therefore, given that the car spent 6 times as much of the total combined time on Segment C as it did on Segment A, it can be calculated that the car spent 0.1 h on Segment A and 0.6 h on Segment C. Because we know that the car was traveling at 140 km/h for 0.1 h on Segment A, we can determine that Segment A was 14 kilometers long.

The correct answer is *14*.

Length of Segment C (kilometers)

As noted in the analysis above, the car spent 0.6 h traveling Segment C. Because we know that the car was traveling at 70 km/h for 0.6 h on Segment C, we can determine that Segment C was 42 kilometers long.

The correct answer is *42*.

440. Let *X*, *Y*, and *Z* denote the number of international students, in thousands, that Company U predicted would be studying in the United States (US) during the school years 2014–2015, 2019–2020, and 2024–2025, respectively. The average (arithmetic mean) of *X*, *Y*, and *Z* is 1,128, and *Y* = 1,124. Company U predicted that there would be more international students studying in the US during the 2024–2025 school year than during the 2014–2015 school year.

In the table, identify a value of X and a value of Z that are jointly consistent with the information provided. Make only two selections, one in each column.

X	Z	
		910
		995
		1,175
		1,350
		1,435

Answer Explanation:

Apply

Infer

The task is to determine values for X and Z, where $X < Z$, such that the arithmetic mean of X, Y, and Z is 1,128 and $Y = 1,124$. Given that the arithmetic mean of X, Y, and Z is 1,128, it follows that $\frac{X+Y+Z}{3}$ and $X + Y + Z = 3(1,128) = 3,384$. If $Y = 1,124$, then $X + Z = 3,384 - 1,124 = 2,260$. Since $X < Z$ and $\frac{2,260}{2}$, it follows that $X < 1,130$ and $Z > 1,130$.

X:

Since $X < 1,130$, the only table values possible are $X = 910$ or $X = 995$. If $X = 910$, then, since $X + Z = 2,260$, $Z = 2,260 - 910 = 1,350$, which is a table entry.

The correct answer is *910*.

Z:

Since $X = 910$ and $X + Z = 2,260$, it follows that $Z = 2,260 - 910 = 1,350$.

The correct answer is *1,350*.

441. Advice from a computer security expert, on passwords used for accessing online accounts follows:

Computer users should use a different password for each online account. They should also use *strong passwords*, which are hard for hackers to decipher.

However, strong passwords are difficult to remember, and this is especially the case for users who have multiple online accounts.

Fortunately, software is available at no cost that can store and encrypt a user's passwords: the user need only remember one password to access the rest. For users willing to take the time to install the software on a computer and enter all the required data, such software provides one way to comply with my advice. Some versions of the software can even be copied to a portable device, such as a USB drive, whereby a user can access passwords from any compatible computer.

For computer users with multiple accounts who would not otherwise use a different strong password on every account, the expert's advice amounts to suggesting that such users make certain sacrifices in order to make certain gains. Indicate by appropriate selections in the first and second column which of the items in the third column such users would sacrifice and which they would gain. Make only two selections, one in each column.

Sacrifice	Gain	
		Money
		Computing speed
		Security
		Number of online accounts
		Time

Answer Explanation:

Infer

Sacrifice:

To be able to follow the computer security expert's advice effectively, the expert acknowledges that computer users with multiple accounts will have to make a sacrifice of time to install the software and input the relevant data.

The correct answer is *Time*.

Gain:

The computer security expert claims that making the sacrifice of time involved in installing the software and inputting the relevant data will result in an increase in security (namely, by making online accounts secure from hacking).

The correct answer is *Security*.

442. Some studies of how it was that Prussia resisted the wave of European democratization in the nineteenth century point to Prussia's unequal distribution of land ownership as the principal explanation. And political figures from areas in Prussia with high inequality in land ownership tended to be the staunchest opponents of democratic reforms.

However, **arguments that focus only on those figures' conflicts with landless people ignore the fact that political figures are not only representatives of socioeconomic interests but also political actors embedded in particular contexts that shape whether they support democratic reforms**. Historians must take such contexts into account if they hope to explain what transpired in Prussia during this period.

Select *Passage* for the statement that best describes the purpose of the passage as a whole, and select *Portion in **Boldface*** for the statement that best describes the purpose of the portion in **boldface**. Make only two selections, one in each column.

Passage	Portion in Boldface	
		To offer an alternative to the standard explanation of a particular historical event
		To provide evidence that economic issues were at the root of a particular historical event
		To criticize a certain type of argument about a particular historical event
		To criticize the motives of political figures involved in a particular historical event
		To encourage historians not to approach a particular historical event from too narrow a perspective

Answer Explanation:

Evaluate

The passage asserts that some studies appeal to the fact that Prussia had significant inequality in land ownership during the nineteenth century to explain why Prussia did not participate in the wave of democratization in that century. Political figures in areas of Prussia with high inequality of land ownership were often most strongly opposed to democratization. The passage, however, asserts (in the **boldfaced** text) that such arguments ignore that these political figures not only represent socioeconomic interests but also are political actors embedded in contexts that affect whether they support democratization. The passage claims that historians must take such contexts into account to arrive at an accurate understanding of Prussia during this period.

Passage:

The passage argues that historians should not focus too narrowly on socioeconomic interests. Instead, the passage asserts that they should think more broadly and consider other contexts.

The correct answer is *To encourage historians not to approach a particular historical event from too narrow a perspective*.

Portion in Boldface:

The portion in **boldface** is critical of arguments that focus only on political figures' conflicts with landless people, saying that such arguments ignore certain key facts about the political figures.

The correct answer is *To criticize a certain type of argument about a particular historical event*.

443. In September 2010, Armando purchased 5 identically priced shirts and 3 identically priced pairs of trousers from a certain department store. Armando paid a total of €28.85 for the shirts and €38.97 for the trousers. In October 2010, the department store held a sale, taking 25% off the September price of everything in the store. Armando returned to the store during the October 2010 sale and bought 11 of the shirts and 7 pairs of the trousers for some friends.

In the table, select how much Armando paid in October for the 11 shirts and 7 pairs of trousers, rounding for each item to the nearest cent. Make only one selection in each column.

Shirts	Trousers	
		€47.60
		€63.51
		€68.20
		€79.39
		€90.91
		€204.54

Answer Explanation:

Infer

Shirts:

In September 2010, Armando purchased 5 identically priced shirts for a total of €28.85. It follows that he paid €$\frac{28.85}{5}$ = €5.77 each. At the sale in October 2010, he purchased 11 of these shirts at a reduced price of 25% off the September 2010 price and paid a total of (€5.77)(0.75)(11) ≈ €47.60.

The correct answer is €47.60.

Trousers:

In September 2010, Armando purchased 3 identically priced pairs of trousers for a total of €38.97. It follows that he paid €$\frac{38.97}{3}$ = €12.99 each. At the sale in October 2010, he purchased 7 of these pairs of trousers at a reduced price of 25% off the September 2010 price and paid a total of (€12.99)(0.75)(7) ≈ €68.20.

The correct answer is €68.20.

444. A city is hosting a table tennis tournament for its residents. Each team has exactly two players, and each player is on exactly one team. In each round, each team plays exactly one other team and either wins or loses. The winning team advances to the next round and the losing team is eliminated. No team

or player drops out except by losing a game. The tournament is in progress, and exactly 512 players participated in the first round.

From the available options, select a number of tournament rounds and a number of teams such that after the specified number of rounds there will be the specified number of teams remaining in the tournament. Make only two selections, one in each column.

Rounds Completed	Teams Remaining	
		2
		4
		8
		16
		32

Answer Explanation:

Apply

Before any rounds are completed, there are 512 players, each on exactly one team of two players. Therefore, there are 256 teams in the competition. After each round, half of the teams are eliminated. The following table summarizes the results after each round of the tournament.

Rounds completed	1	2	3	4	5	6	7	8
Teams remaining	128	64	32	16	8	4	2	1

The only available combination of rounds completed and number of teams remaining is 4 rounds completed and 16 teams remaining.

Rounds completed:

The correct answer is 4.

Teams remaining:

The correct answer is 16.

445. Adiliah, Bao, Davi, Laszlo, Saleema, and Yarah work in a firm's legal department. Adiliah supervises Bao and Davi, Davi supervises Laszlo, and Laszlo supervises Saleema and Yarah. These are the only supervisory

relationships involving these six employees. Each document that the department processes must be initially reviewed by exactly one department member. Each document reviewed by a department member must then be reviewed by that person's supervisor. No other rules require anyone else to review any document. Anyone not required to review a given document will not review it.

Select *Laszlo among reviewers* for the maximum number of department members who could have reviewed a single document if Laszlo was among the reviewers. Select *Adiliah among reviewers* for the maximum number of department members who could have reviewed a single document if Adiliah was among the reviewers. Make only two selections, one in each column.

Laszlo among reviewers	Adiliah among reviewers	
		1
		2
		3
		4
		5
		6

Answer Explanation:

Apply

Laszlo among reviewers:

If Laszlo reviews a document, so must his supervisor, Davi, and Davi's supervisor, Adiliah. If Laszlo is the initial reviewer, then exactly 3 department members would review the document. However, if Laszlo reviews a document but is not the initial reviewer, the initial reviewer must be either Saleema or Yarah for a maximum total of 4 reviewers of the document.

The correct answer is *4*.

Adiliah among reviewers:

If Adiliah reviews a document, no department members will review the document after her.

If Adiliah is the initial reviewer, then exactly 1 department member will review the document. If Bao or Davi is the initial reviewer, then the document will be reviewed by exactly 2 department members. If Laszlo is the initial reviewer, then the document will be reviewed by exactly 3 department members. Finally, if Saleema or Yarah is the initial reviewer, then exactly 4 department members will review the document. Since no one else can be the initial reviewer, 4 must be the maximum number of reviewers of a single document for which Adiliah is among the reviewers.

The correct answer is *4*.

446. Naturalist: The decline of coral reefs has various causes. One contributing factor is predation on coral by organisms such as the crown-of-thorns sea star, whose preferred food source is coral polyps. Human fishing practices have decreased the sea star's predators, such as the harlequin shrimp. It is also possible that runoff containing nutrients for phytoplankton has resulted in larger phytoplankton blooms: the crown-of-thorns sea star gladly eats phytoplankton.

Indicate which cause-and-effect sequence would most likely, according to the naturalist, result in coral reef decline. Make only two selections, one in each column.

Cause	Effect	
		An increase in phytoplankton
		A decrease in phytoplankton
		An increase in crown-of-thorns sea stars
		A decrease in crown-of-thorns sea stars
		An increase in harlequin shrimp

Answer Explanation:

Infer

We are asked to provide a sequence of cause and effect that would (according to the naturalist) result in coral reef decline. The question suggests that the answers will be dependent on one another, in that the correct answer for *Cause* will depend on the correct answer for *Effect*, and vice versa.

The passage states that one factor contributing to coral reef decline is predation on coral by organisms such as the crown-of-thorns sea star. The preferred food source for this organism is coral polyps, and so a causal sequence that has as its effect an increase in crown-of-thorns sea stars may be likely to produce a decline in coral reefs. This suggests that the third option may be the correct response for *Effect*. However, this depends on whether one of the other statements in the table describes a cause suggested by the naturalist to produce this effect.

The last sentence of the naturalist's statement indeed suggests, in the context of the passage, that an increase in phytoplankton blooms would result in greater numbers of crown-of-thorns sea stars. This suggests that the first option may be the correct response for *Cause*. And indeed, according to the naturalist, the crown-of-thorns sea star's preferred food source is coral polyps. All of the naturalist's statement is about possible explanations of the decline of coral reefs. The passage therefore indicates that the naturalist would take an increase in phytoplankton (the first option, *Cause*) to produce an increase in crown-of-thorns sea stars (the third option, *Effect*), and that this causal sequence would likely result in coral reef decline.

Cause:

The correct answer is *An increase in phytoplankton.*

Effect:

The correct answer is *An increase in crown-of-thorns sea stars.*

447. Archaeologist: There were several porcelain-production centers in eighteenth-century Britain, among them Bristol, Plymouth, and New Hall. Each center developed a unique recipe for its porcelain that might include flint glass, soapstone, bone ash, clay, quartz, and so on. We will therefore be able to determine, on the basis of compositional analysis, where the next cup we recover from this archaeological site was made.

Indicate two different statements as follows: one statement identifies an *assumption required* by the

archaeologist's argument, and the other identifies a *possible fact* that would, if true, provide significant logical support for the required assumption. Make only two selections, one in each column.

Assumption Required	Possible Fact	
		Other cups have been recovered from the archeological site, all of which were made of porcelain.
		Some of the cups recovered from the archeological site were not made of porcelain.
		The next cup to be recovered from the site will likely be made of porcelain.
		Porcelain makers often traveled between centers, experimenting with one another's recipes.
		There was considerable overlap of materials in the recipes used by the various centers.
		Most porcelain in eighteenth-century Britain was made at one of the several centers.

Answer Explanation:

Infer

This item asks for a possible fact and an assumption of the argument such that the possible fact supports the assumption. This suggests that the correctness of the answer for one response opportunity could depend on the correctness of the answer for the other.

Assumption Required:

Only one of the statements in the table is an assumption required by the archaeologist's argument. If the next cup recovered from the archaeological site is not made of porcelain, then the evidence provided by the archaeologist has no relevance regarding where the next cup recovered from the site was made. This indicates that the third statement may be the correct response.

In contrast, the first statement, although a strengthener of the argument, is not a required assumption: we could, for example, have other reasons for believing that the next cup will be made of porcelain. The sixth statement would also be an important strengthener, but it is not required for the reasoning of the argument to be sound.

The correct answer is *The next cup to be recovered from the site will likely be made of porcelain.*

Possible Fact:

Given that the third statement is the required assumption within the list in the table, the possible fact asked for in the question must be a possible fact that provides significant logical support for this statement. (Because the question specifies that two *different* statements must be selected, the *possible fact* cannot be the third statement.)

The correct answer is *Other cups have been recovered from the archaeological site, all of which were made of porcelain.*

448. Health advocate: The government's current farm-subsidy system primarily rewards large farms for planting monocultures of corn, soybeans, wheat, and rice. Most of the crops produced in this way go to feed livestock in factory farms, which results in a glut of fatty meats in the marketplace. A large proportion of such crops that are not used to feed livestock are used to make sugary processed foods. These subsidies promote unhealthy diets by making sugary foods and fatty meats artificially cheap. Obviously, it is important for the government to avoid these effects.

On the basis of the information above, select *Recommends* for the option that describes the government action that the health advocate most likely recommends, and select *Intended result* for the option that describes what the health advocate likely hopes will be the result of that action. Make only two selections, one in each column.

Recommends	Intended result	
		Improve the overall quality of livestock feed
		Improve the overall quality of people's diets
		Reduce the overall financial cost of people's diets
		Prevent the manufacture of sugary processed food
		Change the farm-subsidy system

Answer Explanation:

Infer

Recommends:

The health advocate's comments have little or no relevance to overall **quality** of livestock feed, **overall** financial cost of people's diets, or **prevention of the manufacture** of sugary processed food. Of the two remaining options, the health advocate's comments are more appropriate for an argument to change the farm-subsidy system than to improve the overall quality of people's diets, the latter of which the health advocate's last two sentences suggest would be a consequence of changing the farm-subsidy system.

The correct answer is *Change the farm-subsidy system.*

Intended result:

The explanation above shows that, among the options, improving the overall quality of people's diets is the intended result of changing the farm-subsidy system.

The correct answer is *Improve the overall quality of people's diets.*

449. An archaeologist studying Artifacts A–D is interested in whether Artifact C is older than Artifact A.

Select an assertion involving Artifact A and an assertion involving Artifact C that together imply the assertion "Artifact C is older than Artifact A." Make only two selections, one in each column.

Assertion involving Artifact A	Assertion involving Artifact C	
		Artifact A is older than Artifact B.
		Artifact A is older than Artifact D.
		Artifact B is older than Artifact A.
		Artifact B is older than Artifact D.
		Artifact C is older than Artifact D.
		Artifact C is older than Artifact B.

Answer Explanation:

Infer

We are asked to select an assertion pertaining to Artifact A and an assertion pertaining to Artifact C that together imply the assertion *Artifact C is older than Artifact A.*

An assertion that Artifact A is *older* than one of the three other artifacts will not, together with any of the assertions involving Artifact C, imply the assertion *Artifact C is older than Artifact A.* Therefore, the assertion involving Artifact A must be an assertion that one of the other artifacts is older than Artifact A. Only the third option, *Artifact B is older than Artifact A,* is such an assertion.

Given the assertion that *Artifact B is older than Artifact A,* the assertion involving Artifact C that *Artifact C is older than Artifact B* implies that *Artifact C is older than Artifact A.* None of the other pairs of options would together imply that *Artifact C is older than Artifact A.*

Assertion involving Artifact A:

The correct answer is *Artifact B is older than Artifact A.*

Assertion involving Artifact C:

The correct answer is *Artifact C is older than Artifact B.*

450. For a randomly selected day, the probability that a visitor to a certain pond will see at least one swan is 0.35. The probability that a visitor to that pond on a randomly selected day will see at least one heron is 0.2. Furthermore, seeing a swan and seeing a heron are independent of each other.

Based on the information provided, select *Both swan and heron* for the probability that a visitor to the pond will see both at least one swan and at least one heron on any given day, and select *Neither swan nor heron* for the probability that a visitor to the pond will see neither a swan nor a heron on any given day. Make only two selections, one in each column.

Both swan and heron	Neither swan nor heron	
		0.02
		0.07
		0.48
		0.52
		0.70

Answer Explanation:

Apply

Both swan and heron:

We're told that seeing a swan and seeing a heron are independent of each other. The probability that two independent events both occur equals the probability of the first multiplied by the probability of the second. So, the probability that a visitor to the pond will see both at least one swan and at least one heron on any given day is $0.35 \times 0.2 = 0.07$.

The correct answer is *0.07.*

Neither swan nor heron:

If the probability of an event is P, the probability that the event won't occur is 1 – P. So, the probability of a visitor to the pond not seeing a swan on any given day is 1 – 0.35 = 0.65, and the probability of the visitor not seeing a heron on any given day is 1 – 0.2 = 0.8. Since seeing a swan is independent of seeing a heron, not seeing a swan is likewise independent of not seeing a heron. Thus, the probability that a visitor to the pond will see neither a swan nor a heron on any given day is 0.65 × 0.8 = 0.52.

The correct answer is *0.52*.

451. Two primary school teachers are debating the merits of classrooms with highly decorated walls.

Teacher 1: A recent study has shown that highly decorated walls can interfere with learning in the classroom. We should therefore decrease the number of wall decorations in our classrooms.

Teacher 2: The results of that study are correct, but pertain only to the retention of information from single lessons in which the students were in the classroom for only a short period of time. Our students are in the same classroom all day, five days a week. Without some added stimulation, students can become bored and therefore even more distracted than they would be by highly decorated walls. I therefore maintain that highly decorated walls serve to increase learning over the long term.

Select for X and for Y the options such that the following statement, if filled in accordingly, has the most support from the information provided. Make only two selections, one in each column. Teacher 2 suggests that he agrees with Teacher 1 about the effects of wall decorations on ____X____, but disagrees about the effects of wall decorations on ____Y____.

X	Y	
		retention of certain specified types of information
		the effectiveness of teaching methods that eschew rote learning
		the ability of students to maintain skills if practiced in various classrooms
		retention of information from multiple lessons given in the same room over a period of time
		retention of information from lessons given in rooms occupied for only a short time

Answer Explanation:

Infer

X:

Teacher 1 cites a study as having shown that highly decorated walls interfere with classroom learning. Teacher 2 remarks that these study results are correct with regard to retention of information from single, brief lessons. Thus, the two teachers agree that wall decorations interfere with retention of information from lessons given in rooms occupied for only a short time.

The correct answer is *retention of information from lessons given in rooms occupied for only a short time.*

Y:

By citing the study without qualification as a reason to remove classroom wall decorations, Teacher 1 implicitly accepts that the study results hold in general. Thus, Teacher 1 seems to believe that highly decorated walls generally interfere with classroom learning. But Teacher 2 argues that when students are in the same room for many lessons over long periods, decorated walls reduce their boredom and distraction, helping them learn better in the long run. So, the two teachers evidently disagree about whether highly decorated walls interfere with students' retention of information from multiple lessons given in the same room over time.

The correct answer is *retention of information from multiple lessons given in the same room over a period of time.*

452. Natalya put 14 blue marbles, 14 red marbles, and no other marbles into 3 empty cups. She put 2 blue marbles and 6 red marbles in Cup A, 6 blue marbles and 4 red marbles in Cup B, and 6 blue marbles and 4 red marbles in Cup C. After this, Dmitry will randomly pick three marbles, one from each cup.

Consistent with the given information, select for *3 blue* the probability that Dmitry will pick 3 blue marbles, and select for *3 red* the probability that Dmitry will pick 3 red marbles. Make only two selections, one in each column.

3 blue	3 red	
		0.090
		0.120
		0.125
		0.150
		0.250
		0.500

Answer Explanation:

Apply

3 blue:

Using the multiplication rule for independent events, the probability of selecting 3 blue marbles is the probability of selecting 1 blue marble from Cup A times the probability of selecting 1 blue marble from Cup B times the probability of selecting 1 blue marble from Cup C, which is equal to

$$\frac{\text{number of blue marbles in Cup A}}{\text{number of marbles in Cup A}}$$

$$\times \frac{\text{number of blue marbles in Cup B}}{\text{number of marbles in Cup B}}$$

$$\times \frac{\text{number of blue marbles in Cup C}}{\text{number of marbles in Cup C}}$$

$$= \frac{2^1}{8^4} \times \frac{6^3}{10^5} \times \frac{6^3}{10^5} = \frac{9}{100} = 0.09$$

The correct answer is *0.090.*

3 red:

Using the multiplication rule for independent events, the probability of selecting 3 red marbles is the probability of selecting 1 red marble from Cup A times the probability of selecting 1 red marble from Cup B times the probability of selecting 1 red marble from Cup C, which is equal to

$$\frac{\text{number of red marbles in Cup A}}{\text{number of marbles in Cup A}}$$

$$\times \frac{\text{number of red marbles in Cup B}}{\text{number of marbles in Cup B}}$$

$$\times \frac{\text{number of red marbles in Cup C}}{\text{number of marbles in Cup C}}$$

$$= \frac{6^3}{8^1} \times \frac{4^1}{10} \times \frac{4}{10} = \frac{12}{100} = 0.12$$

The correct answer is *0.120.*

453. In recent years, commercial beekeepers have reported *colony collapse*: the disappearance of entire colonies of bees. A biologist, Dr. B, argues that colony collapse is caused by a new parasite to which bees have not acquired immunity. A chemist, Dr. C, argues that colony collapse is caused by genetic damage from pesticides. And an ecologist, Dr. E, argues that 3 specific commercial beekeeping practices—transportation of hives over long distances, indiscriminate medication, and inbreeding—compromise both the immunity and the genetic diversity of bees, leaving them susceptible to mass die-offs from normally benign microbes.

Complete the table based on the stated views of Dr. B, Dr. C, and Dr. E. In the first column, select the factor common to both Dr. B's and Dr. E's accounts of colony collapse. In the second column, select the factor common to both Dr. C's and Dr. E's accounts of colony collapse. Make two selections, one in each column.

Dr. B and Dr. E	Dr. C and Dr. E	Factor
		Genetics
		Immunity
		Medication
		New parasites
		Normally benign microbes
		Pesticides

Answer Explanation:

Strategize

By listing the available factors associated with the information given about the arguments by Dr. B, Dr. C, and Dr. E, we can determine which factor is common to Dr. B and Dr. E and which factor is common to Dr. C and Dr. E.

Dr. B: New parasites, Immunity

Dr. C: Genetics, Pesticides

Dr. E: Medication, Immunity, Genetics, Normally benign microbes

Dr. B and Dr. E:

The factor common to both Dr. B and Dr. E is Immunity.

The correct answer is *Immunity*.

Dr. C and Dr. E:

The factor common to both Dr. C and Dr. E is Genetics.

The correct answer is *Genetics*.

454. Martine is scheduling five contractors (Contractors A through E) to do various tasks during Monday through Friday of the upcoming week. For each day, exactly one contractor will be scheduled to work, and each contractor's task will be completed on the day for which that contractor is scheduled. The scheduling must conform to the following constraints:

Contractor A must be scheduled to work on Monday.

Contractor B must be scheduled to work exactly two days after Contractor A.

Contractor E must be scheduled to work exactly three days after Contractor C.

Statement: Given the constraints, Martine must schedule Contractor B to work on ___1___ and Contractor D to work on ___2___.

Select for *1* and for *2* the options that complete the statement so that it is accurate based on the information provided. Make only two selections, one in each column.

1	2	
		Monday
		Tuesday
		Wednesday
		Thursday
		Friday

Answer Explanation:

Recognize

Using the first two constraints, Contractor A must be scheduled on Monday, and Contractor B must be scheduled two days later, which is on Wednesday.

Monday	Tuesday	Wednesday	Thursday	Friday
A		B		

According to the third constraint, Contractor C can only be scheduled on Monday or Tuesday, since three days later needs to be within the same Monday-through-Friday week. Since Contractor A must be scheduled on Monday, it follows that Contractor C must be scheduled on Tuesday, hence Contractor E must be scheduled three days later, which is on Friday.

Monday	Tuesday	Wednesday	Thursday	Friday
A	C	B		E

Finally, the remaining contractor, Contractor D, must be scheduled on the remaining day, Thursday, since each day exactly one contractor will be scheduled.

Monday	Tuesday	Wednesday	Thursday	Friday
A	C	B	D	E

1:

Using the last table above, Contractor B must be scheduled on Wednesday.

The correct answer is *Wednesday*.

2:

Using the last table above, Contractor D must be scheduled on Thursday.

The correct answer is *Thursday*.

455. Maria and her companion were given a $20 gift certificate for a restaurant. When they dined at the restaurant, the total amount they originally owed consisted of the total cost of the items they ordered plus a 7 percent sales tax and an 18 percent tip, both calculated on the total cost of the items they ordered. They applied the gift certificate and paid the remainder of the total amount they originally owed.

Let P denote the total cost, in dollars, of the items Maria and her companion ordered. Select *Before gift certificate* for the expression that is equivalent, for all $P > 20$, to the total amount they originally owed, before they applied the gift certificate, and select *After gift certificate* for the expression that is equivalent, for all $P > 20$, to the amount they paid after they applied the gift certificate.

Before gift certificate	After gift certificate	Expressions
		$1.25(P - 20)$
		$1.25P + 20$
		$1.25P - 20$
		$P + 0.25P$
		$0.8P + 0.18P + 0.07P$

Answer Explanation:

Infer

The total amount that Maria and her companion owed before applying the gift certificate was the cost of what they ordered ($$P$), plus the 7 percent sales tax on that cost ($$0.07P$), plus the 18 percent tip on that cost ($$0.18P$). So the total amount they owed in dollars before applying the gift certificate was $P + 0.07P + 0.18P = P + 0.25P$.

After applying the $20 gift certificate, they owed $20 less. That is, in dollars they owed $P + 0.25P - 20 = 1.25P - 20$.

Before gift certificate:
The correct answer is $P + 0.25P$.

After gift certificate:
The correct answer is $1.25P - 20$.

Questions 456 to 486 — Difficulty: Medium

456. Supervisor's memo: At the present rate of manufacture we will not have the 1,200 circuit boards assembled in time to ship them to the customer. We currently have 10 workers, all working 8 hours a day at the same hourly rate, assembling the boards, and to date they've assembled 400. In order to finish the customer's order in time, I'll need to have each of the workers work an additional 2 hours for each of the 10 workdays between now and the deadline.

One can determine the hourly rate at which each worker assembled circuit boards up to the date of the supervisor's memo by dividing ___1___ circuit boards by the product of ___2___ worker-hours per day and the number of days since the workers began assembling the circuit boards.

Select *Circuit boards* for the option that fills the blank labeled 1 in the given statement, and select *Worker-hours* for the option that fills the blank labeled 2 in the given statement to create the most accurate statement on the basis of the information provided. Make only two selections, one in each column.

Circuit boards	Worker-hours	
		80
		400
		500
		800
		1,000
		1,200

Answer Explanation:

Strategize

Circuit boards:

The number of circuit boards assembled is the product of the number of workers, the hourly rate per worker, the number of hours worked per day, and the number of days worked. Using the given information, it follows that

(400 boards) = (10 workers)(hourly rate)
(8 hours/day)(number of days)

Now solve for the hourly rate:

$$\text{hourly rate} = \frac{400 \text{ boards}}{(10 \text{ workers})(8 \text{ hours})(\text{number of days})}$$

$$= \frac{400 \text{ boards}}{(80 \text{ worker-hours})(\text{number of days})}$$

The correct answer is *400*.

Worker-hours:

The analysis in Response 1 shows that the number of worker-hours per day is 80.

The correct answer is *80*.

457. In an experiment, one thousand nine-year-old children were allowed to choose whether to participate in a program in which the researchers taught them dance during the daily break from their lessons. Four hundred of the children chose to participate for at least one year. At the end of the year, researchers found that the children who had participated had significantly better balance, on average, than those who had not. The researchers hypothesized that dancing resulted in a sustained improvement in the children's sense of balance.

It would be most helpful in evaluating the researchers' hypothesis to know whether the researchers ___1___ prior to having ___2___.

Select *Researchers* for the phrase that fills the blank labeled 1 in the given statement, and select *Prior to* for the phrase that fills the blank labeled 2 in the given statement to create the most accurate statement on the basis of the information provided. Make only two selections, one in each column.

Researchers	Prior to	
		tested the children's ability to dance
		designed a second experiment
		divided the children into the two experimental groups
		tested the children's sense of balance
		taught dance to the children through the dance program

Answer Explanation:

Evaluate

Researchers and *Prior to*:

Note that because of the relationship between the two answers that complete the sentence, the responses have to be considered together, not separately.

The question asks what would be most helpful to know when evaluating the researchers' hypothesis. To answer this, it is useful to consider some alternative explanations for the better balance of the children who had participated in the program. One alternative would be that the children who had decided to participate in the program already had better balance before participating. Therefore, it would be useful to know whether they actually did have any improvement in their balance. To resolve that issue, it would be helpful if we knew that the researchers had this information, which they could have acquired by testing the children's sense of balance prior to teaching them dance through the dance program.

The correct answer to Response 1 is *tested the children's sense of balance.*

The correct answer to Response 2 is *taught dance to the children through the dance program.*

458. Klaus: Closing our neighborhood's school will mean a major hassle for neighborhood families. Students will have to travel farther to and from school, which means they'll have less time for homework. That will likely affect them academically. Additionally, a vacant school building in our neighborhood is sure to attract crime and drag down home values.

Rena: Our neighborhood's school never had a great reputation anyway. Closing it means students will get to go to a larger school—with a better reputation—just a few kilometers away, where they'll have more opportunities to participate in extracurricular activities. That should make homes here more valuable to potential buyers. And the vacant school building could be converted into a much-needed community center.

Select *Klaus* for the phrase that best describes a factor that is specifically addressed by Klaus but not

by Rena, and select *Rena* for the phrase that best describes a factor that is specifically addressed by Rena but not by Klaus. Make only two selections, one in each column.

Klaus	Rena	
		The vacant school building
		The distance students must travel to school
		Extracurricular activities
		Real estate values
		Students' academic performance

Answer Explanation:

Recognition

Klaus:

Klaus and Rena both specifically mention the vacant school building, the distance students must travel to school, and real estate values. Klaus, unlike Rena, also specifically mentions students' academic performance. (It is possible that when Rena talks about the schools' reputations, the schools' students' academic performance is one of the factors that affects the schools' reputations, but we do not know for certain.)

The correct answer is *Students' academic performance.*

Rena:

Klaus and Rena both specifically mention the vacant school building, the distance students must travel to school, and real estate values. Rena, unlike Klaus, also specifically mentions extracurricular activities.

The correct answer is *Extracurricular activities.*

459. Alfredo: The United States could make significant progress toward becoming independent of petroleum-derived gasoline as a source of energy by diverting a large proportion of corn grown in the US to the production of ethanol for fuel. Brazil is virtually independent of petroleum as a source of fuel because that country has been very successful in ethanol production.

Mavis: Ethanol derived from corn will never be a viable substitute for petroleum-derived gasoline in the US. While it is true that Brazil has been very successful in replacing gasoline with ethanol, Brazil's ethanol is derived from sugarcane, which is very easy to convert to ethanol and, in Brazil, very easy to cultivate. Corn, on the other hand, is difficult to grow, requiring intensive cultivation. Also, the amount of power that can be garnered from the land is much less per square meter for corn ethanol.

In the table, select the statement about which Alfredo and Mavis would most clearly agree and select the statement about which Alfredo and Mavis would most clearly disagree. Make only two selections, one in each column.

Agree with each other about	Disagree with each other about	
		Corn ethanol produces much less power per square meter of cultivated land than does sugarcane ethanol.
		Ethanol is easier to produce from sugarcane than from corn.
		There are no crops, other than corn, for producing ethanol that could viably be grown in the US.
		Brazil has been very successful at replacing petroleum with ethanol.
		Producing corn ethanol is a viable strategy for a nation intent on reducing dependence on petroleum.

Answer Explanation:

Infer

Agree with each other about:

Alfredo and Mavis both accept the claim that Brazil has been very successful at replacing petroleum with ethanol.

The correct answer is *Brazil has been very successful at replacing petroleum with ethanol*.

Disagree with each other about:

Whereas Alfredo believes that Brazil's success at replacing demand for petroleum with ethanol supports the claim that producing corn ethanol is a viable strategy for a nation intent on reducing demand on petroleum, Mavis does not. Mavis points out that producing ethanol from sugarcane, as Brazil does, has very significant advantages over producing ethanol from corn.

The correct answer is *Producing corn ethanol is a viable strategy for a nation intent on reducing dependence on petroleum*.

460. Radhika is refinancing a business loan and is considering 2 different loan offers. Under Offer 1, the loan's initial principal would be $190,000, and she would pay down $1,250 in principal with each monthly payment during the first year of the loan. Under Offer 2, $4,000 in refinancing fees would be added to bring the principal to $194,000, but she would pay down $1,775 in principal with each monthly payment during the first year of the loan.

In the first column of the table, select the amount of principal that would remain after 12 monthly payments under Offer 1. In the second column of the table, select the amount of principal that would remain after 12 monthly payments under Offer 2. Make only two selections, one in each column.

Principal remaining after 12 months under Offer 1	Principal remaining after 12 months under Offer 2	
		$168,700
		$171,000
		$172,700
		$175,000
		$176,700
		$179,000

Answer Explanation:

Apply

Principal remaining after 12 months under Offer 1:

Under Offer 1, the principal would be $190,000, and the monthly payment would be $1,250. The total of 12 monthly payments would be 12($1,250) = $15,000. Therefore, the principal remaining after 12 months under Offer 1 would be $190,000 − $15,000 = $175,000.

The correct answer is *$175,000*.

Principal remaining after 12 months under Offer 2:

Under Offer 2, with the $4,000 refinancing fee added, the principal would be $194,000 and the monthly payment would be $1,775. The total of 12 monthly payments would be 12($1,775) = $21,300. Therefore, the principal remaining after 12 months under Offer 2 would be $194,000 − $21,300 = $172,700.

The correct answer is *$172,700*.

461. Professor A: The field of Artificial Intelligence (AI) was originally aimed exclusively at the construction of *thinking machines*, that is, computer systems with human-like general intelligence. But the difficulty of this goal of general AI has led researchers to shift their focus to producing narrow AI systems: software displaying intelligence regarding specific tasks in relatively narrow domains such as chess. The problem is, narrow AI and general AI are fundamentally and entirely different pursuits. If modeling general intelligence is the objective, AI researchers must redirect themselves toward the original goals of the field and confront the more difficult issues of human-like intelligence.

Professor B: Narrow AI work is producing real results today, such as chess-playing programs that can defeat any human, programs that translate speech to text, and programs that can drive automated vehicles. Achievements in this field will continue to flow, and eventually narrow AI will lead to the creation of systems with general intelligence.

On the basis of the given information, select a claim that *Professor A* would most likely *disagree* with, and select a claim that *Professor B* would most likely *disagree* with. Select only two claims, one in each column.

Professor A disagrees	Professor B disagrees	
		The creation of computer systems that display human-like general intelligence is an important goal.
		The creation of systems that display intelligence regarding specific tasks is an especially important step toward the creation of systems with general intelligence.
		Systems with general intelligence are more difficult to create than are systems with narrow intelligence.
		Research in the narrow AI field is not likely to lead to significant breakthroughs in the general AI field.
		The original aim of AI research was to create systems with general intelligence.
		The research into narrow AI is not producing results that real people can benefit from today.

Answer Explanation:

Infer

Professor A disagrees:

Professor A states that the field of AI (Artificial Intelligence) originally was intended to create thinking machines, that is, computers that could display human-like general intelligence. Professor A then states that over time the field of AI shifted its focus to narrow AI systems, ones that address relatively narrow realms of intelligence, such as chess playing. Professor A states that narrow AI will not aid in being able to produce systems that model general intelligence, because narrow AI and general AI are entirely different pursuits. Therefore, a claim that Professor A would *disagree* with is that the creation of systems that display intelligence regarding specific tasks is an especially important step toward the creation of systems with general intelligence.

The correct answer is *The creation of systems that display intelligence regarding specific tasks is an especially important step toward the creation of systems with general intelligence.*

Professor B disagrees:

Unlike Professor A, Professor B believes that the achievements of narrow AI—of which Professor B says there are many—will eventually lead to the creation of systems with general intelligence. Therefore, a claim that Professor B would *disagree* with is that research in the narrow AI field will not likely lead to significant breakthroughs in the general AI field.

The correct answer is *Research in the narrow AI field is not likely to lead to significant breakthroughs in the general AI field.*

462. Swamp sparrows live in a variety of wetland habitats. Unlike most swamp sparrows, which live in freshwater habitats, the coastal-plain subspecies lives in tidal wetlands, where freshwater and seawater mix and the mud is gray rather than brown. Coastal-plain swamp sparrows differ from all other populations of swamp sparrows in having plumage that is gray-brown rather than rusty brown. DNA analysis indicates several important genetic differences between swamp sparrows that inhabit tidal marshes and other subspecies of swamp sparrows. Therefore, there must have been genetic-selection pressure on swamp sparrows in tidal marshes to become darker and grayer.

Select *Strengthen* for the statement that would, if true, most strengthen the argument, and select *Weaken* for the statement that would, if true, most weaken the argument. Make only two selections, one in each column.

Strengthen	Weaken	
		None of the genetic differences that have been identified in the genomes of coastal-plain swamp sparrows and freshwater swamp sparrows affect plumage color.
		Mud in tidal marshes tends to be grayish because of the presence of iron sulfide, whereas freshwater mud is browner because of the presence of iron oxide.
		Some species of birds that live in tidal marshes do not have gray plumage.
		The diets of both coastal-plain and freshwater swamp sparrows can change significantly from season to season.
		Baby birds of the coastal-plain subspecies and baby birds of a freshwater swamp subspecies, all raised on an identical diet under controlled conditions, grew plumage similar in color to that of their respective parents.

Answer Explanation:

Evaluate

The passage discusses differences among various types of swamp sparrows and their habitats. Most swamp sparrows, which have rusty brown plumage, live in freshwater habitats, where the mud tends to be brown, but coastal-plain swamp sparrows, which have gray-brown plumage, live in tidal wetlands, where the mud tends to be gray. Research on the DNA of these types of birds has discovered important genetic differences between the coastal-plain swamp sparrows and other, freshwater-dwelling swamp sparrows. The passage draws the conclusion from these facts that there was some genetic pressure on coastal-plain swamp sparrows to become darker and grayer.

Strengthen:

The argument concludes that the difference in plumage between tidal-marsh swamp sparrows and other swamp sparrows is genetic rather than, for instance, the direct environment in which an individual sparrow grows up or the sorts of food an individual sparrow consumes. Therefore, the argument in the passage would be strengthened if there were evidence that baby birds of the coastal-plain subspecies and baby birds of the freshwater species had plumage similar in color to their respective parents, even if the baby birds were raised in identical environments and fed the same sorts of food.

The correct answer is *Baby birds of the coastal-plain subspecies and baby birds of a freshwater swamp subspecies, all raised on an identical diet under controlled conditions, grew plumage similar in color to that of their respective parents.*

Weaken:

Part of the evidence for the conclusion that the differences in color are due to genetic pressure is that DNA evidence shows important genetic differences among these subspecies. The argument would therefore be weakened if none of those genetic differences that have been identified has an effect on the color of plumage.

The correct answer is *None of the genetic differences that have been identified in the genomes of coastal-plain swamp sparrows and freshwater swamp sparrows affect plumage color.*

463. Boppo is a game played by 2 teams for a fixed duration (number of minutes). It is played with 8 members of each team on the floor—actually playing the game—at all times. At any time during the game, exactly one player from each team must be off the floor—not actually playing. Thus, by taking a break, by entering the game after it starts, or by leaving before it finishes, every player on each team must spend exactly 5 minutes resting or otherwise not playing.

In the table, identify a number of players per team and a number of minutes per game that are consistent with the given information about Boppo. Make only two selections, one in each column.

Number of players	Number of minutes
	9
	11
	18
	30
	45
	50

Answer Explanation:

Apply

Number of players:

Having $8 + 1 = 9$ players per team is consistent with the requirement that, at any time during the game, 8 players must be on the floor actually playing the game and 1 player must be off the floor—not actually playing the game.

The correct answer is 9.

Number of minutes:

A fixed duration of $9 \times 5 = 45$ minutes per game is consistent with each of the 9 members on a team being required to spend exactly 5 minutes during each game resting or otherwise not playing the game.

The correct answer is 45.

464. Loan X has a principal of $$x$ and a yearly simple interest rate of 4%. Loan Y has a principal of $$y$ and a yearly simple interest rate of 8%. Loans X and Y will be consolidated to form Loan Z with a principal of $$(x + y)$ and a yearly simple interest rate of r%, where $r = \dfrac{4x + 8y}{x + y}$. Select a value for x and a value for y corresponding to a yearly simple interest rate of 5% for the consolidated loan. Make only two selections, one in each column.

x	y	Value
		21,000
		32,000
		51,000
		64,000
		81,000
		96,000

Answer Explanation:

Apply

The task is to determine values of x and y such that $\frac{4x + 8y}{x + y} = 5$.

As shown, algebraic manipulation results in a simple relationship between x and y.

$\frac{4x + 8y}{x + y} = 5$	given
$4x + 8y = 5(x + y)$	multiply both sides by $x + y$
$4x + 8y = 5x + 5y$	apply the distributive property
$4x + 3y = 5x$	subtract $5y$ from both sides
$3y = x$	subtract $4x$ from both sides

x:

Choose a value for x that is 3 times another value in the *Value* column. Since the value for x will be greater than the other value, it is wise to start with the greatest value, which is 96,000. Since 96,000 is 3(32,000), 96,000 is a value for x that is consistent with the given information.

The correct answer is *96,000*.

y:

From the explanation above, the value of y is 32,000.

The correct answer is *32,000*.

465. Perry, Maria, and Lorna are painting rooms in a college dormitory. Working alone, Perry can paint a standard room in 3 hours, Maria can paint a standard room in 2 hours, and Lorna can paint a standard room in 2 hours 30 minutes. Perry, Maria, and Lorna have decided that, to speed up the work, 2 of them will paint a standard room together.

Select the value closest to the shortest time in which a 2-person team could paint a standard room, and select the value closest to the longest time in which a 2-person team could paint a standard room, with each person working at his or her respective rate. Make only two selections, one in each column.

Shortest time	Longest time	
		49 minutes
		1 hour 7 minutes
		1 hour 12 minutes
		1 hour 14 minutes
		1 hour 22 minutes
		1 hour 45 minutes

Answer Explanation:

Apply

Shortest time:

Working together, Lorna and Maria can paint a standard room in the shortest amount of time because individually they can paint a standard room in less time than Perry. Lorna can paint a standard room in $2\frac{1}{2} = \frac{5}{2}$ hours, so she can paint $\frac{2}{5}$ room in 1 hour. Maria can paint a standard room in 2 hours, so she can paint $\frac{1}{2}$ room in 1 hour. Working together, they can paint $\frac{2}{5} + \frac{1}{2} = \frac{9}{10}$ room in 1 hour. It follows that they can paint 1 room in $\frac{10}{9}$ hours, which is equivalent to $1\frac{1}{9}$ hours or about 1 hour 7 minutes.

The correct answer is *1 hour 7 minutes*.

Longest time:

Working together, Lorna and Perry take the longest amount of time to paint a standard room because individually they take more time than Maria to paint a standard room. Lorna can paint a standard room in $2\frac{1}{2} = \frac{5}{2}$ hours, so she can paint $\frac{2}{5}$ room in 1 hour. Perry can paint a standard room in 3 hours, so he can paint $\frac{1}{3}$ room in 1 hour. Working together, they can paint $\frac{2}{5} + \frac{1}{3} = \frac{11}{15}$ room in 1 hour. It follows that they can paint 1 room in $\frac{15}{11}$ hours, which is equivalent to $1\frac{4}{11}$ hours or about 1 hour 22 minutes.

The correct answer is *1 hour 22 minutes*.

466. A dance show will include exactly five pieces, and each piece will be presented only once: Requiem, Smooth Step, Trampoline, Unleashed, and Waltzy. Requiem will be presented immediately before Smooth Step. Unleashed will be presented earlier than Trampoline, with at least one piece in between. Waltzy will not be the final piece presented.

In the table, select a piece that cannot be the second piece presented and a piece that cannot be the third piece presented. Make only two selections, one in each column.

Cannot be presented second	Cannot be presented third	
		Requiem
		Smooth Step
		Trampoline
		Unleashed
		Waltzy

Answer Explanation:

Infer

Cannot be presented second:

One of the conditions states that Unleashed will be presented earlier than Trampoline, with at least one piece in between. It follows from this that the earliest Trampoline can be presented is third, because both Unleashed and at least one of the other pieces must be presented earlier than Trampoline. Therefore, Trampoline cannot be presented first or second.

The correct answer is *Trampoline*.

Cannot be presented third:

Waltzy cannot be presented third. To see this, remember that Requiem must be presented immediately before Smooth Step. If Waltzy were third, then Requiem and Smooth Step would have to be first and second, in that order, or fourth and fifth, in that order. In either of those cases, Unleashed and Trampoline would have to be presented one right after the other—either first and second or fourth and fifth—but that is not allowed; there must be some piece presented between them. Therefore, Waltzy cannot be presented third.

The correct answer is *Waltzy*.

467. An American museum of East Asian art reviewed its acquisitions strategy in 2009. As part of that review, a marketing executive recommended purchasing more ceramics, jades, and paintings of people or landscapes because visitor surveys indicated that those types are of greatest interest to museumgoers in the region. The museum's curator recommended purchasing more twenty-first-century East Asian art—particularly abstract (nonrepresentational) paintings and sculptures—because the museum's collection is weakest in that area.

Among the East Asian works of art described below, select a painting and a sculpture, each of which satisfies at least one of the recommendations made by the marketing executive and at least one of the recommendations made by the curator. Make only two selections, one in each column.

Painting	Sculpture	
		Painting of girl's face, in shades of blue and red, acrylic and oil on canvas, 2006
		Chinese brush painting of fish in a tank, ink on paper, 2002
		Fish-shaped vase with dragon head, jade, 1849
		Abstract sequence of interconnected curves, ceramic, 2008
		Fossil-like, jagged sculpture suspended from cables, stainless steel, aluminum, fiberglass, and cable, 2004

Answer Explanation:

Apply

Painting:

"*Painting of girl's face* …" satisfies the people or landscapes recommendation of the marketing executive and satisfies the twenty-first-century (from 2006) recommendation of the museum's curator.

The correct answer is *Painting of girl's face, in shades of blue and red, acrylic and oil on canvas, 2006*.

Sculpture:

"*Abstract sequence* …" satisfies the ceramic recommendation of the marketing executive and satisfies the twenty-first-century (from 2008) recommendation of the museum's curator.

The correct answer is *Abstract sequence of interconnected curves, ceramic, 2008*.

468. Professor A: The aid industry should begin to focus its efforts to spending on primary schools in the poorest areas, to providing medicines and other basic supplies for health such as mosquito nets, and to a few key agricultural initiatives.

Professor B: Much education work has been ineffective. A village or town with poor schooling may be better off getting a road than a teacher. Once local farmers can transport produce to market, they will be willing to pay for schools—and to make sure the schools succeed.

Suppose that the professors' statements express their genuine opinions. Select statements (1) and (2) as follows: Professor A would likely disagree with (1), and Professor B would take (2) to present logical support for (1). Select only two statements, one per column.

(1)	(2)	
		The aid industry should focus less on the areas of health and agriculture than it now does.
		The aid industry should focus more on primary education than it now does.
		The aid industry should focus its spending less on primary education than it now does.
		Projects in health and agriculture are more likely to be successful if they are not paid for by the aid industry.
		Projects in education are more likely to be successful if they are paid for by the aid industry.
		Projects in education are more likely to be successful if they are paid for by local people.

Answer Explanation:

Infer

The wording of the question suggests that the correctness of an answer for one of the response opportunities will depend on the correctness of the answer to the other. We are to find a statement in the table such that the information indicates Professor A would likely disagree with the first statement and Professor B would take the second statement to present evidence against the first.

1:

The only statement in the table that the dialogue strongly suggests Professor A would disagree with is *The aid industry should focus its spending less on primary education than it now does*. For example, if the relative distribution of spending by the *aid industry* between *primary schools in the poorest areas, medicines, and other basic supplies for health such as mosquito nets,* and the *few key agricultural initiatives* is maintained, while spending in other areas is drastically reduced, then the aid industry will thereby focus its spending more on primary education than it now does.

The correct answer is *The aid industry should focus its spending less on primary education than it now does.*

2:

Given the answer for *1*, the question requires identification of the statement within the table that Professor B would take to be evidence for the statement that the aid industry should focus its spending less on primary education than it now does. The claims attributed to Professor B, in the context of the dialogue with Professor A, strongly suggest that she would take such evidence to be provided by *Projects in education are more likely to be successful if they are paid for by local people.*

The correct answer is *Projects in education are more likely to be successful if they are paid for by local people.*

469. A car is traveling on a straight stretch of roadway, and the speed of the car is increasing at a constant rate with respect to time. At time 0 seconds, the speed of the car is v_0 meters per second; 10 seconds later, the front bumper of the car has traveled 125 meters, and the speed of the car is v_{10} meters per second.

Select values of v_0 and v_{10} that are together consistent with the information provided. Make only two selections, one in each column.

v_0	v_{10}	
		5
		18
		20
		36
		72

Answer Explanation:

Infer

Since the speed of the car increases at a constant rate, the car's average speed, in meters per second, over the 10-second period is equal to $\frac{1}{2}(v_0 + v_{10})$. Thus, the distance the car traveled, in meters, over that period is equal to $\frac{1}{2}(v_0 + v_{10})(10)$, or $5(v_0 + v_{10})$. But this value is given to be 125, so it must be true that $v_0 + v_{10} = \frac{125}{5}$, or 25. Because speed must be positive, both v_0 and v_{10} must be less than 25, ruling out 36 and 72 as possible values.

v_0:

Among the available alternatives—5, 18, and 20—the only pair that sum to 25 are 5 and 20. Since the speed is increasing, it must also be true that $v_0 \le v_{10}$. Therefore, $v_0 = 5$.

The correct answer is *5*.

v_{10}:

Following the analysis for Response 1, the value of v_{10} must correspond to $v_0 = 5$. So, $5 + v_{10} = 25$, and therefore, $v_{10} = 20$.

The correct answer is *20*.

470. For each positive integer n, the quantity s_n is defined such that $s_{n+2} = (s_n)^2 - s_{n+1}$. In addition, $s_2 = 1$.

Select values for s_1 and s_4 that are jointly compatible with these conditions. Select only two values, one in each column.

s_1	s_4	
		−12
		−7
		−3
		−1
		0

First two bars	Third bar	
		0.92
		0.93
		0.94
		0.98
		0.99

Answer Explanation:

Infer

For $n = 1$, the equation $s_{n+2} = (s_n)^2 - s_{n+1}$ is equivalent to $s_3 = (s_1)^2 - s_2$. For $n = 2$, the equation $s_{n+2} = (s_n)^2 - s_{n+1}$ is equivalent to $s_4 = (s_2)^2 - s_3$, and substituting $(s_1)^2 - s_2$ for s_3 yields $s_4 = (s_2)^2 - (s_1)^2 + s_2$. (Continuing in this fashion, it is possible to produce, for each positive integer n, an expression for s_n in terms of s_1 and s_2.) Substituting 1 for s_2 in the equation for s_4, it follows that the values of s_1 and s_4 are related by the equation $s_4 = 2 - (s_1)^2$. One strategy is to substitute each value in the table for s_1 to see if the corresponding value of s_4 is present.

s_1:

Because the value of $(s_1)^2$ is nonnegative and increases rapidly as the absolute value of s_1 increases, it makes sense to begin testing possible values for s_1 at the bottom of the table. When s_1 is equal to 0 or -1, the quantity $2 - (s_1)^2$ is positive, so the corresponding value of s_4 does not appear. When $s_1 = -3$, the corresponding value of s_4 is $2 - (-3)^2 = -7$, which is present in the table. Note that when $s_1 \leq -7$, it follows that $2 - (s_1)^2 \leq 2 - 49$, so the corresponding value of s_4 is less than or equal to -47 and hence cannot appear in the table. So the value of s_1 must be -3.

The correct answer is -3.

s_4:

Following the analysis for Response 1, the value of s_4 must correspond to $s_1 = -3$, and it is given by $s_4 = -7$.

The correct answer is -7.

471. The *finesse* of a gold bar is the weight of the gold present in the bar divided by the total weight of the bar. A jeweler has three gold bars. The three bars have identical weights, and the first two bars have identical finesse. If all three bars were melted and combined into one bar, the finesse of the resulting bar would be 0.96.

Select a finesse of the *First two bars* and a finesse of the *Third bar* that are jointly consistent with the given information. Make only two selections, one in each column.

Answer Explanation:

Infer

First two bars:

According to the text, the finesse of a gold bar is equal to the weight of gold in the bar divided by the total weight of the bar. The text also indicates that the three gold bars have the same weight, that the first two bars have the same finesse, and that melting and combining the three bars would result in a gold bar with a finesse of 0.96. Since the first two bars have identical finesse and identical weight, the weight of the gold present in those bars must also be identical. Let x equal the weight of the gold in each of the first two bars, let y equal the weight of the gold in the third bar, and let w be the total weight of each bar. Then, since the finesse of the combined bar is 0.96, it must be the case that $\frac{2x + y}{3w} = 0.96$, or $2\left(\frac{x}{w}\right) + \left(\frac{y}{w}\right) = (0.96)(3) = 2.88$. But then if $F_1 = \left(\frac{x}{w}\right)$ is the finesse of each of the first two bars, and $F_3 = \left(\frac{y}{w}\right)$ is the finesse of the third bar, then $2F_1 + F_3 = 2.88$. Among the available options, substituting 0.98 for F_1 and 0.92 for F_3 gives us $2(0.98) + 0.92 = 1.96 + 0.92 = 2.88$. No other pair of options yields the correct result.

The correct answer is 0.98.

Third bar:

Based on the explanation for Response 1, the correct answer for Response 2 is 0.92.

The correct answer is 0.92.

472. A fair coin has 2 distinct flat sides—one of which bears the image of a face and the other of which does not—and when the coin is tossed, the probability that the coin will land face up is $\frac{1}{2}$. For certain values of M, N, p, and q, when M fair coins are tossed simultaneously, the probability is p that all M coins land face up, and when N fair coins are tossed simultaneously, the probability is q that all N coins land face up. Furthermore, $M < N$ and $\frac{1}{p} + \frac{1}{q} = 72$.

In the table, select a value for M and a value for N that are jointly consistent with the given information. Make only two selections, one in each column.

M	N	
		2
		3
		4
		5
		6
		7

Answer Explanation:

Infer

If M is a positive integer, then the probability, p, that M fair coins all land face up is $p = \left(\frac{1}{2}\right)^M = \frac{1}{2^M}$

Similarly, if N is a positive integer, then the probability, q, that N fair coins all land face up is

$q = \left(\frac{1}{2}\right)^N = \frac{1}{2^N}$

Since $\frac{1}{p} + \frac{1}{q} = 72$

Then $p = \dfrac{1}{\left(\frac{1}{2^M}\right)} + \dfrac{1}{\left(\frac{1}{2^N}\right)} = 2^M + 2^N = 72$

The task, then, is to find two powers of 2 (an Mth power and an Nth power) that add up to 72. The correct answer for M will be the lesser of the two exponents. Note that for the given options, the only possible powers of 2 are 4, 8, 16, 32, 64, and 128. The only way for two of these to add up to 72 is for one to be $8 = 2^3$ and the other to

be $64 = 2^6$. Since M is to be the lesser of the two exponents and N is to be the greater of the two exponents, it must be that $M = 3$ and $N = 6$.

M:

As noted in the discussion above, $M = 3$.

The correct answer is 3.

N:

As noted in the discussion above, $N = 6$.

The correct answer is 6.

473. Educational policy analyst: To improve the long-term economic benefits that our country's universities provide to their students, the government should provide subsidies enabling the universities to hire more academic staff. Hiring more academic staff would allow smaller class sizes. Statistically, university students in smaller classes tend to receive higher grades than those in larger classes. And on average, a student who earns higher grades in university classes tends to have a higher salary after graduation than a student who earns lower grades. Thus, hiring more academic staff nationwide should improve the economic well-being of graduates nationwide.

Consider the incomplete statement:

According to the analyst's argument, students' ___1___ is bolstered by their ___2___.

Select for *1* and *2* the options that complete the statement in the manner that most accurately reflects the given information. Make only two selections, one in each column.

1	2	
		tendency to earn higher grades in university classes
		economic well-being after graduating from university
		being in larger than average university classes
		receiving better education overall
		learning from a greater number of academic staff

Answer Explanation:

Evaluate

We are asked to complete the statement so that it is an accurate reflection of the information provided in the educational policy analyst's argument.

The educational policy analyst asserts that *hiring more academic staff would allow smaller class sizes*, and that *on average, a student who earns higher grades in university classes tends to have a higher salary after graduation than a student who earns lower grades.* This leads the analyst to conclude that *hiring more academic staff would improve the economic well-being of graduates nationwide.* Given this conclusion in conjunction with the analyst's other assertions, according to the analyst's argument, *students' economic well-being after graduation from university* is bolstered by their *tendency to earn higher grades in university classes.*

The analyst makes no claims about the quality of education overall or the number of academic staff students learn from. Furthermore, the only implication with respect to larger university class sizes is that they would likely not bolster either grades or salaries. Therefore, no other pair of options completes the statement so that it is an accurate reflection of the information provided.

1:

The correct answer is *economic well-being after graduating from university*.

2:

The correct answer is *tendency to earn higher grades in university classes*.

474. The *payload rating* (PR) of a truck is the truck's recommended load weight, which is specified as a number of tonnes (t), where 1 tonne = 1,000 kilograms. A certain truck's PR is a whole number of tonnes. The truck has hauled exactly 7 loads, exactly 3 of which had a greater weight than the truck's PR. The weights of these 7 loads, in tonnes, are as follows:

50, 51, 52, 52, 54, 54, 56.

Select the *Least* and the *Greatest* possible values for the truck's PR, in tonnes. Make only two selections, one in each column.

Least	Greatest	
		49
		50
		51
		52
		53
		54

Answer Explanation:

Apply

Least:

According to the information provided, the PR is a whole number of tonnes, and among the seven loads (weighing 50, 51, 52, 52, 54, 54, and 56 tonnes), exactly three exceeded the truck's PR. Given this, the PR must be a whole number of tonnes less than 54 and no less than 52, so the truck's PR can be either 52 or 53 tonnes. Therefore, the least possible value for the truck's PR is 52 tonnes.

The correct answer is *52*.

Greatest:

Based on the explanation for Response 1, the greatest possible value for the truck's PR is 53 tonnes.

The correct answer is *53*.

475. Each of the species of a certain type of insect has at least one of five significant traits: A, B, C, D, and E. Furthermore, one study has determined that any species with Trait A has at least one of the Traits B and C. Another study has determined that any species with Trait C has at least one of the Traits D and E. And a third study has determined that any of the species with Trait B has Trait C. The results of each study are correct.

Select different options for *X* and for *Y* such that the following statement most accurately describes the passage. Make only two selections, one in each column.

In addition to the relationship between Traits B and C that is stated explicitly with respect to the third study, the passage implies that any of the insects that has Trait ____*X*____ also has Trait ____*Y*____.

X	Y	
		A
		B
		C
		D
		E

Answer Explanation:

Infer

We are asked to identify, in addition to the relationship between Traits B and C, a relationship between two of the five significant traits of a certain type of insect that is implied by the information in the passage.

The passage states that any species of insect with Trait A has at least one of the Traits B and C—any insects with Trait A will have Trait B, Trait C, or both. The passage also states that any of the species with Trait B has Trait C. Taken together, these claims imply that any of the insects that has Trait A also has Trait C—an insect with Trait A will either have Trait C and not Trait B, or it will have both Trait B and Trait C. The passage does not imply any other relationships between the five significant traits such that any insect that has any one of the significant traits must also have another of the significant traits. Therefore, the statement that the passage implies that any of the insects that has Trait A also has Trait C most accurately describes the passage.

X:

The correct answer is *A*.

Y:

The correct answer is *C*.

476. Events A, B, and C have the following probabilities of future occurrence:

A: 20%

B: 50%

C: 80%

On the basis of these probabilities, select for *Both A and B* a description that must be true of the probability that both A and B will occur. And select for *B or C or Both* a description that must be true of the probability that B or C or both will occur. Make only two selections, one in each column.

Both A and B	B or C or Both	
		Must be equal to 40%
		Must be equal to 50%
		Must be equal to 70%
		Must be less than or equal to 20%
		Must be greater than or equal to 80%

Answer Explanation:

Apply

Both A and B:

The probability of two events both occurring never exceeds either individual event's probability of occurring. The probability of A occurring is only 20%, so the probability of both A and B occurring cannot exceed 20%.

The correct answer is *Must be less than or equal to 20%*.

B or C or Both:

The probability that at least one of two events will occur is never less than either individual event's probability of occurring. The probability of C occurring is 80%, so the probability that either B or C or both will occur must be at least 80%.

The correct answer is *Must be greater than or equal to 80%*.

477. Premiolex Corporation spokesperson: In our survey of Premiolex customers, the majority of respondents rated our services as "Excellent," whereas in our competitor Cretazole's survey, the majority of their respondents rated Cretazole's services as "Very good." That's proof that—on average, at least—our customers have a higher opinion of Premiolex's services than Cretazole's customers have of its services.

Skeptic: I don't think the spokesperson's conclusion necessarily follows from the evidence he cites. What if, for example, the Premiolex survey asked participants to choose from among options that weren't all identical to the ones used in Cretazole's survey?

Select for *Premiolex survey* and *Cretazole survey* the options such that, in combination, the Premiolex survey and Cretazole survey would support the skeptic's position and be consistent with the spokesperson's report of the results but indicate that the spokesperson's conclusion does not necessarily follow. Make only two selections, one in each column.

Premiolex Survey	Cretazole Survey	Condition: 1,000 respondents were asked to choose among these survey options	Results: Number of respondents who chose each survey option
		Excellent	517
		Average	482
		Below average	1
		Poor	0
		Unacceptable	0
		Excellent	463
		Average	501
		Below average	0
		Poor	35
		Unacceptable	1

Premiolex Survey	Cretazole Survey	Condition: 1,000 respondents were asked to choose among these survey options	Results: Number of respondents who chose each survey option
		Excellent	454
		Average	511
		Below average	34
		Poor	0
		Unacceptable	1
		Excellent	512
		Average	478
		Below average	10
		Poor	0
		Unacceptable	0
		Excellent	23
		Average	516
		Below average	230
		Poor	231
		Unacceptable	0

Answer Explanation:

Evaluate

Only two selections are consistent with the Premiolex Corporation spokesperson's report that more than half of the respondents to the Premiolex Survey rated Premiolex's services as "Excellent"—the first selection (517 of 1,000 ratings were "Excellent") and the fourth selection (512 of 1,000 ratings were "Excellent"). Also, only slightly more than half for the first selection rated Premiolex's services above average (because the only survey option for above average was "Excellent"), whereas nearly all for the fourth selection rated Premiolex's services above average (512 + 478 = 990 ratings were for above average). Therefore, among these two selections, the choice of the **first selection** for the Premiolex Survey options offers the greater possibility of failure for the spokesperson's conclusion.

Neither the first selection nor the second selection could be the survey options for the Cretazole Survey because neither selection has "Very good" as a survey option. Also, the fourth selection could not be the survey options in the Cretazole Survey because, for this selection, a majority of respondents did not choose "Very good" (478 of 1,000 ratings were "Very good"). Of the two remaining selections for the Cretazole Survey options, the **third selection** offers a greater possibility of failure than the fifth selection, because the fifth selection has a relatively large number of respondents who chose "Poor."

Using the first selection for the Premiolex Survey, the majority of respondents chose "Excellent," and using the third selection for the Cretazole Survey, the majority of respondents chose "Very good." Thus, these two selections are consistent with the spokesperson's report of the results. However, for the first selection, only 517 respondents chose a rating higher than average, whereas for the third selection, 454 + 511 = 965 respondents chose a rating higher than average. Therefore, it is possible that, on average, the Premiolex respondents did NOT have a higher opinion of Premiolex's services than Cretazole's customers had of its services. That is, the spokesperson's conclusion does not necessarily follow.

Premiolex Survey:

The correct answer is *first selection*.

Cretazole Survey:

The correct answer is *third selection*.

478. A satellite is currently in a circular orbit with radius 32,714 km about the center of the earth. (Note: The circumference of a circle is given by $C = 2\pi r$, where r is the radius of the circle and, to the nearest 0.01, $\pi \approx 3.14$.)

Select for *0.5 km* the increase, to the nearest whole kilometer, in the distance the satellite travels about the center of the earth during each revolution if the orbital

radius of the satellite is increased by 0.5 km. And select for *1.5 km* the increase, to the nearest whole kilometer, in the distance the satellite travels about the center of the earth during each revolution if the orbital radius is increased by 1.5 km. Make only two selections, one in each column.

0.5 km	1.5 km	
		3
		9
		27
		81
		150
		450

Answer Explanation:

Infer

(Note: The circumference of a circle is given by $C = 2\pi r$, where r is the radius of the circle and, to the nearest 0.01, $\pi \approx 3.14$.)

0.5 km:

The increase in distance the satellite travels is the increase in the circumference of a circle when the circle's radius is increased from 32,714 km to (32,714 + 0.5) km. Thus, the increase in distance, in kilometers, is

$$2\pi(32{,}714 + 0.5) - 2\pi(32{,}714)$$

$$= 2\pi(32{,}714) + 2\pi(0.5) - 2\pi(32{,}714)$$

$$= 2\pi(0.5) \approx 2(3.14)(0.5), \text{ which is 3 to the}$$

nearest whole number.

The correct answer is 3.

1.5 km:

The increase in distance the satellite travels is the increase in the circumference of a circle when the circle's radius is increased from 32,714 km to (32,714 + 1.5) km. Thus, the increase in distance, in kilometers, is

$2p(32,714 + 1.5) - 2p(32,714)$

$= 2p(32,714) + 2p(1.5) - 2p(32,714)$

$= 2p(0.5) \approx 2(3.14)(1.5)$, which is 9 to the nearest whole number.

The correct answer is 9.

479. Some studies of how Prussia resisted the wave of European democratization in the nineteenth century point to Prussia's unequal distribution of land ownership as the principal explanation. Indeed, political figures from areas in Prussia with high inequality in land ownership tended to be the staunchest opponents of democratic reforms. However, arguments that focus so strongly on those figures' conflicts with landless people tend to ignore the fact that political figures are not merely representatives of socioeconomic interests but are also political actors embedded in particular contexts that shape whether they support democratic reforms. Historians must take such contexts into account if they hope to explain what transpired in Prussia during this period.

This argument would be most strengthened if, in the nineteenth century, there were other European countries that ___1___ despite the fact that those countries ___2___ .

Select for *1* and *2* the options that complete the statement in the manner that most accurately reflects the given information. Make only two selections, one in each column.

1	2	
		enacted more democratic reforms than did Prussia
		enacted fewer democratic reforms than did Prussia
		had similar inequality in land ownership as did Prussia
		had less inequality in land ownership than did Prussia
		had more complex political contexts than did Prussia

Answer Explanation:

Infer

The passage's implicit thesis is that what led Prussia to resist the wave of European democratization in the nineteenth century might have mainly been the political contexts Prussian political figures operated in rather than the unequal distribution of land

ownership. Evidence for this thesis could include examples of other nineteenth-century European countries whose land ownership was also distributed unequally but that did not resist the wave of democratization. In other words, the thesis would be most strengthened if, in the nineteenth century, there were other European countries that enacted more democratic reforms than did Prussia despite the fact that those countries had similar inequality in land ownership as did Prussia.

1:

The correct answer is *enacted more democratic reforms than did Prussia.*

2:

The correct answer is *had similar inequality in land ownership as did Prussia.*

480. Many countries have traditionally used surface-irrigation systems, which use gravity to distribute water over the soil surface. But these systems contribute significantly to groundwater depletion. Many of these countries' governments are not regulating such groundwater extraction properly, resulting in water table depletion in many regions. Therefore governments need to introduce new water-management policies that will curtail such practices, control allocations of water to agriculture and industry, and enable the governments to reduce those allocations when supplies become scarce or demand from other sectors increases.

Select for *Cause* and *Consequence* the options such that the information provided most strongly suggests that if the cause occurs, the consequence is likely to occur. Make only two selections, one in each column.

Cause	Consequence	
		Governments enacting new water-management policies
		Governments failing to enact new water-management policies
		Depletion of groundwater supplies in some regions
		Greater allocation of groundwater for agricultural use than for industrial use
		Agriculture and industry voluntarily curtailing groundwater use

Answer Explanation:

Evaluate

We're told that many countries' governments are not regulating groundwater extraction properly, and that this has resulted in water table depletion in many regions. This strongly suggests that if the governments don't change their water-management policies, the same trend will continue. That is, if these governments fail to enact new water-management policies, the likely consequence will be continued depletion of groundwater supplies in some regions.

Cause:

The correct answer is *Governments failing to enact new water-management policies*.

Consequence:

The correct answer is *Depletion of groundwater supplies in some regions*.

481. A philosophy professor randomly assigned students to either of the two different sides of a debate in an ethics class, regardless of their stance on the issue. The students then researched and prepared arguments for a week. The students had been almost evenly divided on the issue when the assignments were made, according to an anonymous survey, but almost all of the students reported strong agreement with their assigned position in another, postdebate anonymous survey. The professor concluded that the research and preparation for the debate had a polarizing effect, causing many students to change their original positions.

In the columns, select the statement that, if true, would most strengthen the professor's conclusion and the statement that, if true, would most weaken the conclusion. Make only two selections, one in each column.

Strengthens	Weakens	
		Most students learned a great deal about both sides of their debate topic during their week of preparation.
		Most of the students consulted research materials that were outdated and based on incomplete data.
		Prior to the assignment, none of the students had strong feelings about either side of the debate topic.
		By chance, almost all of the students were assigned to the side of the debate that they already agreed with.
		Many students had not reported their original positions to their debate partners at the outset of the project.

Answer Explanation:

Evaluate

The professor's conclusion was that researching and preparing for the debate caused many students to change their original positions on the issue, with a polarizing effect: that is, it made the students develop more intense, polarized opinions than they had at first. We're told that after the debate, almost all the students reported strong agreement with their assigned debate positions. Thus, evidence that none of the students had strong feelings on the issue prior to the assignment would strengthen the professor's conclusion that the assignment both changed and polarized the students' positions.

On the other hand, evidence that almost all the students already agreed with the position they supported during the debate would weaken the professor's conclusion, because this evidence would suggest that the students' opinions were similar before and after the assignment, and thus that the assignment must not have changed their opinions much.

Strengthens:

The correct answer is *Prior to the assignment, none of the students had strong feelings about either side of the debate topic*.

Weakens:

The correct answer is *By chance, almost all of the students were assigned to the side of the debate that they already agreed with.*

482. The results of a large study suggest that television viewers enjoy shows with commercials more than those without them. Test subjects who viewed an episode of a television series with commercials rated it more enjoyable than did subjects who viewed the same episode commercial-free. The study's researchers concluded that a viewer's enjoyment of a program depends a great deal on how well one can maintain attention, reasoning that commercial breaks enable viewers to reset their attention.

In the columns, select the statement that, if true, would most strengthen the argument and the statement that, if true, would most weaken the argument. Make only two selections, one in each column.

Strengthens	Weakens	
		Television programs tend to hold viewers' attention better when they have shorter commercial breaks.
		Television programs with commercial breaks have often been edited to allow time for the insertion of the breaks.
		When the option to pause a commercial-free television program is available, the vast majority of people will do so at least once during a program.
		People shown to have especially long attention spans are no more likely to enjoy commercial-free television programs than are people with short attention spans.
		Commercial-free television programming tends to be of lower production quality than that shown with commercials.

Answer Explanation:

Evaluate

Based on the study's results and an assumption that commercial breaks enable viewers to reset their attention, the researchers argued that viewers' enjoyment of a program depends largely on how well the viewers can maintain attention. A finding that most people pause commercial-free television programs when given the option might suggest that people like to take breaks from viewing to reset their attention, in order to enjoy the programs more. Thus, this finding would strengthen the argument.

On the other hand, a finding that people with especially long attention spans don't enjoy commercial-free television programs any more than people with shorter attention spans do would conflict with the researchers' hypothesis that enjoyment of a program depends on how well one can maintain attention during it. Therefore, this finding would weaken the argument.

Strengthens:

The correct answer is *When the option to pause a commercial-free television program is available, the vast majority of people will do so at least once during a program.*

Weakens:

The correct answer is *People shown to have especially long attention spans are no more likely to enjoy commercial-free television programs than are people with short attention spans.*

483. The workers in an office are placed into three working groups, each containing 20 workers. All workers are in at least one group. Any 2 groups have exactly 10 members in common.

Identify in the table two numbers that are jointly consistent with the given information: the total number of workers in the office, and the number of workers who are members of all three groups. Make only two selections, one in each column.

Total workers	Workers in all three	Number
		4
		8
		10
		18
		34
		45

Answer Explanation:

Infer

For any three sets, $|A| + |B| + |C| - (|A \cap B| + |A \cap C| + |B \cap C|) + |A \cap B \cap C| = |A \cup B \cup C|$. The left side of the equation becomes $20 + 20 + 20 - (10 + 10 + 10) + |A \cap B \cap C|$, which is $30 + |A \cap B \cap C|$. This establishes the desired relationship (the total number of workers is 30 greater than the number of workers in all three).

Total workers:
The correct answer is *34*.

Workers in all three:
The correct answer is *4*.

484. In a study of human behavior, researchers solicited charitable donations from two different groups of people, those having just donated blood and those having just visited a doctor. Contributions from blood donors were significantly less than contributions from people who had visited a doctor. The researchers concluded that people believe their obligation to behave generously is finite. Therefore those who had donated blood, the researchers explained, believed they had temporarily somewhat satisfied their charitable obligations.

Which of the following would, if true, most weaken the researchers' conclusion, and which would, if true, most strengthen it? Make only two selections, one in each column.

Most weakens	Most strengthens	
		Blood donors are generally allowed to donate whole blood only once every two months.
		People report that they are more likely to make charitable donations when the request is made in person than when it is made over the phone.
		People who placed money in a store's charity collection container before shopping bought fewer groceries, on average, than those who did so after shopping.
		People report that making charitable donations causes them to feel better about themselves.
		People tend to give less to charity during weeks in which they help neighbors by providing a needed good or service.
		A different study found that few blood donors consider donating blood to be comparable to "charitable giving."

Answer Explanation:

Evaluate

The researchers explained the study results by positing that the blood donors believed they had temporarily satisfied their charitable obligations by donating blood and thus didn't feel obliged to be as generous with their donations to charity.

But if a different study found that few blood donors consider donating blood to be comparable to charitable giving, that finding would weaken the researchers' hypothesis by suggesting that the blood donors wouldn't be likely to make the posited connection between donating blood and donating to charity.

On the other hand, a finding that people tend to give less to charity during weeks in which they help their neighbors would strengthen the researchers' hypothesis by providing further evidence that people feel both that their obligations to behave generously are finite and that behaving generously in one way temporarily excuses them from behaving generously in other ways.

Most weakens:

The correct answer is *A different study found that few blood donors consider donating blood to be comparable to "charitable giving."*

Most strengthens:

The correct answer is *People tend to give less to charity during weeks in which they help neighbors by providing a needed good or service.*

485. Organization A currently has 1,050 members. Organization B currently has 1,550 members. The number of members of Organization A and the number of members of Organization B are increasing annually, each at its own constant rate. Analysts project that if each of these organizations maintains its constant annual rate of membership increase, five years from now they will for the first time have the same number of members, and in subsequent years Organization A will have more members than Organization B.

In the following table, identify a rate of increase, in members per year, for Organization A and a rate of increase, in members per year, for Organization B that together are consistent with the analysts' projection. Make only one selection in each column.

Organization A	Organization B	Rate of increase (members per year)
		10
		30
		40
		120
		130
		150

Answer Explanation:

Infer

Let x be the annual increase in the number of members of Organization A and y be the annual increase in the number of members of Organization B. The value of x will be the answer in the first column, and the value of y will be the answer in the second column. We're told that five years from now the two organizations will have the same number of members. Thus, $1,050 + 5x = 1,550 + 5y$. It follows that $5x = 500 + 5y$, so $x = 100 + y$. So the correct answer in the first column must be exactly 100 more than the correct answer in the second column. Of the answer options given, the only two satisfying this constraint are 130 in the first column together with 30 in the second column.

Organization A:

The correct answer is *130*.

Organization B:

The correct answer is *30*.

486. A company called the US Copyright Group (USCG) has filed seven lawsuits in Washington, DC, courts, naming over fourteen thousand defendants. The defendants are associated with personal computers implicated in USCG's investigations of unauthorized movie downloads. The USCG contends that the strategy of prosecuting groups makes the most sense because each individual defendant lacks the assets and earning capacity to make individual prosecutions worthwhile financially. The Electronic Frontier Foundation (EFF) claims that USCG's strategy deprives defendants of a fair chance to defend themselves. Because the vast majority of defendants in these cases do not live in Washington, DC—indeed, many live outside the United States—the travel and legal defense costs associated with contesting the charges are likely to be prohibitively high for them.

Select *EFF objects to* for the statement that most accurately describes an aspect of USCG's lawsuits to which the EFF objects; select *On the basis that* for the statement that most accurately describes the EFF's basis for that objection. Make only two selections, one in each column.

EFF objects to	On the basis that	
		The USCG filed multiple cases alleging copyright infringement, rather than naming all individuals in a single case.
		The costs associated with contesting the charges would be high for a large number of the defendants.
		Many defendants named in the cases likely did not infringe on copyrights.
		The USCG investigated IP addresses associated with unauthorized downloading of movies.
		Each of the USCG's suits was filed in a single location and names a large number of defendants in other locations.
		The investigative methods employed by USCG violate the rights of Internet users.

Answer Explanation:

Evaluate

According to the passage, the EFF argues that because the vast majority of the defendants live outside of Washington, DC, where the USCG filed the suits, the travel and legal costs for the defendants to contest the charges would be prohibitively high—depriving the defendants of a fair chance to defend themselves. In other words, the EFF objects to the fact that each of the USCG's suits was filed in the single location of Washington, DC but names a large number of defendants in other locations. And the basis of the EFF's objection to this is that the costs associated with contesting the charges would be high for a large number of the defendants.

EFF objects to:

The correct answer is *Each of the USCG's suits was filed in a single location and names a large number of defendants in other locations*.

On the basis that:

The correct answer is *The costs associated with contesting the charges would be high for a large number of the defendants*.

Questions 487 to 504 — Difficulty: **Hard**

487. Companies A and B are part of the same industry and are located in the same city. For Company A, the average (arithmetic mean) salary of its employees, in United Arab Emirates dirhams (AED), is 10,000 AED higher than that for Company B. However, more than half of the employees at Company A have salaries below the average for Company B.

Statement: If the average salary at Company B is ____1____, then the median salary at Company A is ____2____.

Select for 1 and for 2 the options that complete the statement so that it most accurately reflects the information provided. Make only two selections, one in each column.

1	2	
		(A) greater than 100,000 AED
		(B) less than 100,000 AED
		(C) equal to 110,000 AED
		(D) between 100,000 and 110,000 AED
		(E) greater than 110,000 AED

Answer Explanation:

Infer

Let $med(A)$ be the median of the salaries at Company A and $ave(B)$ be the average of the salaries at Company B. Since more than half of the salaries at Company A are less than $ave(B)$, it follows that $med(A) < ave(B)$. Therefore, if we know that $ave(B)$ is at most some given amount, then $med(A)$ will be less than this amount. In particular, if $ave(B) < 100,000$, then we have $med(A) < ave(B) < 100,000$, and hence $med(A) < 100,000$.

1:

The correct answer is *less than 100,000 AED*.

2:

The correct answer is *less than 100,000 AED*.

488. The following statements describe certain characteristics of a certain pool of candidates for a position. Any candidate who did not meet the minimum qualifications for the position was immediately excluded from consideration. The two candidates who met the minimum qualifications for the position and met all of the desired qualifications also had multiple recommendations. All candidates who received a telephone interview also had extensive experience. All candidates who had extensive experience and impressed the hiring committee during the telephone interview were invited to interview on-site. At least one candidate declined an invitation for an on-site interview, and exactly one candidate was interviewed on-site without receiving a telephone interview.

Consider the following incomplete sentence:

If any candidate ____1____, then that candidate ____2____.

Select for *1* and for *2* two different options that best complete the sentence such that it can be logically inferred from the information provided. Make only two selections, one in each column.

1	2	
		did not meet the minimum qualifications
		had multiple recommendations
		had extensive experience
		impressed the hiring committee during the telephone interview
		interviewed on-site

Answer Explanation:

Infer

If a certain candidate impressed the hiring committee during the telephone interview, then the candidate certainly received a telephone interview. Since all candidates who received a telephone interview also had extensive experience, it follows that the candidate had extensive experience. Therefore, if the candidate impressed the hiring committee during the telephone interview, then the candidate had extensive experience.

1:

The correct answer is *impressed the hiring committee during the telephone interview*.

2:

The correct answer is *had extensive experience*.

489. In Country C, some but not all eligible voters are required to vote. The particulars of the country's laws governing voting are as follows.

Every citizen who is eligible must vote on Election Day.

A person is eligible if (and only if) that person meets the age requirement and is either a citizen or meets the residency requirement for noncitizens.

The age requirement is that every voter must be at least 19 years old on Election Day.

The residency requirement for noncitizens is that the voter must have been a resident of Country C for at least 5 years on Election Day.

Consider the following individuals:

Abigail: a citizen who is currently 19 years old

Barbara: a 7-year resident noncitizen who is currently 19 years old

Charles: a 7-year resident noncitizen who is currently 18 years old

For an election held today, select the individual or individuals who must vote based on the information provided, and select the individual or individuals who must not vote based on the information provided. Make only two selections, one in each column.

Must vote	Must not vote	
		Abigail only
		Barbara only
		Charles only
		Abigail and Barbara only
		Abigail and Charles only
		Barbara and Charles only

Answer Explanation:

Infer

To help with justifying the reasoning that follows without extensively quoting the country's voting laws, let S1, S2, S3, and S4 denote the country's voting laws in the order they are stated above.

Using S2, it follows that Abigail is eligible to vote today because Abigail meets the age requirement today (S3), and Abigail is a citizen. Thus, Abigail is a citizen who is eligible to vote today, and hence by S1, Abigail must vote today.

Using S2, it follows that Barbara is eligible to vote today because Barbara meets the age requirement today (S3), and Barbara meets the residency requirement today (S4). However, there is no requirement that Barbara must vote today, because Barbara is a noncitizen.

Using S3, it follows that Charles must not vote today because Charles does not meet the age requirement.

Must vote:

From the analysis above, only Abigail must vote today.

The correct answer is *Abigail only*.

Must not vote:

From the analysis above, only Charles must not vote today.

The correct answer is *Charles only*.

490. Most of the cubicles in the north wing of the Acme Company headquarters are less than 20 meters from the nearest fire escape, whereas half of the cubicles in the east wing are not. In other words, those same east-wing cubicles and ___1___ half the north-wing cubicles are ___2___ 20 meters from the nearest fire escape.

Select for *1* and for *2* two options to create a sentence that most accurately restates the information given in the first sentence. Make only two selections, one in each column.

1	2	
		at least
		at most
		exactly
		greater than
		less than

Answer Explanation:

Recognize

The phrase "those same east-wing cubicles" refers to the half of the cubicles in the east wing that are NOT less than 20 meters from the nearest fire escape. Thus, these cubicles are greater than or equal to 20 meters from the nearest fire escape, or equivalently, these cubicles are at least 20 meters from the nearest fire escape. Therefore, select "at least" for the second blank.

To determine the option for the first blank, we want a relation that describes the number of cubicles in the north wing that are at least 20 meters from the nearest fire escape. Since more than half of the cubicles in the north wing are less than 20 meters from the nearest fire escape, the remaining cubicles—less than half of the cubicles—are at least 20 meters from the nearest fire escape. Therefore, select "less than" for the first blank.

1:

The correct answer is *less than*.

2:

The correct answer is *at least*.

491. In June 1990, a small academic press published an initial run of 2,500 copies of linguist Chloe Vermeulen's first book, *Speech and Speaking*. Because the first run was selling well, a second, larger run was produced in June 1995. Total sales for the period from June 1995–June 2000 represented an increase of 52 percent over total sales for the preceding five years; by June 2000, Vermeulen's book had sold a total of 3,843 copies. In 2000, *Speech and Speaking* was cited in an influential paper; subsequently, for the period June 2000–June 2005, sales of Vermeulen's book were double the sales for the previous five-year period.

In the table, identify the number of books that most closely approximates the total sales of *Speech and Speaking* for each of the five-year periods June 1990–June 1995 and June 2000–June 2005, based on the information given. Make only two selections, one in each column.

June 1990–June 1995	June 2000–June 2005	Total sales for the period (number of books)
		1,320
		1,530
		2,530
		2,640
		3,800
		4,640

Answer Explanation:

Apply

June 1990–June 1995:

Let N be the total sales for June 1990–June 1995. Then 1.52N is the total sales for June 1995–June 2000 and N + 1.52N = 2.52N is the sales by June 2000. Since the sales by June 2000 is 3,843, it follows that 2.52N = 3,843, or N = 1,525. Among the table values, 1,530 most closely approximates the value of N (total sales for June 1990–June 1995).

The correct answer is *1,530*.

June 2000–June 2005:

From the analysis above, 1.52N = 1.52(1,525) = 2,318 is the total sales for June 1995–June 2000. The total sales for June 2000–June 2005 is double the total sales for June 1995–June 2000, or 2(2,318) = 4,636. Among the table values, 4,640 most closely approximates the total sales for June 2000–June 2005.

The correct answer is *4,640*.

492. Miguel's online banking password is nine characters long and includes at least one character of each of five types: digits, punctuation marks, uppercase (capital) letters, lowercase (noncapital) letters, and certain other characters. The password begins or ends with one of these other characters, of which it contains exactly one. No consecutive characters in the password are of the same one of these types. (For example, no capital letter is preceded or followed by another capital letter.) The password contains more lowercase letters than characters of any one of the other four types. It also contains fewer punctuation marks than digits, lowercase

letters, or uppercase letters. The first three characters of the password are M, ?, and G.

In the table, select a type of character that the fifth character in the password must be and a type of character that the seventh character must be. Make only two selections, one in each column.

Fifth character	Seventh character	
		Digit
		Lowercase letter
		Punctuation mark
		Uppercase letter
		Other character

Answer Explanation:

Apply

The passage indicates that Miguel's password is nine characters long, contains at least one character of each of five different types—digits, punctuation marks, uppercase letters, lowercase letters, and "other characters"—and either begins or ends with one of the "other characters." We are also given the first three characters of the password: M, ?, and G. So, because the password begins with an uppercase letter, it must end with one of the "other characters." We know the password contains more lowercase letters than characters of any of the other types, so it must contain at least three lowercase letters. We also know that there is at least one punctuation mark and fewer punctuation marks than digits, lowercase letters, or uppercase letters, so there must be at least two digits.

Given that the password is nine characters long, we can now determine the distribution of all the characters in the password across all five of the types: one *other character*, one *punctuation mark*, two *digits*, two *uppercase letters*, and three *lowercase letters*. We know that the two uppercase letters and the one punctuation mark are among the first three characters and that the "other character" is the ninth character of the password. Therefore, characters 4 through 8 of the password consist of two digits and three lowercase letters. The passage indicates that no consecutive characters are of the same type, and this provides that characters 4, 6, and 8 are all lowercase letters; otherwise, two or more lowercase letters would appear consecutively. If characters 4, 6, and 8 are all lowercase letters, then both character 5 and character 7 must be digits.

Fifth character:

The correct answer is *Digit*.

Seventh character:

The correct answer is *Digit*.

493. Public health professional: The Happydale Department of Environmental Services (DES) has inspected area beaches for pathogenic bacteria for over 20 years. Currently, DES monitors 50 freshwater beaches and 10 coastal beaches on a weekly basis. Program participation by owners of beaches that are open to the public is voluntary. Beach owners who choose not to participate in the program are allowing the public to recreate on entirely unmonitored beaches. The DES now proposes adoption of the Adopt-a-Beach Program, designed to promote health and environmental education as well as public involvement in the protecting of public beaches. The program would require DES to collect biological data from all area beaches. It will also help reduce the number of beach advisories, whereby the public must be warned of dangerous conditions on certain beaches.

On the basis of the public health professional's statement, indicate in the table which of the following is most likely to result if the DES proposal is successfully adopted, and indicate which is most likely to result if the DES proposal is not adopted. Make only two selections, one in each column.

Adopted	Not adopted	
		Incidents of waterborne disease will increase.
		The number of beach advisories will increase.
		DES will shift its principal priorities from monitoring to education.
		There will be fewer, if any, entirely unmonitored beaches.
		Some beaches will remain entirely unmonitored.

Answer Explanation:

Infer

Adopted:

Currently not all beaches are monitored. Because the proposal calls for the DES to collect data on—that is, monitor—all area beaches, it is reasonable to conclude that there will be fewer, if any, entirely unmonitored beaches in the area.

The correct answer is *There will be fewer, if any, entirely unmonitored beaches*.

Not adopted:

If the proposal requiring that all area beaches be monitored is not adopted, then, barring some other change to the current situation, it is likely that some beaches will remain entirely unmonitored.

The correct answer is *Some beaches will remain entirely unmonitored*.

494. Marco: Giant kangaroos—one of several extinct species of large mammals (megafauna)—went extinct in Australia around 46,000 years ago. The deposits and wear patterns on the teeth of these animals from around the time of their extinction indicate that they fed mostly on saltbrush shrubs. Saltbrush thrives in arid climates, so it is not likely that the kangaroos' food supply was adversely affected by the increasing aridity of the climate at the time. Thus, something else would have to account for their extinction, and the best candidate for that cause is predation by humans.

Fatima: That argument alone is not likely to satisfy many researchers in this field. Have you found any other evidence to bolster your conclusion?

Select *Marco* for the statement that, if true, most justifies Marco's assertions, and select *Fatima* for the statement that, if true, most justifies Fatima's skepticism about Marco's assertions. Make only two selections, one in each column.

Marco	Fatima	
		Giant kangaroos became extinct during a period that was less arid than previous periods they endured.
		Many researchers believe humans first arrived in Australia around 40,000 years ago.
		Approximately 60 different species in Australia died out in the wave of extinctions around 46,000 years ago.
		Fossils of giant kangaroos also show evidence that those animals' diets routinely included plants other than saltbrush.
		Several types of megafauna larger than the giant kangaroo went extinct around 46,000 years ago.

Answer Explanation:

Evaluate

Marco:

Marco argues that increasing aridity is not likely the cause of the giant kangaroos' extinction in Australia. If it is a fact that giant kangaroos endured during even more arid conditions than the conditions at the time of their extinction, this fact would make it less likely that the increasing aridity would be either a direct or indirect cause of their extinction. This would, therefore, help justify Marco's conclusion that something other than increasing aridity led to their extinction.

The correct answer is *Giant kangaroos became extinct during a period that was less arid than previous periods they endured*.

Fatima:

Marco proposes that the most likely cause of the giant kangaroos' extinction is human predation. But giant kangaroos went extinct in Australia about 46,000 years ago. Therefore, if many researchers believe that humans didn't first arrive in Australia until 40,000 years ago, then Fatima has justification for being skeptical about Marco's suggestion that human predation is the best candidate for the cause

of giant kangaroos' extinction in Australia. If these researchers are correct, humans did not arrive in Australia until giant kangaroos had been extinct there for about 6,000 years.

The correct answer is *Many researchers believe humans first arrived in Australia around 40,000 years ago*.

495. A mattress company has two stores, one in City X and the other in City Z. The company has advertised equally in newspapers in both cities but has advertised twice as much on the radio in City Z as in City X. The two cities have similar populations and economies, and the sales at each store have been roughly equal. A consultant claims this shows that the radio advertising has not improved mattress sales. In the table below, select changes that the company could make in City X and City Z, respectively, that together would probably be most helpful in testing the consultant's claim. Make only two selections, one in each column.

City X	City Z	
		Double newspaper advertising
		Eliminate newspaper advertising
		Eliminate radio advertising
		Change the content of radio advertising
		Add television advertising

Answer Explanation:

Strategize

While changes to the newspaper or television advertising strategy may affect mattress sales, those changes would not necessarily clarify the effect radio advertising has had on mattress sales.

Even if changing the content of the radio advertising in either city were to bring about an increase in mattress sales, it may not be possible to determine if the consultant's claim was correct. If the previous content had a negligible or a positive effect on sales, then an increase in sales coinciding with the change of content would be evidence that the consultant's claim is incorrect.

On the other hand, if the previous content had a negative effect on sales, then the new content may simply have had less of a negative effect.

The best way to determine if radio advertising does not improve mattress sales is to eliminate radio advertising in both cities. Any change in sales may be attributed to the radio advertising, indicating whether the consultant's claim was correct. If there was no change, the consultant's claim would be strongly supported.

City X:

The correct answer is *Eliminate radio advertising*.

City Z:

The correct answer is *Eliminate radio advertising*.

496. Metro Ballet Company presents high-quality productions of traditional, classical ballet. For the past several years, however, the company's overall profits have been declining, and ticket sales have been flat. Annual audience surveys indicate that a majority of those who attend Metro Ballet productions consistently enjoy the performances and prefer classical ballet to other forms of dance; almost all of them have been attending Metro Ballet for several years. General surveys of area residents indicate, however, that very few are aware of Metro Ballet productions, and most imagine that the performances are boring and the tickets too expensive. In an effort to appeal to a wider audience, over the past decade the company has spent increasing amounts of money on spectacular stage productions, while lowering ticket prices.

In the first column, select the strategy that, in the absence of the other alternatives listed, would lead most directly to decreasing Metro Ballet's expenses for its classical ballet productions. In the second column, select the strategy that, in the absence of the other alternatives listed, would constitute the most direct approach to solving the problem of increasing audience size for Metro Ballet's classical ballet productions. Make only two selections, one in each column.

Decrease expenses	Increase audience size	
		Obtain public funding to double the spending on stage productions without increasing ticket prices
		Return spending on productions to levels of several years ago
		Expand productions to include modern, folk, and tap dance traditions
		Offer special discounts to reward people who have attended the greatest number of performances
		Mount a local advertising campaign emphasizing the affordability and excitement of Metro Ballet's spectacular stage productions

Answer Explanation:

Strategize

Decrease expenses:

This requires consideration of all the strategy options presented in the table to determine which one would lead most directly to decreasing expenses for Metro Ballet's classical ballet productions. Obtaining public funding to double the spending on stage productions without increasing ticket prices (the first option) would lead to an *increase* in expenses for ballet productions, although those expenses should be offset by public funding. If expanding productions to include modern, folk, and tap dance traditions (the third option) had the effect of decreasing expenses associated with ballet, that effect would be indirect. Offering discounts to reward people who have attended the greatest number of performances (the fourth option) has no clear implication for expenses associated with ballet productions. Mounting an advertising campaign emphasizing the affordability and excitement of the ballet's spectacular productions (the fifth option) should increase expenses in the short term, although it may lead to increased revenue in the long term. Only the strategy of returning spending on productions to the level of several years ago (the second option) has the immediate effect of decreasing expenses associated with classical ballet productions.

The correct answer is *Return spending on productions to levels of several years ago*.

Increase audience size:

It is again necessary to consider all the options. It is unclear how the strategy of doubling spending on stage productions without raising ticket prices (the first option) would address the problem of attracting a larger audience, unless the process of obtaining public funding entailed an advertising campaign. Since the current audience has become accustomed to lavish productions, a reduction in spending on ballet productions (the second option) might actually *reduce* that audience. Expanding productions to include different dance traditions (the third option) might attract a larger audience, but only if these traditions appeal to people not currently attending Metro Ballet, and only if they are made aware of the new productions. Since most people in the current audience have already been attending Metro Ballet productions for a number of years, offering discounts to those who have already attended a great number of performances (the fourth option) may reinforce their loyalty, but it is unlikely to attract people who haven't previously attended. An advertising campaign aimed at addressing the reasons why area residents surveyed don't currently attend (the fifth option), however, would constitute the most direct attempt to increase audience size among the options listed.

The correct answer is *Mount a local advertising campaign emphasizing the affordability and excitement of Metro Ballet's spectacular stage productions*.

497. At XYZ Inc. any employee receives a verbal warning upon accumulating at least 3 unexcused absences within any 365-day period and a written reprimand upon accumulating at least 4 such absences. For any single 8-hour workday, missing between 10 minutes and 2 hours of work counts as one-third of an absence, missing between 2 hours and 4 hours of work counts as half an absence, and missing more than 4 hours counts as a full absence. However, an employee may stay late to make up for up to 1 hour of an unexcused absence on the same day.

The following options are descriptions of the unexcused absences of 5 employees of XYZ Inc. Assume that in each case the employee had no other unexcused absences and made up no other time. Select a description of an employee who qualified for a verbal warning but not a written reprimand, and select a description of an employee who qualified for a written reprimand. Make only two selections, one in each column.

Verbal warning	Written reprimand	
		Absent all day on 5 April 2010, 8 June 2010, 17 April 2011, and 14 June 2011
		Absent 4.5 hours but stayed 1 hour late on 13 May 2010; absent all day on 2 June 2010, 1 May 2011, and 21 July 2011
		Absent 4.5 hours on 19 March 2010; stayed one hour late on 20 March 2010; absent all day on 8 February 2011 and 9 February 2011; arrived 40 minutes late on 17 April 2011
		Absent 3.5 hours on 13 September 2010; absent 1 hour on 15 September 2010; absent 6 hours on 16 September 2010; absent 2.5 hours on 18 September 2010; absent 1 hour on 19 September 2010
		Absent 3 hours on 7 July 2010; absent 2.5 hours on 13 September 2010; absent all day on 31 January 2011 and 4 July 2011; absent 5 hours on 12 March 2011

Answer Explanation:

Apply

Verbal warning:

Each employee description must be checked to see if it meets the criteria for verbal warning, but not for written reprimand: accumulating at least 3, but fewer than 4, unexcused absences within a 365-day period. The employee described in the first option had 4 unexcused absences, but no more than 2 of these occurred within a single 365-day period, so the employee did not qualify for a verbal warning.

Likewise, the employee in the second option did not qualify for a verbal warning: the employee reduced the absence on 13 May 2010 from a full day to half a day by staying late and working an extra hour, and thus had only $2\frac{1}{2}$ absences during the 365-day period beginning 13 May, and no more than 2 absences within any other 365-day period.

In the third option, the 4.5-hour absence on 19 March 2010 counts as a full day's absence and is not offset by the extra hour because it was not worked on the same day. Therefore, the employee in the third option had exactly 3 unexcused absences in the 365-day period beginning on 19 March 2010—enough for a verbal warning, though not a written reprimand.

In the fourth option, the employee was absent between 10 minutes and 2 hours on 15 and 19 September, between 2 hours and 4 hours on 13 and 18 September, and more than 4 hours on 16 September. Thus, in that single 365-day period, the employee accumulated $(2)\left(\frac{1}{3}\right) + (2)\left(\frac{1}{2}\right) + 1$, or $2\frac{2}{3}$, total absences, which falls just short of 3 absences and thus does not qualify for a verbal warning.

In the fifth option, during the 365-day period beginning on 7 July 2010, the employee had a 3-hour (half-day) absence, a 2.5-hour (half-day) absence, two all-day (full-day) absences, and a 5-hour (full-day) absence, for a total of $(2)\left(\frac{1}{2}\right) + (2)(1) + 1$, or 4 absences. This employee meets the criteria for a verbal warning, but also for a written reprimand, and hence the fifth option is not a key.

The correct answer is *Absent 4.5 hours on 19 March 2010; stayed one hour late on 20 March 2010; absent all day on 8 February 2011 and 9 February 2011; arrived 40 minutes late on 17 April 2011.*

Written reprimand:

As noted in the analysis for *Verbal warning*, the employee in the fifth option meets the criteria for both a verbal warning and a written reprimand, and hence this option is the answer. Also by the previous analysis, the employees in the first, second, and fourth options do not meet the criteria for verbal warning, and hence cannot meet the criteria for written reprimand. While a verbal warning is warranted in the third option, the employee has fewer than 4 absences in a 365-day period and thus does not merit a written reprimand.

The correct answer is *Absent 3 hours on 7 July 2010; absent 2.5 hours on 13 September 2010; absent all day on 31 January 2011 and 4 July 2011; absent 5 hours on 12 March 2011.*

498. Marketing strategist: Agency A designed an advertising campaign that our company is about to test with a focus group. We are wondering whether a new ad campaign will increase our name recognition among consumers. As a contingency, we have decided that we might ask Agency B to design an alternate campaign. However, if we find that Agency A's campaign elicits positive responses from the focus group, we will not ask Agency B for a campaign.

A statement that must be true if the marketing strategist's statements are true: After the focus testing is complete, if the company ____1____, then it must also be the case that the company ____2____.

Select for *1 if* and *2 then* the two different options that create a statement that must be true if the marketing strategist's statements are true. Make only two selections, one in each column.

1 if	2 then	
		believes Agency A's campaign will increase the company's name recognition
		believes Agency A's campaign will decrease the company's name recognition
		asks Agency B for a campaign
		asks Agency A for an alternate campaign
		believes the focus group did not respond positively to Agency A's campaign

Answer Explanation:

Infer

The item requires completing a statement such that if a certain claim about a company is true, then a different claim about the company must also be true. The passage indicates that the company will not ask Agency B to design an advertising campaign if Agency A's advertising campaign elicits positive responses from the focus group. Therefore, if the company *asks Agency B for a campaign*, then it must be the case, given the information provided, that the company *believes the focus group did not respond positively to Agency A's campaign*. There are no other relationships between any two answer options that would create a statement that follows logically from the information provided.

1 if:

The correct answer is *asks Agency B for a campaign*.

2 then:

The correct answer is *believes the focus group did not respond positively to Agency A's campaign*.

499. Francois and Pierre each owe Claudine money. Today, Francois will make a payment equal to 50% of the amount he owes Claudine, and Pierre will make a payment equal to 10% of the amount he owes Claudine. Together, the two payments will be equal to 40% of the combined amount that Francois and Pierre owe Claudine.

Select for *Francois* and *Pierre* amounts that Francois and Pierre could owe Claudine that are jointly consistent with the given information. Make only two selections, one in each column.

Francois	Pierre	
		€50
		€250
		€750
		€3,750
		€6,750

Answer Explanation:

Infer

Francois:

Let F and P be the amounts, in euros (€) and respectively, that Francois and Pierre owe Claudine. Then $0.4(F + P)$ is 40% of the total amount they owe Claudine, and $0.5F + 0.1P$ is the total amount they will pay Claudine today.

$0.5F + 0.1P = 0.4(F + P)$	given
$5F + P = 4(F + P)$	multiply both sides by 10
$5F + P = 4F + 4P$	expand right side
$F = 3P$	subtract $4F + P$ from both sides

The table below shows the value of F (which is $3P$) for each possible value of P.

$F = 3P$	P
150	50
750	250
2,250	750
11,250	3,750
20,250	6,750

The only value of $F = 3P$ above that is one of the allowable values is 750.

The correct answer is €750.

Pierre:

The table above shows that 250 is the value of P corresponding to $F = 750$.

The correct answer is €250.

500. Witness testimony: Around 8:00 on the morning of Tuesday, July 6, I saw a man exit from the back entrance of the building. I knew it was McGregor by the man's height and his long, slightly awkward steps, and from the fact that he was wearing a hat—possibly a baseball cap. McGregor always seemed to be wearing some kind of hat. On Tuesdays there are always several groundskeepers scheduled to work on the grounds, and he would very likely have been scheduled that day.

Select *Assumes to be true* for the statement that describes something the testimony implies the witness assumes to be true, and select *Assumes to be false* for the statement that describes something the testimony implies the witness assumes to be false. Make only two selections, one in each column.

Assumes to be true	Assumes to be false	
		McGregor was the only groundskeeper scheduled to work at the building on Tuesday, July 6.
		McGregor exited the rear of the building in question alone at 8:00 on the morning of Tuesday, July 6.
		McGregor was scheduled to work at the building on the morning of Tuesday, July 6.
		McGregor's height, way of walking, and tendency to wear hats distinguish him from the other groundskeepers.
		McGregor often wore a baseball cap prior to the morning of Tuesday, July 6.

Answer Explanation:

Infer

Assumes to be true:

The witness says there are always several groundskeepers scheduled to work on the grounds on Tuesdays. But the witness also claims to have known that the man seen exiting the building on the Tuesday morning was McGregor, based on the man's height, way of walking, and wearing of a hat. Since the witness assumes that these features revealed that it was McGregor rather than another groundskeeper who was seen exiting the building, the witness is also assuming that McGregor's height, way of walking, and tendency to wear hats distinguish him from the other groundskeepers.

The correct answer is *McGregor's height, way of walking, and tendency to wear hats distinguish him from the other groundskeepers.*

Assumes to be false:

The witness claims there are always several groundskeepers scheduled to work on the grounds on Tuesdays. This claim implies that more than one groundskeeper was scheduled to work there on Tuesday, July 6. So, the witness is assuming it's false that McGregor was the only groundskeeper scheduled to work there that day.

The correct answer is *McGregor was the only groundskeeper scheduled to work at the building on Tuesday, July 6.*

501. Ribonucleic acid (RNA) is a molecule built from sequences of smaller molecules called nucleobases. RNA nucleobases are of 4 different types: adenine (A), cytosine (C), guanine (G), and uracil (U). Consider the collection of all possible RNA sequences consisting of 12 nucleobases, 3 of each type. An RNA sequence will be selected at random from this collection and the first 3 nucleobases of the sequence will be detached from the sequence.

In the table, select the probability that the 3 nucleobases are all of the same type, and select the probability that they are of 3 different types. Make only two selections, one in each column.

All the same type	3 different types	
		$\frac{1}{55}$
		$\frac{9}{220}$
		$\frac{9}{110}$
		$\frac{9}{55}$
		$\frac{27}{55}$

Answer Explanation:

Apply

All the same type:

We're considering a randomly ordered sequence of 12 nucleobases, which is made up of 3 of each of the 4 types of nucleobase. The first nucleobase in this sequence must be of the same type as exactly 2 of the remaining 11 nucleobases. So, the probability that the first 2 nucleobases are of the same type is $\frac{2}{11}$. If they are of the same type, then exactly 1 of the remaining 10 nucleobases is also of that type. Thus, the probability that the first 3 nucleobases in the sequence are all of the same type is $\frac{2}{11} \times \frac{1}{10} = \frac{1}{55}$.

The correct answer is $\frac{1}{55}$.

3 different types:

We saw above that the first nucleobase in the sequence is of the same type as exactly 2 of the remaining 11 nucleobases. So, it's of a different type than each of the other 9 of those 11. That means the probability that the first 2 nucleobases are of different types is $\frac{9}{11}$. If the first 2 nucleobases are of different types, then among the 10 remaining nucleobases are still 3 apiece of the other 2 types, making a total of 6 nucleobases that are of types different than either of the first 2

nucleobases' types. In that case, the probability that the third nucleobase in the sequence is of a different type than either of the first 2 is $\frac{6}{10}$. Thus, the probability that the first 3 nucleobases in the sequence are all of different types is

$$\frac{9}{11} \times \frac{6}{10} = \frac{27}{55}.$$

The correct answer is $\frac{27}{55}$.

502. Let S be the set of all 7-digit numbers N such that the sum of the digits of N is divisible by 7.

A and B are two 7-digit numbers:

$A = 4,893,P12$

$B = 5,857,0Q5$

Select a value for P so that A is an element of S. Select a value for Q so that B is an element of S. Make two selections, one in each column.

P	Q	
		4
		5
		6
		7
		8

Answer Explanation:

Apply

P:

The sum of the digits in A other than P is $4 + 8 + 9 + 3 + 1 + 2 = 27$. Since $8 + 27 = 35$, which is divisible by 7, selecting the value 8 for P makes A a 7-digit number whose digits sum to a value divisible by 7. And that makes A an element of S.

The correct answer is *8*.

Q:

The sum of the digits in *B* other than *Q* is 5 + 8 + 5 + 7 + 0 + 5 = 30. Since 5 + 30 = 35, which is divisible by 7, selecting the value 5 for *Q* makes *A* a 7-digit number whose digits sum to a value divisible by 7. And that makes *B* an element of *S*.

The correct answer is *5*.

503. Alfredo: The United States could make significant progress toward becoming independent of petroleum-derived gasoline as a source of energy by diverting a large proportion of corn grown in the US to the production of ethanol for fuel. Brazil is virtually independent of petroleum as a source of fuel because that country has been very successful in ethanol production.

Mavis: Ethanol derived from corn will never be a viable substitute for petroleum-derived gasoline in the US. While it is true that Brazil has been very successful in replacing gasoline with ethanol, the US cannot expect the same degree of success with corn-derived ethanol. Brazil's ethanol is derived from sugarcane, which is very easy to convert to ethanol and, in Brazil, very easy to cultivate. Corn, on the other hand, is difficult to grow, requiring intensive cultivation. Also, the amount of fuel energy that can be garnered from the land is much less per square meter for corn ethanol.

Based on the information provided, select for *Alfredo* the statement that best describes the primary purpose of Alfredo's remarks and select for *Mavis* the statement that best describes the primary purpose of Mavis's remarks. Make only two selections, one in each column.

Alfredo	Mavis	
		Critique a line of reasoning
		Compare two strategies aimed at solving a problem
		Provide an alternative to a given proposal
		Illustrate the details of a particular strategy
		Recommend a course of action for reaching a goal

Answer Explanation:

Apply

Alfredo recommends a course of action, diverting much of the corn grown in the US to produce ethanol for fuel, to reach the goal of making the US less dependent on petroleum-derived gasoline. To support this recommendation, he draws an analogy between the US and Brazil. He asserts that Brazil is already virtually independent of petroleum as a fuel source because it produces a lot of ethanol. He then implies that the US could follow Brazil's lead with similar success.

Mavis critiques Alfredo's line of reasoning by challenging the analogy between the US and Brazil. She lists several factors that would make it much harder for the US to produce large amounts of ethanol than it has been for Brazil to do so.

Alfredo:
The correct answer is *Recommend a course of action for reaching a goal*.

Mavis:
The correct answer is *Critique a line of reasoning*.

504. Company T projected the number of international students studying in the United States (US) for three consecutive school years from 2014–2015 through 2016–2017. The projected numbers for the 2014–2015 school year and during the 2016–2017 school year would be 880,000 and 1,026,080, respectively. Let *X*% and *Y*% denote the company's predicted percentage increase in the number of international students studying in the US from school year 2014–2015 to school year 2015–2016, and from school year 2015–2016 to school year 2016–2017, respectively. Both *X* and *Y* are positive integers, and *X* is less than *Y*.

In the table, identify the value of *X* and the value of *Y*. Make only two selections, one in each column.

X	Y	
		2
		6
		10
		15
		20

Answer Explanation:

Infer

Let A, B, and C be the projected numbers of international students for school years 2014–2015, 2015–2016, and 2016–2017, respectively. Since $A = 880{,}000$ and $C = 1{,}026{,}080$, $C/A = 1{,}026{,}080/880{,}000 = 1.166$. So the percent increase from A to C is $(C/A - 1) \times 100\% = 0.166 \times 100\% = 16.6\%$.

We now want to find percent increases from A to B and from B to C that yield this 16.6% increase from A to C. To do this, first note that since $C/A = B/A \times C/B$, it follows that $1.166 = B/A \times C/B$. Also note that X is the percent increase from A to B, which is $(B/A - 1) \times 100\%$, and that Y is the percent increase from B to C, which is $(C/B - 1) \times 100\%$. Finally, note that we've been told that $X < Y$.

The five answer options 2, 6, 10, 15, and 20 given in the first column, for X, stand for percentage increases of 2%, 6%, 10%, 15%, and 20% from A to B, so these answer options yield the five possible values for B/A of 1.02, 1.06, 1.1, 1.15, and 1.2, respectively. Likewise, the same five answer options given in the second column, for Y, stand for the same five percentage increases from B to C, so they yield the same five possible values of 1.02, 1.06, 1.1, 1.15, and 1.2 for C/B. Therefore, since $1.166 = 1.06 \times 1.1$, the two correct answer options must be 6 and 10. Since we know $X < Y$, this gives us answers of $X = 6$ (corresponding to $B/A = 1.06$) for the first column and $Y = 10$ (corresponding to $C/B = 1.1$) for the second column.

X:

The correct answer is *6*.

Y:

The correct answer is *10*.

7.0   Verbal Review

7.0 Verbal Review

To prepare for the GMAT™ exam's Verbal Reasoning section and Data Insights section, and to succeed in graduate business programs, you need basic skills in analyzing and evaluating texts and the ideas they express. This chapter explains concepts to help you develop these skills. This is only a brief overview. So, if you find unfamiliar terms or concepts, consult outside resources to learn more.

The sections below can help you develop skills you need for the Verbal Reasoning and Data Insights sections of the GMAT exam.

Section 7.1, "Analyzing Passages," includes:

1. Arguments
2. Explanations and Plans
3. Narratives and Descriptions

Section 7.2, "Inductive Reasoning," includes:

1. Inductive Arguments
2. Generalizations and Predictions
3. Causal Reasoning
4. Analogies

Section 7.3, "Deductive Reasoning," includes:

1. Deductive Arguments
2. Logical Operators
3. Reasoning with Logical Operators
4. Necessity, Probability, and Possibility
5. Quantifiers
6. Reasoning with Quantifiers

7.1 Analyzing Passages

1. Arguments

A. An *argument* gives one or more ideas as reasons to accept one or more other ideas. Often some of these ideas are implied but not stated.

Example:

The sidewalk is dry, so it must not have rained last night.

This argument gives the observation that the sidewalk is dry as a reason to accept that it didn't rain last night. The argument implies but doesn't say that rain typically leaves sidewalks wet.

B. A *premise* is an idea that an argument gives as a reason to accept another idea. An argument can have any number of premises.

The words and phrases below often mark premises:

after all	*for one thing*	*moreover*
because	*furthermore*	*seeing that*
for	*given that*	*since*
for the reason that	*in light of the fact that*	*whereas*

Example:

Our mayor shouldn't support the proposal to expand the freeway **because** the expansion's benefits wouldn't justify the costs. **Furthermore**, most voters oppose the expansion.

This is an argument with two stated premises. The word *because* marks the first premise, that the expansion's benefits wouldn't justify the costs. The word *furthermore* marks the second premise, that most voters oppose the expansion. These premises are given as reasons the mayor shouldn't support the proposal.

C. A *conclusion* is an idea an argument supports with one or more premises. An *intermediate conclusion* is a conclusion the argument uses to support another conclusion. A *main conclusion* is a conclusion the argument doesn't use to support any other conclusion.

The words and phrases below often mark conclusions:

clearly	*it follows that*	*suggests that*
entails that	*proves*	*surely*
hence	*shows that*	*therefore*
implies that	*so*	*thus*

Example:

Julia just hiked fifteen kilometers, **so** she must have burned a lot of calories. **Surely**, she's hungry now.

This argument has a premise, an intermediate conclusion, and a main conclusion. The word *so* marks the intermediate conclusion: that Julia must have burned a lot of calories. The word *surely* marks the main conclusion: that Julia is hungry now. The premise that Julia just hiked fifteen kilometers supports the intermediate conclusion, which in turn supports the main conclusion.

Conclusions may be stated before, between, or after premises. Sometimes no marker words show which statements are premises and which are conclusions. To find premises and conclusions without marker words, consider which statements the author gives as reasons to accept which other statements. The reasons given are the premises. The ideas the author tries to persuade readers to accept are the conclusions.

Example:

For healthy eating, Healthful Brand Donuts are the best donuts you can buy. Unlike any other donuts on the market, Healthful Brand Donuts have plenty of fiber and natural ingredients.

In this argument, the author tries to persuade the reader that Healthful Brand Donuts are the best donuts to buy for healthy eating. So, the first sentence is the conclusion. The statement about Healthful Brand Donuts' ingredients is a premise because it's given as a reason to accept the conclusion. Since the author's intent is clear, no marker words are needed.

D. A *valid* argument is one whose conclusions follow from its premises. A valid argument can have false premises and conclusions. In a valid argument with false premises, the conclusion **would** follow if the premises **were** true.

A *sound* argument is a valid argument with true premises. Since a sound argument's premises are true, and its conclusions follow from those premises, its conclusions must also be true.

Examples:

(i) Everyone who tries fried eggplant is guaranteed to love the taste. So, if you try it, you'll love the taste too.

In example (i), the premise is false: not everyone who tries fried eggplant is guaranteed to love the taste. So, example (i) is not a sound argument. But it is a valid argument because if everyone who tried fried eggplant **were** guaranteed to love the taste, it would follow that you, too, would love the taste if **you** tried it.

(ii) Some people who try fried eggplant dislike the taste. So, if you try it, you'll probably dislike the taste too.

In example (ii), the premise is true: some people who try fried eggplant do dislike the taste. However, example (ii) is an invalid argument, so it's not sound. **Some** people dislike the taste of fried eggplant, but that does not mean **you personally** will **probably** dislike the taste.

E. An *assumption* is an idea taken for granted. An assumption may be a premise in an argument, a claim about a cause or effect in a causal explanation, a condition a plan relies on, or any other type of idea taken for granted. A conclusion is never an assumption—an argument doesn't take a conclusion for granted, but rather gives reasons to accept it.

A passage may also have *implicit assumptions* the author considers too obvious to state. These unstated ideas fill logical gaps between the passage's statements.

An argument, plan, or explanation with implausible assumptions is weak and vulnerable to criticism.

F. A *necessary assumption* of an argument is an idea that must be true for the argument's stated premises to be good enough reasons to accept its conclusions. That is, a necessary assumption is one the argument needs in order to work.

Example:

Mario has booked a flight scheduled to arrive at 5:00 p.m.—which should let him get here by around 6:30 p.m. So, by 7:00 p.m. we'll be going out to dinner with Mario.

In this argument, one necessary assumption is that the flight Mario booked will arrive not much later than scheduled. A second necessary assumption is that Mario caught his flight. Unless these and all the argument's other necessary assumptions are true, the argument's stated premises aren't good enough reasons to accept the conclusion.

G. A *sufficient assumption* of an argument is an idea whose truth would make the argument's main conclusion follow from the stated premises. That is, adding a sufficient assumption to an argument makes the argument valid.

Example:

The study of poetry is entirely without value since poetry has no practical use.

In this argument, one sufficient assumption is that studying anything with no practical use is entirely without value. This assumption, together with the argument's stated premise, is enough to make the conclusion follow. If both the premise and the assumption are true, the conclusion must also be true. But this sufficient assumption is not a necessary assumption.

H. Arguments are often classified based on what kinds of conclusions they have.

   i. A *prescriptive* argument has a conclusion about what should or shouldn't be done. Prescriptive arguments may advocate for or against policies, procedures, strategies, goals, laws, or ethical norms.

Example:

Our company's staff is too small to handle our upcoming project. So, to make sure the project succeeds, the company **should** hire more employees.

Another example of a prescriptive argument is shown above in Section 7.1.1.B. That argument is prescriptive because it concludes that the mayor **should not** support the proposed freeway expansion.

   ii. An *evaluative* argument concludes that something is good or bad, desirable or undesirable, without advocating any particular policy or actions.

Example:

This early novel is clearly one of the greatest of all time. Not only did it pioneer brilliantly innovative narrative techniques, but it did so with exceptional grace, subtlety, and sophistication.

   iii. An *interpretive* argument has a conclusion about something's underlying significance. An interpretive argument may be about the meaning, importance, or implications of observations, a theory, an artistic or literary work, or a historical event.

Example:

Many famous authors have commented emphatically on this early novel, either praising or condemning it. This suggests the novel has had an enormous influence on later fiction.

iv. A *causal* argument concludes that one or more factors did or did not contribute to one or more effects. A causal argument may be about the causes, reasons, or motivations for an event, condition, decision, or outcome. For example, a causal argument may support or oppose an account of the influences behind a literary or artistic style or movement.

> *Example:*
>
> Our houseplant started to thrive only when we moved it to a sunny window. So, probably the reason it was sickly before then was that it wasn't getting enough sunlight.
>
> Another causal argument can be found in the example in Section 7.1.1.C above, which concludes that Julia must be hungry now.

v. A basic *factual* argument has a factual conclusion that doesn't fit in any other category explained above.

> *Example:*
>
> All dogs are mammals. Rover is a dog. Therefore, Rover is a mammal.

2. Explanations and Plans

A. A *causal explanation* claims that one or more factors contribute to one or more effects. A causal explanation might not be an argument. It might have no premises or conclusions. But a causal explanation can be a premise or conclusion in an argument.

The words and phrases below often mark a causal explanation:

as a result	*due to*	*results in*
because	*leads to*	*that's why*
causes	*produces*	*thereby*
contributes to	*responsible for*	*thus*

Some of these words can also mark premises or conclusions in arguments. To tell what the words mark, you may have to judge whether the author is giving reasons to accept a conclusion or only saying what causes an effect. If the author is only saying what causes an effect, without trying to persuade the reader that the effect is real, then the passage is a causal explanation but not an argument.

Just as an argument may have premises, intermediate conclusions, and main conclusions, a causal explanation may claim that one or more factors cause one or more intermediate effects that, in turn, cause further effects.

Example:

Julia just hiked fifteen kilometers, **thereby** burning a lot of calories. **That's why** she's hungry now.

This is a causal explanation claiming that a factor (Julia's fifteen-kilometer hike) caused an intermediate effect (Julia burning a lot of calories) that, in turn, caused another effect (Julia being hungry now). The word *thereby* marks the intermediate effect, and the phrase *that's why* marks the final effect. This explanation doesn't try to convince the reader that Julia's hungry. It just explains what made her hungry. So, it's not an argument.

B. An *observation* is a claim that something was observed or is otherwise directly known. In the example of a causal explanation above, the claims that Julia just hiked fifteen kilometers and that she's hungry are observations. But if her burning of calories was not directly known or observed, the claim that she burned a lot of calories is not an observation.

C. A *hypothesis* is a tentative idea neither known nor assumed to be true. A hypothesis can be an argument's conclusion. Causal explanations are often hypotheses. A passage may discuss *alternative hypotheses*, such as competing explanations for the same observation. Sometimes a passage gives pros and cons of alternative hypotheses without arguing for any particular hypothesis as a conclusion.

Example:

A bush in our yard just died. The invasive insects we've seen around the yard lately might be the cause. Or the bush might not have gotten enough water. It's been a dry summer.

This example presents two alternative hypotheses. The first hypothesis gives the observation that invasive insects have been in the yard as a possible causal explanation for the bush's observed death. This hypothesis assumes the insects can hurt bushes like the one in the yard. The second hypothesis provides the observation that it's been a dry summer as an alternative causal explanation for the bush's observed death. This hypothesis assumes dry weather can result in bushes getting too little water. The passage presents observations to tentatively support each hypothesis. But it doesn't argue for either hypothesis as a conclusion.

D. A *plan* describes an imagined set of actions meant to work together to achieve one or more goals. A plan is not itself an argument. Its actions aren't proposed as reasons to accept a goal, but rather as ways to reach the goal. However, a prescriptive argument may recommend or oppose a plan. A plan may also be among an argument's premises.

Just as an argument may have premises, intermediate conclusions, and main conclusions, a plan may suggest actions to reach intermediate goals that, in turn, are meant to help achieve main goals. And like an argument, a plan may have assumptions, including necessary and sufficient assumptions. A necessary assumption of a plan is one that must be true for the plan to achieve its goals. And a sufficient assumption of a plan is one whose truth guarantees the plan would achieve its goals if followed.

A plan is not a causal explanation. The actions a plan suggests haven't been done yet, so they can't have caused anything. However, any plan does assume possible future causal links between its proposed actions and its goals.

Example:

To repaint our house, we'll need to buy gallons of paint. To do that, we could go to the hardware store.

In this plan, going to the hardware store is an action imagined to help reach the intermediate goal of getting gallons of paint. The intermediate goal is imagined to help reach the main goal of repainting the house. This plan isn't itself an argument. But, combined with the premise that we **should** repaint the house, the plan could be part of a prescriptive argument that we **should** go to the hardware store.

3. Narratives and Descriptions

A. A *narrative* describes a sequence of related events. A narrative is not an argument, an explanation, or a plan. But it may contain one or more arguments, causal explanations, or plans—or be contained in them.

The words and phrases below often show narrative sequence:

after	*earlier*	*then*
afterwards	*later*	*thereafter*
before	*previously*	*until*
beforehand	*since*	*while*
during	*subsequently*	*when*

Example:

While Julia was hiking fifteen kilometers, she burned a lot of calories. **Afterwards**, she felt hungry.

This narrative describes a sequence of three events. The word *while* shows that Julia's hike and her burning of calories happened at the same time. The word *afterwards* shows that her hunger arose soon after the first two events. Although you can reasonably assume these events were causally linked, the narrative doesn't say they were. So, it's not an explicit causal explanation. And since the narrative doesn't report the events as reasons to accept a particular conclusion, it's not an argument either.

B. Not all passages are arguments, causal explanations, plans, or narratives. Some passages report on views, findings, innovations, places, societies, artistic works, devices, organisms, etc., without arguing for a conclusion, explaining what caused what, suggesting actions to reach a goal, or narrating what happened.

C. Likewise, not all statements in passages are premises, conclusions, observations to be explained, hypotheses, or reports of events. Statements in passages can also:

- Give background information to help the reader understand the rest of the passage
- Describe details of something that the passage is discussing
- Express the author's attitude toward material in the passage
- Provide examples to illustrate general statements
- Summarize ideas that the passage is arguing against

7.2 Inductive Reasoning

1. Inductive Arguments

A. In an ***inductive argument***, the premises are meant to support a conclusion but not to fully prove it. For example, the premises may just be meant to give evidence that the conclusion is **probably** true, leaving a chance that the conclusion is false despite that evidence.

B. An inductive argument may be ***strengthened*** by adding reasons that directly support the conclusion or that help the argument's premises better support the conclusion. Conversely, an inductive argument may be ***weakened*** by adding reasons that directly cast doubt on the argument's conclusion, or that make the argument's premises less effective at supporting the conclusion. Below, we discuss how various types of inductive arguments are evaluated, strengthened, and weakened.

2. Generalizations and Predictions

A. An argument by ***generalization*** often uses premises about a sample of a population to support a conclusion about the whole population.

> *Example:*
>
> Six of the eight apartments available for lease in this building are studio apartments. So, probably about $\frac{3}{4}$ of all the apartments in the building are studio apartments.
>
> In this example, the whole set of apartments in the building is a population. The apartments available for lease are a ***sample*** of that population. Since six of the eight apartments available for lease are studio apartments, $\frac{3}{4}$ of the apartments in the sample are studio apartments. The argument generalizes from this by assuming the whole population is probably like the sample. It concludes that as in the sample, probably about $\frac{3}{4}$ of the apartments in the population are studio apartments.

B. A similar type of argument by generalization uses premises about a whole population to support a conclusion about part of that population.

> *Example:*
>
> About $\frac{3}{4}$ of all the apartments in the building are studio apartments. So, probably about $\frac{3}{4}$ of the apartments on the building's second floor are studio apartments.
>
> This example uses a premise about the proportion of studio apartments in the population of all the apartments in the building to support the conclusion that there's a similar proportion of studio apartments in just a part of the population—the apartments on the second floor.

C. A ***predictive*** argument by generalization uses a premise about the sample observed so far in a population to support a conclusion about another part of the population.

Example:

Of the eight apartments I've visited in this building so far, six have been studio apartments. So, probably about six out of the next eight apartments I visit in the building will also be studio apartments.

In this example, the apartments the author has visited so far are a sample of the total population of apartments in the building. The observation about the proportion of studio apartments in the sample supports a prediction that roughly the same proportion of studio apartments will be found in another part of the population—the next eight apartments the author will visit in the building.

D. The strength of an argument by generalization partly depends on how similar the sample is to the overall population, or to the unobserved part of the population a prediction is about. A sample chosen in a way likely to make it relevantly different than the population is a ***biased sample***. An argument using a biased sample is flawed.

Example:

In a telephone survey of our city's residents, about four out of every five respondents said they usually answer the phone when it rings. So, about four out of every five residents of our city usually answer the phone when it rings.

In this example, the sample is the respondents to the telephone survey. People who usually answer the phone when it rings are more likely than other people to respond to telephone surveys. Because the sample was selected through a telephone survey, probably a greater proportion of the sample than of all city residents usually answer the phone when it rings. So, the argument is flawed because the sample is biased.

E. The strength of an argument generalizing from a sample also partly depends on the sample's size. The smaller the sample, the weaker the argument. This is because a smaller sample is statistically likely to differ more from the population in its average traits. An argument by generalization that uses too small a sample to justify its conclusion is flawed by ***hasty generalization***.

Example:

A coin came up heads five of the eight times Beth flipped it. This suggests the coin she flipped is weighted to make it come up heads more often than tails.

In this argument, the sample is the eight flips of the coin, and the population is all the potential flips of the same coin. The sample is probably not biased because Beth's flips of the coin are probably no more likely than anyone else's flips of the same coin to come up heads or tails. However, the sample is too small to justify the conclusion that the coin is weighted to favor heads. A fair, unweighted coin flipped eight times usually comes up heads more or fewer than exactly four times—just by chance. So, this argument is flawed by hasty generalization. If Beth and other people flipped the coin thousands or millions of times, and still saw it come up heads in five out of every eight flips, that would strengthen the argument. But no matter how many times the coin was flipped to confirm this pattern, a tiny chance would be left that the coin was not weighted to favor heads and that the results had been purely random.

F. An argument by generalization is weaker when its conclusion is more precise, and stronger when its conclusion is vaguer, given the same premises. That's because a sample usually doesn't precisely match the population it's extracted from. A less precise conclusion allows a larger range of potential mismatches between sample and population. So, it's more likely to be true, given the same evidence. An argument whose conclusion is too precise for its premises to justify is flawed by the ***fallacy of specificity***.

Example:

Biologists carefully caught, weighed, and released fifty frogs out of the hundreds in a local lake. These fifty frogs weighed an average of 32.86 grams apiece. So, the frogs in the lake must also weigh an average of 32.86 grams apiece.

In this example, the sample might be biased because frogs of certain types might have been easier for the biologists to catch. But even if the biologists avoided any sampling bias, the average weight of the fifty sampled frogs probably wouldn't exactly match the average weight of the hundreds of frogs in the lake. The conclusion is too precise, so the argument suffers from the fallacy of specificity. A stronger argument might use the same evidence to conclude less precisely that the frogs in the lake weigh on average between 25 and 40 grams apiece. This less precise conclusion would still be true even if the average weight of the sampled frogs didn't exactly match the average weight of all the frogs in the lake. Since the less precise conclusion is more likely to be true given the same evidence, that evidence justifies it better. That means the argument for the less precise conclusion is stronger.

3. Causal Reasoning

A. Causal arguments use premises about correlations or causal links to support conclusions about causes and effects. Causal reasoning is hard because causal links can't be directly observed. And there's no scientific or philosophical consensus about what causality is. But saying that one type of situation causally contributes to another usually implies that after a situation of the first type, situations of the second type are more likely. It also implies that situations of the first type help to explain situations of the second type.

Example:

Bushes of the species in our yard tend to die after several weeks without water. So, they must need water at least every few weeks to survive.

In this example, the premise is that after situations of one type (bushes of a certain species getting no water for several weeks), situations of another type become more likely (the bushes dying). The conclusion implies that the first type of situation causes the second: getting no water for several weeks causes bushes of that species to die.

B. A causal argument may use a general correlation to support the conclusion that a situation of one type caused a situation of another type.

Example:

A bush in our yard just died. There's been no rain this summer, and no one has been watering the yard. Bushes of the species in our yard tend to die after several weeks without water. So, probably, the bush died because it didn't get enough water.

In this example, the first premises say that a *specific* situation of one type (a bush of a specific species dying) followed a specific situation of another type (the bush going without water for weeks). The final premise says that *in general*, situations of the first type (bushes of that species dying) follow situations of the second type (bushes of that species getting no water for weeks). These premises together support the conclusion that the lack of water caused the bush to die.

C. Causal arguments can be weakened by observations that suggest alternative causal explanations. A way to check which of two competing explanations is stronger is to look at situations with the possible cause from one explanation but not the possible cause from the other.

Example:

Explanation 1: Bushes of this species tend to die after several weeks without water. Maybe the lack of water kills the bushes.

Explanation 2: Bushes of this species grow only in a region where long dry spells are always very hot. Maybe the heat alone kills these bushes during weeks without water.

To check which of these two hypothetical explanations is stronger, we can run two experiments. Each experiment creates a situation with one of the two proposed causes but not the other.

Experiment 1: Water some of the bushes often during weeks of extreme heat and see how well they survive.

Experiment 2: Keep some of the bushes dry in cooler weather and see how well they survive.

Finding that the bushes survive well in Experiment 1 but not in Experiment 2 would support Explanation 1 and cast doubt on Explanation 2.

Finding that the bushes survive well in Experiment 2 but not in Experiment 1 would support Explanation 2 and cast doubt on Explanation 1.

Finding that the bushes always die in both experiments would support both explanations, suggesting either heat or drought alone can kill the bushes.

Finding that the bushes survive well in both experiments would cast doubt on both explanations. It would suggest that something other than drought or heat is killing the bushes—or that drought and heat must occur together to kill the bushes.

D. Experiments to test causal hypotheses shouldn't add or remove possible causal factors other than those tested for.

Examples:

(i) To run Experiment 1 above, a scientist planted some of the bushes in a tropical rainforest where very hot days are usually rainy.

(ii) To run Experiment 2 above, a scientist planted some of the bushes under an awning where rain couldn't reach them in cooler weather.

These versions of the two experiments are problematic because they add other possible causal factors. In example (i), the rainforest's soil type, insects, or humidity might make it harder or easier for the bushes to survive, regardless of the heat and rainfall. In example (ii), putting the bushes under an awning would likely help keep them shaded. That, too, might make it easier or harder for the bushes to survive, regardless of the heat and rainfall. These experimental design flaws cast doubt on any argument that cites these versions of the experiments as evidence to support Explanation 1 or Explanation 2.

Testing a hypothesis through experiments usually means reasoning by generalization: a conclusion about a whole population is reached by observing a sample in the experiment. Causal arguments based on experiments can have the flaws discussed above in Section 7.2.2, "Generalizations and Predictions." A causal argument is weak if it generalizes from a sample that's too small or chosen in a biased way. In small or biased samples, correlations between factors that aren't causally linked often appear just by chance or because of outside factors.

E. Even when two factors clearly are causally linked, it can be hard to tell which causes which, or whether a third, underlying factor causes them both.

Example:

One type of earthworm is far more often found in soil under healthy bushes of a certain species than in soil under sickly bushes of that same species.

Even if the earthworms' presence is causally linked to the bushes' health, the causal link could be that:

(i) the earthworms improve the bushes' health, or

(ii) healthier bushes attract the earthworms, or

(iii) certain soil conditions both improve the bushes' health and attract the earthworms.

More than one of these causal links, and others, may hold at once. A way to untangle the causal links is to find out:

(i) how healthy the bushes are in the same soil conditions without earthworms,

(ii) how attracted the earthworms are to those soil conditions without the bushes, and

(iii) whether the earthworms tend to appear around healthier bushes even in different soil conditions.

F. Even reliable correlations sometimes arise just by chance. One way to check whether a correlation between two types of situations is just a coincidence is to test whether stopping situations of the first type also stops situations of the other type. Even when no test is possible, you can consider whether there's any plausible way either type of situation could cause the other.

> *Example:*
>
> For years, Juan has arrived at work at a hair salon every weekday at exactly 8:00 a.m. Five hundred miles to the north, over the same years, Ashley has arrived at work at a car dealership every weekday at exactly 8:01 a.m. So, Juan's daily arrival at his work must make Ashley arrive at her work a minute later.
>
> In this example, even though for years Ashley has always arrived at work a minute after Juan has, the argument is absurdly weak. That's because Juan's arrival at his work has no apparent way to affect when Ashley arrives at her work. But we could still test the hypothesis in the argument's conclusion. For example, we could persuade Juan to vary his arrival times, then see whether Ashley's arrival times change to match. With no plausible link between the two workers' arrival times, we'd need a lot of evidence like this to reasonably overcome the suspicion that the correlation is pure coincidence. However, finding out that Juan and Ashley know each other and have reasons to coordinate their work schedules could give us a plausible causal link between their arrival times. That would greatly strengthen the argument that their arrival times are indeed causally linked.

4. Analogies

A. An argument by *analogy* starts by saying two or more things are alike in certain ways. The argument then gives a claim about one of those two things as a reason to accept a similar claim about the other.

> *Example:*
>
> Laotian cuisine and Thai cuisine use many of the same ingredients and cooking techniques. Ahmed enjoys Thai cuisine. So, if he tried Laotian cuisine, he'd probably enjoy it.
>
> This example starts by saying how Laotian cuisine and Thai cuisine are alike: they use similar ingredients and cooking techniques. The argument then makes a claim about Thai cuisine: that Ahmed enjoys it. By analogy, these premises support a similar claim about Laotian cuisine: Ahmed would enjoy it if he tried it.

B. For an argument by analogy to work well, the noted similarities must be *relevant* to whether the two things are also similar in the way the conclusion claims. The argument in the example above meets this standard. A cuisine's ingredients and cooking techniques usually affect how much a specific person would enjoy it. Noting that Laotian cuisine and Thai cuisine have similar ingredients and cooking techniques is relevant to whether Ahmed is likely to similarly enjoy the two cuisines.

An argument by analogy is weaker if its premises only note similarities that are less relevant to its conclusion.

> *Example:*
>
> Laotian cuisine and Latvian cuisine both come from nations whose English names start with the letter **L**. Ahmed enjoys Latvian cuisine. So, if he tried Laotian cuisine, he'd probably enjoy it too.
>
> This example notes that Laotian cuisine and Latvian cuisine are similar with respect to the English names of the nations they're from. Since the spelling of a nation's name almost never affects how much anyone enjoys that nation's cuisine, this similarity is irrelevant to whether Ahmed would similarly enjoy the two cuisines. The analogy is absurd, so the argument is flawed. To save the argument, we'd need a good reason why the noted similarity is relevant after all—for example, evidence that Ahmed is an unusual person whose enjoyment of different cuisines depends on English spellings.

C. A reasonable argument by analogy can be strengthened by noting other relevant similarities between the things compared, or weakened by noting relevant dissimilarities.

> *Example:*
>
> Beth and Alan are children living on the same block in the Hazelfern School District. Beth attends Tubman Primary School. Therefore, Alan probably does as well.
>
> Noting that Beth and Alan are both in the same grade would strengthen this moderately reasonable argument, because that similarity increases the odds that they attend the same school. However, noting that Beth is eight years older than Alan would weaken the argument, because that dissimilarity suggests Alan may be too young to attend the school Beth attends.

7.3 Deductive Reasoning

1. Deductive Arguments

A. The premises of a *deductive argument* are given to fully prove its conclusion. A valid deductive argument with only true premises **must** have a true conclusion. An argument presented as deductive is flawed if its premises can all be true while its conclusion is false. However, a flawed deductive argument might still work well as an inductive argument if the author doesn't wrongly present the premises as **proving** the conclusion. Deductive arguments often use *logical operators* or *quantifiers* or both, as explained below.

2. Logical Operators

A. A *logical operator* shows how the truth or falsehood of one or more statements affects the truth or falsehood of a larger statement made from those statements and the operator. The basic logical operators are *negations*, *logical conjunctions*, *disjunctions*, and *implications*.

B. A statement's *negation* is true just when the statement is false. Words and phrases like *not*, *it is false that*, and *it is not the case that* often mark negation.

Statements are often vague, ambiguous, context-sensitive, or subjective. They may be true in one sense and false in another, they may be only partly true, or their truth may be indefinite. If a statement is true only in one way or to a limited degree, its negation is false in the same way and to the same degree.

> *Example:*
>
> "The cat is on the mat" can have the negation "The cat is not on the mat." Either of these statements is true if the other is false—but only when both are about the same cat and the same mat, in the same sense and the same context. If you make the first statement while the cat is sleeping on the mat, but then the cat wakes up and leaves before you make the second statement, the context has changed. Then your second statement isn't the negation of your first. If the cat is only partly on the mat when both statements are made, then the second statement is *partly* false just as much as the first is partly true, and in just the same way.

C. A *logical conjunction* of two statements is true just when both are true. The words and phrases below can mark a logical conjunction of statements *A* and *B*:

A and B	*A even though B*	*not only A but also B*
Although A, B	*A. Furthermore, B.*	*A, whereas B*
A but B	*A, however, B*	

The conjunction markers *and*, *furthermore*, and *not only . . . but also* usually imply that *A* and *B* are relevant to each other or mentioned for similar reasons—for example, that both are premises supporting the same conclusion. On the other hand, the conjunction markers *although*, *but*, *even though*, *however*, and *whereas* suggest tension between *A* and *B*—for example, that it's surprising *A* and *B* are both true, or that *A* and *B* support conflicting conclusions, or that *A* and *B* differ in some other unexpected way.

> *Examples:*
>
> (i) Raul has worked for this company a long time, **and** he's searching for another job.
>
> (ii) **Although** Raul has worked for this company a long time, he's searching for another job.
>
> Both these examples say that Raul has worked for the company a long time, and that he's searching for another job. But in example (ii), *although* suggests Raul's search for another job is **surprising**, given that he's worked for the company a long time. In contrast, the *and* in example (i) suggests Raul's search for another job is **unsurprising** now that he's worked for the company a long time.

D. A *disjunction* of two statements is true only when one of them is true. The words and phrases *A or B*, *either A or B*, and *A unless B* often mark a disjunction of *A* and *B*.

There are two kinds of disjunction. An *inclusive disjunction* of two statements is true when **at least** one of them is true, and **also** when both are. An *exclusive disjunction* of two statements is true just when **exactly** one of them is true—**not** when both are. English disjunctions often aren't clearly inclusive or clearly exclusive. But *A or B or both* clearly means inclusive disjunction. And *A or B but not both* clearly means exclusive disjunction.

Examples:

(i) It will **either** rain **or** snow tomorrow.

(ii) It will rain tomorrow **unless** it snows.

These examples both say that at least one of the statements "It will rain tomorrow" and "It will snow tomorrow" is true. But neither example clearly says whether or not it might *both* rain *and* snow tomorrow. To clarify, we can say:

(iii) Tomorrow, it will rain or snow—or both. (*inclusive disjunction*)

or

(iv) Tomorrow, it will either rain or snow, but not both. (*exclusive disjunction*)

E. A *conditional* says that for one statement to be true, another must be true. In other words, a conditional means the first statement entails the second. The words and phrases below all mark the same conditional link between statements *A* and *B*:

A would mean that B	*B if A*	*A only if B*
If A, then B	*Not A unless B*	*B provided that A*

Conditionals of these forms do not mean that *A* is true, nor that *B* is. They do not give *A* as a reason to accept *B*. So, in a conditional, *A* isn't a premise and *B* isn't a conclusion. That is, a conditional is not an argument. However, the conditional *if A, then B* does mean that correctly assuming *A* as a premise lets you correctly reach *B* as a conclusion.

Examples:

(i) It will snow tonight **only if** the temperature falls below 5 degrees Celsius.

(ii) It **won't** snow tonight **unless** the temperature falls below 5 degrees Celsius.

(iii) **If** it snows tonight, it'll mean the temperature has fallen below 5 degrees Celsius.

These three conditionals all mean the same thing. Each says that snow tonight would require a temperature below 5 degrees Celsius. They do not say that it **will** snow tonight, nor that the temperature **will** be below 5 degrees Celsius. But they do suggest, for example, that seeing it snow tonight would tell you the temperature must be below 5 degrees Celsius.

Although conditionals often make or suggest causal claims, their meaning isn't always causal. The examples above do not mean that snow tonight would **cause** the temperature to fall below 5 degrees Celsius, nor vice versa.

None of these examples imply that it **must** snow if the temperature falls below 5 degrees Celsius tonight. A conditional *if A, then B* does not imply that *if B, then A*.

F. Two *logically equivalent* statements *A and B* are always both true or both false under the same conditions. Each implies the other. That is, *if A, then B*, and *if B, then A*. These two conditionals can be combined as *A if and only if B*.

3. Reasoning with Logical Operators

A. Here's a list of some types of logically equivalent statements made with logical operators. In this list, *not* means negation, *and* means logical conjunction, *or* means inclusive disjunction, and *if... then* means conditional implication.

Logical Equivalences with Logical Operators

A and B	is logically equivalent to	*B and A*
not (A and B)	is logically equivalent to	*not-A or not-B*
A or B	is logically equivalent to	*B or A*
not (A or B)	is logically equivalent to	*not-A and not-B* (in other words, *neither A nor B*)
if A, then B	is logically equivalent to	*if not-B, then not-A*
if A, then (B and C)	is logically equivalent to	(*if A, then B*) *and* (*if A, then C*)
if A, then (B or C)	is logically equivalent to	(*if A, then B*) *or* (*if A, then C*)
if (A or B), then C	is logically equivalent to	(*if A, then C*) *and* (*if B, then C*)

B. Of any two logically equivalent statements, either can be a premise supporting the other as a conclusion in a valid deductive argument. For any line in the list above, a valid deductive argument has a premise of the form on one side and a logically equivalent conclusion of the form on the other side.

Examples:

The second line in the list above says that for any statements *A* and *B*, the statement *not (A and B)* is logically equivalent to *not-A or not-B*. This gives us two valid deductive arguments:

(i) *not (A and B), therefore not-A or not-B*

and

(ii) *not-A or not-B, therefore not (A and B)*

For example, the statement *Ashley and Tim don't both live in this neighborhood* is logically equivalent to *Either Ashley doesn't live in this neighborhood or Tim doesn't*. This lets us make two valid deductive arguments:

(iii) Ashley and Tim don't both live in this neighborhood. Therefore, either Ashley doesn't live in this neighborhood or Tim doesn't.

and

(iv) Either Ashley doesn't live in this neighborhood or Tim doesn't. Therefore, Ashley and Tim don't both live in this neighborhood.

C. Here's a list of some other valid deductive argument forms with logical operators, and of invalid forms often confused with them.

Valid and Invalid Inferences with Logical Operators	
Valid: *A and B, therefore A*	**Invalid:** *A, therefore A and B*
Valid: *A, therefore A or B*	**Invalid:** *A or B, therefore A*
Valid: *not-A and not-B, therefore not (A and B)*	**Invalid:** *not (A and B), therefore not-A and not-B*
Valid: *not (A or B), therefore not-A or not-B*	**Invalid:** *not-A or not-B, therefore not (A or B)*
Valid: *if A, then B; and A; therefore B*	**Invalid:** *if A, then B; and B; therefore A*
Valid: *if A, then B; and not-B; therefore not-A*	**Invalid:** *if A, then B; and not-A; therefore not-B*

Examples:

The third line in the table above says that ***not-A and not-B, therefore not (A and B)*** is valid, but ***not (A and B), therefore not-A and not-B*** is invalid. A simple example of a **valid** argument is:

(i) Ashley doesn't live in this neighborhood, and Tim doesn't either. Therefore, Ashley and Tim don't both live in this neighborhood.

But swapping argument (i)'s premise with its conclusion makes this **invalid** argument:

(ii) Ashley and Tim don't both live in this neighborhood. Therefore, Ashley doesn't live in this neighborhood and Tim doesn't either.

As another example, the table's fifth line says that ***if A, then B; and A; therefore B*** is valid, but ***if A, then B; and B; therefore A*** is invalid. So, another **valid** argument is:

(iii) If Ashley lives in this neighborhood, so does Tim. Ashley does live in this neighborhood. Therefore, Tim also lives in this neighborhood.

However, swapping argument (iii)'s second premise with its conclusion makes this **invalid** argument:

(iv) If Ashley lives in this neighborhood, so does Tim. Tim does live in this neighborhood. Therefore, Ashley lives in this neighborhood.

4. Necessity, Probability, and Possibility

A. Some words and phrases mark how likely a statement is to be true. For example, they may mean that:

- The statement is ***necessarily*** true; that is, there's a 100 percent chance the statement is true; or

- The statement is ***probably*** true; that is, there's a good chance the statement is true;

- The statement is ***possibly*** true; that is, the odds are greater than 0 percent that the statement is true.

Saying a claim is possibly true or probably true usually implies it's not necessarily true.

B. The table below shows three categories of words and phrases that can stand for degrees of probability:

Words Standing for Necessity, Probability, and Possibility		
Necessity	**Probability**	**Possibility**
certainly	*probably*	*can*
clearly	*likely*	*could*
definitely	*more likely than not*	*may*
must		*maybe*
necessarily		*might*
surely		*perhaps*
		possibly

The words ***probably*** and ***likely*** sometimes mean high probability, like a 95 percent chance. Other times they mean a medium chance, even one below 50 percent. Don't give these terms any exact meanings when you find them on the GMAT exam.

C. The table below lists some valid deductive argument forms with necessity, probability, and possibility, as well as invalid forms often confused with them.

Valid and Invalid Inferences with Necessity, Probability, and Possibility	
Valid: *Probably A, therefore possibly A*	**Invalid:** *Possibly A, therefore probably A*
Valid: *Possibly (A and B), therefore possibly A and possibly B*	**Invalid:** *Possibly A and possibly B, therefore possibly (A and B)*
Valid: *Probably (A and B), therefore probably A and probably B*	**Invalid:** *Probably A and probably B, therefore probably (A and B)*
Valid: *Probably A or probably B, therefore probably (A or B)*	**Invalid:** *Probably (A or B), therefore probably A or probably B*
Valid: *Necessarily A or necessarily B, therefore necessarily (A or B)*	**Invalid:** *Necessarily (A or B), therefore necessarily A or necessarily B*

Examples:

The table's second line says that ***possibly (A and B), therefore possibly A and possibly B*** is valid, while ***possibly A and possibly B, therefore possibly (A and B)*** is invalid. A simple **valid** argument is:

(i) Possibly Tim and Ashley both live in this house. So, possibly Tim lives in this house, and possibly Ashley does.

Swapping argument (i)'s premise with its conclusion gives us this **invalid** argument:

(ii) Possibly Tim lives in this house, and possibly Ashley does. So, possibly both Tim and Ashley live in this house.

To see that argument (ii) is invalid, suppose you know only one person lives in the house, but you don't know whether that person is Tim, Ashley, or someone else. Then argument (ii)'s premise would be true, but its conclusion would be false.

5. Quantifiers

A. A *quantifier* is a word or phrase for a proportion, number, or amount. Some basic quantifiers are *all*, *most*, *some*, and *none*.

    i. A quantifier like *all* means 100 percent of the individuals in a category, or the whole of an amount.

    ii. A quantifier like *most* usually means more than half the individuals in a category, or more than half of a whole. *Most* usually implies *not all*, but not always. Writing *most but not all*, or else *most or all*, can clarify the meaning.

    iii. A quantifier like *some* often means one or more individuals in a category, or part of a whole. *Some* usually but not always implies *not all*. However, *only some* clearly does imply *not all*, while *at least some* clearly doesn't. *Some* with a plural usually means *more than one*. In contrast, *some* with a singular usually means *exactly one*. For example, "some dogs" usually means "more than one dog," while "some dog" usually means "exactly one dog." But "some dog or dogs" means "at least one dog."

    iv. A quantifier like *no* or *none of* means something is being denied about all the individuals in a category, or about all of some whole.

    v. Other common quantifiers have more nuanced meanings. For example, *a few* vaguely means a small number more than two. The upper limit of what counts as *a few* depends on context. For example, "a few Europeans" might mean thousands of people (still a tiny part of Europe's population). But "a few residents in our building" might mean only three or four people if the building has only fifteen residents.

B. The table below classifies some quantifier words by their meanings.

Basic Quantifier Words

"All" and similar quantifier words	"Most" and similar quantifier words	"Some" and similar quantifier words	"No" and similar quantifier words
all	*generally*	*a number*	*never*
always	*a majority*	*a portion*	*no*
any	*most*	*any*	*none*
both	*more than half*	*at least one*	*not any*
each	*usually*	*occasionally*	*not one*
every		*one or more*	*nowhere*
everywhere		*some*	
whenever		*sometimes*	
wherever		*somewhere*	

Notice the table shows *any* both as a quantifier like *all* and as a quantifier like *some*. That's because *any* can have either meaning. For example, *Any of the students would prefer chocolate ice cream* means *Each of the students would prefer chocolate ice cream*. However, *I don't know if any of the students would prefer chocolate ice cream* means *I don't know if even one of the students would prefer chocolate ice cream*.

C. A quantifier used with a category usually implies the category isn't empty. But this doesn't always hold in hypothetical statements, in conditionals, or with the quantifier *any*.

Examples:

(i) **All** life forms native to planets other than Earth **are** carbon-based.

(ii) **Any** life forms native to planets other than Earth **would be** carbon-based.

In (i), the words *all* and *are* show the author is claiming there really are life forms native to planets other than Earth. But in (ii), the words *any* and *would be* show the author is carefully avoiding that claim.

D. Statements with two or more quantifiers sometimes look alike but differ in meaning because of word order and phrasing.

Example:

(i) Some beverage must be the favorite of every student in the class.

(ii) Each student in the class must have some favorite beverage.

Statement (i) suggests that every student in the class must have **the same** favorite beverage. In contrast, statement (ii) can be true even if each student has a **different** favorite beverage.

6. Reasoning with Quantifiers

A. Here's a list of some logically equivalent statement forms with quantifiers. In this list, *some* means **one or more**. The forms in the list use plurals, but similar equivalences can hold without plurals. For example, *No water is fire* is logically equivalent to *No fire is water*, even though those two statements don't have plurals like the forms in the list do.

Logical Equivalences with Quantifiers		
All As are Bs	is logically equivalent to	*No As are not Bs.*
Some As are Bs	is logically equivalent to	*Some Bs are As.*
No As are Bs	is logically equivalent to	*No Bs are As.*
Some As are not Bs	is logically equivalent to	*Not all As are Bs.*

However, *All As are Bs* is **not** equivalent to *All Bs are As*. And *Some As are not Bs* is **not** equivalent to *Some Bs are not As*.

Examples:

(i) The true statement *All ostriches are birds* is not equivalent to the false statement *All birds are ostriches*.

(ii) The true statement *Some birds are not ostriches* is not equivalent to the false statement *Some ostriches are not birds*.

B. As explained above, either of two logically equivalent statements can be a premise supporting the other as a conclusion in a valid deductive argument. This works for equivalences with quantifiers just like it does for equivalences with logical operators.

C. A *syllogism* is a type of simple deductive argument whose two premises have one quantifier apiece, and whose conclusion also has one quantifier.

Here's a list of some valid syllogism forms along with invalid forms sometimes confused with them. As above, in this list, *some* means *one or more*.

Valid and Invalid Syllogisms

Valid: *All As are Bs. All Bs are Cs. So, all As are Cs.*	**Invalid:** *All As are Bs. All Bs are Cs. So, all Cs are As.* **Invalid:** *All As are Bs. All Cs are Bs. So, all As are Cs.* **Invalid:** *All Bs are As. All Bs are Cs. So, all As are Cs.*
Valid: *Some As are Bs. All Bs are Cs. So, some As are Cs.*	**Invalid:** *All As are Bs. Some Bs are Cs. So, some As are Cs.* **Invalid:** *Some As are Bs. Some Bs are Cs. So, some As are Cs.*
Valid: *All As are Bs. No Bs are Cs. So, no As are Cs.*	**Invalid:** *No As are Bs. All Bs are Cs. So, no As are Cs.* **Invalid:** *No As are Bs. No Bs are Cs. So, all As are Cs.* **Invalid:** *No As are Bs. All Bs are Cs. So, some As are not Cs.*

Examples:

The list's first line says that **All As are Bs. All Bs are Cs. So, all As are Cs** is valid. And here's a **valid** syllogism of that form:

(i) All the trees in the local park were planted by the town arborist. All the trees the arborist planted have been labeled by her. So, all the trees in the park must have been labeled by the arborist.

A similar-looking but **invalid** syllogism has the form **All As are Bs. All Bs are Cs. So, all Cs are As** from the list's second line:

(ii) All the trees in the local park were planted by the town arborist. All the trees the arborist planted have been labeled by her. So, all the trees the arborist has labeled must be in the park.

To see that argument (ii) is invalid, notice that even if both premises are true, the arborist might also have labeled trees outside the park—maybe even trees she didn't plant.

Another **invalid** syllogism has the form **All As are Bs. All Cs are Bs. So, all As are Cs** from the list's third line:

(iii) All the trees in the local park were planted by the town arborist. All the trees the arborist has labeled are trees she planted. So, all the trees in the park must have been labeled by the arborist.

To see that argument (iii) is invalid, notice that even if both premises are true, the arborist might not have labeled every tree she planted, nor even every tree she planted in the park.

The form in the list's fourth line (**All Bs are As. All Bs are Cs. So, all As are Cs**) gives us yet another **invalid** syllogism:

(iv) All the trees the town arborist has planted are in the local park. All the trees the arborist planted have been labeled by her. So, all the trees in the park must have been labeled by the arborist.

To see that argument (iv) is invalid, notice that even if both premises are true, the park might have many trees that the arborist neither planted nor labeled.

D. Some quantifier words in the table "Basic Quantifier Words" in Section 7.3.5.B above refer to time or place. For example, *whenever* means *every time*, *usually* means *most times*, and *never* means *at no time*. Understanding these meanings can help you rewrite deductive arguments using these words into standard syllogisms to check their validity.

Example:

Max never goes running when the sidewalks are icy. The sidewalks are usually icy on January mornings, so Max must not go running on most January mornings.

We can rewrite this argument in the valid syllogism form *No As are Bs. Most Cs are Bs. So, most Cs are not As*:

No occasions when Max goes running are occasions when the sidewalks are icy. Most January mornings are occasions when the sidewalks are icy. So, most January mornings are not occasions when Max goes running.

Since arguments in this syllogism form are valid, we can tell that the argument in this example is valid.

To register for the GMAT™ exam, go to www.mba.com/register

8.0 Verbal Reasoning

8.0 Verbal Reasoning

The Verbal Reasoning section of the GMAT™ exam uses multiple-choice questions to measure your skill in reasoning, understanding what you read, and evaluating arguments. This section has passages about many topics, but it doesn't assume you already know about the topics. Mingled throughout the section are questions of two main types of questions: Reading Comprehension and Critical Reasoning.

Reading Comprehension questions are based on passages of around 200 to 350 words. With each passage are several questions asking you to understand, analyze, apply, and evaluate that passage's information and concepts. On the left side of your screen, the passage stays visible as you answer the questions about it. On the right side of your screen, one question appears at a time, along with its answer choices. Different passages may have different numbers of questions.

Critical Reasoning questions are based on passages usually of fewer than 100 words. Unlike Reading Comprehension passages, each Critical Reasoning passage has just one question. This question asks you to logically analyze, evaluate, or reason about an argument, situation, or plan the passage presents. Only one passage and its single question appear at a time.

You have 45 minutes to answer the 23 questions in the Verbal Reasoning section, an average of just under two minutes per question.

To prepare for the Verbal Reasoning section, first review basic concepts of text analysis and logical reasoning. Read Chapter 7, "Verbal Review," which briefly covers these concepts. After reviewing, practice on questions from past GMAT exams.

8.1 What Is Measured

The Verbal Reasoning section measures how well you understand, analyze, apply, evaluate, and reason about information and ideas in texts. Specifically, it tests the following skills:

Skill Category	Details	Examples
Recognize stated ideas	Understand, restate, and summarize information and ideas	• Find a passage's overall theme or point • Find a specific detail • Summarize a set of statements • Tell if an idea is stated or implied • Tell what a word or phrase means in context
Analyze reasoning structure	Identify premises, conclusions, explanations, argument techniques, reasons for plans, and background information	• Tell what argument technique someone uses • Tell a statement's role in a passage
Apply ideas in new contexts	Use general ideas in new situations the passage doesn't discuss	• Decide which new situation is most like one in the passage • Tell which new action would follow or break a rule in the passage • Decide which new example would best illustrate an idea in the passage

Skill Category	Details	Examples
Infer	Draw an unstated conclusion from a passage	• Decide which conclusion a passage most strongly supports • Tell what follows logically from information given • Decide what a stated opinion implies • Recognize an author's attitude from word choices
Identify unstated assumptions	Find an assumption that fills a logical gap in an argument, explanation, or plan	• Find an assumption an argument depends on • Find an assumption that makes an argument's conclusion follow logically • Tell what must happen for a plan to succeed
Evaluate hypotheses	Judge explanations for a situation	• Decide what would most help explain why a plan failed • Decide what most likely caused an observed effect
Resolve discrepancies	Explain or justify an apparent conflict between two statements or situations	• Explain why a factor didn't cause its usual effect • Decide which principle resolves a conflict between two opinions
Strengthen or weaken reasoning	Identify new information that either supports or undermines an argument, explanation, plan, or claim	• Tell which discovery would cast the most doubt on an argument's reasoning • Tell what added evidence would best support a causal explanation
Identify reasoning flaws	Identify mistakes such as confusing correlation with causation or confusing a sufficient assumption with a necessary one	• Decide which observation points to a reasoning flaw • Tell which criticism an argument is most vulnerable to
Identify points of disagreement	Tell what two parties disagree about, based on their statements	• Find the main implied point of disagreement in a dialogue
Solve a practical problem	Recognize a good strategy for solving a problem	• Find a way of sampling a population accurately despite an obstacle

8.2 Question Types

Reading Comprehension and Critical Reasoning are the two main Verbal Reasoning question types. Each has several subtypes. During the test, the subtypes aren't labeled. Each question tells you what you need to do.

1. Reading Comprehension

The five Reading Comprehension question subtypes are Main Idea, Supporting Idea, Inference, Application, and Evaluation. Each tests a different main skill, but sometimes the skills overlap. For example, to find a passage's main idea, you must understand the passage's logical and rhetorical structure. To make inferences or apply ideas from a passage, you often must find its main and supporting ideas.

Below, we discuss the Reading Comprehension question subtypes.

A. Main Idea

- In each passage, all the sentences and paragraphs develop one central point or share one overall purpose. A Main Idea question asks you to find this central point or purpose. Sometimes the passage tells you its central point. Other times you must infer it from the passage's structure and content.

- A Main Idea question may ask which answer option best restates the central point, best explains the author's main goal for the passage, or works best as a title for the passage.

- Main Idea questions use phrases like these:

  . . . most accurately expresses the main idea . . . ,

  The primary purpose of the passage as a whole is to . . . , or

  In the passage, the author seeks primarily to. . . .

- The right answer to a Main Idea question about an argumentative passage often restates or describes the main conclusion of the main argument. To find the main conclusion, you must notice which statements in the passage are given as reasons to accept which other statements. The main conclusion is an idea that the whole passage gives reasons to accept, but that isn't in turn given as a reason to accept some further conclusion.

- When the passage isn't argumentative, the right answer to a Main Idea question usually gives the passage's overall theme or purpose. The overall theme is often an idea repeated in different paragraphs. The overall purpose is usually a goal toward which all the paragraphs work. If the passage has no overall theme or purpose, the right answer may just summarize the passage. For example, the right answer to a Main Idea question about a narrative passage might summarize the events described or state their overall outcome.

- Wrong answer choices often repeat passage details that aren't the main point, make claims that look like the main point but are different, or state ideas not mentioned in the passage but related to it.

B. Supporting Idea

- Supporting Idea questions may ask you about anything the passage states except for the main point. To answer a Supporting Idea question, you must understand individual statements and their roles in the passage.

- Answers to Supporting Idea questions almost never directly quote the passage. They usually rephrase statements from the passage or describe them abstractly. A Supporting Idea question may ask which statement plays a specific role in the passage. For example, it may ask you to find a premise, an intermediate conclusion, a described viewpoint, an objection, an example or counterexample, a causal claim, background information, a descriptive detail, or part of an explanation or narrative. Or it may also ask what a word or phrase in the passage means in context.

- Supporting Idea questions often use phrases like these:

  According to the passage . . .,

  Which of the following does the author cite as . . .,

  Which of the following does the author offer as an objection to . . .,

  The passage compares . . .,

  The passage mentions . . ., or

  Which of the following does the author propose. . . .

C. Inference

- Inference questions ask about ideas the passage suggests or supports but doesn't state. Some of these questions ask about ideas the author clearly meant the passage to imply. Others ask about logical implications, which the author may not have noticed.

- An Inference question may ask you to find:

  a likely cause or effect of a situation the passage describes,

  a specific implication of a generalization in the passage, or

  a statement that someone discussed in the passage would likely accept or reject.

- Sometimes the inference follows from one small part of the passage. Other times it depends on several statements scattered through different paragraphs. Sometimes the question says where to look in the passage, but not always.

- Inference questions often use phrases like these:

  Which of the following statements about . . . is most strongly supported by . . .,

  It can be inferred from the passage that . . .,

  If the claims about . . . are true, which of the following is most likely also true?

  The passage implies that . . ., or

  The information in the passage suggests that. . . .

- Wrong answer choices may be true, and related to the passage, but not supported by it. Conversely, the right answer choice may be false but follow logically from false statements in the passage. For example, even if the passage rightly says a theory is mistaken, a question might ask what would follow if the theory were true.

D. Application

- Application questions ask how situations or ideas the passage discusses relate to other situations or ideas the passage doesn't mention.

- Application questions may use words like *would, could, might,* or *should,* or phrases like *most clearly exemplifies, most similar to,* or *most likely ruled out by.*

- Some Application questions ask you to reason by analogy. They may ask which of several roles, methods, goals, or relationships is most like one the passage mentions. Review Section 7.2.4, "Analogies," which explains reasoning by analogy.

- Other Application questions ask you to apply general rules. For example, they may ask:

  which rule's enforcement would help achieve a goal the passage mentions, which principle a judgment in the passage relies on,

which action would break or follow a rule the passage states,

which generalization the evidence in the passage best fits, or

which general strategy could solve a problem the passage describes.

- The third type of Application question asks you to extend the passage. Questions of this type may ask for:

the best topic for a new paragraph added to the end of the passage,

a good example of a point the author makes, or

the author's most likely response to a possible objection.

- The fourth type of Application question asks about "what-if" scenarios. These questions may ask:

how different experimental results might affect a researcher's conclusions,

how a trend the passage mentions might be disrupted, or

how events might have gone differently if a situation had never occurred.

- Don't rule out answer choices just because they're not about the passage. Because Application questions relate the passage to new topics, the right answers are often about topics the passage never mentions. For instance, the right answer to an analogy question about a water-treatment process the passage explains might be about book publishing.

E. Evaluation

- Evaluation questions ask you to assess the passage's organization and logic.
- They often use phrases like these:

The purpose of . . .,

. . . most accurately describes the structure of . . .,

. . . most strengthens . . .,

. . . would most justify . . .,

. . . is most vulnerable to the objection that . . ., or

Which . . . additional information would most help. . . .

- An Evaluation question's answer choices are often abstract. They may not use specific words or ideas from the passage. For example, a question about a paragraph's function might have this answer choice: *It rejects a theory presented in the preceding paragraph and offers some criteria that an alternative theory would need to meet.*

- Some Evaluation questions ask about the roles of different parts of the passage. They may ask:

how the whole passage or part of it is structured,

why the author put a specific detail in the passage,

what purpose a statement in the passage serves,

how the author tries to persuade readers to accept a claim, or

what attitude most likely motivated an opinion the passage mentions.

- Other Evaluation questions ask about:

    the strengths, weaknesses, relevance, or effectiveness of parts of the passage,

    implicit assumptions in the passage,

    what would best resolve apparent conflicts between parts of the passage, or

    potential objections, justifications, supporting evidence, or counterexamples.

These questions are often similar to Critical Reasoning questions, discussed below.

2. Critical Reasoning

The four subtypes of Critical Reasoning question are Analysis, Construction, Critique, and Plan. We discuss each below.

A. Analysis

- Analysis questions ask about a passage's logical structure and the roles that statements play in it.

- Analysis questions often use phrases like these:

    *. . . the two portions in **boldface** play which of the following roles?*

    The argument proceeds by . . .,

    A technique used in the argument is to . . .,

    . . . responds to . . . by . . .,

    The statements above can best serve as part of an argument against . . ., or

    Which of the following is the main point of disagreement between. . . .

- Some Analysis questions ask about the roles of one or two statements in the passage. Often the passage shows these statements in **boldface**.

- Other Analysis questions ask about an argumentative method in the passage. Sometimes the passage itself is an argument, and the question asks how it works. Other times, the passage is a dialogue, and the question asks what argumentative technique one speaker uses in replying to the other.

- Another type of Analysis question asks about an unstated point in the passage. This point may be a conclusion the passage is meant to support. Or it may be a point of agreement or disagreement between the two speakers in a dialogue.

B. Construction

- Construction questions ask how to best complete partial arguments or explanations.

- Construction questions often use phrases like these:

    . . . most logically completes . . .,

    If the statements above are true . . .,

    . . . most strongly support . . .,

    . . . best explains the discrepancy . . .,

    . . . depends on the assumption that . . .,

    . . . enables the conclusion to be properly drawn? or

    . . . provides the strongest justification for. . . .

- Some Construction questions ask what conclusion a set of premises best supports. These questions may ask for a conclusion that logically follows from the premises, or for a conclusion that the premises merely give evidence for.

- Other Construction questions ask for a missing premise to support a given conclusion. A question like this usually says whether the premise must be a necessary assumption, a sufficient assumption, a relevant observation, or a justification for a position. The passage may state only the conclusion, or it may also give other premises to combine with the missing premise.

- Another type of Construction question asks what would best explain either an observation or a puzzling discrepancy between observations.

C. Critique

- Critique questions ask you to judge reasoning in passages, find its strengths or weaknesses, and decide how it could be improved.

- Critique questions often use phrases like these:

   . . . most vulnerable to the criticism that . . . ,

   . . . logically flawed in that . . . ,

   . . . most seriously weakens . . . ,

   . . . casts the most serious doubt on . . . ,

   . . . most strengthens . . . ,

   . . . most strongly supports . . . , or

   . . . would be most useful to know in order to evaluate. . . .

- Some Critique questions ask how an argument is flawed or weak. These questions are often about arguments with standard reasoning flaws, like the flaws discussed in Sections 7.2, "Inductive Reasoning," and 7.3, "Deductive Reasoning." In other cases, the arguments have no standard flaw but don't work because they rely on some obviously implausible assumption.

- Other Critique questions ask what new evidence would most strengthen or weaken an argument. These arguments are always inductive because evidence can't strengthen or weaken a deductive argument. Section 7.2, "Inductive Reasoning," explains how evidence can strengthen and weaken arguments.

- Finally, some Critique questions ask you what would be most helpful to know in order to assess a hypothesis or argument in the passage. The answer choices for these questions start with the word *Whether*, followed by an idea whose truth is unknown. The right answer choice gives the idea whose truth or falsehood would be most helpful to know in order to decide whether the hypothesis in the passage is true. The wrong answer choices give ideas that, whether true or false, are less relevant to the hypothesis.

D. Plan

- Plan questions ask you to construct or judge reasoning about actual or proposed courses of action, or plans. Section 7.1.2.D briefly explains this type of reasoning.

- Plan questions use many of the same phrases found in Construction and Critique questions, but the questions are always about plans, strategies, or courses of action.

- Plan questions may ask:

   what must be true for a plan to succeed,

what conditions would make a plan more or less likely to succeed,

what would be most helpful to know in order to judge a plan,

what evidence would best support an opinion about a plan,

how a plan is flawed,

what strategy would most help overcome a problem,

what policy would most help reach a goal under certain conditions, or

why a plan succeeded, failed, or had some unexpected effect.

8.3 Tips for Answering Verbal Reasoning Questions

1. Answer using only the information given and common knowledge.

The passages and common knowledge tell you everything you need to answer correctly. If you already know about the passage topic, don't use that knowledge to answer. Answer based on what the passage states or implies, and on common knowledge. For example, if the passage says something happened during a snowstorm, you can use common knowledge about snowstorms to infer that the weather wasn't hot.

2. Look for cue words marking statements' roles.

Section 7.1, "Analyzing Passages," explains how certain cue words often mark premises, conclusions, causal explanations, and narrative sequences. These cue words tell you what roles statements near them play. Also notice transition words marking a shift from one topic to another, and how those words suggest the topics are related. Usually, you can tell a statement's role even without a cue word. For example, if the passage clearly gives one statement as a reason to accept another, you don't need cue words to tell that the first statement is a premise and the second a conclusion.

3. Analyze the passage's structure and purpose.

Once you know the roles individual statements play, you can find the passage's overall structure and purpose. Does the passage mainly report facts and events? Does it argue for a conclusion? Does it discuss competing causal explanations? Does it comment on situations or other writers' views? Notice which premises are given to support which conclusions, and which causes are said to produce which effects. Notice also if the passage uses intermediate conclusions to support a main conclusion. Finally, notice any clear but unstated implications of the passage.

4. Use basic principles of good reasoning to judge the passage's reasoning.

Sections 7.2, "Inductive Reasoning," and 7.3, "Deductive Reasoning," review some principles of good reasoning. When a question asks you to judge the reasoning in the passage, use these basic principles. You don't need advanced knowledge of logic or any other subject to answer correctly.

5. Notice exactly what the question asks.

Often the wrong answer to one question would be the right answer to another question that looks similar. You need to pick the right answer to the specific question asked. To do that, focus on the question. For example, if the question asks about one part of the passage, don't pick an answer choice about some other part of the passage. As another example, these two questions could easily be confused:

i) Which of the following crops is grown by *the most farms* in Nation X?

ii) Farms in Nation X grow *the most of* which of the following crops?

The nation's farms may grow the most of a crop that's not grown by the most farms. If many small farms grow potatoes while a few huge farms grow wheat, the right answer to (i) could be *potatoes* even if the right answer to (ii) is *wheat*.

6. Read all the answer choices before picking one.

Verbal Reasoning questions often ask you to pick the best answer choice of those given. To tell which answer choice is best, read them all.

7. If you're not sure which answer choice is right, try ruling out some that are clearly wrong.

Ruling out some clearly wrong answer choices can help you find the right answer choice. If you're still undecided between two answer choices, study the passage again for clues you may have missed.

8. Pace yourself.

You have less than two minutes per question. You need to spend much of that time reading the passages. To avoid running out of time, don't spend too long on any one question. If you get stuck on a question for a couple of minutes after you've ruled out some of the answer choices, just pick the remaining choice that seems best. Then go to the next question.

To register for the GMAT™ exam, go to www.mba.com/register

8.4 Practice Questions: Reading Comprehension

Each of the Reading Comprehension questions is based on the content of a passage. After reading the passage, answer all questions pertaining to it on the basis of what is stated or implied in the passage. For each question, select the best answer of the choices given. On the actual GMAT exam, you will see no more than four questions per passage.

Questions 505–547 — Difficulty: Easy

Line   Scientists long believed that two nerve clusters in
the human hypothalamus, called suprachiasmatic
nuclei (SCNs), were what controlled our circadian
rhythms. Those rhythms are the biological cycles
(5)   that recur approximately every 24 hours in
synchronization with the cycle of sunlight and
darkness caused by Earth's rotation. Studies have
demonstrated that in some animals, the SCNs
control daily fluctuations in blood pressure, body
(10)   temperature, activity level, and alertness, as well as
the nighttime release of the sleep-promoting agent
melatonin. Furthermore, cells in the human retina
dedicated to transmitting information about light
levels to the SCNs have recently been discovered.
(15)   Four critical genes governing circadian cycles
have been found to be active in every tissue,
however, not just the SCNs, of flies, mice, and
humans. In addition, when laboratory rats that
usually ate at will were fed only once a day, peak
(20)   activity of a clock gene in their livers shifted by
12 hours, whereas the same clock gene in the
SCNs remained synchronized with light cycles. While
scientists do not dispute the role of the SCNs in
controlling core functions such as the regulation of
(25)   body temperature and blood pressure, scientists
now believe that circadian clocks in other organs
and tissues may respond to external cues other than
light—including temperature changes—that recur
regularly every 24 hours.

Questions 505–507 refer to the passage.

505. The primary purpose of the passage is to

   (A)   challenge recent findings that appear to
          contradict earlier findings

   (B)   present two sides of an ongoing scientific debate

   (C)   report answers to several questions that have
          long puzzled researchers

   (D)   discuss evidence that has caused a long-
          standing belief to be revised

   (E)   attempt to explain a commonly misunderstood
          biological phenomenon

506. The passage mentions each of the following as a
     function regulated by the SCNs in some animals
     EXCEPT

   (A)   activity level

   (B)   blood pressure

   (C)   alertness

   (D)   vision

   (E)   temperature

507. The author of the passage would probably agree with which of the following statements about the SCNs?

(A)   The SCNs are found in other organs and tissues of the body besides the hypothalamus.

(B)   The SCNs play a critical but not exclusive role in regulating circadian rhythms.

(C)   The SCNs control clock genes in a number of tissues and organs throughout the body.

(D)   The SCNs are a less significant factor in regulating blood pressure than scientists once believed.

(E)   The SCNs are less strongly affected by changes in light levels than they are by other external cues.

Line   In their study of whether offering a guarantee of
        service quality will encourage customers to visit a
        particular restaurant, Tucci and Talaga have found
        that the effect of such guarantees is mixed. For
(5)   higher-priced restaurants, there is some evidence
        that offering a guarantee increases the likelihood of
        customer selection, probably reflecting the greater
        financial commitment involved in choosing an
        expensive restaurant. For lower-priced restaurants,
(10)   where one expects less assiduous service, Tucci and
        Talaga found that a guarantee could actually have a
        negative effect: a potential customer might think that
        a restaurant offering a guarantee is worried about
        its service. Moreover, since customers understand a
(15)   restaurant's product and know what to anticipate in
        terms of service, they are empowered to question its
        quality. This is not generally true in the case of skilled
        activities such as electrical work, where, consequently,
        a guarantee might have greater customer appeal.
(20)   For restaurants generally, the main benefit of
        a service guarantee probably lies not so much in
        customer appeal as in managing and motivating staff.
        Staff members would know what service standards
        are expected of them and also know that the success
(25)   of the business relies on their adhering to those
        standards. Additionally, guarantees provide some
        basis for defining the skills needed for successful
        service in areas traditionally regarded as unskilled,
        such as waiting tables.

Questions 508–510 refer to the passage.

508. The primary purpose of the passage is to

(A) question the results of a study that examined
    the effect of service-quality guarantees in the
    restaurant industry

(B) discuss potential advantages and disadvantages
    of service-quality guarantees in the restaurant
    industry

(C) examine the conventional wisdom regarding
    the effect of service-quality guarantees in the
    restaurant industry

(D) argue that only certain restaurants would benefit
    from the implementation of service-quality
    guarantees

(E) consider the impact that service-quality
    guarantees can have on the service provided by
    a restaurant

509. It can be inferred that the author of the passage would
     agree with which of the following statements about the
     appeal of service guarantees to customers?

(A) Such guarantees are likely to be somewhat more
    appealing to customers of restaurants than to
    customers of other businesses.

(B) Such guarantees are likely to be more appealing
    to customers who know what to anticipate in
    terms of service.

(C) Such guarantees are likely to have less appeal in
    situations where customers are knowledgeable
    about a business's product or service.

(D) In situations where a high level of financial
    commitment is involved, a service guarantee is
    not likely to be very appealing.

(E) In situations where customers expect a high
    level of customer service, a service guarantee is
    likely to make customers think that a business is
    worried about its service.

510. According to the passage, Tucci and Talaga found that service guarantees, when offered by lower-priced restaurants, can have which of the following effects?

    (A) Customers' developing unreasonably high expectations regarding service

    (B) Customers' avoiding such restaurants because they fear that the service guarantee may not be fully honored

    (C) Customers' interpreting the service guarantee as a sign that management is not confident about the quality of its service

    (D) A restaurant's becoming concerned that its service will not be assiduous enough to satisfy customers

    (E) A restaurant's becoming concerned that customers will be more emboldened to question the quality of the service they receive

Line   The argument for "monetizing"—or putting a monetary value on—ecosystem functions may be stated thus: Concern about the depletion of natural resources is widespread, but this concern, in the
(5)   absence of an economic argument for conservation, has not translated into significant conservational progress. Some critics blame this impasse on environmentalists, whom they believe fail to address the economic issues of environmental degradation.
(10)   Conservation can appear unprofitable when compared with the economic returns derived from converting natural assets (pristine coastlines, for example) into explicitly commercial ones (such as resort hotels). But according to David Pearce, that illusion stems
(15)   from the fact that "services" provided by ecological systems are not traded on the commodities market, and thus have no readily *quantifiable* value. To remedy this, says Pearce, one has to show that all ecosystems have economic value—indeed, that all
(20)   ecological services are economic services. Tourists visiting wildlife preserves, for example, create jobs and generate income for national economies; undisturbed forests and wetlands regulate water runoff and act as water-purifying systems, saving
(25)   millions of dollars worth of damage to property and to marine ecosystems. In Gretchen Daily's view, monetization, while unpopular with many environmentalists, reflects the dominant role that economic considerations play in human behavior,
(30)   and the expression of economic value in a common currency helps inform environmental decision-making processes.

Questions 511–514 refer to the passage.

511. Information in the passage suggests that David Pearce would most readily endorse which of the following statements concerning monetization?

(A)   Monetization represents a strategy that is attractive to both environmentalists and their critics.

(B)   Monetization is an untested strategy, but it is increasingly being embraced by environmentalists.

(C)   Monetization should at present be restricted to ecological services and should only gradually be extended to such commercial endeavors as tourism and recreation.

(D)   Monetization can serve as a means of representing persuasively the value of environmental conservation.

(E)   Monetization should inform environmental decision-making processes only if it is accepted by environmentalist groups.

512. Which of the following most clearly represents an example of an "ecological service" as that term is used in line 20?

(A)   A resort hotel located in an area noted for its natural beauty

(B)   A water-purifying plant that supplements natural processes with nontoxic chemicals

(C)   A wildlife preserve that draws many international travelers

(D)   A nonprofit firm that specializes in restoring previously damaged ecosystems

(E)   A newsletter that keeps readers informed of ecological victories and setbacks

513. According to the passage, Daily sees monetization as an indication of which of the following?

   (A)   The centrality of economic interests to people's actions

   (B)   The reluctance of the critics of environmentalism to acknowledge the importance of conservation

   (C)   The inability of financial interests and ecological interests to reach a common ideological ground

   (D)   The inevitability of environmental degradation

   (E)   The inevitability of the growth of ecological services in the future

514. Which of the following can be inferred from the passage concerning the environmentalists mentioned in line 8?

   (A)   They are organized in opposition to the generation of income produced by the sale of ecological services.

   (B)   They are fewer in number but better organized and better connected to the media than their opponents.

   (C)   They have sometimes been charged with failing to use a particular strategy in their pursuit of conservational goals.

   (D)   They have been in the forefront of publicizing the extent of worldwide environmental degradation.

   (E)   They define environmental progress differently and more conservatively than do other organized groups of environmentalists.

Line   Social learning in animals is said to occur when direct or indirect social interaction facilitates the acquisition of a novel behavior. It usually takes the form of an experienced animal (the demonstrator)

(5)   performing a behavior such that the naïve animal (the observer) subsequently expresses the same behavior sooner, or more completely, than it would have otherwise. One example of social learning is the acquisition of preferences for novel foods.

(10)   Some experiments have suggested that among mammals, social learning facilitates the identification of beneficial food items, but that among birds, social learning helps animals avoid toxic substances. For example, one study showed that when red-wing

(15)   blackbirds observed others consuming a colored food or a food in a distinctly marked container and then becoming ill, they subsequently avoided food associated with that color or container. Another experiment showed house sparrows consumed less

(20)   red food after they observed others eating red food that was treated so as to be noxious. Studies on nonavian species have not produced similar results, leading researchers to speculate avian social learning may be fundamentally different from that of mammals.

(25)   But Sherwin's recent experiments with domestic hens do not support the notion that avian social learning necessarily facilitates aversion to novel foods that are noxious or toxic. Even when demonstrator hens reacted with obvious disgust to a specific food

(30)   via vigorous headshaking and bill-wiping, there was no evidence that observers subsequently avoided eating that food. Sherwin's research team speculated that ecological or social constraints during the evolution of this species might have resulted in there being little

(35)   benefit from the social learning of unpalatability. For instance, selective pressures for this mode of learning would be reduced if the birds rarely encountered noxious or toxic food or rarely interacted after eating such food, or if the consequences of ingestion were

(40)   minimal. In a related experiment, the same researchers showed if observer hens watched demonstrator hens react favorably to food of a particular color, then observer hens ate more food of that color than they ate of food of other colors. These results confirmed

(41)   avian species can develop preferences for palatable food through social learning.

Questions 515–518 refer to the passage.

515. Which of the following best describes the main purpose of the first paragraph of the passage?

(A) It explains why a particular behavior discussed in the remainder of the passage is beneficial to the animals that engage in it.

(B) It introduces a concept that has been widely misunderstood among nonscientists.

(C) It outlines the types of studies that have been conducted to investigate a certain animal behavior.

(D) It provides information necessary to understand the nature of the phenomenon discussed in the remainder of the passage.

(E) It describes a viewpoint that is called into question later in the passage.

516. According to the passage, Sherwin's research team speculated the social learning of unpalatability within a particular species might be discouraged if the animals

(A) did not suffer serious effects from any noxious or toxic foods they ingested

(B) consumed food in small quantities throughout the day rather than in a few large feedings

(C) had an unusually large variety of foods available to them

(D) interacted after feeding as well as during feeding

(E) did not show signs of illness until considerable time had passed following the ingestion of noxious or toxic food

517. According to the passage, which of the following is true of the experiments on domestic hens conducted by Sherwin's research team?

    (A) Only a small number of observer hens appeared to learn to avoid food that was demonstrated by other hens to be noxious.

    (B) Observer hens ingested food preferentially only after numerous instances of witnessing demonstrator hens preferentially ingest that type of food.

    (C) Observer hens appeared unable to recognize when demonstrator hens found a particular food especially palatable.

    (D) Demonstrator hens reacted adversely to ingesting certain novel foods.

    (E) Demonstrator hens altered their behavior less obviously in response to noxious foods than in response to highly palatable foods.

518. The passage indicates that which of the following is true about studies of social learning in mammals?

    (A) Such studies have only rarely demonstrated a capacity among mammals to learn to prefer certain foods via observation of other animals.

    (B) Such studies have suggested that in mammals, one function of social learning is to establish preferences for novel foods.

    (C) Such studies have demonstrated some capacity among mammals to learn via observation of other animals to avoid ingestion of toxic substances.

    (D) Such studies have been conducted primarily in the mammals' natural habitats rather than in laboratory settings.

    (E) Such studies have focused primarily on forms of social learning other than the acquisition of preferences for novel foods.

Line   In recent years, Western business managers have been heeding the exhortations of business journalists and academics to move their companies toward long-term, collaborative "strategic partnerships" with
(5)   their external business partners (e.g., suppliers). The experts' advice comes as a natural reaction to numerous studies conducted during the past decade that compared Japanese production and supply practices with those of the rest of the world. The
(10)   link between the success of a certain well-known Japanese automaker and its effective management of its suppliers, for example, has led to an unquestioning belief within Western management circles in the value of strategic partnerships. Indeed, in the automobile
(15)   sector all three United States manufacturers and most of their European competitors have launched programs to reduce their total number of suppliers and move toward having strategic partnerships with a few.
(20)   However, new research concerning supplier relationships in various industries demonstrates that the widespread assumption of Western managers and business consultants that Japanese firms manage their suppliers primarily through strategic
(25)   partnerships is unjustified. Not only do Japanese firms appear to conduct a far smaller proportion of their business through strategic partnerships than is commonly believed, but they also make extensive use of "market-exchange" relationships, in which
(30)   either party can turn to the marketplace and shift to different business partners at will, a practice usually associated with Western manufacturers.

Questions 519–522 refer to the passage.

519. The passage is primarily concerned with

(A)   examining economic factors that may have contributed to the success of certain Japanese companies

(B)   discussing the relative merits of strategic partnerships as compared with those of market-exchange relationships

(C)   challenging the validity of a widely held assumption about how Japanese firms operate

(D)   explaining why Western companies have been slow to adopt a particular practice favored by Japanese companies

(E)   pointing out certain differences between Japanese and Western supplier relationships

520. According to the passage, the advice referred to in line 6 was a response to which of the following?

(A)   A recent decrease in the number of available suppliers within the United States automobile industry

(B)   A debate within Western management circles during the past decade regarding the value of strategic partnerships

(C)   The success of certain European automobile manufacturers that have adopted strategic partnerships

(D)   An increase in demand over the past decade for automobiles made by Western manufacturers

(E)   Research comparing Japanese business practices with those of other nations

521. The author mentions "the success of a certain well-known Japanese automaker" in lines 10–11, most probably in order to

(A) demonstrate some of the possible reasons for the success of a certain business practice

(B) cite a specific case that has convinced Western business experts of the value of a certain business practice

(C) describe specific steps taken by Western automakers that have enabled them to compete more successfully in a global market

(D) introduce a paradox about the effect of a certain business practice in Japan

(E) indicate the need for Western managers to change their relationships with their external business partners

522. Which of the following is cited in the passage as evidence supporting the author's claim about what the new research referred to in line 20 demonstrates?

(A) The belief within Western management circles regarding the extent to which Japanese firms rely on strategic partnerships

(B) The surprising number of European and United States businesses that have strategic partnerships with their suppliers

(C) The response of Western automobile manufacturers to the advice that they adopt strategic partnerships with their suppliers

(D) The prevalence of "market-exchange" relationships between Japanese firms and their suppliers

(E) The success of a particular Japanese automobile manufacturer that favors strategic partnerships with its suppliers

Line   When Jamaican-born social activist Marcus
        Garvey came to the United States in 1916, he
        arrived at precisely the right historical moment.
        What made the moment right was the return of
(5)   African American soldiers from the First World War
        in 1918, which created an ideal constituency for
        someone with Garvey's message of unity, pride,
        and improved conditions for African American
        communities.
(10)   Hoping to participate in the traditional American
        ethos of individual success, many African American
        people entered the armed forces with enthusiasm,
        only to find themselves segregated from white
        troops and subjected to numerous indignities. They
(15)   returned to a United States that was as segregated
        as it had been before the war. Considering similar
        experiences, anthropologist Anthony F. C. Wallace
        has argued that when a perceptible gap arises
        between a culture's expectations and the reality of
(20)   that culture, the resulting tension can inspire a
        revitalization movement: an organized, conscious
        effort to construct a culture that fulfills long-
        standing expectations.
        Some scholars have argued that Garvey created
(25)   the consciousness from which he built, in the
        1920s, the largest revitalization movement in
        African American history. But such an argument
        only tends to obscure the consciousness of identity,
        strength, and sense of history that already existed
(30)   in the African American community. Garvey did not
        create this consciousness; rather, he gave this
        consciousness its political expression.

Questions 523–526 refer to the passage.

523. According to the passage, which of the following
     contributed to Marcus Garvey's success?

   (A) He introduced cultural and historical
        consciousness to the African American
        community.

   (B) He believed enthusiastically in the traditional
        American success ethos.

   (C) His audience had already formed a
        consciousness that made it receptive to his
        message.

   (D) His message appealed to critics of African
        American support for United States military
        involvement in the First World War.

   (E) He supported the movement to protest
        segregation that had emerged prior to his arrival
        in the United States.

524. The passage suggests that many African American
     people responded to their experiences in the armed
     forces in which of the following ways?

   (A) They maintained as civilians their enthusiastic
        allegiance to the armed forces.

   (B) They questioned United States involvement in the
        First World War.

   (C) They joined political organizations to protest the
        segregation of African American troops and the
        indignities they suffered in the military.

   (D) They became aware of the gap between their
        expectations and the realities of American
        culture.

   (E) They repudiated Garvey's message of pride and
        unity.

525. It can be inferred from the passage that the "scholars" mentioned in line 24 believe which of the following to be true?

    (A) Revitalization resulted from the political activism of returning African American soldiers following the First World War.

    (B) Marcus Garvey had to change a number of prevailing attitudes in order for his mass movement to find a foothold in the United States.

    (C) The prevailing sensibility of the African American community provided the foundation of Marcus Garvey's political appeal.

    (D) Marcus Garvey hoped to revitalize consciousness of cultural and historical identity in the African American community.

    (E) The goal of the mass movement that Marcus Garvey helped bring into being was to build on the pride and unity among African Americans.

526. According to the passage, many African American people joined the armed forces during the First World War for which of the following reasons?

    (A) They wished to escape worsening economic conditions in African American communities.

    (B) They expected to fulfill ideals of personal attainment.

    (C) They sought to express their loyalty to the United States.

    (D) They hoped that joining the military would help advance the cause of desegregation.

    (E) They saw military service as an opportunity to fulfill Marcus Garvey's political vision.

Line   The sloth bear, an insect-eating animal native to
          Nepal, exhibits only one behavior that is truly distinct
          from that of other bear species: The females carry
          their cubs (at least part time) until the cubs are
(5)   about nine months old even though the cubs can
          walk on their own at six months. Cub-carrying also
          occurs among some other myrmecophagous (ant-
          eating) mammals; therefore, one explanation is
          cub-carrying is necessitated by myrmecophagy since
(10)   myrmecophagy entails a low metabolic rate and high
          energy expenditure in walking between food patches.
          However, although polar bears' locomotion is similarly
          inefficient, polar bear cubs walk along with their
          mother. Furthermore, the daily movements of sloth
(15)   bears and American black bears—which are similar
          in size to sloth bears and have similarly sized home
          ranges—reveal similar travel rates and distances,
          suggesting if black bear cubs are able to keep up with
          their mother, so too should sloth bear cubs.
(20)   An alternative explanation is defense from
          predation. Black bear cubs use trees for defense,
          whereas brown bears and polar bears, which regularly
          inhabit treeless environments, rely on aggression
          to protect their cubs. Like brown bears and polar
(25)   bears (and unlike other myrmecophagous mammals,
          which are noted for their passivity), sloth bears are
          easily provoked to aggression. Sloth bears also have
          relatively large canine teeth, which appear to be more
          functional for fighting than for foraging. Like brown
(30)   bears and polar bears, sloth bears may have evolved
          in an environment with few trees. They are especially
          attracted to food-rich grasslands; although few
          grasslands persist today on the Indian subcontinent,
          this type of habitat was once widespread there.
(35)   Grasslands support high densities of tigers, which
          fight and sometimes kill sloth bears. Sloth bears also
          coexist with and have been killed by tree-climbing
          leopards and are often confronted and chased by
          rhinoceroses and elephants, which can topple trees.
(40)   Collectively these factors probably selected against
          tree-climbing as a defensive strategy for sloth bear
          cubs. Because sloth bears are smaller than brown
          and polar bears and are under greater threat from
          dangerous animals, they may have adopted the extra
(45)   precaution of carrying their cubs. Although cub-
          carrying may also be adaptive for myrmecophagous
          foraging, the behavior of sloth bear cubs, which climb
          on their mother's back at the first sign of danger,
          suggests that predation was a key stimulus.

Questions 527–531 refer to the passage.

527. The author mentions rhinoceroses and elephants
     (see line 39) primarily in order to

     (A) explain why sloth bears are not successful
          foragers in grassland habitats

     (B) identify the predators that have had the most
          influence on the behavior of sloth bears

     (C) suggest a possible reason that sloth bear cubs
          do not use tree-climbing as a defense

     (D) provide examples of predators that were once
          widespread across the Indian subcontinent

     (E) defend the assertion that sloth bears are under
          greater threat from dangerous animals than are
          other bear species

528. Which of the following, if true, would most weaken the
     author's argument in lines 14–19?

     (A) Cub-carrying behavior has been observed in
          many non-myrmecophagous mammals.

     (B) Many of the largest myrmecophagous mammals
          do not typically exhibit cub-carrying behavior.

     (C) Some sloth bears have home ranges that are
          smaller in size than the average home ranges of
          black bears.

     (D) The locomotion of black bears is significantly
          more efficient than the locomotion of sloth
          bears.

     (E) The habitat of black bears consists of terrain
          that is significantly more varied than that of the
          habitat of sloth bears.

529. Which of the following is mentioned in the passage
     as a way in which brown bears and sloth bears are
     similar?

     (A) They tend to become aggressive when provoked.

     (B) They live almost exclusively in treeless
          environments.

     (C) They are preyed upon by animals that can climb
          or topple trees.

     (D) They are inefficient in their locomotion.

     (E) They have relatively large canine teeth.

530. The author mentions which of the following as evidence for the view that cub-carrying behavior among sloth bears functions primarily as a defense from predation?

    (A) The relative passivity of sloth bears in comparison with other species of bears

    (B) The age at which sloth bear cubs can defend themselves from predators

    (C) The unsuitability of cub-carrying for myrmecophagous foraging

    (D) The behavior of sloth bear cubs when they first perceive danger

    (E) The inefficient locomotion of sloth bears and other myrmecophagous animals

531. The primary purpose of the passage is to

    (A) trace the development of a particular behavioral characteristic of the sloth bear

    (B) explore possible explanations for a particular behavioral characteristic of the sloth bear

    (C) compare the defensive strategies of sloth bear cubs to the defensive strategies of cubs of other bear species

    (D) describe how certain behavioral characteristics of the sloth bear differ from those of other myrmecophagous mammals

    (E) provide an alternative to a generally accepted explanation of a particular behavioral characteristic of myrmecophagous mammals

Line   Biologists have advanced two theories to explain
why schooling of fish occurs in so many fish species.
Because schooling is particularly widespread among
species of small fish, both theories assume that
(5)   schooling offers the advantage of some protection
from predators.

Proponents of theory A dispute the assumption
that a school of thousands of fish is highly visible.
Experiments have shown that any fish can be seen,
(10)   even in very clear water, only within a sphere of
200 meters in diameter. When fish are in a compact
group, the spheres of visibility overlap. Thus the
chance of a predator finding the school is only
slightly greater than the chance of the predator
(15)   finding a single fish swimming alone. Schooling
is advantageous to the individual fish because a
predator's chance of finding any particular fish
swimming in the school is much smaller than its
chance of finding at least one of the same group of
(20)   fish if the fish were dispersed throughout an area.

However, critics of theory A point out that some
fish form schools even in areas where predators
are abundant and thus little possibility of escaping
detection exists. They argue that the school continues
(25)   to be of value to its members even after detection.
They advocate theory B, the "confusion effect," which
can be explained in two different ways.

Sometimes, proponents argue, predators simply
cannot decide which fish to attack. This indecision
(30)   supposedly results from a predator's preference
for striking prey that is distinct from the rest of the
school in appearance. In many schools the fish are
almost identical in appearance, making it difficult for
a predator to select one. The second explanation
(35)   for the "confusion effect" has to do with the sensory
confusion caused by a large number of prey moving
around the predator. Even if the predator makes the
decision to attack a particular fish, the movement
of other prey in the school can be distracting. The
(40)   predator's difficulty can be compared to that of a
tennis player trying to hit a tennis ball when two are
approaching simultaneously.

Questions 532–535 refer to the passage.

532. According to the passage, theory B states that which
of the following is a factor that enables a schooling fish
to escape predators?

(A)   The tendency of fish to form compact groups

(B)   The movement of other fish within the school

(C)   The inability of predators to detect schools

(D)   The ability of fish to hide behind one another in a
school

(E)   The great speed with which a school can
disperse

533. According to the passage, both theory A and theory B
have been developed to explain how

(A)   fish hide from predators by forming schools

(B)   forming schools functions to protect fish from
predators

(C)   schooling among fish differs from other
protective behaviors

(D)   small fish are able to make rapid decisions

(E)   small fish are able to survive in an environment
densely populated by large predators

534. According to one explanation of the "confusion
effect," a fish that swims in a school will have greater
advantages for survival if it

(A)   tends to be visible for no more than 200 meters

(B)   stays near either the front or the rear of a school

(C)   is part of a small school rather than a large
school

(D)   is very similar in appearance to the other fish in
the school

(E)   is medium-sized

535. The author is primarily concerned with

(A)   discussing different theories

(B)   analyzing different techniques

(C)   defending two hypotheses

(D)   refuting established beliefs

(E)   revealing new evidence

Line   Recently, biologist Christopher Imboden proposed
a strategy to correct a major tactical error on the
part of conservation biologists. For the past 25
years, the status of the world's bird species has been
(5)   summarized in so-called Red Data Books, which list
species definitely known to be threatened, thereby
implying that all remaining species are secure.
Imboden now suggests using "green lists" to indicate
those species definitely known to be secure, thereby
(10)   shifting the burden of proof to those who maintain
that all is well. Use of the books is appropriate for
Europe and North America, where armies of amateur
naturalists, field guides in hand, search for rare birds
every weekend; thus, up-to-date information is always
(15)   available on the conservation status of every species.
But most species live in the tropics, where one
cannot assume that lack of bad news about a species
guarantees good news. Nothing is known about the
current status of many tropical species discovered
(20)   long ago, simply because no biologist has visited the
collecting locality since the original description. Given
the small geographical ranges often characteristic
of tropical species, many must have vanished from
formerly forested areas now converted to cropland.
(25)   Hence, Red Data Books for the tropics are minimal
rather than maximal lists of endangered species, and
only case-by-case assessments can show which of
the remaining species actually belong on a green list.
    The real test of whether Red Data Books or green
(30)   lists give a truer picture of the extinction crisis will
come from case-by-case surveys of the world's
most species-rich habitats—the continental tropics.
As one indication of what such surveys may show,
a four-year search for freshwater fish in Malaya
(35)   revealed no evidence for the continued existence
of an astonishing 54 percent of the 266 species
originally recorded. Although those who advocate the
use of Red Data Books claim that 96 percent of the
world's bird species are secure, believing that 87 of
(40)   the approximately 8,000 bird species extant in the
year 1600 are now extinct and that about 283 more
are endangered, Imboden estimates that fewer than
one-third of the world's bird species would qualify for
a green list.

Questions 536–538 refer to the passage.

536. The relationship between which of the following is most closely analogous to the relationship between Red Data Books and green lists, as they are described in the passage?

(A)   A list of reference materials that are important to consult and a list of materials that are less important to consult

(B)   A list of cars in need of major repairs and a list of cars in need of minor repairs

(C)   A list of tours given in Europe and a list of tours given in Africa and Asia

(D)   A list of necessary expenses and a list of expenses that can be eliminated

(E)   A list of items in low supply and a list of items of which there is sufficient stock

537. The author most likely mentions Malayan freshwater fish in order to

(A)   compare the rates of extinction found in fish species with the rates found in bird species

(B)   describe the way in which case-by-case assessment of species was conducted in the past

(C)   emphasize that tropical species are more prone to extinction than species in temperate regions

(D)   provide an example of data revealed by a case-by-case assessment of species

(E)   suggest that more up-to-date information is available for species of fish than for species of birds

538. According to the passage, all of the following are true statements about tropical bird species EXCEPT:

(A)   Current information is not available about the conservation status of many tropical species.

(B)   Biologists have only recently begun to describe and categorize rare tropical species.

(C)   Many tropical species are losing their habitats because of increased cultivation of land.

(D)   Tropical species often inhabit small geographical areas.

(E)   There are more bird species in the tropics than in other parts of the world.

Line   Resin is a plant secretion that hardens when
exposed to air; fossilized resin is called amber.
Although Pliny in the first century recognized that
amber was produced from "marrow discharged by
(5)   trees," amber has been widely misunderstood to be
a semiprecious gem and has even been described
in mineralogy textbooks. Confusion also persists
surrounding the term "resin," which was defined
before rigorous chemical analyses were available.
(10)   Resin is often confused with gum, a substance
produced in plants in response to bacterial infections,
and with sap, an aqueous solution transported
through certain plant tissues. Resin differs from both
gum and sap in that scientists have not determined a
(15)   physiological function for resin.
    In the 1950s, entomologists posited that resin
may function to repel or attract insects. Fraenkel
conjectured that plants initially produced resin in
nonspecific chemical responses to insect attack
(20)   and that, over time, plants evolved that produced
resin with specific repellent effects. But some insect
species, he noted, might overcome the repellent
effects, actually becoming attracted to the resin.
This might induce the insects to feed on those
(25)   plants or aid them in securing a breeding site.
Later researchers suggested that resin mediates
the complex interdependence, or "coevolution," of
plants and insects over time. Such ideas led to the
development of the specialized discipline of chemical
(30)   ecology, which is concerned with the role of plant
chemicals in interactions with other organisms and
with the evolution and ecology of plant antiherbivore
chemistry (plants' chemical defenses against attack
by herbivores such as insects).

Questions 539–540 refer to the passage.

539. The passage is primarily concerned with

(A)   comparing the significance of the physiological
and nonphysiological functions of resin

(B)   introducing the field of chemical ecology and
highlighting some of its applications

(C)   discussing some misconceptions about resin and
presenting a theory about its function

(D)   demonstrating that misinformation concerning
resin and amber can be traced back to the first
century

(E)   suggesting that the study of resin lies properly
in the hands of entomologists rather than
mineralogists or chemists

540. The passage supports each of the following
statements about sap EXCEPT:

(A)   Sap is an aqueous solution.

(B)   Sap and resin are often confused by observers.

(C)   Sap is found less abundantly than resin in most
plants.

(D)   Sap moves through certain tissues of a plant.

(E)   Sap performs a physiological function in plants.

Line   When the history of women began to receive
focused attention in the 1970s, Eleanor Roosevelt
was one of a handful of female Americans who were
well known to both historians and the general public.
(5)   Despite the evidence that she had been important in
social reform circles before her husband was elected
president and that she continued to advocate different
causes than he did, she held a place in the public
imagination largely because she was the wife of a
(10)   particularly influential president. Her own activities
were seen as preparing the way for her husband's
election or as a complement to his programs. Even
Joseph Lash's two volumes of sympathetic biography,
Eleanor and Franklin (1971) and *Eleanor: The Years*
(15)   *Alone* (1972), reflected this assumption.
    Lash's biography revealed a complicated woman
who sought through political activity both to flee
inner misery and to promote causes in which she
passionately believed. However, she still appeared to
(20)   be an idiosyncratic figure, somehow self-generated,
not amenable to any generalized explanation. She
emerged from the biography as a mother to the entire
nation, or as a busybody, but hardly as a social type,
a figure comprehensible in terms of broader social
(25)   developments.
    But more recent work on the feminism of the
post-suffrage years (following 1920) allows us to see
Roosevelt in a different light and to bring her life into
a more richly detailed context. Lois Scharf's *Eleanor*
(30)   *Roosevelt*, written in 1987, depicts a generation of
privileged women, born in the late nineteenth century
and maturing in the twentieth, who made the transition
from old patterns of female association to new ones.
Their views and their lives were full of contradictions.
(35)   They maintained female social networks but began
to integrate women into mainstream politics; they
demanded equal treatment but also argued that
women's maternal responsibilities made them both
wards and representatives of the public interest.
(40)   Thanks to Scharf and others, Roosevelt's activities—
for example, her support both for labor laws
protecting women and for appointments of women to
high public office—have become intelligible in terms
of this social context rather than as the idiosyncratic
(45)   career of a famous man's wife.

Questions 541–542 refer to the passage.

541. According to the passage, Lash's biography of Eleanor
Roosevelt reflects the assumption that

(A)   she was an uncomplicated figure relatively free
of contradiction

(B)   her activities were undertaken primarily in
support of her husband

(C)   she is best understood in terms of the feminist
movement of the post-suffrage years

(D)   she was one of only a few women who were well
known to the public

(E)   her career included the pursuit of aims, many of
which were inconsistent with one another

542. The passage as a whole is primarily concerned with
which of the following?

(A)   Changes in the way in which Eleanor Roosevelt's
life is understood

(B)   Social changes that made possible the role
played by Eleanor Roosevelt in social reform

(C)   Changes in the ways in which historians have
viewed the lives of American women

(D)   Social changes that resulted from the activities
of Eleanor Roosevelt

(E)   Changes in the social roles that American women
have played

Line   Acting on the recommendation of a British
government committee investigating the high
incidence in white lead factories of illness among
employees, most of whom were women, the home
(5)   secretary proposed in 1895 that Parliament enact
legislation that would prohibit women from holding
most jobs in white lead factories. Although the
Women's Industrial Defence Committee (WIDC),
formed in 1892 in response to earlier legislative
(10)   attempts to restrict women's labor, did not discount
the white lead trade's potential health dangers, it
opposed the proposal, viewing it as yet another
instance of limiting women's work opportunities.
Also opposing the proposal was the Society for
(15)   Promoting the Employment of Women (SPEW), which
attempted to challenge it by investigating the causes
of illness in white lead factories. SPEW contended,
and WIDC concurred, that controllable conditions in
such factories were responsible for the development
(20)   of lead poisoning. SPEW provided convincing
evidence that lead poisoning could be avoided
if workers were careful and clean and if already
extant workplace safety regulations were stringently
enforced. However, the Women's Trade Union League
(25)   (WTUL), which had ceased in the late 1880s to
oppose restrictions on women's labor, supported the
eventually enacted proposal, in part because safety
regulations were generally not being enforced in white
lead factories, where there were no unions (and little
(30)   prospect of any) to pressure employers to comply
with safety regulations.

Questions 543–545 refer to the passage.

543. The passage suggests that which of the following
most accurately describes the attitudes of SPEW
and WIDC toward the safety regulations referred to in
lines 28–29?

(A)   They disagreed about whether or not unions
could successfully pressure employers to
comply with such regulations.

(B)   They disagreed about the extent to which the
proposed legislation would strengthen such
regulations.

(C)   They agreed that, while adequate for other types
of factories, extant workplace safety regulations
did not specifically address the conditions unique
to white lead factories.

(D)   They agreed that, if adequately enforced, such
regulations could reduce the incidence of illness
among women working in white lead factories.

(E)   They agreed that the extant workplace safety
regulations had already been effective in
reducing the incidence of lead poisoning in many
white lead factories.

544. According to the passage, the WIDC believed that
the proposed legislation resembled earlier legislation
concerning women's labor in that it

(A)   caused divisiveness among women's
organizations

(B)   sought to protect women's health

(C)   limited women's occupational opportunities

(D)   failed to bolster workplace safety regulations

(E)   failed to make distinctions among types of
factory work

545. The reference to the absence of unions in white lead factories (lines 28 and 29) serves primarily to explain why

    (A) more women than men worked in white lead factories

    (B) previous attempts to restrict women's labor had been successful

    (C) SPEW felt the need to investigate the causes of illness in white lead factories

    (D) WTUL ceased to oppose restrictions on women's labor

    (E) WTUL doubted that safety regulations would be enforced in white lead factories

Line   In *American Genesis*, which covers the century
of technological innovation in the United States
beginning in 1876, Thomas Hughes assigns special
prominence to Thomas Edison as archetype of
(5)   the independent nineteenth-century inventor.
However, Hughes virtually ignores Edison's famous
contemporary and notorious adversary in the field of
electric light and power, George Westinghouse. This
comparative neglect of Westinghouse is consistent
(10)   with other recent historians' works, although it marks
an intriguing departure from the prevailing view during
the inventors' lifetimes (and for decades afterward)
of Edison and Westinghouse as the two "pioneer
innovators" of the electrical industry.
(15)   My recent reevaluation of Westinghouse, facilitated
by materials found in railroad archives, suggests that
while Westinghouse and Edison shared important
traits as inventors, they differed markedly in their
approach to the business aspects of innovation. For
(20)   Edison as an inventor, novelty was always paramount;
the overriding goal of the business of innovation was
simply to generate funding for new inventions. Edison
therefore undertook just enough sales, product
development, and manufacturing to accomplish this.
(25)   Westinghouse, however, shared the attitudes of the
railroads and other industries for whom he developed
innovations: Product development, standardization,
system, and order were top priorities. Westinghouse
thus better exemplifies the systematic approach
(30)   to technological development that would become
a hallmark of modern corporate research and
development.

Questions 546–547 refer to the passage.

546. The passage suggests that Hughes's views regarding
the comparative importance of Westinghouse and
Edison as nineteenth-century inventors are most
consistent with the views expressed by which of the
following?

(A)   Some recent historians

(B)   The author of the passage

(C)   Modern corporate research directors

(D)   Archivists of nineteenth-century railroad records

(E)   Historians during the late nineteenth century

547. Which of the following does the passage suggest was
LEAST important to the railroad industry of the late
nineteenth century?

(A)   Systemization

(B)   Product development

(C)   Standardization

(D)   Innovativeness

(E)   Orderliness

Questions 548–600 — Difficulty: **Medium**

Line   In *Winters v. United States* (1908), the Supreme Court held that the right to use waters flowing through or adjacent to the Fort Berthold Indian Reservation was reserved to American Indians by the treaty

(5) establishing the reservation. Although this treaty did not mention water rights, the Court ruled that the federal government, when it created the reservation, intended to deal fairly with American Indians by reserving for them the waters without which their

(10) lands would have been useless. Later decisions, citing Winters, established that courts can find federal rights to reserve water for particular purposes if (1) the land in question lies within an enclave under exclusive federal jurisdiction; (2) the land has been

(15) formally withdrawn from federal public lands—i.e., withdrawn from the stock of federal lands available for private use under federal land use laws—and set aside or reserved; and (3) the circumstances reveal the government intended to reserve water as well as

(20) land when establishing the reservation.
     Some American Indian tribes have also established water rights through the courts based on their traditional diversion and use of certain waters prior to the United States' acquisition of sovereignty. For

(25) example, the Rio Grande pueblos already existed when the United States acquired sovereignty over New Mexico in 1848. Although they at that time became part of the United States, the pueblo lands never formally constituted a part of federal public

(30) lands; in any event, no treaty, statute, or executive order has ever designated or withdrawn the pueblos from public lands as American Indian reservations. This fact, however, has not barred application of the Winters doctrine. What constitutes an American Indian

(35) reservation is a question of practice, not of legal definition, and the pueblos have always been treated as reservations by the United States. This pragmatic approach is buttressed by *Arizona v. California* (1963), wherein the Supreme Court indicated that

(40) the manner in which any type of federal reservation is created does not affect the application to it of the Winters doctrine. Therefore, the reserved water rights of Pueblo Indians have priority over other citizens' water rights as of 1848, the year in which pueblos

(45) must be considered to have become reservations.

Questions 548–553 refer to the passage.

548. According to the passage, which of the following was true of the treaty establishing the Fort Berthold Indian Reservation?

(A) It was challenged in the Supreme Court a number of times.

(B) It was rescinded by the federal government, an action that gave rise to the Winters case.

(C) It cited American Indians' traditional use of the land's resources.

(D) It failed to mention water rights to be enjoyed by the reservation's inhabitants.

(E) It was modified by the Supreme Court in *Arizona v. California*.

549. The passage suggests that, if the criteria discussed in lines 10–20 of the text were the only criteria for establishing a reservation's water rights, which of the following would be true?

(A) The water rights of the inhabitants of the Fort Berthold Indian Reservation would not take precedence over those of other citizens.

(B) Reservations established before 1848 would be judged to have no water rights.

(C) There would be no legal basis for the water rights of the Rio Grande pueblos.

(D) Reservations other than American Indian reservations could not be created with reserved water rights.

(E) Treaties establishing reservations would have to mention water rights explicitly in order to reserve water for a particular purpose.

550. Which of the following most accurately summarizes the relationship between *Arizona v. California*, as that decision is described in the passage, and the criteria discussed in lines 10–20?

   (A) *Arizona v. California* abolishes these criteria and establishes a competing set of criteria for applying the Winters doctrine.

   (B) *Arizona v. California* establishes that the Winters doctrine applies to a broader range of situations than those defined by these criteria.

   (C) *Arizona v. California* represents the sole example of an exception to the criteria as they were set forth in the Winters doctrine.

   (D) *Arizona v. California* does not refer to the Winters doctrine to justify water rights, whereas these criteria do rely on the Winters doctrine.

   (E) *Arizona v. California* applies the criteria derived from the Winters doctrine only to federal lands other than American Indian reservations.

551. The "pragmatic approach" mentioned in lines 37–38 of the passage is best defined as one that

   (A) grants recognition to reservations that were never formally established but that have traditionally been treated as such

   (B) determines the water rights of all citizens in a particular region by examining the actual history of water usage in that region

   (C) gives federal courts the right to reserve water along with land even when it is clear that the government originally intended to reserve only the land

   (D) bases the decision to recognize the legal rights of a group on the practical effect such a recognition is likely to have on other citizens

   (E) dictates that courts ignore precedents set by such cases as *Winters v. United States* in deciding what water rights belong to reserved land

552. It can be inferred from the passage that the Winters doctrine has been used to establish which of the following?

   (A) A rule that the government may reserve water only by explicit treaty or agreement

   (B) A legal distinction between federal lands reserved for American Indians and federal lands reserved for other purposes

   (C) Criteria governing when the federal government may set land aside for a particular purpose

   (D) The special status of American Indian tribes' rights to reserved land

   (E) The federal right to reserve water implicitly as well as explicitly under certain conditions

553. The author cites the fact that the Rio Grande pueblos were never formally withdrawn from public lands primarily in order to do which of the following?

   (A) Suggest why it might have been argued that the Winters doctrine ought not to apply to pueblo lands

   (B) Imply that the United States never really acquired sovereignty over pueblo lands

   (C) Argue that the pueblo lands ought still to be considered part of federal public lands

   (D) Support the argument that the water rights of citizens other than American Indians are limited by the Winters doctrine

   (E) Suggest that federal courts cannot claim jurisdiction over cases disputing the traditional diversion and use of water by Pueblo Indians

Line   In corporate purchasing, competitive scrutiny is typically limited to suppliers of items that are directly related to end products. With "indirect" purchases (such as computers, advertising, and legal services),
(5)   which are not directly related to production, corporations often favor "supplier partnerships" (arrangements in which the purchaser forgoes the right to pursue alternative suppliers), which can inappropriately shelter suppliers from rigorous
(10)   competitive scrutiny that might afford the purchaser economic leverage. There are two independent variables—availability of alternatives and ease of changing suppliers—that companies should use to evaluate the feasibility of subjecting suppliers of
(15)   indirect purchases to competitive scrutiny. This can create four possible situations.
        In Type 1 situations, there are many alternatives and change is relatively easy. Open pursuit of alternatives—by frequent competitive bidding, if
(20)   possible—will likely yield the best results. In Type 2 situations, where there are many alternatives but change is difficult—as for providers of employee health care benefits—it is important to continuously test the market and use the results to secure
(25)   concessions from existing suppliers. Alternatives provide a credible threat to suppliers, even if the ability to switch is constrained. In Type 3 situations, there are few alternatives, but the ability to switch without difficulty creates a threat that companies
(30)   can use to negotiate concessions from existing suppliers. In Type 4 situations, where there are few alternatives and change is difficult, partnerships may be unavoidable.

Questions 554–558 refer to the passage.

554. Which of the following can be inferred about supplier partnerships, as they are described in the passage?

(A)   They cannot be sustained unless the goods or services provided are available from a large number of suppliers.

(B)   They can result in purchasers paying more for goods and services than they would in a competitive-bidding situation.

(C)   They typically are instituted at the urging of the supplier rather than the purchaser.

(D)   They are not feasible when the goods or services provided are directly related to the purchasers' end products.

(E)   They are least appropriate when the purchasers' ability to change suppliers is limited.

555. Which of the following best describes the relation of the second paragraph to the first?

(A)   The second paragraph offers proof of an assertion made in the first paragraph.

(B)   The second paragraph provides an explanation for the occurrence of a situation described in the first paragraph.

(C)   The second paragraph discusses the application of a strategy proposed in the first paragraph.

(D)   The second paragraph examines the scope of a problem presented in the first paragraph.

(E)   The second paragraph discusses the contradictions inherent in a relationship described in the first paragraph.

556. It can be inferred that the author of the passage would be most likely to make which of the following recommendations to a company purchasing health care benefits for its employees?

(A) Devise strategies for circumventing the obstacles to replacing the current provider of health care benefits.

(B) Obtain health care benefits from a provider that also provides other indirect products and services.

(C) Obtain bids from other providers of health care benefits in order to be in a position to negotiate a better deal with the current provider.

(D) Switch providers of health care benefits whenever a different provider offers a more competitive price.

(E) Acknowledge the difficulties involved in replacing the current provider of health care benefits and offer to form a partnership with the provider.

557. Which of the following is one difference between Type 2 situations and Type 4 situations, as they are described in the passage?

(A) The number of alternative suppliers available to the purchaser

(B) The most effective approach for the purchaser to use in obtaining competitive bids from potential suppliers

(C) The degree of difficulty the purchaser encounters when changing suppliers

(D) The frequency with which each type of situation occurs in a typical business environment

(E) The likelihood that any given purchase will be an indirect purchase

558. According to the passage, which of the following factors distinguishes an indirect purchase from other purchases?

(A) The ability of the purchasing company to subject potential suppliers of the purchased item to competitive scrutiny

(B) The number of suppliers of the purchased item available to the purchasing company

(C) The methods of negotiation that are available to the purchasing company

(D) The relationship of the purchased item to the purchasing company's end product

(E) The degree of importance of the purchased item in the purchasing company's business operations

Line   Linda Kerber argued in the mid-1980s that after
the American Revolution (1775–1783), an ideology
of "republican motherhood" resulted in a surge of
educational opportunities for women in the United

(5)   States. Kerber maintained that the leaders of
the new nation wanted women to be educated in
order to raise politically virtuous sons. A virtuous
citizenry was considered essential to the success
of the country's republican form of government;

(10)   virtue was to be instilled not only by churches and
schools, but by families, where the mother's role
was crucial. Thus, according to Kerber, motherhood
became pivotal to the fate of the republic, providing
justification for an unprecedented attention to female

(15)   education.
    Introduction of the "republican motherhood"
thesis dramatically changed historiography. Prior
to Kerber's work, educational historians barely
mentioned women and girls; Thomas Woody's

(20)   1929 work is the notable exception. Examining
newspaper advertisements for academies, Woody
found that educational opportunities increased for
both girls and boys around 1750. Pointing to "An
Essay on Woman" (1753) as reflecting a shift in

(25)   view, Woody also claimed that practical education
for females had many advocates before the
Revolution. Woody's evidence challenges the notion
that the Revolution changed attitudes regarding
female education, although it may have accelerated

(30)   earlier trends. Historians' reliance on Kerber's
"republican motherhood" thesis may have obscured
the presence of these trends, making it difficult
to determine to what extent the Revolution really
changed women's lives.

Questions 559–563 refer to the passage.

559. According to the passage, Kerber maintained that
which of the following led to an increase in educational
opportunities for women in the United States after the
American Revolution?

(A)   An unprecedented demand by women for
greater educational opportunities in the decades
following the Revolution

(B)   A new political ideology calling for equality of
opportunity between women and men in all
aspects of life

(C)   A belief that the American educational system
could be reformed only if women participated
more fully in that system

(D)   A belief that women needed to be educated if
they were to contribute to the success of the
nation's new form of government

(E)   A recognition that women needed to be educated
if they were to take an active role in the nation's
schools and churches

560. According to the passage, within the field of
educational history, Thomas Woody's 1929 work was

(A)   innovative because it relied on newspaper
advertisements as evidence

(B)   exceptional in that it concentrated on the period
before the American Revolution

(C)   unusual in that it focused on educational
attitudes rather than on educational practices

(D)   controversial in its claims regarding educational
opportunities for boys

(E)   atypical in that it examined the education of girls

561. The passage suggests that Woody would have agreed with which of the following claims regarding "An Essay on Woman"?

  (A) It expressed attitudes concerning women's education that were reflected in new educational opportunities for women after 1750.

  (B) It persuaded educators to offer greater educational opportunities to women in the 1750s.

  (C) It articulated ideas about women's education that would not be realized until after the American Revolution.

  (D) It offered one of the most original arguments in favor of women's education in the United States in the eighteenth century.

  (E) It presented views about women's education that were still controversial in Woody's own time.

562. The passage suggests that, with regard to the history of women's education in the United States, Kerber's work differs from Woody's primarily concerning which of the following?

  (A) The extent to which women were interested in pursuing educational opportunities in the eighteenth century

  (B) The extent of the support for educational opportunities for girls prior to the American Revolution

  (C) The extent of public resistance to educational opportunities for women after the American Revolution

  (D) Whether attitudes toward women's educational opportunities changed during the eighteenth century

  (E) Whether women needed to be educated in order to contribute to the success of a republican form of government

563. According to the passage, Kerber argued that political leaders thought that the form of government adopted by the United States after the American Revolution depended on which of the following for its success?

  (A) Women assuming the sole responsibility for instilling political virtue in children

  (B) Girls becoming the primary focus of a reformed educational system that emphasized political virtue

  (C) The family serving as one of the primary means by which children were imbued with political virtue

  (D) The family assuming many of the functions previously performed by schools and churches

  (E) Men and women assuming equal responsibility for the management of schools, churches, and the family

Line Years before the advent of plate tectonics—the widely accepted theory, developed in the mid-1960s, that holds the major features of Earth's surface are created by the horizontal motions
(5) of Earth's outer shell, or lithosphere—a similar theory was rejected by the geological community. In 1912, Alfred Wegener proposed, in a widely debated theory that came to be called continental drift, that Earth's continents were mobile. To most
(10) geologists today, Wegener's *The Origin of Continents and Oceans* appears an impressive and prescient document, containing several of the essential presumptions underlying plate tectonics theory: the horizontal mobility of pieces of Earth's crust; the
(15) essential difference between oceanic and continental crust; and a causal connection between horizontal displacements and the formation of mountain chains. Yet despite the considerable overlap between Wegener's concepts and the later widely embraced
(20) plate tectonics theory, and despite the fact that continental drift theory presented a possible solution to the problem of the origin of mountains at a time when existing explanations were seriously in doubt, in its day Wegener's theory was rejected by the vast
(25) majority of geologists.

Most geologists and many historians today believe Wegener's theory was rejected because of its lack of an adequate mechanical basis. A group of researchers argues continental drift theory was
(30) rejected because it did not explain how continents could move through an apparently solid oceanic floor. However, as Anthony Hallam has pointed out, many scientific phenomena, such as the ice ages, have been accepted before they could be fully
(35) explained. The most likely cause for the rejection of continental drift—a cause that has been largely ignored because we consider Wegener's theory to have been validated by the theory of plate tectonics—is the nature of the evidence that was put forward
(40) to support it. Most of Wegener's evidence consisted of homologies—similarities of patterns and forms based on direct observations of rocks in the field, supported by the use of hammers, hand lenses, and field notebooks. In contrast, the data supporting
(45) plate tectonics were impressively geophysical: instrumental determinations of the physical properties of Earth garnered through the use of seismographs and magnetometers.

Questions 564–568 refer to the passage.

564. It can be inferred from the passage that geologists today would be most likely to agree with which of the following statements about Wegener's *The Origin of Continents and Oceans*?

(A) It was a worthy scientific effort that was ahead of its time.

(B) It was based on evidence that was later disproved.

(C) It was directly responsible for the acceptance of the theory of plate tectonics.

(D) It has been disproved by continental drift theory.

(E) It misrepresented how horizontal displacements cause the formation of mountain chains.

565. The author of the passage suggests the most likely explanation for the geological community's response to continental drift theory in its day was that the theory

(A) was in conflict with certain aspects of plate tectonics theory

(B) failed to account for how mountains were formed

(C) did not adequately explain how continents moved through the ocean floor

(D) was contradicted by the geophysical data of the time

(E) was based on a kind of evidence that was considered insufficiently convincing

566. The author of the passage probably refers to the "considerable overlap" (see line 18) between the continental drift theory and plate tectonics theory in order to

(A) suggest that plate tectonics theory is derived from Wegener's work

(B) introduce a discussion comparing the elements of the two theories

(C) examine the question of whether continental drift theory was innovative in its time

(D) provide a reason why it might seem surprising that continental drift theory was not more widely embraced by geologists

(E) cite an explanation that has been frequently offered for Wegener's high standing among geologists today

567. The author cites Hallam (see line 32) on the ice ages primarily in order to

   (A)   provide an example of a geologic phenomenon with precise causes that are not fully understood by geologists today

   (B)   criticize the geological community for an apparent lack of consistency in its responses to new theories

   (C)   offer evidence held to undermine a common view of why Wegener's theory was not accepted in its day

   (D)   give an example of a modern scientist who believes Wegener's theory was rejected because it failed to adequately explain the mechanical basis of continental drift

   (E)   support some researchers' rationale for why Wegener's theory was rejected by most geologists in the early twentieth century

568. The author of the passage most likely discusses the "essential presumptions" (see lines 12–13) of *The Origin of Continents and Oceans* in order to

   (A)   indicate features of Wegener's theory that caused it to be doubted in its day

   (B)   show why Wegener's theory is now regarded as prescient

   (C)   indicate differences between plate tectonics and the theory of continental drift

   (D)   cite features of the theory of continental drift for which no evidence was available in Wegener's day

   (E)   point out aspects of Wegener's theory that were accepted well before the advent of plate tectonics

Line   Resin is a plant secretion that hardens when
        exposed to air; fossilized resin is called amber.
        Although Pliny in the first century recognized that
        amber was produced from "marrow discharged by
(5)   trees," amber has been widely misunderstood to be
        a semiprecious gem and has even been described
        in mineralogy textbooks. Confusion also persists
        surrounding the term "resin," which was defined
        before rigorous chemical analyses were available.
(10)   Resin is often confused with gum, a substance
        produced in plants in response to bacterial infections,
        and with sap, an aqueous solution transported
        through certain plant tissues. Resin differs from both
        gum and sap in that scientists have not determined a
(15)   physiological function for resin.
            In the 1950s, entomologists posited that resin
        may function to repel or attract insects. Fraenkel
        conjectured that plants initially produced resin in
        nonspecific chemical responses to insect attack
(20)   and that, over time, plants evolved that produced
        resin with specific repellent effects. But some insect
        species, he noted, might overcome the repellent
        effects, actually becoming attracted to the resin.
        This might induce the insects to feed on those
(25)   plants or aid them in securing a breeding site.
        Later researchers suggested that resin mediates
        the complex interdependence, or "coevolution," of
        plants and insects over time. Such ideas led to the
        development of the specialized discipline of chemical
(30)   ecology, which is concerned with the role of plant
        chemicals in interactions with other organisms and
        with the evolution and ecology of plant antiherbivore
        chemistry (plants' chemical defenses against attack
        by herbivores such as insects).

Questions 569–572 refer to the passage.

569. According to the passage, which of the following is
     true of plant antiherbivore chemistry?

     (A)   Changes in a plant's antiherbivore chemistry may
           affect insect feeding behavior.

     (B)   A plant's repellent effects often involve
           interactions between gum and resin.

     (C)   A plant's antiherbivore responses assist in
           combating bacterial infections.

     (D)   Plant antiherbivore chemistry plays only a minor
           role in the coevolution of plants and insects.

     (E)   Researchers first studied repellent effects in
           plants beginning in the 1950s.

570. Of the following topics, which would be most likely to
     be studied within the discipline of chemical ecology as
     it is described in the passage?

     (A)   Seeds that become attached to certain insects,
           which in turn carry away the seeds and aid in
           the reproductive cycle of the plant species in
           question

     (B)   An insect species that feeds on weeds
           detrimental to crop health and yield, and how
           these insects might aid in agricultural production

     (C)   The effects of deforestation on the life cycles
           of subtropical carnivorous plants and the insect
           species on which the plants feed

     (D)   The growth patterns of a particular species of
           plant that has proved remarkably resistant to
           herbicides

     (E)   Insects that develop a tolerance for feeding on a
           plant that had previously been toxic to them, and
           the resultant changes within that plant species

571. The author refers to "bacterial infections" (see line 11) most likely in order to

(A) describe the physiological function that gum performs in plants

(B) demonstrate that sap is not the only substance that is transported through a plant's tissues

(C) explain how modern chemical analysis has been used to clarify the function of resin

(D) show that gum cannot serve as an effective defense against herbivores

(E) give an example of how confusion has arisen with regard to the nature of resin

572. The author of the passage refers to Pliny most probably in order to

(A) give an example of how the nature of amber has been misunderstood in the past

(B) show that confusion about amber has long been more pervasive than confusion about resin

(C) make note of the first known reference to amber as a semiprecious gem

(D) point out an exception to a generalization about the history of people's understanding of amber

(E) demonstrate that Pliny believed amber to be a mineral

Line

Resin is a plant secretion that hardens when exposed to air. Fossilized resin is called amber.

(5) Although Pliny in the first century recognized that amber was produced by trees, amber has been widely misunderstood to be a semiprecious gem, and has even been described in mineralogy textbooks. Confusion also persists

(10) surrounding the term "resin," which was defined before rigorous chemical analyses were available. Resin is often confused with gum, a substance produced in plants in response to bacterial infections, and with sap, an aqueous solution transported

(15) through a plant's tissues. Resin differs from both gum and sap in that scientists have not determined a physiological function for resin.

In the 1980s, entomologists posited that resin may function to attract insects. Researchers

(20) opined that plants initially produced resin in nonspecific chemical responses to insect attack and that, over time, plants evolved that produced resin with an insect-repellent effect—but some insect species, in turn, might have become more resilient,

(25) actually becoming attracted to the resin. This might influence the insects tied to those insects or tied to them in a deeper food chain.

Later, researchers suggested that resin regulates the complex interdependence, or "coevolution," of

(30) plants and insects over time. Such ideas led to the development of the specialized discipline of chemical ecology, which is concerned with the role of plant chemicals in interactions with other organisms and with the evolution and ecology of plant chemicals—primarily a plant's chemical defenses against attack by herbivores such as insects.

Line During the 1980s, many economic historians studying Latin America focused on the impact of the Great Depression of the 1930s. Most of these historians argued that although the Depression
(5) began earlier in Latin America than in the United States, it was less severe in Latin America and did not significantly impede industrial growth there. The historians' argument was grounded in national government records concerning tax revenues and
(10) exports and in government-sponsored industrial censuses, from which historians have drawn conclusions about total manufacturing output and profit levels across Latin America. However, economic statistics published by Latin American
(15) governments in the early twentieth century are neither reliable nor consistent; this is especially true of manufacturing data, which were gathered from factory owners for taxation purposes and which therefore may well be distorted. Moreover,
(20) one cannot assume a direct correlation between the output level and the profit level of a given industry, as these variables often move in opposite directions. Finally, national and regional economies are composed of individual firms and industries,
(25) and relying on general, sweeping economic indicators may mask substantial variations among these different enterprises. For example, recent analyses of previously unexamined data on textile manufacturing in Brazil and Mexico suggest that the
(30) Great Depression had a more severe impact on this Latin American industry than scholars had recognized.

Questions 573–575 refer to the passage.

573. The primary purpose of the passage is to

(A) compare the impact of the Great Depression on Latin America with its impact on the United States

(B) criticize a school of economic historians for failing to analyze the Great Depression in Latin America within a global context

(C) illustrate the risks inherent in comparing different types of economic enterprises to explain economic phenomena

(D) call into question certain scholars' views concerning the severity of the Great Depression in Latin America

(E) demonstrate that the Great Depression had a more severe impact on industry in Latin America than in certain other regions

574. Which of the following conclusions about the Great Depression is best supported by the passage?

(A) It did not impede Latin American industrial growth as much as historians had previously thought.

(B) It had a more severe impact on the Brazilian and the Mexican textile industries than it had on Latin America as a region.

(C) It affected the Latin American textile industry more severely than it did any other industry in Latin America.

(D) The overall impact on Latin American industrial growth should be reevaluated by economic historians.

(E) Its impact on Latin America should not be compared with its impact on the United States.

575. Which of the following, if true, would most strengthen the author's assertion regarding economic indicators in lines 25–27?

(A) During an economic depression, European textile manufacturers' profits rise while their industrial output remains steady.

(B) During a national economic recession, United States microchips manufacturers' profits rise sharply while United States steel manufacturers' profits plunge.

(C) During the years following a severe economic depression, textile manufacturers' output levels and profit levels increase in Brazil and Mexico but not in the rest of Latin America.

(D) Although Japanese industry as a whole recovers after an economic recession, it does not regain its previously high levels of production.

(E) While European industrial output increases in the years following an economic depression, total output remains below that of Japan or the United States.

Line   Among the myths taken as fact by the
environmental managers of most corporations is
the belief that environmental regulations affect all
competitors in a given industry uniformly. In reality,
(5)   regulatory costs—and therefore compliance—
fall unevenly, economically disadvantaging some
companies and benefiting others. For example, a
plant situated near a number of larger
noncompliant competitors is less likely to attract
(10)   the attention of local regulators than is an isolated
plant, and less attention means lower costs.
        Additionally, large plants can spread compliance
costs such as waste treatment across a larger
revenue base; on the other hand, some smaller
(15)   plants may not even be subject to certain
provisions such as permit or reporting
requirements by virtue of their size. Finally, older
production technologies often continue to generate
toxic wastes that were not regulated when the
(20)   technology was first adopted. New regulations
have imposed extensive compliance costs on
companies still using older industrial coal-fired
burners that generate high sulfur dioxide and
nitrogen oxide outputs, for example, whereas new
(25)   facilities generally avoid processes that would
create such waste products. By realizing that they
have discretion and that not all industries are
affected equally by environmental regulation,
environmental managers can help their companies
(30)   to achieve a competitive edge by anticipating
regulatory pressure and exploring all possibilities for
addressing how changing regulations will affect their
companies specifically.

Questions 576–579 refer to the passage.

576. It can be inferred from the passage that a large plant
might have to spend more than a similar but smaller
plant on environmental compliance because the larger
plant is

(A)   more likely to attract attention from local
regulators

(B)   less likely to be exempt from permit and
reporting requirements

(C)   less likely to have regulatory costs passed on to
it by companies that supply its raw materials

(D)   more likely to employ older production
technologies

(E)   more likely to generate wastes that are more
environmentally damaging than those generated
by smaller plants

577. According to the passage, which of the following
statements about sulfur dioxide and nitrogen oxide
outputs is true?

(A)   Older production technologies cannot be
adapted so as to reduce production of these
outputs as waste products.

(B)   Under the most recent environmental regulations,
industrial plants are no longer permitted to
produce these outputs.

(C)   Although these outputs are environmentally
hazardous, some plants still generate them as
waste products despite the high compliance
costs they impose.

(D)   Many older plants have developed innovative
technological processes that reduce the
amounts of these outputs generated as waste
products.

(E)   Since the production processes that generate
these outputs are less costly than alternative
processes, these less expensive processes are
sometimes adopted despite their acknowledged
environmental hazards.

578. Which of the following best describes the relationship of the statement about large plants (lines 12–17) to the passage as a whole?

   (A) It presents a hypothesis that is disproved later in the passage.

   (B) It highlights an opposition between two ideas mentioned in the passage.

   (C) It provides examples to support a claim made earlier in the passage.

   (D) It exemplifies a misconception mentioned earlier in the passage.

   (E) It draws an analogy between two situations described in the passage.

579. The primary purpose of the passage is to

   (A) address a widespread environmental management problem and suggest possible solutions

   (B) illustrate varying levels of compliance with environmental regulation among different corporations

   (C) describe the various alternatives to traditional methods of environmental management

   (D) advocate increased corporate compliance with environmental regulation

   (E) correct a common misconception about the impact of environmental regulations

Line   Findings from several studies on corporate
mergers and acquisitions during the 1970s and
1980s raise questions about why firms initiate and
consummate such transactions. One study showed,
(5)   for example, that acquiring firms were on average
unable to maintain acquired firms' pre-merger levels
of profitability. A second study concluded that
post-acquisition gains to most acquiring firms were
not adequate to cover the premiums paid to obtain
(10)   acquired firms. A third demonstrated that, following
the announcement of a prospective merger, the stock
of the prospective acquiring firm tends to increase in
value much less than does that of the firm for which it
bids. Yet mergers and acquisitions remain common,
(15)   and bidders continue to assert that their objectives
are economic ones. Acquisitions may well have the
desirable effect of channeling a nation's resources
efficiently from less to more efficient sectors of its
economy, but the individual executives arranging
(20)   these deals must see them as advancing either their
own or their companies' private economic interests. It
seems that factors having little to do with corporate
economic interests explain acquisitions. These
factors may include the incentive compensation of
(25)   executives, lack of monitoring by boards of directors,
and managerial error in estimating the value of firms
targeted for acquisition. Alternatively, the acquisition
acts of bidders may derive from modeling: a manager
does what other managers do.

Questions 580–583 refer to the passage.

580. The primary purpose of the passage is to

(A) review research demonstrating the benefits of
corporate mergers and acquisitions and examine
some of the drawbacks that acquisition behavior
entails

(B) contrast the effects of corporate mergers and
acquisitions on acquiring firms and on firms that
are acquired

(C) report findings that raise questions about a
reason for corporate mergers and acquisitions
and suggest possible alternative reasons

(D) explain changes in attitude on the part of acquiring
firms toward corporate mergers and acquisitions

(E) account for a recent decline in the rate of
corporate mergers and acquisitions

581. It can be inferred from the passage that the author
would be most likely to agree with which of the
following statements about corporate acquisitions?

(A) Their known benefits to national economies
explain their appeal to individual firms during the
1970s and 1980s.

(B) Despite their adverse impact on some firms,
they are the best way to channel resources from
less to more productive sectors of a nation's
economy.

(C) They are as likely to occur because of poor
monitoring by boards of directors as to be
caused by incentive compensation for managers.

(D) They will be less prevalent in the future, since
their actual effects will gain wider recognition.

(E) Factors other than economic benefit to the
acquiring firm help to explain the frequency with
which they occur.

582. The author of the passage mentions the effect of acquisitions on national economies most probably in order to

(A) provide an explanation for the mergers and acquisitions of the 1970s and 1980s overlooked by the findings discussed in the passage

(B) suggest that national economic interests played an important role in the mergers and acquisitions of the 1970s and 1980s

(C) support a noneconomic explanation for the mergers and acquisitions of the 1970s and 1980s that was cited earlier in the passage

(D) cite and point out the inadequacy of one possible explanation for the prevalence of mergers and acquisitions during the 1970s and 1980s

(E) explain how modeling affected the decisions made by managers involved in mergers and acquisitions during the 1970s and 1980s

583. The author of the passage implies that which of the following is a possible partial explanation for acquisition behavior during the 1970s and 1980s?

(A) Managers wished to imitate other managers primarily because they saw how financially beneficial other firms' acquisitions were.

(B) Managers miscalculated the value of firms that were to be acquired.

(C) Lack of consensus within boards of directors resulted in their imposing conflicting goals on managers.

(D) Total compensation packages for managers increased during that period.

(E) The value of bidding firms' stock increased significantly when prospective mergers were announced.

Line   Historical documents have revealed that among the Timucua of Florida, a Native American people, the best from the hunt or the harvest was given to families of high social status, even in times

(5)   of economic stress. Archaeological research suggests a similar relationship between social status and diet in the Dallas communities of eastern Tennessee, prehistoric Native American groups with a social organization and economy similar to

(10)   that of the Timucua. The first real clue came when archaeologists discovered that skeletons of higher-status individuals tended to be several centimeters taller than those of people of lower status.

    In the largest Dallas communities, some individuals

(15)   were buried in the earthen mounds that served as substructures for buildings important to civic and religious affairs. These burials included quantities of finely crafted items made of nonlocal material, denoting the high political standing of those interred.

(20)   Burials of lower-status individuals contained primarily utilitarian items such as cooking vessels and chipped stone tools and are located in more remote sections of the settlements. The burials actually formed a pattern, the tallest skeletons being found in the

(25)   mounds, and the heights declining as burials became more distant from the mounds. While it is possible that taller people were simply more successful in achieving high social standing, it is more likely that a number of stresses, including those resulting from a

(30)   relatively poor diet, which could affect stature, were common among the lower-status groups.

    Excavations indicate that three food categories made up the bulk of the population's diet: agricultural crops cultivated in the fertile alluvial soils where the

(35)   communities were located, game, and wild edible plants, primarily nuts. Information about dietary variation among community members is derived by analyzing trace elements in human bone. Higher than normal levels of manganese, strontium, and vanadium

(40)   probably indicate a less nutritious diet heavily dependent on edible plants. Very low concentrations of vanadium, which is scarce in meats and somewhat lower in nuts than in other plant resources, are good evidence of meat consumption and thus a better

(45)   balanced diet. As expected, vanadium was found in considerably greater quantities in skeletons in the burials of lower-status groups.

Questions 584–587 refer to the passage.

584. According to the passage, which of the following statements regarding earthen mounds in the Dallas communities is accurate?

    (A)   They served primarily as burial grounds.

    (B)   They were constructed in key locations on the perimeter of the village.

    (C)   They were elements in important structures in the community.

    (D)   They were used as storehouses for keeping valuable possessions safe.

    (E)   They contained utilitarian items made of nonlocal materials.

585. In lines 26–28, the author of the passage raises the possibility that taller people achieved greater success most probably in order to

    (A)   suggest that two explanations for a phenomenon are equally plausible

    (B)   introduce empirical data supporting a position

    (C)   anticipate an objection to an argument

    (D)   question the usefulness of relying solely on physical evidence

    (E)   point out a weakness in a traditional argument

586. The passage suggests that the "relationship" mentioned in line 6 was initially recognized when archaeologists

    (A)   attempted to trace the ancestry of the Timucua of Florida

    (B)   discovered a height differential among members of subgroups in the Dallas community

    (C)   realized that the Dallas communities endured periods of nutritional deprivation

    (D)   began to compare the social organization and economies of the Timucua with that of the Dallas communities

    (E)   became curious about differences in trace elements found in the bones of Dallas community members

587. The passage suggests which of the following about the diet of the Dallas communities?

(A) Wild edible plants were a relatively minor element in the diet.

(B) Game was less likely to be available to lower-status individuals than were edible plants.

(C) The diet was composed primarily of agricultural crops when game was scarce.

(D) The diet was obtained entirely from local food sources.

(E) The diet was well balanced, especially at harvest-time.

Line   Historically, relations between workers and
employers in the United States have often been
characterized by the employment-at-will doctrine,
according to which the duration of employment is
(5)   determined by the employer and the grounds for
termination are limited only by the provisions of
contracts and specific statutes. Many state courts
and legislatures have reevaluated this doctrine
and have modified it by expanding the concept of
(10)   wrongful termination, thereby increasing employer
liability. Some economic theorists suggest that such
changes tend to reduce employment in states that
enact them, because protecting workers against
wrongful termination raises the cost of labor to
(15)   employers: firms will tend to spend more time and
money screening potential employees, be reluctant to
terminate less-productive workers, and incur greater
legal expenses. In a study that took into account
differences among states, researchers Dertouzos and
(20)   Karoly concluded that states with wrongful-termination
laws experienced a 2 percent to 5 percent drop in
their employment rate as a result of adopting these
laws. They also found that the impact on employment
appears to be smallest in manufacturing, where
(25)   unions have already institutionalized similar protection,
and in small firms, perhaps because those firms'
lesser ability to pay damages makes it less profitable
for employees to file wrongful-termination lawsuits
against them.

Questions 588–590 refer to the passage.

588. The primary purpose of the passage is to

(A)   explore the legal consequences of terminating a
worker's employment

(B)   define the employment-at-will doctrine and
chronicle its historical evolution

(C)   examine reasons underlying a trend away from
the employment-at-will doctrine

(D)   advocate increased protection for workers
against wrongful termination by employers

(E)   discuss a possible drawback of state laws
intended to protect workers against wrongful
termination

589. Which of the following best describes the organization
of the passage?

(A)   An idea is proposed and arguments against it are
examined and then refuted.

(B)   A doctrine is defined and reasons for favoring its
adoption are listed.

(C)   A doctrine is criticized, several possible
alternatives are outlined, and one is endorsed.

(D)   An idea is described, its antithesis is presented,
and a synthesis of the two is proposed.

(E)   A doctrine is defined, a revision to it is described,
and the implications of that revision are discussed.

590. The passage suggests which of the following regarding
wrongful-termination lawsuits?

(A)   States that do not implement wrongful-
termination laws will probably see an increase in
wrongful-termination lawsuits.

(B)   It is less profitable to file wrongful-termination
lawsuits against unionized companies than
against companies without unions.

(C)   A wrongful-termination lawsuit is less costly to a
company than continuing the employment of an
unproductive worker.

(D)   Obtaining financial compensation is an important
motivation for filing wrongful-termination lawsuits.

(E)   Those who file wrongful-termination lawsuits are
likely to be awarded larger settlements under the
employment-at-will doctrine than under wrongful-
termination laws.

Line   The incentives for developing vaccines for plants
have never been greater. The world's farmers are
spending about $25 billion per year on chemical
sprays, yet diseases still destroy about twelve
(5)   percent of the total harvest of food. When we want
to protect children against disease, we use vaccines
that stimulate their immune systems, but plants
we simply douse in noxious chemicals. Spraying
chemical agents to kill off crop diseases is so central
(10)   to modern agriculture that the idea of vaccinating a
plant seems thoroughly alien. However, biologists are
now learning how to stimulate the natural biochemical
mechanisms by which plants defend themselves from
disease.
(15)   A variety of "resistance genes" enable plants to
detect particular infectious agents. A plant having
the appropriate resistance gene will respond by
instructing cells near the site of infection to die off.
Cells around the infection die rapidly, depriving the
(20)   invader of food, while cells immediately outside the
dead area produce chemicals that thicken their walls.
In a few days, the infection is isolated by a layer of
dead cells. Plants will also actively attack infectious
agents by producing compounds toxic to invading
(25)   organisms or by producing enzymes that degrade the
invader's cell walls.
    Plants that do not possess resistance genes
against a particular infectious organism can still, like
animals, acquire immunity through being exposed to
(30)   the organism. Unlike animals, plants infected with one
disease can also acquire immunity to a wide range
of other diseases. Immunologists have demonstrated
that infecting cucumber seedlings with a controlled
anthracnose fungus infection protected the seedlings
(35)   against more severe infections for up to six
weeks, radically reduced damage from subsequent
anthracnose infections, and protected plants against
twelve other bacterial, viral, and fungal diseases. The
treatment did not, however, protect against powdery
(40)   mildew.
    Unfortunately, immunization can also inhibit plant
growth, presumably because defense mechanisms
divert food resources. When deployed too vigorously,
defense mechanisms may also damage the plant
(45)   itself. Some substances made in response to disease
are toxic to the plants that produce them, as well
as to infectious organisms. Biologists will have to
overcome these side effects if immunization is going
to replace chemical spraying.

Questions 591–593 refer to the passage.

591. According to the passage, an unwanted side effect of
plant immunization is that immunized plants

(A)   become more susceptible to certain infections,
such as powdery mildew

(B)   become more vulnerable to uncontrolled
infections from the same infectious agent used
to immunize the plants

(C)   produce substances that are toxic to organisms
that are beneficial to the plant

(D)   produce enzymes that can degrade the plants'
cell walls

(E)   focus their resources on fighting invading
organisms, thereby impeding other plant
processes

592. According to the passage, biologists can immunize a
plant against an infectious organism by doing which of
the following?

(A)   Manipulating the plant's genetic code in order to
give it the appropriate resistance genes

(B)   Exposing the plant to a controlled infection of the
organism

(C)   Killing off cells near the site of the infection

(D)   Applying enzymes to the infectious organism in
order to degrade its cell walls

(E)   Treating the plant with chemicals that thicken the
plant's cell walls

593. Which of the following best states the function of the
first paragraph?

(A)   It presents an example to help illustrate a
problem.

(B)   It discusses the history of a problem and its
present implications.

(C)   It describes a situation and introduces a possible
solution.

(D)   It reconciles two conflicting solutions to a problem.

(E)   It evaluates a possible solution to a problem.

Line   A recent study has provided clues to predator-prey dynamics in the late Pleistocene era. Researchers compared the number of tooth fractures in present-day carnivores with tooth fractures in carnivores
(5)   that lived 36,000 to 10,000 years ago and that were preserved in the Rancho La Brea tar pits in Los Angeles. The breakage frequencies in the extinct species were strikingly higher than those in the present-day species.

(10)   In considering possible explanations for this finding, the researchers dismissed demographic bias because older individuals were not overrepresented in the fossil samples. They rejected preservational bias because a total absence of breakage in two extinct
(15)   species demonstrated that the fractures were not the result of abrasion within the pits. They ruled out local bias because breakage data obtained from other Pleistocene sites were similar to the La Brea data. The explanation they consider most plausible is
(20)   behavioral differences between extinct and present-day carnivores—in particular, more complete contact between the teeth of predators and the bones of prey due to more thorough consumption of carcasses by the extinct species. Such thorough carcass
(25)   consumption implies to the researchers either that prey availability was low, at least seasonally, or that there was intense competition over kills and a high rate of carcass theft due to relatively high predator densities.

Questions 594–596 refer to the passage.

594. The behavioral differences explanation discussed in the passage would be most seriously weakened if which of the following were true?

(A)   Pleistocene carnivores were more likely to starve to death due to tooth fractures than are present-day carnivores.

(B)   Interactions among Pleistocene carnivore species were more complex than are interactions among present-day carnivore species.

(C)   The teeth of many Pleistocene carnivores were significantly weaker than are the teeth of present-day carnivores.

(D)   The primary cause of death for Pleistocene carnivores was a shortage of prey.

(E)   The availability of prey for Pleistocene carnivores in the La Brea area was much greater in summer than in winter.

595. The primary purpose of the passage is to

(A)   present several explanations for a well-known fact

(B)   suggest alternative methods for resolving a debate

(C)   argue in favor of a controversial theory

(D)   question the methodology used in a study

(E)   discuss the implications of a research finding

596. The passage suggests that, compared with Pleistocene carnivores in other areas, Pleistocene carnivores in the La Brea area

(A)   included the same species, in approximately the same proportions

(B)   had a similar frequency of tooth fractures

(C)   populated the La Brea area more densely

(D)   consumed their prey more thoroughly

(E)   found it harder to obtain sufficient prey

Line   After the Second World War, unionism in the
Japanese auto industry was company-based, with
separate unions in each auto company. Most
company unions played no independent role in
(5)   bargaining shop-floor issues or pressing autoworkers'
grievances. In a 1981 survey, for example, less
than 1 percent of workers said they sought union
assistance for work-related problems, while 43
percent said they turned to management instead.
(10)   There was little to distinguish the two in any case:
Most union officers were foremen or middle-level
managers, and the union's role was primarily one
of passive support for company goals. Conflict
occasionally disrupted this cooperative relationship—
(15)   one company union's opposition to the productivity
campaigns of the early 1980s has been cited as
such a case. In 1986, however, a caucus led by the
Foreman's Association forced the union's leadership
out of office and returned the union's policy to one
(20)   of passive cooperation. In the United States, the
potential for such company unionism grew after
1979, but it had difficulty taking hold in the auto
industry, where a single union represented workers
from all companies, particularly since federal law
(25)   prohibited foremen from joining or leading industrial
unions.
       The Japanese model was often invoked as one
in which authority decentralized to the shop floor
empowered production workers to make key
(30)   decisions. What these claims failed to recognize was
that the actual delegation of authority was to the
foreman, not the workers. The foreman exercised
discretion over job assignments, training, transfers,
and promotions; worker initiative was limited to
(35)   suggestions that fine-tuned a management-controlled
production process. Rather than being proactive,
Japanese workers were forced to be reactive, the
range of their responsibilities being far wider than
their span of control. For example, the founder
(40)   of one production system, Taichi Ohno, routinely
gave department managers only 90 percent of
the resources needed for production. As soon
as workers could meet production goals without
working overtime, 10 percent of remaining resources
(45)   would be removed. Because the "OH! NO!" system
continually pushed the production process to the
verge of breakdown in an effort to find the minimum
resource requirement, critics described it as
"management by stress."

Questions 597–599 refer to the passage.

597. It can be inferred that which of the following is most
likely to have been a goal of the Foreman's Association
(line 18)?

(A)   Increasing the range of responsibilities of plant
workers

(B)   Communicating autoworkers' grievances to plant
management

(C)   Introducing company unionism into a plant

(D)   Supporting the policies of plant management

(E)   Reducing bureaucratic layers of management

598. The passage is primarily concerned with

(A)   contrasting the role of unions in the Japanese
auto industry with the role of unions in the
United States auto industry after the Second
World War

(B)   describing unionism and the situation of workers
in the Japanese auto industry after the Second
World War

(C)   providing examples of grievances of Japanese
auto workers against the auto industry after the
Second World War

(D)   correcting a misconception about the
role of the foreman in the Japanese auto
industry's union system after the Second
World War

(E)   reasserting the traditional view of the company's
role in Japanese auto workers' unions after the
Second World War

599. According to the passage, a foreman in a United States auto company differed from a foreman in a Japanese auto company in that the foreman in the United States would

   (A) not have been a member of an auto workers' union

   (B) have been unlikely to support the goals of company management

   (C) have been able to control production processes to a large extent

   (D) have experienced greater stress

   (E) have experienced less conflict with workers

Line In *American Genesis*, which covers the century
of technological innovation in the United States
beginning in 1876, Thomas Hughes assigns special
prominence to Thomas Edison as archetype of
(5) the independent nineteenth-century inventor.
However, Hughes virtually ignores Edison's famous
contemporary and notorious adversary in the field of
electric light and power, George Westinghouse. This
comparative neglect of Westinghouse is consistent
(10) with other recent historians' works, although it marks
an intriguing departure from the prevailing view during
the inventors' lifetimes (and for decades afterward)
of Edison and Westinghouse as the two "pioneer
innovators" of the electrical industry.
(15) My recent reevaluation of Westinghouse, facilitated
by materials found in railroad archives, suggests that
while Westinghouse and Edison shared important
traits as inventors, they differed markedly in their
approach to the business aspects of innovation. For
(20) Edison as an inventor, novelty was always paramount;
the overriding goal of the business of innovation
was simply to generate funding for new inventions.
Westinghouse, however, shared the attitudes of the
railroads and other industries for whom he developed
(25) innovations: Product development, standardization,
system, and order were top priorities. Westinghouse
thus better exemplifies the systematic approach
to technological development that would become
a hallmark of modern corporate research and
(30) development.

Questions 600–601 refer to the passage.

600. Which of the following best describes the organization
of the passage?

(A) A theory is examined, the assumptions
underlying the theory are evaluated, and the
theory is modified.

(B) A hypothesis is suggested, evidence challenging
the hypothesis is presented and rejected, and a
new hypothesis is offered.

(C) A range of views is considered, evidence
in support of each view is examined, and a
hypothesis based on one of the views is offered.

(D) Different points of view are contrasted, evidence
to support a new perspective is presented, and a
conclusion based on that evidence is drawn.

(E) Two conflicting views are introduced, evidence
supporting each view is examined, and the two
views are reconciled.

601. According to the passage, during his lifetime
Westinghouse was regarded as

(A) the archetype of the independent nineteenth-
century inventor

(B) Edison's equal as an innovator in the field of
electric light and power

(C) less innovative than Edison as an inventor but
more astute as a businessman

(D) more important as an innovator in the field of
electric light and power than historians in the
decades following his death considered him to
be

(E) less important as an innovator in the field of
electric light and power than recent historians
have portrayed him to be

Questions 602–644 — Difficulty: **Hard**

Line   Acting on the recommendation of a British government committee investigating the high incidence in white lead factories of illness among employees, most of whom were women, the Home

(5) Secretary proposed in 1895 that Parliament enact legislation that would prohibit women from holding most jobs in white lead factories. Although the Women's Industrial Defence Committee (WIDC), formed in 1892 in response to earlier legislative

(10) attempts to restrict women's labor, did not discount the white lead trade's potential health dangers, it opposed the proposal, viewing it as yet another instance of limiting women's work opportunities.

    Also opposing the proposal was the Society for

(15) Promoting the Employment of Women (SPEW), which attempted to challenge it by investigating the causes of illness in white lead factories. SPEW contended, and WIDC concurred, that controllable conditions in such factories were responsible for

(20) the development of lead poisoning. SPEW provided convincing evidence that lead poisoning could be avoided if workers were careful and clean and if already extant workplace safety regulations were stringently enforced. However, the Women's Trade

(25) Union League (WTUL), which had ceased in the late 1880s to oppose restrictions on women's labor, supported the eventually enacted proposal, in part because safety regulations were generally not being enforced in white lead factories, where there were

(30) no unions (and little prospect of any) to pressure employers to comply with safety regulations.

602. The passage suggests that WIDC differed from WTUL in which of the following ways?

(A) WIDC believed that the existing safety regulations were adequate to protect women's health, whereas WTUL believed that such regulations needed to be strengthened.

(B) WIDC believed that unions could not succeed in pressuring employers to comply with such regulations, whereas WTUL believed that unions could succeed in doing so.

(C) WIDC believed that lead poisoning in white lead factories could be avoided by controlling conditions there, whereas WTUL believed that lead poisoning in such factories could not be avoided no matter how stringently safety regulations were enforced.

(D) At the time that the legislation concerning white lead factories was proposed, WIDC was primarily concerned with addressing health conditions in white lead factories, whereas WTUL was concerned with improving working conditions in all types of factories.

(E) At the time that WIDC was opposing legislative attempts to restrict women's labor, WTUL had already ceased to do so.

603. Which of the following, if true, would most clearly support the contention attributed to SPEW in lines 17–20?

(A) Those white lead factories that most strongly enforced regulations concerning worker safety and hygiene had the lowest incidences of lead poisoning among employees.

(B) The incidence of lead poisoning was much higher among women who worked in white lead factories than among women who worked in other types of factories.

(C) There were many household sources of lead that could have contributed to the incidence of lead poisoning among women who also worked outside the home in the late nineteenth century.

(D) White lead factories were more stringent than were certain other types of factories in their enforcement of workplace safety regulations.

(E) Even brief exposure to the conditions typically found in white lead factories could cause lead poisoning among factory workers.

604. The passage is primarily concerned with

(A) presenting various groups' views of the motives of those proposing certain legislation

(B) contrasting the reasoning of various groups concerning their positions on certain proposed legislation

(C) tracing the process whereby certain proposed legislation was eventually enacted

(D) assessing the success of tactics adopted by various groups with respect to certain proposed legislation

(E) evaluating the arguments of various groups concerning certain proposed legislation

Line   It is an odd but indisputable fact that the seventeenth-century English women who are generally regarded as among the forerunners of modern feminism are almost all identified with the
(5)   Royalist side in the conflict between Royalists and Parliamentarians known as the English Civil Wars. Since Royalist ideology is often associated with the radical patriarchalism of seventeenth-century political theorist Robert Filmer—a patriarchalism
(10)   that equates family and kingdom and asserts the divinely ordained absolute power of the king and, by analogy, of the male head of the household— historians have been understandably puzzled by the fact that Royalist women wrote the earliest
(15)   extended criticisms of the absolute subordination of women in marriage and the earliest systematic assertions of women's rational and moral equality with men. Some historians have questioned the facile equation of Royalist ideology with Filmerian
(20)   patriarchalism; and indeed, there may have been no consistent differences between Royalists and Parliamentarians on issues of family organization and women's political rights, but in that case one would expect early feminists to be equally divided
(25)   between the two sides.
    Catherine Gallagher argues that Royalism engendered feminism because the ideology of absolute monarchy provided a transition to an ideology of the absolute self. She cites the example
(30)   of the notoriously eccentric author Margaret Cavendish (1626–1673), duchess of Newcastle. Cavendish claimed to be as ambitious as any woman could be, but knowing that as a woman she was excluded from the pursuit of power in the real
(35)   world, she resolved to be mistress of her own world, the "immaterial world" that any person can create within her own mind—and, as a writer, on paper. In proclaiming what she called her "singularity," Cavendish insisted that she was a
(40)   self-sufficient being within her mental empire, the center of her own subjective universe rather than a satellite orbiting a dominant male planet. In justifying this absolute singularity, Cavendish repeatedly invoked the model of the absolute
(45)   monarch, a figure that became a metaphor for the self-enclosed, autonomous nature of the individual person. Cavendish's successors among early feminists retained her notion of woman's sovereign self, but they also sought to break free from the
(50)   complete political and social isolation that her absolute singularity entailed.

Questions 605–610 refer to the passage.

605. The author of the passage refers to Robert Filmer (see line 9) primarily in order to

(A)   show that Royalist ideology was somewhat more radical than most historians appear to realize

(B)   qualify the claim that patriarchalism formed the basis of Royalist ideology

(C)   question the view that most early feminists were associated with the Royalist faction

(D)   highlight an apparent tension between Royalist ideology and the ideas of early feminists

(E)   argue that Royalists held conflicting opinions on issues of family organization and women's political rights

606. The passage suggests which of the following about the seventeenth-century English women mentioned in line 2?

(A)   Their status as forerunners of modern feminism is not entirely justified.

(B)   They did not openly challenge the radical patriarchalism of Royalist Filmerian ideology.

(C)   Cavendish was the first among these women to criticize women's subordination in marriage and assert women's equality with men.

(D)   Their views on family organization and women's political rights were diametrically opposed to those of both Royalist and Parliamentarian ideology.

(E)   Historians would be less puzzled if more of them were identified with the Parliamentarian side in the English Civil Wars.

607. The passage suggests that Margaret Cavendish's decision to become an author was motivated, at least in part, by a desire to

   (A) justify her support for the Royalist cause

   (B) encourage her readers to work toward eradicating Filmerian patriarchalism

   (C) persuade other women to break free from their political and social isolation

   (D) analyze the causes for women's exclusion from the pursuit of power

   (E) create a world over which she could exercise total control

608. The phrase "a satellite orbiting a dominant male planet" (lines 41–42) refers most directly to

   (A) Cavendish's concept that each woman is a sovereign self

   (B) the complete political and social isolation of absolute singularity

   (C) the immaterial world that a writer can create on paper

   (D) the absolute subordination of women in a patriarchal society

   (E) the metaphorical figure of the absolute monarch

609. The primary purpose of the passage is to

   (A) trace the historical roots of a modern sociopolitical movement

   (B) present one scholar's explanation for a puzzling historical phenomenon

   (C) contrast two interpretations of the ideological origins of a political conflict

   (D) establish a link between the ideology of an influential political theorist and that of a notoriously eccentric writer

   (E) call attention to some points of agreement between opposing sides in an ideological debate

610. Which of the following, if true, would most clearly undermine Gallagher's explanation of the link between Royalism and feminism?

   (A) Because of their privileged backgrounds, Royalist women were generally better educated than were their Parliamentarian counterparts.

   (B) Filmer himself had read some of Cavendish's early writings and was highly critical of her ideas.

   (C) Cavendish's views were highly individual and were not shared by the other Royalist women who wrote early feminist works.

   (D) The Royalist and Parliamentarian ideologies were largely in agreement on issues of family organization and women's political rights.

   (E) The Royalist side included a sizable minority faction that was opposed to the more radical tendencies of Filmerian patriarchalism.

Line   There are recent reports of apparently drastic
declines in amphibian populations and of extinctions
of a number of the world's endangered amphibian
species. These declines, if real, may be signs of a
(5)   general trend toward extinction, and many
environmentalists have claimed that immediate
environmental action is necessary to remedy
this "amphibian crisis," which, in their view, is an
indicator of general and catastrophic environmental
(10)   degradation due to human activity.
        To evaluate these claims, it is useful to make a
preliminary distinction that is far too often ignored.
A declining population should not be confused with
an endangered one. An endangered population is
(15)   always rare, almost always small, and, by definition,
under constant threat of extinction even without a
proximate cause in human activities. Its disappearance,
however unfortunate, should come as no great
surprise. Moreover, chance events—which may
(20)   indicate nothing about the direction of trends in
population size—may lead to its extinction. The
probability of extinction due to such random factors
depends on the population size and is independent of
the prevailing direction of change in that size.
(25)   For biologists, population declines are potentially
more worrisome than extinctions. Persistent
declines, especially in large populations, indicate a
changed ecological context. Even here, distinctions
must again be made among declines that are only
(30)   apparent (in the sense that they are part of habitual
cycles or of normal fluctuations), declines that take
a population to some lower but still acceptable
level, and those that threaten extinction (e.g., by
taking the number of individuals below the minimum
(35)   viable population). Anecdotal reports of population
decreases cannot distinguish among these
possibilities, and some amphibian populations have
shown strong fluctuations in the past.
        It is indisputably true that there is simply not
(40)   enough long-term scientific data on amphibian
populations to enable researchers to identify real
declines in amphibian populations. Many fairly
common amphibian species declared all but extinct
after severe declines in the 1950s and 1960s
(45)   have subsequently recovered, and so might
the apparently declining populations that have
generated the current appearance of an amphibian
crisis. Unfortunately, long-term data will not soon
be forthcoming, and postponing environmental
(50)   action while we wait for it may doom species and
whole ecosystems to extinction.

Questions 611–616 refer to the passage.

611. The primary purpose of the passage is to

(A)   assess the validity of a certain view

(B)   distinguish between two phenomena

(C)   identify the causes of a problem

(D)   describe a disturbing trend

(E)   allay concern about a particular phenomenon

612. It can be inferred from the passage that the author
believes which of the following to be true of the
environmentalists mentioned in lines 5–6?

(A)   They have wrongly chosen to focus on anecdotal
reports rather than on the long-term data that
are currently available concerning amphibians.

(B)   Their recommendations are flawed because
their research focuses too narrowly on a single
category of animal species.

(C)   Their certainty that population declines in general
are caused by environmental degradation is not
warranted.

(D)   They have drawn premature conclusions
concerning a crisis in amphibian populations
from recent reports of declines.

(E)   They have overestimated the effects of chance
events on trends in amphibian populations.

613. It can be inferred from the passage that the author
believes which of the following to be true of the
amphibian extinctions that have recently been
reported?

(A)   They have resulted primarily from human
activities causing environmental degradation.

(B)   They could probably have been prevented if
timely action had been taken to protect the
habitats of amphibian species.

(C)   They should not come as a surprise, because
amphibian populations generally have been
declining for a number of years.

(D)   They have probably been caused by a
combination of chance events.

(E)   They do not clearly constitute evidence of
general environmental degradation.

614. According to the passage, each of the following is true of endangered amphibian species EXCEPT:

(A)   They are among the rarest kinds of amphibians.

(B)   They generally have populations that are small in size.

(C)   They are in constant danger of extinction.

(D)   Those with decreasing populations are the most likely candidates for immediate extinction.

(E)   They are in danger of extinction due to events that sometimes have nothing to do with human activities.

615. Which of the following most accurately describes the organization of the passage?

(A)   A question is raised, a distinction regarding it is made, and the question is answered.

(B)   An interpretation is presented, its soundness is examined, and a warning is given.

(C)   A situation is described, its consequences are analyzed, and a prediction is made.

(D)   Two interpretations of a phenomenon are described, and one of them is rejected as invalid.

(E)   Two methods for analyzing a phenomenon are compared, and further study of the phenomenon is recommended.

616. Which of the following best describes the function of the sentence in lines 35–38?

(A)   To give an example of a particular kind of study

(B)   To cast doubt on an assertion made in the previous sentence

(C)   To raise an objection to a view presented in the first paragraph

(D)   To provide support for a view presented in the first paragraph

(E)   To introduce an idea that will be countered in the following paragraph

Line   While the most abundant and dominant species
within a particular ecosystem is often crucial in
perpetuating the ecosystem, a "keystone" species,
here defined as one whose effects are much larger
(5)   than would be predicted from its abundance, can
also play a vital role. But because complex species
interactions may be involved, identifying a keystone
species by removing the species and observing
changes in the ecosystem is problematic. It might
(10)   seem that certain traits would clearly define a species
as a keystone species; for example,
Pisaster ochraceus is often a keystone predator
because it consumes and suppresses mussel
populations, which in the absence of this starfish
(15)   can be a dominant species. But such predation on a
dominant or potentially dominant species occurs in
systems that do as well as in systems that do not
have species that play keystone roles. Moreover,
whereas *P. ochraceus* occupies an unambiguous
(20)   keystone role on wave-exposed rocky headlands,
in more wave-sheltered habitats the impact of
P. ochraceus predation is weak or nonexistent,
and at certain sites sand burial is responsible for
eliminating mussels. Keystone status appears to
(25)   depend on context, whether of particular
geography or of such factors as community
diversity (for example, a reduction in species
diversity may thrust more of the remaining species
into keystone roles) and length of species
(30)   interaction (since newly arrived species in particular
may dramatically affect ecosystems).

Questions 617–620 refer to the passage.

617. The passage mentions which of the following as
a factor that affects the role of *P. ochraceus* as a
keystone species within different habitats?

(A) The degree to which the habitat is sheltered from
waves

(B) The degree to which other animals within a
habitat prey on mussels

(C) The fact that mussel populations are often not
dominant within some habitats occupied by
P. ochraceus

(D) The size of the *P. ochraceus* population within
the habitat

(E) The fact that there is great species diversity
within some habitats occupied by *P. ochraceus*

618. Which of the following hypothetical experiments most
clearly exemplifies the method of identifying species'
roles that the author considers problematic?

(A) A population of seals in an Arctic habitat is
counted in order to determine whether it is the
dominant species in that ecosystem.

(B) A species of fish that is a keystone species in
one marine ecosystem is introduced into another
marine ecosystem to see whether the species
will come to occupy a keystone role.

(C) In order to determine whether a species of
monkey is a keystone species within a particular
ecosystem, the monkeys are removed from that
ecosystem and the ecosystem is then studied.

(D) Different mountain ecosystems are compared to
determine how geography affects a particular
species' ability to dominate its ecosystem.

(E) In a grassland experiencing a changing climate,
patterns of species extinction are traced in order
to evaluate the effect of climate changes on
keystone species in that grassland.

619. Which of the following, if true, would most clearly support the argument about keystone status advanced in the last sentence of the passage (lines 24–31)?

(A) A species of bat is primarily responsible for keeping insect populations within an ecosystem low, and the size of the insect population in turn affects bird species within that ecosystem.

(B) A species of iguana occupies a keystone role on certain tropical islands but does not play that role on adjacent tropical islands that are inhabited by a greater number of animal species.

(C) Close observation of a savannah ecosystem reveals that more species occupy keystone roles within that ecosystem than biologists had previously believed.

(D) As a keystone species of bee becomes more abundant, it has a larger effect on the ecosystem it inhabits.

(E) A species of moth that occupies a keystone role in a prairie habitat develops coloration patterns that camouflage it from potential predators.

620. The passage suggests which of the following about the identification of a species as a keystone species?

(A) Such an identification depends primarily on the species' relationship to the dominant species.

(B) Such an identification can best be made by removing the species from a particular ecosystem and observing changes that occur in the ecosystem.

(C) Such an identification is likely to be less reliable as an ecosystem becomes less diverse.

(D) Such an identification seems to depend on various factors within the ecosystem.

(E) Such an identification can best be made by observing predation behavior.

Line   Conodonts, the spiky phosphatic remains (bones and teeth composed of calcium phosphate) of tiny marine animals that probably appeared about 520 million years ago, were once among the most

(5) controversial of fossils. Both the nature of the organism to which the remains belonged and the function of the remains were unknown. However, since the 1981 discovery of fossils preserving not just the phosphatic elements but also other remains

(10) of the tiny soft-bodied animals (also called conodonts) that bore them, scientists' reconstructions of the animals' anatomy have had important implications for hypotheses concerning the development of the vertebrate skeleton.

(15)   The vertebrate skeleton had traditionally been regarded as a defensive development, champions of this view postulating that it was only with the much later evolution of jaws that vertebrates became predators. The first vertebrates, which were soft-

(20) bodied, would have been easy prey for numerous invertebrate carnivores, especially if these early vertebrates were sedentary suspension feeders. Thus, traditionalists argued, these animals developed coverings of bony scales or plates, and teeth were

(25) secondary features, adapted from the protective bony scales. Indeed, external skeletons of this type are common among the well-known fossils of ostracoderms, jawless vertebrates that existed from approximately 500 to 400 million years ago.

(30) However, other paleontologists argued that many of the definitive characteristics of vertebrates, such as paired eyes and muscular and skeletal adaptations for active life, would not have evolved unless the first vertebrates were predatory. Teeth were more

(35) primitive than external armor according to this view, and the earliest vertebrates were predators.

    The stiffening notochord along the back of the body, V-shaped muscle blocks along the sides, and posterior tail fins help to identify conodonts as

(40) among the most primitive of vertebrates. The lack of any mineralized structures apart from the elements in the mouth indicates that conodonts were more primitive than the armored jawless fishes such as the ostracoderms. It now appears that the hard parts that

(45) first evolved in the mouth of an animal improved its efficiency as a predator, and that aggression rather than protection was the driving force behind the origin of the vertebrate skeleton.

Questions 621–623 refer to the passage.

621. According to the passage, the anatomical evidence provided by the preserved soft bodies of conodonts led scientists to conclude that

(A) conodonts had actually been invertebrate carnivores

(B) conodonts' teeth were adapted from protective bony scales

(C) conodonts were primitive vertebrate suspension feeders

(D) primitive vertebrates with teeth appeared earlier than armored vertebrates

(E) scientists' original observations concerning the phosphatic remains of conodonts were essentially correct

622. The second paragraph in the passage serves primarily to

(A) outline the significance of the 1981 discovery of conodont remains to the debate concerning the development of the vertebrate skeleton

(B) contrast the traditional view of the development of the vertebrate skeleton with a view derived from the 1981 discovery of conodont remains

(C) contrast the characteristics of the ostracoderms with the characteristics of earlier soft-bodied vertebrates

(D) explain the importance of the development of teeth among the earliest vertebrate predators

(E) present the two sides of the debate concerning the development of the vertebrate skeleton

623. It can be inferred that on the basis of the 1981 discovery of conodont remains, paleontologists could draw which of the following conclusions?

(A) The earliest vertebrates were sedentary suspension feeders.

(B) Ostracoderms were not the earliest vertebrates.

(C) Defensive armor preceded jaws among vertebrates.

(D) Paired eyes and adaptations for activity are definitive characteristics of vertebrates.

(E) Conodonts were unlikely to have been predators.

Line   Because the framers of the United States
        Constitution (written in 1787) believed that protecting
        property rights relating to inventions would encourage
        the new nation's economic growth, they gave
(5)   Congress—the national legislature—a constitutional
        mandate to grant patents for inventions. The resulting
        patent system has served as a model for those in
        other nations. Recently, however, scholars have
        questioned whether the American system helped
(10)   achieve the framers' goals. These scholars have
        contended that from 1794 to roughly 1830, American
        inventors were unable to enforce property rights
        because judges were "antipatent" and routinely
        invalidated patents for arbitrary reasons. This
(15)   argument is based partly on examination of court
        decisions in cases where patent holders ("patentees")
        brought suit alleging infringement of their patent
        rights. In the 1820s, for instance, 75 percent
        of verdicts were decided against the patentee.
(20)   The proportion of verdicts for the patentee began to
        increase in the 1830s, suggesting to these scholars
        that judicial attitudes toward patent rights began
        shifting then.
            Not all patent disputes in the early nineteenth
(25)   century were litigated, however, and litigated
        cases were not drawn randomly from the
        population of disputes. Therefore, the rate of
        verdicts in favor of patentees cannot be used
        by itself to gauge changes in judicial attitudes
(30)   or enforceability of patent rights. If early judicial
        decisions were prejudiced against patentees, one
        might expect that subsequent courts—allegedly
        more supportive of patent rights—would reject
        the former legal precedents. But pre-1830
(35)   cases have been cited as frequently as later
        decisions, and they continue to be cited today,
        suggesting that the early decisions, many of
        which clearly declared that patent rights were
        a just recompense for inventive ingenuity,
(40)   provided a lasting foundation for patent law.
        The proportion of judicial decisions in favor of
        patentees began to increase during the 1830s
        because of a change in the underlying population
        of cases brought to trial. This change was partly
(45)   due to an 1836 revision to the patent system:
        an examination procedure, still in use today, was
        instituted in which each application is scrutinized
        for its adherence to patent law. Previously,
        patents were automatically granted upon payment
(50)   of a $30 fee.

Questions 624–628 refer to the passage.

624. The passage implies that which of the following was a reason that the proportion of verdicts in favor of patentees began to increase in the 1830s?

(A)   Patent applications approved after 1836 were more likely to adhere closely to patent law.

(B)   Patent laws enacted during the 1830s better defined patent rights.

(C)   Judges became less prejudiced against patentees during the 1830s.

(D)   After 1836, litigated cases became less representative of the population of patent disputes.

(E)   The proportion of patent disputes brought to trial began to increase after 1836.

625. The passage implies that the scholars mentioned in line 8 would agree with which of the following criticisms of the American patent system before 1830?

(A)   Its definition of property rights relating to inventions was too vague to be useful.

(B)   Its criteria for the granting of patents were not clear.

(C)   It made it excessively difficult for inventors to receive patents.

(D)   It led to excessive numbers of patent-infringement suits.

(E)   It failed to encourage national economic growth.

626. It can be inferred from the passage that the frequency with which pre-1830 cases have been cited in court decisions is an indication that

(A)   judicial support for patent rights was strongest in the period before 1830

(B)   judicial support for patent rights did not increase after 1830

(C)   courts have returned to judicial standards that prevailed before 1830

(D)   verdicts favoring patentees in patent-infringement suits did not increase after 1830

(E)   judicial bias against patentees persisted after 1830

627. It can be inferred from the passage that the author and the scholars referred to in line 21 disagree about which of the following aspects of the patents defended in patent-infringement suits before 1830?

   (A) Whether the patents were granted for inventions that were genuinely useful

   (B) Whether the patents were actually relevant to the growth of the United States economy

   (C) Whether the patents were particularly likely to be annulled by judges

   (D) Whether the patents were routinely invalidated for reasons that were arbitrary

   (E) Whether the patents were vindicated at a significantly lower rate than patents in later suits

628. The author of the passage cites which of the following as evidence challenging the argument referred to in lines 14–15?

   (A) The proportion of cases that were decided against patentees in the 1820s

   (B) The total number of patent disputes that were litigated from 1794 to 1830

   (C) The fact that later courts drew upon the legal precedents set in pre-1830 patent cases

   (D) The fact that the proportion of judicial decisions in favor of patentees began to increase during the 1830s

   (E) The constitutional rationale for the 1836 revision of the patent system

Line Jacob Burckhardt's view that Renaissance European women "stood on a footing of perfect equality" with Renaissance men has been repeatedly cited by feminist scholars as a prelude to their
(5) presentation of rich historical evidence of women's inequality. In striking contrast to Burckhardt, Joan Kelly in her famous 1977 essay, "Did Women Have a Renaissance?" argued that the Renaissance was a period of economic and social decline for women
(10) relative both to Renaissance men and to medieval women. Recently, however, a significant trend among feminist scholars has entailed a rejection of both Kelly's dark vision of the Renaissance and Burckhardt's rosy one. Many recent works by these
(15) scholars stress the ways in which differences among Renaissance women—especially in terms of social status and religion—work to complicate the kinds of generalizations both Burckhardt and Kelly made on the basis of their observations about
(20) upper-class Italian women.

The trend is also evident, however, in works focusing on those middle- and upper-class European women whose ability to write gives them disproportionate representation in the historical
(25) record. Such women were, simply by virtue of their literacy, members of a tiny minority of the population, so it is risky to take their descriptions of their experiences as typical of "female experience" in any general sense. Tina Krontiris, for example, in
(30) her fascinating study of six Renaissance women writers, does tend at times to conflate "women" and "women writers," assuming that women's gender, irrespective of other social differences, including literacy, allows us to view women as a homogeneous
(35) social group and make that group an object of analysis. Nonetheless, Krontiris makes a significant contribution to the field and is representative of those authors who offer what might be called a cautiously optimistic assessment of Renaissance
(40) women's achievements, although she also stresses the social obstacles Renaissance women faced when they sought to raise their "oppositional voices." Krontiris is concerned to show women intentionally negotiating some power for themselves
(45) (at least in the realm of public discourse) against potentially constraining ideologies, but in her sober and thoughtful concluding remarks, she suggests that such verbal opposition to cultural stereotypes was highly circumscribed; women seldom attacked
(50) the basic assumptions in the ideologies that oppressed them.

Questions 629–635 refer to the passage.

629. The author of the passage discusses Krontiris primarily to provide an example of a writer who

(A) is highly critical of the writings of certain Renaissance women

(B) supports Kelly's view of women's status during the Renaissance

(C) has misinterpreted the works of certain Renaissance women

(D) has rejected the views of both Burckhardt and Kelly

(E) has studied Renaissance women in a wide variety of social and religious contexts

630. According to the passage, Krontiris's work differs from that of the scholars mentioned in line 12 in which of the following ways?

(A) Krontiris's work stresses the achievements of Renaissance women rather than the obstacles to their success.

(B) Krontiris's work is based on a reinterpretation of the work of earlier scholars.

(C) Krontiris's views are at odds with those of both Kelly and Burkhardt.

(D) Krontiris's work focuses on the place of women in Renaissance society.

(E) Krontiris's views are based exclusively on the study of a privileged group of women.

631. According to the passage, feminist scholars cite Burckhardt's view of Renaissance women primarily for which of the following reasons?

(A) Burckhardt's view forms the basis for most arguments refuting Kelly's point of view.

(B) Burckhardt's view has been discredited by Kelly.

(C) Burckhardt's view is one that many feminist scholars wish to refute.

(D) Burckhardt's work provides rich historical evidence of inequality between Renaissance women and men.

(E) Burckhardt's work includes historical research supporting the arguments of the feminist scholars.

632. It can be inferred that both Burckhardt and Kelly have been criticized by the scholars mentioned in line 12 for which of the following?

(A) Assuming that women writers of the Renaissance are representative of Renaissance women in general

(B) Drawing conclusions that are based on the study of an atypical group of women

(C) Failing to describe clearly the relationship between social status and literacy among Renaissance women

(D) Failing to acknowledge the role played by Renaissance women in opposing cultural stereotypes

(E) Failing to acknowledge the ways in which social status affected the creative activities of Renaissance women

633. The author of the passage suggests that Krontiris incorrectly assumes that

(A) social differences among Renaissance women are less important than the fact that they were women

(B) literacy among Renaissance women was more prevalent than most scholars today acknowledge

(C) during the Renaissance, women were able to successfully oppose cultural stereotypes relating to gender

(D) Renaissance women did not face many difficult social obstacles relating to their gender

(E) in order to attain power, Renaissance women attacked basic assumptions in the ideologies that oppressed them

634. The last sentence in the passage serves primarily to

(A) suggest that Krontiris's work is not representative of recent trends among feminist scholars

(B) undermine the argument that literate women of the Renaissance sought to oppose social constraints imposed on them

(C) show a way in which Krontiris's work illustrates a "cautiously optimistic" assessment of Renaissance women's achievements

(D) summarize Krontiris's view of the effect of literacy on the lives of upper- and middle-class Renaissance women

(E) illustrate the way in which Krontiris's study differs from the studies done by Burckhardt and Kelly

635. The author of the passage implies that the women studied by Krontiris are unusual in which of the following ways?

(A) They faced obstacles less formidable than those faced by other Renaissance women.

(B) They have been seen by historians as more interesting than other Renaissance women.

(C) They were more concerned about recording history accurately than were other Renaissance women.

(D) Their perceptions are more likely to be accessible to historians than are those of most other Renaissance women.

(E) Their concerns are likely to be of greater interest to feminist scholars than are the ideas of most other Renaissance women.

Line   When asteroids collide, some collisions cause
an asteroid to spin faster; others slow it down. If
asteroids are all monoliths—single rocks—undergoing
random collisions, a graph of their rotation rates
(5)   should show a bell-shaped distribution with statistical
"tails" of very fast and very slow rotators. If asteroids
are rubble piles, however, the tail representing the
very fast rotators would be missing, because any
loose aggregate spinning faster than once every few
(10)   hours (depending on the asteroid's bulk density)
would fly apart. Researchers have discovered that
all but five observed asteroids obey a strict limit on
rate of rotation. The exceptions are all smaller than
200 meters in diameter, with an abrupt cutoff for
(15)   asteroids larger than that.
    The evident conclusion—that asteroids larger than
200 meters across are multicomponent structures or
rubble piles—agrees with recent computer modeling
of collisions, which also finds a transition at that
(20)   diameter. A collision can blast a large asteroid to bits,
but after the collision, those bits will usually move
slower than their mutual escape velocity. Over several
hours, gravity will reassemble all but the fastest
pieces into a rubble pile. Because collisions among
(25)   asteroids are relatively frequent, most large bodies
have already suffered this fate. Conversely, most
small asteroids should be monolithic, because impact
fragments easily escape their feeble gravity.

Questions 636–639 refer to the passage.

636. The passage implies which of the following about the five asteroids mentioned in line 12?

(A)   Their rotation rates are approximately the same.

(B)   They have undergone approximately the same number of collisions.

(C)   They are monoliths.

(D)   They are composed of fragments that have escaped the gravity of larger asteroids.

(E)   They were detected only recently.

637. The discovery of which of the following would call into question the conclusion mentioned in line 16?

(A)   An asteroid 100 meters in diameter rotating at a rate of once per week

(B)   An asteroid 150 meters in diameter rotating at a rate of 20 times per hour

(C)   An asteroid 250 meters in diameter rotating at a rate of once per week

(D)   An asteroid 500 meters in diameter rotating at a rate of once per hour

(E)   An asteroid 1,000 meters in diameter rotating at a rate of once every 24 hours

638. According to the passage, which of the following is a prediction that is based on the strength of the gravitational attraction of small asteroids?

(A)   Small asteroids will be few in number.

(B)   Small asteroids will be monoliths.

(C)   Small asteroids will collide with other asteroids very rarely.

(D)   Most small asteroids will have very fast rotation rates.

(E)   Almost no small asteroids will have very slow rotation rates.

639. The author of the passage mentions "escape velocity" (see line 22) in order to help explain which of the following?

(A) The tendency for asteroids to become smaller rather than larger over time

(B) The speed with which impact fragments reassemble when they do not escape an asteroid's gravitational attraction after a collision

(C) The frequency with which collisions among asteroids occur

(D) The rotation rates of asteroids smaller than 200 meters in diameter

(E) The tendency for large asteroids to persist after collisions

Line   Most attempts by physicists to send particles faster than the speed of light involve a remarkable phenomenon called quantum tunneling, in which particles travel through solid barriers that appear

(5) to be impenetrable. If you throw a ball at a wall, you expect it to bounce back, not to pass straight through it. Yet subatomic particles perform the equivalent feat. Quantum theory says that there is a distinct, albeit small, probability that such a particle

(10) will tunnel its way through a barrier; the probability declines exponentially as the thickness of the barrier increases. Though the extreme rapidity of quantum tunneling was noted as early as 1932, not until 1955 was it hypothesized—by Wigner and

(15) Eisenbud—that tunneling particles sometimes travel faster than light. Their grounds were calculations that suggested that the time it takes a particle to tunnel through a barrier increases with the thickness of the barrier until tunneling time

(20) reaches a maximum; beyond that maximum, tunneling time stays the same regardless of barrier thickness. This would imply that once maximum tunneling time is reached, tunneling speed will increase without limit as barrier thickness increases. Several recent

(25) experiments have supported this hypothesis that tunneling particles sometimes reach superluminal speed. According to measurements performed by Raymond Chiao and colleagues, for example, photons can pass through an optical filter at 1.7 times the

(30) speed of light.

Questions 640–642 refer to the passage.

640. The author of the passage mentions calculations about tunneling time and barrier thickness in order to

    (A)   suggest that tunneling time is unrelated to barrier thickness

    (B)   explain the evidence by which Wigner and Eisenbud discovered the phenomenon of tunneling

    (C)   describe data recently challenged by Raymond Chiao and colleagues

    (D)   question why particles engaged in quantum tunneling rarely achieve extremely high speeds

    (E)   explain the basis for Wigner and Eisenbud's hypothesis

641. The passage implies that if tunneling time reached no maximum in increasing with barrier thickness, then

    (A)   tunneling speed would increase with barrier thickness

    (B)   tunneling speed would decline with barrier thickness

    (C)   tunneling speed would vary with barrier thickness

    (D)   tunneling speed would not be expected to increase without limit

    (E)   successful tunneling would occur even less frequently than it does

642. Which of the following statements about the earliest scientific investigators of quantum tunneling can be inferred from the passage?

    (A)   They found it difficult to increase barrier thickness continually.

    (B)   They anticipated the later results of Chiao and his colleagues.

    (C)   They did not suppose that tunneling particles could travel faster than light.

    (D)   They were unable to observe instances of successful tunneling.

    (E)   They made use of photons to study the phenomenon of tunneling.

Line   Economic historians usually assume that the size
of animal herds maintained by medieval European
farmers was inversely related to medieval cereal
production: Land devoted to crop farming could

(5)   not be used for pasturing animals, and vice versa.
Thus, one historian has postulated a pastoral
crisis in thirteenth-century Europe, arguing that the
amount of pastureland, and hence herd size, must
have diminished during the period, since cereal

(10)   harvests are known to have increased. However, the
rising costs of pasturage in the thirteenth century,
which this historian cites as evidence of a shortage
caused by declines in pastureland acreage, could
have resulted instead from increased demand for

(15)   pasturage as wool prices rose and sheep flocks
grew. In fact, although one study did find high
volumes of cereal production together with low ratios
of pastureland to cropland in some regions in the
thirteenth century, these higher cereal yields could

(20)   have resulted from new institutional arrangements
governing agricultural work rather than from increases
in cropland acreage. Furthermore, even a decrease in
pastureland acreage may be an ambiguous indicator
of herd sizes—for example, as the medieval economy

(25)   became increasingly oriented to markets, farmers
may have expanded production of cereals such as
oats to feed the working draft animals (oxen and
horses) they needed to haul their crops to market.

Questions 643–644 refer to the passage.

643. In lines 10–16, the author mentions possible rises in
wool prices primarily in order to

(A)   identify a factor capable of causing declines
in total pastureland acreage without causing
declines in herd sizes in the thirteenth century

(B)   provide an example of a likely market response
to a thirteenth-century pastoral crisis that
reduced pastureland acreage

(C)   identify a possible area of disagreement between
most economic historians and the historians
who postulate a pastoral crisis in the thirteenth
century

(D)   suggest a reason why the cost of pastureland
could have risen in the thirteenth century even
without declines in pasture acreage

(E)   cite evidence supporting the conclusion that herd
sizes increased during the thirteenth century

644. Which of the following, if true, would cast most doubt
on the argument of the historian mentioned in
lines 10–16

(A)   The thirteenth century was a comparatively
prosperous period during which population
increased and new markets for agricultural
goods emerged in Europe.

(B)   During the medieval period, wool prices in
Europe tended to rise slightly in response to
decreases in herd sizes.

(C)   New institutional arrangements governing
agricultural work were not established in the
thirteenth century in areas of Europe until the
fourteenth century.

(D)   Most farmers in thirteenth-century Europe would
not have been able to afford draft animals to
transport their crops to market.

(E)   The clearing of forests and the draining of
swamps significantly increased the total acreage
of land available to European farmers in the
thirteenth century.

8.5 Answer Key: Reading Comprehension

505.	D	533.	B	561.	A	589.	E	617.	A
506.	D	534.	D	562.	B	590.	D	618.	C
507.	B	535.	A	563.	C	591.	E	619.	B
508.	B	536.	E	564.	A	592.	B	620.	D
509.	C	537.	D	565.	E	593.	C	621.	D
510.	C	538.	B	566.	D	594.	C	622.	E
511.	D	539.	C	567.	C	595.	E	623.	B
512.	C	540.	C	568.	B	596.	B	624.	A
513.	A	541.	B	569.	A	597.	D	625.	E
514.	C	542.	A	570.	E	598.	B	626.	B
515.	D	543.	D	571.	A	599.	A	627.	D
516.	A	544.	B	572.	D	600.	D	628.	C
517.	D	545.	E	573.	D	601.	B	629.	D
518.	B	546.	A	574.	D	602.	E	630.	B
519.	C	547.	D	575.	B	603.	A	631.	C
520.	E	548.	B	576.	B	604.	B	632.	B
521.	B	549.	C	577.	C	605.	D	633.	A
522.	D	550.	B	578.	C	606.	E	634.	C
523.	C	551.	A	579.	E	607.	E	635.	D
524.	D	552.	E	580.	C	608.	D	636.	C
525.	B	553.	A	581.	E	609.	B	637.	D
526.	B	554.	B	582.	D	610.	C	638.	B
527.	C	555.	C	583.	B	611.	A	639.	E
528.	D	556.	C	584.	C	612.	D	640.	E
529.	A	557.	A	585.	C	613.	B	641.	C
530.	D	558.	D	586.	B	614.	D	642.	C
531.	B	559.	D	587.	B	615.	B	643.	D
532.	B	560.	E	588.	E	616.	C	644.	E

8.6 Answer Explanations: Reading Comprehension

The following discussion of Reading Comprehension is intended to familiarize you with the most efficient and effective approaches to the kinds of problems common to Reading Comprehension. The particular questions in this chapter are generally representative of the kinds of Reading Comprehension questions you will encounter on the GMAT exam. Remember that it is the problem-solving strategy that is important, not the specific details of a particular question.

Questions 505–547 — Difficulty: Easy

Questions 505–507 refer to the passage on page 458.

505. The primary purpose of the passage is to

    (A) challenge recent findings that appear to contradict earlier findings

    (B) present two sides of an ongoing scientific debate

    (C) report answers to several questions that have long puzzled researchers

    (D) discuss evidence that has caused a long-standing belief to be revised

    (E) attempt to explain a commonly misunderstood biological phenomenon

Main Idea

This question depends on understanding the passage as a whole. The passage begins by describing a long-held belief regarding humans' circadian rhythms: that the SCNs control them. It then goes on to explain that new findings have led scientists to believe that other organs and tissues may be involved in regulating the body's circadian rhythms as well.

A   The passage does not challenge the more-recent findings. Furthermore, the recent findings that the passage recounts do not contradict earlier findings; rather, when placed alongside those earlier findings, they have led scientists to reach additional conclusions.

B   The passage does not discuss a two-sided debate; no findings or conclusions are disputed by any figures in the passages.

C   There is only one question at issue in the passage: whether the SCN alone control human circadian rhythms. Furthermore, nothing in the passage suggests that researchers have been puzzled for a long time about this.

D   **Correct.** The new evidence regarding circadian rhythm–related gene activity in all the body's tissue has led scientists to revise their long-standing belief that the SCN alone control circadian rhythms.

E   The biological phenomenon of circadian rhythms is not, at least as far as the passage is concerned, misunderstood. Its causes are being investigated and refined.

The correct answer is D.

506. The passage mentions each of the following as a function regulated by the SCNs in some animals EXCEPT:

    (A) activity level

    (B) blood pressure

    (C) alertness

    (D) vision

    (E) temperature

Supporting Idea

This question asks about what is NOT specifically mentioned in the passage with regard to functions regulated by the SCN. Those functions, as identified in the passage, are blood pressure, body temperature, activity level, alertness, and the release of melatonin.

A   The passage includes activity level in its list of functions regulated by the SCN.

B   The passage includes blood pressure in its list of functions regulated by the SCN.

C   The passage includes alertness in its list of functions regulated by the SCN.

D   Correct. While the passage does say that cells in the human retina transmit information to the SCN, there is no suggestion that the SCN reciprocally control vision.

E   The passage includes temperature in its list of functions regulated by the SCN.

The correct answer is D.

507.   The author of the passage would probably agree with which of the following statements about the SCNs?

(A)   The SCNs are found in other organs and tissues of the body besides the hypothalamus.

(B)   The SCNs play a critical but not exclusive role in regulating circadian rhythms.

(C)   The SCNs control clock genes in a number of tissues and organs throughout the body.

(D)   The SCNs are a less significant factor in regulating blood pressure than scientists once believed.

(E)   The SCNs are less strongly affected by changes in light levels than they are by other external cues.

Application

The author of the passage states in the second paragraph, *Four critical genes governing circadian cycles have been found to be active in every tissue, however, not just in the SCNs, of flies, mice, and humans.* The author goes on in that paragraph to point out that though scientists still accept the role of SCNs in *controlling core functions,* they *now believe that circadian clocks in other organs and tissues may respond to external cues other than light . . . that recur regularly every 24 hours.* The author nowhere disputes these beliefs, and so it is reasonable to conclude that the author of the passage agrees that these beliefs are true.

A   The author states that the SCNs are nerve clusters in the hypothalamus, and nothing in the passage contradicts or undermines the supposition that they are only in the hypothalamus.

B   Correct. The author indicates in the second paragraph that while scientists still believe that the SCNs control core circadian function, they also believe that circadian clocks found elsewhere in the body have an effect as well. Because the author nowhere disputes these beliefs, it is reasonable to conclude that the author would agree that SCNs play a critical but not exclusive role in regulating circadian rhythms.

C   The evidence offered in the second paragraph about the activity of the clock gene in rat livers suggests that these clock genes are not under the SCNs' control. The passage does not suggest that the SCNs control any of the non-SCN controllers of circadian rhythms.

D   The author states in the second paragraph that scientists do not dispute the idea that the SCNs regulate blood pressure.

E   The first paragraph indicates that the SCNs respond to light levels; clock genes in other tissues are the ones that may respond to other external cues.

The correct answer is B.

Questions 508–510 refer to the passage on page 460.

508. The primary purpose of the passage is to

(A) question the results of a study that examined the effect of service-quality guarantees in the restaurant industry

(B) discuss potential advantages and disadvantages of service-quality guarantees in the restaurant industry

(C) examine the conventional wisdom regarding the effect of service-quality guarantees in the restaurant industry

(D) argue that only certain restaurants would benefit from the implementation of service-quality guarantees

(E) consider the impact that service-quality guarantees can have on the service provided by a restaurant

Main Idea

This question depends on understanding the passage as a whole. The first paragraph describes Tucci and Talaga's findings regarding the effect of service-quality guarantees: that they have different, more positive results for higher-priced restaurants than for lower-priced ones, which could be affected negatively. The second paragraph explains that a particular benefit from service guarantees could accrue to restaurants generally.

A   The passage does not question the results of Tucci and Talaga's study; rather, the passage appears to accept the results of the study as accurate.

B   **Correct.** The potential advantages involve the management and motivation of service staff, as well as, for higher-priced restaurants, a greater likelihood of being selected by customers over other restaurants. Potential disadvantages for lower-priced restaurants include the possibility that potential customers may believe that such restaurants are concerned about the quality of their service.

C   The passage does not indicate whether there is any conventional wisdom regarding service-quality guarantees in the restaurant industry.

D   The second paragraph of the passage suggests that restaurants in general could potentially enjoy some benefits from the implementation of service-quality guarantees. For lower-priced restaurants, these benefits could offset the possible negative effects of service-quality guarantees described in the first paragraph.

E   The second paragraph of the passage indicates an effect that service-quality guarantees could have on a restaurant's staff and the service that the staff provides, but this is only one of the subsidiary points contributing to the focus of the passage as a whole. The first is more concerned with the question of what effect these guarantees would have on whether customers choose to patronize that restaurant.

The correct answer is B.

509. It can be inferred that the author of the passage would agree with which of the following statements about the appeal of service guarantees to customers?

(A) Such guarantees are likely to be somewhat more appealing to customers of restaurants than to customers of other businesses.

(B) Such guarantees are likely to be more appealing to customers who know what to anticipate in terms of service.

(C) Such guarantees are likely to have less appeal in situations where customers are knowledgeable about a business's product or service.

(D) In situations where a high level of financial commitment is involved, a service guarantee is not likely to be very appealing.

(E) In situations where customers expect a high level of customer service, a service guarantee is likely to make customers think that a business is worried about its service.

Inference

This question asks for an inference from the passage about the author's view of why and how service guarantees would appeal to customers. The question does not ask specifically about service guarantees in the context of restaurants, but rather service guarantees in general. The end of the first paragraph addresses this general question: a service guarantee may appeal most to customers in the case of activities whose quality they are less likely to know how to question.

A   The author states that a service guarantee might have greater appeal in the case of skilled activities than it would for restaurant customers.

B   According to the author, customers who know what to expect in terms of service—a group that includes restaurant customers— would likely find service guarantees less appealing.

C   **Correct.** The author makes clear that service guarantees would be less appealing to restaurant customers when they know what to expect in terms of the quality of service.

D   The passage provides some evidence that where a high level of financial commitment is involved, a service guarantee may be more rather than less appealing than in other situations. In discussing higher-priced restaurants, which require a relatively high level of financial commitment, the author states that Tucci and Talaga found evidence that a service guarantee would likely appeal to customers.

E   The author implies that customers of higher-priced restaurants expect a high level of service, certainly a level higher than that expected by customers of lower-priced restaurants. But it is at lower-priced restaurants that Tucci and Talaga found that a service guarantee makes customers think a given restaurant is concerned about its service.

The correct answer is C.

510. According to the passage, Tucci and Talaga found that service guarantees, when offered by lower-priced restaurants, can have which of the following effects?

(A)   Customers' developing unreasonably high expectations regarding service

(B)   Customers' avoiding such restaurants because they fear that the service guarantee may not be fully honored

(C)   Customers' interpreting the service guarantee as a sign that management is not confident about the quality of its service

(D)   A restaurant's becoming concerned that its service will not be assiduous enough to satisfy customers

(E)   A restaurant's becoming concerned that customers will be more emboldened to question the quality of the service they receive

Supporting Idea

This question requires identifying Tucci and Talaga's findings regarding service guarantees offered by lower-priced restaurants. The passage states directly that these researchers found in these situations that a guarantee could lead potential customers to think that the restaurant has concerns about its service.

A   The passage does not report that Tucci and Talaga found that service guarantees create unreasonably high expectations regarding service.

B   The passage does not report that Tucci and Talaga found that customers doubted that service guarantees would be honored.

C   **Correct.** The passage explicitly indicates that Tucci and Talaga found that potential customers of lower-priced restaurants could interpret service guarantees as indicating worries about the quality of service.

D   The passage indicates that Tucci and Talaga found that customers might think that lower-priced restaurants are offering service guarantees because they are concerned that the quality of their service is too low, but the passage does not indicate that service guarantees lead such restaurants to have concerns about the quality of their service, and in fact it may be that such guarantees could lead to improvements in service.

E   The passage indicates that service guarantees offered at lower-priced restaurants may empower customers to question the quality of service, but it does not indicate that service guarantees lead restaurants to have concerns about this.

The correct answer is C.

Questions 511–514 refer to the passage on page 462.

Main Idea Summary

The passage as a whole functions as an introduction to the notion of monetizing (i.e., putting a monetary value on) ecosystem functions. The passage begins by considering the argument for monetizing such functions and then considers David Pearce's claim that all ecosystems have economic value and that, by showing this, we can help overcome the illusion that conservation is relatively unprofitable. The passage concludes with Gretchen Daily's view that monetization will help inform environmental decision-making.

511. Information in the passage suggests that David Pearce would most readily endorse which of the following statements concerning monetization?

(A)   Monetization represents a strategy that is attractive to both environmentalists and their critics.

(B)   Monetization is an untested strategy, but it is increasingly being embraced by environmentalists.

(C)   Monetization should at present be restricted to ecological services and should only gradually be extended to such commercial endeavors as tourism and recreation.

(D)   Monetization can serve as a means of representing persuasively the value of environmental conservation.

(E)   Monetization should inform environmental decision-making processes only if it is accepted by environmentalist groups.

Inference

This question requires an understanding of David Pearce's view of monetization. According to the passage, Pearce finds the idea that conservation is unprofitable to be an illusion. He argues for showing the economic value of ecosystems in order to make progress in conserving those ecosystems.

A   The passage attributes to Gretchen Daily the view that monetization is unpopular with environmentalists. The passage gives no reason to believe that Pearce would endorse the idea that environmentalists currently find monetization attractive.

B   The passage gives no indication that monetization is increasingly being embraced by environmentalists, even if Pearce thinks it should be.

C   The passage indicates Pearce's belief that some types of tourism are also types of ecological services that have economic value and that they should be monetized.

D   Correct. Pearce believes that monetization quantifies the value of the services provided by ecological systems—and if that value is quantified, people are more likely to be persuaded to conserve those systems.

E   Pearce is arguing, against some environmentalists, that monetization should inform the decision-making process with regard to preserving ecosystems.

The correct answer is D.

512. Which of the following most clearly represents an example of an "ecological service" as that term is used in line 20?

(A)   A resort hotel located in an area noted for its natural beauty

(B)   A water-purifying plant that supplements natural processes with nontoxic chemicals

(C)   A wildlife preserve that draws many international travelers

(D)   A nonprofit firm that specializes in restoring previously damaged ecosystems

(E)   A newsletter that keeps readers informed of ecological victories and setbacks

Application

Based on the passage, *ecological services* are services provided by natural assets that have not been converted into commercial assets. Thus, any example of such an ecological service requires that the area providing it is natural.

A The passage mentions resort hotels as an example of explicitly commercial assets. Although some hotels might be situated in ecologically valuable natural environments, any ecological services in such cases would be contributed by the natural environments, not by the hotels themselves.

B Water purifying is an ecological service if it is supplied by *undisturbed forests and wetlands*. The word *plant* here must mean a technological installation, not a botanical organism, because it is said to supplement— not to be part of—the natural processes. Thus, it is not a natural asset and therefore does not provide an ecological service as described in the passage.

C **Correct.** The passage states that a wildlife preserve that creates jobs and generates income would be providing an ecological service.

D A nonprofit firm that restores damaged ecosystems would be performing a valuable ecology-related service, but it would not itself be an example of a natural asset providing an ecological service.

E Environmentalists and others would most likely find such a newsletter informative, but it would not be an ecological service, because it is not a service provided by a natural asset.

The correct answer is C.

513. According to the passage, Daily sees monetization as an indication of which of the following?

(A) The centrality of economic interests to people's actions

(B) The reluctance of the critics of environmentalism to acknowledge the importance of conservation

(C) The inability of financial interests and ecological interests to reach a common ideological ground

(D) The inevitability of environmental degradation

(E) The inevitability of the growth of ecological services in the future

Supporting Idea

This question asks about Daily's view of monetization, and according to the passage, she sees monetization as a practice that *reflects the dominant role that economic decisions play in human behavior.*

A **Correct.** According to the passage, Daily believes that economic interests are central to people's actions, and monetization of ecological services would take that central role realistically into account.

B The passage gives no evidence of this. It says nothing about how the concept of monetization relates to critics of environmentalism or about what Daily's opinion regarding such a relationship might be. It is reasonable to suppose that some critics of environmentalism would oppose the move to monetize the values of ecosystem functions because they believe that many ecosystem functions do not have true monetary value. However, the passage mentions Daily's views on the topic only as they relate to environmentalists, not to critics of environmentalism.

C This is the opposite of what, according to the passage, Daily says can be a benefit of monetization. For Daily, monetization represents a way for financial interests and ecological interests to reach a common ground; by using this common currency, both sides can make good decisions about the environment.

D Monetization, in Daily's view, would help to prevent environmental degradation; the passage does not suggest that she regards such degradation as at all inevitable.

E Daily does not see monetization as inevitably spurring the growth of ecological services but as more likely preventing their decline by leaving those services undisturbed.

The correct answer is A.

514. Which of the following can be inferred from the passage concerning the environmentalists mentioned in line 8?

(A) They are organized in opposition to the generation of income produced by the sale of ecological services.

(B) They are fewer in number but better organized and better connected to the media than their opponents.

(C) They have sometimes been charged with failing to use a particular strategy in their pursuit of conservational goals.

(D) They have been in the forefront of publicizing the extent of worldwide environmental degradation.

(E) They define environmental progress differently and more conservatively than do other organized groups of environmentalists.

Inference

The sentence in question states that critics blame environmentalists for their failure *to address the economic issues of environmental degradation.*

A   The passage states that, in the absence of monetization, conservation can appear unprofitable. But this does not mean that the environmentalists in question are opposed to conservation generating income.

B   The passage does not address the issue of the number of environmentalists in question, the number of those opposed to them, or whether either group is better connected to the media.

C   **Correct.** The passage indicates that critics of the environmentalists in question believe environmentalists are to blame for not using an effective economics-based strategy to promote conservation.

D   Although it may be the case that the environmentalists in question have been prominent in publicizing worldwide environmental degradation, the passage does not provide grounds for inferring that the possibility is necessarily true.

E   The passage suggests that certain critics consider environmentalists in general to be at fault for failing to address economic issues. In this respect, the passage makes no distinctions among different environmentalist groups, organized or otherwise, yet this answer choice is based on the assumption that the passage has made this distinction. Therefore, this answer choice cannot be inferred from the passage.

The correct answer is C.

Questions 515–518 refer to the passage on page 464.

Main Idea Summary

The passage provides a definition of social learning and utilizes an animal's acquisition for preferences of novel foods as an example of social learning. The focus is on the similarities and differences between how birds and other animals acquire novel foods and theorizes that avian social learning differs from that of other mammals. Several studies including Sherwin's recent studies with domestic hens are featured.

515. Which of the following best describes the main purpose of the first paragraph of the passage?

(A) It explains why a particular behavior discussed in the remainder of the passage is beneficial to the animals that engage in it.

(B) It introduces a concept that has been widely misunderstood among nonscientists.

(C) It outlines the types of studies that have been conducted to investigate a certain animal behavior.

(D) It provides information necessary to understand the nature of the phenomenon discussed in the remainder of the passage.

(E) It describes a viewpoint that is called into question later in the passage.

Inference

The passage discusses how, if at all, social learning may affect the development of food preferences among avian species. The first paragraph functions to orient the reader by introducing and clarifying the concept of social learning.

A   The main purpose of the first paragraph is not to explain why social learning would benefit animals engaging in it.

B   Nothing in the passage states or implies that any concept introduced in the first paragraph has been widely misunderstood among nonscientists.

C   The first paragraph provides no information about studies that have investigated an animal behavior.

D   Correct. The information in the first paragraph is needed for readers to understand the main topic of discussion in the passage.

E   The first paragraph consists of factual assertions about social learning but contains no viewpoint that the passage provides reason to reject.

The correct answer is D.

516. According to the passage, Sherwin's research team speculated the social learning of unpalatability within a particular species might be discouraged if the animals

(A)   did not suffer serious effects from any noxious or toxic foods they ingested

(B)   consumed food in small quantities throughout the day rather than in a few large feedings

(C)   had an unusually large variety of foods available to them

(D)   interacted after feeding as well as during feeding

(E)   did not show signs of illness until considerable time had passed following the ingestion of noxious or toxic food

Supporting Idea

Sherwin's research is discussed in the final paragraph of the passage. Sherwin's research team speculated about conditions that could have minimized any increase in survival value derivable from social learning of unpalatability. This could occur if little or no harm resulted from ingesting noxious or toxic food.

A   Correct. If noxious or toxic foods were consumed by animals without causing death or significant illness, observer animals might not learn to avoid those foods.

B   Animals' consumption of only a small quantity of a toxic or noxious food at one time is not mentioned as a condition that Sherwin's research team speculated could impede social learning of the food's unpalatability.

C   The passage does not mention availability of a large variety of foods as a condition that Sherwin's team speculated could impede social learning about the unpalatability of a noxious or toxic food.

D   The passage does not mention interaction after feeding as a condition that Sherwin's team speculated could impede social learning about the unpalatability of a noxious or toxic food.

E   A long time-lapse after eating an unpalatable food before illness appeared is not mentioned in the passage as a condition that Sherwin's team speculated could impede social learning about the unpalatability of the food.

The correct answer is A.

517. According to the passage, which of the following is true of the experiments on domestic hens conducted by Sherwin's research team?

(A)   Only a small number of observer hens appeared to learn to avoid food that was demonstrated by other hens to be noxious.

(B)   Observer hens ingested food preferentially only after numerous instances of witnessing demonstrator hens preferentially ingest that type of food.

(C)   Observer hens appeared unable to recognize when demonstrator hens found a particular food especially palatable.

(D)   Demonstrator hens reacted adversely to ingesting certain novel foods.

(E) Demonstrator hens altered their behavior less obviously in response to noxious foods than in response to highly palatable foods.

Evaluation

The passage describes experiments on social learning in domestic hens done by Sherwin's research team. We are asked to select a statement that accurately characterizes the experiments based on the information given. Two different kinds of experiments were conducted: one kind in which a demonstrator tried eating a new food and reacted negatively, and another kind in which the demonstrator reacted favorably.

A The passage suggests that no evidence was found of observer hens avoiding a novel food that a demonstrator hen had found unpalatable.

B Nothing in the passage indicates that before developing a preference for a particular type of food, observer hens needed to see several instances of a demonstrator hen preferring food of that type.

C Nothing in the passage indicates that observer hens were unable to interpret the aversive responses of demonstrator hens to a food as indicating unpalatability.

D Correct. The passage's third paragraph indicates that there were some instances in which demonstrator hens "reacted with obvious disgust" to a novel food that was noxious or toxic.

E The passage's description of the Sherwin experiments makes clear that demonstrator hens showed obvious aversion to noxious or toxic foods. However, the passage neither states nor implies any comparison of the obviousness of such responses with that of responses to highly palatable foods.

The correct answer is D.

518. The passage indicates that which of the following is true about studies of social learning in mammals?

(A) Such studies have only rarely demonstrated a capacity among mammals to learn to prefer certain foods via observation of other animals.

(B) Such studies have suggested that in mammals, one function of social learning is to establish preferences for novel foods.

(C) Such studies have demonstrated some capacity among mammals to learn via observation of other animals to avoid ingestion of toxic substances.

(D) Such studies have been conducted primarily in the mammals' natural habitats rather than in laboratory settings.

(E) Such studies have focused primarily on forms of social learning other than the acquisition of preferences for novel foods.

Supporting Idea

This question asks us to identify a general idea the passage conveys about social learning in mammals. The passage, which is largely concerned with social learning in avian species, addresses mammalian learning only in passing at the start and at the end of the second paragraph.

A The first sentence of the second paragraph tells us that some studies have "suggested" that mammals can learn to prefer certain foods through social learning. It does not tell us such an ability was "demonstrated," even rarely.

B Correct. We read: "Some experiments have suggested that among mammals, social learning facilitates the identification of beneficial food items . . . ."

C The final sentence of the second paragraph tells us that researchers think mammalian social learning may differ fundamentally from avian social learning. Elsewhere in the passage, we are told that studies suggest mammalian social learning primarily teaches how to identify beneficial foods rather than how to avoid toxic foods.

D The passage provides no information that compares the relative extent of laboratory studies with that of habitat-based studies in investigations of social learning in animals.

E   The contrary is suggested in the passage. See the explanation for (B) above. The passage does not mention any studies of mammalian social learning other than those regarding development of preferences for beneficial foods.

The correct answer is B.

Questions 519–522 refer to the passage on page 466.

519. The passage is primarily concerned with

(A)   examining economic factors that may have contributed to the success of certain Japanese companies

(B)   discussing the relative merits of strategic partnerships as compared with those of market-exchange relationships

(C)   challenging the validity of a widely held assumption about how Japanese firms operate

(D)   explaining why Western companies have been slow to adopt a particular practice favored by Japanese companies

(E)   pointing out certain differences between Japanese and Western supplier relationships

Main Idea

This question asks for an assessment of what the passage as a whole is doing. The passage discusses how Western business managers have been following the advice of academics and journalists to pursue strategic partnerships with their suppliers. The advice is based on studies comparing Japanese production and supply practices with those of the rest of the world. Newer research, however, indicates that Japanese practices actually differ from those indicated in the earlier studies and are not significantly different from practices associated with Western manufacturers.

A   The passage is not primarily concerned with economic factors contributing to the success of Japanese companies, but rather with whether Japanese relationships with suppliers conform to the practices recently adopted by Western business manufacturers.

B   Although the passage discusses strategic partnerships and market-exchange relationships, it does not discuss their relative merits.

C   **Correct.** The passage does question the view promoted by several studies regarding the relationship Japanese firms have with their suppliers.

D   The passage does not indicate that Western companies have been slow to adopt any particular practice favored by Japanese companies.

E   Rather than pointing out differences between Japanese and Western supplier relationships, it actually suggests that they are more similar than generally realized.

The correct answer is C.

520. According to the passage, the advice referred to in line 6 was a response to which of the following?

(A)   A recent decrease in the number of available suppliers within the United States automobile industry

(B)   A debate within Western management circles during the past decade regarding the value of strategic partnerships

(C)   The success of certain European automobile manufacturers that have adopted strategic partnerships

(D)   An increase in demand over the past decade for automobiles made by Western manufacturers

(E)   Research comparing Japanese business practices with those of other nations

Supporting Idea

This question is concerned with identifying what the passage says about certain experts' advice. The passage indicates that the experts' advice is based on numerous studies carried out over the previous decade that compared Japanese manufacturing and supply practices with those of the rest of the world.

A   The passage indicates that the major automobile manufacturers in the United States have decreased the number of suppliers they deal with, but the experts' advice was not in response to such a decrease; rather, the decrease was in response to the manufacturers' adoption of the experts' advice.

B   The passage does not say anything about a debate within Western management circles regarding management partnerships.

C   The passage mentions that European manufacturers have adopted strategic partnerships, but it does not indicate how successful those manufacturers have been.

D   The passage does not indicate whether demand for automobiles has increased over the past decade.

E   **Correct.** The passage indicates that the experts' advice was made in reaction to studies that compared Japanese business practices regarding production and suppliers with those of other companies.

The correct answer is E.

521. The author mentions "the success of a certain well-known Japanese automaker" in lines 10–11, most probably in order to

(A)   demonstrate some of the possible reasons for the success of a certain business practice

(B)   cite a specific case that has convinced Western business experts of the value of a certain business practice

(C)   describe specific steps taken by Western automakers that have enabled them to compete more successfully in a global market

(D)   introduce a paradox about the effect of a certain business practice in Japan

(E)   indicate the need for Western managers to change their relationships with their external business partners

Evaluation

The question requires the test-taker to determine the author's reason for mentioning *the success of a certain well-known Japanese automaker*. Most likely, the author wishes to present

a specific case that was crucial in leading Western management circles to value strategic partnerships.

A   The passage does not discuss reasons for the success of the business practice.

B   **Correct.** The success of a certain well-known Japanese automaker is offered as a reason for Western management circles to believe in the value of the business practice of forming strategic partnerships.

C   Although the passage does indicate that Western automakers have adopted strategic partnerships with suppliers, it does not indicate whether this has enabled them to become more successful globally.

D   The passage does not specifically discuss any paradox related to the effects of Japanese business practices.

E   Although the passage does give reason to think that the changes adopted by Western managers may have made their relationships with external business partners less, rather than more, like the relationships Japanese managers have, the passage does not indicate whether the Western managers need to make any further changes.

The correct answer is B.

522. Which of the following is cited in the passage as evidence supporting the author's claim about what the new research referred to in line 20 demonstrates?

(A)   The belief within Western management circles regarding the extent to which Japanese firms rely on strategic partnerships

(B)   The surprising number of European and United States businesses that have strategic partnerships with their suppliers

(C)   The response of Western automobile manufacturers to the advice that they adopt strategic partnerships with their suppliers

(D)   The prevalence of "market-exchange" relationships between Japanese firms and their suppliers

(E)   The success of a particular Japanese automobile manufacturer that favors strategic partnerships with its suppliers

Supporting Idea

To answer this question, you must identify what evidence is cited in the passage regarding the author's claim that new research casts doubt on the widespread view that Japanese firms primarily manage their supplier relationships through strategic partnerships. To support this claim regarding the new research, the author points out that Japanese firms make extensive use of "market-exchange" relationships, which are alternatives to the strategic relationships discussed in the preceding paragraph.

A   This is the belief that the author claims that the new research casts doubt on, so it would not make sense for the author to cite this as evidence for the author's claim.

B   This is cited as a result of the belief that the author claims the new research casts doubt on, not as evidence for the author's claim.

C   The new research undermines the basis of the advice referred to here—advice that the Western automobile manufacturers heed—so it would make little sense for the author to cite this as evidence in support of the author's claim about the new research.

D   **Correct.** The passage does cite this prevalence as evidence for the author's claim that the new research casts doubt on the widely held view about Japanese firms.

E   Citing this firm's success would tend to support the widespread view about Japanese firms, not undermine that view.

The correct answer is D.

Questions 523–526 refer to the passage on page 468.

Main Idea Summary

The passage is primarily concerned with Marcus Garvey's role in the African American revitalization movement of the early twentieth century. The passage's first paragraph states that the return of African American soldiers from the First World War created an ideal constituency for Garvey's message of pride and unity among African Americans. The second paragraph describes the disillusionment of these soldiers upon their return and discusses

Anthony F. C. Wallace's idea that the tension between a culture's expectations and reality can inspire a revitalization movement. The final paragraph argues that Garvey did not create the consciousness on which he built his movement, but merely gave it its political expression.

523.   According to the passage, which of the following contributed to Marcus Garvey's success?

(A)   He introduced cultural and historical consciousness to the African American community.

(B)   He believed enthusiastically in the traditional American success ethos.

(C)   His audience had already formed a consciousness that made it receptive to his message.

(D)   His message appealed to critics of African American support for United States military involvement in the First World War.

(E)   He supported the movement to protest segregation that had emerged prior to his arrival in the United States.

Supporting Idea

To answer this question, find what the passage states explicitly about how Marcus Garvey achieved his success. The passage begins by stating that Garvey arrived at the right time: that returning African American soldiers were primed to receive what he had to say about the African American community. These soldiers already held strong beliefs about their rights to opportunities for success; the passage concludes that the divide between the soldiers' expectations and their experiences led to Garvey's success.

A   The passage states that African American people were in possession of a strong cultural and historical consciousness prior to Garvey's arrival in the United States.

B   The passage attributes belief in the traditional American success ethos to African American people who joined the armed forces; it does not mention Garvey's beliefs on this subject.

C   **Correct.** African American soldiers who had experienced segregation during the First World War were ready to hear what Garvey had to say.

D   Critics of African American support for United States involvement in the First World War are not mentioned in the passage.

E   While Garvey most likely would have supported a movement to protest segregation, such a movement is not discussed in the passage.

The correct answer is C.

524. The passage suggests that many African American people responded to their experiences in the armed forces in which of the following ways?

(A)   They maintained as civilians their enthusiastic allegiance to the armed forces.

(B)   They questioned United States involvement in the First World War.

(C)   They joined political organizations to protest the segregation of African American troops and the indignities they suffered in the military.

(D)   They became aware of the gap between their expectations and the realities of American culture.

(E)   They repudiated Garvey's message of pride and unity.

Inference

According to the passage, African Americans enthusiastically joined the armed services but were confronted with continued segregation, both in the military and when they returned home. The passage does not explicitly state their response to these experiences, but a response can be inferred. The second paragraph refers to anthropologist Anthony F. C. Wallace, who argued that a revitalization movement may be brought about by the perception of a gap between expectations and reality, and such a revitalization did occur in African American communities following the First World War; thus, many African American people may have become aware of a gap such as Wallace described.

A   The passage states that African American troops experienced segregation and other indignities while in the military; these experiences could reasonably be inferred to have dampened their enthusiasm for the armed forces. Regardless, the passage does not suggest an enthusiastic allegiance.

B   The passage describes African American people's enthusiasm about joining the military. Although they experienced segregation and other indignities while in the military, the passage does not suggest that their opinion about involvement in the war changed.

C   While African American troops may have joined political organizations, the passage does not provide any actual evidence of this having occurred.

D   **Correct.** The fact that, as the passage states, a revitalization movement occurred in the African American community following the First World War suggests that the returning soldiers did become aware of the gap between their expectations of an improved situation with regard to segregation and the reality of continued segregation in the United States.

E   The passage does not suggest that African American troops repudiated Garvey's message. On the contrary, it states that Garvey built *the largest revitalization movement in African American history*. This suggests that the members of the African American community, including the returning soldiers, were extremely receptive to Garvey's message.

The correct answer is D.

525. It can be inferred from the passage that the "scholars" mentioned in line 24 believe which of the following to be true?

(A)   Revitalization resulted from the political activism of returning African American soldiers following the First World War.

(B)   Marcus Garvey had to change a number of prevailing attitudes in order for his mass movement to find a foothold in the United States.

(C) The prevailing sensibility of the African American community provided the foundation of Marcus Garvey's political appeal.

(D) Marcus Garvey hoped to revitalize consciousness of cultural and historical identity in the African American community.

(E) The goal of the mass movement that Marcus Garvey helped bring into being was to build on the pride and unity among African Americans.

Inference

To determine what it is logical to infer regarding the scholars discussed in the third paragraph, look at the context in which they are mentioned. According to the passage, these scholars argue that Garvey was responsible for creating a particular consciousness within the African American community, a consciousness that the passage identifies as *identity, strength, and [a] sense of history*. Unlike the passage author, these scholars believe strongly in Garvey's responsibility for this consciousness, so they would most likely reject any suggestion that it existed prior to his arrival and activism.

A According to the passage, the scholars believe that Garvey was responsible for the creation of the consciousness that led to revitalization, which suggests that revitalization resulted from Garvey's activism, not soldiers' activism.

B **Correct.** According to the passage, the scholars believe that Garvey created the consciousness that led to his revitalization movement. This suggests that he had to change prevailing attitudes in order to foster this new consciousness.

C According to the passage, the scholars believe that Garvey created a new consciousness in the African American community; thus, the prevailing sensibility could not have provided a foundation for his appeal.

D According to the passage, the scholars believe that Garvey built his revitalization movement on a new consciousness of cultural and historical identity, not a previously existing one.

E According to the passage, the scholars' position is that Garvey's movement was built on a new sense of pride and unity that he provided, and that that sense did not precede Garvey's work.

The correct answer is B.

526. According to the passage, many African American people joined the armed forces during the First World War for which of the following reasons?

(A) They wished to escape worsening economic conditions in African American communities.

(B) They expected to fulfill ideals of personal attainment.

(C) They sought to express their loyalty to the United States.

(D) They hoped that joining the military would help advance the cause of desegregation.

(E) They saw military service as an opportunity to fulfill Marcus Garvey's political vision.

Supporting Idea

This question depends on identifying what the passage states directly about African American people's reasons for joining the armed forces. The reason offered by the passage is that the African American people who entered the armed forces did so because they were *hoping to participate in the traditional American ethos of individual success*.

A Although this is a plausible reason for entering the armed forces, the passage does not discuss economic conditions.

B **Correct.** The passage states that African American people who joined the armed forces during the First World War wanted to achieve individual success.

C The passage does not discuss African American people's loyalty to the United States.

D The passage states that African American troops experienced segregation, but it does not suggest that they had hoped their joining the military would promote desegregation.

E The passage suggests that African American troops did not become aware of Marcus Garvey's political vision until after they returned from the First World War.

The correct answer is B.

Questions 527–531 refer to the passage on page 470.

527. The author mentions rhinoceroses and elephants (see line 39) primarily in order to

(A) explain why sloth bears are not successful foragers in grassland habitats

(B) identify the predators that have had the most influence on the behavior of sloth bears

(C) suggest a possible reason that sloth bear cubs do not use tree-climbing as a defense

(D) provide examples of predators that were once widespread across the Indian subcontinent

(E) defend the assertion that sloth bears are under greater threat from dangerous animals than are other bear species

Supporting Idea

Sloth bear females sometimes carry their cubs during their first nine months even while foraging, even though the cubs learn to walk at six months. The passage seeks to explain how that behavior may have evolved and argues that the evolution of sloth bears likely selected against climbing trees for defense. Among the reasons suggested is that climbing trees offered sloth bears no protection against predators or other animals, including rhinoceroses and elephants.

A The passage suggests the contrary, stating that sloth bears are "especially attracted to food-rich grasslands."

B The passage suggests that a variety of predators posed a threat to sloth bears. It indicates that rhinoceroses and elephants have a hostile relationship with sloth bears but does not characterize that relationship as predatory.

C **Correct.** The fact that rhinoceroses and elephants could topple trees minimized the protection climbing trees could offer to sloth bear cubs confronted by predators or tree-toppling animals.

D The passage does not characterize rhinoceroses and elephants as predators that were once especially widespread across all of India.

E This assertion is to be found in the passage, but defending it is not the primary purpose of line 39.

The correct answer is C.

528. Which of the following, if true, would most weaken the author's argument in lines 14–19?

(A) Cub-carrying behavior has been observed in many nonmyrmecophagous mammals.

(B) Many of the largest myrmecophagous mammals do not typically exhibit cub-carrying behavior.

(C) Some sloth bears have home ranges that are smaller in size than the average home ranges of black bears.

(D) The locomotion of black bears is significantly more efficient than the locomotion of sloth bears.

(E) The habitat of black bears consists of terrain that is significantly more varied than that of the habitat of sloth bears.

Evaluation

The argument in lines 14–19 is meant to support the claim that the cubs of sloth bears should be able to walk fast enough to keep up with their mother. The support provided relies on indicating relevant similarities between American black bears and sloth bears. What new information, if true, would undermine this argument?

A The argument hinges on a comparison regarding range size and locomotion rather than the presence or absence of ant-eating. The information given in this option is logically irrelevant to the argument.

B This information does not undermine support for the claim that sloth bear cubs should be just as able to keep pace with their mother as American black bear cubs.

C It is to be expected that home-range size would vary for individuals in both species of bears. This fact is consistent with the information given in lines 14–19 and lacks any weakening effect on the support provided for the argument's conclusion.

D **Correct.** If the locomotion of sloth bears is less efficient than that of black bears, then expenditure of energy over a given distance would be greater for sloth bear cubs. This information, if true, would cast doubt on support for the conclusion that sloth bear cubs should be able to walk fast enough to keep pace with their mother.

E If this is true, the terrain traversed by black bear cubs would likely be more challenging than that traversed by sloth bear cubs. The addition of such information would tend to strengthen rather than weaken support for the argument's conclusion.

The correct answer is D.

529. Which of the following is mentioned in the passage as a way in which brown bears and sloth bears are similar?

(A) They tend to become aggressive when provoked.

(B) They live almost exclusively in treeless environments.

(C) They are preyed upon by animals that can climb or topple trees.

(D) They are inefficient in their locomotion.

(E) They have relatively large canine teeth.

Supporting Idea

Note what is being asked: What does the passage state is a resemblance between sloth bears and brown bears?

A **Correct.** The passage states that "brown bears … rely on aggression to protect their cubs" and sloth bears, "[l]ike brown bears," are "easily provoked to aggression."

B The passage states that brown bears and sloth bears may have evolved in relatively treeless environments but does not assert that almost all current habitats of sloth bears lack trees.

C The passage indicates that some grassland habitats of sloth bears have tree-climbing animals that may prey on them. Even if this is also true of brown bears, the passage does not mention it.

D The passage does not explicitly characterize the locomotion of both brown bears and sloth bears as inefficient.

E The passage states that sloth bears have relatively large canine teeth but does not attribute this to brown bears.

The correct answer is A.

530. The author mentions which of the following as evidence for the view that cub-carrying behavior among sloth bears functions primarily as a defense from predation?

(A) The relative passivity of sloth bears in comparison with other species of bears

(B) The age at which sloth bear cubs can defend themselves from predators

(C) The unsuitability of cub-carrying for myrmecophagous foraging

(D) The behavior of sloth bear cubs when they first perceive danger

(E) The inefficient locomotion of sloth bears and other myrmecophagous animals

Logical Structure

The question asks what characteristic of sloth bears is evidence that cub-carrying behavior evolved primarily as an adaptive strategy to defend against predation.

A Sloth bears are not characterized as more passive than other bear species. On the contrary, the author describes them as "easily provoked to aggression."

B The passage gives no information regarding the age at which bear cubs become able to defend themselves against predators.

C One explanation for cub-carrying that the passage considers but rejects is that cub-carrying may be needed for myrmecophagy.

D **Correct.** The passage states that sloth bear cubs "climb on their mother's back at the first sign of danger." The author infers that this behavior may have originated mainly as an adaptive strategy to defend against predation.

E   The inefficient locomotion of sloth bears is not mentioned as evidence that cub-carrying evolved as a defense against predation. To suggest that inefficient locomotion is not a sufficient explanation for cub-carrying, the author notes that although the locomotion of polar bears, like that of sloth bears, is inefficient, polar bear cubs walk along with their mother.

The correct answer is D.

531. The primary purpose of the passage is to

(A) trace the development of a particular behavioral characteristic of the sloth bear

(B) explore possible explanations for a particular behavioral characteristic of the sloth bear

(C) compare the defensive strategies of sloth bear cubs to the defensive strategies of cubs of other bear species

(D) describe how certain behavioral characteristics of the sloth bear differ from those of other myrmecophagous mammals

(E) provide an alternative to a generally accepted explanation of a particular behavioral characteristic of myrmecophagous mammals

Main Idea

The passage is focused on a puzzling behavior of sloth bears: females carrying their cubs even after the cubs have become able to walk on their own. The goal is to explain how such behavior would have evolved. Behaviors evolve if they promote the survival of a species.

A   Tracing the development of a puzzling behavior is distinct from explaining the survival function served by that behavior and explaining why sloth bears evolved with that behavior.

B   **Correct.** The passage consists of a consideration of explanations for how cub-carrying could have served a survival function for sloth bears and arguing for the preferability of one of those explanations.

C   Some comparisons are briefly made (e.g., "black bear cubs use trees for defense"), but any such comparison is subordinate to the main purpose of the passage.

D   A brief allusion is made in passing to the fact that other myrmecophagous species also engage in cub-carrying, but the making of any such comparison cannot plausibly be regarded as the primary purpose of the passage.

E   No such "generally accepted explanation" is described in the passage, so the primary purpose of the passage cannot be to provide an alternative to such an explanation.

The correct answer is B.

Questions 532–535 refer to the passage on page 472.

532. According to the passage, theory B states that which of the following is a factor that enables a schooling fish to escape predators?

(A) The tendency of fish to form compact groups

(B) The movement of other fish within the school

(C) The inability of predators to detect schools

(D) The ability of fish to hide behind one another in a school

(E) The great speed with which a school can disperse

Supporting Idea

This question depends on understanding what the passage states about theory B, the "confusion effect." One element of theory B is that predators may experience sensory confusion created by large numbers of moving fish in a school.

A   The compactness of groups of schooling fish is an element of theory A, not theory B.

B   **Correct.** It is the movement of schooling fish around a predator that creates sensory confusion in the predator; this movement may distract the predator and help to protect individual fish in the school.

C   According to the passage's description of theory A, predators are actually slightly more likely to detect schools than they are to detect individual fish.

D   Theory B does not involve fish hiding behind one another, but rather moving around the predator.

E   The passage does not discuss the speed of dispersal of schools of fish.

The correct answer is B.

533.   According to the passage, both theory A and theory B have been developed to explain how

(A)   fish hide from predators by forming schools

(B)   forming schools functions to protect fish from predators

(C)   schooling among fish differs from other protective behaviors

(D)   small fish are able to make rapid decisions

(E)   small fish are able to survive in an environment densely populated by large predators

Supporting Idea

The passage states in its first paragraph that two theories were developed to explain why schooling occurs in so many fish species and that they both assume that schooling helps protect fish from predators.

A   While theory A involves an explanation of how schooling makes an individual fish less likely to be found by predators, theory B explains how schooling protects fish even when they are detected by predators.

B   Correct. Both theory A and theory B begin with the assumption that schooling provides protection from predators, and each theory offers a different explanation for how that protection occurs.

C   The passage does not discuss protective behaviors other than schooling.

D   The decision-making ability of predators, not schooling fish, is discussed in the passage; schooling is presented as an instinctive behavior.

E   The passage suggests that only theory B helps explain schooling behavior in environments where many predators, large or otherwise, are found, and that theory A explains schooling in areas where predators are not as abundant.

The correct answer is B.

534.   According to one explanation of the "confusion effect," a fish that swims in a school will have greater advantages for survival if it

(A)   tends to be visible for no more than 200 meters

(B)   stays near either the front or the rear of a school

(C)   is part of a small school rather than a large school

(D)   is very similar in appearance to the other fish in the school

(E)   is medium-sized

Inference

The "confusion effect" is discussed in the third and fourth paragraphs. The first explanation of the "confusion effect" proposes that because predators prefer to select distinctive prey, they find it difficult to select one fish from among many that look the same.

A   The 200-meter visibility of fish is part of the explanation for theory A, not theory B (the "confusion effect").

B   The location of an individual fish within a school is not discussed in the passage as being important to the "confusion effect."

C   The size of a school of fish is not discussed as an element of the "confusion effect."

D   Correct. Because predators, according to the "confusion effect," prefer to select prey that is distinct from the rest of the school, a fish that is similar in appearance to the other fish in its school would most likely enjoy a survival advantage.

E   The size of a fish relative to the other fish in its school would most likely contribute to its ability to survive: that is, if it resembled other fish in size, it would be safer, based on what the passage says about the "confusion effect." Furthermore, the passage gives no reason to think that merely being medium-sized would confer any advantage (unless the other fish were medium-sized as well).

The correct answer is D.

535. The author is primarily concerned with

(A) discussing different theories

(B) analyzing different techniques

(C) defending two hypotheses

(D) refuting established beliefs

(E) revealing new evidence

Main Idea

Determining the author's primary concern depends on understanding the focus of the passage as a whole. The author presents two theories that purport to account for why fish, particularly small fish, tend to school, and explains the arguments of proponents of each theory.

A **Correct.** The author discusses two theories—identified as theory A and theory B—that account for the tendency of fish to school.

B The author is not concerned with different techniques in the passage.

C The two theories of why fish school could be referred to as hypotheses, but the author is not primarily concerned with defending them; rather, the passage explains how each attempts to account for the phenomenon in question.

D The author presents, rather than refutes, beliefs about why fish tend to school.

E The author reveals no evidence, new or otherwise, in the passage. The passage is a general discussion of scientific opinions based on existing evidence.

The correct answer is A.

Questions 536–538 refer to the passage on page 473.

536. The relationship between which of the following is most closely analogous to the relationship between Red Data Books and green lists, as they are described in the passage?

(A) A list of reference materials that are important to consult and a list of materials that are less important to consult

(B) A list of cars in need of major repairs and a list of cars in need of minor repairs

(C) A list of tours given in Europe and a list of tours given in Africa and Asia

(D) A list of necessary expenses and a list of expenses that can be eliminated

(E) A list of items in low supply and a list of items of which there is sufficient stock

Evaluation

The question asks for an analogy that best matches the relationship between Red Data Books and green lists as presented in the passage. The core relationship is a change in default assumption or burden of proof. The Red Data Book lists the exceptions that are negatively defined: threatened species, or low numbers of the birds in question. This implies that other species are in the default state of security. The green lists, by contrast, attempt to actively affirm which bird species are secure, or sufficient. Therefore the closest analogy will refer to parallel methods of assessment: a list of things that are insufficient, or in low supply, compared to a list of things that are sufficient.

A This option describes two levels of importance, not two opposing states (threatened vs. secure) that redefine the default assumption.

B Both lists represent cars in a problematic state (in need of repair). The original lists represent opposing states: problem (threatened) vs. success (secure).

C This option represents two mutually exclusive geographical categories; it does not present a relationship of opposite status or a change in an underlying, default assumption.

D This option describes two distinct categories of expenses; it does not reflect the structural, inverse relationship where one list's existence changes the assumption about everything else.

E **Correct.** This analogy perfectly mirrors the relationship. Red Data Book is parallel to a "List of items in low supply." Both reflect the negative, potentially problematic state of scarcity. The green list is analogous to a "List of items of which there is sufficient stock." Both reflect the positive, desired state of sufficiency.

The correct answer is E.

537. The author most likely mentions Malayan freshwater fish in order to

    (A) compare the rates of extinction found in fish species with the rates found in bird species

    (B) describe the way in which case-by-case assessment of species was conducted in the past

    (C) emphasize that tropical species are more prone to extinction than species in temperate regions

    (D) provide an example of data revealed by a case-by-case assessment of species

    (E) suggest that more up-to-date information is available for species of fish than for species of birds

Purpose

The author's viewpoint that green lists would give a more useful picture than do the Red Data Books of the status of the world's bird species is suggested in the first sentence, which describes green lists as a way to "correct a major tactical error." A green list, or a list of species that are demonstrably secure, would rely on case-by-case assessments of specific species; the Red Data Books, by contrast, merely list species which are known to be threatened but employ no case-by-case examinations of the health of individual species. The author states that evidence favoring one approach over the other can come from examining other case-by-case surveys of species. The author cites the survey of Malayan freshwater fish "as one indication of what such surveys may show"; in other words, the author is using it as an example of the data offered by the case-by-case approach.

A   The author's point is that rates of extinction in bird species are obscured by a lack of data; there is no implicit or explicit comparison of such rates between birds and fish.

B   There is no discussion of how the survey of Malayan fish species was conducted, so a description of methods cannot be the author's purpose in referring to that survey.

C   The author suggests that extinctions of tropical species may be more likely to

occur *unobserved* than those of European and North American species, not that tropical species are more likely to go extinct; therefore, this study is not cited to emphasize the greater vulnerability of tropical species.

D   **Correct.** The author explicitly states that the survey of Malayan fish is "one indication" of the data that can be gained through case-by-case assessments of species, a method which the author believes should be used for birds.

E   While the study might suggest that there is more up-to-date data regarding *some* species of fish than for many species of birds, especially tropical birds, nothing in the passage implies that data for fish in general is more current than data for birds in general.

The correct answer is D.

538. According to the passage, all of the following are true statements about tropical bird species EXCEPT:

    (A) Current information is not available about the conservation status of many tropical species.

    (B) Biologists have only recently begun to describe and categorize rare tropical species.

    (C) Many tropical species are losing their habitats because of increased cultivation of land.

    (D) Tropical species often inhabit small geographical areas.

    (E) There are more bird species in the tropics than in other parts of the world.

Supporting Idea

This item requires the identification of a claim that is clearly not included in the passage. The passage explicitly includes the information that most bird species live in the tropics, often in small geographical ranges, and are likely in many cases to have lost habitats that were converted to farmland; it further states that biologists have not gathered recent data for many species. Moreover, the passage emphasizes that biologists discovered many tropical bird species "long ago."

A The passage explicitly states, "Nothing is known about the current status of many tropical species."

B **Correct.** The passage explicitly states that many rare tropical species were discovered "long ago," so it cannot be the case that biologists have begun to identify such rare species only recently.

C The passage refers to "many" species losing their habitats owing to "forested areas now converted to cropland."

D The passage states that "small geographical ranges" are "often characteristic" of tropical species.

E The passage mentions that "most" bird species live in the tropics; in other words, there are more bird species in the tropics than in other regions.

The correct answer is B.

Questions 539–540 refer to the passage on page 474.

539. The passage is primarily concerned with

(A) comparing the significance of the physiological and nonphysiological functions of resin

(B) introducing the field of chemical ecology and highlighting some of its applications

(C) discussing some misconceptions about resin and presenting a theory about its function

(D) demonstrating that misinformation concerning resin and amber can be traced back to the first century

(E) suggesting that the study of resin lies properly in the hands of entomologists rather than mineralogists or chemists

Main Idea

The question asks for the primary concern or main focus of the entire passage. Determining the author's primary concern depends on understanding the nature of the content covered in each section of the passage and identifying the idea that connects the parts. The first paragraph discusses misconceptions about resin and its fossilized form (amber), noting its confusion with gum and sap, and clarifying that a physiological function for resin has not been

determined. The second paragraph presents the theory proposed by Fraenkel regarding resin's possible role in repelling or attracting insects and later researchers' ideas regarding resin's role in coevolution. These theories attempt to assign a function to resin.

A The passage explicitly states scientists have *not* determined a physiological function for resin. Therefore, it cannot compare the significance of a known physiological function with a nonphysiological one.

B Chemical ecology is mentioned only in the final sentence as the *result* of ideas about resin's function. The passage's focus is on the substance (resin) that led to the field, not primarily on the field itself or its broad applications.

C **Correct.** The passage begins by correcting misconceptions (resin vs. amber, resin vs. gum/sap). It then dedicates the second half to introducing and detailing the leading theory about resin's function (insect attractant/repellent, coevolution mediator). This accurately covers the content flow, and therefore the primary concern, of the passage.

D The passage *mentions* Pliny in the first century, but the passage mainly focuses on modern-day confusion and the development of a functional theory, not on a historical tracing of misinformation.

E While the passage focuses on entomological theories, the passage never makes a prescriptive statement about which discipline *should* properly study resin.

The correct answer is C.

540. The passage supports each of the following statements about sap EXCEPT:

(A) Sap is an aqueous solution.

(B) Sap and resin are often confused by observers.

(C) Sap is found less abundantly than resin in most plants.

(D) Sap moves through certain tissues of a plant.

(E) Sap performs a physiological function in plants.

Supporting Idea

The question asks which statement about sap is NOT supported by the passage. The passage clearly states that sap is often confused with resin and that it is a solution transported through plant tissues; it also strongly implies that sap has a physiological function. It does not, however, compare sap and resin in other key respects, such as their relative abundance in plants.

A   The passage defines sap as "an aqueous solution" transported through certain plant tissues.

B   The passage notes that confusion "persists surrounding the term 'resin'" and that "Resin is often confused with gum, . . . and with sap. . . ."

C   Correct. The passage describes the chemical and functional differences between sap and resin, but it makes no statement about their relative abundance or quantity in plants. Therefore a claim regarding the relative abundance of sap and resin is not supported by the passage.

D   The passage defines sap as "an aqueous solution transported through certain plant tissues."

E   The passage states that scientists have "not determined a physiological function for resin." Because resin is explicitly contrasted with sap and gum in this respect, the passage implies that sap (and gum) *do* perform determined physiological functions.

The correct answer is C.

Questions 541–542 refer to the passage on page 475.

541. According to the passage, Lash's biography of Eleanor Roosevelt reflects the assumption that

(A)   she was an uncomplicated figure relatively free of contradiction

(B)   her activities were undertaken primarily in support of her husband

(C)   she is best understood in terms of the feminist movement of the post-suffrage years

(D)   she was one of only a few women who were well known to the public

(E)   her career included the pursuit of aims, many of which were inconsistent with one another

Supporting Idea

The item asks what assumption Lash's 1970s biography of Eleanor Roosevelt reflects, according to the passage. This depends on noting that the passage directly states that the initial historical view, which Lash's work reflected, was that Eleanor Roosevelt "held a place in the public imagination largely because she was the wife of a particularly influential president" and that her "own activities were seen as preparing the way for her husband's election or as a complement to his programs."

A   The passage states the opposite; namely, that Lash's biography "revealed a complicated woman" and that her life was "full of contradictions."

B   Correct. This claim directly reflects Lash's assumption that her actions were fundamentally in support of or complementary to her husband's career.

C   This claim summarizes the newer, more recent view that the passage contrasts with the earlier historical interpretation, which Lash's work reflected.

D   The passage states that she *was* one of a handful of well-known women, but this is a fact noted by the author, not an assumption reflected by Lash's biography regarding the *meaning* or *source* of her activities.

E   This view aligns with the newer interpretation (Scharf's view) of the generation of women who were full of "contradictions"; nothing in the passage suggests that Lash viewed Eleanor Roosevelt's aims as inconsistent.

The correct answer is B.

542. The passage as a whole is primarily concerned with which of the following?

(A)   Changes in the way in which Eleanor Roosevelt's life is understood

(B)   Social changes that made possible the role played by Eleanor Roosevelt in social reform

(C)   Changes in the ways in which historians have viewed the lives of American women

(D)   Social changes that resulted from the activities of Eleanor Roosevelt

(E)   Changes in the social roles that American women have played

Main Idea

The item asks for the primary concern of the passage as a whole. This is revealed by the passage's structure as a comparison between the older view (1970s, Lash's work), which saw Eleanor Roosevelt primarily as the President's wife and an "idiosyncratic figure," and the newer view (1987, Scharf's work), which sees her as a figure "comprehensible in terms of broader social developments" by placing her within the context of the post-suffrage feminist generation.

A   Correct. The passage is structured as a comparison between two distinct historical views of Eleanor Roosevelt.

B   The passage mentions "broader social developments" (post-suffrage feminism) as the context Scharf used to *understand* Roosevelt's role, but the main focus is on the *historians' understanding* of the role, not a detailed analysis of the social changes themselves.

C   While the passage uses the shift in understanding Roosevelt as an *example* of how historians are now viewing the lives of American women (specifically, post-suffrage feminists), the passage's primary and constant subject is Roosevelt herself, making (A) a more precise summary of the text's focus.

D   The passage is concerned with the historical interpretation of her activities, not the *results* of her activities (the social changes she caused).

E   The passage describes a generation of women making a "transition from old patterns . . . to new ones," which implies a change in social roles. However, this information is introduced solely to serve as the *context* for reinterpreting Eleanor Roosevelt's life, not as the central topic of the passage as a whole.

The correct answer is A.

Questions 543–545 refer to the passage on page 476.

543.   The passage suggests that which of the following most accurately describes the attitudes of SPEW and WIDC toward the safety regulations referred to in lines 28–29?

(A)   They disagreed about whether or not unions could successfully pressure employers to comply with such regulations.

(B)   They disagreed about the extent to which the proposed legislation would strengthen such regulations.

(C)   They agreed that, while adequate for other types of factories, extant workplace safety regulations did not specifically address the conditions unique to white lead factories.

(D)   They agreed that, if adequately enforced, such regulations could reduce the incidence of illness among women working in white lead factories.

(E)   They agreed that the extant workplace safety regulations had already been effective in reducing the incidence of lead poisoning in many white lead factories.

Inference

The passage outlines the positions of various groups on this proposal. Proponents (home secretary/government) supported the ban due to the high incidence of illness among predominantly female workers. Opponents (WIDC and SPEW) opposed the ban, seeing it as a limit on women's opportunities. They argued that the illness was due to controllable factors, such as workers' care and cleanliness and lack of enforcement of existing safety regulations. WTUL, by contrast, supported the ban because safety regulations were generally not enforced in non-unionized white lead factories, leaving the women vulnerable. The item asks what the passage suggests about the shared attitudes of the SPEW and WIDC regarding the extant (existing) safety regulations.

A   The passage gives no information on whether SPEW and WIDC agreed or disagreed on the potential role of unions.

B   The passage states both groups *opposed* the legislation because it limited women's job opportunities. Their focus was on enforcement, not the law itself.

C   The groups' argument was that lead poisoning "could be avoided" if the regulations were enforced. This implies the extant regulations *were* adequate for white lead factories, provided they were followed, rather than being inadequate or too general.

D   **Correct.** The passage states that the SPEW provided "convincing evidence that lead poisoning could be avoided . . . if already extant workplace safety regulations were *stringently enforced*." Crucially, the WIDC "concurred" with the SPEW's overall contention that "controllable conditions" (which included the lack of stringent enforcement) were responsible for the illness. Therefore, both groups agreed that enforcing the existing rules was the solution to reducing illness.

E   The initial premise of the entire debate is the "high incidence" of illness. The groups argued the regulations *could* be effective if enforced, but the current reality was the opposite, suggesting the regulations had not been effective due to non-enforcement.

The correct answer is D.

544. According to the passage, the WIDC believed that the proposed legislation resembled earlier legislation concerning women's labor in that it

(A)   caused divisiveness among women's organizations

(B)   sought to protect women's health

(C)   limited women's occupational opportunities

(D)   failed to bolster workplace safety regulations

(E)   failed to make distinctions among types of factory work

Supporting Idea

The item asks why the WIDC (Women's Industrial Defence Committee) opposed the 1895 white lead factory legislation, specifically how they viewed it in relation to earlier legislation concerning women's labor.

A   The passage shows that the proposal *did* cause divisiveness (WIDC and SPEW vs. WTUL), but the WIDC's stated reason for opposing the legislation was that it restricted opportunities, not that it caused internal conflict.

B   While the earlier legislation may have also been framed as a health measure (just as the white lead proposal was), the WIDC's reason for *opposing* the measure was not its goal but its *effect* (limiting opportunities).

C   **Correct.** The passage directly states that the WIDC "opposed the proposal, viewing it as yet another instance of limiting women's work opportunities." The phrase "yet another instance" shows the WIDC saw a clear resemblance to earlier legislation, which had also been aimed at restricting women's labor.

D   The WIDC and SPEW argued that the law should focus on enforcing existing regulations, but the WIDC's primary stated opposition to *this* legislation (and, by extension, earlier similar legislation) was based on limiting job opportunities.

E   The legislation was specifically targeted at the white lead trade, meaning it *did* make distinctions. There is no information that the WIDC criticized the law for being overly broad or failing to make distinctions.

The correct answer is C.

545. The reference to the absence of unions in white lead factories (lines 28 and 29) serves primarily to explain why

(A)   more women than men worked in white lead factories

(B)   previous attempts to restrict women's labor had been successful

(C)   SPEW felt the need to investigate the causes of illness in white lead factories

(D)   WTUL ceased to oppose restrictions on women's labor

(E)   WTUL doubted that safety regulations would be enforced in white lead factories

Evaluation

The item asks for the primary purpose of the reference to the absence of unions in white lead factories. Understanding the purpose of the reference to the absence of unions depends on understanding their traditional role in advocating for adherence to safety regulations, and then connecting that to the WTUL's position.

A   The passage mentions that most workers were women, but it does not connect this gender disparity to the absence of unions.

B   The passage only mentions the WTUL's change of heart ("ceased . . . to oppose restrictions") in the late 1880s, but the lack of unions is used to explain why the WTUL supported the *current* 1895 proposal, not why *previous* attempts to restrict women's labor participation succeeded.

C   SPEW's investigation was prompted by the high incidence of illness and their desire to challenge the legislative ban, but the passage does not link the lack of unions to the SPEW's decision to investigate.

D   The WTUL "ceased . . . to oppose restrictions" in the late 1880s, *before* the 1895 proposal. The lack of unions is a reason for their support of the *specific* 1895 proposal, not a reason for the original, prior shift in their general policy.

E   **Correct.** The passage explains the WTUL's position: it supported the ban "in part because safety regulations were generally not being enforced in white lead factories, where there were no unions (and little prospect of any) to pressure employers to comply with safety regulations." The reference to the absence of unions is the direct causal reason for the WTUL's doubt about enforcement, which in turn explains why the WTUL supported the legislation (unlike WIDC and SPEW).

The correct answer is E.

Questions 546–547 refer to the passage on page 478.

546. The passage suggests that Hughes's views regarding the comparative importance of Westinghouse and Edison as nineteenth-century inventors are most consistent with the views expressed by which of the following?

(A)   Some recent historians

(B)   The author of the passage

(C)   Modern corporate research directors

(D)   Archivists of nineteenth-century railroad records

(E)   Historians during the late nineteenth century

Supporting Idea

The item asks which group's views align with those of Thomas Hughes, who is cited in the passage as assigning "special prominence to Thomas Edison" while virtually ignoring George Westinghouse. Hughes's view emphasizes Edison's importance and tends to disregard Westinghouse; this emphasis on Edison is explicitly compared to the views of recent historians.

A   **Correct.** The passage states that Hughes's comparative neglect of Westinghouse "is consistent with other recent historians' works." This observation directly indicates that Hughes's view, which elevates Edison and minimizes Westinghouse, is shared by some recent historians.

B   The author's view is that Westinghouse has been *neglected* and his importance should be *reevaluated*, which contrasts sharply with Hughes's lack of interest in Westinghouse.

C   The passage states that Westinghouse's systematic approach better exemplifies the approach that would become a hallmark of modern corporate research and development. This suggests modern corporate research directors would likely value Westinghouse's methods, in contrast to Hughes's neglect of him.

D   The author's reevaluation of Westinghouse was facilitated by materials found in railroad archives. While these archives provided the *evidence* for the author's argument for Westinghouse's importance, the passage does not suggest that the archivists themselves hold a specific view regarding the comparative importance of the two inventors.

E   The passage explicitly notes that Hughes's neglect of Westinghouse "marks an intriguing departure from the prevailing view during the inventors' lifetimes (and for decades afterward)" which saw Edison and Westinghouse as the two "pioneer innovators." The historians of the late nineteenth century (during the inventors' lifetimes) saw both men as important, which is inconsistent with Hughes's focus on Edison.

The correct answer is A.

547. Which of the following does the passage suggest was LEAST important to the railroad industry of the late nineteenth century?

(A)   Systemization

(B)   Product development

(C)   Standardization

(D)   Innovativeness

(E)   Orderliness

Supporting Idea

The item asks which factor was *least* important to the railroad industry of the late nineteenth century, based on the information in the passage. The key sentence is in the second paragraph: "Westinghouse, however, shared the attitudes of the railroads and other industries for whom he developed innovations: product development, standardization, system, and order were top priorities."

A   The passage states that Westinghouse shared the attitudes of the railroads, for whom *system* was a "top priority."

B   The passage states that product development was a "top priority" for the railroads.

C   The passage states that standardization was a "top priority" for the railroads.

D   **Correct.** The passage focuses on Edison's paramount goal being *novelty* (a synonym for innovativeness) and contrasts this with Westinghouse's focus on system and standardization, which he shared with the railroads. While the railroads certainly needed innovation, the passage explicitly lists "product development, standardization, system, and order" as their *top priorities*. *Innovativeness* (or novelty) is the only concept *not* explicitly called a "top priority."

E   The passage states that order was a "top priority" for the railroads.

The correct answer is D.

Questions 548–600 — Difficulty: **Medium**

Questions 548–553 refer to the passage on page 479.

548. According to the passage, which of the following was true of the treaty establishing the Fort Berthold Indian Reservation?

(A)   It was challenged in the Supreme Court a number of times.

(B)   It was rescinded by the federal government, an action that gave rise to the Winters case.

(C)   It cited American Indians' traditional use of the land's resources.

(D)   It failed to mention water rights to be enjoyed by the reservation's inhabitants.

(E)   It was modified by the Supreme Court in *Arizona v. California*.

Supporting Idea

This question depends on recognizing what the passage says about the treaty that established the Fort Berthold Indian Reservation. The passage indicates that the treaty does not mention water rights, but the federal government had intended, according to the Supreme Court, to reserve for the inhabitants of the reservation the waters that were essential to the usefulness of the land.

A   The passage does discuss Supreme Court cases, but it does not explicitly mention any challenges in the Supreme Court to the treaty.

B   The passage does not state that the federal government rescinded the treaty.

C   The passage does not indicate that the treaty made any reference to the traditional use of the land's resources.

D   Correct. The passage indicates that the treaty does not mention water rights.

E   The passage's reference to *Arizona v. California* relates to the treaty that established the Fort Berthold Indian Reservation only in that *Arizona v. California* refers to the Winters doctrine, which was established in a case regarding that treaty; *Arizona v. California* does not modify that treaty in any way.

The correct answer is D.

549. The passage suggests that, if the criteria discussed in lines 10–20 of the text were the only criteria for establishing a reservation's water rights, which of the following would be true?

(A)   The water rights of the inhabitants of the Fort Berthold Indian Reservation would not take precedence over those of other citizens.

(B)   Reservations established before 1848 would be judged to have no water rights.

(C)   There would be no legal basis for the water rights of the Rio Grande pueblos.

(D)   Reservations other than American Indian reservations could not be created with reserved water rights.

(E)   Treaties establishing reservations would have to mention water rights explicitly in order to reserve water for a particular purpose.

Inference

The question requires you to make an inference based on a hypothetical situation in which the criteria discussed in lines 10–20 are the only criteria relevant to establishing a reservation's water rights. These criteria relate to any reservation that has been formally withdrawn from federal public lands, in which the circumstances of that withdrawal make clear that the government had intended to reserve both water and land when the reservation was established. Because the Rio Grande pueblos never formally constituted a part of federal public lands, they were never formally withdrawn from these lands, and so this set of criteria does not apply to these pueblos. Thus, if these were the only legal criteria for establishing water rights, then there would be no legal basis for water rights for the Rio Grande pueblos.

A   The criteria, which were established on the precedent set in the *Winters v. United States* ruling, all apply to the Fort Berthold Indian Reservation.

B   Although in actual fact there were no Indian reservations formally established before 1848, nothing in the passage suggests that there were not any, or that none would have met the criteria.

C   Correct. If the criteria were the only criteria relevant for establishing water rights, then the passage suggests that, because the Rio Grande pueblos were never formally withdrawn from federal public lands, there would be no legal basis for water rights for these pueblos.

D   The criteria as expressed in the passage do not restrict the type of reservation covered to American Indian reservations.

E   The criteria are meant to cover any circumstances in which the government intended to reserve water rights, whether water rights are explicitly mentioned or not.

The correct answer is C.

550. Which of the following most accurately summarizes the relationship between *Arizona v. California*, as that decision is described in the passage, and the criteria discussed in lines 10–20?

(A) *Arizona v. California* abolishes these criteria and establishes a competing set of criteria for applying the Winters doctrine.

(B) *Arizona v. California* establishes that the Winters doctrine applies to a broader range of situations than those defined by these criteria.

(C) *Arizona v. California* represents the sole example of an exception to the criteria as they were set forth in the Winters doctrine.

(D) *Arizona v. California* does not refer to the Winters doctrine to justify water rights, whereas these criteria do rely on the Winters doctrine.

(E) *Arizona v. California* applies the criteria derived from the Winters doctrine only to federal lands other than American Indian reservations.

Evaluation

This question requires you to determine how *Arizona v. California*, as it is described in the passage, relates to the criteria discussed in lines 10–20. Those criteria, which were established in various decisions based on the precedent of *Winters v. United States*, lay down conditions under which courts can uphold federal rights to reserve water. One of the criteria is related to land formally withdrawn from federal public lands. *Arizona v. California* establishes that the Winters doctrine—which stipulates that water rights need not have been granted explicitly—applies to a broader range of situations than those defined by the criteria. For instance, the doctrine can apply in cases in which the land in question was never formally withdrawn from public lands.

A   The passage does not indicate that *Arizona v. California* abolishes these criteria. It merely indicates that *Arizona v. California* recognizes further situations to which the Winters doctrine can apply.

B   Correct. The passage indicates that *Arizona v. California* applies the Winters doctrine to a situation that falls outside these criteria.

C   The passage does not indicate that there are no other exceptions besides *Arizona v. California* to these criteria.

D   The passage indicates that *Arizona v. California* does refer to the Winters doctrine to justify water rights.

E   The passage does not indicate that *Arizona v. California* applies these criteria at all; instead, *Arizona v. California* broadens the range of situations to which the Winters doctrine applies.

The correct answer is B.

551. The "pragmatic approach" mentioned in lines 37–38 of the passage is best defined as one that

(A) grants recognition to reservations that were never formally established but that have traditionally been treated as such

(B) determines the water rights of all citizens in a particular region by examining the actual history of water usage in that region

(C) gives federal courts the right to reserve water along with land even when it is clear that the government originally intended to reserve only the land

(D) bases the decision to recognize the legal rights of a group on the practical effect such a recognition is likely to have on other citizens

(E) dictates that courts ignore precedents set by such cases as *Winters v. United States* in deciding what water rights belong to reserved land

Evaluation

This question depends on determining how the term *pragmatic approach* is used in lines 37–38. The passage states that what constitutes an American Indian reservation is a matter not of legal definition, but of practice. The Rio Grande pueblos, though they were never formally established by a withdrawal from federal public lands, have always been treated in practice as reservations. This is what is described in the passage as a *pragmatic approach*.

A **Correct.** The passage refers to the idea that *[w]hat constitutes an American Indian reservation is a question of practice, not of legal definition* as a *pragmatic approach.* Thus, the pragmatic approach does not require that a reservation has been formally established, but only that it has been traditionally treated as such.

B The passage does not concern itself with the water rights of all citizens.

C The passage clearly indicates that determining whether the government intended to reserve water along with the land is crucial for courts.

D The passage does not specifically consider the likely practical effect of recognizing a particular group's legal rights on other citizens.

E The passage indicates that the pragmatic approach is supported by *Arizona v. California*, which used, and expanded on, the precedent set by *Winters v. United States*.

The correct answer is A.

552. It can be inferred from the passage that the Winters doctrine has been used to establish which of the following?

(A) A rule that the government may reserve water only by explicit treaty or agreement

(B) A legal distinction between federal lands reserved for American Indians and federal lands reserved for other purposes

(C) Criteria governing when the federal government may set land aside for a particular purpose

(D) The special status of American Indian tribes' rights to reserved land

(E) The federal right to reserve water implicitly as well as explicitly under certain conditions

Inference

This question requires you to make an inference based on facts the passage cites regarding the Winters doctrine. The passage indicates that the Supreme Court ruled in *Winters v. United States* that, despite the fact that the treaty establishing the Berthold Indian Reservation made no explicit mention of water rights, the federal government had intended to reserve such rights to the American Indians living on that reservation. Later court rulings that cited the Winters ruling as precedent further refined this doctrine such that water rights can be reserved implicitly if *circumstances reveal [that] the government intended to reserve water as well as land when establishing the reservation.*

A The passage states that the Winters doctrine ruled that even if a treaty has not explicitly reserved water, water may be reserved if conditions reveal that the reservation of water had been intended.

B The passage indicates that the Winters doctrine presupposes such a legal distinction; it does not establish it.

C The passage does not give any information that suggests that the Winters doctrine has been used to establish any criteria governing when the federal government may set land aside for a particular purpose.

D The passage indicates that the Winters doctrine gives special status to the water flowing through reserved lands, but it does not suggest that the doctrine has been used to establish any special status of American Indian tribes' rights to those lands.

E **Correct.** The passage provides information suggesting that the Winters doctrine has been used to establish a federal right to implicitly reserve water under certain conditions.

The correct answer is E.

553. The author cites the fact that the Rio Grande pueblos were never formally withdrawn from public lands primarily in order to do which of the following?

(A) Suggest why it might have been argued that the Winters doctrine ought not to apply to pueblo lands

(B) Imply that the United States never really acquired sovereignty over pueblo lands

(C) Argue that the pueblo lands ought still to be considered part of federal public lands

(D) Support the argument that the water rights of citizens other than American Indians are limited by the Winters doctrine

(E)   Suggest that federal courts cannot claim jurisdiction over cases disputing the traditional diversion and use of water by Pueblo Indians

Evaluation

The passage in the first paragraph outlines a set of criteria that, through various court decisions using the Winters decision as precedent, refined what came to be known as the Winters doctrine. These decisions established that courts can uphold federal rights to reserve water (specifically, for use by American Indians) if, among other conditions, *the land has been formally withdrawn from federal public lands*. Because the Rio Grande pueblos never formally constituted a part of federal public lands, it might appear that the Winters doctrine would not apply to them. The passage indicates, however, that *Arizona v. California* established that this doctrine did apply to them.

A   Correct. Because the Rio Grande pueblo lands were never formally withdrawn from federal public lands—because they never were a part of federal public lands—it might have appeared that the Winters doctrine did not apply to them, because that doctrine had traditionally been taken to apply only to land that had been formally withdrawn from federal public lands.

B   The passage does suggest that the federal government never acquired sovereignty over the Rio Grande pueblos. But the passage indicates this not by citing the fact that the pueblos were never formally withdrawn from public lands, but by pointing out that these pueblos were never part of federal public lands in the first place.

C   The passage states that the pueblo lands were never considered to be part of federal public lands.

D   It is not the fact that these lands were never withdrawn from federal public lands that is cited in support of this argument; it is, rather, the fact that these lands were never part of federal public lands that is cited for this purpose.

E   The passage actually suggests the opposite of what this says, namely, that federal courts can claim jurisdiction over such cases.

The correct answer is A.

Questions 554–558 refer to the passage on page 481.

Main Idea Summary

The passage seeks to provide guidance about when companies should subject their suppliers to "competitive scrutiny" (readily comparing suppliers to provide the purchaser with economic leverage) and when they should accept "supplier partnerships" (arrangements in which the purchaser forgoes the right to pursue alternative suppliers). It does this primarily by distinguishing among four types of situations, each with its own set of implications for which approach is likely to be more advantageous.

554. Which of the following can be inferred about supplier partnerships, as they are described in the passage?

(A)   They cannot be sustained unless the goods or services provided are available from a large number of suppliers.

(B)   They can result in purchasers paying more for goods and services than they would in a competitive-bidding situation.

(C)   They typically are instituted at the urging of the supplier rather than the purchaser.

(D)   They are not feasible when the goods or services provided are directly related to the purchasers' end products.

(E)   They are least appropriate when the purchasers' ability to change suppliers is limited.

Inference

According to the passage, in supplier partnerships a corporate purchaser forgoes the right to pursue alternative suppliers for certain goods or services. This tends to reduce or eliminate the threat of competition for the supplier in the partnership. It can be inferred that the corporate purchaser in a supplier partnership risks paying more for goods or services than it would if the supplier had to compete for the business.

A   The passage suggests something incompatible with this, i.e., that availability of the relevant goods or services from many suppliers would undermine rather than strengthen a supplier partnership.

B   Correct. The passage indicates that supplier partnerships, by definition, reduce the supplier's exposure to competition, and it can be inferred from this that a purchaser in such a partnership could sometimes pay more for the supplied goods or services than if not in the partnership.

C   The passage is silent on how supplier partnerships are initiated, and the passage gives no reason to believe that these would usually be initiated by suppliers.

D   The passage indicates that supplier partnerships are usually instituted for the supply of goods or services that do not contribute directly to the company's end products, though the passage gives no reason to believe that such partnerships would never make sense for supply of items directly related to end products.

E   The passage states that where alternative suppliers for certain goods or services are few and change from an existing supplier is difficult, *partnerships may be unavoidable.* This seems to imply that in such cases, supplier partnerships are the most appropriate.

The correct answer is B.

555. Which of the following best describes the relation of the second paragraph to the first?

(A)   The second paragraph offers proof of an assertion made in the first paragraph.

(B)   The second paragraph provides an explanation for the occurrence of a situation described in the first paragraph.

(C)   The second paragraph discusses the application of a strategy proposed in the first paragraph.

(D)   The second paragraph examines the scope of a problem presented in the first paragraph.

(E)   The second paragraph discusses the contradictions inherent in a relationship described in the first paragraph.

Evaluation

The first paragraph recommends that a corporate purchaser of certain categories of goods and services should consider two variables to evaluate how, if at all, it might exert pressure on a supplier to gain economic advantage. Applying the two variables, the second paragraph identifies four different scenarios and, for each scenario, explains how the purchaser can gain some economic advantage.

A   The second paragraph is not focused on proving anything; rather, it conducts an analysis of the ways in which, under various conditions, a corporate purchaser can gain economic advantage from a supplier.

B   The second paragraph conducts an analysis of various situations affecting the feasibility of a purchaser's exerting pressure to gain economic advantage from a supplier; it is not focused on explaining what causes the occurrence of any situation mentioned in the first paragraph.

C   Correct. The first paragraph recommends that corporate purchasers consider two variables in analyzing the feasibility of exerting pressure on suppliers with a view to economic advantage; the second paragraph shows how purchasers can apply those variables to identify four different types of situations affecting the degree to which economic advantage can be gained by exerting competitive pressure.

D   The first paragraph is not focused on presenting a problem, but rather on indicating an approach that purchasers might use in evaluating the feasibility of exerting economic pressure on suppliers with a view to economic advantage. The second paragraph elaborates on the suggested approach.

E   The second paragraph does not characterize as contradictory any relationship involved in the four types of situations it discusses. The first paragraph discusses supplier partnerships and identifies a disadvantage that they sometimes involve for purchasers, but the discussion in the second paragraph does not focus exclusively on situations that involve a supplier partnership.

The correct answer is C.

556. It can be inferred that the author of the passage would be most likely to make which of the following recommendations to a company purchasing health care benefits for its employees?

(A)   Devise strategies for circumventing the obstacles to replacing the current provider of health care benefits.

(B)   Obtain health care benefits from a provider that also provides other indirect products and services.

(C)   Obtain bids from other providers of health care benefits in order to be in a position to negotiate a better deal with the current provider.

(D)   Switch providers of health care benefits whenever a different provider offers a more competitive price.

(E)   Acknowledge the difficulties involved in replacing the current provider of health care benefits and offer to form a partnership with the provider.

Inference

In the passage, health care benefits are used as an example of a Type 2 situation, where there are many competing providers but changing from one provider to another is difficult. In Type 2 situations, the author of the passage recommends that the corporate purchaser examine the alternative providers to provide leverage in bargaining with the existing provider.

A   Presumably handling any obstacles to replacement would be necessary if a corporate purchaser had decided to change providers. The author of the passage does not preclude the possibility that this may sometimes be a reasonable decision but does not recommend it.

B   The author of the passage does not consider such a possibility and does not even recommend switching from the existing provider in a Type 2 situation.

C   **Correct.** The recommendation offered in the passage is to review competitive alternatives to the existing provider, with a view to bargaining effectively for better terms with the existing provider.

D   As already noted, the author of the passage does not recommend switching from the existing provider, but rather recommends reviewing competitive alternatives to exert pressure on the existing provider to grant more favorable terms.

E   The author of the passage does not recommend this course of action in a Type 2 situation, which the corporate purchase of health care benefits exemplifies. The only situation in which the author views a supplier partnership as possibly the best of a set of bad options is a Type 4 situation, where there are few competitive alternatives available and change is difficult.

The correct answer is C.

557. Which of the following is one difference between Type 2 situations and Type 4 situations, as they are described in the passage?

(A)   The number of alternative suppliers available to the purchaser

(B)   The most effective approach for the purchaser to use in obtaining competitive bids from potential suppliers

(C)   The degree of difficulty the purchaser encounters when changing suppliers

(D)   The frequency with which each type of situation occurs in a typical business environment

(E)   The likelihood that any given purchase will be an indirect purchase

Evaluation

According to the passage, Type 2 situations are those where there are several competitive alternative suppliers available but changing from the existing supplier would be difficult. Type 4 situations are those where there are few competitive alternative suppliers and changing from the existing supplier would be difficult.

A   **Correct.** The two types of situations differ in the number of competitive alternatives to the existing supplier that are available: in Type 2 situations there are several; in Type 4 situations there are few.

B   How should the prospective purchaser ensure that potential suppliers submit truly competitive bids, or can a prospective purchaser even ensure it? The passage gives no answer to such questions that helps to identify a difference between the two types of situations.

C   In both types of situations as described in the passage, changing to a new supplier is difficult, and no difference in the degree of difficulty is mentioned.

D   How frequently each of the two types of situations typically occurs is not addressed in the passage.

E   Indirect purchases, as described in the passage, are goods or services that are not embodied in the corporation's end products. Many corporate producers currently make indirect purchases such as computers or business consultancy services. The passage does not compare the proportion of a corporation's total purchases that are indirect (the proportion would presumably vary widely depending on the nature of a corporation's production), so the passage provides no rational basis for estimating a universally applicable likelihood that a given purchase would be indirect.

The correct answer is A.

558. According to the passage, which of the following factors distinguishes an indirect purchase from other purchases?

(A)   The ability of the purchasing company to subject potential suppliers of the purchased item to competitive scrutiny

(B)   The number of suppliers of the purchased item available to the purchasing company

(C)   The methods of negotiation that are available to the purchasing company

(D)   The relationship of the purchased item to the purchasing company's end product

(E)   The degree of importance of the purchased item in the purchasing company's business operations

Supporting Idea

The passage characterizes a purchase of goods or services as indirect when the goods or services are not directly related to the end products of the purchasing corporation. Examples given are computers, advertising, and legal services. By implication, direct purchases by an automobile manufacturer could include steel, batteries, and tires: these would obviously be inputs embodied in the final products.

A   The passage suggests that competitive scrutiny is typically applied only to suppliers of direct purchases, but it makes the case that it could also be applied to suppliers of indirect purchases. The exposure to competitive scrutiny is not the characteristic that the passage uses to distinguish direct from indirect purchases.

B   The number of available suppliers clearly can vary for both direct purchases and indirect purchases, and the passage provides no reason to think otherwise.

C   The passage provides no information about the methods of negotiation that are available for direct purchases. The passage does not base the distinction between direct and indirect purchases on differences in methods of negotiation.

D   **Correct.** The passage defines direct purchases as those directly related to the purchasing firm's end products; indirect purchases are purchases that are not related to the end products.

E   The type of purchase—direct or indirect—is not, according to the passage, determined by the degree of importance of the purchase in facilitating the purchasing firm's business operations. For example, purchase of advertising by an accounting firm could be critically important for success of the firm's business operations, but such a purchase would likely count as indirect, given the way the passage defines indirect purchases.

The correct answer is D.

Questions 559–563 refer to the passage on page 483.

Main Idea Summary

The passage is a discussion of historian Linda Kerber's "republican motherhood" thesis, according to which the American Revolution led to an increase in educational opportunities for women and girls in the United States in the late eighteenth century. Kerber's work was influential at least partly because she explored a topic (female education) that historians had largely ignored. However, the passage cites an earlier historian who had provided evidence that the trend toward greater educational opportunities for women and girls had begun decades before the American Revolution. The main idea of the passage is that the influence of the "republican motherhood" thesis may have led historians to overlook evidence that the trend Kerber describes was already underway before the American Revolution.

559. According to the passage, Kerber maintained that which of the following led to an increase in educational opportunities for women in the United States after the American Revolution?

(A) An unprecedented demand by women for greater educational opportunities in the decades following the Revolution

(B) A new political ideology calling for equality of opportunity between women and men in all aspects of life

(C) A belief that the American educational system could be reformed only if women participated more fully in that system

(D) A belief that women needed to be educated if they were to contribute to the success of the nation's new form of government

(E) A recognition that women needed to be educated if they were to take an active role in the nation's schools and churches

Supporting Idea

The passage ascribes to Linda Kerber the claim that there was *a surge of educational opportunities for women in the United States* after the American Revolution, and that this surge resulted from a new ideology of "republican motherhood."

According to the passage, Kerber argued that the nation's leaders advocated education for women to equip them, in their family role, to raise politically virtuous sons.

A   The passage attributes no claim to Kerber concerning a demand by women for education.

B   The passage attributes no claim to Kerber concerning a new ideology calling for equality between women and men.

C   Kerber's argument as represented in the passage did not claim that an increase in education opportunities for women resulted from a belief that such an increase was required for successful reform of the American educational system.

D   Correct. According to the passage, Kerber argued that educational opportunities for women increased because the nation's leaders believed that successful democratic government would require that women raise politically virtuous sons within their families, and that women could do so only if they had access to education themselves.

E   According to the passage, Kerber's thesis primarily concerns the roles that it was believed educated women could play in raising politically virtuous sons in the context of the family, not in the nation's schools or churches.

The correct answer is D.

560. According to the passage, within the field of educational history, Thomas Woody's 1929 work was

(A) innovative because it relied on newspaper advertisements as evidence

(B) exceptional in that it concentrated on the period before the American Revolution

(C) unusual in that it focused on educational attitudes rather than on educational practices

(D) controversial in its claims regarding educational opportunities for boys

(E) atypical in that it examined the education of girls

Supporting Idea

According to the passage, Woody's work was a *notable exception* as contrast to the work of other educational historians, who *barely mentioned women and girls*.

A   Other historians prior to Woody's 1929 work may have used newspaper advertisements as evidence, but the passage provides no information as to whether this was so.

B   The passage is silent as to whether educational historians besides Woody concentrated on the period before the American Revolution.

C   The passage does not provide information as to the extent to which either Woody or other historians focused on educational attitudes as opposed to educational practices.

D   According to the passage, Woody noted that educational opportunities increased for both girls and boys around 1750. But the passage does not indicate that this claim, or any other claim Woody may have made about educational opportunities for boys, was controversial.

E   **Correct.** As stated above, the passage describes Woody's work as a *notable exception*, i.e., atypical, with respect to his discussion of education for girls.

The correct answer is E.

561. The passage suggests that Woody would have agreed with which of the following claims regarding "An Essay on Woman"?

(A)   It expressed attitudes concerning women's education that were reflected in new educational opportunities for women after 1750.

(B)   It persuaded educators to offer greater educational opportunities to women in the 1750s.

(C)   It articulated ideas about women's education that would not be realized until after the American Revolution.

(D)   It offered one of the most original arguments in favor of women's education in the United States in the eighteenth century.

(E)   It presented views about women's education that were still controversial in Woody's own time.

Application

According to the passage, Woody characterized "An Essay on Woman" (1753) as reflecting a shift in view, and the context indicates that this shift concerned new attitudes that accompanied increased opportunities after 1750 for girls to become educated women.

A   **Correct.** Based on the passage, this is a claim with which Woody would likely have agreed.

B   The passage represents Woody as claiming that "An Essay on Woman" reflected changes that had already occurred around 1750. The passage does not indicate whether Woody would have agreed with this claim about a persuasive effect on educators.

C   Nothing in the passage represents Woody as thinking that "An Essay on Woman" had ideas about women's education that did not come to fruition until after the American Revolution. The tenor of Woody's thinking, as the passage represents it, is that the essay reflected changes already occurring.

D   The passage indicates that Woody characterizes "An Essay on Woman" as *reflecting* a view that had already gained some currency, so it is unlikely that Woody saw the essay as offering any highly original arguments in favor of women's education.

E   It may be true that "An Essay on Woman" presented some views that were at least somewhat controversial even around 1929, but the passage provides no information that addresses this point.

The correct answer is A.

562. The passage suggests that, with regard to the history of women's education in the United States, Kerber's work differs from Woody's primarily concerning which of the following?

(A)   The extent to which women were interested in pursuing educational opportunities in the eighteenth century

(B)   The extent of the support for educational opportunities for girls prior to the American Revolution

(C)   The extent of public resistance to educational opportunities for women after the American Revolution

(D)   Whether attitudes toward women's educational opportunities changed during the eighteenth century

(E)   Whether women needed to be educated in order to contribute to the success of a republican form of government

Evaluation

The passage represents Kerber as claiming that the American Revolution led to a surge in educational opportunities for women because the nation's leaders believed women needed to be educated if they were to raise politically virtuous sons. Woody, however, is represented as claiming that there was a significant increase in such opportunities and significant advocacy for women's education well before the Revolution.

A   The passage does not represent either Kerber or Woody as addressing the extent to which women were interested in pursuing educational opportunities in the eighteenth century.

B   Correct. The passage attributes to Woody the view that *practical education for females had many advocates before the Revolution*, notably in the 1750s, and that the Revolution at most accelerated an earlier trend of changing attitudes. This is contrary to the views attributed to Kerber.

C   The passage gives no information as to whether Kerber or Woody addresses this issue, nor does it discuss to what extent, if any, such resistance may have occurred.

D   The passage indicates that Kerber and Woody hold that there was a change in attitudes toward women's educational opportunities during the eighteenth century, disagreeing, however, as to whether the most significant change occurred before or after the Revolution.

E   Neither Kerber nor Woody is represented by the passage as holding divergent views on this point, and it would be reasonable to think that they may have agreed.

The correct answer is B.

563. According to the passage, Kerber argued that political leaders thought that the form of government adopted by the United States after the American Revolution depended on which of the following for its success?

(A)   Women assuming the sole responsibility for instilling political virtue in children

(B)   Girls becoming the primary focus of a reformed educational system that emphasized political virtue

(C)   The family serving as one of the primary means by which children were imbued with political virtue

(D)   The family assuming many of the functions previously performed by schools and churches

(E)   Men and women assuming equal responsibility for the management of schools, churches, and the family

Supporting Idea

The passage attributes to Kerber the claim that the nation's leaders believed a virtuous citizenry was essential to the success of the nation's republican form of government, and that women would play a primary role in raising future citizens who would be politically virtuous.

A   According to the passage, Kerber indicates that the nation's leaders believed churches and schools, as well as families, would work to imbue political virtue, though they emphasized the crucial role of families.

B   Kerber argues that the educational system underwent reform in the sense that educational opportunities for women increased but does not claim that schools or families would change focus to imbue girls with political virtue.

C   Correct. Kerber argues that political leaders emphasized the family as the primary means by which future citizens would be imbued with political virtue.

D   Kerber does not claim the nation's leaders proposed that the family would take over functions previously fulfilled by schools and churches.

E   Kerber does not attribute to the nation's leaders the view that men and women would exercise equal roles in managing schools, churches, and the family.

The correct answer is C.

Questions 564–568 refer to the passage on page 485.

564. It can be inferred from the passage that geologists today would be most likely to agree with which of the following statements about Wegener's *The Origin of Continents and Oceans*?

   (A) It was a worthy scientific effort that was ahead of its time.

   (B) It was based on evidence that was later disproved.

   (C) It was directly responsible for the acceptance of the theory of plate tectonics.

   (D) It has been disproved by continental drift theory.

   (E) It misrepresented how horizontal displacements cause the formation of mountain chains.

Inference

Notice what is asserted in the passage's first paragraph about the attitudes or beliefs of today's geologists. We read that most geologists today consider Wegener's book "an impressive and prescient document" because its ideas significantly overlap with those of plate tectonics, the theory accepted by most geologists today. But the passage stops short of attributing the development of plate tectonics to Wegener's ideas, which were widely rejected by Wegener's peer geologists.

A **Correct.** The passage tells us that today's geologists find Wegener's book to be impressive, i.e., respectable as a work of science, as well as "prescient," i.e., it anticipated some of the key assumptions of plate tectonics.

B Nowhere in the passage is it asserted that Wegener's evidence was "disproved," though the passage indicates that Wegener's evidence and his theoretical findings were largely rejected by his geological contemporaries. The passage does not suggest that the rejection was based on countervailing evidence.

C The word "directly" in this option is unwarranted by any information provided in the passage, even though the passage notes an important conceptual kinship between Wegener's theories and plate tectonics.

D The passage tells us that the content of Wegener's book focused on what was later called continental drift theory. Rather than supporting the claim that continental drift theory disproved the major ideas in Wegener's book, it shows the absurdity of such a claim.

E This option suggests that today's geologists assume Wegener's theory lacked an adequate account of mountain range formation. The passage suggests that today's geologists believe Wegener's theory lacked "an adequate mechanical basis." In other words, it provided no plausible mechanism to adequately explain how continental drift produced mountain ranges. This is distinct from misrepresenting the process, i.e., providing an account of the process that was false or misleading.

The correct answer is A.

565. The author of the passage suggests the most likely explanation for the geological community's response to continental drift theory in its day was that the theory

   (A) was in conflict with certain aspects of plate tectonics theory

   (B) failed to account for how mountains were formed

   (C) did not adequately explain how continents moved through the ocean floor

   (D) was contradicted by the geophysical data of the time

   (E) was based on a kind of evidence that was considered insufficiently convincing

Supporting Idea

Why did Wegener's scientific peers reject his continental drift theory? In the passage's second paragraph, the author suggests that the most likely cause was "the nature of the evidence" Wegener offered in support of it. Wegener's evidence was derived from "direct observations of rocks in the field" using simple tools such as hammers and hand lenses, whereas plate tectonics used technically sophisticated instruments.

A   The passage indicates that the primary motivation for the rejection of continental drift theory by Wegener's peers was not theoretical incompatibility with plate tectonic theory. The passage emphasizes the significant overlaps in the "presumptions" of both theories.

B   The passage states that Wegener's theory was rejected despite providing a possible explanation for mountain formation, not because it failed to do so.

C   The author of the passage signals disagreement with the view of a number of other researchers that Wegener's peers rejected continental drift theory because it failed to explain how continents could move through the ocean floor.

D   The passage neither states nor implies that continental drift theory conflicted, or was perceived to conflict, with geophysical data available around 1912 when Wegener's book was published.

E   **Correct.** The passage contrasts the kind of data related to "similarities of patterns and forms" with the more precise kind of data that plate tectonics collected. Wegener's data was collected using hammers and hand lenses, whereas the data collected by plate tectonics used technical instruments. This difference is offered to explain why Wegener's peers found his data less convincing. According to the author, this likely led to their rejection of continental drift theory.

The correct answer is E.

566. The author of the passage probably refers to the "considerable overlap" (See line 18) between the continental drift theory and plate tectonics theory in order to

(A)   suggest that plate tectonics theory is derived from Wegener's work

(B)   introduce a discussion comparing the elements of the two theories

(C)   examine the question of whether continental drift theory was innovative in its time

(D)   provide a reason why it might seem surprising that continental drift theory was not more widely embraced by geologists

(E)   cite an explanation that has been frequently offered for Wegener's high standing among geologists today

Supporting Idea

The sentence in line 18 has the following structure: Despite X and despite Y, what occurred was Z. The point being made is that it was surprising that Z occurred when X and Y would have led us to expect that Z would not occur. More concretely: Despite continental drift's overlap with plate tectonics and its initially plausible explanation for the origin of mountains, it was surprising that Wegener's peer geologists largely rejected continental drift theory.

A   The author does not imply anywhere that the plate tectonics were derived from continental drift theory. In fact, the passage describes a difference in the kind of data and collection methods used by the two theories.

B   No such discussion occurs following the phrase in line 18.

C   The passage suggests that continental drift theory was innovative in 1912, but there is no discussion in the context of line 18 as to whether, or in what respects, it was innovative.

D   **Correct.** See the introductory analysis above. The sentence in line 18 provides two reasons why one would expect that continental drift theory would have gained acceptance among Wegener's peer geologists. Surprisingly, it did not.

E   The context of line 18 focuses on explaining the surprising nonacceptance of Wegener's continental drift theory by his contemporaries in geology. That context does not address Wegener's standing among today's geologists.

The correct answer is D.

567. The author cites Hallam (see line 32) on the ice ages primarily in order to

(A) provide an example of a geologic phenomenon with precise causes that are not fully understood by geologists today

(B) criticize the geological community for an apparent lack of consistency in its responses to new theories

(C) offer evidence held to undermine a common view of why Wegener's theory was not accepted in its day

(D) give an example of a modern scientist who believes Wegener's theory was rejected because it failed to adequately explain the mechanical basis of continental drift

(E) support some researchers' rationale for why Wegener's theory was rejected by most geologists in the early twentieth century

Evaluation

The point attributed to Hallam is that the acceptance of a new scientific phenomenon by the scientific community has often not required that the phenomenon have a satisfactory explanation provided for it. What is the author's purpose in citing this point? The point immediately preceding this one is that most of today's geologists and historians of science believe that Wegener's continental drift theory was rejected because it was deficient in explaining some of the phenomena it cited. The author disagrees with this view and cites Hallam as evidence to counter this widely held view of why Wegener's theory was not accepted by his contemporaries in geology.

A   The passage does not provide any example of a phenomenon, the occurrence of which Wegener established and today's geologists regard as not yet having received an adequate causal explanation.

B   The passage asserts that geologists and historians today believe that what caused the nonacceptance of Wegener's theory after 1912 was a deficiency in its explanatory power. But the point attributed to Hallam suggests that this historical account is inadequate. The author cites Hallam not primarily to "criticize" the geological community for a general lack of consistency in "responses to new theories," but to help

show the inadequacy of a widely accepted historical explanation.

C   **Correct.** The purpose of the citation of Hallam is to help show the inadequacy of a widely accepted historical explanation concerning the nonacceptance of Wegener's theory by his contemporaries.

D   The citation of Hallam, a twentieth-century geologist, indicates that he probably did not endorse the historical explanation, which is widely accepted by most of today's geologists and science historians, of why Wegener's theory was not accepted.

E   The citation of Hallam is intended to cast doubt on the historical explanation offered by other researchers, not to support it.

The correct answer is C.

568. The author of the passage most likely discusses the "essential presumptions" (see lines 12–13) of *The Origin of Continents and Oceans* in order to

(A) indicate features of Wegener's theory that caused it to be doubted in its day

(B) show why Wegener's theory is now regarded as prescient

(C) indicate differences between plate tectonics and the theory of continental drift

(D) cite features of the theory of continental drift for which no evidence was available in Wegener's day

(E) point out aspects of Wegener's theory that were accepted well before the advent of plate tectonics

Evaluation

According to the passage, Wegener's book is regarded as "prescient" by most geologists today. This point is supported by detailing three "essential presumptions" of Wegener's theory that are shared by plate tectonics. Thus, the author aims to show that most geologists see Wegener's theory as anticipating, in some important respects, the scientific advances achieved by plate tectonics.

A   The passage does not suggest that the presumptions that Wegener's theory shared with plate tectonics were the cause of the nonacceptance of the theory by Wegener's contemporary peers in geology.

B **Correct.** The context of the phrase "essential presumptions" indicates that the author's purpose is to show how Wegener anticipated some of the important ideas in plate tectonics and was therefore prescient.

C   The passage indicates that there were such differences, but that is not the author's goal in mentioning the "essential presumptions" shared by plate tectonics and continental drift theory.

D   The passage suggests that the kind of evidence given by Wegener for continental drift theory differed from that on which plate tectonics relied, but the author's purpose in citing the "essential presumptions" is not to indicate deficiencies in the evidence for claims made by continental drift theory.

E   The passage does not tell us whether the "essential presumptions" cited were or were not accepted by Wegener's contemporaries in geology.

The correct answer is B.

Questions 569–572 refer to the passage on page 487.

Main Idea Summary

The primary purpose of the passage is to describe resin and discuss a theory on its biological function. The first paragraph identifies some of the characteristics of resin and distinguishes it from gum and sap; one way in which resin differs from these two substances is that its physiological function is not clearly understood. The second paragraph considers whether resin may function to repel or attract insects, and indicates that the consideration of such issues led to the development of the discipline of chemical ecology.

569. According to the passage, which of the following is true of plant antiherbivore chemistry?

(A)   Changes in a plant's antiherbivore chemistry may affect insect feeding behavior.

(B)   A plant's repellent effects often involve interactions between gum and resin.

(C)   A plant's antiherbivore responses assist in combating bacterial infections.

(D)   Plant antiherbivore chemistry plays only a minor role in the coevolution of plants and insects.

(E)   Researchers first studied repellent effects in plants beginning in the 1950s.

Supporting Idea

This question addresses what the information in the passage indicates about plant antiherbivore chemistry—that is, plants' chemical defenses against herbivore attacks. The second paragraph of the passage cites the views of various scientists regarding the possible role of resin in antiherbivore chemistry; plants could have evolved resin specifically to repel insects.

A **Correct.** According to the second paragraph, various scientists have suggested that a change in antiherbivore chemistry, here specifically involving resin, could repel insects; alternatively, some insects could have been attracted to resin, feeding more heavily on plants that produced it. Other researchers have suggested that even if resin does not directly repel or attract insects, it may indirectly affect insect-feeding behavior by mediating changes in plants' antiherbivore chemistry.

B   The first paragraph states that plants produce gum in response to bacterial infections. Although this does not rule out the hypothesis that gum also contributes to plants' antiherbivore chemistry, the passage provides no evidence that it does so.

C   According to the passage, a plant's antiherbivore responses have developed to combat predators, such as insects, that eat plants. The passage provides no evidence that such responses also combat bacterial infections.

D   The second paragraph indicates that plant antiherbivore chemistry plays a major role in the discipline of chemical ecology, and chemical ecology concerns itself with coevolution of plants and insects.

E   According to the passage, it was in the 1950s that entomologists began discussing resin's possible role in repelling and attracting insects. The passage does not suggest that this marked the beginning of their study of repellent effects more generally.

The correct answer is A.

570. Of the following topics, which would be most likely to be studied within the discipline of chemical ecology as it is described in the passage?

(A)   Seeds that become attached to certain insects, which in turn carry away the seeds and aid in the reproductive cycle of the plant species in question

(B)   An insect species that feeds on weeds detrimental to crop health and yield, and how these insects might aid in agricultural production

(C)   The effects of deforestation on the life cycles of subtropical carnivorous plants and the insect species on which the plants feed

(D)   The growth patterns of a particular species of plant that has proved remarkably resistant to herbicides

(E)   Insects that develop a tolerance for feeding on a plant that had previously been toxic to them, and the resultant changes within that plant species

Application

The discipline of chemical ecology, as it is described in the passage, deals with how plants use chemicals to interact with other organisms—in particular, how they defend against attack—and how those interactions have evolved. To be studied within that discipline, a specific topic would need to address some aspect of that chemical interaction.

A   The passage provides no reason to suppose that the topic of seeds and how they travel would be studied within chemical ecology, given that it does not discuss how chemicals might be involved in the reproductive cycle.

B   The passage provides no indication that chemical ecology would be concerned with how weed-destroying insects would aid agricultural production.

C   The passage provides no indication that deforestation would involve plant chemicals or that its effects would be studied in chemical ecology.

D   The passage provides no indication that a plant's resistance to herbicides would be studied in chemical ecology, but the passage does suggest that the focus of chemical ecology is on how plants chemically interact with other organisms.

E   **Correct.** Chemical ecology developed to deal with the interdependence between plants and insects. Insects' developing a tolerance for feeding on a once-toxic plant, and the plants' resultant changes, is a situation of just such interdependence: plants and insects coevolving.

The correct answer is E.

571. The author refers to "bacterial infections" (see line 11) most likely in order to

(A)   describe the physiological function that gum performs in plants

(B)   demonstrate that sap is not the only substance that is transported through a plant's tissues

(C)   explain how modern chemical analysis has been used to clarify the function of resin

(D)   show that gum cannot serve as an effective defense against herbivores

(E)   give an example of how confusion has arisen with regard to the nature of resin

Evaluation

The author mentions *bacterial infections* in the first paragraph as the reason why plants produce the substance known as gum.

A   **Correct.** The author states directly that plants produce gum in response to bacterial infections.

B   The author states directly that sap is transported through plant tissues. The passage does not address the question of whether bacterial infections or anything related to them are similarly transported.

C   The passage indicates that rigorous chemical analysis is now available, but scientists still do not know resin's function. The reference to bacterial infections is related to gum, not resin.

D   The reference to bacterial infections indicates the actual purpose served by gum; it does not function to show ways in which gum is inadequate.

E   Gum itself serves as an example of the confusion surrounding the nature of resin; bacterial infections, to which gum production is a response, do not serve as that example.

The correct answer is A.

572. The author of the passage refers to Pliny most probably in order to

(A)   give an example of how the nature of amber has been misunderstood in the past

(B)   show that confusion about amber has long been more pervasive than confusion about resin

(C)   make note of the first known reference to amber as a semiprecious gem

(D)   point out an exception to a generalization about the history of people's understanding of amber

(E)   demonstrate that Pliny believed amber to be a mineral

Evaluation

The passage states generally that *amber has been widely misunderstood* but cites Pliny as noting correctly, in the first century, that amber resulted from a substance discharged by trees.

A   Pliny's observation was, according to the author, accurate and not a misunderstanding.

B   The author equates confusion about amber with confusion about resin; the reference to Pliny does not indicate which of the two, amber or resin, has been more widely misunderstood.

C   The author indicates that others, not Pliny, mischaracterized amber as a semiprecious gem—and when that mischaracterization first occurred is not identified.

D   **Correct.** Pliny's recognition that amber came from a substance discharged by trees stands, in the author's account, as an exception to the widespread incorrect identifications of the substance.

E   Others held the belief that amber was a mineral. The passage indicates that Pliny recognized that amber came from trees but provides no evidence that he also considered it a mineral.

The correct answer is D.

Questions 573–575 refer to the passage on page 489.

573. The primary purpose of the passage is to

(A)   compare the impact of the Great Depression on Latin America with its impact on the United States

(B)   criticize a school of economic historians for failing to analyze the Great Depression in Latin America within a global context

(C)   illustrate the risks inherent in comparing different types of economic enterprises to explain economic phenomena

(D)   call into question certain scholars' views concerning the severity of the Great Depression in Latin America

(E)   demonstrate that the Great Depression had a more severe impact on industry in Latin American than in certain other regions

Main Idea

This question depends on understanding the passage as a whole. The passage first describes the view of many economic historians of the 1980s. It next describes the evidence on which that view is based. The remainder of the passage raises issues about the rationale for that view.

A   The comparison between Latin America and the United States is only a small part of a larger argument analyzing studies of the Great Depression in Latin America.

B   The passage does not discuss a global context for the Great Depression.

C   The passage does not primarily aim to illustrate risks that may be generally inherent in explaining economic phenomena.

D   **Correct.** The passage claims that certain scholars underestimate the severity of the Great Depression in Latin America.

E   The passage does not claim that the impact of the Great Depression on Latin American industry was generally more severe than its impact on industry elsewhere.

The correct answer is D.

574. Which of the following conclusions about the Great Depression is best supported by the passage?

(A)   It did not impede Latin American industrial growth as much as historians had previously thought.

(B)   It had a more severe impact on the Brazilian and the Mexican textile industries than it had on Latin America as a region.

(C)   It affected the Latin American textile industry more severely than it did any other industry in Latin America.

(D)   The overall impact on Latin American industrial growth should be reevaluated by economic historians.

(E)   Its impact on Latin America should not be compared with its impact on the United States.

Inference

This question asks which conclusion is most strongly supported by the passage. The passage presents the rationale of some historians for their conclusion that the Great Depression did not significantly interfere with economic growth in Latin America. It then critiques that rationale and conclusion. By questioning the historians' claims, the passage suggests that a reevaluation of the Great Depression's effect on Latin America is needed.

A   The passage does not significantly support this. The passage indicates that, in fact, the Great Depression impeded Latin American economic development more than some historians had thought.

B   The passage does not significantly support this. The passage does not compare the impact on the Brazilian and Mexican textile industries to the impact on the Latin American region.

C   The passage does not significantly support this. The passage does not compare the effect of the Great Depression on the textile industry to its effect on other industries.

D   **Correct.** As presented in the passage, the passage author's critique of the historians' rationale for their claims provides significant support for the conclusion that their claims should be reevaluated.

E   The passage does not significantly support the claim that the comparison in question should not be made.

The correct answer is D.

575. Which of the following, if true, would most strengthen the author's assertion regarding economic indicators in lines 25–27?

(A)   During an economic depression, European textile manufacturers' profits rise while their industrial output remains steady.

(B)   During a national economic recession, United States microchips manufacturers' profits rise sharply while United States steel manufacturers' profits plunge.

(C)   During the years following a severe economic depression, textile manufacturers' output levels and profit levels increase in Brazil and Mexico but not in the rest of Latin America.

(D)   Although Japanese industry as a whole recovers after an economic recession, it does not regain its previously high levels of production.

(E)   While European industrial output increases in the years following an economic depression, total output remains below that of Japan or the United States.

Application

The question involves applying information from outside the passage to a claim made by the author. The text in lines 25–27 asserts that broad economic indicators pertaining to a nation or region can obscure differences between individual firms or industries within that nation or region. The question asks which evidence would most strengthen the support for that conclusion.

A   This refers only to the relationship between a single industry's profits and its output, not to general economic indicators.

B Correct. The phrase *a national recession* refers to a general economic indicator. Suppose that in a situation described as a national recession, one industry (microchip manufacturing) prospers while another industry (steel manufacturing) does not. This would provide some additional support, over and above that given in the passage, for the assertion that broad economic indicators may mask differences between industries.

C Economic differences between countries do not strengthen the support for the author's assertion regarding variations among different firms and industries in one country or region.

D This has no obvious bearing on how sweeping economic indicators can mask differences between industries or enterprises in a single country or region.

E A comparison of different countries does not pertain to the assertion regarding variation among firms and industries in the same country.

The correct answer is B.

Questions 576–579 refer to the passage on page 491.

576. It can be inferred from the passage that a large plant might have to spend more than a similar but smaller plant on environmental compliance because the larger plant is

(A) more likely to attract attention from local regulators

(B) less likely to be exempt from permit and reporting requirements

(C) less likely to have regulatory costs passed on to it by companies that supply its raw materials

(D) more likely to employ older production technologies

(E) more likely to generate wastes that are more environmentally damaging than those generated by smaller plants

Inference

This item depends on understanding the implications of the passage's discussion of differences between large and small plants. It asks what might be true of a larger plant that would compel it to spend more than a smaller plant on environmental compliance. The passage addresses this issue by stating that smaller plants are often not subject to the same permit or reporting requirements that larger plants are.

A The likelihood of attracting regulatory attention is discussed only in the context of comparing plants that are *isolated* with small plants that are near large noncompliant ones. The passage does not suggest that size is generally the crucial determining factor in attracting regulatory attention.

B Correct. According to the passage, certain permit or reporting requirements may not apply to smaller plants; this suggests that larger plants are less likely than smaller plants to be exempt from these requirements, and thus that the larger plants would have to spend more to comply.

C The passage does not discuss the passing on of regulatory costs from suppliers to plants.

D The passage does not suggest that larger plants are any more likely than smaller plants to employ older production technologies.

E The passage does not distinguish between the types of wastes emitted by larger plants and those emitted by smaller plants.

The correct answer is B.

577. According to the passage, which of the following statements about sulfur dioxide and nitrogen oxide outputs is true?

(A) Older production technologies cannot be adapted so as to reduce production of these outputs as waste products.

(B) Under the most recent environmental regulations, industrial plants are no longer permitted to produce these outputs.

(C) Although these outputs are environmentally hazardous, some plants still generate them as waste products despite the high compliance costs they impose.

(D) Many older plants have developed innovative technological processes that reduce the amounts of these outputs generated as waste products.

(E) Since the production processes that generate these outputs are less costly than alternative processes, these less expensive processes are sometimes adopted despite their acknowledged environmental hazards.

Supporting Idea

This item depends on identifying what the passage states explicitly about outputs of sulfur dioxide and nitrogen oxide. The passage says that plants that produce these outputs are those that use older industrial coal-fired burners, and that such plants are subject to extensive compliance costs imposed by new regulations.

A The passage does not address the question of whether older production technologies might be adapted to reduce outputs of sulfur dioxide and nitrogen oxide.

B The passage states that new regulations have imposed high compliance costs on companies that produce sulfur dioxide and nitrogen oxide outputs, not that these outputs are prohibited.

C **Correct.** The passage states that some companies are still using the older kinds of burners that generate sulfur dioxide and nitrogen oxide outputs, and that new regulations have imposed high compliance costs on these companies.

D The passage does not address the question of whether older plants have developed new processes to reduce the amounts of sulfur dioxide and nitrogen oxide they produce.

E Sulfur dioxide and nitrogen oxide outputs, the passage suggests, are produced only by older industrial coal-fired burners; newer facilities (using alternative processes) do not employ this technology, the expense of which is not mentioned in the passage.

The correct answer is C.

578. Which of the following best describes the relationship of the statement about large plants (lines 12–17) to the passage as a whole?

(A) It presents a hypothesis that is disproved later in the passage.

(B) It highlights an opposition between two ideas mentioned in the passage.

(C) It provides examples to support a claim made earlier in the passage.

(D) It exemplifies a misconception mentioned earlier in the passage.

(E) It draws an analogy between two situations described in the passage.

Evaluation

This question asks about the role played in the passage by the following statement: *Additionally, large plants can spread compliance costs such as waste treatment across a larger revenue base; on the other hand, some smaller plants may not even be subject to certain provisions such as permit or reporting requirements by virtue of their size.* This statement describes situations in which compliance costs for plants of different sizes may differ, which serve as evidence in support of the passage's main claim: that environmental regulations do *not* affect all competitors in a given industry uniformly.

A The statement in question is not a hypothesis; rather, it reports factors that are known to affect the varying impact of environmental regulations.

B This is too vague to be a good description of the kind of relationship the question asks about. The statement in question does present a contrast—it suggests that larger plants' compliance costs are lower under some circumstances, while smaller plants' compliance costs are lower under other circumstances. But this purports to state two facts rather than mere *ideas*; they are contrasting facts but not in any meaningful sense *opposed*, since they can easily coexist.

C   **Correct.** The statement provides examples to support the initial claim made in the passage that regulatory costs fall unevenly on competitors in an industry: large plants can spread compliance costs around, and smaller plants may not even have to pay certain costs.

D   This statement helps to dispel, not exemplify, a misconception mentioned earlier in the passage—i.e., the myth that environmental regulations affect all companies in an industry the same way.

E   The statement does not suggest that the situation of larger and smaller plants is similar (or analogous) to any other situation mentioned in the passage.

The correct answer is C.

579. The primary purpose of the passage is to

(A)   address a widespread environmental management problem and suggest possible solutions

(B)   illustrate varying levels of compliance with environmental regulation among different corporations

(C)   describe the various alternatives to traditional methods of environmental management

(D)   advocate increased corporate compliance with environmental regulation

(E)   correct a common misconception about the impact of environmental regulations

Main Idea

This question depends on understanding the passage as a whole. Its first sentence indicates its main purpose: to dispel a myth about environmental regulations that is often taken as fact.

A   The passage is not about the management of any environmental problem, which would be a problem about how to prevent or undo damage to the environment. The passage primarily aims to dispel a belief that the passage says is widely held by environmental managers.

B   The passage refers to variations in firms' levels of compliance with environmental regulations, but its primary purpose is not to illustrate those varying levels, nor does it do so.

C   The passage suggests that most environmental managers are mistaken about a key concept; its primary purpose is not to describe traditional methods of environmental management or alternatives to those traditional methods, nor does it do so.

D   The passage takes no position on whether companies should increase their compliance with environmental regulation.

E   **Correct.** The passage primarily aims to dispel the belief that environmental regulations affect all companies in an industry uniformly.

The correct answer is E.

Questions 580–583 refer to the passage on page 493.

580. The primary purpose of the passage is to

(A)   review research demonstrating the benefits of corporate mergers and acquisitions and examine some of the drawbacks that acquisition behavior entails

(B)   contrast the effects of corporate mergers and acquisitions on acquiring firms and on firms that are acquired

(C)   report findings that raise questions about a reason for corporate mergers and acquisitions and suggest possible alternative reasons

(D)   explain changes in attitude on the part of acquiring firms toward corporate mergers and acquisitions

(E)   account for a recent decline in the rate of corporate mergers and acquisitions

Main Idea

This question requires understanding what the passage as a whole is trying to do. The passage begins by citing three studies that demonstrate that when firms acquire other firms, there is not necessarily a worthwhile economic gain. The passage then cites economic interests as the reason given by firms when they acquire other firms but calls into question the veracity of this reasoning. The passage then goes on to speculate as to why mergers and acquisitions occur.

A   The research cited in the passage calls into question whether mergers and acquisitions are beneficial to firms.

B   The passage is not concerned with comparing the relative effects of mergers and acquisitions on the acquired and acquiring firms.

C   **Correct.** The passage surveys reports that question the reason given by firms when they acquire other firms and suggests other reasons for these acquisitions.

D   The passage does not indicate that there has been a change in the attitude of acquiring firms toward mergers and acquisitions.

E   The passage does not indicate that there has been a decline in the rate of mergers and acquisitions.

The correct answer is C.

581. It can be inferred from the passage that the author would be most likely to agree with which of the following statements about corporate acquisitions?

(A)   Their known benefits to national economies explain their appeal to individual firms during the 1970s and 1980s.

(B)   Despite their adverse impact on some firms, they are the best way to channel resources from less to more productive sectors of a nation's economy.

(C)   They are as likely to occur because of poor monitoring by boards of directors as to be caused by incentive compensation for managers.

(D)   They will be less prevalent in the future, since their actual effects will gain wider recognition.

(E)   Factors other than economic benefit to the acquiring firm help to explain the frequency with which they occur.

Inference

This question requires understanding what view the author has about a particular issue. The three studies cited by the passage all suggest that mergers and acquisitions do not necessarily bring economic benefit to the acquiring firms. The author concludes therefore that *factors having little to do with corporate economic interests explain*

acquisitions and then goes on to speculate as to what the reasons may actually be.

A   The passage indicates that while mergers and acquisitions may benefit the national economy, the appeal of mergers and acquisitions must be tied to companies' *private economic interests*.

B   The passage makes no judgment as to the best way for firms to channel resources from less to more efficient economic sectors.

C   The passage makes no comparison between the influence of poor monitoring by boards and that of executive incentives.

D   The passage makes no prediction as to future trends in the market for mergers and acquisitions.

E   **Correct.** The passage states that factors other than economic interests drive mergers and acquisitions.

The correct answer is E.

582. The author of the passage mentions the effect of acquisitions on national economies most probably in order to

(A)   provide an explanation for the mergers and acquisitions of the 1970s and 1980s overlooked by the findings discussed in the passage

(B)   suggest that national economic interests played an important role in the mergers and acquisitions of the 1970s and 1980s

(C)   support a noneconomic explanation for the mergers and acquisitions of the 1970s and 1980s that was cited earlier in the passage

(D)   cite and point out the inadequacy of one possible explanation for the prevalence of mergers and acquisitions during the 1970s and 1980s

(E)   explain how modeling affected the decisions made by managers involved in mergers and acquisitions during the 1970s and 1980s

Evaluation

This question requires understanding why a piece of information is included in the passage. After the passage cites the results of the three studies on mergers and acquisitions, which call into question the economic benefits of acquisitions, it indicates that firms nonetheless claim that their objectives are economic. The passage then states that while acquisitions *may well have* a desirable effect on national economies, the results of the studies suggest that factors other than economic interest must drive executives to arrange mergers and acquisitions.

A   The passage does not mention national economies as part of an explanation for the occurrence of mergers and acquisitions.

B   The passage suggests that the effect of acquisitions on national economies is not tied to any explanations for why acquisitions occur.

C   The effect of acquisitions on national economies is not mentioned in the passage as an explanation for why acquisitions occur.

D   **Correct.** The passage uses the mention of national economies as part of a larger point questioning the stated motivations behind firms' efforts to acquire other firms.

E   In the passage, modeling is unrelated to the idea that acquisitions may have a desirable effect on national economies.

The correct answer is D.

583. The author of the passage implies that which of the following is a possible partial explanation for acquisition behavior during the 1970s and 1980s?

(A)   Managers wished to imitate other managers primarily because they saw how financially beneficial other firms' acquisitions were.

(B)   Managers miscalculated the value of firms that were to be acquired.

(C)   Lack of consensus within boards of directors resulted in their imposing conflicting goals on managers.

(D)   Total compensation packages for managers increased during that period.

(E)   The value of bidding firms' stock increased significantly when prospective mergers were announced.

Inference

This question requires recognizing what can be inferred from the information in the passage. After providing the results of the studies of mergers and acquisitions, the author concludes that even though acquiring firms state that their objectives are economic, *factors having little to do with corporate economic interests explain acquisitions* (lines 10–11). Among alternative explanations, the author points to *managerial error in estimating the value of firms targeted for acquisition* (lines 12–13) as possibly contributing to acquisition behavior in the 1970s and 1980s.

A   While the passage indicates that managers may have modeled their behavior on other managers, it does not provide a reason for why this would be so.

B   **Correct.** The author states that one explanation for acquisition behavior may be that managers erred when they estimated the value of firms being acquired.

C   The author discusses a lack of monitoring by boards of directors but makes no mention of consensus within these boards.

D   The author does not discuss compensation packages for managers.

E   The passage does not state how significantly the value of the bidding firm's stock increased upon announcing a merger but only that it increased less in value than did the stock of the prospective firm being acquired.

The correct answer is B.

Questions 584–587 refer to the passage on page 495.

584. According to the passage, which of the following statements regarding earthen mounds in the Dallas communities is accurate?

(A)   They served primarily as burial grounds.

(B)   They were constructed in key locations on the perimeter of the village.

(C)   They were elements in important structures in the community.

(D)   They were used as storehouses for keeping valuable possessions safe.

(E)   They contained utilitarian items made of nonlocal materials.

Supporting Idea

This question requires recognizing what claim the passage makes about the earthen mounds in the Dallas communities. The passage states that in the largest Dallas communities, earthen mounds served as substructures for buildings that were important for civic and religious affairs.

A   The passage does indicate that some individuals were buried in the mounds, but the mounds are also described as having served as substructures for buildings important to civic and religious affairs. The passage does not indicate whether either of these purposes was primary.

B   The fact that the mounds served as substructures for important civic and religious buildings does not suggest that they were located on the perimeter of villages.

C   **Correct.** The mounds are described in the passage as substructures for buildings that were important to civic and religious affairs.

D   Valuable possessions are not described as being stored in the mounds for safekeeping, but rather as being buried there along with the high-status people interred there.

E   The items described as being made of nonlocal materials are not utilitarian objects but rather finely crafted items that denoted the high political status of the people interred in the mounds.

The correct answer is C.

585. In lines 26–28, the author of the passage raises the possibility that taller people achieved greater success most probably in order to

(A)   suggest that two explanations for a phenomenon are equally plausible

(B)   introduce empirical data supporting a position

(C)   anticipate an objection to an argument

(D)   question the usefulness of relying solely on physical evidence

(E)   point out a weakness in a traditional argument

Evaluation

This question requires recognizing what role the author intends lines 26–28 to play in the context of the passage. The passage points out that the burials of the Dallas communities formed a pattern, with the tallest skeletons being interred in the mounds, and progressively smaller skeletons interred progressively more distant from the mounds. The passage infers from this that the people buried further from the mounds were of lower status, and their lower status—because of a relatively poor diet—led to these people being less tall. Lines 26–28—stating that it is possible that taller people had greater success in attaining high status—is presented as an alternative possible explanation, thus a potential objection to the implication the author makes.

A   The passage does not suggest that two explanations are equally plausible, and in fact suggests one explanation is superior to the one expressed in lines 26–28.

B   Lines 26–28 does not serve as empirical data supporting a position, but rather as a potential objection to the position the author supports.

C   **Correct.** In lines 26–28, the author presents an explanation that is an alternative to the one the author proposes, thereby anticipating an objection to the author's argument.

D   The author throughout the passage argues solely on the basis of physical evidence and does not question the usefulness of such evidence at this or any point.

E   Nowhere is any argument characterized as a traditional argument.

The correct answer is C.

586. The passage suggests that the "relationship" mentioned in line 6 was initially recognized when archaeologists

(A)   attempted to trace the ancestry of the Timucua of Florida

(B)   discovered a height differential among members of subgroups in the Dallas community

(C)   realized that the Dallas communities endured periods of nutritional deprivation

(D)   began to compare the social organization and economies of the Timucua with that of the Dallas communities

(E)   became curious about differences in trace elements found in the bones of Dallas community members

Supporting Idea

This question requires recognizing what the passage suggests about the relationship mentioned in line 6. The passage begins with a brief mention of the Timucua of Florida, among whom the best food derived from harvesting and hunting went to families of high social status. The passage then shifts to its main focus, a similar relationship between diet and social status among the Dallas communities. Evidence for this relationship first came when archaeologists discovered that higher-status individuals in the Dallas community tended to be significantly taller than lower-status individuals.

A   The passage makes no mention of attempts to trace the ancestry of the Timucua of Florida.

B   **Correct.** The passage asserts that the first clue regarding the relationship between diet and social status in Dallas communities came when archaeologists noted the height differences between members of different socioeconomic subgroups.

C   The passage makes no mention of periods of nutritional deprivation in the Dallas communities. It does mention times of economic stress among the Timucua, but this is not related to the recognition of the relationship between social status and diet in Dallas communities.

D   The passage does mention similarities between the social organization and economies of the Timucua and those of the Dallas communities, but there is no indication in the passage of whether these comparisons were first made before or after the discovery of the relationship between status and diet among the Dallas communities.

E   The fact that there are differences in trace elements found in Dallas community members is mentioned in the passage, and it is used as evidence for the existence of the relationship between social status and diet.

Curiosity about these differences in trace elements, however, is not what the passage identifies as the first real clue about the existence of this relationship.

The correct answer is B.

587.   The passage suggests which of the following about the diet of the Dallas communities?

(A)   Wild edible plants were a relatively minor element in the diet.

(B)   Game was less likely to be available to lower-status individuals than were edible plants.

(C)   The diet was composed primarily of agricultural crops when game was scarce.

(D)   The diet was obtained entirely from local food sources.

(E)   The diet was well balanced, especially at harvest-time.

Inference

Answering this question requires recognizing something that is suggested by the passage. The passage indicates that high levels of vanadium in human bone indicate a less nutritious diet that is heavily dependent on edible plants. A low level of vanadium, which is scarce in meat, would serve as evidence for a higher proportion of meat in an individual's diet. The passage also indicates that among the Dallas communities, game, rather than domestic animals, served as the source of meat. The other primary food sources were agricultural crops and wild edible plants, primarily nuts. Finally, the passage indicates high levels of vanadium in the skeletons of lower-status individuals of the Dallas communities. All this information taken together suggests that game was less likely to be available to such lower-status individuals than were edible plants.

A   The passage indicates that wild edible plants were one of the three primary elements in the diet of the Dallas communities.

B   **Correct.** The passage suggests that game was less available to lower-status individuals, and implies this from the fact that bones found in the burials of lower-status individuals contained greater quantities of vanadium.

C   The passage does not indicate whether, when game was scarce, the diet of the Dallas communities relied on agricultural crops more than on wild edible plants.

D   The passage does not indicate whether all of the Dallas communities' food was locally sourced, which leaves open the possibility that some of their food came from elsewhere.

E   The passage provides support for the claim that, among the lower-status individuals in the Dallas communities, the diet was not well balanced; furthermore, the passage provides no evidence as to whether the diet of these communities became any more or less balanced at harvest-time.

The correct answer is B.

Questions 588–590 refer to the passage on page 497.

588. The primary purpose of the passage is to

(A)   explore the legal consequences of terminating a worker's employment

(B)   define the employment-at-will doctrine and chronicle its historical evolution

(C)   examine reasons underlying a trend away from the employment-at-will doctrine

(D)   advocate increased protection for workers against wrongful termination by employers

(E)   discuss a possible drawback of state laws intended to protect workers against wrongful termination

Main Idea

This question requires understanding the passage as a whole. The passage discusses the consequences that result from the enactment by state legislatures of laws that expand the concept of wrongful termination. It considers whether protecting workers against wrongful termination raises employers' labor costs, resulting in a reduction in employment in those states. A study by Dertouzos and Karoly confirmed that these laws do have such an effect.

A   The passage considers the effect on employment rates of expanding the concept of wrongful termination, not the legal consequences of terminating a worker's employment.

B   The passage does define the employment-at-will doctrine and discusses one change made to that doctrine by certain states, but it does not recount a series of specific changes that would constitute an account of its historical evolution.

C   The passage simply asserts that some states have made a specific type of change to the employment-at-will doctrine; it does not examine reasons why the change has been made.

D   The passage does not advocate increased protection for workers against wrongful termination by employers, but rather indicates that one study has found that certain negative consequences arise from such increased protection.

E   **Correct.** The passage describes the findings of a study showing that state laws intended to protect workers against wrongful termination led to modest declines in employment in that state, indicating a possible drawback to such state laws.

The correct answer is E.

589. Which of the following best describes the organization of the passage?

(A)   An idea is proposed and arguments against it are examined and then refuted.

(B)   A doctrine is defined and reasons for favoring its adoption are listed.

(C)   A doctrine is criticized, several possible alternatives are outlined, and one is endorsed.

(D)   An idea is described, its antithesis is presented, and a synthesis of the two is proposed.

(E)   A doctrine is defined, a revision to it is described, and the implications of that revision are discussed.

Logical Structure

The passage begins by introducing and defining a doctrine that has historically prevailed in the United States, the doctrine of employment-at-will. The passage then goes on to consider a modification of the doctrine that has been implemented, namely, an expansion of the concept of wrongful termination. Finally, the passage presents the results of a study showing some negative implications of this modification of the doctrine.

A   Though the passage does provide some negative effects of the expansion of wrongful termination that could be used in an argument against that expansion, the passage does not refute such an argument.

B   The passage does define a doctrine, but the doctrine is already widely implemented, and the passage does not list reasons favoring its adoption.

C   The passage does not criticize the doctrine of employment-at-will, though it does present some negative information about a modification of it—the expansion of the concept of wrongful termination. But the passage does not list several alternatives either to the doctrine or to its modification.

D   Even if one could describe the discussion of the expansion of wrongful termination as the "antithesis" of the doctrine of employment-at-will—a description that is not well supported—the passage does not propose any synthesis of the two.

E   **Correct.** A doctrine (employment-at-will) is defined, a revision—the expansion of the concept of wrongful termination—is discussed, and evidence of negative effects of the revision is discussed.

The correct answer is E.

590. The passage suggests which of the following regarding wrongful-termination lawsuits?

(A)   States that do not implement wrongful-termination laws will probably see an increase in wrongful-termination lawsuits.

(B)   It is less profitable to file wrongful-termination lawsuits against unionized companies than against companies without unions.

(C)   A wrongful-termination lawsuit is less costly to a company than continuing the employment of an unproductive worker.

(D)   Obtaining financial compensation is an important motivation for filing wrongful-termination lawsuits.

(E)   Those who file wrongful-termination lawsuits are likely to be awarded larger settlements under the employment-at-will doctrine than under wrongful-termination laws.

Inference

Answering this question requires recognizing what the passage suggests regarding wrongful-termination lawsuits. The passage does not directly state that one of the motivations for filing wrongful-termination lawsuits is obtaining financial compensation, but there are suggestions that this is the case. For instance, the passage discusses the increased cost of labor to employers due to the expansion of the concept of wrongful termination. The threat of wrongful-termination lawsuits leads employers to spend more time and money screening potential employees, suggesting that the cost to employers of successfully being sued for wrongful termination would likely involve some financial payout—or compensation—to the former employees who sue them. Additionally, the passage mentions the various degrees of profitability for employees who file wrongful-termination lawsuits, which results in various degrees of motivation to file such suits, suggesting that financial compensation is a crucial motivation for filing these suits.

A   The passage gives no indication that states that do not implement such laws would likely see an increase in wrongful-termination lawsuits.

B   The passage does indicate that the reduction in employment due to a state's expansion of the concept of wrongful termination would be smaller for unionized companies than for nonunionized companies. However, the passage suggests that this is because unions have already implemented protection from wrongful termination—and so there would not be much of a change from current practice—and not because the lawsuits would be less profitable.

C   The passage states that economic theorists suggest that expanding the concept of wrongful termination will lead firms to be reluctant to terminate less-productive workers, which would not be the case if such lawsuits were less costly than retaining such workers.

D   Correct. As discussed above, the passage strongly implies that financial compensation is a significant motivation for such lawsuits.

E   If this were the case, the expansion of the concept of wrongful termination would not lead to increased employment costs and a reduction in employment.

The correct answer is D.

Questions 591–593 refer to the passage on page 498.

591. According to the passage, an unwanted side effect of plant immunization is that immunized plants

   (A)   become more susceptible to certain infections, such as powdery mildew

   (B)   become more vulnerable to uncontrolled infections from the same infectious agent used to immunize the plants

   (C)   produce substances that are toxic to organisms that are beneficial to the plant

   (D)   produce enzymes that can degrade the plants' cell walls

   (E)   focus their resources on fighting invading organisms, thereby impeding other plant processes

Supporting Idea

The question requires identification of a detail explicitly addressed in the passage. While the passage overall treats the positive effects of immunizing plants, it also mentions drawbacks, or unwanted effects, that can result from immunization. The passage states that the resource demands of plants' defense mechanisms following immunization can lead to inhibited growth; in other words, focusing their resources on defense against invading organisms can impede other processes, namely growth.

A   The passage states that the specific cucumber treatment "did not, however, protect against powdery mildew." But this only indicates a lack of protection (a limitation), not an increased susceptibility (a negative side effect).

B   The passage states that immunization "radically reduced damage from subsequent anthracnose infections," which is the opposite of becoming more vulnerable.

C   The text mentions that some defense substances are "toxic to infectious organisms" and sometimes "toxic to the plant itself," but it makes no mention of them being toxic to organisms beneficial to the plant, such as pollinators.

D   The passage mentions that plants attack invaders by "producing enzymes that *degrade the invader's cell walls*." This attack is a beneficial part of the defense mechanism, not an unwanted side effect on the plant itself.

E   Correct. The final paragraph explicitly describes this side effect: "Immunization can also inhibit plant growth, presumably because defense mechanisms divert food resources." The diversion of food resources (focusing resources on fighting) and the resulting inhibition of growth (impeding other plant processes) is a clear, undesirable side effect discussed in the passage.

The correct answer is E.

592. According to the passage, biologists can immunize a plant against an infectious organism by doing which of the following?

   (A)   Manipulating the plant's genetic code in order to give it the appropriate resistance genes

   (B)   Exposing the plant to a controlled infection of the organism

   (C)   Killing off cells near the site of the infection

   (D)   Applying enzymes to the infectious organism in order to degrade its cell walls

   (E)   Treating the plant with chemicals that thicken the plant's cell walls

Supporting Idea

This item requires the identification of information explicitly presented in the passage. The third paragraph includes a description of how biologists have induced plants, namely cucumber seedlings, to acquire immunity to a specific infectious organism, namely anthracnose fungus, by exposing the seedlings to a controlled infection with that organism.

A   While the passage states that resistance genes can enable plants to fight infection, there is no mention of biologists manipulating plants' genetic code to produce such genes.

B **Correct.** The third paragraph of the passage explicitly describes biologists exposing cucumber seedlings to a specific infectious organism, a fungus, in order to induce immunity to that organism.

C While the passage states that plants kill off cells around the site of an infection as a means of isolating and eliminating that infection, there is nothing to suggest that biologists employ this method to immunize plants.

D Producing enzymes that degrade the cell walls of pathogens is mentioned as one of the ways that plants fight infection, not as a way that biologists create immunity in plants.

E The passage states that plants may produce chemicals to thicken their own cellular walls in response to infection, but it says nothing about biologists treating plants with such chemicals.

The correct answer is B.

593. Which of the following best states the function of the first paragraph?

(A) It presents an example to help illustrate a problem.

(B) It discusses the history of a problem and its present implications.

(C) It describes a situation and introduces a possible solution.

(D) It reconciles two conflicting solutions to a problem.

(E) It evaluates a possible solution to a problem.

Evaluation

The question asks for the best statement describing the function of the first paragraph. The first paragraph describes a problematic situation, namely that farmers spend $25 billion yearly on chemical sprays, yet diseases still destroy 12 percent of the harvest. The current method of fighting plant pests (spraying chemicals) is standard but "noxious" and not fully effective. The paragraph then introduces a possible solution. It contrasts the current method of protecting plants with the method used for protecting children from disease (vaccines) and

notes that biologists are now "learning how to stimulate the natural biochemical mechanisms by which plants defend themselves from disease," thus introducing the potentially beneficial approach of plant immunization, or vaccination.

A The paragraph presents the *statistics* ($25 billion, 12 percent loss) of the problem and the analogy of human vaccines to introduce the solution. It does not spend the majority of its time illustrating the problem with a detailed example (like a specific crop disease).

B The paragraph mentions the current state of the problem (chemical dependence) but does not discuss the *history* of the problem (e.g., how long spraying has been used or how losses have changed over time).

C **Correct.** The paragraph effectively sets the stage by describing the unsatisfactory situation in modern agriculture (high cost, high loss from disease) and then introduces the topic of plant vaccines as a possible solution to replace the noxious chemicals.

D It presents two solutions—chemical spraying and immunization—but it emphasizes the contrast and the drawbacks of the first, arguing for the second. It does not try to show how the two solutions can be brought together or reconciled.

E The paragraph only introduces the possible solution (vaccines); it does not evaluate its effectiveness or drawbacks. The evaluation (e.g., resistance genes, acquired immunity, growth inhibition) occurs in the subsequent paragraphs.

The correct answer is C.

Questions 594–596 refer to the passage on page 499.

594. The behavioral differences explanation discussed in the passage would be most seriously weakened if which of the following were true?

(A) Pleistocene carnivores were more likely to starve to death due to tooth fractures than are present-day carnivores.

(B) Interactions among Pleistocene carnivore species were more complex than are interactions among present-day carnivore species.

(C)   The teeth of many Pleistocene carnivores were significantly weaker than are the teeth of present-day carnivores.

(D)   The primary cause of death for Pleistocene carnivores was a shortage of prey.

(E)   The availability of prey for Pleistocene carnivores in the La Brea area was much greater in summer than in winter.

Evaluation

The passage describes the finding that extinct carnivores had strikingly higher tooth fracture frequencies. Proposed explanations relating to various kinds of bias (demographic, preservational, and local) were ruled out, in favor of a more plausible explanation involving behavioral differences, specifically more thorough consumption of carcasses, which would have caused more tooth-to-bone contact. This thorough consumption suggests either low prey availability (at least seasonally) or intense competition resulting from high predator densities. The item asks which statement would most seriously weaken the researchers' preferred explanation for the high rate of tooth fractures in Pleistocene carnivores. To weaken that preferred explanation, a fact is needed that suggests the high fracture rate was not due to this tooth-to-bone behavior, but rather due to a different factor.

A   This effect would be a *consequence* of the high fracture rate, not an alternative cause. If they fractured their teeth more often (for whatever reason), they would logically be more likely to starve.

B   More complex interactions might well involve increased competition and carcass theft, which is one of the behavioral implications the researchers use to support their hypothesis (high competition implies thorough consumption, which implies high fractures). Therefore this fact would tend to slightly support, not weaken, the researchers' explanation.

C   **Correct.** If the teeth of the extinct carnivores were physiologically weaker than those of their modern counterparts, they would naturally fracture more often, *regardless* of their feeding behavior. This alternative, non-behavioral explanation

directly undermines the researchers' conclusion that the cause must be a behavioral difference (i.e., having to chew more bone).

D   A shortage of prey is one of the two underlying causes that the thorough carcass consumption behavior implies ("prey availability was low, at least seasonally"). If this claim were true, it would tend to *support*, not undermine, the proposed behavioral difference which the researchers consider most plausible.

E   The researchers state that the thorough consumption implies prey availability was low, "at least seasonally." This statement merely provides a specific instance of seasonal variation, which is perfectly consistent with and, therefore, does not weaken the "behavioral differences" explanation.

The correct answer is C.

595. The primary purpose of the passage is to

(A)   present several explanations for a well-known fact

(B)   suggest alternative methods for resolving a debate

(C)   argue in favor of a controversial theory

(D)   question the methodology used in a study

(E)   discuss the implications of a research finding

Purpose

The passage introduces a specific research finding, namely that fossils of Pleistocene predators tend to show more tooth fractures than are found in contemporary predators. The passage goes on to consider, and dismiss, various possibilities that would suggest the data might be flawed. It then discusses an explanation for why Pleistocene predators might have suffered tooth fractures at a higher rate than modern ones do, namely that they consumed prey more thoroughly. It further discusses how that fact in turn would carry implications regarding either prey availability or predator density. Therefore, the passage's purpose is to explore the implications of the initial finding.

A   The passage does indeed discuss several explanations for the high rate of tooth fractures found in Pleistocene predators, but nothing suggests that this fact is especially well-known.

B   The passage makes no mention of methods for resolving a debate, so suggesting such methods cannot be its purpose.

C   Nothing suggests that the theory under discussion in the passage—that Pleistocene predators damaged their teeth by biting into bone—is controversial.

D   The passage does suggest that the researchers who made the finding under discussion carefully considered their own methodology, but the passage itself is not concerned with questioning their methodology.

E   **Correct.** The passage discusses the ramifications of the initial research finding regarding tooth damage among Pleistocene predators, concluding that such damage likely implies either a shortage of prey or high predator densities at the time.

The correct answer is E.

596. The passage suggests that, compared with Pleistocene carnivores in other areas, Pleistocene carnivores in the La Brea area

(A)   included the same species, in approximately the same proportions

(B)   had a similar frequency of tooth fractures

(C)   populated the La Brea area more densely

(D)   consumed their prey more thoroughly

(E)   found it harder to obtain sufficient prey

Inference

The item requires identifying an implication made by the passage concerning Pleistocene predators in the La Brea area compared to Pleistocene predators in other areas. The passage is mainly concerned with a different comparison, specifically between Pleistocene predators and modern ones. However, the passage does discuss La Brea Pleistocene predators in relation to Pleistocene predators from other areas in one instance: when it states that researchers "ruled

out local bias" in their data by comparing it with "breakage data obtained from other Pleistocene sites," which presented similar findings. That similarity to the data from other areas implies that Pleistocene predators from La Brea had tooth fracture rates similar to those of Pleistocene predators in other locations.

A   The passage suggests nothing about proportions of specific Pleistocene species in different regions.

B   **Correct.** The passage states that "breakage data obtained from other Pleistocene sites were similar to the La Brea data." This similarity suggests that La Brea Pleistocene predators suffered tooth fractures at a frequency similar to that of other Pleistocene predators.

C   The passage suggests that there may have been high predator densities during the Pleistocene but does not suggest those densities were higher in La Brea than in other areas.

D   The passage suggests that Pleistocene predators probably consumed their prey more thoroughly than do modern predators, but it does not suggest that La Brea predators were especially thorough consumers relative to other predators of their time.

E   The passage refers to the possibility that Pleistocene predators consumed their prey more thoroughly owing to a dearth of prey, but it does not suggest that such a dearth affected La Brea predators more than those in other areas.

The correct answer is B.

Questions 597–599 refer to the passage on page 500.

597. It can be inferred that which of the following is most likely to have been a goal of the Foreman's Association (line 18)?

(A)   Increasing the range of responsibilities of plant workers

(B)   Communicating autoworkers' grievances to plant management

(C)   Introducing company unionism into a plant

(D)   Supporting the policies of plant management

(E)   Reducing bureaucratic layers of management

Inference

The item asks for an inference about the most likely goal of the Foreman's Association based on its actions described in the passage. Regarding the Foreman's Association, the passage says: "In 1986, however, a caucus led by the Foreman's Association forced the union's leadership out of office and returned the union's policy to one of passive cooperation." The action was to enforce a policy of "passive cooperation" with management. The fact that the caucus was *led by the Foreman's Association* and resulted in the union becoming more supportive of the company's existing policies suggests their goal was to maintain or re-establish a cooperative, management-aligned union structure.

A   The passage notes that management's (and therefore the foreman's) goal was to limit worker initiative to "fine-tun[ing]" and force them to be "reactive," rather than proactive. Increasing worker responsibility is counter to the management-controlled system the foremen would likely support.

B   The passage highlights that, historically, the union (which foremen led) played "no independent role in bargaining shop-floor issues or pressing autoworkers' grievances." Returning the policy to "passive cooperation" would further limit, not promote, the communication of grievances.

C   Company unionism was the *existing* structure in the Japanese auto industry ("unionism . . . was company-based"). The Foreman's Association acted to restore the union's *passive* nature after a disruption, not to introduce the structure itself.

D   **Correct.** The goal of the caucus was to return the union's policy to "passive cooperation," that is, being passively supportive of company goals and management policy. Since foremen themselves were often union officers and middle-level managers, it's highly likely the Foreman's Association would want the union to align with management rather than act as an independent voice for workers.

E   The foremen were part of the existing management structure. There is no information that they sought to reduce the layers of management. Their goal was political control of the union to ensure compliance with the existing management-controlled production system.

The correct answer is D.

598.   The passage is primarily concerned with

(A)   contrasting the role of unions in the Japanese auto industry with the role of unions in the United States auto industry after the Second World War

(B)   describing unionism and the situation of workers in the Japanese auto industry after the Second World War

(C)   providing examples of grievances of Japanese auto workers against the auto industry after the Second World War

(D)   correcting a misconception about the role of the foreman in the Japanese auto industry's union system after the Second World War

(E)   reasserting the traditional view of the company's role in Japanese auto workers' unions after the Second World War

Main Idea

The passage discusses the Japanese auto industry after the Second World War, presenting an overview of the role of unions and the expectations, pressures, and responsibilities under which the auto workers labored. Other topics are mentioned in relationship to these primary concerns.

A   While the role of auto unions in the United States is mentioned in relation to the role of such unions in Japan, this comparison is a detail and not the primary concern of the passage.

B   **Correct.** The passage is focused on a detailed discussion of two aspects of the Japanese auto industry after the Second World War: the role played by unions and the condition of the workers.

C   While the passage does discuss management techniques that negatively impacted workers, providing specific examples of workers' grievances is not the passage's main concern.

D   The passage does suggest that there have been misconceptions regarding the role of foremen in the Japanese auto industry at that time, but such misconceptions are a supporting detail and not the primary focus of the passage.

E   The passage does not reassert a traditional view of the role played by Japanese auto companies relative to unions.

The correct answer is B.

599. According to the passage, a foreman in a United States auto company differed from a foreman in a Japanese auto company in that the foreman in the United States would

(A)   not have been a member of an auto workers' union

(B)   have been unlikely to support the goals of company management

(C)   have been able to control production processes to a large extent

(D)   have experienced greater stress

(E)   have experienced less conflict with workers

Supporting Idea

The item requires the identification of a difference—between foremen in Japan's postwar auto industry and those in the United States' postwar auto industry—that was explicitly stated in the passage. The passage notes that most union officers in Japan's auto industry were company foremen or managers; in the United States, by contrast, the passage states that foremen were prohibited by law from joining industrial unions.

A   **Correct.** The passage explicitly states that in the United States, "federal law prohibited foremen from joining or leading industrial unions," and contrasts that prohibition with the situation in Japan, where many union officers were also company foremen.

B   Nothing in the passage states that United States foremen differed from those in Japan in their support for company goals.

C   The passage states that Japanese foremen had significant control over production and mentions nothing about whether or not United States foremen had any such control.

D   The passage makes no reference to the stress experienced by United States foremen and certainly does not say their stress exceeded the stress of foremen in Japan.

E   There is no comparison drawn in the passage regarding conflict levels between workers and foremen in the United States as opposed to Japan.

The correct answer is A.

Questions 600–601 refer to the passage on page 502.

600. Which of the following best describes the organization of the passage?

(A)   A theory is examined, the assumptions underlying the theory are evaluated, and the theory is modified.

(B)   A hypothesis is suggested, evidence challenging the hypothesis is presented and rejected, and a new hypothesis is offered.

(C)   A range of views is considered, evidence in support of each view is examined, and a hypothesis based on one of the views is offered.

(D)   Different points of view are contrasted, evidence to support a new perspective is presented, and a conclusion based on that evidence is drawn.

(E)   Two conflicting views are introduced, evidence supporting each view is examined, and the two views are reconciled.

Logical Structure

The item asks for the organization of the passage, which can be summarized as consisting of 1) the introduction of contrasting points of view on the relative merits of Edison and Westinghouse; 2) a new perspective based on a reevaluation in light of new evidence from railroad archives; and 3) the conclusion that Westinghouse's systematic approach "better exemplifies the systematic approach to technological development that would become a hallmark of modern corporate research and development."

A   No single, formal "theory" is examined and modified. The passage contrasts historical views of two individuals. While the author presents a new perspective, they do not evaluate the assumptions of a central theory.

B   Evidence challenging the prevailing view that Westinghouse was relatively unimportant is not rejected. Rather it is contrasted with an earlier view. The author then offers a new perspective, not a new hypothesis suggested *after* rejecting a challenge.

C   While a range of views is considered, the author does not examine evidence *for* Hughes's view or the "prevailing view" of the time. The author presents new evidence only to support their own perspective on Westinghouse.

D   **Correct.** The passage starts by contrasting different points of view: Hughes and recent historians vs. earlier historians. It then presents evidence (railroad archives) to support the author's new perspective (the reevaluation of Westinghouse). Finally, a conclusion is drawn: that Westinghouse better exemplifies the systematic R&D approach of the modern era.

E   The two views (Edison-focused vs. dual pioneer) are contrasted, but they are not reconciled. The author essentially sides with the earlier view, presenting evidence that supports the importance of Westinghouse, which runs counter to the view of "recent historians." Reconciling would mean finding common ground, which the author does not do.

The correct answer is D.

601. According to the passage, during his lifetime Westinghouse was regarded as

(A)   the archetype of the independent nineteenth-century inventor

(B)   Edison's equal as an innovator in the field of electric light and power

(C)   less innovative than Edison as an inventor but more astute as a businessman

(D)   more important as an innovator in the field of electric light and power than historians in the decades following his death considered him to be

(E)   less important as an innovator in the field of electric light and power than recent historians have portrayed him to be

Supporting Idea

The item asks how George Westinghouse was regarded during his lifetime, based only on the information provided in the passage. The passage explicitly states that during the two inventors' lifetimes, they were regarded as "pioneer innovators," or peers in the field of electrical invention.

A   The passage states that Thomas Hughes assigns the archetype role to Thomas Edison, not to Westinghouse.

B   **Correct.** The passage notes that Hughes's neglect of Westinghouse "marks an intriguing departure from the prevailing view during the inventors' lifetimes (and for decades afterward) of Edison and Westinghouse as the two 'pioneer innovators' of the electrical industry." Being described as one of the two pioneers suggests he was regarded as Edison's equal (or near-equal) as an innovator in their shared field.

C   The passage does contrast the two inventors, stating that Westinghouse "better exemplifies the systematic approach" to business, but it does *not* state that people during his lifetime regarded him as *less* innovative than Edison. In fact, the prevailing view saw them as co-equal "pioneer innovators."

D   The passage states that the "prevailing view" lasted "for decades afterward" (after their lifetimes), meaning for a significant time after his death, historians *still* regarded Westinghouse highly; nothing suggests a view that Westinghouse was *more* important than those historians believed.

E   The view of Westinghouse as less important is attributed to recent historians (Hughes and others), whose view the author is trying to counteract. During his lifetime, he was regarded instead as one of the two "pioneer innovators."

The correct answer is B.

Questions 602–644 — Difficulty: **Hard**

Questions 602–604 refer to the passage on page 503.

602. The passage suggests that WIDC differed from WTUL in which of the following ways?

(A) WIDC believed that the existing safety regulations were adequate to protect women's health, whereas WTUL believed that such regulations needed to be strengthened.

(B) WIDC believed that unions could not succeed in pressuring employers to comply with such regulations, whereas WTUL believed that unions could succeed in doing so.

(C) WIDC believed that lead poisoning in white lead factories could be avoided by controlling conditions there, whereas WTUL believed that lead poisoning in such factories could not be avoided no matter how stringently safety regulations were enforced.

(D) At the time that the legislation concerning white lead factories was proposed, WIDC was primarily concerned with addressing health conditions in white lead factories, whereas WTUL was concerned with improving working conditions in all types of factories.

(E) At the time that WIDC was opposing legislative attempts to restrict women's labor, WTUL had already ceased to do so.

Inference

To answer this question, you need to understand the differences between WIDC and WTUL as they are described in the passage. The only information about WTUL in the passage is that it had stopped opposing restrictions on women's labor in the late 1880s, and that, because existing safety regulations were not being enforced, it supported the proposal to prohibit women from working in white lead factories. WIDC, on the other hand, was formed in 1892 specifically to oppose restrictions on women's labor, and it opposed the proposal.

A According to the passage, WIDC did believe that existing safety regulations, if enforced, could prevent lead poisoning. WTUL may or may not have believed that the safety regulations needed to be

strengthened; all the passage states is that WTUL did not believe that the safety regulations were likely to be enforced.

B The passage states that WTUL believed that because there were no unions to pressure employers, the employers would not comply with safety regulations. The passage does not present any information on which to base a conclusion about WIDC's beliefs regarding union pressure on employers.

C Based on information in the passage, both WIDC and SPEW believed that enforcing safety regulations could protect women against lead poisoning. WIDC supported SPEW's position on the matter. WTUL believed that safety regulations were unlikely to be enforced because of the lack of unions.

D The passage states that WIDC viewed the proposal to restrict women's employment in white lead factories as an instance of legislation designed to limit women's work opportunities—precisely the legislation that WIDC was formed to oppose. Thus, WIDC was not primarily concerned with the factories' health conditions.

E **Correct.** WIDC began opposing legislative attempts to restrict women's labor in 1892 and continued to do so through at least 1895, when the Home Secretary proposed prohibiting women from working in white lead factories. WTUL stopped opposing restrictions on women's labor in the late 1880s, before WIDC was even founded. Thus, the passage suggests that WTUL had stopped opposing restrictions on women's labor well before WIDC worked to oppose such legislation.

The correct answer is E.

603. Which of the following, if true, would most clearly support the contention attributed to SPEW in lines 17–20?

(A) Those white lead factories that most strongly enforced regulations concerning worker safety and hygiene had the lowest incidences of lead poisoning among employees.

(B)   The incidence of lead poisoning was much higher among women who worked in white lead factories than among women who worked in other types of factories.

(C)   There were many household sources of lead that could have contributed to the incidence of lead poisoning among women who also worked outside the home in the late nineteenth century.

(D)   White lead factories were more stringent than were certain other types of factories in their enforcement of workplace safety regulations.

(E)   Even brief exposure to the conditions typically found in white lead factories could cause lead poisoning among factory workers.

Evaluation

This question requires the reader to find a statement that would provide additional support for the contention made in the following statement: *SPEW contended, and WIDC concurred, that controllable conditions in such factories were responsible for the development of lead poisoning.* Information suggesting that when conditions were controlled, lead poisoning was less likely to develop would provide support for SPEW's contention.

A   Correct. If incidences of lead poisoning were low in those factories that enforced hygiene and safety regulations, that would suggest that lead poisoning was not an inevitable result of working in a white lead factory—but rather that lead poisoning was the result of poor hygiene and safety practices.

B   It would not be particularly surprising for the incidence of lead poisoning to be higher among women working in white lead factories than among women working in other kinds of factories—but such a finding would say nothing about whether controllable conditions had any effect on the development of lead poisoning.

C   The existence of household sources of lead that might contribute to lead poisoning would weaken, not support,

SPEW's contention that controllable factory conditions were responsible for the development of lead poisoning.

D   If white lead factories enforced workplace safety regulations more stringently than did some other types of factories, it might be the case that SPEW's contention was incorrect: that even controlled conditions could not prevent a high incidence of lead poisoning.

E   If the conditions typically found in white lead factories were particularly bad with regard to safety and hygiene, it could conceivably be the case that SPEW's contention was true— that is, that the conditions that caused lead poisoning were controllable. But it might also be the case that an uncontrollable aspect of those conditions caused lead poisoning. Thus, this neither supports nor undermines SPEW's contention clearly.

The correct answer is A.

604. The passage is primarily concerned with

(A)   presenting various groups' views of the motives of those proposing certain legislation

(B)   contrasting the reasoning of various groups concerning their positions on certain proposed legislation

(C)   tracing the process whereby certain proposed legislation was eventually enacted

(D)   assessing the success of tactics adopted by various groups with respect to certain proposed legislation

(E)   evaluating the arguments of various groups concerning certain proposed legislation

Main Idea

Answering this question depends on identifying the overall point of the passage. The passage is mainly concerned with explaining the reasons behind the positions taken by WIDC and SPEW, which opposed the proposal to enact legislation prohibiting women from holding most white lead factory jobs, and the reasoning of WTUL, which supported the proposal.

A   The passage explains how WIDC viewed the proposal, but it does not indicate what any of the groups believed about the motivations of the Home Secretary, who made the proposal.

B **Correct.** The passage contrasts the reasoning of the WIDC and SPEW, both of which believed that enforcing safety regulations would make the proposed legislation unnecessary, with the reasoning of WTUL, which thought that safety regulations were unlikely to be enforced and thus supported the proposal.

C The passage simply states that the proposal was eventually enacted; it does not trace the process by which this occurred.

D The passage implies that WIDC and SPEW were unsuccessful in their opposition to the proposed legislation, but it identifies only one tactic used in opposition to it: SPEW's attempt to challenge it by investigating the causes of lead poisoning.

E The passage does not evaluate the groups' arguments concerning the proposed legislation; rather, it presents those arguments without comment on their quality or value.

The correct answer is B.

Questions 605–610 refer to the passage on page 505.

605. The author of the passage refers to Robert Filmer (see line 9) primarily in order to

(A) show that Royalist ideology was somewhat more radical than most historians appear to realize

(B) qualify the claim that patriarchalism formed the basis of Royalist ideology

(C) question the view that most early feminists were associated with the Royalist faction

(D) highlight an apparent tension between Royalist ideology and the ideas of early feminists

(E) argue that Royalists held conflicting opinions on issues of family organization and women's political rights

Evaluation

This question asks about the role of Filmer in the passage. The author states that Filmer's radical patriarchalism is associated with Royalist ideology and then goes on to define radical patriarchalism as an ideology that asserts the power of the

king and the male head of the household. Early feminists, however, questioned the subordination of women in marriage. Thus, there seems to be a conflict between these two sets of ideas.

A Although the passage refers to Filmer's view as *radical patriarchalism*, it provides no evidence regarding any differences in the degrees to which historians consider that view, or Royalism in general, to be radical.

B Filmer's work supports the claim that patriarchalism was the basis of Royalist ideology; it does not qualify such a claim.

C That Filmer's approach was one of radical patriarchalism makes it surprising that early feminists were associated with the Royalist faction, but it does not provide any grounds for questioning whether they were so associated.

D **Correct.** There is apparent tension between Filmer's radical patriarchalism, if that is indeed essential to Royalist ideology, and the ideas of early feminists, who questioned such patriarchalism.

E The author refers to Filmer in order to suggest, initially, a uniformity among Royalists regarding family and women; it is only later in the passage that this view becomes more complicated.

The correct answer is D.

606. The passage suggests which of the following about the seventeenth-century English women mentioned in line 2?

(A) Their status as forerunners of modern feminism is not entirely justified.

(B) They did not openly challenge the radical patriarchalism of Royalist Filmerian ideology.

(C) Cavendish was the first among these women to criticize women's subordination in marriage and assert women's equality with men.

(D) Their views on family organization and women's political rights were diametrically opposed to those of both Royalist and Parliamentarian ideology.

(E) Historians would be less puzzled if more of them were identified with the Parliamentarian side in the English Civil Wars.

Inference

The first sentence of the passage refers to women who are both regarded as forerunners of modern feminism and identified as Royalists. The passage goes on to suggest that, given Royalist ideology's association with Filmer's radical patriarchalism (equating absolute power of the king with absolute power of the male head of household), it is surprising that feminism would find any footing within such an ideology.

A   Nothing in the passage disputes the idea that the seventeenth-century English women in question should be considered the forerunners of modern feminism.

B   Gallagher provides the example of Margaret Cavendish as a writer who did openly challenge radical patriarchalism—albeit only in her writings.

C   The passage states that Cavendish had successors among early feminists, but it does not indicate whether she herself was the first seventeenth-century English woman to assert women's equality.

D   The passage does not indicate what the Parliamentarian view of family organization and women's political rights was, so there is no way to determine whether the Royalist forerunners of modern feminism were opposed to that view.

E   **Correct.** The basic puzzle the passage sets out to solve is why the forerunners of modern feminism would have been associated with the Royalist side, which seems to have been based on radical patriarchalism. Historians would most likely have been less surprised if these women had been identified with the Parliamentarian side, which presumably did not embrace radical patriarchalism.

The correct answer is E.

607.   The passage suggests that Margaret Cavendish's decision to become an author was motivated, at least in part, by a desire to

(A)   justify her support for the Royalist cause

(B)   encourage her readers to work toward eradicating Filmerian patriarchalism

(C)   persuade other women to break free from their political and social isolation

(D)   analyze the causes for women's exclusion from the pursuit of power

(E)   create a world over which she could exercise total control

Inference

This question asks about Margaret Cavendish's reasons for becoming an author. The second paragraph describes her as someone who *insisted that she was a self-sufficient being*; she understood that, given the real-world strictures in place, she could achieve this self-sufficiency in her own mind and on paper as a writer. So her decision to become a writer can be inferred to be motivated by her desire to exercise power and control.

A   The passage states that Cavendish justified her being the center of her own universe by invoking the Royalist figure of the absolute monarch; there is no suggestion in the passage that Cavendish felt the need to justify any support for the actual Royalist cause.

B   The passage gives no direct indication that Cavendish was even aware of Filmerian patriarchalism.

C   The second paragraph states that Cavendish's idea of absolute singularity carried with it the idea of social and political isolation; Cavendish was most likely not motivated by a desire to persuade other women to break free from such isolation.

D   Cavendish took the exclusion of women from the pursuit of power for granted; the passage does not suggest that she was concerned with its causes.

E   **Correct.** According to the passage, Cavendish considered herself a self-sufficient being who was at the center of her own universe; in her writing, she wanted to create a world in which this was also true.

The correct answer is E.

608.   The phrase "a satellite orbiting a dominant male planet" (lines 41–42) refers most directly to

(A)   Cavendish's concept that each woman is a sovereign self

(B)   the complete political and social isolation of absolute singularity

(C)   the immaterial world that a writer can create on paper

(D)   the absolute subordination of women in a patriarchal society

(E)   the metaphorical figure of the absolute monarch

Evaluation

The phrase in question is *a satellite orbiting a dominant male planet.* The passage states that this was the idea that Cavendish was reacting against; she preferred instead the idea that she was the center of her own universe, her own sovereign, subject to no one.

A   The idea of a satellite orbiting a dominant male planet refers not to Cavendish's idea that each woman is a sovereign self, but rather to the idea directly opposed to that: each woman must submit to a dominant male.

B   A *satellite orbiting a dominant male planet* is by definition not isolated, nor is it singular.

C   According to the passage, Cavendish wished to create her own world as a writer so that she did not have to be a *satellite*.

D   Correct. The phrase refers to the idea that in a patriarchal society, women are as satellites to men, who are the dominant planets.

E   While radical patriarchy does equate the monarch with the male head of the household, the phrase in question is most directly about the relationship, under patriarchy, between women and men.

The correct answer is D.

609.   The primary purpose of the passage is to

(A)   trace the historical roots of a modern sociopolitical movement

(B)   present one scholar's explanation for a puzzling historical phenomenon

(C)   contrast two interpretations of the ideological origins of a political conflict

(D)   establish a link between the ideology of an influential political theorist and that of a notoriously eccentric writer

(E)   call attention to some points of agreement between opposing sides in an ideological debate

Main Idea

This question asks about the passage as a whole. The passage is mainly concerned with outlining Catherine Gallagher's attempt to explain why, given Royalist ideology's apparent association with radical patriarchalism, Royalist women offered feminist critiques of women's subordination in marriage and asserted their equality with men.

A   The passage makes no connection between early feminism and its modern form.

B   Correct. The passage presents a puzzling historical phenomenon, that Royalist women critiqued patriarchalism, in the first paragraph, and then presents Catherine Gallagher's explanation for that phenomenon in the second paragraph.

C   While the passage discusses the political conflict between the Royalists and Parliamentarians in the English Civil Wars in the first paragraph, neither this conflict, nor its ideological origins are the focus of the passage. Furthermore, the passage does not offer any interpretations of the origins of the conflict.

D   The passage attempts to unlink the ideology of political theorist Robert Filmer and the eccentric author Margaret Cavendish by suggesting that Filmer's radical patriarchalism was not the only way of understanding Royalist ideology. Cavendish provided a different understanding entirely.

E   While both sides of the ideological debate did agree on the absolute monarchy, the passage as a whole does not focus on this agreement, but rather on the disagreement about where, theoretically, the idea of absolute monarchy leads.

The correct answer is B.

610.   Which of the following, if true, would most clearly undermine Gallagher's explanation of the link between Royalism and feminism?

(A)   Because of their privileged backgrounds, Royalist women were generally better educated than were their Parliamentarian counterparts.

(B)   Filmer himself had read some of Cavendish's early writings and was highly critical of her ideas.

(C)   Cavendish's views were highly individual and were not shared by the other Royalist women who wrote early feminist works.

(D)   The Royalist and Parliamentarian ideologies were largely in agreement on issues of family organization and women's political rights.

(E)   The Royalist side included a sizable minority faction that was opposed to the more radical tendencies of Filmerian patriarchalism.

Inference

This question asks about how to undermine the way in which Gallagher connects Royalism and feminism. According to Gallagher, Cavendish's work exemplifies the connection between these ideas, because Cavendish took the idea of absolute monarchy and extended that to the idea of absolute self, an idea that should, Cavendish believed, apply to women as well as men.

A   Gallagher's explanation of the link between Royalism and feminism does not depend on the education level of Royalist women relative to Parliamentarian women.

B   Filmer most likely would have been critical of Cavendish's ideas, had he encountered them, but the passage does not indicate that Gallagher's argument had anything to do with whether Filmer read Cavendish's writings.

C   **Correct.** Gallagher uses Cavendish's work to explain how Royalism gave rise to feminism, but if Cavendish's views were completely atypical of other Royalist women, then those views cannot explain the link as Gallagher suggests they do.

D   The passage states in the first paragraph that if the Royalists and Parliamentarians were in agreement *on issues of family organization and women's political rights*, then feminists should have been divided between the two sides— but they were not. So this idea, if true, would undermine that statement, but not Gallagher's argument about the link between Royalists and feminists.

E   If more Royalists were opposed to Filmer's radical patriarchalism, then Cavendish's

writings would seem to be more representative of tendencies in Royalist ideology, thus making Gallagher's case stronger, not weaker.

The correct answer is C.

Questions 611–616 refer to the passage on page 507.

611.   The primary purpose of the passage is to

(A)   assess the validity of a certain view

(B)   distinguish between two phenomena

(C)   identify the causes of a problem

(D)   describe a disturbing trend

(E)   allay concern about a particular phenomenon

Main Idea

This question requires understanding, in general terms, the purpose of the passage as a whole. The first paragraph identifies an area of concern: declines in amphibian populations may constitute a crisis, one that indicates humans' catastrophic effects on the environment. The rest of the passage then goes on to evaluate, as the second paragraph states, whether claims of crisis-level extinctions as a result of human activity are valid. In making this evaluation, the passage discusses the possible causes of extinctions, biologists' prioritization of population declines over extinctions, and the fact that we lack extensive long-term data on amphibian populations.

A   **Correct.** The passage's main purpose is to assess whether the view that humans are causing crisis-level declines in amphibian populations is valid.

B   The passage takes care, particularly in the third paragraph, to distinguish between population declines and extinctions, but this is not its primary purpose.

C   The passage makes clear that it is difficult to identify the real extent of the problem facing amphibian populations, much less identify its causes.

D   The first paragraph notes what may seem to be a disturbing trend—the decline in amphibian populations—but the rest of the passage is concerned not with describing that trend in greater detail, but rather with determining whether it is in fact occurring.

E   While the passage provides possible grounds for concluding that concern about declining amphibian populations is overblown, it concludes by suggesting that we might, because we lack data, doom species and ecosystems to extinction. Thus, the overall purpose is not to allay concern.

The correct answer is A.

612.   It can be inferred from the passage that the author believes which of the following to be true of the environmentalists mentioned in lines 5–6?

(A)   They have wrongly chosen to focus on anecdotal reports rather than on the long-term data that are currently available concerning amphibians.

(B)   Their recommendations are flawed because their research focuses too narrowly on a single category of animal species.

(C)   Their certainty that population declines in general are caused by environmental degradation is not warranted.

(D)   They have drawn premature conclusions concerning a crisis in amphibian populations from recent reports of declines.

(E)   They have overestimated the effects of chance events on trends in amphibian populations.

Inference

This question asks about the author's view of the environmentalists mentioned in the first paragraph. These environmentalists have claimed, based on amphibian population declines, that the situation is a crisis and that immediate action must be taken. The author, however, states that the declines are only *apparently* drastic and questions whether they are real, thus suggesting that the environmentalists are drawing conclusions in the absence of a complete consideration of the situation.

A   The passage indicates that anecdotal reports are insufficient, but so too are other resources. The fourth paragraph of the passage makes clear that there is not enough long-term data available on which to base conclusions about amphibian populations.

B   The passage does not indicate that the environmentalists under discussion have conducted research on any animal species.

C   The passage does not indicate that the environmentalists in question hold, with certainty, any particular view regarding population declines in general.

D   Correct. The author argues that the recent declines may have several different causes, and that environmentalists have jumped to a conclusion about the cause of the declines as well as their significance.

E   The environmentalists, in attributing population declines to intentional human activity, have more likely underestimated than overestimated the effects of chance events on amphibian populations.

The correct answer is D.

613.   It can be inferred from the passage that the author believes which of the following to be true of the amphibian extinctions that have recently been reported?

(A)   They have resulted primarily from human activities causing environmental degradation.

(B)   They could probably have been prevented if timely action had been taken to protect the habitats of amphibian species.

(C)   They should not come as a surprise, because amphibian populations generally have been declining for a number of years.

(D)   They have probably been caused by a combination of chance events.

(E)   They do not clearly constitute evidence of general environmental degradation.

Inference

The author suggests throughout the passage that recently reported amphibian extinctions may have several different causes: they may be due to any number of chance events, for example, or may simply be the result of a small population that finds itself unable to continue under difficult conditions, whatever causes those conditions.

A   The author states in the second paragraph that extinctions may occur without a proximate cause in human activities and does not make a commitment to any particular explanation of the amphibian extinctions.

B   That chance events can cause extinctions suggests that even if habitats had been protected, extinctions still might have occurred.

C   In the second paragraph, the author says that extinctions *should come as no great surprise*, but this option is imprecise. The amphibian populations have not generally *been declining for a number of years*. The author says in the third paragraph that amphibian populations show strong fluctuations; further, in the fourth paragraph, the author says that there is insufficient long-term data to conclude that amphibian populations have been, or are, in decline.

D   The author suggests that the extinctions may have been caused by chance events, but there is not enough data to know whether or not this is probable.

E   **Correct.** The reported extinctions could have resulted from several different causes; thus, they are not clear evidence of general environmental degradation.

The correct answer is E.

614. According to the passage, each of the following is true of endangered amphibian species EXCEPT:

(A)   They are among the rarest kinds of amphibians.

(B)   They generally have populations that are small in size.

(C)   They are in constant danger of extinction.

(D)   Those with decreasing populations are the most likely candidates for immediate extinction.

(E)   They are in danger of extinction due to events that sometimes have nothing to do with human activities.

Application

This question asks what the passage does not say is true of endangered amphibian species. The second paragraph discusses endangered species, stating that they are *always rare, almost always small, and, by definition, under constant threat of extinction*, which may be caused by chance events. The possibility of their extinction, the passage states, depends

only on the population size, and not whether that population is increasing or decreasing.

A   The second paragraph mentions rarity as a characteristic of endangered amphibian species.

B   According to the second paragraph, endangered amphibian species are generally those of small populations.

C   The second paragraph states that an endangered population is under constant threat of extinction.

D   **Correct.** The last sentence of the second paragraph states that the probability of extinction due to chance events is independent of how a population changes in size. Immediate extinction would more likely come from such events, whereas population decline is gradual, even if fairly rapid.

E   Endangered species, according to the second paragraph, may become extinct due to chance events—that is, events that have nothing to do with human activities.

The correct answer is D.

615. Which of the following most accurately describes the organization of the passage?

(A)   A question is raised, a distinction regarding it is made, and the question is answered.

(B)   An interpretation is presented, its soundness is examined, and a warning is given.

(C)   A situation is described, its consequences are analyzed, and a prediction is made.

(D)   Two interpretations of a phenomenon are described, and one of them is rejected as invalid.

(E)   Two methods for analyzing a phenomenon are compared, and further study of the phenomenon is recommended.

Evaluation

This question asks about the organization of the passage as a whole. In the first paragraph, the author tells about a situation that has been interpreted in a particular way by environmentalists. The passage then proceeds to consider whether that interpretation is valid, and while it does not come to a definitive conclusion on that point, the final paragraph warns about the possible consequences of not taking the action recommended by the environmentalists.

A   The passage does initially raise a question regarding whether the environmentalists' interpretation of events is valid, but it does not answer that question, for the appropriate long-term data are not available.

B   Correct. The passage presents environmentalists' interpretation of recent news regarding amphibians, then examines the soundness of that interpretation. Finally, the author warns that postponing environmental action may have disastrous consequences.

C   The first paragraph describes a situation of possibly drastic declines in amphibian populations but does not follow this description with an analysis of its consequences.

D   The passage suggests that apparent declines in amphibian populations may or may not constitute a crisis, but it does not reject either idea.

E   While the passage does imply, in its final paragraph, that long-term data on amphibian populations should be collected, the passage does not compare two methods for analyzing amphibian populations or population declines in those populations.

The correct answer is B.

616. Which of the following best describes the function of the sentence in lines 35–38?

(A)   To give an example of a particular kind of study

(B)   To cast doubt on an assertion made in the previous sentence

(C)   To raise an objection to a view presented in the first paragraph

(D)   To provide support for a view presented in the first paragraph

(E)   To introduce an idea that will be countered in the following paragraph

Evaluation

The sentence in question discusses the way in which anecdotal reports of population decreases cannot help biologists determine whether

those decreases are normal fluctuations, take populations to lower levels that are not actually worrisome, or actually threaten extinctions. This indicates that the view mentioned in the first paragraph—reports of declines indicate a catastrophic crisis—may be mistaken.

A   The sentence does not address a particular kind of study; it objects to the use of anecdotal reports in place of actual study.

B   The previous sentence describes the possibilities referred to in the sentence in question. The sentence does not cast doubt on any of those possibilities.

C   Correct. The view that reports of amphibian population declines indicate a crisis, as presented in the first paragraph, is countered by the objection here that there are several possible causes for population declines, and anecdotal reports cannot distinguish among those possibilities.

D   The first paragraph is concerned with articulating the view that amphibian population declines constitute a crisis. This sentence does not support that view; instead, it offers reason to question it.

E   The sentence introduces the idea that amphibian populations have fluctuated in the past, and the following paragraph supports this idea by stating that several amphibian species that appeared almost extinct in the 1950s and 1960s have recovered. Thus, the paragraph does not counter the sentence.

The correct answer is C.

Questions 617–620 refer to the passage on page 509.

Main Idea Summary

The main idea of the passage is that attempts to identify keystone species are complicated by multiple factors, including the difficulty of directly testing for keystone status with controlled experiments and the fact that keystone status appears to depend in complex ways on the contexts in which the species are found. The passage defines a keystone species as one whose effects on its ecosystem *are much larger than would be predicted from its abundance.* It notes that testing for keystone status by removing species from their environment and observing the effects of their absence is problematic. It then discusses one species of starfish to exemplify the difficulties inherent in determining whether a species is a keystone one. Drawing on those examples, the passage describes some ways in which keystone status depends on species' contexts.

617. The passage mentions which of the following as a factor that affects the role of *P. ochraceus* as a keystone species within different habitats?

(A) The degree to which the habitat is sheltered from waves

(B) The degree to which other animals within a habitat prey on mussels

(C) The fact that mussel populations are often not dominant within some habitats occupied by *P. ochraceus*

(D) The size of the *P. ochraceus* population within the habitat

(E) The fact that there is great species diversity within some habitats occupied by *P. ochraceus*

Supporting Idea

This question depends on recognizing what the passage states about the factors affecting *P. ochraceus*'s role as a keystone species, which is different in different habitats. According to the passage, *P. ochraceus* consumes and suppresses mussel populations in some habitats—specifically, those that are wave-exposed—making it a keystone predator in those habitats. But in wave-sheltered habitats, *P. ochraceus* does not play the same role in suppressing mussel populations.

A **Correct.** The passage clearly states that *P. ochraceus*'s role in wave-exposed habitats differs from its role in wave-sheltered habitats.

B The passage says that the impact of *P. ochraceus* predation on mussels is not strong in wave-sheltered habitats, but this is not the case—at least not at all sites—because other animals are preying on the mussels; rather, at least at some sites, it is because mussels are controlled by sand burial.

C The passage does not suggest that mussel populations are dominant in any habitats occupied by *P. ochraceus*.

D The size of the *P. ochraceus* population affects the size of the mussel population within wave-exposed habitats, but the passage does not suggest that *P. ochraceus*'s role as a keystone species depends on the size of its population within those habitats.

E The only other species the passage mentions in conjunction with *P. ochraceus* habitats is the mussel; the passage does not address species diversity in these habitats.

The correct answer is A.

618. Which of the following hypothetical experiments most clearly exemplifies the method of identifying species' roles that the author considers problematic?

(A) A population of seals in an Arctic habitat is counted in order to determine whether it is the dominant species in that ecosystem.

(B) A species of fish that is a keystone species in one marine ecosystem is introduced into another marine ecosystem to see whether the species will come to occupy a keystone role.

(C) In order to determine whether a species of monkey is a keystone species within a particular ecosystem, the monkeys are removed from that ecosystem and the ecosystem is then studied.

(D) Different mountain ecosystems are compared to determine how geography affects a particular species' ability to dominate its ecosystem.

(E) In a grassland experiencing a changing climate, patterns of species extinction are traced in order to evaluate the effect of climate changes on keystone species in that grassland.

Application

Answering this question depends on recognizing what the author says about identifying species' roles in habitats and then extending that to another situation. The author considers a particular method of studying keystone species problematic: removing a suspected keystone species from its habitat and observing what happens to the ecosystem. The author finds this problematic because interactions among species are complex.

A The author does not discuss counting the members of a population as a problematic way of determining whether that population is a dominant species.

B   The method that the author finds problematic has to do with observing what happens to an ecosystem when a keystone species is removed from it, not with observing what happens to a different ecosystem when the species is introduced into it.

C   **Correct.** The author states explicitly that removing a species from a habitat in order to determine its keystone status is problematic. Removing the monkeys from their habitat is a clear example of this problematic practice.

D   Comparison of habitats in order to determine geography's effect on a particular species' dominance would most likely find favor with the author, for this is the approach the author seems to advocate in investigating *P. ochraceus*'s keystone status.

E   The author does not discuss tracing patterns of extinction or changing climates in the passage.

The correct answer is C.

619. Which of the following, if true, would most clearly support the argument about keystone status advanced in the last sentence of the passage (lines 24–31)?

(A)   A species of bat is primarily responsible for keeping insect populations within an ecosystem low, and the size of the insect population in turn affects bird species within that ecosystem.

(B)   A species of iguana occupies a keystone role on certain tropical islands but does not play that role on adjacent tropical islands that are inhabited by a greater number of animal species.

(C)   Close observation of a savannah ecosystem reveals that more species occupy keystone roles within that ecosystem than biologists had previously believed.

(D)   As a keystone species of bee becomes more abundant, it has a larger effect on the ecosystem it inhabits.

(E)   A species of moth that occupies a keystone role in a prairie habitat develops coloration patterns that camouflage it from potential predators.

Evaluation

To answer this question, focus on the argument advanced in the last sentence of the passage and identify what information would support that argument. In the last sentence of the passage, the author claims that keystone status depends on context. The author then offers three contextual factors that may affect a species' keystone status: geography, community diversity (i.e., the number of species in a given habitat), and length of species interaction. Evidence supporting this argument would show that context is important to a species' keystone status.

A   This scenario does not indicate anything about keystone status; this is simply a description of how species populations in a single ecosystem affect one another.

B   **Correct.** That the iguana is a keystone species in a location that has limited species diversity but not a keystone species in a location that has greater species diversity suggests that keystone status does indeed depend on context. Thus, this example supports the author's argument in the last sentence of the passage.

C   That biologists were mistaken about keystone species in a particular ecosystem does not have a bearing on whether keystone status is context dependent.

D   It is not surprising that an increase in a species' population would lead to that species having a larger effect on its ecosystem—but this does not speak directly to the question of whether keystone status itself depends on context.

E   A keystone species enhancing its ability to survive in a single ecosystem does not lend any support to the idea that keystone status depends on context. The moth's keystone status would have to undergo some change for this to have a bearing on the question of context.

The correct answer is B.

620. The passage suggests which of the following about the identification of a species as a keystone species?

(A) Such an identification depends primarily on the species' relationship to the dominant species.

(B) Such an identification can best be made by removing the species from a particular ecosystem and observing changes that occur in the ecosystem.

(C) Such an identification is likely to be less reliable as an ecosystem becomes less diverse.

(D) Such an identification seems to depend on various factors within the ecosystem.

(E) Such an identification can best be made by observing predation behavior.

Inference

Answering this question requires identifying how the passage suggests that keystone species should be identified. The passage identifies a particular way in which keystone status should *not* be determined: removing a species and observing what happens to the ecosystem. The passage also argues that keystone status depends strongly on context: that is, an ecosystem's characteristics, including its geography and inhabitants, determine its keystone species.

A   While the passage uses an example of a keystone species, *P. ochraceus*, which preys on a species that would, in the keystone species' absence, be dominant, there is nothing to suggest that a keystone species *must* have a particular relationship with the dominant, or potentially dominant, species in an ecosystem.

B   The passage explicitly states that this method of identification would be problematic.

C   A reduction in an ecosystem's diversity might alter which species occupy keystone roles in that ecosystem, the passage suggests, but there is no indication that identifying such species would become more difficult.

D   **Correct.** If, as the passage suggests, keystone status for any given species depends on the context of the ecosystem in which it lives,

then it is likely that identifying keystone species depends strongly on understanding what factors of the ecosystem contribute to creating keystone status. The passage lists such factors as geography, community diversity, and species interaction.

E   While the passage uses a predator, *P. ochraceus*, as its example of a keystone species, there is no indication that predation is an essential component of the actual definition of keystone species (*one whose effects are much larger than would be predicted from its abundance*).

The correct answer is D.

Questions 621–623 refer to the passage on page 511.

Main Idea Summary

The first paragraph of the passage indicates that the 1981 discovery of fossil remains of the tiny soft-bodied animals known as conodonts shed light on hypotheses regarding the development of vertebrate skeletons. The second paragraph states that the traditional view was that the vertebrate skeleton had developed as a defensive mechanism and that teeth were secondary features. The paragraph mentions, however, that other paleontologists argued that certain characteristics of vertebrates would not have evolved had the vertebrates not been predators and that teeth were more primitive than external armor. The final paragraph argues that certain features of conodonts suggest that hard parts first evolved in the mouth to improve predation, and aggression rather than protection drove the origin of the vertebrate skeleton. Supporting these latter claims is the primary purpose of the passage.

621. According to the passage, the anatomical evidence provided by the preserved soft bodies of conodonts led scientists to conclude that

(A) conodonts had actually been invertebrate carnivores

(B) conodonts' teeth were adapted from protective bony scales

(C) conodonts were primitive vertebrate suspension feeders

(D) primitive vertebrates with teeth appeared earlier than armored vertebrates

(E) scientists' original observations concerning the phosphatic remains of conodonts were essentially correct

Supporting Idea

This question depends on understanding how a particular type of evidence—the preserved soft bodies of conodonts—supports a particular conclusion stated in the passage. The third paragraph makes this relationship explicit, explaining that certain features of conodonts show them to be more primitive than other vertebrates. Further, those features indicate that they came before ostracoderms and other armored jawless fishes. These remains support the conclusion stated in the second paragraph regarding teeth being more primitive than external armor.

A   The passage states explicitly that conodonts were not invertebrates but rather vertebrates.

B   This view is attributed to certain traditionalists but is contradicted by other paleontological evidence presented in the second and third paragraphs. According to the third paragraph, the evidence provided by the preserved soft bodies of conodonts undermines this traditional view.

C   The final sentence of the passage indicates that the evidence in question supports the conclusion that conodonts were predators rather than suspension feeders.

D   **Correct.** The third paragraph explains how conodonts' remains support the conclusion that teeth were more primitive than external armor.

E   The second paragraph explains that originally, scientists thought that early vertebrates were not predators—but the remainder of the passage indicates that this idea is inconsistent with more recent evidence described in the passage.

The correct answer is D.

622. The second paragraph in the passage serves primarily to

(A) outline the significance of the 1981 discovery of conodont remains to the debate concerning the development of the vertebrate skeleton

(B) contrast the traditional view of the development of the vertebrate skeleton with a view derived from the 1981 discovery of conodont remains

(C) contrast the characteristics of the ostracoderms with the characteristics of earlier soft-bodied vertebrates

(D) explain the importance of the development of teeth among the earliest vertebrate predators

(E) present the two sides of the debate concerning the development of the vertebrate skeleton

Evaluation

This question depends on understanding the second paragraph in the context of the passage as a whole. The second paragraph begins by noting the traditional view of the vertebrate skeleton—that it was a defense against predators—and then goes on to explain that other paleontologists argued against this idea, claiming instead that vertebrates began as predators and that teeth were a more primary feature than external armor.

A   The second paragraph focuses on describing the debate rather than on the distinctive contribution of the 1981 discovery to that debate.

B   The second paragraph does not explicitly indicate whether the opposition to the traditional view originally rested on the 1981 discovery of conodont remains. In fact, the surrounding discussion, in the first and third paragraphs, suggests that the discovery in 1981 turned out to support the opposing view, which some paleontologists already held at that time.

C   The mention of ostracoderms in the second paragraph merely serves to indicate how the traditionalists' arguments might have seemed plausible. The paragraph as a whole is not devoted to contrasting the ostracoderms with earlier soft-bodied vertebrates.

D   The development of teeth figures in the second paragraph, but this development is mentioned first as a feature that some believed to have been adapted from protective scales; only the final sentence of the paragraph connects teeth to early vertebrate predators.

E   Correct. According to the passage, the debate concerning the development of the vertebrate skeleton hinges on whether vertebrates began as predators, with teeth, or whether skeletal defenses such as external armor evolved first. The primary purpose of the second paragraph is to distinguish these two sides.

The correct answer is E.

623. It can be inferred that on the basis of the 1981 discovery of conodont remains, paleontologists could draw which of the following conclusions?

(A)   The earliest vertebrates were sedentary suspension feeders.

(B)   Ostracoderms were not the earliest vertebrates.

(C)   Defensive armor preceded jaws among vertebrates.

(D)   Paired eyes and adaptations for activity are definitive characteristics of vertebrates.

(E)   Conodonts were unlikely to have been predators.

Inference

What could paleontologists conclude, based on the 1981 discovery of conodont remains? That discovery, according to the passage, supported the view of certain paleontologists that the earliest vertebrates were predators with teeth—unlike the ostracoderms, which had no jaws.

A   According to the second paragraph, traditionalists believed that early vertebrates were sedentary suspension feeders. But the 1981 discovery supported the hypothesis that early vertebrates were predators instead.

B   Correct. According to the third paragraph, the conodonts' body structures indicated that they were more primitive than the ostracoderms, so the ostracoderms must not have been the earliest vertebrates.

C   Traditionalists argued that teeth were adapted from bony scales that provided defensive armor, but the 1981 discovery suggested that teeth preceded such scales.

D   Paleontologists knew prior to the 1981 discovery that paired eyes and other adaptations are characteristics of vertebrates. They used this knowledge to help them interpret the 1981 discovery.

E   The third paragraph indicates that conodonts, given their teeth, were most likely predators.

The correct answer is B.

Questions 624–628 refer to the passage on page 513.

Main Idea Summary

The central question addressed by the passage is whether, during the period 1794 to 1830, judges in the United States were prejudiced against patent holders. After a brief introduction to the history of patents, the author presents some purported evidence that the courts during this period had an antipatent bias. The passage then presents some considerations that weigh against such a conclusion. The main idea of the passage, implied in the chain of reasoning in the second paragraph but not explicitly stated, is that the pattern of judgments against patentees during the period in question was probably due to the fact that many patents had been awarded without merit rather than to an antipatent bias of the judges.

624. The passage implies that which of the following was a reason that the proportion of verdicts in favor of patentees began to increase in the 1830s?

(A)   Patent applications approved after 1836 were more likely to adhere closely to patent law.

(B)   Patent laws enacted during the 1830s better defined patent rights.

(C)   Judges became less prejudiced against patentees during the 1830s.

(D)   After 1836, litigated cases became less representative of the population of patent disputes.

(E)   The proportion of patent disputes brought to trial began to increase after 1836.

(D)   It led to excessive numbers of patent-infringement suits.

(E)   It failed to encourage national economic growth.

Inference

This question asks about a statement implied by the passage. The scholars mentioned in line 8 question whether U.S. patent law achieved its goal. That goal is described in the first sentence of the passage: to encourage America's economic growth. Thus, it is reasonable to conclude that the scholars would criticize the pre-1830 patent system for failing to encourage economic growth.

A   The scholars contend that judges rejected patents for arbitrary reasons, not because the definition of property rights was vague.

B   The passage does not indicate that the scholars were critical of the criteria for granting patents.

C   The scholars are concerned with inventors' attempts to protect their patents, not the difficulty of acquiring a patent in the first place.

D   The passage does not imply that the scholars in question believed that too many patent-infringement suits were brought to court, but rather that too few succeeded.

E   **Correct.** The scholars doubt that patent law helped to achieve its goal, which was to encourage economic growth.

The correct answer is E.

626. It can be inferred from the passage that the frequency with which pre-1830 cases have been cited in court decisions is an indication that

(A)   judicial support for patent rights was strongest in the period before 1830

(B)   judicial support for patent rights did not increase after 1830

(C)   courts have returned to judicial standards that prevailed before 1830

(D)   verdicts favoring patentees in patent-infringement suits did not increase after 1830

(E)   judicial bias against patentees persisted after 1830

Inference

The question asks which statement can be reasonably inferred, from information provided in the passage, to be a reason for the increase in proportion of verdicts favoring patentees, starting in the 1830s. The second paragraph argues that what changed in that decade was not judges' attitudes toward patent law but the types of patent cases that were litigated. It explains that a law passed in 1836 required that, for the first time in U.S. history, applications for patents had to be examined for their adherence to patent law before a patent would be issued. This information implies that patents granted after 1836 were more likely to adhere to patent law and were thus more likely to be upheld in court.

A   **Correct.** The passage implies that patents granted after the 1836 law went into effect were more likely to adhere to patent law.

B   The passage does not indicate that any law mentioned made changes to the definition of patent rights; rather, the passage indicates that the patent system was revised to require that patent applications be reviewed for adherence to existing law.

C   The passage rejects the explanation that judges' attitudes toward patent rights became more favorable.

D   The passage indicates that the population of disputes that were litigated changed after 1836, but it does not suggest that the population of litigated disputes differed from that of patent disputes as a whole.

E   The passage does not indicate any change in the proportion of patent disputes brought to trial.

The correct answer is A.

625. The passage implies that the scholars mentioned in line 8 would agree with which of the following criticisms of the American patent system before 1830?

(A)   Its definition of property rights relating to inventions was too vague to be useful.

(B)   Its criteria for the granting of patents were not clear.

(C)   It made it excessively difficult for inventors to receive patents.

Inference

The question asks what is indicated by the frequency with which pre-1830 cases have been cited in court decisions. The second paragraph rejects some scholars' claims that judges prior to the 1830s were *antipatent*, while judges after that time were more accepting of patent rights. The passage supports its critique by pointing out that decisions made by judges before the 1830s have been cited as precedents by later judges just as frequently as post-1830s decisions have been. This implies that later judges' attitudes toward patent rights were similar to those of pre-1830s judges. Thus, there is no reason to believe judges' attitudes toward patent rights changed at that time.

A   The passage argues that judicial support for patents did not change in the 1830s.

B   Correct. Pre-1830s court decisions have been cited as frequently as later decisions, suggesting no change in judges' attitudes.

C   The passage does not indicate that judicial standards changed from, and then returned to, those that prevailed before 1830.

D   Although actual numbers of favorable verdicts are not mentioned, the passage indicates that the proportion of verdicts decided in favor of patentees did, in fact, increase beginning in the 1830s.

E   The passage rejects the notion that judges were biased against patentees either before or after 1830.

The correct answer is B.

627. It can be inferred from the passage that the author and the scholars referred to in line 21 disagree about which of the following aspects of the patents defended in patent-infringement suits before 1830?

(A)   Whether the patents were granted for inventions that were genuinely useful

(B)   Whether the patents were actually relevant to the growth of the United States economy

(C)   Whether the patents were particularly likely to be annulled by judges

(D)   Whether the patents were routinely invalidated for reasons that were arbitrary

(E)   Whether the patents were vindicated at a significantly lower rate than patents in later suits

Inference

The question depends on recognizing differences between two explanations—one favored by the scholars mentioned in line 21, the other favored by the author—for the frequency with which patents were invalidated in U.S. courts prior to 1830. The first paragraph describes the scholars' view that judges before 1830 were *antipatent* and rejected patentees' claims for *arbitrary reasons*. The author of the passage rejects that view. As an alternate explanation, the author implies in the second paragraph that earlier patents often violated copyright law; this view is supported with reference to an 1836 revision to the patent system which instituted a procedure by which patent applications were inspected to ensure adherence to patent law.

A   The author and the scholars are both focused on protecting inventors' property rights, not with their inventions' utility.

B   Although the passage suggests that the scholars thought America's patent system did not help encourage economic growth, there is no suggestion that either the scholars or the author believes actual patents defended in court were irrelevant to economic growth.

C   Both the scholars and the author believe that patents defended in court prior to 1830 were more likely to be invalidated than were patents in later legal disputes.

D   Correct. The scholars claim that judges before 1830 decided against patentees for arbitrary reasons, but the passage suggests that the patents may have been invalidated because they failed to adhere to patent law.

E   Both the scholars and the author accept that patents were upheld in court less often before 1830 than after.

The correct answer is D.

628. The author of the passage cites which of the following as evidence challenging the argument referred to in lines 14–15?

(A)   The proportion of cases that were decided against patentees in the 1820s

(B)   The total number of patent disputes that were litigated from 1794 to 1830

(C) The fact that later courts drew upon the legal precedents set in pre-1830 patent cases

(D) The fact that the proportion of judicial decisions in favor of patentees began to increase during the 1830s

(E) The constitutional rationale for the 1836 revision of the patent system

Supporting Idea

The question asks what evidence the author brings to bear against the argument referred to in lines 14–15. In the first paragraph, the author summarizes scholars' arguments to the conclusion that judges' attitudes toward patent rights shifted in the 1830s, based on the fact that judges earlier had routinely ruled against patentees in lawsuits whereas judges after that time provided more protection for patent rights. In the second paragraph, the author challenges the claim that judges' attitudes shifted. The author provides evidence that judges after the 1830s cited legal precedents set in pre-1830s cases, suggesting that their views had not changed.

A The proportion of cases decided against patentees in the 1920s is cited as evidence that supports the scholars' argument in the first paragraph, not as evidence challenging their views.

B The total number of disputes litigated is not mentioned in the passage.

C **Correct.** The fact that judges after 1830 cited earlier cases as precedents is used as evidence to challenge scholars' claims that judges' attitudes shifted around 1830.

D The change in the proportion of decisions in favor of patentees is a fact that both the scholars and the author of the passage attempt to explain.

E No constitutional rationale for the 1836 law is mentioned in the passage.

The correct answer is C.

Questions 629–635 refer to the passage on page 515.

Main Idea Summary

The passage is primarily concerned with surveying various views of the social standing of European women during the Renaissance. The first paragraph discusses Jacob Burckhardt's view that the Renaissance was a period in which women had equality with men; Joan Kelly's contrary view that the Renaissance was a period in which women's status relative both to men and to medieval women was in decline; and a more complex view, held by various feminist scholars, who suggest that Burckhardt and Kelly each drew too heavily on observations of upper-class Italian women. The second paragraph warns of the risks of conflating "women" and "women writers" in studying the status of Renaissance women, but, despite such a caveat regarding Tina Krontiris's research, praises her contributions to the field. The author sees her as representative of a cautiously optimistic assessment of Renaissance women's achievements while stressing the social obstacles Renaissance women faced and the caution they exercised when opposing cultural stereotypes.

629. The author of the passage discusses Krontiris primarily to provide an example of a writer who

(A) is highly critical of the writings of certain Renaissance women

(B) supports Kelly's view of women's status during the Renaissance

(C) has misinterpreted the works of certain Renaissance women

(D) has rejected the views of both Burckhardt and Kelly

(E) has studied Renaissance women in a wide variety of social and religious contexts

Evaluation

This question focuses on the author's reason for mentioning Krontiris's work. The passage states that Krontiris, in her discussion of six Renaissance women writers, is an example of scholars who are optimistic about women's achievements but also suggest that these women faced significant obstacles. She is a writer who, in other words, agrees with neither Kelly's negative views nor Burckhardt's positive approach.

A   The passage indicates that Krontiris uses the Renaissance women writers' works as historical evidence, not that she offered any criticism of the works themselves.

B   Krontiris's work, according to the author, is cautiously optimistic about women's achievements during the Renaissance. This contradicts Kelly's view that the status of women declined during this time.

C   The author suggests that Krontiris may have erred in taking her six subjects as representative of all women during the Renaissance, not that she made any misinterpretations of their actual writing.

D   **Correct.** The author uses Krontiris as an example of those feminist scholars who have rejected the overgeneralized approaches of both Kelly and Burckhardt.

E   The author makes clear that Krontiris's study focuses on literate Renaissance women, who constituted a small minority.

The correct answer is D.

630. According to the passage, Krontiris's work differs from that of the scholars mentioned in line 12 in which of the following ways?

(A)   Krontiris's work stresses the achievements of Renaissance women rather than the obstacles to their success.

(B)   Krontiris's work is based on a reinterpretation of the work of earlier scholars.

(C)   Krontiris's views are at odds with those of both Kelly and Burkhardt.

(D)   Krontiris's work focuses on the place of women in Renaissance society.

(E)   Krontiris's views are based exclusively on the study of a privileged group of women.

Supporting Idea

This question asks what the passage directly states about the difference between Krontiris's work and the feminist scholars mentioned in the first paragraph. The feminist scholars mentioned in the first paragraph explore differences among Renaissance women, particularly their social status and religion, and thus complicate Burckhardt's and Kelly's generalizations. Krontiris's work, on the other hand, focuses on Renaissance women writers, who are a distinctly privileged and small social group.

A   The second paragraph makes clear that Krontiris addresses the obstacles faced by Renaissance women.

B   The passage does not suggest that Krontiris is reinterpreting or drawing on reinterpretations of the work of earlier scholars.

C   The second paragraph shows that Krontiris's work does complicate both Burckhardt's and Kelly's views, but in this, she is in agreement with the feminist scholars mentioned in the first paragraph.

D   Both Krontiris and the feminist scholars mentioned in the first paragraph are concerned with the place of women in Renaissance society.

E   **Correct.** The feminist scholars mentioned in the first paragraph are concerned with women of different social classes and religions, whereas Krontiris's work focuses on a limited social group.

The correct answer is E.

631. According to the passage, feminist scholars cite Burckhardt's view of Renaissance women primarily for which of the following reasons?

(A)   Burckhardt's view forms the basis for most arguments refuting Kelly's point of view.

(B)   Burckhardt's view has been discredited by Kelly.

(C) Burckhardt's view is one that many feminist scholars wish to refute.

(D) Burckhardt's work provides rich historical evidence of inequality between Renaissance women and men.

(E) Burckhardt's work includes historical research supporting the arguments of the feminist scholars.

Supporting Idea

This question asks what the passage says explicitly about why feminist scholars reference Burckhardt's view of Renaissance women. The first paragraph states that Burckhardt's view is that Renaissance women enjoyed *perfect equality* with men, and then follows that by noting how feminist scholars have *repeatedly cited* this view to contrast it with extensive evidence of women's inequality during the Renaissance.

A   The passage does not indicate that any feminist scholars cite Burckhardt to refute Kelly's view. It uses Krontiris as an example of scholars who refute Kelly's point of view to a certain degree, but Krontiris does not use Burckhardt's view as her basis for doing so; Krontiris argues against Burckhardt as well.

B   According to the first paragraph, Kelly's work was in certain ways inconsistent with Burckhardt's view, but that is not a reason why Burckhardt's view is cited by feminist scholars. Rather, according to the passage, they cite it in order to argue against it.

C   **Correct.** Many feminist scholars wish to refute Burckhardt's view that Renaissance women and men were equal.

D   As the first paragraph makes clear, Burckhardt's work emphasizes equality, not inequality, between Renaissance women and men.

E   The passage does not discuss the historical research on which Burckhardt based his work.

The correct answer is C.

632. It can be inferred that both Burckhardt and Kelly have been criticized by the scholars mentioned in line 12 for which of the following?

(A) Assuming that women writers of the Renaissance are representative of Renaissance women in general

(B) Drawing conclusions that are based on the study of an atypical group of women

(C) Failing to describe clearly the relationship between social status and literacy among Renaissance women

(D) Failing to acknowledge the role played by Renaissance women in opposing cultural stereotypes

(E) Failing to acknowledge the ways in which social status affected the creative activities of Renaissance women

Inference

Line 12 refers to feminist scholars who have rejected both Kelly's and Burckhardt's views of the status of Renaissance women. The next sentence states that the feminist scholars use class and religious differences among Renaissance women to argue against Kelly's and Burckhardt's generalizations, which were based on upper-class Italian women.

A   The second paragraph suggests that Krontiris at times conflates Renaissance women writers and women in general, but the passage does not indicate that the feminist scholars believe this of Kelly or Burckhardt.

B   **Correct.** The feminist scholars mentioned study different types of Renaissance women and so reject Kelly's and Burckhardt's conclusions that were based on a group that was not in fact typical.

C   Krontiris, not Kelly and Burckhardt, is the scholar who, according to the passage, fails to address the relationship between literacy and social status.

D   The passage provides no grounds for determining whether Kelly, Burckhardt, or the feminist scholars mentioned in the first paragraph dealt with Renaissance women's opposition to cultural stereotypes; Krontiris's work is concerned with this question.

E   The first paragraph suggests that feminist scholars criticized Kelly and Burckhardt for failing to acknowledge the ways in which social status complicates any generalizations that can be made about Renaissance women's lives, not their creative activities specifically.

The correct answer is B.

633. The author of the passage suggests that Krontiris incorrectly assumes that

(A)   social differences among Renaissance women are less important than the fact that they were women

(B)   literacy among Renaissance women was more prevalent than most scholars today acknowledge

(C)   during the Renaissance, women were able to successfully oppose cultural stereotypes relating to gender

(D)   Renaissance women did not face many difficult social obstacles relating to their gender

(E)   in order to attain power, Renaissance women attacked basic assumptions in the ideologies that oppressed them

Inference

The first statement the author makes about Krontiris, in the second paragraph, concerns what the author characterizes as a problem with Krontiris's work. Krontiris takes the Renaissance women writers she studies as representative of all Renaissance women; the author says that designating *women* as the most important grouping fails to consider whether other social differences might make for differences in experience.

A   **Correct.** The author indicates that Krontiris's error lies in assuming that women's identity as women trumps social and other differences.

B   The author does not suggest that Krontiris assumes inappropriate literacy levels among Renaissance women, but rather that Krontiris does not give sufficient consideration to the idea that women who could read and write most likely led lives very different from those of women who could not read and write.

C   The author says that Krontiris suggests that there were many cultural stereotypes that women were not able to oppose effectively.

D   Krontiris, according to the author, acknowledges the many social obstacles faced by women on the basis of their gender.

E   According to the author, Krontiris's concluding remarks suggest that Renaissance women *seldom attacked the basic assumptions in the ideologies that oppressed them.*

The correct answer is A.

634. The last sentence in the passage serves primarily to

(A)   suggest that Krontiris's work is not representative of recent trends among feminist scholars

(B)   undermine the argument that literate women of the Renaissance sought to oppose social constraints imposed on them

(C)   show a way in which Krontiris's work illustrates a "cautiously optimistic" assessment of Renaissance women's achievements

(D)   summarize Krontiris's view of the effect of literacy on the lives of upper- and middle-class Renaissance women

(E)   illustrate the way in which Krontiris's study differs from the studies done by Burckhardt and Kelly

Evaluation

The function of the final sentence of the passage is to indicate how Krontiris's work takes neither a completely positive nor completely negative view of Renaissance women's experiences—i.e., how her work is representative of those authors who are cautiously optimistic about the achievements of Renaissance women.

A   The passage discusses Krontiris's work as an example of the trend described in the latter part of the first paragraph and mentioned in the first line of the second paragraph. The last sentence in the passage shows that Krontiris's work is in fact representative of recent trends among feminist scholars.

B   The last sentence in the passage states that Renaissance women's opposition to cultural stereotypes was circumscribed, but it also suggests that these women did gain some power for themselves. Thus, the sentence does not serve primarily to undermine the argument that the women sought to oppose social constraints.

C   **Correct.** Krontiris's work illustrates the "cautiously optimistic" view by embracing both the idea that Renaissance women could gain a certain amount of power and the idea that the extent of their opposition was limited.

D   The last sentence in the passage summarizes Krontiris's view, but that view does not, according to the passage, take into account the effect of literacy on the members of a particular social class.

E   The main function of the final sentence of the passage is to take up the idea of the "cautiously optimistic" assessment offered in the penultimate sentence. This does mark a significant departure from both Burckhardt and Kelly, but the distinction between their work and that of other feminist scholars is marked more clearly earlier in the passage.

The correct answer is C.

635. The author of the passage implies that the women studied by Krontiris are unusual in which of the following ways?

(A)   They faced obstacles less formidable than those faced by other Renaissance women.

(B)   They have been seen by historians as more interesting than other Renaissance women.

(C)   They were more concerned about recording history accurately than were other Renaissance women.

(D)   Their perceptions are more likely to be accessible to historians than are those of most other Renaissance women.

(E)   Their concerns are likely to be of greater interest to feminist scholars than are the ideas of most other Renaissance women.

Inference

The women Krontiris studied are unusual, the author suggests, because they were literate, thus putting them among the minority of Renaissance women. That they could write, however, means that their written reflections are part of the historical record, whereas the direct impressions of experiences had by Renaissance women who could not write about their lives are lost to history.

A   The author implies that the obstacles faced by Krontiris's subjects may have been different from those faced by other women, not that they were less formidable.

B   The author does not imply that the women studied by Krontiris are seen as more interesting; rather, the author indicates that their work is that which is available for study.

C   The women Krontiris studies were able to record their own history because they, unlike most other Renaissance women, were literate. This does not imply that they were more concerned with recording history accurately.

D   **Correct.** Because Krontiris's subjects were literate, they were able to write down, and thus preserve for historians, their perceptions in a way that most other Renaissance women were not.

E   The author does not suggest that feminist scholars in general are more interested in the concerns of middle- and upper-class literate women than they are with women of other classes.

The correct answer is D.

Questions 636–639 refer to the passage on page 517.

Main Idea Summary

The main idea of the passage is that observations of asteroid collisions and computer simulations of such collisions indicate that most observed asteroids are loose collections of rocks and only small asteroids are individual, solid rocks. The passage begins by describing how, in theory, one could determine the structure of asteroids by observing the rates at which they spin after collisions. The passage then reports that, using this method, scientists have found that most observed asteroids spin in ways that are inconsistent with their being solid rocks. The second paragraph indicates that the conclusions are supported by computer modeling and then presents a causal explanation for the observed phenomena.

636. The passage implies which of the following about the five asteroids mentioned in line 12?

(A) Their rotation rates are approximately the same.

(B) They have undergone approximately the same number of collisions.

(C) They are monoliths.

(D) They are composed of fragments that have escaped the gravity of larger asteroids.

(E) They were detected only recently.

Inference

In line 12, *five observed asteroids* refers to the five asteroids whose rotation rates are exceptions to the strict limit on the rate of rotation found in all other observed asteroids. These five asteroids all have diameters smaller than 200 meters. The passage indicates that if asteroids were all monoliths—that is, single rocks—then their rotation rates would form a bell curve when graphed, but if asteroids were piles of rubble, the tail of the bell curve indicating very fast rotation rates would be missing. Among asteroids larger than 200 meters, this tail is missing, and only the five asteroids described as exceptions have rotation rates falling at the very high end of the bell curve.

A All that the passage states about the rotation rates of these five asteroids is that they do not obey a strict limit. The passage does not rule out that their rates of rotation are significantly different from one another.

B According to the passage, frequent collisions occur among asteroids. But the passage does not suggest that asteroids that are of similar sizes, or that have particularly high rotation rates, will be similar in terms of the number of collisions that they have undergone to reach those distinctive states.

C **Correct.** The second paragraph states that *most small asteroids* should be monolithic, and the five observed asteroids are all smaller than 200 meters in diameter.

D The five asteroids are most likely not composed of fragments because, as the passage states, small asteroids should be monoliths.

E The passage notes that researchers have observed these five asteroids, along with others, but it does not indicate when these asteroids were originally detected.

The correct answer is C.

637. The discovery of which of the following would call into question the conclusion mentioned in line 16?

(A) An asteroid 100 meters in diameter rotating at a rate of once per week

(B) An asteroid 150 meters in diameter rotating at a rate of 20 times per hour

(C) An asteroid 250 meters in diameter rotating at a rate of once per week

(D) An asteroid 500 meters in diameter rotating at a rate of once per hour

(E) An asteroid 1,000 meters in diameter rotating at a rate of once every 24 hours

Application

The conclusion that the text in line 16 points to is that asteroids with diameters greater than 200 meters are *multicomponent structures or rubble piles.* To call that conclusion into question, an observation would have to suggest that asteroids larger than 200 meters across are not such multicomponent structures. According to the first paragraph, rubble piles cannot be fast rotators: spinning faster than once every few hours would make them fly apart.

A   Nothing in the passage suggests that the behavior of an asteroid 100 meters in diameter is relevant to a conclusion about the behavior of asteroids greater than 200 meters in diameter.

B   Nothing in the passage suggests that the behavior of an asteroid 150 meters in diameter would have any effect on a conclusion about the constitution of asteroids with diameters greater than 200 meters.

C   An asteroid 250 meters in diameter rotating at a rate of once per week would be rotating at a slow enough rate to hold together a pile of rubble. Thus, this observation would be entirely consistent with the conclusion about asteroids larger than 200 meters in diameter.

D   Correct. Assuming that an asteroid composed of a pile of rubble is of a great enough density, a rotation rate greater than one revolution every few hours would make it fly apart. So a 500-meter asteroid rotating at a rate of once per hour—that is, faster than the crucial speed—would fly apart if it were not a monolith. The conclusion states that all asteroids larger than 200 meters are multicomponent structures—that is, are not monoliths—so the discovery of a 500-meter asteroid rotating at a rate of once an hour would call into question that conclusion.

E   An asteroid rotating at a rate of once every 24 hours would, regardless of size, be rotating much more slowly than the *once every few hours* that the passage claims would make a pile of rubble of a sufficient density fly apart. So an asteroid with a diameter of 1,000 meters that rotated once per day could be a pile of rubble and not conflict with the conclusion.

The correct answer is D.

638.   According to the passage, which of the following is a prediction that is based on the strength of the gravitational attraction of small asteroids?

(A)   Small asteroids will be few in number.

(B)   Small asteroids will be monoliths.

(C)   Small asteroids will collide with other asteroids very rarely.

(D)   Most small asteroids will have very fast rotation rates.

(E)   Almost no small asteroids will have very slow rotation rates.

Supporting Idea

Regarding small asteroids, the second paragraph states that they have feeble gravity. Any fragments from impacts would escape that gravity, and thus, the passage states, the small asteroids *should be monolithic.*

A   Small asteroids could be few in number, but the passage does not offer such a prediction.

B   Correct. This prediction is offered in the second paragraph, based on the fact that small asteroids do not have strong gravitational attraction. Any impact fragments will easily escape the weak gravitational attraction of the small asteroids.

C   The passage discusses large asteroids collisions in more detail than small-asteroid collisions, but it provides no basis for predicting how often large and small asteroids will, comparatively, be involved in such collisions.

D   The first paragraph indicates that the rotation rates of small asteroids can exceed the upper limit on the rotation rates of large asteroids, but it does not indicate that most small asteroids have rotation rates that exceed this upper limit.

E   The passage only indicates that there are few observed exceptions to the upper limit on rotation rates of large asteroids, and these exceptions are all smaller than 200 meters in diameter; the passage does not indicate that there are few small asteroids that have very slow rotation rates.

The correct answer is B.

639. The author of the passage mentions "escape velocity" (see line 22) in order to help explain which of the following?

(A) The tendency for asteroids to become smaller rather than larger over time

(B) The speed with which impact fragments reassemble when they do not escape an asteroid's gravitational attraction after a collision

(C) The frequency with which collisions among asteroids occur

(D) The rotation rates of asteroids smaller than 200 meters in diameter

(E) The tendency for large asteroids to persist after collisions

Evaluation

This question asks about the purpose of the author's use of the phrase *escape velocity* in the second paragraph. The author is discussing what occurs after an asteroid collision, in which a large asteroid might be blasted to bits. The bits, according to the author, will move slower than their *mutual escape velocity*—that is, the speed at which they would have to move to get away from each other and not reassemble, under the influence of gravity, into a rubble pile.

A   The author is emphasizing the asteroid bits that do not escape rather than those that do. Asteroids may become smaller over time, but the fact that most bits move slower than their escape velocity would not help to explain this shrinkage.

B   That the bits of asteroid move slower than their escape velocity helps explain why the fragments reassemble, but it does not help explain the speed with which they reassemble.

C   According to the author, asteroid collisions occur frequently, but the escape velocity of the resulting fragments does not help to explain that frequency.

D   The concept of escape velocity may help explain why small asteroids are monoliths, but it has no relevance, at least as far as the passage indicates, to those asteroids' rotation rates.

E   **Correct.** After a collision, it is the asteroid fragments' failure to reach escape velocity that allows the fragments' gravitational pull to reassemble them into a rubble pile.

The correct answer is E.

Questions 640–642 refer to the passage on page 519.

Main Idea Summary

The primary purpose of the passage is to discuss the theory underlying attempts to get particles to travel faster than the speed of light by means of quantum tunneling. The passage states that quantum theory implies that there is a small probability that a particle can tunnel through a solid barrier. The time it takes a particle to tunnel through a barrier increases as the thickness of the barrier increases, but only up to a maximum amount of time; beyond that maximum, the amount of time does not vary no matter the thickness of the barrier. This implies that, given a certain thickness, the particle will exceed the speed of light, and this has received some empirical support.

640. The author of the passage mentions calculations about tunneling time and barrier thickness in order to

(A) suggest that tunneling time is unrelated to barrier thickness

(B) explain the evidence by which Wigner and Eisenbud discovered the phenomenon of tunneling

(C) describe data recently challenged by Raymond Chiao and colleagues

(D) question why particles engaged in quantum tunneling rarely achieve extremely high speeds

(E) explain the basis for Wigner and Eisenbud's hypothesis

Evaluation

This question asks why the author discusses calculations about tunneling time and barrier thickness. According to the passage, these calculations provided the grounds for Wigner and Eisenbud's hypothesis that tunneling particles may travel faster than light.

A   The passage states that tunneling time is related to barrier thickness, up to the point at which tunneling time reaches a maximum.

B   The passage indicates that the phenomenon of tunneling was noted at least as early as 1932. It provides no evidence that Wigner and Eisenbud discovered it.

C   The passage uses Chiao's work to support the idea that tunneling particles may move faster than light, not challenge it.

D   The author describes calculations about tunneling time and barrier thickness in order to explain that particles engaged in quantum tunneling may in fact achieve extremely high speeds, not to explain the rarity of the phenomenon.

E   **Correct.** The calculations about tunneling time and barrier thickness supported Wigner and Eisenbud's hypothesis that quantum tunneling could occur at speeds faster than that of light.

The correct answer is E.

641. The passage implies that if tunneling time reached no maximum in increasing with barrier thickness, then

    (A)   tunneling speed would increase with barrier thickness

    (B)   tunneling speed would decline with barrier thickness

    (C)   tunneling speed would vary with barrier thickness

    (D)   tunneling speed would not be expected to increase without limit

    (E)   successful tunneling would occur even less frequently than it does

Inference

The passage states that because tunneling time reaches a maximum, then tunneling speed must increase as barrier thickness increases. But if tunneling time did not reach such a maximum, then speed need not increase without limit; the particle could have as low a speed in thicker barriers as in thinner ones and take longer to tunnel through a barrier.

A   If tunneling time could not reach a maximum, then speed might increase, decrease, or remain the same as barrier thickness increases.

B   If tunneling time could not reach a maximum, then speed might increase, decrease, or remain the same as barrier thickness increases.

C   Tunneling speed could vary with barrier thickness if tunneling time could not reach a maximum, but there is no basis in the passage on which to conclude that this is definitely so.

D   **Correct.** The tunneling particle could have as low a speed in thicker barriers as in thinner ones and simply take longer to make its way through a thicker barrier.

E   The passage states that the probability of successful tunneling declines as the thickness of the barrier increases. However, it does not address the issue of whether the differences in probability of successful tunneling are due to the greater time required to go through thicker barriers.

The correct answer is D.

642. Which of the following statements about the earliest scientific investigators of quantum tunneling can be inferred from the passage?

    (A)   They found it difficult to increase barrier thickness continually.

    (B)   They anticipated the later results of Chiao and his colleagues.

    (C)   They did not suppose that tunneling particles could travel faster than light.

    (D)   They were unable to observe instances of successful tunneling.

    (E)   They made use of photons to study the phenomenon of tunneling.

Inference

This question asks about the earliest investigators of quantum tunneling. The passage notes that quantum tunneling's *extreme rapidity* was observed in 1932; thus, the earliest investigators of this phenomenon knew of its existence at that time. Not until 1955 did Wigner and Eisenbud hypothesize that the particles traveled faster than light. Thus, it is logical to infer that the earliest investigators did not imagine such a speed.

A   There is nothing in the passage to suggest that the earliest investigators of quantum tunneling had difficulty manipulating barrier thickness.

B   The passage states that Chiao and his colleagues measured photons moving at 1.7 times the speed of light—but the passage does not provide evidence that the earliest investigators anticipated such speeds.

C   **Correct.** The passage suggests that prior to 1955, investigators of quantum tunneling had not hypothesized that the particles could travel faster than the speed of light.

D   The passage indicates that by 1932, investigators had noted the rapidity of quantum tunneling; although this does not entail that they observed the phenomenon, it is consistent with their having been able to do so.

E   The passage indicates that Chiao's work involves photons, but it does not indicate the type of particles used or observed by the earliest investigators of the phenomenon.

The correct answer is C.

Questions 643–644 refer to the passage on page 520.

643. In lines 10–16, the author mentions possible rises in wool prices primarily in order to

(A)   identify a factor capable of causing declines in total pastureland acreage without causing declines in herd sizes in the thirteenth century

(B)   provide an example of a likely market response to a thirteenth-century pastoral crisis that reduced pastureland acreage

(C)   identify a possible area of disagreement between most economic historians and the historians who postulate a pastoral crisis in the thirteenth century

(D)   suggest a reason why the cost of pastureland could have risen in the thirteenth century even without declines in pasture acreage

(E)   cite evidence supporting the conclusion that herd sizes increased during the thirteenth century

Purpose

The author is arguing against a view, common to economic historians, that increasing cereal production in thirteenth-century Europe necessarily implies a corresponding drop in herd sizes, since land used for agriculture could not be used for pasture. The author refers to one historian's argument that increasing costs for pasturage in thirteenth-century Europe are clear evidence for a shortage of pasturage. The author then proposes an alternative explanation for those rising prices: instead of the price of pasturage going up because of reduced supply, it could have gone up because of increased demand. The reference to rising prices for wool suggests a mechanism for such increased demand: high wool prices would incentivize farmers to raise more sheep, and therefore those farmers would require more pasturage.

A   There is no reason to suppose that rising prices for wool could produce declines in pastureland acreage, so identifying wool prices as the cause of such a decline cannot be the author's purpose.

B   While it is plausible that a reduction in pasturage, and hence in the number of sheep, could lead to rising wool prices, the author refers to rising wool prices as a *cause* for "increased demand for pasturage" and not as an *effect* of a pastoral crisis.

C   Nothing in the passage suggests that wool prices are an area of possible disagreement between most economic historians and those historians who believe there was a pastoral crisis in thirteenth-century Europe.

D   **Correct.** The author is disputing the claim that rising prices for pasturage clearly indicate that pasturage was in short supply. Rising demand for pasturage would provide an alternative explanation for those rising prices, so the author's reference to high wool prices at that time suggests a reason why demand might have increased, bringing higher prices for pasturage with it, regardless of whether available pasturage diminished.

E   The author makes no argument that herd sizes *increased* in the thirteenth century but rather argues that such herd sizes did not necessarily *decrease*; the reference to wool prices cannot support a nonexistent conclusion.

The correct answer is D.

644. Which of the following, if true, would cast most doubt on the argument of the historian mentioned in lines 10–16?

(A)   The thirteenth century was a comparatively prosperous period during which population increased and new markets for agricultural goods emerged in Europe.

(B)   During the medieval period, wool prices in Europe tended to rise slightly in response to decreases in herd sizes.

(C)   New institutional arrangements governing agricultural work were not established in the thirteenth century in areas of Europe until the fourteenth century.

(D)   Most farmers in thirteenth-century Europe would not have been able to afford draft animals to transport their crops to market.

(E)   The clearing of forests and the draining of swamps significantly increased the total acreage of land available to European farmers in the thirteenth century.

Evaluation

The historian referred to in lines 10–16 has argued that because cereal harvests in thirteenth-century Europe increased, it must mean that more land was used for agriculture; therefore, it follows that there must have been a corresponding reduction in the amount of available pastureland, and thus in the number

of domestic herd animals. This argument relies on the assumption that any additional land used for agriculture must have been subtracted from land used for pasture. If, therefore, there was some additional factor that would explain how cereal production could have increased *without* subtracting from the total amount of pastureland—for example, if more land became available from other sources—then that new fact would significantly weaken the historian's argument.

A   An increased demand for agricultural products in thirteenth-century Europe would have no bearing on the historian's central argument: that increased agriculture necessarily implies reduced pasturage and also reductions in the herds that depend on pasturage.

B   While wool prices might be expected to rise if herds of sheep diminished and wool became relatively scarce, that relationship would not affect the amount of land available for agriculture.

C   Arrangements regarding agricultural work are not relevant to the central issue: whether increased agriculture necessarily implies decreased pasturage and herds.

D   Whether or not most farmers at the time could afford draft animals is a question that does not affect the relationship between land used for agriculture and land used for pasturage.

E   **Correct.** If the amount of land available for farming increased significantly during the thirteenth century, then the amount of land used for agriculture, and the resulting grain harvests, could very well have increased without diminishing the amount of land available for pasturage; therefore, this additional fact would cast considerable doubt on the historian's central argument.

The correct answer is E.

8.7 Practice Questions: Critical Reasoning

Each of the Critical Reasoning questions is based on a short argument, a set of statements, or a plan of action. For each question, select the best answer of the choices given.

Questions 645–707 — Difficulty: **Easy**

645. Ramirez: The film industry claims that pirated DVDs, which are usually cheaper than legitimate DVDs and become available well before a film's official DVD release date, adversely affect its bottom line. But the industry should note what the spread of piracy indicates: consumers want lower prices and faster DVD releases. Lowering prices of DVDs and releasing them sooner would mitigate piracy's negative effect on film industry profits.

The argument above relies on which of the following assumptions?

(A) Releasing legitimate DVDs earlier would not cause any reduction in the revenue the film industry receives from the films' theatrical release.

(B) Some people who would otherwise purchase pirated DVDs would be willing to purchase legitimate DVDs if they were less expensive and released earlier than they are now.

(C) The film industry will in the future be able to produce DVDs more cheaply than is currently the case.

(D) Some current sellers of pirated DVDs would likely discontinue their businesses if legitimate DVDs were released faster and priced lower.

(E) Current purchasers of pirated DVDs are aware that those DVDs are not authorized by the film industry.

646. Harunia Province has a relatively dry climate and is attracting a fast-growing population that has put increasing demands on its water supply. The two companies that supply water to the region have struggled to keep up with demand and still remain profitable. Yet now they are asking Harunian authorities to write residential water-use regulations that could reduce their revenues and restrict their future flexibility in supplying water profitably.

Which of the following would, if true, most logically help explain why the water-supply companies are asking the authorities to regulate residential water use?

(A) The companies are planning large water-transportation and irrigation systems that require the approval of neighboring provinces.

(B) The companies believe regulation is inevitable and that having it in place now will allow better planning and thus future profitability.

(C) Few, if any, Harunian government officials have investments in the companies or serve on their boards of directors.

(D) The companies believe that the population is not likely to continue to grow.

(E) Long-term climate projections suggest that greater rainfall will eventually increase the amount of water available.

647. Loss of the Gocha mangrove forests has caused coastal erosion, reducing fish populations and requiring the Gocha Fishing Cooperative (GFC) to partially fund dredging and new shore facilities. However, as part of its subsidiary businesses, the GFC has now invested in a program to replant significant parts of the coast with mangrove trees. Given income from a controlled harvest of wood with continuing replanting, the mangrove regeneration effort makes it more likely that the cooperative will increase its net income.

Which of the following, if true, would most strengthen the argument that mangrove replanting will increase the Gocha cooperative's net income?

(A) The cost of dredging and shore facilities was shared with the local government.

(B) The GFC will be able to hire local workers to assist with the mangrove replanting.

(C) The GFC derives 10 percent of its revenue from salt-production facilities in an area previously cleared of mangroves.

(D) Mangrove forests tend to increase the commercial fish populations in coastal fishing grounds.

(E) A controlled harvesting of mangrove wood by the GFC would have little effect on coastal erosion.

648. Executives at the Fizzles Beverage Company plan to boost profits in Country X on their range of fruit-flavored drinks by introducing new flavors based on tropical fruits that are little known there. The executives reason that since the fruit drinks of other companies have none of these flavors, Fizzles will not have to compete for customers and thus will be able to sell the drinks at a higher price.

Which of the following, if true, presents the most serious potential weakness of the plan?

(A) The new fruit drinks would be priced significantly higher than other Fizzles fruit drinks with more conventional flavors.

(B) In a telephone survey, at least one of the consumers contacted said that they preferred many of the new flavors to all of the more familiar flavors.

(C) To build widespread demand for the new flavors, Fizzles would have to launch an advertising campaign to familiarize consumers with them.

(D) Consumers choosing among fruit-flavored drinks of different brands generally buy on the basis of name recognition and price rather than the specific fruit flavor.

(E) Few consumers who are loyal to a specific brand of fruit-flavored drinks would willingly switch to another brand that costs more.

649. Economist: In 2015, the average per-person amount paid for goods and services purchased by consumers in Country X was the equivalent of $17,570 in United States dollars, just 30 percent of the corresponding figure of $58,566 for Country Y. Yet in 2015, there was already a substantial middle class in Country X that had discretionary income for middle-class consumer goods such as new vehicles, computers, or major household appliances, while a significant portion of the middle class in Country Y did not have sufficient income to purchase such items.

Which of the following, if true, most helps explain the discrepancy in the relationships described by the economist?

(A) There are many consumer goods, such as household appliances, that are produced in Country X to be sold in the Country Y market.

(B) The volume of trade between Country X and Country Y is increasing rapidly in both directions.

(C) The economy of Country Y is recovering from a downturn that affected both Country Y and Country X.

(D) Country X residents pay much less than their Country Y counterparts for housing, transportation, and child care.

(E) In Country Y as well as in Country X, there are few assembly-line jobs in factories that pay a middle-class wage.

650. Neuroscientist: Memory evolved to help animals react appropriately to situations they encounter by drawing on the past experience of similar situations. But this does not require that animals perfectly recall every detail of all their experiences. Instead, to function well, memory should generalize from past experiences that are similar to the current one.

The neuroscientist's statements, if true, most strongly support which of the following conclusions?

(A) At least some animals perfectly recall every detail of at least some past experiences.

(B) Perfectly recalling every detail of all their past experiences could help at least some animals react more appropriately than they otherwise would to new situations they encounter.

(C) Generalizing from past experiences requires clear memories of most if not all the details of those experiences.

(D) Recalling every detail of all past experiences would be incompatible with any ability to generalize from those experiences.

(E) Animals can often react more appropriately than they otherwise would to situations they encounter if they draw on generalizations from past experiences of similar situations.

651. In Country X's last election, the Reform Party beat its main opponent, the Conservative Party, although pollsters, employing in-person interviews shortly before the vote, had projected a Conservative Party victory. Afterward, the pollsters determined that, unlike Conservative Party supporters, Reform Party supporters were less likely to express their party preference during in-person interviews than they were during telephone interviews. Therefore, using only telephone interviews instead would likely result in more accurate projections for the next election.

Which of the following statements, if true, would most support the argument in the passage?

(A) The number of voters in Country X's next election will be significantly larger than the number of voters in the last election.

(B) The Conservative Party will win the next election.

(C) For each person interviewed in telephone polls before the next election, pollsters will be able to reasonably determine the likelihood of that person voting.

(D) People who expressed no party preference during the in-person interviews shortly before Country X's last election did not outnumber the people who expressed a preference for the Conservative Party.

(E) In the next election, pollsters will be able to conduct more in-person interviews than telephone interviews.

652. A company that manufactures plastic products from recyclable plastic is, surprisingly, unconcerned that economic conditions may worsen, despite analysts' belief that consumers would then consider ecofriendly plastic products an expensive luxury. But the company reasons that it will be able to lower its prices because, in a weakened economy, other ecofriendly plastic manufacturers are likely to fail. Demand among manufacturers for recyclable plastics as raw materials would then plummet, creating an oversupply of such materials, making them less expensive for the manufacturer to purchase and thus lowering the company's costs.

Which of the following, if true, most weakens the company's reasoning?

(A) Smaller ecofriendly plastic manufacturers are more likely to fail in a weakened economy than larger ecofriendly manufacturers are.

(B) Some retailers whose sales include various companies' ecofriendly plastic products have struggled in recent years despite the overall good economy.

(C) Consumers would likely soon learn of the oversupply of recyclable plastics and cease recycling them, significantly raising manufacturers' raw-material costs.

(D) Retailers, including retailers that cater to consumers seeking certain types of ecofriendly products, may lose some business if economic conditions worsen.

(E) The plastics used by the company in its products were, after a recent investigation by a regulatory body, declared to be safe for consumers.

653. Researchers asked volunteers to imagine they were running a five-kilometer race against 50 people and then against 500 people, races in each of which the top 10 percent would receive a $1,000 prize. Asked about the effort they would apply in the respective cases, the volunteers indicated, on average, that they would run slower in the race against the greater number of people. A likely explanation of this result is that those of the volunteers who were most *comparatively inclined*— those who most tended to compare themselves with others in the social environment—determined (perhaps unconsciously) that extreme effort would not be worthwhile in the 500-competitor race.

Which of the following would, if known to be true, most help justify the explanation offered above?

(A) The volunteers who were most comparatively inclined were also those who had the greatest desire to win a $1,000 prize.

(B) The volunteers who were the least comparatively inclined had no greater desire to win the $1,000 than those who were the most comparatively inclined.

(C) The volunteers who were most comparatively inclined were likely to indicate that they would run the two races at the same speed.

(D) The most comparatively inclined volunteers believed that they were significantly less likely to finish in the top 10 percent in the race against 500 than in the race against 50.

(E) Volunteers were chosen for participation in the study on the basis of answers to various questions designed to measure the degree to which the volunteers were comparatively inclined.

654. According to a study, after a week of high-altitude living, twenty men had slimmed down. The men, middle-aged residents of low-altitude areas, had been taken to a research station at 2,650 meters (8,694 feet) above sea level. They had unrestricted access to food and were forbidden vigorous exercise, yet they lost an average of 1.5 kilograms (3.3 pounds) during their one-week stay. Clearly, the lower availability of oxygen at higher altitudes, or hypobaric hypoxia, can be said to have caused the weight loss, since _____.

Which of the following would, if true, most logically complete the argument?

(A) a decrease in oxygen intake has been shown to depress appetite

(B) the men all participated in the same kinds of exercise during their stay

(C) the foods available to the men had fewer calories than the foods they usually ate

(D) exercise at higher altitudes is more difficult than exercise at lower altitudes is

(E) several weeks after returning home, the men still weighed less than they had before the study

655. Editorial: Our city's public transportation agency is facing a budget shortfall. The fastest-growing part of the budget has been employee retirement benefits, which are exceptionally generous. Unless the budget shortfall is resolved, transportation service will be cut, and many transportation employees will lose their jobs. Thus, it would be in the employees' best interest for their union to accept cuts in retirement benefits.

Which of the following is an assumption the editorial's argument requires?

(A) The transportation employees' union should not accept cuts in retirement benefits if doing so would not be in the employees' best interest.

(B) The only feasible way for the agency to resolve the budget shortfall would involve cutting transportation service and eliminating jobs.

(C) Other things being equal, it is in the transportation employees' interest to have exceptionally generous retirement benefits.

(D) Cutting the retirement benefits would help resolve the agency's budget shortfall.

(E) The transportation employees' union will not accept cuts in retirement benefits if doing so will not allow more transportation employees to keep their jobs.

656. Researchers hope to find clues about the A'mk peoples who lived in the Kaumpta region about one thousand years ago but who left few obvious traces. The researchers plan to hire the few remaining shamans of the modern-day indigenous people in Kaumpta, who are believed to be descended from the A'mk, to lead them to ancestral sites that may be the remains of A'mk buildings or ceremonial spaces. The shamans were taught the location of such sites as part of their traditional training as youths, and their knowledge of traditional Kaumpta customs may help determine the nature of any sites the researchers find.

Which of the following is an assumption on which the success of the plan depends?

(A) The researchers have reliable evidence that the A'mk of one thousand years ago built important ceremonial spaces.

(B) The shamans have a reasonably accurate memory of A'mk sites they learned about as youths.

(C) Kaumpta shamans are generally held in high esteem for their traditional knowledge.

(D) Modern technologies available to the researchers are likely to be able to find some A'mk sites easily.

(E) Most or all A'mk sites are likely to be found within the Kaumpta region.

657. Astronomer: Most stars are born in groups of thousands, each star in a group forming from the same parent cloud of gas. Each cloud has a unique, homogeneous chemical composition. Therefore, whenever two stars have the same chemical composition as each other, they must have originated from the same cloud of gas.

Which of the following, if true, would most strengthen the astronomer's argument?

(A) In some groups of stars, not every star originated from the same parent cloud of gas.

(B) Clouds of gas of similar or identical chemical composition may be remote from each other.

(C) Whenever a star forms, it inherits the chemical composition of its parent cloud of gas.

(D) Many stars in vastly different parts of the universe are quite similar in their chemical compositions.

(E) Astronomers can at least sometimes precisely determine whether a star has the same chemical composition as its parent cloud of gas.

658. With employer-paid training, workers have the potential to become more productive not only in their present employment but also in any number of jobs with different employers. To increase the productivity of their workforce, many firms are planning to maintain or even increase their investments in worker training. But some training experts object that if a trained worker is hired away by another firm, the employer that paid for the training has merely subsidized a competitor. They note that such hiring has been on the rise in recent years.

Which of the following would, if true, contribute most to defeating the training experts' objection to the firms' strategy?

(A) Firms that promise opportunities for advancement to their employees get, on average, somewhat larger numbers of job applications from untrained workers than do firms that make no such promise.

(B) In many industries, employees who take continuing-education courses are more competitive in the job market.

(C) More and more educational and training institutions are offering reduced tuition fees to firms that subsidize worker training.

(D) Research shows that workers whose training is wholly or partially subsidized by their employer tend to get at least as much training as do workers who pay for all their own training.

(E) For most firms that invest in training their employees, the value added by that investment in employees who stay exceeds the value lost through other employees' leaving to work for other companies.

659. In emerging economies in Africa and other regions, large foreign banks that were set up during the colonial era have long played a major economic role. These institutions have tended to confine their business to the wealthier of banks' potential customers. But development of these countries' economies requires financing of the small businesses that dominate their manufacturing, farming, and services sectors. So economic growth will be likely to occur if local banks take on this portion of the financial services markets, since _____.

Which of the following completions would produce the strongest argument?

(A) local banks tend not to strive as much as large foreign banks to diversify their investments

(B) small farming and manufacturing businesses contribute to economic growth if they obtain adequate investment capital

(C) large foreign banks in emerging economies could, with local employees and appropriate local consultation, profitably expand their business to less wealthy clients

(D) some small businesses are among the wealthier customers of foreign banks in emerging economies

(E) local banks in emerging economies tend to be less risk-averse than foreign banks

660. Exporters in Country X are facing lower revenues due to a shortage of the large metal shipping containers in which they send their goods by sea to other countries. Fewer containers arrive in Country X due to reductions in imports. This has meant lost orders, costly delays, and a scramble for alternatives, such as air freight, all of which are costlier. Moreover, the revenues of exporters in Country X will probably continue to decline in the near future. This is because other countries are likely to find it increasingly unprofitable to export their goods to Country X, and because _____.

Which of the following would most logically complete the passage?

(A) production of shipping containers in Country X is growing rapidly as a response to the shortage

(B) shipping companies are willing to move containers from country to country only when the containers are full

(C) the cost of shipping alternatives such as air freight is likely to stabilize in the near future

(D) consumers in Country X are purchasing more products than ever before

(E) the worldwide demand for goods made in Country X has only recently begun to rise after a long decline

661. In order to reduce the number of items damaged while in transit to customers, packaging consultants recommended the TrueSave mail-order company increase the amount of packing material so as to fill any empty spaces in its cartons. Accordingly, TrueSave officials instructed the company's packers to use more packing material than before, and the packers zealously acted on these instructions and used as much as they could. Nevertheless, customer reports of damaged items rose somewhat.

Which of the following, if true, most helps to explain why acting on the consultants' recommendation failed to achieve its goal?

(A) The change in packing policy led to an increase in expenditure on packing material and labor.

(B) When packing material is compressed too densely, it loses some of its capacity to absorb shock.

(C) The amount of packing material used in a carton does not significantly influence the ease with which a customer can unpack the package.

(D) Most of the goods TrueSave ships are electronic products that are highly vulnerable to being damaged in transit.

(E) TrueSave has lost some of its regular customers as a result of the high number of damaged items they received.

662. An unusually severe winter occurred in Europe after the continent was blanketed by a blue haze resulting from the eruption of the Laki Volcano in the European republic of Iceland in the summer of 1984. Thus, it is evident that major eruptions cause the atmosphere to become cooler than it would be otherwise.

Which of the following statements, if true, most seriously weakens the argument above?

(A) The cooling effect triggered by volcanic eruptions in 1985 was counteracted by an unusual warming of Pacific waters.

(B) There is a strong statistical link between volcanic eruptions and the severity of the rainy season in India.

(C) A few months after El Chichón's large eruption in April 1982, air temperatures throughout the region remained higher than expected given the long-term weather trends.

(D) The climatic effects of major volcanic eruptions can temporarily mask the general warming trend resulting from an excess of carbon dioxide in the atmosphere.

(E) Three months after an early springtime eruption in South America during the late nineteenth century, sea surface temperatures near the coast began to fall.

663. Political theorist: Even with the best spies, area experts, and satellite surveillance, foreign policy assessments can still lack important information. In such circumstances intuitive judgment is vital. A national leader with such judgment can make good decisions about foreign policy even when current information is incomplete, since _____.

Which of the following, if true, most logically completes the argument?

(A) the central reason for failure in foreign policy decision making is the absence of critical information

(B) those leaders whose foreign policy decisions have been highly ranked have also been found to have good intuitive judgment

(C) both intuitive judgment and good information are required for sound decision-making

(D) good foreign policy decisions often lead to improved methods of gathering information

(E) intuitive judgment can produce good decisions based on past experience, even when there are important gaps in current information

664. Supply shortages and signs of growing demand are driving cocoa prices upward. Unusually severe weather in cocoa-producing regions—too much rain in Brazil and too little in West Africa—has limited production. Further, Europe and North America recently reported stronger demand for cocoa. In the first quarter, grinding of cocoa beans—the first stage in processing cocoa for chocolate—rose 8.1 percent in Europe and 16 percent in North America. Analysts have concluded that cocoa's price will continue to rise at least into the near future.

Which of the following would, if true, most strengthen the reasoning above?

(A) Ground cocoa beans can be stored for long periods before they spoil.

(B) Several European and North American manufacturers that use cocoa have recently improved their processing capacity.

(C) It takes new cocoa trees five or six years before they start bearing fruit.

(D) Governments in Europe and North America are likely to change current restrictions on cocoa imports.

(E) Historically, cocoa production has varied widely from year to year.

665. A popular beach has long had a dolphin-feeding program in which fish are given to dolphins several times a day. Many dolphins get as much as half of their food each day there. Although dolphins that first benefit from the program as adults are healthy and long-lived, their offspring have a lower life expectancy than offspring of dolphins that feed exclusively in the wild.

Which of the following, if true, most helps to explain the lower life expectancy of offspring of dolphins feeding at the beach compared to other young dolphins?

(A) Sharks that prey on dolphins are less common in the open seas off the beach than in many other areas of the open seas where dolphins congregate.

(B) Many of the adult dolphins that feed at the beach are females that nurse their offspring there.

(C) The fish given to the dolphins at the beach are the same types of fish that dolphins typically catch in the wild.

(D) Many dolphins that feed at the beach with their offspring come to the beach only a few times a month.

(E) Adult dolphins that feed at the beach spend much less time teaching their offspring how to catch fish in the wild than do other adult dolphins.

666. **Plant scientists have used genetic engineering on seeds to produce crop plants that are highly resistant to insect damage.** Unfortunately, the seeds themselves are quite expensive, and the plants require more fertilizer and water to grow well than normal ones. Accordingly, **for most farmers the savings on pesticides would not compensate for the higher seed costs and the cost of additional fertilizer.** However, since consumer demand for grains, fruits, and vegetables grown without the use of pesticides continues to rise, the use of genetically engineered seeds of this kind is likely to become widespread.

In the argument given, the two portions in **boldface** play which of the following roles?

(A) The first supplies a context for the argument; the second is the argument's main conclusion.

(B) The first introduces a development that the argument predicts will have a certain outcome; the second is a state of affairs that, according to the argument, contributes to bringing about that outcome.

(C) The first presents a development that the argument predicts will have a certain outcome; the second acknowledges a consideration that tends to weigh against that prediction.

(D) The first provides evidence to support a prediction that the argument seeks to defend; the second is that prediction.

(E) The first and the second each provide evidence to support the argument's main conclusion.

667. Which of the following most logically completes the passage?

Leptin, a protein occurring naturally in the blood, appears to regulate how much fat the body carries by speeding up the metabolism and decreasing the appetite when the body has too much fat. Mice that do not naturally produce leptin have more fat than other mice, but they lose fat rapidly when they are given leptin injections. Unfortunately, however, leptin cannot be used as a dietary supplement to control fat, since _____.

(A) the digestive system breaks down proteins before they can enter the bloodstream

(B) there are pharmaceuticals already available that can contribute to weight loss by speeding up the metabolism

(C) people with unusually low levels of leptin in their blood tend to have a high percentage of body fat

(D) the mice that do not naturally produce leptin were from a specially bred strain of mice

(E) mice whose bodies did produce leptin also lost some of their body fat when given leptin injections

668. Large national budget deficits do not cause large trade deficits. If they did, countries with the largest budget deficits would also have the largest trade deficits. In fact, when deficit figures are adjusted so different countries are reliably comparable to each other, there is no such correlation.

If the statements above are all true, which of the following can properly be inferred on the basis of them?

(A) Countries with large national budget deficits tend to restrict foreign trade.

(B) Reliable comparisons of the deficit figures of one country with those of another are impossible.

(C) Reducing a country's national budget deficit will not necessarily result in a lowering of any trade deficit that country may have.

(D) When countries are ordered from largest to smallest in terms of population, the smallest countries generally have the smallest budget and trade deficits.

(E) Countries with the largest trade deficits never have similarly large national budget deficits.

669. Archaeologists use technology to analyze ancient sites. It is likely that this technology will advance considerably in the near future, allowing archaeologists to gather more information than is currently possible. If they study certain sites now, they risk contaminating or compromising them for future studies. Therefore, in order to maximize the potential for gathering knowledge in the long run, a team of archaeologists plans to delay the examination of a newly excavated site.

Which of the following would be most useful to investigate for the purpose of evaluating the plan's prospects for achieving its goal?

(A) Whether any of the contents of the site will significantly deteriorate before the anticipated technology is available

(B) Whether there will continue to be improvements on the relevant technology

(C) Whether the team can study a site other than the newly excavated site for the time being

(D) Whether the site was inhabited by a very ancient culture

(E) Whether the anticipated technology will damage objects under study

670. More and more law firms specializing in corporate taxes are paid on a contingency-fee basis. Under this arrangement, if a case is won, the firm usually receives more than it would have received if it had been paid on the alternate hourly rate basis. If the case is lost, the firm receives nothing. Most firms are likely to make more under the contingency-fee arrangement.

Which of the following, if true, would most strengthen the prediction above?

(A) Firms that work exclusively under the hourly rate arrangement spend, on average, fewer hours on cases that are won than on cases that are lost.

(B) Some litigation can last for years before any decision is reached, and, even then, the decision may be appealed.

(C) Firms under the contingency-fee arrangement still pay their employees on an hourly basis.

(D) Since the majority of firms specialize in certain kinds of cases, they are able to assess accurately their chances of winning each potential case.

(E) Firms working under the contingency-fee arrangement take in fewer cases per year than do firms working under the hourly rate arrangement.

671. Pretzel vendor: The new license fee for operating a pretzel stand outside the art museum is prohibitively expensive. Charging typical prices, I would need to sell an average of 25 pretzels per hour to break even. At my stand outside City Hall, with about as many passers-by as at the art museum, I average only 15 per hour. So I could not break even running a stand outside the art museum, much less turn a profit.

Which of the following, if true, most seriously weakens the pretzel vendor's argument?

(A) The pretzel vendor does not sell anything other than pretzels.

(B) People who visit the art museum are more likely to buy pretzels than are people who go to City Hall.

(C) The license fee for operating a pretzel stand outside City Hall will not increase.

(D) People who buy pretzels at pretzel stands are more likely to do so during the lunch hour than at other times.

(E) The city will grant more licenses for pretzel stands outside the art museum than the number it grants for stands outside City Hall.

672. Beginning in 1966, all new cars sold in Morodia were required to have safety belts and power steering. Previously, most cars in Morodia were without these features. Safety belts help to prevent injuries in collisions, and power steering helps to avoid collisions in the first place. But even though in 1966 one-seventh of the cars in Morodia were replaced with new cars, the number of car collisions and collision-related injuries did not decline.

Which of the following, if true about Morodia, most helps to explain why the number of collisions and collision-related injuries in Morodia failed to decline in 1966?

(A)   Because of a driver-education campaign, most drivers and passengers in cars that did have safety belts used them in 1966.

(B)   Most of the new cars bought in 1966 were bought in the months of January and February.

(C)   In 1965, substantially more than one-seventh of the cars in Morodia were replaced with new cars.

(D)   An excessive reliance on the new safety features led many owners of new cars to drive less cautiously in 1966 than before.

(E)   The seat belts and power steering put into new cars sold in 1966 had to undergo strict quality-control inspections by manufacturers, whether the cars were manufactured in Morodia or not.

673. Manufacturers of mechanical pencils make most of their profit on pencil leads rather than on the pencils themselves. The Write Company, which cannot sell its leads as cheaply as other manufacturers can, plans to alter the design of its mechanical pencil so that it will accept only a newly designed Write Company lead, which will be sold at the same price as the Write Company's current lead.

Which of the following, if true, most strongly supports the Write Company's projection that its plan will lead to an increase in its sales of pencil leads?

(A)   The new Write Company pencil will be introduced at a price higher than the price the Write Company charges for its current model.

(B)   In the foreseeable future, manufacturers of mechanical pencils will probably have to raise the prices they charge for mechanical pencils.

(C)   The newly designed Write Company lead will cost somewhat more to manufacture than the Write Company's current lead does.

(D)   A rival manufacturer recently announced similar plans to introduce a mechanical pencil that would accept only the leads produced by that manufacturer.

(E)   In extensive test marketing, mechanical-pencil users found the new Write Company pencil markedly superior to other mechanical pencils they had used.

674. Enterprise Bank currently requires customers with checking accounts to maintain a minimum balance or pay a monthly fee. Enterprise plans to offer accounts with no monthly fee and no minimum-balance requirement; to cover their projected administrative costs of $3 per account per month, they plan to charge $30 for overdrawing an account. Since each month on average slightly more than 10 percent of Enterprise's customers overdraw their accounts, bank officials predict the new accounts will generate a profit.

Which of the following, if true, most strongly supports the bank officials' prediction?

(A)   Some of Enterprise Bank's current checking account customers are expected to switch to the new accounts once they are offered.

(B)   One-third of Enterprise Bank's revenues are currently derived from monthly fees tied to checking accounts.

(C)   Many checking account customers who occasionally pay a fee for not maintaining a minimum balance in their account generally maintain a balance well above the minimum.

(D)   Customers whose checking accounts do not have a minimum-balance requirement are more likely than others to overdraw their checking accounts.

(E)   Customers whose checking accounts do not have a minimum-balance requirement are more likely than others to write checks for small amounts.

675. Highway official: When resurfacing our concrete bridges, we should use electrically conductive concrete (ECC) rather than standard concrete. In the winter, ECC can be heated by passing an electric current through it, thereby preventing ice buildup. The cost of the electricity needed is substantially lower than the cost of the deicing salt we currently use.

Taxpayer: But ECC is vastly more expensive than standard concrete, so your proposal is probably not justifiable on economic grounds.

Which of the following, if true, could best be used by the highway official to support the official's proposal in the face of the taxpayer's objection?

(A)   The use of deicing salt causes corrosion of reinforcing steel in concrete bridge decks and damage to the concrete itself, thereby considerably shortening the useful life of concrete bridges.

(B)   Severe icing conditions can cause power outages and slow down the work of emergency crews trying to get power restored.

(C) In weather conditions conducive to icing, ice generally forms on the concrete surfaces of bridges well before it forms on parts of the roadway that go over solid ground.

(D) Aside from its potential use for deicing bridges, ECC might also be an effective means of keeping other concrete structures such as parking garages and airport runways ice free.

(E) If ECC were to be used for a bridge surface, the electric current would be turned on only at times at which ice was likely to form.

676. In virtually any industry, technological improvements increase labor productivity, which is the output of goods and services per person-hour worked. In Parland's industries, labor productivity is significantly higher than it is in Vergia's industries. Clearly, therefore, Parland's industries must, on the whole, be further advanced technologically than Vergia's are. The argument is most vulnerable to which of the following criticisms?

(A) It offers a conclusion that is no more than a paraphrase of one of the pieces of information provided in its support.

(B) It presents as evidence in support of a claim information that is inconsistent with other evidence presented in support of the same claim.

(C) It takes one possible cause of a condition to be the actual cause of that condition without considering any other possible causes.

(D) It takes a condition to be the effect of something that happened only after the condition already existed.

(E) It makes a distinction that presupposes the truth of the conclusion that is to be established.

677. Chaco Canyon, a settlement of the ancient Anasazi culture in North America, had massive buildings. **It must have been a major Anasazi center.** Analysis of wood samples shows that some of the timber for the buildings came from the Chuska and San Mateo mountains, 50 miles from Chaco Canyon. **Only a major cultural center would have the organizational power to import timber from 50 miles away.**

In the argument given, the two portions in **boldface** play which of the following roles?

(A) The first is a premise used to support the argument's main conclusion; the second is the argument's main conclusion.

(B) The first is the argument's main conclusion; the second is a premise used to support that conclusion.

(C) The first is one of two premises used to support the argument's main conclusion; the second is the other of those two premises.

(D) The first is a premise used to support the argument's main conclusion; the second is a premise used to support another conclusion drawn in the argument.

(E) The first is inferred from another statement in the argument; the second is inferred from the first.

678. Regulations will not allow a pesticide that is toxic to humans to be used inside houses unless the pesticide will dissipate completely from the air within eight hours after its application. One test pesticide manufacturers typically use to determine how quickly anti-termite pesticides dissipate involves spraying the pesticides on the walls of room-sized plywood boxes and then timing their dissipation.

Which of the following would it be most useful to know in order to evaluate whether a dissipation time of just under eight hours on the manufacturers' test indicates an anti-termite pesticide that is toxic to humans obeys regulations for use in houses?

(A) Whether anti-termite pesticides dissipate more slowly in furnished rooms than in plywood boxes

(B) Whether people who apply anti-termite pesticides typically wear protective equipment that prevents them from being exposed to the pesticide

(C) Whether people whose houses are being treated with anti-termite pesticide generally know they should remain out of their house during the hours immediately after the pesticide's application

(D) Whether there are anti-termite pesticides toxic to humans that, when subjected to the manufacturers' test, dissipate completely from the air in the boxes in well under eight hours

(E) Whether anti-termite pesticides that are not toxic to humans tend to take longer to dissipate than those that are toxic

679. Which of the following most logically completes the argument?

In a typical year, Innovair's airplanes are involved in 35 collisions while parked or being towed in airports, with a resulting yearly cost of $1,000,000 for repairs.

To reduce the frequency of ground collisions, Innovair will begin giving its ground crews additional training, at an annual cost of $500,000. Although this will cut the number of ground collisions by about half at best, the drop in repair costs can be expected to be much greater, since _____.

(A) most ground collisions happen when ground crews are rushing to minimize the time a delayed airplane spends on the ground

(B) a ground collision typically occurs when there are no passengers on the airplane

(C) the additional training will focus on helping ground crews avoid those kinds of ground collisions that cause the most costly damage

(D) the $500,000 cost figure for the additional training of ground crews includes the wages that those crews will earn during the time spent in actual training

(E) most ground collisions have been caused by the least experienced ground-crew members

680. Scientists propose placing seismic stations on the floor of the Pacific Ocean to warn threatened coastal communities on the northwestern coast of the United States of approaching tidal waves caused by earthquakes. Since forewarned communities could take steps to evacuate, many of the injuries and deaths that would otherwise occur could be avoided if the government would implement this proposal.

The answer to which of the following questions would be most important in determining whether implementing the proposal would be likely to achieve the desired result?

(A) When was the last time that the coastal communities were threatened by an approaching tidal wave?

(B) How far below sea level would the stations be located?

(C) Would there be enough time after receiving warning of an approaching tidal wave for communities to evacuate safely?

(D) How soon after a tidal wave hits land is it safe for evacuees to return to their communities?

(E) Can the stations be equipped to collect and relay information about phenomena other than tidal waves caused by earthquakes?

681. Only a reduction of 10 percent in the number of scheduled flights using Greentown's airport will allow the delays that are so common there to be avoided. Hevelia airstrip, 40 miles away, would, if upgraded and expanded, be an attractive alternative for fully 20 percent of the passengers using Greentown airport. Nevertheless, experts reject the claim that turning Hevelia into a full-service airport would end the chronic delays at Greentown.

Which of the following, if true, most helps to justify the experts' position?

(A) Turning Hevelia into a full-service airport would require not only substantial construction at the airport itself but also the construction of new access highways.

(B) A second largely undeveloped airstrip close to Greentown airport would be a more attractive alternative than Hevelia for many passengers who now use Greentown.

(C) Hevelia airstrip lies in a relatively undeveloped area but would, if it became a full-service airport, be a magnet for commercial and residential development.

(D) If an airplane has to wait to land, the extra jet fuel required adds significantly to the airline's costs.

(E) Several airlines use Greentown as a regional hub, so that most flights landing at Greentown have many passengers who then take different flights to reach their final destinations.

682. Farmer: Worldwide, just three grain crops—rice, wheat, and corn—account for most human caloric intake. To maintain this level of caloric intake and also keep pace with global population growth, yields per acre from each of these crops will have to increase at least 1.5 percent every year, given that the supply of cultivated land is diminishing. Therefore, the government should increase funding for research into new ways to improve yields.

Which of the following is an assumption on which the farmer's argument depends?

(A) It is solely the government's responsibility to ensure that the amount of rice, wheat, and corn produced worldwide keeps pace with global population growth.

(B)   Increasing government funding for research into new ways to improve the yields per acre of rice, wheat, and corn crops would help to increase total worldwide annual production of food from these crops.

(C)   Increasing the yields per acre of rice, wheat, and corn is more important than increasing the yields per acre of other crops.

(D)   Current levels of funding for research into ways of improving grain crop yields per acre have enabled grain crop yields per acre to increase by more than 1.5 percent per year worldwide.

(E)   In coming decades, rice, wheat, and corn will become a minor part of human caloric intake, unless there is government-funded research to increase their yields per acre.

683.   The air quality board recently informed Coffee Roast, a small coffee roasting firm, of a complaint regarding the smoke from its roaster. Recently enacted air quality regulations require machines roasting more than 10 pounds of coffee to be equipped with expensive smoke-dissipating afterburners. The firm, however, roasts only 8 pounds of coffee at a time. Nevertheless, the company has decided to purchase and install an afterburner.

Which of the following, if true, most strongly supports the firm's decision?

(A)   Until settling on the new air quality regulations, the board had debated whether to require afterburners for machines roasting more than 5 pounds of coffee at a time.

(B)   Coffee roasted in a machine equipped with an afterburner has its flavor subtly altered.

(C)   The cost to the firm of an afterburner is less than the cost of replacing its roaster with a smaller one.

(D)   Fewer complaints are reported in areas that maintain strict rules regarding afterburners.

(E)   The firm has reason to fear that negative publicity regarding the complaints could result in lost sales.

684.   A study compared a sample of Swedish people older than 75 who needed in-home assistance with a similar sample of Israeli people. The people in the two samples received both informal assistance, provided by family and friends, and formal assistance, professionally provided. Although Sweden and Israel have equally well-funded and comprehensive systems for providing formal assistance, the study found that the people in the Swedish sample received more formal assistance, on average, than those in the Israeli sample.

Which of the following, if true, does most to explain the difference that the study found?

(A)   A companion study found that among children needing special in-home care, the amount of formal assistance they received was roughly the same in Sweden as in Israel.

(B)   More Swedish than Israeli people older than 75 live in rural areas where formal assistance services are sparse or nonexistent.

(C)   Although in both Sweden and Israel much of the funding for formal assistance ultimately comes from the central government, the local structures through which assistance is delivered are different in the two countries.

(D)   In recent decades, the increase in life expectancy of someone who is 75 years old has been greater in Israel than in Sweden.

(E)   In Israel, people older than 75 tend to live with their children, whereas in Sweden people of that age tend to live alone.

685.   Film director: It is true that certain characters and plot twists in my newly released film *The Big Heist* are similar to characters and plot twists in *Thieves*, a movie that came out last year. Pointing to these similarities, the film studio that produced *Thieves* is now accusing me of taking ideas from that film. The accusation is clearly without merit. All production work on *The Big Heist* was actually completed months before *Thieves* was released.

Which of the following, if true, provides the strongest support for the director's position?

(A)   Before *Thieves* began production, its script had been circulating for several years among various film studios, including the studio that produced *The Big Heist*.

(B)   The characters and plot twists that are most similar in the two films have close parallels in many earlier films of the same genre.

(C)   The film studio that produced *Thieves* seldom produces films in this genre.

(D)   The director of *Thieves* worked with the director of *The Big Heist* on several earlier projects.

(E)   Production work on *Thieves* began before production work on *The Big Heist* was started.

686. In Mernia, commercial fossil hunters often sell important fossils they have found, not to universities or museums but to individual collectors, who pay much better but generally do not allow researchers access to their collections. To increase the number of fossils available for research, some legislators propose requiring all fossils that are found in Mernia to be sold only to universities or museums.

Which of the following, if true, most strongly indicates that the legislators' proposal will fail to achieve its goal?

(A) Some fossil hunters in Mernia are not commercial fossil hunters, but rather are amateurs who keep the fossils that they find.

(B) Most fossils found in Mernia are common types that have little scientific interest.

(C) Commercial fossil hunters in Mernia currently sell some of the fossils they find to universities and museums.

(D) Many universities in Mernia do not engage in fossil research.

(E) Most fossils are found by commercial fossil hunters, and they would give up looking for fossils if they were no longer allowed to sell to individual collectors.

687. Brown tides are growths of algae on the sea's surface that prevent sunlight from reaching marine plants below, thereby destroying not only the plants but also the shellfish that live off these plants. Biologists recently isolated a virus that, when added to seawater, kills the algae that cause brown tides. Adding large quantities of this virus to waters affected by brown tides will therefore make it possible to save the populations of shellfish that inhabit those waters.

Which of the following, if true, provides the most support for the conclusion of the argument?

(A) When applied in large quantities, the virus not only kills the algae that cause brown tides but also many harmless kinds of algae.

(B) Marine animals that prey on shellfish avoid areas of the sea in which brown tides are occurring.

(C) The number of different kinds of viruses present in seawater is far greater than many marine biologists had, until recently, believed.

(D) The presence of large quantities of the virus in seawater does not adversely affect the growth of marine plants.

(E) The amount of the virus naturally present in seawater in which brown tides occur is neither significantly greater nor significantly less than the amount present in seawater in which brown tides do not occur.

688. Educational theorist: Recent editorials have called for limits on the amount of homework assigned to schoolchildren younger than 12. They point out that free-time activities play an important role in childhood development and that homework in large quantities can severely restrict children's free time, hindering their development. But the actual average homework time for children under 12—little more than 30 minutes per night—leaves plenty of free time. In reality, therefore, the editorials' rationale cannot justify the restriction they advocate.

Which of the following, if true, would most seriously call into question the educational theorist's conclusion?

(A) Some teachers give as homework assignments work of a kind that research suggests is most effective educationally when done in class.

(B) For children younger than 12, regularly doing homework in the first years of school has no proven academic value, but many educators believe that it fosters self-discipline and time management.

(C) Some homework assignments are related to free-time activities that children engage in, such as reading or hobbies.

(D) A substantial proportion of schoolchildren under 12, particularly those in their first few years of school, have less than 10 minutes of homework assigned per night.

(E) Some free-time activities teach children skills or information that they later find useful in their schoolwork.

689. Thyrian lawmaker: Thyria's Cheese Importation Board inspects all cheese shipments to Thyria and rejects shipments not meeting specified standards. Yet only 1 percent is ever rejected. Therefore, since the health consequences and associated economic costs of not rejecting that 1 percent are negligible, whereas the board's operating costs are considerable, for economic reasons alone the board should be disbanded.

Consultant: I disagree. The threat of having their shipments rejected deters many cheese exporters from shipping substandard product.

The consultant responds to the lawmaker's argument by

(A) rejecting the lawmaker's argument while proposing that the standards according to which the board inspects imported cheese should be raised

(B) providing evidence that the lawmaker's argument has significantly overestimated the cost of maintaining the board

(C) objecting to the lawmaker's introducing into the discussion factors that are not strictly economic

(D) pointing out a benefit of maintaining the board which the lawmaker's argument has failed to consider

(E) shifting the discussion from the argument at hand to an attack on the integrity of the cheese inspectors

690. The tulu, a popular ornamental plant, does not reproduce naturally and is only bred and sold by specialized horticultural companies. Unfortunately, the tulu is easily devastated by a contagious fungal rot. The government ministry plans to reassure worried gardeners by requiring all tulu plants to be tested for fungal rot before being sold. However, infected plants less than 30 weeks old have generally not built up enough fungal rot in their systems to be detected reliably. And many tulu plants are sold before they are 24 weeks old.

Which of the following, if performed by the government ministry, could logically be expected to overcome the problem with their plan to test for the fungal rot?

(A) Releasing a general announcement that tulu plants less than 30 weeks old cannot be effectively tested for fungal rot

(B) Requiring all tulu plants less than 30 weeks old to be labeled as such

(C) Researching possible ways to test tulu plants less than 24 weeks old for fungal rot

(D) Ensuring that tulu plants are not sold before they are 30 weeks old

(E) Quarantining all tulu plants from horticultural companies at which any case of fungal rot has been detected until those tulu plants can be tested for fungal rot

691. Secret passwords are often used to control access to computers.

When employees select their own passwords, they frequently choose such easily guessed passwords as their initials or birth dates. To improve security, employers should assign randomly generated passwords to employees rather than allowing employees to make up their own.

Which of the following, if true, most seriously undermines the conclusion drawn above?

(A) If passwords are generated randomly, it is theoretically possible that employees will be assigned passwords that they might have selected on their own.

(B) Randomly generated passwords are so difficult for employees to recall that they often record the passwords in places where the passwords could be easily seen by others.

(C) Computer systems protected by passwords are designed to ignore commands that are entered by employees or others who use invalid passwords.

(D) In general, the higher the level of security maintained at the computer system, the more difficult it is for unauthorized users to obtain access to the system.

(E) Control of physical access to computers by the use of locked doors and guards should be used in addition to passwords in order to maintain security.

692. The economy around Lake Paqua depends on fishing of the lake's landlocked salmon population. In recent years, scarcity of food for salmon there has caused a decline in both the number and the size of the adult salmon in the lake. As a result, the region's revenues from salmon fishing have declined significantly. To remedy this situation, officials plan to introduce shrimp, which can serve as a food source for adult salmon, into Lake Paqua.

Which of the following, if true, most seriously calls into question the plan's chances for success?

(A) Salmon is not a popular food among residents of the Lake Paqua region.

(B) Tourists coming to fish for sport generate more income for residents of the Lake Paqua region than does commercial fishing.

(C)   The shrimp to be introduced into Lake Paqua are of a variety that is too small to be harvested for human consumption.

(D)   The primary food for both shrimp and juvenile salmon is plankton, which is not abundant in Lake Paqua.

(E)   Fishing regulations prohibit people from keeping any salmon they have caught in Lake Paqua that are smaller than a certain minimum size.

693.   Certainly, pesticides can adversely affect the environment in localities distant from where the pesticide has actually been used. Nevertheless, **regulation of pesticide use should not take place at the national level but at the local level.** It is in the areas where pesticides are actually applied that they have their most serious effects. Just how serious these effects are depends on local conditions such as climate, soil type, and water supply. And **local officials are much more likely than national legislators to be truly knowledgeable about such local conditions.**

In the argument given, the two **boldface** portions play which of the following roles?

(A)   The first provides support for the conclusion of the argument; the second states that conclusion.

(B)   The first states the conclusion of the argument; the second provides support for that conclusion.

(C)   The first identifies grounds for a potential objection to the conclusion of the argument; the second states that conclusion.

(D)   The first identifies grounds for a potential objection to the conclusion of the argument; the second provides support for that conclusion.

(E)   Each provides support for the conclusion of the argument.

694.   Which of the following most logically completes the passage?

Concerned about the well-being of its elderly citizens, the government of Runagia decided two years ago to increase by 20 percent the government-provided pension paid to all Runagians over 65. The annual rate of inflation since then has been below 5 percent, and the increase has been duly received by all eligible Runagians. Nevertheless, many of them are no better off than they were before the increase, in large part because _____.

(A)   they rely entirely on the government pension for their income

(B)   Runagian banks are so inefficient that it can take up to three weeks to cash a pension check

(C)   the prices of goods and services for special needs of elderly people have increased at a rate much higher than the rate of inflation

(D)   the pension was increased at the time when the number of elderly Runagians below the poverty level reached an all-time high

(E)   the increase was only the second such increase in the last ten years

695.   Museums that house Renaissance oil paintings typically store them in environments that are carefully kept within narrow margins of temperature and humidity to inhibit any deterioration. Recent laboratory tests have shown that **the oil paint used in these paintings actually adjusts to climatic changes quite well**. Assuming paint to be the most sensitive substance in these works, some museum directors now argue that museums can reduce energy costs without risking damage to these paintings by relaxing the standards for temperature and humidity control. Museums would be rash to relax those standards, however, since results of preliminary tests indicate that **gesso, a compound routinely used by Renaissance artists to help paint adhere to the canvas, is unable to withstand significant variations in humidity**.

In the argument above, the two portions in **boldface** play which of the following roles?

(A)   The first is evidence that has been used to support a position that the argument calls into question; the second is that position.

(B)   The first is evidence that has been used to support a position that the argument calls into question; the second is a claim, the accuracy of which is questioned in the argument.

(C)   The first is evidence that has been used to support a position that the argument calls into question; the second is a preliminary finding used by the argument to weaken the force of that evidence.

(D)   The first is the main conclusion of the argument; the second is a preliminary finding used by the argument to weaken the force of evidence that has been used to support a position that the argument calls into question.

(E) The first is an objection that has been raised against the position taken by the argument; the second is that position.

696. People get more than pleasure from seeing trees. Seeing trees can be good for people's physical health. That this is so is shown by a comparison of a large group of hospital patients who had a view of trees from their rooms and a similarly large group of hospital patients who did not. The patients with a view of trees returned to health faster.

Which of the following would it be most useful to establish in order to evaluate the argument above?

(A) Whether the trees that could be seen from the hospital rooms were, for the most part, equally healthy and well grown

(B) Whether the two groups of patients were well matched with respect to the nature and severity of the conditions for which they were hospitalized

(C) Whether the patients in both groups knew that their recovery times were being compared

(D) What proportion of all of the patients contracted an infection while in the hospital

(E) What proportion of all of the rooms in the hospitals from which the two groups were drawn had a view of trees

697. Because the cork stoppers in wine bottles can leak, crumble, or become moldy, winemakers must often discard a significant proportion of their inventory of bottled wine. **Bottlemasters, Inc., produces a plastic stopper that cannot leak, crumble, or mold.** Bottlemasters's plastic stopper is available to winemakers for a price only slightly higher than that of traditional cork stoppers, and **cork prices are expected to rise considerably in the near future.** Therefore, the Bottlemasters plastic stopper will most probably increase its share of the market for wine-bottle stoppers.

In the argument given, the two portions in **boldface** play which of the following roles?

(A) The first and the second each provide evidence to support the conclusion of the argument.

(B) The first provides evidence to support the main conclusion of the argument; the second is that main conclusion.

(C) The first provides evidence to support the main conclusion of the argument; the second is an objection that has been raised against that main conclusion.

(D) The first and the second are each claims that have been advanced in support of a position that the argument opposes.

(E) The first is evidence that has been used to support a position that the argument opposes; the second is a claim advanced in support of the main conclusion of the argument.

698. Which of the following most logically completes the argument?

A significant number of Qualitex Corporation's department heads are due to retire this year. The number of employees other than current department heads who could take on the position of department head is equal to only about half of the expected vacancies. Qualitex is not going to hire department heads from outside the company or have current department heads take over more than one department, so some departments will be without department heads next year unless Qualitex _____.

(A) promotes some current department heads to higher-level managerial positions

(B) raises the salary for department heads

(C) reduces the number of new employees it hires next year

(D) reduces the average number of employees per department

(E) reduces the number of its departments

699. It is crucially important to farmers that the herbicides they use to control weeds not damage their crops. One very effective herbicide is safe for corn, but soybeans are damaged even by the herbicide's residue, which remains in the soil more than a year after the herbicide is applied. Soybeans and corn are not sown together in the same field; nevertheless, most farmers are reluctant to use the herbicide on their corn.

Which of the following, if true, provides the strongest justification for the farmers' reluctance?

(A) The residue of the herbicide in the soil a year after application is not enough to control most weeds effectively.

(B) To maintain the nutrients in the soil, corn and soybeans are often planted in a field in alternate years.

(C) The demand for soybeans is growing faster than is the demand for corn.

(D) For maximum yield, soybean plants are grown closer together than are corn plants.

(E) The application of herbicides is less critical for soybeans than for corn crops.

700. Last August most gasoline stations in the XT chain of gasoline stations participated in a temporary sales promotion that XT sponsored. In the promotion, any customers who purchased ten or more gallons of gasoline were entitled to a free car wash. For the month of August, the XT chain's gasoline sales were five percent higher than in August the previous year. Evidently the promotion was successful as a means of boosting sales.

Which of the following, if true, most strengthens the argument?

(A) During last August, some of XT's competitors also had sales promotions in effect and also experienced sales increases as compared to the previous August.

(B) The money that XT earned from the increase in gasoline sales was not enough to offset the cost of providing free car washes during the promotion.

(C) Some customers who took advantage of the promotion would have made smaller but more frequent gasoline purchases at XT gasoline stations if the promotion had not been in effect.

(D) XT gasoline stations that participated in the promotion but did not have car wash facilities on their premises gave vouchers that could be used at a nearby car wash.

(E) Last August the XT gasoline stations that did not participate in the promotion had no increase in gasoline sales as compared to their sales the previous August.

701. Airlines are considering applying a new plastic film to airplanes instead of paint. It is clear that airlines should adopt this new technology right away, since **it would reduce the time that an airplane is out of service for maintenance.** When an airplane is taken out of service for maintenance, it is often repainted. During repainting, no other maintenance work can be done on the plane, but other maintenance tasks can be done while the nontoxic plastic film is being applied. In addition, **switching to the film would not increase maintenance costs in labor and materials**, since the film is as quick to apply as paint without being more expensive.

In the argument given, the two portions in **boldface** play which of the following roles?

(A) The first is the main position that the argument seeks to establish; the second is a consideration put forward in support of that position.

(B) The first and the second are each considerations that are put forward in support of the position that the argument seeks to establish.

(C) The first is a consideration that is put forward in support of the position that the argument seeks to establish; the second is an assumption for which no justification is offered.

(D) The first is presented as an advantage of following the recommendation made by the argument; the second is presented as a drawback to following that recommendation.

(E) The first and the second are each presented as a drawback to following the recommendation made by the argument.

702. Early in the twentieth century, Lake Konfa became very polluted. Recently fish populations have recovered as release of industrial pollutants has declined and the lake's waters have become cleaner. Fears are now being voiced that the planned construction of an oil pipeline across the lake's bottom might revive pollution and cause the fish population to decline again. However, a technology for preventing leaks is being installed. Therefore, provided this technology is effective, those fears are groundless.

The argument depends on assuming which of the following?

(A) Apart from development related to the pipeline, there will be no new industrial development around the lake that will create renewed pollution in its waters.

(B) Other than the possibility of a leak, there is no realistic pollution threat posed to the lake by the pipeline's construction.

(C) There is no reason to believe that the leak-preventing technology would be ineffective when installed in the pipeline in Lake Konfa.

(D) Damage to the lake's fish populations would be the only harm that a leak of oil from the pipeline would cause.

(E) The species of fish that are present in Lake Konfa now are the same as those that were in the lake before it was affected by pollution.

703. As a large corporation in a small country, Hachnut values having managers with international experience, so each year it sponsors management education abroad for a few management trainees. Although many who receive the sponsorship leave Hachnut soon after completing the sponsorship, Hachnut executives plan to continue the sponsorship program despite this problem.

Which of the following, if true, provides the strongest reason for Hachnut to continue the sponsorship program despite the problem cited above?

(A) Since Hachnut is heavily involved in foreign markets and has large operations abroad, its managers can gain international experience without taking advantage of the sponsorship program.

(B) The Hachnut managers who are citizens of countries other than Hachnut's home country are, for the most part, people who were recruited by Hachnut after working for other firms.

(C) The managers who leave Hachnut soon after receiving the sponsorship generally achieve about the same level of success in their careers as do the sponsored managers who do not leave Hachnut.

(D) Hachnut relies on performance during the education abroad to select candidates for promotion to higher management positions.

(E) The managers who leave Hachnut soon after receiving the sponsorship generally accept jobs in the country where they receive management education.

704. The country of Rowolia has, until now, been narrowly self-sufficient in both grain and meat. However, with growing prosperity in Rowolia has come a steadily increasing per capita consumption of meat, and it takes several pounds of grain to produce one pound of meat. Therefore, since Rowolian per capita income is almost certain to rise further and increases in domestic grain production are highly unlikely, Rowolia will soon need to import grain.

Which of the following is an assumption on which the argument depends?

(A) When people's consumption of meat increases, their consumption of grains and other foodstuffs tends to fall.

(B) Future demands for meat by Rowolians over and above current consumption levels will not be satisfied by the importation of meat from other countries.

(C) There are currently no laws in Rowolia prohibiting the importation of meat from abroad, nor will such laws be enacted in the near future.

(D) The per capita consumption of meat in Rowolia is roughly the same across all income levels.

(E) In Rowolia, meat is subject to strict government price controls but grain is not.

705. Which of the following most logically completes the argument below?

Papoose River farmers are deciding whether to plant winter wheat or spring wheat. The two types of wheat are usually about equally profitable and cannot both be grown in the same year. This year much lower yields per acre are expected for winter wheat because of new government restrictions on the use of Papoose River water for irrigation. Therefore, planting spring wheat will be more profitable than planting winter wheat, since _____.

(A) in the Papoose River region, spring wheat is not dependent on irrigation

(B) new crops of spring wheat must be planted before standing crops of winter wheat are ready to be harvested

(C) the spring wheat that farmers in the Papoose River region plant is well adapted to the soil of the region

(D) spring wheat has uses that are different from those of winter wheat

(E) planting spring wheat is more profitable than planting certain other crops, such as corn

706. Plant scientists have been able to genetically engineer seeds to produce crops that are highly resistant to insect damage. Farmers planting such seeds can use much less pesticide. Although these seeds currently cost significantly more than nonengineered seeds, their cost is likely to decline. Since these seeds produce crop yields as high as those produced by nonengineered seeds, the use of genetically engineered seeds is likely to become increasingly common.

Which of the following, if true, most strengthens the argument?

(A) Plant scientists have not yet developed insect-resistant seeds for all commercially grown food crops.

(B) Consumers prefer to buy grains, fruits, and vegetables that have been grown using little or no pesticide.

(C) Traditional methods of plant breeding have also resulted in some insect-resistant strains of plants.

(D) Crops grown from seeds that are genetically engineered to produce insect resistance will still be vulnerable to other types of pests.

(E) The cost of many commonly used agricultural pesticides is likely to decline as the use of genetically engineered seeds increases.

707. Over the past five years, the price gap between name-brand cereals and less expensive store-brand cereals has become so wide that consumers have been switching increasingly to store brands despite the name brands' reputation for better quality. To attract these consumers back, several manufacturers of name-brand cereals plan to narrow the price gap between their cereals and store brands to less than what it was five years ago.

Which of the following, if true, most seriously calls into question the likelihood that the manufacturers' plan will succeed in attracting back a large percentage of consumers who have switched to store brands?

(A) There is no significant difference among manufacturers of name-brand cereals in the prices they charge for their products.

(B) Consumers who have switched to store-brand cereals have generally been satisfied with the quality of those cereals.

(C) Many consumers would never think of switching to store-brand cereals because they believe the name-brand cereals to be of better quality.

(D) Because of lower advertising costs, stores are able to offer their own brands of cereals at significantly lower prices than those charged for name-brand cereals.

(E) Total annual sales of cereals—including both name-brand and store-brand cereals—have not increased significantly over the past five years.

Questions 708–777 — Difficulty: **Medium**

708. Although the school would receive financial benefits if it had soft drink vending machines in the cafeteria, we should not allow them. Allowing soft drink machines there would not be in our students' interest. If our students start drinking more soft drinks, they will be less healthy.

The argument depends on which of the following?

(A) If the soft drink vending machines were placed in the cafeteria, students would consume more soft drinks as a result.

(B) The amount of soft drinks that most students at the school currently drink is not detrimental to their health.

(C) Students are apt to be healthier if they do not drink soft drinks at all than if they just drink small amounts occasionally.

(D) Students will not simply bring soft drinks from home if the soft drink vending machines are not placed in the cafeteria.

(E) The school's primary concern should be to promote good health among its students.

709. Historian: Fifteenth-century advances in mapmaking contributed to the rise of modern nation-states. In medieval Europe (from the fifth to the fifteenth century), sovereignty centered in cities and towns and radiated outward, with boundaries often ambiguously defined. The conceptual shift toward the modern state began in the late fifteenth century, when mapmakers learned to reflect geography accurately by basing maps on latitude-longitude grids. By the mid-seventeenth century, nearly all maps showed boundary lines.

Which of the following would, if true, most strengthen the historian's reasoning?

(A) Borders did not become codified in Europe until certain treaties were signed in the early nineteenth century.

(B) During the medieval period, various authorities in Europe claimed power over collections of cities and towns, not contiguous territories.

(C) Many members of the political elite collected maps as a hobby during the late sixteenth and early seventeenth centuries.

(D) Seventeenth-century treatises and other sources of political authority describe areas of sovereignty rather than illustrate them using maps.

(E) During the fifteenth century in Europe, mapmakers simplified the borders of sovereignty by drawing clear lines of demarcation between political powers.

710. Sascha: The attempt to ban parliament's right to pass directed-spending bills—bills that contain provisions specifically funding the favorite projects of some powerful politicians—is antidemocratic. Our nation's constitution requires that money be drawn from our treasury only when so stipulated by laws passed by parliament, the branch of government most directly representative of the citizens. This requirement is based on the belief that exercising the power to spend public resources involves the ultimate exercise of state authority and that therefore _____.

Which of the following most logically completes Sascha's argument?

(A) designating funding specifically for the favorite projects of some powerful politicians should be considered antidemocratic

(B) the right to exercise such a power should belong exclusively to the branch of government most directly representative of the citizens

(C) exercising the power to spend public resources is in most cases—but not all—protected by the constitution

(D) modifications to any spending bills should be considered expenditures authorized by law

(E) only officials who are motivated by concerns for reelection should retain that power

711. Boreal owls range over a much larger area than do other owls of similar size. Scientists have hypothesized that **it is scarcity of prey that leads the owls to range so widely.** This hypothesis would be hard to confirm directly, since it is not possible to produce a sufficiently accurate count of the populations of small mammals inhabiting the forests where boreal owls live. Careful study of owl behavior has, however, shown that **boreal owls do range over larger areas when they live in regions where food of the sort eaten by small mammals is comparatively sparse.** This indicates that the scientists' hypothesis is not sheer speculation.

In the argument given, the two **boldfaced** portions play which of the following roles?

(A) The first presents an explanatory hypothesis; the second states the main conclusion of the argument.

(B) The first presents an explanatory hypothesis; the second presents evidence tending to support this hypothesis.

(C) The first presents an explanatory hypothesis; the second presents evidence to support an alternative explanation.

(D) The first describes a position that the argument opposes; the second presents evidence to undermine the support for the position being opposed.

(E) The first describes a position that the argument opposes; the second states the main conclusion of the argument.

712. Cognitive scientist: Using the pioneering work of comparative psychologist Gordon Gallup as a model, several studies have investigated animals' capacity for mirror self-recognition (MSR). Most animals exposed to a mirror respond only with social behavior, such as aggression. However, in the case of the great apes, repeated exposure to mirrors leads to self-directed behaviors, such as exploring the inside of the mouth, suggesting that these animals recognize the reflection as an image of self. The implication of these studies is that the great apes have a capacity for self-awareness unique among nonhuman species.

The cognitive scientist makes which of the following assumptions in the argument above?

(A) Gallup's work has established that the great apes have a capacity for MSR unique among nonhuman species.

(B) If an animal does not have the capacity for MSR, it does not have the capacity for self-awareness.

(C) If a researcher exposes an animal to a mirror and that animal exhibits social behavior, that animal is incapable of being self-aware.

(D) When exposed to a mirror, all animals display either social behavior or self-directed behavior.

(E) Animals that do not exhibit MSR may demonstrate a capacity for self-awareness in other ways.

713. A study of ticket sales at a summer theater festival found that people who bought tickets to individual plays had a no-show rate of less than 1 percent, while those who paid in advance for all ten plays being performed that summer had a no-show rate of nearly 30 percent. This may be at least in part because the greater the awareness customers retain about the cost of an item, the more likely they are to use it.

Which of the following would, if true, best serve as an alternative explanation of the results of the study?

(A) The price per ticket was slightly cheaper for those who bought all ten tickets in advance.

(B) Many people who attended the theater festival believed strongly that they should support it financially.

(C) Those who attended all ten plays became eligible for a partial refund.

(D) Usually, people who bought tickets to individual plays did so immediately prior to each performance that they attended.

(E) People who arrived just before the performance began could not be assured of obtaining seats in a preferred location.

714. Although there is no record of poet Edmund Spenser's parentage, we do know that as a youth, Spenser attended the Merchant Tailors' School in London for a period between 1560 and 1570. Records from this time indicate that the Merchant Tailors' Guild then had only three members named Spenser: Robert Spenser, listed as a gentleman; Nicholas Spenser, elected the Guild's Warden in 1568; and John Spenser, listed as a "journeyman cloth-maker." Of these, the last was likely the least affluent of the three—and most likely Edmund's father, since school accounting records list Edmund as a scholar who attended the school at a reduced fee.

Which of the following is an assumption on which the argument depends?

(A) Anybody in sixteenth-century London who made clothing professionally would have had to be a member of the Merchant Tailors' Guild.

(B) The fact that Edmund Spenser attended the Merchant Tailors' School did not necessarily mean that he planned to become a tailor.

(C) No member of the Guild could become Guild warden in sixteenth-century London unless he was a gentleman.

(D) Most of those whose fathers were members of the Merchant Tailors' Guild were students at the Merchant Tailors' School.

(E) The Merchant Tailors' School did not reduce its fees for the children of the more affluent Guild members.

715. Hea Sook: One should not readily believe urban legends. Most legends are propagated because the moral lesson underlying them supports a political agenda. People will repeat a tale if it fits their purpose. They may not deliberately spread untruths, but neither are they particularly motivated to investigate deeply to determine if the tale they are telling is true.

Kayla: But people would not repeat stories that they did not believe were true. Therefore, one can safely assume that if a story has been repeated by enough people, then it is more likely to be true.

Kayla's reply is most vulnerable to the criticism that it

(A) does not specify how many people need to repeat a story before someone is justified in believing it

(B) overstates the significance of political agendas in the retelling of stories

(C) fails to address the claim that people will not verify the truth of a story that fits their purpose

(D) implicitly supports the claim that the people repeating legends are not deliberately spreading untruths

(E) cannot distinguish people's motivations for repeating urban legends from their motivations for repeating other types of story

716. Rainwater contains hydrogen of a heavy form called deuterium. The deuterium content of wood reflects the deuterium content of rainwater available to trees during their growth. Wood from trees that grew between 16,000 and 24,000 years ago in North America contains significantly more deuterium than wood from trees growing today. But water trapped in several North American caves that formed during that same early period contains significantly less deuterium than rainwater in North America contains today.

Which of the following, if true, most helps to reconcile the two findings?

(A) There is little deuterium in the North American caves other than the deuterium in the water trapped there.

(B) Exposure to water after a tree has died does not change the deuterium content of the wood.

(C) Industrialization in North America over the past 100 years has altered the deuterium content of rain.

(D) Trees draw on shallow groundwater from rain that falls during their growth, whereas water trapped in caves may have fallen as rainwater thousands of years before the caves formed.

(E) Wood with a high deuterium content is no more likely to remain preserved for long periods than is wood with a low deuterium content.

717. Enforcement of local speed limits through police monitoring has proven unsuccessful in the town of Ardane. In many nearby towns, speed humps (raised areas of pavement placed across residential streets, about 300 feet apart) have reduced traffic speeds on residential streets by 20 to 25 percent. In order to reduce traffic speed and thereby enhance safety in residential neighborhoods, Ardane's transportation commission plans to install multiple speed humps in those neighborhoods.

Which of the following, if true, identifies a potentially serious drawback to the plan for installing speed humps in Ardane?

(A) On residential streets without speed humps, many vehicles travel at speeds more than 25 percent above the posted speed limit.

(B) Because of their high weight, emergency vehicles such as fire trucks and ambulances must slow almost to a stop at speed humps.

(C) The residential speed limit in Ardane is higher than that of the nearby towns where speed humps were installed.

(D) Motorists who are not familiar with the streets in Ardane's residential districts would be likely to encounter the speed humps unawares unless warned by signs and painted indicators.

(E) Bicyclists generally prefer that speed humps be constructed so as to leave a space on the side of the road where bicycles can travel without going over the humps.

718. Which of the choices most logically completes the following argument?

NowNews, although still the most popular magazine covering cultural events in Kalopolis, has recently suffered a significant drop in advertising revenue because of falling circulation. Many readers have begun buying a competing magazine that, at 50 cents per copy, costs less than *NowNews* at $1.50 per copy. In order to boost circulation and thus increase advertising revenue, *NowNews*'s publisher has proposed making it available at no charge. However, this proposal has a serious drawback, since

_____.

(A) those Kalopolis residents with the greatest interest in cultural events are regular readers of both magazines

(B)   one reason *NowNews's* circulation fell was that its competitor's reporting on cultural events was superior

(C)   the newsstands and stores that currently sell *NowNews* will no longer carry it if it is being given away for free

(D)   at present, 10 percent of the total number of copies of each issue of *NowNews* are distributed free to students on college campuses in the Kalopolis area

(E)   *NowNews's* competitor would begin to lose large amounts of money if it were forced to lower its cover price

719. Over the last five years, demand for hotel rooms in Cenopolis has increased significantly, as has the average price Cenopolis hotels charge for rooms. These trends are projected to continue for the next several years. In response to this economic forecast, Centennial Commercial, a real estate developer, is considering a plan to convert several unoccupied office buildings it owns in Cenopolis into hotels in order to maximize its revenues from these properties.

Which of the following would it be most useful for Centennial Commercial to know in evaluating the plan it is considering?

(A)   Whether the population of Cenopolis is expected to grow in the next several years

(B)   Whether demand for office space in Cenopolis is projected to increase in the near future

(C)   Whether the increased demand for hotel rooms, if met, is likely to lead to an increase in the demand for other travel-related services

(D)   Whether demand for hotel rooms has also increased in other cities where Centennial Commercial owns office buildings

(E)   Whether, on average, hotels that have been created by converting office buildings have fewer guest rooms than do hotels that were built as hotels

720. Economist: The most economically efficient way to reduce emissions of air pollutants is to tax them in proportion to the damage they are likely to cause. But in Country Y, many serious pollutants are untaxed and unregulated, and policy makers strongly oppose new taxes. Therefore, the best way to achieve a reduction in air pollutant emissions in Country Y would be to institute fixed upper limits on them.

Which of the following is an assumption of the economist's argument?

(A)   Policy makers in Country Y oppose all new taxes equally strongly, regardless of any benefits they may provide.

(B)   Country Y's air pollutant emissions would not fall significantly if they were taxed in proportion to the damage they are likely to cause.

(C)   Policy makers in Country Y strongly favor reductions in air pollutant emissions.

(D)   Country Y's policy makers believe that air pollutant emissions should be reduced with maximum economic efficiency.

(E)   Policy makers in Country Y do not oppose setting fixed upper limits on air pollutant emissions as strongly as they oppose new taxes.

721. A study of high blood pressure treatments found certain meditation techniques and the most commonly prescribed drugs are equally effective if the selected treatment is followed as directed over the long term. Half the patients given drugs soon stop taking them regularly, whereas 80 percent of the study's participants who were taught meditation techniques were still regularly using them five years later. Therefore, the meditation treatment is the one likely to produce the best results.

Which of the following, if true, most seriously weakens the argument?

(A)   People who have high blood pressure are usually advised by their physicians to make changes in diet that have been found in many cases to reduce the severity of the condition.

(B)   The participants in the study were selected in part on the basis of their willingness to use meditation techniques.

(C)   Meditation techniques can reduce the blood pressure of people who do not suffer from high blood pressure.

(D)   Some of the participants in the study whose high blood pressure was controlled through meditation techniques were physicians.

(E)   Many people with dangerously high blood pressure are unaware of their condition.

722. Many industrialized nations are trying to reduce atmospheric concentrations of carbon dioxide, a gas released by the burning of fossil fuels. One proposal is to replace conventional cement, which is made with calcium carbonate, by a new "eco-cement." This new cement, made with magnesium carbonate, absorbs large amounts of carbon dioxide when exposed to the atmosphere. Therefore, using eco-cement for new concrete building projects will significantly help reduce atmospheric concentrations of carbon dioxide.

Which of the following, if true, most strengthens the argument?

(A) The cost of magnesium carbonate, currently greater than the cost of calcium carbonate, probably will fall as more magnesium carbonate is used in cement manufacture.

(B) Eco-cement is strengthened when absorbed carbon dioxide reacts with the cement.

(C) Before the development of eco-cement, magnesium-based cement was considered too susceptible to water erosion to be of practical use.

(D) The manufacture of eco-cement uses considerably less fossil fuel per unit of cement than the manufacture of conventional cement does.

(E) Most building-industry groups are unaware of the development or availability of eco-cement.

723. Advertisement: When your car's engine is running at its normal operating temperature, any major brand of motor oil will protect it about as well as Tuff does. When the engine is cold, it is a different story: Tuff motor oil flows better at lower temperatures than its major competitors do. So, if you want your car's engine to have maximum protection, you should use Tuff.

Which of the following, if true, most strengthens the argument in the advertisement?

(A) Tuff motor oil provides above-average protection for engines that happen to overheat.

(B) Tuff motor oil is periodically supplied free of charge to automobile manufacturers to use in factory-new cars.

(C) Tuff motor oil's share of the engine oil market peaked three years ago.

(D) Tuff motor oil, like any motor oil, is thicker and flows less freely at cold temperatures than at hot temperatures.

(E) Tuff motor oil is manufactured at only one refinery and shipped from there to all markets.

724. Linguist: In English, the past is described as "behind" and the future "ahead," whereas in Aymara, the past is "ahead" and the future "behind." Research indicates that English speakers sway backward when discussing the past and forward when discussing the future. Conversely, Aymara speakers gesture forward with their hands when discussing the past and backward when discussing the future. These bodily movements, therefore, suggest that the language one speaks affects how one mentally visualizes time.

The linguist's reasoning depends on assuming which of the following?

(A) At least some Aymara speakers sway forward when discussing the past and backward when discussing the future.

(B) Most people mentally visualize time as running either forward or backward.

(C) Not all English and Aymara speakers tend to sway or gesture forward or backward when discussing the present.

(D) How people move when discussing the future correlates to some extent with how they mentally visualize time.

(E) The researchers also examined the movements of at least some speakers of languages other than English and Aymara discussing the past and the future.

725. *The Testament of William Thorpe* was published around 1530 as an appendix to Thorpe's longer *Examination*. Many scholars, however, doubt the attribution of the *Testament* to Thorpe because, whereas the *Examination* is dated 1406, the *Testament* is dated 1460. One scholar has recently argued that the 1460 date be amended to 1409, based on the observation that when these numbers are expressed as Roman numerals, MCCCCLX and MCCCCIX, it becomes easy to see how the dates might have become confused through scribal error.

Which of the following, if true, would most support the scholar's hypothesis concerning the date of the *Testament*?

(A) The sole evidence that historians have had that William Thorpe died no earlier than 1460 was the presumed date of publication of the *Testament*.

(B) In the preface to the 1530 publication, the editor attributes both works to William Thorpe.

(C) Few writers in fifteenth-century England marked dates in their works using only Roman numerals.

(D) The *Testament* alludes to a date, "Friday, September 20," as apparently contemporaneous with the writing of the *Testament*, and September 20 fell on a Friday in 1409 but not in 1460.

(E) The *Testament* contains few references to historical events that occurred later than 1406.

726. A prominent investor who holds a large stake in the Burton Tool Company has recently claimed that the company is mismanaged, citing as evidence the company's failure to slow down production in response to a recent rise in its inventory of finished products. It is doubtful whether an investor's sniping at management can ever be anything other than counterproductive, but in this case, it is clearly not justified. It is true that **an increased inventory of finished products often indicates that production is outstripping demand**, but in Burton's case it indicates no such thing. Rather, **the increase in inventory is entirely attributable to products that have already been assigned to orders received from customers.**

In the argument given, the two **boldfaced** portions play which of the following roles?

(A) The first states a generalization that underlies the position that the argument as a whole opposes; the second provides evidence to show that the generalization does not apply in the case at issue.

(B) The first states a generalization that underlies the position that the argument as a whole opposes; the second clarifies the meaning of a specific phrase as it is used in that generalization.

(C) The first provides evidence to support the conclusion of the argument as a whole; the second is evidence that has been used to support the position that the argument as a whole opposes.

(D) The first provides evidence to support the conclusion of the argument as a whole; the second states that conclusion.

(E) The first and the second each provide evidence against the position that the argument as a whole opposes.

727. Kate: The recent decline in numbers of the Tennessee warbler, a North American songbird that migrates each fall to coffee plantations in South America, is due to the elimination of the dense tree cover that formerly was a feature of most South American coffee plantations.

Scott: The population of the spruce budworm, the warbler's favorite prey in North America, has been dropping. This is a more likely explanation of the warbler's decline.

Which of the following, if true, most seriously calls Scott's hypothesis into question?

(A) The numbers of the Baltimore oriole, a songbird that does not eat budworms but is as dependent on South American coffee plantations as is the Tennessee warbler, are declining.

(B) The spruce budworm population has dropped because of a disease that can infect budworms but not Tennessee warblers.

(C) The drop in the population of the spruce budworm is expected to be only temporary.

(D) Many Tennessee warblers have begun migrating in the fall to places other than traditional coffee plantations.

(E) Although many North American songbirds have declined in numbers, no other species has experienced as great a decline as the Tennessee warbler.

728. Advertising by mail has become much less effective, with fewer consumers responding. Because consumers are increasingly overwhelmed by the sheer amount of junk mail they receive, most discard almost all offers without considering them. Thus, an effective way for corporations to improve response rates would be to more carefully target the individuals to whom they mail advertising, thereby cutting down on the amount of junk mail each consumer receives.

Which of the following, if true, would most support the recommendation above?

(A) There are cost-effective means by which corporations that currently advertise by mail could improve response rates.

(B) Many successful corporations are already carefully targeting the individuals to whom they mail advertising.

(C) Any consumer who, immediately after receiving an advertisement by mail, merely glances at it is very likely to discard it.

(D)   Improvements in the quality of the advertising materials used in mail that is carefully targeted to individuals can improve the response rate for such mail.

(E)   Response rates to carefully targeted advertisements by mail are considerably higher, on average, than response rates to most other forms of advertising.

729. A company has developed a new sensing device that, according to the company's claims, detects weak, ultralow-frequency electromagnetic signals associated with a beating heart. These signals, which pass through almost any physical obstruction, are purportedly detected by the device even at significant distances. Therefore, if the company's claims are true, their device will radically improve emergency teams' ability to locate quickly people who are trapped within the wreckage of collapsed buildings.

Which of the following, if true, most strengthens the argument?

(A)   People trapped within the wreckage of collapsed buildings usually have serious injuries that require prompt medical treatment.

(B)   The device gives a distinctive reading when the signals it detects come from human beings rather than from any other living beings.

(C)   Most people who have survived after being trapped in collapsed buildings were rescued within two hours of the building's collapse.

(D)   Ultralow-frequency signals are not the only electromagnetic signals that can pass through almost any physical obstruction.

(E)   Extensive training is required in order to operate the device effectively.

730. Economist: The price of tap water in our region should be raised drastically. **Supplies in local freshwater reservoirs have been declining for years** because water is being used faster than it can be replenished. Since the price of tap water has been low, **few users have bothered to adopt even easy conservation measures.**

The two sections in **boldface** play which of the following roles in the economist's argument?

(A)   The first is a conclusion for which support is provided, and which in turn supports the main conclusion; the second is the main conclusion.

(B)   The first is an observation for which the second provides an explanation; the second is the main conclusion but not the only conclusion.

(C)   The first is a premise supporting the argument's main conclusion; so is the second.

(D)   The first is the only conclusion; the second provides an explanation for the first.

(E)   The first is the main conclusion; the second is a conclusion for which support is provided, and which in turn supports the first.

731. Maize contains the vitamin niacin, but not in a form the body can absorb. Pellagra is a disease that results from niacin deficiency. When maize was introduced into southern Europe from the Americas in the eighteenth century, it quickly became a dietary staple, and many Europeans who came to subsist primarily on maize developed pellagra. Pellagra was virtually unknown at that time in the Americas, however, even among people who subsisted primarily on maize.

Which of the following, if true, most helps to explain the contrasting incidence of pellagra described above?

(A)   Once introduced into southern Europe, maize became popular with landowners because of its high yields relative to other cereal crops.

(B)   Maize grown in the Americas contained more niacin than maize grown in Europe did.

(C)   Traditional ways of preparing maize in the Americas convert maize's niacin into a nutritionally useful form.

(D)   In southern Europe, many of the people who consumed maize also ate niacin-rich foods.

(E)   Before the discovery of pellagra's link with niacin, it was widely believed the disease was an infection that could be transmitted from person to person.

732. Mayor: False alarms from home security systems waste so much valuable police time that in many communities, police have stopped responding to alarms from homes whose systems frequently produce false alarms. This policy reduces wastage of police time but results in a loss of protection for some residents. To achieve a comparable reduction in wastage without reducing protection for residents, the council has enacted a measure to fine residents for repeated false alarms.

Which of the following, if true, casts the most doubt on whether the measure enacted by the council will achieve its goal?

(A) A fine in the amount planned by the council will not cover the expenses police typically incur when they respond to a false alarm.

(B) Homes equipped with security systems are far less likely to be broken into than are homes without security systems.

(C) The threat of fines is likely to cause many residents to deactivate their security systems.

(D) The number of home security systems is likely to increase dramatically over the next five years.

(E) Many home security systems have never produced false alarms.

733. Excavation of the house of a third-century Camarnian official revealed that he had served four magistrates—public officials who administer the law—over his thirty-year public career, in four provincial capital cities. However, given the Camarnian administrative system of that era, it is unclear whether he served them simultaneously, as a traveling administrator living for part of the year in each provincial capital, or else did so sequentially, leaving one magistrate after several years to join another.

Which of the following would, if found in the excavation, most likely help reveal the pattern of the official's administrative service?

(A) Maps and documents describing each of the four provincial capitals

(B) A cache of the official's documents related to work from early in his career

(C) A set of cups of a type made only in the city of the first magistrate whom the official is known to have served

(D) Several pieces of furniture in the styles of two of the provincial capital cities

(E) Heavy clothing appropriate only for the coldest of the four cities

734. In 1563, in Florence's Palazzo Vecchio, Giorgio Vasari built in front of an existing wall a new wall on which he painted a mural. Investigators recently discovered a gap between Vasari's wall and the original, large enough to have preserved anything painted on the original. Historians believe that Leonardo da Vinci had painted, but left unfinished, a mural on the original wall; some historians had also believed that by 1563, the mural had been destroyed. However, it is known that in the late 1560s, when renovating another building, Santa Maria Novella, Vasari built a façade over its frescoes, and the frescoes were thereby preserved. Thus, Leonardo's Palazzo Vecchio mural probably still exists behind Vasari's wall.

Which of the following is an assumption on which the argument depends?

(A) Leonardo rarely if ever destroyed artworks that he left unfinished.

(B) Vasari was likely unaware that the mural in the Palazzo Vecchio had willingly been abandoned by Leonardo.

(C) Vasari probably would not have built the Palazzo Vecchio wall with a gap behind it except to preserve something behind the new wall.

(D) Leonardo would probably have completed the Palazzo Vecchio mural if he had had the opportunity to do so.

(E) When Vasari preserved the frescoes of Santa Maria Novella he did so secretly.

735. Coffee shop owner: A large number of customers will pay at least the fair market value for a cup of coffee, even if there is no formal charge. Some will pay more than this out of appreciation of the trust that is placed in them. And our total number of customers is likely to increase. We could therefore improve our net cash flow by implementing an honor system in which customers pay what they wish for coffee by depositing money in a can.

Manager: We're likely to lose money on this plan. Many customers would cheat the system, paying a very small sum or nothing at all.

Which of the following, if true, would best support the owner's plan, in light of the manager's concern?

(A) The new system, if implemented, would increase the number of customers.

(B) By roasting its own coffee, the shop has managed to reduce the difficulties (and cost) of maintaining an inventory of freshly roasted coffee.

(C)   Many customers stay in the cafe for long stretches of time.

(D)   The shop makes a substantial profit from pastries and other food bought by the coffee drinkers.

(E)   No other coffee shop in the area has such a system.

736. Certain groups of Asian snails include both "left-handed" and "right-handed" species, with shells coiling to the left and right, respectively. Some left-handed species have evolved from right-handed ones. Also, researchers found that snail-eating snakes in the same habitat have asymmetrical jaws, allowing them to grasp right-handed snail shells more easily. If these snakes ate more right-handed snails over time, this would have given left-handed snails an evolutionary advantage over right-handed snails, with the left-handed snails eventually becoming a new species. Thus, the snakes' asymmetrical jaws probably helped drive the emergence of the left-handed snail species.

Which of the following would, if true, most strengthen the argument that asymmetrical snake jaws helped drive left-handed snail evolution?

(A)   In one snake species, the snakes with asymmetrical jaws eat snails, while the snakes with symmetrical jaws do not eat snails.

(B)   Some species of Asian snails contain either all right-handed snails or all left-handed snails.

(C)   Anatomical differences prevent left-handed snails from mating easily with right-handed snails.

(D)   Some right-handed snails in this habitat have shells with a very narrow opening that helps prevent snakes from extracting the snails from inside their shells.

(E)   Experiments show that the snail-eating snakes in this habitat fail more often in trying to eat left-handed snails than in trying to eat right-handed snails.

737. A moderately large city is redesigning its central downtown area and is considering a plan that would reduce the number of lanes for automobiles and trucks and increase those for bicycles and pedestrians. The intent is to attract more workers and shoppers to downtown businesses by making downtown easier to reach and more pleasant to move around in.

Which of the following would, if true, most strongly support the prediction that the plan would achieve its goal?

(A)   People who make a habit of walking or bicycling whenever feasible derive significant health benefits from doing so.

(B)   Most people who prefer to shop at suburban malls instead of downtown urban areas do so because parking is easier and cheaper at the former.

(C)   In other moderately sized cities where measures were taken to make downtowns more accessible for walkers and cyclists, downtown businesses began to thrive.

(D)   If the proposed lane restrictions on drivers are rigorously enforced, more people will likely be attracted to downtown businesses than would otherwise be.

(E)   Most people who own and frequently ride bicycles for recreational purposes live at a significant distance from downtown urban areas.

738. Previously, Autoco designed all of its cars itself and then contracted with specialized parts suppliers to build parts according to its specifications. Now it plans to include its suppliers in designing the parts they are to build. Since many parts suppliers have more designers with specialized experience than Autoco has, Autoco expects this shift to reduce the overall time and cost of the design of its next new car.

Which of the following, if true, most strongly supports Autoco's expectation?

(A)   When suppliers provide their own designs, Autoco often needs to modify its overall design.

(B)   In order to provide designs for Autoco, several of the parts suppliers will have to add to their existing staffs of designers.

(C)   Parts and services provided by outside suppliers account for more than 50 percent of Autoco's total costs.

(D)   When suppliers built parts according to specifications provided by Autoco, the suppliers competed to win contracts.

(E)   Most of Autoco's suppliers have on hand a wide range of previously prepared parts designs that can readily be modified for a new car.

739. In response to viral infection, the immune systems of mice typically produce antibodies that destroy the virus by binding to proteins on its surface. Mice infected with the herpesvirus generally develop keratitis, a degenerative disease affecting part of the eye. Since proteins on the surface of cells in this part of the eye closely resemble those on the herpesvirus surface, scientists hypothesize that these cases of keratitis are caused by antibodies to the herpesvirus.

Which of the following, if true, most helps to support the scientists' reasoning?

(A) Other types of viruses have surface proteins that closely resemble proteins found in various organs of mice.

(B) Mice that are infected with the herpesvirus but do not develop keratitis produce as many antibodies as infected mice that do develop keratitis.

(C) Mice infected with a new strain of the herpesvirus that has different surface proteins did not develop keratitis.

(D) Mice that have never been infected with the herpesvirus can sometimes develop keratitis.

(E) There are mice that are unable to form antibodies in response to herpes infections, and these mice contract herpes at roughly the same rate as other mice.

740. One might expect that within a particular species, any individuals that managed to slow down the aging process would leave more offspring. Natural selection should therefore favor extreme longevity—but this does not seem to be the case. A possible explanation is that aging is a product of the inevitable wear and tear of living, similar to how household appliances generally accumulate faults that lead to their eventual demise. However, most researchers do not find this analogy satisfactory as an explanation.

Which of the following would, if true, provide the strongest explanation for the researchers' reaction?

(A) Some organisms are capable of living much longer than other organisms.

(B) Some organisms reproduce very quickly despite having short lifespans.

(C) There are several ways of defining "extreme longevity," and according to some definitions it occurs frequently.

(D) Organisms are capable of maintenance and self-repair and can remedy much of the damage that they accumulate.

(E) Some organisms generate much more wear and tear on their bodies than others.

741. In Stenland, many workers have been complaining that they cannot survive on minimum wage, the lowest wage an employer is permitted to pay. The government is proposing to raise the minimum wage. Many employers who pay their workers the current minimum wage argue that if it is raised, unemployment will increase because they will no longer be able to afford to employ as many workers.

Which of the following, if true in Stenland, most strongly supports the claim that raising the minimum wage there will not have the effects that the employers predict?

(A) For any position with wages below a living wage, the difficulty of finding and retaining employees adds as much to employment costs as would raising wages.

(B) Raising the minimum wage does not also increase the amount employers have to contribute in employee benefits.

(C) When inflation is taken into account, the proposed new minimum wage is not as high as the current one was when it was introduced.

(D) Many employees currently being paid wages at the level of the proposed new minimum wage will demand significant wage increases.

(E) Many employers who pay some workers only the minimum wage also pay other workers wages that are much higher than the minimum.

742. Biologists with a predilection for theory have tried—and largely failed—to define what it is that makes something a living thing. Organisms take in energy-providing materials and excrete waste products, but so do automobiles. Living things replicate and take part in evolution, but so do some computer programs. We must be open to the possibility that there are living things on other planets. Therefore, we will not be successful in defining what it is that makes something a living thing merely by examining living things on Earth—the only ones we know. Trying to do so is analogous to trying to specify _____.

Which of the following most logically completes the passage?

(A) the laws of physics by using pure mathematics

(B) what a fish is by listing its chemical components

(C) what an animal is by examining a plant

(D) what a machine is by examining a sketch of it

(E) what a mammal is by examining a zebra

743. For the period from the eighth century through the eleventh century, the shifting boundaries between Kingdom F and Kingdom G have not been well charted. Although a certain village in a border region between the two kingdoms usually belonged to Kingdom G, ninth-century artifacts found in the village were in the typical Kingdom F style of that time. It is unclear whether the village was actually a part of Kingdom F in the ninth century or whether it was a part of Kingdom G but had merely adopted Kingdom F's artistic styles under Kingdom F's cultural influence.

Which of the following would, if found in ninth-century sites in the village, best help in determining whether the village was a part of Kingdom F or Kingdom G in the ninth century?

(A) A trading contract written in the Kingdom G dialect

(B) A drawing of a dwelling complex known to have existed on the border of Kingdom F and Kingdom G in the ninth century

(C) Knives and other utensils made from metal typical of ninth-century mining sites in Kingdom F

(D) Some fragments of pottery made in the Kingdom G style from the seventh century out of materials only found in Kingdom F

(E) Numerous teeth from the ninth century with a chemical signature typical only of teeth from people who had grown up in the heart of Kingdom F

744. Sammy: For my arthritis, I am going to try my aunt's diet: large amounts of wheat germ and garlic. She was able to move more easily right after she started that diet.

Pat: When my brother began that diet, his arthritis got worse. But he has been doing much better since he stopped eating vegetables in the nightshade family, such as tomatoes and peppers.

Which of the following, if true, would provide a basis for explaining the fact that Sammy's aunt and Pat's brother had contrasting experiences with the same diet?

(A) A change in diet, regardless of the nature of the change, frequently brings temporary relief from arthritis symptoms.

(B) The compounds in garlic that can lessen the symptoms of arthritis are also present in tomatoes and peppers.

(C) Arthritis is a chronic condition whose symptoms improve and worsen from time to time without regard to diet.

(D) In general, men are more likely to have their arthritis symptoms alleviated by avoiding vegetables in the nightshade family than are women.

(E) People who are closely related are more likely to experience the same result from adopting a particular diet than are people who are unrelated.

745. In the 1960s, surveys of Florida's alligator population indicated that the population was dwindling rapidly. Hunting alligators was banned. By the early 1990s, the alligator population had recovered, and restricted hunting was allowed. Over the course of the 1990s, reports of alligators appearing on golf courses and lawns increased dramatically. Therefore, in spite of whatever alligator hunting went on, the alligator population must have increased significantly over the decade of the 1990s.

Which of the following, if true, most seriously weakens the argument?

(A) The human population of Florida increased significantly during the 1990s.

(B) The hunting restrictions applied to commercial as well as private hunters.

(C) The number of sightings of alligators in lakes and swamps increased greatly in Florida during the 1990s.

(D) Throughout the 1990s, selling alligator products was more strictly regulated than hunting was.

(E) Most of the sightings of alligators on golf courses and lawns in the 1990s occurred at times at which few people were present on those golf courses and lawns.

746. Infotek, a computer manufacturer in Katrovia, has just introduced a new personal computer model that sells for significantly less than any other model. Market research shows, however, that very few Katrovian households without personal computers would buy a computer, regardless of its price. Therefore, introducing the new model is unlikely to increase the number of computers in Katrovian homes.

Which of the following is an assumption on which the argument depends?

(A) Infotek achieved the lower price of the new model by using components of lower quality than those used by other manufacturers.

(B) The main reason cited by consumers in Katrovia for replacing a personal computer is the desire to have an improved model.

(C) Katrovians in households that already have computers are unlikely to purchase the new Infotek model as an additional computer for home use.

(D) The price of other personal computers in Katrovia is unlikely to drop below the price of Infotek's new model in the near future.

(E) Most personal computers purchased in Katrovia are intended for home use.

747. Fast-food restaurants make up 45 percent of all restaurants in Canatria. Customers at these restaurants tend to be young; in fact, studies have shown that the older people get, the less likely they are to eat in fast-food restaurants. Since the average age of the Canatrian population is gradually rising and will continue to do so, the number of fast-food restaurants is likely to decrease.

Which of the following, if true, most seriously weakens the argument?

(A) Fast-food restaurants in Canatria are getting bigger, so each one can serve more customers.

(B) Some older people eat at fast-food restaurants more frequently than the average young person.

(C) Many people who rarely eat in fast-food restaurants nevertheless eat regularly in restaurants.

(D) The overall population of Canatria is growing steadily.

(E) As the population of Canatria gets older, more people are eating at home.

748. Transportation expenses accounted for a large portion of the total dollar amount spent on trips for pleasure by residents of the United States in 1997, and about half of the total dollar amount spent on transportation was for airfare. However, the large majority of United States residents who took trips for pleasure in 1997 did not travel by airplane but used other means of transportation.

If the statements above are true, which of the following must also be true about United States residents who took trips for pleasure in 1997?

(A) Most of those who traveled by airplane did so because the airfare to their destination was lower than the cost of other available means of transportation.

(B) Most of those who traveled by airplane did so because other means of transportation to their destination were unavailable.

(C) Per mile traveled, those who traveled by airplane tended to spend more on transportation to their destination than did those who used other means of transportation.

(D) Overall, people who did not travel by airplane had lower average transportation expenses than people who did.

(E) Those who traveled by airplane spent about as much, on average, on other means of transportation as they did on airfare.

749. Voters commonly condemn politicians for being insincere, but politicians often must disguise their true feelings when they make public statements. If they expressed their honest views—about, say, their party's policies—then achieving politically necessary compromises would be much more difficult. Clearly, the very insincerity that people decry shows that our government is functioning well.

Which of the following, if true, most seriously undermines this reasoning?

(A) Achieving political compromises is not all that is necessary for the proper functioning of a government.

(B) Some political compromises are not in the best long-term interest of the government.

(C) Voters often judge politicians by criteria other than the sincerity with which they express their views.

(D) A political party's policies could turn out to be detrimental to the functioning of a government.

(E) Some of the public statements made by politicians about their party's policies could in fact be sincere.

750. One summer, floods covered low-lying garlic fields situated in a region with a large mosquito population. Since mosquitoes lay their eggs in standing water, flooded fields would normally attract mosquitoes, yet no mosquitoes were found in the fields. Diallyl sulfide, a major component of garlic, is known to repel several species of insects, including mosquitoes, so it is likely that diallyl sulfide from the garlic repelled the mosquitoes.

Which of the following, if true, most strengthens the argument?

(A) Diallyl sulfide is also found in onions but at concentrations lower than in garlic.

(B) The mosquito population of the region as a whole was significantly smaller during the year in which the flooding took place than it had been in previous years.

(C) By the end of the summer, most of the garlic plants in the flooded fields had been killed by waterborne fungi.

(D) Many insect species not repelled by diallyl sulfide were found in the flooded garlic fields throughout the summer.

(E) Mosquitoes are known to be susceptible to toxins in plants other than garlic, such as marigolds.

751. The population of desert tortoises in Targland's Red Desert has declined, partly because they are captured for sale as pets and partly because people riding all-terrain vehicles have damaged their habitat. Targland plans to halt this population decline by blocking the current access routes into the desert and announcing

new regulations to allow access only on foot. Targland's officials predict that these measures will be adequate, since it is difficult to collect the tortoises without a vehicle.

Which of the following would it be most important to establish in order to evaluate the officials' prediction?

(A) Whether possessing the tortoises as pets remains legally permissible in Targland

(B) Whether Targland is able to enforce the regulations with respect to all-terrain vehicle entry at points other than the current access routes

(C) Whether the Red Desert tortoises are most active during the day or at night

(D) Whether people who travel on foot in the Red Desert often encounter the tortoises

(E) Whether the Targland authorities held public hearings before restricting entry by vehicle into the Red Desert

752. Yeasts capable of leavening bread are widespread, and in the many centuries during which the ancient Egyptians made only unleavened bread, such yeasts must frequently have been mixed into bread doughs accidentally. The Egyptians, however, did not discover leavened bread until about 3000 B.C. That discovery roughly coincided with the introduction of a wheat variety that was preferable to previous varieties because its edible kernel could be removed from the husk without first toasting the grain.

Which of the following, if true, provides the strongest evidence that the two developments were causally related?

(A) Even after the ancient Egyptians discovered leavened bread and the techniques for reliably producing it were well known, unleavened bread continued to be widely consumed.

(B) Only when the Egyptians stopped the practice of toasting grain were their stone-lined grain-toasting pits available for baking bread.

(C) Heating a wheat kernel destroys its gluten, a protein that must be present in order for yeast to leaven bread dough.

(D)   The new variety of wheat, which had a more delicate flavor because it was not toasted, was reserved for the consumption of high officials when it first began to be grown.

(E)   Because the husk of the new variety of wheat was more easily removed, flour made from it required less effort to produce.

753.   That the application of new technology can increase the productivity of existing coal mines is demonstrated by the case of Tribnia's coal industry. Coal output per miner in Tribnia is double what it was five years ago even though no new mines have opened.

Which of the following can be properly concluded from the statement about coal output per miner in the passage?

(A)   If the number of miners working in Tribnian coal mines has remained constant in the past five years, Tribnia's total coal production has doubled in that period of time.

(B)   Any individual Tribnian coal mine that achieved an increase in overall output in the past five years has also experienced an increase in output per miner.

(C)   If any new coal mines had opened in Tribnia in the past five years, then the increase in output per miner would have been even greater than it actually was.

(D)   If any individual Tribnian coal mine has not increased its output per miner in the past five years, then that mine's overall output has declined or remained constant.

(E)   In Tribnia, the cost of producing a given quantity of coal has declined over the past five years.

754.   Shipping clerk: The five specially ordered shipments sent out last week were sent out on Thursday. Last week, all of the shipments sent out on Friday consisted entirely of building supplies, and the shipping department then closed for the weekend. Four shipments were sent to Truax Construction last week, only three of which consisted of building supplies.

If the shipping clerk's statements are true, which of the following must also be true?

(A)   At least one of the shipments sent to Truax Construction last week was specially ordered.

(B)   At least one of last week's specially ordered shipments did not consist of building supplies.

(C)   At least one of the shipments sent to Truax Construction was not sent out on Thursday of last week.

(D)   At least one of the shipments sent out on Friday of last week was sent to Truax Construction.

(E)   At least one of the shipments sent to Truax Construction last week was sent out before Friday.

755.   In Kravonia, the average salary for jobs requiring a college degree has always been higher than the average salary for jobs that do not require a degree. Current enrollments in Kravonia's colleges indicate that over the next four years, the percentage of the Kravonian workforce with college degrees will increase dramatically. Therefore, the average salary for all workers in Kravonia is likely to increase over the next four years.

Which of the following is an assumption on which the argument depends?

(A)   Kravonians with more than one college degree earn more, on average, than do Kravonians with only one college degree.

(B)   The percentage of Kravonians who attend college in order to earn higher salaries is higher now than it was several years ago.

(C)   The higher average salary for jobs requiring a college degree is not due largely to a scarcity among the Kravonian workforce of people with a college degree.

(D)   The average salary in Kravonia for jobs that do not require a college degree will not increase over the next four years.

(E)   Few members of the Kravonian workforce earned their degrees in other countries.

756.   Charcoal from a hearth site in Colorado, 2,000 miles south of Alaska, is known to be 11,200 years old. Siberia is located in northeast Russia, and Alaska is located in northwest America. Researchers reasoned since glaciers prevented human migration south from the Alaska-Siberia land bridge between 18,000 and 11,000 years ago, humans must have come to the Americas more than 18,000 years ago.

Which of the following pieces of new evidence would cast doubt on the conclusion drawn above?

(A) Using new radiocarbon dating techniques, it was determined the charcoal from the Colorado site was at least 11,400 years old.

(B) Another campsite was found in New Mexico with remains dated at 16,000 years old.

(C) A computer simulation of glacial activity showed it would already have been impossible for humans to travel south overland from Alaska 18,500 years ago.

(D) Using new radiocarbon dating techniques, it was proven that an ice-free corridor allowed passage south from the Alaska-Siberia land bridge approximately 11,400 years ago.

(E) Studies of various other hunting-gathering populations showed convincingly that once the glaciers allowed passage, humans could have migrated from Alaska to Colorado in about 20 years.

757. A group of children of various ages was read stories in which people caused harm, with some of those people doing so intentionally and some accidentally. When asked about appropriate punishments for those who had caused harm, the younger children, unlike the older ones, assigned punishments that did not vary according to whether the harm was done intentionally or accidentally. Younger children, then, do not regard people's intentions as relevant to punishment.

Which of the following, if true, would most seriously weaken the conclusion above?

(A) In interpreting these stories, the listeners had to draw on a relatively mature sense of human psychology in order to tell whether harm was produced intentionally or accidentally.

(B) In these stories, the severity of the harm produced was clearly stated.

(C) Younger children are as likely to produce harm unintentionally as older children.

(D) The older children assigned punishment in a way that closely resembled the way adults had assigned punishment in a similar experiment.

(E) The younger children assigned punishments that varied according to the severity of the harm done by the agents in the stories.

758. Mansour: We should both plan to change some of our investments from coal companies to less polluting energy companies, and here's why: Consumers are increasingly demanding nonpolluting energy, and energy companies are increasingly supplying it.

Therese: I'm not sure we should do what you suggest. As demand for nonpolluting energy increases relative to supply, its price will increase, and then the more polluting energy will cost relatively less. Demand for the cheaper, dirtier energy forms will then increase, as will the stock values of the companies that produce them.

Therese responds to Mansour's proposal by doing which of the following?

(A) Advocating that consumers use less expensive forms of energy

(B) Implying that not all uses of coal for energy are necessarily polluting

(C) Disagreeing with Mansour's claim that consumers are increasingly demanding nonpolluting energy

(D) Suggesting that leaving their existing energy investments unchanged could be the better course

(E) Providing a reason to doubt Mansour's assumption that supply of nonpolluting energy will increase in line with demand

759. The earliest Mayan pottery found at Colha in Belize is about 3,000 years old. Recently, however, 4,500-year-old stone agricultural implements were unearthed at Colha. These implements resemble Mayan stone implements of a much later period, also found at Colha. Moreover, the implements' designs are strikingly different from the designs of stone implements produced by other cultures known to have inhabited the area in prehistoric times. Therefore, there were surely Mayan settlements in Colha 4,500 years ago.

Which of the following, if true, most seriously weakens the argument?

(A) Ceramicware is not known to have been used by the Mayans to make agricultural implements.

(B) Carbon dating of corn pollen in Colha indicates agriculture began there around 4,500 years ago.

(C)   Archaeological evidence indicates some of the oldest stone implements found at Colha were used to cut away vegetation after controlled burning of trees to open areas of swampland for cultivation.

(D)   Successor cultures at a given site often adopt the style of agricultural implements used by earlier inhabitants of the same site.

(E)   Many religious and social institutions of the Mayan people who inhabited Colha 3,000 years ago relied on a highly developed system of agricultural symbols.

760.   That the application of new technology can increase the productivity of existing coal mines is demonstrated by the case of Tribnia's coal industry. Coal output per miner in Tribnia is double what it was five years ago, even though no new mines have opened.

Which of the following, if true, most seriously weakens the argument in the passage?

(A)   The most efficient mining technology is specifically designed for open-pit mines, the type of mine prevalent in Tribnia.

(B)   The new mining technology can be successfully applied in most coal mines, but not in such mines as metal-ore mines, for example.

(C)   New coal mines that opened in a country bordering Tribnia have lower productivity than is currently achieved in the Tribnian mines that are highest in productivity.

(D)   In the last three years several of the Tribnian coal mines that were lowest in productivity have been closed down.

(E)   Tribnia's coal output is not sufficient to satisfy domestic demand, which has increased in the last five years.

761.   Migratory North American songbirds like the Tennessee warbler and the Baltimore oriole depend on the dense tree cover that has long been a feature of South American coffee plantations. This tree cover is being eliminated. Yet a population decline among Tennessee warblers is being attributed to a temporary drop in the population of spruce budworms, the warbler's favorite North American prey. Baltimore orioles, however, do not eat budworms and are also experiencing a population decline.

The information above, if accurate, could best serve as part of an argument that

(A)   the decline in the numbers of the Tennessee warbler is responsible for the decline in the population of the spruce budworm

(B)   the Tennessee warbler population will not rebound when the spruce budworm population returns to normal

(C)   variations in the population of the Tennessee warbler influence the numbers of the Baltimore oriole

(D)   the population of Tennessee warblers can reasonably be expected to increase in the near future

(E)   the population of Tennessee warblers is declining less sharply than the population of Baltimore orioles

762.   Historian: Newton developed mathematical concepts and techniques that are fundamental to modern calculus. Leibniz developed closely analogous concepts and techniques. It has traditionally been thought that these discoveries were independent. Researchers have, however, recently discovered notes of Leibniz's that discuss one of Newton's books on mathematics. Several scholars have argued that since the book includes a presentation of Newton's calculus concepts and techniques, and since **the notes were written before Leibniz's own development of calculus concepts and techniques**, it is virtually certain that the traditional view is false. **A more cautious conclusion than this is called for**, however. Leibniz's notes are limited to early sections of Newton's book, sections that precede the ones in which Newton's calculus concepts and techniques are presented.

In the historian's reasoning, the two **boldfaced** portions play which of the following roles?

(A)   The first provides evidence in support of the general position that the historian defends; the second reports the doubts of others concerning that position.

(B)   The first states a conclusion drawn as part of an argument that the historian criticizes; the second is that conclusion.

(C) The first is evidence that has been used to support a conclusion that the historian criticizes; the second is the judgment reached by the historian about that conclusion.

(D) The first identifies grounds for a potential objection to the conclusion of the argument; the second is the judgment reached by the argument concerning the accuracy of the finding.

(E) The first is a claim, the explanation of which is at issue in the argument; the second brings evidence that has been used to support that explanation.

763. Any machine that could be used to keep fields free of weeds without manual weeding or the use of herbicides would have a large market among farmers. A company has developed a prototype weeding machine that distinguishes between plants on the basis of their color and can remove any plant that falls outside a predetermined color range. The company is presently considering whether to go ahead with full-scale production of this weeding machine.

Which of the following, if true, is the strongest consideration in favor of the company's going into full-scale production?

(A) There is a considerable degree of variation in color among weeds of different species.

(B) For many crops, weeds pose a greater threat to high yields than insect pests do.

(C) When crops are weeded manually, color is often a major factor in distinguishing agricultural plants from weeds.

(D) Selection and genetic manipulation allow nearly all agricultural plants to be economically bred to have a distinctive shade of color without altering their other characteristics.

(E) The last time the company decided to go ahead with full-scale production of a machine for which they had developed a prototype, the venture proved far more profitable than the company had anticipated.

764. Charcoal from a hearth site in Colorado, 2,000 miles south of Alaska, is known to be 11,200 years old. Researchers reasoned that, since glaciers prevented human migration south from the Alaska–Siberia land bridge between 18,000 and 11,000 years ago, humans must have come to the Americas more than 18,000 years ago.

The argument above relies on which of the following assumptions?

(A) The earliest controlled use of fire on the American continents occurred around 11,200 years ago.

(B) Any humans who came to the Americas more than 11,000 years ago came via the Alaska–Siberia land bridge.

(C) The Alaska–Siberia land bridge was the result of the uptake of seawater by the continental glaciers.

(D) Early human inhabitants of the Americas were hunters whose diet consisted primarily of meat, rather than gatherers who subsisted on fruit and seeds.

(E) Early humans tended to migrate to warmer climates, even those who were accustomed to living in cold, harsh climates.

765. Advertisement for ShopEx Supermarkets: Dozens of shoppers, chosen at random, were asked as they came out of their ShopEx stores what they had purchased. The prices of the very same items at the nearest PriceKing store were totaled and compared with the ShopEx total. At ShopEx, the totals averaged five percent less than at PriceKing. So, for overall savings on their food bills, shoppers should go to ShopEx instead of PriceKing.

Which of the following, if true, most seriously undermines the argument of the advertisement?

(A) When more than 20 items were selected, the PriceKing totals averaged more than five percent higher than the ShopEx totals.

(B) Many shoppers consider additional factors other than price in choosing the supermarket at which they shop most regularly.

(C) Virtually every grocery item that can be found at PriceKing can also be found at ShopEx.

(D) When purchasing items in a grocery store, shoppers tend to select those items that are on sale, and different stores have sales on different items.

(E) Most of the shoppers who were stopped on their way out of ShopEx said that they shopped at PriceKing either regularly or occasionally.

766. The earliest surviving Greek inscriptions written in an alphabet date from the eighth century B.C. Some of these inscriptions are written from right to left, others from left to right. The alphabet they employ clearly derives from Phoenician writing, but by the eighth century B.C., Phoenician was consistently written from right to left, and had been for about two centuries. Therefore, the Greeks must have adopted alphabetic writing no later than the tenth century B.C.

Which of the following is an assumption on which the argument depends?

(A) Greek inscriptions from the eighth century B.C. that are written from right to left were not translations of Phoenician inscriptions.

(B) In Greece, the adoption of an alphabetic writing system supplanted a writing system in which Greek was written from right to left.

(C) When the Greeks adopted alphabetic writing, they also adopted the Phoenician practices of the time with respect to the direction in which texts were written.

(D) After adopting alphabetic writing, the Greeks had no exposure to Phoenician inscriptions for at least two centuries.

(E) Apart from Greek, all languages whose alphabets derived from Phoenician writing were consistently written from right to left.

767. Generalization: The more viewers a television show attracts, the greater the advertising revenue it generates.

Situation: Production costs for *Starlight*, the VNT network's most popular weekly show, are very high and rising. The advertising revenue *Starlight* generates minus the show's production costs is below average for VNT shows and is declining.

Judgment: VNT's profits would be better protected by retaining *Starlight* than by replacing it with a show of average popularity and average production costs.

Which of the following, if true, provides the strongest reason for considering the judgment to be well founded?

(A) The average profits of VNT shows have increased in each of the last three years.

(B) Shows that occupy time slots immediately before and after a very popular show tend to have far more viewers than they otherwise would.

(C) *Starlight* currently has the highest production costs of all VNT shows.

(D) Last year VNT lost money on a weekly show that was substantially similar to *Starlight* but was broadcast on a different day of the week than *Starlight* is.

(E) *Starlight*'s high production costs are a direct result of its format and content and cannot be reduced without fundamentally changing the show.

768. Last year a record number of new manufacturing jobs were created. Will this year bring another record? Well, **any new manufacturing job is created either within an existing company or by the start-up of a new company.** Within existing firms, new jobs have been created this year at well below last year's record pace. At the same time, there is considerable evidence that the number of new companies starting up will be no higher this year than it was last year, and there is no reason to think that **the new companies starting up this year will create more jobs per company than did last year's start-ups.** So clearly, the number of new jobs created this year will fall short of last year's record.

In the argument given, the two portions in **boldface** play which of the following roles?

(A) The first is presented as an obvious truth on which the argument is based; the second is a claim advanced in support of the conclusion of the argument.

(B) The first is presented as an obvious truth on which the argument is based; the second presents a possible objection that the argument discounts.

(C) The first provides evidence in support of the conclusion of the argument; the second is a prediction that, if accurate, would provide further support for that conclusion.

(D) The first is a generalization that the argument seeks to establish; the second is a claim that has been advanced in support of a position that the argument opposes.

(E) The first is a generalization that the argument seeks to establish; the second is a claim that has been advanced in order to challenge that generalization.

769. Business Consultant: Some corporations shun the use of executive titles because they fear that **the use of titles indicating position in the corporation tends to inhibit communication up and down the corporate hierarchy.** Since an executive who uses a title is treated with more respect by outsiders, however, **use of a title can facilitate an executive's dealings with external businesses.** The obvious compromise is for these executives to use their corporate titles externally but not internally, since even if it is widely known that the corporation's executives use executive titles outside their organization, this knowledge does not by itself inhibit communication within the corporation.

In the consultant's reasoning, the two portions in **boldface** play which of the following roles?

(A) The first presents an obstacle to achieving a certain goal; the second presents a reason for considering that goal to be undesirable.

(B) The first is a consideration that has led to the adoption of a certain strategy; the second presents a reason against adopting that strategy.

(C) The first describes a concern that the consultant dismisses as insignificant; the second is a consideration that serves as the basis for that dismissal.

(D) The first is a belief for which the consultant offers support; the second is part of that support.

(E) The first is a belief against which evidence is offered; the second is part of the evidence offered against that belief.

770. Since it has become known that several of a bank's top executives have been buying shares in their own bank, the bank's depositors, who had been worried by rumors that the bank faced impending financial collapse, have been greatly relieved. They reason that since **top executives evidently have faith in the bank's financial soundness**, those worrisome rumors must be false. The depositors might well be over-optimistic, however, since **corporate executives have been known to buy shares in their own company in a calculated attempt to dispel negative rumors about the company's health.**

In the argument given, the two **boldfaced** portions play which of the following roles?

(A) The first describes evidence used in the reasoning that the argument calls into question; the second gives information about the source of that evidence.

(B) The first describes evidence used in the reasoning that the argument calls into question; the second states the conclusion of the argument as a whole.

(C) The first is an intermediate conclusion that forms part of the reasoning that the argument calls into question; the second is evidence that undermines the support for this intermediate conclusion.

(D) The first is an intermediate conclusion that forms part of the reasoning that the argument calls into question; the second states the conclusion of the argument as a whole.

(E) The first is an intermediate conclusion that forms part of the reasoning that the argument calls into question; the second states a further conclusion supported by this intermediate conclusion.

771. Throughout May, crabs arrive on Delaware's beaches to lay eggs. Migrating shorebirds that rely on these eggs for food stop there before continuing to their northern breeding grounds. The earlier in the season they reach those breeding grounds, the greater their likelihood of breeding successfully. Because the crab population was much smaller this year than last, the shorebirds lengthened their Delaware stay considerably in order to consume enough crab eggs to permit completion of their migration.

For which of the following hypotheses does the information given above provide the strongest support?

(A) The shorebirds will leave their northern breeding grounds earlier this year than they have in years past.

(B) The decline in the crab population was largely due to the shorebirds' consumption of crab eggs in years past.

(C) The average number of eggs laid per egg-laying crab will be significantly lower next year than this year.

(D) The proportion of the migratory shorebirds that breed successfully will be lower this year than it was last year.

(E) Many fewer of the shorebirds will reach their northern breeding grounds this year than did last year.

772. Surveys in Lynzia indicate that while more than half of all Lynzians over thirty read a newspaper regularly, only 10 percent of Lynzians in their twenties do. Since the mean age of Lynzia's population is quite low, with people in their twenties constituting a large proportion of the population, it is safe to predict that the percentage of Lynzians who regularly read a newspaper will be much lower ten years from now than it is today.

Which of the following, if true, casts most doubt on the prediction?

(A) The number of Lynzians in their twenties is less than the number of Lynzians over thirty.

(B) The surveys counted someone as reading a newspaper regularly if that person read a newspaper more than four times a month.

(C) The proportion of Lynzians who regularly read a newspaper was higher 20 years ago than it is today.

(D) The proportion of Lynzians in their twenties who regularly read a newspaper has always been low.

(E) The number of newspapers published in Lynzia has been gradually diminishing over the last several decades.

773. Inscorp, a manufacturer, wishes to make its information booth at an industry convention more productive, in terms of boosting sales. The booth offers information introducing the company's new products and services. To achieve the desired result, Inscorp's marketing department will attempt to attract more people to the booth. The marketing director's first measure was to instruct each salesperson to call five ex-customers and personally invite them to visit the booth.

Which of the following, if true, most strongly calls into question the effectiveness of the marketing director's first measure as a step toward the goal of boosting sales?

(A) In past years, the information booth was not well attended.

(B) The ex-customers most likely to act on Inscorp's invitation are ones who hope to use the booth to resolve long-standing complaints on which Inscorp is unlikely to give them satisfaction.

(C) Many of Inscorp's competitors believe that by making their information booths more distinctive they can increase the number of potential customers who will visit their booths at the convention.

(D) Inscorp's best customers regularly receive special discounts on large orders placed with Inscorp.

(E) Inscorp has more new products and services available this year than it had in previous years.

774. Fish currently costs about the same at seafood stores throughout Eastville and its surrounding suburbs. Seafood stores buy fish from the same wholesalers and at the same prices, and other business expenses have also been about the same. But new tax breaks will substantially lower the cost of doing business within the city. Therefore, in the future, profit margins will be higher at seafood stores within the city than at suburban seafood stores.

For the purposes of evaluating the argument, it would be most useful to know whether

(A) more fish wholesalers are located within the city than in the surrounding suburbs

(B) any people who currently own seafood stores in the suburbs surrounding Eastville will relocate their businesses nearer to the city

(C) the wholesale price of fish is likely to fall in the future

(D) fish has always cost about the same at seafood stores throughout Eastville and its surrounding suburbs

(E) seafood stores within the city will in the future set prices that are lower than those at suburban seafood stores

775. **During the past year, Pro-Tect Insurance Company's total payouts on car-theft claims were larger than the company can afford to sustain.** Pro-Tect cannot reduce the number of car-theft policies it carries, so it cannot protect itself against continued large payouts that way. Therefore, **Pro-Tect has decided to offer a discount to holders of car-theft policies whose cars have antitheft devices.** Many policyholders will respond to the discount by installing antitheft devices, since the amount of the discount will within two years typically more than cover the cost of installation. Thus, because cars with antitheft devices are rarely stolen, Pro-Tect's plan is likely to reduce its annual payouts.

In the argument above, the two portions in **boldface** play which of the following roles?

(A) The first provides evidence in support of the main conclusion of the argument; the second is that conclusion.

(B) The first presents a problem a response to which the argument assesses; the second is that response.

(C) The first poses a problem for which the argument suggests a possible solution; the second is a conclusion that the argument draws in the course of supporting that possible solution.

(D) The first raises a consideration that the argument takes as weighing against the effectiveness of a certain policy; the second is that policy.

(E) The first presents a circumstance whose explanation is the issue the argument addresses; the second is an explanation that the argument rejects.

776. Ecologist: The Scottish Highlands were once the site of extensive forests, but these forests have mostly disappeared and been replaced by peat bogs. The common view is that **the Highlands' deforestation was caused by human activity, especially agriculture.** However, agriculture began in the Highlands less than 2,000 years ago. Peat bogs, which consist of compressed decayed vegetable matter, build up by only about one foot per 1,000 years and,

throughout the Highlands, remains of trees in peat bogs are almost all at depths greater than four feet. Since climate changes that occurred between 7,000 and 4,000 years ago favored the development of peat bogs rather than the survival of forests, the deforestation was more likely the result of natural processes than of human activity.

In the ecologist's argument, the two portions in **boldface** play which of the following roles?

(A) The first is a position that the ecologist rejects; the second is evidence offered in support of that rejection.

(B) The first is a position that the ecologist rejects; the second is evidence that has been used to support the position the ecologist rejects.

(C) The first is a position that the ecologist seeks to defend; the second is evidence that has been used against that position.

(D) The first is a position that the ecologist seeks to defend; the second provides evidence in support of that position.

(E) The first is an explanation, rejected by the ecologist, that has been offered for a certain finding; the second is that finding.

777. In Gandania, where the government has a monopoly on tobacco sales, the incidence of smoking-related health problems has risen steadily for the last twenty years, and health care costs to the government have risen correspondingly. The health secretary recently proposed a series of laws aimed at halting tobacco use in Gandania. Fully ten percent of the annual revenues Gandania receives come from tobacco sales, however, so Gandania cannot afford to institute the proposed laws.

Which of the following is an assumption on which the argument depends?

(A) If the health secretary's proposal is not implemented, the health secretary will be obliged in the near future either to resign or to present an alternative proposal.

(B) If smoking is halted in Gandania, Gandania's smoking-related health care costs will not soon decrease enough to offset the projected loss of revenue from tobacco sales.

(C)   The proposed laws are not likely to cause a significant decrease in the amount of tobacco Gandania exports.

(D)   The percentage of revenue Gandania receives from tobacco sales has remained relatively stable in recent years.

(E)   In Gandania, government revenue from tobacco sales far surpasses that from any other source.

Questions 778–850 — Difficulty: Hard

778. Duckbill dinosaurs, like today's monitor lizards, had particularly long tails, which they could whip at considerable speed. Monitor lizards use their tails to strike predators. However, although duckbill tails were otherwise very similar to those of monitor lizards, the duckbill's tailbones were proportionately much thinner and thus more delicate. Moreover, to ward off their proportionately much larger predators, duckbills would have had to whip their tails considerably faster than monitor lizards do.

The information given, if accurate, provides the strongest support for which of the following hypotheses?

(A)   If duckbills whipped their tails faster than monitor lizards do, the duckbill's tail would have been effective at warding off the duckbills' fiercest predators.

(B)   Duckbills used their tails to strike predators, and their tailbones were frequently damaged from the impact.

(C)   Using their tails was not the only means duckbills had for warding off predators.

(D)   Duckbills were at much greater risk of being killed by a predator than monitor lizards are.

(E)   The tails of duckbills, if used to ward off predators, would have been more likely than the tails of monitor lizards to sustain damage from the impact.

779. In an attempt to produce a coffee plant that would yield beans containing no caffeine, the synthesis of a substance known to be integral to the initial stages of caffeine production was blocked either in the beans, in the leaves, or both. For those plants in which synthesis of the substance was blocked only in the leaves, the resulting beans contained no caffeine.

Any of the following, if true, would provide the basis for an explanation of the observed results EXCEPT:

(A)   In coffee plants, the substance is synthesized only in the leaves and then moves to the beans, where the initial stages of caffeine production take place.

(B)   In coffee plants, the last stage of caffeine production takes place in the beans using a compound that is produced only in the leaves by the substance.

(C)   In coffee plants, the initial stages of caffeine production take place only in the beans, but later stages depend on another substance that is synthesized only in the leaves and does not depend on the blocked substance.

(D)   In coffee plants, caffeine production takes place only in the leaves, but the caffeine then moves to the beans.

(E)   Caffeine was produced in the beans of the modified coffee plants, but all of it moved to the leaves, which normally produce their own caffeine.

780. Which of the following most logically completes the passage?

Laminated glass is much harder to break than the glass typically used in the windows of cars driven in Relnia. It is more difficult for thieves to break into cars with laminated glass windows than into cars with ordinary glass windows, and laminated glass windows are less likely to break in a collision. Nevertheless, considerations of security and safety do not unambiguously support a proposal to require that in Relnia all glass installed in cars be laminated glass, since _____.

(A)   most people cannot visually distinguish laminated glass from the glass typically used for car windows

(B)   a significant proportion of cars driven in Relnia are manufactured elsewhere

(C)   some cars in Relnia already have laminated glass in their windows

(D)   the rates of car theft and of collisions have both fallen slightly in Relnia in recent years

(E)   there are times when breaking a car's window is the best way to provide timely help for people trapped inside

781. Consultant: **Ace Repairs ends up having to redo a significant number of the complex repair jobs it undertakes, but when those repairs are redone, they are invariably done right.** Since we have established that there is no systematic difference between the mechanics who are assigned to do the initial repairs and those who are assigned to redo unsatisfactory jobs, we must reject the hypothesis that mistakes made in the initial repairs are due to the mechanics' lack of competence. Rather, it is likely that **complex repairs require a level of focused attention that the company's mechanics apply consistently only to repair jobs that have not been done right on the first try.**

In the consultant's reasoning, the two portions in **boldface** play which of the following roles?

(A) The first is the consultant's main conclusion; the second provides evidence in support of that main conclusion.

(B) The first is evidence that serves as the basis for rejecting one explanation of a certain finding; the second is the consultant's own explanation of that finding.

(C) The first is a claim whose truth is at issue in the reasoning; the second provides evidence to show that the claim is true.

(D) The first presents a contrast whose explanation is at issue in the reasoning; the second is the consultant's explanation of that contrast.

(E) The first presents a contrast whose explanation is at issue in the reasoning; the second is evidence that has been used to challenge the consultant's explanation of that contrast.

782. To reduce waste of raw materials, the government of Sperland is considering requiring household appliances to be broken down for salvage when discarded. To cover the cost of salvage, the government is planning to charge a fee, which would be imposed when the appliance is first sold. Imposing the fee at the time of salvage would reduce waste more effectively, however, because consumers tend to keep old appliances longer if they are faced with a fee for discarding them.

Which of the following, if true, most seriously weakens the argument?

(A) Increasing the cost of disposing of an appliance properly increases the incentive to dispose of it improperly.

(B) The fee provides manufacturers with no incentive to produce appliances that are more durable.

(C) For people who have bought new appliances recently, the salvage fee would not need to be paid for a number of years.

(D) People who sell their used, working appliances to others would not need to pay the salvage fee.

(E) Many nonfunctioning appliances that are currently discarded could be repaired at relatively little expense.

783. Increased use of incineration is sometimes advocated as a safe way to dispose of chemical waste. But opponents of incineration point to the 40 incidents involving unexpected releases of dangerous chemical agents that were reported just last year at two existing incinerators commissioned to destroy a quantity of chemical waste material. Since designs for proposed new incinerators include no additional means of preventing such releases, leaks will only become more prevalent if use of incineration increases.

Which of the following, if true, most seriously weakens the argument?

(A) At the two incinerators at which leaks were reported, staff had had only cursory training on the proper procedures for incinerating chemical waste.

(B) Other means of disposing of chemical waste, such as chemical neutralization processes, have not been proven safer than incineration.

(C) The capacity of existing incinerators is sufficient to allow for increased incineration of chemical waste without any need for new incinerators.

(D) The frequency of reports of unexpected releases of chemical agents at newly built incinerators is about the same as the frequency at older incinerators.

(E) In only three of the reported incidents of unexpected chemical leaks did the releases extend outside the property on which the incinerators were located.

784. Public health expert: **Increasing the urgency of a public health message may be counterproductive.** In addition to irritating the majority who already behave responsibly, **it may undermine all government pronouncements on health by convincing people that such messages are overly cautious.** And there is no reason to believe that those who ignore measured voices will listen to shouting.

The two sections in **boldface** play which of the following roles in the public health expert's argument?

(A) The first is a conclusion for which support is provided, but it is not the argument's main conclusion; the second is an unsupported premise supporting the argument's main conclusion.

(B) The first is a premise supporting the only explicit conclusion; so is the second.

(C) The first is the argument's main conclusion; the second supports that conclusion and is itself a conclusion for which support is provided.

(D) The first is a premise supporting the argument's only conclusion; the second is that conclusion.

(E) The first is the argument's only explicit conclusion; the second is a premise supporting that conclusion.

785. Which of the following most logically completes the passage?

According to the last pre-election poll in Whippleton, most voters believe that the three problems government needs to address, in order of importance, are pollution, crime, and unemployment. Yet in the election, candidates from parties perceived as strongly against pollution were defeated, while those elected were all from parties with a history of opposing legislation designed to reduce pollution. These results should not be taken to indicate that the poll was inaccurate, however, since _____.

(A) some voters in Whippleton do not believe that pollution needs to be reduced

(B) every candidate who was defeated had a strong antipollution record

(C) there were no issues other than crime, unemployment, and pollution on which the candidates had significant differences of opinion

(D) all the candidates who were elected were perceived as being stronger against both crime and unemployment than the candidates who were defeated

(E) many of the people who voted in the election refused to participate in the poll

786. Manufacturing plants in Arundia have recently been acquired in substantial numbers by investors from abroad. Arundian politicians are proposing legislative action to stop such investment, justifying the proposal by arguing that foreign investors, opportunistically exploiting a recent fall in the value of the Arundian currency, were able to buy Arundian assets at less than their true value.

Which of the following, if true, casts the most serious doubt on the adequacy of the Arundian politicians' justification for the proposed legislation?

(A) The Arundian government originally welcomed the fall in the value of the Arundian currency because the fall made Arundian exports more competitive on international markets.

(B) Foreign investors who acquired Arundian manufacturing plants generally did so with no intention of keeping and running those plants over the long term.

(C) Without the recent fall in the value of the Arundian currency, many of the Arundian assets bought by foreign investors would have been beyond the financial reach of those investors.

(D) In Concordia, a country broadly similar to Arundia, the share of manufacturing assets that is foreign-controlled is 60 percent higher than it is in Arundia.

(E) The true value of an investment is determined by the value of the profits from it, and the low value of the Arundian currency has depressed the value of any profits earned by foreign investors from Arundian assets.

787. Proposed new safety rules for Beach City airport would lengthen considerably the minimum time between takeoffs from the airport. In consequence, the airport would be able to accommodate 10 percent fewer flights than currently use the airport daily. The city's operating budget depends heavily on taxes generated by tourist spending, and most of the tourists come by plane. Therefore, the proposed new safety rules, if adopted, will reduce the revenue available for the operating budget.

The argument depends on assuming which of the following?

(A)   There are no periods of the day during which the interval between flights taking off from the airport is significantly greater than the currently allowed minimum.

(B)   Few, if any, of the tourists who use Beach City airport do so when their main destination is a neighboring community and not Beach City itself.

(C)   If the proposed safety rules are adopted, the reduction in tourist numbers will not result mainly from a reduction in the number of tourists who spend relatively little in Beach City.

(D)   Increasing the minimum time between takeoffs is the only way to achieve necessary safety improvements without a large expenditure by the city government on airport enhancements.

(E)   The response to the adoption of the new safety rules would not include a large increase in the number of passengers per flight.

788. The introduction of new drugs into the market is frequently prevented by a shortage of human subjects for the clinical trials needed to show that the drugs are safe and effective. Since the lives and health of people in future generations may depend on treatments that are currently experimental, practicing physicians are morally in the wrong when, in the absence of any treatment proven to be effective, they fail to encourage suitable patients to volunteer for clinical trials.

Which of the following, if true, casts most doubt on the conclusion of the argument?

(A)   Many drugs undergoing clinical trials are intended for the treatment of conditions for which there is currently no effective treatment.

(B)   Patients do not share the physician's professional concern for public health, but everyone has a moral obligation to alleviate suffering when able to do so.

(C)   Usually, half the patients in a clinical trial serve as a control group and receive a nonactive drug in place of the drug being tested.

(D)   An experimental drug cannot legally be made available to patients unless those patients are subjects in clinical trials of the drug.

(E)   Physicians have an overriding moral and legal duty to care for the health and safety of their current patients.

789. As a construction material, bamboo is as strong as steel and sturdier than concrete. Moreover, in tropical areas, bamboo is a much less expensive construction material than either steel or concrete and is always readily available. In tropical areas, therefore, building with bamboo makes better economic sense than building with steel or concrete, except where land values are high.

Which of the following, if true, most helps to explain the exception noted above?

(A)   Buildings constructed of bamboo are less likely to suffer earthquake damage than are steel and concrete buildings.

(B)   Bamboo is unsuitable as a building material for multistory buildings.

(C)   In order to protect it from being damaged by termites and beetles, bamboo must be soaked, at some expense, in a preservative.

(D)   In some tropical areas, bamboo is used to make the scaffolding that is used during large construction projects.

(E)   Bamboo growing in an area where land values are increasing is often cleared to make way for construction.

790. Newspaper editors should not allow reporters to write the headlines for their own stories. The reason for this is that, while the headlines that reporters themselves write are often clever, what typically makes them clever is that they allude to little-known information that is familiar to the reporter but that never appears explicitly in the story itself.

Which of the following, if true, most strengthens the argument?

(A)   The reporter who writes a story is usually better placed than the reporter's editor is to judge what the story's most newsworthy features are.

(B)   To write a headline that is clever, a person must have sufficient understanding of the story that the headline accompanies.

(C) Most reporters rarely bother to find out how other reporters have written stories and headlines about the same events that they themselves have covered.

(D) For virtually any story that a reporter writes, there are at least a few people who know more about the story's subject matter than does the reporter.

(E) The kind of headlines that newspaper editors want are those that anyone who has read a reporter's story in its entirety will recognize as clever.

791. Advertisement: Our competitors' computer salespeople are paid according to the value of the products they sell, so they have a financial incentive to convince you to buy the most expensive units—whether you need them or not. But here at Comput-o-Mart, our salespeople are paid a salary that is not dependent on the value of their sales, so they won't try to tell you what to buy. That means when you buy a computer at Comput-o-Mart, you can be sure you're not paying for computing capabilities you don't need.

Which of the following would, if true, most weaken the advertisement's reasoning?

(A) Some less-expensive computers actually have greater computing power than more expensive ones.

(B) Salespeople who have a financial incentive to make sales generally provide more attentive service than do other salespeople.

(C) Extended warranties purchased for less-expensive computers can cost nearly as much as the purchase price of the computer.

(D) Comput-o-Mart is open only limited hours, which makes it more difficult for many shoppers to buy computers there than at other retail stores.

(E) Comput-o-Mart does not sell any computers that support only basic computing.

792. Proponents of the recently introduced tax on sales of new luxury boats had argued that a tax of this sort would be an equitable way to increase government revenue because the admittedly heavy tax burden would fall only on wealthy people, and neither they nor anyone else would suffer any economic hardship. In fact, however, 20 percent of the workers employed by manufacturers of luxury boats have lost their jobs as a direct result of this tax.

The information given, if true, most strongly supports which of the following?

(A) The market for luxury boats would have collapsed even if the new tax on luxury boats had been lower.

(B) The new tax would produce a net gain in tax revenue for the government only if the yearly total revenue that it generates exceeds the total of any yearly tax-revenue decrease resulting from the workers' loss of jobs.

(C) Because many people never buy luxury items, imposing a sales tax on luxury items is the kind of legislative action that does not cost incumbent legislators much popular support.

(D) Before the tax was instituted, luxury boats were largely bought by people who were not wealthy.

(E) Taxes can be equitable only if their burden is evenly distributed over the entire population.

793. In the past, the country of Malvernia has relied heavily on imported oil. Malvernia recently implemented a program to convert heating systems from oil to natural gas. Malvernia currently produces more natural gas each year than it uses, and oil production in Malvernian oil fields is increasing at a steady pace. If these trends in fuel production and usage continue, therefore, Malvernian reliance on foreign sources for fuel is likely to decline soon.

Which of the following would it be most useful to establish in evaluating the argument?

(A) When, if ever, will production of oil in Malvernia outstrip production of natural gas?

(B) Is Malvernia among the countries that rely most on imported oil?

(C) What proportion of Malvernia's total energy needs is met by hydroelectric, solar, and nuclear power?

(D) Is the amount of oil used each year in Malvernia for generating electricity and fuel for transportation increasing?

(E) Have any existing oil-burning heating systems in Malvernia already been converted to natural-gas-burning heating systems?

794. Exposure to certain chemicals commonly used in elementary schools as cleaners or pesticides causes allergic reactions in some children. Elementary school nurses in Renston report that the proportion of schoolchildren sent to them for treatment of allergic reactions to those chemicals has increased significantly over the past ten years. Therefore, either Renston's schoolchildren have been exposed to greater quantities of the chemicals or they are more sensitive to them than schoolchildren were ten years ago.

Which of the following is an assumption on which the argument depends?

(A) The number of school nurses employed by Renston's elementary schools has not decreased over the past ten years.

(B) Children who are allergic to the chemicals are no more likely than other children to have allergies to other substances.

(C) Children who have allergic reactions to the chemicals are not more likely to be sent to a school nurse now than they were ten years ago.

(D) The chemicals are not commonly used as cleaners or pesticides in houses and apartment buildings in Renston.

(E) Children attending elementary school do not make up a larger proportion of Renston's population now than they did ten years ago.

795. Lockeport's commercial fishing boats use gill nets, which kill many of the netted fish, including some fish of endangered species. The fishing commission has proposed requiring the use of tent nets, which do not kill fish; boat crews would then throw back fish of endangered species. Profitable commercial fishing boats in similar areas have already switched over to tent nets. The proposal can therefore be implemented without economic harm to Lockeport's commercial fishing boat operators.

Which of the following, if true, casts the most serious doubt on the argument made for the proposal?

(A) In places where the use of tent nets has been mandated, there are typically fewer commercial fishing boats in operation than there were before tent nets came into use.

(B) Even when used properly, gill nets require many more repairs than do tent nets.

(C) Recreational anglers in Lockeport catch more fish of endangered species than do commercial fishing boats.

(D) The endangered species of fish in Lockeport's commercial fishing area did not become endangered as a result of the use of gill nets by fishing fleets.

(E) The endangered species of fish caught by Lockeport's commercial fishing fleet are of no commercial value.

796. Last year Comfort Airlines had twice as many delayed flights as the year before, but the number of complaints from passengers about delayed flights went up three times. It is unlikely that this disproportionate increase in complaints was rooted in an increase in overall dissatisfaction with the service Comfort Airlines provides, since the airline made a special effort to improve other aspects of its service last year.

Which of the following, if true, most helps to explain the disproportionate increase in customer complaints?

(A) Comfort Airlines had more flights last year than the year before.

(B) Last year a single period of unusually bad weather caused a large number of flights to be delayed.

(C) Some of the improvements that Comfort Airlines made in its service were required by new government regulations.

(D) The average length of a flight delay was greater last year than it was the year before.

(E) The average number of passengers per flight was no higher last year than the year before.

797. Last year a global disturbance of weather patterns disrupted harvests in many of the world's important agricultural areas. Worldwide production of soybeans, an important source of protein for people and livestock alike, was not adversely affected, however. Indeed, last year's soybean crop was actually slightly larger than average. Nevertheless, the weather phenomenon is probably responsible for a recent increase in the world price of soybeans.

Which of the following, if true, provides the strongest justification for the attribution of the increase in soybean prices to the weather phenomenon?

(A)   Last year's harvest of anchovies, which provide an important protein source for livestock, was disrupted by the effects of the weather phenomenon.

(B)   Most countries that produce soybeans for export had above-average harvests of a number of food crops other than soybeans last year.

(C)   The world price of soybeans also rose several years ago, immediately after an earlier occurrence of a similar global weather disturbance.

(D)   Heavy rains attributable to the weather phenomenon improved grazing pastures last year, allowing farmers in many parts of the world to reduce their dependence on supplemental feed.

(E)   Prior to last year, soybean prices had been falling for several years.

798. Most of the year, the hermit thrush, a North American songbird, eats a diet consisting mainly of insects, but in autumn, as the thrushes migrate to their Central and South American wintering grounds, they feed almost exclusively on wild berries. Wild berries, however, are not as rich in calories as insects, yet thrushes need to consume plenty of calories in order to complete their migration. One possible explanation is that berries contain other nutrients that thrushes need for migration and that insects lack.

Which of the following, if true, most seriously calls into question the explanation given for the thrush's diet during migration?

(A)   Hermit thrushes, if undernourished, are unable to complete their autumn migration before the onset of winter.

(B)   Insect species contain certain nutrients that are not found in wild berries.

(C)   For songbirds, catching insects requires the expenditure of significantly more calories than eating wild berries does.

(D)   Along the hermit thrushes' migration routes, insects are abundant throughout the migration season.

(E)   There are some species of wild berries that hermit thrushes generally do not eat, even though these berry species are exceptionally rich in calories.

799. The kinds of hand and wrist injuries that result from extended use of a computer while maintaining an incorrect posture are common among schoolchildren in Harnville. Computers are important to the school curriculum there, so instead of reducing the amount of time their students use computers, teachers plan to bring about a sharp reduction in the number of these injuries by carefully monitoring their students' posture when using computers in the classroom.

Which of the following would it be most useful to know in order to assess the likelihood that the teachers' plan will be successful?

(A)   Whether extended use of a computer while maintaining incorrect posture can cause injuries other than hand and wrist injuries

(B)   Whether hand and wrist injuries not caused by computer use are common among schoolchildren in Harnville

(C)   What proportion of schoolchildren in Harnville with hand and wrist injuries use computers extensively outside the classroom

(D)   Whether changes in the curriculum could reduce the schools' dependence on computers

(E)   What proportion of schoolchildren in Harnville already use correct posture while using a computer

800. Many people suffer an allergic reaction to certain sulfites, including those that are commonly added to wine as preservatives. However, since there are several winemakers who add sulfites to none of the wines they produce, people who would like to drink wine but are allergic to sulfites can drink wines produced by these winemakers without risking an allergic reaction to sulfites.

Which of the following is an assumption on which the argument depends?

(A)   These winemakers have been able to duplicate the preservative effect produced by adding sulfites by means that do not involve adding any potentially allergenic substances to their wine.

(B)   Not all forms of sulfite are equally likely to produce the allergic reaction.

(C)   Wine is the only beverage to which sulfites are commonly added.

(D)   Apart from sulfites, there are no substances commonly present in wine that give rise to an allergic reaction.

(E)   Sulfites are not naturally present in the wines produced by these winemakers in amounts large enough to produce an allergic reaction in someone who drinks these wines.

801.   A new law gives ownership of patents—documents providing exclusive right to make and sell an invention—to universities, not the government, when those patents result from government-sponsored university research. Administrators at Logos University plan to sell any patents they acquire to corporations in order to fund programs to improve undergraduate teaching.

Which of the following, if true, would cast the most doubt on the viability of the college administrators' plan described above?

(A)   Profit-making corporations interested in developing products based on patents held by universities are likely to try to serve as exclusive sponsors of ongoing university research projects.

(B)   Corporate sponsors of research in university facilities are entitled to tax credits under new federal tax-code guidelines.

(C)   Research scientists at Logos University have few or no teaching responsibilities and participate little if at all in the undergraduate programs in their field.

(D)   Government-sponsored research conducted at Logos University for the most part duplicates research already completed by several profitmaking corporations.

(E)   Logos University is unlikely to attract corporate sponsorship of its scientific research.

802.   Between 1980 and 2000, the sea otter population of the Aleutian Islands declined precipitously. There were no signs of disease or malnutrition, so there was probably an increase in the number of otters being eaten by predators. Orcas will eat otters when seals, their normal prey, are unavailable, and the Aleutian Islands seal population declined dramatically in the 1980s. Therefore, orcas were most likely the immediate cause of the otter population decline.

Which of the following, if true, most strengthens the argument?

(A)   The population of sea urchins, the main food of sea otters, has increased since the sea otter population declined.

(B)   Seals do not eat sea otters, nor do they compete with sea otters for food.

(C)   Most of the surviving sea otters live in a bay that is inaccessible to orcas.

(D)   The population of orcas in the Aleutian Islands has declined since the 1980s.

(E)   An increase in commercial fishing near the Aleutian Islands in the 1980s caused a slight decline in the population of the fish that seals use for food.

803.   Political strategist: The domestic policies of our opponents in Party X are contrary to the priorities of many middle-class voters. Yet some of these same voters are supporters of Party X and its candidates due to the party's appeals about foreign policy. In order to win these voters back, we in Party Y must prove to middle-class voters that Party X does not represent their priorities with respect to domestic policy.

Which of the following would, if true, most strongly suggest that the political strategist's plan is unlikely to succeed?

(A)   Many in the middle class who support Party X for its foreign policies also support its domestic policies and are fully aware of the implications of those policies.

(B)   Most middle-class supporters of Party X care about foreign policy and know very little about its domestic policies.

(C)   Long-term domestic policy sometimes conflicts with short-term domestic policy.

(D)   There are topics on which Party X and Party Y have significant agreement.

(E)   Some middle-class voters are concerned about both domestic and foreign policy.

804. Studies in restaurants show that the tips left by customers who pay their bill in cash tend to be larger when the bill is presented on a tray that bears a credit-card logo. Consumer psychologists hypothesize that simply seeing a credit-card logo makes many credit-card holders willing to spend more because it reminds them that their spending power exceeds the cash they have immediately available.

Which of the following, if true, most strongly supports the psychologists' interpretation of the studies?

(A) The effect noted in the studies is not limited to patrons who have credit cards.

(B) Patrons who are under financial pressure from their credit-card obligations tend to tip less when presented with a restaurant bill on a tray with a credit-card logo than when the tray has no logo.

(C) In virtually all of the cases in the studies, the patrons who paid bills in cash did not possess credit cards.

(D) In general, restaurant patrons who pay their bills in cash leave larger tips than do those who pay by credit card.

(E) The percentage of restaurant bills paid with a given brand of credit card increases when that credit card's logo is displayed on the tray with which the bill is presented.

805. In an experiment, each volunteer was allowed to choose between an easy task and a hard task and was told that another volunteer would do the other task. Each volunteer could also choose to have a computer assign the two tasks randomly. Most volunteers chose the easy task for themselves and under questioning later said they had acted fairly. But when the scenario was described to another group of volunteers, almost all said choosing the easy task would be unfair. This shows that most people apply weaker moral standards to themselves than to others.

Which of the following is an assumption required by this argument?

(A) At least some volunteers who said they had acted fairly in choosing the easy task would have said that it was unfair for someone else to do so.

(B) The most moral choice for the volunteers would have been to have the computer assign the two tasks randomly.

(C) There were at least some volunteers who were assigned to do the hard task and felt that the assignment was unfair.

(D) On average, the volunteers to whom the scenario was described were more accurate in their moral judgments than the other volunteers were.

(E) At least some volunteers given the choice between assigning the tasks themselves and having the computer assign them felt that they had made the only fair choice available to them.

806. Country X's recent stock-trading scandal should not diminish investors' confidence in the country's stock market. For one thing, **the discovery of the scandal confirms that Country X has a strong regulatory system**, as the following considerations show. In any stock market, some fraudulent activity is inevitable. If a stock market is well regulated, any significant stock-trading fraud in it will very likely be discovered. This deters potential perpetrators and facilitates improvement in regulatory processes.

In the argument, the portion in **boldface** plays which of the following roles?

(A) It is the argument's only conclusion.

(B) It is a conclusion for which the argument provides support and which itself is used to support the argument's main conclusion.

(C) It is the argument's main conclusion and is supported by another explicitly stated conclusion for which further support is provided.

(D) It is an assumption for which no explicit support is provided and is used to support the argument's only conclusion.

(E) It is a compound statement containing both the argument's main conclusion and an assumption used to support that conclusion.

807. **Delta Products Inc. has recently switched at least partly from older technologies using fossil fuels to new technologies powered by electricity.** The question has been raised whether it can be concluded that **for a given level of output, Delta's operation now causes less fossil fuel to be consumed than it did formerly.** The answer, clearly, is yes, since the amount of fossil fuel used to generate the electricity needed to power the new technologies is less than the amount needed to power the older technologies, provided level of output is held constant.

In the argument given, the two **boldfaced** portions play which of the following roles?

(A)   The first identifies the content of the conclusion of the argument; the second provides support for that conclusion.

(B)   The first provides support for the conclusion of the argument; the second identifies the content of that conclusion.

(C)   The first states the conclusion of the argument; the second calls that conclusion into question.

(D)   The first provides support for the conclusion of the argument; the second calls that conclusion into question.

(E)   Each provides support for the conclusion of the argument.

808.   Theater critic: The play *La Finestrina*, now at Central Theater, was written in Italy in the eighteenth century. The director claims that this production is as similar to the original production as is possible in a modern theater. Although the actor who plays Harlequin the clown gives a performance very reminiscent of the twentieth-century American comedian Groucho Marx, Marx's comic style was very much within the comic acting tradition that had begun in sixteenth-century Italy.

The considerations given best serve as part of an argument that

(A)   modern audiences would find it hard to tolerate certain characteristics of a historically accurate performance of an eighteenth-century play

(B)   Groucho Marx once performed the part of the character Harlequin in *La Finestrina*

(C)   in the United States, the training of actors in the twentieth century is based on principles that do not differ radically from those that underlay the training of actors in eighteenth-century Italy

(D)   the performance of the actor who plays Harlequin in *La Finestrina* does not serve as evidence against the director's claim

(E)   the director of *La Finestrina* must have advised the actor who plays Harlequin to model his performance on comic performances of Groucho Marx

809.   Although the discount stores in Goreville's central shopping district are expected to close within five years as a result of competition from a SpendLess discount department store that just opened, those locations will not stay vacant for long. In the five years since the opening of Colson's, a nondiscount department store, a new store has opened at the location of every store in the shopping district that closed because it could not compete with Colson's.

Which of the following, if true, most seriously weakens the argument?

(A)   Many customers of Colson's are expected to do less shopping there than they did before the SpendLess store opened.

(B)   Increasingly, the stores that have opened in the central shopping district since Colson's opened have been discount stores.

(C)   At present, the central shopping district has as many stores operating in it as it ever had.

(D)   Over the course of the next five years, it is expected that Goreville's population will grow at a faster rate than it has for the past several decades.

(E)   Many stores in the central shopping district sell types of merchandise that are not available at either SpendLess or Colson's.

810.   Last year all refuse collected by Shelbyville city services was incinerated. This incineration generated a large quantity of residual ash. In order to reduce the amount of residual ash Shelbyville generates this year to half of last year's total, the city has revamped its collection program. This year city services will separate for recycling enough refuse to reduce the number of truckloads of refuse to be incinerated to half of last year's number.

Which of the following is required for the revamped collection program to achieve its aim?

(A)   This year no materials that city services could separate for recycling will be incinerated.

(B)   Separating recyclable materials from materials to be incinerated will cost Shelbyville less than half what it cost last year to dispose of the residual ash.

(C)   Refuse collected by city services will contain a larger proportion of recyclable materials this year than it did last year.

(D)   The refuse incinerated this year will generate no more residual ash per truckload incinerated than did the refuse incinerated last year.

(E)   The total quantity of refuse collected by Shelbyville city services this year will be no greater than that collected last year.

811. Veterinarians generally derive some of their income from selling several manufacturers' lines of pet-care products. Knowing that pet owners rarely throw away mail from their pet's veterinarian unread, one manufacturer of pet-care products offered free promotional materials on its products to veterinarians for mailing to their clients. Very few veterinarians accepted the offer, however, even though the manufacturer's products are of high quality.

Which of the following, if true, most helps to explain the veterinarians' reaction to the manufacturer's promotional scheme?

(A)   Most of the veterinarians to whom the free promotional materials were offered were already selling the manufacturer's pet-care products to their clients.

(B)   The special promotional materials were intended as a supplement to the manufacturer's usual promotional activities rather than as a replacement for them.

(C)   The manufacturer's products, unlike most equally good competing products sold by veterinarians, are also available in pet stores and in supermarkets.

(D)   Many pet owners have begun demanding quality in products they buy for their pets that is as high as that in products they buy for themselves.

(E)   Veterinarians sometimes recommend that pet owners use products formulated for people when no suitable product specially formulated for animals is available.

812. The average hourly wage of television assemblers in Vernland has long been significantly lower than that in neighboring Borodia. Since Borodia dropped all tariffs on Vernlandian televisions three years ago, the number of televisions sold annually in Borodia has not changed. However, recent statistics show a drop in the number of television assemblers in Borodia. Therefore, updated trade statistics will probably indicate that the number of televisions Borodia imports annually from Vernland has increased.

Which of the following is an assumption on which the argument depends?

(A)   The number of television assemblers in Vernland has increased by at least as much as the number of television assemblers in Borodia has decreased.

(B)   Televisions assembled in Vernland have features that televisions assembled in Borodia do not have.

(C)   The average number of hours it takes a Borodian television assembler to assemble a television has not decreased significantly during the past three years.

(D)   The number of televisions assembled annually in Vernland has increased significantly during the past three years.

(E)   The difference between the hourly wage of television assemblers in Vernland and the hourly wage of television assemblers in Borodia is likely to decrease in the next few years.

813. Guidebook writer: I have visited hotels throughout the country and have noticed that in those built before 1930 the quality of the original carpentry work is generally superior to that in hotels built afterward. Clearly, carpenters working on hotels before 1930 typically worked with more skill, care, and effort than carpenters who have worked on hotels built subsequently.

Which of the following, if true, most seriously weakens the guidebook writer's argument?

(A)   The quality of original carpentry in hotels is generally far superior to the quality of original carpentry in other structures, such as houses and stores.

(B)   Hotels built since 1930 can generally accommodate more guests than those built before 1930.

(C)   The materials available to carpenters working before 1930 were not significantly different in quality from the materials available to carpenters working after 1930.

(D)   The better the quality of original carpentry in a building, the less likely that building is to fall into disuse and be demolished.

(E)   The average length of apprenticeship for carpenters has declined significantly since 1930.

814. Most of Western music since the Renaissance has been based on a seven-note scale known as the diatonic scale, but when did the scale originate? A fragment of a bone flute excavated at a Neanderthal campsite has four holes, which are spaced in exactly the right way for playing the third through sixth notes of a diatonic scale. **The entire flute must surely have had more holes**, and the flute was made from a bone that was long enough for these additional holes to have allowed a complete diatonic scale to be played. Therefore, **the Neanderthals who made the flute probably used a diatonic musical scale**.

In the argument given, the two portions in **boldface** play which of the following roles?

(A) The first is presented as evidence that is confirmed by data presented elsewhere in the argument given; the second states a hypothesis this evidence is used to undermine.

(B) The first is an opinion for which no supporting evidence is presented in the argument given, which is used to support the main conclusion of the argument; the second is that main conclusion.

(C) The first describes a discovery as undermining the position against which the argument is directed; the second states the main conclusion of the argument.

(D) The first is a preliminary conclusion drawn on the basis of evidence presented elsewhere in the argument given; the second is the main conclusion this preliminary conclusion supports.

(E) The first provides evidence to support the main conclusion of the argument; the second states a subsidiary conclusion that is drawn in order to support the main conclusion stated earlier in the argument.

815. NorthAir charges low fares for its economy-class seats, but it provides very cramped seating and few amenities. Market research shows that economy passengers would willingly pay more for wider seating and better service, and additional revenue provided by these higher ticket prices would more than cover the additional cost of providing these amenities. Even though NorthAir is searching for ways to improve its profitability, it has decided not to make these improvements.

Which of the following, if true, would most help to explain NorthAir's decision in light of its objectives?

(A) None of NorthAir's competitors offers significantly better seating and service to economy-class passengers than NorthAir does.

(B) On many of the routes that NorthAir flies, it is the only airline to offer direct flights.

(C) A few of NorthAir's economy-class passengers are satisfied with the service they receive, given the low price they pay.

(D) Very few people avoid flying on NorthAir because of the cramped seating and poor service offered in economy class.

(E) The number of people who would be willing to pay the high fares NorthAir charges for its business-class seats would decrease if its economy-class seating were more acceptable.

816. Which of the following most logically completes the argument given?

Asthma, a chronic breathing disorder, is significantly more common today among adult competitive swimmers than it is among competitive athletes who specialize in other sports. Although chlorine is now known to be a lung irritant and swimming pool water is generally chlorinated, it would be rash to assume that frequent exposure to chlorine is the explanation of the high incidence of asthma among these swimmers, since _____.

(A) young people who have asthma are no more likely to become competitive athletes than are young people who do not have asthma

(B) competitive athletes who specialize in sports other than swimming are rarely exposed to chlorine

(C) competitive athletes as a group have a significantly lower incidence of asthma than do people who do not participate in competitive athletics

(D) until a few years ago, physicians routinely recommended competitive swimming to children with asthma, in the belief that this form of exercise could alleviate asthma symptoms

(E) many people have asthma without knowing they have it and thus are not diagnosed with the condition until they begin engaging in very strenuous activities, such as competitive athletics

817. In the country of Marut, the Foreign Trade Agency's records were reviewed in 1994 in light of information then newly available about neighboring Goro. The review revealed that in every year since 1963, the agency's projection of what Goro's gross national product (GNP) would be five years later was a serious underestimate. The review also revealed that in every year since 1963, the agency estimated Goro's GNP for the previous year—a Goro state secret—very accurately.

Of the following claims, which is most strongly supported by the statements given?

(A) Goro's GNP fluctuated greatly between 1963 and 1994.

(B) Prior to 1995, Goro had not released data intended to mislead the agency in making its five-year projections.

(C) The amount by which the agency underestimated the GNP it projected for Goro tended to increase over time.

(D) Even before the new information came to light, the agency had reason to think that at least some of the five-year projections it had made were inaccurate.

(E) The agency's five-year projections of Goro's GNP had no impact on economic planning in Marut.

818. In Colorado subalpine meadows, nonnative dandelions co-occur with a native flower, the larkspur. Bumblebees visit both species, creating the potential for interactions between the two species with respect to pollination. In a recent study, researchers selected 16 plots containing both species; all dandelions were removed from eight plots; the remaining eight control plots were left undisturbed. The control plots yielded significantly more larkspur seeds than the dandelion-free plots, leading the researchers to conclude that the presence of dandelions facilitates pollination (and hence seed production) in the native species by attracting more pollinators to the mixed plots.

Which of the following, if true, most seriously undermines the researchers' reasoning?

(A) Bumblebees preferentially visit dandelions over larkspurs in mixed plots.

(B) In mixed plots, pollinators can transfer pollen from one species to another to augment seed production.

(C) If left unchecked, nonnative species like dandelions quickly crowd out native species.

(D) Seed germination is a more reliable measure of a species' fitness than seed production.

(E) Soil disturbances can result in fewer blooms, and hence lower seed production.

819. Paleontologist: About 2.8 million years ago, many species that lived near the ocean floor suffered substantial population declines. These declines coincided with the onset of an ice age. The notion that cold killed those bottom-dwelling creatures outright is misguided, however; temperatures near the ocean floor would have changed very little. Nevertheless, **the cold probably did cause the population declines, though indirectly**. Many bottom-dwellers depended on plankton, small organisms that lived close to the surface and sank to the bottom when they died, for food. **Most probably, the plankton suffered a severe population decline as a result of sharply lower temperatures at the surface,** depriving many bottom-dwellers of food.

In the paleontologist's reasoning, the two portions in **boldface** play which of the following roles?

(A) The first introduces the hypothesis proposed by the paleontologist; the second is a judgment offered in spelling out that hypothesis.

(B) The first introduces the hypothesis proposed by the paleontologist; the second is a position the paleontologist opposes.

(C) The first is an explanation challenged by the paleontologist; the second is an explanation proposed by the paleontologist.

(D) The first is a judgment advanced in support of a conclusion reached by the paleontologist; the second is that conclusion.

(E) The first is a generalization put forward by the paleontologist; the second presents certain exceptional cases in which that generalization does not hold.

820. With seventeen casinos, Moneyland operates the most casinos in a certain state. Although intent on expanding, it was outmaneuvered by Apex Casinos in negotiations to acquire the Eldorado chain. To complete its acquisition of Eldorado, Apex must sell five casinos to comply with a state law forbidding any owner to operate more than one casino per county. Since Apex will still be left operating twenty casinos in the state, it will then have the most casinos in the state.

Which of the following, if true, most seriously undermines the prediction?

(A) Apex, Eldorado, and Moneyland are the only organizations licensed to operate casinos in the state.

(B) The majority of Eldorado's casinos in the state will need extensive renovations if they are to continue to operate profitably.

(C) Some of the state's counties do not permit casinos.

(D) Moneyland already operates casinos in the majority of the state's counties.

(E) Apex will use funds it obtains from the sale of the five casinos to help fund its acquisition of the Eldorado chain.

821. It is widely assumed that people need to engage in intellectual activities such as solving crossword puzzles or mathematics problems in order to maintain mental sharpness as they age. In fact, however, simply talking to other people—that is, participating in social interaction, which engages many mental and perceptual skills—suffices. Evidence to this effect comes from a study showing that the more social contact people report, the better their mental skills.

Which of the following, if true, most seriously weakens the force of the evidence cited?

(A) As people grow older, they are often advised to keep exercising their physical and mental capacities in order to maintain or improve them.

(B) Many medical conditions and treatments that adversely affect a person's mental sharpness also tend to increase that person's social isolation.

(C) Many people are proficient both in social interactions and in solving mathematical problems.

(D) The study did not itself collect data but analyzed data bearing on the issue from prior studies.

(E) The tasks evaluating mental sharpness for which data were compiled by the study were more akin to mathematics problems than to conversation.

822. In the United States, of the people who moved from one state to another when they retired, the percentage who retired to Florida has decreased by three percentage points over the past ten years. Since many local businesses in Florida cater to retirees, these declines are likely to have a noticeably negative economic effect on these businesses and therefore on the economy of Florida.

Which of the following, if true, most seriously weakens the argument given?

(A) People who moved from one state to another when they retired moved a greater distance, on average, last year than such people did ten years ago.

(B) People were more likely to retire to North Carolina from another state last year than people were ten years ago.

(C) The number of people who moved from one state to another when they retired has increased significantly over the past ten years.

(D) The number of people who left Florida when they retired to live in another state was greater last year than it was ten years ago.

(E) Florida attracts more people who move from one state to another when they retire than does any other state.

823. Which of the following most logically completes the passage?

The figures in portraits by the Spanish painter El Greco (1541–1614) are systematically elongated. In El Greco's time, the intentional distortion of human figures was unprecedented in European painting. Consequently, some critics have suggested that El Greco had an astigmatism, a type of visual impairment, that resulted in people appearing to him in the distorted way that is characteristic of his paintings. However, this suggestion cannot be the explanation, because _____.

(A) several twentieth-century artists have consciously adopted from El Greco's paintings the systematic elongation of the human form

(B)   some people do have elongated bodies somewhat like those depicted in El Greco's portraits

(C)   if El Greco had an astigmatism, then, relative to how people looked to him, the elongated figures in his paintings would have appeared to him to be distorted

(D)   even if El Greco had an astigmatism, there would have been no correction for it available in the period in which he lived

(E)   there were non-European artists, even in El Greco's time, who included in their works human figures that were intentionally distorted

824. Museums that house Renaissance oil paintings typically store them in environments that are carefully kept within narrow margins of temperature and humidity to inhibit any deterioration. Laboratory tests have shown that the kind of oil paint used in these paintings actually adjusts to climatic changes quite well. If, as some museum directors believe, **paint is the most sensitive substance in these works**, then by relaxing the standards for temperature and humidity control, **museums can reduce energy costs without risking damage to these paintings.** Museums would be rash to relax those standards, however, since results of preliminary tests indicate that gesso, a compound routinely used by Renaissance artists to help paint adhere to the canvas, is unable to withstand significant variations in humidity.

In the argument above, the two portions in **boldface** play which of the following roles?

(A)   The first is an objection that has been raised against the position taken by the argument; the second is the position taken by the argument.

(B)   The first is the position taken by the argument; the second is the position that the argument calls into question.

(C)   The first is a judgment that has been offered in support of the position that the argument calls into question; the second is a circumstance on which that judgment is, in part, based.

(D)   The first is a judgment that has been offered in support of the position that the argument calls into question; the second is that position.

(E)   The first is a claim that the argument calls into question; the second is the position taken by the argument.

825. Excavations of the Roman city of Sepphoris have uncovered numerous detailed mosaics depicting several readily identifiable animal species: a hare, a partridge, and various Mediterranean fish. Oddly, most of the species represented did not live in the Sepphoris region when these mosaics were created. Since identical motifs appear in mosaics found in other Roman cities, however, the mosaics of Sepphoris were very likely created by traveling artisans from some other part of the Roman Empire.

Which of the following is an assumption on which the argument depends?

(A)   The Sepphoris mosaics are not composed exclusively of types of stones found naturally in the Sepphoris area.

(B)   There is no single region to which all the species depicted in the Sepphoris mosaics are native.

(C)   No motifs appear in the Sepphoris mosaics that do not also appear in the mosaics of some other Roman city.

(D)   All of the animal figures in the Sepphoris mosaics are readily identifiable as representations of known species.

(E)   There was not a common repertory of mosaic designs with which artisans who lived in various parts of the Roman Empire were familiar.

826. As a large corporation in a small country, Hachnut wants its managers to have international experience, so **each year it sponsors management education abroad for its management trainees.** Hachnut has found, however, that the attrition rate of graduates from this program is very high, with many of them leaving Hachnut to join competing firms soon after completing the program. Hachnut does use performance during the program as a criterion in deciding among candidates for management positions, but **both this function and the goal of providing international experience could be achieved in other ways.** Therefore, if the attrition problem cannot be successfully addressed, Hachnut should discontinue the sponsorship program.

In the argument given, the two **boldfaced** portions play which of the following roles?

(A)   The first describes a practice that the argument seeks to justify; the second states a judgment that is used in support of a justification for that practice.

(B)   The first describes a practice that the argument seeks to explain; the second presents part of the argument's explanation of that practice.

(C)   The first introduces a practice that the argument seeks to evaluate; the second provides grounds for holding that the practice cannot achieve its objective.

(D)   The first introduces a policy that the argument seeks to evaluate; the second provides grounds for holding that the policy is not needed.

(E)   The first introduces a consideration supporting a policy that the argument seeks to evaluate; the second provides evidence for concluding that the policy should be abandoned.

827.   Letter to the editor: If the water level in the Searle River Delta continues to drop, the rising sea level will make the water saltier and less suitable for drinking. Currently, 40 percent of the water from upstream tributaries is diverted to neighboring areas. To keep the delta's water level from dropping any further, we should end all current diversions from the upstream tributaries. Neighboring water utilities are likely to see higher costs and diminished water supplies, but these costs are necessary to preserve the delta.

Which of the following would, if true, indicate a serious potential weakness of the suggested plan of action?

(A)   Desalination equipment would allow water from the delta to be used for drinking even it if became saltier.

(B)   Water level is only one factor that affects salinity in the delta.

(C)   The upstream tributaries' water levels are controlled by systems of dams and reservoirs.

(D)   Neighboring areas have grown in population since the water was first diverted from upstream tributaries.

(E)   Much of the recent drop in the delta's water level can be attributed to a prolonged drought that has recently ended.

828.   In 1960s studies of rats, scientists found that crowding increases the number of attacks among the animals significantly. But in recent experiments in which rhesus monkeys were placed in crowded conditions, although there was an increase in instances of "coping" behavior—such as submissive gestures and avoidance of dominant individuals—attacks did not become any more frequent. Therefore it is not likely that, for any species of monkey, crowding increases aggression as significantly as was seen in rats.

Which of the following, if true, most strengthens the argument?

(A)   All the observed forms of coping behavior can be found among rhesus monkeys living in uncrowded conditions.

(B)   In the studies of rats, nondominant individuals were found to increasingly avoid dominant individuals when the animals were in crowded conditions.

(C)   Rhesus monkeys respond with aggression to a wider range of stimuli than any other monkeys do.

(D)   Some individual monkeys in the experiments were involved in significantly more attacks than the other monkeys were.

(E)   Some of the coping behavior displayed by rhesus monkeys is similar to behavior rhesus monkeys use to bring to an end an attack that has begun.

829.   **In countries where automobile insurance includes compensation for whiplash injuries sustained in automobile accidents, reports of having suffered such injuries are twice as frequent as they are in countries where whiplash is not covered.** Presently, no objective test for whiplash exists, so it is true that spurious reports of whiplash injuries cannot be readily identified. Nevertheless, **these facts do not warrant a conclusion that has been drawn by some commentators:** that in the countries with the higher rates of reported whiplash injuries, half of the reported cases are spurious. Clearly, in countries where automobile insurance does not include compensation for whiplash, people often have little incentive to report whiplash injuries that they actually have suffered.

In the argument given, the two **boldfaced** portions play which of the following roles?

(A) The first is a claim that the argument disputes; the second is a conclusion that has been based on that claim.

(B) The first is a claim that has been used to support a position that the argument accepts; the second is a position that the argument rejects.

(C) The first is a finding whose accuracy is evaluated in the argument; the second is the judgment reached by the argument concerning the accuracy of the finding.

(D) The first is a finding whose implications are at issue in the argument; the second is the judgment reached by the argument concerning one alleged implication.

(E) The first is a finding, the explanation of which is at issue in the argument; the second is an objection that has been raised against the explanation that the argument defends.

830. Twenty years ago, Balzania put in place regulations requiring operators of surface mines to pay for the reclamation of mined-out land. Since then, reclamation technology has not improved. Yet, the average reclamation cost for a surface coal mine being reclaimed today is only four dollars per ton of coal that the mine produced, less than half what it cost to reclaim surface mines in the years immediately after the regulations took effect.

Which of the following, if true, most helps to account for the drop in reclamation costs described?

(A) Even after Balzania began requiring surface mine operators to pay reclamation costs, coal mines in Balzania continued to be less expensive to operate than coal mines in almost any other country.

(B) Even after Balzania began requiring surface mine operators to pay reclamation costs, surface mines continued to produce coal at a lower total cost than underground mines.

(C) As compared to 20 years ago, a greater percentage of the coal mined in Balzania today comes from surface mines.

(D) Over the last 20 years, mine operators have generally located new surface coal mines in areas with flat terrain that makes reclamation easy.

(E) In the 20 years since the regulations took effect, the use of coal as a fuel has declined from the level it was at in the previous 20 years.

831. In a study conducted in Pennsylvania, servers in various restaurants wrote "Thank you" on randomly selected bills before presenting the bills to their customers. Tips on these bills were an average of three percentage points higher than tips on bills without the message. Therefore, if all servers in Pennsylvania regularly wrote "Thank you" on restaurant bills, tips left in Pennsylvania would increase by about three percentage points, on average.

Which of the following is an assumption on which the argument relies?

(A) No more than a small proportion of food servers in Pennsylvania currently write "Thank you" on restaurant bills.

(B) Most patrons of Pennsylvania restaurants will notice the written "Thank you" on their bills.

(C) The written "Thank you" reminds restaurant patrons that tips constitute a significant part of the income of many food servers.

(D) The rate at which people tip food servers in Pennsylvania does not vary with how expensive a restaurant is.

(E) The "Thank you" messages will have the same impact on regular restaurant patrons as they will on occasional patrons.

832. Historian: In the Drindian Empire, a census was conducted annually to determine the adult population of each village. Until 1700, the central government used annual census figures to assess the tax a village owed. Since an increase in population would mean an increase in tax, villages would have a strong economic incentive to try to minimize the number of people recorded. Therefore, it was probably common for census figures from a village to underreport its population significantly.

Which of the following, if true, most strengthens the historian's argument?

(A) After 1700, the census figures for the adult populations of villages did not rise faster than would be expected as a result of normal population growth.

(B) Before 1700, increases in tax rates were often followed by a larger-than-usual number of villages reporting a lower population than the year before.

(C) The official tax and census records for a village in the Drindian Empire were never stored in that village.

(D) Pre-1700 census figures from individual villages sometimes show significant declines in the adult population from one year to the next.

(E) It would have been impossible for villages to conceal from the central government's census takers all additions to their village's population.

833. Advertisement: Ten years ago, the Cormond Hotel's lobby was carpeted with Duratex carpet, and the lobby of the Bromley Hotel was carpeted with our competitor's most durable carpet. Since then, thousands more people have stayed at the Cormond than at the Bromley, yet the carpet in the Bromley lobby has worn out, while the Cormond's Duratex carpeting has years of wear left in it. Clearly, Duratex is more durable than any of our competitor's carpets.

Which of the following, if true, most strengthens the argument of the advertisement?

(A) Duratex is the most durable kind of carpet that its manufacturer makes.

(B) In neither the Bromley nor the Cormond is the lobby used heavily by people who are not staying at the hotel.

(C) On average, carpeting in hotel lobbies wears out in seven years.

(D) At a third hotel, carpet of the same kind as that installed in the lobby of the Bromley ten years ago is being replaced after only five years of use.

(E) The Bromley is not only going to have its lobby carpeting replaced, but is also going to have its lobby remodeled.

834. Lyme disease is caused by a bacterium transmitted to humans by deer ticks. Generally deer ticks pick up the bacterium while in the larval stage from feeding on infected white-footed mice. However, certain other species on which the larvae feed do not harbor the bacterium. Therefore, if the population of these other species were increased, the number of ticks acquiring the bacterium—and hence the number of people contracting Lyme disease—would likely decline.

Which of the following, if true, most strengthens the argument?

(A) Ticks do not suffer any adverse consequences from carrying the bacterium that causes Lyme disease in humans.

(B) There are no known cases of a human's contracting Lyme disease through contact with white-footed mice.

(C) A deer tick feeds only once while in the larval stage.

(D) A single host animal can be the source of bacteria for many tick larvae.

(E) None of the other species on which deer tick larvae feed harbor other bacteria that ticks transmit to humans.

835. Museums that house Renaissance oil paintings typically store them in environments that are carefully kept within narrow margins of temperature and humidity to inhibit any deterioration. Laboratory tests have shown that the kind of oil paint used in these paintings actually adjusts to climatic changes quite well. If paint is the most sensitive substance in these works, then by relaxing the standards for temperature and humidity control as some museum directors suggest, **museums can reduce energy costs without risking damage to these paintings**. Museums would be rash to relax those standards, however, since results of preliminary tests indicate that **gesso, a compound routinely used by Renaissance artists to help paint adhere to the canvas, is unable to withstand significant variations in humidity**.

In the argument above, the two portions in **boldface** play which of the following roles?

(A) The first is a position that the argument calls into question; the second is an alternative position endorsed by the argument.

(B)   The first is a position that the argument calls into question; the second is evidence put forward by the argument to challenge that position.

(C)   The first is a position that the argument calls into question; the second is evidence that has been used to support that position.

(D)   The first is the position taken by the argument; the second provides evidence to support that position.

(E)   The first is the position taken by the argument; the second is evidence that has been used to challenge that position.

836. Most of Western music since the Renaissance has been based on a seven-note scale known as the diatonic scale, but when did the scale originate? A fragment of a bone flute excavated at a Neanderthal campsite has four holes, which are spaced in exactly the right way for playing the third through sixth notes of a diatonic scale. **The entire flute must surely have had more holes**, and examination of the find shows that **the flute was made from a bone that was long enough for these additional holes to have allowed a complete diatonic scale to be played**. Therefore, the Neanderthals who made the flute probably used a diatonic musical scale.

In the argument given, the two portions in **boldface** play which of the following roles?

(A)   The first states the hypothesis that the argument seeks to support; the second presents evidence to support a conclusion that, in turn, supports the argument's main conclusion.

(B)   The first states the hypothesis that the argument seeks to support; the second introduces evidence that has been used to argue against the argument's main conclusion.

(C)   The first is a judgment that is used to support the main conclusion of the argument; the second introduces evidence to support that conclusion.

(D)   The first is a judgment that is used to support the main conclusion of the argument; the second presents evidence restricting the scope of that judgment.

(E)   The first is a conclusion drawn on the basis of evidence stated elsewhere in the argument; the second is the argument's main conclusion.

837. Woodco Plywood Manufacturer: Ten years ago a study linked the high rates of respiratory ailments in Loganville to airborne pollutants released in the manufacture of plywood. In response, the city government imposed strict regulations on emissions from our plant, which we have followed at great cost to our production capacity. But after an initial dip, the rate of respiratory ailments rose to new levels, so the high rate was never a result of pollution from our plant.

Which of the following, if true, most seriously weakens the argument?

(A)   Over the last decade, a series of studies linking respiratory ailments to dietary deficiencies has been published.

(B)   Seven years ago, the Woodco plant installed equipment to increase production capacity without increasing annual pollutant emissions.

(C)   Pollutant emissions at Woodco plywood plants in other towns have declined during the past twelve years.

(D)   Nine years ago, a competing plywood manufacturer opened a plant just across the river from Woodco's plant.

(E)   There are more facilities for treating respiratory ailments in Loganville today than there were eleven years ago.

838. Journalist: **Every election year at this time the state government releases the financial disclosures that potential candidates must make in order to be eligible to run for office.** Among those making a financial disclosure this year is, for the first time ever, the prominent local businessman Arnold Bergeron. There has often been talk in the past of Mr. Bergeron's running for governor, not least from Mr. Bergeron himself. This year it is likely he finally will, since even supporters of a Bergeron candidacy always conceded that **the necessity of making financial disclosures might have proved an insuperable obstacle.**

In the journalist's argument, the two **boldfaced** portions play which of the following roles?

(A)   The first provides information without which the argument lacks force; the second states the journalist's conclusion.

(B)   The first provides information without which the argument lacks force; the second identifies a position that the journalist argues against.

(C)   The first provides information without which the argument lacks force; the second provides information that reinforces the journalist's argument.

(D)   The first provides evidence in support of the journalist's conclusion; the second states that conclusion.

(E)   The first provides evidence in support of the journalist's conclusion; the second provides evidence bearing against that conclusion.

839.   Rabbits were introduced to Numa Island in the nineteenth century. Overgrazing by the enormous population of rabbits now menaces the island's agriculture. The government proposes to reduce the population by using a virus that has caused devastating epidemics in rabbit populations elsewhere. There is, however, a chance that the virus will infect the bilby, an endangered native marsupial. The government's plan, therefore, may serve the interests of agriculture but will clearly increase the threat to native wildlife.

Which of the following, if true, most seriously weakens the argument?

(A)   There is less chance that the virus will infect domestic animals on Numa than that it will infect bilbies.

(B)   There are no species of animals on the island that prey on the rabbits.

(C)   Overgrazing by rabbits endangers many of the plants on which bilbies feed.

(D)   The virus that the government proposes to use has been successfully used elsewhere to control populations of rabbits.

(E)   There is no alternative means of reducing the rabbit population that would involve no threat to the bilby.

840.   Although utilities pay less for low-quality coal per ton delivered than for high-quality coal, more low-quality coal must be burned to generate the same amount of electricity. Therefore, the proper basis for a cost comparison at any given time is the relative cost, at that time, of purchasing the amount of coal a utility

needs to buy in order to generate a given amount of electricity.

Which of the following, if true, casts the most serious doubt on the accuracy of the conclusion above?

(A)   Per ton of coal burned, low-quality coal generates more ash than does high-quality coal, and the disposal of ash is becoming more expensive.

(B)   Many large industrial centers are located closer to geological deposits of high-quality coal than they are to geological deposits of low-quality coal.

(C)   Known reserves of low-quality coal are many times larger than known reserves of high-quality coal.

(D)   The price per ton of high-quality coal has been rising faster than the price per ton for low-quality coal, and this trend will continue.

(E)   Coal-fired power plants that burn low-quality coal efficiently also burn high-quality coal efficiently.

841.   Newspaper article: Pecan growers get a high price for their crop when pecans are comparatively scarce, but the price drops sharply when pecans are abundant. Thus, in high-yield years, growers often hold back part of their crop in refrigerated warehouses until after the following year's harvest, hoping for higher prices then. This year's pecan crop was the smallest in five years. It is unlikely, therefore, that any of this year's crop will be held back.

Which of the following, if true, most seriously weakens the argument?

(A)   Each of the last two years produced record-breaking pecan yields, and an unusually high percentage of last year's crop was held back.

(B)   The quality of this year's pecan crop is typical of the quality of the pecan crops of the previous five years.

(C)   Because of the practice of holding back part of the crop from especially high-yield years, pecan prices have not been subject to sharp fluctuations in recent years.

(D) For some pecan growers, this year's crop was no smaller than last year's.

(E) The last time the pecan crop was as small as it was this year, the practice of holding back part of one year's crop in anticipation of higher prices the next year had not yet become widespread.

842. **For most scientists, the period of highest creativity occurs before the age of forty.** It is commonly thought that this happens because the aging process brings about a loss of creative capacity. However, it turns out that almost all scientists who produce highly creative work beyond the age of forty entered their field late, less than a dozen years before their creative breakthroughs. Since **creative breakthroughs by scientists under forty also generally occur within a dozen years of the scientist's entry into the field,** it is most likely that the real reason why scientists over forty rarely produce highly creative work is not that they are too old but rather that they generally have spent too long in a given field.

In the argument given, the two portions in **boldface** play which of the following roles?

(A) The first presents a state of affairs, the explanation of which is at issue in the argument; the second provides evidence in support of the explanation that the argument seeks to establish.

(B) The first presents a state of affairs, the explanation of which is at issue in the argument; the second presents evidence that has been used to challenge the explanation that the argument favors.

(C) The first is the main conclusion of the argument; the second provides evidence in support of that main conclusion.

(D) The first is a claim that the argument seeks to refute; the second provides evidence in support of an alternative claim that the argument seeks to establish.

(E) The first is a generalization that, according to the argument, has exceptions; the second presents some of those exceptions.

843. Though sucking zinc lozenges has been promoted as a treatment for the common cold, research has revealed no consistent effect. Recently, however, a zinc gel applied nasally has been shown to greatly reduce the duration of colds. Since the gel contains zinc in the same form and concentration as the lozenges, the greater effectiveness of the gel must be due to the fact that cold viruses tend to concentrate in the nose, not the mouth.

In order to evaluate the argument, it would be most helpful to determine which of the following?

(A) Whether zinc is effective only against colds, or also has an effect on other virally caused diseases

(B) Whether there are remedies that do not contain zinc but that, when taken orally, can reduce the duration of colds

(C) Whether people who frequently catch colds have a zinc deficiency

(D) Whether either the zinc gel or the lozenges contain ingredients that have an impact on the activity of the zinc

(E) Whether the zinc gel has an effect on the severity of cold symptoms, as well as on their duration

844. An Italian map labeled "Mappamundi" ("Map of the world") is undated, but, based on its contents, was probably drawn sometime in the years 1488 to 1493. The map accurately depicts the western coast of Africa down to the Cape of Good Hope, which European explorers first reached in 1488, but it shows none of the islands of the West Indies visited by Columbus on his first voyage, from which he returned to Europe in early 1493.

Which of the following, if true, most strengthens the argument?

(A) European ships of the period required nearly a year to make the voyage to the Cape of Good Hope and back.

(B) Columbus published a widely read account of his first voyage immediately after his return.

(C) European authorities who sponsored expeditions often tried to keep information gained by those expeditions secret for as long as possible.

(D) A map as complicated as the map in question would have taken a cartographer of the 1400s several months to finish.

(E)   During his first voyage, Columbus was able to sail from the West Indies back to Europe in less than three months.

845.   In the year following an eight-cent increase in the federal tax on a pack of cigarettes, sales of cigarettes fell ten percent. In contrast, in the year prior to the tax increase, sales had fallen one percent. The volume of cigarette sales is therefore strongly related to the after-tax price of a pack of cigarettes.

The argument above requires which of the following assumptions?

(A)   During the year following the tax increase, the pretax price of a pack of cigarettes did not increase by as much as it had during the year prior to the tax increase.

(B)   The one percent fall in cigarette sales in the year prior to the tax increase was due to a smaller tax increase.

(C)   The pretax price of a pack of cigarettes gradually decreased throughout the year before and the year after the tax increase.

(D)   For the year following the tax increase, the pretax price of a pack of cigarettes was not eight or more cents lower than it had been the previous year.

(E)   As the after-tax price of a pack of cigarettes rises, the pretax price also rises.

846.   Which of the following most logically completes the argument below?

According to promotional material published by the city of Springfield, more tourists stay in hotels in Springfield than stay in the neighboring city of Harristown. A brochure from the largest hotel in Harristown claims that more tourists stay in that hotel than stay in the Royal Arms Hotel in Springfield. If both of these sources are accurate, however, the county's "Report on Tourism" must be in error in indicating that _____.

(A)   more tourists stay in hotel accommodations in Harristown than stay in the Royal Arms Hotel

(B)   the Royal Arms Hotel is the only hotel in Springfield

(C)   there are several hotels in Harristown that are larger than the Royal Arms Hotel

(D)   some of the tourists who have stayed in hotels in Harristown have also stayed in the Royal Arms Hotel

(E)   some hotels in Harristown have fewer tourist guests each year than the Royal Arms Hotel has

847.   The composer Pescard (1400–1474) is known to have been prolific, but little appears to have survived from the middle of Pescard's career (1440–1450). There are, however, many anonymous musical compositions from that decade, and modern scholarship has tentatively attributed several of them to Pescard. The recent attribution of one such piece, a particularly fine large-scale work, seems secure, being based on a newly discovered theoretical treatise from 1560 that names Pescard as that work's composer.

Which of the following, if true, would provide the most justification for judging secure modern scholarship's attribution of the large-scale work to Pescard?

(A)   The 1560 treatise considers many works from the 1400s about whose authorship modern scholars had reached agreement before the treatise was discovered, and its attribution of these works to composers never disagrees with that of modern scholars.

(B)   The 1560 treatise itself says that authorship of the work at issue is in dispute and attributes it to Pescard on the basis of a few stylistic features that turn out to be equally characteristic of other composers of the period.

(C)   There are many other compositions from the 1400s whose authorship is in dispute among modern scholars that the 1560 treatise attributes to named composers.

(D)   Around the time that the treatise was written, works were frequently attributed to prestigious composers, such as Pescard, simply because the person making the attribution thought well of the work.

(E)   There are stylistic features of the work at issue that although first appearing in Pescard's early works also appear both in works of Pescard's contemporaries and in later works by Pescard.

848. **Plant scientists have used genetic engineering on seeds to produce crop plants that are highly resistant to insect damage.** Unfortunately, the seeds themselves are quite expensive, and the plants require more fertilizer and water to grow well than normal ones. Thus, for most farmers the savings on pesticides would not compensate for the higher seed costs and the cost of additional fertilizer. However, since **consumer demand for grains, fruits, and vegetables grown without the use of pesticides continues to rise,** the use of genetically engineered seeds of this kind is likely to become widespread.

In the argument given, the two portions in **boldface** play which of the following roles?

(A) The first supplies a context for the argument; the second is evidence that would, if not offset by other evidence, call the conclusion of the argument into question.

(B) The first presents a situation that the argument assumes will develop in certain ways; the second is one of those ways.

(C) The first introduces a development that the argument predicts will have a certain impact; the second is a consideration on which that prediction is based.

(D) The first provides evidence to support a prediction defended by the argument; the second acknowledges a trend that could undermine the force of that evidence.

(E) The first provides evidence to support a prediction defended by the argument; the second is that prediction.

849. The percentage of households with an annual income of more than $40,000 is higher in Merton County than in any other county. However, the percentage of households with an annual income of $60,000 or more is highest in Sommer County.

If the statements above are true, which of the following can properly be concluded on the basis of them?

(A) No household in Merton County has an annual income of $60,000 or more.

(B) Some households in Merton County have an annual income between $40,000 and $60,000.

(C) The number of households with an annual income of more than $40,000 is greater in Merton than in Sommer County.

(D) Average annual household income is higher in Sommer than in Merton County.

(E) The percentage of households with an annual income of $80,000 is higher in Sommer than in Merton County.

850. The Shoemaker–Levy comet broke into fragments before colliding with Jupiter in 1994, but astronomers are uncertain of the fragments' size. Analysis of the ammonia clouds of Jupiter's outer atmosphere at the impact point showed traces of sulfur not normally present there. Since astronomers believe that the layer of clouds just below the outer atmosphere does contain sulfur, they concluded that the fragments must have been big enough to travel through the outer atmosphere before burning up.

Determining which of the following would be most useful in evaluating the astronomers' argument?

(A) Whether the ammonia clouds of Jupiter's outer atmosphere were of at least average thickness at the point of impact

(B) Whether the traces of sulfur detected in 1994 in the ammonia clouds have since disappeared

(C) Whether comets the size of Shoemaker–Levy typically break into fragments before colliding with a planet

(D) Whether comet fragments can release sulfur when they burn up

(E) Whether the comet fragments would have burned up sooner if they had struck at a different angle

8.8 Answer Key: Critical Reasoning

645. B	683. B	719. B	756. D	793. D	830. D
646. B	683. B	720. E	757. A	794. A	831. A
647. D	684. E	721. B	758. A	795. A	832. B
648. D	685. B	722. D	759. D	796. C	833. D
649. D	686. E	723. A	760. D	797. A	834. C
650. E	687. D	724. A	761. B	798. C	835. B
651. C	688. B	725. D	762. C	799. D	836. C
652. C	689. D	726. A	763. D	800. C	837. D
653. D	690. D	727. A	764. B	801. D	838. C
654. A	691. B	728. E	765. D	802. C	839. C
655. D	692. A	729. B	766. D	803. B	840. A
656. B	693. B	730. C	767. B	804. C	841. A
657. C	694. C	731. D	768. B	805. A	842. A
658. E	695. C	732. C	769. B	806. C	843. D
659. B	696. C	733. B	770. C	807. B	844. B
660. B	697. A	734. C	771. D	808. D	845. A
661. B	698. E	735. D	772. D	809. B	846. B
662. C	699. B	736. E	773. B	810. B	847. A
663. E	700. E	737. C	774. E	811. A	848. C
664. C	701. B	738. D	775. B	812. C	849. B
665. E	702. C	739. C	776. A	813. A	850. D
666. C	703. D	740. D	777. B	814. B	
667. A	704. B	741. A	778. E	815. E	
668. C	705. A	742. E	779. C	816. C	
669. A	706. B	743. E	780. E	817. D	
670. D	707. C	744. C	781. D	818. E	
671. B	708. A	745. A	782. D	819. D	
672. D	709. E	746. C	783. A	820. A	
673. E	710. E	747. B	784. B	821. C	
674. D	711. B	748. D	785. A	822. A	
675. A	712. E	749. B	786. E	823. C	
676. C	713. D	750. D	787. E	824. A	
677. B	714. E	751. B	788. E	825. A	
678. A	715. C	752. C	789. B	826. D	
679. C	716. B	753. D	790. E	827. A	
680. C	717. C	754. E	791. D	828. C	
681. E	718. C	755. C	792. B	829. D	

8.9 Answer Explanations: Critical Reasoning

The following discussion is intended to familiarize you with the most efficient and effective approaches to Critical Reasoning questions. The particular questions in this chapter are generally representative of the kinds of Critical Reasoning questions you will encounter on the GMAT exam. Remember that it is the problem-solving strategy that is important, not the specific details of a particular question.

Questions 645–707 — Difficulty: Easy

645. Ramirez: The film industry claims that pirated DVDs, which are usually cheaper than legitimate DVDs and become available well before a film's official DVD release date, adversely affect its bottom line. But the industry should note what the spread of piracy indicates: consumers want lower prices and faster DVD releases. Lowering prices of DVDs and releasing them sooner would mitigate piracy's negative effect on film industry profits.

The argument above relies on which of the following assumptions?

(A) Releasing legitimate DVDs earlier would not cause any reduction in the revenue the film industry receives from the films' theatrical release.

(B) Some people who would otherwise purchase pirated DVDs would be willing to purchase legitimate DVDs if they were less expensive and released earlier than they are now.

(C) The film industry will in the future be able to produce DVDs more cheaply than is currently the case.

(D) Some current sellers of pirated DVDs would likely discontinue their businesses if legitimate DVDs were released faster and priced lower.

(E) Current purchasers of pirated DVDs are aware that those DVDs are not authorized by the film industry.

Argument Construction

Situation Pirated DVDs of films are released earlier than the film's official DVD release day. They are also sold more cheaply. These practices cut into the revenue expected from a film's official DVD sales. According to Ramirez, the prevalence of piracy indicates that consumers want lower prices and earlier releases. Ramirez concludes that if the official DVDs were sold more cheaply and released earlier, the impact of piracy on film industry profits might be reduced.

Reasoning *What must Ramirez assume for the argument to be logically correct?* To evaluate which answer choice the argument relies on assuming, ask yourself about each answer choice, "If this statement were false, then would the argument's conclusion also have to be false?" If the answer is yes, then the argument must be making that assumption. For example, suppose the statement made in answer choice B were false. That would mean that none of the people who would otherwise purchase pirated DVDs would be willing to purchase legitimate DVDs even if these were released earlier and at a significantly lower price. If that were so, then the measures Ramirez suggests would not mitigate piracy.

A This does not have to be assumed for Ramirez's reasoning to be logically good. Earlier release of the official DVDs at a lower price could somewhat reduce revenue from movie theater showings of the films. But if the revenue from official DVDs released earlier and priced lower were greatly boosted through greatly increased official DVD sales, overall revenue for each film could be higher than would be the case with widespread piracy.

B **Correct.** If all existing purchasers of pirated film DVDs continued to purchase such DVDs even after implementation of the changes Ramirez advocates, then the changes would not mitigate the destructive consequences of piracy. Thus, Ramirez's reasoning must assume that the recommended changes would cause at least some former purchasers of pirated DVDs to begin purchasing the official DVDs.

C This might improve profits provided revenue did not also decline. Ramirez's argument does not depend on the assumption that the cost of producing DVDs will decline. Ramirez's reasoning assumes that total sales volume for official DVDs would increase if piracy were reduced.

D   Ideally, this would occur with the change Ramirez recommends, but it does not have to be assumed for Ramirez's reasoning to be logically sound. For example, the result Ramirez predicts could occur if all existing sellers of pirated DVDs continued to sell them but sold fewer.

E   This is likely true but is not an assumption that Ramirez needs to make for the reasoning to be logically sound. Even if some DVDs sold by DVD sellers were pirated without the sellers being aware of it, e.g., if they purchased them from a fraudulent wholesaler, the fact that the pirated DVDs are sold more cheaply and before the release of the official DVD would reduce the filmmakers' total revenue.

The correct answer is B.

646. Harunia Province has a relatively dry climate and is attracting a fast-growing population that has put increasing demands on its water supply. The two companies that supply water to the region have struggled to keep up with demand and still remain profitable. Yet now they are asking Harunian authorities to write residential water-use regulations that could reduce their revenues and restrict their future flexibility in supplying water profitably.

Which of the following would, if true, most logically help explain why the water-supply companies are asking the authorities to regulate residential water use?

(A) The companies are planning large water-transportation and irrigation systems that require the approval of neighboring provinces.

(B) The companies believe regulation is inevitable and that having it in place now will allow better planning and thus future profitability.

(C) Few, if any, Harunian government officials have investments in the companies or serve on their boards of directors.

(D) The companies believe that the population is not likely to continue to grow.

(E) Long-term climate projections suggest that greater rainfall will eventually increase the amount of water available.

Argument Construction

Situation   Two water-supply companies are asking the authorities in Harunia Province to regulate residential water use, even though regulation could reduce their revenues and restrict their flexibility in supplying water profitably in the future.

Reasoning   *Which piece of information would most help explain why the companies are advocating water-use regulations that would restrict their operations?* The companies are already struggling to keep up with demand from a fast-growing population in the region. So why would they advocate regulations that could, at least in the immediate term, reduce their profits and restrict them? Is there any advantage that the companies perceive—an advantage that would outweigh any disadvantages—in getting regulations instituted soon?

A   It is unclear how this information bears on the companies' request for regulations in Harunia Province, since neighboring provinces seem primarily involved.

B   **Correct.** The companies presumably must strategically plan their capital investments to cope with increasing water demand in Harunia Province and to receive adequate return on that investment. In that context it seems critically important for the companies to have certainty at the planning stage about future regulatory requirements. Moreover, given possible shortfalls in water supply, the companies would reasonably expect government regulation even if they did not request it.

C   This suggests that, in framing water regulations, Harunian government officials will not be influenced by financial interests, so the companies cannot expect to obtain special favors from the regulatory authorities in the framing of water regulations.

D   If anything, this suggests that the companies could continue to operate without any regulatory regime that might restrict their operations.

E   This would presumably result in a weakening of the case for residential water-use regulation and would also make it easier for the water-supply companies to meet demand.

The correct answer is B.

647. Loss of the Gocha mangrove forests has caused coastal erosion, reducing fish populations and requiring the Gocha Fishing Cooperative (GFC) to partially fund dredging and new shore facilities. However, as part of its subsidiary businesses, the GFC has now invested in a program to replant significant parts of the coast with mangrove trees. Given income from a controlled harvest of wood with continuing replanting, the mangrove regeneration effort makes it more likely that the cooperative will increase its net income.

Which of the following, if true, would most strengthen the argument that mangrove replanting will increase the Gocha cooperative's net income?

(A) The cost of dredging and shore facilities was shared with the local government.

(B) The GFC will be able to hire local workers to assist with the mangrove replanting.

(C) The GFC derives 10 percent of its revenue from salt-production facilities in an area previously cleared of mangroves.

(D) Mangrove forests tend to increase the commercial fish populations in coastal fishing grounds.

(E) A controlled harvesting of mangrove wood by the GFC would have little effect on coastal erosion.

Argument Evaluation

Situation   A subsidiary business of the Gocha Fishing Cooperative (GFC) has invested in a program to replant significant parts of the coast with mangrove trees.

Reasoning   *What additional information, if true, would most strengthen the argument's support for the conclusion that the mangrove regeneration effort will increase the GFC's net income?* If the regeneration effort helped the GFC's fishing operations, this could lead to an increase in GFC's income.

A   If the local government helped with the cost of dredging and shore facilities, that would help reduce the GFC's costs, but that is not directly related to the impact of the GFC's mangrove regeneration effort on GFC's net income.

B   It is unclear whether hiring local workers to assist with mangrove replanting would be less costly than hiring workers from elsewhere, so it is unclear whether this would help the GFC increase its net income.

C   The information provided does not indicate whether the mangrove regeneration effort will have any effect on its salt-production facilities, or any revenue or profit that it derives from these facilities, so this does not strengthen the argument.

D   Correct. If the mangrove restoration effort helps increase the commercial fish population in coastal fishing grounds, then there is a good chance that the GFC's income from its fishing operations will increase as a result.

E   The information provided does not indicate what, if any, effect coastal erosion has on GFC's net income, so the fact that controlled harvesting of mangrove wood would have little effect on coastal erosion does not strengthen the argument.

The correct answer is D.

648. Executives at the Fizzles Beverage Company plan to boost profits in Country X on their range of fruit-flavored drinks by introducing new flavors based on tropical fruits that are little known there. The executives reason that since the fruit drinks of other companies have none of these flavors, Fizzles will not have to compete for customers and thus will be able to sell the drinks at a higher price.

Which of the following, if true, presents the most serious potential weakness of the plan?

(A) The new fruit drinks would be priced significantly higher than other Fizzles fruit drinks with more conventional flavors.

(B) In a telephone survey, at least one of the consumers contacted said that they preferred many of the new flavors to all of the more familiar flavors.

(C) To build widespread demand for the new flavors, Fizzles would have to launch an advertising campaign to familiarize consumers with them.

(D) Consumers choosing among fruit-flavored drinks of different brands generally buy on the basis of name recognition and price rather than the specific fruit flavor.

(E) Few consumers who are loyal to a specific brand of fruit-flavored drinks would willingly switch to another brand that costs more.

Evaluation of a Plan

Situation   Fizzle Beverage Company's executives plan to offer drinks with tropical fruit flavors that are little known in Country X in the hope that doing so will boost profits in that country. They reason that because their competitors in that country do not offer drinks with these flavors, Fizzle will be able to sell the drinks at a premium price.

Reasoning   *What casts the most doubt on the claim that the executives' plan will effectively allow them to sell fruit-flavored drinks at a higher price?* The executives believe that the lack of a direct competitor to these drinks will allow the company to sell the drinks for a higher price. But any information indicating that something other than the specific fruit flavor of the drink drives sales of fruit-flavored drinks would cast doubt on the plan.

A   We have already been told that the prices will be higher. The question is whether they will be able to sell the drink successfully at these higher prices as a result of the plan.

B   This provides at least some very slight support for the belief that the plan would succeed (if no one at all preferred the new drinks, then the plan would almost certainly fail); however, the question asks for something that would cast doubt on the effectiveness of the plan.

C   When introducing a new product, companies usually have to launch advertising campaigns, and quite frequently such campaigns effectively create demand for the product, so the fact that Fizzles will have to launch an advertising campaign does not cast doubt on the plan.

D   **Correct.** The plan depends on consumers wanting the drinks because of their unique, unfamiliar flavors, and being willing to pay a higher price for them because of their uniqueness in the market. If price (presumably a lower one) and name recognition, rather than the specific fruit flavor, are what generally drive sales, then it seems unlikely that the executives' plan will succeed.

E   Nothing in the information provided indicates how many consumers are loyal to any specific brand of fruit-flavored drinks. Perhaps the vast majority of consumers are willing to switch brands. If that is so, then the fact that the very few who are loyal to a specific brand would not be willing to switch would not cast much doubt on the effectiveness of the plan.

The correct answer is D.

649. Economist: In 2015, the average per-person amount paid for goods and services purchased by consumers in Country X was the equivalent of $17,570 in United States dollars, just 30 percent of the corresponding figure of $58,566 for Country Y. Yet in 2015, there was already a substantial middle class in Country X that had discretionary income for middle-class consumer goods such as new vehicles, computers, or major household appliances, while a significant portion of the middle class in Country Y did not have sufficient income to purchase such items.

Which of the following, if true, most helps explain the discrepancy in the relationships described by the economist?

(A) There are many consumer goods, such as household appliances, that are produced in Country X to be sold in the Country Y market.

(B) The volume of trade between Country X and Country Y is increasing rapidly in both directions.

(C) The economy of Country Y is recovering from a downturn that affected both Country Y and Country X.

(D) Country X residents pay much less than their Country Y counterparts for housing, transportation, and child care.

(E) In Country Y as well as in Country X, there are few assembly-line jobs in factories that pay a middle-class wage.

Argument Construction

Situation   An economist points out that even though in 2015 the average per-person amount paid for goods and services in Country X was only 30 percent of the corresponding figure in Country Y, a substantial middle class in Country X had discretionary income for consumer goods, whereas a substantial portion of the middle class in Country Y did not.

Reasoning   *What, if true, would most help explain the discrepancies described by the economist?* Information indicating that residents in Country X pay much less for nondiscretionary items than do residents of Country Y would help explain why, even though people in Country Y pay on average three times more for goods and services than people in Country X, Country X has a more substantial middle class capable of buying discretionary goods than does Country Y.

A   That many consumer goods produced in Country X are intended to be sold in Country Y does not help explain why many people in Country Y are not able to afford such goods.

B   An increasing volume of trade between Country X and Country Y—which, for all we know, is perfectly balanced—would not help explain any discrepancies between the two countries.

C   That the economies of both Country X and Country Y suffered a downturn, and Country Y is recovering, could not plausibly explain why many people in Country Y have trouble paying for discretionary goods unless we had the information that Country Y's recovery was significantly slower than Country X's. But we do not have that information.

D   **Correct.** That people in one nation pay far less for nondiscretionary goods than people in another nation would potentially be helpful in explaining how the people in the former nation would more easily be able to afford discretionary goods.

E   If a claim is true of both Country X and Country Y, it would not help explain a discrepancy between the two countries.

The correct answer is D.

650. Neuroscientist: Memory evolved to help animals react appropriately to situations they encounter by drawing on the past experience of similar situations. But this does not require that animals perfectly recall every detail of all their experiences. Instead, to function well, memory should generalize from past experiences that are similar to the current one.

The neuroscientist's statements, if true, most strongly support which of the following conclusions?

(A) At least some animals perfectly recall every detail of at least some past experiences.

(B) Perfectly recalling every detail of all their past experiences could help at least some animals react more appropriately than they otherwise would to new situations they encounter.

(C) Generalizing from past experiences requires clear memories of most if not all the details of those experiences.

(D) Recalling every detail of all past experiences would be incompatible with any ability to generalize from those experiences.

(E) Animals can often react more appropriately than they otherwise would to situations they encounter if they draw on generalizations from past experiences of similar situations.

Argument Construction

Situation A neuroscientist claims that memory evolved to help animals learn how to react appropriately by generalizing from past experiences but that this does not require animals to remember all details of those experiences.

Reasoning *What conclusion would the neuroscientist's theory about memory most strongly support?* The neuroscientist asserts that the evolutionary function of memory is to help animals learn to react appropriately by drawing on generalizations from similar experiences they have had. If memory is to serve this function, drawing on generalizations must actually help animals learn to react more appropriately than they otherwise would, even when they do not remember all the details of past experiences.

A Even if no animal ever recalls all the details of any past experience, animals could still learn through generalizations, as the neuroscientist claims.

B This statement could be false even if all of what the neuroscientist says is true. Even if it were never helpful for any animal to recall every detail of all its past experiences, animals could still benefit by learning through generalizations.

C Generalizations from experiences might be made while the experiences are occurring, so that only the generalizations and not the details need to be remembered.

D The neuroscientist only claims that remembering perfect details is not required for memory to serve its function, not that such perfect recall is incompatible with memory serving its function.

E **Correct.** If the evolutionary function of memory is to help animals react more appropriately by drawing on generalizations from past experiences, it follows that animal memories can often successfully serve this function in this manner.

The correct answer is E.

651. In Country X's last election, the Reform Party beat its main opponent, the Conservative Party, although pollsters, employing in-person interviews shortly before the vote, had projected a Conservative Party victory. Afterward, the pollsters determined that, unlike Conservative Party supporters, Reform Party supporters were less likely to express their party preference during in-person interviews than they were during telephone interviews. Therefore, using only telephone interviews instead would likely result in more accurate projections for the next election.

Which of the following statements, if true, would most support the argument in the passage?

(A) The number of voters in Country X's next election will be significantly larger than the number of voters in the last election.

(B) The Conservative Party will win the next election.

(C) For each person interviewed in telephone polls before the next election, pollsters will be able to reasonably determine the likelihood of that person voting.

(D) People who expressed no party preference during the in-person interviews shortly before Country X's last election did not outnumber the people who expressed a preference for the Conservative Party.

(E) In the next election, pollsters will be able to conduct more in-person interviews than telephone interviews.

Argument Evaluation

Situation   Pollsters, using in-person interviews shortly before the last election in Country X, incorrectly predicted that the Conservative Party would win that election, whereas the Reform Party won instead. The pollsters determined that Reform Party supporters, unlike Conservative Party supporters, are less likely to give their party preference in person than in telephone interviews.

Reasoning   *What additional information, if true, would most strengthen the support, in light of the given information, for the prediction that using only telephone interviews would result in more accurate projections in the next election in Country X?* Even if in telephone interviews pollsters are more likely to get accurate information about which party a person interviewed supports, the pollsters' projections may not be accurate if the pollsters are unable to determine whether that person is actually likely to vote. So, information indicating that pollsters will be able to determine the likelihood that a person will vote would strengthen support for the conclusion.

A   If this larger number of voters in the next election is not anticipated by pollsters, then it may affect the accuracy of their predictions. However, the effect would likely be a decrease, rather than an increase, in accuracy. If the pollsters are able to accurately predict voter turnout, then their predictions for the next election could be more accurate. But we have no indication as to whether their turnout predictions will be accurate.

B   If the Conservative Party will win the next election, an underestimate of Reform Party support will be less important for the accuracy of the projection of which party will win.

C   **Correct.** It would certainly be helpful if the pollsters were able to determine how likely the person they were interviewing would be to vote.

D   This is irrelevant to the argument. The conclusion concerns the relative accuracy of telephone interviews in predicting voting numbers in the next election.

E   If pollsters are able to do more in-person interviews than telephone interviews for the next election, that at least weakly suggests that they might not be able to conduct a sufficient number of telephone interviews to get a representative sample—which would weaken support for the conclusion, not strengthen it.

The correct answer is C.

652. A company that manufactures plastic products from recyclable plastic is, surprisingly, unconcerned that economic conditions may worsen, despite analysts' belief that consumers would then consider ecofriendly plastic products an expensive luxury. But the company reasons that it will be able to lower its prices because, in a weakened economy, other ecofriendly plastic manufacturers are likely to fail. Demand among manufacturers for recyclable plastics as raw materials would then plummet, creating an oversupply of such materials, making them less expensive for the manufacturer to purchase and thus lowering the company's costs.

Which of the following, if true, most weakens the company's reasoning?

(A) Smaller ecofriendly plastic manufacturers are more likely to fail in a weakened economy than larger ecofriendly manufacturers are.

(B) Some retailers whose sales include various companies' ecofriendly plastic products have struggled in recent years despite the overall good economy.

(C) Consumers would likely soon learn of the oversupply of recyclable plastics and cease recycling them, significantly raising manufacturers' raw-material costs.

(D) Retailers, including retailers that cater to consumers seeking certain types of ecofriendly products, may lose some business if economic conditions worsen.

(E) The plastics used by the company in its products were, after a recent investigation by a regulatory body, declared to be safe for consumers.

Argument Evaluation

Situation   A company that manufactures products from recyclable plastics believes that if economic conditions worsen, it will be able to lower its prices. It believes its costs will decline because other ecofriendly plastic manufacturers will fail, thereby reducing the demand for recyclable plastics as raw materials.

Reasoning   *What would most weaken the reasoning?* Suppose the company's costs did not decline and the company consequently could not reduce its prices. Even if demand for recyclable plastics as raw materials weakens in an economic downturn, the company's costs may nonetheless not decline if for some reason the supply of recyclable plastics also declines. If so, then the company may well not be able to lower its prices and stay profitable.

A   We are not told whether the company in question is a smaller ecofriendly plastic manufacturer or a larger one. Given that, the fact that smaller such companies are more likely to fail than larger ones may strengthen the argument rather than weaken it (assuming the company in question is a larger such company).

B   If some retailers whose sales include various companies' ecofriendly plastic products have struggled in a healthy economy, they may well struggle even more in a weak economy. This could help drive the company's competitors out of business, which is what the company argues is likely to happen in an economic downturn. So, rather than weakening the argument, this arguably strengthens it.

C   **Correct.** Suppose consumers learn of the oversupply of recyclable plastics and stop recycling them as a result; the oversupply may therefore not last long, and indeed a shortage might arise. This would lead not to lower raw-material costs, as the company argues, but to higher raw-material costs.

D   The information that retailers' lost business might result in a decrease in sales of the competing products does not weaken the argument. A loss of business due to worsening economic conditions is a presupposition of the argument.

E   The fact that the plastics used by the company have been declared safe has probably helped boost demand for the company's products, and perhaps for the competing products as well, yet an economic downturn could still hurt the company's competitors. So, this does little to weaken the company's argument.

The correct answer is C.

653. Researchers asked volunteers to imagine they were running a five-kilometer race against 50 people and then against 500 people, races in each of which the top 10 percent would receive a $1,000 prize. Asked about the effort they would apply in the respective cases, the volunteers indicated, on average, that they would run slower in the race against the greater number of people. A likely explanation of this result is that those of the volunteers who were most *comparatively inclined*—those who most tended to compare themselves with others in the social environment—determined (perhaps unconsciously) that extreme effort would not be worthwhile in the 500-competitor race.

Which of the following would, if known to be true, most help justify the explanation offered above?

(A) The volunteers who were most comparatively inclined were also those that had the greatest desire to win a $1,000 prize.

(B) The volunteers who were the least comparatively inclined had no greater desire to win the $1,000 than those who were the most comparatively inclined.

(C) The volunteers who were most comparatively inclined were likely to indicate that they would run the two races at the same speed.

(D) The most comparatively inclined volunteers believed that they were significantly less likely to finish in the top 10 percent in the race against 500 than in the race against 50.

(E) Volunteers were chosen for participation in the study on the basis of answers to various questions designed to measure the degree to which the volunteers were comparatively inclined.

Argument Construction

Situation   Volunteers were asked how much effort they would expend when running a five-kilometer race against 50 people and how much they would expend in such a race against 500 people, when the prize for each race is $1,000 for finishing in the top 10 percent. The volunteers indicated, on average, that they would run more slowly in the race against 500 people than in the race against 50 people. This result is likely because comparatively inclined volunteers believed that extreme effort would not have been worthwhile in the race against 500 competitors.

Reasoning   *What would most help to justify the explanation proposed above?* If comparatively inclined volunteers thought it was at least as likely that they would finish in the top 10 percent in the race against 500 as in the race against 50, the proposed explanation would fail. Thus, it would help justify the explanation if we knew that the comparatively inclined volunteers believed they were less likely to win in the race against 500 than in the race against 50.

A   If one knew that the volunteers who were most comparatively inclined had the greatest desire to win the $1,000, one might actually be more puzzled about why these volunteers said they would expend less effort against the 500 competitors. If they expended less effort, they would probably be less likely to finish in the top 10 percent.

B   If one knew that the volunteers who were more comparatively inclined had no less desire to win a $1,000 prize than those who were least comparatively inclined, one would have at least some reason to think the comparatively inclined volunteers wanted to win the $1,000; this clearly cannot explain why they would not expend as much effort in the 500-competitor race as in the 50-competitor race.

C   The claim that one would run the two races at the same speed contradicts the position expressed on average by the group as a whole (that they would run more slowly against the larger group of contestants). Therefore, if the most comparatively inclined volunteers said that they would run the two races at the same speed, their position would be inconsistent with that of the group as a whole. So, if this answer choice were true, it would weaken, rather than strengthen, the explanation that the views of the most comparatively inclined volunteers account for the fact that the volunteers said, on average, that they would run more slowly against the greater number of contestants.

D   **Correct.** If the most comparatively inclined volunteers believed they would be far less likely to finish in the top 10 percent in the race against 500 than in the race against 50, then they would likely believe that extreme effort would not be worthwhile in the race with more people. This therefore is likely to be at least part of the explanation.

E   Even if volunteers were chosen on the basis of answers to questions designed to measure how comparatively inclined they were, we are not told whether the volunteers were chosen because of the degree to which they were comparatively inclined.

The correct answer is D.

654. According to a study, after a week of high-altitude living, twenty men had slimmed down. The men, middle-aged residents of low-altitude areas, had been taken to a research station at 2,650 meters (8,694 feet) above sea level. They had unrestricted access to food and were forbidden vigorous exercise, yet they lost an average of 1.5 kilograms (3.3 pounds) during their one-week stay. Clearly, the lower availability of oxygen at higher altitudes, or hypobaric hypoxia, can be said to have caused the weight loss, since _____.

Which of the following would, if true, most logically complete the argument?

(A) a decrease in oxygen intake has been shown to depress appetite

(B) the men all participated in the same kinds of exercise during their stay

(C) the foods available to the men had fewer calories than the foods they usually ate

(D) exercise at higher altitudes is more difficult than exercise at lower altitudes is

(E) several weeks after returning home, the men still weighed less than they had before the study

Argument Construction

Situation   Twenty middle-aged men lived at a high-altitude research station for one week. They had unrestricted access to food but did no vigorous exercise. By the end of their stay, they had lost an average 1.5 kilograms (3.3 pounds) of weight.

Reasoning   *Which additional information, if true, would most help support the claim that lower availability of oxygen at higher altitudes caused the weight loss?* The puzzlement arises from the fact that the twenty men had free access to food and did no vigorous exercise. And consuming less of the types of food they would normally eat would have caused weight loss. But suppose one or both of these behaviors had not occurred?

A   **Correct.** This information helps support the explanatory hypothesis that lower oxygen levels accounted for the weight loss. The men's intake of oxygen certainly decreased at an altitude of 2,650 meters (8694 feet), since they normally lived in low-altitude areas. Moreover, reduced appetite would provide a mechanism by which weight loss could have occurred.

B   The men were forbidden vigorous exercise, and we can assume that, in a research context, they followed this restriction. Mild exercise would be unlikely to explain the weight loss.

C   This does not support the explanatory hypothesis concerning the role of oxygen reduction in the weight loss.

D   Even if this is generally true, it does not support the hypothesis that lower oxygen levels accounted for the weight loss.

E   This provides no support for the explanatory hypothesis that lower oxygen levels accounted for the weight loss. It might even cast some doubt on the hypothesis, since over a period of several weeks following the study, the men's weight did not increase with their return to their normal oxygen levels.

The correct answer is A.

655. Editorial: Our city's public transportation agency is facing a budget shortfall. The fastest growing part of the budget has been employee retirement benefits, which are exceptionally generous. Unless the budget shortfall is resolved, transportation service will be cut, and many transportation employees will lose their jobs. Thus, it would be in the employees' best interest for their union to accept cuts in retirement benefits.

Which of the following is an assumption the editorial's argument requires?

(A) The transportation employees' union should not accept cuts in retirement benefits if doing so would not be in the employees' best interest.

(B) The only feasible way for the agency to resolve the budget shortfall would involve cutting transportation service and eliminating jobs.

(C) Other things being equal, it is in the transportation employees' interest to have exceptionally generous retirement benefits.

(D) Cutting the retirement benefits would help resolve the agency's budget shortfall.

(E) The transportation employees' union will not accept cuts in retirement benefits if doing so will not allow more transportation employees to keep their jobs.

Argument Construction

Situation An editorial indicates that the fastest growing part of a particular city's public transportation agency's budget is employee retirement benefits. The agency's budget has a shortfall. If the shortfall is not resolved, transportation service will be cut, and many of the employees will lose their jobs.

Reasoning *What must be true if we are to accept the editorial's conclusion, that it is in the employees' best interest to accept cuts in retirement benefits?* If cutting the employees' retirement benefits would not be sufficient to resolve the budget shortfall, then it may well not be in the employees' best interest to accept such cuts. The reasons given for accepting the cuts are related to the undesirable consequences of a continued shortfall.

A   The argument is about whether the union's accepting the cuts is in fact in the employees' best interest and does not require any assumption about whether employees should accept what is in their best interest.

B   This is incompatible with an assumption made by the argument. The argument assumes that cutting the retirement benefits of the employees would help resolve the budget shortfall.

C   The argument would actually be stronger if it were NOT the case that it is in the employees' best interest to have exceptionally generous retirement benefits.

D   Correct. If cutting retirement benefits would not help resolve the agency's budget shortfall, then cutting those benefits would not help the employees avoid job cuts.

E   The argument does not depend on assuming anything regarding what factors would motivate the union's acceptance.

The correct answer is D.

656. Researchers hope to find clues about the A'mk peoples who lived in the Kaumpta region about one thousand years ago but who left few obvious traces. The researchers plan to hire the few remaining shamans of the modern-day indigenous people in Kaumpta, who are believed to be descended from the A'mk, to lead them to ancestral sites that may be the remains of A'mk buildings or ceremonial spaces. The shamans were taught the location of such sites as part of their traditional training as youths, and their knowledge of traditional Kaumpta customs may help determine the nature of any sites the researchers find.

Which of the following is an assumption on which the success of the plan depends?

(A) The researchers have reliable evidence that the A'mk of one thousand years ago built important ceremonial spaces.

(B) The shamans have a reasonably accurate memory of A'mk sites they learned about as youths.

(C) Kaumpta shamans are generally held in high esteem for their traditional knowledge.

(D) Modern technologies available to the researchers are likely to be able to find some A'mk sites easily.

(E) Most or all A'mk sites are likely to be found within the Kaumpta region.

Evaluation of a Plan

Situation Researchers wish to find sites of an ancient people, the A'mk, who lived in the Kaumpta region one thousand years ago. Indigenous people believed to be descended from the A'mk live in that region today. Their shamans, as youths, were taught about such sites. To discover some of these sites, the researchers plan to hire the shamans.

Reasoning *What must be true for the success of the researchers' plan to find the sites by relying on the shamans' assistance?* The plan would fail, for example, if there were no such sites in the Kaumpta region. Therefore, the researchers' plan depends on assuming that Kaumpta have some such sites—but not that most of the sites are there. The plan also requires that the shamans collectively have reasonably accurate recall of what they learned about the sites as youths.

A The researchers hope to find buildings or ceremonial spaces or both. However, the plan does not require ceremonial spaces to be found or that the researchers have evidence of them.

B **Correct.** If the shamans collectively have no "reasonably accurate memory" of what they learned of the location of such sites, then the researchers' plan is not a useful one and can have no reasonable expectation of success.

C This is likely to be so if the indigenous group from which they come is still committed to maintaining their traditional knowledge. But the plan does not rely on the shamans being honored among their own people. It must be assumed, of course, that the shamans currently possess "traditional knowledge" and are willing to share it.

D The researchers' reliance on the shamans' assistance suggests that it is not so easy for the researchers to rely entirely on "modern technologies" in this case.

E The plan can succeed even if this is not correct. What must be assumed is that at least some of the A'mk sites are within the Kaumpta region; it need not be assumed that most or all are.

The correct answer is B.

657. Astronomer: Most stars are born in groups of thousands, each star in a group forming from the same parent cloud of gas. Each cloud has a unique, homogeneous chemical composition. Therefore, whenever two stars have the same chemical composition as each other, they must have originated from the same cloud of gas.

Which of the following, if true, would most strengthen the astronomer's argument?

(A) In some groups of stars, not every star originated from the same parent cloud of gas.

(B) Clouds of gas of similar or identical chemical composition may be remote from each other.

(C) Whenever a star forms, it inherits the chemical composition of its parent cloud of gas.

(D) Many stars in vastly different parts of the universe are quite similar in their chemical compositions.

(E) Astronomers can at least sometimes precisely determine whether a star has the same chemical composition as its parent cloud of gas.

Argument Evaluation

Situation   Most stars are born in groups, any one of which forms from a parent gas cloud with a unique, homogenous chemical composition.

Reasoning   *What would be additional evidence that any two stars with the same chemical composition originated from the same gas cloud?* The implicit reasoning is that since the chemical composition of each gas cloud is unique and homogenous, any two stars that formed from gas with the same chemical composition must have originated from the same cloud. The astronomer then infers that if two stars have the same composition now, they must have originated from the same cloud. This inference requires the assumption that the composition each star has now depends only on the composition of the cloud in which it originated. Any evidence that supports this assumption will strengthen the argument.

A   Whether or not stars born in different clouds of gas are ever in the same "group" is not clearly relevant to whether or not they ever have the same chemical composition.

B   How remote clouds of similar compositions are from each other is not clearly relevant to whether stars that have the same chemical composition may have formed from different clouds of gas. Also, the suggestion that different gas clouds may have identical compositions conflicts with the astronomer's premise that the composition of each cloud from which stars form is unique.

C   **Correct.** If each star's composition is identical to that of its parent cloud, and each cloud's composition is unique, then any two stars identical in composition must have formed from the same parent cloud.

D   If anything, this would suggest that stars with the same composition might have formed from different clouds, so it would weaken rather than strengthen the argument.

E   If astronomers could do this, they might be able to obtain additional evidence for or against the position taken in the argument, but the mere fact that they can do this does not, in itself, provide any support for the astronomer's argument because it tells us nothing about whether two stars with the same chemical composition as one another actually did originate from the same parent cloud of gas.

The correct answer is C.

658. With employer-paid training, workers have the potential to become more productive not only in their present employment but also in any number of jobs with different employers. To increase the productivity of their workforce, many firms are planning to maintain or even increase their investments in worker training. But some training experts object that if a trained worker is hired away by another firm, the employer that paid for the training has merely subsidized a competitor. They note that such hiring has been on the rise in recent years.

Which of the following would, if true, contribute most to defeating the training experts' objection to the firms' strategy?

(A) Firms that promise opportunities for advancement to their employees get, on average, somewhat larger numbers of job applications from untrained workers than do firms that make no such promise.

(B) In many industries, employees that take continuing-education courses are more competitive in the job market.

(C) More and more educational and training institutions are offering reduced tuition fees to firms that subsidize worker training.

(D) Research shows that workers whose training is wholly or partially subsidized by their employer tend to get at least as much training as do workers who pay for all their own training.

(E) For most firms that invest in training their employees, the value added by that investment in employees who stay exceeds the value lost through other employees' leaving to work for other companies.

Evaluation of a Plan

Situation   Many firms pay to train their workers in order to increase their workforces' productivity. But in recent years, firms have been increasingly hiring away from each other workers who have had such training.

Reasoning   *What would most help address the concern that firms that pay to train workers are thereby subsidizing competitors that hire away those workers?* In order for the employer-paid training to be worthwhile for a given firm despite the risk of subsidizing competitors that may hire away the trained workers, that firm has to gain more benefits from the training than it loses by subsidizing such competitors. Any evidence that this is true for most firms would help to address the experts' concern.

A   A typical firm does not necessarily want larger numbers of applications from unqualified workers. And if hired, those workers can still be hired away by competitors after the firm has paid to train them, just as the experts warned.

B   This suggests that in many industries, companies, rather than investing in employee training, prefer to hire employees who already have specifically relevant training (perhaps funded by other companies). If anything, this slightly supports, rather than defeats, the training experts' view. No firm has an interest in making its own employees more competitive in the job market unless the firm is likely to benefit from their being so.

C   Even firms that pay reduced tuition fees for worker training may lose the money they pay for those fees and effectively subsidize competitors that hire the trained employees away. So this does not defeat the training experts' objection.

D   The more highly trained workers—regardless of whether their training was company subsidized or not—would presumably be prime targets for recruitment by competing firms, just as the experts warned. The research finding in question does not help defeat the experts' objection.

E   **Correct.** This explicitly indicates that most firms gain more than they lose from the general practice of firms paying to train their workers.

The correct answer is E.

659. In emerging economies in Africa and other regions, large foreign banks that were set up during the colonial era have long played a major economic role. These institutions have tended to confine their business to the wealthier of banks' potential customers. But development of these countries' economies requires financing of the small businesses that dominate their manufacturing, farming, and services sectors. So economic growth will be likely to occur if local banks take on this portion of the financial services markets, since _____.

Which of the following completions would produce the strongest argument?

(A)   local banks tend not to strive as much as large foreign banks to diversify their investments

(B)   small farming and manufacturing businesses contribute to economic growth if they obtain adequate investment capital

(C)   large foreign banks in emerging economies could, with local employees and appropriate local consultation, profitably expand their business to less wealthy clients

(D)   some small businesses are among the wealthier customers of foreign banks in emerging economies

(E)   local banks in emerging economies tend to be less risk-averse than foreign banks

Argument Construction

Situation   Large foreign banks have long played an economic role in emerging economies, but they have typically confined their business to wealthier customers. Economic development in these countries requires the financing of small businesses that dominate their manufacturing, farming, and services sectors.

Reasoning   *What would most help support the claim that growth in emerging economies will likely occur if local banks help finance small businesses in the relevant sectors of these emerging markets?* If it were the case that these small businesses would actually be likely to contribute to economic growth, given adequate investment capital, then economic growth would indeed be likely to occur if local banks provided the investment capital.

A   It could be the case that whatever sorts of investments local banks make—diversified or not—economic growth will not tend to occur; for instance, it could be that the businesses they invest in do not use the capital wisely. So, this claim does not help support the conclusion.

B   **Correct.** If small farming and manufacturing businesses will contribute to economic growth if they obtain adequate investment capital, then we have fairly good reason to think that economic growth is likely to occur if local banks take on the financing of such small businesses (we merely need to also assume that they will provide adequate investment capital when they take on this financing).

C   Even if large foreign banks could profitably expand their businesses to less-wealthy clients, we have been given no reason to think they will. Furthermore, the claim in need of support is that economic growth will occur if local, rather than foreign, banks financially support these small businesses.

D   The claim that economic growth will occur if local banks finance small businesses in certain sectors is not supported by the claim that there are some small businesses supported by foreign banks. If these businesses are already financially supported and yet there is not the sort of economic growth discussed, then that might even suggest that economic growth is unlikely to occur.

E   It could be that, if local banks are less risk-averse than foreign banks, they will invest in risky businesses that fail, which would not tend to support the claim that economic growth will likely result if local banks in emerging counties provide financial support for the relevant sectors.

The correct answer is B.

660. Exporters in Country X are facing lower revenues due to a shortage of the large metal shipping containers in which they send their goods by sea to other countries. Fewer containers arrive in Country X due to reductions in imports. This has meant lost orders, costly delays, and a scramble for alternatives, such as air freight, all of which are costlier. Moreover, the revenues of exporters in Country X will probably continue to decline in the near future. This is because other countries are likely to find it increasingly unprofitable to export their goods to Country X, and because _____.

Which of the following would most logically complete the passage?

(A) production of shipping containers in Country X is growing rapidly as a response to the shortage

(B) shipping companies are willing to move containers from country to country only when the containers are full

(C) the cost of shipping alternatives such as air freight is likely to stabilize in the near future

(D) consumers in Country X are purchasing more products than ever before

(E) the worldwide demand for goods made in Country X has only recently begun to rise after a long decline

Argument Construction

Situation   Exporters in Country X are finding that there is an insufficient number of shipping containers for them to use for their exports, because the number of such containers arriving in Country X has declined because of reduced imports. Also, alternative methods of shipping are relatively costly. Furthermore, other countries will likely find shipping goods to Country X to be less and less profitable.

Reasoning   *What would most support the prediction that Country X's exporters' revenues will likely see further declines in revenue in the near future?* If the number of shipping containers available to exporters is likely to decrease, then the prediction would have further support. We know that other countries exporting to Country X will find it increasingly unprofitable, so there is reason to believe their exports will decline further—meaning there will be fewer imports into Country X, which means fewer shipping containers arriving in Country X carrying imported goods, unless the shipping containers shipped in the future are less full than when they are shipped now. If shipping companies are willing to move such containers to another country only when the containers are full, then that will not occur.

A   If production of shipping containers in Country X were rapidly increasing, then the reason given for the decline in revenue for exporters in Country X—that there is an insufficient number of shipping containers—would be undermined, and so therefore would be the conclusion.

B   Correct. If shipping companies are unwilling to move containers from country to country unless the containers are full, then, given Country X's decline in imports, there will likely be fewer shipping containers available to Country X's exporters, which provides support for the claim that their revenues will likely decline.

C   If the cost of shipping alternatives such as air freight is likely to stabilize, then those alternative methods of shipping might become economically viable, which would undermine rather than support the conclusion.

D   The fact that consumers in Country X are purchasing more goods than ever before does not affect how much revenue is generated by exporting goods from Country X.

E   If there is increased demand for goods from Country X, then the price of such goods might increase sufficiently to make alternative methods of shipping economically viable, which would undermine rather than support the conclusion.

The correct answer is B.

661. In order to reduce the number of items damaged while in transit to customers, packaging consultants recommended the TrueSave mail-order company increase the amount of packing material so as to fill any empty spaces in its cartons. Accordingly, TrueSave officials instructed the company's packers to use more packing material than before, and the packers zealously acted on these instructions and used as much as they could. Nevertheless, customer reports of damaged items rose somewhat.

Which of the following, if true, most helps to explain why acting on the consultants' recommendation failed to achieve its goal?

(A) The change in packing policy led to an increase in expenditure on packing material and labor.

(B) When packing material is compressed too densely, it loses some of its capacity to absorb shock.

(C) The amount of packing material used in a carton does not significantly influence the ease with which a customer can unpack the package.

(D) Most of the goods TrueSave ships are electronic products that are highly vulnerable to being damaged in transit.

(E) TrueSave has lost some of its regular customers as a result of the high number of damaged items they received.

Argument Construction

Situation   TrueSave company followed consultants' recommendations to decrease damage to its shipments by increasing the amount of packing material. Workers stuffed in as much material as they could, but the number of items damaged in shipping increased rather than decreased.

Reasoning   *What would cause a correlation between increased packing materials and increased rates of damaged items?* Using more packing material might be ineffective at preventing damage to shipped items if such tightly packed materials had unforeseen effects. Identifying such an effect could help explain why the consultants' recommendation to use more materials backfired.

A   Increased expenditure on packing materials and labor would not explain why more items were damaged during shipping after the recommendations were put into practice.

B   **Correct.** If densely compressed packing material is less effective at absorbing shock, then excessive use of packing materials could backfire by transmitting more shock, not less, to packed items. If TrueSave's workers are stuffing in packing materials too vigorously, that would help explain why the recommendation to use more materials has led to somewhat increased rates of damaged shipments.

C   The ease of unpacking TrueSave's shipments is not relevant to the question of why items are damaged during shipping.

D   If TrueSave primarily ships fragile electronic goods, that would not explain why more of those fragile goods were damaged after TrueSave began using more packing materials than before.

E   The loss of customers due to damaged shipments does nothing to explain why those shipments were damaged in the first place.

The correct answer is B.

662. An unusually severe winter occurred in Europe after the continent was blanketed by a blue haze resulting from the eruption of the Laki Volcano in the European republic of Iceland in the summer of 1984. Thus, it is evident that major eruptions cause the atmosphere to become cooler than it would be otherwise.

Which of the following statements, if true, most seriously weakens the argument above?

(A) The cooling effect triggered by volcanic eruptions in 1985 was counteracted by an unusual warming of Pacific waters.

(B) There is a strong statistical link between volcanic eruptions and the severity of the rainy season in India.

(C) A few months after El Chichón's large eruption in April 1982, air temperatures throughout the region remained higher than expected given the long-term weather trends.

(D) The climatic effects of major volcanic eruptions can temporarily mask the general warming trend resulting from an excess of carbon dioxide in the atmosphere.

(E) Three months after an early springtime eruption in South America during the late nineteenth century, sea surface temperatures near the coast began to fall.

Argument Evaluation

Situation   A volcanic eruption in Iceland was followed a few months later by an unusually cold winter in Europe, possibly due to atmospheric haze from the eruption. The author posits this cooling demonstrates that large volcanic eruptions in general cause atmospheric cooling.

Reasoning   *What would weaken the argument that major eruptions result in colder weather?* The argument draws a general conclusion—major volcanic eruptions cause atmospheric cooling—from a single example: cold weather following the eruption of Laki Volcano in 1984. Thus, any examples of volcanic eruptions that do *not* show a similar effect on atmospheric temperatures would tend to weaken the argument that such atmospheric cooling is a general result of major eruptions.

A   The fact that cooling resulting from other eruptions was countered by a separate trend of oceanic warming would not weaken the argument that major volcanic eruptions in general cool the atmosphere.

B   A correlation between major eruptions and severe rainy seasons in India has no bearing on the argument that major eruptions have a cooling effect on climate.

C   **Correct.** If a different major volcanic eruption was followed by unexpectedly warm weather, rather than by cooling, that would tend to weaken the argument that major volcanic eruptions produce colder weather as a rule.

D   Even if atmospheric cooling caused by volcanoes could mask the warming caused by excessive atmospheric carbon dioxide, that has no bearing on the question of whether large eruptions in general cause cooling.

E   Oceanic cooling following an eruption has no bearing on the argument's claim regarding atmospheric cooling.

The correct answer is C.

663. Political theorist: Even with the best spies, area experts, and satellite surveillance, foreign policy assessments can still lack important information. In such circumstances intuitive judgment is vital. A national leader with such judgment can make good decisions about foreign policy even when current information is incomplete, since _____.

Which of the following, if true, most logically completes the argument?

(A)   the central reason for failure in foreign policy decision making is the absence of critical information

(B)   those leaders whose foreign policy decisions have been highly ranked have also been found to have good intuitive judgment

(C)   both intuitive judgment and good information are required for sound decision-making

(D)   good foreign policy decisions often lead to improved methods of gathering information

(E)   intuitive judgment can produce good decisions based on past experience, even when there are important gaps in current information

Argument Construction

Situation   National leaders sometimes must make foreign policy decisions while lacking important information.

Reasoning   *What would most help support the claim that a national leader with intuitive judgment can make good foreign policy decisions without complete information?* The word *since* preceding the blank indicates that the blank should be filled with a premise supporting the statement immediately before the blank. So, an observation that supports the claim that a national leader with intuitive judgment can make good foreign policy decisions without complete information would logically complete the argument.

A   This gives us no reason to suppose that intuitive judgment helps national leaders avoid such failures.

B   This does not specify who ranked the foreign policy decisions, nor how they determined the rankings, so it gives us no reason to accept those rankings. For all we know, the anonymous rankers may have used the dubious rankings they created as the sole evidence for their so-called findings about which leaders have good intuitive judgment.

C   This implies that intuitive judgment alone is inadequate without good information, so it undermines rather than supports the claim that national leaders can make good foreign policy decisions with intuitive judgment while lacking complete information.

D   This gives us no reason to suppose that good foreign policy decisions can be made in the first place by leaders lacking important information.

E   **Correct.** This suggests that national leaders can make good foreign policy decisions using intuitive judgment based on their past foreign policy experience, even without complete information about the current situations they're facing.

The correct answer is E.

664. Supply shortages and signs of growing demand are driving cocoa prices upward. Unusually severe weather in cocoa-producing regions—too much rain in Brazil and too little in West Africa—has limited production. Further, Europe and North America recently reported stronger demand for cocoa. In the first quarter, grinding of cocoa beans—the first stage in processing cocoa for chocolate—rose 8.1 percent in Europe and 16 percent in North America. Analysts have concluded that cocoa's price will continue to rise at least into the near future.

Which of the following would, if true, most strengthen the reasoning above?

(A) Ground cocoa beans can be stored for long periods before they spoil.

(B) Several European and North American manufacturers that use cocoa have recently improved their processing capacity.

(C) It takes new cocoa trees five or six years before they start bearing fruit.

(D) Governments in Europe and North America are likely to change current restrictions on cocoa imports.

(E) Historically, cocoa production has varied widely from year to year.

Argument Evaluation

Situation   There has been limited production of cocoa beans due to severe weather and also increased demand for cocoa; as a result, cocoa prices have risen.

Reasoning   *What would help support the analysts' inference that cocoa prices will continue to rise at least into the near future?* If the price of cocoa is to continue to rise, then the conditions that have led to the recent increase in price must not be ameliorated. They would be ameliorated if demand for cocoa beans declined, e.g., because price increases made people less likely to want ground cocoa; they would also be ameliorated if supply increased, e.g., because many new cocoa trees were planted and very quickly started bearing fruit. If we had reason to believe that one or more of these ameliorating factors is unlikely to happen, then we have more reason to think that prices might stay high, and possibly even rise further.

A   That ground cocoa beans can be stored for long periods without spoiling does not tell us whether supply and demand conditions will stay stable, improve, or get worse.

B   The fact that these manufacturers have recently improved their processing capacity might help explain why the grinding of cocoa beans has increased recently, but it does not indicate that this increased capacity will be fully utilized. Often, if end-product demand decreases, industrial capacity will become underutilized.

C   **Correct.** If it takes new cocoa trees several years to start bearing fruit, then it is less likely that supply can quickly be increased, which in turn makes it less likely that supply can quickly meet any increased demand and thereby relieve pricing pressures.

D   These governments may change current restrictions on cocoa imports, but for all we know, they may make them more restrictive rather than less restrictive. If they made them more restrictive, demand might decrease, in which case prices might actually fall.

E   If cocoa production varies from year to year, it could be that next year cocoa production increases, in which case, as long as demand does not increase as well, prices might fall.

The correct answer is C.

665. A popular beach has long had a dolphin-feeding program in which fish are given to dolphins several times a day. Many dolphins get as much as half of their food each day there. Although dolphins that first benefit from the program as adults are healthy and long-lived, their offspring have a lower life expectancy than offspring of dolphins that feed exclusively in the wild.

Which of the following, if true, most helps to explain the lower life expectancy of offspring of dolphins feeding at the beach compared to other young dolphins?

(A) Sharks that prey on dolphins are less common in the open seas off the beach than in many other areas of the open seas where dolphins congregate.

(B) Many of the adult dolphins that feed at the beach are females that nurse their offspring there.

(C) The fish given to the dolphins at the beach are the same types of fish that dolphins typically catch in the wild.

(D) Many dolphins that feed at the beach with their offspring come to the beach only a few times a month.

(E) Adult dolphins that feed at the beach spend much less time teaching their offspring how to catch fish in the wild than do other adult dolphins.

Argument Construction

Situation   A program that feeds dolphins fish at a beach has no negative effect on adult dolphins, but the offspring of the human-fed dolphins generally have shorter lives than the offspring of dolphins that hunt their own food.

Reasoning   *What factor would explain why the dolphin-feeding program negatively affects the offspring of dolphin recipients?* The dolphin-feeding program produces no problems for adults that eat fish provided by humans, but their young fare worse than the young of dolphins that catch all their own fish. Therefore, some additional complication of the program is likely to explain these negative effects.

A   Fewer sharks preying on dolphins near the beach would be expected to increase, not reduce, the life expectancy of young dolphins that frequent that area.

B   The proportion of nursing females among the fed dolphins has no bearing on why their offspring have reduced life expectancy.

C   The fact that fed dolphins and freely hunting dolphins eat the same types of fish does nothing to explain why the offspring of the first group have generally shorter lives than the second group.

D   The frequency with which dolphins take advantage of the feeding program would not explain why the offspring of fed dolphins have worse outcomes.

E   **Correct.** The passage states that the fed dolphins derive at most half their total food from the feeding program, so if fed dolphins spend less time teaching their young to hunt on their own, then those young would be at a serious disadvantage relative to the well-taught young of wild-feeding dolphins. Therefore, such an effect of the feeding program would explain the negative impact on life expectancy among the offspring.

The correct answer is E.

666. **Plant scientists have used genetic engineering on seeds to produce crop plants that are highly resistant to insect damage.** Unfortunately, the seeds themselves are quite expensive, and the plants require more fertilizer and water to grow well than normal ones. Accordingly, **for most farmers the savings on pesticides would not compensate for the higher seed costs and the cost of additional fertilizer.** However, since consumer demand for grains, fruits, and vegetables grown without the use of pesticides continues to rise, the use of genetically engineered seeds of this kind is likely to become widespread.

In the argument given, the two portions in **boldface** play which of the following roles?

(A)   The first supplies a context for the argument; the second is the argument's main conclusion.

(B)   The first introduces a development that the argument predicts will have a certain outcome; the second is a state of affairs that, according to the argument, contributes to bringing about that outcome.

(C)   The first presents a development that the argument predicts will have a certain outcome; the second acknowledges a consideration that tends to weigh against that prediction.

(D)   The first provides evidence to support a prediction that the argument seeks to defend; the second is that prediction.

(E)   The first and the second each provide evidence to support the argument's main conclusion.

Argument Construction

Situation   Seeds genetically engineered by plant scientists produce crops that are highly resistant to insect damage, and such crops can be grown with less use of pesticides. The seeds would be costly to use, and the savings on pesticides would not be sufficient, in themselves, to increase most farmers' profitability. Nonetheless, consumer demand for pesticide-free food materials is increasing, so genetically engineered seeds are likely to become widely used.

Reasoning   *What function is served by the statement that plant scientists have used genetic engineering on seeds to produce insect-resistant crop plants? What function is served by the statement that for most farmers the savings on pesticides would not outweigh other associated costs?* The first statement describes an innovation—genetically engineered seeds—that allows crops to be grown with little or no use of pesticides. The second statement notes that savings on pesticide use would not outweigh the higher costs of the genetically engineered seeds. The argument's main conclusion, however, is the prediction, expressed in the second clause of the final sentence of the passage, that use of such genetically engineered seeds will become widespread.

A   The second statement is not the main conclusion. Instead, it is an intermediate conclusion, which is based on the preceding statements. The main conclusion is presented in the final clause of the passage.

B   This correctly characterizes the first statement but not the second. The second statement is not meant to indicate a factor that contributes to the predicted outcome; instead, it indicates a factor that could hypothetically count against the argument's prediction.

C   **Correct.** The first **boldfaced** portion reports a development in agricultural technology. In the final sentence, the argument goes on to predict that an outcome of this development will be the widespread adoption of insect-resistant genetically engineered seeds. The second **boldfaced** portion acknowledges a financial consideration that would tend to count against that prediction.

D   The first statement does provide partial support for the prediction stated in the argument's main conclusion. The second statement does not provide any support for the prediction that the argument seeks to defend. That prediction is expressed in the final clause of the passage and is the main conclusion of the argument.

E   The second statement cannot accurately be described as giving evidence to support the prediction stated in the argument's main conclusion. Instead, it tangentially acknowledges a consideration that could plausibly be thought to count against the conclusion.

The correct answer is C.

667. Which of the following most logically completes the passage?

Leptin, a protein occurring naturally in the blood, appears to regulate how much fat the body carries by speeding up the metabolism and decreasing the appetite when the body has too much fat. Mice that do not naturally produce leptin have more fat than other mice, but they lose fat rapidly when they are given leptin injections. Unfortunately, however, leptin cannot be used as a dietary supplement to control fat, since _____.

(A) the digestive system breaks down proteins before they can enter the bloodstream

(B) there are pharmaceuticals already available that can contribute to weight loss by speeding up the metabolism

(C) people with unusually low levels of leptin in their blood tend to have a high percentage of body fat

(D) the mice that do not naturally produce leptin were from a specially bred strain of mice

(E) mice whose bodies did produce leptin also lost some of their body fat when given leptin injections

Argument Construction

Situation   Leptin, a protein naturally occurring in the bloodstream, speeds up metabolism to induce loss of excessive fat. Mice that lack leptin have more fat than other mice, but they lose fat when given leptin injections. However, leptin cannot be used as a dietary supplement to control fat.

Reasoning   *What would explain the fact that a dietary supplement of leptin will not help to control fat?* Leptin injected into the bloodstream—but not leptin taken as a dietary supplement—helps control fat. So, leptin taken as a dietary supplement is either inactivated in the gastrointestinal system or for some other reason fails to enter the bloodstream.

A   **Correct.** The digestive system breaks down proteins and would therefore break down leptin, which is a protein. This means that leptin given as a dietary supplement would never reach the bloodstream.

B   The question concerns leptin alone, and this new information fails to explain why leptin cannot help control fat if administered as a dietary supplement.

C   It is unsurprising that this would be so, but this information does nothing to explain why leptin consumed as a supplement would fail to control fat.

D   Presumably leptin administered as a dietary supplement was first tested on mice bred to lack leptin. However, the question about leptin does not concern only mice but presumably humans and other mammals.

E   This suggests that boosting existing normal leptin levels with injections can induce further fat loss. However, this has no obvious relevance to the question raised about why dietary supplements of leptin fail to produce fat loss.

The correct answer is A.

668. Large national budget deficits do not cause large trade deficits. If they did, countries with the largest budget deficits would also have the largest trade deficits. In fact, when deficit figures are adjusted so different countries are reliably comparable to each other, there is no such correlation.

If the statements above are all true, which of the following can properly be inferred on the basis of them?

(A) Countries with large national budget deficits tend to restrict foreign trade.

(B) Reliable comparisons of the deficit figures of one country with those of another are impossible.

(C) Reducing a country's national budget deficit will not necessarily result in a lowering of any trade deficit that country may have.

(D) When countries are ordered from largest to smallest in terms of population, the smallest countries generally have the smallest budget and trade deficits.

(E) Countries with the largest trade deficits never have similarly large national budget deficits.

Argument Construction

Situation   Large trade deficits are not the result of large national budget deficits. When adjustments are made so that different countries can be compared to one another, no correlation between greater budget deficits and greater trade deficits appears in the data.

Reasoning   *What inference would logically follow from the information?* If it is true that there is not a causal relationship between the size of a nation's budget deficit and the size of its trade deficit, then it can be inferred that reducing a budget deficit will not necessarily result in a lower trade deficit.

A   The passage implies nothing about the trade policies of countries with large budget deficits.

B   The passage states adjustments *can* be made to allow reliable comparisons between the deficits of different countries; it does not suggest reliable comparisons are impossible.

C   **Correct.** If there is no causal relationship between budget deficits and trade deficits, then one can infer that lowering the former would not necessarily have any effect on the latter.

D   The passage implies nothing about a relationship between a nation's population and its deficits.

E   The passage states there is no *general* correlation between high budget deficits and high trade deficits; it does not imply *specific* countries never have both.

The correct answer is C.

669. Archaeologists use technology to analyze ancient sites. It is likely that this technology will advance considerably in the near future, allowing archaeologists to gather more information than is currently possible. If they study certain sites now, they risk contaminating or compromising them for future studies. Therefore, in order to maximize the potential for gathering knowledge in the long run, a team of archaeologists plans to delay the examination of a newly excavated site.

Which of the following would be most useful to investigate for the purpose of evaluating the plan's prospects for achieving its goal?

(A) Whether any of the contents of the site will significantly deteriorate before the anticipated technology is available

(B) Whether there will continue to be improvements on the relevant technology

(C) Whether the team can study a site other than the newly excavated site for the time being

(D) Whether the site was inhabited by a very ancient culture

(E) Whether the anticipated technology will damage objects under study

Evaluation of a Plan

Situation   To avoid prematurely compromising a newly excavated site, an archaeological team plans to postpone examining it until more advanced technology is developed that will let them gather more information from it. Their goal is to maximize the potential for gathering knowledge.

Reasoning   *What would be most helpful to investigate in order to assess how likely it is that delaying examination of the site will maximize the potential for gathering knowledge from it?* In order to maximize (or even increase) the potential for gathering knowledge from the site by delaying its examination, the risk of compromising the site by examining it now has to be greater than the risk that the site will be compromised as much or more by delaying the examination. The delay might also increase the risk that the site will never be examined at all—for example, the team might lose its funding while it delays, or changes in local political conditions might prevent the site's future examination. Investigating any of these risks could be helpful in assessing the likelihood that the team's plan will achieve its goal.

A   **Correct.** If any of the site's contents will significantly deteriorate before the technology becomes available, that could reduce the ability to gather future information from the site even more than examining and compromising the site now would.

B   The passage already tells us that it is likely the technology *will advance considerably in the near future*. Given this information, further inquiry into whether there will be any ongoing (perhaps minor) improvements is somewhat redundant and probably of minimal value with respect to evaluating the plan's likelihood of success.

C   Even if the team can study a second site in the meantime, they might maximize the overall potential for gathering knowledge by delaying the examination of either site, both sites, or neither site until more advanced technology is available.

D   The age of the culture that inhabited the site is irrelevant to assessing the risks of delaying the site's examination until more advanced technology is available.

E   Even if the anticipated technology will damage or destroy the objects under study, it might still maximize the amount of knowledge that can be gathered from those objects. Without any comparison between the damage risk that would be incurred by proceeding with the current technology and the damage risk that would be incurred by waiting, the mere fact that some damage would occur is irrelevant.

The correct answer is A.

670. More and more law firms specializing in corporate taxes are paid on a contingency-fee basis. Under this arrangement, if a case is won, the firm usually receives more than it would have received if it had been paid on the alternate hourly rate basis. If the case is lost, the firm receives nothing. Most firms are likely to make more under the contingency-fee arrangement.

Which of the following, if true, would most strengthen the prediction above?

(A) Firms that work exclusively under the hourly rate arrangement spend, on average, fewer hours on cases that are won than on cases that are lost.

(B) Some litigation can last for years before any decision is reached, and, even then, the decision may be appealed.

(C) Firms under the contingency-fee arrangement still pay their employees on an hourly basis.

(D) Since the majority of firms specialize in certain kinds of cases, they are able to assess accurately their chances of winning each potential case.

(E) Firms working under the contingency-fee arrangement take in fewer cases per year than do firms working under the hourly rate arrangement.

Argument Evaluation

Situation Law firms of a certain type are increasingly working on a contingency-fee basis, whereby the firm is only paid if the case is won. For the individual cases that are thus taken and won, the payments are generally greater than the total payments would have been if the firms had been paid on an hourly basis. Furthermore, although cases taken on a contingency-fee basis present a significant risk of working for many hours on a case and not being paid, the passage claims that most firms are likely to make more money, on average, than they would if they took their cases on an hourly basis.

Reasoning *What would most strongly indicate that, despite the risks, the law firms working on a contingency-fee basis are likely to make more money, on average, than they would have otherwise?* Our task is to find the statement that would most strongly support this prediction. A primary risk of using contingency fees is that a firm might have so many unsuccessful cases that the average revenue (and profit) is less than it would have been with hourly fees. Anything indicating that the firms might be able to reduce that risk would provide some support for the prediction that they would make more money with contingency fees than with hourly fees.

A Supposing that the firms mentioned in this option changed from working on an hourly rate basis to working on a contingency-fee basis, we would not have enough information to predict what the results would be. For example, we may have no reason to expect that the firm would accept the same cases that they would have accepted if they were working on an hourly rate basis. As such, patterns of work on cases taken on an hourly rate basis may be irrelevant for determining how much the firms would make if they were to take their cases on a contingency-fee basis.

B This answer choice indicates that firms taking cases on a contingency-fee basis can work on the cases for years without payment. Rather than supporting the point that firms would make more money if they worked on a contingency-fee basis, the option illustrates an aspect of the risks associated with this payment arrangement.

C This answer choice does not support the prediction that *most firms are likely to make more*; it could mean either that they are likely to have greater total revenue or that they are likely to have a greater amount of profit. With regard to gross revenue, the cost of staff time tells us nothing about how much money the firms are likely to take in. With regard to profits, the need to pay employees even for work on unsuccessful cases slightly weakens the prediction: all else being equal, profits would be higher if employees were not paid for work on such cases. However, we are given no information about whether firms might be able to have some alternative arrangement whereby they pay employees only for successful cases, or about whether they would have to pay considerably more with such arrangements.

D **Correct.** This answer choice suggests that firms working on a contingency-fee basis would be able to select cases that they would be likely to win and therefore be paid for. Thus, they could mitigate the risk of having too few successful cases to offset the lack of income from the unsuccessful ones. This increases the probability that the firms would be able to bring in more total revenue in the long run with a contingency-fee system than they would if they charged hourly fees. And since we are given no evidence that the ability to select high-win-probability cases would lead to greater costs, this also tends slightly to strengthen the prediction that the firms' profits would be greater in the long run.

E Although the difference in numbers of cases described in this option could, given certain possible facts, be relevant to the prediction made by the argument, we have not been given any such facts.

The correct answer is D.

671. Pretzel vendor: The new license fee for operating a pretzel stand outside the art museum is prohibitively expensive. Charging typical prices, I would need to sell an average of 25 pretzels per hour to break even. At my stand outside City Hall, with about as many passers-by as at the art museum, I average only 15 per hour. So I could not break even running a stand outside the art museum, much less turn a profit.

Which of the following, if true, most seriously weakens the pretzel vendor's argument?

(A) The pretzel vendor does not sell anything other than pretzels.

(B) People who visit the art museum are more likely to buy pretzels than are people who go to City Hall.

(C) The license fee for operating a pretzel stand outside City Hall will not increase.

(D) People who buy pretzels at pretzel stands are more likely to do so during the lunch hour than at other times.

(E) The city will grant more licenses for pretzel stands outside the art museum than the number it grants for stands outside City Hall.

Argument Evaluation

Situation Because of a new license fee for operating a pretzel stand outside the art museum, a pretzel vendor would have to sell on average 25 pretzels per hour to break even, which is 10 more on average than the vendor sells outside City Hall. But the museum would have no more passers-by than City Hall has. The vendor concludes that a pretzel stand outside the museum would not break even.

Reasoning *What additional information, if true, would most weaken the support, in light of the given information, for the prediction that the vendor would not break even running a stand outside the art museum?* The vendor's prediction that a pretzel stand outside the art museum would not break even is based on the following considerations: (1) the vendor would have to sell 10 more pretzels on average per hour than the vendor sells outside City Hall, and (2) there are no more passers-by outside the museum than outside City Hall. But what matters is not how many *potential* customers pass by the art museum. What matters is how many *actual* customers there will be. If the people who pass by the stand outside the museum are more likely to buy pretzels than the people who pass by the stand at City Hall are, the prediction might fail.

A This would be more likely to strengthen the argument than weaken it. If the vendor did sell something other than pretzels outside the museum but not outside City Hall, then it is possible that this product would help the vendor at least break even. But this answer choice tells us that the vendor sells only pretzels.

B **Correct.** If the people who visit the museum are more likely to buy pretzels than the people who go to City Hall are, then it could be that the vendor will be able to sell 25 pretzels per hour on average. This could be true even if there are not more people outside the art museum than outside City Hall.

C The vendor's prediction is only about whether a stand outside the art museum could break even, not about whether the business in the current location would continue to break even. For that prediction, it does not matter whether there will be a fee for a stand outside City Hall.

D The vendor's argument does not include or depend on anything about when the pretzels are sold at the stand. So, a claim that more pretzels are sold during the lunch hour than at any other time does not weaken the argument.

E This claim strengthens the argument instead of weakening it. If there are more pretzel stands outside the art museum than there are outside City Hall, then there would be more competition. That might make it harder to sell even 15 pretzels per hour, let alone 25.

The correct answer is B.

672. Beginning in 1966, all new cars sold in Morodia were required to have safety belts and power steering. Previously, most cars in Morodia were without these features. Safety belts help to prevent injuries in collisions, and power steering helps to avoid collisions in the first place. But even though in 1966 one-seventh of the cars in Morodia were replaced with new cars, the number of car collisions and collision-related injuries did not decline.

Which of the following, if true about Morodia, most helps to explain why the number of collisions and collision-related injuries in Morodia failed to decline in 1966?

(A) Because of a driver-education campaign, most drivers and passengers in cars that did have safety belts used them in 1966.

(B) Most of the new cars bought in 1966 were bought in the months of January and February.

(C) In 1965, substantially more than one-seventh of the cars in Morodia were replaced with new cars.

(D) An excessive reliance on the new safety features led many owners of new cars to drive less cautiously in 1966 than before.

(E) The seat belts and power steering put into new cars sold in 1966 had to undergo strict quality-control inspections by manufacturers, whether the cars were manufactured in Morodia or not.

Argument Construction

Situation Starting in 1966, new cars sold in Morodia were required to have safety belts and power steering. But the numbers of car collisions and collision-related injuries did not decline that year.

Reasoning *What could explain why the newly required safety features did not reduce the numbers of collisions and collision-related injuries in 1966?* The passage says that power steering helps to prevent collisions and that safety belts help to prevent collision-related injuries. Since most Morodian cars previously lacked these features, and one-seventh of them were replaced with new cars in 1966, the proportion of cars with these features must have increased that year. This should have reduced the numbers of collisions and collision-related injuries unless some other factor counteracted the reductions. Evidence of any such countervailing factor would help to explain why the numbers did not decrease.

A Increased usage of safety belts should have reduced the number of collision-related injuries, so it would not help explain why this number did not decrease.

B If the new cars bought in 1966 were mostly purchased early in the year, the increased proportion of cars with the newly required safety features should have started more significantly reducing the numbers of collisions and collision-related injuries early in the year, producing greater reductions for the year as a whole.

C However many cars were replaced in the year before the safety features were required, in 1966 the replacement of one-seventh of all Morodian cars should still have increased the overall proportion of Morodian cars with the safety features and thus reduced the numbers of collisions and collision-related injuries.

D **Correct.** If many owners of the cars with the new safety features drove less cautiously, their recklessness could have increased the overall numbers of collisions and collision-related injuries despite any benefits from the safety features.

E Strict quality-control inspections should have made the safety features more reliable, further reducing the numbers of collisions and collision-related injuries.

The correct answer is D.

673. Manufacturers of mechanical pencils make most of their profit on pencil leads rather than on the pencils themselves. The Write Company, which cannot sell its leads as cheaply as other manufacturers can, plans to alter the design of its mechanical pencil so that it will accept only a newly designed Write Company lead, which will be sold at the same price as the Write Company's current lead.

Which of the following, if true, most strongly supports the Write Company's projection that its plan will lead to an increase in its sales of pencil leads?

(A) The new Write Company pencil will be introduced at a price higher than the price the Write Company charges for its current model.

(B) In the foreseeable future, manufacturers of mechanical pencils will probably have to raise the prices they charge for mechanical pencils.

(C) The newly designed Write Company lead will cost somewhat more to manufacture than the Write Company's current lead does.

(D) A rival manufacturer recently announced similar plans to introduce a mechanical pencil that would accept only the leads produced by that manufacturer.

(E) In extensive test marketing, mechanical-pencil users found the new Write Company pencil markedly superior to other mechanical pencils they had used.

Argument Evaluation

Situation   The Write Company makes mechanical pencils and pencil-lead refills. Companies in this type of business make most of their profits from selling the leads, but the Write Company's leads cost more than leads made by other firms, so the refills are not selling well. The company plans to alter the design of its pencil and leads so that only the company's leads will fit. The new leads will be sold at the same price as the existing ones. The company projects that its plan will lead to an increase in the sale of its leads.

Reasoning   *Which of the stated pieces of additional information most strongly supports the company's projection of an increase in sales of leads?* Presumably, because of the price difference, users of Write Company pencils are often refilling them with competitors' cheaper leads instead of Write Company leads. If the number of sales of the company's redesigned pencil did not drop significantly below the number of sales for its original pencil, a likely consequence would be a significant increase in refill sales for the redesigned pencil, because users would no longer have the option of using competitors' leads. The pencil would have to be priced competitively and function well.

A   This slightly weakens support for the company's projection because it suggests that the redesigned pencil might not sell sufficiently well to boost lead sales unless the redesigned pencil is perceived by potential buyers as being worth the higher price.

B   It is not clear whether, if this predicted outcome were to occur, it would help or hinder the Write Company in selling more of its pencil leads. For all we know, the Write Company's pencil and leads could become less price-competitive compared with those of other firms.

C   Since the new lead will cost the same as the current one, the increased unit cost would, all else being equal, tend to reduce profits unless this reduction were compensated for by increased sales volume. Given that the price to consumers would stay the same, the lower profit per lead does not suggest that consumers would buy more of the leads.

D   This provides too little information to tell what the effect of the competitor's action might be. For one thing, we have no information about whether the competitor would continue to sell its leads at a lower price than that of Write Company leads. The competitor's action might create additional competition for the Write Company's new products, increasing the risk that the Write Company's plan will fail. On the other hand, the competitor's pencils would have a similar potential drawback to that of the new Write Company pencils (restriction on the choice of refill leads), so it might tend to reduce the number of consumers who would avoid the new Write Company pencils in favor of the competitor's product.

E   **Correct.** This information suggests that sales of the Write Company's redesigned pencil may increase (or at least will probably not significantly decrease), that many consumers will find the company's pencils worth the additional expense of refilling them with Write Company leads, and that consequently the company's plan to increase lead sales will succeed.

The correct answer is E.

674. Enterprise Bank currently requires customers with checking accounts to maintain a minimum balance or pay a monthly fee. Enterprise plans to offer accounts with no monthly fee and no minimum-balance requirement; to cover their projected administrative costs of $3 per account per month, they plan to charge $30 for overdrawing an account. Since each month on average slightly more than 10 percent of Enterprise's customers overdraw their accounts, bank officials predict the new accounts will generate a profit.

Which of the following, if true, most strongly supports the bank officials' prediction?

(A) Some of Enterprise Bank's current checking account customers are expected to switch to the new accounts once they are offered.

(B) One-third of Enterprise Bank's revenues are currently derived from monthly fees tied to checking accounts.

(C) Many checking account customers who occasionally pay a fee for not maintaining a minimum balance in their account generally maintain a balance well above the minimum.

(D) Customers whose checking accounts do not have a minimum-balance requirement are more likely than others to overdraw their checking accounts.

(E) Customers whose checking accounts do not have a minimum-balance requirement are more likely than others to write checks for small amounts.

Evaluation of a Plan

Situation   Enterprise Bank gives customers checking accounts with no monthly fee provided they maintain a certain minimum balance. However, the bank plans to offer accounts with no minimum-balance requirement and no monthly fee. It plans to cover the bank's $3 per account per month administrative cost by charging a $30 penalty for overdrafts. Only slightly more than 10 percent of customers, on average, overdraw their accounts in a month. The bank officials predict the new accounts will generate a profit.

Reasoning   *What new information, if accurate, would most strongly support the prediction?* If about only one customer in ten, on average, currently has an overdraft in a month, and if this trend continues among customers who sign up for the new account, then the proposed $30 penalty per overdraft will cover the $30 cost of maintaining checking accounts for 10 customers per month. Would removing the minimum-balance requirement significantly increase the 10 percent overdraft rate? If so, then significantly more than one in ten customers, on average, would pay a $30 penalty. If this were so, then the new plan would yield a profit, as predicted.

A   "Some" might mean only a few, and this would probably not be sufficient to make the new plan significantly profitable.

B   This suggests that many customers with the current minimum-balance no-monthly-fee account do not maintain the minimum-balance requirement and pay fees instead. However, this information by itself seems to have little bearing on the new plan.

C   Such customers would be likely to overdraw their accounts less frequently. This suggests that if a preponderance of the customers for the proposed new account were such customers, the overdraft rate would decrease, and the proposed new account would be less profitable, or even unprofitable.

D   **Correct.** This information provides strong support for the bank officials' prediction. It indicates that the currently roughly 10 percent overdraft rate might increase drastically with the no-minimum-balance account and, on average, cause the imposition of a $30 penalty on significantly more than 10 percent of customers per month. This would make the new account significantly profitable.

E   This suggests that a check written by one of these customers is more likely to be for a small amount and is therefore somewhat less likely to cause an overdraft (unless such customers typically have small checking balances, which we are not told). If there were many such customers for the proposed new account, the overdraft rate might be less than 10 percent; this would indicate that the new account might not turn out to be profitable.

The correct answer is D.

675. Highway official: When resurfacing our concrete bridges, we should use electrically conductive concrete (ECC) rather than standard concrete. In the winter, ECC can be heated by passing an electric current through it, thereby preventing ice buildup. The cost of the electricity needed is substantially lower than the cost of the deicing salt we currently use.

Taxpayer: But ECC is vastly more expensive than standard concrete, so your proposal is probably not justifiable on economic grounds.

Which of the following, if true, could best be used by the highway official to support the official's proposal in the face of the taxpayer's objection?

(A) The use of deicing salt causes corrosion of reinforcing steel in concrete bridge decks and damage to the concrete itself, thereby considerably shortening the useful life of concrete bridges.

(B) Severe icing conditions can cause power outages and slow down the work of emergency crews trying to get power restored.

(C) In weather conditions conducive to icing, ice generally forms on the concrete surfaces of bridges well before it forms on parts of the roadway that go over solid ground.

(D) Aside from its potential use for deicing bridges, ECC might also be an effective means of keeping other concrete structures such as parking garages and airport runways ice free.

(E) If ECC were to be used for a bridge surface, the electric current would be turned on only at times at which ice was likely to form.

Evaluation of a Plan

Situation A highway official recommends using electrically conductive concrete (ECC) for resurfacing concrete bridges. This would allow the transmission of an electric current to prevent ice buildup in winter. The highway official supports the proposal by stating that the cost of the electricity used would be substantially lower than the cost of the deicing salt used at present. A taxpayer objects that ECC is much more expensive than standard concrete.

Reasoning *Which piece of additional information would most logically address the objection of the taxpayer?* Consider whether there could be other, indirect or long-term, costs associated with either of the two deicing methods (salt, electricity). For example, would use of ECC involve installation of additional infrastructure to provide electric power to the bridges—and, if so, how would the total costs compare with total existing costs? What are the cost implications of the current use of deicing salt? Any additional information that addresses these questions will be relevant. Note that the taxpayer's objection primarily concerns the capital cost of ECC bridge surfacing.

A **Correct.** The use of deicing salt causes corrosion that considerably shortens the useful life of the bridge. Clearly, replacement of a bridge would involve a large capital expenditure. This is a major reason for reconsidering the use of deicing salt. Of course, absent additional information about total costs of installation and use of each deicing method, it is not a conclusive reason to discontinue using deicing salt.

B Power outages in severe icing conditions would cause dangerous road-surface conditions on bridges surfaced with ECC, thus requiring a backup method of deicing in such circumstances. This would probably require road maintenance systems to use an auxiliary power backup or deicing salt in rare cases. However, this provides no evidence that the cost of emergency backup measures would exceed the overall savings available with the use of ECC.

C This is a reason for ensuring that deicing of bridges is given priority over deicing other places, but this prioritization can be done whatever method of deicing is used.

D The issues raised by the statements of the highway official and the taxpayer concern only the use of ECC for deicing bridges, so the information in this answer choice has no clear or direct relevance to that issue.

E This most likely offers no relevant additional information, since it is presumably already taken into account in the claim that the cost of electricity for deicing is lower than the cost of deicing salt. So, this merely acknowledges one way to help optimize the costs associated with ECC deicing, but it is not, by itself, a substantial refutation of the taxpayer's objection.

The correct answer is A.

676. In virtually any industry, technological improvements increase labor productivity, which is the output of goods and services per person-hour worked. In Parland's industries, labor productivity is significantly higher than it is in Vergia's industries. Clearly, therefore, Parland's industries must, on the whole, be further advanced technologically than Vergia's are. The argument is most vulnerable to which of the following criticisms?

(A) It offers a conclusion that is no more than a paraphrase of one of the pieces of information provided in its support.

(B) It presents as evidence in support of a claim information that is inconsistent with other evidence presented in support of the same claim.

(C) It takes one possible cause of a condition to be the actual cause of that condition without considering any other possible causes.

(D) It takes a condition to be the effect of something that happened only after the condition already existed.

(E) It makes a distinction that presupposes the truth of the conclusion that is to be established.

Argument Evaluation

Situation   Technological improvements in nearly every industry increase labor productivity, which is the output of goods and services per person-hour worked. Because labor productivity is significantly higher in Parland than Vergia, Parland's industries are, in general, more technologically advanced than Vergia's.

Reasoning   *To which criticism is the argument most vulnerable?* Though one factor, such as technological advancements, may lead to greater labor productivity, it may not be the only such factor, or even a necessary factor, leading to greater labor productivity. Therefore, the mere fact that one region's labor is more productive than another's is not sufficient to establish that the former region is more technologically advanced than the latter region is.

A   The conclusion is not merely a paraphrase of the pieces of information provided in its support. Indeed, the problem with the argument is that the conclusion goes too far beyond what the premises merit.

B   The premises of the argument are not inconsistent with one another.

C   **Correct.** This accurately describes the flaw in the argument because the reasons given in the argument for its conclusion would be good reasons only if there were no other plausible explanations for Parland's greater labor productivity.

D   The argument does not mention how long Parland has had more productive labor, or when technological improvements would have occurred.

E   Neither of the premises contains anything that presupposes the conclusion to be true. The argument's two premises are *Technological improvements in nearly every industry increase labor productivity* and *Labor productivity is significantly higher in Parland than Vergia.* The argument's conclusion states *Parland's industries must, on the whole, be further advanced than Vergia's are.* If anything in the premises presupposed that conclusion, the conclusion could not be false if the premises were true. But the conclusion can be false even if both premises are true. Suppose, for instance, that Parland and Vergia engage in different industries and Parland's industries inherently have greater labor productivity. That might not be because Parland's industries are more technologically advanced than Vergia's are, but only because of the nature of the different industries. Yet it can nonetheless be true that technological improvements increase labor productivity.

The correct answer is C.

677. Chaco Canyon, a settlement of the ancient Anasazi culture in North America, had massive buildings. **It must have been a major Anasazi center.** Analysis of wood samples shows that some of the timber for the buildings came from the Chuska and San Mateo mountains, 50 miles from Chaco Canyon. **Only a major cultural center would have the organizational power to import timber from 50 miles away.**

In the argument given, the two portions in **boldface** play which of the following roles?

(A) The first is a premise used to support the argument's main conclusion; the second is the argument's main conclusion.

(B) The first is the argument's main conclusion; the second is a premise used to support that conclusion.

(C) The first is one of two premises used to support the argument's main conclusion; the second is the other of those two premises.

(D) The first is a premise used to support the argument's main conclusion; the second is a premise used to support another conclusion drawn in the argument.

(E) The first is inferred from another statement in the argument; the second is inferred from the first.

Argument Construction

Situation   The ancient Anasazi settlement at Chaco Canyon had massive buildings, for which some of the timber came from mountains 50 miles away.

Reasoning   *What roles do the statement that Chaco Canyon must have been a major Anasazi center and the statement that only a major center would have the organizational power to import timber from 50 miles away play in the argument?* The first and third sentences in the passage are both factual observations. Since no further support is provided for either of them, neither can be a conclusion in the argument. The final sentence (i.e., the second **boldfaced** portion of the argument) is a speculative generalization about major cultural centers. None of the other statements gives us any reason to think this generalization is true, so it cannot be a conclusion in the argument either. However, the third and fourth sentences together imply that Chaco Canyon was a major cultural center, and the first sentence indicates that it was Anasazi. So, together, the first, third, and fourth sentences all support the claim that Chaco Canyon was a major Anasazi cultural center and thus more generally a major Anasazi center, as the second sentence asserts. Therefore, the first, third, and fourth sentences are all premises that jointly support the second sentence (i.e., the first **boldfaced** portion of the argument) as a conclusion.

A   As explained above in the Reasoning section, the first **boldfaced** sentence is a conclusion supported by the second **boldfaced** sentence, not the other way around.

B   **Correct.** As explained above in the Reasoning section, the first **boldfaced** sentence is the argument's only stated conclusion, and thus is its main conclusion, while all the other sentences are premises used to support it; therefore, the second **boldfaced** sentence (*Only a major cultural center . . . 50 miles away*) is a premise used to support the conclusion.

C   As explained above in the Reasoning section, the first **boldfaced** sentence is the argument's conclusion, not a premise used to support the conclusion.

D   As explained above in the Reasoning section, the first **boldfaced** sentence is the argument's only stated conclusion, and there is no reason to suppose that the argument is intended to lead to any other tacit conclusion that the second **boldfaced** sentence is intended to support.

E   As explained above in the Reasoning section, the first **boldfaced** sentence is inferred from the three other statements in the argument together, not from any one of them alone. The second **boldfaced** sentence is a speculative generalization that cannot be, and is not meant to be, inferred from the first **boldfaced** sentence or from any other statement in the argument.

The correct answer is B.

678. Regulations will not allow a pesticide that is toxic to humans to be used inside houses unless the pesticide will dissipate completely from the air within eight hours after its application. One test pesticide manufacturers typically use to determine how quickly anti-termite pesticides dissipate involves spraying the pesticides on the walls of room-sized plywood boxes and then timing their dissipation.

Which of the following would it be most useful to know in order to evaluate whether a dissipation time of just under eight hours on the manufacturers' test indicates an anti-termite pesticide that is toxic to humans obeys regulations for use in houses?

(A) Whether anti-termite pesticides dissipate more slowly in furnished rooms than in plywood boxes

(B) Whether people who apply anti-termite pesticides typically wear protective equipment that prevents them from being exposed to the pesticide

(C) Whether people whose house is being treated with anti-termite pesticide generally know they should remain out of their house during the hours immediately after the pesticide's application

(D) Whether there are anti-termite pesticides toxic to humans that, when subjected to the manufacturers' test, dissipate completely from the air in the boxes in well under eight hours

(E) Whether anti-termite pesticides that are not toxic to humans tend to take longer to dissipate than those that are toxic

Evaluation of a Plan

Situation   Pesticides toxic to humans are not approved for residential use unless they dissipate completely within eight hours after being sprayed. To determine whether certain pesticides dissipate within the required timeframe and so meet regulations, manufacturers spray them in plywood boxes and then check to see if they have dissipated eight hours later.

Reasoning   *What additional factor could affect the question of whether the pesticides meet regulations?* The manufacturers' test relies on the assumption that the pesticides behave the same way in a plywood box as they would in a typical residence. It would therefore be helpful to know if that assumption is accurate, or if conditions in a residence might affect the speed at which pesticides dissipate.

A   **Correct.** If the pesticides dissipate more slowly under typical residential conditions, such as furniture being present, then pesticides that dissipate in slightly less than eight hours in a plywood box might take longer than that to dissipate in a home and would therefore not meet regulations.

B   The regulations in question do not concern the exposure of the workers who apply pesticides, so whether or not they wear protective gear is not helpful in determining if those regulations are met.

C   The knowledge of people in houses treated with pesticides affects their exposure to those pesticides, not whether the pesticides meet regulations.

D   The fact that some pesticides dissipate faster than others is not relevant to the question asked. That question is: What additional information would be useful in evaluating pesticides that barely succeed in meeting the manufacturer's eight-hour test?

E   The relative dissipation rates of toxic versus nontoxic pesticides are not relevant to the question of whether the toxic pesticides meet regulations.

The correct answer is A.

679. Which of the following most logically completes the argument?

In a typical year, Innovair's airplanes are involved in 35 collisions while parked or being towed in airports, with a resulting yearly cost of $1,000,000 for repairs.

To reduce the frequency of ground collisions, Innovair will begin giving its ground crews additional training, at an annual cost of $500,000. Although this will cut the number of ground collisions by about half at best, the drop in repair costs can be expected to be much greater, since _____.

(A) most ground collisions happen when ground crews are rushing to minimize the time a delayed airplane spends on the ground

(B) a ground collision typically occurs when there are no passengers on the airplane

(C) the additional training will focus on helping ground crews avoid those kinds of ground collisions that cause the most costly damage

(D) the $500,000 cost figure for the additional training of ground crews includes the wages that those crews will earn during the time spent in actual training

(E) most ground collisions have been caused by the least experienced ground-crew members

Evaluation of a Plan

Situation An airline will give its ground crews additional training to reduce the frequency of the collisions its airplanes are involved in while parked or being towed in airports.

Reasoning *What premise would most logically support the conclusion that the additional training will reduce repair costs from ground collisions much more than it reduces the number of such collisions?* The key word *since* before the blank shows that the argument should be completed with a premise that supports the preceding claim that the *drop in repair costs can be expected to be much greater.* What statement would support that claim? Note that the annual cost of training, $500,000, is half as much as the yearly cost of the repairs needed as a result of ground collisions, $1,000,000. We are told that the training will cut the number of ground collisions by at most about half, so if the drop in repair costs will be much greater than half, which would need to be the case to make the training worthwhile, what would have to be true of the ground collisions that the training will help the ground crews avoid? Presumably, they would have to be among the higher repair cost collisions, as opposed to the less serious collisions that result in lower repair costs. That is, the collisions that are avoided would have to make up more than half of the repair costs, so they would have to be costlier than average, given that the number of collisions avoided is no more than half. Thus, it would be quite useful to include in the argument a premise providing evidence that the training will help avoid the sorts of ground collisions that lead to above average repair costs.

A We are given no reason to believe that the additional training would affect how much ground crews rush to minimize delays.

B The number of passengers is not clearly relevant to the repair costs resulting from a ground collision and in any case would not be affected by additional ground crew training.

C **Correct.** If the training especially helps the ground crews avoid those kinds of collisions that cause the most costly damage—that is, damage from ground collisions that has higher repair costs than the average repair costs for damage from ground collisions—then it will probably reduce repair costs by more than half.

D Whether the cited expense for training includes wages is irrelevant to whether the training will reduce repair costs more than it reduces the number of collisions.

E This suggests that the additional training may help reduce the number of collisions, not that it will reduce repair costs more than it reduces the number of collisions.

The correct answer is C.

680. Scientists propose placing seismic stations on the floor of the Pacific Ocean to warn threatened coastal communities on the northwestern coast of the United States of approaching tidal waves caused by earthquakes. Since forewarned communities could take steps to evacuate, many of the injuries and deaths that would otherwise occur could be avoided if the government would implement this proposal.

The answer to which of the following questions would be most important in determining whether implementing the proposal would be likely to achieve the desired result?

(A) When was the last time that the coastal communities were threatened by an approaching tidal wave?

(B) How far below sea level would the stations be located?

(C) Would there be enough time after receiving warning of an approaching tidal wave for communities to evacuate safely?

(D) How soon after a tidal wave hits land is it safe for evacuees to return to their communities?

(E) Can the stations be equipped to collect and relay information about phenomena other than tidal waves caused by earthquakes?

Evaluation of a Plan

Situation   In order to provide advance warning of tidal waves threatening coastal communities, scientists suggest the government should install stations to measure seismic activity on the ocean floor. The passage argues the advance warning provided by these stations would allow communities to evacuate and therefore prevent significant numbers of deaths and injuries.

Reasoning   *What would affect the question of whether the seismic stations would effectively prevent deaths and injuries?* The proposed seismic stations will only achieve their intended result—preventing significant numbers of deaths and injuries in coastal communities—if the warnings from those stations arrive far enough in advance of an oncoming tidal wave to allow the affected communities to evacuate in time. A warning that comes too late will be unhelpful.

A   The time elapsed since the *last* tidal wave has no bearing on whether or not seismic stations will prevent deaths from the *next* tidal wave.

B   The depth at which undersea stations are placed is not obviously relevant to the question of whether those stations will achieve their intended result.

C   **Correct.** If warnings from the seismic stations arrive too late for communities to evacuate safely, then those stations might not prevent many deaths and injuries among the affected population and could conceivably even make the situation worse—for example, by creating traffic jams on vulnerable coastal roads.

D   The question of when evacuees could return has no bearing on whether the seismic stations would have the desired effect of preventing deaths.

E   The stations are intended to protect against tidal waves specifically, so other data those stations provide might be useful but are not relevant to whether the stations achieve their intended purpose.

The correct answer is C.

681. Only a reduction of 10 percent in the number of scheduled flights using Greentown's airport will allow the delays that are so common there to be avoided. Hevelia airstrip, 40 miles away, would, if upgraded and expanded, be an attractive alternative for fully 20 percent of the passengers using Greentown airport. Nevertheless, experts reject the claim that turning Hevelia into a full-service airport would end the chronic delays at Greentown.

Which of the following, if true, most helps to justify the experts' position?

(A) Turning Hevelia into a full-service airport would require not only substantial construction at the airport itself but also the construction of new access highways.

(B) A second largely undeveloped airstrip close to Greentown airport would be a more attractive alternative than Hevelia for many passengers who now use Greentown.

(C) Hevelia airstrip lies in a relatively undeveloped area but would, if it became a full-service airport, be a magnet for commercial and residential development.

(D) If an airplane has to wait to land, the extra jet fuel required adds significantly to the airline's costs.

(E) Several airlines use Greentown as a regional hub, so that most flights landing at Greentown have many passengers who then take different flights to reach their final destinations.

Evaluation of a Plan

Situation To avoid the delays now common at Greentown's airport, the number of scheduled flights there would need to be reduced by 10 percent. If the nearby Hevelia airstrip were expanded and upgraded, it would be an attractive alternative for 20 percent of Greentown airport's passengers. Still, experts do not believe that the delays at Greentown would end even if Hevelia were turned into a full-service airport.

Reasoning *Which statement most supports the experts' position?* If the number of flights at Greentown's airport did not drop by at least 10 percent, despite the fact that 20 percent of the passengers who currently use Greentown's airport would find nearby Hevelia airstrip an attractive alternative, then the delays would not be avoided. Airlines generally use certain airports as regional hubs—an airport through which an airline routes most of its traffic—so, even if many passengers would be willing to use Hevelia airstrip, the number of flights at Greentown may not decline significantly, or at all.

A The experts' position concerns what would happen to the flight delays at Greentown airport if the Hevelia airstrip were converted into a full-service airport. So, the fact that there are great costs involved in making such a conversion—possibly making it unlikely—has no bearing on the effects such a conversion would have on flight delays at Greentown if it were to be carried out.

B This statement indicates that the undeveloped airstrip near Greentown might be a better way to alleviate flight delays at Greentown, but it tells us nothing about the effects that converting the Hevelia airstrip to a full-service airport would have were it to be carried out.

C This in no way explains why converting the Hevelia airstrip into a full-service airport would not alleviate the problem with flight delays at Greentown.

D This provides a reason to think that reducing the number of flights at Greentown might make the airport more efficient. But that has no bearing on the effect that converting the Hevelia airstrip to a full-service airport might have on flight delays at Greentown.

E **Correct.** This statement provides support for the experts' position because it gives a reason for thinking that the number of scheduled flights at Greentown would not be reduced, even if Hevelia airstrip became an attractive alternative for some 20 percent of Greentown's passengers.

The correct answer is E.

682. Farmer: Worldwide, just three grain crops—rice, wheat, and corn—account for most human caloric intake. To maintain this level of caloric intake and also keep pace with global population growth, yields per acre from each of these crops will have to increase at least 1.5 percent every year, given that the supply of cultivated land is diminishing. Therefore, the government should increase funding for research into new ways to improve yields.

Which of the following is an assumption on which the farmer's argument depends?

(A) It is solely the government's responsibility to ensure that the amount of rice, wheat, and corn produced worldwide keeps pace with global population growth.

(B) Increasing government funding for research into new ways to improve the yields per acre of rice, wheat, and corn crops would help to increase total worldwide annual production of food from these crops.

(C) Increasing the yields per acre of rice, wheat, and corn is more important than increasing the yields per acre of other crops.

(D) Current levels of funding for research into ways of improving grain crop yields per acre have enabled grain crop yields per acre to increase by more than 1.5 percent per year worldwide.

(E) In coming decades, rice, wheat, and corn will become a minor part of human caloric intake, unless there is government-funded research to increase their yields per acre.

Argument Construction

Situation   The farmer states that although the worldwide human population is increasing, the supply of cultivated land is decreasing. We thus need to increase yields for the food crops that account for most of human caloric intake—rice, wheat, and corn—if we are to maintain our existing caloric intake. The increase in yields, according to the farmer, would need to be at least 1.5 percent every year.

Reasoning   *What must be true if we are to accept the farmer's conclusion, that the government should increase funding for research into new ways to improve crop yields, on the basis of the above statements?* The farmer uses the above statements as premises of an argument for an increase in government funding for research on crop yields. Supposing that the farmer's statements are true, we need to find in the available options the statement that, if added to the argument, may allow us to accept the farmer's conclusion, based on the argument.

A   Whether or not nongovernmental entities such as NGOs (nongovernmental organizations) are responsible for helping to ensure that humans have an adequate amount of food, governments may or may not also have this responsibility.

B   **Correct.** If government funding of this research does not increase crop yields, then the premises of the argument provide no support for the conclusion that the government should provide such funding. The cogency of the argument thus depends on this statement.

C   Crops in addition to rice, wheat, and corn could also be very important, and perhaps essential for human existence. However, this would not diminish the importance of food crops such as rice, wheat, and corn.

D   This option may suggest that current levels of funding of research into crop yields are sufficient for purposes of our obtaining the necessary crop yields.

E   This option suggests that rice, wheat, and corn may be replaced by other crops, because the other crops have better yields. Because we might thus have a means for increasing crop yields that does not involve an increase in government research funding, this option may actually decrease the support for the conclusion.

The correct answer is B.

683. The air quality board recently informed Coffee Roast, a small coffee roasting firm, of a complaint regarding the smoke from its roaster. Recently enacted air quality regulations require machines roasting more than 10 pounds of coffee to be equipped with expensive smoke-dissipating afterburners. The firm, however, roasts only 8 pounds of coffee at a time. Nevertheless, the company has decided to purchase and install an afterburner.

Which of the following, if true, most strongly supports the firm's decision?

(A) Until settling on the new air quality regulations, the board had debated whether to require afterburners for machines roasting more than 5 pounds of coffee at a time.

(B) Coffee roasted in a machine equipped with an afterburner has its flavor subtly altered.

(C) The cost to the firm of an afterburner is less than the cost of replacing its roaster with a smaller one.

(D) Fewer complaints are reported in areas that maintain strict rules regarding afterburners.

(E) The firm has reason to fear that negative publicity regarding the complaints could result in lost sales.

Evaluation of a Plan

Situation   After being informed of a complaint about smoke from its coffee roaster, a firm decided to purchase and install an afterburner to reduce or eliminate emissions of smoke, even though the roaster roasts too little coffee at a time for an afterburner to be legally required.

Reasoning   *What would have been a good reason for the firm to buy and install the afterburner?* The only factors mentioned that might give the firm reason to buy an afterburner are the complaint about smoke and the regulations requiring an afterburner. Since the regulations do not apply in this case, the complaint is more likely to have motivated the firm's decision. Any serious potential consequences the firm might have faced from failure to address the complaint could have provided a good reason to buy and install the afterburner.

A   If this debate had still been ongoing when the firm made its decision, uncertainty about the pending regulations might have justified the decision. But the debate had already been settled before the firm decided to purchase the afterburner, and the regulations clearly did not require one.

B   An unspecified alteration in flavor is not clearly a good reason to use an afterburner—the afterburner might worsen the flavor.

C   The firm's roaster was already small enough that the regulations did not require it to be replaced, even without an afterburner.

D   This reason relates only to rules regarding afterburners, not to Coffee Roast's purchase of an afterburner, which was not mandated by regulations. Furthermore, it could be that the air quality regulations recently enacted are among the strictest in any region, which could result in fewer complaints regardless of whether Coffee Roast installs an afterburner.

E   **Correct.** Since installing an afterburner is a plausible way to address the complaint and prevent future complaints, the firm has plausible reasons to believe this strategy will help it avoid the negative publicity and lost sales it fears. These considerations could have reasonably justified its decision.

The correct answer is E.

684. A study compared a sample of Swedish people older than 75 who needed in-home assistance with a similar sample of Israeli people. The people in the two samples received both informal assistance, provided by family and friends, and formal assistance, professionally provided. Although Sweden and Israel have equally well-funded and comprehensive systems for providing formal assistance, the study found that the people in the Swedish sample received more formal assistance, on average, than those in the Israeli sample.

Which of the following, if true, does most to explain the difference that the study found?

(A) A companion study found that among children needing special in-home care, the amount of formal assistance they received was roughly the same in Sweden as in Israel.

(B) More Swedish than Israeli people older than 75 live in rural areas where formal assistance services are sparse or nonexistent.

(C) Although in both Sweden and Israel much of the funding for formal assistance ultimately comes from the central government, the local structures through which assistance is delivered are different in the two countries.

(D) In recent decades, the increase in life expectancy of someone who is 75 years old has been greater in Israel than in Sweden.

(E) In Israel, people older than 75 tend to live with their children, whereas in Sweden people of that age tend to live alone.

Argument Construction

Situation   A study of elder care in Israel and Sweden found that in Sweden, of the total amount of care that people older than 75 and needing in-home assistance received, the proportion of care that was formal, i.e., provided by professional care personnel, was greater than in Israel. Both Sweden and Israel had equally good systems for providing formal care, and in both countries, the elderly also received informal care, i.e., care provided by friends and family.

Reasoning   *Among the factors given, which would most contribute to explaining the difference the study found between Sweden and Israel with respect to elder care?* A good guess would be that there is a difference in some societal factor that affects the difference the study found. For example, perhaps elders in one of the countries regard maintaining independence as a higher priority than elders in the other and consequently try to rely less on friends and family? Perhaps patterns of decline in ability to remain independent are different in the two countries? Or perhaps a greater proportion of elders live alone in one of the countries than in the other?

A   The difference to be explained concerns only elder care, not care of children.

B   The fact that formal elder care is less available in Swedish rural areas than in Israeli rural areas might suggest that there would be a greater reliance on informal care in such areas in Sweden. But this new information throws little light on how the overall proportions of formal and informal care in each country would be affected.

C   This information is not specific enough to help explain the precise difference found in the study. It is reasonable to assume that the study was conducted with sufficient rigor to take account of any relevant structural differences in the delivery of formal elder care.

D   This could suggest either that the greater proportion of informal elder care in Israel contributes to greater life expectancy or that greater life expectancy signals greater fitness during old age that would make it more practical for friends and family to provide informal elder care.

E   **Correct.** The prevalence in Israel of elders living in family settings—in contrast to Sweden, where elders tend to live alone—offers a plausible explanation of the difference that the study found in the patterns of elder care in Israel and Sweden. It seems reasonable to think that, all things being equal, elders living alone would use formal elder care services more often than elders living with friends or family.

The correct answer is E.

685. Film director: It is true that certain characters and plot twists in my newly released film *The Big Heist* are similar to characters and plot twists in *Thieves*, a movie that came out last year. Pointing to these similarities, the film studio that produced *Thieves* is now accusing me of taking ideas from that film. The accusation is clearly without merit. All production work on *The Big Heist* was actually completed months before *Thieves* was released.

Which of the following, if true, provides the strongest support for the director's position?

(A) Before *Thieves* began production, its script had been circulating for several years among various film studios, including the studio that produced *The Big Heist*.

(B) The characters and plot twists that are most similar in the two films have close parallels in many earlier films of the same genre.

(C) The film studio that produced *Thieves* seldom produces films in this genre.

(D) The director of *Thieves* worked with the director of *The Big Heist* on several earlier projects.

(E) Production work on *Thieves* began before production work on *The Big Heist* was started.

Argument Evaluation

Situation   The director of the film *The Big Heist* has been accused, by the studio that produced the film *Thieves*, of taking ideas from the film. The director responds that the accusation lacks merit, since all production work on *The Big Heist* was completed before *Thieves* appeared last year in theaters.

Reasoning   *Which of the five statements most strongly supports the director's position?* Crime thrillers, as a film genre, are likely to have stock characters and plot lines that reflect a long tradition. So, it would be no surprise if some of the characters or plot twists in one such film would resemble, to a greater or lesser extent, the characters and plot twists in another. The studio might be correct in identifying such resemblances between *The Big Heist* and *Thieves*. But it would not necessarily be correct that characters or plot lines in *The Big Heist* were derived from *Thieves*.

A   This undercuts the director's position, since it provides information that indicates an opportunity for the director to copy ideas from the script for *Thieves*.

B   Correct. This information strengthens the support for the director's claim that the studio's accusation lacks merit. Since both *Thieves* and *The Big Heist* fall within a long tradition of crime thriller films, the characters and plot lines in both films reflect that tradition, and so any resemblances do not imply deliberate copying of the ideas in *Thieves* by the director of *The Big Heist*.

C   This information seems largely irrelevant to the issue raised and does not strengthen support for the director's conclusion.

D   This does little to indicate that the director's conclusion is correct. For example, the then-future director of *Thieves* might have discussed with the future director of *The Big Heist* specific ideas about character and plot for a planned crime thriller film.

E   This does not support the director's claim. For example, it raises the possibility that information about *Thieves* leaked during the early stages of production—information that could have been exploited in the production of *The Big Heist*.

The correct answer is B.

686. In Mernia, commercial fossil hunters often sell important fossils they have found, not to universities or museums, but to individual collectors, who pay much better but generally do not allow researchers access to their collections. To increase the number of fossils available for research, some legislators propose requiring all fossils that are found in Mernia to be sold only to universities or museums.

Which of the following, if true, most strongly indicates that the legislators' proposal will fail to achieve its goal?

(A) Some fossil hunters in Mernia are not commercial fossil hunters, but rather are amateurs who keep the fossils that they find.

(B) Most fossils found in Mernia are common types that have little scientific interest.

(C) Commercial fossil hunters in Mernia currently sell some of the fossils they find to universities and museums.

(D) Many universities in Mernia do not engage in fossil research.

(E) Most fossils are found by commercial fossil hunters, and they would give up looking for fossils if they were no longer allowed to sell to individual collectors.

Evaluation of a Plan

Situation Fossil hunters in Mernia often sell important fossils to collectors who do not make them accessible to researchers. To increase the number of fossils available for research, some legislators propose requiring all fossils found in Mernia to be sold only to universities or museums.

Reasoning *What would most strongly suggest that requiring all fossils found in Mernia to be sold only to universities or museums would not increase the number of fossils available for research?* To increase the number of fossils available for research, the proposed requirement will have to be implemented and effectively enforced. It will presumably have to increase the total number of fossils sold to universities and museums. And those institutions will have to make more of the fossils in their collections available to researchers than the private collectors do. Evidence that any of those conditions will not be fulfilled would suggest that the legislators' proposal will fail to achieve its goal.

A Even if the legislation does not affect fossils kept by amateurs, it might still result in many more fossils being sold to universities or museums rather than to private collectors, and thus might still increase the number of fossils available for research.

B Even if few Mernian fossils are interesting to researchers, the legislation could still achieve its goal of making more fossils available for research.

C Even if commercial fossil hunters already sell a few fossils to universities and museums, the legislation could encourage them to sell many more fossils.

D The universities that do not engage in fossil research presumably will not be interested in buying fossils even if the legislation passes. But the fossil hunters can just sell their fossils to other universities and museums that do engage in fossil research.

E **Correct.** This suggests that if the legislation passes, fossils will simply be left in the ground rather than sold to private collectors. That would not increase the total number of fossils available for research.

The correct answer is E.

687. Brown tides are growths of algae on the sea's surface that prevent sunlight from reaching marine plants below, thereby destroying not only the plants but also the shellfish that live off these plants. Biologists recently isolated a virus that, when added to seawater, kills the algae that cause brown tides. Adding large quantities of this virus to waters affected by brown tides will therefore make it possible to save the populations of shellfish that inhabit those waters.

Which of the following, if true, provides the most support for the conclusion of the argument?

(A) When applied in large quantities, the virus not only kills the algae that cause brown tides but also many harmless kinds of algae.

(B) Marine animals that prey on shellfish avoid areas of the sea in which brown tides are occurring.

(C) The number of different kinds of viruses present in seawater is far greater than many marine biologists had, until recently, believed.

(D) The presence of large quantities of the virus in seawater does not adversely affect the growth of marine plants.

(E) The amount of the virus naturally present in seawater in which brown tides occur is neither significantly greater nor significantly less than the amount present in seawater in which brown tides do not occur.

Argument Evaluation

Situation   Brown tides—growths of algae on the sea's surface—kill the marine plants on which certain shellfish depend, by depriving them of sunlight. Biologists have discovered a virus that, if added to seawater in large quantities, can kill the algae. An author argues that this can be a means of saving the shellfish populations.

Reasoning   *Which of the answer choices most strongly supports the conclusion of the argument?* The argument concludes that adding large quantities of the virus to seawater infected by brown tides will help the shellfish survive. Any new information suggesting that the virus would, directly or indirectly, help the shellfish survive supports the conclusion. But the conclusion would be questionable if the virus could directly or indirectly harm the shellfish in a way that would outweigh any benefits the virus provides. New information indicating that this would not occur could provide support for the argument.

A   This information suggests that deployment of the virus could have undesirable side effects, but it neither supports nor casts doubt on the conclusion. We have no information suggesting that killing algae other than those that produce brown tides would, directly or indirectly, help the shellfish survive.

B   This information neither supports nor casts doubt on the conclusion. It indicates a way in which brown tides indirectly provide a benefit to shellfish, even if the indirect harm they cause to shellfish outweighs that benefit.

C   This information indicates that certain viruses can survive in seawater environments, but this information, by itself, neither supports nor casts doubt on the conclusion.

D   Correct. This information indicates that the virus the biologists isolated does not directly harm the marine plants on which shellfish depend. Therefore, it provides significant support for the conclusion by indicating that the virus will not harm the shellfish indirectly by harming their food source.

E   This information suggests that only large quantities of the virus the biologists isolated will be effective in eliminating brown tides. But the conclusion of the argument specifies that the virus would need to be added in *large quantities*, so the information given in this answer choice provides no additional support for the conclusion.

The correct answer is D.

688. Educational theorist: Recent editorials have called for limits on the amount of homework assigned to schoolchildren younger than 12. They point out that free-time activities play an important role in childhood development and that homework in large quantities can severely restrict children's free time, hindering their development. But the actual average homework time for children under 12—little more than 30 minutes per night—leaves plenty of free time. In reality, therefore, the editorials' rationale cannot justify the restriction they advocate.

Which of the following, if true, would most seriously call into question the educational theorist's conclusion?

(A) Some teachers give as homework assignments work of a kind that research suggests is most effective educationally when done in class.

(B) For children younger than 12, regularly doing homework in the first years of school has no proven academic value, but many educators believe that it fosters self-discipline and time management.

(C) Some homework assignments are related to free-time activities that children engage in, such as reading or hobbies.

(D) A substantial proportion of schoolchildren under 12, particularly those in their first few years of school, have less than 10 minutes of homework assigned per night.

(E) Some free-time activities teach children skills or information that they later find useful in their schoolwork.

Argument Evaluation

Situation   An educational theorist points out that recent editorials have called for limits on the amount of homework assigned to children under the age of 12, since large amounts of homework can restrict the sort of free-time activities that are crucial to their development. The theorist argues that such restrictions are not justified, because children under 12 spend on average only 30 minutes on homework. That leaves plenty of time for other activities.

Reasoning   *What would most seriously call the theorist's conclusion into question?* The theorist gives only the average amount of time children under the age of 12 spend on homework. However, the editorials advocated a limit on the maximum amount of homework assigned, not on the average amount across all schoolchildren. There could be a wide variation among the amounts of time different children spend on homework. While a large number of children may spend only a short amount of time on homework, some children may spend much longer. For those who have the greater amounts of homework, this might leave little time for important free-time activities.

A   This claim, if true, may suggest that certain types of homework that teachers assign would be better done in class. It might be best not to give such assignments for homework, but that does not give us much reason to think that the *amount* of homework should be restricted.

B   This choice indicates that, despite a possible objection to assigning homework, homework does have value. That does not tell us, though, whether the maximum amount of homework that is assigned is too much, too little, or just right.

C   This claim could be true and yet children could still be left with too little time for important free-time activities.

D   Correct. As explained in the Reasoning section above, the educational theorist draws a conclusion regarding whether there should be a limit on the *maximum* amount of homework assigned to children under 12 and bases this conclusion solely on the *average* amount of time children under the age of 12 spend on homework. This conclusion would not be well supported if there is a wide variation in the amount of time children under the age of 12 spend on homework and if some—perhaps in the lower grades—spend only a very short amount of time on it. Suppose, for instance, as this answer choice has, that less than 10 minutes of homework is assigned to some of these children each night. If that were the case, then because the average amount of time schoolchildren under the age of 12 spend on homework each night is 30 minutes, that would mean that many schoolchildren may be spending far more than 30 minutes a night on homework. If so, then those children may not have enough free time for other important activities. That might mean that it would be appropriate to put limits on the amount of homework assigned to children under the age of 12.

E   This claim shows that some free-time activities are important for schoolwork later in life. But that does not tell us whether the maximum amount of homework that is assigned is too much, too little, or just right.

The correct answer is D.

689. Thyrian lawmaker: Thyria's Cheese Importation Board inspects all cheese shipments to Thyria and rejects shipments not meeting specified standards. Yet only 1 percent is ever rejected. Therefore, since the health consequences and associated economic costs of not rejecting that 1 percent are negligible, whereas the board's operating costs are considerable, for economic reasons alone the board should be disbanded.

Consultant: I disagree. The threat of having their shipments rejected deters many cheese exporters from shipping substandard product.

The consultant responds to the lawmaker's argument by

(A) rejecting the lawmaker's argument while proposing that the standards according to which the board inspects imported cheese should be raised

(B) providing evidence that the lawmaker's argument has significantly overestimated the cost of maintaining the board

(C) objecting to the lawmaker's introducing into the discussion factors that are not strictly economic

(D) pointing out a benefit of maintaining the board which the lawmaker's argument has failed to consider

(E) shifting the discussion from the argument at hand to an attack on the integrity of the cheese inspectors

Argument Construction

Situation   The Thyrian lawmaker argues that the Cheese Importation Board should be disbanded, because its operating costs are high and it rejects only a small percentage of the cheese it inspects. The consultant disagrees, pointing out that the board's inspections deter those who export cheese to Thyria from shipping substandard cheese.

Reasoning   *What strategy does the consultant use in the counterargument?* The consultant indicates to the lawmaker that there is a reason to retain the board that the lawmaker has not considered. The benefit the board provides is not that it identifies a great deal of substandard cheese and rejects it (thus keeping the public healthy), but that the possibility that their cheese could be found substandard is what keeps exporters from attempting to export low-quality cheese to Thyria.

A   The consultant does reject the lawmaker's argument, but the consultant does not propose higher standards. Indeed, in suggesting that the board should be retained, the consultant implies that the board's standards are appropriate.

B   The consultant does not provide any evidence related to the board's cost.

C   The only point the lawmaker raises that is not strictly economic is about the health consequences of disbanding the board, but the consultant does not address this point at all.

D   **Correct.** This statement properly identifies the strategy the consultant employs in his or her counterargument. The consultant points out that the board provides a significant benefit that the lawmaker did not consider.

E   The consultant does not attack the integrity of the cheese inspectors; to the contrary, the consultant says that their inspections deter the cheese exporters from shipping substandard cheese.

The correct answer is D.

690. The tulu, a popular ornamental plant, does not reproduce naturally and is only bred and sold by specialized horticultural companies. Unfortunately, the tulu is easily devastated by a contagious fungal rot. The government ministry plans to reassure worried gardeners by requiring all tulu plants to be tested for fungal rot before being sold. However, infected plants less than 30 weeks old have generally not built up enough fungal rot in their systems to be detected reliably. And many tulu plants are sold before they are 24 weeks old.

Which of the following, if performed by the government ministry, could logically be expected to overcome the problem with their plan to test for the fungal rot?

(A) Releasing a general announcement that tulu plants less than 30 weeks old cannot be effectively tested for fungal rot

(B) Requiring all tulu plants less than 30 weeks old to be labeled as such

(C) Researching possible ways to test tulu plants less than 24 weeks old for fungal rot

(D) Ensuring that tulu plants are not sold before they are 30 weeks old

(E) Quarantining all tulu plants from horticultural companies at which any case of fungal rot has been detected until those tulu plants can be tested for fungal rot

Evaluation of a Plan

Situation   There is a contagious fungal rot that devastates the tulu, a popular ornamental plant. To reassure worried gardeners, the government ministry plans to require that tulu plants be tested for the rot before being sold. However, many tulu plants are sold before they are 24 weeks old, yet fungal rot in plants less than 30 weeks old generally cannot be detected reliably.

Reasoning   *What could the government ministry do to overcome the problem?* The problem arises from the fact that tulu plants are frequently sold before they are 24 weeks old, which is too soon for any fungal rot that is present to have built up enough in their root systems to be detected. Since the goal of the testing is to ensure that infected tulu plants are not sold, an obvious solution would be to make sure that no plants are sold before they are old enough for fungal rot to have built up to a detectable level. Thus, tulu plants should not be sold before they are 30 weeks old.

A   Releasing such an announcement would help overcome the problem if it guaranteed that no one would buy or sell tulu plants before the plants were 30 weeks old, but it is far from certain that it would guarantee this.

B   Similar to A, introducing such labeling would help overcome the problem if it guaranteed that no one would buy or sell tulu plants before the plants were 30 weeks old, but it is far from certain that it would guarantee this.

C   There is no guarantee that such research will be successful at reducing the age at which tulu plants can be reliably tested.

D   Correct. If the government *ensures* that no tulu plants less than 30 weeks of age are sold, then the specific problem mentioned in the passage would be overcome.

E   This will not help overcome the problem. Such a quarantine program might lead horticultural companies to start selling tulu plants *only* if they are less than 24 weeks old, thereby minimizing the chance of quarantine by minimizing the chance of detection.

The correct answer is D.

691. Secret passwords are often used to control access to computers. When employees select their own passwords, they frequently choose such easily guessed passwords as their initials or birth dates. To improve security, employers should assign randomly generated passwords to employees rather than allowing employees to make up their own.

Which of the following, if true, most seriously undermines the conclusion drawn above?

(A) If passwords are generated randomly, it is theoretically possible that employees will be assigned passwords that they might have selected on their own.

(B) Randomly generated passwords are so difficult for employees to recall that they often record the passwords in places where the passwords could be easily seen by others.

(C) Computer systems protected by passwords are designed to ignore commands that are entered by employees or others who use invalid passwords.

(D) In general, the higher the level of security maintained at the computer system, the more difficult it is for unauthorized users to obtain access to the system.

(E) Control of physical access to computers by the use of locked doors and guards should be used in addition to passwords in order to maintain security.

Argument Evaluation

Situation Passwords are intended to control access to computers, limiting access only to intended users. Employees often choose easily guessed passwords. To improve security, therefore, employers should assign randomly generated passwords.

Reasoning *What would significantly undermine the argument's conclusion?* Any evidence that suggests that assigning randomly generated passwords would be no more likely to be secure than employee-generated passwords would undermine the conclusion.

A Even if in theory a randomly generated password could assign an employee a password the employee might have selected, that in actuality is extremely improbable.

B **Correct.** If employees frequently record their randomly generated passwords where people who are not intended to have access to their computers can easily see them, as this option indicates, then such randomly generated passwords might in such cases reduce rather than increase security.

C This detail is irrelevant because the issue is whether an unauthorized user can easily enter a valid password, not an invalid one.

D This does not undermine the conclusion because the issue is whether the proposed plan does in fact increase the level of security maintained at the computer system.

E This does not undermine the conclusion because this simply details a possible security measure that could be employed in addition to passwords.

The correct answer is B.

692. The economy around Lake Paqua depends on fishing of the lake's landlocked salmon population. In recent years, scarcity of food for salmon there has caused a decline in both the number and the size of the adult salmon in the lake. As a result, the region's revenues from salmon fishing have declined significantly. To remedy this situation, officials plan to introduce shrimp, which can serve as a food source for adult salmon, into Lake Paqua.

Which of the following, if true, most seriously calls into question the plan's chances for success?

(A) Salmon is not a popular food among residents of the Lake Paqua region.

(B) Tourists coming to fish for sport generate more income for residents of the Lake Paqua region than does commercial fishing.

(C) The shrimp to be introduced into Lake Paqua are of a variety that is too small to be harvested for human consumption.

(D) The primary food for both shrimp and juvenile salmon is plankton, which is not abundant in Lake Paqua.

(E) Fishing regulations prohibit people from keeping any salmon they have caught in Lake Paqua that are smaller than a certain minimum size.

Evaluation of a Plan

Situation   In recent years, scarcity of food for landlocked salmon in Lake Paqua has led to a decline in number and size of the salmon there, leading to a decline in revenues from salmon fishing, on which the area's economy depends. Officials plan to remedy this situation by introducing shrimp, a common food source for adult salmon, into Lake Paqua.

Reasoning   *What would seriously undermine the plan's chances for success?* Note that shrimp are described as a food source for *adult* salmon. If there were good reason to think that shrimp cannot serve as a significant source of food for juvenile salmon—or that shrimp would not be able to live sustainably in the lake—there would be reason to be skeptical of the plan's eventual success.

A   Whether salmon is a popular food among residents around Lake Paqua is not particularly relevant to the question of whether introducing shrimp will help the salmon population there rebound.

B   Nothing in the plan depends on whether salmon fishing's primary contribution to the economy of the Lake Paqua region comes from tourists fishing or from commercial fishing.

C   The plan does not depend on the shrimp being usable as a human food source, only on their utility as food for salmon.

D   Correct. If the plan does not resolve the food source problem for juvenile shrimp, then the salmon may not survive to adulthood. Furthermore, because shrimp depend on plankton, which are not plentiful in the lake, any relief that the introduction of shrimp may provide will likely not be sustainable.

E   If anything, this would seem likely to assist the plan, by aiding in restoring the salmon population in the lake.

The correct answer is D.

693. Certainly, pesticides can adversely affect the environment in localities distant from where the pesticide has actually been used. Nevertheless, **regulation of pesticide use should not take place at the national level but at the local level.** It is in the areas where pesticides are actually applied that they have their most serious effects. Just how serious these effects are depends on local conditions such as climate, soil type, and water supply. And **local officials are much more likely than national legislators to be truly knowledgeable about such local conditions.**

In the argument given, the two **boldface** portions play which of the following roles?

(A) The first provides support for the conclusion of the argument; the second states that conclusion.

(B) The first states the conclusion of the argument; the second provides support for that conclusion.

(C) The first identifies grounds for a potential objection to the conclusion of the argument; the second states that conclusion.

(D) The first identifies grounds for a potential objection to the conclusion of the argument; the second provides support for that conclusion.

(E) Each provides support for the conclusion of the argument.

Argument Construction

Situation   The argument addresses the proper level of government (national vs. local) for regulating pesticide use. The author argues against national-level regulation, conceding only that pesticides can cause problems far from the application site. The core of the argument rests on two premises: the most serious effects are local, and the severity of these local effects depends on local conditions.

Reasoning   *What function is served by the two **boldfaced** portions?* The first **boldfaced** portion expresses the argument's main conclusion, a judgment or recommendation that the rest of the passage is designed to support. The second portion provides a piece of evidence that directly supports the conclusion; establishing that local officials possess the superior knowledge required to make effective regulations that account for variable local conditions, thereby justifying the call for local-level regulation.

A   The first **boldfaced** portion *is* the conclusion, not support for a conclusion, and the second is a fact that provides support for that conclusion.

B   **Correct.** The first **boldfaced** portion is the main claim the argument seeks to establish (the conclusion). The second **boldfaced** portion explains *why* the local level is the appropriate place for regulation.

C   The first **boldfaced** portion is the conclusion, not an objection. The objection is the preceding sentence about distant effects. Moreover, the second portion is not the conclusion, but support.

D   The first **boldfaced** portion is the conclusion, not grounds for a potential objection. The second portion, however, is indeed support.

E   The first **boldfaced** portion is the main conclusion; it is not support for itself. The second **boldfaced** portion is support.

The correct answer is B.

694. Which of the following most logically completes the passage?

Concerned about the well-being of its elderly citizens, the government of Runagia decided two years ago to increase by 20 percent the government-provided pension paid to all Runagians over 65. The annual rate of inflation since then has been below 5 percent, and the increase has been duly received by all eligible Runagians. Nevertheless, many of them are no better off than they were before the increase, in large part because _____.

(A) they rely entirely on the government pension for their income

(B) Runagian banks are so inefficient that it can take up to three weeks to cash a pension check

(C) the prices of goods and services for special needs of elderly people have increased at a rate much higher than the rate of inflation

(D) the pension was increased at the time when the number of elderly Runagians below the poverty level reached an all-time high

(E) the increase was only the second such increase in the last ten years

Argument Construction

Situation   The government of Runagia increased the pension for citizens over 65 by 20 percent. The general annual inflation rate has been less than 5 percent. Despite receiving this increase, many elderly citizens are no better off than they were before the pension hike.

Reasoning   *What additional factor would account for the limited effect of the pension increase?* The argument presents a paradox: the pension increased significantly (20%), far outpacing general inflation (under 5%), yet the beneficiaries feel no improvement in their financial well-being. To logically complete the argument, the missing piece must be a factor that accounts for this discrepancy. Specifically, we need an explanation for a hidden, high rate of financial erosion or increased costs that has effectively nullified the 20% gain for the elderly population. A factor showing that the specific goods and services the elderly rely on have seen price increases significantly higher than 20% would resolve this paradox.

A   This fact describes *who* receives the income and *how much* they rely on it, but it does not explain why an increased pension amount (20%) would be offset when general inflation is low (under 5%). If anything, this suggests they should notice the increase more, making the lack of improvement even more puzzling.

B   This fact explains a *delay* in accessing the money, but it does not explain a *reduction* in the money's purchasing power once it is received. The argument is about being "no better off," implying a loss of value or purchasing power, not a delay in receipt.

C   **Correct.** This option resolves the paradox. While the general inflation rate is low, if the *specific* goods and services that the elderly disproportionately purchase (like specialized healthcare, housing assistance, or mobility aids) have increased in price by, say, 25% or more, then their 20% pension increase may have been entirely or even more than entirely nullified, leaving them "no better off" or potentially worse off.

D   This high rate of poverty provides context about the timing of the increase and the general need, but it is not a mechanism that could cause the 20% increase to be negated. The poverty level is an effect of low income, not a cause of reduced purchasing power following an increase.

E   The historical frequency of past increases is irrelevant to the current situation. The argument is concerned with the discrepancy between the *current* 20% raise and the *current* low inflation rate, and how that discrepancy resulted in no benefit for the recipients.

The correct answer is C.

695. Museums that house Renaissance oil paintings typically store them in environments that are carefully kept within narrow margins of temperature and humidity to inhibit any deterioration. Recent laboratory tests have shown that **the oil paint used in these paintings actually adjusts to climatic changes quite well**. Assuming paint to be the most sensitive substance in these works, some museum directors now argue that museums can reduce energy costs without risking damage to these paintings by relaxing the standards for temperature and humidity control. Museums would be rash to relax those standards, however, since results of preliminary tests indicate that **gesso, a compound routinely used by Renaissance artists to help paint adhere to the canvas, is unable to withstand significant variations in humidity**.

In the argument above, the two portions in **boldface** play which of the following roles?

(A) The first is evidence that has been used to support a position that the argument calls into question; the second is that position.

(B) The first is evidence that has been used to support a position that the argument calls into question; the second is a claim, the accuracy of which is questioned in the argument.

(C) The first is evidence that has been used to support a position that the argument calls into question; the second is a preliminary finding used by the argument to weaken the force of that evidence.

(D) The first is the main conclusion of the argument; the second is a preliminary finding used by the argument to weaken the force of evidence that has been used to support a position that the argument calls into question.

(E) The first is an objection that has been raised against the position taken by the argument; the second is that position.

Argument Construction

Situation   Museums currently maintain strict temperature and humidity controls to protect Renaissance oil paintings. Laboratory tests indicate the oil paint handles climatic changes well. Based on this, some museum directors conclude they can relax climate standards to save energy without resulting damage to the paintings. The historian's argument criticizes this proposal, stating it would be rash, because a different component of the paintings, gesso, is highly sensitive to humidity variations.

Reasoning   *What roles do the two **boldfaced** portions play in the argument?* The argument follows a pattern of presenting a finding, outlining a conclusion drawn from that finding (the position being criticized), and then introducing new information to support the argument's main position. The first **boldfaced** portion is the evidence derived from "recent laboratory tests." This evidence directly supports the museum directors' proposal to relax standards. Since the historian argues against relaxing the standards ("Museums would be rash . . ."), the first portion is evidence for the position the argument calls into question. The second **boldfaced** portion is a new piece of evidence cited by the author to support their own position and undermine the premise of the directors' proposal. The directors assume paint is the most sensitive substance; but the second **boldfaced** portion shows that gesso is more sensitive, proving that even if the paint would not be damaged by looser climate controls, the paintings would nonetheless be at risk. This additional evidence successfully weakens the force of the evidence presented in the first portion.

A   The first portion is indeed evidence for the opposed position. The second portion is evidence for the argument's position, not the position or main conclusion itself, which is that relaxing standards would be rash.

B   The first portion is indeed evidence for the opposing position. However, the accuracy of the second portion (the gesso finding) is not questioned; it is the foundation upon which the argument's criticism rests.

C   **Correct.** The first portion is evidence used to support the directors' position that relaxing standards would be safe, a position the argument calls into question. The second portion, the gesso finding, is the new information used by the argument to weaken the force of the paint evidence by showing that paint's stability is irrelevant if another crucial component, namely gesso, is highly sensitive.

D   The first portion is evidence, not the main conclusion. The second portion, however, is characterized accurately.

E   The first portion is evidence supporting the position the argument opposes (the directors' view), not an objection against the historian's final conclusion. The second portion is evidence for the argument's conclusion, not the conclusion itself.

The correct answer is C.

696. People get more than pleasure from seeing trees. Seeing trees can be good for people's physical health. That this is so is shown by a comparison of a large group of hospital patients who had a view of trees from their rooms and a similarly large group of hospital patients who did not. The patients with a view of trees returned to health faster.

Which of the following would it be most useful to establish in order to evaluate the argument above?

(A) Whether the trees that could be seen from the hospital rooms were, for the most part, equally healthy and well grown

(B) Whether the two groups of patients were well matched with respect to the nature and severity of the conditions for which they were hospitalized

(C) Whether the patients in both groups knew that their recovery times were being compared

(D) What proportion of all of the patients contracted an infection while in the hospital

(E) What proportion of all of the rooms in the hospitals from which the two groups were drawn had a view of trees

Argument Evaluation

Situation   The argument claims that seeing trees is good for people's physical health. The evidence is a comparison between two large groups of hospital patients: one group had a view of trees from their rooms, and the other did not. The finding is that the patients with the view of trees returned to health faster.

Reasoning   *What additional factor would affect the conclusion that seeing trees aids recovery?* The argument uses a correlation, namely that a view of trees correlates with faster recovery, in order to establish a causal link, namely that seeing trees *causes* better health. For this causal link to be sound, the two groups being compared must be identical in all respects *except* for the variable being studied: the view of trees. The most serious threat to the argument's validity is the possibility of an alternative cause or a pre-existing difference between the two groups. If the patients with the tree view were already less sick, younger, had better care, or were recovering from less severe procedures, the entire causal claim is undermined. Therefore, to evaluate the argument, we must establish whether the two groups were matched for the relevant medical factors.

A   The argument is about the therapeutic effect of *seeing* trees. Whether the trees were healthy or well-grown is a minor detail and unlikely to be the primary factor in recovery speed.

B   Correct. This is the most crucial piece of information. If the group with the tree view was, for instance, recovering from minor elective surgery, and the group without the view was recovering from major trauma or chronic illness, the faster recovery time would be fully explained by the difference in medical condition, not the view. If the groups *were* well-matched, the argument is strengthened; if they *were not* well-matched, the argument is severely weakened.

C   Knowledge of the study might introduce a Hawthorne effect (people behave differently when they know they are being observed), but this effect would apply equally to both groups, so it would not explain the observed difference in recovery time between the two groups.

D   While infection rates are critical to health, they would need to be compared *between the two groups* (view vs. no-view), not against the total patient population. Knowing the overall proportion is not useful for evaluating the difference between the two study groups.

E   This fact is irrelevant to the comparison. The argument only relies on the fact that one group *did* have the view and the other group *did not*. The total number of rooms with views does not affect the validity of the comparison between the two large study groups.

The correct answer is B.

697. Because the cork stoppers in wine bottles can leak, crumble, or become moldy, winemakers must often discard a significant proportion of their inventory of bottled wine. **Bottlemasters, Inc., produces a plastic stopper that cannot leak, crumble, or mold.** Bottlemasters's plastic stopper is available to winemakers for a price only slightly higher than that of traditional cork stoppers, and **cork prices are expected to rise considerably in the near future.** Therefore, the Bottlemasters plastic stopper will most probably increase its share of the market for wine-bottle stoppers.

In the argument given, the two portions in **boldface** play which of the following roles?

(A) The first and the second each provide evidence to support the conclusion of the argument.

(B) The first provides evidence to support the main conclusion of the argument; the second is that main conclusion.

(C) The first provides evidence to support the main conclusion of the argument; the second is an objection that has been raised against that main conclusion.

(D) The first and the second are each claims that have been advanced in support of a position that the argument opposes.

(E) The first is evidence that has been used to support a position that the argument opposes; the second is a claim advanced in support of the main conclusion of the argument.

Argument Construction

Situation   Cork stoppers for wine bottles can lead to spoiled wine by leaking, crumbling, or growing mold, which causes lost inventory for winemakers. Bottlemasters, Inc. manufactures a slightly more expensive plastic stopper that lacks the problems that lead to spoilage; moreover, the price of cork is expected to increase soon. The argument concludes that Bottlemasters's plastic stoppers are very likely to gain market share.

Reasoning   *How do the two* **boldface** *portions function in relation to the argument that Bottlemasters's plastic stoppers will gain market share?* The first portion states that the plastic stoppers do not have the drawbacks associated with cork stoppers; that is, that Bottlemasters makes a superior product which can solve the problem of spoilage. These superior stoppers are slightly more expensive than cork stoppers, but the second **boldfaced** portion addresses that issue by stating that cork's price is expected to increase "significantly," a rise that would be likely to make the price of the plastic stoppers more competitive. It is therefore reasonable to expect that this better product at a more competitive price will gain a larger share of the market for bottle stoppers.

A   **Correct.** The first portion establishes that the plastic stoppers are superior to cork stoppers in an important respect; the second portion suggests that, since cork is likely to become more expensive, the price of plastic stoppers will probably become more competitive. Both of these facts are reasonable, if indirect, evidence for the conclusion that plastic stoppers will be likely to claim a greater share of the market for bottle stoppers.

B   The first portion is evidence for the conclusion that plastic stoppers will gain market share, but the second portion—which states that cork prices are expected to rise soon—is not a conclusion but rather evidence implying that cork stoppers could become as, or more, expensive than the plastic stoppers, and thereby lose their advantage in terms of price.

C   The first portion is indeed evidence for the conclusion, but the second portion further supports the conclusion rather than forming an objection against it.

D   Neither the first nor the second portion supports a position the argument opposes; rather, both support the idea that plastic stoppers will probably gain market share.

E   The first portion, like the second, provides support for the argument's conclusion, not support for an opposing position.

The correct answer is A.

698. Which of the following most logically completes the argument?

A significant number of Qualitex Corporation's department heads are due to retire this year. The number of employees other than current department heads who could take on the position of department head is equal to only about half of the expected vacancies. Qualitex is not going to hire department heads from outside the company or have current department heads take over more than one department, so some departments will be without department heads next year unless Qualitex _____.

(A) promotes some current department heads to higher-level managerial positions

(B) raises the salary for department heads

(C) reduces the number of new employees it hires next year

(D) reduces the average number of employees per department

(E) reduces the number of its departments

Argument Construction

Situation   Qualitex Corporation expects a significant number of department heads to retire this year. Only roughly half of those positions can be filled by current employees who are not department heads; moreover, Qualitex will not fill the vacancies with external candidates or make current department heads lead more than one department. Therefore some departments will lack department heads next year unless Qualitex does something to prevent that situation from occurring.

Reasoning   *What is the most logical way for Qualitex to avoid having departments without department heads?* The information presented establishes that Qualitex will have more departments than it will have department heads. Since the company does not want to take steps such as hiring external candidates to increase the number of department heads, it follows that they will have to reduce the number of total departments in order to eliminate the disparity.

A   Promoting current department heads to other positions would exacerbate, not solve, the shortage of department heads relative to departments.

B   Raising the salary for department heads might be helpful if the company was willing to hire external candidates; however, because the company is not open to that solution, raising department heads' salaries will not eliminate the problem of having more departments than department heads.

C   Hiring fewer employees would not solve the disparity between the number of departments and the number of department heads.

D   Reducing the number of employees per department would do nothing to address the problem of having more departments than available department heads.

E   **Correct.** Since Qualitex does not want to take measures such as bringing in new department heads from outside the company, the most logical way it can address the imbalance between department heads and departments is by eliminating some of the latter.

The correct answer is E.

699. It is crucially important to farmers that the herbicides they use to control weeds not damage their crops. One very effective herbicide is safe for corn, but soybeans are damaged even by the herbicide's residue, which remains in the soil more than a year after the herbicide is applied. Soybeans and corn are not sown together in the same field; nevertheless, most farmers are reluctant to use the herbicide on their corn.

Which of the following, if true, provides the strongest justification for the farmers' reluctance?

(A)   The residue of the herbicide in the soil a year after application is not enough to control most weeds effectively.

(B)   To maintain the nutrients in the soil, corn and soybeans are often planted in a field in alternate years.

(C)   The demand for soybeans is growing faster than is the demand for corn.

(D)   For maximum yield, soybean plants are grown closer together than are corn plants.

(E)   The application of herbicides is less critical for soybeans than for corn crops.

Argument Evaluation

Situation   Farmers want herbicides that kill weeds but do not harm crops. One herbicide is safe for corn but harmful to soybeans; the residue from the herbicide persists for over a year in quantities sufficient to harm soybeans. Even though the two crops are not planted together, most farmers do not want to use this herbicide on their corn.

Reasoning   *Why are farmers resistant to using the herbicide on their corn?* The information provided establishes that the herbicide is safe and effective for corn crops, but harmful to soybeans planted in the treated soil for a considerable time afterward. Therefore it would be logical for farmers to avoid this herbicide if they were likely to plant soybeans in the same soil during the period—over one year—that the herbicide lingers.

A   The fact that the herbicide might need to be reapplied annually to control weeds adequately would not, in itself, account for farmers' unwillingness to use it.

B   **Correct.** The information establishes that the herbicide will continue harming soybeans for over a year after application; if, then, soybean and corn are planted on the same land in alternating years, using the herbicide on corn would damage the following year's soybean crops, making it logical for farmers to avoid its use.

C   Increasing demand for soybeans would not explain why farmers prefer not to use the herbicide on their corn crops.

D   The relative planting densities of soybean and corn crops has no bearing on the question of why farmers prefer to avoid use of the herbicide.

E   The fact that herbicides are more important for growing corn crops than for growing soybeans does nothing to explain why farmers would avoid using a specific herbicide on their corn.

The correct answer is B.

700. Last August most gasoline stations in the XT chain of gasoline stations participated in a temporary sales promotion that XT sponsored. In the promotion, any customers who purchased ten or more gallons of gasoline were entitled to a free car wash. For the month of August, the XT chain's gasoline sales were five percent higher than in August the previous year. Evidently the promotion was successful as a means of boosting sales.

Which of the following, if true, most strengthens the argument?

(A) During last August, some of XT's competitors also had sales promotions in effect and also experienced sales increases as compared to the previous August.

(B) The money that XT earned from the increase in gasoline sales was not enough to offset the cost of providing free car washes during the promotion.

(C) Some customers who took advantage of the promotion would have made smaller but more frequent gasoline purchases at XT gasoline stations if the promotion had not been in effect.

(D) XT gasoline stations that participated in the promotion but did not have car-wash facilities on their premises gave vouchers that could be used at a nearby car wash.

(E) Last August the XT gasoline stations that did not participate in the promotion had no increase in gasoline sales as compared to their sales the previous August.

Argument Evaluation

Situation   Some of the gas stations belonging to a chain called XT participated in a promotion during the month of August: a free car wash with the purchase of ten or more gallons of gasoline. Sales of gasoline in that month were five percent higher than in the same month the year previous. The author concludes that the promotion was successful.

Reasoning   *What would strengthen the argument that the promotion, and not some other factor, was the cause of the sales increase?* The author concludes that the sales promotion was successful because of the five percent increase in sales, but such a conclusion cannot be definitive unless there is some way to pinpoint the promotion as the cause of that increase; the five percent sales increase could have some other cause or could simply be coincidence. Therefore, a comparison with a group of gas stations that did not run the same promotion would strengthen the argument by isolating the relevant factor: the sales promotion.

A   While the fact that some XT competitors also had sales promotions and concurrent sales increases might appear to support the idea that sales promotions are effective, it does not isolate the sales promotions as the reason for the increase; perhaps there was another reason for the increase across multiple gas station chains, for example a large number of people traveling for a nearby festival, or a strong overall economy.

B   The fact that the promotion was not cost-effective for XT is not relevant to the question of whether the promotion was directly responsible for the increased sales.

C   If customers would have made smaller, but more frequent, purchases without the promotion in effect, it suggests only that the promotion may have been effective in persuading customers to buy more gasoline per visit, not in increasing gasoline sales overall.

D   The location of the carwashes has no bearing on the question of whether offering free carwashes was an effective way of increasing sales of gasoline.

E   **Correct.** If XT gas stations that *did not* run the promotion *did not* see increased sales compared to the same period the year previous, and gas stations that *did* run the promotion *did* see increased sales, then that would strengthen the conclusion that the sales promotions were effective by isolating those promotions as the distinguishing factor between gas stations in the two groups: those with higher sales, and those without.

The correct answer is E.

701. Airlines are considering applying a new plastic film to airplanes instead of paint. It is clear that airlines should adopt this new technology right away, since **it would reduce the time that an airplane is out of service for maintenance.** When an airplane is taken out of service for maintenance, it is often repainted. During repainting, no other maintenance work can be done on the plane, but other maintenance tasks can be done while the nontoxic plastic film is being applied. In addition, **switching to the film would not increase maintenance costs in labor and materials**, since the film is as quick to apply as paint without being more expensive.

In the argument given, the two portions in **boldface** play which of the following roles?

(A) The first is the main position that the argument seeks to establish; the second is a consideration put forward in support of that position.

(B) The first and the second are each considerations that are put forward in support of the position that the argument seeks to establish.

(C) The first is a consideration that is put forward in support of the position that the argument seeks to establish; the second is an assumption for which no justification is offered.

(D) The first is presented as an advantage of following the recommendation made by the argument; the second is presented as a drawback to following that recommendation.

(E) The first and the second are each presented as a drawback to following the recommendation made by the argument.

Argument Construction

Situation Airlines may switch from using paint on their planes to using a new plastic film. The plastic film reduces the amount of time a plane must be grounded for maintenance, since unlike paint it can be applied while other maintenance work is being done. In other respects, namely speed of application and cost, the film is comparable to paint. The author concludes that airlines should switch to using the plastic film.

Reasoning *What role do the two **boldfaced** portions play in the argument that airlines should switch from paint to plastic film?* The first portion presents an advantage of switching to plastic film: reduced time required for maintenance. The second portion presents a respect in which the proposed switch is neutral: the film would not incur higher costs for materials and labor. This second consideration eliminates a possible concern, so like the first consideration it argues for the overall conclusion: that switching to the plastic film is advisable.

A The first portion is supporting evidence for the main position, not the position itself: that airlines should switch to using plastic film; the second portion is a consideration that supports the conclusion, not a consideration supporting the claim that the film reduces maintenance time.

B **Correct.** The first portion states a consideration in favor of switching to plastic film, as the argument endorses; the second portion presents a consideration that eliminates a possible reason *not* to make the switch, and thereby also argues for the position that the switch is advisable overall.

C The first portion does state a consideration in support of the main position; however, the second portion, the claim that the film would not increase maintenance costs from parts and labor, is not without justification, since the information states that the film is equal to or better than paint in terms of cost and application time.

D The first portion does indeed describe an advantage of following the recommendation to switch to plastic film; however, the second portion describes an aspect in which that switch would be neutral, not disadvantageous.

E Neither the first nor the second portion presents a drawback to following the recommendation to switch to plastic film.

The correct answer is B.

702. Early in the twentieth century, Lake Konfa became very polluted. Recently fish populations have recovered as release of industrial pollutants has declined and the lake's waters have become cleaner. Fears are now being voiced that the planned construction of an oil pipeline across the lake's bottom might revive pollution and cause the fish population to decline again. However, a technology for preventing leaks is being installed. Therefore, provided this technology is effective, those fears are groundless.

The argument depends on assuming which of the following?

(A) Apart from development related to the pipeline, there will be no new industrial development around the lake that will create renewed pollution in its waters.

(B) Other than the possibility of a leak, there is no realistic pollution threat posed to the lake by the pipeline's construction.

(C) There is no reason to believe that the leak-preventing technology would be ineffective when installed in the pipeline in Lake Konfa.

(D) Damage to the lake's fish populations would be the only harm that a leak of oil from the pipeline would cause.

(E) The species of fish that are present in Lake Konfa now are the same as those that were in the lake before it was affected by pollution.

Argument Evaluation

Situation   Lake Konfa has been recovering from a period of severe pollution, and its fish populations have rebounded as a result of the reduced pollution. There are plans to construct an oil pipeline across the lake, and this plan has provoked concerns that it will produce new pollution and thereby damage the reviving fish populations. Leak-prevention technology is being used on the pipeline, so the argument dismisses concerns regarding the pollution that the pipeline might cause.

Reasoning   *What implicit assumption underlies the claim that concerns regarding pollution are invalid?* The concerns regarding pollution produced by the pipeline are general and not limited to any single way in which the pipeline might cause pollution. However, the argument addresses only one possible source of pollution the pipeline might cause, namely leaks, and then concludes that *all* concerns about pollution are groundless. The argument therefore depends on an unstated assumption that leaks are the *only* way in which the pipeline might cause pollution.

A   The argument dismisses concerns regarding pollution caused by the pipeline specifically, not pollution from additional sources, so the argument does not depend on this assumption.

B   **Correct.** The argument dismisses concerns about pollution from the pipeline by addressing only one possible source of such pollution, namely leaks. Therefore, the argument relies on the assumption that the pipeline will not pollute the lake in any other way.

C   The argument includes the explicit caveat that its conclusion depends on the effectiveness of the leak-prevention technology, so its effectiveness, or otherwise, is not an implicit assumption.

D   Damage beyond the damage to Lake Konfa's fish populations is not at issue in the argument, and therefore is not an assumption of that argument.

E   The particular species of fish in the lake are not relevant to the claim that concerns regarding pollution from the pipeline are groundless.

The correct answer is B.

703. As a large corporation in a small country, Hachnut values having managers with international experience, so each year it sponsors management education abroad for a few management trainees. Although many who receive the sponsorship leave Hachnut soon after completing the sponsorship, Hachnut executives plan to continue the sponsorship program despite this problem.

Which of the following, if true, provides the strongest reason for Hachnut to continue the sponsorship program despite the problem cited above?

(A) Since Hachnut is heavily involved in foreign markets and has large operations abroad, its managers can gain international experience without taking advantage of the sponsorship program.

(B) The Hachnut managers who are citizens of countries other than Hachnut's home country are, for the most part, people who were recruited by Hachnut after working for other firms.

(C) The managers who leave Hachnut soon after receiving the sponsorship generally achieve about the same level of success in their careers as do the sponsored managers who do not leave Hachnut.

(D) Hachnut relies on performance during the education abroad to select candidates for promotion to higher management positions.

(E) The managers who leave Hachnut soon after receiving the sponsorship generally accept jobs in the country where they receive management education.

Argument Evaluation

Situation Hachnut is a company that prefers its managers to have international experience, and therefore pays for some trainees to study internationally. An unspecified percentage of such trainees then leave the company. Hachnut intends to continue sponsoring study abroad despite this attrition.

Reasoning *What benefit does Hachnut derive from sponsoring international training?* The fact that an unspecified but significant percentage of international trainees leave the company after completing their training diminishes the program's usefulness for achieving its first stated goal: producing managers with international experience. That diminished usefulness might still be adequate as a reason for maintaining the program, or it might not. If, however, the sponsorship program offered some further benefit to Hachnut, that benefit would provide an additional reason to continue the program, and perhaps tip the balance in the program's favor if its usefulness in other respects was marginal.

A If there are other ways to achieve the goal of having managers with international experience, then that would diminish, not increase, the company's motivation for maintaining the sponsorship program.

B Whether or not Hachnut's international employees previously worked for other firms has no bearing on the sponsorship program's usefulness.

C The future success of the sponsored trainees is not relevant to the question of how the sponsorship benefits Hachnut.

D Correct. If the sponsorship is useful to Hachnut in helping it determine whom to promote, then that additional benefit of the sponsorship program would compensate to some degree for its diminished usefulness in reaching Hachnut's goal of gaining managers with international experience.

E Where the sponsored trainees who quit the company end up working is not relevant to the question of how the sponsorship program benefits Hachnut.

The correct answer is D.

704. The country of Rowolia has, until now, been narrowly self-sufficient in both grain and meat. However, with growing prosperity in Rowolia has come a steadily increasing per capita consumption of meat, and it takes several pounds of grain to produce one pound of meat. Therefore, since Rowolian per capita income is almost certain to rise further and increases in domestic grain production are highly unlikely, Rowolia will soon need to import grain.

Which of the following is an assumption on which the argument depends?

(A) When people's consumption of meat increases, their consumption of grains and other foodstuffs tends to fall.

(B) Future demands for meat by Rowolians over and above current consumption levels will not be satisfied by the importation of meat from other countries.

(C) There are currently no laws in Rowolia prohibiting the importation of meat from abroad, nor will such laws be enacted in the near future.

(D) The per capita consumption of meat in Rowolia is roughly the same across all income levels.

(E) In Rowolia, meat is subject to strict government price controls but grain is not.

Argument Evaluation

Situation Rowolia has produced enough meat and grain to satisfy domestic demand, but because of a growing demand for meat it seems likely that demand will start to outstrip supply. Because several pounds of grain are required to produce one pound of meat, and because the country is unlikely to produce more grain domestically, the argument concludes that to meet the growing demand for meat Rowolia will need to import grain.

Reasoning *What assumption underlies the argument?* The argument states that Rowolia's demand for meat will soon outstrip its domestic supply of meat, and then infers from this fact that the country will need to import *grain* in order to produce that additional meat. This points to an underlying assumption that the country will not simply import meat directly in response to rising domestic demand.

A   The argument does not depend on an assumption that increasing meat consumption will lead to decreasing grain consumption; a potential reduction in demand for grain does not suggest a need for grain imports.

B   **Correct.** The argument suggests that increasing demand for meat will require grain imports in order to produce that meat; the argument therefore depends on an assumption that the demand for meat will not be met by meat imports.

C   Because the argument never suggests that meat imports are an option, it does not require any assumptions about whether such imports are legal.

D   The argument does indeed suggest that rising income levels have led to greater demand for meat, but it does not assume that demand for meat is equal per capita across income levels; if anything, it might imply the contrary.

E   The argument that Rowolia will need to import grain in order to satisfy domestic demand for meat does not rest on assumptions of any kind regarding price controls; although such price controls could conceivably make the Rowolian market less attractive to meat importers, and thereby provide an underlying reason why importing meat is not mentioned as a possibility, there are other possible reasons for not importing meat and instead producing it domestically.

The correct answer is B.

705. Which of the following most logically completes the argument below?

Papoose River farmers are deciding whether to plant winter wheat or spring wheat. The two types of wheat are usually about equally profitable and cannot both be grown in the same year. This year much lower yields per acre are expected for winter wheat because of new government restrictions on the use of Papoose River water for irrigation. Therefore, planting spring wheat will be more profitable than planting winter wheat, since _____.

(A) in the Papoose River region, spring wheat is not dependent on irrigation

(B) new crops of spring wheat must be planted before standing crops of winter wheat are ready to be harvested

(C) the spring wheat that farmers in the Papoose River region plant is well adapted to the soil of the region

(D) spring wheat has uses that are different from those of winter wheat

(E) planting spring wheat is more profitable than planting certain other crops, such as corn

Argument Construction

Situation   Farmers must choose between planting spring or winter wheat this year in the Papoose River region. While the two types of wheat typically bring in comparable profits, this year new limitations on the use of the Papoose River for irrigation are expected to reduce yields of winter wheat and therefore implicitly winter wheat's profitability as well. The argument concludes that planting spring wheat will be the more profitable choice.

Reasoning   *What would account for the expectation that spring wheat's profitability will be higher than winter wheat's profitability?* The argument suggests that limits on irrigation will reduce the profitability of winter wheat. Since there is nothing to suggest that these limits on irrigation apply only at certain times of year, it would be logical to conclude that, since spring wheat is expected to be more profitable than winter wheat under the new restrictions, spring wheat is less dependent than is winter wheat on irrigation from the Papoose River. Therefore a statement about spring wheat's lesser dependence on irrigation would logically complete the argument.

A   **Correct.** If spring wheat in the Papoose River region does not require irrigation, that would provide a logical basis for the expectation that spring wheat's profitability will exceed that of winter wheat: spring wheat will not be negatively affected by the irrigation restrictions, but winter wheat will be. Therefore this explanation logically completes the sentence.

B   This fact would not explain the expectation that spring wheat will be more profitable than winter wheat; it only explains why farmers must choose to plant one or the other.

C   Since spring wheat and winter wheat were formerly equally profitable for Papoose River farmers, the fact that spring wheat grows well in the region's soil would not explain the expectation that spring wheat will be more profitable *this year*.

D   The uses of the two types of wheat has no bearing on the question of why one type would be more profitable than the other for farmers.

E   The relative profitability of spring wheat compared to other non-wheat crops is not relevant to a choice between spring wheat and winter wheat specifically.

The correct answer is A.

706. Plant scientists have been able to genetically engineer seeds to produce crops that are highly resistant to insect damage. Farmers planting such seeds can use much less pesticide. Although these seeds currently cost significantly more than nonengineered seeds, their cost is likely to decline. Since these seeds produce crop yields as high as those produced by nonengineered seeds, the use of genetically engineered seeds is likely to become increasingly common.

Which of the following, if true, most strengthens the argument?

(A) Plant scientists have not yet developed insect-resistant seeds for all commercially grown food crops.

(B) Consumers prefer to buy grains, fruits, and vegetables that have been grown using little or no pesticide.

(C) Traditional methods of plant breeding have also resulted in some insect-resistant strains of plants.

(D) Crops grown from seeds that are genetically engineered to produce insect resistance will still be vulnerable to other types of pests.

(E) The cost of many commonly used agricultural pesticides is likely to decline as the use of genetically engineered seeds increases.

Argument Evaluation

Situation   Scientists have successfully genetically engineered seeds for strong insect-resistance in the resulting crops. These seeds greatly reduce the need for pesticides, but are more expensive than ordinary seeds. Further, the modified seeds will probably come down in price and produce comparable yields. The argument concludes that it is probable that the engineered seeds will be used more widely.

Reasoning   *What would strengthen the argument that the genetically modified seeds will be used more widely?* The information includes a number of points of comparison between the engineered seeds and ordinary seeds: engineered seeds are much better for insect resistance and reducing pesticide, significantly higher in price although likely to become less expensive in the future, and comparable in yields produced. Any information, then, that suggested an additional reason why engineered seeds' positive traits were desirable would tend to strengthen the argument, by showing that farmers have a further incentive to choose them.

A   The fact that scientists have not yet developed insect-resistant seeds for all crops does not strengthen the argument that such seeds will gain popularity.

B   **Correct.** If consumers prefer food grown with little to no pesticide, then that demand would create an added incentive for farmers to grow modified crops that require little pesticide, and thereby strengthen the argument that the seeds probably will be used more commonly.

C   The fact that there may be other methods of creating insect-resistant plants would slightly weaken the argument if anything, not strengthen it.

D   The fact that the insect-resistant seeds would still have other vulnerabilities does not strengthen the argument that those seeds will gain popularity.

E   If pesticide prices decline, then that would tend to decrease the incentive to reduce pesticide use by choosing engineered seeds, and thereby weaken rather than strengthen the argument.

The correct answer is B.

707. Over the past five years, the price gap between name-brand cereals and less expensive store-brand cereals has become so wide that consumers have been switching increasingly to store brands despite the name brands' reputation for better quality. To attract these consumers back, several manufacturers of name-brand cereals plan to narrow the price gap between their cereals and store brands to less than what it was five years ago.

Which of the following, if true, most seriously calls into question the likelihood that the manufacturers' plan will succeed in attracting back a large percentage of consumers who have switched to store brands?

(A) There is no significant difference among manufacturers of name-brand cereals in the prices they charge for their products.

(B) Consumers who have switched to store-brand cereals have generally been satisfied with the quality of those cereals.

(C) Many consumers would never think of switching to store-brand cereals because they believe the name-brand cereals to be of better quality.

(D) Because of lower advertising costs, stores are able to offer their own brands of cereals at significantly lower prices than those charged for name-brand cereals.

(E) Total annual sales of cereals—including both name-brand and store-brand cereals—have not increased significantly over the past five years.

Argument Evaluation

Situation   A widening price gap between expensive name-brand cereals and cheaper store-brand cereals has led increasing numbers of consumers to opt for the store brands, even though name brands are generally held to be superior. To regain consumers who have defected to store brands, makers of name-brand cereal plan to reduce—though not to eliminate—the price gap.

Reasoning   *What factor would undermine the effectiveness of the plan to win back cereal buyers with lower prices?* There is a key phrase in the information given: it states that consumers have been changing from name brands to store brands despite name brands' reputation for better quality. If, then, consumers who switch to store brands discover that that reputation is unfounded, and the store brands' quality is in fact similar or at least perfectly acceptable, then those consumers may well be disinclined to switch back to name brands, which will still be more expensive—even if the difference in cost becomes less drastic.

A   Variations in price among name-brand cereals are not relevant to the plan to win back cereal buyers who have switched to *store* brands.

B   **Correct.** The information suggests that a major reason consumers have bought name-brand cereals—despite their higher prices—is that such cereals have a reputation for quality superior to that of the store brands. If, therefore, consumers who have switched to store brands are generally happy with their quality, they will quite probably be disinclined to switch back to more-expensive name brands, even if those brands lower their prices to some degree. The satisfactory quality of the store brands is therefore a factor that would call into question the likelihood that the cereal manufacturers' plan will succeed.

C   The fact that many consumers would not switch to store brands has no bearing on a plan to win back consumers who already have switched.

D   The reason *why* store brands are priced lower than name brands has no relevance to a plan to win back consumers who switched to store brands.

E   Overall rates of cereal sales have no bearing on the cereal manufacturers' plan's odds of success.

The correct answer is B.

Questions 708–777 — Difficulty: **Medium**

708. Although the school would receive financial benefits if it had soft drink vending machines in the cafeteria, we should not allow them. Allowing soft drink machines there would not be in our students' interest. If our students start drinking more soft drinks, they will be less healthy.

The argument depends on which of the following?

(A) If the soft drink vending machines were placed in the cafeteria, students would consume more soft drinks as a result.

(B) The amount of soft drinks that most students at the school currently drink is not detrimental to their health.

(C) Students are apt to be healthier if they do not drink soft drinks at all than if they just drink small amounts occasionally.

(D) Students will not simply bring soft drinks from home if the soft drink vending machines are not placed in the cafeteria.

(E) The school's primary concern should be to promote good health among its students.

Argument Construction

Situation   Allowing soft drink vending machines in a school cafeteria would financially benefit the school, but students who drink more soft drinks would become less healthy.

Reasoning   *What must be true in order for the claim that students drinking more soft drinks would cause them to become less healthy to justify the conclusion that soft drink vending machines should not be allowed in the cafeteria?* The argument is that because drinking more soft drinks would be unhealthy for the students, allowing the vending machines would not be in the students' interest, so the vending machines should not be allowed. This reasoning depends on the implicit factual assumption that allowing the vending machines would result in the students drinking more soft drinks. It also depends on the implicit value judgment that receiving financial benefits should be less important to the school than preventing a situation that would make the students less healthy.

A   **Correct.** If the cafeteria vending machines would not result in students consuming more soft drinks, then allowing the machines would not harm the students' health in the way the argument assumes.

B   Even if the amount of soft drinks the students currently drink were unhealthy, enabling the students to drink more could make them even less healthy.

C   Even if drinking small amounts of soft drinks occasionally would not harm the students, vending machines in the cafeteria could lead the students to drink excessive amounts.

D   Even if students who cannot buy soft drinks in the cafeteria sometimes bring them from home instead, adding vending machines in the cafeteria could increase the students' overall soft drink consumption.

E   A concern does not have to be the primary one in order to be valid and important. It could be held that promoting students' good health should not be the schools' primary concern but should still be a more important concern than the financial benefits from the vending machines.

The correct answer is A.

709. Historian: Fifteenth-century advances in mapmaking contributed to the rise of modern nation-states. In medieval Europe (from the fifth to the fifteenth century), sovereignty centered in cities and towns and radiated outward, with boundaries often ambiguously defined. The conceptual shift toward the modern state began in the late fifteenth century, when mapmakers learned to reflect geography accurately by basing maps on latitude-longitude grids. By the mid-seventeenth century, nearly all maps showed boundary lines.

Which of the following would, if true, most strengthen the historian's reasoning?

(A) Borders did not become codified in Europe until certain treaties were signed in the early nineteenth century.

(B) During the medieval period, various authorities in Europe claimed power over collections of cities and towns, not contiguous territories.

(C) Many members of the political elite collected maps as a hobby during the late sixteenth and early seventeenth centuries.

(D) Seventeenth-century treatises and other sources of political authority describe areas of sovereignty rather than illustrate them using maps.

(E) During the fifteenth century in Europe, mapmakers simplified the borders of sovereignty by drawing clear lines of demarcation between political powers.

Argument Evaluation

Situation   A historian claims that fifteenth-century advances in mapmaking contributed to the rise of modern nation-states. In earlier centuries, boundaries of sovereignty in Europe were poorly defined, but in the fifteenth century, maps were made based on grids showing latitude and longitude.

Reasoning   *What additional piece of information, if true and added to the argument, would most improve the support offered for the conclusion that improved mapping contributed to the rise of nation-states?* The historian claims that there was a cause-effect relationship between progress in mapmaking and the rise of the nation-state. This claim is supported by information that territories of sovereignty were vague and ill-defined before the fifteenth century, when latitude-longitude grids began to allow progressively greater accuracy in the delineation of territories on maps. The argument assumes that the rise of nation-states would have required a high degree of clarity about each state's nonoverlapping area of sovereignty.

A   This indicates the role of treaties in the evolution of nation-states but provides no additional support for the historian's causal claim.

B   This information is consistent with the historian's belief that nothing resembling the modern state existed before the fifteenth century, but it provides no additional support for the historian's causal claim.

C   The relevance of this information to the argument is tenuous at best. There could be many nonpolitical explanations for the interest of political elites in collecting maps. Many people other than political elites may also have collected maps during the period mentioned.

D   This information tends to minimize the role of maps in defining areas of sovereignty and to cast some doubt on the historian's causal claim.

E   **Correct.** This information makes explicit the role of mapmakers in providing clarity about the geographical boundaries of each political entity's sovereignty. It thus provides additional evidence for the historian's causal claim and strengthens the historian's reasoning.

The correct answer is E.

710. Sascha: The attempt to ban parliament's right to pass directed-spending bills—bills that contain provisions specifically funding the favorite projects of some powerful politicians—is antidemocratic. Our nation's constitution requires that money be drawn from our treasury only when so stipulated by laws passed by parliament, the branch of government most directly representative of the citizens. This requirement is based on the belief that exercising the power to spend public resources involves the ultimate exercise of state authority and that therefore _____.

Which of the following most logically completes Sascha's argument?

(A) designating funding specifically for the favorite projects of some powerful politicians should be considered antidemocratic

(B) the right to exercise such a power should belong exclusively to the branch of government most directly representative of the citizens

(C) exercising the power to spend public resources is in most cases—but not all—protected by the constitution

(D) modifications to any spending bills should be considered expenditures authorized by law

(E) only officials who are motivated by concerns for reelection should retain that power

Argument Construction

Situation   According to Sascha, restricting parliament's ability to direct public money to the projects favored by powerful politicians would be undemocratic. Sascha argues that such a restriction on directed spending would be inconsistent with constitutional requirements.

Reasoning   *What piece of information would most logically complete Sascha's argument?* What piece of information would most strongly associate parliament's spending authority with the concept of democracy? A good guess would be: some information that connects parliament's public representation role with its spending authority.

A   Sascha believes that democratic constitutional principles require that parliament remain free to do what is described in this sentence.

B   **Correct.** This statement makes explicit the connection, implicitly relied on by Sascha's argument, between parliament's spending authority and its role in representing the public.

C   This statement may be true but fails to associate parliament's spending authority under the constitution with the notion of democracy.

D   Bills are merely works-in-progress, texts of proposed laws. Modifications of bills do not in themselves provide legal authority for any public spending item.

E   Sascha opposes restrictions on parliament's spending power, and this would seem to imply that Sascha believes every parliamentary representative should be free to vote on such measures regardless of their levels of concern for reelection.

The correct answer is B.

711. Boreal owls range over a much larger area than do other owls of similar size. Scientists have hypothesized that **it is scarcity of prey that leads the owls to range so widely.** This hypothesis would be hard to confirm directly, since it is not possible to produce a sufficiently accurate count of the populations of small mammals inhabiting the forests where boreal owls live. Careful study of owl behavior has, however, shown that **boreal owls do range over larger areas when they live in regions where food of the sort eaten by small mammals is comparatively sparse.** This indicates that the scientists' hypothesis is not sheer speculation.

In the argument given, the two **boldfaced** portions play which of the following roles?

(A) The first presents an explanatory hypothesis; the second states the main conclusion of the argument.

(B) The first presents an explanatory hypothesis; the second presents evidence tending to support this hypothesis.

(C) The first presents an explanatory hypothesis; the second presents evidence to support an alternative explanation.

(D) The first describes a position that the argument opposes; the second presents evidence to undermine the support for the position being opposed.

(E) The first describes a position that the argument opposes; the second states the main conclusion of the argument.

Argument Construction

Situation   Boreal owls range over a much larger area than other owls of similar size. Scientists hypothesize that they do so because of prey scarcity. Counting the owls' prey—small mammals—in the boreal owls' habitat is inherently difficult. This makes the scientists' hypothesis hard to confirm directly. However, it has been found that boreal owls range widely when they inhabit regions that have relatively little food for the small mammals they prey on.

Reasoning   *What function is served by the statement that it is scarcity of prey that leads the owls to range so widely? What function is served by the statement that boreal owls range widely if food for their small-mammal prey is relatively sparse in the region they inhabit?* The first **boldfaced** statement expresses an explanatory hypothesis. The passage explicitly says that this is a hypothesis and indicates that scientists have proposed this hypothesis as a tentative explanation for the comparatively wide range of boreal owls. The second **boldfaced** statement provides some indirect evidence for the scientists' hypothesis. The final sentence of the passage says that the immediately preceding idea (expressed in the second **boldfaced** portion) indicates that the scientists' hypothesis (the first **boldfaced** portion) is not mere speculation. The evidence expressed in this second **boldfaced** portion is indirect in that it depends heavily on further assumptions and is not sufficient to prove the hypothesis.

A   The main conclusion of the argument is that the scientists' hypothesis is not sheer speculation, i.e., that the scientists have based their hypothesis on some evidence that they have discovered. The first statement presents the scientists' hypothesis. The second statement cites some evidence for the hypothesis and is not the main conclusion of the argument.

B   **Correct.** As explained above, the first statement presents an explanatory hypothesis, while the second cites some indirect evidence for the hypothesis.

C   The second statement cites some indirect evidence for the scientists' hypothesis, not for some other hypothesis.

D   The argument does not oppose the scientists' hypothesis, presented in the first statement; the second statement cites evidence for the hypothesis and does not cite evidence for any position the argument opposes.

E   The second statement does not present the argument's main conclusion. The main conclusion is that the scientists' hypothesis is not mere speculation.

The correct answer is B.

712. Cognitive scientist: Using the pioneering work of comparative psychologist Gordon Gallup as a model, several studies have investigated animals' capacity for mirror self-recognition (MSR). Most animals exposed to a mirror respond only with social behavior, such as aggression. However, in the case of the great apes, repeated exposure to mirrors leads to self-directed behaviors, such as exploring the inside of the mouth, suggesting that these animals recognize the reflection as an image of self. The implication of these studies is that the great apes have a capacity for self-awareness unique among nonhuman species.

The cognitive scientist makes which of the following assumptions in the argument above?

(A) Gallup's work has established that the great apes have a capacity for MSR unique among nonhuman species.

(B) If an animal does not have the capacity for MSR, it does not have the capacity for self-awareness.

(C) If a researcher exposes an animal to a mirror and that animal exhibits social behavior, that animal is incapable of being self-aware.

(D) When exposed to a mirror, all animals display either social behavior or self-directed behavior.

(E) Animals that do not exhibit MSR may demonstrate a capacity for self-awareness in other ways.

Argument Construction

Situation   A cognitive scientist claims that several studies, modeled on Gordon Gallup's work, have investigated animals' capacity for mirror self-recognition (MSR) and found that, whereas most animals exposed to a mirror exhibit only social behavior in response, great apes can come to respond with self-directed behavior. The cognitive scientist infers from this that the great apes, unique among nonhumans, have a capacity for self-awareness.

Reasoning   *What must be true for the studies to support the cognitive scientist's conclusion?* The implicit reasoning is that an animal has self-awareness only if the animal has the capacity for MSR; if the latter is lacking, so is the capacity for self-awareness.

A   The studies the cognitive scientist's inference is based on were not necessarily conducted by Gallup himself. We are told only that they are modeled on his work.

B   Correct. If it were possible for an animal to have the capacity for self-awareness even if the animal lacks the capacity for MSR, then the studies would not imply that the great apes have a capacity for self-awareness that other nonhuman animal species lack.

C   The cognitive scientist's reasoning does not require that an animal with the capacity for self-awareness never exhibits social behavior when exposed to a mirror; it merely requires that it does not exhibit only such behavior.

D   The cognitive scientist's reasoning is compatible with an animal's displaying no behavior in response to exposure to a mirror.

E   The cognitive scientist's reasoning is compatible with the claim that an animal that does not exhibit MSR has no capacity at all for self-awareness.

The correct answer is B.

713. A study of ticket sales at a summer theater festival found that people who bought tickets to individual plays had a no-show rate of less than 1 percent, while those who paid in advance for all ten plays being performed that summer had a no-show rate of nearly 30 percent. This may be at least in part because the greater the awareness customers retain about the cost of an item, the more likely they are to use it.

Which of the following would, if true, best serve as an alternative explanation of the results of the study?

(A) The price per ticket was slightly cheaper for those who bought all ten tickets in advance.

(B) Many people who attended the theater festival believed strongly that they should support it financially.

(C) Those who attended all ten plays became eligible for a partial refund.

(D) Usually, people who bought tickets to individual plays did so immediately prior to each performance that they attended.

(E) People who arrived just before the performance began could not be assured of obtaining seats in a preferred location.

Argument Construction

Situation People who bought tickets to individual plays at a theater festival had a much lower no-show rate than did people who paid in advance for all ten plays.

Reasoning *What factor other than greater awareness of the ticket costs could explain why people who bought tickets individually were more likely to attend the plays?* The passage suggests that people who bought tickets individually were more likely to attend the plays because they were more vividly aware of what they had paid for each ticket. But there are other possible explanations—perhaps the people who bought the tickets individually were more eager to attend each play for its own sake, or they had other characteristics or incentives that made them more likely to attend the plays.

A A slight price difference would not plausibly explain why the no-show rate was thirty times greater among those who bought all the tickets in advance than among those who bought them individually.

B This could be true of many people who bought their tickets individually as well as many who bought them in advance.

C This would provide an added incentive for those who bought tickets in advance to attend all the plays.

D Correct. If people who bought individual tickets usually did so right before each performance, they would have much less time after buying the tickets to change their minds about whether to attend than would people who bought all the tickets in advance.

E If anything, this might present an additional difficulty for those who bought individual tickets without advance planning, so it would not help to explain the lower no-show rate among buyers of individual tickets.

The correct answer is D.

714. Although there is no record of poet Edmund Spenser's parentage, we do know that as a youth Spenser attended the Merchant Tailors' School in London for a period between 1560 and 1570. Records from this time indicate that the Merchant Tailors' Guild then had only three members named Spenser: Robert Spenser, listed as a gentleman; Nicholas Spenser, elected the Guild's Warden in 1568; and John Spenser, listed as a "journeyman cloth-maker." Of these, the last was likely the least affluent of the three—and most likely Edmund's father, since school accounting records list Edmund as a scholar who attended the school at a reduced fee.

Which of the following is an assumption on which the argument depends?

(A)   Anybody in sixteenth-century London who made clothing professionally would have had to be a member of the Merchant Tailors' Guild.

(B)   The fact that Edmund Spenser attended the Merchant Tailors' School did not necessarily mean that he planned to become a tailor.

(C)   No member of the Guild could become Guild warden in sixteenth-century London unless he was a gentleman.

(D)   Most of those whose fathers were members of the Merchant Tailors' Guild were students at the Merchant Tailors' School.

(E)   The Merchant Tailors' School did not reduce its fees for the children of the more affluent Guild members.

Argument Construction

Situation   Records indicate that the poet Edmund Spenser attended the Merchant Tailors' School for a reduced fee as a youth. There is no record of his parentage, but at the time, the Merchant Tailors' Guild had only three members named Spenser, of whom the least affluent was probably John Spenser.

Reasoning   *What must be true in order for the cited facts to support the conclusion that John Spenser was probably Edmund Spenser's father?* The implicit reasoning is that since Edmund Spenser attended the Merchant Tailors' School at a reduced fee, his father must have been poor. And since John Spenser was probably the poorest of the three men named Spenser in the Merchant Tailors' Guild, he was probably Edmund Spenser's father. This reasoning assumes that only the children of poor parents had reduced fees at the Merchant Tailors' School, that the children at the school generally had fathers in the Merchant Tailors' Guild, that children in that time and place generally shared their fathers' surnames, and that the two other Spensers in the Merchant Tailors' Guild were not poor enough for their children to qualify for reduced fees.

A   John Spenser, as a tailor and member of the Guild, could have been Edmund Spenser's father even if some other professional tailors did not belong to the Guild and did not have children at the school.

B   Although Edmund Spenser became a poet as an adult, he and all his classmates might have attended the school as children because they planned to become tailors.

C   The argument assumes that a Guild's Warden probably would have been wealthier than a journeyman cloth-maker, but that might have been probable even if the Guild's Warden were not a "gentleman."

D   Even if most children of fathers in the Guild did not attend the school, all the children who did attend the school might have had fathers in the Guild.

E   **Correct.** If the school reduced its fees for children of wealthier Guild members, then the fact that Edmund Spenser's fees were reduced would not provide evidence that his father was the poorest of the three Spensers in the Guild, as the argument requires.

The correct answer is E.

715. Hea Sook: One should not readily believe urban legends. Most legends are propagated because the moral lesson underlying them supports a political agenda. People will repeat a tale if it fits their purpose. They may not deliberately spread untruths, but neither are they particularly motivated to investigate deeply to determine if the tale they are telling is true.

Kayla: But people would not repeat stories that they did not believe were true. Therefore, one can safely assume that if a story has been repeated by enough people, then it is more likely to be true.

Kayla's reply is most vulnerable to the criticism that it

(A) does not specify how many people need to repeat a story before someone is justified in believing it

(B) overstates the significance of political agendas in the retelling of stories

(C) fails to address the claim that people will not verify the truth of a story that fits their purpose

(D) implicitly supports the claim that the people repeating legends are not deliberately spreading untruths

(E) cannot distinguish people's motivations for repeating urban legends from their motivations for repeating other types of story

Argument Evaluation

Situation   Hea Sook and Kayla have a difference of opinion on how likely urban legends are to be true.

Reasoning   *What criticism is Kayla's reply most vulnerable to?* Hea Sook argues that because urban legends generally are propagated for political purposes, people are not particularly motivated to carefully investigate whether the story they are telling is true. These people may not be deliberately telling an untruth, but they have not taken care to establish whether the story is true. Kayla responds that people would not repeat a story that they did not believe to be true, but Hea Sook not only does not attempt to deny that, but she suggests that it may be true. Kayla ignores the fact that sometimes people believe that something is true without carefully determining whether it actually is true, and that they are less likely to verify whether it is true when the story fits their purposes.

A   Kayla does not specify how many people need to repeat a story before one is justified in believing it, but she does not need to. Her claim—that there is some number sufficient for such belief to be justified—could be true even if she does not specify what that number is.

B   It is Hea Sook, not Kayla, who asserts that political agendas are a significant factor in whether one retells a story.

C   **Correct.** Kayla does not address whether people are unlikely to verify whether a story is true if the story fits their purpose.

D   Kayla does not merely implicitly claim that people who repeat legends are not deliberately spreading untruths; she explicitly states this, but in this she and Hea Sook agree.

E   We have no reason to think that Kayla cannot distinguish people's motivations for repeating urban legends from their motivations for repeating other types of stories. She may well be able to do this.

The correct answer is C.

716. Rainwater contains hydrogen of a heavy form called deuterium. The deuterium content of wood reflects the deuterium content of rainwater available to trees during their growth. Wood from trees that grew between 16,000 and 24,000 years ago in North America contains significantly more deuterium than wood from trees growing today. But water trapped in several North American caves that formed during that same early period contains significantly less deuterium than rainwater in North America contains today.

Which of the following, if true, most helps to reconcile the two findings?

(A) There is little deuterium in the North American caves other than the deuterium in the water trapped there.

(B) Exposure to water after a tree has died does not change the deuterium content of the wood.

(C) Industrialization in North America over the past 100 years has altered the deuterium content of rain.

(D) Trees draw on shallow groundwater from rain that falls during their growth, whereas water trapped in caves may have fallen as rainwater thousands of years before the caves formed.

(E) Wood with a high deuterium content is no more likely to remain preserved for long periods than is wood with a low deuterium content.

Argument Construction

Situation In North America, wood from trees that grew 16,000 to 24,000 years ago contains more deuterium than wood from trees growing today. But water in caves that formed during that same period contains less deuterium than rainwater contains today.

Reasoning *What could explain the puzzling discrepancy between the observed deuterium levels in wood and in caves?* Since the deuterium content of wood from trees reflects the deuterium content of rainwater available to the trees while they grew, the deuterium levels observed in wood suggests that North American rainwater contained more deuterium 16,000 to 24,000 years ago than it contains today. But this conclusion seems at odds with the low deuterium levels in water in caves that formed 16,000 to 24,000 years ago. Several factors might explain the discrepancy: the water in those caves might not be rainwater from the period when the caves formed; or some natural process might have altered the deuterium levels in the cave water or the wood; or the wood or caves in which deuterium levels were measured might be statistically abnormal somehow.

A If the caves had absorbed deuterium out of the rainwater trapped in them, there would probably be deuterium in the cave walls. So, the observation that there is little deuterium in the caves apart from that in the water eliminates one possible explanation for the oddly low deuterium levels in the cave water.

B This suggests that the deuterium levels in the wood accurately reflect higher deuterium levels in rainwater that fell 16,000 to 24,000 years ago, but it does not explain why the deuterium levels are so low in water in the caves that formed then.

C This could explain why deuterium levels in rainwater have changed, but it does not help explain the discrepancy between the high deuterium levels in the wood and the low deuterium levels in the cave water.

D **Correct.** If the water in the caves fell as rainwater thousands of years before the caves formed, it may date from a period when rainwater contained much less deuterium than during the period 16,000 to 24,000 years ago, and much less than today.

E If wood with high deuterium content were more likely to be preserved, then wood from 16,000 to 24,000 years ago might have a high deuterium content even if the rainwater then had a low deuterium content. So the observation that wood with more deuterium is not more likely to be preserved eliminates one possible explanation for the discrepancy.

The correct answer is D.

717. Enforcement of local speed limits through police monitoring has proven unsuccessful in the town of Ardane. In many nearby towns, speed humps (raised areas of pavement placed across residential streets, about 300 feet apart) have reduced traffic speeds on residential streets by 20 to 25 percent. In order to reduce traffic speed and thereby enhance safety in residential neighborhoods, Ardane's transportation commission plans to install multiple speed humps in those neighborhoods.

Which of the following, if true, identifies a potentially serious drawback to the plan for installing speed humps in Ardane?

(A) On residential streets without speed humps, many vehicles travel at speeds more than 25 percent above the posted speed limit.

(B) Because of their high weight, emergency vehicles such as fire trucks and ambulances must slow almost to a stop at speed humps.

(C) The residential speed limit in Ardane is higher than that of the nearby towns where speed humps were installed.

(D) Motorists who are not familiar with the streets in Ardane's residential districts would be likely to encounter the speed humps unawares unless warned by signs and painted indicators.

(E) Bicyclists generally prefer that speed humps be constructed so as to leave a space on the side of the road where bicycles can travel without going over the humps.

Evaluation of a Plan

Situation   Ardane's difficulty in getting compliance with speed limits has led it to propose the installation of speed humps to slow traffic. In nearby towns, speed humps have reduced speeds in residential areas by up to 25 percent.

Reasoning   *Which one of the statements presented identifies a major disadvantage of the proposed installation of speed humps?* Is it possible that they might slow traffic too much? Clearly, there is a general need for traffic to flow smoothly. Would speed humps affect all types of traffic equally? Perhaps not. For example, certain emergency vehicles must sometimes need to travel quickly through residential neighborhoods. A problem with speed humps is that some heavier vehicles must go very slowly over speed humps.

A   This indicates a drawback of not installing speed humps.

B   **Correct.** This information indicates a significant drawback—possibly leading to loss of life and property—of the plan to install the speed humps.

C   This suggests that installing speed humps might lower speeds significantly below the current speed limits. If speeds became very low, the result could be traffic gridlock that would have unforeseen consequences. However, we have insufficient information to evaluate such possibilities.

D   This is unlikely to be a drawback, since such warning signs are typically put in place whenever speed humps are installed.

E   This information provides no evidence of a drawback in Ardane's plan for speed humps, since the design of Ardane's planned speed humps is not indicated.

The correct answer is B.

718. Which of the following most logically completes the argument below?

NowNews, although still the most popular magazine covering cultural events in Kalopolis, has recently suffered a significant drop in advertising revenue because of falling circulation. Many readers have begun buying a competing magazine that, at 50 cents per copy, costs less than *NowNews* at $1.50 per copy. In order to boost circulation and thus increase advertising revenue, *NowNews*'s publisher has proposed making it available at no charge, but this proposal has a serious drawback, since _____.

(A) those Kalopolis residents with the greatest interest in cultural events are regular readers of both magazines

(B) one reason *NowNews*'s circulation fell was that its competitor's reporting on cultural events was superior

(C) the newsstands and stores that currently sell *NowNews* will no longer carry it if it is being given away for free

(D) at present, 10 percent of the total number of copies of each issue of *NowNews* are distributed free to students on college campuses in the Kalopolis area

(E) *NowNews*'s competitor would begin to lose large amounts of money if it were forced to lower its cover price

Argument Construction

Situation   *NowNews* is suffering declines in circulation and advertising revenue due to competition from a lower-priced magazine. The publisher proposes offering *NowNews* for free to reverse these declines.

Reasoning   *What would suggest that the publisher's proposal will fail to increase circulation and advertising revenue?* The proposal's intended effect is simply to increase advertising revenue by increasing circulation. Any evidence that offering the magazine for free will not result in more copies being circulated or will not attract advertisers would therefore be evidence of a drawback in the proposal. So, a statement offering such evidence would logically complete the argument.

A   The fact that certain highly motivated Kalopolis residents still read *NowNews* even at a cost of $1.50 per issue leaves open the possibility that providing the magazine free might still boost readership.

B   This suggests that improving its cultural reporting might help *NowNews* increase its circulation, not that the publisher's proposal will fail to do so.

C   **Correct.** If the proposal leads newsstands and stores to stop carrying *NowNews*, circulation and advertising revenue would probably decline as a result.

D   Even if 10 percent of the copies of *NowNews* are already distributed for free, distributing the remaining 90 percent for free could still increase circulation and advertising revenue as the publisher intends.

E   Forcing a competing magazine to lower its cover price and lose lots of money would be an advantage rather than a drawback of the proposal, as far as the publisher of *NowNews* is concerned.

The correct answer is C.

719. Over the last five years, demand for hotel rooms in Cenopolis has increased significantly, as has the average price Cenopolis hotels charge for rooms. These trends are projected to continue for the next several years. In response to this economic forecast, Centennial Commercial, a real estate developer, is considering a plan to convert several unoccupied office buildings it owns in Cenopolis into hotels in order to maximize its revenues from these properties.

Which of the following would it be most useful for Centennial Commercial to know in evaluating the plan it is considering?

(A) Whether the population of Cenopolis is expected to grow in the next several years

(B) Whether demand for office space in Cenopolis is projected to increase in the near future

(C) Whether the increased demand for hotel rooms, if met, is likely to lead to an increase in the demand for other travel-related services

(D) Whether demand for hotel rooms has also increased in other cities where Centennial Commercial owns office buildings

(E) Whether, on average, hotels that have been created by converting office buildings have fewer guest rooms than do hotels that were built as hotels

Argument Construction

Situation   Cenopolis has seen rising demand for hotel rooms over the past five years, and a corresponding rise in prices for such rooms; moreover, these prices seem likely to keep increasing. Centennial Commercial is considering converting vacant office buildings in its possession into hotels to make those properties more profitable.

Reasoning   *What factor would affect the plan to maximize profits by converting the buildings?* Since Centennial Commercial is seeking to maximize profits from its buildings, it would be helpful for the company to have information that could affect the relative profitability of its options: to convert the buildings to hotels or to keep them as office space.

A   Demand for hotel rooms in Cenopolis is already projected to grow regardless of changes in the size of its population, so projected population increases have little bearing on the advantages of converting the buildings into hotels.

B   **Correct.** If demand for office space in Cenopolis increased significantly in coming years, then that demand would affect Centennial Commercial's ability to profit off its office buildings without converting them into hotels. Depending on the extent of increasing demand, it might be more profitable to keep the buildings as they are, so having information regarding future need for office space would be very helpful in evaluating the plan to convert the buildings.

C   The plan concerns the possible profitability of converting the office buildings into hotels, and demand for other travel-related services has no bearing on that issue.

D   Demand for hotel rooms in other cities where Centennial Commercial owns office buildings is not relevant to the question of whether or not the company can maximize profits by converting its buildings in Cenopolis.

E   The average number of hotel rooms in converted office buildings versus the number in preexisting hotels does not affect the question of whether or not converting Centennial Commercial's buildings would be the best way to make them profitable, though the number of rooms that could be created in these particular buildings would be relevant.

The correct answer is B.

720. Economist: The most economically efficient way to reduce emissions of air pollutants is to tax them in proportion to the damage they are likely to cause. But in Country Y, many serious pollutants are untaxed and unregulated, and policy makers strongly oppose new taxes. Therefore, the best way to achieve a reduction in air pollutant emissions in Country Y would be to institute fixed upper limits on them.

Which of the following is an assumption of the economist's argument?

(A) Policy makers in Country Y oppose all new taxes equally strongly, regardless of any benefits they may provide.

(B) Country Y's air pollutant emissions would not fall significantly if they were taxed in proportion to the damage they are likely to cause.

(C) Policy makers in Country Y strongly favor reductions in air pollutant emissions.

(D) Country Y's policy makers believe that air pollutant emissions should be reduced with maximum economic efficiency.

(E) Policy makers in Country Y do not oppose setting fixed upper limits on air pollutant emissions as strongly as they oppose new taxes.

Argument Construction

Situation   Although taxing air pollution emissions in proportion to the damage they cause is the most economically efficient way to reduce those emissions, many serious pollutants in Nation Y are untaxed and unregulated, and the nation's policy makers strongly oppose new taxes. Therefore, fixed upper limits on such emissions would more effectively reach this goal.

Reasoning   *What must be true in order for the factors the economist cites to support the claim that fixing upper limits on air pollutant emissions in Nation Y would be the best way to reduce those emissions?* Political opposition to taxation in Nation Y is the only factor the economist cites to support the argument's conclusion that it would be best to institute fixed upper limits on air pollutants. In order for the premise to support the conclusion, there must be less political opposition in Nation Y to instituting such limits than there would be to the proportional taxation approach the economist prefers.

A   Even if the policy makers oppose some new taxes less than others, they could still oppose the proportional taxation approach strongly enough for it to be utterly infeasible.

B   Even if the proportional taxation scheme would significantly reduce emissions, it still might not be the best approach for Nation Y if it would generate too much political opposition to be viable there.

C   Even if policy makers in Nation Y do not strongly favor reducing emissions, fixing upper limits on emissions might still be a better and more politically feasible way to reduce emissions than any alternative is.

D   Since fixing upper emissions limits would be no more economically efficient than the proportional taxation scheme, the policy makers' support for economic efficiency would not make the former approach any more politically feasible than the latter.

E   **Correct.** If the policy makers opposed fixing upper emissions limits as strongly as they oppose new taxes, then their opposition to new taxes would no longer support the conclusion that fixing the emissions limits is a better way to reduce emissions.

The correct answer is E.

721. A study of high blood pressure treatments found certain meditation techniques and the most commonly prescribed drugs are equally effective if the selected treatment is followed as directed over the long term. Half the patients given drugs soon stop taking them regularly, whereas 80 percent of the study's participants who were taught meditation techniques were still regularly using them five years later. Therefore, the meditation treatment is the one likely to produce the best results.

Which of the following, if true, most seriously weakens the argument?

(A) People who have high blood pressure are usually advised by their physicians to make changes in diet that have been found in many cases to reduce the severity of the condition.

(B) The participants in the study were selected in part on the basis of their willingness to use meditation techniques.

(C) Meditation techniques can reduce the blood pressure of people who do not suffer from high blood pressure.

(D) Some of the participants in the study whose high blood pressure was controlled through meditation techniques were physicians.

(E) Many people with dangerously high blood pressure are unaware of their condition.

Argument Evaluation

Situation In a study of treatments for high blood pressure, meditation and medication both worked equally well at managing the condition as long as patients adhered to their treatment plan. However, patients prescribed meditation were significantly more likely to continue the treatment than patients prescribed medication, so the author concludes that meditation is likely to be more effective.

Reasoning *What factor would undermine the contention that meditation is the better treatment for high blood pressure?* Since the argument that meditation is better than medication depends on study participants' good adherence to a program of meditation, the argument would be weakened by evidence that the general population might not be as likely to continue meditating as the participants were.

A   The fact that high blood pressure patients are usually advised to change their diets has no bearing on the efficacy of other methods of managing high blood pressure.

B   **Correct.** If study participants were selected partly on the basis of their willingness to practice meditation, then those participants might have better adherence to a meditation program than the general population, who might well be less willing or less able to meditate consistently over long periods of time. Such a discrepancy between the study participants and other patients would seriously undermine the argument that meditation will work better than medication since that argument depends entirely on the contention that more patients will continue with meditation than with medication.

C   The fact that meditation techniques can lower blood pressure in people whose levels are healthy does not undermine the argument that meditation is the best treatment for those whose levels are unhealthy.

D   The fact that some of the participants who benefited from meditation were physicians does not undermine the argument that meditation will be the best treatment for blood pressure patients who may not be physicians. It does not, by itself, indicate the sample studied was unrepresentative.

E   People with high blood pressure being unaware of their condition reduces the likelihood that they will be treated, but it does not undermine the argument that one treatment is better than another.

The correct answer is B.

722. Many industrialized nations are trying to reduce atmospheric concentrations of carbon dioxide, a gas released by the burning of fossil fuels. One proposal is to replace conventional cement, which is made with calcium carbonate, by a new "eco-cement." This new cement, made with magnesium carbonate, absorbs large amounts of carbon dioxide when exposed to the atmosphere. Therefore, using eco-cement for new concrete building projects will significantly help reduce atmospheric concentrations of carbon dioxide.

Which of the following, if true, most strengthens the argument?

(A) The cost of magnesium carbonate, currently greater than the cost of calcium carbonate, probably will fall as more magnesium carbonate is used in cement manufacture.

(B) Eco-cement is strengthened when absorbed carbon dioxide reacts with the cement.

(C) Before the development of eco-cement, magnesium-based cement was considered too susceptible to water erosion to be of practical use.

(D) The manufacture of eco-cement uses considerably less fossil fuel per unit of cement than the manufacture of conventional cement does.

(E) Most building-industry groups are unaware of the development or availability of eco-cement.

Argument Evaluation

Situation   Many nations are trying to reduce atmospheric concentrations of carbon dioxide. One proposed method is to use a new type of "eco-cement" that absorbs carbon dioxide from air.

Reasoning   *What evidence, combined with the cited facts, would most support the prediction that using eco-cement will significantly help reduce atmospheric concentrations of carbon dioxide?* The prediction assumes that the use of eco-cement would be an effective way to reduce carbon dioxide levels. Any evidence supporting this assumption will support the prediction.

A   Since eco-cement uses magnesium carbonate, the prediction that magnesium carbonate prices will fall suggests that a potential financial barrier to widespread eco-cement use will diminish. However, those prices may not fall enough to make eco-cement cost-competitive with regular cement.

B   Even if absorbed carbon dioxide strengthens eco-cement, the strengthened eco-cement might still be much weaker than regular cement and thus might never become widely used, in which case it will not significantly help reduce atmospheric concentrations of carbon dioxide.

C   Even if eco-cement is less susceptible to water erosion than earlier forms of magnesium-based cement were, it might still be much more susceptible to water erosion than regular cement is, and thus might never become widely used.

D   Correct. This suggests that manufacturing eco-cement produces much less carbon dioxide than manufacturing regular cement does, so it supports the claim that widespread use of eco-cement would be an effective way to reduce carbon dioxide levels.

E   If anything, this lack of awareness makes it less likely that eco-cement will become widely used, which in turn makes it less likely that eco-cement will significantly help reduce atmospheric concentrations of carbon dioxide.

The correct answer is D.

723. Advertisement: When your car's engine is running at its normal operating temperature, any major brand of motor oil will protect it about as well as Tuff does. When the engine is cold, it is a different story: Tuff motor oil flows better at lower temperatures than its major competitors do. So, if you want your car's engine to have maximum protection, you should use Tuff.

Which of the following, if true, most strengthens the argument in the advertisement?

(A) Tuff motor oil provides above-average protection for engines that happen to overheat.

(B) Tuff motor oil is periodically supplied free of charge to automobile manufacturers to use in factory-new cars.

(C) Tuff motor oil's share of the engine oil market peaked three years ago.

(D) Tuff motor oil, like any motor oil, is thicker and flows less freely at cold temperatures than at hot temperatures.

(E) Tuff motor oil is manufactured at only one refinery and shipped from there to all markets.

Argument Evaluation

Situation   An advertisement argues that since Tuff motor oil flows better than its major competitors at low temperatures and works about as well as they do at normal temperatures, it provides *maximum protection* for car engines.

Reasoning   *What additional evidence would suggest that Tuff motor oil provides the best available protection for car engines?* The argument requires the assumptions that no type of motor oil other than the "major brands" provides superior protection, that flowing better at lower temperatures ensures superior protection at those temperatures, and that Tuff protects car engines at least as well as its competitors do at above-normal temperatures. Any evidence supporting any of these assumptions would strengthen the argument.

A   **Correct.** If Tuff provides above-average protection when engines overheat, in addition to the solid protection it provides at normal and low temperatures, it may well provide the best available protection overall.

B   The company that makes Tuff might give automobile manufacturers free motor oil as a promotional gimmick even if Tuff is an inferior product.

C   Tuff's sales might have declined over the past three years because consumers have realized that Tuff is an inferior product.

D   The similar responses of Tuff and other motor oils to temperature changes do not suggest that Tuff provides better protection overall than those other motor oils do.

E   Even if Tuff is manufactured at only one refinery, it may still be an inferior product.

The correct answer is A.

724. Linguist: In English, the past is described as "behind" and the future "ahead," whereas in Aymara, the past is "ahead" and the future "behind." Research indicates that English speakers sway backward when discussing the past and forward when discussing the future. Conversely, Aymara speakers gesture forward with their hands when discussing the past and backward when discussing the future. These bodily movements, therefore, suggest that the language one speaks affects how one mentally visualizes time.

The linguist's reasoning depends on assuming which of the following?

(A)   At least some Aymara speakers sway forward when discussing the past and backward when discussing the future.

(B)   Most people mentally visualize time as running either forward or backward.

(C)   Not all English and Aymara speakers tend to sway or gesture forward or backward when discussing the present.

(D)   How people move when discussing the future correlates to some extent with how they mentally visualize time.

(E)   The researchers also examined the movements of at least some speakers of languages other than English and Aymara discussing the past and the future.

Argument Construction

Situation   A linguist argues that the language one speaks affects how one mentally visualizes time. The linguist's argument is based on the fact that English speakers, who refer to the past as "behind" and the future as "ahead," display backward and forward bodily movements when speaking of the past and the future, while speakers of Aymara, who refer to the past as "ahead" and the future as "behind," display correspondingly different body movements.

Reasoning   *What must be true if we are to accept the linguist's conclusion from the given information that the language one speaks affects how one mentally visualizes time?* The linguist's evidence will support the conclusion only if there is some correlation between people's bodily movements and how they mentally visualize time. So, the linguist's reasoning requires an assumption to that effect.

A   The linguist's reasoning is based on the differences in bodily movements discussed in the argument—that is, that Aymara speakers gesture in certain ways and that English speakers sway in certain ways; thus, the linguist's reasoning does not require that Aymara speakers sway in any way whatsoever when they discuss the past or future.

B   The linguist's reasoning is based only on speakers of English and Aymara, so no claim related to speakers of other languages—who make up a majority of people—is required.

C   The linguist's argument would actually be stronger if all English and Aymara speakers sway or gesture in the ways discussed, so the argument certainly does not depend on assuming that not all such speakers sway or gesture in these ways.

D   **Correct.** The fact that English and Aymara speakers sway or gesture in the ways described would be irrelevant to the linguist's conclusion if how people move when discussing the future does not correlate at least to some extent with how they visualize time.

E   It might be helpful to the linguist's argument to examine the movements of speakers of other languages when they discuss the past and the future, but the linguist's argument does not require this.

The correct answer is D.

725. *The Testament of William Thorpe* was published around 1530 as an appendix to Thorpe's longer *Examination*. Many scholars, however, doubt the attribution of the *Testament* to Thorpe because, whereas the *Examination* is dated 1406, the *Testament* is dated 1460. One scholar has recently argued that the 1460 date be amended to 1409, based on the observation that when these numbers are expressed as Roman numerals, MCCCCLX and MCCCCIX, it becomes easy to see how the dates might have become confused through scribal error.

Which of the following, if true, would most support the scholar's hypothesis concerning the date of the *Testament*?

(A) The sole evidence that historians have had that William Thorpe died no earlier than 1460 was the presumed date of publication of the *Testament*.

(B) In the preface to the 1530 publication, the editor attributes both works to William Thorpe.

(C) Few writers in fifteenth-century England marked dates in their works using only Roman numerals.

(D) The *Testament* alludes to a date, "Friday, September 20," as apparently contemporaneous with the writing of the *Testament*, and September 20 fell on a Friday in 1409 but not in 1460.

(E) The *Testament* contains few references to historical events that occurred later than 1406.

Argument Construction

Situation *The Testament of William Thorpe*, dated 1460, was published around 1530 as an appendix to Thorpe's *Examination*, dated 1406. But when expressed in Roman numerals, 1460 could easily be confused with 1409.

Reasoning *Given the facts cited, what would provide additional evidence that Thorpe's* Testament *dates from 1409 rather than 1460?* The scholar's hypothesis that the work dates from 1409 is based on the observation that in Roman numerals, 1409 might easily have been improperly transcribed as 1460. What evidence would support this hypothesis? Any independent evidence that 1409 is a more likely date for the *Testament* than 1460 would certainly help. For instance, if some event or date that occurred in 1409 but not in 1460 is referred to in the *Testament* as being recent or contemporaneous, this would lend significant support to the hypothesis. For instance, if the *Testament* indicated that some day of the month had just fallen on a given day of the week, and that date fell on that day in 1409 but not in 1460, this would support the hypothesis significantly.

A Suppose there is no reason to think that Thorpe was still alive in 1460 other than the presumption that the *Testament* was published in that year. That gives us no more reason to accept the scholar's hypothesis about a scribal error in reporting the date than to accept the other scholars' hypothesis that the *Testament* is improperly ascribed to Thorpe. Furthermore, it provides very little reason to support either of these hypotheses, because the mere lack of evidence, other than the purported 1460 date of creation, that Thorpe died no earlier than 1460 does not provide us with any evidence that he *did* die earlier than 1460.

B The editor of the 1530 publication could easily have been mistaken about the authorship of one or both works. And even if the editor were correct, Thorpe might have lived long enough to write one work in 1406 and the other in 1460.

C This would cast doubt on the scholar's argument by providing evidence that the original manuscripts were not dated only in Roman numerals.

D **Correct.** As explained in the Reasoning section above, this provides strong evidence directly supporting the hypothesis that the *Testament* dates from 1409 specifically.

E Even if the *Testament* contained only one reference to a historical event that occurred later than 1406 (for example, one event in 1459), that reference alone could provide strong evidence that the work dates from 1460 rather than 1409.

The correct answer is D.

726. A prominent investor who holds a large stake in the Burton Tool Company has recently claimed that the company is mismanaged, citing as evidence the company's failure to slow down production in response to a recent rise in its inventory of finished products. It is doubtful whether an investor's sniping at management can ever be anything other than counterproductive, but in this case, it is clearly not justified. It is true that **an increased inventory of finished products often indicates that production is outstripping demand**, but in Burton's case it indicates no such thing. Rather, **the increase in inventory is entirely attributable to products that have already been assigned to orders received from customers.**

In the argument given, the two **boldfaced** portions play which of the following roles?

(A) The first states a generalization that underlies the position that the argument as a whole opposes; the second provides evidence to show that the generalization does not apply in the case at issue.

(B) The first states a generalization that underlies the position that the argument as a whole opposes; the second clarifies the meaning of a specific phrase as it is used in that generalization.

(C) The first provides evidence to support the conclusion of the argument as a whole; the second is evidence that has been used to support the position that the argument as a whole opposes.

(D) The first provides evidence to support the conclusion of the argument as a whole; the second states that conclusion.

(E) The first and the second each provide evidence against the position that the argument as a whole opposes.

Argument Construction

Situation An investor has criticized a company, based on the company's recent increase in inventory and on its not decreasing production as a result of this increase.

Reasoning *What roles do the two **boldfaced** statements play in the argument?* The argument suggests that the investor's criticism is based on a principle that increased inventory of finished products often indicates that production is faster than it should be, given the existing demand for a company's products. However, the argument then states that the increase in inventory at the company in question is *entirely attributable* to existing orders of products. The argument thus suggests that the investor's criticism is misplaced, based on a suggestion as to (1) a principle that the investor could be using to support her argument and (2) an explanation as to why the principle does not apply to the company. The two **boldfaced** portions state these respective elements.

A Correct. The first **boldfaced** portion states the principle that may provide the basis of the investor's criticism, which the argument as a whole opposes. The second **boldfaced** portion is a statement that, if true, shows the generalization would not apply to the company in question.

B This option correctly describes the first of the **boldfaced** portions. However, rather than clarifying an aspect of the meaning of the first generalization, the second **boldfaced** portion indicates why the first generalization may not apply to the company.

C This option incorrectly describes both of the **boldfaced** portions. The first **boldfaced** portion states a general principle that could support the position that the argument *opposes*. The second **boldfaced** portion then criticizes the application of the principle.

D Because the second **boldfaced** portion describes a fundamental premise rather than the conclusion, the description in this option of the second **boldfaced** portion is incorrect.

E If we think of an argument as a set of statements that are meant to support, or provide evidence for, a conclusion, then, because the **boldfaced** statements are indeed part of the argument, they may be seen as providing evidence for the position the argument opposes. However, a description of the roles of the **boldfaced** statements in this argument would need to provide more detail, such as what option A provides.

The correct answer is A.

727. Kate: The recent decline in numbers of the Tennessee warbler, a North American songbird that migrates each fall to coffee plantations in South America, is due to the elimination of the dense tree cover that formerly was a feature of most South American coffee plantations.

Scott: The population of the spruce budworm, the warbler's favorite prey in North America, has been dropping. This is a more likely explanation of the warbler's decline.

Which of the following, if true, most seriously calls Scott's hypothesis into question?

(A) The numbers of the Baltimore oriole, a songbird that does not eat budworms but is as dependent on South American coffee plantations as the Tennessee warbler, are declining.

(B) The spruce budworm population has dropped because of a disease that can infect budworms but not Tennessee warblers.

(C) The drop in the population of the spruce budworm is expected to be only temporary.

(D) Many Tennessee warblers have begun migrating in the fall to places other than traditional coffee plantations.

(E) Although many North American songbirds have declined in numbers, no other species has experienced as great a decline as the Tennessee warbler.

Argument Evaluation

Situation Scott and Kate are arguing about the reason for declining numbers of Tennessee warblers. Kate believes that loss of habitat, specifically tree cover in South American coffee plantations, is to blame. Scott, by contrast, posits that the declining population of North American spruce budworms, which the warblers eat, is more likely to be to blame.

Reasoning *What would undermine the argument that declining numbers of budworms have caused declining numbers of Tennessee warblers?* Scott and Kate have identified two possible causes for the warblers' decline: loss of habitat and loss of prey. If other species that depend on the same habitat but not on the same prey are shown to be suffering similar decline, that fact would tend to support Kate's argument that habitat loss is the main issue and to undermine Scott's argument that prey loss is the main issue.

A Correct. If the Baltimore oriole, a species that relies on the same habitat as the Tennessee warbler but not on the same food sources, is also declining, then that fact would call into question Scott's hypothesis that not habitat loss but rather loss of food, specifically spruce budworm, is probably the reason for the warblers' decline.

B The reason behind declining numbers of spruce budworm does not affect the question of whether fewer budworms are the main cause of fewer warblers.

C The fact that budworm populations are expected to rebound has no bearing on whether or not budworm population decline is the main cause of warbler population decline.

D If Tennessee warblers have begun migrating to habitats other than South American coffee plantations, then if the new habitats lack the dense tree cover traditional in South American coffee plantations, that fact would tend to undermine Kate's argument, not Scott's.

E The greater decline of Tennessee warbler populations relative to those of other songbirds has no direct bearing on the cause of the warblers' decline.

The correct answer is A.

728. Advertising by mail has become much less effective, with fewer consumers responding. Because consumers are increasingly overwhelmed by the sheer amount of junk mail they receive, most discard almost all offers without considering them. Thus, an effective way for corporations to improve response rates would be to more carefully target the individuals to whom they mail advertising, thereby cutting down on the amount of junk mail each consumer receives.

Which of the following, if true, would most support the recommendation above?

(A) There are cost-effective means by which corporations that currently advertise by mail could improve response rates.

(B) Many successful corporations are already carefully targeting the individuals to whom they mail advertising.

(C) Any consumer who, immediately after receiving an advertisement by mail, merely glances at it is very likely to discard it.

(D) Improvements in the quality of the advertising materials used in mail that is carefully targeted to individuals can improve the response rate for such mail.

(E) Response rates to carefully targeted advertisements by mail are considerably higher, on average, than response rates to most other forms of advertising.

Evaluation of a Plan

Situation Advertising by mail has become less effective because consumers overwhelmed with the amount of junk mail they receive discard almost all of it without considering it.

Reasoning *What would most help to support the claim that making mail advertising more carefully targeted would improve response rates?* The passage recommends targeted advertising, reasoning that since targeted advertising would reduce the total amount of junk mail consumers receive, it would generate higher response rates. Any additional evidence for the claim that carefully targeted advertising would improve response rates would support this recommendation.

A   Even if targeted advertising and every other means of improving response rates were too expensive to be cost-effective, targeted advertising could still be effective for any corporation willing to pay the expense.

B   If many corporations already mail targeted advertising, and mail advertising is nonetheless yielding declining response rates, that suggests that targeted mail is an ineffective way to increase response rates.

C   This could be equally true for targeted and untargeted mail advertising, so it does not suggest that the former is more effective.

D   The question under consideration is whether more carefully targeted mail advertising would in itself increase response rates, not whether higher quality advertising would do so.

E   **Correct.** This provides some evidence that carefully targeted mail advertising is associated with higher response rates than untargeted mail advertising is, and therefore that targeting mail advertising more carefully would improve response rates.

The correct answer is E.

729. A company has developed a new sensing device that, according to the company's claims, detects weak, ultralow-frequency electromagnetic signals associated with a beating heart. These signals, which pass through almost any physical obstruction, are purportedly detected by the device even at significant distances. Therefore, if the company's claims are true, their device will radically improve emergency teams' ability to locate quickly people who are trapped within the wreckage of collapsed buildings.

Which of the following, if true, most strengthens the argument?

(A) People trapped within the wreckage of collapsed buildings usually have serious injuries that require prompt medical treatment.

(B) The device gives a distinctive reading when the signals it detects come from human beings rather than from any other living beings.

(C) Most people who have survived after being trapped in collapsed buildings were rescued within two hours of the building's collapse.

(D) Ultralow-frequency signals are not the only electromagnetic signals that can pass through almost any physical obstruction.

(E) Extensive training is required in order to operate the device effectively.

Argument Evaluation

Situation   A new sensing device can detect—at significant distances and even behind obstructions such as walls—weak, ultralow-frequency electromagnetic signals that are characteristic of heartbeats. It is predicted, based on this information, that the new device will shorten the time it currently takes to locate people buried under collapsed buildings but still alive.

Reasoning   *What new information, if accurate, would provide further evidence that would support the prediction?* The existing evidence fails to tell us whether the new device can distinguish between human heartbeats and heartbeats from other species. If the device does not allow the user to distinguish between the heartbeats of humans and those of animals of other species, then the prediction might not be correct, because if there are any nonhuman animals in the building, emergency teams may believe they have located a trapped human and begin a rescue effort, when in fact they have merely located an animal of some other species. Any new information that implies the device can help the user to discern between signals associated with a human heartbeat and signals associated with the heartbeats of animals of other species will strengthen support for the prediction.

A   This implies that prompt rescue of people trapped under collapsed buildings is vitally important. The prediction is that the new device will speed rescue of such people, but the new information here does nothing to indicate that the prediction is accurate.

B   Correct. As explained in the Reasoning section above, there is a crucial gap in the argument: The argument does not indicate whether the device allows the user to distinguish between signals associated with human heartbeats and signals associated with the heartbeats of other species. This information fills that gap.

C   Even if this is true, shortening the time for locating and rescuing people from collapsed buildings would clearly be beneficial. However, the new information given here does not make it more likely that the prediction is correct.

D   If this is correct, then, if anything, it somewhat undermines the evidence given for the prediction, since it raises the possibility that the detection ability of the device might be impeded by "noise" from irrelevant electromagnetic signals near the collapsed building.

E   This could lead to practical obstacles when using the device even in emergency situations, with the result that the device might never actually be used by competent personnel to "improve emergency teams' ability" because the "extensive training" would cost too much.

The correct answer is B.

730. Economist: The price of tap water in our region should be raised drastically. **Supplies in local freshwater reservoirs have been declining for years** because water is being used faster than it can be replenished. Since the price of tap water has been low, **few users have bothered to adopt even easy conservation measures.**

The two sections in **boldface** play which of the following roles in the economist's argument?

(A) The first is a conclusion for which support is provided, and which in turn supports the main conclusion; the second is the main conclusion.

(B) The first is an observation for which the second provides an explanation; the second is the main conclusion but not the only conclusion.

(C) The first is a premise supporting the argument's main conclusion; so is the second.

(D) The first is the only conclusion; the second provides an explanation for the first.

(E) The first is the main conclusion; the second is a conclusion for which support is provided, and which in turn supports the first.

Argument Construction

Situation   Local water supplies have been declining for years because of excessive water use and low prices. Few users have adopted even easy conservation measures.

Reasoning   *What roles do the two **boldfaced** statements play in the argument?* Both are factual observations. Since no further evidence or support is provided for either, neither can be a conclusion in the argument. However, interconnected causal explanations, signaled by *because* and *since*, are provided for both. The observation in the first **boldfaced** statement is causally explained by the further observation that water is being used faster than it can be replenished, which in turn is causally explained by the entire final sentence. The observation in the second **boldfaced** statement is causally explained by the observation that the price of tap water has been low. The only remaining portion of the argument is the initial sentence, a recommendation supported by these four observations together, and by the causal claims in which they are embedded. Thus, the four observations (including the two **boldfaced** statements) and the causal claims containing them are all premises, and the initial statement is the argument's only conclusion.

A   As explained in the Reasoning section above, the two **boldfaced** statements are premises of the argument. Although causal explanations are provided for both, no support or evidence is provided for either. Neither statement is inferred from anything else in the argument, so neither can be a conclusion in the argument.

B   As explained in the Reasoning section above, the second **boldfaced** statement does provide part of the causal explanation for the observation in the first **boldfaced** statement. But the second is not a conclusion. It is not inferred from anything else in the argument, so it cannot be a conclusion in the argument.

C   **Correct.** As explained in the Reasoning section above, each of the statements is a premise that serves along with other claims to support the recommendation in the initial sentence, which is the argument's only conclusion, and in that sense its main conclusion.

D   As explained in the Reasoning section above, the second **boldfaced** statement does provide part of the causal explanation for the observation in the first **boldfaced** statement. But the first is not a conclusion. It is not inferred from anything else in the argument, so it cannot be a conclusion in the argument.

E   As explained in the Reasoning section above, the two **boldfaced** statements are premises of the argument. Although causal explanations are provided for both, no support or evidence is provided for either. Neither statement is inferred from anything else in the argument, so neither can be a conclusion in the argument.

The correct answer is C.

731. Maize contains the vitamin niacin, but not in a form the body can absorb. Pellagra is a disease that results from niacin deficiency. When maize was introduced into southern Europe from the Americas in the eighteenth century, it quickly became a dietary staple, and many Europeans who came to subsist primarily on maize developed pellagra. Pellagra was virtually unknown at that time in the Americas, however, even among people who subsisted primarily on maize.

Which of the following, if true, most helps to explain the contrasting incidence of pellagra described above?

(A) Once introduced into southern Europe, maize became popular with landowners because of its high yields relative to other cereal crops.

(B) Maize grown in the Americas contained more niacin than maize grown in Europe did.

(C) Traditional ways of preparing maize in the Americas convert maize's niacin into a nutritionally useful form.

(D) In southern Europe, many of the people who consumed maize also ate niacin-rich foods.

(E) Before the discovery of pellagra's link with niacin, it was widely believed the disease was an infection that could be transmitted from person to person.

Argument Construction

Situation Maize contains niacin in a form the body cannot readily utilize, and pellagra is a disease that results from niacin deficiency. In southern Europe a diet heavily dependent on maize resulted in a high incidence of pellagra, whereas in the Americas a diet similarly dependent on maize had no such effect.

Reasoning *What would account for the differing effects of a maize-dependent diet in Europe versus the Americas?* A diet primarily consisting of maize resulted in widespread niacin deficiency, and consequent pellagra, in southern Europe, where maize was introduced, but had no such effect in the Americas, where that diet was traditional. Identifying a factor that would account for why people in the Americas were getting more niacin from the same staple food would explain that discrepancy.

A An explanation for why maize became popular does nothing to explain the differing effects of a maize-dependent diet in Europe as opposed to the Americas.

B Because the passage specifies the niacin in maize is not accessible to the body, higher levels of niacin would still be inaccessible and therefore would not explain the differing incidence of pellagra in the Americas versus Europe.

C **Correct.** If methods of preparing maize in the Americas converted maize's niacin into a form the body can absorb and European cooking techniques did not, that would explain the differing incidence of a disease caused by niacin deficiency in the two regions.

D Consumption of niacin-rich foods in southern Europe would be expected to lower the incidence of pellagra in the region and therefore would not explain why that incidence was higher there.

E Mistaken beliefs about the causes of pellagra do nothing to explain its relative frequency in Europe versus the Americas.

The correct answer is C.

732. Mayor: False alarms from home security systems waste so much valuable police time that in many communities, police have stopped responding to alarms from homes whose systems frequently produce false alarms. This policy reduces wastage of police time but results in a loss of protection for some residents. To achieve a comparable reduction in wastage without reducing protection for residents, the council has enacted a measure to fine residents for repeated false alarms.

Which of the following, if true, casts the most doubt on whether the measure enacted by the council will achieve its goal?

(A) A fine in the amount planned by the council will not cover the expenses police typically incur when they respond to a false alarm.

(B) Homes equipped with security systems are far less likely to be broken into than are homes without security systems.

(C) The threat of fines is likely to cause many residents to deactivate their security systems.

(D) The number of home security systems is likely to increase dramatically over the next five years.

(E) Many home security systems have never produced false alarms.

Evaluation of a Plan

Situation   In many communities, police have been responding to false home-security alarms but have ceased to respond to alarms from homes that often have such false alarms. To reduce wastage of police time without compromising residents' home protection, one town council has enacted a new measure that will fine home residents for repeated false alarms.

Reasoning   *What fact or occurrence would most reduce the likelihood that the town council's newly enacted measure would achieve its goal, which is to reduce wastage of police time without compromising home protection? Note that the goal is not to eliminate all wastage of police time or to pay all the costs of it; some random wastage is to be expected. But if many residents deactivated their security alarms (even well-functioning systems) because they wish to avoid being fined, this could reduce the level of home protection for those residents.*

A   The goal is to reduce wastage of police time resulting from false security-system alarms, not necessarily to cover all the costs in police time for such alarms.

B   This seems obviously true, but it is also irrelevant to the frequency of false home-security alarms. It is therefore irrelevant, also, to whether the council's measure will effectively address wastage of police time stemming from such alarms.

C   **Correct.** If this occurred, it would result in a lower level of home protection for some residents and would mean that the town council's measure would have failed to achieve its goal.

D   This scenario does not make the council's measure more likely to fail to achieve its goal. If the increase in alarm systems occurs, it will likely result in more protection for the homes of more residents. Assuming vigorous enforcement of the new measure, we have no reason to believe that the number of false alarms would increase.

E   This has little bearing on the likelihood of the council's measure succeeding. Any home security system that has never produced a false alarm could do so tomorrow, for all kinds of reasons.

The correct answer is C.

733. Excavation of the house of a third-century Camarnian official revealed that he had served four magistrates—public officials who administer the law—over his thirty-year public career, in four provincial capital cities. However, given the Camarnian administrative system of that era, it is unclear whether he served them simultaneously, as a traveling administrator living for part of the year in each provincial capital, or else did so sequentially, leaving one magistrate after several years to join another.

Which of the following would, if found in the excavation, most likely help reveal the pattern of the official's administrative service?

(A) Maps and documents describing each of the four provincial capitals

(B) A cache of the official's documents related to work from early in his career

(C) A set of cups of a type made only in the city of the first magistrate whom the official is known to have served

(D) Several pieces of furniture in the styles of two of the provincial capital cities

(E) Heavy clothing appropriate only for the coldest of the four cities

Argument Construction

Situation   Evidence from an excavation makes clear that a particular third-century Camarnian official served four magistrates in four provincial capitals over his thirty-year career, but it is unclear whether he served the magistrates simultaneously or sequentially.

Reasoning   *What evidence, if it were also found in the excavation, would be most helpful in determining whether the official served the magistrates simultaneously or sequentially?* It would be helpful to find documents from throughout the magistrate's career indicating at what times he worked for each magistrate, or even documents from just one period, as long as there were a large number, because this would likely show whether he was working for just one magistrate or for all four.

A   We already know that the official worked in each of the four capitals. The fact that maps and documents describing the capitals were at his house tells us nothing about whether he worked for magistrates in these capitals simultaneously or not.

B   **Correct.** Presumably, the work-related documents would show whom he was working for at the time, and for how long—and would provide evidence as to whether he was working for multiple magistrates or for just one.

C   Merely finding a set of cups made only in one of the cities tells us little. Even if we knew when he acquired the set, he need not have been working for the magistrate of that city at the time he acquired it; perhaps he had simply traveled to that city.

D   One frequently moves furniture when moving from one city to another, so the fact that the official had pieces of furniture that may have come from different cities does not give us any indication of whether the official worked for all four magistrates simultaneously or not.

E   The fact that heavy clothing appropriate only for the coldest of the four cities was found in the excavation of the official's house does not imply that other clothing, appropriate for one or more of the other cities, was not found. Consistent with the finding of the heavy clothing, the official may have worked exclusively in the city for which that clothing was appropriate, or worked intermittently in this city.

The correct answer is B.

734. In 1563, in Florence's Palazzo Vecchio, Giorgio Vasari built in front of an existing wall a new wall on which he painted a mural. Investigators recently discovered a gap between Vasari's wall and the original, large enough to have preserved anything painted on the original. Historians believe that Leonardo da Vinci had painted, but left unfinished, a mural on the original wall; some historians had also believed that by 1563, the mural had been destroyed. However, it is known that in the late 1560s, when renovating another building, Santa Maria Novella, Vasari built a façade over its frescoes, and the frescoes were thereby preserved. Thus, Leonardo's Palazzo Vecchio mural probably still exists behind Vasari's wall.

Which of the following is an assumption on which the argument depends?

(A) Leonardo rarely if ever destroyed artworks that he left unfinished.

(B) Vasari was likely unaware that the mural in the Palazzo Vecchio had willingly been abandoned by Leonardo.

(C) Vasari probably would not have built the Palazzo Vecchio wall with a gap behind it except to preserve something behind the new wall.

(D) Leonardo would probably have completed the Palazzo Vecchio mural if he had had the opportunity to do so.

(E) When Vasari preserved the frescoes of Santa Maria Novella he did so secretly.

Argument Construction

Situation   Georgio Vasari built a new wall in front of an existing wall in the Palazzo Vecchio that historians believe had had an unfinished mural by Leonardo da Vinci painted on it. Some historians, however, believe the mural had been destroyed by the time Vasari built the new wall. There is a gap between the old and new wall, large enough to have preserved anything painted on it, as there is in Santa Maria Novella, where Vasari also constructed a new wall in front of an old wall; on that wall, the building's frescoes were preserved.

Reasoning   *What claim needs to be true for the cited facts to support the conclusion that Leonardo's Palazzo Vecchio mural likely still exists behind Vasari's wall?* If there are other equally likely reasons that Vasari would have left a gap between the old wall and a new wall, besides preserving any painting on the old wall, the stated facts would not support the conclusion. After all, it may be only fortuitous that the frescoes in the Santa Maria Novella were preserved when Vasari built the new wall with a gap between it and the old wall. Therefore, the argument depends on assuming that it is unlikely that Vasari would have created a gap between the old and new walls unless he had been trying to preserve something painted on the old wall.

A   The argument does not depend on the claim that Leonardo rarely if ever destroyed his unfinished artworks. Obviously, it does depend on the claim that he did not always do so, but even if he fairly regularly destroyed unfinished artworks, this mural could be one of the ones he did not—perhaps the reason the mural was left unfinished was that he died before completing it.

B   The argument does not depend on Vasari knowing that Leonardo had willingly abandoned the mural. Even if Leonardo did willingly leave it unfinished, Vasari could nonetheless have thought the mural was of value and wanted to preserve it.

C   **Correct.** If there had been other likely reasons for Vasari to have built a gap behind the new wall other than to preserve something painted on the old wall, the cited facts would not be a good reason to believe that Vasari built the gap for the purpose of preserving anything painted on it.

D   Leonardo may have had no interest in finishing the mural. Vasari could nevertheless have thought that there was value in preserving it.

E   There is no need to assume that Vasari preserved the frescoes at Santa Maria Novella secretly. Even if he did not do so in this instance, he could have preserved other paintings secretly by the same means, or he may have let others know that he was preserving Leonardo's mural, although there is no historical record that he did let them know.

The correct answer is C.

735. Coffee shop owner: A large number of customers will pay at least the fair market value for a cup of coffee, even if there is no formal charge. Some will pay more than this out of appreciation of the trust that is placed in them. And our total number of customers is likely to increase. We could therefore improve our net cash flow by implementing an honor system in which customers pay what they wish for coffee by depositing money in a can.

Manager: We're likely to lose money on this plan. Many customers would cheat the system, paying a very small sum or nothing at all.

Which of the following, if true, would best support the owner's plan, in light of the manager's concern?

(A)   The new system, if implemented, would increase the number of customers.

(B)   By roasting its own coffee, the shop has managed to reduce the difficulties (and cost) of maintaining an inventory of freshly roasted coffee.

(C)   Many customers stay in the cafe for long stretches of time.

(D)   The shop makes a substantial profit from pastries and other food bought by the coffee drinkers.

(E)   No other coffee shop in the area has such a system.

Evaluation of a Plan

Situation   The owner and the manager of a coffee shop disagree about whether allowing customers to pay for coffee on an honor system would increase or decrease profits.

Reasoning   *What would be the best evidence that the honor-system plan would increase profits even if many customers cheated the system?* The owner argues that profits would increase because many customers will choose to pay as much or more than before and the total number of customers will likely increase. But the manager points out that many customers would also choose to pay little or nothing. Assuming that the manager is correct about that, what further support could the owner present for the claim that the plan would still be profitable?

A   Since the owner has already basically asserted this, asserting it again would not provide any significant additional support for the plan.

B   This suggests that the shop is already profitable, not that the honor-system plan would make it more profitable.

C   Customers who stay in the cafe for long stretches would not necessarily pay any more per cup on the honor-system plan than other customers would.

D   Correct. If the customer base increases (as both the owner and the manager seem to agree), more customers will likely purchase highly profitable pastries and other foods, thus boosting profits.

E   The reason no other coffee shop in the area has an honor system may be that their owners and managers have determined that it would not be profitable.

The correct answer is D.

736. Certain groups of Asian snails include both "left-handed" and "right-handed" species, with shells coiling to the left and right, respectively. Some left-handed species have evolved from right-handed ones. Also, researchers found that snail-eating snakes in the same habitat have asymmetrical jaws, allowing them to grasp right-handed snail shells more easily. If these snakes ate more right-handed snails over time, this would have given left-handed snails an evolutionary advantage over right-handed snails, with the left-handed snails eventually becoming a new species. Thus, the snakes' asymmetrical jaws probably helped drive the emergence of the left-handed snail species.

Which of the following would, if true, most strengthen the argument that asymmetrical snake jaws helped drive left-handed snail evolution?

(A) In one snake species, the snakes with asymmetrical jaws eat snails, while the snakes with symmetrical jaws do not eat snails.

(B) Some species of Asian snails contain either all right-handed snails, or all left-handed snails.

(C) Anatomical differences prevent left-handed snails from mating easily with right-handed snails.

(D) Some right-handed snails in this habitat have shells with a very narrow opening that helps prevent snakes from extracting the snails from inside their shells.

(E) Experiments show that the snail-eating snakes in this habitat fail more often in trying to eat left-handed snails than in trying to eat right-handed snails.

Argument Evaluation

Situation There are both Asian snails with shells that coil to the right and Asian snails with shells that coil to the left, and the latter have evolved from the former; furthermore, there are snakes that have asymmetrical jaws that allow the snakes to grasp the snails with right-coiled shells more easily.

Reasoning *What fact would help support the claim that the snakes' asymmetrical jaws helped drive the emergence of species of snails with left-coiled shells?* We are told that if over time the snakes with asymmetrical jaws ate more snails with right-coiled shells than snails with left-coiled shells, then this would give snails with left-coiled shells an evolutionary survival advantage. So, if some evidence showed that the snakes with such jaws in fact were more likely to have successfully eaten the snails with the right-coiled shells, then we would have good reason to think the snakes' asymmetrical jaws helped drive the emergence of snails with left-coiled shells.

A The fact that snakes with asymmetrical jaws eat snails and other snakes do not does not give any indication as to whether snails with left-coiled shells have any evolutionary advantages over snails with right-coiled shells. At best it only tells us that if snakes drove the evolution of snails with left-coiled shells, it would likely have been the snakes with asymmetrical jaws.

B The fact that some species of Asian snails have no variation in the direction in which their shells coil tells us nothing about what, if any, evolutionary advantages they have relative to other snails, or whether the snakes' asymmetrical jaws had any effect on any such evolutionary advantages.

C The inability of snails with left-coiled shells to mate easily with snails with right-coiled shells in and of itself tells us nothing about whether the snakes' asymmetrical jaws had any effect on the emergence of snails with left-coiled shells. Although it does suggest a different factor that could have contributed to the emergence of the snail species with left-coiled shells, it does not exclude the possibility that the snakes were also a factor.

D The fact that snakes cannot extract some snails with right-coiled shells from their shells would suggest that these snails might have an evolutionary advantage, but the argument's conclusion is about an evolutionary advantage that snails with left-coiled shells presumably have, not an advantage that snails with right-coiled shells would have.

E **Correct.** The fact that experiments show that the snakes are more successful at eating snails with right-coiled shells than they are at eating snails with left-coiled shells would support the claim that these snakes did in fact eat more snails with right-coiled shells, and hence the snails with left-coiled shells would as a result have an evolutionary advantage.

The correct answer is E.

737. A moderately large city is redesigning its central downtown area and is considering a plan that would reduce the number of lanes for automobiles and trucks and increase those for bicycles and pedestrians. The intent is to attract more workers and shoppers to downtown businesses by making downtown easier to reach and more pleasant to move around in.

Which of the following would, if true, most strongly support the prediction that the plan would achieve its goal?

(A) People who make a habit of walking or bicycling whenever feasible derive significant health benefits from doing so.

(B) Most people who prefer to shop at suburban malls instead of downtown urban areas do so because parking is easier and cheaper at the former.

(C) In other moderately sized cities where measures were taken to make downtowns more accessible for walkers and cyclists, downtown businesses began to thrive.

(D) If the proposed lane restrictions on drivers are rigorously enforced, more people will likely be attracted to downtown businesses than would otherwise be.

(E) Most people who own and frequently ride bicycles for recreational purposes live at a significant distance from downtown urban areas.

Evaluation of a Plan

Situation   A moderately large city desires to attract more workers and shoppers to downtown businesses by making the downtown area more pleasant and easier to travel to. In light of this goal, the city is considering a plan that would reduce the number of lanes for automobiles and trucks and increase those for bicycles and pedestrians.

Reasoning   *What would most strongly support the prediction that reducing the number of lanes for automobiles and trucks and increasing those for bicycles and pedestrians would achieve the goal of attracting more people to downtown businesses?* If other moderately sized cities that have improved the accessibility of their downtown areas to pedestrians and cyclists have seen increased downtown business, then it is reasonable to think that the city in question will have improved downtown business as well.

A   If people who make a habit of walking or bicycling derive significant health benefits from doing so, that would provide further motivation for trying to encourage people to walk or ride a bicycle, but it does not provide much support for the claim that adding lanes for pedestrians and cyclists will successfully bring people to shop or work more in the city's downtown. Perhaps people will merely use the new lanes for exercise but not to get to the downtown area to do business.

B   Because the plan as described does not provide for additional parking, the fact that parking is a major concern motivating people to shop at suburban malls does not give us good reason to think that the city's plan will help achieve the city's goal.

C   **Correct.** If other moderately sized cities that have made their downtown areas more accessible to pedestrians and cyclists have seen their downtown businesses begin to thrive soon afterward, this is evidence—even if not conclusive—that the changes produced the thriving. Consequently, it is reasonable to think that the same will result for the city in question.

D   It might be the case that rigorously enforcing lane restrictions will attract more people to downtown businesses than would otherwise be the case, but the information provided does not indicate how strictly lane restrictions will be enforced.

E   The city's plan is aimed at increasing the use of bicycles for the purposes of shopping or getting to work, not only for recreational purposes. And even if people who use their bicycles for recreational purposes would also be likely to use them for shopping or getting to work, the fact that most recreational cyclists live at a significant distance from the city's downtown area may suggest that the city's plan will not be successful, because the cyclists may live too far away to use their bicycles for these purposes, even if it would be somewhat easier for them to do so once the plan has been implemented.

The correct answer is C.

738. Previously, Autoco designed all of its cars itself and then contracted with specialized parts suppliers to build parts according to its specifications. Now it plans to include its suppliers in designing the parts they are to build. Since many parts suppliers have more designers with specialized experience than Autoco has, Autoco expects this shift to reduce the overall time and cost of the design of its next new car.

Which of the following, if true, most strongly supports Autoco's expectation?

(A) When suppliers provide their own designs, Autoco often needs to modify its overall design.

(B) In order to provide designs for Autoco, several of the parts suppliers will have to add to their existing staffs of designers.

(C) Parts and services provided by outside suppliers account for more than 50 percent of Autoco's total costs.

(D) When suppliers built parts according to specifications provided by Autoco, the suppliers competed to win contracts.

(E) Most of Autoco's suppliers have on hand a wide range of previously prepared parts designs that can readily be modified for a new car.

Evaluation of a Plan

Situation A car manufacturer plans to have its parts suppliers start helping to design the parts they build for the manufacturer. Many parts suppliers have more designers with specialized experience than the manufacturer has.

Reasoning *What would make it more likely that having the parts suppliers help design the parts will reduce the time and cost of designing the manufacturer's next new car?* In order for the change to reduce the time and cost, the parts suppliers involved in designing the next car will probably have to do their portion of the design process faster and cheaper than the manufacturer would have, and the design collaboration process will have to avoid producing substantial new inefficiencies.

A The additional need to modify the overall design would probably make the design process slower and more expensive, not faster and cheaper.

B The additional need to hire more designers would probably increase design costs, not reduce them.

C Although this suggests that the change is likely to substantially affect the design's expense, it does not indicate whether the expense will increase or decrease.

D If anything, this competition probably made Autoco's previous design process cheaper. It does not suggest that the new design process, which may involve less competition, will be faster or cheaper than the previous one.

E **Correct.** Modifying the previously prepared parts designs will probably be faster and cheaper than creating new designs from scratch.

The correct answer is E.

739. In response to viral infection, the immune systems of mice typically produce antibodies that destroy the virus by binding to proteins on its surface. Mice infected with the herpesvirus generally develop keratitis, a degenerative disease affecting part of the eye. Since proteins on the surface of cells in this part of the eye closely resemble those on the herpesvirus surface, scientists hypothesize that these cases of keratitis are caused by antibodies to the herpesvirus.

Which of the following, if true, most helps to support the scientists' reasoning?

(A) Other types of viruses have surface proteins that closely resemble proteins found in various organs of mice.

(B) Mice that are infected with the herpesvirus but do not develop keratitis produce as many antibodies as infected mice that do develop keratitis.

(C) Mice infected with a new strain of the herpesvirus that has different surface proteins did not develop keratitis.

(D) Mice that have never been infected with the herpesvirus can sometimes develop keratitis.

(E) There are mice that are unable to form antibodies in response to herpes infections, and these mice contract herpes at roughly the same rate as other mice.

Argument Evaluation

Situation   Mice infected with the herpesvirus tend to develop keratitis, an eye disease. The surface of the eye cells has proteins that resemble those on the herpesvirus surface. Based on this finding, scientists have hypothesized that keratitis develops in mice because antibodies that attack herpesvirus surface proteins can also attack eyes.

Reasoning   *What other information, if correct, would provide the strongest support for the scientists' hypothesis?* The clue that led the scientists to form their hypothesis was the close resemblance of the proteins on the mouse eye surface to those on the herpesvirus surface. The resemblance could cause antibodies to bind to both types of proteins, in one case eliminating the herpesvirus and in the other case causing keratitis.

A   Even if this is correct, we lack information as to whether the antibodies to those other types of virus can damage the organs that display the closely resembling proteins. If such a damage process were confirmed, it could count as evidence—even if not sufficient—to confirm the scientists' hypothesis.

B   If anything, this would, absent further information, raise doubts about the correctness of the scientists' proposed explanation.

C   **Correct.** This provides strong confirmation of the scientists' hypothesis. The proteins on the new strain of the herpesvirus no longer sufficiently resemble the proteins on the eye surface to cause the antibodies to attack those proteins and cause keratitis.

D   For all we know, keratitis may have multiple independent causes and may sometimes be caused by processes other than the protein misidentification hypothesized by the scientists. This information neither confirms nor refutes the scientists' hypothesis.

E   The rates at which mice contract herpes is not discussed. We lack any information as to whether mice that lack antibodies to the herpesvirus sometimes contract keratitis along with herpes infection.

The correct answer is C.

740. One might expect that within a particular species, any individuals that managed to slow down the aging process would leave more offspring. Natural selection should therefore favor extreme longevity—but this does not seem to be the case. A possible explanation is that aging is a product of the inevitable wear and tear of living, similar to how household appliances generally accumulate faults that lead to their eventual demise. However, most researchers do not find this analogy satisfactory as an explanation.

Which of the following would, if true, provide the strongest explanation for the researchers' reaction?

(A)   Some organisms are capable of living much longer than other organisms.

(B)   Some organisms reproduce very quickly despite having short lifespans.

(C)   There are several ways of defining "extreme longevity," and according to some definitions it occurs frequently.

(D)   Organisms are capable of maintenance and self-repair and can remedy much of the damage that they accumulate.

(E)   Some organisms generate much more wear and tear on their bodies than others.

Argument Construction

Situation   One possible explanation for the fact that natural selection does not favor extreme longevity, despite the fact that a slowed-down aging process would leave more offspring, is that aging is the product of wear and tear, much like how household appliances eventually no longer function because of wear and tear; most researchers, however, reject this analogy as an explanation.

Reasoning   *What would explain the researchers' rejection of the explanation?* The explanation is based on analogy between organisms and household appliances. If there were a crucial difference between appliances and organisms, such as the fact that organisms are capable of self-repair in a way that household appliances are not, then it would be reasonable for the researchers to reject the explanation.

A   The fact that some organisms can live much longer than other organisms is not a good reason to reject the analogy; after all, some household appliances may last much longer than others, perhaps because they receive a different amount of wear and tear.

B   Even if some organisms reproduce very quickly despite having short lifespans, that does not mean that they would not have even more offspring if they lived longer; also, this is irrelevant as to whether the analogy between the aging process and the wear and tear on household appliances is any good.

C   It is unclear what these different ways of defining "extreme longevity" are—perhaps the definition is merely a relative one; some organisms live much longer than others, and those that do have "extreme longevity." But presumably, some household appliances last much longer than others, so this would not indicate a difference, and thus would not explain why most researchers reject the analogy.

D   Correct. Household appliances cannot repair themselves as organisms can, so the wear and tear of living is quite different from the wear and tear in household appliances.

E   Presumably, some household appliances receive much more wear and tear than other household appliances, so the fact that some organisms generate more wear and tear on their bodies than others does not indicate a difference between appliances and organisms, and thus does not explain why the researchers reject the analogy.

The correct answer is D.

741. In Stenland, many workers have been complaining that they cannot survive on minimum wage, the lowest wage an employer is permitted to pay. The government is proposing to raise the minimum wage. Many employers who pay their workers the current minimum wage argue that if it is raised, unemployment will increase because they will no longer be able to afford to employ as many workers.

Which of the following, if true in Stenland, most strongly supports the claim that raising the minimum wage there will not have the effects that the employers predict?

(A) For any position with wages below a living wage, the difficulty of finding and retaining employees adds as much to employment costs as would raising wages.

(B) Raising the minimum wage does not also increase the amount employers have to contribute in employee benefits.

(C) When inflation is taken into account, the proposed new minimum wage is not as high as the current one was when it was introduced.

(D) Many employees currently being paid wages at the level of the proposed new minimum wage will demand significant wage increases.

(E) Many employers who pay some workers only the minimum wage also pay other workers wages that are much higher than the minimum.

Argument Evaluation

Situation   Stenland's government proposes to raise the minimum wage because many workers have complained they cannot survive on it. But many employers claim that raising the minimum wage will increase unemployment.

Reasoning   *What evidence would most strongly suggest that raising the minimum wage will not increase unemployment?* The employers with minimum-wage workers implicitly reason that because raising the minimum wage will increase the wages they have to pay each worker, it will reduce the number of workers they can afford to employ, and thus will increase unemployment. Evidence that the increased wage would not actually increase the employers' expenses per employee would cast doubt on their prediction, as would evidence that reducing the number of minimum-wage workers would not increase the nation's overall unemployment rate.

A   **Correct.** This suggests that raising the minimum wage would make it easier for employers to find and retain minimum-wage employees, and that the savings would fully offset the cost of paying the higher wages. If there were such offsetting savings, the employers should still be able to afford to employ as many workers as they currently do.

B   Even if raising the minimum wage does not increase employers' costs for employee benefits, paying the higher wage might still in itself substantially increase employers' overall costs per employee.

C   For all we know, the current minimum wage might have substantially increased unemployment when it was introduced.

D   These additional demands would probably raise employers' overall costs per employee, making it more likely that increasing the minimum wage would increase overall unemployment.

E   Even if some workers receive more than the minimum wage, raising that wage could still raise employers' expenses for employing low-wage workers, making it too expensive for the employers to employ as many workers overall.

The correct answer is A.

742. Biologists with a predilection for theory have tried—and largely failed—to define what it is that makes something a living thing. Organisms take in energy-providing materials and excrete waste products, but so do automobiles. Living things replicate and take part in evolution, but so do some computer programs. We must be open to the possibility that there are living things on other planets. Therefore, we will not be successful in defining what it is that makes something a living thing merely by examining living things on Earth—the only ones we know. Trying to do so is analogous to trying to specify _____.

Which of the following most logically completes the passage?

(A) the laws of physics by using pure mathematics

(B) what a fish is by listing its chemical components

(C) what an animal is by examining a plant

(D) what a machine is by examining a sketch of it

(E) what a mammal is by examining a zebra

Argument Construction

Situation   Some biologists have tried, unsuccessfully, to find a theoretically defensible account of what it means for something to be a living thing. Some of the suggested definitions are too broad because they include things that we would not regard as living. To find life on other planets, we must not narrow our conception of life by basing it simply on the kinds of life encountered on Earth.

Reasoning   *Which of the answer choices would be the logically most appropriate completion of the argument?* The argument points out that life-forms elsewhere in the universe may be very different from any of the life-forms on Earth. Both life-forms on Earth and life-forms discovered elsewhere would all qualify as members of a very large class, the class of all life-forms. Taking life-forms on Earth, a mere subset of the class of all life-forms, as representative of all life-forms would be a logical mistake and might not lead to success in defining what it means for something to be a living thing. The correct answer choice, therefore, would involve a case of specifying what some general class of things is by examining the members of only a small, and not necessarily representative, subset of that class of things. In other words, the correct answer choice will involve the logical mistake of taking a subset as representative of a larger class.

A   Pure mathematics is not a subset of the law of physics, so this does not involve the logical mistake of taking a subset as representative of a larger class.

B   The chemical components of a fish are what make up the fish; they are not a small subset of the fish, so this does not involve the logical mistake of taking a subset as representative of a larger class.

C   Plants are not a subset of the class of animals, so this does not involve the logical mistake of taking a subset as representative of a larger class.

D   A sketch of a machine is not a subclass of the machine itself, so this does not involve the logical mistake of taking a subset as representative of a larger class.

E   **Correct.** This involves the logical mistake of taking the class of zebras, a subclass of the class of mammals, as representative of the class of all mammals. Logically, it resembles taking the class of life-forms on Earth as representative of the class of all life-forms.

The correct answer is E.

743. For the period from the eighth century through the eleventh century, the shifting boundaries between Kingdom F and Kingdom G have not been well charted. Although a certain village in a border region between the two kingdoms usually belonged to Kingdom G, ninth-century artifacts found in the village were in the typical Kingdom F style of that time. It is unclear whether the village was actually a part of Kingdom F in the ninth century or whether it was a part of Kingdom G but had merely adopted Kingdom F's artistic styles under Kingdom F's cultural influence.

Which of the following would, if found in ninth-century sites in the village, best help in determining whether the village was a part of Kingdom F or Kingdom G in the ninth century?

(A) A trading contract written in the Kingdom G dialect

(B) A drawing of a dwelling complex known to have existed on the border of Kingdom F and Kingdom G in the ninth century

(C) Knives and other utensils made from metal typical of ninth-century mining sites in Kingdom F

(D) Some fragments of pottery made in the Kingdom G style from the seventh century out of materials only found in Kingdom F

(E) Numerous teeth from the ninth century with a chemical signature typical only of teeth from people who had grown up in the heart of Kingdom F

Argument Construction

Situation From the eighth century to the eleventh century, the boundaries between two kingdoms, F and G, shifted, but these shifts are not well documented. A certain village in a border region was usually part of Kingdom G, but ninth-century artifacts in the village are typical of the style of ninth-century artifacts from Kingdom F.

Reasoning *What evidence, if it were found in the ninth-century sites in the village, would be most helpful in determining which of the two kingdoms the village was a part of during that century?* Information strongly indicating that during the ninth century the village was primarily settled by people clearly from Kingdom F would lend support to the claim that the village was part of Kingdom F in the ninth century.

A A trading contract found at a ninth-century site in the village written in Kingdom G dialect would not settle whether the village was part of Kingdom G, because it could be the case that such a document would be written in that dialect even if the village were part of Kingdom F but regularly traded with Kingdom G.

B Finding at a ninth-century site in the village a drawing of a dwelling complex known to have been on the border of Kingdom F and Kingdom G would not be useful in determining to which kingdom the village belonged at the time. We are not told in which kingdom that dwelling complex existed, and even if we were told, it could be that a villager in the other kingdom had a drawing of that complex for some reason (e.g., the villager could have had it because that complex was going to be attacked in a skirmish between the kingdoms).

C Because there could have been trade between Kingdom F and Kingdom G, the fact that utensils made from metal typical of ninth-century mining sites in Kingdom F would not be very helpful in determining to which of the two kingdoms the village belonged in that century.

D If fragments of pottery from the seventh century made in the Kingdom G style but from materials found only in Kingdom F were discovered, it would be unclear in which kingdom the pottery had been made. Given that the fragments may be from two centuries earlier than the period in question, and that we do not even know what kingdom the pottery was created in, these fragments would be of no use in determining to which kingdom the village belonged in the ninth century.

E   **Correct.** Although the mere presence of people from Kingdom F in the village would not provide strong support for the claim that the village was part of Kingdom F during the ninth century—the village could have shifted from Kingdom F to Kingdom G while maintaining much of its Kingdom F population—the presence of significant numbers of people from the heart of Kingdom F would support the claim that there was widespread migration of people from Kingdom F to the village. This is what one might reasonably expect if the village was part of Kingdom F during the ninth century. The discovery of numerous teeth that clearly belonged to people who grew up in the heart of Kingdom F in the ninth century would support the claim that many such people lived in the village during that century.

The correct answer is E.

744. Sammy: For my arthritis, I am going to try my aunt's diet: large amounts of wheat germ and garlic. She was able to move more easily right after she started that diet.

Pat: When my brother began that diet, his arthritis got worse. But he has been doing much better since he stopped eating vegetables in the nightshade family, such as tomatoes and peppers.

Which of the following, if true, would provide a basis for explaining the fact that Sammy's aunt and Pat's brother had contrasting experiences with the same diet?

(A) A change in diet, regardless of the nature of the change, frequently brings temporary relief from arthritis symptoms.

(B) The compounds in garlic that can lessen the symptoms of arthritis are also present in tomatoes and peppers.

(C) Arthritis is a chronic condition whose symptoms improve and worsen from time to time without regard to diet.

(D) In general, men are more likely to have their arthritis symptoms alleviated by avoiding vegetables in the nightshade family than are women.

(E) People who are closely related are more likely to experience the same result from adopting a particular diet than are people who are unrelated.

Argument Construction

Situation   Sammy's aunt's arthritis apparently improved after she consumed large amounts of wheat germ and garlic. Pat's brother's arthritis deteriorated after he followed the same diet. Since he stopped eating vegetables in the nightshade family, such as tomatoes and peppers, his arthritis has improved.

Reasoning   *What could account for the fact that Sammy's aunt's arthritis improved and Pat's brother's arthritis got worse after they both followed the wheat germ and garlic diet?* The fact that a person has a health improvement following a diet is, by itself, very weak evidence for the claim that the diet caused the improvement. More generally, the fact that one event follows another is seldom, by itself, evidence that the earlier event caused the later. This applies to both the experience of Sammy's aunt and that of Pat's brother with the wheat germ and garlic diet.

A   In theory, this could be somewhat relevant to Sammy's aunt's experience but not to Pat's brother's experience. It is, however, insufficient to explain either.

B   Even if this is true, it might be the case that a large quantity of the compounds in question must be consumed in concentrated form to benefit arthritis. No evidence is given to indicate whether this is so. Regardless, the puzzle as to why the wheat germ and garlic diet was followed by arthritis improvement in one case and not in the other remains.

C   **Correct.** If we know there are typically fluctuations in the severity of arthritis symptoms and these can occur independent of diet, then the divergent experiences of the two people can be attributed to such fluctuations—even if it is conceded that some diets can affect arthritis symptoms in some manner. The wheat germ and garlic diet may, or may not, be such a diet.

D   This could throw light on Pat's brother's experience but not on Sammy's aunt's experience.

E   If this is correct, it is still far too general to provide a basis for explaining why the experiences of the two people were different. Does it apply to arthritis? We're not told. Nor are we told that it applies to the wheat germ and garlic diet. Is Pat's brother closely related to Sammy's aunt? We don't know.

The correct answer is C.

745. In the 1960s, surveys of Florida's alligator population indicated that the population was dwindling rapidly. Hunting alligators was banned. By the early 1990s, the alligator population had recovered, and restricted hunting was allowed. Over the course of the 1990s, reports of alligators appearing on golf courses and lawns increased dramatically. Therefore, in spite of whatever alligator hunting went on, the alligator population must have increased significantly over the decade of the 1990s.

Which of the following, if true, most seriously weakens the argument?

(A) The human population of Florida increased significantly during the 1990s.

(B) The hunting restrictions applied to commercial as well as private hunters.

(C) The number of sightings of alligators in lakes and swamps increased greatly in Florida during the 1990s.

(D) Throughout the 1990s, selling alligator products was more strictly regulated than hunting was.

(E) Most of the sightings of alligators on golf courses and lawns in the 1990s occurred at times at which few people were present on those golf courses and lawns.

Argument Evaluation

Situation   In the 1960s, hunting alligators was banned in Florida to allow the alligator population to recover—as it did by the early 1990s. Then restricted hunting was allowed. But over the decade, reports of alligators appearing on golf courses and lawns increased greatly. The author of the argument concludes from this information that the alligator population must have increased significantly during the 1990s.

Reasoning   *What new piece of information would seriously weaken the argument?* Increased sightings of alligators could occur either because there are more alligators or because more people are seeing the ones that are there. Any information indicating an increase in the ratio of people to alligators in locations where the two species coexist could offer an alternative to the hypothesis that the alligator population increased.

A   **Correct.** The argument suggests that Florida is an area in which golf courses and lawns are common. A large rapid increase in the human population of such an area would probably lead to a significant increase in the number of golf courses and lawns, some of which would encroach on the alligators' habitats. Even without any increase in the overall number of alligators, this could lead to an increase in both the percentage of alligators that venture onto golf courses and lawns and the number of people who happen to be in such locations when alligators are present.

B   This information is peripheral to the issue we are being asked to address; it neither weakens nor strengthens the argument.

C   This information tends to strengthen, not weaken, the argument; it suggests that the frequency of reported sightings in other places was reliable and that the sightings indicated a surge in the alligator population.

D   To the extent that this is relevant, it could provide some weak support for the argument. Strictly regulating the sale of alligator products could deter alligator hunting by making it less profitable and could thus allow further increases in the alligator population.

E   Without further evidence, the net effect of this information cannot be reliably determined. On the one hand, if *sightings* is understood as elliptical for *reports of seeing alligators*, this could suggest that some of the reports may be dubious because they are not corroborated by additional observers. On the other hand, it suggests that the alligator population may in fact have increased. Times when few people are present are also times when wildlife such as alligators would be more likely to venture onto lawns and golf courses. Without any evidence that sightings before the 1990s did not typically occur in such conditions, this suggests that the number of alligators observable at those times increased in the 1990s.

The correct answer is A.

746. Infotek, a computer manufacturer in Katrovia, has just introduced a new personal computer model that sells for significantly less than any other model. Market research shows, however, that very few Katrovian households without personal computers would buy a computer, regardless of its price. Therefore, introducing the new model is unlikely to increase the number of computers in Katrovian homes.

Which of the following is an assumption on which the argument depends?

(A) Infotek achieved the lower price of the new model by using components of lower quality than those used by other manufacturers.

(B) The main reason cited by consumers in Katrovia for replacing a personal computer is the desire to have an improved model.

(C) Katrovians in households that already have computers are unlikely to purchase the new Infotek model as an additional computer for home use.

(D) The price of other personal computers in Katrovia is unlikely to drop below the price of Infotek's new model in the near future.

(E) Most personal computers purchased in Katrovia are intended for home use.

Argument Construction

Situation   In Katrovia, a new personal computer model costs less than any other model. But market research shows that very few Katrovian households without personal computers would buy even cheap ones.

Reasoning   *What must be true in order for the stated facts to support the conclusion that introducing the new computer model is unlikely to increase the overall number of computers in Katrovian homes?* The market research supports the conclusion that no new computer model is likely to significantly increase the number of computers in Katrovian homes that currently lack computers. But the overall number of computers in Katrovian homes will still increase if Katrovian homes that already have computers buy additional computers while keeping their existing ones. So, the argument has to assume that the new computer model will not increase the number of additional computers purchased for Katrovian homes that already have computers.

A   Even if Infotek used high-quality components in the new computer model, Katrovians might still refuse to buy it.

B   Replacing a personal computer does not change the overall number of personal computers in homes, so Katrovians' motives for replacing their computers are irrelevant to the argument.

C   **Correct.** As explained above, unless computers of the new model are purchased as additional computers for Katrovian homes that already have computers, the new model's introduction is unlikely to increase the overall number of computers in Katrovian homes.

D   The assumption that other personal computer prices would stay relatively high does not help establish the link between its premises and its conclusion. If answer choice D were false, the argument would be no weaker than it is without any consideration of other computers' potential prices.

E   If most personal computers purchased in Katrovia were not intended for home use, then the new model's introduction would be even less likely to increase the number of personal computers in Katrovian homes. So, the argument does not depend on assuming that most of the computers purchased are for home use.

The correct answer is C.

747. Fast-food restaurants make up 45 percent of all restaurants in Canatria. Customers at these restaurants tend to be young; in fact, studies have shown that the older people get, the less likely they are to eat in fast-food restaurants. Since the average age of the Canatrian population is gradually rising and will continue to do so, the number of fast-food restaurants is likely to decrease.

Which of the following, if true, most seriously weakens the argument?

(A)   Fast-food restaurants in Canatria are getting bigger, so each one can serve more customers.

(B)   Some older people eat at fast-food restaurants more frequently than the average young person.

(C)   Many people who rarely eat in fast-food restaurants nevertheless eat regularly in restaurants.

(D)   The overall population of Canatria is growing steadily.

(E)   As the population of Canatria gets older, more people are eating at home.

Argument Evaluation

Situation   In Canatria, the older people get, the less likely they are to eat in fast-food restaurants. The average age of Canatrians is increasing.

Reasoning   *What evidence would most weaken the support provided by the cited facts for the prediction that the number of fast-food restaurants in Canatria is likely to decrease?* The argument implicitly reasons that since studies have shown that Canatrians tend to eat in fast-food restaurants less as they get older, and since Canatrians are getting older on average, the proportion of Canatrians eating in fast-food restaurants will decline. The argument assumes that this means the overall number of fast-food restaurant customers will decline and that demand will decrease enough to reduce the number of fast-food restaurants that can sustain profitability. Consequently, fewer new fast-food restaurants will open or more old ones will close, or both. Thus, the number of fast-food restaurants in Canatria will fall. Any evidence casting doubt on any inference in this chain of implicit reasoning will weaken the argument.

A   This strengthens the argument by providing additional evidence that the total number of fast-food restaurants will decrease. If the average number of customers per fast-food restaurant is increasing, then fewer fast-food restaurants will be needed to serve the same—or a lesser—number of customers.

B   Even if a few individuals do not follow the general trends described, those trends could still reduce the overall demand for and number of fast-food restaurants.

C   The argument is only about fast-food restaurants, not restaurants of other types.

D   **Correct.** This suggests that even if the proportion of Canatrians eating at fast-food restaurants declines, the total number doing so may not decline. Thus, the total demand for and profitability of fast-food restaurants may not decline either, so the total number of fast-food restaurants in Canatria may not decrease.

E   If anything, this strengthens the argument by pointing out an additional trend likely to reduce the demand for, and thus the number of, fast-food restaurants in Canatria.

The correct answer is D.

748. Transportation expenses accounted for a large portion of the total dollar amount spent on trips for pleasure by residents of the United States in 1997, and about half of the total dollar amount spent on transportation was for airfare. However, the large majority of United States residents who took trips for pleasure in 1997 did not travel by airplane but used other means of transportation.

If the statements above are true, which of the following must also be true about United States residents who took trips for pleasure in 1997?

(A) Most of those who traveled by airplane did so because the airfare to their destination was lower than the cost of other available means of transportation.

(B) Most of those who traveled by airplane did so because other means of transportation to their destination were unavailable.

(C) Per mile traveled, those who traveled by airplane tended to spend more on transportation to their destination than did those who used other means of transportation.

(D) Overall, people who did not travel by airplane had lower average transportation expenses than people who did.

(E) Those who traveled by airplane spent about as much, on average, on other means of transportation as they did on airfare.

Argument Construction

Situation   In 1997, about half of total transportation spending by U.S. residents taking trips for pleasure was for airfare. But the large majority of U.S. residents who took trips for pleasure in 1997 did not travel by airplane.

Reasoning   *What can be deduced from the stated facts?* The information provided indicates that among U.S. residents who took trips for pleasure in 1997, those who traveled by airplane were a small minority. Yet this small minority's spending for airfare accounted for half of all transportation spending among residents taking trips for pleasure. It follows that on average, those who traveled by airplane must have spent far more per person on transportation than those who did not travel by airplane.

A   This does not follow logically from the information given. Most of those who traveled by airplane may have done so even if flying was more expensive than other modes of transportation—for example, because flying was faster or more comfortable.

B   This does not follow from the information given. Most of those who traveled by airplane may have done so even if many other modes of transportation were available—the other modes may all have been less desirable.

C   This does not follow from the information given. Those who traveled by airplane may have traveled much farther on average than those who used other means of transportation, so their transportation spending per mile traveled need not have been greater.

D   Correct. As explained above, those who traveled by airplane must have spent more per person on transportation than those who did not travel by airplane, on average. In other words, those who did not travel by airplane must have had lower average transportation expenses than those who did.

E   This does not follow from the information given. Although half the total dollar spending on transportation was for airfare, much of the transportation spending that was not for airfare was by the large majority of U.S. residents who did not travel by airplane.

The correct answer is D.

749. Voters commonly condemn politicians for being insincere, but politicians often must disguise their true feelings when they make public statements. If they expressed their honest views—about, say, their party's policies—then achieving politically necessary compromises would be much more difficult. Clearly, the very insincerity that people decry shows that our government is functioning well.

Which of the following, if true, most seriously undermines this reasoning?

(A) Achieving political compromises is not all that is necessary for the proper functioning of a government.

(B) Some political compromises are not in the best long-term interest of the government.

(C) Voters often judge politicians by criteria other than the sincerity with which they express their views.

(D) A political party's policies could turn out to be detrimental to the functioning of a government.

(E) Some of the public statements made by politicians about their party's policies could in fact be sincere.

Argument Evaluation

Situation   Politicians must often make insincere public statements because expressing their true feelings would make it harder for them to achieve politically necessary compromises.

Reasoning   *What would suggest that the argument's premises do not establish that politicians' insincerity shows our government is functioning well?* The implicit reasoning is that insincerity helps politicians achieve politically necessary compromises, and these compromises help our government to function well, so insincerity must show that our government is functioning well. Evidence that these necessary compromises do not ensure that our government functions well would undermine the argument's reasoning, as would evidence that politicians' insincerity has other substantial effects that hinder the government's functioning.

A **Correct.** If governments may function poorly even when insincerity allows necessary political compromises to be made, then the argument's premises do not establish that politicians' insincerity shows our government is functioning well.

B The argument does not require that all political compromises help government to function well, only that politically necessary compromises do.

C Even if voters often judge politicians by criteria other than their sincerity, they may also often decry politicians' insincerity, not realizing or caring that such insincerity helps the government function well.

D Even if a political party's policies impair the government's functioning, politically necessary compromises by politicians in that party could improve the government's functioning.

E Even if politicians sometimes speak sincerely about their party's policies, their general willingness to be insincere as needed to achieve politically necessary compromises could be a sign that the government is functioning well.

The correct answer is A.

750. One summer, floods covered low-lying garlic fields situated in a region with a large mosquito population. Since mosquitoes lay their eggs in standing water, flooded fields would normally attract mosquitoes, yet no mosquitoes were found in the fields. Diallyl sulfide, a major component of garlic, is known to repel several species of insects, including mosquitoes, so it is likely that diallyl sulfide from the garlic repelled the mosquitoes.

Which of the following, if true, most strengthens the argument?

(A) Diallyl sulfide is also found in onions but at concentrations lower than in garlic.

(B) The mosquito population of the region as a whole was significantly smaller during the year in which the flooding took place than it had been in previous years.

(C) By the end of the summer, most of the garlic plants in the flooded fields had been killed by waterborne fungi.

(D) Many insect species not repelled by diallyl sulfide were found in the flooded garlic fields throughout the summer.

(E) Mosquitoes are known to be susceptible to toxins in plants other than garlic, such as marigolds.

Argument Evaluation

Situation   When summer floods covered garlic fields in an area with many mosquitoes, no mosquitoes were found in the fields, even though flooded fields would normally attract mosquitoes to lay their eggs in the water. Diallyl sulfide, which is found in garlic, repels mosquitoes and some other insect species and likely accounts for the lack of mosquitoes in the area.

Reasoning   *Given the facts cited, what would provide additional evidence that diallyl sulfide from the garlic made mosquitoes avoid the flooded fields?* The argument would be strengthened by any independent evidence suggesting that diallyl sulfide pervaded the flooded fields or excluding other factors that might explain the absence of mosquitoes in the fields.

A   This could strengthen the argument if mosquitoes also avoid flooded onion fields, but we do not know whether they do.

B   This would weaken the argument by suggesting that the general mosquito population decline, rather than the diallyl sulfide, could explain the absence of mosquitoes in the fields.

C   It is not clear how this would affect the amount of diallyl sulfide in the flooded fields, so this does not provide evidence that the diallyl sulfide repelled the mosquitoes.

D   **Correct.** This provides evidence that there was no factor other than diallyl sulfide that reduced insect populations in the flooded garlic fields.

E   If anything, this would weaken the argument, since it is at least possible that some of these toxins were present in the flooded fields.

The correct answer is D.

751. The population of desert tortoises in Targland's Red Desert has declined, partly because they are captured for sale as pets and partly because people riding all-terrain vehicles have damaged their habitat. Targland plans to halt this population decline by blocking the current access routes into the desert and announcing new regulations to allow access only on foot. Targland's officials predict that these measures will be adequate, since it is difficult to collect the tortoises without a vehicle.

Which of the following would it be most important to establish in order to evaluate the officials' prediction?

(A) Whether possessing the tortoises as pets remains legally permissible in Targland

(B) Whether Targland is able to enforce the regulations with respect to all-terrain vehicle entry at points other than the current access routes

(C) Whether the Red Desert tortoises are most active during the day or at night

(D) Whether people who travel on foot in the Red Desert often encounter the tortoises

(E) Whether the Targland authorities held public hearings before restricting entry by vehicle into the Red Desert

Argument Evaluation

Situation   Desert tortoises in Targland's Red Desert have been captured for sale as pets. Furthermore, these tortoises' habitat has been damaged by people riding all-terrain vehicles. These factors have led to the decline of the tortoise population in the Red Desert, a decline Targland plans to halt by blocking current access and announcing new regulations limiting access to only by foot. Officials predict these will be adequate because prohibiting vehicles will make it harder to collect tortoises.

Reasoning   *What would be most useful to know in order to evaluate the officials' prediction?* If Targland's new restrictions are not enforceable, then there is good reason to doubt the officials' prediction that these restrictions will be adequate to protect the tortoises. Thus, it would be useful to know whether either or both of the new restrictions can be enforced.

A   The prediction is not based on whether it is legally permissible to possess the tortoises as pets, but rather on whether people will be as capable of collecting them.

B   **Correct.** The prediction is based on whether Targland can effectively restrict access to foot traffic. If it cannot, and people can still gain entry to the desert using all-terrain vehicles at points other than the current access routes, then the fact that they would still be able to gain access casts doubt on the officials' prediction.

C   The prediction in no way depends on whether the tortoises are most active during the day or at night.

D   The prediction is based on the difficulty of collecting tortoises without a vehicle—presumably because it would be harder to transport them. Therefore, it is not particularly relevant whether people on foot in the Red Desert often encounter tortoises.

E   The prediction would be just as likely to be accurate whether or not the Targland authorities held public hearings before restricting entry by vehicle to the desert. All that matters is whether the restrictions are effectively communicated and enforced.

The correct answer is B.

752. Yeasts capable of leavening bread are widespread, and in the many centuries during which the ancient Egyptians made only unleavened bread, such yeasts must frequently have been mixed into bread doughs accidentally. The Egyptians, however, did not discover leavened bread until about 3000 B.C. That discovery roughly coincided with the introduction of a wheat variety that was preferable to previous varieties because its edible kernel could be removed from the husk without first toasting the grain.

Which of the following, if true, provides the strongest evidence that the two developments were causally related?

(A) Even after the ancient Egyptians discovered leavened bread and the techniques for reliably producing it were well known, unleavened bread continued to be widely consumed.

(B) Only when the Egyptians stopped the practice of toasting grain were their stone-lined grain-toasting pits available for baking bread.

(C) Heating a wheat kernel destroys its gluten, a protein that must be present in order for yeast to leaven bread dough.

(D) The new variety of wheat, which had a more delicate flavor because it was not toasted, was reserved for the consumption of high officials when it first began to be grown.

(E) Because the husk of the new variety of wheat was more easily removed, flour made from it required less effort to produce.

Argument Construction

Situation Because they were widespread, yeasts capable of leavening bread most likely were occasionally accidentally mixed into the doughs of the unleavened bread made by ancient Egyptians. Despite this, Egyptians did not discover leavened bread until about 3000 B.C., around the time of the introduction of an improved variety of wheat that had kernels that could be removed from the husk without toasting.

Reasoning *What evidence would suggest these developments were causally linked?* If one of these two developments would not have been possible without the other, there is reason to think that the developments were causally linked in some way.

A Continued consumption of unleavened bread tells us nothing about the improved variety of wheat and so provides no evidence regarding a causal link between that variety of wheat and the ancient Egyptians' discovery of leavened bread.

B The availability of the pits for baking bread does not indicate that leavened bread could not have been discovered, and then baked, in the ovens that were used previously to bake unleavened bread.

C **Correct.** Because gluten is destroyed when a wheat kernel is toasted and gluten is necessary for yeast to be able to leaven dough, leavened dough was directly enabled by the introduction of the improved wheat variety.

D The new variety of wheat could have been reserved for high officials because of its delicate flavor even if the ancient Egyptians had never discovered leavened bread, so it does not imply a causal link.

E There is no evidence to suggest that the discovery of leavened bread was in any way linked to flour becoming easier to produce.

The correct answer is C.

753. That the application of new technology can increase the productivity of existing coal mines is demonstrated by the case of Tribnia's coal industry. Coal output per miner in Tribnia is double what it was five years ago even though no new mines have opened.

Which of the following can be properly concluded from the statement about coal output per miner in the passage?

(A) If the number of miners working in Tribnian coal mines has remained constant in the past five years, Tribnia's total coal production has doubled in that period of time.

(B) Any individual Tribnian coal mine that achieved an increase in overall output in the past five years has also experienced an increase in output per miner.

(C) If any new coal mines had opened in Tribnia in the past five years, then the increase in output per miner would have been even greater than it actually was.

(D) If any individual Tribnian coal mine has not increased its output per miner in the past five years, then that mine's overall output has declined or remained constant.

(E) In Tribnia, the cost of producing a given quantity of coal has declined over the past five years.

Argument Construction

Situation   Tribnia's coal industry provides an example of the increased productivity enabled by new technology. In the past five years, coal output per miner has doubled. No new mines have opened in the same period.

Reasoning   *What conclusion can be drawn from the information regarding average output per miner?* If coal output per miner has doubled in five years, then that increase would produce a corresponding change in overall output factored by the number of miners.

A   **Correct.** The passage states that output per miner has doubled in five years. If the total number of miners is the same, it would necessarily follow that overall output has doubled in five years.

B   While this is plausible, individual mines may have experienced the same or lower output per miner regardless of their overall output; they could have simply hired more miners to increase output.

C   There is no reason to conclude that new mines would have increased the output per miner.

D   It does not follow that a lack of increased output per miner implies a similar lack of overall increase; individual mines could have increased total output with more hiring.

E   While increased productivity might imply declining costs, such a decline does not necessarily follow—for example, savings in labor costs might be offset by the cost of the new technology.

The correct answer is A.

754. Shipping clerk: The five specially ordered shipments sent out last week were sent out on Thursday. Last week, all of the shipments sent out on Friday consisted entirely of building supplies, and the shipping department then closed for the weekend. Four shipments were sent to Truax Construction last week, only three of which consisted of building supplies.

If the shipping clerk's statements are true, which of the following must also be true?

(A) At least one of the shipments sent to Truax Construction last week was specially ordered.

(B) At least one of last week's specially ordered shipments did not consist of building supplies.

(C) At least one of the shipments sent to Truax Construction was not sent out on Thursday of last week.

(D) At least one of the shipments sent out on Friday of last week was sent to Truax Construction.

(E) At least one of the shipments sent to Truax Construction last week was sent out before Friday.

Argument Construction

Situation   A shipping clerk states five specially ordered shipments went out on Thursday. Moreover, all the Friday shipments exclusively contained building supplies; no shipments went out after Friday. Truax was sent four shipments, and only three of those shipments were building supplies.

Reasoning   *What follows from the facts presented?* The clerk states Truax was sent four shipments, of which three were building supplies. Some or all of those three shipments could have been sent on Friday since *only* building supplies went out that day. That leaves at least one shipment to Truax unaccounted for. Since no shipments went out *after* Friday, it follows that at least one shipment to Truax must have been sent *before* Friday.

A   It does not follow that any of Truax's shipments were specially ordered; they could have been shipped before Thursday.

B   There is not enough information provided to conclude anything about the nature of Thursday's specially ordered shipments.

C   We can only conclude that *at least one* Truax shipment went out before Friday; if Truax's shipments were specially ordered, it is quite possible they all went out on Thursday.

D   All of the Truax shipments could have gone out on any day before Friday of that week, so we cannot conclude one shipment to Truax must have gone on Friday.

E   **Correct.** Since only building materials went out on Friday and three out of four of Truax's shipments contained building materials, it follows that at least one of Truax's shipments cannot have been sent on Friday and therefore must have been shipped on one of the days before.

The correct answer is E.

755. In Kravonia, the average salary for jobs requiring a college degree has always been higher than the average salary for jobs that do not require a degree. Current enrollments in Kravonia's colleges indicate that over the next four years, the percentage of the Kravonian workforce with college degrees will increase dramatically. Therefore, the average salary for all workers in Kravonia is likely to increase over the next four years.

Which of the following is an assumption on which the argument depends?

(A) Kravonians with more than one college degree earn more, on average, than do Kravonians with only one college degree.

(B) The percentage of Kravonians who attend college in order to earn higher salaries is higher now than it was several years ago.

(C) The higher average salary for jobs requiring a college degree is not due largely to a scarcity among the Kravonian workforce of people with a college degree.

(D) The average salary in Kravonia for jobs that do not require a college degree will not increase over the next four years.

(E) Few members of the Kravonian workforce earned their degrees in other countries.

Argument Construction

Situation   In Kravonia, average salaries for college graduates are higher than for nongraduates. High enrollment in Kravonia's colleges will result in a far greater share of workers with college degrees in coming years. Overall average salaries will therefore increase.

Reasoning   *What must be true for the conclusion to follow?* A growing percentage of higher-paid workers would indeed be expected to raise average salaries in Kravonia, but that average increase will follow only if college graduates *continue* to command high salaries even when their numbers increase dramatically. Therefore, the argument relies on the assumption that greater numbers of degreed workers will not increase competition for degree-dependent jobs and thereby lower their average salaries.

A   While this might be the case, the argument does not depend on relative salaries for workers with multiple degrees.

B   The conclusion does not rely on the motivations of Kravonians for attending college.

C   **Correct.** The argument relies on the assumption that college graduates have not received high salaries owing to the relative scarcity of degreed workers; if scarcity is the reason for those high salaries, an abundance of new college graduates entering the job market will lower their salaries and therefore lower the average Kravonian salaries overall.

D   The conclusion may rely on the assumption that salaries for nondegree jobs will not decline significantly since that would depress the average, but it does not rely on such salaries *not* rising.

E   The argument states that national enrollment figures indicate the percentage of all graduates will rise dramatically; there is no reason to believe the expectation of rising overall salaries depends on a low number of foreign degrees.

The correct answer is C.

756. Charcoal from a hearth site in Colorado, 2,000 miles south of Alaska, is known to be 11,200 years old. Siberia is located in northeast Russia, and Alaska is located in northwest America. Researchers reasoned since glaciers prevented human migration south from the Alaska-Siberia land bridge between 18,000 and 11,000 years ago, humans must have come to the Americas more than 18,000 years ago.

Which of the following pieces of new evidence would cast doubt on the conclusion drawn above?

(A) Using new radiocarbon dating techniques, it was determined the charcoal from the Colorado site was at least 11,400 years old.

(B) Another campsite was found in New Mexico with remains dated at 16,000 years old.

(C) A computer simulation of glacial activity showed it would already have been impossible for humans to travel south overland from Alaska 18,500 years ago.

(D) Using new radiocarbon dating techniques, it was proved that an ice-free corridor allowed passage south from the Alaska-Siberia land bridge approximately 11,400 years ago.

(E) Studies of various other hunting-gathering populations showed convincingly that once the glaciers allowed passage, humans could have migrated from Alaska to Colorado in about 20 years.

Argument Evaluation

Situation A hearth site in Colorado is 11,200 years old. Glaciers obstructed human migration from Siberia to Alaska, and therefore to the rest of North America, during a period lasting from 18,000 to 11,000 years ago, so researchers concluded human migration must have occurred before the glaciers blocked the land bridge—that is, before 18,000 years ago.

Reasoning *What would have made it possible for humans to migrate more recently?* The researchers' conclusion that humans must have come to North America prior to the obstruction caused by the glaciers 18,000 years ago is reasonable unless new evidence calls their premises into question. If, for example, evidence suggested the land bridge was open at any more recent date before the date of the hearth site, that would imply humans could have arrived later and therefore cast doubt on the researchers' conclusion.

A If the hearth site is at least 11,400 years old, it would still fall in or prior to the interval when the land bridge was obstructed and therefore suggest humans must have arrived before the obstruction; therefore, that fact would not cast doubt on the conclusion.

B A much earlier campsite would tend to support the researchers' conclusion, not cast doubt on it.

C While this fact would imply an even earlier date of human migration, it would not cast doubt on the conclusion that such migration occurred *more than* 18,000 years ago.

D **Correct.** Evidence of a corridor that allowed human migration 11,400 years ago—200 years before the date of the campsite—would cast doubt on the conclusion that humans necessarily must have arrived in North America much earlier.

E The fact that hunter-gatherers could have made the journey to Colorado in twenty years has no bearing on whether they could have made that journey more recently than 18,000 years ago.

The correct answer is D.

757. A group of children of various ages was read stories in which people caused harm, with some of those people doing so intentionally, and some accidentally. When asked about appropriate punishments for those who had caused harm, the younger children, unlike the older ones, assigned punishments that did not vary according to whether the harm was done intentionally or accidentally. Younger children, then, do not regard people's intentions as relevant to punishment.

Which of the following, if true, would most seriously weaken the conclusion above?

(A) In interpreting these stories, the listeners had to draw on a relatively mature sense of human psychology in order to tell whether harm was produced intentionally or accidentally.

(B) In these stories, the severity of the harm produced was clearly stated.

(C) Younger children are as likely to produce harm unintentionally as older children.

(D) The older children assigned punishment in a way that closely resembled the way adults had assigned punishment in a similar experiment.

(E) The younger children assigned punishments that varied according to the severity of the harm done by the agents in the stories.

Argument Evaluation

Situation Children of mixed ages heard stories about people causing harm; in some cases the harm was caused deliberately, and in other cases it was caused accidentally. When the children were asked what punishments would be appropriate, younger children, unlike older ones, assigned equal punishments regardless of whether the harm was intentional. This leads to the conclusion that younger children do not think intentions should matter when determining punishment.

Reasoning *What would undermine support for the conclusion that young children regard intention as irrelevant?* If the younger children had difficulty discerning whether or not the harmful acts in the stories were intentional, that would weaken support for the conclusion that these children think intention should not matter.

A **Correct.** If it required maturity to evaluate whether the harm caused was intentional or accidental, that fact might suggest the younger children simply could not make that determination, not that they believed intention should not affect punishment as the argument concludes.

B The argument rests on children's understanding of the intention behind the harm, not on their understanding the severity of the harm itself.

C The relative rates at which younger and older children accidentally cause harm are not relevant to the conclusion.

D The similarity between older children's responses and those of adults has no bearing on the beliefs of younger children regarding the relationship between intentionality and guilt.

E The fact that younger children took the severity of harm into account does not affect the conclusion that these children believed intention *should not* be taken into account.

The correct answer is A.

758. Mansour: We should both plan to change some of our investments from coal companies to less polluting energy companies, and here's why: Consumers are increasingly demanding nonpolluting energy, and energy companies are increasingly supplying it.

Therese: I'm not sure we should do what you suggest. As demand for nonpolluting energy increases relative to supply, its price will increase, and then the more polluting energy will cost relatively less. Demand for the cheaper, dirtier energy forms will then increase, as will the stock values of the companies that produce them.

Therese responds to Mansour's proposal by doing which of the following?

(A) Advocating that consumers use less expensive forms of energy

(B) Implying that not all uses of coal for energy are necessarily polluting

(C) Disagreeing with Mansour's claim that consumers are increasingly demanding nonpolluting energy

(D) Suggesting that leaving their existing energy investments unchanged could be the better course

(E) Providing a reason to doubt Mansour's assumption that supply of nonpolluting energy will increase in line with demand

Evaluation of a Plan

Situation   Therese and Mansour are discussing what energy investments will be more profitable. Mansour claims the most profitable course is to move their investments from dirty to clean energy because consumer demand for clean energy is increasing. Therese counters with the claim that demand for clean energy will outstrip supply and thereby raise prices for such energy; that in turn will make dirty energy comparatively cheap, driving demand back in its direction and thereby making investments in dirty energy more profitable once again.

Reasoning   *What function does Therese's argument perform?* Mansour argues they should switch to investing in clean energy as he believes it will be more profitable. Therese argues shifting demand will ultimately make dirty energy more profitable; this in turn implies keeping their investments in dirty energy will be the superior course.

A   Therese anticipates consumers will choose cheaper energy but does not advocate for such a choice.

B   Therese does not imply there are some uses of coal for energy that may not be polluting, only that investing in coal is likely to be profitable.

C   Therese does not dispute Mansour's claim that demand for clean energy is rising; rather, she anticipates rising demand will lead to rising prices.

D   Correct. Therese's argument suggests their current investments in dirty energy will ultimately become more profitable, and therefore it would be better not to switch to investing in clean energy.

E   Mansour may well assume the supply of clean energy will increase in line with demand, and Therese assumes supply *will not* meet demand, but she offers no evidence that her position is the correct one.

The correct answer is D.

759. The earliest Mayan pottery found at Colha in Belize is about 3,000 years old. Recently, however, 4,500-year-old stone agricultural implements were unearthed at Colha. These implements resemble Mayan stone implements of a much later period, also found at Colha. Moreover, the implements' designs are strikingly different from the designs of stone implements produced by other cultures known to have inhabited the area in prehistoric times. Therefore, there were surely Mayan settlements in Colha 4,500 years ago.

Which of the following, if true, most seriously weakens the argument?

(A) Ceramicware is not known to have been used by the Mayans to make agricultural implements.

(B) Carbon dating of corn pollen in Colha indicates agriculture began there around 4,500 years ago.

(C) Archaeological evidence indicates some of the oldest stone implements found at Colha were used to cut away vegetation after controlled burning of trees to open areas of swampland for cultivation.

(D) Successor cultures at a given site often adopt the style of agricultural implements used by earlier inhabitants of the same site.

(E) Many religious and social institutions of the Mayan people who inhabited Colha 3,000 years ago relied on a highly developed system of agricultural symbols.

Evaluation of a Plan

Situation   Mayan pottery found at Colha dates back as far as 3,000 years. Stone agricultural implements at the same site date back 4,500 years. These implements are similar to later Mayan ones and dissimilar to implements from other cultures in the region. This leads to the conclusion that the Mayans *surely* lived in Colha 4,500 years ago.

Reasoning   *What factor would suggest that the stone implements might not be Mayan?* The claim that the Mayans lived at Colha 4,500 years ago rests entirely on the fact that stone agricultural implements from that date and place resemble later Mayan implements and do not resemble those of other nearby cultures. Therefore, if some other explanation could account for that resemblance that would weaken the argument that the Mayans must have lived at Colha 4,500 years ago.

A   The agricultural implements under discussion are stone, not ceramic, so this point is irrelevant.

B   The date at which agriculture began at Colha has no bearing on whether or not those farmers were Mayan.

C   The purpose for which the stone implements were used does not suggest the users might not have been Mayan.

D   **Correct.** If cultures often copy the agricultural implements of those who preceded them at the same location, that fact would suggest the possibility that the Mayans of 3,000 years ago could have copied implements made by a different, earlier culture at the site. This possibility would not disprove the hypothesis that the Colha farmers of 4,500 years ago were Mayan, but it would weaken the argument that they were *surely* Mayan.

E   The highly developed agricultural symbols used by the Mayans 3,000 years ago at Colha do not weaken the argument that the Mayans were *surely* already at Colha 4,500 years ago; if anything, they provide modest support for that argument by suggesting the Mayans probably had lived there for some time.

The correct answer is D.

760. That the application of new technology can increase the productivity of existing coal mines is demonstrated by the case of Tribnia's coal industry. Coal output per miner in Tribnia is double what it was five years ago, even though no new mines have opened.

Which of the following, if true, most seriously weakens the argument in the passage?

(A) The most efficient mining technology is specifically designed for open-pit mines, the type of mine prevalent in Tribnia.

(B) The new mining technology can be successfully applied in most coal mines, but not in such mines as metal-ore mines, for example.

(C) New coal mines that opened in a country bordering Tribnia have lower productivity than is currently achieved in the Tribnian mines that are highest in productivity.

(D) In the last three years several of the Tribnian coal mines that were lowest in productivity have been closed down.

(E) Tribnia's coal output is not sufficient to satisfy domestic demand, which has increased in the last five years.

Argument Evaluation

Situation   The argument attempts to demonstrate a causal link between the application of new technology and increased productivity in existing coal mines, using Tribnia as evidence. Coal output per miner in Tribnia has doubled over the last five years, and no new mines have opened. The conclusion is that the increase in productivity must be the result of applying new technology. The argument commits a version of the fallacy of False Cause (or *post hoc ergo propter hoc*). It observes a correlation (new technology together with increased productivity) and asserts causation, but it fails to eliminate other possible causes for the observed effect.

Reasoning   *What alternative factor could account for the increased coal output per miner?* The argument would be weakened by introducing a piece of information that makes the conclusion less likely to be true by suggesting an alternative cause for the observed effect or by showing the cause and effect are unrelated. We are looking for an answer that suggests that the doubling of output per miner (the observed effect) was due to something other than the new technology.

A   This fact would confirm that the new technology is particularly well-suited for Tribnia's mines, making it *more likely* that the technology caused the observed increase.

B   The fact that the technology is not suited to metal-ore mines has no bearing on whether it was the cause of productivity gains in Tribnia's coal mines.

C   Comparing Tribnia's productivity to that of a neighboring country provides no insight into the *cause* of Tribnia's productivity increase over the last five years.

D   Correct. This fact would provide a powerful alternative explanation for the doubling of output per miner. If the least productive mines have been *closed down*, the average output of the *remaining* miners (those working in the more efficient mines) will automatically rise, even if the technology or efficiency in any single mine hasn't changed at all. This suggests that the increase in the average productivity statistic may be due to attrition/selection bias, not technology, thereby weakening the argument's conclusion.

E   Domestic demand for coal does not affect the calculation of output per miner. This information is about the market and has no bearing on the cause of the productivity statistic change.

The correct answer is D.

761. Migratory North American songbirds like the Tennessee warbler and the Baltimore oriole depend on the dense tree cover that has long been a feature of South American coffee plantations. This tree cover is being eliminated. Yet a population decline among Tennessee warblers is being attributed to a temporary drop in the population of spruce budworms, the warbler's favorite North American prey. Baltimore orioles, however, do not eat budworms and are also experiencing a population decline.

The information above, if accurate, could best serve as part of an argument that

(A) the decline in the numbers of the Tennessee warbler is responsible for the decline in the population of the spruce budworm

(B) the Tennessee warbler population will not rebound when the spruce budworm population returns to normal

(C) variations in the population of the Tennessee warbler influence the numbers of the Baltimore oriole

(D) the population of Tennessee warblers can reasonably be expected to increase in the near future

(E) the population of Tennessee warblers is declining less sharply than the population of Baltimore orioles

Argument Construction

Situation
The argument presents several facts concerning two migratory songbirds: Tennessee warblers and Baltimore orioles, and their winter habitat in South American coffee plantations.

Fact 1: Both warblers and orioles rely on dense tree cover in South American coffee plantations.

Fact 2: This dense tree cover is being eliminated.

Fact 3: The warbler's decline is being attributed to a temporary drop in its favorite North American prey, the spruce budworm (a cause specific to the warbler).

Fact 4: The oriole, which does not eat budworms, is also experiencing a population decline.

Reasoning
What argument would be best supported by the evidence presented? The central inconsistency lies between Fact 3 (Warbler decline is due to budworms) and Fact 4 (Oriole decline, which is *not* linked to budworms). Since both birds are experiencing decline and share a threatened winter habitat (Fact 2), the information strongly suggests that the common factor—the loss of the South American tree cover—is the true cause of the decline for *both* species. The information specifically undermines the budworm explanation for the warbler's decline because a parallel decline is occurring in a bird not affected by budworms. Therefore, the set of facts can best be used to support an argument that the budworm explanation for the warbler's decline is incorrect or insufficient, and that the real cause is the loss of the shared winter habitat.

However, the options provided are not about the habitat directly. We must choose the option that is most strongly suggested by the rejection of the budworm theory. Since the budworm theory is challenged by the oriole's parallel decline, the most logical inference is to shift focus away from the budworm explanation for the warbler. The facts challenge the causal attribution in Fact 3.

Fact 3 states the warbler's decline is attributed to a *temporary* drop in budworms. If the decline were *only* due to a temporary factor, the warbler population would be expected to rebound when the budworms do. However, the oriole's decline suggests a more fundamental, non-temporary issue is at play, namely the loss of habitat. Therefore, the facts best serve an argument that the warbler's decline is driven by a more persistent problem, in which case it will probably not rebound just because the budworms return.

A
The argument states the budworm decline is being identified as the cause of the warbler decline. Reversing this causality is not supported or suggested by the evidence.

B   **Correct.** The evidence challenges the simple, temporary budworm explanation by noting the oriole's parallel decline, which has no budworm link. This strongly suggests that a deeper, shared problem (habitat loss) is causing the warbler's decline. If the root cause is habitat loss, a non-temporary factor, rather than the temporary budworm drop, the warbler population cannot reasonably be expected to recover just because budworms return.

C   The text only suggests that the two species share a common problem, namely habitat loss. There is no evidence they interact or influence each other's population dynamics.

D   The evidence suggests the true cause is habitat loss (a negative, persistent factor), not just a temporary drop in prey. This makes an increase in the warbler population *less likely*, not more likely.

E   The passage only states that both populations are declining. It provides no comparative data on the *rate* or *sharpness* of the decline for either species.

The correct answer is B.

762. Historian: Newton developed mathematical concepts and techniques that are fundamental to modern calculus. Leibniz developed closely analogous concepts and techniques. It has traditionally been thought that these discoveries were independent. Researchers have, however, recently discovered notes of Leibniz's that discuss one of Newton's books on mathematics. Several scholars have argued that since the book includes a presentation of Newton's calculus concepts and techniques, and since **the notes were written before Leibniz's own development of calculus concepts and techniques**, it is virtually certain that the traditional view is false. **A more cautious conclusion than this is called for,** however. Leibniz's notes are limited to early sections of Newton's book, sections that precede the ones in which Newton's calculus concepts and techniques are presented.

In the historian's reasoning, the two **boldfaced** portions play which of the following roles?

(A) The first provides evidence in support of the general position that the historian defends; the second reports the doubts of others concerning that position.

(B) The first states a conclusion drawn as part of an argument that the historian criticizes; the second is that conclusion.

(C) The first is evidence that has been used to support a conclusion that the historian criticizes; the second is the judgment reached by the historian about that conclusion.

(D) The first identifies grounds for a potential objection to the conclusion of the argument; the second is the judgment reached by the argument concerning the accuracy of the finding.

(E) The first is a claim, the explanation of which is at issue in the argument; the second brings evidence that has been used to support that explanation.

Argument Construction

Situation   A historian is discussing the origin of calculus concepts developed by Newton and Leibniz. The traditional view is that their discoveries were made independently. Recent evidence, namely Leibniz's notes on Newton's book in which he presented ideas regarding calculus, has led "several scholars" to argue that the traditional view is false. But the historian argues that this conclusion is too strong.

Reasoning   *What roles do the two **boldfaced** portions play in the argument?* The first portion is evidence used by "several scholars" to support their conclusion. It establishes the *timing* necessary to suggest influence (i.e., Leibniz read it *before* his discovery). The second portion is the historian's main conclusion or judgment on the scholars' conclusion. It explicitly states that the historian finds the scholars' conclusion unwarranted or too strong, based on the counter-evidence that Leibniz's notes are limited to early sections of Newton's book *before* the calculus sections, undermining the scholars' claim of influence. Thus, the first **boldfaced** portion is *evidence* used to support a conclusion, and the second excerpt is the *historian's judgment* or criticism of that conclusion.

A   The first **boldfaced** portion is evidence used by the scholars to support the conclusion that the traditional view is false. The historian *defends* the traditional view (or at least defends a more cautious conclusion), so the first portion does *not* support the historian's position. The second **boldfaced** portion is the historian's own judgment, not the reported doubts of others.

B   The first **boldfaced** portion is a premise/evidence (about the timing of the notes), not a conclusion. The second portion correctly gives the historian's evaluation of the scholars' conclusion.

C   **Correct.** The first **boldfaced** portion is evidence (Leibniz wrote notes *before* his discovery) used to support the conclusion that the traditional view is false. The historian then criticizes this conclusion by stating it is too strong and offering counter-evidence. The second **boldfaced** portion is the historian's judgment ("A more cautious conclusion . . . is called for") regarding the criticized conclusion.

D   The first **boldfaced** portion is evidence used to support a claim the historian argues against. However, the second excerpt is the main conclusion/judgment of the historian's argument, not an intermediate step.

E   The historian does not *dispute the accuracy* of the first **boldfaced** portion, which states that the notes predate Leibniz's discovery. The historian accepts this fact but disputes the conclusion drawn from it. The second **boldfaced** portion is a judgment about the scholars' *conclusion*, not a judgment about the first claim itself.

The correct answer is C.

763. Any machine that could be used to keep fields free of weeds without manual weeding or the use of herbicides would have a large market among farmers. A company has developed a prototype weeding machine that distinguishes between plants on the basis of their color and can remove any plant that falls outside a predetermined color range. The company is presently considering whether to go ahead with full-scale production of this weeding machine.

Which of the following, if true, is the strongest consideration in favor of the company's going into full-scale production?

(A)   There is a considerable degree of variation in color among weeds of different species.

(B)   For many crops, weeds pose a greater threat to high yields than insect pests do.

(C)   When crops are weeded manually, color is often a major factor in distinguishing agricultural plants from weeds.

(D)   Selection and genetic manipulation allow nearly all agricultural plants to be economically bred to have a distinctive shade of color without altering their other characteristics.

(E)   The last time the company decided to go ahead with full-scale production of a machine for which they had developed a prototype, the venture proved far more profitable than the company had anticipated.

Argument Evaluation

Situation   A company has developed a prototype weeding machine that uses color to distinguish between weeds and crop plants, allowing it to remove any plant outside a predetermined color range. The company is deciding whether to begin full-scale production. The market is known to be large if the machine works.

Reasoning   *What additional factor would suggest that the machine will successfully identify weeds as opposed to crop plants?* The machine's success hinges entirely on its ability to reliably distinguish between desirable crop plants and undesirable weeds based on color. For the company to proceed with full-scale production, the strongest consideration in its favor would be one that guarantees or highly increases the reliability and practicality of the color-based distinction in a real-world farming context. If the crops can be easily and economically made to have a unique color that weeds *cannot* match, the machine's effectiveness is confirmed, strongly favoring production.

A   This observation would act as a consideration *against* the machine's effectiveness. If weed colors vary widely, it makes it harder to set a color range for the crop that successfully excludes *all* weeds, potentially leading to the machine missing some weeds or pulling up some crop plants.

B   This fact confirms the existence of a large market, but it does not address the crucial question of whether the machine itself will work effectively using its color-based technology. Therefore, it does not strengthen the decision to proceed with *this specific* machine.

C   This describes the process of manual weeding and the factors *human* workers use to recognize weeds. It doesn't confirm that the simple, automated color-range technology of the machine will be successful, as humans can use subtle cues and complex judgment that the machine cannot.

D   **Correct.** This is the strongest consideration in favor of production. If farmers can economically ensure their crops have a distinctive, uniform color, then the machine's color recognition presumably could be calibrated to avoid pulling up plants of that precise shade. This would make the machine highly reliable and practical, providing a strong reason to go into full-scale production.

E   This fact is irrelevant historical information about the company's past successes. While it speaks to the company's general entrepreneurial skill, it provides no information about the technical feasibility or market viability of *this specific* weeding machine.

The correct answer is D.

764. Charcoal from a hearth site in Colorado, 2,000 miles south of Alaska, is known to be 11,200 years old. Researchers reasoned that, since glaciers prevented human migration south from the Alaska–Siberia land bridge between 18,000 and 11,000 years ago, humans must have come to the Americas more than 18,000 years ago.

The argument above relies on which of the following assumptions?

(A) The earliest controlled use of fire on the American continents occurred around 11,200 years ago.

(B) Any humans who came to the Americas more than 11,000 years ago came via the Alaska–Siberia land bridge.

(C) The Alaska–Siberia land bridge was the result of the uptake of seawater by the continental glaciers.

(D) Early human inhabitants of the Americas were hunters whose diet consisted primarily of meat, rather than gatherers who subsisted on fruit and seeds.

(E) Early humans tended to migrate to warmer climates, even those who were accustomed to living in cold, harsh climates.

Argument Construction

Situation   Charcoal found in Colorado, 2,000 miles south of Alaska, is dated to 11,200 years ago. Glaciers are known to have blocked the primary migratory route, the Alaska–Siberia land bridge, between 18,000 and 11,000 years ago.

Reasoning   *What implicit assumption underlies the argument?* The argument concludes that humans must have arrived in the Americas more than 18,000 years ago. The reasoning is a two-step causal chain: humans were in Colorado 11,200 years ago; migration was impossible between 18,000 and 11,000 years ago; therefore, humans must have migrated *before* the blockade began, i.e., more than 18,000 years ago. The core assumption required to link the evidence to the conclusion is that the only possible way for humans to have reached Colorado was by migrating south from the Alaska-Siberia land bridge. If there were any other viable route (e.g., crossing by boat or migrating south along the Pacific coast *before* the inland ice-free corridor formed), the conclusion that they must have come before 18,000 years ago is undermined. The argument assumes that the glaciers blocked the only path.

A   The argument concerns *migration timing*, not the *earliest use of fire*. If fire was used earlier, the conclusion (*more than 18,000 years ago*) is still valid. If it was used later, the charcoal dating is inaccurate, but the assumption doesn't help the existing argument.

B   **Correct.** This is the necessary assumption. The argument explicitly relies on the land bridge being the sole route and the glaciers blocking it being the only impediment. If humans could have migrated by another means, such as boats, during the 18,000- to 11,000-year period, they would not necessarily have had to arrive before 18,000 years ago, thus undermining the conclusion. By assuming the land bridge was the only way, the researchers force the arrival date to predate the glacial blockade.

C   This fact explains the *cause* of the land bridge, which is irrelevant to the timing of human migration or the existence of the glacial blockade.

D   The argument is based on migration routes and dates, not diet. This fact has no bearing on the logic used.

E   The reason *why* they migrated is irrelevant. The argument only concerns *when* they migrated based on *when* the route was open.

The correct answer is B.

765. Advertisement for ShopEx Supermarkets: Dozens of shoppers, chosen at random, were asked as they came out of their ShopEx stores what they had purchased. The prices of the very same items at the nearest PriceKing store were totaled and compared with the ShopEx total. At ShopEx, the totals averaged five percent less than at PriceKing. So, for overall savings on their food bills, shoppers should go to ShopEx instead of PriceKing.

Which of the following, if true, most seriously undermines the argument of the advertisement?

(A) When more than 20 items were selected, the PriceKing totals averaged more than five percent higher than the ShopEx totals.

(B) Many shoppers consider additional factors other than price in choosing the supermarket at which they shop most regularly.

(C) Virtually every grocery item that can be found at PriceKing can also be found at ShopEx.

(D) When purchasing items in a grocery store, shoppers tend to select those items that are on sale, and different stores have sales on different items.

(E) Most of the shoppers who were stopped on their way out of ShopEx said that they shopped at PriceKing either regularly or occasionally.

Argument Evaluation

Situation   A study compared the prices of items purchased by a random sample of ShopEx shoppers with the prices of the same items at a competitor, PriceKing. The ShopEx totals averaged five percent less than the PriceKing totals for those specific purchased items.

Reasoning   *What additional factor would suggest that ShopEx's overall prices are not necessarily lower than PriceKing's?* The argument concludes that shoppers should go to ShopEx instead of PriceKing for overall savings on their food bills. The conclusion makes a leap from savings on a specific selection of items (the ones the surveyed shoppers happened to buy) to savings on a customer's entire food bill. The argument assumes that the five percent savings found in the survey is representative of the relative prices of *all* grocery items at the two stores, or at least the items that make up a shopper's overall food bill. To undermine the argument, we must show that the survey results are skewed or unrepresentative of typical, comprehensive shopping habits. This would suggest that the five percent savings is misleading when applied to overall food bills.

A   This fact merely suggests that the savings at ShopEx might be *greater* than five percent for larger purchases, which strengthens the conclusion rather than weakening it.

B   The conclusion is about *overall savings*, which is strictly related to price. While other factors such as convenience, cleanliness, etc. may affect where shoppers choose to go, this does not undermine the claim about which store offers better savings.

C   This fact merely confirms that the two stores offer comparable selections, which does not undermine the price comparison.

D   Correct. This most seriously undermines the argument. The surveyed shoppers were stopped *coming out of ShopEx*. Because shoppers tend to buy items that are on sale, the surveyed selections would likely represent items that were priced lowest at ShopEx on that specific day. If the PriceKing total had been based on the items that were *on sale at PriceKing* that day, the results would likely be different. By measuring the price of only those items that ShopEx's shoppers were incentivized to buy at ShopEx, the survey is inherently biased and unrepresentative of the prices for a customer's overall food bill.

E   This fact confirms that the shoppers are familiar with both stores, which makes them informed consumers, but it does not invalidate the price comparison or the logic used to draw the conclusion about overall savings.

The correct answer is D.

766. The earliest surviving Greek inscriptions written in an alphabet date from the eighth century B.C. Some of these inscriptions are written from right to left, others from left to right. The alphabet they employ clearly derives from Phoenician writing, but by the eighth century B.C., Phoenician was consistently written from right to left and had been for about two centuries. Therefore, the Greeks must have adopted alphabetic writing no later than the tenth century B.C.

Which of the following is an assumption on which the argument depends?

(A) Greek inscriptions from the eighth century B.C. that are written from right to left were not translations of Phoenician inscriptions.

(B) In Greece, the adoption of an alphabetic writing system supplanted a writing system in which Greek was written from right to left.

(C) When the Greeks adopted alphabetic writing, they also adopted the Phoenician practices of the time with respect to the direction in which texts were written.

(D) After adopting alphabetic writing, the Greeks had no exposure to Phoenician inscriptions for at least two centuries.

(E) Apart from Greek, all languages whose alphabets derived from Phoenician writing were consistently written from right to left.

Argument Construction

Situation   The earliest Greek inscriptions date from the eighth century B.C., and some are written right-to-left, while others are left-to-right. The Greek alphabet derives from the Phoenician script. By the eighth century B.C., Phoenician writing had been consistently right-to-left for about two centuries (i.e., since the tenth century B.C.).

Reasoning   *What assumption underlies the argument regarding the date of Greeks' adoption of alphabetic writing?* The argument concludes that the Greeks must have adopted alphabetic writing no later than the tenth century B.C.: that is, before Phoenician standardized its direction. The conclusion bridges a gap between the evidence—namely that the earliest known Greek inscriptions show variation in direction, but the source script, Phoenician, had long since standardized—and the conclusion regarding the adoption date. The core assumption is that when the Greeks initially adopted the Phoenician script, they adopted the writing conventions of the Phoenicians at that specific time. If, at the time of adoption, the Phoenician script itself still showed variation in writing direction (i.e., before 10th century B.C.), this would explain why the earliest Greek scripts also show variation. Conversely, the argument assumes that the Greeks would not have created their own, unique directional variation after adopting a standardized Phoenician script. Therefore, the argument depends on the assumption that the Greek practice of varying the writing direction was a direct inheritance from the Phoenician script *before* it standardized its direction.

A   Even if they were translations, the variation (right-to-left *and* left-to-right) suggests the Greeks had not yet standardized their *own* direction, which is the key point. The argument does not depend on whether the inscriptions are translations or originals.

B   This fact is irrelevant. The argument concerns the transition from Phoenician practices to Greek practices, not what preceding Greek writing system may have existed.

C   **Correct.** This is the necessary assumption. If the Greeks adopted the Phoenician script but then spontaneously created their own directional variation (right-to-left *and* left-to-right) *after* the Phoenician direction was already standardized (after 10th century B.C.), the conclusion is invalid. The argument must assume that the observed Greek variation reflects the earlier Phoenician practice before the 10th century B.C. standardization.

D   Continued exposure would tend to make the argument *weaker*, as the Greeks might have adopted the standardized right-to-left practice later on. The argument does not rely on a lack of exposure.

E   The practices of *other* derivative languages are irrelevant; the argument focuses only on the relationship between Greek and its direct source, Phoenician.

The correct answer is C.

767. Generalization: The more viewers a television show attracts, the greater the advertising revenue it generates.

Situation: Production costs for *Starlight*, the VNT network's most popular weekly show, are very high and rising. The advertising revenue *Starlight* generates minus the show's production costs is below average for VNT shows and is declining.

Judgment: VNT's profits would be better protected by retaining *Starlight* than by replacing it with a show of average popularity and average production costs.

Which of the following, if true, provides the strongest reason for considering the judgment to be well founded?

(A) The average profits of VNT shows have increased in each of the last three years.

(B) Shows that occupy time slots immediately before and after a very popular show tend to have far more viewers than they otherwise would.

(C) *Starlight* currently has the highest production costs of all VNT shows.

(D) Last year VNT lost money on a weekly show that was substantially similar to *Starlight* but was broadcast on a different day of the week than *Starlight* is.

(E) *Starlight*'s high production costs are a direct result of its format and content and cannot be reduced without fundamentally changing the show.

Argument Construction

Situation The argument presents a Generalization that more viewers equals greater revenue, and the Situation of a specific show, *Starlight*: it's the network's most popular show, but its net profitability (revenue minus costs) is below average and declining due to high and rising production costs.

Reasoning *What additional factor would support the idea that Starlight contributes more to profits than its net profitability would suggest?* The Judgment, or conclusion, is that VNT's profits would be better protected by retaining *Starlight* than by replacing it with an average show. This judgment seems counterintuitive, as *Starlight*'s profitability is low and falling. To provide the strongest reason that the judgment is well-founded, we need to find a factor that demonstrates *Starlight* contributes significantly to VNT's overall profits in a way that is not captured by looking solely at *Starlight*'s individual net income. In other words, we need to show that *Starlight* generates a positive externality (a benefit to other shows) that would be lost if the show were replaced by an average performer.

A General network data is irrelevant to the specific comparison between keeping *Starlight* and replacing it with an average show.

B **Correct.** This provides the necessary positive externality. If *Starlight* (VNT's most popular show) significantly boosts the viewership of the shows surrounding it, then replacing *Starlight* with an average show would cause a sharp drop in viewership—and thus in advertising revenue—for two or more adjacent shows. This potential massive loss in revenue across the entire prime-time lineup makes the retention of the less profitable *Starlight* a much better strategy for protecting overall VNT profits.

C This fact merely reinforces the problem stated in the Situation section, explaining *why* the show's profitability is low. It does not provide a reason why retaining the show is the better financial decision.

D This fact merely suggests that a show similar to *Starlight* failed in a different time slot, which might discourage replacement with a similar show but does not explain the unique, positive value of *retaining* the current *Starlight* in its current time slot.

E This fact reinforces the idea that the show's low profitability is permanent, which makes the decision to retain it *less* logical. It doesn't offer a hidden benefit that justifies retention.

The correct answer is B.

768. Last year a record number of new manufacturing jobs were created. Will this year bring another record? Well, **any new manufacturing job is created either within an existing company or by the start-up of a new company.** Within existing firms, new jobs have been created this year at well below last year's record pace. At the same time, there is considerable evidence that the number of new companies starting up will be no higher this year than it was last year, and there is no reason to think that **the new companies starting up this year will create more jobs per company than did last year's start-ups.** So clearly, the number of new jobs created this year will fall short of last year's record.

In the argument given, the two portions in **boldface** play which of the following roles?

(A) The first is presented as an obvious truth on which the argument is based; the second is a claim advanced in support of the conclusion of the argument.

(B) The first is presented as an obvious truth on which the argument is based; the second presents a possible objection that the argument discounts.

(C) The first provides evidence in support of the conclusion of the argument; the second is a prediction that, if accurate, would provide further support for that conclusion.

(D) The first is a generalization that the argument seeks to establish; the second is a claim that has been advanced in support of a position that the argument opposes.

(E) The first is a generalization that the argument seeks to establish; the second is a claim that has been advanced in order to challenge that generalization.

Argument Construction

Situation   A record number of manufacturing jobs were created in the year previous. For this year to set a new record, manufacturing jobs must be created in greater numbers by the two sources of such jobs taken together: established companies and start-up companies. Established companies are creating fewer manufacturing jobs than they did the year previous; moreover, because companies are starting up at the same, or lower, rate than they did the year previous, and because there is no evidence that these start-ups will create jobs at a higher rate per company than did companies that started up the year previous, the author concludes that the total of new manufacturing jobs will be fewer this year than last year.

Reasoning   *How do the two* **boldfaced** *portions function in relation to the argument that fewer manufacturing jobs will be created this year than last?* The first portion states that new jobs can come from only two sources: existing companies and start-up companies. This is presented as an obvious, common-sense fact, and the rest of the argument depends on it. The second portion relates to the fact that, because start-up companies are forming at a rate no greater than last year's, the only way there could be more manufacturing jobs created this year would be if this year's start-ups created more jobs per company; if that were the case, it would undermine that author's conclusion that "clearly" fewer manufacturing jobs will be created this year. This potential objection is presented in the second **boldfaced** portion. However, the author discounts this possibility by stating that there is "no reason" to believe it is true.

A   While the first portion is indeed presented as an obvious truth, the second portion, if true, would undermine rather than support the argument's conclusion.

B   **Correct.** The first portion consists of the claim the new manufacturing jobs must come from either existing companies or new ones, and this presents as an obvious fact on which the remainder of the argument rests; the second portion describes a possible avenue by which more jobs *could* be created this year than last, and so it amounts to a potential objection to the conclusion that fewer jobs will be created this year. However, the author dismisses this potential objection by stating that there is "no reason" to believe it is the case.

C   The first portion is a common-sense assertion, not evidence per se; the second portion presents a prediction that, if accurate, would undermine rather than support the conclusion.

D   The first portion is a statement that the argument relies on but does nothing to establish beyond simply asserting it to be true; the second is a claim that *could be* advanced in support of an opposed position, but there is no evidence to suggest it actually *has been* advanced.

E   The first portion is a statement that the argument relies on but does nothing to establish beyond simply asserting it to be true; the second does not in any way contest that statement: that new jobs must come from either existing companies or new ones.

The correct answer is B.

769. Business Consultant: Some corporations shun the use of executive titles because they fear that **the use of titles indicating position in the corporation tends to inhibit communication up and down the corporate hierarchy.** Since an executive who uses a title is treated with more respect by outsiders, however, **use of a title can facilitate an executive's dealings with external businesses.** The obvious compromise is for these executives to use their corporate titles externally but not internally, since even if it is widely known that the corporation's executives use executive titles outside their organization, this knowledge does not by itself inhibit communication within the corporation.

In the consultant's reasoning, the two portions in **boldface** play which of the following roles?

(A) The first presents an obstacle to achieving a certain goal; the second presents a reason for considering that goal to be undesirable.

(B) The first is a consideration that has led to the adoption of a certain strategy; the second presents a reason against adopting that strategy.

(C) The first describes a concern that the consultant dismisses as insignificant; the second is a consideration that serves as the basis for that dismissal.

(D) The first is a belief for which the consultant offers support; the second is part of that support.

(E) The first is a belief against which evidence is offered; the second is part of the evidence offered against that belief.

Argument Construction

Situation   A business consultant presents the possible concern that the use of executive titles may impede vertical communication within a company; the drawback to simply dropping such titles, as some companies have done, is that such titles are useful in dealing with external businesses. The consultant proposes a solution: Use such executive titles with outsiders, but not with fellow employees of the company. The consultant asserts that awareness of such externally used titles does not have an inhibiting effect on company communications.

Reasoning   *What role do the two* **boldfaced** *portions play in the consultant's discussion of the best way to use executive titles?* The first portion states the concern that executive titles may inhibit vertical communication within a company; the surrounding context includes the information that concern regarding such inhibition has led some companies to avoid executive titles. The second portion states that having an executive title can help an executive in their dealings with external businesses: that is, it points to a drawback in the strategy of simply eliminating titles and therefore a reason not to adopt it.

A   The first portion does discuss the idea that titles may impede communication within a company, and it is reasonable to assume that good communication may be a goal of most companies; however, the second portion in no way suggests that good vertical communication is undesirable.

B   **Correct.** The first portion presents the reason some companies have dropped the use of executive titles: their concern that such titles inhibit communication. The second portion presents a reason that this strategy of simply eliminating titles may not be the best choice: namely, that such impressive titles are useful in dealing with outsiders.

C   The consultant does not dismiss the concern regarding poor communication, described in the first portion, as insignificant, nor does the second portion provide a basis for a dismissal that is not present in the text.

D   The first portion does describe a belief, not a confirmed fact, since no evidence is offered for the idea that executive titles inhibit communication; however, the consultant advances no support for that belief anywhere, including in the second portion.

E   No evidence is offered against the belief that executive titles inhibit communication, so this is incorrect in regard to both **boldfaced** portions of the text.

The correct answer is B.

770. Since it has become known that several of a bank's top executives have been buying shares in their own bank, the bank's depositors, who had been worried by rumors that the bank faced impending financial collapse, have been greatly relieved. They reason that since **top executives evidently have faith in the bank's financial soundness**, those worrisome rumors must be false. The depositors might well be over-optimistic, however, since **corporate executives have been known to buy shares in their own company in a calculated attempt to dispel negative rumors about the company's health.**

In the argument given, the two **boldfaced** portions play which of the following roles?

(A) The first describes evidence used in the reasoning that the argument calls into question; the second gives information about the source of that evidence.

(B) The first describes evidence used in the reasoning that the argument calls into question; the second states the conclusion of the argument as a whole.

(C) The first is an intermediate conclusion that forms part of the reasoning that the argument calls into question; the second is evidence that undermines the support for this intermediate conclusion.

(D) The first is an intermediate conclusion that forms part of the reasoning that the argument calls into question; the second states the conclusion of the argument as a whole.

(E) The first is an intermediate conclusion that forms part of the reasoning that the argument calls into question; the second states a further conclusion supported by this intermediate conclusion.

Argument Construction

Situation   A bank's depositors are concerned that the bank may be failing but are reassured to learn that the bank's executives are buying shares in the bank. The depositors believe that these purchases show that the bank must be sound. The argument calls their belief into question by stating that executives sometimes purchase stocks in their own company merely to create the appearance of corporate health.

Reasoning   *What role do the two **boldfaced** portions play in the argument that the bank's depositors may have been misled into believing the bank is sound?* The first portion states an intermediate conclusion drawn by the depositors: that "evidently" the bank's executives believe the bank is sound, as demonstrated by their stock purchases. The argument, however, describes this reasoning as overly optimistic. The second portion offers evidence that undermines the support for the intermediate conclusion: executives may not necessarily buy stock out of faith in their company, but rather to create a misleading public impression of such faith.

A   The first portion does describe evidence used in the reasoning that the argument calls into question, namely that the stock purchases by executives demonstrate their faith in the company; however, the second portion is opposing evidence, not information regarding the source of the earlier evidence.

B   The first portion does describe evidence supporting a belief that the argument views as misguided, namely the belief that rumors the bank is collapsing must be false; however, the second portion is not the overall conclusion, but support for that conclusion: that the depositors may be mistaken in believing the bank is sound after all.

C   **Correct.** The first portion describes the intermediate conclusion drawn by the depositors: the executives clearly believe the bank is healthy. The argument immediately calls this conclusion into question by calling it overly optimistic, then, in the second portion, offers evidence against the support used by the depositors in drawing their hopeful conclusion: executives' stock purchases may derive not from genuine faith in their company, but rather from a desire to create the illusion of such faith.

D   The first portion does describe the intermediate conclusion drawn by the depositors, namely that the executives have faith in the bank's health; however, the second portion is not the overall conclusion but support for that conclusion: that the depositors may be overly optimistic in taking the executives' purchases as reassurance.

E   The first portion does describe the intermediate conclusion drawn by the depositors, namely that the executives have faith in the bank's health; the second portion, however, is evidence against that intermediate conclusion, not a further conclusion it supports.

The correct answer is C.

771. Throughout May, crabs arrive on Delaware's beaches to lay eggs. Migrating shorebirds that rely on these eggs for food stop there before continuing to their northern breeding grounds. The earlier in the season they reach those breeding grounds, the greater their likelihood of breeding successfully. Because the crab population was much smaller this year than last, the shorebirds lengthened their Delaware stay considerably in order to consume enough crab eggs to permit completion of their migration.

For which of the following hypotheses does the information given above provide the strongest support?

(A)   The shorebirds will leave their northern breeding grounds earlier this year than they have in years past.

(B)   The decline in the crab population was largely due to the shorebirds' consumption of crab eggs in years past.

(C)   The average number of eggs laid per egg-laying crab will be significantly lower next year than this year.

(D)   The proportion of the migratory shorebirds that breed successfully will be lower this year than it was last year.

(E)   Many fewer of the shorebirds will reach their northern breeding grounds this year than did last year.

Argument Evaluation

Situation   Crabs lay eggs on Delaware's beaches every May, and migrating shorebirds depend on these eggs for sufficient food to reach their northern breeding grounds. Reaching those breeding grounds early increases the chance of successful breeding; however, this year a dearth of crabs, and therefore of crab eggs, forced the shorebirds to search longer for adequate food and thereby delayed their migration significantly in comparison with the year previous.

Reasoning   *What is likely to be the result of the shorebirds' delayed migration?* The information states that early migration is key to successful breeding, so it can be inferred that a delayed migration this year will lead to a corresponding reduction in the proportion of migratory shorebirds that can breed successfully this year, compared to those who bred successfully last year.

A   There is no support for the hypothesis that a delayed migration north will lead to an early migration south.

B   There is no evidence for any specific hypothesis regarding the reason for declining crab populations; since the shorebirds eat the crab eggs every year, there is no obvious reason why that consumption would affect crab populations now, and not formerly.

C   There is no support for the idea that the number of eggs produced per crab will change in any way.

D   **Correct.** If early migration is key to successful breeding, and most of the shorebirds migrated much later this year than last year, then those facts taken together support the hypothesis that a lower proportion of shorebirds will breed successfully this year as compared to last year.

E   While it is possible that some of the shorebirds could not find enough food to complete their migration north, the information given suggests that their migration was delayed by the shortage of crab eggs, not that the shortage was so severe that many of the birds could not migrate at all.

The correct answer is D.

772. Surveys in Lynzia indicate that while more than half of all Lynzians over thirty read a newspaper regularly, only 10 percent of Lynzians in their twenties do. Since the mean age of Lynzia's population is quite low, with people in their twenties constituting a large proportion of the population, it is safe to predict that the percentage of Lynzians who regularly read a newspaper will be much lower ten years from now than it is today.

Which of the following, if true, casts most doubt on the prediction?

(A) The number of Lynzians in their twenties is less than the number of Lynzians over thirty.

(B) The surveys counted someone as reading a newspaper regularly if that person read a newspaper more than four times a month.

(C) The proportion of Lynzians who regularly read a newspaper was higher 20 years ago than it is today.

(D) The proportion of Lynzians in their twenties who regularly read a newspaper has always been low.

(E) The number of newspapers published in Lynzia has been gradually diminishing over the last several decades.

Argument Evaluation

Situation   Ten percent of Lynzians in their twenties habitually read newspapers, in contrast to Lynzians over thirty, of whom a majority read newspapers. Lynzians in their twenties make up a large percentage of the population overall. The argument infers from these facts that in ten years the percentage of Lynzians who read newspapers habitually will have fallen significantly.

Reasoning   *What additional factor would undermine the conclusion that the percentage of newspaper-readers in Lynzia will fall?* The argument is based on the assumption that Lynzians in their twenties will maintain their low rates of newspaper-reading as they age: As older newspaper-readers die, they will be replaced by nonreaders, and the percentage of newspaper-readers overall will fall. However, if an additional fact cast doubt on that assumption—for example, by suggesting that newspaper-reading habits are not necessarily static as Lynzians age—then that additional fact would undermine the prediction that the percentage of Lynzians who regularly read newspapers will have fallen steeply in ten years.

A   The fact that there are fewer Lynzians in their twenties than the total of Lynzians over thirty would not affect the implicit assumption underlying the argument: that non-readers will replace readers over time and therefore become a larger percentage of the total population.

B   The way in which regular newspaper readers are defined has no bearing on the prediction that the total percentage of those who meet that definition will fall.

C   If the proportion of newspaper readers in Lynzia has fallen over the last twenty years, then that fact would tend to support, not undermine, the prediction that it will continue to fall.

D   Correct. The information states that most Lynzians over thirty read newspapers regularly; if, then, the percentage of Lynzians in their twenties who read newspapers has always been low, that would mean that many older newspaper-readers must have taken up newspaper reading as they matured. Because the argument rests on the assumption that newspaper reading habits are necessarily static—that a non-reader will remain a non-reader—this additional fact casts doubt on the prediction that the percentage of newspaper readers will fall steeply. Instead, an unknown percentage of younger Lynzians may simply begin reading newspapers regularly as they grow older, and the percentage of the overall population that reads newspapers may grow, remain constant, or diminish to only a modest degree.

E   The number of newspapers published in Lynzia is not relevant to the question of what percentage of Lynzians will read them in ten years.

The correct answer is D.

773. Inscorp, a manufacturer, wishes to make its information booth at an industry convention more productive in terms of boosting sales. The booth offers information introducing the company's new products and services. To achieve the desired result, Inscorp's marketing department will attempt to attract more people to the booth. The marketing director's first measure was to instruct each salesperson to call five ex-customers and personally invite them to visit the booth.

Which of the following, if true, most strongly calls into question the effectiveness of the marketing director's first measure as a step toward the goal of boosting sales?

(A) In past years, the information booth was not well attended.

(B) The ex-customers most likely to act on Inscorp's invitation are ones who hope to use the booth to resolve long-standing complaints on which Inscorp is unlikely to give them satisfaction.

(C) Many of Inscorp's competitors believe that by making their information booths more distinctive they can increase the number of potential customers who will visit their booths at the convention.

(D) Inscorp's best customers regularly receive special discounts on large orders placed with Inscorp.

(E) Inscorp has more new products and services available this year than it had in previous years.

Argument Evaluation

Situation   Inscorp would like its information booth at a convention to increase sales. To that end, they intend to directly invite former customers to visit the booth.

Reasoning   *What would be likely to make booth visits from ex-customers ineffective for boosting sales?* The plan to increase sales by inviting former customers to the booth will be effective only if those former customers are inclined to buy from Inscorp again. If, therefore, there is reason to believe that such ex-customers may not be so inclined, then that would call the plan's chance of success into question.

A   Past attendance at the information booth has no bearing on plans to use that booth to produce sales this year.

B   **Correct.** If the ex-customers most likely to visit the booth are already dissatisfied with Inscorp, and are likely to remain dissatisfied, then they will probably lack enthusiasm for buying more Inscorp products, and the plan to leverage their visits as a means of increasing sales will be quite likely to fail.

C   The beliefs of Inscorp's competitors are irrelevant to the question of whether soliciting visits from ex-customers will be a good way to boost sales.

D   Discounts for Inscorp's customers have no bearing on whether inviting ex-customers to visit will produce sales.

E   Inscorp's new products and services may conceivably help boost sales, but that fact does not cast doubt on the effectiveness of the plan to invite former customers to the booth.

The correct answer is B.

774. Fish currently costs about the same at seafood stores throughout Eastville and its surrounding suburbs. Seafood stores buy fish from the same wholesalers and at the same prices, and other business expenses have also been about the same. But new tax breaks will substantially lower the cost of doing business within the city. Therefore, in the future, profit margins will be higher at seafood stores within the city than at suburban seafood stores.

For the purposes of evaluating the argument, it would be most useful to know whether

(A) more fish wholesalers are located within the city than in the surrounding suburbs

(B) any people who currently own seafood stores in the suburbs surrounding Eastville will relocate their businesses nearer to the city

(C) the wholesale price of fish is likely to fall in the future

(D) fish has always cost about the same at seafood stores throughout Eastville and its surrounding suburbs

(E) seafood stores within the city will in the future set prices that are lower than those at suburban seafood stores

Argument Evaluation

Situation   Fish costs are comparable at stores within the city of Eastville and stores in its suburbs. In other respects, namely wholesale prices and other expenses, stores in the two categories are also comparable. However, new tax breaks will lower costs for businesses in the city, so the argument concludes that fish stores within the city will soon have higher profit margins than those outside.

Reasoning   *What additional factor could affect the prediction that seafood stores in the city will soon have higher profit margins than suburban stores do?* The prediction is based on a single factor: stores in the city will get tax breaks that lower their costs. If all other factors affecting profit margins remained constant, then it would be reasonable to conclude that lower costs would lead to higher profits. If, on the other hand, other factors changed along with the changing costs—for example, if the city stores passed on their new savings to customers in the form of lower prices—then that would tend to undermine the argument's prediction.

A   The number of wholesalers in each location has no bearing on the profit margins of city versus suburban stores.

B   Moving suburban stores closer to the city would have no effect, since the tax break only applies within city limits, nor would it affect the profit margins of city stores.

C   Falling wholesale fish prices would benefit both city and suburban stores and therefore not affect the argument that city stores will have higher profit margins than suburban stores will.

D   The prices of fish in the past would not inform the prediction that city stores will gain higher profit margins because of the tax break.

E   **Correct.** In order to evaluate the argument, it would be helpful to know if there are any other potential changes *besides* the tax breaks that could affect the city stores' profit margins relative to those of suburban stores. If, for example, the city stores lower their prices in response to the decrease in their costs, and suburban stores don't lower prices, then their relative profit margins might stay constant.

The correct answer is E.

775. **During the past year, Pro-Tect Insurance Company's total payouts on car-theft claims were larger than the company can afford to sustain.** Pro-Tect cannot reduce the number of car-theft policies it carries, so it cannot protect itself against continued large payouts that way. Therefore, **Pro-Tect has decided to offer a discount to holders of car-theft policies whose cars have antitheft devices.** Many policyholders will respond to the discount by installing antitheft devices, since the amount of the discount will within two years typically more than cover the cost of installation. Thus, because cars with antitheft devices are rarely stolen, Pro-Tect's plan is likely to reduce its annual payouts.

In the argument above, the two portions in **boldface** play which of the following roles?

(A) The first provides evidence in support of the main conclusion of the argument; the second is that conclusion.

(B) The first presents a problem a response to which the argument assesses; the second is that response.

(C) The first poses a problem for which the argument suggests a possible solution; the second is a conclusion that the argument draws in the course of supporting that possible solution.

(D) The first raises a consideration that the argument takes as weighing against the effectiveness of a certain policy; the second is that policy.

(E) The first presents a circumstance whose explanation is the issue the argument addresses; the second is an explanation that the argument rejects.

Argument Construction

Situation An insurance company has been obliged to pay car-theft claims at a rate it cannot afford to continue. Because carrying fewer car-theft policies is not an option, the company has decided instead to offer incentives for policy-holders to install antitheft devices. The incentive is sufficient to make the installation cost-effective within two years, and is therefore likely to be popular with policy-holders. The argument concludes that, because the antitheft devices are quite effective, the insurance company's plan is likely to succeed in reducing its annual payouts for car theft.

Reasoning *What role do the portions in* **boldface** *play relative to the argument that the plan will probably succeed?* The first portion states the problem confronting the insurance company: it cannot afford to continue paying out car-theft claims at the same rate. The argument goes on to assess a possible response to the problem, namely incentivizing policy-holders to install antitheft devices in their cars; this response is described in the second **boldfaced** portion.

A The first portion states the problem rather than presenting evidence for anything; the second portion outlines a solution for the problem rather than being the conclusion.

B **Correct.** The first portion states the problem confronting the insurance company: unaffordable payouts for car theft. The second portion states a response the company hopes will solve that problem: incentivizing antitheft devices. The argument assesses that proposed solution and concludes it is likely to succeed.

C The first portion does state a problem for which the argument discusses a solution, but the second portion is not a conclusion; rather it is the proposed solution itself.

D The first portion, which outlines the problem of unaffordable payouts, does not weigh against the effectiveness of the proposed policy, designed to reduce those payouts, which is described in the second portion.

E The argument in no way attempts to explain the reason for the high payouts for car theft, and the second portion does nothing to explain why the payouts are so high in any case.

The correct answer is B.

776. Ecologist: The Scottish Highlands were once the site of extensive forests, but these forests have mostly disappeared and been replaced by peat bogs. The common view is that **the Highlands' deforestation was caused by human activity, especially agriculture.** However, agriculture began in the Highlands less than 2,000 years ago. Peat bogs, which consist of compressed decayed vegetable matter, build up by only about one foot per 1,000 years and, **throughout the Highlands, remains of trees in peat bogs are almost all at depths greater than four feet.** Since climate changes that occurred between 7,000 and 4,000 years ago favored the development of peat bogs rather than the survival of forests, the deforestation was more likely the result of natural processes than of human activity.

In the ecologist's argument, the two portions in **boldface** play which of the following roles?

(A) The first is a position that the ecologist rejects; the second is evidence offered in support of that rejection.

(B) The first is a position that the ecologist rejects; the second is evidence that has been used to support the position the ecologist rejects.

(C) The first is a position that the ecologist seeks to defend; the second is evidence that has been used against that position.

(D) The first is a position that the ecologist seeks to defend; the second provides evidence in support of that position.

(E) The first is an explanation, rejected by the ecologist, that has been offered for a certain finding; the second is that finding.

Argument Construction

Situation An ecologist states that the formerly widespread forests of the Scottish Highlands have largely been replaced by peat bogs. The usual explanation for this change is that the forests were destroyed by human actions, especially clearing land for farming. The ecologist counters this explanation by stating that agriculture began in the region less than two thousand years ago, peat bogs accumulate at a rate of roughly one foot per thousand years, and tree remnants in the Scottish peat bogs are generally found deeper than four feet. The ecologist further states that climatic shifts over four thousand years ago were more favorable to the creation of peat bogs than to the continuation of forests, and concludes that natural forces, not human actions, were probably the cause of the change.

Reasoning *What role do the two **boldfaced** portions play in the argument that natural forces, not human activity, were likely the cause of the Highlands' deforestation?* The first portion is the position contested in the remainder of the argument, namely the claim that human activity, especially agriculture, was responsible for the Highlands' deforestation. The second portion is evidence that the position stated in the first portion is likely incorrect: the fact that tree remnants are typically found at depths greater than four feet in the peat strongly suggests that the deforestation occurred at least four thousand years ago, well before the advent of agriculture in the region.

A **Correct.** The first portion is an explanation for the Highlands' deforestation, namely human activity, that is contested in the remainder of the argument; the second portion provides a basis for rejecting that explanation: the evidence suggests that deforestation occurred too early for agriculture to have been the cause.

B The first portion is an explanation for the Highlands' deforestation, namely human activity, that the argument rejects, but the second portion supports the argument's position and not the opposing position.

C The ecologist rejects, not defends, the position advanced in the first portion, but the second portion is indeed evidence against that position.

D The ecologist rejects, not defends, the position advanced in the first portion, and the second portion is evidence against, not for, that position.

E The first portion is indeed an explanation rejected by the ecologist, namely that humans caused deforestation, though deforestation is not a "finding" per se but a readily observable fact; the second portion can be characterized as a finding, but the first portion does not explain it.

The correct answer is A.

777. In Gandania, where the government has a monopoly on tobacco sales, the incidence of smoking-related health problems has risen steadily for the last twenty years, and health care costs to the government have risen correspondingly. The health secretary recently proposed a series of laws aimed at halting tobacco use in Gandania. Fully ten percent of the annual revenues Gandania receives come from tobacco sales, however, so Gandania cannot afford to institute the proposed laws.

Which of the following is an assumption on which the argument depends?

(A) If the health secretary's proposal is not implemented, the health secretary will be obliged in the near future either to resign or to present an alternative proposal.

(B) If smoking is halted in Gandania, Gandania's smoking-related health care costs will not soon decrease enough to offset the projected loss of revenue from tobacco sales.

(C) The proposed laws are not likely to cause a significant decrease in the amount of tobacco Gandania exports.

(D) The percentage of revenue Gandania receives from tobacco sales has remained relatively stable in recent years.

(E) In Gandania, government revenue from tobacco sales far surpasses that from any other source.

Argument Evaluation

Situation The Gandanian government has a monopoly on tobacco sales; tobacco-related health problems have been increasing, and this increase has obliged the government to pay for the resulting health care costs. There is a proposal from the health secretary intended to stop tobacco use in Gandania; however, because the government budget depends significantly on tobacco sales, the argument concludes that ending such sales would be unaffordable.

Reasoning *What assumption is implied by the conclusion that ending tobacco sales would be unaffordable?* The argument makes a logical leap: because the government relies financially on tobacco sales, ending such sales would be unaffordable. This leap implies the assumption that ending tobacco sales would not have financial *benefits* sufficient to offset the lost revenue.

A   There are no implicit assumptions regarding the fate of the health secretary.

B   **Correct.** The argument concludes that, because the government relies financially on tobacco sales, it cannot afford to discontinue them; however, the information mentions that the tobacco sales also lead to significant health care costs for the government. The argument therefore depends on an assumption that the savings derived from paying less for the treatment of tobacco-related illness would not be sufficient to offset the income lost from ending tobacco sales.

C   If the proposed laws increased tobacco exports, then that would undermine and not support the conclusion that the laws are unaffordable; however the argument makes no assumptions *specifically* regarding exports.

D   The argument does not rely on an assumption that tobacco sales have been stable, although there may be very slight support for that possibility implied by the degree to which the government depends on such sales.

E   The information states that ten percent of the government's income derives from tobacco sales, and it is not germane to the argument if other sources of income approach or surpass that figure.

The correct answer is B.

Questions 778–850 — Difficulty: **Hard**

778. Duckbill dinosaurs, like today's monitor lizards, had particularly long tails, which they could whip at considerable speed. Monitor lizards use their tails to strike predators. However, although duckbill tails were otherwise very similar to those of monitor lizards, the duckbill's tailbones were proportionately much thinner and thus more delicate. Moreover, to ward off their proportionately much larger predators, duckbills would have had to whip their tails considerably faster than monitor lizards do.

The information given, if accurate, provides the strongest support for which of the following hypotheses?

(A)   If duckbills whipped their tails faster than monitor lizards do, the duckbill's tail would have been effective at warding off the duckbills' fiercest predators.

(B)   Duckbills used their tails to strike predators, and their tailbones were frequently damaged from the impact.

(C)   Using their tails was not the only means duckbills had for warding off predators.

(D)   Duckbills were at much greater risk of being killed by a predator than monitor lizards are.

(E)   The tails of duckbills, if used to ward off predators, would have been more likely than the tails of monitor lizards to sustain damage from the impact.

Argument Construction

Situation   Duckbill dinosaur tails were like the tails of contemporary monitor lizards in that they were very long. They differed, though, in that their tailbones were much thinner and more delicate than monitor lizards' tailbones. Monitor lizards use their tails to strike predators. If duckbills did so, they would have had to whip their tails much faster, as their predators were proportionately much larger.

Reasoning   *Which hypothesis is most strongly supported by the given information?* The information states that duckbills would have had to whip their tails much faster than monitor lizards do to ward off their proportionately larger predators, but their tailbones were more delicate. It would be reasonable to conclude, then, that duckbills' tails would have been more likely to sustain damage if used to ward off predators than monitor lizards' tails are.

A   The information gives us little reason to be confident that duckbills would have been effective at warding off their fiercest predators even if they whipped their tails faster than monitor lizards do. Note that we are not even told how effective monitor lizards are at warding off particularly fierce predators.

B   The information gives us both a reason to think that duckbills might have used their tails to strike predators—their tails are similar in length to the tails of monitor lizards, which are used to strike predators—and reasons to think they might not have done so—their tailbones were much thinner and more delicate than monitor lizards' tailbones, and they would have had to whip their tails much faster than monitor lizards whip theirs. Therefore, the support for this answer choice is not very strong.

C   The information does give some modest support for the claim that duckbills' tails would not provide a particularly good defense against their predators. This suggests weakly that they had other defenses against their predators. Note, though, that this answer choice, as worded, entails that duckbills *did* use their tails as a defense; it was simply not the only defense. But the information on which we are to base the hypothesis is compatible with duckbills not having used their tails to ward off predators.

D   The information does not give much support for this answer choice. It could be that duckbills had other effective defenses against their predators. Perhaps they were fast or had sharp claws.

E   **Correct.** As noted above, duckbills would have had to whip their tails much faster than monitor lizards do to ward off their proportionately larger predators, but their tailbones were more delicate, so duckbills' tails would have been more likely to sustain damage if used to ward off predators than monitor lizards' tails are.

The correct answer is E.

779. In an attempt to produce a coffee plant that would yield beans containing no caffeine, the synthesis of a substance known to be integral to the initial stages of caffeine production was blocked either in the beans, in the leaves, or both. For those plants in which synthesis of the substance was blocked only in the leaves, the resulting beans contained no caffeine.

Any of the following, if true, would provide the basis for an explanation of the observed results EXCEPT:

(A)   In coffee plants, the substance is synthesized only in the leaves and then moves to the beans, where the initial stages of caffeine production take place.

(B)   In coffee plants, the last stage of caffeine production takes place in the beans using a compound that is produced only in the leaves by the substance.

(C)   In coffee plants, the initial stages of caffeine production take place only in the beans, but later stages depend on another substance that is synthesized only in the leaves and does not depend on the blocked substance.

(D)   In coffee plants, caffeine production takes place only in the leaves, but the caffeine then moves to the beans.

(E)   Caffeine was produced in the beans of the modified coffee plants, but all of it moved to the leaves, which normally produce their own caffeine.

Argument Evaluation

Situation   The synthesis of a substance integral to the initial production of caffeine was blocked only in the beans of some coffee plants, only in the leaves of others, and in both the beans and leaves of yet other coffee plants. No caffeine was found in beans from the plants in which the synthesis of the substance was blocked only in the leaves.

Reasoning   *Which claim would NOT form the basis for an explanation of the observed results?* There are many possible explanations. For instance, the results could be explained by any claim that indicates (1) that the substance integral to the initial production of caffeine is synthesized only in the leaves, or (2) that the substance is also produced in the beans but, when it is blocked from being produced in the leaves, that substance or the caffeine that is produced in the beans is entirely depleted from the beans. However, the observed results would *not* be explained by any claim that (1) indicates that the early stages of caffeine synthesis can occur in the beans, entailing that the crucial substance is present in the beans even when it is blocked in the leaves, and (2) provides no explanation for why blocking the crucial substance in the leaves would prevent the completion of the caffeine synthesis in the beans.

A   If a substance that is integral to the initial production of caffeine is produced only in the leaves, and that production has been blocked, then the observed results are to be expected.

B   If the last stage of caffeine production requires a compound that is produced in the leaves by a substance the synthesis of which is blocked in the leaves, then the observed results are to be expected.

C   Correct. Suppose the initial stages of caffeine production take place in the beans. The substance integral to those initial stages must therefore be present in the beans. But this does not tell us whether that substance is synthesized in the beans or elsewhere. It does tell us that some other substance that plays a part in the production of caffeine is synthesized in the leaves, but we are not told that the synthesis of that substance is blocked. Therefore, this answer choice does not give us reason to expect the observed results, and so does not serve as the basis for an explanation of those results.

D   Suppose we know that caffeine production in coffee plants takes place entirely in the leaves but at least some of the caffeine migrates from there to the beans. Then, if the synthesis of a substance that is integral to the initial production of caffeine is blocked in the leaves, it seems reasonable to expect the observed results.

E   If caffeine is normally produced in both the leaves and the beans of a coffee plant, but all the caffeine produced in the beans will migrate from the beans to the leaves if for any reason caffeine is not produced in the leaves, then it is reasonable to expect the observed results.

The correct answer is C.

780. Which of the following most logically completes the passage?

Laminated glass is much harder to break than the glass typically used in the windows of cars driven in Relnia. It is more difficult for thieves to break into cars with laminated glass windows than into cars with ordinary glass windows, and laminated glass windows are less likely to break in a collision. Nevertheless, considerations of security and safety do not unambiguously support a proposal to require that in Relnia all glass installed in cars be laminated glass, since _____.

(A) most people cannot visually distinguish laminated glass from the glass typically used for car windows

(B) a significant proportion of cars driven in Relnia are manufactured elsewhere

(C) some cars in Relnia already have laminated glass in their windows

(D) the rates of car theft and of collisions have both fallen slightly in Relnia in recent years

(E) there are times when breaking a car's window is the best way to provide timely help for people trapped inside

Argument Construction

Situation   Laminated glass is much more difficult to break than the glass that is typically used in car windows in Relnia and, when used in a car window, makes it harder for thieves to break into the car and is less likely to shatter in collisions.

Reasoning   *What claim, despite the given information, most helps support the conclusion that considerations of security and safety do not unambiguously support a proposal to require that in Relnia all glass installed in cars be laminated glass?* If there are any significant safety or security problems that would arise from having laminated glass, this would count against the proposal. For instance, sometimes it is essential to break a car's window to help people trapped in the car.

A   None of the security- or safety-related characteristics of laminated glass discussed in the argument depend on laminated glass being visually distinguishable from the glass typically used for car windows. Therefore, this answer choice does not help justify the conclusion and so would not logically complete the passage.

B   Even if most cars in Relnia are manufactured elsewhere, there may be no reason not to require that all glass installed in cars in Relnia be laminated glass.

C   Whether some cars, no cars, or all cars currently in Relnia have laminated glass in their windows is irrelevant to whether it is a good idea to require that all glass installed in cars in Relnia be laminated glass.

D   Even if rates of car theft and of collision have fallen, that does not mean they could not fall further if laminated glass were required. In fact, we are not told why they fell. Could it be that more cars in Relnia had windows made of laminated glass, and that this led to these reduced rates?

E   **Correct.** This answer choice provides a reason to think that sometimes, for the security or safety of passengers in cars, it might be better not to have all the windows of every car made of laminated glass. Therefore, it logically completes the passage.

The correct answer is E.

781. Consultant: **Ace Repairs ends up having to redo a significant number of the complex repair jobs it undertakes, but when those repairs are redone, they are invariably done right.** Since we have established that there is no systematic difference between the mechanics who are assigned to do the initial repairs and those who are assigned to redo unsatisfactory jobs, we must reject the hypothesis that mistakes made in the initial repairs are due to the mechanics' lack of competence. Rather, it is likely that **complex repairs require a level of focused attention that the company's mechanics apply consistently only to repair jobs that have not been done right on the first try.**

In the consultant's reasoning, the two portions in **boldface** play which of the following roles?

(A) The first is the consultant's main conclusion; the second provides evidence in support of that main conclusion.

(B) The first is evidence that serves as the basis for rejecting one explanation of a certain finding; the second is the consultant's own explanation of that finding.

(C) The first is a claim whose truth is at issue in the reasoning; the second provides evidence to show that the claim is true.

(D) The first presents a contrast whose explanation is at issue in the reasoning; the second is the consultant's explanation of that contrast.

(E) The first presents a contrast whose explanation is at issue in the reasoning; the second is evidence that has been used to challenge the consultant's explanation of that contrast.

Argument Construction

Situation   The following information is attributed to a consultant: Some complex repair jobs done by Ace Repairs have to be redone. The repairs, when redone, are usually successful. But the mechanics who do the initial repairs and any others who redo those repairs are, overall, competent to do the repairs successfully.

Reasoning   *What role in the consultant's reasoning do the **boldfaced** statements play?* The consultant's first sentence describes a phenomenon that could be puzzling and needs explanation. One might be inclined to argue that the mechanics who redo the repairs are more competent than those who did the initial repairs. But the second **boldfaced** statement rebuts this explanation by telling us that it has been *established* that there are no systematic differences in competence. The final sentence of the consultant's reasoning puts forward another explanation: that the redoing of a repair elicits from mechanics a higher level of focused attention than did the performance of the initial repair.

A   The first describes a puzzling phenomenon for which the consultant seeks an explanation. It is not presented as a conclusion, i.e., a statement that is asserted on the basis of other statements. The second is not a statement presented *in support of* the first; it gives an explanation offered by the consultant for the puzzling phenomenon described in the first **boldfaced** portion.

B   The first describes a puzzling phenomenon for which the consultant seeks an explanation, and it is not offered to show that a certain explanation does not fit. The second gives the consultant's own explanation of that finding.

C   The reasoning does not question the accuracy of the first **boldfaced** portion; that portion is a description of a phenomenon that the consultant believes needs explanation. The second is not meant as evidence to indicate that the first is true; rather, it is offered as an explanation for the puzzling phenomenon described in the first.

D   **Correct.** The first **boldfaced** portion contrasts the success of repairs that are redone with the failure of those repairs when they were first done. The second gives an explanation proposed by the consultant for the difference.

E   The first contrasts the success of repairs that are redone with the failure of those repairs when they were first done. Rather than giving evidence to challenge the consultant's explanation, the second provides that explanation itself.

The correct answer is D.

782. To reduce waste of raw materials, the government of Sperland is considering requiring household appliances to be broken down for salvage when discarded. To cover the cost of salvage, the government is planning to charge a fee, which would be imposed when the appliance is first sold. Imposing the fee at the time of salvage would reduce waste more effectively, however, because consumers tend to keep old appliances longer if they are faced with a fee for discarding them.

Which of the following, if true, most seriously weakens the argument?

(A) Increasing the cost of disposing of an appliance properly increases the incentive to dispose of it improperly.

(B) The fee provides manufacturers with no incentive to produce appliances that are more durable.

(C) For people who have bought new appliances recently, the salvage fee would not need to be paid for a number of years.

(D) People who sell their used, working appliances to others would not need to pay the salvage fee.

(E) Many nonfunctioning appliances that are currently discarded could be repaired at relatively little expense.

Evaluation of a Plan

Situation A government is considering requiring household appliances to be broken down for salvage when discarded. To cover the salvage costs, the government plans to charge a fee on appliance sales.

Reasoning *What would suggest that charging the fee at the time of salvage would less effectively reduce waste than charging the fee at the time of sale would?* The argument is that charging the fee at the time of salvage would reduce waste of raw materials because it would encourage consumers to keep their appliances longer before salvaging them. This argument could be weakened by pointing out other factors that might increase waste if the fee is charged at the time of salvage or reduce waste if the fee is charged at the time of sale.

A **Correct.** This suggests that charging the fee at the time of salvage rather than the time of sale would encourage consumers to discard their appliances illegally, thereby increasing waste of raw materials by reducing the proportion of discarded appliances that are salvaged.

B This factor would remain the same regardless of whether the fee was charged at the time of sale or the time of salvage.

C This might be a reason for consumers to prefer the fee be charged at the time of salvage rather than the time of sale, but it does not suggest that charging the fee at the time of salvage would reduce waste less effectively.

D This provides an additional reason to expect that charging the fee at the time of salvage would help reduce waste, so it strengthens rather than weakens the argument.

E This would give consumers an additional reason to keep using their old appliances and postpone paying a fee at the time of salvage, so it strengthens rather than weakens the argument.

The correct answer is A.

783. Increased use of incineration is sometimes advocated as a safe way to dispose of chemical waste. But opponents of incineration point to the 40 incidents involving unexpected releases of dangerous chemical agents that were reported just last year at two existing incinerators commissioned to destroy a quantity of chemical waste material. Since designs for proposed new incinerators include no additional means of preventing such releases, leaks will only become more prevalent if use of incineration increases.

Which of the following, if true, most seriously weakens the argument?

(A) At the two incinerators at which leaks were reported, staff had had only cursory training on the proper procedures for incinerating chemical waste.

(B) Other means of disposing of chemical waste, such as chemical neutralization processes, have not been proven safer than incineration.

(C) The capacity of existing incinerators is sufficient to allow for increased incineration of chemical waste without any need for new incinerators.

(D) The frequency of reports of unexpected releases of chemical agents at newly built incinerators is about the same as the frequency at older incinerators.

(E) In only three of the reported incidents of unexpected chemical leaks did the releases extend outside the property on which the incinerators were located.

Argument Evaluation

Situation   Last year, at two chemical waste incinerators, there were forty reported incidents involving unexpected releases of dangerous chemicals. Designs for proposed new incinerators include no additional safeguards against such releases. Therefore, increased use of incineration will likely make such releases more prevalent.

Reasoning   *What would undermine the support provided for the conclusion that leaks will become more prevalent if more chemical waste is disposed of through incineration?* The argument draws a general conclusion about chemical waste incineration from evidence about only two particular incinerators. This reasoning would be undermined by any evidence that the leaks at those two incinerators were the result of something other than insufficient safeguards against such releases.

A   **Correct.** If the staff training at the two incinerators was cursory, then the leaks may have been the results of staff not knowing how to use safeguards with which the incinerators are equipped that, if properly used, would have prevented the release of dangerous chemicals. Therefore, if staff at newer incinerators will be better trained, leaks might not become more prevalent even if chemical waste incineration becomes more common.

B   Other chemical waste disposal methods may be safer than incineration even if no one has proven so, and even if they're not safer overall, they may involve fewer leaks.

C   Continuing to use existing incinerators might well produce just as many leaks as switching to new incinerators would.

D   This suggests that new incinerators produce as many leaks as older incinerators do, a finding that provides additional evidence that increased incineration even with proposed new incinerators would lead to more leaks.

E   The argument is not about how far the releases from leaks extend, only about how many of them are likely to occur.

The correct answer is A.

784. Public health expert: **Increasing the urgency of a public health message may be counterproductive.** In addition to irritating the majority who already behave responsibly, **it may undermine all government pronouncements on health by convincing people that such messages are overly cautious.** And there is no reason to believe that those who ignore measured voices will listen to shouting.

The two sections in **boldface** play which of the following roles in the public health expert's argument?

(A) The first is a conclusion for which support is provided, but it is not the argument's main conclusion; the second is an unsupported premise supporting the argument's main conclusion.

(B) The first is a premise supporting the only explicit conclusion; so is the second.

(C) The first is the argument's main conclusion; the second supports that conclusion and is itself a conclusion for which support is provided.

(D) The first is a premise supporting the argument's only conclusion; the second is that conclusion.

(E) The first is the argument's only explicit conclusion; the second is a premise supporting that conclusion.

Argument Construction

Situation   A public health expert argues against increasing the urgency of public health messages by pointing out negative effects that may arise from such an increase, as well as by questioning its efficacy.

Reasoning   *What roles are played in the argument by the two claims in* **boldface**? The first claim in **boldface** states that increasing the urgency of public health messages may be counterproductive. After making this claim, the public health expert mentions two specific reasons this could be so: it could irritate people who already behave responsibly, and it could convince people that all public health messages are too cautious (the latter reason in the second claim in **boldface**.) The phrase *[i]n addition to* indicates that neither claim in the second sentence is intended to support or explain the other. However, since each claim in the second sentence gives a reason to believe the claim in the first sentence, each independently supports the first sentence as a conclusion. The word *[a]nd* beginning the third sentence reveals that its intended role in the argument is the same as that of the two claims in the second sentence.

A   Everything stated after the first sentence is intended to help support it, so the first sentence is the argument's main conclusion.

B   Everything stated after the first sentence is intended to help support it, so the first sentence is a conclusion, not a premise.

C   Each of the three claims in the second and third sentences is presented as an independent reason to accept the general claim in the first sentence. Therefore, nothing in the passage is intended to support the second statement in **boldface** as a conclusion.

D   Everything stated after the first sentence is intended to help support it, so the first sentence is a conclusion, not a premise.

E   **Correct.** Each of the three claims in the second and third sentences is presented as an independent reason to accept the general claim in the first sentence. Thus, each of those claims is a premise supporting the claim in the first sentence as the argument's only conclusion.

The correct answer is E.

785. Which of the following most logically completes the passage?

According to the last pre-election poll in Whippleton, most voters believe that the three problems government needs to address, in order of importance, are pollution, crime, and unemployment. Yet in the election, candidates from parties perceived as strongly against pollution were defeated, while those elected were all from parties with a history of opposing legislation designed to reduce pollution. These results should not be taken to indicate that the poll was inaccurate, however, since _____.

(A)   some voters in Whippleton do not believe that pollution needs to be reduced

(B)   every candidate who was defeated had a strong antipollution record

(C)   there were no issues other than crime, unemployment, and pollution on which the candidates had significant differences of opinion

(D)   all the candidates who were elected were perceived as being stronger against both crime and unemployment than the candidates who were defeated

(E)   many of the people who voted in the election refused to participate in the poll

Argument Construction

Situation   A pre-election poll indicated that most voters believed the three problems government needs to address, in order of importance, are pollution, crime, and unemployment. But in the election, candidates from parties with a history of opposing antipollution legislation beat candidates from parties perceived as more strongly against pollution.

Reasoning   *What would most help explain how the poll might have been accurate despite the election results?* Since the poll indicated that voters were most concerned about pollution, it suggested that candidates from antipollution parties would be more likely to be elected, other things being equal—and yet those candidates were not elected. There are many possible explanations for this outcome that are compatible with the poll having been accurate. For example, voters might have been swayed by the candidates' personalities, qualifications, or advertising more than by their positions on the issues. Or some candidates might have convinced voters that their personal positions on the issues were different from those of their parties. Or voters might have chosen candidates based on their positions on crime and unemployment, considering those issues together more important than pollution alone. Any statement suggesting that any such factors explained the election results would logically complete the passage by providing a reason to believe that the poll could have been accurate despite those results.

A   If the number of voters who did not believe that pollution needed to be reduced was large enough to explain the election results, then the poll was probably inaccurate. So, this does not explain how the poll might have been accurate despite those results.

B   This eliminates the possibility that candidates were defeated for having weak antipollution records conflicting with their parties' antipollution stances, so it eliminates one explanation of how the poll might have been accurate despite the election results. Thus, it slightly weakens the conclusion of the argument instead of providing a premise to support it.

C   This eliminates the possibility that differences of opinion among the candidates on these other issues might explain the election results, but it does not explain how the poll could have been accurate despite the election results.

D   Correct. The poll indicated that voters believed that the government needs to address crime and unemployment as well as pollution. So, if the poll was accurate, the election outcome might have resulted from voters considering candidates' positions on crime and unemployment to be jointly more important than their positions on pollution.

E   If anything, this provides a reason to doubt that the poll accurately reflected voters' opinions. It does not explain how the poll might have accurately reflected those opinions despite the election results.

The correct answer is D.

786. Manufacturing plants in Arundia have recently been acquired in substantial numbers by investors from abroad. Arundian politicians are proposing legislative action to stop such investment, justifying the proposal by arguing that foreign investors, opportunistically exploiting a recent fall in the value of the Arundian currency, were able to buy Arundian assets at less than their true value.

Which of the following, if true, casts the most serious doubt on the adequacy of the Arundian politicians' justification for the proposed legislation?

(A) The Arundian government originally welcomed the fall in the value of the Arundian currency because the fall made Arundian exports more competitive on international markets.

(B) Foreign investors who acquired Arundian manufacturing plants generally did so with no intention of keeping and running those plants over the long term.

(C) Without the recent fall in the value of the Arundian currency, many of the Arundian assets bought by foreign investors would have been beyond the financial reach of those investors.

(D) In Concordia, a country broadly similar to Arundia, the share of manufacturing assets that is foreign-controlled is 60 percent higher than it is in Arundia.

(E) The true value of an investment is determined by the value of the profits from it, and the low value of the Arundian currency has depressed the value of any profits earned by foreign investors from Arundian assets.

Argument Evaluation

Situation After a recent fall in the value of Arundian currency, foreign investors have been acquiring many Arundian manufacturing plants. Arundian politicians are proposing legislation to stop such investment.

Reasoning *What would most undermine the Arundian politicians' justification for the proposed legislation?* The politicians are justifying their proposal by claiming that foreign investors have been exploiting the fall in the currency's value by buying Arundian assets at less than their *true value* (whatever that means). Any evidence that their claim is false or meaningless would undermine their justification for the proposal, as would any evidence that the claim, even if true, does not provide a good reason to stop the foreign investments.

A This suggests that the foreign investors got a good deal on the manufacturing plants, since it provides evidence that those plants will now be more competitive and profitable. So, if anything, it supports the politicians' justification for their proposal rather than undermining it.

B This suggests that the foreign investors generally believe the manufacturing plants are undervalued and intend to sell them at a profit as soon as the currency rises enough. So, it supports the politicians' justification for their proposal rather than undermining it.

C This suggests that the recent fall in the currency's value made Arundian assets cost less than usual for foreign investors, thus arguably allowing the investors to buy the assets at less than their *true value*. So, if anything, it supports the politicians' justification for their proposal rather than undermining it.

D The Arundian politicians might consider the example of Concordia to be a warning of the disaster that could befall Arundia unless the legislation is enacted. So, the situation in Concordia might be cited as support for the politicians' justification of their proposal.

E **Correct.** This implies that the fall in the Arundian currency's value has reduced the *true value* of Arundian manufacturing plants and any profits they may make, so it undermines the politicians' claim that the foreign investors exploited the fall in the currency's value to acquire the plants for less than their *true value*.

The correct answer is E.

787. Proposed new safety rules for the Beach City airport would lengthen considerably the minimum time between takeoffs from the airport. In consequence, the airport would be able to accommodate 10 percent fewer flights than currently use the airport daily. The city's operating budget depends heavily on taxes generated by tourist spending, and most of the tourists come by plane. Therefore, the proposed new safety rules, if adopted, will reduce the revenue available for the operating budget.

The argument depends on assuming which of the following?

(A) There are no periods of the day during which the interval between flights taking off from the airport is significantly greater than the currently allowed minimum.

(B) Few, if any, of the tourists who use the Beach City airport do so when their main destination is a neighboring community and not Beach City itself.

(C) If the proposed safety rules are adopted, the reduction in tourist numbers will not result mainly from a reduction in the number of tourists who spend relatively little in Beach City.

(D) Increasing the minimum time between takeoffs is the only way to achieve necessary safety improvements without a large expenditure by the city government on airport enhancements.

(E) The response to the adoption of the new safety rules would not include an increase in the number of passengers per flight.

Argument Construction

Situation   Proposed safety rules for a city airport would reduce the number of daily flights the airport can accommodate. The city's operating budget depends heavily on taxes generated by tourists, who mostly come by plane. Therefore, adopting the safety rules will result in lower revenue available for the operating budget.

Reasoning   *What must be true in order for the cited facts to support the conclusion that the proposed rules would reduce the revenue for the operating budget?* The implicit reasoning is that since the rules would reduce the number of flights that can be accommodated, they would thereby reduce the number of tourists arriving by plane, which in turn would reduce the tax revenue that tourist spending generates for the operating budget. This assumes that the actual number of daily flights would fall along with the number that the airport can accommodate; that fewer daily flights would mean fewer people flying into the airport; that fewer people flying into the airport would mean fewer tourists flying into the airport; that fewer tourists flying into the airport would mean fewer tourists visiting the city; that fewer tourists visiting the city would mean less taxable spending by tourists; and that less taxable spending by tourists would mean less revenue overall for the operating budget.

A   Even if flights depart the airport less frequently during some periods of the day, increasing the minimum time between flights at busy times of day could reduce the total number of daily flights from the airport.

B   Even if half the tourists flying into the airport were bound for other nearby towns, the other half could still spend enough in town to generate lots of revenue for the operating budget.

C   It is possible that most tourists spend relatively little in the city, but a few spend a lot. In that case, even if a reduction in tourist numbers resulted mainly from a declining number of tourists who spend relatively little, it could also greatly reduce the already small number of tourists who spend a lot.

D   This suggests that the proposed rules might be financially better for the city than any alternative way to improve safety, whereas the argument's conclusion is that the proposed rules are financially disadvantageous.

E   **Correct.** If adopting the proposed rules would result in a large increase in the number of passengers per flight, fewer daily flights would not necessarily mean fewer passengers or fewer tourists overall.

The correct answer is E.

788. The introduction of new drugs into the market is frequently prevented by a shortage of human subjects for the clinical trials needed to show that the drugs are safe and effective. Since the lives and health of people in future generations may depend on treatments that are currently experimental, practicing physicians are morally in the wrong when, in the absence of any treatment proven to be effective, they fail to encourage suitable patients to volunteer for clinical trials.

Which of the following, if true, casts most doubt on the conclusion of the argument?

(A) Many drugs undergoing clinical trials are intended for the treatment of conditions for which there is currently no effective treatment.

(B) Patients do not share the physician's professional concern for public health, but everyone has a moral obligation to alleviate suffering when able to do so.

(C) Usually, half the patients in a clinical trial serve as a control group and receive a nonactive drug in place of the drug being tested.

(D) An experimental drug cannot legally be made available to patients unless those patients are subjects in clinical trials of the drug.

(E) Physicians have an overriding moral and legal duty to care for the health and safety of their current patients.

Argument Evaluation

Situation A shortage of human subjects for clinical trials needed to show that new drugs are safe and effective often prevents those drugs from being introduced into the market. The lives and health of future generations may depend on treatments that are now experimental.

Reasoning *What would cast doubt on the judgment that doctors are morally obligated to encourage their patients to volunteer for clinical trials?* Note that the argument's conclusion, unlike its premises, is a moral judgment. This judgment could be cast into doubt by a moral principle that would be likely to conflict with it under the conditions described. For example, a principle suggesting that it is sometimes morally unacceptable for doctors to encourage their patients to volunteer for clinical trials would also suggest that they are not morally obligated to encourage their patients to volunteer for clinical trials, since anything morally obligatory must also be morally acceptable.

A If anything, this highlights how important it is to ensure that these drugs undergo clinical trials to benefit future generations, so it supports rather than casts doubt on the argument's conclusion.

B This suggests that patients are morally obligated to volunteer for clinical trials to help prevent suffering in future generations. If anything, this supports the claim that doctors are morally obligated to encourage their patients to volunteer.

C The clinical trial will probably not harm any patients in the control group, yet their participation will benefit future generations. So, if anything, this supports the claim that doctors should encourage their patients to volunteer.

D This legal barrier makes it even more essential for the drugs to undergo clinical trials in order to benefit patients, so it supports rather than casts doubt on the argument's conclusion.

E **Correct.** Since the experimental drugs' safety is being tested during the trials, the drugs may prove unsafe for subjects in the trials. If doctors have an overriding moral duty to keep their current patients safe, then it may be morally unacceptable for them to encourage those patients to volunteer for the trials.

The correct answer is E.

789. As a construction material, bamboo is as strong as steel and sturdier than concrete. Moreover, in tropical areas, bamboo is a much less expensive construction material than either steel or concrete and is always readily available. In tropical areas, therefore, building with bamboo makes better economic sense than building with steel or concrete, except where land values are high.

    Which of the following, if true, most helps to explain the exception noted above?

    (A) Buildings constructed of bamboo are less likely to suffer earthquake damage than are steel and concrete buildings.

    (B) Bamboo is unsuitable as a building material for multistory buildings.

    (C) In order to protect it from being damaged by termites and beetles, bamboo must be soaked, at some expense, in a preservative.

    (D) In some tropical areas, bamboo is used to make the scaffolding that is used during large construction projects.

    (E) Bamboo growing in an area where land values are increasing is often cleared to make way for construction.

Argument Construction

Situation Bamboo is as strong as steel and sturdier than concrete when used as a construction material. In tropical areas, bamboo is much less expensive and is always readily available.

Reasoning *What explains the exception specified in the conclusion?* The argument's conclusion is that in tropical areas, bamboo is a more economical building material than steel or concrete, *except where land values are high*. The information in the passage makes clear why bamboo is a more economical building material in tropical areas than are concrete or steel. So the question is: Why must an exception be made for areas where land values are high? Multistory buildings are particularly desirable in areas where land values are high, but bamboo may not be suitable for such buildings.

A   This explains why bamboo would be preferable to steel or concrete in tropical areas especially prone to earthquakes. However, there is no clear connection to be made between areas where land values are high and areas especially prone to earthquakes.

B   Correct. Multistory buildings provide a greater area of floor space for a given site area, and in that sense are more economical. A single-story building with the same floor space will occupy a much bigger site, so the higher the land values, the more likely it is that a multistory building will be built on that land. Thus, given this information, bamboo is less suitable for areas where land values are high.

C   This undermines, to some extent, the claim that bamboo is an economical building material. But it does nothing to explain why it would be less economical specifically in areas where land values are high.

D   This is irrelevant. Bamboo is used to build scaffolding for construction projects and as a building material for permanent structures. There is no way to infer from this that bamboo is less economical specifically in areas where land values are high.

E   The fact that bamboo is cleared from an area to make room for construction in no way implies that bamboo would not be a suitable and economical building material for the area once it has been cleared.

The correct answer is B.

790. Newspaper editors should not allow reporters to write the headlines for their own stories. The reason for this is that, while the headlines that reporters themselves write are often clever, what typically makes them clever is that they allude to little-known information that is familiar to the reporter but that never appears explicitly in the story itself.

Which of the following, if true, most strengthens the argument?

(A) The reporter who writes a story is usually better placed than the reporter's editor is to judge what the story's most newsworthy features are.

(B) To write a headline that is clever, a person must have sufficient understanding of the story that the headline accompanies.

(C) Most reporters rarely bother to find out how other reporters have written stories and headlines about the same events that they themselves have covered.

(D) For virtually any story that a reporter writes, there are at least a few people who know more about the story's subject matter than does the reporter.

(E) The kind of headlines that newspaper editors want are those that anyone who has read a reporter's story in its entirety will recognize as clever.

Argument Evaluation

Situation   The headlines newspaper reporters write for their own stories are often clever only because they allude to little-known information that never appears explicitly in the stories themselves.

Reasoning   *What would most help the argument support the conclusion that newspaper editors should not allow reporters to write headlines for their own stories?* The argument's only explicit premise is that the headlines newspaper reporters write for their own stories are often clever only because they allude to little-known information that never appears explicitly in the stories themselves. In order for this premise to support the conclusion that newspaper editors should not allow reporters to write their own headlines, it would be helpful to be given a reason why editors should avoid headlines alluding to such little-known information.

A   This suggests that reporters are likely to write better headlines for their stories than editors are, so it weakens the argument that editors should not allow reporters to write their own headlines.

B   Since a reporter who wrote a story is likely to understand that story well, this does not provide a reason why editors should not allow reporters to write their own headlines.

C   If most reporters did what is suggested, they could perhaps hone their headline-writing skills—unless almost all reporters are weak in such skills, as suggested in the given information. The fact that they do not bother to do so may help explain why reporters' headline-writing skills are weak. An explanation of why this is so does not provide additional support for the argument's conclusion.

D   The people who know more about a story's subject matter than the reporter writing the story might be just as likely to see the cleverness of allusions to little-known information as the reporters are. So, to the extent that this is relevant at all, it slightly weakens the argument by suggesting that obscurely clever headlines sometimes function as intended.

E   **Correct.** The argument's explicit premise suggests that typically a reporter's headline for his or her own story cannot be recognized as clever by a reader who has read the whole story. So, if editors want headlines that anyone who has read the accompanying stories would recognize as clever, they have a reason not to let reporters write the headlines.

The correct answer is E.

791. Advertisement: Our competitors' computer salespeople are paid according to the value of the products they sell, so they have a financial incentive to convince you to buy the most expensive units—whether you need them or not. But here at Comput-o-Mart, our salespeople are paid a salary that is not dependent on the value of their sales, so they won't try to tell you what to buy. That means when you buy a computer at Comput-o-Mart, you can be sure you're not paying for computing capabilities you don't need.

Which of the following would, if true, most weaken the advertisement's reasoning?

(A) Some less-expensive computers actually have greater computing power than more expensive ones.

(B) Salespeople who have a financial incentive to make sales generally provide more attentive service than do other salespeople.

(C) Extended warranties purchased for less-expensive computers can cost nearly as much as the purchase price of the computer.

(D) Comput-o-Mart is open only limited hours, which makes it more difficult for many shoppers to buy computers there than at other retail stores.

(E) Comput-o-Mart does not sell any computers that support only basic computing.

Argument Evaluation

Situation   An advertisement states that other computer stores pay salespeople on commission. Since these salespeople receive a percentage of total sales, they have a motive to sell the most expensive computers possible to customers who might require only cheaper, and presumably less powerful, computers. Because Comput-o-Mart pays salaries rather than commissions, their salespeople are not motivated to sell unnecessarily expensive machines. Therefore, Comput-o-Mart shoppers can feel confident they are buying a machine targeted to their needs rather than a pointlessly powerful and more expensive model.

Reasoning   *What would undermine the argument that customers at Comput-o-Mart will not pay for needless computing power?* The advertisement relies on the suggestion that Comput-o-Mart will sell inexpensive, basic computers to those customers whose needs are basic. That argument is therefore weakened if Comput-o-Mart does not offer such basic, low-cost computers for sale.

A   The fact that price does not always correlate with computing power would not affect the argument that Comput-o-Mart will not sell needlessly expensive machines to its customers.

B   The fact that salaried salespeople might be less attentive has no bearing on the argument that such employees will not attempt to sell unnecessarily expensive computers.

C   The cost of warranties is not relevant to the argument that Comput-o-Mart will not upsell.

D   The relative business hours of different stores have no bearing on the question of whether Comput-o-Mart will sell basic machines to customers who require nothing more powerful.

E   **Correct.** The advertisement relies on the suggestion that Comput-o-Mart will sell a basic machine to a customer with basic needs rather than trying to induce them to buy a fancier, more expensive model; that argument is undermined if Comput-o-Mart has no such basic computers available for purchase.

The correct answer is E.

792. Proponents of the recently introduced tax on sales of new luxury boats had argued that a tax of this sort would be an equitable way to increase government revenue because the admittedly heavy tax burden would fall only on wealthy people, and neither they nor anyone else would suffer any economic hardship. In fact, however, 20 percent of the workers employed by manufacturers of luxury boats have lost their jobs as a direct result of this tax.

The information given, if true, most strongly supports which of the following?

(A) The market for luxury boats would have collapsed even if the new tax on luxury boats had been lower.

(B) The new tax would produce a net gain in tax revenue for the government only if the yearly total revenue that it generates exceeds the total of any yearly tax-revenue decrease resulting from the workers' loss of jobs.

(C) Because many people never buy luxury items, imposing a sales tax on luxury items is the kind of legislative action that does not cost incumbent legislators much popular support.

(D) Before the tax was instituted, luxury boats were largely bought by people who were not wealthy.

(E) Taxes can be equitable only if their burden is evenly distributed over the entire population.

Argument Construction

Situation   Proponents of a recently introduced tax on sales of new luxury boats argued that it would be an equitable way to increase government revenue because the tax would fall only on the wealthy and cause no economic hardship. But because of the tax, 20 percent of luxury-boat manufacturing workers have lost their jobs.

Reasoning   *What conclusion do the statements about the proponents' argument and the tax's effects support?* Since the tax caused many workers to lose their jobs, apparently the proponents were incorrect in asserting that it would cause no one to suffer any economic hardship. Thus, their justification for concluding that the tax is an equitable way to increase government revenue is factually inaccurate, casting doubt on that conclusion.

A   The passage indicates that the tax directly caused a significant decrease (though not necessarily a collapse) in the market for luxury boats. But the passage contains no evidence about whether such a decrease might not have occurred if the new tax had been somewhat lower.

B   Correct. Since the tax caused the workers to lose their jobs, it might have made the government lose revenue from payroll taxes that the laid-off workers would have paid if they had kept their jobs. So, if the yearly total revenue generated directly and indirectly by the tax were less than those total yearly payroll taxes and any other tax revenue that was lost as a result of the tax, the tax would have caused a net loss in tax revenue.

C   The passage contains no information about what types of legislative actions cost, or do not cost, incumbent legislators popular support.

D   Although the passage suggests that some of the tax proponents' assumptions were wrong, it contains no information suggesting that those proponents were wrong in thinking that luxury boats are purchased mainly by wealthy people.

E   The passage does not provide any basis for determining what makes a tax equitable or about whether the luxury boat tax is equitable. The tax's proponents evidently felt that a tax whose burden falls only on the wealthy rather than evenly on the entire population can be equitable.

The correct answer is B.

793. In the past, the country of Malvernia has relied heavily on imported oil. Malvernia recently implemented a program to convert heating systems from oil to natural gas. Malvernia currently produces more natural gas each year than it uses, and oil production in Malvernian oil fields is increasing at a steady pace. If these trends in fuel production and usage continue, therefore, Malvernian reliance on foreign sources for fuel is likely to decline soon.

Which of the following would it be most useful to establish in evaluating the argument?

(A) When, if ever, will production of oil in Malvernia outstrip production of natural gas?

(B) Is Malvernia among the countries that rely most on imported oil?

(C) What proportion of Malvernia's total energy needs is met by hydroelectric, solar, and nuclear power?

(D) Is the amount of oil used each year in Malvernia for generating electricity and fuel for transportation increasing?

(E) Have any existing oil-burning heating systems in Malvernia already been converted to natural-gas-burning heating systems?

Argument Evaluation

Situation   Malvernia has relied heavily on imported oil but recently began a program to convert heating systems from oil to natural gas. Malvernia produces more natural gas than it uses. Furthermore, Malvernia's oil production is expanding. Therefore, Malvernia will probably reduce its reliance on imported oils if these trends continue.

Reasoning   *Which option provides the information that it would be most useful to know in evaluating the argument?* In other words, we are looking for the option which—depending on whether it was answered yes or no—would either most weaken or most strengthen the argument. The argument indicates that Malvernia will be using less oil for heating and will be producing more oil domestically. But the conclusion that Malvernia's reliance on foreign oil will decline, assuming the current trends mentioned continue, would be undermined if there was something in the works that could offset these trends—for instance, if it turned out that the country's need for oil was going to rise in the coming years.

A   Since both domestic oil production and domestic natural gas production counteract the need for imported oil, it makes little difference to the argument whether domestic oil production exceeds domestic natural gas.

B   Whether there are many countries that rely more on foreign oil than Malvernia would have little impact on whether Malvernia's need for foreign oil can be expected to decline.

C   Since there is no information in the argument about whether Malvernia can expect an increase or decrease from these other energy sources, it does not matter how much they now provide.

D   Correct. This option provides the information that it would be most useful to know in evaluating the argument. As explained in the Reasoning section above, if Malvernia's need for oil rises in the coming years, the conclusion that Malvernia's reliance on foreign oil will decline is undermined.

E   The argument tells us that a program has begun *recently* to convert heating systems from oil to gas. So, even if no such conversions have been completed, the argument still indicates that they can be expected to occur.

The correct answer is D.

794. Exposure to certain chemicals commonly used in elementary schools as cleaners or pesticides causes allergic reactions in some children. Elementary school nurses in Renston report that the proportion of schoolchildren sent to them for treatment of allergic reactions to those chemicals has increased significantly over the past ten years. Therefore, either Renston's schoolchildren have been exposed to greater quantities of the chemicals or they are more sensitive to them than schoolchildren were ten years ago.

Which of the following is an assumption on which the argument depends?

(A) The number of school nurses employed by Renston's elementary schools has not decreased over the past ten years.

(B) Children who are allergic to the chemicals are no more likely than other children to have allergies to other substances.

(C) Children who have allergic reactions to the chemicals are not more likely to be sent to a school nurse now than they were ten years ago.

(D) The chemicals are not commonly used as cleaners or pesticides in houses and apartment buildings in Renston.

(E) Children attending elementary school do not make up a larger proportion of Renston's population now than they did ten years ago.

Argument Construction

Situation   Some children have allergic reactions to some of the chemicals commonly used in elementary schools as cleaners and pesticides. The number of children sent to elementary school nurses in Renston for allergic reactions to such chemicals has risen significantly over the past ten years.

Reasoning   *What must the argument assume?* The argument's conclusion presents just two alternatives: either the children are exposed to more of the chemicals than children in earlier years *or* they are more sensitive. But there is a third possible explanation for the significant increase in school-nurse visits that the school nurses have reported: that children are just more inclined to go to the school nurse when they experience an allergic reaction than were children several years ago. For the conclusion to follow from its premises, the argument must assume that this is not the correct explanation.

A   If the number of school nurses in Renston elementary schools had decreased over the past ten years, that would in no way explain the rise in the proportion of children reporting to school nurses for allergic reactions.

B   Only school-nurse visits for allergic reactions to the cleaners and pesticides used in elementary schools are in question in the argument. Of course there could be school-nurse visits for allergic reactions to other things, but that issue does not arise in the argument.

C   **Correct.** This can be seen by considering whether the argument would work if we assume that this were false, i.e., that a school-nurse visit *is* more likely in such cases. As noted above, this provides an alternative to the two explanations that the conclusion claims are the sole possibilities.

D   This does not need to be assumed by the argument. The argument's conclusion suggests that children may in recent years have had greater exposure to the chemicals, not that this exposure has occurred exclusively in the schools. The argument does not rely on this latter assumption.

E   The argument does not need to make this assumption. The argument is framed in terms of proportions of children having school-nurse visits for certain allergic reactions. *How many* children there are or what proportion such children are of Renston's total population is not directly relevant to the argument.

The correct answer is C.

795. Lockeport's commercial fishing boats use gill nets, which kill many of the netted fish, including some fish of endangered species. The fishing commission has proposed requiring the use of tent nets, which do not kill fish; boat crews would then throw back fish of endangered species. Profitable commercial fishing boats in similar areas have already switched over to tent nets. The proposal can therefore be implemented without economic harm to Lockeport's commercial fishing boat operators.

Which of the following, if true, casts the most serious doubt on the argument made for the proposal?

(A) In places where the use of tent nets has been mandated, there are typically fewer commercial fishing boats in operation than there were before tent nets came into use.

(B) Even when used properly, gill nets require many more repairs than do tent nets.

(C) Recreational anglers in Lockeport catch more fish of endangered species than do commercial fishing boats.

(D) The endangered species of fish in Lockeport's commercial fishing area did not become endangered as a result of the use of gill nets by fishing fleets.

(E) The endangered species of fish caught by Lockeport's commercial fishing fleet are of no commercial value.

Evaluation of a Plan

Situation   Gill nets, used by Lockeport's commercial fishing boats, kill some fish of endangered species. The fishing commission has proposed requiring the use of tent nets, which do not kill fish. This would allow the fish of endangered species to be thrown back. It is argued that the proposed requirement will not harm commercial fishing boat operators, since commercial fishing boats in other similar places are using tent nets and are profitable.

Reasoning   *What new piece of information would weaken the argument for the proposed requirement?* The crucial support given for the argument is that in other similar places, commercial fishing boats that use tent nets and not gill nets are profitable. But if, in places where only tent nets are now used, the numbers of commercial fishing boats diminished, it would be reasonable to suspect that switching entirely to tent nets may have driven some of the fishing operations out of business or caused them to move to other areas in which there was no expectation that they would use only tent nets.

A   **Correct.** This is new information. As explained above, it would justify doubt about the argument made in favor of the proposal.

B   This suggests that implementation of the proposed requirement could, over time, lower a certain type of operational costs for commercial fishing boats using tent nets. This would provide a new reason in support of the proposed requirement, not a reason to doubt the argument for it.

C   This suggests that perhaps recreational fishing in Lockeport needs to be regulated more strictly, but that is a separate issue from the one addressed in the argument for the proposed tent-net requirement.

D   This information casts no doubt on the relevance of the stated information that using gill nets contributes to undermining populations of at least some of the endangered fish species in Lockeport. If the species are currently endangered, they may need protection regardless of how they became endangered.

E   This information suggests that fish of the endangered species in Lockeport cannot profitably be sold. It does not cast doubt on the argument made in favor of the proposed requirement. Neither does it cast doubt on the practicality or the desirability of the proposed requirement.

The correct answer is A.

796. Last year Comfort Airlines had twice as many delayed flights as the year before, but the number of complaints from passengers about delayed flights went up three times. It is unlikely that this disproportionate increase in complaints was rooted in an increase in overall dissatisfaction with the service Comfort Airlines provides, since the airline made a special effort to improve other aspects of its service last year.

Which of the following, if true, most helps to explain the disproportionate increase in customer complaints?

(A) Comfort Airlines had more flights last year than the year before.

(B) Last year a single period of unusually bad weather caused a large number of flights to be delayed.

(C) Some of the improvements that Comfort Airlines made in its service were required by new government regulations.

(D) The average length of a flight delay was greater last year than it was the year before.

(E) The average number of passengers per flight was no higher last year than the year before.

Argument Construction

Situation Last year Comfort Airlines had twice as many delayed flights as it did the year before but three times as many passenger complaints about delayed flights. The airline made a special effort to improve other aspects of its service last year.

Reasoning *What could explain why the number of complaints about delayed flights increased disproportionately to the number of delayed flights last year?* In other words, why did the average number of passenger complaints per delayed flight go up last year? One obvious possibility is that the average number of passengers per delayed flight was greater last year than it had been the year before. Another is that the flight delays tended to cause worse problems for passengers last year than they had the year before, so that on average each delay was more upsetting for the passengers.

A   This helps explain why the airline had more delayed flights last year, but not why the increase in complaints about delayed flights was disproportionate to the increase in delayed flights.

B   This helps explain why the airline had more delayed flights last year. But, if anything, the situation should have reduced the number of passenger complaints per delayed flight, since many passengers should have realized that the unusually bad weather was not the airline's fault.

C   If any of the improvements concerned handling of flight delays, for example, and passengers were aware that government regulations addressed this, then passengers might have complained more than previously. But the information we are given here is too general and too vague to explain the disproportionate increase in complaints.

D   Correct. Longer flight delays would have more severely inconvenienced passengers and thus would probably have generated more passenger complaints per delay.

E   This rules out the possibility that an increased number of passengers per delayed flight could have caused the disproportionate increase in the number of complaints about delayed flights. But no alternative explanation is offered.

The correct answer is D.

797. Last year a global disturbance of weather patterns disrupted harvests in many of the world's important agricultural areas. Worldwide production of soybeans, an important source of protein for people and livestock alike, was not adversely affected, however. Indeed, last year's soybean crop was actually slightly larger than average. Nevertheless, the weather phenomenon is probably responsible for a recent increase in the world price of soybeans.

Which of the following, if true, provides the strongest justification for the attribution of the increase in soybean prices to the weather phenomenon?

(A) Last year's harvest of anchovies, which provide an important protein source for livestock, was disrupted by the effects of the weather phenomenon.

(B) Most countries that produce soybeans for export had above-average harvests of a number of food crops other than soybeans last year.

(C) The world price of soybeans also rose several years ago, immediately after an earlier occurrence of a similar global weather disturbance.

(D) Heavy rains attributable to the weather phenomenon improved grazing pastures last year, allowing farmers in many parts of the world to reduce their dependence on supplemental feed.

(E) Prior to last year, soybean prices had been falling for several years.

Argument Construction

Situation   A weather disturbance last year disrupted harvests worldwide but did not reduce production of soybeans, a protein source for both people and livestock. Soybean prices increased nonetheless, likely a result of the weather.

Reasoning   *What evidence would suggest that the weather disturbance caused the increase in soybean prices even though it did not reduce soybean production?* Prices tend to increase when the supply of a product falls relative to the demand for the product. But the production of soybeans did not fall. Evidence that the weather disturbance either hindered the global distribution of soybeans or increased global demand for soybeans could support the claim that the weather disturbance caused the increase in soybean prices.

A   **Correct.** If the weather disturbance reduced the anchovy harvest, and anchovies provide protein for livestock just as soybeans do, then more soybeans for livestock feed would be needed to compensate for the lack of anchovies. The resulting increase in demand for soybeans could thus have increased global soybean prices.

B   This is not surprising, given that the weather disturbance did not severely affect the soybean-producing countries, but it does not explain how the weather disturbance could have caused soybean prices to increase.

C   The rise in soybean prices after the earlier weather disturbance could easily have been a coincidence. Or, unlike last year's disturbance, the earlier disturbance could have reduced soybean production.

D   This suggests that demand for soybeans should have fallen as a result of the weather disturbance, so it does not explain why soybean prices rose.

E   If soybean prices were unusually low for some temporary reason when the weather disturbance occurred, they might have been likely to rise back to normal levels even without the weather disturbance.

The correct answer is A.

798. Most of the year, the hermit thrush, a North American songbird, eats a diet consisting mainly of insects, but in autumn, as the thrushes migrate to their Central and South American wintering grounds, they feed almost exclusively on wild berries. Wild berries, however, are not as rich in calories as insects, yet thrushes need to consume plenty of calories in order to complete their migration. One possible explanation is that berries contain other nutrients that thrushes need for migration and that insects lack.

Which of the following, if true, most seriously calls into question the explanation given for the thrush's diet during migration?

(A) Hermit thrushes, if undernourished, are unable to complete their autumn migration before the onset of winter.

(B) Insect species contain certain nutrients that are not found in wild berries.

(C) For songbirds, catching insects requires the expenditure of significantly more calories than eating wild berries does.

(D) Along the hermit thrushes' migration routes, insects are abundant throughout the migration season.

(E) There are some species of wild berries that hermit thrushes generally do not eat, even though these berry species are exceptionally rich in calories.

Argument Evaluation

Situation   Hermit thrushes are songbirds that usually eat insects but switch to eating berries when migrating. The thrushes need lots of calories to migrate, but berries contain fewer calories than insects do. Perhaps the berries contain nutrients that insects do not provide.

Reasoning   *What would cast doubt on the claim that the thrushes switch to berries because berries contain nutrients that insects lack and that the thrushes need for their migration?* Evidence that berries do not contain such nutrients or that thrushes do not decrease their net calorie consumption by eating berries would cast doubt on the proposed explanation. So would any evidence that supported an alternative explanation for the diet change during migration—for example, seasonal or regional differences in the amount or quality of berries or insects available for the thrushes to consume.

A   Even if thrushes need to be well-nourished to finish migrating before winter, extra nutrients found in berries but not insects might help provide the nourishment they need.

B   Even if insects contain *certain nutrients* not found in wild berries, those specific nutrients may not be the ones the thrushes need for their migration.

C   **Correct.** This suggests that the thrushes might gain more net calories from eating berries than from eating insects, which could explain why they switch to eating berries even if the berries contain no extra nutrients.

D   By ruling out a lack of insects to eat while migrating as an alternative explanation for why the thrushes switch to eating berries, this would support the proposed explanation.

E   The calorie-rich species of berries the thrushes do not eat might be poisonous or indigestible for them, even if the species of berries the thrushes do eat contain nutrients they need to migrate.

The correct answer is C.

799. The kinds of hand and wrist injuries that result from extended use of a computer while maintaining an incorrect posture are common among schoolchildren in Harnville. Computers are important to the school curriculum there, so instead of reducing the amount of time their students use computers, teachers plan to bring about a sharp reduction in the number of these injuries by carefully monitoring their students' posture when using computers in the classroom.

Which of the following would it be most useful to know in order to assess the likelihood that the teachers' plan will be successful?

(A) Whether extended use of a computer while maintaining incorrect posture can cause injuries other than hand and wrist injuries

(B) Whether hand and wrist injuries not caused by computer use are common among schoolchildren in Harnville

(C) What proportion of schoolchildren in Harnville with hand and wrist injuries use computers extensively outside the classroom

(D) Whether changes in the curriculum could reduce the schools' dependence on computers

(E) What proportion of schoolchildren in Harnville already use correct posture while using a computer

Evaluation of a Plan

Situation   Hand and wrist injuries from using computers while maintaining poor posture are common among schoolchildren in Harnville. Teachers plan to greatly reduce the number of such injuries by monitoring their students' posture while the students use computers in the classroom.

Reasoning   *What would be most helpful to know to determine the likelihood that the teachers' plan will succeed?* The primary concern is the *posture* students adopt while using computers. To succeed, the teachers' plan must reduce the time students spend with poor posture while using computers and reduce it enough to greatly reduce the number of injuries. To know how likely this is, it would help to know how effectively the teachers will be able to monitor and improve their students' posture inside the classroom. But how many of the students use computers *outside of school* while maintaining poor posture, and how often do they do so? If many students do so quite often, they may develop hand and wrist injuries regardless of what happens in school.

A   The teachers do not plan to reduce any injuries other than hand and wrist injuries, so whether computer use with poor posture causes any such other injuries is irrelevant to the likelihood that their plan will produce its intended effect.

B   The plan being discussed concerns only the reduction of hand and wrist injuries caused specifically by computer use with poor posture, so the frequency of hand and wrist injuries from other causes is irrelevant to the likelihood that the plan will produce its intended effect.

C   **Correct.** If the students' school use of computers is a large part of their overall computer use, any retraining that accompanies the monitoring might have some effect on their posture and related injury rates overall. However, the greater the proportion of children with hand and wrist injuries who use computers extensively outside the classroom, the more children are likely to keep developing the injuries regardless of any monitoring at school, so the less effective the teachers' plan involving only computer use at school is likely to be.

D   Knowing whether this is the case might help in developing a potential alternative to the teachers' plan, but if it did, this would not help significantly toward assessing the likelihood that the actual plan will succeed. The teachers' actual plan involves monitoring computer use in school without reducing such use. Other possible means of achieving the plan's goal are not part of the plan and are therefore irrelevant to the likelihood that the teachers' actual plan will succeed.

E   The passage indicates that the proportion of the schoolchildren maintaining poor posture while using computers is high enough for many to develop hand and wrist injuries as a result. Whatever the exact proportion is, the teachers' plan may or may not succeed in reducing it.

The correct answer is C.

800. Many people suffer an allergic reaction to certain sulfites, including those that are commonly added to wine as preservatives. However, since there are several winemakers who add sulfites to none of the wines they produce, people who would like to drink wine but are allergic to sulfites can drink wines produced by these winemakers without risking an allergic reaction to sulfites.

Which of the following is an assumption on which the argument depends?

(A) These winemakers have been able to duplicate the preservative effect produced by adding sulfites by means that do not involve adding any potentially allergenic substances to their wine.

(B) Not all forms of sulfite are equally likely to produce the allergic reaction.

(C) Wine is the only beverage to which sulfites are commonly added.

(D) Apart from sulfites, there are no substances commonly present in wine that give rise to an allergic reaction.

(E) Sulfites are not naturally present in the wines produced by these winemakers in amounts large enough to produce an allergic reaction in someone who drinks these wines.

Argument Construction

Situation   People who are allergic to certain sulfites can avoid risking an allergic reaction by drinking wine from one of the several producers that does not add sulfites.

Reasoning   *On what assumption does the argument depend?* Drinking wine to which no sulfites have been *added* will not prevent exposure to sulfites if, for instance, sulfites occur naturally in wines. In particular, if the wines that do not have sulfites added have sulfites present naturally in quantities sufficient to produce an allergic reaction, drinking these wines will not result in an allergic reaction. The argument therefore depends on assuming that this is not the case.

A   The argument does not require this because the conclusion does not address allergic reactions to substances other than sulfites.

B   The argument specifically refers to "certain sulfites" producing allergic reactions. It is entirely compatible with certain other forms of sulfites not producing allergic reactions in anyone.

C   This is irrelevant. The argument does not claim that one can avoid having an allergic reaction to sulfites *from any source* just by restricting one's wine consumption to those varieties to which no sulfites have been added.

D   Once again, the argument's conclusion does not address allergic reactions to substances other than sulfites in wine.

E   **Correct.** As explained in the Reasoning section above, the argument relies on the assumption that sulfites are not naturally present, in quantities sufficient to cause allergic reactions, in the wines to which no sulfites are added. If this assumption is not made, then the fact that no sulfites are added to certain wines is not a good reason to believe that people with sulfite allergies who consume the wines will not have an allergic reaction; if there are enough sulfites that naturally occur in the wine, people who consume the wine may well have an allergic reaction despite the fact that no sulfites have been added.

The correct answer is E.

801. A new law gives ownership of patents—documents providing exclusive right to make and sell an invention—to universities, not the government, when those patents result from government-sponsored university research. Administrators at Logos University plan to sell any patents they acquire to corporations in order to fund programs to improve undergraduate teaching.

Which of the following, if true, would cast the most doubt on the viability of the college administrators' plan described above?

(A) Profit-making corporations interested in developing products based on patents held by universities are likely to try to serve as exclusive sponsors of ongoing university research projects.

(B) Corporate sponsors of research in university facilities are entitled to tax credits under new federal tax-code guidelines.

(C) Research scientists at Logos University have few or no teaching responsibilities and participate little if at all in the undergraduate programs in their field.

(D) Government-sponsored research conducted at Logos University for the most part duplicates research already completed by several profit-making corporations.

(E) Logos University is unlikely to attract corporate sponsorship of its scientific research.

Evaluation of a Plan

Situation   Universities own the patents resulting from government-sponsored research at their institutions. One university plans to sell its patents to corporations and use the proceeds to fund a program to improve teaching.

Reasoning   *What would cast doubt on the university's plan?* The plan assumes that the university has been granted, and/or will be granted, patents for its inventions; that there will be a market for its patents; and that corporations will want to buy them. What might make this untrue? For example, the university's inventions might have no practical value or might be useful only for government agencies, and if some of the corporations have already done the same or similar research, they will likely not be prospective buyers of the university's patents.

A   This point is irrelevant to the plan to sell patents in order to fund a program.

B   The university plans to sell the patents to the corporations, not to invite the corporations to sponsor research.

C   This point is irrelevant to the university's plan to sell off patents since the plan does not specify that the research scientists will be involved in the programs to improve undergraduate teaching.

D   Correct. This statement properly identifies a factor that casts doubt on the university's plan. The plan presupposes that corporations will want to buy the rights to the inventions. If some of the corporations have already done the same or similar research, they would likely have developed ways of achieving what the university's inventions promise to achieve. In the case of potential future patents, they might even have already patented the inventions that the university would develop, in which case the university would be unable to patent them. Or the corporations might have developed similar, but not identical, inventions that serve the same purpose. In such cases, they probably would not need the university's inventions.

E   The plan concerns selling patents resulting from government-sponsored research, not attracting corporate sponsorship for research.

The correct answer is D.

802. Between 1980 and 2000, the sea otter population of the Aleutian Islands declined precipitously. There were no signs of disease or malnutrition, so there was probably an increase in the number of otters being eaten by predators. Orcas will eat otters when seals, their normal prey, are unavailable, and the Aleutian Islands seal population declined dramatically in the 1980s. Therefore, orcas were most likely the immediate cause of the otter population decline.

Which of the following, if true, most strengthens the argument?

(A) The population of sea urchins, the main food of sea otters, has increased since the sea otter population declined.

(B) Seals do not eat sea otters, nor do they compete with sea otters for food.

(C) Most of the surviving sea otters live in a bay that is inaccessible to orcas.

(D) The population of orcas in the Aleutian Islands has declined since the 1980s.

(E) An increase in commercial fishing near the Aleutian Islands in the 1980s caused a slight decline in the population of the fish that seals use for food.

Argument Evaluation

Situation   A sea otter population declined even though there were no signs of disease or malnutrition. The local seal population also declined. Orcas eat otters when seals are unavailable, and thus are probably the cause of the decline in the otter population.

Reasoning   *What would be evidence that predation by orcas reduced the sea otter population?* Disease and malnutrition are ruled out as alternative explanations of the decline in the sea otter population. The argument could be further strengthened by casting doubt on other possible explanations, such as predation by other animals, or by presenting observations that predation of otters by orcas would help to explain.

A   Regardless of whether or not orcas ate the sea otters, the sea urchin population would most likely have increased when the population of sea otters preying on them decreased.

B   Because the seal population declined during the initial years of the otter population decline, predation by and competition with seals were already implausible explanations of the otter population decline.

C   Correct. Orcas eating most of the accessible otters could plausibly explain this observation, which therefore provides additional evidence that orca predation reduced the sea otter population.

D   If the orca population declined at the same time as the sea otter population, it would be less likely that increasing predation by orcas reduced the otter population.

E   Since the sea otters showed no signs of malnutrition, they were probably getting enough fish. But if they were not, commercial fishing rather than orcas might have caused the otter population decline.

The correct answer is C.

803. Political strategist: The domestic policies of our opponents in Party X are contrary to the priorities of many middle-class voters. Yet some of these same voters are supporters of Party X and its candidates due to the party's appeals about foreign policy. In order to win these voters back, we in Party Y must prove to middle-class voters that Party X does not represent their priorities with respect to domestic policy.

Which of the following would, if true, most strongly suggest that the political strategist's plan is unlikely to succeed?

(A) Many in the middle class who support Party X for its foreign policies also support its domestic policies and are fully aware of the implications of those policies.

(B) Most middle-class supporters of Party X care about foreign policy and know very little about its domestic policies.

(C) Long-term domestic policy sometimes conflicts with short-term domestic policy.

(D) There are topics on which Party X and Party Y have significant agreement.

(E) Some middle-class voters are concerned about both domestic and foreign policy.

Evaluation of a Plan

Situation   A political strategist for Party Y notes that the domestic policies of Party X are contrary to the priorities of middle-class voters. Many middle-class voters nonetheless support Party X because of its foreign policy. The strategist argues that to win these voters back, Party Y should prove to middle-class voters that Party X's domestic policies do not represent their priorities.

Reasoning   *What claim would most strongly suggest that the strategist's plan will not succeed?* Suppose that a large number of the middle-class voters who support Party X's foreign policies also support its domestic policies, despite the fact that the domestic policies are contrary to their priorities. If that were true, then Party Y might well be unable to win back these voters by following the strategist's plan.

A   **Correct.** As noted above, if many middle-class voters who support Party X's foreign policies also support its domestic policies, the strategy of attempting to show these voters that there is a conflict between their priorities and Party X's domestic policies may well fail to get them to vote for Party Y. Presumably, these voters are aware of the conflict and support Party X nonetheless—perhaps because Party Y's domestic policies conflict with their priorities even more.

B   If most middle-class supporters of Party X know little about its domestic policies, Party Y may well be able to win them back simply by showing them the inconsistencies between those policies and their own priorities.

C   A conflict between long-term domestic policy and short-term domestic policy tells us nothing about whether educating middle-class voters about conflicts between their priorities and Party X's domestic policies would help win them back to Party Y.

D   The fact that the two parties have significant agreement on certain topics does not suggest the strategist's plan will not succeed. In fact, if the parties agreed on very little, the strategy of pointing only to issues related to domestic policy might be less likely to work. Therefore, this answer choice helps rule out a reason for thinking that the plan might not work.

E   If anything, this would help support the claim that the strategist's plan will succeed.

The correct answer is A.

804. Studies in restaurants show that the tips left by customers who pay their bill in cash tend to be larger when the bill is presented on a tray that bears a credit-card logo. Consumer psychologists hypothesize that simply seeing a credit-card logo makes many credit-card holders willing to spend more because it reminds them that their spending power exceeds the cash they have immediately available.

Which of the following, if true, most strongly supports the psychologists' interpretation of the studies?

(A) The effect noted in the studies is not limited to patrons who have credit cards.

(B) Patrons who are under financial pressure from their credit-card obligations tend to tip less when presented with a restaurant bill on a tray with a credit-card logo than when the tray has no logo.

(C) In virtually all of the cases in the studies, the patrons who paid bills in cash did not possess credit cards.

(D) In general, restaurant patrons who pay their bills in cash leave larger tips than do those who pay by credit card.

(E) The percentage of restaurant bills paid with a given brand of credit card increases when that credit card's logo is displayed on the tray with which the bill is presented.

Argument Evaluation

Situation Studies have found that restaurant customers give more generous tips when their bills are brought on trays bearing a credit-card logo. Psychologists speculate that this is because the logo reminds customers of their ability to spend more money than they have.

Reasoning *Which of the options most helps to support the psychologists' explanation of the studies?* The psychologists' hypothesis is that the credit-card logos on the trays bring to the minds of those who tip more the fact that they have more purchasing power than merely the cash that they have at hand. This explanation would not be valid even if those people who are not reminded of their own excess purchasing power—if in fact they have any such power—when they see such a logo nonetheless tip more in such trays. Thus, if restaurant patrons who are under financial pressure from their credit-card obligations do not tip more when their bills are presented on trays bearing credit-card logos, then the psychologists' interpretation of the studies is supported.

A This undermines the psychologists' interpretation, for it shows that the same phenomenon occurs even when the alleged cause has been removed.

B **Correct.** If the consumer psychologists' hypothesis is true, it implies that only those who do, in fact, have additional spending power in the form of credit will be influenced by the logos to leave larger tips. If those who do not have such additional spending power are influenced in the same way, the hypothesis is flawed. Answer choice B indicates that the hypothesis is not flawed in this way, so it thereby tends to strengthen the hypothesis. It also strengthens the hypothesis by weakening some alternative hypotheses such as the following: Most of the customers who pay with cash do so because they have excessive credit-card debt and cannot use a credit card. However, seeing a credit-card logo makes them wonder whether credit-card customers may leave larger tips, and to avoid displeasing the server by leaving a small tip, they decide to leave a larger tip than they might otherwise have done.

C This undermines the psychologists' interpretation by showing that the same phenomenon occurs even when the alleged cause has been removed; patrons cannot be reminded of something that is not there.

D To the extent that this bears on the interpretation of the study, it weakens it. Patrons using credit cards are surely aware that they have credit, and yet they spend less generously.

E This does not support the idea that being reminded that one has a credit card induces one to be more generous, only that it induces one to use that credit card.

The correct answer is B.

805. In an experiment, each volunteer was allowed to choose between an easy task and a hard task and was told that another volunteer would do the other task. Each volunteer could also choose to have a computer assign the two tasks randomly. Most volunteers chose the easy task for themselves and under questioning later said they had acted fairly. But when the scenario was described to another group of volunteers, almost all said choosing the easy task would be unfair. This shows that most people apply weaker moral standards to themselves than to others.

Which of the following is an assumption required by this argument?

(A) At least some volunteers who said they had acted fairly in choosing the easy task would have said that it was unfair for someone else to do so.

(B) The most moral choice for the volunteers would have been to have the computer assign the two tasks randomly.

(C) There were at least some volunteers who were assigned to do the hard task and felt that the assignment was unfair.

(D) On average, the volunteers to whom the scenario was described were more accurate in their moral judgments than the other volunteers were.

(E) At least some volunteers given the choice between assigning the tasks themselves and having the computer assign them felt that they had made the only fair choice available to them.

Argument Construction

Situation In an experiment, most volunteers chose to do an easy task themselves and leave a hard task for someone else. They later said they had acted fairly, but almost all volunteers in another group to which the scenario was described said choosing the easy task would be unfair, indicating that most people apply weaker moral standards to themselves.

Reasoning *What must be true in order for the facts presented to support the conclusion that most people apply weaker moral standards to themselves than to others?* One set of volunteers said they had acted fairly in taking the easy task, whereas different volunteers said that doing so would be unfair. In neither case did any of the volunteers actually judge their own behavior differently from how they judged anyone else's. So, the argument implicitly infers from the experimental results that most of the volunteers would judge their own behavior differently from someone else's if given the chance. This inference assumes that the volunteers in the second group would have applied the same moral standards that those in the first group did if they had been in the first group's position, and vice versa.

A **Correct.** If none of the volunteers who said their own behavior was fair would have judged someone else's similar behavior as unfair, then their relaxed moral judgment of themselves would not suggest that they applied weaker moral standards to themselves than to others.

B Even if this is so, the experimental results could still suggest that the volunteers would apply weaker moral standards to themselves than to others.

C The argument would be equally strong even if volunteers who were assigned the hard task did not know that someone else had gotten an easier task—or even if no volunteers were actually assigned the hard task at all.

D Even if the moral standards applied by the volunteers who judged themselves were as accurate as those applied by the volunteers to whom the scenario was described, the former standards were still weaker.

E Even if all the volunteers in the first group had felt that all the choices available to them would have been fair for them to make personally, they might have applied stricter moral standards to someone else in the same position.

The correct answer is A.

806. Country X's recent stock-trading scandal should not diminish investors' confidence in the country's stock market. For one thing, **the discovery of the scandal confirms that Country X has a strong regulatory system**, as the following considerations show. In any stock market, some fraudulent activity is inevitable. If a stock market is well regulated, any significant stock-trading fraud in it will very likely be discovered. This deters potential perpetrators and facilitates improvement in regulatory processes.

In the argument, the portion in **boldface** plays which of the following roles?

(A) It is the argument's only conclusion.

(B) It is a conclusion for which the argument provides support and which itself is used to support the argument's main conclusion.

(C) It is the argument's main conclusion and is supported by another explicitly stated conclusion for which further support is provided.

(D) It is an assumption for which no explicit support is provided and is used to support the argument's only conclusion.

(E) It is a compound statement containing both the argument's main conclusion and an assumption used to support that conclusion.

Argument Construction

Situation   Country X recently had a stock-trading scandal.

Reasoning   *What role does the statement that the scandal's discovery confirms that Country X has a strong regulatory system play in the argument?* In the sentence containing the **boldfaced** statement, the phrase *For one thing* indicates that the statement is being used to justify the claim in the preceding sentence. Thus, the **boldfaced** statement must support that preceding sentence as a conclusion. Directly after the **boldfaced** statement, the phrase *as the following considerations show* indicates that the subsequent sentences are being used to support the **boldfaced** statement. Thus, the **boldfaced** statement is a conclusion supported by the sentences following it, and this statement itself supports the sentence preceding it, which must be the argument's main conclusion.

A   As explained above, the **boldfaced** statement supports the claim in the preceding sentence, so it cannot be the argument's only conclusion.

B   **Correct.** As explained above, the **boldfaced** statement is supported by the statements following it and in turn is used to support the argument's main conclusion in the statement preceding it.

C   As explained above, the **boldfaced** statement cannot be the argument's main conclusion, because it supports a further conclusion presented in the sentence preceding it.

D   As explained above, the sentences following the **boldfaced** statement are the explicit support provided for it.

E   As explained above, the argument's main conclusion is stated only in the first sentence, which precedes the **boldfaced** statement. It is not repeated anywhere in the **boldfaced** statement.

The correct answer is B.

807. **Delta Products Inc. has recently switched at least partly from older technologies using fossil fuels to new technologies powered by electricity.** The question has been raised whether it can be concluded that, **for a given level of output, Delta's operation now causes less fossil fuel to be consumed than it did formerly.** The answer, clearly, is yes, since the amount of fossil fuel used to generate the electricity needed to power the new technologies is less than the amount needed to power the older technologies, provided level of output is held constant.

In the argument given, the two **boldfaced** portions play which of the following roles?

(A) The first identifies the content of the conclusion of the argument; the second provides support for that conclusion.

(B) The first provides support for the conclusion of the argument; the second identifies the content of that conclusion.

(C) The first states the conclusion of the argument; the second calls that conclusion into question.

(D) The first provides support for the conclusion of the argument; the second calls that conclusion into question.

(E) Each provides support for the conclusion of the argument.

Argument Evaluation

Situation   Delta switched from technologies using fossil fuels to ones using electricity. It has been asked whether this results in less fossil fuel used per level of output. The answer is that it does.

Reasoning   *What roles do the two **boldfaced** portions play in the argument?* The first **boldfaced** statement is simply asserted by the passage; no premise, or reason, is given to support it. But the second **boldfaced** statement, when it is first introduced, is not asserted to be true, but rather is identified as something that might be inferred from the first statement. By the end of the passage, the argument concludes that the second statement is true.

A   This option simply reverses the roles that the statements play in the argument.

B   **Correct.** This option identifies the roles the **boldfaced** portions play: The second statement is not, on its own, the conclusion, because the argument initially merely *asks* whether it can be concluded on the basis of the first statement—that is, it asks whether the first **boldfaced** statement provides support for it. The conclusion of the argument is actually the statement *The answer, clearly, is yes.* The word *yes* is elliptical for *Yes, it can be concluded that for a given level of output, Delta's operation now causes less fossil fuel to be consumed than it did formerly.* The **boldfaced** portion tells us what can be concluded, and thus it can accurately be described as the content of the conclusion.

C   Nothing in the passage is intended to support the first statement, and the second statement is not supposed to call the first into question.

D   This correctly identifies the role of the first statement, but the second **boldfaced** portion does not call the argument's conclusion into question—it is part of a sentence that refers to the question whether that conclusion can be drawn from the first statement.

E   Again, this is only half right. The second **boldfaced** portion is not offered as support for the conclusion; if it were offered as such support, the argument would be guilty of circular reasoning, since the second **boldfaced** portion states exactly what the argument concludes.

The correct answer is B.

808. Theater critic: The play *La Finestrina*, now at Central Theater, was written in Italy in the eighteenth century. The director claims that this production is as similar to the original production as is possible in a modern theater. Although the actor who plays Harlequin the clown gives a performance very reminiscent of the twentieth-century American comedian Groucho Marx, Marx's comic style was very much within the comic acting tradition that had begun in sixteenth-century Italy.

The considerations given best serve as part of an argument that

(A) modern audiences would find it hard to tolerate certain characteristics of a historically accurate performance of an eighteenth-century play

(B) Groucho Marx once performed the part of the character Harlequin in *La Finestrina*

(C) in the United States, the training of actors in the twentieth century is based on principles that do not differ radically from those that underlay the training of actors in eighteenth-century Italy

(D) the performance of the actor who plays Harlequin in *La Finestrina* does not serve as evidence against the director's claim

(E) the director of *La Finestrina* must have advised the actor who plays Harlequin to model his performance on comic performances of Groucho Marx

Argument Construction

Situation   The director of the local production of *La Finestrina* says it is as similar to the original production as is possible in a modern theater. The actor playing Harlequin gives a performance reminiscent of Groucho Marx, whose comic style falls within an acting tradition which began in sixteenth-century Italy.

Reasoning   *For which of the options would the consideration given best serve as an argument?* The actor's performance was reminiscent of someone who fell within a tradition going back to sixteenth-century Italy. The play was written, and therefore was likely first performed, in eighteenth-century Italy. All of this suggests that there could be a similarity between the performances of Harlequin in the local production and in the original production. While the two performances *might* have been quite dissimilar, there is nothing *here* that supports that.

A   Regardless of how plausible this option might be on its own merits, the passage provides no support for it because the passage provides no information about the characteristics of a historically accurate performance of an eighteenth-century play.

B   The passage neither says this nor implies it.

C   The passage says nothing about the training of actors, so this option would be supported by the passage only in a very roundabout, indirect way.

D   **Correct.** This is the option that the considerations most support.

E   That the performance reminded the theater critic of Groucho Marx hardly shows that the similarity was intentional, let alone that it was at the director's instruction.

The correct answer is D.

809. Although the discount stores in Goreville's central shopping district are expected to close within five years as a result of competition from a SpendLess discount department store that just opened, those locations will not stay vacant for long. In the five years since the opening of Colson's, a nondiscount department store, a new store has opened at the location of every store in the shopping district that closed because it could not compete with Colson's.

Which of the following, if true, most seriously weakens the argument?

(A) Many customers of Colson's are expected to do less shopping there than they did before the SpendLess store opened.

(B) Increasingly, the stores that have opened in the central shopping district since Colson's opened have been discount stores.

(C) At present, the central shopping district has as many stores operating in it as it ever had.

(D) Over the course of the next five years, it is expected that Goreville's population will grow at a faster rate than it has for the past several decades.

(E) Many stores in the central shopping district sell types of merchandise that are not available at either SpendLess or Colson's.

Argument Evaluation

Situation   Due to competition from a recently opened SpendLess discount department store, discount stores in Goreville's central shopping district are expected to close within five years. But those locations will not be vacant long, for new stores have replaced all those that closed because of the opening five years ago of a Colson's nondiscount department store.

Reasoning   *Which option would most weaken the argument?* The arguer infers that stores that leave because of the SpendLess will be replaced in their locations by other stores because that is what happened after the Colson's department store came in. Since the reasoning relies on a presumed similarity between the two cases, any information that brings to light a relevant dissimilarity would weaken the argument. If the stores that were driven out by Colson's were replaced mostly by discount stores, that suggests that the stores were replaced because of a need that no longer exists after the opening of SpendLess.

A   The fact that Colson's may be seeing fewer customers does not mean that the discount stores that close will not be replaced; they might be replaced by stores that in no way compete with Colson's or SpendLess.

B   **Correct.** As explained in the Reasoning section above, the reasoning in the argument relies on a presumed similarity between the two cases, so any information that brings to light a relevant dissimilarity would weaken the argument. In the previous five years, the stores that went out of business were apparently direct competitors of Colson's, whereas their replacements were of a different type. In contrast, in the predicted scenario, the stores that are expected to go out of business are apparently direct competitors of the new SpendLess discount store. Furthermore, if there has been a significant increase in the number of discount stores in the shopping district, the market for discount stores may well be nearly saturated, so that few, if any, new ones can survive.

C   If anything, this strengthens the argument by indicating that Goreville's central shopping district is thriving.

D   This strengthens the argument because one is more likely to open a new store in an area with a growing population.

E   Because this statement does not indicate whether any of these stores that offer goods not sold at SpendLess or Colson's will be among those that are closing, it is not possible to determine what effect it has on the strength of the argument.

The correct answer is B.

810. Last year all refuse collected by Shelbyville city services was incinerated. This incineration generated a large quantity of residual ash. In order to reduce the amount of residual ash Shelbyville generates this year to half of last year's total, the city has revamped its collection program. This year city services will separate for recycling enough refuse to reduce the number of truckloads of refuse to be incinerated to half of last year's number.

Which of the following is required for the revamped collection program to achieve its aim?

(A) This year no materials that city services could separate for recycling will be incinerated.

(B) Separating recyclable materials from materials to be incinerated will cost Shelbyville less than half what it cost last year to dispose of the residual ash.

(C) Refuse collected by city services will contain a larger proportion of recyclable materials this year than it did last year.

(D) The refuse incinerated this year will generate no more residual ash per truckload incinerated than did the refuse incinerated last year.

(E) The total quantity of refuse collected by Shelbyville city services this year will be no greater than that collected last year.

Argument Construction

Situation   To cut in half the residual ash produced at its incinerator, the city will separate, for recycling, enough refuse to cut in half the number of truckloads of refuse going to the incinerator.

Reasoning   *Which option is required if the city's revamped collection program is to achieve its aim?* Cutting the number of truckloads of refuse in half must reduce the amount of residual ash to half last year's level. But if removal of the recycled refuse does not proportionately reduce the amount of ash, this will not happen. So, if the amount of residual ash produced per truckload increases after recycling, then the amount of ash produced will not be cut in half by cutting in half the number of truckloads.

A   This merely indicates that no further reduction of ash through recycling could be achieved this year; it indicates nothing about how much the ash will be reduced.

B   This suggests a further benefit from recycling but does not bear on the amount of ash that will be produced.

C   Since no information is provided about how much, if any, recyclable materials were removed from the refuse last year, this does not affect the reasoning.

D   **Correct.** This states a requirement for the collection program to achieve its aim. To see why this is required, assume this were not true. Suppose, instead, that the refuse incinerated this year would generate more residual ash per truckload incinerated than the refuse incinerated last year did. If that were the case, then cutting in half the truckloads to be incinerated would not cut in half the amount of residual ash generated by incineration.

E   This is not a requirement because even if the city collects more refuse this year, it could still cut in half the amount of residual ash by cutting in half the number of truckloads going to the incinerator.

The correct answer is D.

811. Veterinarians generally derive some of their income from selling several manufacturers' lines of pet-care products. Knowing that pet owners rarely throw away mail from their pet's veterinarian unread, one manufacturer of pet-care products offered free promotional materials on its products to veterinarians for mailing to their clients. Very few veterinarians accepted the offer, however, even though the manufacturer's products are of high quality.

Which of the following, if true, most helps to explain the veterinarians' reaction to the manufacturer's promotional scheme?

(A) Most of the veterinarians to whom the free promotional materials were offered were already selling the manufacturer's pet-care products to their clients.

(B) The special promotional materials were intended as a supplement to the manufacturer's usual promotional activities rather than as a replacement for them.

(C) The manufacturer's products, unlike most equally good competing products sold by veterinarians, are also available in pet stores and in supermarkets.

(D) Many pet owners have begun demanding quality in products they buy for their pets that is as high as that in products they buy for themselves.

(E) Veterinarians sometimes recommend that pet owners use products formulated for people when no suitable product specially formulated for animals is available.

Evaluation of a Plan

Situation   Veterinarians generally derive some income from selling various manufacturers' pet-care products, but very few veterinarians accepted free promotional materials from one such manufacturer to mail to their clients.

Reasoning   *What would most help explain why so few veterinarians accepted the free promotional materials to mail to their clients?* The passage says that veterinarians generally derive income from selling pet-care products, which suggests that it should have been in many veterinarians' financial interest to accept and mail out the free promotional materials to increase sales. Any evidence that mailing out these specific promotional materials from this manufacturer would not actually have been in many veterinarians' financial interest could help explain why so few veterinarians accepted the materials.

A   This suggests that most of the veterinarians should have had a financial interest in accepting and mailing out the promotional materials in order to increase their sales of the manufacturer's products.

B   Even if the promotional materials supplemented the manufacturer's usual promotional activities, they could still have increased the veterinarians' sales of the manufacturer's products and thus generated more income for the veterinarians.

C   **Correct.** If this manufacturer's products are available in pet stores and supermarkets but most other products sold by veterinarians are not, then distributing the manufacturer's promotional materials could have encouraged customers to buy this manufacturer's products from pet stores and supermarkets rather than to buy competing products from the veterinarians. Thus, the veterinarians may have been concerned that the promotions would reduce their profits.

D   The passage says the manufacturer's products are of high quality, so we have no reason to suppose that clients' demand for quality products would discourage veterinarians from accepting the manufacturer's promotional materials.

E   Presumably the manufacturer's products are specially formulated for pets, so any products veterinarians recommend only when no specially formulated pet-care products are available would not reduce the veterinarians' interest in promoting the manufacturer's products.

The correct answer is C.

812. The average hourly wage of television assemblers in Vernland has long been significantly lower than that in neighboring Borodia. Since Borodia dropped all tariffs on Vernlandian televisions three years ago, the number of televisions sold annually in Borodia has not changed. However, recent statistics show a drop in the number of television assemblers in Borodia. Therefore, updated trade statistics will probably indicate that the number of televisions Borodia imports annually from Vernland has increased.

Which of the following is an assumption on which the argument depends?

(A) The number of television assemblers in Vernland has increased by at least as much as the number of television assemblers in Borodia has decreased.

(B) Televisions assembled in Vernland have features that televisions assembled in Borodia do not have.

(C) The average number of hours it takes a Borodian television assembler to assemble a television has not decreased significantly during the past three years.

(D) The number of televisions assembled annually in Vernland has increased significantly during the past three years.

(E) The difference between the hourly wage of television assemblers in Vernland and the hourly wage of television assemblers in Borodia is likely to decrease in the next few years.

Argument Construction

Situation   Television assemblers in Vernland are paid less than those in neighboring Borodia. The number of televisions sold in Borodia has not dropped since its tariffs on Vernlandian TVs were lowered three years ago, but the number of TV assemblers in Borodia has. So, TV imports from Vernland have likely increased.

Reasoning   *What assumption does the argument depend on?* The fact that fewer individuals in Borodia are working as TV assemblers is offered as evidence that TV imports from Vernland into Borodia have likely increased. That piece of evidence is relevant only as an indication that the number of TVs being produced within Borodia has decreased. But a drop in the number of TV assemblers does not indicate a drop in the number of TVs being assembled if the number of TVs an average assembler puts together has increased. Thus, the argument must be assuming that the average time it takes an assembler to put together a TV has not significantly decreased.

A   The argument does not rely on any information about the number of television assemblers in Vernland nor, for that matter, on the number of TVs assembled in Vernland.

B   The argument need not assume there is any difference in the features of the TVs produced in the two countries. Increased sales of Vernlandian TVs in Borodia could be due to any number of other reasons, such as price or quality.

C   **Correct.** If the average productivity of TV assemblers had increased significantly, the fact that there are fewer Borodian TV assemblers would not strongly support the conclusion that there has been a decrease in the number of TVs assembled in Borodia and an increase in imports; fewer assemblers may be producing just as many TVs as before. Therefore, for the argument to work, it needs to assume that productivity per assembler in Borodia has not decreased significantly.

D   The argument does not depend upon this being so: Vernland's domestic TV sales (or perhaps its exports to countries other than Borodia) may have decreased by more than its exports to Borodia have increased.

E   The argument's conclusion addresses what has happened; the argument in no way relies on any assumptions about what may or may not happen in the coming years.

The correct answer is C.

813. Guidebook writer: I have visited hotels throughout the country and have noticed that in those built before 1930 the quality of the original carpentry work is generally superior to that in hotels built afterward. Clearly, carpenters working on hotels before 1930 typically worked with more skill, care, and effort than carpenters who have worked on hotels built subsequently.

Which of the following, if true, most seriously weakens the guidebook writer's argument?

(A) The quality of original carpentry in hotels is generally far superior to the quality of original carpentry in other structures, such as houses and stores.

(B) Hotels built since 1930 can generally accommodate more guests than those built before 1930.

(C) The materials available to carpenters working before 1930 were not significantly different in quality from the materials available to carpenters working after 1930.

(D) The better the quality of original carpentry in a building, the less likely that building is to fall into disuse and be demolished.

(E) The average length of apprenticeship for carpenters has declined significantly since 1930.

Argument Evaluation

Situation   The original carpentry in hotels built before 1930 shows superior care, skill, and effort to that in hotels built after 1930. This leads to the conclusion that carpenters working on hotels before 1930 were superior in skill, care, and effort to those who came after.

Reasoning   *Which option most seriously weakens the argument?* The argument draws an inference from a comparison between carpentry in hotels of different eras to a judgment about the carpenters working on hotels in those eras. One way to weaken this inference is by finding some way in which the carpentry in the hotels may be unrepresentative of the skill, care, and effort of the carpenters working in the eras. The comparison is between the carpentry evident in hotels of the two eras *that still exist*. Thus, if there is some reason to think that hotels with good carpentry survive longer than those with bad carpentry, then still-existing hotels from the older era will have disproportionately more good carpentry, even assuming no difference between the skill, care, and effort of the carpenters from the two eras.

A   This option applies equally to both eras, so it has no bearing on the argument.

B   It is not clear whether carpenters working on larger hotels would exercise more, less, or the same skill and care as those working on smaller hotels; thus, this option does not weaken the argument.

C   The argument does not rely, even implicitly, on there being any difference in the quality of materials used in the two eras, so it does not weaken the argument to point out that no such difference exists.

D   **Correct.** This weakens the reasoning in the argument by showing a respect in which the comparison between *existing* hotels may be unrepresentative. Specifically, the comparison may be unrepresentative in that still-existing hotels that were built prior to 1930 may well have been better built than most hotels built prior to 1930 were; the hotels that did not have unusually high-quality carpentry work may have all fallen into disuse and been demolished.

E   The longer a carpenter works as an apprentice, the more skill he or she is apt to have upon becoming a full-fledged carpenter. So, this option would tend to slightly strengthen rather than weaken the argument.

The correct answer is D.

814. Most of Western music since the Renaissance has been based on a seven-note scale known as the diatonic scale, but when did the scale originate? A fragment of a bone flute excavated at a Neanderthal campsite has four holes, which are spaced in exactly the right way for playing the third through sixth notes of a diatonic scale. **The entire flute must surely have had more holes**, and the flute was made from a bone that was long enough for these additional holes to have allowed a complete diatonic scale to be played. Therefore, **the Neanderthals who made the flute probably used a diatonic musical scale**.

In the argument given, the two portions in **boldface** play which of the following roles?

(A) The first is presented as evidence that is confirmed by data presented elsewhere in the argument given; the second states a hypothesis this evidence is used to undermine.

(B) The first is an opinion for which no supporting evidence is presented in the argument given, which is used to support the main conclusion of the argument; the second is that main conclusion.

(C) The first describes a discovery as undermining the position against which the argument is directed; the second states the main conclusion of the argument.

(D) The first is a preliminary conclusion drawn on the basis of evidence presented elsewhere in the argument given; the second is the main conclusion this preliminary conclusion supports.

(E) The first provides evidence to support the main conclusion of the argument; the second states a subsidiary conclusion that is drawn in order to support the main conclusion stated earlier in the argument.

Argument Evaluation

Situation Western music has generally relied on the seven-note diatonic scale for centuries. A piece of Neanderthal bone flute has holes corresponding to part, but not all, of a diatonic scale. Because the fragment suggests a longer bone, the author infers that there must have been more holes corresponding to more notes and concludes the Neanderthal flute-makers probably employed a full diatonic scale.

Reasoning *Two key phrases are in **boldface**: What function does each phrase perform?* The first phrase in **boldface** states the original flute "surely" had more holes corresponding to more notes. While this is a plausible inference, the word *surely* overstates the case. There is no convincing evidence provided to support the idea that the flute certainly had the extra holes before it was broken, and thereby that the original flute likely played a diatonic scale. The second **boldface** phrase concludes this particular group of Neanderthals likely used a diatonic scale; this conclusion relies entirely on the first, unsupported, assertion.

A The first phrase is not supported by concrete data, only by the intuitive belief that the extra holes must have existed, and it supports rather than undermines the second phrase.

B **Correct.** No actual evidence is presented for the assertion that the flute *surely* had more holes, making the first phrase an unsupported opinion; the second phrase concludes these Neanderthals likely used a diatonic scale, and that conclusion rests entirely on the assertion that the broken flute played such a scale in its complete form.

C The first phrase constitutes an assertion, not a description of a discovery, and it supports rather than undermines the conclusion in the second phrase.

D While the first phrase is a preliminary conclusion, it rests on the author's intuitive belief that there were *surely* more holes when the flute was complete rather than on actual evidence that such holes existed—those missing holes and their corresponding notes are possible, but far from certain. The second phrase is a final conclusion based on that previous overstatement of the case.

E The first phrase presents an assertion, not evidence, and the second phrase is a final rather than subsidiary conclusion.

The correct answer is B.

815. NorthAir charges low fares for its economy-class seats, but it provides very cramped seating and few amenities. Market research shows that economy passengers would willingly pay more for wider seating and better service, and additional revenue provided by these higher ticket prices would more than cover the additional cost of providing these amenities. Even though NorthAir is searching for ways to improve its profitability, it has decided not to make these improvements.

Which of the following, if true, would most help to explain NorthAir's decision in light of its objectives?

(A) None of NorthAir's competitors offers significantly better seating and service to economy-class passengers than NorthAir does.

(B) On many of the routes that NorthAir flies, it is the only airline to offer direct flights.

(C) A few of NorthAir's economy-class passengers are satisfied with the service they receive, given the low price they pay.

(D) Very few people avoid flying on NorthAir because of the cramped seating and poor service offered in economy class.

(E) The number of people who would be willing to pay the high fares NorthAir charges for its business-class seats would decrease if its economy-class seating were more acceptable.

Evaluation of a Plan

Situation   Market research shows that improving some amenities for economy-class passengers would allow NorthAir to raise its economy ticket prices more than enough to cover the additional cost of providing those amenities. But NorthAir has decided not to improve those amenities, even though it is looking for ways to improve its profitability.

Reasoning   *What would most help explain why NorthAir decided not to improve the seating and other amenities, even though the resulting increase in economy-class ticket prices would more than cover the expense?* NorthAir is looking for ways to improve its profitability. Making improvements that would increase ticket prices enough to generate more revenue than they cost should improve profitability, other things being equal. But if improving the amenities would generate side effects that reduced profitability, those side effects would provide a good reason for NorthAir's decision not to improve the amenities and hence would help explain why NorthAir made that decision.

A   The passage says that for NorthAir, the cost of providing better economy seating and other amenities would be more than met by the increased revenue from the higher ticket prices that passengers would be willing to pay. This could give NorthAir a competitive edge, with improved profitability.

B   Even if NorthAir faces little or no competition on certain routes, offering extra amenities might increase passengers' interest in flying those routes. It might also lead passengers to choose NorthAir on other routes that competing airlines also serve. Both of these effects could improve NorthAir's profitability.

C   Even if a few NorthAir economy passengers would not pay more for extra amenities, the market research indicates that most of them would, so offering the amenities could still improve NorthAir's profits attributable to economy-class seating.

D   This suggests that improving the amenities would not increase the total number of NorthAir passengers. But improving the amenities might still enable the airline to increase its ticket prices per passenger enough to improve its profitability.

E   **Correct.** This suggests that improving the economy-class amenities would reduce NorthAir's revenue from sales of business-class tickets, which are likely much more expensive than economy-class tickets. This reduction in revenue could be enough to reduce NorthAir's total profitability despite the increased revenue from economy-class ticket sales.

The correct answer is E.

816. Which of the following most logically completes the argument given?

Asthma, a chronic breathing disorder, is significantly more common today among adult competitive swimmers than it is among competitive athletes who specialize in other sports. Although chlorine is now known to be a lung irritant and swimming pool water is generally chlorinated, it would be rash to assume that frequent exposure to chlorine is the explanation of the high incidence of asthma among these swimmers, since _____.

(A) young people who have asthma are no more likely to become competitive athletes than are young people who do not have asthma

(B) competitive athletes who specialize in sports other than swimming are rarely exposed to chlorine

(C) competitive athletes as a group have a significantly lower incidence of asthma than do people who do not participate in competitive athletics

(D) until a few years ago, physicians routinely recommended competitive swimming to children with asthma, in the belief that this form of exercise could alleviate asthma symptoms

(E) many people have asthma without knowing they have it and thus are not diagnosed with the condition until they begin engaging in very strenuous activities, such as competitive athletics

Argument Construction

Situation   Asthma is more common among competitive swimmers than among other competitive athletes. Chlorine is a lung irritant generally present in swimming pool water.

Reasoning   *What would cast doubt on the hypothesis that exposure to chlorine in swimming pools accounts for the high incidence of asthma among adult competitive swimmers?* Evidence of any other factor that would provide an alternative explanation of why asthma is more common among adult competitive swimmers than among other competitive athletes would make it rash to assume that frequent exposure to chlorine explains the high incidence of asthma among these swimmers, so a statement providing such evidence would logically fill in the blank at the end of the passage to complete the argument.

A   This might help explain why competitive athletes in general are not especially likely to have asthma, but it does not explain why adult competitive swimmers are more likely to have asthma than other competitive athletes are.

B   This provides additional evidence that exposure to chlorine explains why adult competitive swimmers are more likely to have asthma than other competitive athletes are, so it does not cast doubt on that hypothesis.

C   A lower incidence of asthma among competitive athletes than among nonathletes does not help explain the higher incidence of asthma among adult competitive swimmers than among other competitive athletes.

D   **Correct.** Routinely encouraging children with asthma to take up competitive swimming would likely have made the proportion of adult competitive swimmers with asthma exceed the proportion of other competitive athletes with asthma, even if chlorine in swimming pool water never causes asthma in swimmers.

E   This might help explain why people with asthma are just as likely as other people to become competitive athletes, but it does not help explain why adult competitive swimmers are more likely to have asthma than other competitive athletes are.

The correct answer is D.

817. In the country of Marut, the Foreign Trade Agency's records were reviewed in 1994 in light of information then newly available about neighboring Goro. The review revealed that in every year since 1963, the agency's projection of what Goro's gross national product (GNP) would be five years later was a serious underestimate. The review also revealed that in every year since 1963, the agency estimated Goro's GNP for the previous year—a Goro state secret—very accurately.

Of the following claims, which is most strongly supported by the statements given?

(A) Goro's GNP fluctuated greatly between 1963 and 1994.

(B) Prior to 1995, Goro had not released data intended to mislead the agency in making its five-year projections.

(C) The amount by which the agency underestimated the GNP it projected for Goro tended to increase over time.

(D) Even before the new information came to light, the agency had reason to think that at least some of the five-year projections it had made were inaccurate.

(E) The agency's five-year projections of Goro's GNP had no impact on economic planning in Marut.

Argument Construction

Situation   A review in 1994 revealed that every year since 1963, Marut's Foreign Trade Agency had seriously underestimated what Goro's GNP would be five years later but accurately estimated what Goro's GNP had been the previous year.

Reasoning   *What conclusion do the stated facts most strongly support?* Goro's GNP in each year at least from 1969 through 1993 had been seriously underestimated by the agency five years in advance, yet was then accurately estimated by the agency one year after the fact. It follows that for each of these years, the agency's earlier projection of Goro's GNP must have been much lower than its later estimate.

A   This is not supported by the information given. The fact that the agency consistently underestimated each year's GNP in its five-year projections and then correctly estimated it after the fact does not indicate that Goro's GNP fluctuated greatly.

B   This is not supported by the information given. The reason the agency's five-year projections were inaccurate might well have been that Goro deliberately released data intended to mislead the agency in making those projections.

C   This is not supported by the information given. The fact that the underestimates remained large throughout the years in question does not indicate that the underestimates increased over time.

D   Correct. As explained above, for many years there were serious discrepancies between the agency's five-year projections of Goro's GNP and its retrospective estimates of each previous year's trade. In any year at least from 1970 through 1993, these discrepancies, if noticed, would have given the agency reason to doubt some of the five-year projections.

E   This is not supported by the information given. Even though at least some of the five-year projections were eventually known to be serious underestimates, they could still have affected Marut's economic planning. The economic planners might have retained an unreasonable faith in the accuracy of the most recent projections.

The correct answer is D.

818. In Colorado subalpine meadows, nonnative dandelions co-occur with a native flower, the larkspur. Bumblebees visit both species, creating the potential for interactions between the two species with respect to pollination. In a recent study, researchers selected 16 plots containing both species; all dandelions were removed from eight plots; the remaining eight control plots were left undisturbed. The control plots yielded significantly more larkspur seeds than the dandelion-free plots, leading the researchers to conclude that the presence of dandelions facilitates pollination (and hence seed production) in the native species by attracting more pollinators to the mixed plots.

Which of the following, if true, most seriously undermines the researchers' reasoning?

(A) Bumblebees preferentially visit dandelions over larkspurs in mixed plots.

(B) In mixed plots, pollinators can transfer pollen from one species to another to augment seed production.

(C) If left unchecked, nonnative species like dandelions quickly crowd out native species.

(D) Seed germination is a more reliable measure of a species' fitness than seed production.

(E) Soil disturbances can result in fewer blooms, and hence lower seed production.

Argument Evaluation

Situation   Bumblebees visit both larkspur and dandelions in certain meadows. A study found that more larkspur seeds were produced in meadow plots in which both larkspur and dandelions grew than in similar plots from which all dandelions had been removed. The researchers inferred that dandelions facilitate larkspur pollination.

Reasoning   *What evidence would cast the most doubt on the inference from the study's findings to the conclusion that dandelions facilitate larkspur pollination by attracting more pollinators?* The argument assumes that the only relevant difference between the two types of plots was whether dandelions were present. Evidence that the plots differed in some other way that could provide a plausible alternative explanation of why more larkspur seeds were produced in the plots with dandelions would weaken the argument.

A   This would suggest that the larkspur pollination should have been lower in the plots with dandelions, so it does not provide a plausible alternative explanation for the study's findings.

B   This is fully compatible with the claim that the dandelions attracted more pollinators to the mixed plots, and it would also help to support the argument's conclusion that dandelions facilitated larkspur pollination in those plots.

C   Although this suggests that the mixed plots won't remain mixed for long, it does not provide a plausible alternative explanation for the study's finding that larkspur seed production was higher in the mixed plots.

D   The argument is not about how fit larkspurs are as a species but about why they produced different numbers of seeds in the different plots.

E   **Correct.** This provides a plausible alternative explanation for why larkspur seed production was lower in the plots from which dandelions had been removed, since digging them out would have disturbed the soil.

The correct answer is E.

819. Paleontologist: About 2.8 million years ago, many species that lived near the ocean floor suffered substantial population declines. These declines coincided with the onset of an ice age. The notion that cold killed those bottom-dwelling creatures outright is misguided, however; temperatures near the ocean floor would have changed very little. Nevertheless, **the cold probably did cause the population declines, though indirectly**. Many bottom-dwellers depended on plankton, small organisms that lived close to the surface and sank to the bottom when they died, for food. **Most probably, the plankton suffered a severe population decline as a result of sharply lower temperatures at the surface,** depriving many bottom-dwellers of food.

In the paleontologist's reasoning, the two portions in **boldface** play which of the following roles?

(A) The first introduces the hypothesis proposed by the paleontologist; the second is a judgment offered in spelling out that hypothesis.

(B) The first introduces the hypothesis proposed by the paleontologist; the second is a position the paleontologist opposes.

(C) The first is an explanation challenged by the paleontologist; the second is an explanation proposed by the paleontologist.

(D) The first is a judgment advanced in support of a conclusion reached by the paleontologist; the second is that conclusion.

(E) The first is a generalization put forward by the paleontologist; the second presents certain exceptional cases in which that generalization does not hold.

Evaluation of a Plan

Situation   At the beginning of an ice age roughly 2.8 million years ago, many species of deep-sea animals suffered sharp drops in population. Because temperatures at those depths would have been very modestly affected, the author rejects the conclusion that cold killed these animals directly. Rather, the author suggests cold had an indirect impact by killing off surface-dwelling plankton since the bottom-dwelling animals relied on dead plankton drifting downward for food. The author concludes that sharp declines in plankton populations near the ocean surface likely led to population declines among species far below.

Reasoning   *Two key phrases are in* **boldface***: What function does each phrase perform?* The first phrase states the cold probably had an indirect impact on populations of deep-sea animals. This constitutes a hypothesis proposed by the author to explain the correlation between the beginning of an ice age and sharp drops in population among bottom-dwelling animals. The second phrase states the cold probably killed a large proportion of plankton near the surface. This is a judgment spelling out the hypothesis that cold was indirectly responsible for deep-sea population declines by identifying a mechanism that would show how cold could have that effect.

A   Correct. The first phrase presents the author's hypothesis that cold indirectly caused population declines among deep-sea species; the second phrase, that the cold likely killed a large proportion of the plankton, is a judgment regarding probable effects of the cold that spells out the details of how that hypothesis would work.

B   While the first phrase is the author's hypothesis, the author endorses rather than opposes the position in the second phrase—that cold probably killed off a large proportion of the plankton.

C   The author challenges the explanation that cold was *directly* responsible for population declines among deep-sea species; the first phrase, that cold was *indirectly* responsible, is the explanation the author proposes, and the second phrase elaborates on that explanation.

D   The first phrase is a hypothesis, not a judgment; the second phrase develops that hypothesis rather than drawing a conclusion.

E   The first phrase presents a hypothesis, not a generalization, and the second phrase develops that hypothesis rather than saying anything about exceptional cases.

The correct answer is A.

820. With seventeen casinos, Moneyland operates the most casinos in a certain state. Although intent on expanding, it was outmaneuvered by Apex Casinos in negotiations to acquire the Eldorado chain. To complete its acquisition of Eldorado, Apex must sell five casinos to comply with a state law forbidding any owner to operate more than one casino per county. Since Apex will still be left operating twenty casinos in the state, it will then have the most casinos in the state.

Which of the following, if true, most seriously undermines the prediction?

(A) Apex, Eldorado, and Moneyland are the only organizations licensed to operate casinos in the state.

(B) The majority of Eldorado's casinos in the state will need extensive renovations if they are to continue to operate profitably.

(C) Some of the state's counties do not permit casinos.

(D) Moneyland already operates casinos in the majority of the state's counties.

(E) Apex will use funds it obtains from the sale of the five casinos to help fund its acquisition of the Eldorado chain.

Argument Evaluation

Situation   Moneyland operates seventeen casinos, the most in a certain state, and is intent on expanding. Another operator, Apex Casinos, is acquiring the Eldorado casino chain but must sell five casinos to comply with a state law forbidding any owner to operate more than one casino per county. After these transactions, Apex will operate twenty casinos in the state.

Reasoning   *What observation would cast the most doubt on the prediction that Apex will have the most casinos in the state after the transactions?* Apex will operate twenty casinos, whereas Moneyland now operates just seventeen, and no one else operates even that many. It follows that Apex will operate more casinos after its transactions than Moneyland or any other one owner now operates. However, if Moneyland also acquires three or more casinos during the transactions, then Apex will not have the most casinos in the state afterward. Thus, any observation suggesting that Moneyland is about to acquire several casinos would undermine the prediction.

A   **Correct.** Since Apex is acquiring Eldorado, Moneyland and Apex will be the only remaining licensed casino operators in the state. Therefore, Moneyland is the only likely buyer for the five casinos Apex needs to sell. So, Moneyland is likely to acquire the five casinos during the sale and end up with twenty-two casinos—more than Apex.

B   This does not undermine the prediction. Even if the Eldorado casinos cannot operate profitably for long without extensive renovations, Apex will still have twenty casinos immediately after its transactions.

C   This supports rather than undermines the prediction. If fewer counties permit casinos, there will be fewer opportunities for Moneyland or any other operator to acquire more casinos to surpass the twenty Apex will own.

D   This supports rather than undermines the prediction. If Moneyland's seventeen casinos are in most of the state's counties already, then there are fewer counties in which Moneyland could acquire additional casinos to surpass the twenty Apex will own.

E   This supports rather than undermines the prediction. Apex's use of the funds from selling the five casinos to acquire the Eldorado chain will not help anyone else to acquire more casinos to surpass the twenty Apex will own.

The correct answer is A.

821. It is widely assumed that people need to engage in intellectual activities such as solving crossword puzzles or mathematics problems in order to maintain mental sharpness as they age. In fact, however, simply talking to other people—that is, participating in social interaction, which engages many mental and perceptual skills—suffices. Evidence to this effect comes from a study showing that the more social contact people report, the better their mental skills.

Which of the following, if true, most seriously weakens the force of the evidence cited?

(A) As people grow older, they are often advised to keep exercising their physical and mental capacities in order to maintain or improve them.

(B) Many medical conditions and treatments that adversely affect a person's mental sharpness also tend to increase that person's social isolation.

(C) Many people are proficient both in social interactions and in solving mathematical problems.

(D) The study did not itself collect data but analyzed data bearing on the issue from prior studies.

(E) The tasks evaluating mental sharpness for which data were compiled by the study were more akin to mathematics problems than to conversation.

Argument Evaluation

Situation   A study shows that the more social contact people report, the better their mental skills are, so engaging in social interaction is sufficient for maintaining mental sharpness.

Reasoning   *What would suggest that the study does not establish the truth of the conclusion?* The study shows a correlation between mental sharpness and social interaction but does not indicate why this correlation exists. Evidence that mental sharpness contributes to social interaction, or that some third factor affects both mental sharpness and social interaction, could provide an alternative explanation for the correlation and thus cast doubt on the explanation that social interaction contributes to mental sharpness.

A   People are often wrongly advised to do things that are not actually beneficial. And even if exercising mental capacities does help to maintain them, the passage says that social interaction provides such exercise.

B   **Correct.** This provides evidence that the correlation observed in the study results from mental sharpness facilitating social interaction, in which case the study results do not indicate that social interaction facilitates mental sharpness.

C   This would be expected, given the argument's conclusion that social interaction helps to maintain better mental skills overall.

D   A study that analyzes data from prior studies can provide evidence just as well as a study that collects its own data can.

E   The argument's conclusion would be compatible with this observation and would then suggest that social interaction contributes to the mental sharpness needed for tasks similar to math problems.

The correct answer is B.

822. In the United States, of the people who moved from one state to another when they retired, the percentage who retired to Florida has decreased by three percentage points over the past ten years. Since many local businesses in Florida cater to retirees, these declines are likely to have a noticeably negative economic effect on these businesses and therefore on the economy of Florida.

Which of the following, if true, most seriously weakens the argument given?

(A) People who moved from one state to another when they retired moved a greater distance, on average, last year than such people did ten years ago.

(B) People were more likely to retire to North Carolina from another state last year than people were ten years ago.

(C) The number of people who moved from one state to another when they retired has increased significantly over the past ten years.

(D) The number of people who left Florida when they retired to live in another state was greater last year than it was ten years ago.

(E) Florida attracts more people who move from one state to another when they retire than does any other state.

Argument Evaluation

Situation   Of those people who move to another state when they retire, the percentage moving to Florida has declined. This trend is apt to harm Florida's economy because many businesses there cater to retirees.

Reasoning   *Which of the options most weakens the argument?* The argument draws its conclusion from data about the *proportion* of emigrating retirees moving to Florida. Yet what matters more directly to the conclusion (and to Florida's economy) is the *absolute number* of retirees immigrating to Florida. That number could have remained constant, or even risen, if the absolute number of emigrating retirees itself increased while the proportion going to Florida decreased.

A   This has no obvious bearing on the argument one way or another. It makes it more likely, perhaps, that a person in a distant state will retire to Florida but less likely that one in a neighboring state will do so.

B   This has no bearing on whether fewer people have been retiring to Florida over the last ten years.

C   **Correct.** This is the option that most seriously weakens the argument.

D   This makes it *more* likely that Florida's economy will be harmed because of decreasing numbers of retirees, but it has no real bearing on the argument which concludes specifically that *declines in the proportion of emigrating retirees moving to Florida* will have a negative effect on the state's economy.

E   This is irrelevant. At issue is how the numbers of retirees in Florida from one year compare to the next, not how those numbers compare with numbers of retirees in other states.

The correct answer is C.

823. Which of the following most logically completes the passage?

The figures in portraits by the Spanish painter El Greco (1541–1614) are systematically elongated. In El Greco's time, the intentional distortion of human figures was unprecedented in European painting. Consequently, some critics have suggested that El Greco had an astigmatism, a type of visual impairment, that resulted in people appearing to him in the distorted way that is characteristic of his paintings. However, this suggestion cannot be the explanation, because _____.

(A) several twentieth-century artists have consciously adopted from El Greco's paintings the systematic elongation of the human form

(B) some people do have elongated bodies somewhat like those depicted in El Greco's portraits

(C) if El Greco had an astigmatism, then, relative to how people looked to him, the elongated figures in his paintings would have appeared to him to be distorted

(D) even if El Greco had an astigmatism, there would have been no correction for it available in the period in which he lived

(E) there were non-European artists, even in El Greco's time, who included in their works human figures that were intentionally distorted

Argument Evaluation

Situation Figures in portraits by the Spanish painter El Greco are elongated. Some critics infer that this was because El Greco suffered from an astigmatism that made people appear elongated to him. But this explanation cannot be correct.

Reasoning *Which option would most logically complete the argument?* We need something that provides the best reason for thinking that the explanation suggested by critics—astigmatism—cannot be right. The critics' explanation might seem to work because ordinarily an artist would try to paint an image of a person so that the image would have the same proportions as the perceived person. So, if people seemed to El Greco to have longer arms and legs than they actually had, the arms and legs of the painted figures should appear to others to be longer than people's arms and legs normally are. This is how the explanation seems to make sense. But if astigmatism were the explanation, then the elongated images in his pictures should have appeared to El Greco to be too long: he would have perceived the images as longer than they actually are—and therefore as inaccurate representations of what he perceived. So, astigmatism cannot be a sufficient explanation for the elongated figures in his paintings.

A Even if subsequent artists intentionally depicted human forms as more elongated than human figures actually are, and they did so to mimic El Greco's painted figures, that does not mean that El Greco's figures were intentionally elongated.

B Although this option provides another possible explanation for El Greco's elongated figures, it provides no evidence that the people El Greco painted had such elongated figures.

C **Correct.** El Greco would have perceived the images of people in his paintings as too long, relative to his perception of the people themselves. This means that even if El Greco did have astigmatism, that factor would not provide an answer to the question, "Why did El Greco paint images that he knew were distorted?"

D The absence of an ability to correct astigmatism in El Greco's day does not undermine the hypothesis that it was astigmatism that caused El Greco to paint elongated figures.

E Again, this suggests another possible explanation for the distortion—namely, that El Greco did it deliberately—but it does not provide any reason to think that this is the correct explanation (and that the critics' explanation is actually incorrect).

The correct answer is C.

824. Museums that house Renaissance oil paintings typically store them in environments that are carefully kept within narrow margins of temperature and humidity to inhibit any deterioration. Laboratory tests have shown that the kind of oil paint used in these paintings actually adjusts to climatic changes quite well. If, as some museum directors believe, **paint is the most sensitive substance in these works**, then by relaxing the standards for temperature and humidity control, **museums can reduce energy costs without risking damage to these paintings.** Museums would be rash to relax those standards, however, since results of preliminary tests indicate that gesso, a compound routinely used by Renaissance artists to help paint adhere to the canvas, is unable to withstand significant variations in humidity.

In the argument above, the two portions in **boldface** play which of the following roles?

(A) The first is an objection that has been raised against the position taken by the argument; the second is the position taken by the argument.

(B) The first is the position taken by the argument; the second is the position that the argument calls into question.

(C) The first is a judgment that has been offered in support of the position that the argument calls into question; the second is a circumstance on which that judgment is, in part, based.

(D) The first is a judgment that has been offered in support of the position that the argument calls into question; the second is that position.

(E) The first is a claim that the argument calls into question; the second is the position taken by the argument.

Argument Evaluation

Situation   Museums house Renaissance paintings under strictly controlled climatic conditions to prevent deterioration. This is costly. But the paint in these works actually adjusts well to climate changes. On the other hand, another compound routinely used in these paintings, gesso, does not react well to changes in humidity.

Reasoning   *What roles do the two **boldfaced** statements play in the argument?* The first statement is not asserted by the author of the argument, but rather attributed as a belief to some museum directors. What the argument itself asserts is that IF this belief is true, THEN the second **boldfaced** statement is true. But the argument then goes on to offer evidence that the first statement is false and so concludes that museum directors would be ill-advised to assume that the second statement was true.

A   This option mistakenly claims that the argument adopts the second statement as its position, when in fact the argument calls this position into question.

B   Rather than adopting the first statement, the argument offers evidence that calls it into question.

C   This option contends that the first statement is a judgment that is based on the second; in fact, the opposite is true.

D   **Correct.** This option properly identifies the roles the two portions in **boldface** play in the argument.

E   While the argument does call the first statement into question, it also calls the second statement into question as well.

The correct answer is D.

825. Excavations of the Roman city of Sepphoris have uncovered numerous detailed mosaics depicting several readily identifiable animal species: a hare, a partridge, and various Mediterranean fish. Oddly, most of the species represented did not live in the Sepphoris region when these mosaics were created. Since identical motifs appear in mosaics found in other Roman cities, however, the mosaics of Sepphoris were very likely created by traveling artisans from some other part of the Roman Empire.

Which of the following is an assumption on which the argument depends?

(A) The Sepphoris mosaics are not composed exclusively of types of stones found naturally in the Sepphoris area.

(B) There is no single region to which all the species depicted in the Sepphoris mosaics are native.

(C) No motifs appear in the Sepphoris mosaics that do not also appear in the mosaics of some other Roman city.

(D) All of the animal figures in the Sepphoris mosaics are readily identifiable as representations of known species.

(E) There was not a common repertory of mosaic designs with which artisans who lived in various parts of the Roman Empire were familiar.

Argument Construction

Situation   Mosaics uncovered at the site of the Roman city of Sepphoris depict animals that did not live in Sepphoris. Because identical motifs appear in other Roman cities, traveling artisans from elsewhere in the Roman Empire likely created the mosaics of Sepphoris.

Reasoning   *What assumption underlies this argument?* The argument implicitly assumes that the artisans who created the mosaics had seen the animals depicted firsthand. This suggests that the artisans had been to the regions where these animals live and then traveled to Sepphoris to create the mosaics depicting non-native animals. This, in turn, suggests the assumption that the artisans were not including these motifs based solely on familiarity with motifs common throughout the Empire.

A   The argument draws its conclusion based on subjects of the mosaics, not on the types of stones used in the mosaics, so the origin of the stone is irrelevant.

B   The argument does not rely on the assumption that the species depicted in the Sepphoris mosaics are native to disparate regions, only on the idea that traveling artisans must have seen such species.

C   Nothing in the argument relies on whether or not any of the motifs appear exclusively in Sepphoris. The argument relies only on the fact that there are motifs depicting animals not native to Sepphoris.

D   The argument requires only that at least some of the animals in the mosaics are identifiable as known species that are non-native to Sepphoris.

E   **Correct.** If there was a common repertory of mosaic designs with which artisans who lived in various parts of the Roman Empire were familiar, then it could well be that artisans native to Sepphoris would have been familiar with these designs and could have produced them without ever having seen for themselves animals of the species depicted and without having been the same artisans who created the mosaics elsewhere. Therefore, the argument must assume that such a common repertory did not exist.

The correct answer is E.

826. As a large corporation in a small country, Hachnut wants its managers to have international experience, so **each year it sponsors management education abroad for its management trainees.** Hachnut has found, however, that the attrition rate of graduates from this program is very high, with many of them leaving Hachnut to join competing firms soon after completing the program. Hachnut does use performance during the program as a criterion in deciding among candidates for management positions, but **both this function and the goal of providing international experience could be achieved in other ways.** Therefore, if the attrition problem cannot be successfully addressed, Hachnut should discontinue the sponsorship program.

In the argument given, the two **boldfaced** portions play which of the following roles?

(A) The first describes a practice that the argument seeks to justify; the second states a judgment that is used in support of a justification for that practice.

(B) The first describes a practice that the argument seeks to explain; the second presents part of the argument's explanation of that practice.

(C) The first introduces a practice that the argument seeks to evaluate; the second provides grounds for holding that the practice cannot achieve its objective.

(D) The first introduces a policy that the argument seeks to evaluate; the second provides grounds for holding that the policy is not needed.

(E) The first introduces a consideration supporting a policy that the argument seeks to evaluate; the second provides evidence for concluding that the policy should be abandoned.

Argument Construction

Situation   One of Hachnut's goals is for its managers to have international experience, so it sponsors education abroad for management trainees. Graduates of this program, however, frequently leave the company soon after the training to work for competitors. Even though Hachnut uses trainees' performance in the program to make placement decisions, it should discontinue the sponsorship program, because both achievement of international experience and assistance in making placement decisions can be achieved in other ways.

Reasoning   *What role do the two portions in **boldface** play in the argument?* The first **boldfaced** portion introduces the policy of sponsorship of management training abroad. The argument goes on to evaluate this policy in light of the second **boldfaced** portion—which states that there are alternative ways of accomplishing what the sponsorship is intended to do—and concludes that the program should be discontinued.

A   The argument does not seek to justify the practice described in the first **boldfaced** portion, and the second portion argues against the practice, not for it.

B   The argument does not seek to explain the practice, but rather to evaluate whether it should be retained.

C   Although the first **boldfaced** portion does introduce a practice that the argument seeks to evaluate, the second does not provide grounds for holding that the practice cannot achieve its objective, but rather states that there are other means of achieving that objective.

D   **Correct.** The first **boldfaced** portion introduces a policy the argument seeks to evaluate. The second states that there are alternative ways to achieve the goal, which provides grounds for holding that the policy is not needed.

E   Although the second **boldfaced** portion does provide a reason to abandon the policy the argument evaluates, the first does not introduce a consideration supporting that policy, but rather introduces the policy itself.

The correct answer is D.

827. Letter to the editor: If the water level in the Searle River Delta continues to drop, the rising sea level will make the water saltier and less suitable for drinking. Currently, 40 percent of the water from upstream tributaries is diverted to neighboring areas. To keep the delta's water level from dropping any further, we should end all current diversions from the upstream tributaries. Neighboring water utilities are likely to see higher costs and diminished water supplies, but these costs are necessary to preserve the delta.

Which of the following would, if true, indicate a serious potential weakness of the suggested plan of action?

(A) Desalination equipment would allow water from the delta to be used for drinking even it if became saltier.

(B) Water level is only one factor that affects salinity in the delta.

(C) The upstream tributaries' water levels are controlled by systems of dams and reservoirs.

(D) Neighboring areas have grown in population since the water was first diverted from upstream tributaries.

(E) Much of the recent drop in the delta's water level can be attributed to a prolonged drought that has recently ended.

Evaluation of a Plan

Situation   A letter states that progressively lower levels in the Searle River Delta will raise the salt content of its water and make that water less fit for human consumption. Because 40 percent of the water flowing to the delta from upstream is diverted for the use of upstream communities, the letter proposes reclaiming that diverted water regardless of negative impacts on upstream communities in order to protect the delta's water levels from dropping further.

Reasoning   *What would weaken the argument for this plan?* The argument for the plan to end diversion of water rests on the assumption that if diversion continues, water levels in the Searle River Delta will likewise continue to drop. If some additional factor suggested water levels in the delta might hold steady or rebound *even if* upstream communities continue to divert water, then that new fact would weaken the argument that the plan is necessary to protect the delta.

A   The fact that desalination equipment could create drinking water would argue against the necessity of the plan *specifically* for providing drinking water, but it would not weaken the argument that the plan is necessary to protect the delta's water levels per se.

B   Even if factors other than water level affect the delta's salinity, that would not weaken the argument that the plan is necessary to defend the delta's water levels.

C   A system of dams upstream would not affect the argument that upstream communities should no longer be allowed to divert water because that water is needed in the Searle River Delta.

D   Growing need for water upstream would increase the negative impact of the plan, but it would not undermine the claim that the plan is necessary to protect the delta.

E   **Correct.** If the drop in the delta's water level was largely caused by a drought, and if that drought has ended, then the water level in the delta might stay constant or rise even without the plan to end water diversion by upstream communities. Water flowing into the delta from increased rain would weaken the argument that the plan is necessary to defend the delta.

The correct answer is E.

828. In 1960s studies of rats, scientists found that crowding increases the number of attacks among the animals significantly. But in recent experiments in which rhesus monkeys were placed in crowded conditions, although there was an increase in instances of "coping" behavior—such as submissive gestures and avoidance of dominant individuals—attacks did not become any more frequent. Therefore it is not likely that, for any species of monkey, crowding increases aggression as significantly as was seen in rats.

Which of the following, if true, most strengthens the argument?

(A) All the observed forms of coping behavior can be found among rhesus monkeys living in uncrowded conditions.

(B) In the studies of rats, nondominant individuals were found to increasingly avoid dominant individuals when the animals were in crowded conditions.

(C) Rhesus monkeys respond with aggression to a wider range of stimuli than any other monkeys do.

(D) Some individual monkeys in the experiments were involved in significantly more attacks than the other monkeys were.

(E) Some of the coping behavior displayed by rhesus monkeys is similar to behavior rhesus monkeys use to bring to an end an attack that has begun.

Argument Evaluation

Situation Crowding among rats was found to significantly increase attacks. Among rhesus monkeys, however, crowding increased coping behavior such as submissive gestures, avoidance, but resulted in no increase in attacks. The author concludes that it's unlikely, for any species of monkey, that crowding increases aggression as significantly as was seen in rats.

Reasoning *What fact would most strongly support the author's conclusion?* The argument is based on an assumption that the behavior observed in rhesus monkeys is representative of how all species of monkeys would react to crowding. To strengthen this argument, we need evidence that either reinforces the relevance of rhesus monkeys as representatives for the broader group ("any species of monkey"), or rules out an alternative explanation for the low aggression in rhesus monkeys.

A The presence of coping behavior in *uncrowded* conditions would not explain why attacks *didn't increase* in *crowded* conditions. It fails to address the effect of crowding on aggression.

B The fact that rats also exhibited avoidance to cope with crowding does not support the implied contention that rhesus monkeys' behavior under crowded conditions can serve as a reliable indicator of all monkeys' behavior under such conditions.

C **Correct.** This fact would suggest that rhesus monkeys, when compared to other monkey species, are more prone to aggression (they respond aggressively to a wider range of stimuli). If a species *more prone* to aggression shows no increase in attacks when crowded, then it is even less likely that a *less aggressive* monkey species would show a significant increase. It strengthens the argument by ruling out the possibility that rhesus monkeys are unusually non-aggressive, and thereby making it more plausible that their non-aggression would be representative of monkeys in general.

D The distribution of attacks among individuals (some aggressive, some not) doesn't suggest anything about whether the overall behavior of crowded rhesus monkeys reliably indicates how other monkey species would behave in response to crowding.

E If the coping behaviors are a way of *stopping* aggression, that would imply the possibility that aggression *was* present and had to be halted. This fact could be interpreted as an alternative explanation for why the attack rate didn't *rise* dramatically, rather than supporting the idea that the aggression wasn't there in the first place. However, it is not relevant to the main conclusion regarding aggression across all monkey species.

The correct answer is C.

829. **In countries where automobile insurance includes compensation for whiplash injuries sustained in automobile accidents, reports of having suffered such injuries are twice as frequent as they are in countries where whiplash is not covered.** Presently, no objective test for whiplash exists, so it is true that spurious reports of whiplash injuries cannot be readily identified. Nevertheless, **these facts do not warrant a conclusion that has been drawn by some commentators:** that in the countries with the higher rates of reported whiplash injuries, half of the reported cases are spurious. Clearly, in countries where automobile insurance does not include compensation for whiplash, people often have little incentive to report whiplash injuries that they actually have suffered.

In the argument given, the two **boldfaced** portions play which of the following roles?

(A) The first is a claim that the argument disputes; the second is a conclusion that has been based on that claim.

(B) The first is a claim that has been used to support a position that the argument accepts; the second is a position that the argument rejects.

(C) The first is a finding whose accuracy is evaluated in the argument; the second is the judgment reached by the argument concerning the accuracy of the finding.

(D) The first is a finding whose implications are at issue in the argument; the second is the judgment reached by the argument concerning one alleged implication.

(E) The first is a finding, the explanation of which is at issue in the argument; the second is an objection that has been raised against the explanation that the argument defends.

Argument Construction

Situation   The argument begins with an observed correlation: In countries that compensate for whiplash injuries, people report them twice as frequently as in countries that do not compensate. This finding, combined with the difficulty of objectively testing for whiplash, has led "some commentators" to conclude that half the reported cases in compensating countries must be spurious. The overall purpose of the argument is to reject this specific conclusion drawn by the commentators.

Reasoning   *What roles do the two **boldfaced** portions play in the argument?* The first portion presents the central piece of statistical evidence or finding upon which the entire discussion is based. The proper interpretation of this finding is the central issue debated in the argument: Are the comparatively greater number of reports due to fraud, or due to a lack of incentive to report in non-compensating countries?

This second **boldfaced** statement is the argument's rejection of the specific inference drawn from the finding. The conclusion drawn by commentators is that "half of the reported cases are spurious." The second portion explicitly states that the evidence does not justify this conclusion. Therefore, it is the judgment reached by the argument regarding the validity of a specific implication, namely the conclusion that half of the reports are spurious.

A   The argument *accepts* the accuracy of the claim in the first portion; it only disputes its *implication*. The second portion is a *rejection* of a conclusion, not the conclusion itself.

B   The claim in the first portion has been used to support a position the argument rejects, not that it accepts: the commentators' conclusion. The second portion is the argument's judgment *against* the rejected position, not a position it rejects.

C   The argument accepts the accuracy of the finding stated in the first portion rather than evaluating it. The second portion is a judgment regarding the *implication* of the finding, not its accuracy.

D   Correct. The first portion states a finding whose implication is being debated. The second portion presents the argument's judgment: a rejection of the specific implication drawn by commentators that half the cases are spurious.

E   The first portion does state a finding whose explanation is at issue; the second portion, however, is a judgment, not an objection against the explanation the argument ultimately favors.

The correct answer is D.

830. Twenty years ago, Balzania put in place regulations requiring operators of surface mines to pay for the reclamation of mined-out land. Since then, reclamation technology has not improved. Yet, the average reclamation cost for a surface coal mine being reclaimed today is only four dollars per ton of coal that the mine produced, less than half what it cost to reclaim surface mines in the years immediately after the regulations took effect.

Which of the following, if true, most helps to account for the drop in reclamation costs described?

(A) Even after Balzania began requiring surface mine operators to pay reclamation costs, coal mines in Balzania continued to be less expensive to operate than coal mines in almost any other country.

(B) Even after Balzania began requiring surface mine operators to pay reclamation costs, surface mines continued to produce coal at a lower total cost than underground mines.

(C) As compared to 20 years ago, a greater percentage of the coal mined in Balzania today comes from surface mines.

(D) Over the last 20 years, mine operators have generally located new surface coal mines in areas with flat terrain that makes reclamation easy.

(E) In the 20 years since the regulations took effect, the use of coal as a fuel has declined from the level it was at in the previous 20 years.

Argument Evaluation

Situation   Twenty years ago, Balzania mandated that surface mine operators pay for land reclamation. Since then, two facts are observed: reclamation technology has not improved, and the average reclamation cost per ton of coal produced has dropped by more than half (from over eight dollars to four dollars per ton). The task is to find a factor that helps account for this significant cost reduction, despite the lack of technological improvement.

Reasoning   *What additional factor could account for the drop in reclamation costs?* The observed effect is a large drop in average reclamation cost per ton. Since the technology itself hasn't improved, the reduction must be due to a change in *what is being mined or how the mines are being operated and reclaimed.* Specifically, the cost is calculated as average cost per ton = total reclamation cost / total tons produced So a drop in this average means either the total reclamation cost dropped significantly, or the total tons produced increased significantly relative to the cost, or the drop could result from the cost per unit of production dropping for new mines. For example, a reason why the *difficulty* or *effort* (and therefore the cost) required for reclamation might have decreased could account for the fall in cost relative to total tons mined.

A   This claim compares Balzania's costs to other countries' costs. It does not explain the *drop* in Balzania's own costs over the last 20 years.

B   This claim compares surface mines to underground mines. It does not explain the drop in reclamation costs *for surface mines* over time.

C   This is a change in the *mix* of mining (more surface mining), but it provides no information about *why* the cost per ton for surface mine reclamation itself has decreased.

D   **Correct.** This provides a powerful, external reason for the observed cost drop. By locating new mines in areas that are inherently easier, and therefore less costly, to reclaim due to flat terrain, the mine operators have successfully reduced the input effort and cost required for reclamation, even without new technology. This directly accounts for the significant drop in the average cost per ton.

E   The decline in coal *use*, or demand, does not explain the decline in the *cost per ton* of reclaiming the mines that are still being operated.

The correct answer is D.

831. In a study conducted in Pennsylvania, servers in various restaurants wrote "Thank you" on randomly selected bills before presenting the bills to their customers. Tips on these bills were an average of three percentage points higher than tips on bills without the message. Therefore, if all servers in Pennsylvania regularly wrote "Thank you" on restaurant bills, tips left in Pennsylvania would increase by about three percentage points, on average.

Which of the following is an assumption on which the argument relies?

(A) No more than a small proportion of food servers in Pennsylvania currently write "Thank you" on restaurant bills.

(B) Most patrons of Pennsylvania restaurants will notice the written "Thank you" on their bills.

(C) The written "Thank you" reminds restaurant patrons that tips constitute a significant part of the income of many food servers.

(D) The rate at which people tip food servers in Pennsylvania does not vary with how expensive a restaurant is.

(E) The "Thank you" messages will have the same impact on regular restaurant patrons as they will on occasional patrons.

Argument Construction

Situation   A study observed that tips on restaurant bills with a handwritten "Thank you" were, on average, three percentage points higher than tips on bills without the message. The argument extrapolates from this study to conclude that if all servers in Pennsylvania adopted this practice, the average tip rate across Pennsylvania would increase by about three percentage points.

Reasoning   *What assumption underlies the conclusion that the three percent increase could be replicated at a large scale?* The argument observes an effect (*increased tips*) in a controlled, small-scale study where the "Thank you" messages were applied to randomly selected bills. It then concludes that the *entire population* of Pennsylvania servers can replicate this effect. A core principle of generalizing a study's finding is that the effect being studied must not already be widespread in the population to which the conclusion applies. If a significant proportion of Pennsylvania servers already write "Thank you" on their bills, then the overall average tips for the state would already be inflated by the current use of "Thank you," meaning implementing it statewide would only capture the remaining servers, leading to a smaller than three-percentage-point increase in the state average. Therefore, the argument must assume that the observed effect would be a *novel* change for the majority of Pennsylvania's servers. It assumes that the current tipping rate in Pennsylvania is not already significantly boosted by the practice being widespread.

A   **Correct.** This is the necessary assumption. If the majority of servers already wrote "Thank you" (meaning the practice was *widespread*), the overall average tipping rate in the state would already reflect the benefit of the message. In that case, having the remaining few adopt the practice would cause a tip increase much smaller than three percentage points for the state average. For the argument's conclusion (a three-point *increase* across the entire state) to hold, the practice must not already be common.

B   It is not necessary that "most" patrons outside the study will notice the message, only that enough will notice to replicate the three-point increase. The primary assumption gap is *generalizability* across the state, not *observability* by customers.

C   This claim proposes a *mechanism* for why the practice works. The argument doesn't need to assume this specific mechanism is correct; it only needs to assume the *effect* (higher tips) will be replicated when generalized.

D   The study used *various restaurants*, which suggests the average increase of three points already accounts for this variation. The argument only needs to assume the average effect holds true for the statewide implementation.

E   Because the study was conducted on random patrons, not on regular or occasional patrons specifically, there is no necessary assumption that regular and occasional patrons will respond similarly to the message. The argument relies on the *average* effect holding true statewide, not that every sub-group responds identically.

The correct answer is A.

832. Historian: In the Drindian Empire, a census was conducted annually to determine the adult population of each village. Until 1700, the central government used annual census figures to assess the tax a village owed. Since an increase in population would mean an increase in tax, villages would have a strong economic incentive to try to minimize the number of people recorded. Therefore, it was probably common for census figures from a village to underreport its population significantly.

Which of the following, if true, most strengthens the historian's argument?

(A) After 1700, the census figures for the adult populations of villages did not rise faster than would be expected as a result of normal population growth.

(B) Before 1700, increases in tax rates were often followed by a larger-than-usual number of villages reporting a lower population than the year before.

(C) The official tax and census records for a village in the Drindian Empire were never stored in that village.

(D) Pre-1700 census figures from individual villages sometimes show significant declines in the adult population from one year to the next.

(E) It would have been impossible for villages to conceal from the central government's census takers all additions to their village's population.

Argument Evaluation

Situation   The historian argues that a specific economic setup created a strong motive for deception, leading to systematic underreporting of the population. The economic situation was that until 1700, the central government used the annual census figures to determine a village's tax burden. The result was that an increase in population meant an increase in tax. The historian's conclusion is that villages had a strong economic incentive (a lower tax burden) to underreport their population, and therefore, it was probably common for census figures to underreport significantly.

Reasoning   *What additional evidence would tend to confirm the claim that the taxes led to underreported population figures?* To strengthen the argument, we need evidence that confirms the causal link between the tax disincentive relative to reported population and the underreporting outcome. A strong example of such evidence would show that when the incentive became stronger, the alleged effect (underreporting) also became more pronounced.

A   The argument concerns the period *before* 1700. Post-1700 data is only relevant if it establishes a comparison, but this choice only says the post-1700 figures were *normal*, which doesn't confirm that pre-1700 figures were *abnormal*, or underreported.

B   **Correct.** This fact provides direct evidence of the mechanism in action. When tax rates increased (making the economic incentive to underreport stronger), the frequency of villages reporting a population *decline* (a sign of deliberate underreporting) also increased. This links the strength of the incentive directly to the alleged dishonest outcome, clearly strengthening the historian's claim that the system led to underreporting.

C   Where the records were stored doesn't affect whether the village reported accurate numbers to the census taker initially. The issue is reporting, not storage location.

D   Significant declines from year to year are *expected* in census figures due to migration, disease, or famine. This information is consistent with *accurate* reporting of *fluctuating* populations. To strengthen the argument, we need evidence of *systematic dishonesty*, not expected natural variation.

E   The argument is not that *all* additions to population were concealed, but rather that the population was *significantly underreported*. An inability to conceal every single person would not rule out the ability to conceal a large number of people.

The correct answer is B.

833. Advertisement: Ten years ago, the Cormond Hotel's lobby was carpeted with Duratex carpet, and the lobby of the Bromley Hotel was carpeted with our competitor's most durable carpet. Since then, thousands more people have stayed at the Cormond than at the Bromley, yet the carpet in the Bromley lobby has worn out, while the Cormond's Duratex carpeting has years of wear left in it. Clearly, Duratex is more durable than any of our competitor's carpets.

Which of the following, if true, most strengthens the argument of the advertisement?

(A) Duratex is the most durable kind of carpet that its manufacturer makes.

(B) In neither the Bromley nor the Cormond is the lobby used heavily by people who are not staying at the hotel.

(C) On average, carpeting in hotel lobbies wears out in seven years.

(D) At a third hotel, carpet of the same kind as that installed in the lobby of the Bromley ten years ago is being replaced after only five years of use.

(E) The Bromley is not only going to have its lobby carpeting replaced, but is also going to have its lobby remodeled.

Argument Evaluation

Situation   An advertisement attempts to draw a general conclusion about Duratex carpet's superior durability based on a single comparative case. The argument compares the wear of two different carpets in two different hotel lobbies over a ten-year period. Duratex carpet was installed at the Cormond; the competitor's most durable carpet was installed at the Bromley; thousands more people have stayed at Cormond than Bromley; and the carpet at the Bromley wore out, while the Cormond's Duratex carpet *has years left*. The advertisement concludes that Duratex carpet is more durable than any of their competitor's carpets. The argument makes a crucial assumption: that the comparison between the two hotels is fair and representative. Specifically, it assumes that the use and wear conditions (besides the number of guests) are similar enough to attribute the difference in wear solely to the carpets themselves.

Reasoning   *What would support the contention that Duratex carpet is more durable than its competitor?* To strengthen the argument, we need evidence that either reinforces the fairness of the comparison by showing that factors *other than* carpet type did not favor the Duratex carpet; or evidence that generalizes the finding beyond the Bromley, broadening the limited evidence that the competitor's carpet is inferior.

A   This only compares Duratex to other carpets *by the same manufacturer*. It has no bearing on the comparison against the competitor's carpet, which is the focus of the argument.

B   If the lobby is used *only* by hotel guests, this means the Cormond (with "thousands more guests") had an even greater disparity in traffic than assumed, which slightly strengthens the conclusion, as the Duratex withstood higher use. However, it doesn't provide the best support.

C   Knowing the average wear time (seven years) doesn't help compare the two specific carpets against each other, nor does it address the cause of the wear differences observed in the two hotels.

D   Correct. This fact significantly generalizes the finding. By showing that the competitor's carpet failed quickly in a *third, separate location* (only five years), it reinforces the conclusion that the competitor's product is inherently inferior and not just that the Bromley was a uniquely bad installation. It suggests the poor performance of the competitor's carpet is systemic, not isolated.

E   The Bromley's decision to remodel its lobby along with replacing the carpet is a business decision that does not affect the physical durability comparison between the two carpets.

The correct answer is D.

834. Lyme disease is caused by a bacterium transmitted to humans by deer ticks. Generally deer ticks pick up the bacterium while in the larval stage from feeding on infected white-footed mice. However, certain other species on which the larvae feed do not harbor the bacterium. Therefore, if the population of these other species were increased, the number of ticks acquiring the bacterium—and hence the number of people contracting Lyme disease—would likely decline.

Which of the following, if true, most strengthens the argument?

(A) Ticks do not suffer any adverse consequences from carrying the bacterium that causes Lyme disease in humans.

(B) There are no known cases of a human's contracting Lyme disease through contact with white-footed mice.

(C) A deer tick feeds only once while in the larval stage.

(D) A single host animal can be the source of bacteria for many tick larvae.

(E) None of the other species on which deer tick larvae feed harbor other bacteria that ticks transmit to humans.

Argument Evaluation

Situation The argument proposes a method for reducing the incidence of Lyme disease in humans by manipulating the ecological environment of the deer tick. Lyme disease is caused by bacterium transmitted by deer ticks, and larval deer ticks usually get the bacterium by feeding on infected white-footed mice. Other species the larvae feed on do not harbor the bacterium. So the proposed intervention is to increase the population of these other species, thereby providing more non-infected hosts. Then the number of ticks acquiring the bacterium, and consequently, the number of people contracting Lyme disease, would likely decline.

Reasoning *What additional fact would reinforce the argument that greater availability of non-infected hosts would reduce the transmission of Lyme?* The argument relies on the assumption that if more non-infected hosts are available, the ticks will simply switch hosts, thereby diluting the rate of infection in the tick population. To strengthen this dilution effect argument, we need a piece of information that confirms the larvae will have only one chance to become infected. If a tick larva could feed multiple times, its exposure to an infected mouse would be higher, making the dilution effect less reliable.

A The tick's health is not a factor in whether it transmits the bacterium to humans.

B The argument concerns tick-to-human transmission, not mouse-to-human transmission. This fact is already implicitly assumed by the focus on the tick vector.

C **Correct.** This strengthens the argument by validating the mechanism of the proposed solution. If a deer tick feeds **only once** while in the larval stage, then being exposed to one of the non-infected species guarantees the tick will **not** acquire the Lyme bacterium during its crucial larval feeding period. This maximizes the proposed "dilution effect" and makes the intervention much more likely to succeed.

D If a single mouse can infect many larvae, it means the host population of the mouse is highly efficient at spreading the bacterium. This suggests that even a small population of mice could offset the dilution effect from the increased "other species," making the intervention less effective; therefore this fact would tend to weaken the argument.

E Whether the non-infected species harbor *other* bacteria is outside the scope of the argument, which is focused solely on the Lyme disease bacterium.

The correct answer is C.

835. Museums that house Renaissance oil paintings typically store them in environments that are carefully kept within narrow margins of temperature and humidity to inhibit any deterioration. Laboratory tests have shown that the kind of oil paint used in these paintings actually adjusts to climatic changes quite well. If paint is the most sensitive substance in these works, then by relaxing the standards for temperature and humidity control as some museum directors suggest, **museums can reduce energy costs without risking damage to these paintings**. Museums would be rash to relax those standards, however, since results of preliminary tests indicate that **gesso, a compound routinely used by Renaissance artists to help paint adhere to the canvas, is unable to withstand significant variations in humidity**.

In the argument above, the two portions in **boldface** play which of the following roles?

(A) The first is a position that the argument calls into question; the second is an alternative position endorsed by the argument.

(B) The first is a position that the argument calls into question; the second is evidence put forward by the argument to challenge that position.

(C) The first is a position that the argument calls into question; the second is evidence that has been used to support that position.

(D) The first is the position taken by the argument; the second provides evidence to support that position.

(E) The first is the position taken by the argument; the second is evidence that has been used to challenge that position.

Argument Construction

Situation   Museums currently maintain strict temperature and humidity controls to protect Renaissance oil paintings. Laboratory tests indicate the oil paint handles climatic changes well. Based on this, some museum directors conclude they can relax climate standards to save energy without damage to the paintings. The historian's argument criticizes this proposal, stating it would be rash, because a different component of the paintings, gesso, is highly sensitive to humidity variations.

Reasoning   *What roles do the two **boldfaced** portions play in the argument?* The first **boldfaced** portion is the position or conclusion derived by the museum directors whom the historian's argument implicitly criticizes. It is the conclusion of a conditional statement that *if* paint is the most sensitive material in the paintings, controls could be relaxed without resulting harm. Since the historian immediately follows this with the counter-argument ("Museums would be rash . . . however . . ."), the first portion represents the position that the argument calls into question. This is followed by the second **boldfaced** portion, which is the evidence the historian uses to support their main conclusion that relaxing standards would be rash. This new information directly refutes the directors' crucial assumption that paint is the most sensitive substance, thus showing why their position, stated in the first **boldfaced** portion, is risky. The second portion therefore acts as a challenge or counter-evidence to the position in the first portion.

A   The first portion does state the position called into question. The second portion, however, is *evidence*, not an alternative position.

B   **Correct.** The first portion states the directors' proposed conclusion: a position the argument calls into question. The second portion, the discovery about gesso, is the *evidence* offered by the argument to directly *challenge* or undermine the directors' position.

C   The first portion does state the position called into question. However, the second portion is *evidence that challenges* the directors' position, not evidence used to *support* it.

D   The first portion is the position *rejected* by the argument, not the position taken by the argument. The second portion is evidence for an opposing position: the position taken by the argument.

E   The first portion is the position *rejected* by the argument. The second portion, however, is indeed evidence that challenges the position stated in the first portion.

The correct answer is B.

836. Most of Western music since the Renaissance has been based on a seven-note scale known as the diatonic scale, but when did the scale originate? A fragment of a bone flute excavated at a Neanderthal campsite has four holes, which are spaced in exactly the right way for playing the third through sixth notes of a diatonic scale. **The entire flute must surely have had more holes**, and examination of the find shows that **the flute was made from a bone that was long enough for these additional holes to have allowed a complete diatonic scale to be played**. Therefore, the Neanderthals who made the flute probably used a diatonic musical scale.

In the argument given, the two portions in **boldface** play which of the following roles?

(A) The first states the hypothesis that the argument seeks to support; the second presents evidence to support a conclusion that, in turn, supports the argument's main conclusion.

(B) The first states the hypothesis that the argument seeks to support; the second introduces evidence that has been used to argue against the argument's main conclusion.

(C) The first is a judgment that is used to support the main conclusion of the argument; the second introduces evidence to support that conclusion.

(D) The first is a judgment that is used to support the main conclusion of the argument; the second presents evidence restricting the scope of that judgment.

(E) The first is a conclusion drawn on the basis of evidence stated elsewhere in the argument; the second is the argument's main conclusion.

Argument Construction

Situation   The argument investigates the origin of the diatonic (seven-note) musical scale, which forms the basis of most Western music. The evidence is a fragment of a Neanderthal bone flute with four holes spaced correctly to play the third through sixth notes of this scale. The argument concludes that Neanderthals likely used the diatonic scale.

Reasoning   *What roles do the two **boldfaced** portions play in the argument?* The argument uses a chain of inference to bridge the archaeological evidence of the fragmentary flute to the final conclusion that Neanderthals probably used the diatonic scale. The initial evidence is the fact that four holes are spaced correctly for notes 3–6 of the diatonic scale. The first **boldfaced** portion is the first inference or judgment in the chain. It is based on the initial evidence of a fragment, suggesting the original flute was complete and functional. This judgment is essential because a flute with only four holes cannot play a full diatonic scale. The second **boldfaced** portion is the evidence that supports the judgment in the first portion. The bone's sufficient length supports the idea that the "more holes" mentioned in the first portion could have existed and served the necessary function of playing the complete scale. So the second portion supports the first portion, and the first portion is an intermediate step supporting the main conclusion, namely that the Neanderthals who made the flute probably used a diatonic musical scale.

A   The main hypothesis the argument seeks to support is the final conclusion (Neanderthals used the diatonic scale), not the claim stated in the first portion, namely that the flute "surely" had more holes. The second portion is not support for a preliminary conclusion, but rather evidence that makes the claim in the first portion more plausible.

B   The first portion states an intermediate judgment, not the main hypothesis. The second is evidence *for* the main conclusion, not against it.

C   **Correct.** The first portion is a judgment ("must surely have had more holes") that is a necessary intermediate step used to support the main conclusion that the Neanderthals used the diatonic scale. The second portion is the evidence: the bone was long enough; that evidence directly supports the immediate conclusion/judgment made in the first portion. This description captures the support relationship where the second supports the first, and the first supports the overall conclusion.

D   While the first portion is fairly characterized here, the second portion *supports* the judgment in the first by confirming the physical possibility that there were "more holes"; it does not restrict its scope.

E   While the first portion is an intermediate conclusion, the second portion is *evidence*, not the main conclusion, which can be found in the final sentence.

The correct answer is C.

837. Woodco Plywood Manufacturer: Ten years ago a study linked the high rates of respiratory ailments in Loganville to airborne pollutants released in the manufacture of plywood. In response, the city government imposed strict regulations on emissions from our plant, which we have followed at great cost to our production capacity. But after an initial dip, the rate of respiratory ailments rose to new levels, so the high rate was never a result of pollution from our plant.

Which of the following, if true, most seriously weakens the argument?

(A) Over the last decade, a series of studies linking respiratory ailments to dietary deficiencies has been published.

(B) Seven years ago, the Woodco plant installed equipment to increase production capacity without increasing annual pollutant emissions.

(C) Pollutant emissions at Woodco plywood plants in other towns have declined during the past twelve years.

(D) Nine years ago, a competing plywood manufacturer opened a plant just across the river from Woodco's plant.

(E) There are more facilities for treating respiratory ailments in Loganville today than there were eleven years ago.

Argument Evaluation

Situation   Ten years ago, a study linked Loganville's high rate of respiratory ailments to airborne pollutants from the Woodco Plywood plant. The city imposed strict, costly emission regulations on Woodco, which the company followed. After an initial drop, however, the rate of ailments returned to and then exceeded previous levels.

Reasoning   *What additional factor would tend to confirm that plywood manufacture is linked to respiratory illness?* Woodco concludes that since the ailment rate ultimately rose despite their compliance with regulations, their plant's pollution was never the cause of the high rate of respiratory disease. The argument attempts to demonstrate that the supposed cause (Woodco's pollution) and effect (high ailment rate) are not linked because when the cause was removed (Woodco's emissions reduced), the effect did not permanently disappear. To weaken this conclusion, we must introduce a factor that explains *why* the ailment rate increased *despite* Woodco's compliance, in a way that maintains the possibility that Woodco's pollution was indeed the original cause. This factor must be a new or continuing source of pollution or a new factor increasing the disease rate that appeared *after* the initial dip.

A   This link introduces an alternative cause for the high rates of illness, but it doesn't strengthen the link to Woodco specifically. It supports the possibility that Woodco may not have been the cause, making it a weak *strengthener* for the argument, not a weakener.

B   This fact explains a change in Woodco's operations but confirms that their emissions remained compliant with the regulations, which is a fact already acknowledged by the argument. It doesn't explain the rise in ailments.

C   The argument is concerned only with the rates and emissions in Loganville. Emissions in other towns are irrelevant.

D   **Correct.** This is the strongest weakener. The argument is based on the premise that Woodco's compliance *should* have solved the problem if Woodco was the cause. This option introduces a new source of airborne pollution—a competing plant—which opened *after* Woodco reduced its emissions. This new plant could have increased its pollution over time, or its addition may have simply outweighed Woodco's reduction. This provides a strong alternative explanation for why the ailment rate rose again, allowing the initial link between "plywood manufacture pollution" and "respiratory ailments" to remain valid.

E   An increase in treatment facilities would likely lead to better diagnosis and *reporting* of ailments, but it would not account for the pollutants that *cause* the ailments, nor would it affect the overall rate of sickness.

The correct answer is D.

838. Journalist: **Every election year at this time the state government releases the financial disclosures that potential candidates must make in order to be eligible to run for office.** Among those making a financial disclosure this year is, for the first time ever, the prominent local businessman Arnold Bergeron. There has often been talk in the past of Mr. Bergeron's running for governor, not least from Mr. Bergeron himself. This year it is likely he finally will, since even supporters of a Bergeron candidacy always conceded that **the necessity of making financial disclosures might have proved an insuperable obstacle.**

In the journalist's argument, the two **boldfaced** portions play which of the following roles?

(A) The first provides information without which the argument lacks force; the second states the journalist's conclusion.

(B) The first provides information without which the argument lacks force; the second identifies a position that the journalist argues against.

(C) The first provides information without which the argument lacks force; the second provides information that reinforces the journalist's argument.

(D) The first provides evidence in support of the journalist's conclusion; the second states that conclusion.

(E) The first provides evidence in support of the journalist's conclusion; the second provides evidence bearing against that conclusion.

Argument Construction

Situation   The state government releases financial disclosures required for political candidates every election year. This year, prominent local businessman Arnold Bergeron has made a disclosure for the first time. There has been ongoing speculation about Bergeron running for governor.

Reasoning   *What roles are played by the two **boldfaced** portions?* The journalist argues that Bergeron is likely to run for governor this year. The reasoning connects the new evidence of Bergeron's disclosure with past speculation regarding his interest in running for the office. The first **boldfaced** portion establishes the context under which the key piece of evidence (Bergeron's disclosure) gains its significance. Without knowing that this disclosure is required for eligibility, the fact that Bergeron made one would not support the conclusion that he is likely to run. Thus, the first portion provides necessary background information, or context, for the central piece of evidence. The second **boldfaced** portion identifies the obstacle that had previously prevented Bergeron from running. Since the journalist points out that Bergeron has now overcome this specific obstacle by making the disclosure, this information strongly supports the journalist's conclusion that Bergeron will finally run this year. It reinforces the idea that the removal of this barrier is the key catalyst for his candidacy.

A   The first portion provides necessary context. However, the second portion identifies the *past obstacle*, not the journalist's conclusion, namely that Bergeron will run this year.

B   The first portion provides necessary context. The second portion identifies a possible reason why he *didn't* run before, which the argument leverages; it is not a position the journalist argues *against*.

C   **Correct.** The first portion provides the context (the disclosure rule) without which the evidence (Bergeron disclosing) is meaningless—thus, the argument would lack force in its absence. The second portion identifies the precise *obstacle* that the journalist then shows has been overcome, thereby reinforcing the argument that Bergeron will run now.

D   The first portion is a rule that provides context, not primary evidence; the disclosure itself is the evidence. The second portion describes an *obstacle*, but does not present the conclusion.

E   The first portion is a rule that provides context, not primary evidence. The second portion provides information that *supports* the conclusion by explaining why the candidate is now free to run, not evidence against the conclusion.

The correct answer is C.

839. Rabbits were introduced to Numa Island in the nineteenth century. Overgrazing by the enormous population of rabbits now menaces the island's agriculture. The government proposes to reduce the population by using a virus that has caused devastating epidemics in rabbit populations elsewhere. There is, however, a chance that the virus will infect the bilby, an endangered native marsupial. The government's plan, therefore, may serve the interests of agriculture but will clearly increase the threat to native wildlife.

Which of the following, if true, most seriously weakens the argument?

(A) There is less chance that the virus will infect domestic animals on Numa than that it will infect bilbies.

(B) There are no species of animals on the island that prey on the rabbits.

(C) Overgrazing by rabbits endangers many of the plants on which bilbies feed.

(D) The virus that the government proposes to use has been successfully used elsewhere to control populations of rabbits.

(E) There is no alternative means of reducing the rabbit population that would involve no threat to the bilby.

Argument Evaluation

Situation   Rabbits, introduced to Numa Island in the nineteenth century, are now an enormous population whose overgrazing menaces agriculture. The government plans to use a virus known to cause rabbit epidemics to reduce the population. There is a chance this virus could also infect the endangered native bilby.

Reasoning   *What additional factor would tend to counteract the argument that the virus would increase the overall threat to the bilby?* The argument concludes that the government's plan "will clearly increase the threat to native wildlife" (specifically the bilby), even if it helps agriculture. The logic relies on a direct link: the plan has a risk of directly harming the bilby via the virus, therefore the plan increases the threat to native wildlife. To weaken this conclusion, we must show that, despite the risk posed by the virus, the government's plan *does not* increase the overall threat to native wildlife, or perhaps even decreases it. This can be achieved by showing that the current, untreated problem, namely the rabbits, already poses a significant, and perhaps greater, threat to the bilby.

A   This fact is irrelevant. The argument is concerned with the threat to native wildlife (the bilby), not to domestic animals. This comparison does not affect the risk/benefit analysis for the bilby.

B   This fact explains *why* the rabbit population is so large, which is background information. It doesn't alter the conclusion about whether the virus increases the threat to the bilby.

C   **Correct.** This most seriously weakens the argument. If the rabbits are destroying the bilbies' food source, they are already posing a severe and potentially greater threat to the bilby population's survival than the chance of the virus infecting them. The government's plan, by successfully reducing the rabbit population, could effectively preserve the bilbies' food supply, thus *reducing* the overall threat to the bilby species. The plan then does not "clearly increase the threat," but rather introduces one risk factor in exchange for a major benefit.

D   This statement strengthens the argument's feasibility in regard to *rabbits* but does not address the conclusion about the increased threat to bilbies.

E   This fact merely suggests the government's choice is pressing, but it doesn't affect the claim that releasing the virus "will clearly increase the threat." It doesn't introduce a mitigating factor that reduces the *net* threat, which is necessary to weaken the conclusion.

The correct answer is C.

840. Although utilities pay less for low-quality coal per ton delivered than for high-quality coal, more low-quality coal must be burned to generate the same amount of electricity. Therefore, the proper basis for a cost comparison at any given time is the relative cost, at that time, of purchasing the amount of coal a utility needs to buy in order to generate a given amount of electricity.

Which of the following, if true, casts the most serious doubt on the accuracy of the conclusion above?

(A) Per ton of coal burned, low-quality coal generates more ash than does high-quality coal, and the disposal of ash is becoming more expensive.

(B) Many large industrial centers are located closer to geological deposits of high-quality coal than they are to geological deposits of low-quality coal.

(C) Known reserves of low-quality coal are many times larger than known reserves of high-quality coal.

(D) The price per ton of high-quality coal has been rising faster than the price per ton for low-quality coal, and this trend will continue.

(E) Coal-fired power plants that burn low-quality coal efficiently also burn high-quality coal efficiently.

Argument Evaluation

Situation   The argument compares two types of coal: low-quality coal, which costs less per ton but requires more tons to generate a given amount of electricity; and high-quality coal, which costs more per ton but requires fewer tons to generate the same amount of electricity.

Reasoning   *What additional factor would suggest that the purchase price of the coal needed to generate a specific amount of electricity is not the best basis for comparison between the two types of coal?* The argument concludes that the proper basis for a cost comparison is the relative cost of purchasing the required amount of coal (i.e., comparing the cost of the *fuel itself* needed to generate the same amount of electricity). The reasoning is that since more low-quality coal is needed, the comparison should be based on the total cost of the required quantity of each type of fuel. To weaken this conclusion, we must introduce a factor that shows the purchase price of the fuel is *not* the proper or sole basis for cost comparison. This factor may be a significant, hidden cost associated with burning one type of coal that is excluded from the conclusion's comparison standard.

A   **Correct.** This introduces a significant and rising cost that is directly linked to the *amount* of coal burned. Since generating the same amount of electricity requires more tons of low-quality coal (and therefore generates more ash), the overall operational cost of using low-quality coal will be much higher than a comparison based solely on the purchase price of the fuel would suggest. The increasing cost of ash disposal means that the purchase price comparison alone is an inaccurate basis for the true economic comparison, thus seriously weakening the conclusion.

B   This statement introduces a possible factor, namely transportation costs, but its effect is ambiguous. If industrial centers are closer to high-quality coal, the transportation cost of low-quality coal would be higher, which only serves to *strengthen* the argument that high-quality coal is the better option and does not undermine the *basis of comparison*.

C   This statement presents a consideration of *future supply* and *long-term price stability*, not the cost comparison at any given time, which is the focus of the conclusion.

D   This information only helps utilities project *future* costs and suggests that low-quality coal may eventually become the cheaper option. It does not undermine the basis of comparison itself, which the argument states should be cost per amount of energy generated.

E   This statement confirms that plant efficiency is not a variable affecting the comparison. It neither strengthens nor weakens the conclusion.

The correct answer is A.

841. Newspaper article: Pecan growers get a high price for their crop when pecans are comparatively scarce, but the price drops sharply when pecans are abundant. Thus, in high-yield years, growers often hold back part of their crop in refrigerated warehouses until after the following year's harvest, hoping for higher prices then. This year's pecan crop was the smallest in five years. It is unlikely, therefore, that any of this year's crop will be held back.

Which of the following, if true, most seriously weakens the argument?

(A) Each of the last two years produced record-breaking pecan yields, and an unusually high percentage of last year's crop was held back.

(B) The quality of this year's pecan crop is typical of the quality of the pecan crops of the previous five years.

(C) Because of the practice of holding back part of the crop from especially high-yield years, pecan prices have not been subject to sharp fluctuations in recent years.

(D) For some pecan growers, this year's crop was no smaller than last year's.

(E) The last time the pecan crop was as small as it was this year, the practice of holding back part of one year's crop in anticipation of higher prices the next year had not yet become widespread.

Argument Evaluation

Situation   Pecan prices are high when scarce and low when abundant. In high-yield years when prices are low, growers often hold back part of their crop for the next year, hoping for better prices. This year's crop was the smallest in five years.

Reasoning   *What additional factor would make it more likely that part of this year's pecan crop will be held in reserve?* The argument concludes that probably none of this year's crop will be held back. The reasoning relies on the following chain of logic: the smallest crop in five years means the crop is scarce; scarce crops lead to high prices; growers typically hold back crops only in high-yield/low-price years; therefore since this is a low-yield/high-price year, the incentive to hold back is gone, so growers won't hold back the crop. To weaken this conclusion, we need a factor showing that growers will still hold back the crop *despite* the high price caused by the small yield. This could be due to an even stronger expectation of high prices next year, or, more simply, that there is already an abundant or excessive supply of pecans for some other reason, such as bumper crops in the preceding years. Alternatively, if the current high price is still lower than the price expected next year, the incentive to hold back remains.

A   **Correct.** This statement provides the crucial missing context: the refrigerated warehouses are likely full of old, unsold pecans from the last two record-breaking years. If there is already a surfeit of available pecans from *previous* years, that abundance will tend to lower the price even in this current low-yield year. That lower price in turn would suggest that growers may sell the old pecans and choose to hold part of this year's crop in reserve.

B   Quality is not a factor mentioned in the argument's logic, which is based purely on price fluctuation and yield size. This information does not affect the incentive to hold back the crop.

C   If fluctuations have been minimized, it actually weakens the incentive to hold back in *any* year, which slightly strengthens the argument that holding back won't happen now.

D   The argument is about the total crop size and the resulting market price. Even if a few growers had a normal yield, the *overall* market remains scarcity-driven, and prices will be high. This exception does not weaken the main conclusion about the general market behavior.

E   This historical fact about past market behavior has no bearing on the current incentive structure or storage constraints facing growers today. It is irrelevant to the current year's decision.

The correct answer is A.

842. **For most scientists, the period of highest creativity occurs before the age of forty.** It is commonly thought that this happens because the aging process brings about a loss of creative capacity. However, it turns out that almost all scientists who produce highly creative work beyond the age of forty entered their field late, less than a dozen years before their creative breakthroughs. Since **creative breakthroughs by scientists under forty also generally occur within a dozen years of the scientist's entry into the field,** it is most likely that the real reason why scientists over forty rarely produce highly creative work is not that they are too old but rather that they generally have spent too long in a given field.

In the argument given, the two portions in **boldface** play which of the following roles?

(A) The first presents a state of affairs, the explanation of which is at issue in the argument; the second provides evidence in support of the explanation that the argument seeks to establish.

(B) The first presents a state of affairs, the explanation of which is at issue in the argument; the second presents evidence that has been used to challenge the explanation that the argument favors.

(C) The first is the main conclusion of the argument; the second provides evidence in support of that main conclusion.

(D) The first is a claim that the argument seeks to refute; the second provides evidence in support of an alternative claim that the argument seeks to establish.

(E) The first is a generalization that, according to the argument, has exceptions; the second presents some of those exceptions.

Argument Construction

Situation   Scientists generally achieve their major creative breakthroughs before they turn forty. However, because most older scientists who achieve major creative breakthroughs became scientists later in life, the author argues that it is not age, but the amount of time spent in the field, that is probably the factor defining a scientist's period of greatest creativity, and further suggests that the twelve years after becoming a scientist constitute that especially creative period.

Reasoning   *How do the two **boldfaced** portions of the text relate to the argument that the reason scientists over forty produce fewer breakthroughs is not their age but rather the duration of their careers in science?* The first portion establishes that most highly creative work is produced by scientists under forty; the argument disputes the assumption that older scientists are simply less creative by offering an alternative explanation for that fact. The second portion points out that younger scientists generally achieve their creative breakthroughs within a dozen years of entering a scientific field, that fact is presented as evidence in support of the author's contention that the highly creative period is probably the dozen years after entering a scientific field, not the years before turning forty.

A   **Correct.** The first portion presents the information that most creative breakthroughs are achieved by scientists under forty; the argument disputes the common explanation that younger scientists are more creative than older ones. The second portion provides evidence for the argument's alternative explanation: that the creative period is probably the dozen years after entering the field, rather than simply the period before age forty.

B   While the first portion does indeed present a situation whose usual explanation is at issue in the argument, the second portion is evidence for, not against, the explanation advanced by the argument: that the creative period is probably the dozen years after entering a scientific field.

C   The first portion is not a conclusion but rather an observed fact that the argument seeks to explain; the second portion in no way provides evidence for the statement that most scientists achieve their creative breakthroughs before turning forty, but merely observes that that period coincides, for most scientists, with their first twelve years in the field.

D   The argument does not seek to refute the claim in the first portion but rather to propose an explanation for that claim; the second portion provides evidence for the alternative *explanation* for that initial claim, not for an alternative claim per se.

E   While the first portion is indeed a generalization subject to exceptions, the second portion in no way presents those exceptions: namely highly creative scientists over forty.

The correct answer is A.

843. Though sucking zinc lozenges has been promoted as a treatment for the common cold, research has revealed no consistent effect. Recently, however, a zinc gel applied nasally has been shown to greatly reduce the duration of colds. Since the gel contains zinc in the same form and concentration as the lozenges, the greater effectiveness of the gel must be due to the fact that cold viruses tend to concentrate in the nose, not the mouth.

In order to evaluate the argument, it would be most helpful to determine which of the following?

(A) Whether zinc is effective only against colds, or also has an effect on other virally caused diseases

(B) Whether there are remedies that do not contain zinc but that, when taken orally, can reduce the duration of colds

(C) Whether people who frequently catch colds have a zinc deficiency

(D) Whether either the zinc gel or the lozenges contain ingredients that have an impact on the activity of the zinc

(E) Whether the zinc gel has an effect on the severity of cold symptoms, as well as on their duration

Argument Evaluation

Situation Sucking zinc lozenges in not effective for treating colds, but nasal application of zinc gel is effective. Because the zinc is equal in form and concentration in both treatments, the argument concludes that the gel's effectiveness derives from the fact that it is applied to the nose, where cold viruses congregate, instead of the mouth, where they are less prevalent.

Reasoning *Is there an additional factor that could affect the relative effectiveness of zinc gel as compared to zinc lozenges?* The argument rules out two factors that might influence the relative effectiveness of gel versus lozenges: the form and concentration of the zinc itself. It then concludes that the only remaining relevant factor is the application site, nose or mouth. To determine whether this conclusion is sound, it would be helpful to know if there might be additional factors which the argument has overlooked that could plausibly influence the relative effectiveness of gel versus lozenges.

A The effectiveness of zinc for treating other viruses is not relevant to the question of why zinc gel is better than zinc lozenges for treating the cold virus.

B The possible effectiveness of other oral cold treatments has no bearing on the question of why zinc gel works better than zinc lozenges; such other treatments might have a different mechanism entirely.

C If people who frequently catch colds have a zinc deficiency, then that fact might help explain why zinc is an effective treatment, but it would not be relevant to the question of why zinc gel is more effective than zinc lozenges.

D **Correct.** The argument assumes that it has isolated the single factor that could explain the relative effectiveness of gel versus lozenges: the treatment site for each. To evaluate whether this assumption is correct, it would be helpful to know if there could be additional factors overlooked by the argument: if either the gel or the lozenges contain other ingredients that either promote or inhibit zinc's activity, then that fact could provide an alternative explanation for the gel's greater effectiveness and thereby undermine the argument, but if there are no such ingredients, that fact would tend to support the argument.

E The effectiveness of zinc gel for treating cold symptoms is not relevant to the question of why zinc gel is more effective than zinc lozenges for treating colds overall.

The correct answer is D.

844. An Italian map labeled "Mappamundi" ("Map of the world") is undated, but, based on its contents, was probably drawn sometime in the years 1488 to 1493. The map accurately depicts the western coast of Africa down to the Cape of Good Hope, which European explorers first reached in 1488, but it shows none of the islands of the West Indies visited by Columbus on his first voyage, from which he returned to Europe in early 1493.

Which of the following, if true, most strengthens the argument?

(A) European ships of the period required nearly a year to make the voyage to the Cape of Good Hope and back.

(B) Columbus published a widely read account of his first voyage immediately after his return.

(C) European authorities who sponsored expeditions often tried to keep information gained by those expeditions secret for as long as possible.

(D) A map as complicated as the map in question would have taken a cartographer of the 1400s several months to finish.

(E) During his first voyage, Columbus was able to sail from the West Indies back to Europe in less than three months.

Argument Evaluation

Situation   An undated Italian map, "Mappamundi," depicts specific landmasses that suggest it was created between 1488 and 1493. It shows the coast of Africa as far as the Cape of Good Hope; since European explorers first voyaged that far in 1488, that fact establishes 1488 as the first year the map could have been created. The conclusion that it was made before 1493 is based on the fact that the West Indies are missing from the map: because Columbus returned from a voyage which included the West Indies that year, the argument rests on the assumption that the mapmaker would have known about the West Indies after that date.

Reasoning   *What would tend to strengthen the claim that the map was drawn between 1488 and 1493?* The depiction of the African coast clearly establishes the start date of 1488. The evidence supporting the end date, 1493, is less conclusive: the absence of the West Indies on the map. Columbus returned to Europe with knowledge of the West Indies in 1493, but the argument relies on the assumption that this information likely would have reached the mapmaker the same year. Therefore any additional information which explains *why* the mapmaker could be expected to have learned about the West Indies in 1493 would tend to strengthen the argument.

A   A return journey of half a year from the Cape of Good Hope in 1488 would allow that information to reach the mapmaker within the same year, so this information does not weaken the argument that 1488 is the earliest plausible date for the map's creation, but neither does it strengthen it.

B   **Correct.** If Columbus published a widely-read account of his voyage immediately after his return in early 1493, then that fact would tend to strengthen the argument that the map was drawn *before* that text became available; if Columbus's account, including his description of the West Indies, became well-known after that date, then the mapmaker probably would have included the islands.

C   If the information gathered by Columbus was indeed kept secret, then that fact would tend to weaken, not strengthen, the argument: the mapmaker might have drawn the map after 1493, and failed to include the islands simply because information about them was suppressed.

D   The amount of time spent on the map does not strengthen the argument that the map was created during a specific period.

E   The duration of Columbus's voyage is not relevant to the question of when information about that voyage would have reached the mapmaker.

The correct answer is B.

845. In the year following an eight-cent increase in the federal tax on a pack of cigarettes, sales of cigarettes fell ten percent. In contrast, in the year prior to the tax increase, sales had fallen one percent. The volume of cigarette sales is therefore strongly related to the after-tax price of a pack of cigarettes.

The argument above requires which of the following assumptions?

(A) During the year following the tax increase, the pretax price of a pack of cigarettes did not increase by as much as it had during the year prior to the tax increase.

(B) The one percent fall in cigarette sales in the year prior to the tax increase was due to a smaller tax increase.

(C) The pretax price of a pack of cigarettes gradually decreased throughout the year before and the year after the tax increase.

(D) For the year following the tax increase, the pretax price of a pack of cigarettes was not eight or more cents lower than it had been the previous year.

(E) As the after-tax price of a pack of cigarettes rises, the pretax price also rises.

Argument Evaluation

Situation After a tax increase on cigarettes of eight cents a pack, sales dropped by ten percent compared to the previous year, when sales had dropped by a single percent. The argument concludes that cigarette sales have an inverse correlation with the after-tax price.

Reasoning: *What assumption underlies the argument?* The argument bases its conclusion regarding the correlation between cigarette sales and their after-tax price on two points: an eight-cent tax increase on cigarettes followed by a ten percent drop in sales. If, however, that eight-cent tax increase *did not* produce a rise in the after-tax price, then there would be no such correlation. Therefore the argument assumes that the pretax price of cigarettes did not fall by an amount sufficient to offset the new tax.

A The argument makes no assumption regarding the rates of pretax inflation on cigarettes; it merely assumes that cigarette prices did not *fall* by an amount sufficient to cancel out the new tax.

B The argument concerns a *correlation* between rising cigarette prices and falling sales; it makes no assumption that any decrease in sales must be *caused* by a price increase.

C An unspecified, slow decrease in pretax cigarette prices would offset the new tax to some unknown degree, but the argument makes no assumption that anything has occurred to counteract the effects of the new tax.

D Correct. The argument relies on a logical leap: from a tax increase on cigarettes to the conclusion that *after-tax* prices have an inverse correlation with cigarette sales. This correlation holds only if there has been no *pretax* price decrease sufficient to cancel out the new tax.

E The argument requires only that the total, after-tax price of cigarettes has gone up at the same time that sales have gone down; it does not depend on an assumption that the pretax price increases along with the after-tax price.

The correct answer is D.

846. Which of the following most logically completes the argument below?

According to promotional material published by the city of Springfield, more tourists stay in hotels in Springfield than stay in the neighboring city of Harristown. A brochure from the largest hotel in Harristown claims that more tourists stay in that hotel than stay in the Royal Arms Hotel in Springfield. If both of these sources are accurate, however, the county's "Report on Tourism" must be in error in indicating that _____.

(A)   more tourists stay in hotel accommodations in Harristown than stay in the Royal Arms Hotel

(B)   the Royal Arms Hotel is the only hotel in Springfield

(C)   there are several hotels in Harristown that are larger than the Royal Arms Hotel

(D)   some of the tourists who have stayed in hotels in Harristown have also stayed in the Royal Arms Hotel

(E)   some hotels in Harristown have fewer tourist guests each year than the Royal Arms Hotel has

Argument Construction

Situation   Sources claim that more tourists stay in Springfield hotels overall than in Harristown hotels overall, but also that more tourists stay at a particular hotel in Harristown than at a particular hotel—the Royal Arms—in Springfield. If both these claims are correct, then together they would indicate that a third claim stated in a report on tourism in the area must be incorrect.

Reasoning   *What claim would be disproved by the two facts about Springfield versus Harristown hotels taken together?* If Springfield is greater than Harristown in overall hotel stays, but also Harristown's largest hotel exceeds Springfield's Royal Arms in hotel stays, then it follows that there must be tourists staying in Springfield hotels *other* than the Royal Arms: otherwise Harristown would come in first overall solely on the basis of its largest hotel. Therefore the "Report on Tourism" must be wrong in stating that the Royal Arms is the only hotel in Springfield.

A   Since more tourists stay in a single hotel in Harristown than in the Royal Arms, there can be no mistake in claiming that more tourists stay in Harristown hotels *in total* than in the Royal Arms.

B   **Correct.** Since the largest hotel in Harristown exceeds Springfield's Royal Arms in the number of tourists' hotel stays, it follows that Springfield must have at least one other hotel in order to have the greater *total* number of hotel stays. Therefore a claim that the Royal Arms is the only hotel in Springfield must be false.

C   It would not necessarily be false to say that Harristown has multiple hotels larger than Springfield's Royal Arms: the question does not concern the relative hotel *capacity* of the two towns, but rather the number of tourists who actually stay in those hotels. Harristown's large hotels might sit empty.

D   The two claims about hotel stays in Harristown versus Springfield imply nothing regarding where particular tourists have, or have not, stayed at different times.

E   The two claims about hotel stays in Harristown versus Springfield do not suggest that Harristown could not have hotels with fewer guests than the Royal Arms, only that the Royal Arms cannot be the sole hotel in Springfield.

The correct answer is B.

847. The composer Pescard (1400–1474) is known to have been prolific, but little appears to have survived from the middle of Pescard's career (1440–1450). There are, however, many anonymous musical compositions from that decade, and modern scholarship has tentatively attributed several of them to Pescard. The recent attribution of one such piece, a particularly fine large-scale work, seems secure, being based on a newly discovered theoretical treatise from 1560 that names Pescard as that work's composer.

Which of the following, if true, would provide the most justification for judging secure modern scholarship's attribution of the large-scale work to Pescard?

(A) The 1560 treatise considers many works from the 1400s about whose authorship modern scholars had reached agreement before the treatise was discovered, and its attribution of these works to composers never disagrees with that of modern scholars.

(B) The 1560 treatise itself says that authorship of the work at issue is in dispute and attributes it to Pescard on the basis of a few stylistic features that turn out to be equally characteristic of other composers of the period.

(C) There are many other compositions from the 1400s whose authorship is in dispute among modern scholars that the 1560 treatise attributes to named composers.

(D) Around the time that the treatise was written, works were frequently attributed to prestigious composers, such as Pescard, simply because the person making the attribution thought well of the work.

(E) There are stylistic features of the work at issue that although first appearing in Pescard's early works also appear both in works of Pescard's contemporaries and in later works by Pescard.

Argument Evaluation

Situation The fact that there are few extant mid-career works by the fifteenth-century composer Pescard may be counteracted by scholars cautiously attributing anonymous works from the same period to Pescard. A large-scale work has been attributed to Pescard because a treatise from 1560 states that Pescard was the work's composer, and the argument considers the attribution to be "secure" owing to that evidence.

Reasoning *What would support the conclusion that the large-scale work's attribution to Pescard is definitive?* The argument offers a single piece of evidence in support of the attribution: the attribution derives from claims in the 1560 treatise. Therefore any evidence that the treatise is a generally reliable source would provide justification for the claim that the attribution is sound, just as any evidence that the treatise is unreliable would undermine that claim.

A **Correct.** The attribution is based entirely on the 1560 treatise, so evidence that the treatise is reliable—i.e., its claims consistently align with the consensus reached by modern scholars regarding other works—would provide some justification for regarding that attribution as "secure."

B Since that attribution is based entirely on the 1560 treatise, it would in no way justify that attribution if even the 1560 treatise described it as disputed and further advanced only dubious stylistic evidence on its behalf.

C If modern scholars continue to dispute the authorship of works despite the fact that the 1560 treatise names authors for those works, then that would suggest that those scholars do not regard the treatise as a definitive source; that fact would in turn cast doubt on the attribution of the large-scale work to Pescard, not justify claims regarding that attribution's soundness.

D If it was common practice at the time the treatise was written to make attributions on such a trivial basis, then that fact could potentially suggest that the treatise is unreliable, and thereby undermine, not justify, a conclusion based on its claims.

E The fact that the work contains features common to both Pescard and to other composers would provide no support for the claim that the work's attribution to Pescard is secure.

The correct answer is A.

848. **Plant scientists have used genetic engineering on seeds to produce crop plants that are highly resistant to insect damage.** Unfortunately, the seeds themselves are quite expensive, and the plants require more fertilizer and water to grow well than normal ones. Thus, for most farmers the savings on pesticides would not compensate for the higher seed costs and the cost of additional fertilizer. However, since **consumer demand for grains, fruits, and vegetables grown without the use of pesticides continues to rise,** the use of genetically engineered seeds of this kind is likely to become widespread.

In the argument given, the two portions in **boldface** play which of the following roles?

(A) The first supplies a context for the argument; the second is evidence that would, if not offset by other evidence, call the conclusion of the argument into question.

(B) The first presents a situation that the argument assumes will develop in certain ways; the second is one of those ways.

(C) The first introduces a development that the argument predicts will have a certain impact; the second is a consideration on which that prediction is based.

(D) The first provides evidence to support a prediction defended by the argument; the second acknowledges a trend that could undermine the force of that evidence.

(E) The first provides evidence to support a prediction defended by the argument; the second is that prediction.

Argument Construction

Situation   Scientists have genetically engineered seeds for common crops for insect resistance. The engineered seeds are expensive and the plants they produce need extra water and fertilizer; these additional costs generally exceed the savings on pesticides that result from the enhanced resistance to insects. The argument concludes that the use of genetically engineered seeds will probably increase, despite these drawbacks, in response to the demand for food grown without pesticides.

Reasoning   *How do the two **boldfaced** portions of the text relate to the argument that farmers probably will grow genetically engineered crops despite the greater expenses they incur?* The first portion describes a development, namely the creation of seeds engineered to produce insect-resistant plants; the argument predicts such seeds probably will be widely used. The second portion refers to rising consumer demand for foods grown without pesticides; because it would be easier to grow food crops without pesticides if those crops were engineered to resist pests on their own, that rising demand provides a basis for the prediction that use of the seeds will increase.

A   While the first portion does supply a context for the argument, the second portion is evidence in support of the argument's conclusion, not evidence that could call the conclusion into question.

B   The first portion does present a situation, namely the development of genetically engineered seeds; however, the second portion, which describes rising consumer demand for pesticide-free foods, is not a way in which the existence of genetically engineered seeds could develop, but rather a reason why they might become more popular with farmers.

C   **Correct.** The first portion describes a development: the creation of genetically engineered seeds. The author predicts such seeds will be widely used by farmers. That prediction is based on information set out in the second portion, which states that there is rising demand for the pesticide-free foods whose production is enabled by the seeds.

D   The first portion is not evidence for a prediction, but rather a development on which a prediction rests: that is, the seeds must exist before their use can become widespread. The second portion does describe a trend, but that trend does not undermine anything presented in the first portion.

E   The first portion cannot be evidence for a prediction made in the second portion, because the second portion is not a prediction but rather an observed trend.

The correct answer is C.

849. The percentage of households with an annual income of more than $40,000 is higher in Merton County than in any other county. However, the percentage of households with an annual income of $60,000 or more is highest in Sommer County.

If the statements above are true, which of the following can properly be concluded on the basis of them?

(A)   No household in Merton County has an annual income of $60,000 or more.

(B)   Some households in Merton County have an annual income between $40,000 and $60,000.

(C)   The number of households with an annual income of more than $40,000 is greater in Merton than in Sommer County.

(D)   Average annual household income is higher in Sommer than in Merton County.

(E)   The percentage of households with an annual income of $80,000 is higher in Sommer than in Merton County.

Argument Evaluation

Situation   Merton County has the highest percentage, of any county, of households with an annual income of $40,000, but Sommer County has the highest percentage of households with an annual income over $60,000.

Reasoning   *What can be inferred from the information regarding the two counties?* From the information presented we can conclude that, since Merton County has the highest percentage of households earning over $40,000 annually, but Sommer County has the highest percentage earning over $60,000 annually, some households in Merton County must make more than $40,000 and less than $60,000. If all of Merton's households earning over $40,000 were, in fact, households earning over $60,000, then it would necessarily have the highest percentage of such households, and Sommer would not.

A   Merton County could very well have households with an income over $60,000, just as long as it has a lower *percentage* of such households than does Sommer County.

B   **Correct.** Because Merton County has the highest percentage of households earning over $40,000, it follows that if *all* those households earned over $60,000, Merton would necessarily have the highest percentage of over-$60,000 households as well. But the information states that Sommer has the highest percentage of over-$60,000 households. Therefore Merton must have some households whose income falls between $40,000 and $60,000 annually.

C   Because there is no information given about the total population of either county, it is impossible to conclude anything about the absolute numbers of households earning over $40,000 in either county.

D   Sommer County might not have higher average household income that Merton County if Sommer has higher income disparity.

E   There is not enough information to support any conclusion regarding households earning over $80,000; either county could have a higher percentage of such households, or there could be no such households at all.

The correct answer is B.

850. The Shoemaker–Levy comet broke into fragments before colliding with Jupiter in 1994, but astronomers are uncertain of the fragments' size. Analysis of the ammonia clouds of Jupiter's outer atmosphere at the impact point showed traces of sulfur not normally present there. Since astronomers believe that the layer of clouds just below the outer atmosphere does contain sulfur, they concluded that the fragments must have been big enough to travel through the outer atmosphere before burning up.

Determining which of the following would be most useful in evaluating the astronomers' argument?

(A) Whether the ammonia clouds of Jupiter's outer atmosphere were of at least average thickness at the point of impact

(B) Whether the traces of sulfur detected in 1994 in the ammonia clouds have since disappeared

(C) Whether comets the size of Shoemaker–Levy typically break into fragments before colliding with a planet

(D) Whether comet fragments can release sulfur when they burn up

(E) Whether the comet fragments would have burned up sooner if they had struck at a different angle

Argument Evaluation

Situation   The Shoemaker–Levy comet shattered before it entered Jupiter's atmosphere, but astronomers were unsure regarding the size of the comet's pieces. Analysis of clouds in Jupiter's outer atmosphere found evidence of sulfur in the locations struck by the comet's fragments. Because astronomers believe that the inner layers of Jupiter's atmosphere may contain sulfur, they concluded that the presence of sulfur was probably due to fragments of the comet striking the clouds of the inner atmosphere, and therefore that those fragments were large enough to reach that layer without burning away.

Reasoning   *What additional factor would affect the conclusion that the sulfur came from Jupiter's inner atmosphere, and therefore that the fragments pierced as far as the inner atmosphere?* The astronomers' conclusion that the comet fragments were big enough to reach the inner atmosphere depends on the belief that the sulfur they observed must have come from that inner atmosphere. Therefore, in order to evaluate the argument, it would be helpful to know if there could be any other plausible source for that sulfur.

A   The thickness of the ammonia clouds of the outer atmosphere has no bearing on the central question: whether the sulfur the astronomers observed came from the inner atmosphere, or could have had some other source.

B   The dissipation of the traces of sulfur is not relevant to the question of where that sulfur came from.

C   Whether or not the fragmentation of the Shoemaker–Levy comet was typical for comets of its size does not affect the question of whether its fragments were big enough to dislodge sulfur from Jupiter's inner atmosphere.

D   Correct. If comet fragments can release sulfur as they burn up, then that would provide an alternative explanation for the sulfur observed in the outer atmosphere, and undermine the argument that the sulfur was likely dislodged from the inner atmosphere by large fragments; if, on the other hand, comet fragments do *not* release sulfur, that would strengthen the argument by eliminating an alternative explanation for the data. Therefore clarifying this point would be helpful for evaluating the argument.

E   Whether the comet fragments would have burned up sooner under hypothetical conditions is not relevant to the question of how far the fragments pierced into Jupiter's atmosphere under *actual* conditions.

The correct answer is D.

To register for the GMAT™ exam, go to www.mba.com/register

9.0   GMAT™ Official Guide Question Index

9.0 GMAT™ Official Guide Question Index

The Official Guide Index is organized by the section, difficulty level, and then by mathematical or verbal concepts in this book. The question number, page number, and answer explanation page number are listed so that questions within the book can be easily located.

Quantitative Reasoning — Chapter 4 – Page 78

Difficulty	Concept	Question #	Question ID #	Page	Answer Explanation Page
Easy	Absolute Value	79	102023	94	154
Easy	Algebraic Expressions	54	100973	90	145
Easy	Algebraic Expressions	62	100685	91	148
Easy	Algebraic Expressions	81	100224	94	155
Easy	Applied Problems	4	100933	82	130
Easy	Applied Problems	17	102007	84	134
Easy	Applied Problems	19	102008	85	134
Easy	Applied Problems	21	102009	85	135
Easy	Applied Problems	23	101006	85	136
Easy	Applied Problems	25	100235	86	136
Easy	Applied Problems	30	102010	86	138
Easy	Applied Problems	32	100275	87	138
Easy	Applied Problems	41	100172	88	141
Easy	Applied Problems	47	100858	89	143
Easy	Applied Problems	50	100968	89	144
Easy	Applied Problems	57	100222	90	146
Easy	Applied Problems	60	100606	91	147
Easy	Applied Problems	61	100716	91	148
Easy	Applied Problems	64	102018	91	148
Easy	Applied Problems	66	100199	92	149
Easy	Applied Problems	89	101035	95	157
Easy	Applied Problems; First-Degree Equations	85	100885	95	156

(Continued)

Difficulty	Concept	Question #	Question ID #	Page	Answer Explanation Page
Easy	Applied Problems; First-Degree Equations	92	101041	96	157
Easy	Applied Problems; First-Degree Equations	102	101209	97	161
Easy	Applied Problems; Percents	94	101043	96	158
Easy	Applied Problems; Properties of Numbers	14	100679	84	133
Easy	Applied Problems; Sequences	68	100523	92	150
Easy	Equations	49	102016	89	144
Easy	Estimation	28	100856	86	137
Easy	Estimation	33	102011	87	139
Easy	Estimation	46	100902	89	143
Easy	Estimation	48	100108	89	143
Easy	Estimation	51	100987	89	144
Easy	Exponents	38	100836	87	140
Easy	First-Degree Equations	10	100276	83	132
Easy	First-Degree Equations	20	100232	85	135
Easy	First-Degree Equations	22	100218	85	135
Easy	First-Degree Equations	63	100658	91	148
Easy	First-Degree Equations	80	100834	94	154
Easy	Formulas	67	102020	92	149
Easy	Formulas	69	102021	92	150
Easy	Formulas	96	101045	96	159
Easy	Fractions	77	100214	94	153
Easy	Fractions	101	101041	97	160
Easy	Functions	87	101011	95	156
Easy	Inequalities	26	100804	86	136
Easy	Inequalities	55	100768	90	145
Easy	Inequalities	73	100123	93	151
Easy	Inequalities	84	100835	95	155
Easy	Inequalities	99	100577	97	160

Difficulty	Concept	Question #	Question ID #	Page	Answer Explanation Page
Easy	Interpretation of Tables; Applied Problems	13	100838	84	132
Easy	Measurement Conversion	82	100741	94	155
Easy	Negative Exponents	91	101040	96	157
Easy	Number Line	9	102005	83	131
Easy	Operations with Integers	27	100410	86	137
Easy	Operations with Integers	74	100206	93	152
Easy	Operations with Radical Expressions	71	100161	93	151
Easy	Operations with Rational Numbers	8	100863	83	131
Easy	Operations with Rational Numbers	11	100718	83	132
Easy	Operations with Rational Numbers	18	100717	85	134
Easy	Operations with Rational Numbers	40	100213	88	141
Easy	Order	93	101042	96	158
Easy	Percents	16	100212	84	134
Easy	Percents	34	102012	87	139
Easy	Percents	39	102013	88	140
Easy	Percents	42	102014	88	142
Easy	Percents	45	102015	89	142
Easy	Percents	59	100152	91	147
Easy	Percents	75	100941	94	153
Easy	Percents	86	100952	95	156
Easy	Percents	88	102025	95	156
Easy	Percents	90	101036	96	157
Easy	Probability	24	100713	86	136
Easy	Profit and Loss	35	100709	87	139
Easy	Properties of Numbers	52	100966	90	144

(Continued)

Difficulty	Concept	Question #	Question ID #	Page	Answer Explanation Page
Easy	Properties of Numbers	70	100761	92	150
Easy	Properties of Numbers	76	100923	94	153
Easy	Rate	58	100928	91	147
Easy	Ratio and Proportion	12	100978	84	132
Easy	Ratio and Proportion	15	102006	84	133
Easy	Ratio and Proportion	37	100189	87	140
Easy	Ratio and Proportion	44	100202	88	142
Easy	Ratio and Proportion	65	102019	92	149
Easy	Ratios	95	101044	96	159
Easy	Sequences	53	100295	90	145
Easy	Series and Sequences	100	100806	97	160
Easy	Simplifying Algebraic Expressions	36	100162	87	139
Easy	Simplifying Algebraic Expressions	78	100163	94	154
Easy	Simplifying Algebraic Expressions; Percents	31	100254	87	138
Easy	Simultaneous Equations	43	100720	88	142
Easy	Simultaneous Equations	83	102024	95	155
Easy	Simultaneous First-Degree Equations	29	100219	86	138
Easy	Statistics	1	102001	82	129
Easy	Statistics	2	102002	82	129
Easy	Statistics	3	100100	82	130
Easy	Statistics	5	102003	82	130
Easy	Statistics	6	100739	83	130
Easy	Statistics	7	102004	83	131
Easy	Statistics	56	100114	90	145
Easy	Statistics	72	102022	93	151
Easy	Statistics	97	100062	96	159
Easy	Statistics	98	100318	97	159
Easy	Statistics	103	101356	97	161
Medium	Absolute Value; Number Line	137	100974	103	173

Difficulty	Concept	Question #	Question ID #	Page	Answer Explanation Page
Medium	Algebraic Expressions	108	100788	98	163
Medium	Applied Problems	117	100964	100	166
Medium	Applied Problems	123	101008	101	168
Medium	Applied Problems	126	102030	101	169
Medium	Applied Problems	134	100990	102	172
Medium	Applied Problems	142	102032	104	175
Medium	Applied Problems	148	100828	105	177
Medium	Applied Problems	149	100158	105	177
Medium	Applied Problems	151	100578	105	178
Medium	Applied Problems	173	102039	108	185
Medium	Applied Problems	181	102042	110	188
Medium	Applied Problems	183	102044	110	189
Medium	Applied Problems	188	102789	111	190
Medium	Applied Problems; Average	187	102667	110	190
Medium	Applied Problems; Percents	165	101049	107	183
Medium	Elementary Combinatorics	161	100103	107	181
Medium	Equations	154	102034	106	179
Medium	Equations	162	102035	107	182
Medium	Equations	167	101051	108	183
Medium	Equations	178	101062	109	187
Medium	Equations	185	102421	110	189
Medium	Equations; Factoring	176	101060	109	186
Medium	Estimation	150	100893	105	178
Medium	Estimation; Exponents	153	100154	105	179
Medium	Exponents	133	100135	102	172
Medium	First-Degree Equations	120	100591	100	167
Medium	Formulas	107	100772	98	163
Medium	Formulas	111	100183	99	164
Medium	Formulas	114	102029	99	165
Medium	Fractions	191	102990	111	191

(Continued)

Difficulty	Concept	Question #	Question ID #	Page	Answer Explanation Page
Medium	Functions	147	100111	104	177
Medium	Functions	175	101059	109	186
Medium	Inequalities	138	100892	103	173
Medium	Measurement Conversion	109	100816	98	163
Medium	Measurement Conversion	122	100734	101	168
Medium	Measurement Conversion	145	100138	104	176
Medium	Measurement Conversion	174	101058	109	186
Medium	Number Line	182	102043	110	188
Medium	Operations on Integers	136	100719	103	173
Medium	Operations with Decimals; Place Value	160	100710	107	181
Medium	Operations with Integers	124	100697	101	168
Medium	Operations with Integers	158	100737	106	181
Medium	Order	169	101053	108	184
Medium	Percents	116	100869	100	166
Medium	Percents	143	100216	104	175
Medium	Percents	155	100797	106	180
Medium	Percents	177	102040	109	187
Medium	Percents	180	102041	109	188
Medium	Percents	189	102856	111	191
Medium	Percents; First-Degree Equations	125	100822	101	169
Medium	Percents; Ratio and Proportion	127	100105	101	170
Medium	Place Value	139	100116	103	174
Medium	Probability	152	100676	105	179
Medium	Properties of Integers; Series	163	101047	107	182
Medium	Properties of Integers; Series	184	102294	110	189
Medium	Properties of Numbers	144	100735	104	176
Medium	Ratio and Proportion	113	100823	99	165
Medium	Ratio and Proportion	170	102036	108	185
Medium	Remainders	119	100136	100	167

Difficulty	Concept	Question #	Question ID #	Page	Answer Explanation Page
Medium	Second-Degree Equations	115	100935	99	166
Medium	Second-Degree Equations	130	100125	102	171
Medium	Second-Degree Equations	146	100732	104	177
Medium	Series and Sequences	121	100153	100	168
Medium	Series and Sequences	172	102038	108	185
Medium	Series and Sequences; Decimals	166	101050	107	183
Medium	Sets	106	100678	98	162
Medium	Sets	132	100900	102	171
Medium	Sets	140	100809	103	174
Medium	Sets	141	100898	103	175
Medium	Sets (Venn Diagrams)	164	101048	107	183
Medium	Sets; Interpretation of Tables	135	100889	103	172
Medium	Simplifying Algebraic Expressions	110	100165	98	164
Medium	Simplifying Algebraic Expressions	157	100274	106	180
Medium	Simplifying Algebraic Expressions; Operations on Rational Numbers	129	101007	102	170
Medium	Simultaneous Equations	128	100997	102	170
Medium	Simultaneous Equations; Computation	179	101063	109	187
Medium	Simultaneous Equations; Inequalities	159	100740	107	181
Medium	Statistics	104	102026	98	162
Medium	Statistics	105	102027	98	162
Medium	Statistics	112	102028	99	164
Medium	Statistics	118	100221	100	167
Medium	Statistics	131	102031	102	171
Medium	Statistics	156	100132	106	180
Medium	Statistics	171	102037	108	185
Medium	Statistics	190	102913	111	191
Medium	Statistics; Applied Problems	186	102538	110	189

(Continued)

Difficulty	Concept	Question #	Question ID #	Page	Answer Explanation Page
Medium	Work Problem	168	101052	108	184
Hard	Applied Problems	192	100252	111	192
Hard	Applied Problems	196	100253	112	193
Hard	Applied Problems	203	100708	113	196
Hard	Applied Problems	209	100257	114	198
Hard	Applied Problems	216	100913	115	201
Hard	Applied Problems	226	100149	116	206
Hard	Applied Problems	230	100944	117	207
Hard	Applied Problems	236	100261	118	210
Hard	Applied Problems	237	100262	118	210
Hard	Applied Problems	245	100241	119	212
Hard	Applied Problems	254	100982	120	216
Hard	Applied Problems	264	100267	122	220
Hard	Applied Problems	265	100268	122	221
Hard	Applied Problems	271	100243	123	224
Hard	Applied Problems	283	101071	125	229
Hard	Applied Problems; Estimation	278	101066	124	227
Hard	Applied Problems; First-Degree Equations	281	101069	125	228
Hard	Applied Problems; Formulas	291	101905	126	232
Hard	Applied Problems; Simultaneous Equations	232	100242	117	208
Hard	Elementary Combinatorics	193	100186	111	192
Hard	Elementary Combinatorics	199	100971	112	194
Hard	Elementary Combinatorics	229	100156	117	207
Hard	Elementary Combinatorics	247	100616	119	213
Hard	Elementary Combinatorics	260	100721	121	218
Hard	Elementary Combinatorics	284	101072	125	229
Hard	Equations	227	100925	116	207
Hard	Equations	288	101498	126	231
Hard	Estimation	238	100263	118	210

Difficulty	Concept	Question #	Question ID #	Page	Answer Explanation Page
Hard	Estimation; Operations on Radical Expressions	285	101073	125	230
Hard	Exponents	276	101064	124	226
Hard	Fractions; Decimals	275	100992	124	226
Hard	Inequalities	231	100911	117	208
Hard	Inequalities	239	100264	118	211
Hard	Inequalities	272	100273	123	224
Hard	Interpretation of Graphs and Tables; Statistics	213	100572	114	200
Hard	Negative Exponents	255	100830	120	216
Hard	Negative Exponents	274	100954	124	225
Hard	Operations on Rational Numbers	212	100912	114	199
Hard	Operations on Rational Numbers	233	100259	117	208
Hard	Operations on Rational Numbers	243	100244	119	212
Hard	Operations on Rational Numbers	248	100184	119	214
Hard	Operations on Rational Numbers	261	100852	121	219
Hard	Operations on Rational Numbers	268	100271	123	222
Hard	Operations on Rational Numbers	269	100272	123	222
Hard	Operations with Integers	222	100831	116	205
Hard	Operations with Integers	250	100776	120	215
Hard	Operations with Rational Numbers	210	100258	114	199
Hard	Percents	204	100240	113	196
Hard	Percents	218	100888	115	201
Hard	Percents	221	100173	115	204
Hard	Percents	253	100986	120	215
Hard	Percents	256	100785	121	217
Hard	Percents	262	100617	122	219
Hard	Probability	195	100712	112	192
Hard	Probability	211	100245	114	199

(Continued)

Difficulty	Concept	Question #	Question ID #	Page	Answer Explanation Page
Hard	Probability	219	100955	115	202
Hard	Probability	266	100269	122	221
Hard	Probability; Elementary Combinatorics	277	101065	124	227
Hard	Profit and Loss	242	100887	118	212
Hard	Properties of Integers	279	101067	124	228
Hard	Properties of Integers	282	101070	125	229
Hard	Properties of Integers	293	102168	126	233
Hard	Properties of Integers; Series	289	101622	126	231
Hard	Properties of Numbers	194	100120	111	192
Hard	Properties of Numbers	205	100122	113	196
Hard	Properties of Numbers	223	100907	116	205
Hard	Properties of Numbers	224	100333	116	206
Hard	Properties of Numbers	225	100829	116	206
Hard	Properties of Numbers	228	100192	116	207
Hard	Properties of Numbers	235	100942	117	209
Hard	Properties of Numbers	241	100266	118	211
Hard	Properties of Numbers	246	100983	119	213
Hard	Properties of Numbers	259	100246	121	218
Hard	Properties of Numbers; Decimals	198	100614	112	194
Hard	Property of Numbers	214	101075	114	200
Hard	Rate	251	100217	120	215
Hard	Second-Degree Equations	217	100940	115	201
Hard	Second-Degree Equations	234	100260	117	208
Hard	Second-Degree Equations	267	100270	122	221
Hard	Second-Degree Equations	270	100699	123	223
Hard	Second-Degree Equations; Simultaneous Equations	206	100256	113	197
Hard	Sequences	252	100908	120	215
Hard	Series and Sequences	287	102045	125	231

Difficulty	Concept	Question #	Question ID #	Page	Answer Explanation Page
Hard	Series and Sequences; First-Degree Equations	286	101074	125	230
Hard	Sets	273	100197	123	225
Hard	Sets (Venn Diagrams)	290	101774	126	232
Hard	Simplifying Algebraic Expressions	244	100910	119	212
Hard	Simplifying Algebraic Expressions	258	100818	121	218
Hard	Simplifying Expressions; Arithmetic Computation with Integers	249	101001	119	214
Hard	Simultaneous Equations	200	100748	112	195
Hard	Simultaneous Equations; Inequalities	207	100832	113	197
Hard	Statistics	197	100937	112	193
Hard	Statistics	202	100791	113	195
Hard	Statistics	208	100250	113	197
Hard	Statistics	215	100969	114	201
Hard	Statistics	220	100901	115	203
Hard	Statistics	257	100946	121	217
Hard	Statistics	280	101068	124	228
Hard	Statistics	292	102037	126	232
Hard	Statistics; Applied Problems	240	100265	118	211
Hard	Statistics; Applied Problems; Simultaneous Equations	263	100760	122	220
Hard	Systems of Equations	201	100251	113	195

Data Insights — Chapter 6 – Page 256

Data Sufficiency – Page 268

Difficulty	Concept	Question #	Question ID #	Page	Answer Explanation Page
Easy	Applied Problems	294	100109	268	286
Easy	Applied Problems	296	100886	268	287
Easy	Applied Problems	307	100967	269	292
Easy	Applied Problems	309	100919	269	292
Easy	Applied Problems	310	100655	269	293
Easy	Applied Problems	321	100722	270	297
Easy	Applied Problems	324	100782	271	298
Easy	Applied Problems	335	101080	272	302
Easy	Applied Problems	336	101081	272	303
Easy	Applied Problems	337	101082	272	303
Easy	Applied Problems	338	101083	272	304
Easy	Applied Problems	339	101084	272	304
Easy	Applied Problems	340	101085	272	305
Easy	Applied Problems	341	100083	272	305
Easy	Applied Problems	342	100274	272	305
Easy	Applied Problems	343	100561	273	306
Easy	Applied Problems	344	100799	273	306
Easy	Equations	311	102046	269	293
Easy	Equations	314	102047	270	294
Easy	Estimation	323	102051	271	298
Easy	Evaluation	332	101077	271	301
Easy	Inequalities	325	100731	271	298
Easy	Inference	331	101076	271	301
Easy	Inference	333	101078	272	302
Easy	Inference	334	101079	272	302
Easy	Order	318	100137	270	296
Easy	Order; Ratio	303	100759	269	290

Difficulty	Concept	Question #	Question ID #	Page	Answer Explanation Page
Easy	Percents	329	100247	271	300
Easy	Probability	322	100805	270	297
Easy	Rate Problem	330	100238	271	300
Easy	Ratio and Proportion	295	100794	268	286
Easy	Ratio and Proportion	298	100150	268	287
Easy	Ratio and Proportion	300	100231	268	288
Easy	Ratio and Proportion	306	100728	269	291
Easy	Ratios	301	100198	268	288
Easy	Sets	313	100962	270	294
Easy	Sets	319	100169	270	296
Easy	Sets	320	100696	270	297
Easy	Simultaneous Equations	299	100960	268	288
Easy	Simultaneous Equations	308	100145	269	292
Easy	Simultaneous Equations	312	100985	270	294
Easy	Simultaneous Equations	326	100282	271	299
Easy	Simultaneous Equations	327	100283	271	299
Easy	Simultaneous Equations	328	100285	271	299
Easy	Statistics	297	100770	268	287
Easy	Statistics	302	100861	269	289
Easy	Statistics	304	100505	269	290
Easy	Statistics	305	100117	269	290
Easy	Statistics	315	102048	270	295
Easy	Statistics	316	102049	270	295
Easy	Statistics	317	102050	270	295
Medium	Applied Problems	354	100210	274	310
Medium	Applied Problems	362	100724	274	313
Medium	Applied Problems	363	100680	275	313
Medium	Applied Problems	367	100873	275	315
Medium	Applied Problems	373	100155	276	318

(*Continued*)

Difficulty	Concept	Question #	Question ID #	Page	Answer Explanation Page
Medium	Applied Problems	375	100207	276	319
Medium	Applied Problems	378	101086	276	320
Medium	Applied Problems	380	101088	277	321
Medium	Applied Problems	381	101089	277	321
Medium	Applied Problems	383	101091	277	322
Medium	Applied Problems	385	101093	277	323
Medium	Applied Problems	387	101095	277	324
Medium	Applied Problems	388	101902	278	324
Medium	Applied Problems; Percents	370	100825	275	316
Medium	Applied Problems; Percents	371	100972	276	317
Medium	Applied Problems; Proportions	351	100975	273	308
Medium	Applied Problems	386	101094	277	323
Medium	Computation with Integers	366	100813	275	315
Medium	Computation with Integers	372	100670	276	317
Medium	Evaluation	382	101090	277	322
Medium	First-Degree Equations	357	100228	274	311
Medium	First-Degree Equations	365	100230	275	314
Medium	Inequalities	369	100171	275	316
Medium	Inference	379	101087	276	320
Medium	Inference	384	101092	277	322
Medium	Operations with Integers; Order	359	100190	274	312
Medium	Percents	355	102054	274	310
Medium	Place Value	352	102052	273	309
Medium	Properties of Integers	377	100215	276	319
Medium	Ratio and Proportion	353	102053	274	310
Medium	Ratios	349	100284	273	308
Medium	Ratios; Simultaneous Equations	348	100281	273	307
Medium	Sets	364	100897	275	314
Medium	Simultaneous Equations	345	100792	273	306
Medium	Simultaneous Equations	346	100279	273	307

Difficulty	Concept	Question #	Question ID #	Page	Answer Explanation Page
Medium	Simultaneous Equations	347	100280	273	307
Medium	Simultaneous Equations	350	100286	273	308
Medium	Simultaneous Equations	358	100278	274	312
Medium	Simultaneous Equations	368	102058	275	315
Medium	Statistics	356	102055	274	311
Medium	Statistics	360	102056	274	312
Medium	Statistics	361	102057	274	313
Medium	Statistics	374	100857	276	318
Medium	Statistics	376	100895	276	319
Hard	Applied Problems	393	100874	278	326
Hard	Applied Problems	395	100877	278	327
Hard	Applied Problems	396	100963	278	327
Hard	Applied Problems	403	100644	279	330
Hard	Applied Problems	407	100248	280	332
Hard	Applied Problems	414	100715	281	335
Hard	Applied Problems	416	100821	281	336
Hard	Applied Problems	418	100249	281	338
Hard	Applied Problems; Estimating	410	100996	280	333
Hard	Computation with Integers	394	100758	278	327
Hard	Equations	401	102059	279	329
Hard	Exponents	432	102060	283	346
Hard	Inequalities	400	101004	279	316
Hard	Inequalities	406	100536	279	331
Hard	Inference	420	101021	281	339
Hard	Inference	421	101022	282	339
Hard	Inference	422	101023	282	340
Hard	Inference	423	101024	282	340
Hard	Inference	424	101025	282	341
Hard	Inference	425	101026	282	342

(Continued)

Difficulty	Concept	Question #	Question ID #	Page	Answer Explanation Page
Hard	Inference	426	101027	282	342
Hard	Inference	427	101028	283	343
Hard	Inference	428	101029	283	344
Hard	Inference	429	101030	283	344
Hard	Inference	430	101031	283	345
Hard	Inference	431	101032	283	345
Hard	Operations on Rational Numbers	411	100694	280	334
Hard	Percents	389	100673	278	325
Hard	Percents	391	100239	278	326
Hard	Percents	397	100204	279	328
Hard	Percents	434	102062	284	347
Hard	Probability	392	100806	278	326
Hard	Properties of Numbers	413	100540	280	335
Hard	Proportions	419	100255	281	338
Hard	Rate Problems	398	100905	279	328
Hard	Ratio and Proportion	405	100662	279	331
Hard	Sets	390	100755	278	325
Hard	Sets	404	100140	279	330
Hard	Sets	412	100853	280	334
Hard	Simultaneous Equations	399	100277	279	328
Hard	Simultaneous Equations	402	100692	279	330
Hard	Statistics	408	100143	280	332
Hard	Statistics	409	100695	280	332
Hard	Statistics	415	100131	281	336
Hard	Statistics	417	100698	281	337
Hard	Statistics	433	102061	284	346
Hard	Statistics	435	102063	284	347
Hard	Statistics	436	101489	284	348

Two-Part Analysis – Page 349

Difficulty	Concept	Question #	Question ID #	Page	Answer Explanation Page
Easy	Apply	438	100357	349	375
Easy	Apply	440	100364	350	376
Easy	Apply	444	100389	351	379
Easy	Apply	445	100390	351	379
Easy	Apply	450	101096	353	383
Easy	Apply	452	102064	354	385
Easy	Evaluate	442	100373	350	378
Easy	Infer	437	100354	349	375
Easy	Infer	441	100367	350	377
Easy	Infer	443	100377	351	378
Easy	Infer	446	100398	352	380
Easy	Infer	447	100399	352	381
Easy	Infer	448	100429	352	382
Easy	Infer	449	100504	353	383
Easy	Infer	451	101097	353	384
Easy	Recognition	454	102066	354	386
Easy	Strategize	439	100359	349	376
Easy	Strategize	453	102065	354	385
Easy	Strategize	455	101018	355	387
Medium	Apply	460	100322	357	390
Medium	Apply	463	100360	358	393
Medium	Apply	464	100365	358	393
Medium	Apply	465	100374	358	394
Medium	Apply	467	100392	359	395
Medium	Apply	476	101098	362	401
Medium	Evaluate	457	100307	355	388
Medium	Evaluate	462	100355	357	392
Medium	Evaluate	473	100451	361	399

(Continued)

Difficulty	Concept	Question #	Question ID #	Page	Answer Explanation Page
Medium	Evaluate	477	102067	362	402
Medium	Evaluate	480	101342	363	404
Medium	Evaluate	481	102045	364	405
Medium	Evaluate	482	102173	364	406
Medium	Evaluate	484	102428	365	407
Medium	Evaluate	486	102701	365	408
Medium	Infer	459	100315	356	389
Medium	Infer	461	100332	357	391
Medium	Infer	466	100378	359	395
Medium	Infer	468	100400	359	396
Medium	Infer	469	100401	360	397
Medium	Infer	470	100402	360	397
Medium	Infer	471	100426	360	398
Medium	Infer	472	100444	360	399
Medium	Infer	474	100474	361	400
Medium	Infer	475	100506	361	400
Medium	Infer	478	102068	363	403
Medium	Infer	479	101167	363	404
Medium	Infer	483	102306	364	406
Medium	Infer	485	102559	365	408
Medium	Recognition	458	100308	356	389
Medium	Strategize	456	100301	355	388
Hard	Apply	490	102072	367	411
Hard	Apply	491	100314	367	411
Hard	Apply	492	100324	368	412
Hard	Apply	497	100404	370	416
Hard	Apply	501	101100	371	419
Hard	Apply	502	101101	371	420
Hard	Apply	503	101633	372	421
Hard	Evaluate	494	100371	368	413

Difficulty	Concept	Question #	Question ID #	Page	Answer Explanation Page
Hard	Infer	487	102069	366	409
Hard	Infer	488	102070	366	410
Hard	Infer	489	102071	367	410
Hard	Infer	493	100331	368	413
Hard	Infer	498	100428	370	417
Hard	Infer	499	100437	370	418
Hard	Infer	500	101099	371	419
Hard	Infer	504	101758	372	421
Hard	Strategize	495	100391	369	414
Hard	Strategize	496	100403	369	415

Verbal Reasoning — Chapter 8 – Page 448

Reading Comprehension – Page 458

Difficulty	Concept	Question #	Question ID #	Page	Answer Explanation Page
Easy	Application	507	100597	459	523
Easy	Application	512	100542	462	526
Easy	Evaluation	517	102075	465	529
Easy	Evaluation	521	100589	467	532
Easy	Evaluation	528	102078	470	536
Easy	Evaluation	536	100047	473	540
Easy	Evaluation	545	100668	477	545
Easy	Inference	509	100604	460	524
Easy	Inference	511	100541	462	526
Easy	Inference	514	100544	463	528
Easy	Inference	515	102073	464	528
Easy	Inference	524	100303	468	534
Easy	Inference	525	100304	469	534
Easy	Inference	534	100481	472	539
Easy	Inference	543	100614	476	544
Easy	Logical Structure	530	102080	471	537
Easy	Main Idea	505	100596	458	522
Easy	Main Idea	508	100603	460	524
Easy	Main Idea	519	100587	466	531
Easy	Main Idea	531	102081	471	538
Easy	Main Idea	535	100482	472	540
Easy	Main Idea	539	100393	474	542
Easy	Main Idea	542	100478	475	543
Easy	Purpose	537	100089	473	541
Easy	Supporting Idea	506	100598	458	522
Easy	Supporting Idea	510	100605	461	525
Easy	Supporting Idea	513	100543	463	527
Easy	Supporting Idea	516	102074	464	529

Difficulty	Concept	Question #	Question ID #	Page	Answer Explanation Page
Easy	Supporting Idea	518	102076	465	530
Easy	Supporting Idea	520	100588	466	531
Easy	Supporting Idea	522	100590	467	532
Easy	Supporting Idea	523	100302	468	533
Easy	Supporting Idea	526	100305	469	535
Easy	Supporting Idea	527	102077	470	536
Easy	Supporting Idea	529	102079	470	537
Easy	Supporting Idea	532	100479	472	538
Easy	Supporting Idea	533	100480	472	539
Easy	Supporting Idea	538	100110	473	541
Easy	Supporting Idea	540	100432	474	542
Easy	Supporting Idea	541	100443	475	543
Easy	Supporting Idea	544	100655	476	545
Easy	Supporting Idea	546	100822	478	546
Easy	Supporting Idea	547	100860	478	547
Medium	Application	561	100547	484	556
Medium	Application	570	100494	487	562
Medium	Application	575	100539	490	564
Medium	Evaluation	550	100340	480	549
Medium	Evaluation	551	100341	480	549
Medium	Evaluation	553	100343	480	550
Medium	Evaluation	555	100561	481	552
Medium	Evaluation	557	100563	482	553
Medium	Evaluation	562	100548	484	556
Medium	Evaluation	567	102087	486	560
Medium	Evaluation	568	102088	486	560
Medium	Evaluation	571	100495	488	562
Medium	Evaluation	572	100496	488	563
Medium	Evaluation	578	100509	492	566

(Continued)

Difficulty	Concept	Question #	Question ID #	Page	Answer Explanation Page
Medium	Evaluation	582	100329	494	568
Medium	Evaluation	585	101103	495	570
Medium	Evaluation	593	100388	498	575
Medium	Evaluation	594	100716	499	575
Medium	Inference	549	100339	479	548
Medium	Inference	552	100342	480	550
Medium	Inference	554	100560	481	551
Medium	Inference	556	100562	482	553
Medium	Inference	564	102084	485	558
Medium	Inference	574	100538	489	564
Medium	Inference	576	100507	491	565
Medium	Inference	581	100328	493	568
Medium	Inference	583	100330	494	569
Medium	Inference	587	101105	496	571
Medium	Inference	590	101108	497	573
Medium	Inference	596	100727	499	577
Medium	Inference	597	100751	500	577
Medium	Logical Structure	589	101107	497	572
Medium	Logical Structure	600	100832	502	579
Medium	Main Idea	573	100537	489	563
Medium	Main Idea	579	100510	492	567
Medium	Main Idea	580	100327	493	567
Medium	Main Idea	588	101106	497	572
Medium	Main Idea	598	100799	500	578
Medium	Purpose	595	100720	499	576
Medium	Supporting Idea	548	100338	479	547
Medium	Supporting Idea	558	100564	482	554
Medium	Supporting Idea	559	100545	483	555
Medium	Supporting Idea	560	100546	483	555
Medium	Supporting Idea	563	100549	484	557

Difficulty	Concept	Question #	Question ID #	Page	Answer Explanation Page
Medium	Supporting Idea	565	102085	485	558
Medium	Supporting Idea	566	102086	485	559
Medium	Supporting Idea	569	100493	487	561
Medium	Supporting Idea	577	100508	491	565
Medium	Supporting Idea	584	101102	495	569
Medium	Supporting Idea	586	101104	495	570
Medium	Supporting Idea	591	100290	498	574
Medium	Supporting Idea	592	100386	498	574
Medium	Supporting Idea	599	100820	501	579
Hard	Application	614	100500	508	588
Hard	Application	618	100608	509	590
Hard	Application	637	100600	517	602
Hard	Evaluation	603	100612	504	581
Hard	Evaluation	605	100579	505	583
Hard	Evaluation	608	100582	506	584
Hard	Evaluation	615	100501	508	588
Hard	Evaluation	616	100502	508	589
Hard	Evaluation	619	100609	510	591
Hard	Evaluation	622	100369	511	593
Hard	Evaluation	629	100529	515	597
Hard	Evaluation	634	100534	516	600
Hard	Evaluation	639	100602	518	604
Hard	Evaluation	640	100522	519	604
Hard	Evaluation	644	102095	520	607
Hard	Inference	602	100611	503	581
Hard	Inference	606	100584	505	583
Hard	Inference	607	100580	506	584
Hard	Inference	610	100583	506	585
Hard	Inference	612	100498	507	587

(Continued)

Difficulty	Concept	Question #	Question ID #	Page	Answer Explanation Page
Hard	Inference	613	100499	507	587
Hard	Inference	620	100610	510	592
Hard	Inference	623	100370	512	594
Hard	Inference	624	100634	513	594
Hard	Inference	625	100635	513	595
Hard	Inference	626	100636	513	595
Hard	Inference	627	100637	514	596
Hard	Inference	632	100532	516	599
Hard	Inference	633	100533	516	600
Hard	Inference	635	100535	516	601
Hard	Inference	636	100599	517	602
Hard	Inference	641	100521	519	605
Hard	Inference	642	100520	519	605
Hard	Main Idea	604	100613	504	582
Hard	Main Idea	609	100581	506	585
Hard	Main Idea	611	100497	507	586
Hard	Purpose	643	102089	520	606
Hard	Supporting Idea	601	100847	502	580
Hard	Supporting Idea	617	100607	509	590
Hard	Supporting Idea	621	100368	511	592
Hard	Supporting Idea	628	100638	514	596
Hard	Supporting Idea	630	100530	515	598
Hard	Supporting Idea	631	100531	515	598
Hard	Supporting Idea	638	100601	517	603

Critical Reasoning – Page 608

Difficulty	Concept	Question #	Question ID #	Page	Answer Explanation Page
Easy	Argument Construction	645	100181	608	672
Easy	Argument Construction	646	100194	608	674
Easy	Argument Construction	649	100237	609	677
Easy	Argument Construction	650	101005	609	678
Easy	Argument Construction	653	100200	610	681
Easy	Argument Construction	654	100195	611	682
Easy	Argument Construction	655	100211	611	683
Easy	Argument Construction	659	100201	612	687
Easy	Argument Construction	660	100223	612	688
Easy	Argument Construction	661	102097	612	689
Easy	Argument Construction	663	100146	613	691
Easy	Argument Construction	665	102099	614	693
Easy	Argument Construction	666	100848	614	694
Easy	Argument Construction	667	100814	614	695
Easy	Argument Construction	668	102100	614	696
Easy	Argument Construction	672	100645	615	701
Easy	Argument Construction	677	100979	617	706
Easy	Argument Construction	682	100954	618	711
Easy	Argument Construction	684	100811	619	713
Easy	Argument Construction	689	100654	620	719
Easy	Argument Construction	693	100873	622	723
Easy	Argument Construction	694	101081	622	724
Easy	Argument Construction	695	101228	622	725
Easy	Argument Construction	697	101819	623	728
Easy	Argument Construction	698	101937	623	729
Easy	Argument Construction	701	102109	624	732
Easy	Argument Construction	705	102458	625	736
Easy	Argument Evaluation	647	100220	608	675

(Continued)

Difficulty	Concept	Question #	Question ID #	Page	Answer Explanation Page
Easy	Argument Evaluation	651	100236	609	679
Easy	Argument Evaluation	652	100226	610	680
Easy	Argument Evaluation	657	101014	611	685
Easy	Argument Evaluation	662	102098	613	690
Easy	Argument Evaluation	664	100196	613	692
Easy	Argument Evaluation	670	100665	615	698
Easy	Argument Evaluation	671	100800	615	700
Easy	Argument Evaluation	673	100771	616	702
Easy	Argument Evaluation	676	102101	617	705
Easy	Argument Evaluation	685	100847	619	714
Easy	Argument Evaluation	687	100641	620	716
Easy	Argument Evaluation	688	100807	620	717
Easy	Argument Evaluation	691	101109	621	721
Easy	Argument Evaluation	696	101617	623	727
Easy	Argument Evaluation	699	101954	623	730
Easy	Argument Evaluation	700	101998	624	731
Easy	Argument Evaluation	702	102267	624	733
Easy	Argument Evaluation	703	102308	625	734
Easy	Argument Evaluation	704	102367	625	735
Easy	Argument Evaluation	706	102794	626	737
Easy	Evaluation of a Plan	648	100225	609	676
Easy	Evaluation of a Plan	656	100175	611	684
Easy	Evaluation of a Plan	658	100965	612	686
Easy	Evaluation of a Plan	669	101013	615	697
Easy	Evaluation of a Plan	674	100839	616	703
Easy	Evaluation of a Plan	675	100769	616	704
Easy	Evaluation of a Plan	678	102103	617	707
Easy	Evaluation of a Plan	679	100705	618	708
Easy	Evaluation of a Plan	680	102104	618	709
Easy	Evaluation of a Plan	681	100820	618	710

Difficulty	Concept	Question #	Question ID #	Page	Answer Explanation Page
Easy	Evaluation of a Plan	683	100988	619	712
Easy	Evaluation of a Plan	686	100864	620	715
Easy	Evaluation of a Plan	690	100938	621	720
Easy	Evaluation of a Plan	692	101111	621	722
Medium	Argument Construction	708	100989	626	739
Medium	Argument Construction	710	100227	627	741
Medium	Argument Construction	711	100714	627	742
Medium	Argument Construction	712	100187	628	743
Medium	Argument Construction	713	100958	628	744
Medium	Argument Construction	714	100142	628	745
Medium	Argument Construction	716	100790	629	747
Medium	Argument Construction	718	100642	629	749
Medium	Argument Construction	719	102106	630	750
Medium	Argument Construction	720	100999	630	751
Medium	Argument Construction	724	100209	631	755
Medium	Argument Construction	725	100168	631	756
Medium	Argument Construction	726	100647	632	757
Medium	Argument Construction	730	100134	633	761
Medium	Argument Construction	731	102110	633	762
Medium	Argument Construction	733	100203	634	764
Medium	Argument Construction	734	100178	634	765
Medium	Argument Construction	740	100191	636	771
Medium	Argument Construction	742	100959	637	773
Medium	Argument Construction	743	100208	637	774
Medium	Argument Construction	744	100741	637	776
Medium	Argument Construction	746	100883	638	778
Medium	Argument Construction	748	100789	638	780
Medium	Argument Construction	752	101113	639	784
Medium	Argument Construction	753	102112	640	785

(*Continued*)

Difficulty	Concept	Question #	Question ID #	Page	Answer Explanation Page
Medium	Argument Construction	754	102114	640	786
Medium	Argument Construction	755	102115	640	787
Medium	Argument Construction	761	101019	642	793
Medium	Argument Construction	762	101086	642	795
Medium	Argument Construction	764	101358	643	798
Medium	Argument Construction	766	101456	644	800
Medium	Argument Construction	767	101532	644	801
Medium	Argument Construction	768	101739	644	802
Medium	Argument Construction	769	102027	645	804
Medium	Argument Construction	770	102116	645	805
Medium	Argument Construction	775	102851	647	811
Medium	Argument Construction	776	102929	647	812
Medium	Argument Evaluation	707	102823	626	738
Medium	Argument Evaluation	709	100229	627	740
Medium	Argument Evaluation	715	100188	628	746
Medium	Argument Evaluation	721	102107	630	752
Medium	Argument Evaluation	722	100842	631	753
Medium	Argument Evaluation	723	100657	631	754
Medium	Argument Evaluation	727	102108	632	758
Medium	Argument Evaluation	729	100688	633	760
Medium	Argument Evaluation	736	100205	635	767
Medium	Argument Evaluation	739	100742	636	770
Medium	Argument Evaluation	741	100653	636	772
Medium	Argument Evaluation	745	100781	637	777
Medium	Argument Evaluation	747	100867	638	779
Medium	Argument Evaluation	749	100144	638	781
Medium	Argument Evaluation	750	100659	639	782
Medium	Argument Evaluation	751	101112	639	783
Medium	Argument Evaluation	756	102116	640	788
Medium	Argument Evaluation	757	102117	641	789
Medium	Argument Evaluation	760	100951	642	792

Difficulty	Concept	Question #	Question ID #	Page	Answer Explanation Page
Medium	Argument Evaluation	763	101257	643	797
Medium	Argument Evaluation	765	101432	643	799
Medium	Argument Evaluation	771	102137	645	807
Medium	Argument Evaluation	772	102156	646	808
Medium	Argument Evaluation	773	102321	646	809
Medium	Argument Evaluation	774	102328	646	810
Medium	Evaluation of a Plan	717	100841	629	748
Medium	Evaluation of a Plan	728	102109	632	759
Medium	Evaluation of a Plan	732	100778	634	763
Medium	Evaluation of a Plan	735	101002	634	766
Medium	Evaluation of a Plan	737	100182	635	768
Medium	Evaluation of a Plan	738	100640	635	769
Medium	Evaluation of a Plan	758	102118	641	790
Medium	Evaluation of a Plan	759	102119	641	791
Hard	Argument Construction	778	100917	648	814
Hard	Argument Construction	780	100927	648	816
Hard	Argument Construction	781	100757	649	817
Hard	Argument Construction	784	100102	650	820
Hard	Argument Construction	785	100677	650	821
Hard	Argument Construction	787	100844	650	823
Hard	Argument Construction	789	100681	651	825
Hard	Argument Construction	792	100865	652	828
Hard	Argument Construction	794	100780	653	830
Hard	Argument Construction	796	100799	653	832
Hard	Argument Construction	797	100686	653	833
Hard	Argument Construction	800	100683	654	836
Hard	Argument Construction	805	100133	656	841
Hard	Argument Construction	806	100981	656	842
Hard	Argument Construction	808	100658	657	844
Hard	Argument Construction	810	100878	657	846

(Continued)

Difficulty	Concept	Question #	Question ID #	Page	Answer Explanation Page
Hard	Argument Construction	812	100648	658	848
Hard	Argument Construction	816	100646	659	852
Hard	Argument Construction	817	100682	660	853
Hard	Argument Construction	825	101110	662	861
Hard	Argument Construction	826	101115	662	862
Hard	Argument Construction	829	100876	663	865
Hard	Argument Construction	831	100965	664	867
Hard	Argument Construction	835	101247	665	871
Hard	Argument Construction	836	101311	666	872
Hard	Argument Construction	838	101436	666	875
Hard	Argument Construction	842	102005	668	879
Hard	Argument Construction	846	102314	669	883
Hard	Argument Construction	848	102757	670	885
Hard	Argument Evaluation	777	102935	647	813
Hard	Argument Evaluation	779	100918	648	815
Hard	Argument Evaluation	783	100840	649	819
Hard	Argument Evaluation	786	100668	650	822
Hard	Argument Evaluation	788	100664	651	824
Hard	Argument Evaluation	790	100649	651	826
Hard	Argument Evaluation	791	102122	652	827
Hard	Argument Evaluation	793	100872	652	829
Hard	Argument Evaluation	798	100777	654	834
Hard	Argument Evaluation	802	100899	655	838
Hard	Argument Evaluation	804	100891	656	840
Hard	Argument Evaluation	807	100875	656	843
Hard	Argument Evaluation	809	100930	657	845
Hard	Argument Evaluation	813	100879	658	849
Hard	Argument Evaluation	814	102123	659	850
Hard	Argument Evaluation	818	101012	660	854
Hard	Argument Evaluation	820	100672	661	856

Difficulty	Concept	Question #	Question ID #	Page	Answer Explanation Page
Hard	Argument Evaluation	821	100850	661	857
Hard	Argument Evaluation	822	100652	661	858
Hard	Argument Evaluation	823	100691	661	859
Hard	Argument Evaluation	824	100693	662	860
Hard	Argument Evaluation	828	100867	663	864
Hard	Argument Evaluation	830	100918	664	866
Hard	Argument Evaluation	832	100970	664	868
Hard	Argument Evaluation	833	101011	665	869
Hard	Argument Evaluation	834	101194	665	870
Hard	Argument Evaluation	837	101401	666	874
Hard	Argument Evaluation	839	101445	667	876
Hard	Argument Evaluation	840	101616	667	877
Hard	Argument Evaluation	841	101688	667	878
Hard	Argument Evaluation	843	102275	668	880
Hard	Argument Evaluation	844	102280	668	881
Hard	Argument Evaluation	845	102290	669	882
Hard	Argument Evaluation	847	102666	669	884
Hard	Argument Evaluation	849	102779	670	886
Hard	Argument Evaluation	850	102795	670	887
Hard	Evaluation of a Plan	782	100914	649	818
Hard	Evaluation of a Plan	795	100725	653	831
Hard	Evaluation of a Plan	799	100706	654	835
Hard	Evaluation of a Plan	801	100128	655	837
Hard	Evaluation of a Plan	803	100233	655	839
Hard	Evaluation of a Plan	811	100702	658	847
Hard	Evaluation of a Plan	815	100796	659	851
Hard	Evaluation of a Plan	819	102124	660	855
Hard	Evaluation of a Plan	827	102125	663	863

To register for the GMAT™ exam, go to www.mba.com/register

Appendix A   Answer Sheets

Quantitative Reasoning Answer Sheet

1.	33.	65.	97.	129.
2.	34.	66.	98.	130.
3.	35.	67.	99.	131.
4.	36.	68.	100.	132.
5.	37.	69.	101.	133.
6.	38.	70.	102.	134.
7.	39.	71.	103.	135.
8.	40.	72.	104.	136.
9.	41.	73.	105.	137.
10.	42.	74.	106.	138.
11.	43.	75.	107.	139.
12.	44.	76.	108.	140.
13.	45.	77.	109.	141.
14.	46.	78.	110.	142.
15.	47.	79.	111.	143.
16.	48.	80.	112.	144.
17.	49.	81.	113.	145.
18.	50.	82.	114.	146.
19.	51.	83.	115.	147.
20.	52.	84.	116.	148.
21.	53.	85.	117.	149.
22.	54.	86.	118.	150.
23.	55.	87.	119.	151.
24.	56.	88.	120.	152.
25.	57.	89.	121.	153.
26.	58.	90.	122.	154.
27.	59.	91.	123.	155.
28.	60.	92.	124.	156.
29.	61.	93.	125.	157.
30.	62.	94.	126.	158.
31.	63.	95.	127.	159.
32.	64.	96.	128.	160.

161.	188.	215.	242.	269.
162.	189.	216.	243.	270.
163.	190.	217.	244.	271.
164.	191.	218.	245.	272.
165.	192.	219.	246.	273.
166.	193.	220.	247.	274.
167.	194.	221.	248.	275.
168.	195.	222.	249.	276.
169.	196.	223.	250.	277.
170.	197.	224.	251.	278.
171.	198.	225.	252.	279.
172.	199.	226.	253.	280.
173.	200.	227.	254.	281.
174.	201.	228.	255.	282.
175.	202.	229.	256.	283.
176.	203.	230.	257.	284.
177.	204.	231.	258.	285.
178.	205.	232.	259.	286.
179.	206.	233.	260.	287.
180.	207.	234.	261.	288.
181.	208.	235.	262.	289.
182.	209.	236.	263.	290.
183.	210.	237.	264.	291.
184.	211.	238.	265.	292.
185.	212.	239.	266.	293.
186.	213.	240.	267.	
187.	214.	241.	268.	

Data Sufficiency Answer Sheet

294.	323.	352.	381.	410.
295.	324.	353.	382.	411.
296.	325.	354.	383.	412.
297.	326.	355.	384.	413.
298.	327.	356.	385.	414.
299.	328.	357.	386.	415.
300.	329.	358.	387.	416.
301.	330.	359.	388.	417.
302.	331.	360.	389.	418.
303.	332.	361.	390.	419.
304.	333.	362.	391.	420.
305.	334.	363.	392.	421.
306.	335.	364.	393.	422.
307.	336.	365.	394.	423.
308.	337.	366.	395.	424.
309.	338.	367.	396.	425.
310.	339.	368.	397.	426.
311.	340.	369.	398.	427.
312.	341.	370.	399.	428.
313.	342.	371.	400.	429.
314.	343.	372.	401.	430.
315.	344.	373.	402.	431.
316.	345.	374.	403.	432.
317.	346.	375.	404.	433.
318.	347.	376.	405.	434.
319.	348.	377.	406.	435.
320.	349.	378.	407.	436.
321.	350.	379.	408.	
322.	351.	380.	409.	

Two-Part Analysis Answer Sheet

437.	451.	465.	479.	493.
438.	452.	466.	480.	494.
439.	453.	467.	481.	495.
440.	454.	468.	482.	496.
441.	455.	469.	483.	497.
442.	456.	470.	484.	498.
443.	457.	471.	485.	499.
444.	458.	472.	486.	500.
445.	459.	473.	487.	501.
446.	460.	474.	488.	502.
447.	461.	475.	489.	503.
448.	462.	476.	490.	504.
449.	463.	477.	491.	
450.	464.	478.	492.	

Reading Comprehension Answer Sheet

505.	533.	561.	589.	617.
506.	534.	562.	590.	618.
507.	535.	563.	591.	619.
508.	536.	564.	592.	620.
509.	537.	565.	593.	621.
510.	538.	566.	594.	622.
511.	539.	567.	595.	623.
512.	540.	568.	596.	624.
513.	541.	569.	597.	625.
514.	542.	570.	598.	626.
515.	543.	571.	599.	627.
516.	544.	572.	600.	628.
517.	545.	573.	601.	629.
518.	546.	574.	602.	630.
519.	547.	575.	603.	631.
520.	548.	576.	604.	632.
521.	549.	577.	605.	633.
522.	550.	578.	606.	634.
523.	551.	579.	607.	635.
524.	552.	580.	608.	636.
525.	553.	581.	609.	637.
526.	554.	582.	610.	638.
527.	555.	583.	611.	639.
528.	556.	584.	612.	640.
529.	557.	585.	613.	641.
530.	558.	586.	614.	642.
531.	559.	587.	615.	643.
532.	560.	588.	616.	644.

Critical Reasoning Answer Sheet

645.	677.	709.	741.	773.
646.	678.	710.	742.	774.
647.	679.	711.	743.	775.
648.	680.	712.	744.	776.
649.	681.	713.	745.	777.
650.	682.	714.	746.	778.
651.	683.	715.	747.	779.
652.	684.	716.	748.	780.
653.	685.	717.	749.	781.
654.	686.	718.	750.	782.
655.	687.	719.	751.	783.
656.	688.	720.	752.	784.
657.	689.	721.	753.	785.
658.	690.	722.	754.	786.
659.	691.	723.	755.	787.
660.	692.	724.	756.	788.
661.	693.	725.	757.	789.
662.	694.	726.	758.	790.
663.	695.	727.	759.	791.
664.	696.	728.	760.	792.
665.	697.	729.	761.	793.
666.	698.	730.	762.	794.
667.	699.	731.	763.	795.
668.	700.	732.	764.	796.
669.	701.	733.	765.	797.
670.	702.	734.	766.	798.
671.	703.	735.	767.	799.
672.	704.	736.	768.	800.
673.	705.	737.	769.	801.
674.	706.	738.	770.	802.
675.	707.	739.	771.	803.
676.	708.	740.	772.	804.

805.

806.

807.

808.

809.

810.

811.

812.

813.

814.

815.

816.

817.

818.

819.

820.

821.

822.

823.

824.

825.

826.

827.

828.

829.

830.

831.

832.

833.

834.

835.

836.

837.

838.

839.

840.

841.

842.

843.

844.

845.

846.

847.

848.

849.

850.

Notes

Notes

Notes

Notes

GMAT Exam

Elevate your prep with our free resources

 1

GMAT Official Starter Kit

Sample 70+ real GMAT questions, a guided review, and Official Practice Exams 1 & 2, which simulate the real exam format and test-taking experience.

 2

GMAT 6-Week Study Planner

Gain exclusive insights and strategies directly from the creators of the GMAT Exam. Utilize this guide to maintain a structured schedule, inform your activities, and monitor your progress.

GMAT Official Starter Kit

GMAT 6-Week Study Planner